Infant Development

A Topical Approach

Alan Fogel
University of Utah

2011
Sloan Publishing
Cornwall-on-Hudson, NY 12520

Library of Congress Cataloging-in-Publication Data

Fogel, Alan.
Infant development : a topical approach / Alan Fogel.
p. cm.
ISBN 978-1-59738-025-6
1. Infants--Development. 2. Infant psychology. I. Title.
RJ134.F64 2011
618.92--dc22
2010001450

Cover photo by Studio Yancey Hughes
Cover design by K&M Design

Sloan Publishing, LLC
220 Maple Road
Cornwall-on-Hudson, NY 12520

Printed in USA

10 9 8 7 6 5 4 3 2

To the well-being of infants and their families.

About the Author

Alan Fogel is a professor of psychology at the University of Utah. Born in Miami, Florida, he earned his B.S. in physics at the University of Miami (1967, Coral Gables, FL) and his M.A. in physics at Columbia University (1968, New York, NY) where he was a Faculty Fellow. During his three-year term with the United States Peace Corps in Bogota, Columbia, Fogel taught physics and worked on developing physics curricula for high schools. Through this experience, Fogel became interested in how people learn, which led to his completion of a Ph.D. in education, in 1976, with a focus on early childhood development, at the University of Chicago.

Dr. Fogel is active as a researcher and author. He is the author of *Infancy: Infant, family, and society, 5th Edition* (Sloan Publishing, 2009). He has written books on early social and communicative development, *Developing through Relationships* (University of Chicago Press, 1993) and *Change Processes in Relationships: A Relational-Historical Research Approach* (with A. Garvey, H. Hsu, & D. West-Stroming, Cambridge University Press, 2006). His most recent book, T*he psychophysiology of self-awareness: Rediscovering the lost art of body sense* (W. W. Norton, 2009), is about the development of body sense, the awareness of our sensations and emotions, how the body sense develops from infancy to adulthood, and body-centered treatments for impairments in body sense. Dr. Fogel writes a blog on body sense for *Psychology Today* magazine (http://www.psychologytoday.com/blog/body-sense).

He has co-edited multiple books on research in child development: *Emotion and Early Interaction* (with Tiffany Field, 1982), *Origins of Nurturance: Biological, Cultural, and Developmental Perspectives in Caregiving* (with Gail F. Melson, 1985), and *Dynamics and Indeterminism in Social and Developmental Processes* (with Maria Lyra and Jaan Valsiner, 1997), the *Handbook of Infant Development* (with Gavin Bremner, 2001), and *Human*

Development in the 21st Century: Visionary Policy Ideas from Systems Scientists (with Barbara King and Stuart Shanker, 2008). He has also written an undergraduate text on child development, *Child Development: Individual, Family, and Society* (with Gail F. Melson).

Fogel's scholarly papers on development in infancy, which includes studies of emotional development, social and communicative development in relation to parents and to peers, and topics of infant development of concern to health care providers and early childhood educators, have been published in *Child Development, Developmental Psychology, Developmental Science, Early Development and Parenting, Infant Behavior and Development, Infancy, Infant and Child Development, International Journal of Behavioral Development, Journal of Developmental Processes,* and *Social Development.* More information, along with free downloads of many of these publications, can be found at http://www.psych.utah.edu/lab/somatics.

Fogel has been supported in his research through grants from the National Science Foundation, the National Institutes of Health, the National Institute of Mental Health, the National March of Dimes Foundation, the Nancy Lurie Marks Family Foundation, the Institute for Research on Unlimited Love, and the United States Department of Agriculture. He has lectured widely in the United States, Japan (where he spent the 1983–1984 academic year as a senior research scholar under a Fulbright fellowship), Brazil, and Europe (where he was a visiting professor at the Free University in Amsterdam in 1990 and again in 1995, at the University of Florence in Italy in 1996, and the University of Rome in 1999).

Brief Contents

Contents

Preface

Babies evoke mixed feelings in almost everyone. Common descriptions of babies range from wonderful, cute, delightful, cuddly, soft, and warm on the positive side to noisy, smelly, demanding, and frustrating on the negative side. The way we feel about babies usually depends on how much experience we have had with them, our relationship to the baby, how old we are, what kind of mood we happen to be in, and what we have heard from others about babies.

Everyone has a relationship with infancy, if only because everyone has been a baby. All of us cried, wet our diapers, and felt tiny and dependent on those whom we trusted to provide everything we needed. Because all of us have a different experience as a baby and different experiences with babies, there cannot be a single truth about babies. Babies mean different things to different people.

This book is about what babies mean to me and the experiences I have had with them as a behavioral scientist, friend, uncle, father, and grandfather. This book draws heavily on infancy research that has been conducted in the past 35 years and provides a scientifically based account of infant development. Science has a lot to offer our relationship with infants, but it is not the only source of evidence. The research results reported in this book, combined with your own experience with infants, should lead you closer to an understanding of what babies are for you.

This book is designed not only to report the facts about infants but also to convey the vitality of infants as developing human beings. I have also endeavored to include research that describes what infants actually do, think, and feel and on how they behave in everyday contexts.

You can take a look at the current syllabus I use when I teach a course called *Infancy and Early Childhood* using this book. The syllabus is available free on my website at: *http://www.psych.utah.edu/lab/somatics* under the "university classes" link. My course focuses primarily on social and emotional development (which you can see from the study questions included in the syllabus) and I also assign supplementary readings in addition to the textbook. I also use many of the experiential exercises contained in this book (see next section) both inside and outside of the classroom.

PEDAGOGICAL FEATURES

Unlike its companion book, *Infancy: Infant, family, and society, 5th Edition* (Sloan Publishing, 2009) which is organized by age period, this book is organized according to topics. While some instructors find the "ages and stages" organization useful, others prefer to focus on particular topics and to cover the age changes over the first three years within each topic. The topical approach used here allows for a coherent organization within domains such as sensorimotor, cognitive, emotional, social and communicative development in infancy. In addition, there are chapters that cover health and risk, and family and culture. Chapters on research methods, theory, prenatal development and childbirth are similar to those found in *Infancy: Infant, family, and society*. As in the past, chapters are introduced with a set of thought-provoking questions, and there are brief summaries at the end of every chapter.

This book, like *Infancy*, contains an "Experiential Exercises" section that appears in most chapters. The "Experiential Exercises" sections contain brief and simple instructions that may help readers to approximate the infant's psychological experience. Instructions for doing the exercises are given below. These are entirely optional and may not fit with the teaching style of many instructors.

If you choose to do the exercises, on your own or as part of the class, it helps to have someone read the steps while you do the exercises, or you could record them and then follow the recording. They can also be led by the instructor and done in a classroom. The reader should take each step slowly, giving the student time to fully experience. Examples of pre-recorded exercises are given on my web site at *http://www.psych.utah.edu/lab/somatics* under the link "audio and video."

In my classes, I allow students about 10-15 minutes to write down their experiences in a journal. Following that, there is a class discussion in which students are encouraged to share what they did and felt. This is useful to highlight the wide range of individual differences, some of which may come from each person's infancy and early childhood past (see the concept of "participatory memory," Chapter 2).

- Instructors must do the exercises themselves at least several times before teaching them, in order to empathize with the students and to understand the effects

- Students should be as comfortable as possible, nothing should be physically painful

- Students should dress comfortably and may want to remove belts, shoes, or jewelry

- The room should have carpet and variable lighting if possible

- Distractions should be reduced as much as possible to encourage relaxation and engagement

- Accommodations need to be made for pregnant women and other physical limitations

- Students should be told to "take care of yourself" and not follow any instruction that may be difficult or painful

- Each instruction must be spoken clearly and slowly and students must be given plenty of time to feel, sense, and move
- The focus is on somatic and emotional awareness and not on conceptual awareness, thinking, evaluating or judging, i.e., the focus is on cultivating "babymind"
- Instructors should also cultivate their own non-conceptual "babymind" awareness in themselves and in empathy with the students, both in their own embodied practice and while teaching
- Encourage students to focus on their whole body and any feelings, leaving full pauses between each step for them to do this
- Do not talk constantly when leading the exercises: allow for silences
- In the discussion that follows the exercise, avoid judging or evaluating what students say; simply comment about infant experience in general or acknowledge their own experience or just say "thank you"
- There is no wrong way to do these exercises, or to experience them
- Create an atmosphere of relaxation, comfort, and acceptance of each person's point of view
- Students are taking a "risk" to act like a baby and to allow themselves to be vulnerable and the sense of that must be implicit in the instructor's behavior

TEACHING SUPPLEMENTS

Two teaching supplements are available for instructors who adopt *Infant Development: A Topical Approach* : a Test Bank prepared by Dr. Denise Bodman of Arizona State University provides approximately 80 multiple-choice, true-false, matching, and essay questions per chapter; and an extensive set of *Powerpoint™ Lecture Slides* for each chapter prepared by Dr. Ilse de Koeyer of the University of Utah.

ACKNOWLEGEMENTS

I would like to thank the following consultants for their important and thoughtful written contributions to this book: Dr. Mark Reese (Feldenkrais practitioner and teacher, deceased; Experiential Exercises), Dr. Ilse de Koeyer (Adjunct Assistant Professor, Department of Psychology, University of Utah; Experiential Exercises), Eileen Rojas (Modern Dancer; Experiential Exercise), Dr. LaDonna Atkins (Associate Professor, Department of Family and Child Studies, University of Central Oklahoma; section on Infant-Parent Mental Health Consusltants), and Mark E. Ludwig (Associate Professor, California Institute of Integral Studies; section on Infant-Parent Mental Health), as well as the publisher's reviewers: Dr. Carolyn A. Johnson (the Pennsylvania State University), Dr. Chryle A. Elieff (the University of Illinois, Urbana), and Dr. Jeanne M. Stolzer (the University of Nebraska, Kearney).

In addition, Dr. Carolyn A. Johnson provided a number of valuable suggestions for Chapters 3, 4, and 9.

I had excellent research assistants, all from the Department of Psychology at the University of Utah, Salt Lake City: Natasha Carrera, Ryan Garcia, Bridget Gauthier, Taralee Hulme, Jurg Schmid, Snowowl Sor-Lokken, Lynda St. Dennis, Allison Van Vooren, and Brandon Whiting. I am indebted to my editorial assistant, Vito Rontino, who put in long hours on this project helping to organize the references. Finally, thanks to my wife—Jacqueline—for providing me the time, space, love, and support to accomplish the task.

Chapter 1

Basic Concepts of Infant Behavior and Development

CHAPTER OUTLINE AND OVERVIEW

The Importance of Infancy	*What can be gained from the study of infants? What can be learned by reading this book?*
A Brief History of Babies	*How have responses to and ideas about infants changed historically? What are the historical origins of our current ideas about infants?*
Infants Enter the World of Science	*What is the current scientific conception of infants? How does it change our view of infancy?*
Research Methods in Developmental Science	*What are the main scientific approaches to the study of human development? Is science a viable source of information about infants?*
Experimental Research Methods	*What are the possibilities and limits of controlled experiments with infants? How can experimental research help us understand how infants think, perceive, or feel?*
Observational Research Methods	*What can be learned from the observation of naturally occurring infant behavior? How has video and computer technology contributed to the accuracy of observation?*
Qualitative Research Methods	*What is the infant's experience of the world? What does it mean when a baby cries or smiles? What are the advantages and sources of bias that occur when adults try to answer these questions from their own point of view?*

Have you ever wondered about the details of your own birth? Do you think it was painful or pleasurable? Did you cry a lot? Do you remember learning to crawl or to walk? What was the first word you ever said? If you know the answer to any of these questions, it is likely you have asked or were told about it by someone who was an adult when you were a baby. Infancy is mysterious to us. We appear to have no memory of our own infancy; we must rely on the memory of others who were there. And babies themselves cannot tell us what they feel, at least not in words. The mystery of the infant's mind has intrigued parents, philosophers, and theologians for thousands of years.

The twentieth century, however, has given us powerful new methods for understanding infancy. Scientific research has helped us understand the limits and possibilities of the infant's ability to sense, move, and feel. We now know some types of environments and forms of care that are conducive to the development of healthy and happy babies. Advanced technologies allow us to monitor the brain's development and to observe the stages of prenatal growth. The fields of Infant Mental Health and Early Childhood Education have developed techniques to improve the lives of many infants and their parents. These methods have generated strong public interest in babies. Why are babies so interesting?

THE IMPORTANCE OF INFANCY

If you read the newspapers or watch television news programs, you will recognize some of these headlines and advertisement leads:

Discoveries allow for the prenatal detection of genetic disorders.

Sixty-year-old women can give birth to their own babies.

Mothers may transmit AIDS to their babies through breast milk.

Parents can recognize their newborn infants by touch alone.

Day care may have harmful effects on the mother-infant relationship.

You can teach your infant to read before the age of two.

Inadequate parenting of infants causes lasting psychological damage.

If these statements are correct, they have a profound impact on our lives and on society. A sixty-year-old mother may die before the child is an adolescent or become too frail to care for the child. If day care is harmful to infants, we will have to reassess the value of parental work. But are these statements correct? In fact, there is some truth to all of them—but only under certain special conditions. A sixty-year-old can give birth by having a fertilized ovum implanted into her uterus, but only if she is in good health and can tolerate taking supplemental hormones. Day care can be harmful in settings where teachers are poorly trained and facilities are inadequate, or when infants are too young to tolerate the demands of a complex social environment; otherwise, it can have some beneficial effects, such as giving children advanced social skills with their peers.

AIDS can be transmitted through breast milk, but this can be prevented by using formula. Parents, especially mothers, appear to be able to distinguish their own newborn from another simply by touching each of the babies, although there are individual differences. If a mother cannot do this, it bears no relationship at all to her ability to become attached or to provide adequate maternal care. New research has shown that overuse of language videos and computer games in children under two years of age can actually have a harmful effect! For every hour per day that a baby spent watching videos such as "Baby Einstein" and "Brainy Baby," they understood about 6 to 8 words fewer at age 2 years than babies who did not watch these videos (Zimmerman, Christakis, & Meltzoff, 2007). In general, TV is not very helpful and may even be harmful for babies.

By the end of this book, you should have a much better idea about how to evaluate claims such as the ones listed above. You will read about these and other issues and learn ways to understand research, so you can look up the answers for yourself. The study of infancy is important for many reasons. A few will be listed here, and you may be able to add some of your own.

The Experience of the Body and Its Movements and Senses

ex: thirst, walk, hot

The consciousness of young infants is almost entirely occupied with bodily sensations, movements, and sensory experiences . Once children acquire the ability to talk, think, and conceptualize, they acquire an intellectual power that distinguishes humans from other animals. On the other hand, the preverbal experience of being a baby in a baby's body is also uniquely human. After infancy, many physical and mental disorders of children and adults can be traced to their having lost touch with their own body, emotions, and senses. Cultural values can often run contrary to the needs of the body, as when work or family stresses cause muscular tension (headaches or backaches, for example) or when cultural ideals of physical beauty lead a person to eat less than her or his own body uniquely requires. Most healthy infants are flexible and soft, they breathe fully and deeply, and they love to be held and touched.

For a baby, losing touch with the body would be nearly impossible. For a baby, after all, what else is there? As you study this book and learn more about infancy, allow yourself to appreciate and to reexperience what is really special about being a baby. It can feel like a breath of fresh air.

In Chapter 4, you will read about research on the sensorimotor world of the infant. This, and other chapters, include brief Experiential Exercises you can do to appreciate the actual experience of being a baby, or at least of your own body as you move it in a more babylike way. With practice, these exercises may allow you to step back from thinking, reasoning, judging, and evaluating, and simply be present to your senses and movements.

Infants have Complex Emotional Lives

Infancy is a special time in one's life. This is not only because it is the earliest stage of life, but because all of life's stages are unique. Each has its pleasures and problems. For the first few years of 2life, infants are almost totally dependent on their caregivers for all their needs. Most of what happens to them is not within their understanding or control. As we'll see in Chapter 7 on emotional development, infants cry easily and feel their pain deeply. They get frustrated with their own clumsiness and relative incompetence to achieve their goals. For reasons we do not fully understand, nature has required all humans to pass through this period and to experience its total reliance on others, its helpless emotional lows and its carefree emotional highs.

Babyhood has a number of high points. Infants can spend hours immersed in the pleasure of play and exploration. They are not plagued by self-doubt, worries, bills to pay, and the other things that can distract adults from living in the moment.

Parent, Caregiver, and Clinician Education

Infants require adult guidance, love, and support. For a young couple ready to provide this care, their first baby can be both rewarding and anxiety provoking. What is the best way to feed babies? How much sleep do they need? Can babies be spoiled with too much holding and affection? What does it mean if a baby cries for long periods? You will find some answers to these questions in this book. Aside from information about infants, some of the chapters review research on the experiences and development of parents. Generally speaking, the more parents know about infants and children, the less anxious they will be, and the better the outcomes will be for the child. Although they cannot substitute for direct experience with infants, books like this one can provide valuable information that enhances the parenting experience. Infant caregivers—such as day care providers, grandparents, and other relatives—can also profit from this book. Infant mental health workers and other clinicians, such as nurses who work with infants and their parents or who work with adult clients and want to know more about the lasting impact of infant experiences on the adult psyche, will also find this book helpful.

Improving Health by Early Prevention

Many of the diseases of childhood and adulthood have their origins in the prenatal period and infancy. During prenatal development, for example, the brain is highly vulnerable to disease, malnutrition, and toxic substances to which the mother may be exposed. Many disorders can be prevented by changing maternal behavior during pregnancy, such as by eating properly, avoiding particular drugs and chemicals, and reducing stress (see Chapters 3 and 9). In addition, medical research has discovered remarkable new treatments for prenatal and infant disorders. In the most serious cases, parents may choose to terminate the pregnancy. In a growing number of cases, however, treatments given to fetuses directly can permanently eliminate the effects of such disorders. Due to advances in medical technology, premature infants are more likely to survive and live normal lives than ever before. In poor nations, simple treatments for combating infant death, caused primarily by diarrhea, are saving millions of lives.

If infants from a wealthy nation survive past birth, the chances that they will die from a serious disease are extremely small due to widespread immunizations and health care, explained in Chapter 9. Public health officials are beginning to make progress in reducing the largest cause of infant death in these countries: accidents. Parent education in infant health and safety, safer toys, better infant restraints for automobiles (more infants and children lose their lives in auto accidents in North America than from all other causes of death combined), and better enforcement of seat belt laws are all helping to reduce injury and mortality.

Reexperiencing Infant-like States Can Be Healing and Rejuvenating

Infants have an ability to take life as it comes, be fully "present" to their experiences, and take joy in everyday actions and sensations (Schafer, 2004). Movement, body awareness, and dance educators often use infant-like movements to help children and adults develop an awareness of their body and a sense of calm. These procedures have proved useful in expanding the range of movement for all individuals. Regular practice of these types of movements may promote relaxation and personal growth. Movement education based on a re-learning of infant patterns of movement works especially well with people who are afflicted with muscular disorders, such as cerebral palsy, and with those who have suffered accidents and injuries. It is also helpful for the relief of everyday tension and muscular pains.

Some psychotherapeutic techniques recreate within the patient-therapist relationship the innocence and trust found in healthy parent-infant relationships. Some touch therapies use gentle, noninvasive contact to create the type of relaxation and self-awareness that babies experience in their mother's arms. Practitioners from all these therapeutic and educational methods assume that there will be a healing effect of recreating—in a safe and protected setting—some of the conditions of being a baby. Reexperiencing some of the traumas of one's own infancy, especially within the supportive contexts of these treatment approaches, can also be therapeutic. Such clinical methods will be discussed in more detail in Chapter 2 and the Experiential Exercises found at the ends of chapters give examples of how to do this.

Informed Public Policy

Because of infants' vulnerability, many social and medical problems could be prevented by making sure that they receive proper care and that young parents receive all the support necessary to provide the best environment for their children. Society can take positive steps toward the achievement of such goals. Citizens who are knowledgeable about the possibilities and risks of prenatal and infant development can make better-informed decisions when asked to vote—as lawmakers or as part of the electorate—on legislation regarding infant, family, and child welfare. Should all families with infants be guaranteed the right to housing, proper nutrition, medical care, and parent education? Currently, these are not guaranteed rights in the United States. They are guaranteed, however, in northern European countries such as Sweden and the Netherlands. Because the quality of day care influences infant development and the parent-child relationship, should there be national standards for day care providers? The United States is one of the few industrialized countries without such standards. You can read more about public policy issues in Chapters 8 and 9.

Origins of Individual Differences

Each human being is different. A lot of these differences come from experiences as a child and adult, such as one's school experience, the effects of family and friends, the world of work, and unplanned opportunities and losses that occur during one's life. But do any of the differences between people have their origins in early infancy? If so, which parts of one's uniqueness are most likely connected to what happened to one as a baby? This is an extremely difficult question to answer because early experiences are rarely preserved in some pure form, but rather combine in complex ways with later experiences. Nonetheless, many differences between people during the prenatal and infancy periods do have a lasting impact. In Chapter 10 you will discover what is known and what is yet to be discovered about the infantile origins of differences between people.

The importance of studying about infants, as illustrated by each of the topics above, may seem self-evident. The importance of infancy, however, is not always appreciated. An infant born into today's world may experience poverty or wealth, love or abuse, health or disease. More must be done to educate parents and political leaders about the need for protecting infants, who cannot protect themselves.

Was it always this way in the life of infants—this mixture of good and bad? In general, yes. In all periods of the past for which there are archaeological or historical sources, we can find evidence of both kindness to and neglect of infants. Nevertheless, there is more money, time, and care devoted to infants today than at any other known period of history. How-to articles, products, and books on child rearing, pregnancy, and childbirth are squeezing other items off store shelves. Most large supermarkets in Europe, Asia, and North America devote an entire aisle to baby products: diapers, oils, powders, foods, furniture, toys, designer clothing, strollers, packs, books, and magazines. In wealthy countries, it is not unusual for infants to be dressed in expensive high-tech running shoes and athletic clothes before they can even walk! More seriously, many countries devote a portion of their tax revenues to fund scientific research on the medical and psychological aspects of infancy, research that has led to many of the findings reported in this book.

To give you some insight into why infancy has become so important, the next section reviews some of the historical trends in the role of the infant in society. Because of limitations of space, the focus will be on the history of Western cultures (European and American). The heightened importance of infancy in today's Western society began in the eighteenth century, with an increase in pediatric medical practice, advice for parents, parental devotion to the individuality of each child, children's books, and other infant care products and resources. Readers are encouraged to integrate what is known about their own cultural history into this story.

A BRIEF HISTORY OF BABIES

Early Civilizations

As far back as there are recorded documents, history reveals a mixture of beliefs and practices about infants: love and cruelty, freedom and restriction, tolerance and intolerance (French, 2002). The history and literature of the ancient Greeks and Romans (200 B.C.–300 A.D.) indicates that they advocated a rather harsh upbringing for infants. Shows of affection were avoided, and infants were wrapped tightly in swaddling bands in order to mold the child's body into one worthy of a citizen. Cold water was used to bathe the child to prevent the child from becoming too soft. Babies hated their baths all the more because nurses would press on the child's skull to make it as round as possible and pull and stretch other body parts in order to shape them.

Similar beliefs in shaping the physical body of the adult by binding and manipulating the infant can be seen in such non-Western ancient practices as the foot binding of girls in China (which made their feet small but deformed). Head binding among both the ancient Maya of Mexico and among eighteenth-century Europeans was used to give the head an oblong shape (Johnson, 1992).

While it may seem surprising to people today, Roman parents felt this treatment to be an expression of their love. They wanted their children to grow up strong, their bodies nicely proportioned and held in a proper posture. Roman literature, in fact, testifies to a strong devotion between parents and children, especially among the wealthy classes, and attests to the importance of hugging, kissing, and affection after infancy, as the child grew older and began to form his or her own character (Dupont, 1989; Gies & Gies, 1987). Historians of ancient Egypt (2,000–100 B.C.) and Greece (800–200 B.C.) have found evidence of toys and games for children and written documents describing the need to love and protect infants (Greenleaf, 1978).

The recognition of the role of the body in the development of the person is an important aspect of Westerners' Greco-Roman heritage. Both Greeks and Romans believed that exercises for the body led to the development of a strong moral character. Upper-class boys learned athletics and gymnastics, while girls learned music and dance.

Many early civilizations, such as ancient Rome, practiced **infanticide**, the deliberate killing of unwanted infants. This was partly because Roman laws considered the child as the property of parents, and also made parents responsible for raising healthy and productive heirs (Borstelmann, 1983). It was the duty of the head of the family to decide if a newborn should live or die. This practice eliminated infants who were malformed, but many healthy babies too were left to die because the family was poor or the child unwanted (Dupont, 1989). Infanticide continued in Europe throughout the Middle Ages, and some societies today still practice it (see the section on family planning in Chapter 3).

The ancient Isrealites' practices of childrearing are known primarily through the Old Testament. The biblical period dates from 2000 B.C.E. to 500 B.C.E. There are many stories in the Old Testament that reflect the importance of infants and children. Hannah, for example, prayed and made vows to God so that she might conceive and give birth to Samuel. Unlike Rome and Greece, children were not considered the property of parents, but rather as a gift from God who needed to be protected, loved, and educated. There is no evidence of infanticide among the ancient Hebrews.

The Bible also gives detailed—and medically informed—prescriptions regarding women's behavior during menstruation, pregnancy, and childbirth. Direct descriptions of infancy are rare in the Bible, but many stories imply that infants should receive loving care, appropriate blessings for a good and holy life, and that male infants should be circumcised. Parental devotion was evident in stories of the suffering of parents who were asked to sacrifice their infants. When two mothers claimed to be the parent of the same child, Solomon's threat to kill the child revealed the true mother, whose pain was sincere. The Hebrew slave revolt in Egypt, which led to the Exodus and return to the promised land, was precipitated by an Egyptian law to kill Hebrew first-born sons meant to limit the slave population. In order to save Moses, his heartbroken family sent him floating down the Nile, to be adopted with love by Egyptian royal women and actually nursed by his own mother. This story suggests a comparison between the concept of human freedom from slavery in general with the act of saving a single infant from death (Frymer-Kensky, 1995).

The Bible asks parents not only to love but to educate their children. Abraham was told to "instruct" his children (Genesis 18:19). Regarding the important facets of Hebrew culture, parents were asked to "teach them intently to your children ... when you sit in your home" (Deuteronomy 6:7). Childrearing involved discipline accompanied by respect for the child, as the following passages illustrate: "Train a child in his own way, and even when he is old, he will not depart from it" (Proverbs 22:6); "Foolishness is bound in the heart of the child but the rod of correction shall drive it from him" (Proverbs 22:15); and "Chasten your son for there is hope, but set not your heart on his destruction" (Proverbs 19:18). While some have interpreted these statements as grounds for justifying corporal punishment, the Old Testament does not specify the type of punishment, but rather makes clear the need for discipline in the context of love. Other Bible stories reveal the undesirable outcomes when discipline is too harsh or nonexistent or when parents fail to educate their children about the stories, rituals, ideals, and history of the culture.

The Middle Ages and the Renaissance

Following the Greek and Romans, a mix of concern for children coexisted with what people today would consider to be harshness and deprivation throughout recorded Western history. The early Middle Ages in Europe (300–1100 A.D.) began with the fall of the Roman empire and the gradual spread of Christianity throughout the continent. The largely rural population began to move in large numbers to cities and towns. At the same time, the political boundaries changed frequently as empires dissolved and local powers asserted themselves. These social changes contributed to an increasingly educated urban population, on the one hand, and to the growth of a class of urban poor who suffered from disease, malnutrition,

pollution, and ignorance, on the other. The poor people in the cities lived in much more unhealthy conditions than did the poor in the countryside.

Because of inadequate sanitation and other sources of urban pollution (pollution is not a new problem), infants of the urban poor were more likely to die or to suffer birth defects than those from rural areas. Because cities drew people away from family roots and because disease claimed the lives not only of infants but of mothers in childbirth, many orphaned children walked the streets as beggars, thieves, and prostitutes. As you can see, childhood among the urban poor then was not too much different from what it is today. This is especially true in the large and growing slums found in many of the "megacities" of the twenty-first century (defined as cities with more than 10 million people) such as Lagos (Nigeria), Bombay (India), and Mexico City. This does not mean that poverty inevitably causes problems for parents and children, but it does increase the risk that problems will occur.

The Christian church began to have an impact on the beliefs and practices of European child rearing after around 400 A.D. Christians, following the ancient Hebrew beliefs and practices, advocated parental love and worked to protect children from infanticide, abortion, and maltreatment. Gravestones for infants began to appear at this time, as well as special penances if a parent had done some wrong to a child (Gies & Gies, 1987).

During the late Middle Ages (1100–1300 A.D.), a few written medical texts giving advice on childbirth and early infant care appeared. Trotola, a female physician in twelfth-century Italy, advised rubbing the newborn's palate with honey, protecting the infant from bright lights and loud noises, and stimulating the infant's senses with cloths of various colors and textures and with "songs and gentle voices" (Gies & Gies, 1987). In England during the same period, birth often occurred in a warm chamber with plenty of bathwater, accompanied by the scent of olives, herbs, and roses. It was attended by a female midwife and female friends wishing mother and baby good fortune and joy (Hanawalt, 1993).

Painting from the late Middle Ages depicting Christ as an infant, but in stylized clothing with adult-like features and gestures.
Source: Art Resource.

Infanticide, however, was still practiced. Although parents had to suffer penances, it was not a crime equivalent to homicide, as it is in most countries today. By the thirteenth century, some cities in Europe had created church-run hospices to adopt orphaned children as an alternative to infanticide. This was partly because of the belief that all life is sacred, and also, according to medieval church doctrine, a child who died unbaptized was barred from heaven for all eternity (Le Goff, 1987). In some countries today, because of urban stress and poverty, infants are left in woods, rivers, and trash bins. Some cities in the United States have begun programs that allow mothers to drop off unwanted infants at local hospitals without fear of prosecution. Social workers then help to find foster homes for these children. Times may have changed, but the problem of unwanted children still remains.

Not until the European Renaissance (1450–1650) do we begin to see the emergence of written philosophies of child rearing in Western cultures. Writers, mostly from the church, condemned the ancient practice of giving children to wet nurses from the poorer classes (a wet nurse was a woman who was paid to nurse the child with her own milk to spare wealthy women the task of nursing the baby themselves) because the child could pick up the habits and diseases of the nurse. The famous Renaissance artist Michelangelo jokingly claimed that his skill in sculpture came from his wet nurse, who was the wife of a stonecutter (Gies & Gies, 1987).

During the early Middle Ages, religious paintings depicted Christ as an adult. By the late Middle Ages, interest in children was growing, and Christ began to appear as an infant. However, the infant Christ in medieval art is typically shown in stylized clothing, with adult facial features and mannerisms. One painting depicts Christ as an infant making the Catholic gesture of benediction to a group of people kneeling before him. In Renaissance art, by contrast, infants and children began to look and behave differently from adults. Children were sometimes shown playing with toys (Koops, 1996). Not only does the infant Christ begin to look more like a real baby, but we also see the emergence of secular paintings of everyday family life and portraits of individual children.

The Enlightenment

By the eighteenth century, new ideas about the value of human life, dignity, and freedom had begun to emerge, a shift of consciousness called the Enlightenment. In France, for example, Jean-Jacques Rousseau (1712–1778) argued that childhood was a time of special privilege, that children bring goodness, not original sin, into the world, and that education should be sensitive to the needs and inclinations of the infant and young child. The social movement Rousseau represented was called **romanticism**. Its followers included such great English romantic poets as William Wordsworth (1770–1850), who wrote of childhood in idealized terms.

> Behold the Child among his new-born blisses,
> A six years' darling of pygmy size!
> See, where 'mid work of his own hand he lies,
> Fretted by sallies of his mother's kisses,
> With light upon him from his father's eyes!
>
> (From "Intimations of Immortality from
> Recollections of Early Childhood," in
> Williams 1952, 263)

William Blake (1757–1827), another English poet, rejected these simple romantic notions of innocence. In a poem called "The Scoffers," Blake suggested that the scientific achievements of Sir Isaac Newton were far more lasting intellectual milestones than the mocking voice of Rousseau. Charles Dickens was another author who rejected romanticism. Instead of depicting childhood in nineteenth-century England as a time of happy contentment, in *Oliver Twist* and other famous stories he courageously exposed the effects of disease, poverty, child abuse, and child labor for all to see.

All of these writers revealed a new concern for the individual and for the value of children, but they disagreed about what was "natural" compared to what needed to be provided for the child's healthy development. The English philosopher John Locke (1632–1704) accepted the importance of early education for children but believed that children needed more structure than the romantics advocated. Locke is known for his rational approach to education, which was decidedly not a romantic one, because he thought children needed specific guidance and discipline. Beginning with the assumption that the infant's mind is a *tabula rasa*, a blank slate on which anything could be written, Locke argued that education should provide the skills to make rational choices. The philosophical movement to which he belonged is called **empiricism**.

Both Rousseau and Locke revived the ancient Greek ideals of the body's importance in healthy moral development. Locke wrote that "a sound mind in a sound body, is a short but full description of a happy state in this world." Rousseau suggested that children should "run, jump, and shout to their heart's content." Their ideas were carried into educational practice by nineteenth-century educational reformers in Europe and North America, who made sure that school curricula offered art, music, and physical education (Friedrich-Cofer, 1986).

The romantic ideas of freedom and happiness combined with the empiricist ideas of reason and realism to create the philosophical foundations for the revolutions in France and the United States. This period also saw the rise in society of the value of the individual. It had been the custom in the past to give a newborn the same name as an older sibling, or the name of a sibling who had died. Such practices gave way in the eighteenth century to a newfound respect for the individuality of the child. Not only did advice books for parents proliferate, but by 1800 a wide range of inexpensive books were being published exclusively for young children. There was a corresponding recognition of the importance of the nuclear family and the maintenance of a private and sacred family home.

Domesticity became a value for the first time. During the American colonial period, the main value of the family was to raise children according to the family's particular beliefs and values. Many of these families came to the New World specifically to practice their own beliefs, away from the conservatism and religious persecution then pervasive in Europe (Clarke-Stewart, 1998). These values of individuality, autonomy, and self- determination had never before existed in the history of the world, and they changed how adults conceptualized the meaning and value of infancy and childhood.

These ideas also led in the nineteenth century to the growth of social responsibility toward infants and children and the rise of the idea of the child as an integral part of the definition of the family. The "discovery" of the child was due to urban forces in Europe and North America that segregated the family from the workplace, defined the mother's role as major supervisor of the domestic scene, and allowed love or sentiment (rather than family inheritance or economic well-being) to be the bond holding the family together (Hareven, 1985).

Educators in the nineteenth century continued to emphasize the importance of the young child's body in the development of the whole individual. Children who were obese, physically awkward, or handicapped could expect to get guidance from the school. The curriculum included free expression and creativity for the body, such as gymnastics and dance. Team sports and other exercise programs were meant to lay the foundation for the continuation of physical exercise through adulthood. Students were expected to understand the principles of health and hygiene. These programs grew out of the Greco-Roman and Enlightenment emphasis on the importance of the body as well as the mind (Friedrich-Cofer, 1986).

Not only did the child emerge as an individual during this period, but the role of full-time mother and housewife appeared on the historical stage for the very first time. It may be shocking for people in Western cultures in the twenty-first century to realize that the idea of a loving mother taking full-time care of an infant is a very recent cultural invention brought about by the rise of the nuclear family. For most of human history, infants were raised by many different caregivers, such as nurses, siblings, and other relatives.

It should be noted, however, that the development of this segregated nuclear family and its full-time mother was at first confined to the white middle class. Families from other classes and ethnic and racial groups preserved the preindustrial extended family, in which love, work, and education all took place within the home, and child care was shared by all family members. Women worked in the fields and in the home in the company of their babies, just as they had done for most of human history. Changes in the family have not occurred uniformly in all parts of American society, and these cultural patterns still account for many of the differences among families today (Hareven, 1982). Other cultural and economic forces have led most recently to the decline of the nuclear family, the reemergence of extended families and communal living, non-parental childcare, and the rise of single-parent families.

Social changes in the nineteenth century led to the growing awareness of the public's responsibility for the welfare and development of infants. Although the first English- language pediatric textbook appeared in 1545, welfare and medical institutions devoted exclusively to children did not open in Europe and the United States until the 1850s, around the same time as the rise of immunization and the pasteurization of milk. Maternal deaths during childbirth declined in this period due to the invention of anesthesia and procedures for sterilizing medical instruments (Greenleaf, 1978).

These medical advances further solidified the family by reducing infant mortality. As each child could be counted on to live a healthy life, families began to consciously reduce the number of children so as to invest more emotional energy in each child. By the middle of the nineteenth century, infancy and childhood had emerged in the public mind as a separate and valuable stage of life (Hareven, 1985). Manufactured baby dolls first appeared in Europe in 1825. In 1840, half of all three-year-olds in Massachusetts were attending infant schools, a practice that later declined because experts began to doubt the wisdom of sending such young children to school (Clarke-Stewart, 1998). The first public playground was developed in Boston in 1885 (a few heaps of sand dumped in a vacant lot), but by 1915, there were well-planned public playgrounds in 430 U.S. cities (Blank & Klig, 1982; Greenleaf, 1978; Zeitz, 1969).

Imagine what it must have been like to raise a baby in North America or Europe before 1850. The pain of childbirth could be helped by home remedies and the advice of a midwife, but there was no protection from serious problems and severe pain. Women could not be sure if they would survive childbirth, and many husbands were left without a wife and mother to raise the new baby. Infants died frequently of unknown (at the time) causes. Daily life with the baby was also much harder than it is today. There were no disposable diapers, no manufactured toys, and no baby foods you could buy. Parents had to make the infant's clothing, diapers, toys, and food from scratch. A baby gets a lot of diapers dirty in a day, and there were no washers and driers. In fact, cotton fabric did not become widely available until the early nineteenth century (the textile mills of that period contributed to the exploitation of child labor, as depicted in the novels of Charles Dickens, among others). Most clothing before that time was made of wool and was hot and heavy. If you were among the few who were wealthy, you could hire a servant and a wet nurse to care for and feed the baby, although wet-nursing declined rapidly at the end of the nineteenth century because maternal love was deemed better for children. For most families, however, having a baby affected all aspects of their lives. There were no readily available forms of contraception, so most women gave birth regularly every three to five years.

INFANTS ENTER THE WORLD OF SCIENCE

The beginning of the twentieth century saw the rise of the scientific study of infant development. Earlier debates over romanticism versus empiricism were replaced by discussions about the contributions to development of **nature** (genes) versus **nurture** (environments). (See Chapter 2 for a discussion of the role of genes and environments in the emergence of individual differences between infants.) Arnold Lucius Gesell (1880–1961), working out of the romantic tradition, thought that the orderly changes seen in early development were specified by the genes. In this regard, Gesell also followed the ideas of Charles Darwin, whose theory of the evolution of species will be discussed in greater detail in Chapter 2. The genetic timetable for the patterning of development was called **maturation**. Gesell made a career out of the careful measurements of developmental changes in size, motor skill, and behavior in infants and young children. He was the first scientist to use a one-way mirror to observe infants unobtrusively and the first to use film to record their behavior.

Because Gesell believed in genetic maturation, he cared little about individual differences and focused instead on the "average" child. This created anxiety in parents who read his works and discovered that their own children walked or talked later than the average child. Even today, most parents want their babies to be above average. We now know that babies vary widely in the ages at which they attain developmental milestones, and that most babies—whether slow or fast—develop normally. There is, in fact, no such thing as an "average child," since all children are unique, according to the perspective of the European Enlightenment. The normal and expected variability between infants will be discussed in later chapters.

all children are unique

Albert Baby

A North American family and their baby in 1913. Note the children's elegant clothing. well-educated parents probably were aware of the competing ideas of Watson's behaviorism and Gesell's maturationism.

Photo: Corbis

In the empiricist tradition, and contrary to Gesell, John B. Watson (1878–1958) believed that children could be trained to do almost anything, given the right kind of "nurture." He demonstrated this by doing studies in which he taught small children to be afraid of cuddly animals by making loud noises whenever they touched the animals. This type of research would be considered unethical today. Nevertheless, Watson's work suggested that all our behavior, even the most basic and innocent, could possibly be controlled by outside forces. This kind of belief, in extreme form, still persists in some science fiction stories of a future in which an all-powerful government manipulates every aspect of learning and development to produce robot-like citizens who are slaves to the rulers. Recently developed dynamic systems theories (see Chapter 2), on the contrary, suggest that not all behavior can be controlled or predicted. Human life is full of surprises and unexpected twists and turns.

Watson nevertheless left a lasting imprint on North American society. The waves of immigrants who landed on the shores of the United States and Canada all believed that they could make a new life for themselves and their children. Watson's idea that anyone could succeed regardless of past history or genetic heritage sustained the hopes of many of the new arrivals. Watson placed responsibility for a child's outcome directly on the shoulders of the parents; if the child failed, it was the parents' fault. He encouraged parents to avoid kissing and holding their babies in order to make them independent individuals. Today we recognize that a wide range of parenting styles is acceptable and appropriate for babies, and later chapters review individual and cultural differences in infant-care patterns. Systems theories of development (Chapter 2) propose that the family, parent, and infant all make important contributions to developmental outcomes. Human development is not so simple that blame or credit can be assigned to a single individual.

Sigmund Freud (1856–1939) presented strong counterarguments to Watson and Gesell. Freud focused on psychological experience rather than on behavior. He recognized that all infants expe rienced emotional highs and lows and that even infants felt the need for love and possessed pow erful desires. Freud's daughter, Anna, devoted most of her life to bringing her father's insights out of the adult psychoanalytic session and into the real lives of parents and children. Anna Freud taught parents to hold and cuddle babies and to be patient while babies discovered and tried to manage their own desires in appropriate ways (A. Freud, 1965). Nurture was important here too, but only to the extent that it encouraged the child's nature to blossom. Unfortunately, Anna Freud too faulted parents for their children's developmental problems—in this case, for giving them too little attention and affection and for "selfishly" not understanding the situation from the child's point of view. Even the most understanding parent sometimes has bad days, and there are many times when infants are in fact incomprehensible. Sigmund Freud will be discussed more in Chapter 2.

The scientific theories of infant care and infant development spread rapidly through Western culture in the nineteenth and twentieth centuries because of the rise of the mass media and electronic communication. Urbanization and the automobile created an increasingly mobile and nuclear family, separated from grandparents and dependent on the advice of child-care experts. Society thus created a demand for better trained and better supported behavioral scientists who could share their expertise with a public hungry for rational approaches to child rearing.

Let us return to the question raised earlier in the chapter. Why is infancy even more in the public mind today than it was fifty years ago? Although there is no single answer, it may be a reaction to the rapid growth of scientific approaches to psychology and human development since the 1960s. This growth was inspired in part by the Cold War, when Western leaders decided that the education and training of their citizens was the best way to combat the technological threats of advanced weapon systems.

The scientific revolution in behavioral research on infancy during these years was very much in the empiricist tradition, but unlike Locke's focus on the whole child's mind and body, the research of the 1970s emphasized infant learning and cognitive development. Cognitive and learning theories rose in importance. The publication in 1973 of Stone, Smith, and Murphy's *The Competent Infant* reflected a desire to discover ever-earlier signs of intelligence in infants. Parents strove to train their infants to achieve the maximum mental potential at the earliest possible age. This was based on the belief that education, rather than natural endowment, was the best guarantee of child success (Clarke-Stewart, 1998). Many parents placed their infants into tightly structured study programs to teach them reading, word learning, music, and mathematics before they reached the age of three years.

This new scientific focus on childhood, for all its benefits, came at a price for children. The research became more focused on using quantitative measures of children's growth and on reporting statistical averages. Much of the research on children in the nineteenth and early twentieth centuries had focused on individual children using qualitative case studies (see the Research Methods section in this chapter). The individual child became lost in the quest for scientific generalizability and validity.

Another consequence that affected the lives of children directly is that the emphasis on intelligence and mental development led to a steady decline in a balanced view of the whole child as needing education not only for mind but for body, emotions, and social connections. According to one historian, "as the individual child and adolescent with bodies faded from view, many of the humanistic ties which bound scientist, teacher, family, and child faded with them" (Friedrich-Cofer, 1986, p. 133). Children's progress began to be reported in the form of standardized test scores, rather than individualized assessment of mental and physical health. Physical education, music, and art programs that had been created for all children declined or disappeared entirely from schools, replaced by competitive athletics and music programs designed for an elite group of talented students. This pattern continues today in the United States with the federal No Child Left Behind (NCLB) Act, which mandates that students need to have a minimum score on standardized tests for the school to qualify for federal funding. This policy has created more drop-outs, especially of minority youth, in order for the school to maintain its scores, with a continued erosion of programs for the enrichment of the body and spirit (Cofer, 2008).

This focus on the early structuring of the infant's intellectual growth was followed in the 1980s by an interest in targeting infants who were at risk for developmental difficulties, such as those who were premature, handicapped, or victims of abuse. The focus on risk was associated with the idea that all humans could become perfect if given the right kind of child rearing. For healthy and wealthy infants, this meant a quest for developing a "superbaby" and giving children a "head start" (Clarke-Stewart, 1998). It also brought the ideal of a "supermom," who could be employed outside the home and at the same time be a great mother and a wonderful and loving wife. The 1980s also saw a rise in the amount of time fathers spent with their babies.

More recently, however, romantic ideas have returned to scientific studies in psychology and in infant development (Schneider, 1998). Perhaps in reaction to what was seen as an overemphasis on intellectual achievement, since the 1990s we have seen a rise in studies of parent-child relationships, emotional development and attachment, the role of the body and touch, and communication and language. Of course, the more rational approaches to infant development continue to grow in such fields as cognitive neuroscience and behavior genetics. On the other hand, some of the trends of the 1970s and 1980s, which focused on babies growing up and getting smart as quickly as possible, were replaced by ideas about slowing down and appreciating the beauty of each phase

of a baby's life and the specialness of being a baby.

It may be enlightening to realize that the view of science as quantitative and the focus on the study of the mind to the exclusion of that of the body is a relatively recent cultural invention that temporarily replaced a long Western cultural history of belief and practice in the holistic integration of body and mind. In the next few sections, a conceptualization of infancy based on these scientific approaches will be discussed, followed by a review of some of the research methods that have been devised for the study of infant development.

Conceptualizing Infancy

How you conceptualize infancy depends on what you want to know about infants. If you are a painter, a poet, or a filmmaker, infants may serve as metaphors for divinity or innocence. If you are a clinician, contacting one's infancy experiences and traumas is a source of healing and new psychological and physical growth. Scientists strive to understand infants in their own right, detached from social and cultural conceptions about infancy. Many scientists admit that they, as products of their own society and culture, can never rid themselves completely of cultural bias. Later in this chapter, I will discuss different scientific methods that either ignore the cultural beliefs of the researcher or take them explicitly into account.

Stages and Changes in Infant Development

The definition of infancy includes how we mark the important developmental transition points during the infancy period. In reality, infancy is a slow and continuous process of **developmental change**. Not all changes that we observe in infants are developmental changes. A baby can change from being happy to being angry, but we would not call such changes developmental, since the child frequently changes back and forth between these two emotions. Developmental change is characterized by the following three features:

- *Developmental changes are <u>not reversible</u>*. Developmental change is a reorganization of the entire person such that the earlier patterns of behavior, thought, and feeling cannot be easily recognized or recaptured.

- *Developmental changes are <u>stable</u>*. Organized patterns that emerge in development persist over relatively long periods of months or years.

- *Developmental changes <u>occur in sequence</u>*. Development occurs in an orderly sequence that is similar across infants.

The progression of language development—for example, crying, cooing, babbling, one-word speech, and multiword speech—has all the required features of developmental change. These changes reflect a reorganization of the whole infant in relation to the social world. Once babies learn to talk, for example, they can express their needs more clearly and participate more fully as partners in relationships. They can acquire conceptual thinking and social understanding. The change is not reversible, since babies rarely go back to simply crying when they need something. The only <u>evidence for reversibility</u> in development would be in the case of <u>neurological damage</u> due to <u>accident or disease</u>. Even here, what is occurring is not, strictly speaking, reversibility, but rather a different reorganization of the whole person that takes account of the deficit.

The developmental progression from crying to speaking also shows stable and persistent patterns called **developmental stages** that last for long periods. The period during which infants cry to get their needs met lasts for three or four months at the beginning of the first year. One-word speech begins around ten months and lasts almost one year for most babies. Even though development is a continuous process of change, people can recognize that there also appear to be persistent stages. Stages also have the characteristic of occurring in an ordered sequence. Few infants can speak in whole sentences without first passing through the period of one-word speech.

Each culture views the stage divisions of an infant's life differently. The Alor people of the Lesser Sundra Islands do not even count the infant's development in days or months, but rather in terms of a series of stages of development. The first stage lasts from birth to the first smile, the second from smiling to sitting up alone or crawling, and the third from this point to the onset of walking. The Chagga of Tanganyika apply different names to infants depending upon their stage of development. A newborn is called *mnangu*, or "incomplete," a *mkoku* is "one who fills the lap," and a *mwana* is an infant before the age of three years (Mead & Newton, 1967). These linguistic labels are comparable to the terms *newborn*, *infant*, and *toddler* in English.

Parents and other infant caregivers may use another type of division for the first three years. They may be more concerned about the ages at which infants become capable of independent play with other infants, the age of the beginning of toilet training and the onset of bowel control, or the age at which infants become more relaxed when separated from their parents. Developmental scientists tend to divide stages according to milestones having to do with one of the areas mentioned in the last section, such as the progression in communication from crying to speech. Another example is the motor development sequence.

RESEARCH METHODS IN DEVELOPMENTAL SCIENCE

What causes people to develop along different pathways and to acquire different ways of experiencing the world? Each culture has its own theory of the formation of individual differences. As explained earlier, for example, the ancient Greeks and Romans believed that exposing an infant to a variety of fearful and stressful events early in life would make the child less fearful and more emotionally balanced later. Nineteenth-century Europeans believed just the opposite—that protecting the child from fear-producing experiences was the best way to create an outgoing child (Kagan, Kearsley, & Zelazo, 1978). Which one of these "folk" theories is more correct? How could you decide?

The position taken in this book is that while folk theories are important parts of people's beliefs that structure the way people behave, scientific theories are a viable alternative for conceptualizing the processes that create developmental change and individual differences. The reason is that the scientist relies on many sources of evidence (folk theories may be based only on experience within one's own family), tries to separate what is repeatable and stable from what is coincidental (folk theories tend to infer general patterns from a small number of instances), and attempts to rid observations of bias (folk theories often embody what the observer hopes to see or believes should occur, rather than what actually does happen).

This does not mean that scientists always succeed in reaching these ideals. As research in the behavioral sciences has returned to a more romantic approach, many scientists are beginning to question this ideal. No scientific study can be flawless, and all science is infused with the values and perspectives of individual scientists. Some scientists have attempted to put themselves into a scientific study as participant observers using qualitative, as contrasted with quantitative, research methods.

Quantitative research methods represent complex behavioral processes using a numerical index called a variable. **Qualitative research**, on the other hand, attempts to capture the meaning or quality of the behavior. Qualitative researchers use verbal or pictorial descriptions of behavior rather than numbers, and they try to understand how their own perspectives influence the subjects and shape the findings and interpretations. They make explicit the idea that science is one type of human interpersonal relationship. These qualitative researchers are like folk theorists in that they do not divorce their own beliefs from the observations, but they maintain a scientific stance by taking multiple perspectives and entertaining alternative interpretations. In the following sections, traditional quantitative research methods will be discussed, including methods for experimental and observational research. This will be followed by a section that discusses qualitative research methods.

Jean Piaget (1896–1980), one of the founders of the field of developmental psychology (Chapter 2), began his career in research on children by making extensive written notes, often on a daily basis, about the behavior of his three infant children. Piaget not only observed natural behavior, but tried out little experiments to test alternate interpretations of what the children could do. At one point, Piaget tried to determine whether his eight-month-old daughter Jacqueline (J.) was capable of imitating mouth movements and sounds.

In the following example, Jacqueline seemed to imitate her father's biting movements. Or did she? Piaget was not sure whether Jacqueline only appeared to imitate him because he had started out by imitating movements she could already make.

J. was moving her lips as she bit on her jaws. I did the same thing, and she stopped and watched me attentively…. J. began to imitate me an hour later…. In order to understand this new development, two circumstances must be noted. Firstly, for some days she had not merely imitated sounds for their own sake but had watched the mouth of the model with great attention. Secondly, as she moved her lips, J. began by making a slight noise with her saliva… and I had imitated this sound at the outset. Her interest in the movements of the mouth was thus clearly due to interest in the production of sound. [Three days later] I resumed the experiment without making any sound and without J. herself having made the movement beforehand. She watched my lips moving and then distinctly imitated me three times, keeping her eyes fixed on my mouth. (Piaget, 1962, pp. 30–31)

EXPERIMENTAL RESEARCH METHODS

In this example, Piaget combined observational research with an experiment. An **experiment** is a research study in which one aspect of the situation is manipulated while all other aspects are held constant or controlled. In this case, in order to discover Jacqueline's ability to imitate mouth movements on her own, Piaget waited for a time when Jacqueline had not made the movement spontaneously for some time, and he did not produce any sound when he made the movements himself. The prior condition (the child makes no similar spontaneous movement and the adult does not imitate the child) and the presentation of the adult model (absence of sound) were controlled. The experimental manipulation is the presence or absence of a movement-only adult model.

In modern versions of Piaget's famous imitation experiment, many other aspects of the situation are controlled: the position in which the child is sitting, the behavior of the adult model, the familiarity of the infant with the adult, and the observation procedures. The following are some standard experimental procedures.

Control groups that do not receive any manipulation are compared to a group of infants who receive the experimental manipulation. Alternatively, different groups can be compared if each receives a different type of manipulation. These are called **contrast groups**. In imitation research, for example, different contrast groups of infants are presented with a different model (tongue protrusion, mouth movement, or a facial expression). If imitation occurs, the frequency of tongue protrusion following the model should be highest in the group that has seen the tongue-protrusion model. This procedure controls for the fact that most babies produce tongue protrusion spontaneously, so that some tongue protrusion would be seen in all the groups.

Random assignment is used to determine which subjects belong to each experimental group. A flip of a coin or some other random process is used to assign subjects to groups. In some cases, it is unethical to use random assignment in a study. For example, suppose we want to compare the effects on language development of differences between mothers in their speech to infants. We obviously cannot randomly assign mothers to infants.

Experiments generally have two important measures, also called variables. The **independent variable** is that which is controlled or manipulated by the experimenter. In the case of imitation studies, the independent variable is the type of model given to the infant. The independent variable is the presumed cause of the phenomenon; that is, different types of models are presumed to cause the infant to imitate different movements. The **dependent variable** is the presumed effect or outcome behavior that is observed in response to the changes in the independent variable. In the case of the imitation study, the dependent variable is the frequency of different actions of the infant, such as the frequency of mouth movements or tongue protrusions. The dependent variable is presumed to be affected by the causal independent variable such that manipulations of the independent variable should lead to systematic changes in the dependent variable.

Infants are not as easily studied as older children or adults. Infants cannot describe their inner states, take standardized written tests, or respond to interview questions. Because of the difficulty of working with infants, special procedures have been devised to measure their behavior.

Standardized Experimental Procedures for Use with Infants

In **paired-preference procedures**, infants are shown two visual stimuli side by side, or they hear sounds presented to one or the other ear. Researchers then try to determine which of the two stimuli is preferred by the infants. During such procedures, infants are either held quietly by their mothers or sit in an infant seat in a darkened room to reduce competing sources of stimulation. Directly in front of the infant there is usually a blank screen on which is mounted a display of flashing lights. A small peephole in this screen, invisible to the infant, allows an observer to look directly at the infant's face and judge where the infant is looking and for how long (Fantz, 1961). In a more sophisticated variation of this procedure, an invisible infrared light is reflected off the infant's cornea, and the angle of reflection is detected by an electronic sensor. The angle of reflection can be translated electrically to determine the precise position of the infant's gaze (Haith, Bergman, & Moore, 1977). The latter procedure has also been used to examine the developmental changes in the way infants scan visual objects.

At the beginning of an experimental trial (a presentation of one pair of stimuli), the light display flashes to attract the infant's attention to the center. When the infant is judged to be looking at the center, the flashing lights are turned off and the paired visual display is presented, usually by a rear-screen slide projector (for example, mother on left, stranger on right). The length of time the infant looks left or right is recorded before the visual displays go off. On the next trial, the flashing lights are again used. After the infant looks to the center, the mother appears on the right and the stranger on the left. The order of presentation of the stimuli is counterbalanced across trials to eliminate any bias due to an infant's preference for turning to one side or another. Preference is determined by the average across trials of the length of time the infant looks to its mother and to a stranger.

Paired-preference methods have been used in many research studies that will be reviewed in this book. Using this method, for example, infants in the first month of life have been found to prefer the sound of their mother's voice to that of another woman and the odor of their mother's breast milk to the milk smell of another woman (Chapter 4). Five-month-old infants prefer a video image of their own legs as they would appear normally to the infant, compared to a manipulated video image in which the left and right legs have been reversed.

A second procedure for the assessment of infant psychological experience uses repeated exposure to the same visual or auditory stimulus. Each time the stimulus is repeated is one trial. If a researcher repeatedly shows the same picture to a baby—say, a picture of a face with a sad expression—the baby spends less and less time looking at the picture with each new presentation, acting

as though he was getting bored with the same old thing. The gradual decline in looking time over repeated trials of the same stimulus is known as **habituation**, which results from increasing familiarity with the stimulus.

Researchers select some minimum amount of looking time as the criterion to decide when the baby has become habituated to a stimulus. For example, if the baby's initial looks at a facial expression last about thirty seconds, a reasonable habituation criterion for subsequent trials might be five seconds. Once the baby has reached the criterion looking time, researchers change the picture or sound; in our example, from the face with a sad expression to the same face with a happy expression. If the baby cannot tell the difference between the two expressions, he or she will go on looking at the happy expression for durations shorter than the habituation criterion. However, if the baby can detect a change, the infant will begin to look longer at the happy face than at the last presentation of the sad face. This abrupt increase in looking time after a change in the stimulus is called **recovery**. Field et al. (1982) used this technique with newborns to see if they could differentiate between happy, sad, and surprised facial expressions. Remarkably, they could.

A final standardized procedure we will review is called the **response-contingent procedure**, which is often used in studies of auditory and taste perception. In this technique, infants are trained to change their behavior if they can detect certain features of the sounds or tastes. Once taught, infants will alter their behavior in order to hear their favorite sound or to receive their preferred taste.

DeCasper and Fifer (1980) used this technique with an automatic suck recorder. The suck recorder is a pacifier that is connected to a pressure transducer (which converts varying degrees of pressure into electrical impulses), which in turn is connected to recording equipment. Each infant in the study was equipped with a set of headphones and a suck recorder. After a two-minute adjustment period, the infant's sucking was recorded for five minutes with no sounds coming through the headphones.

During this period, the experimenter computed the median duration of the pauses between sucking bouts (see Chapter 4). If you make a list of the durations of all the pauses observed for the infant, the median is the duration at the midpoint of the list: half the durations are above the median and half below.

In the experimental period, infants sucked as usual, such that half of their pauses were below the median and half above. When the experimenters detected a pause that was longer than the median interval, they presented the infants with the recorded voice of either their mother (reading a segment of a Dr. Seuss story) or a stranger (reading the same segment). Five of the infants were randomly assigned to a group that could evoke their mother's voice by pausing their sucking for longer than the median pause length and evoke the stranger's voice by pausing for less than the median pause interval. The other five infants had the reverse conditions.

Because the presentation of the adult voices was made contingent upon the duration of the sucking pause, infants quickly learned that by speeding up or slowing down their sucking, they could produce one or the other voice. If the infants had a preference for one or the other voice, they could then systematically shift their pause length to "suck for" that voice. Eight of the ten infants showed a tendency to shift their pause length to produce their own mother's voice. Four of the infants were retested twenty-four hours later in a situation in which the criterion for obtaining the mother's voice was reversed from the previous day. All four continued to suck for their mother's voice.

Babies can tell us very little about themselves using ordinary means of communication. These remarkably creative research methods, therefore, are very useful for finding out more about what infants know. The main problem with all these techniques is that the failure of an infant to respond does not necessarily mean the infant *cannot* respond. The infant may recognize the difference and *choose* not to respond. Thus, it is necessary to test the same infants repeatedly. One could also use a relatively large sample of infants with the expectation that if a sizable number of infants at a particular age can detect a difference, then infants at that age are in general capable of detecting a difference.

Physiological Recording

Because infants cannot report on their internal states, physiological activity is one method of discovering more about what is going on inside the baby. Please note, however, that physiological recording can be used for both experimental and observational research. The level of arousal in the autonomic nervous system (ANS) can be measured with a variety of techniques. Heart rate recordings tell us about the level of the infant's physiological arousal associated with particular types of observed behavior and in different situations. An example of the use of heart rate in research is in the measurement of whether infants can perceive depth. Gibson and Walk (1960) discovered that infants older than six months would not continue to crawl to their mothers if they suddenly saw a deep drop-off between themselves and the mother. The drop-off was created by a trough several feet deep that interrupted the surface on which the infant was crawling. To protect unwary infants from harm, the researchers covered the trough with plexiglass, creating the so-called "visual cliff" device.

The visual cliff could not be used to study depth perception in infants under six months because it required that the infants be able to crawl. When attached to heart rate monitors and placed next to the visual cliff, however, infants as young as two months showed some changes in their heart rate indicating moderate arousal (though not fear) and thus perception of the depth (Campos, Langer, & Krowitz, 1970). It was not until infants began to crawl that they showed heart rate changes similar to those measured during a fearful response. Thus, although two-month-olds perceive the depth, they must have the experience of crawling around in the real world to be able to appreciate the depth with an appropriate level of fear (Campos, 1976).

Behavior can be automatically recorded using a number of techniques. Gross motor activity has been recorded with a device called an actometer, which can be fixed to the infant's clothing or attached to a crib mattress. It records the number of position shifts made by the infant as a function of time. Infant sounds can be studied with a sound spectrograph that shows the duration, pitch, and frequency of vocalizations. Changes in sucking, respiration, and gaze direction can also be detected by electronic devices and recorded as a continuous function of time.

Hormonal activity can be recorded from blood tests, but some hormones can be detected more easily from saliva. Saliva contains the hormone cortisol, which has been shown to increase in response to environmental stresses, such as during medical treatments, and to decrease during periods of relaxation.

Central nervous system (CNS) activity has been measured with a variety of techniques. Electrodes are fastened to the infant's scalp with a small amount of petroleum jelly. The electrodes detect the minute changes in electrical activity inside the brain without hurting the infant. Because the currents generated in the brain are small, infants must be presented with a particular stimulus—a sound or a visual object—many times, and the electrical responses must be averaged by a computer in order to detect the existence of the "signal" of the response to the stimulus against the "noise" of normal spontaneous brain activity. The resulting averages are called averaged **event-related potentials** (ERPs). Although such techniques cannot be used to monitor an infant's ongoing mental state, they can tell us whether there is a general ability to detect a stimulus. ERP methods have also been used to diagnose brain disorders in the form of abnormal patterns of electrical activity or lack of predicted responses.

One advantage of ERP research is that it shows the amount of brain activity when the infant is doing ordinary tasks. Other methods, called **neuroimaging** techniques, create pictures of the brain showing where in the brain an activity is taking place. Two commonly used methods are CT (computed tomography) and fMRI (functional magnetic resonance) to track changes in the brain's metabolic function. CT scans are gradually being replaced by fMRI for infancy research and diagnosis of brain damage. CT scans use X-rays but do not require sedation of the infant. fMRI requires the infant to be sedated in order to lie completely still inside of a large tubular chamber with a great deal of noise, but the resolution is considerably better (Hoon & Melhem, 2000).

Although physiological recording devices allow us to detect information we could not otherwise observe, and although they reduce human error, they have important limitations. For one thing, we can never be sure of the precise meaning of a change in a physiological measure. Many events other than emotion or perception could trigger a change in heart rate or brain activity. Second, physiological activity is itself a response. Just because the heart rate changes when the infant is afraid does not mean the heart is the source of the emotion. All bodily systems are intimately linked together as a complex system such that small changes in one part can have major repercussions throughout the entire system. There is no way to say when and where a response originates or is encoded in the body.

OBSERVATIONAL RESEARCH METHODS

The inability to randomly assign subjects to groups is a major limitation in the application of the experimental method to infant studies. Many of the important questions in infancy research—such as the effects of prematurity and of variations in parental styles of child care—cannot be studied experimentally. We cannot randomly assign infants to be premature, and we cannot randomly assign particular types of parents to particular types of infants. We use, instead, the natural variations within the existing population of infants and mothers.

Methods that rely on natural variations rather than random assignment to create contrast groups

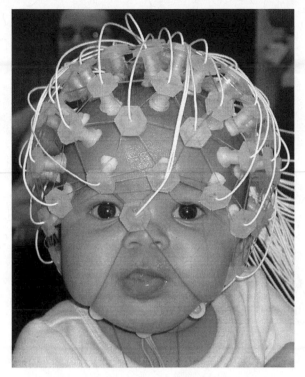

Neuroimaging techniques for use with infants need to be safe and easy to use with a baby. This cap measures ERPs.

Photo courtesy of Charles Nelson, Developmental Medicine Laboratory of Cognitive Neuroscience, Harvard University Children's Hospital.

are called **observational research** methods. The obvious advantage of observational research is that we can study many issues of grave importance to our understanding of early human development that would be unethical or impossible to study experimentally. The problem with observational studies is that the variable on which the groups are assigned (the style of parental child rearing) may also correlate with other factors (such as the mother's social skills and general expressiveness). If this occurs, it is impossible to say which factor—child rearing, social skills, or expressiveness—is the cause of differences in infant behavior.

In most cases involving human infancy, however, observational studies are all we can do. As discussed later in this book, researchers have developed ways to examine the mutual influences of many potential causes that enter into an observational study. Observational studies can be either longitudinal or cross-sectional. In a **longitudinal study**, researchers follow the same group of children as they get older. Longitudinal studies are important for determining how particular early experiences of individuals affect their later devel-

opment and also for revealing patterns of change over time. Change is measured against the individual's own record of growth. The disadvantage is that the researcher must wait for the child to grow, although this takes less time for infants than for older children because infants grow at a faster rate; few researchers can find the research funding to support such long-term efforts. Another problem is **attrition,** which occurs when subjects of a longitudinal study drop out of the study before they complete the entire period of observation. Not only does attrition lower the number of subjects in a study, but researchers worry whether the subjects who remain are different from those who drop out, making the study less representative of the larger population.

One of the methods most commonly used today to study developmental change is a **cross-sectional study**, in which the researcher selects a different group of children at each age period of interest. Cross-sectional studies have the advantage of giving us a sense of age change in development without having to wait for the children to grow up. An additional advantage is that researchers who observe children from only two or three different age groups have more time to collect data from a large number of children and thus may find patterns of between-individual variation in behavioral characteristics and age of attainment of developmental milestones. Thus, while cross-sectional studies allow us to make generalizations about groups of infants, they cannot tell us how individual infants develop over time.

Observational research, like experimental research, can be quantitative. This means that observations are transformed in numerical indices called variables. The variable that is the presumed cause—such as child-rearing styles—is called the **predictor variable**. The presumed effect—child behavior—is called the **outcome variable**. There is an analogy between independent variables and predictor variables, and between dependent variables and outcome variables.

Reducing Bias in Research

Regardless of whether one does observational or experimental research, caution must be taken to assure that variables reflect accurate and unbiased measures of the phenomenon. **Reliability** and validity procedures are ways of attempting to reduce bias in quantitative research. Reliability is a measure of the consistency with which an assessment procedure is applied. If one is trying to measure an infant's preference for looking at her mother compared to an unfamiliar woman, observers may be asked to record the duration of time the infant spends looking at each adult. If two people, working independently, are asked to judge the duration of the same event, the measurement of duration is reliable to the extent that the two observers agree with each other.

Validity is the degree to which the procedure accurately measures what it is intended to measure. For example, one might ask if the duration of time the infant spends looking at the mother versus that spent looking at the stranger is a valid measure of the infant's preference for one or the other. A baby may look longer at an unfamiliar face because it is

new and the baby is curious about it, not because the baby prefers to look at that face. In this case, the duration of time the infant looks at the stranger would not be a valid measure of preference for the stranger. To test whether the duration of the infant's looking is a valid measure of preference or of curiosity, one would have to compare this measure with other measures of preference and curiosity. An additional measure of preference might be the duration of time the infant smiles at and vocalizes to each adult. An additional measure of curiosity might be the duration of time the infant looks at pictures of novel compared to familiar objects.

To test the validity of the measure, a group of infants would have to be assessed on that measure and also on the other validating measures. The same infants, for example, would be tested to measure the duration of time they looked at the stranger compared to their mother. In addition, measures would be taken of the duration of time spent smiling at the stranger (a preference measure) and the duration of time spent looking at unfamiliar objects (a curiosity measure). If the babies who had high durations of time spent looking at the stranger also had high durations of time spent smiling at her, but low durations of time spent looking at unfamiliar objects (a curiosity measure), one could conclude that the duration measure of an infant's looking at a stranger is a valid measure of preference for the stranger. It could also turn out that high durations of time spent looking at the stranger are related to high durations of time spent looking at novel objects, suggesting that looking at the stranger is a valid measure of curiosity. Finally, it may be that there is no consistent relationship between the duration of time the infant looks at the stranger and the durations of the other two measures. If this happens, it means that looking at the stranger may sometimes reflect preference and sometimes curiosity. It cannot, therefore, be considered a valid measure of either one.

Another means of lowering research bias is to protect the outcomes of a study from the unintended influence of the subjects on the experimenters. This is usually accomplished by assuring that both the subjects and the experimenters are blind to the specific purpose of the research and to the group assignment of the subjects. **Blindness** in quantitative research refers to limiting the access of researchers and participants to knowledge that may bias the outcomes of the study. In a study on the relationship between infant language and mother's speech, for instance, experimenters who administer the tests of infant language should not be the same as those who observe the mother's speech, and they should not know anything about the mother's speech score. The mothers should not be aware of the precise measures and relationships being tested, although they might be told that they are participating in a study on infant language development.

Finally, bias in research can be reduced by assuring that the group of infants and parents who participate in a research study is representative of the larger population of infants (**representative research**). A study is representative if its conclusions can be applied to infants who were not direct participants in the study. Most infancy research is done with white, middle-class North American and European infants. It is important to ask whether these findings apply equally to infants from other ethnic groups, cultures, and socioeconomic groups. Research grants from the National Institutes of Health in the United States, which funds both medical and behavioral research on human subjects, cannot be obtained unless the subjects of the study represent both genders and a cross-section of ethnic groups.

Research Ethics and Informed Consent

Research ethics adopted by most institutions in North America require that human subjects give their informed consent to participate in research. **Informed consent** is a voluntary agreement to participate in a research study. It must be based on accurate information about the purpose, procedures, risks, and benefits of the research study

(Keith-Spiegel, 1983). Special provisions are required for research subjects who cannot give consent for themselves, specifically infants and small children. In these cases, one or both parents must sign the consent to participate. Parents are told about the possible risks and benefits of the research, both for themselves and for their infants.

In order to meet requirements of informed consent as well as the scientific requirement that subjects be blind to the purpose of the research, researchers usually tell subjects about the general purpose of the study but not about the specific measures to be used. Subjects must be told about all the procedures, but they need not be told about the specific purpose of the procedures. Most researchers will provide a debriefing session for subjects following the completion of their participation. During the debriefing, more details are provided, and all the subjects' questions should be answered frankly. In research using human subjects, researchers have the responsibility of designing studies of lasting value to society and respecting the rights and dignity of the individuals who volunteer their time to participate. Due to these ethical considerations in research, some of the early studies of infant behavior and development—such as John Watson's research in which he made infants fear cuddly animals—would not be allowed today.

Researchers must pledge to keep the subjects' identity confidential and to limit access to their data only to those persons directly involved with the research. There are several situations, however, in which confidentiality cannot be assured. In the event that the researchers observe behavior constituting child abuse, they are required by law to report it to the appropriate community agency. Also, researchers cannot protect their data if they are subpoenaed in a child-custody dispute. Parents need to be informed about these limits to confidentiality before they agree to participate. Fortunately, these situations rarely occur. In the past thirty-five years of doing infancy research with many hundreds of families, I have never had to violate a subject's confidentiality for these or any other reasons.

Methods of Observational Research

A large portion of research on infants involves the observation of their behavior in relatively natural circumstances without experimental control. Observing the ongoing behavior of infants is difficult because many things are happening at the same time. Imagine trying to write down everything that happens during a social interaction between two partners in the exact sequence in which it occurs, including not only what they say to each other, but all of the nonverbal social behaviors, such as looking, facial expressions, gestures, and body movements. **Microanalysis** is a research approach that focuses on recording and analyzing minute changes in behavior as they occur over some pre- determined period of time during an observation session.

Researchers have developed a number of techniques to simplify the task of microanalysis and to increase accuracy. First of all, it is important to be selective in what you want to observe. Since you cannot see everything, your choice should be guided by some conceptual framework. Suppose, for example, you wanted to observe how an infant interacted with her mother before and during the approach of an unfamiliar person. Based on the theory of infant attachment, we expect that the presence of a stranger may be associated with behavior categories such as the child approaching the mother, following the mother, and staying near the mother's side. Older infants may also ask about the stranger or ask to be picked up and held.

After choosing a list of relevant behavioral categories, the observer is trained to recognize each category until an acceptable level of inter-rater reliability can be obtained. **Coding** is the process by which observers record the presence or absence of the predefined categories as they are watching the research subjects during an observation session.

One relatively easy coding strategy is pencil-and-paper recording of live observations. When any one of the categories is seen, it is checked off on a sheet of paper on which the categories have been listed. Audio and video recordings can improve the accuracy of observational data. Once behavior is recorded on tape, observers can replay the tape as often as necessary to code the entire observation period. Videotapes can be made with a digital clock image in the corner of the screen so that elapsed time between behavior onsets and offsets can be recorded.

In addition to increasing the accuracy of observational research, videotape has been revolutionary in showing us things babies do that are not apparent in live observations. Hand movements and facial expressions of two-month-old infants often give a picture of disorganized or chaotic movement. Looking at them in slow motion on a videotape, however, one can see recognizable patterns of smiling, eyebrow raising, and finger pointing. Computers can be electronically interfaced with videotape players. A timing signal is recorded on the videotape. When the observer presses a key representing a particular behavior category, the computer automatically records and saves the category and the time of onset. The observer can ask the computer to fast-forward through the tape, stopping at all previously coded events in order to compare them or to do more detailed coding.

New methods have been devised for using the computer to automatically identify behavior from a videotape recording, without the need for an observer. The computer is programmed to recognize particular images, such as when an infant smiles, frowns, or moves his or her body in a particular way, and to record the onset and offset time as well as dynamic changes in intensity (Tian & Kanade, 2001). This is similar to the voice recognition programs often used in automatic telephone answering systems. Scientists hope that by using these tools for microanalysis, they will be better able to understand the complexity and dynamic changes in human communication.

A final type of observational research, called **macroanalysis**, focuses on the overall or summary features of behavior, rather than its details and sequences of occurrences. Macroanalysis is usually done with the use of a **rating scale**. A rating scale is a list of categories, usually ordered in a numerical sequence, which allows observers to differentiate the amount or quality of a particular type of observed behavior. In the example of a stranger approaching an infant described earlier, the microanalytic coding categories were discrete behaviors: approaching, following, and staying near the mother when a stranger is present. The observer recorded each category separately whenever it occurred and noted the onset and offset times. A macroanalytic rating scale for the entire interaction could be devised that would eliminate the need for detailed behavior records. For example, after watching the entire observation session of the infant with mother and stranger, an observer might rate the child on a scale of 1 to 5, where 1 is comfort with the stranger (not approaching or following the mother), 3 is some discomfort (maintaining a moderate distance from the mother), and 5 is extreme anxiety (clinging to the mother and following her closely).

Macroanalytic ratings are effective when the measure of interest to the research need not be equated to specific behaviors—in this case, only the overall level of comfort versus anxiety. Ratings are easier to do, but they often require more coder training since they are open to subjective interpretation. Microanalytic behavior codes are often simpler to learn but require more coder time since they must be assessed continuously during an observation period. Microanalysis is necessary when one is interested in the dynamics of behavior—in how it unfolds over time.

Using macroanalysis, an infant's social play might be assessed according to Mildred Parten's (1932) rating scale of mutual involvement in play (see Table 1.1). One could observe children and rate the highest level of play. A rating of 3, for example, means that children have achieved associative but not cooperative play. Bakeman and Brownlee (1980) used Parten's coding categories but did a microanalysis. They observed three-year-old children in out-of-doors free play. Instead of rating, they recorded the presence or absence of each category of play during successive fifteen-second time intervals for about a hundred minutes.

Besides learning about the overall level of play in the children, Bakeman and Brownlee were interested in the sequence of play. For example, when did parallel play occur in relationship to group play? It could be that parallel play occurred during the first half of the observation, and then group play took over. However, the microanalysis revealed that parallel play was sandwiched between episodes of group play.

What does it mean for the children that parallel play occurs between episodes of group play? The microanalysis and macroanalysis are not sufficient to answer this question. In order to find out, it is

TABLE 1.1   Types of Play Between Young Children

Type of Play	Description	Example
Solitary play	Child plays alone.	A child sits alone in a sandbox and fills a pail with sand.
Parallel play	Play in close proximity to other children but without interaction.	Two children sit next to each other in a sandbox, each filling a pail.
Associative play	Children respond to each other during play but maintain separate goals.	Two children talk to each other while playing with sand in a sandbox.
Cooperative play	Play is organized around joint activities.	Two children work together to build a sand castle.

Source: Adapted from M. B. Parten, Social participation among preschool children, 1932. *Journal of Abnormal and Social Psychology, 27*, 243–269.

necessary to observe what happens during these periods of parallel play. What happens when the children change to group play? The authors took their findings from the quantitative microanalysis and went back to the playground to observe the situation without focusing on a particular type of behavior. They discovered that for children of this age, parallel play was a "time out" from group play. During periods of parallel play, children could relax, work momentarily on their own, or observe each other's behavior before reentering the mainstream of group activity. This type of research, which focuses on the meaning of the behaviors for the participants, is called *qualitative research*.

QUALITATIVE RESEARCH METHODS

The previous sections covered quantitative research using experimental and observational methods. In quantitative studies, the phenomenon is measured—that is, it is coded into a number or category. The number could be an onset time, a duration, a frequency, or a score on a rating scale. Qualitative research, on the other hand, does not use quantity or number. It is characterized by one or both of the following features.

1. The observers focus on the meaning of the situation for the participants.
2. The role of the researcher in the situation is taken explicitly into account.

To infer the meaning of the situation and to take account of the observer as part of the situation, qualitative research needs to examine the situation in its broader context. The child is observed in relation to the setting, the actors, the sequences of behavior, the history of previous encounters in similar situations, and the presence of the observer. If the researcher is part of the observation situation as a **participant observer**, he or she has a direct effect on the people being studied and they have an effect on the researcher. If the

observer is watching a videotape or some other already collected data, the researcher's interpretations play a role in deciding what the participant's behaviors mean.

One example of qualitative research is the final part of the study by Bakeman and Brownlee (1980). This part of the study fits the first characteristic of qualitative research: a focus on the meaning of the behavior for the participants. The study done by Piaget on Jacqueline's imitation was described earlier as an example of quantitative research, in the sense that Piaget counted the number of times Jacqueline imitated him under different experimental conditions. It is also an example of qualitative research, because he used a verbal narrative of the whole situation to highlight the broader meaning to Jacqueline of the behavior. Piaget also was explicit about taking account of his own role in the outcome. Having recognized the possible effects of his own behavior on his daughter, he was better able to sort out the possible causes and effects, which led him to design a better experiment.

The earliest known systematic observation and recording of infant behavior, done by educated European and North American parents during the eighteenth and nineteenth centuries, is an example of qualitative research. Some of these parents kept a daily dairy about their baby's life, a **baby biography**. These diaries satisfied the first characteristic of qualitative research: they were narratives intended to understand the meaning of infant behavior rather than to measure it. The German philosopher Dietrich Tiedemann (1748–1803), for example, recorded the development of motor skills, language, thinking abilities, and social behavior in his infant son. Tiedemann described what we now call the Moro reflex (see Chapter 4) as follows:

If he was held in arms and then suddenly lowered from a considerable height, he strove to hold himself with his hands, to save himself from falling; and he did not like to be lifted very high. Since he could not possibly have any conception of fall-ing, his fear was unquestionably a purely mechanical sensation, such as older persons feel at a steep and unaccustomed height, something akin to dizziness. (Tiedemann, 1927, p. 216)

Notice that Tiedemann not only described his son's behavior in the manner of observational research, but also interpreted the meaning of the behavior for the infant when he speculated that the infant's experience was "purely mechanical." Tiedemann may have been an accurate observer of the outward behavior of the baby, but he would not be considered a good qualitative researcher by today's standards. Although we readers can see that his interpretations of the meaning of the child's behavior is based on his own point of view as an adult, Teidemann did not take explicit account of his role in the interpretive process. He was not, in other words, aware of his own biases. Those biases seem to reflect his view that babies of this age are not capable of feeling emotions, which today we know to be inaccurate.

Charles Darwin, whose theory of natu-ral selection will be discussed in Chapter 2, was also a baby biographer. Darwin was very aware of his role in the interpretive process. When his son, William, was only a few months old, Darwin was a relatively objective observer. But as Wil-liam became more active and expressive, Darwin added more references to himself and his affec-tions for William. Because Darwin thought these references to himself were unscientific, however, they were deleted in the versions of his diary that he published (Conrad, 1998). Darwin also made explicit mention of his own point of view in a memorial he wrote at the time of the death of his daughter, Anne, when she was 10 years old (Conrad, 2004).

Qualitative researchers today do not think it is unscientific for observers to take account of their own reactions. They suggest that a deeper under-standing of the meaning of behavior for the sub-jects can only come from a deeper self-awareness of the researchers about their own reactions and biases (Moustakas, 1994). Perhaps the only way to get to know another person meaningfully is to share a long-term relationship full of emotions, opinions, and attachments.

Researchers always have some kind of rela-tionship with their subjects. In the quantitative approach, the relationship is one of keeping a dis-tance and remaining objective as an observer. In qualitative research, observers allow themselves to experience some of the feelings of participa-tion that might be present in any interpersonal relationship (Aureli, 1997). Their training and self-awareness, however, allow them to use their own feelings to enhance their understanding of the subject's perspective. On the other hand, quantita-tive researchers also have biases, which they quan-tify by means of reliability and validity measures. Each type of research has its advantages and dis-advantages.

The assessment of a student's performance in school, for example, can occur through either a distant or a close teacher-student relationship. In large classes, a quantitative approach is most typically used. Instructors use primarily numeri-cal and presumably objective indices of student performance, based on exams and other graded assignments. In small classes, on the other hand, evaluations are based not only on grades but also on a more in-depth interpersonal relationship between teachers and students. In this situation, the teacher has an opportunity to get to know each student. Experienced teachers are able to develop meaningful interpersonal relationships with their students while maintaining the ability to judge the student's performance and guide her or his learn-ing. Experienced clinicians, such as psychothera-pists, also have this skill of being able to evaluate their client's progress while maintaining a strong interpersonal relationship.

Validity in quantitative research is based on comparing different types of numerical measure-ments with each other. It is an assessment of the quality of the measurement instrument, such as an automatic recording device or category of behavior. In qualitative research, *the researcher is the instrument of observation*. Credibility in qualitative research is similar to validity in quantitative research. A researcher has more **credibility** if the researcher is highly trained, has spent many hours doing comparable observations, and/or has had a prolonged engagement with the particular subjects of the study (Denzin & Lincoln, 1994). This is true for Piaget, since he was a trained scientist and he obviously had prolonged contact with his own children. In the example of teaching, more experienced teachers tend to be more credible.

Even if researchers are credible, however, they can still be biased, because the interpretation of meaning is always from their own point of view. Qualitative researchers feel there is a trade-off between the accurate but limited scope of a quantitative measure compared to the flexibility, human insight, and awareness of broad meaning of a highly trained qualitative observer (Patton, 1990). In some qualitative research methods, the researcher allows the subjects to give feedback and to play a role in the interpretation of the data. This is impossible with infant subjects, but sometimes parents can participate as co-researchers.

In quantitative research, reliability is assessed by comparing the coding or rating of behavior between two independent observers. In qualitative research, on the other hand, reliability assessment is replaced by the **constant comparative method** in which the same observers go over the same data many times in order to check and revise their interpretation of the meaning of the behavior for the participants (Strauss & Corbin, 1990). Revisions are repeated until the observers feel confident that the interpretations are consistent throughout, and new interpretations do not emerge during the process (Patton, 1990).

Because prolonged engagement with data is important to assure the credibility of the observer, and also in order to use the constant comparative method, many qualitative researchers use case studies. In a **case study**, the same subjects are observed over a long period of time, as in the baby biographies and Piaget's studies of his own chil-

dren. Case studies are often used as a means for gathering data on individuals in their real-life contexts. They are also used to study changes in individuals over time. Generally, case studies provide more detail about individuals than can be obtained using quantitative methods on large groups of individuals.

Generalizability is when the results of a research study can be applied to people other than the ones who were observed. Research that is done on many individuals using representative samples of subjects is more likely to be generalizable. On the other hand, if there are a lot of subjects, the research can only obtain a limited amount of quantitative information about each individual. When researchers focus on a few cases, they can obtain a more detailed picture of the lives of those individuals and the meaning of their behavior, but the results may not be generalizable to a larger group. Once again, there is a trade-off between the kind of meaning and detail in a case study compared to the generalizability of a large-sample quantitative study.

Which is better, qualitative or quantitative research? Many people believe research is not scientific unless one uses quantitative methods such as representative samples, control groups, random assignment, and reliable and valid measures. Others believe that a scientific approach is not defined by a particular type of method, but rather by the flexible combination of different methods that best allow the scientist to appreciate the beauty and complexity of nature. Qualitative researchers are also scientists who need special training and plenty of experience in order to establish a long-term relationship with particular infants and family while retaining a questioning stance.

As a consumer of research information, you can train yourself to respect your human attachments and needs while at the same time remaining open to sources of data that may contradict your beliefs. It is important to remember that research on infants is, above all, a human enterprise, a relationship between scientist-persons and subject-persons. Every research study is, therefore, a particular point of view on nature, a point of view at the intersection of the scientist's focus of attention and what that scientist has allowed herself or himself to be taught by the subjects.

A single study on a topic is always limited in this way. More information can be gained by reading different studies that use a variety of different measures and research methods. A study on infants from one culture many not apply to another. Research on normal children may not apply to children who are at risk because of poverty, abuse, or prematurity. Reading this book may give you at least some training in how to decide whether research results can be applied to your personal or professional situation.

EXPERIENTIAL EXERCISE

Observing Children using Qualitative Observational Research Methods
by Alan Fogel

Naturalistic observation is the practice of studying real-world situations as they unfold naturally. Following the principles of qualitative research (see Chapter 1), this form of observation is non-manipulative, unobtrusive and non-controlling. It is open to whatever emerges, and as such must be lacking in predetermined constraints on outcomes. In contrast, experimental research attempts to control conditions through manipulating, changing, or holding constant external influences, and in which a very limited set of outcome variables are measured. Qualitative observation is a "discovery-oriented" approach. It focuses on capturing process, documenting variations, and exploring important individual differences in experiences and outcomes. Thus, an important part of qualitative methods includes the investigator's personal experiences and insights. It is important to understand and acknowledge your own history and influence in the existing system during your direct participation (Patton, 1990).

Arrange to observe at a day care center, nursery school or a home where there are children aged 2 to 4 years. At some locations you can choose to observe only or participate with the children. In either case, plan on spending 2 to 3 hours in observation.

During your observation or following your participation at one of the sites, record field notes about your observations. Emphasize your experience as a participant and as an observer, even if you are not in direct contact with the children. Report any insights that you may have about personal experiences or memories that are elicited through your observations. This is a very free format, so be open to any thoughts, feelings, or ideas that come up for you. This is an opportunity to reflect on your own experience and think critically about its direct relevance to you personally and to how you interpret the behavior of the children you observe. Using the definition given in this chapter, how would you rate your credibility as an observer?

SUMMARY

The Importance of Infancy

- Prenatal and infant development are frequent topics in the news, on television, and in the movies today.
- The more a parent knows about infants and children, the lower his or her anxiety will be, and the better the outcomes will be for the child.
- Infancy is a unique stage in the life course. This is not only because it is the earliest stage of life, but because all life's stages are unique.
- The preverbal experience of the body is uniquely human. After infancy, many physical and mental disorders of children and adults can be traced to a person's losing touch with his or her own body.
- Practitioners from different therapeutic and educational methods assume that a healing effect will

ensue from recreating— in a safe and protected set-ting—some of the conditions of being a baby.

- Many disorders can be prevented by changing mater-nal behavior during pregnancy. Advances have been made in the treatment of prenatal disorders and in the care of premature and sick infants.

- Because of the vulnerability of infants, many social and medical problems could be prevented by making sure that infants receive proper care and that young parents receive all the support necessary to provide the best environment for their children.

- Many differences between people during the prena-tal and infancy periods have a lasting impact on later individual differences.

A Brief History of Babies

- During all periods of recorded history, some infants and children have received love and care while others have been abused or neglected.

- Beginning in the Middle Ages, urbanization brought about changes in the family and in the health and safety of infants.

- In the eighteenth century, the ideas of romanticism and empiricism marked the beginning of philosophi-cal and educational efforts directed toward infants.

- In the nineteenth century, the development of the nuclear family, along with advances in infant medical care, led to the discovery of infancy as an important period in the life course.

The Scientific Perspective on Infancy

- In the nineteenth and twentieth centuries, infants became the subjects of scientific study sparked by the debate over whether nature or nurture has the most influence on behavioral development.

- Developmental changes are nonreversible and per-manent, and they occur in a sequence.

- The division of infancy into stages of development is somewhat arbitrary and depends on the purposes of the culture or group.

Research Methods in Developmental Science

- Individual differences between infants may or may not be stable over the course of infancy. Scientists

are still trying to determine whether these differences are due to genetic or environmental factors.

- Scientists rely on many sources of evidence, try to separate what is repeatable and stable from what is coincidental, and attempt to rid observations of bias.

Experimental Research Methods

- An experiment is a research study in which one aspect of the situation is manipulated while all other aspects are held constant or controlled.

- The independent variable is that which is controlled or manipulated by the experimenter. The indepen-dent variable is the presumed cause of the phe-nomenon. The dependent variable is the outcome behavior that is observed in response to the changes in the independent variable.

- Automatic recording of behavior involves measure-ments of heart rate, respiration, brain activity, and aspects of behavior.

- Paired-preference tests, habituation procedures, and response-contingent procedures are techniques for testing perception and cognition in infants.

Observational Research Methods

- Methods that rely on natural variations rather than random assignment to create contrast groups are called observational research methods.

- Longitudinal studies follow the same children at dif-ferent ages, while cross- sectional studies use differ-ent children at different ages.

- In observational studies, the variable that is the pre-sumed cause is called the predictor variable. The pre-sumed effect is called the outcome variable. There is an analogy between independent variables and predictor variables, and between dependent variables and outcome variables.

- Bias is reduced in research by attention to reliability, validity, observer bias, and representativeness.

- Since infants cannot provide informed consent to participate in research, their parents must do so. Researchers need to observe ethical guidelines when using human subjects in research.

- Research focusing on minute changes in behavior is called microanalysis.

- Macroanalysis focuses on the overall or summary features of behavior rather than its details and sequences of occurrences. Macroanalysis is usually done with the use of rating scales.

Qualitative Research Methods

• Qualitative research does not use quantity or number. It is characterized by one or both of the following features: (1) the observers focus on the meaning of the situation for the participants; and (2) the role of the researcher in the situation is explicitly taken into account.

• Qualitative researchers' credibility depends upon their skill, experience, and rigor.

• Using the constant comparative method in qualitative research, the same observers go over the same data many times in order to check and revise their interpretation of the meaning of the behavior for the participants.

• In a case study, the same subjects are observed over a long period of time.

Chapter 2

Theories of Infant Development

CHAPTER OUTLINE AND OVERVIEW

Learning Theories   *How do infants learn? What are the conditions most conducive to infant learning?*

Cognitive Theories   *What are the developmental origins of perceiving, remembering, thinking, and speaking? Are infants intelligent before they can speak?*

Systems Theories   *In what ways do fetuses differ? What are the major causes of these individual differences?*

Clinical Theories   *What has therapy with adults and children revealed about how infancy contributes to psychological development? What are the therapeutic effects when adults reexperience the feelings and movements of normal infant behavior and development?*

People acquire a personal theory about infants in the course of working with infants or raising one of their own. A scientific theory differs from personal theories in several ways. A **scientific theory** is a set of concepts that explains the observable world with structures, processes, or mechanisms that are presumed to exist but that cannot be observed directly.

1. A scientific theory helps to organize observations derived from systematic research, using accepted methods of observation and assessment.

2. A scientific theory is phrased in terms of general principles that can be applied to specific research findings and applications.

3. A scientific theory should accurately predict future observations in a majority of cases. A theory whose predictions are not confirmed should be changed or abandoned.

Scientific theories of human development focus on describing and predicting the ways in which children change over time and the origins of individual differences. Why does one child become adept at language skills from an early age, for example, while another is slow to pick up these abilities?

In this chapter, we shall examine a variety of theories of human development that have been applied to infancy: biological, learning, cognitive, systems, and clinical theories. The main principles and concepts of each theory are described, the historical trends within each are reviewed, and the contributions of the theory to contemporary research are outlined. Finally, the main limitations of the theory are discussed.

BIOLOGICAL APPROACHES

genes

Biological approaches are based on the work of Charles Darwin, who theorized that differences between species and between individuals are shaped by whether or not the individual has the ability to survive long enough to reproduce. In a

"Survival of the fittest"

process called **natural selection**, the individuals who can successfully adapt to the environment will live long enough to reproduce and pass some of their characteristics down to the next generation. Thus, the environment influences which types of characteristics will survive and continue to evolve (Darwin, 1859).

Part of what gets passed down between generations is the genetic code. In sexually reproducing species, each parent passes half of his or her genetic code to the offspring (see Chapter 3). The genetic code is a set of chemical instructions for producing proteins in the nucleus of a living cell. This raw genetic code, made up of large molecules of deoxyribonucleic acid (DNA), is called the **genotype**. Every cell in a person's body contains the same exact genotype. In order for different cells to take on different functions—such as the neural, skeletal, muscular, and other tissues that underlie mental and behavioral abilities—the environment of the cell and of the organism as a whole affects the actions of the genotype. This occurs via the **epigenome**, a set of biochemical markers that are responsive to the environment and that literally turn on or turn off the actions of particular genes within each cell (see Chapter 3).

The other part of what gets passed down between generations is a particular type of environment, including the physical and social environment. Children inherit not only the parent's genes but also the parent's environment. Prenatal development, for example, could not occur outside of the special environment of the female reproductive system. The temperature, chemistry, biology, and physics of that environment are just as important for the development of the individual and the evolution of the species as the composition of the DNA. Individual differences in that environment are just as important as individual differences in the DNA in the formation of the next generation (Hernández, Blasi & Bjorklund, 2003; Lickliter, 2008; see Chapter 3).

The outcomes of the genotype-environment interactions—the resultant products—are called **phenotypes** and include not only tissues but also behaviors, intelligence, and temperament. Thus, it is important to understand that the genotype does not directly determine the phenotype; rather, *the genotype determines the opportunities by which the environment may have an influence on the phenotype* (Gottlieb, 1991b). Natural selection, then, does not operate on the genetic code directly. Natural selection operates on the phenotypes, the characteristics of the individual in his or her environment. In this section, we will review two biological approaches: behavior ecology theory and behavior genetics.

Behavior Ecology Theory

Species-specific behavior.   Behavior ecology theory is the study of behavior from an evolutionary perspective. Drawing upon Darwin's ideas, behavior ecology theory suggests that all animals have **species-specific behaviors** that evolved through the process of natural selection. Species-specific behaviors are those that are seen in only one species, such as chimpanzee calls or human speech. Although these two behaviors are species-specific, both are examples of a more general function of communication. The selection of a specific form of communication in a species is presumably related to the survival of its members over many generations and the maintenance of a particular environment—including the interindividual social environment—in which that form of communication can flourish.

Another example of a general cross-species behavior related to survival is the attachment bond between parent and infant seen in most mammalian species, but each species shows this in different ways. Mother cats lick and nuzzle their infants, while mother monkeys groom and cuddle their babies and carry them around. All mammals nurse their young, but the styles of nursing differ between species. In dogs, the mother lies on her side while her puppies nurse. The mother does not look at her babies, but she may lick them and smell them.

Critical periods.   Another aspect of behavior ecology theory is the prediction that species-specific behaviors are enhanced and modified in specific environments and at specific times during the life course. In many animal species, the young are biologically more susceptible to the acquisition of new behavior than older individuals. Often there is a limited period of time early in life during which environmental input can make a difference in later behavior. This period of maximum susceptibility is called a **critical period** and is a relatively short (compared to the individual's life span) and clearly demarcated period of time in which learning can occur and during which whatever the animal learns has a permanent and irreversible effect.

In some species of birds, for example, attachment of the infant to an adult occurs only during a period of about two hours, several days after hatching. If a gosling follows its mother around during the critical period, it will develop a preference for the mother over other adults and will stay close to her after the critical period ends and for a long time afterward. This learning of preferences for particular adults is called **imprinting**.

Konrad Lorenz (1965) found that goslings could become imprinted on a number of different objects during this period. Lorenz made goslings imprint on flashlights, electric trains, and even himself. He would walk near the goslings during the critical period, squatting and honking like a mother goose. In his description of these early studies, he wrote, "In the interest of science, I submitted myself literally for hours on end to this ordeal" (Lorenz, 1952, p. 42). For this and other work, Lorenz won a Nobel Prize in 1973. He is one of only three behavioral scientists to have received this honor. The other two—Niko Tinbergen and Karl von Frisch—were also behavior ecologists.

A large number of studies—mostly with mallard ducklings—have been done on imprinting since Lorenz's classic work. One of the main findings is that imprinting occurs only after the ducklings leave the nest and only if they can follow a moving adult duck that is calling to them (Bateson, 1966; Hess, 1959). One study (Dyer, Lickliter, & Gottlieb, 1989) suggests that before imprinting, ducklings may be more sensitive to the visual images of their walking siblings than to the mother duck. Ducklings may initially leave the nest as they see other ducklings doing so. Once this happens, the ducklings will respond as a group to the mother duck's call, follow her as a group, and thus become imprinted. Other environmental factors also affect the imprinting process. Ducklings need to hear their own call prior to hatching. In experiments in which duck embryos were made unable to vocalize, they did not recognize the mother's call after hatching (Gottlieb, 1991a). If quail chicks are exposed to patterned light during the first days after birth, instead of seeing their mothers or siblings, they will not imprint even if they can hear the mother's call (Lickliter & Hellewell, 1992).

In birds, critical periods occur in infancy that set down a behavioral pathway for the remainder of their lives. Cow bird males, for example, can either become aggressive and competitive in finding a single mate in their adult sexual behavior, or they can be egalitarian and choose among multiple mates with no competition. It all depends upon whether, as infants, they hear competitive versus egalitarian adult males singing in their environment, since there is a difference in the singing of these two types of adult male (White et al., 2007). We shall see in Chapter 5 that gender stereotypical play in human children depends in part on the behavior of adults in their environment during the period between 2 and 4 years of age, particularly the behavior of the adult males (Hernández, Blasi & Bjorklund, 2003).

The picture of imprinting that emerges from these studies is that a series of related environmental events must be tied together. Imprinting involves age mates, locomotion, and auditory and visual perception and cannot be thought of as simple photographic images of the mother printed on the duckling's brain. Imprinting does not occur in humans and other primate species because the infants are too immature to follow their parents around. Human parents, therefore, play a greater role in the mutual maintenance of proximity. The lasting emotional tie that promotes this proximity is called **attachment** (see Chapter 7). Also, the critical period for human attachment in humans, monkeys and apes is longer and the environmental

conditions under which attachment may occur are more complex.

If there is severe deprivation of parental care, the critical period for attachment is easier to observe. Studies of infants reared with little adult interaction in orphanages in Eastern Europe and in the Middle East showed that these children developed severe symptoms of withdrawal and have life-long socioemotional impairments. Infant monkeys reared without adults tend to show similar symptoms: rocking, head banging, extreme fear in the presence of strangers, and an inability to form relationships with other individuals (Harlow & Harlow, 1965; Spitz, 1965).

Even with these clear deprivations, the situation is more complicated than it may seem. Some of the early orphanage studies have been criticized for confusing the symptoms of malnutrition—common in those institutions—with those predicted for maternal deprivation. Since research that deliberately deprives infants of their mothers is ethically forbidden with humans, researchers have used nonhuman primates for this research. Follow-up studies on monkeys deprived of their mothers early in life showed that some social experiences—in particular, interactions between the deprived monkeys and monkeys younger than themselves—provided when the deprived monkeys were juveniles had the effect of partially reversing the social withdrawal (Suomi & Harlow, 1972). Gorilla infants who are raised by humans develop more aggressive and antisocial behaviors than do gorillas raised with gorilla parents. After spending time in a group of gorilla peers, however, human-reared juvenile gorillas will act more like those who were reared by their own mothers (Meder, 1989). Like the duckling studies, attachment during the critical period of infancy depends upon multiple factors.

Another potential example of a human critical period is the development of language in the first three years of life. Again, severe deprivation is found in the case of a girl named Genie, who was found in 1970 at the age of thirteen after having been isolated in a small room since infancy. Her father, apparently a psychotic who hated children,

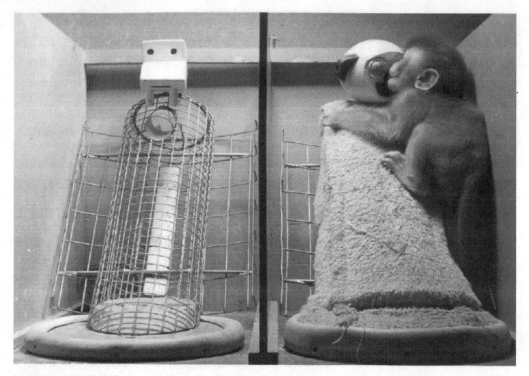

In research by the Harlows, infant monkeys preferred the substitute mother that was covered with a soft cloth, rather than the wire mother to which the food was attached. This study showed that attachment in monkeys is more related to contact comfort than to feeding. In humans, attachment is related to play and communication. Courtesy of the University of Wisconsin Primate Laboratory.

forced Genie to remain in a closet and refused to let anyone speak to her. Susan Curtiss, a developmentalist who spent many years trying to help Genie recover, reported that Genie learned some language (Curtiss, 1977) and after several years of practice could string up to three words together to make her intentions and thoughts known. But she never seemed to grasp the idea of grammar, and she never learned to ask questions.

The problem with this single case study is that we have no way of knowing whether Genie suffered from some form of brain damage or other impairment early in life. Such an organic deficit might be the real cause of Genie's language retardation. Ethically, we cannot do language deprivation experiments on groups of healthy children.

In summary, critical periods exist for humans but they depend upon a complex network of environmental factors. The clearest example of a criti-cal period in human development is the first six months of prenatal development. Environmental influences—such as maternal nutrition and environmental toxins—can have severe effects on the health, physiological and brain development, and behavior that last for a lifetime. These processes will be reviewed in detail in Chapter 9.

Behavior Genetic Theory

Behavior ecology approaches typically focus on species-wide patterns, but what accounts for differences between individuals? **Behavior genetics** is the study of possible environmental and genetic explanations for individual differences in behavior and personality characteristics. In doing research in behavior genetics, it is essential to know how individuals are genetically related to each other and whether the environments in which they are raised are similar or different. A typical research strategy is to observe behavior, such as intelligence or temperament (a word researchers use to talk about infant personality; see Chapter 7), in identical compared to fraternal twins. Identical twins have the same set of genes, while fraternal twins share only a portion of their genes. Thus, if identical twins reared at home are more similar to each other than are fraternal twins reared at home, it is possible to conclude that at least some portion of the observed behavior is explained by a genetic contribution, since identical twins have more genes in common than fraternal twins, who are no more related to each other than any two siblings in a family.

Another research approach is to study identical twins who are adopted at birth and raised in different families. They will have the same genes but be reared in different environments. Twins reared together will be more similar than twins reared apart, showing that some of the similarity between identical twins is due to the fact that they are raised in the same **shared environment** rather than to their genetic similarity. The shared environment of identical twins can be observed because twins look alike and are the same sex, so they are more likely to be treated alike by parents than fraternal twins. Identical twins may be dressed alike and encouraged to spend time together, creating opportunities for mutual imitation and similar experiences. Even in the same home, however, each twin may have somewhat different experiences, called the **nonshared environment** (Loehlin, 1989; Plomin, 1994).

The study of similarities in characteristics between family members is another approach to behavior genetic research (Lemery & Goldsmith, 1999). This kind of study is useful if a particular trait, such as a suspected genetically caused disease, occurs disproportionately within particular families. Identical twins share 100 percent of their genetic material, while other siblings from the same parents share 50 percent of their genetic material, the same amount shared by parents with their children. Uncles and nephews, aunts and nieces, grandparents and grandchildren, and half

siblings share 25 percent of their genetic material. If genetics plays a role for a characteristic, there should be a decreased probability of the occurrence of that characteristic in family members who are more distantly related and an increased probability of occurrence among those who are more closely related.

The **heritability** of the observed behavior measures the extent to which individual differences in the behavior are due to genetic factors. Heritability is usually expressed in terms of a percentage, the percentage of variability between individuals that can be explained by genetic variability. It varies between 0 and 1.00. Research findings show modest heritability (about 30 percent, on average) for some measures of intelligence, temperamental inhibition, empathy, self-esteem, and the ways in which individuals select, modify, create, or avoid specific features of their environments (Plomin, 1994; Robinson et al., 1992; Scarr, 1993; Zahn-Waxler, Robinson, & Emde, 1992). This means that 30 percent of the differences between people in these characteristics can be explained by genetic variability.

Because heritability is expressed as a percentage, results from behavior genetic research are **probabilistic**. That is, if you possess a particular set of genes, you have a higher probability of developing a particular kind of behavioral characteristic than a person without those same genes. The action of the genes is not deterministic, since there are environments that might lessen the impact of those genes on the behavioral outcome (Scarr, 1993; Scarr & McCartney, 1983).

Some genetic predispositions, for example, may never appear in the phenotype because the genotype is never exposed to a "needed" environmental resource at a particular time in life (Turkheimer et al., 2003). Thus, a gosling will never manifest its species-typical attachment behaviors if it is not exposed to an adult goose during the critical period for imprinting. This is an example of a genetic predisposition that is easily influenced by the environment. In this case, *environmental variability has a larger probability of predicting individual phenotypes than does genetic variability*. In fact, genetic variability usually accounts for only a small proportion of behavioral variability. Many genes, each with a small influence, rather than a single gene, are typically involved in influencing behavior (Plomin, 1990, 1994).

Other genotypes may be less susceptible to variations in the environment. If infants have a color blindness genotype, variability in the amount of exposure to visual stimuli will have little influence on the phenotype of color blindness. In this case, *genetic variability between individuals* (inheriting or not inheriting color blindness genes) *has a larger probability of predicting individual phenotypes than does environmental variability.*

No genes and no environments are 100 percent deterministic. Some genetic disorders can be eliminated in the phenotype through surgery, by drug treatments, or by avoiding certain environmental factors (e.g., controlling diabetes through diet). There is also hope that some will be "cured" by as yet undiscovered techniques (see Chapter 9). The increased used of molecular biological methods in behavior genetic research also provides hope for the discovery of particular gene-environment interaction processes that can be more easily regulated to prevent or treat serious physical, behavioral, and psychological disorders (Plomin et al., 2003).

In some cases, genetic variability may predict variability in phenotypes early in life but not later. A stable pattern of temperamental withdrawal tends to be correlated with eye color (withdrawn infants are more represented in the group of blue-eyed infants than would be expected by chance) during the first three years of life. During the preschool period and later, there is no correlation between eye color and temperament (Kagan, Reznick, & Snidman, 1987). These findings suggest that temperamental withdrawal may be genetically based, but after several years, the variability of that phenotype in the population is better predicted by environmental rather than genetic variability. The opposite could also be true: a genetically based skill in language might account for between-infant differences at age three, but not earlier in infancy (Fagard & Jacquet, 1989; Ramsay, 1980).

The relationship between genes and environments is made more complicated because they influence each other. People with a particular genetic predisposition—for temperamental withdrawal, for example—may prefer to be with one or two other people rather than in large groups. Their choice of environments, or preference for particular behaviors, then influences the kinds of skills they can later develop (Karmiloff-Smith, 2007; Scarr & McCartney, 1983).

It is generally assumed that the environment of the home is independent of the child's genetic predispositions. Studies based on parents who are identical and fraternal twins, however, reveal that parental warmth and affection are partly heritable. If the child inherits similar genes from genetically more affectionate parents, the environment created by those parents is also to some extent genetically determined (Losoya et al., 1997). Behavior genetic research is still in its early stages, but it promises to provide important new ways of understanding the origins of differences between people.

What Are the Problems with Biological Approaches?

Behavior ecology theory assumes that all behavior evolved through natural selection. While this may seem clear for species-specific behaviors such as attachment and language, the evolutionary basis of the effects of television on infants or their preference for one storybook over another is a more difficult theoretical problem. Because televisions and books were not in the environment in which the current species-typical characteristics evolved, they are not easily understood from this perspective. It may be, however, that our inherited ability as humans to invent tools and technologies underlies the more specific abilities. This allows us to do things that did not evolve by natural selection, things that are nevertheless adaptive and enhance our ability to pass these characteristics to the next generation (Buss & Goldsmith, 1998).

One criticism of behavior genetics is that in most human situations, it is extremely difficult to sort out the relative effects of genetic and environmental variability. It is difficult to find cases of identical twins reared apart. Even when this happens, the reasons for the twins' separation at birth may make them unrepresentative of the rest of the population. Also, adoptions tend to occur within similar racial, ethnic, and social-class groupings, increasing the degree of shared environment, which may account for the twins' similarity (Baumrind, 1993; Jackson, 1993).

Another problem with behavior genetic research is that while it gives some numerical estimate of genetic and environmental influences for groups of people, it does not tell us anything about a particular individual and his or her probability of inheriting the genetic potential or showing the characteristic in the phenotype (Gottlieb, 1995). Also, behavior genetic research tells us nothing at all about the ways in which the genes and environment act to produce a phenotype, so it gives no guidelines for intervention should a genetic problem be suspected, nor for how to enhance the development of a particular child (Baumrind, 1993). As the future brings more technological advances in the field of molecular biology, it may be possible to find the particular genes associated with those characteristics that have been shown to have a higher heritability (Plomin, 1994; Plomin & Rutter, 1998).

LEARNING THEORIES

Traditionally, learning theories have been contrasted with evolutionary theories as being on opposite sides in the nature-versus-nurture debate. Learning theories suggest that the environment is the most potent influence, while evolutionary theories dwell on genetic influences. As we saw in the section on behavior ecology theory, this simple characterization is not accurate. There is no clear separation between nature (the views of Rousseau and Gesell) and nurture (the views of Locke and Watson).

Evolutionary theory researchers believe that *the genes regulate the kinds of learning possible in a species and the ages at which it can take place* (Richardson, 2008). Often, their research methods are nearly identical to those of learning theorists: both are studying the conditions under which learning takes place. On the other hand, learning theorists are cognizant of species differences in learning, since the vast majority of work based on learning theory has been done with nonhuman species.

Learning theory researchers have contributed to our understanding of development in several ways. First, they have discovered simple yet powerful ways to enhance learning. Second, they have shown that with the proper kinds of environmental supports, individuals and species can be trained to achieve considerably more than what might have been expected from evolutionary models of species-typical behavior. We might say that learning researchers work at the upper end of a species's range of abilities as they search for more optimal strategies to enhance learning skills.

Classical Conditioning

The Russian physiologist Ivan Pavlov (1849–1936) published one of the first demonstrations of learning as a result of systematic environmental manipulation. Pavlov attempted to teach dogs to salivate on cue, not simply in the presence of food. He discovered that if a bell was rung every time a hungry dog was presented with food, the dog would later salivate at the sound of the bell without any food present. This process, called **classical conditioning**, or **learning by association**, is illustrated in Figure 2.1.

In classical conditioning, there must be an unconditioned stimulus that induces the unconditioned response. An example from human infancy is the fear (unconditioned response) induced by strangers in strange places (unconditioned stimulus). Learning occurs when the unconditioned stimulus occurs at the same time as some new conditioned stimulus. Following repeated exposure to this pairing of conditioned and unconditioned stimuli, the unconditioned response will occur in the presence of the conditioned stimulus. For example, if the infant's doctor wears a white coat, the fear of the strangeness of the doctor's office may become associated with white coats. Thus, the infant may later cry

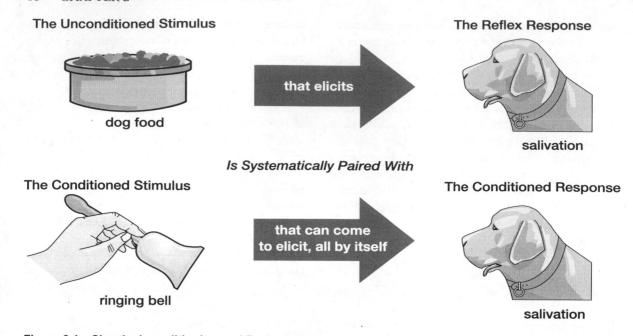

The Unconditioned Stimulus

dog food

that elicits

The Reflex Response

salivation

Is Systematically Paired With

The Conditioned Stimulus

ringing bell

that can come to elicit, all by itself

The Conditioned Response

salivation

Figure 2.1   Classical conditioning and Pavlov's dog.
Adapted from J. P. Dworetzky & N. J. Davis, *Human Development: A Life Span Approach*, 1989, p. 34. St. Paul, MN: West.

at the sight of anyone—even a familiar person—wearing a white coat.

Operant Conditioning

In an experiment that led to a later development in learning theory, B. F. Skinner (1938) tried to condition birds. Since classical conditioning theory assumes that all unconditioned responses must be related to unconditioned stimuli, Skinner faced a problem. He could not discover the unconditioned stimuli for most of the animal's actions: it seemed to emit behavior spontaneously without any obvious external stimulation. Skinner referred to these spontaneously emitted actions as *operants*. Pigeons, for example, peck (the operant) even when not eating. Skinner was not interested in what caused the operants, and he accepted the fact that each different species will have different types of operants. His goal was to change the way in which the animal emitted the operants.

Skinner discovered that the rate of emitted behavior could be controlled by the consequences of the behavior; that is, by what happened in the environment immediately following the operant's occurrence. In one experiment, a pigeon was placed in a cage with no food tray. On the side of the cage was a colored disk. As the pigeon in the cage emitted the operant of pecking, it pecked at all the parts of the cage at random. When the bird happened to peck the colored disk, a small bit of food was dropped into the cage. Over time, the bird began to narrow down its pecking to the region of the cage containing the disk, and eventually it pecked exclusively at the disk: the animal discovered the contingency between its own operant, the disk, and the food. This is similar to our description of the response-contingent method of infant research (see Chapter 1). The process by which the frequency of an operant is controlled by its consequences is called **operant conditioning**.

Consequences that increase the frequency of the preceding operant are called **reinforcers**. A **positive reinforcer** is an action or reward that follows the operant and increases its frequency. In some cases, the frequency of an operant is increased following the removal of an aversive stimulus. Thus, the absence of a consequence that increases the frequency of the operant is called a **negative reinforcer**.

Suppose an infant performs some action that the parents would like to encourage, such as drinking all his or her milk. Parents can increase the frequency with which this happens by praising the child after he or she has finished the milk (a positive reinforcer). On the other hand, the child may increase the frequency with which he or she finishes the milk to avoid being scolded for not finishing it. The absence of scolding becomes a negative reinforcer. A negative reinforcer is not negative in the sense of being bad or unrewarding, but rather in the sense of being absent. Not getting scolded is a rewarding consequence for the child.

Unrewarding consequences have the effect of decreasing rather than increasing the frequency of a particular behavior. An unrewarding consequence that decreases the frequency of an operant is called a **punishment**. In the above example, the scolding may act as a punishment to decrease the probability of the child's *not* finishing the milk.

Another way to decrease the frequency of a behavior is by **extinction**. This is the process by which the frequency of an operant decreases when a reinforcing consequence is removed. In the first few months of life, it is important to respond promptly to an infant's crying. This response, however, may increase the frequency with which the infant cries (although the intensity and duration of the crying episodes may decline over time). When the infant is several months older and is better able to tolerate distress, parents may want the infant to calm down on his or her own. Parents can extinguish crying by not responding to it as frequently or as promptly as before.

Both classical and operant conditioning are able to explain particular learning phenomena in infancy, especially in situations in which there are repeated opportunities for exposure to similar environmental consequences. There are, however, developmental differences in an infant's susceptibility to conditioning and to the types of environmental stimuli and conditions that are most likely to serve as reinforcers or punishers. Unfortunately, learning theory cannot explain how these individual differences and development changes are caused.

Social Learning Theory

Researchers began to notice that simple conditioning was not enough to explain patterns of behavior seen in infants and children. Several theoretical developments led to social learning theory. First of all, researchers discovered that as infants change their behavior to adjust to the contingencies between their behavior and the environment, the infants seek to change the environment to preserve or enhance the same pattern of contingencies. Thus, infants come to control not only their behavior but also the behavior of other people around them (Bijou & Baer, 1965).

Suppose, for example, a parent reinforces the child every time the child asks for help and ignores the child whenever the child whines or cries to get help. The child is likely to increase the frequency of verbal requests for help, but in addition, the child will come to expect help whenever it is asked for in the appropriate way. On the parent's side, when the child asks for help verbally and without whining, the parent is more likely to provide the assistance. Thus, the increase in the child's verbal requests will condition the parent to increase the frequency with which he or she gives help. As a result of this complex social process, the child's recognition of the contingency has ultimately changed that child's social environment.

A second theoretical development was the discovery that infants could change their behavior in ways that had nothing to do with conditioning. Entirely new behaviors could be acquired almost immediately through **observational learning** (Bandura, 1977). Just by watching an adult or peer model, an infant could imitate the behavior and incorporate that imitated act into the infant's own goals.

A final theoretical advance of social learning theory is the idea that infants are more likely to acquire new behaviors in some situations than in others. Both conditioning and observational learning are more likely to occur if infants are moti-vated to pay attention to the consequences of their action or to the model. Thus, an infant's goals help to organize the way in which he or she picks up information from the environment. In a word, social learning theory introduced the self (includ-ing cognitions and motivations) as an intelligent actor and organizer of information. As Figure 2.2 shows, learning is an interaction between the behavior to be learned (is it easy or difficult to mas-ter?), the environment in which it is learned (does the environment support or inhibit the learning?), and the factors the person brings to the situation (is the person motivated to learn?).

If someone gives the infant a task to learn and models a behavior that is too difficult for the infant, if the infant is not interested at that moment in learning, or if consistent and positive help from others is not provided, this affects not only learning but the infant's emotional experience as well. If the infant's experiences are contingent upon his or her actions, and if those actions subsequently change the behavior of others in ways that accord with the infant's goals, a feeling of self-efficacy emerges (Bandura, 1989). If, on the other hand, the infant's goals are typically thwarted and the social environ-ment behaves capriciously, feelings of helplessness and despair emerge (Seligman & Maier, 1967).

Social learning theory has been applied to a wide variety of issues in infant development. It sug-gests that environments can be structured in ways that are conducive to infant learning and to longer-term feelings of self-efficacy. The theory focuses on the immediate context of behavior and shows the importance of the environment's being respon-sive to the infant's current goals and needs and not merely a mechanical producer of reinforcers.

In the first few months, infants are largely dependent upon the pushes and pulls of their emotions. Later, they develop the ability to self-regulate their emotions through a process of social learning. Infants come to identify particular feel-ings with particular expressions and verbal labels. In this view, infants have feelings that they do not understand or recognize. Through a process of parental labeling of their feelings (e.g., say-ing things like "You must be angry" or "Why are you sad today?"), children learn to construct the social meaning of their emotions. Children also imitate adults' use of emotion expressions in par-ticular situations. If adults are smiling, the infant will also smile. In the process, the infant comes to associate the inner feelings of enjoyment with the expression of smiling in others and with the typi-cal situations in which such feelings tend to occur. In addition, strong emotions become less fre-quent with age and are expressed in more socially appropriate forms, by saying, "I'm really angry," as opposed to screaming and hitting (Izard & Malat-esta, 1987; Lewis & Michalson, 1983).

(handwritten margin note:) of cost parents—modeling

(handwritten note:) goals more successfully reached when infants percieved able

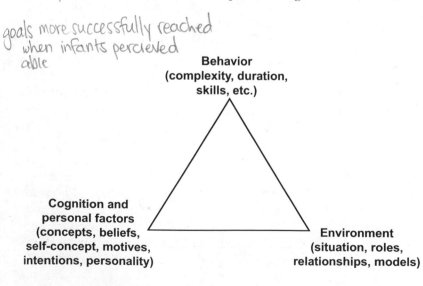

Behavior
(complexity, duration, skills, etc.)

Cognition and personal factors (concepts, beliefs, self-concept, motives, intentions, personality)

Environment (situation, roles, relationships, models)

Figure 2.2 Diagram of Triadic Reciprocality
The triadic relationship between behavior, cognition and personal factors, and environmental con-texts determines social learning.

Source: Adapted from A. Bandura, *Social foundations of thought and action: A social cognitive theory*, 1986, p. 24. Englewood Cliffs, NJ: Prentice Hall. Reprinted by permission.

What Are the Problems with Learning Theory?

Although learning theory has had remarkable success in predicting infant behavior during controlled laboratory experiments, real-life environments are never so simple or so contingent. Many processes, including genetic contributions, may influence the way behavior is acquired. Because learning theory focuses on the immediate conditions of learning, it appears to suggest that an infant can acquire any behavior at any age if the environmental and motivational conditions are right. Since this is clearly not the case, learning theory cannot explain the sequence and timing of developmental stages in infancy. Although learning theorists deny that stages exist, insisting instead that behavior is acquired gradually and cumulatively, the existence of universal developmental sequences cannot be denied. Learning theory also cannot explain the spontaneous emergence of new behaviors, such as stranger anxiety even when children have no prior experience with a stranger, or smiling in blind infants. Cognitive-constructivist theory, to be reviewed next, provides one explanation for the developmental stages of infancy.

COGNITIVE THEORIES

Cognitive developmental theories focus on the mental experience of the person. The goal is to understand intelligence: how people of different ages know about, perceive, plan, and remember their experiences. In cognitive theory, behavior is considered to be a form of intelligence because most of what people do is goal directed and depends upon their knowing what to do under particular circumstances. In this book, I focus on cognitive theories that have been applied to the study of developmental change in infancy.

Constructivist Theory

One of the central theories of infant cognitive development is that of Jean Piaget (1896– 1980), who was trained as an invertebrate biologist before he became interested in the study of human development. Biologists used evolutionary theory to study development from the point of view of each individual's **adaptation** to the environment. Adaptation is a change in an individual's functioning that makes the individual better suited to survive in a particular environment. Piaget's contribution to cognitive development was to conceptualize human intelligence as a form of adaptation to the environment. In his view, even small infants can act in intelligent ways, not by thinking but by acting physically on the environment in order to meet their own goals (Piaget, 1952).

For Piaget, an infant who is touching an object is developing an intelligent way of "knowing" that object. Knowledge is conceived of not as a static library of information but as an active process of **co-construction** between the knower and what is to be known. Co-construction means that what one knows depends upon how one acts on the environment and how the environment responds to those actions. Imagine what you would know about an object if all you could do were grasp it and bring it to your mouth, like a four-month-old. You don't have the skill to shake or bang the object, and you do not have sufficient fine motor coordination to inspect its details with your fingers. But you can sense texture, hardness, shape, and the different feelings that come from touching the object with your mouth compared to your hand. All complex forms of knowing develop out of simpler actions found in infants, such as sucking, chewing, touching, seeing, and hearing.

Piaget brought two principles of biological adaptation into his study of the development of intelligent action: **assimilation** and **accommodation**. Assimilation refers to the process by which individuals use their existing abilities in response to challenges from the environment. It is the application of what one already knows or does to the current situation. Accommodation is the alteration of existing abilities to better fit the requirements of the task or situation. Accommodation is more likely to occur if assimilation does not result in an effective adaptation to the environment.

Jean Piaget is known for his theoretical contributions and also for his empathetic sensitivity with young children. His many experiments with his own three infants take account of his effects on them and were embedded into the infants' daily activities.

Photo: Bill Anderson/Photo Researchers, Inc.

Typically, most actions involve both assimilation and accommodation. Between the ages of six and twelve months, human infants must learn to eat solid foods. This is not an easy task, because the infant's tongue is not yet coordinated enough to keep food in the mouth. While sucking on a breast or a bottle, the baby's tongue moves in and out like a piston. When a baby is first given solid food on a spoon, the baby's response is to move the tongue as if he or she were sucking, which has the effect of expelling food from the mouth. Thus, the infant assimilates the tongue and mouth actions of sucking to the eating of solids. Since this simple assimilation leaves the infant hungry, the child must accommodate mouth and tongue movements so they are better adapted to the shape of the spoon and the consistency of the solid foods. The infant's knowledge about food, therefore, is a co-construction between assimilation and accommodation, as each process influences the other to create the resulting action.

Piaget's main goal was to apply his theory to the development of human intelligence, and he looked for the origins of intelligence in human infancy. He referred to the first two years of life as the **sensorimotor substage** because at that age infants were primarily involved in explorations involving their movements and senses. The main feature of sensorimotor development is the growth of infants' understanding of their bodies and how their bodies relate to other things in the environment (Piaget & Inhelder, 1969). Piaget divided the sensorimotor stage into six substages. We will discuss substages 1 to 6 in Chapter 5. These are described in Table 2.1. Although they will not be discussed in this book, Piaget's discoveries of stages beyond the infancy period are summarized in Table 2.2. The sensorimotor stage was thought to contain the seeds for the post-infancy development of thought, language, social skills, and morality.

Three basic principles about human infants characterize Piaget's theory:

Individuals play an active role in their own development. The major motivation for develop-

TABLE 2.1 Piaget's Substages of Sensorimotor Development

Approximate Age (Months)	Stage	Description
0–2	Reflect schemes	Inborn reflexes such as sucking, looking, and crying establish the infant's first connection to the world.
2–5	Primary circular reactions	Repeated actions (circular) that involve connections within the infant's own body (primary) such as cooing and coordinating arm movements with the mouth to suck on the thumb, initial occurrence of the behavior is discovered by chance.
6–9	Secondary circular reactions	Repeated actions (circular) that involve the connection between the infant and the environment (secondary) such as kicking the crib to make a mobile move or smiling to get another person to smile back. Initial occurrence is discovered by chance.
10–12	Coordination of secondary circular reactions	First sign of goal-directed behavior not motivated by chance occurrences. Combining different circular reactions to achieve goals, such as using one hand to hold an object while the other explores it, or using one object to retrieve or to act on another one.
12–18	Tertiary circular reactions	The use of familiar secondary circular reactions to make new things happen, such as when the child explores how different objects fall from his or her high-chair table, creates new relationships between different objects in play, or uses trial-and-error problem solving.
18–24	Invention of new means through mental combinations	The ability to think before acting by representing actions as mental pictures and symbols. The infant can solve problems without trial and error.

mental change comes from the individual's failure to reach an adaptation to the environment. This experience of failure, when accommodation and assimilation fall short of adaptation, is called **disequilibrium**. Since disequilibrium is defined in relation to what each individual wants to accomplish, it cannot be imposed from the outside: babies seek knowledge about those things that they most want to figure out or accomplish.

Infants develop knowledge by means of their own actions on the environment. The accommodation process literally changes the infant's view of the world, since, by altering his or her own actions, the child comes to "know" new uses for the same objects. Through action, individuals create knowledge. Since knowledge is an active process of creation, this is often referred to as **constructivist theory**, according to which knowledge is built up—constructed—by the child's own action rather than imposed on the child from the outside.

Infants will learn better from experiences if those experiences can be assimilated to their current developmental level. The currently available set of skills and knowledge is known as the infant's **schemes**. Schemes can be sensorimotor, that is, involving physical actions such as reaching and chewing. Schemes can also be conceptual, involving ideas, concepts, or thoughts. In order for accommodation to occur, the infant has to assimilate the existing set of schemes to the environment. For

TABLE 2.2   Piaget's Cognitive-Developmental Stages of Child Development

Approximate Age (Months)	Stage	Description
0–2	Sensorimotor	Infants learn through direct experience of the senses and by handling objects and moving them around. They do not understand that things exist outside their own actions.
3–7	Pre-operational	Ability to form mental representations, language, thinking as internalized action but centered on the self's perspective; inability to think logically.
7–11	Concrete operational	Thinking takes the perspective of others and is logical with respect to concrete actions and objects such as the rules of a game; inability to think about abstract things.
12–adult	Formal operational	Thinking about non-concrete, abstract things; ability to solve word problems, form a coherent system of thought relating many ideas, and think about future possibility.

Source: A. Fogel & G. F. Melson, *Child Development*, 1988, p. 39. St. Paul, MN: West. Copyright © by West Publishing Company. Reprinted by permission. All rights reserved.

this to happen, the environment should present challenges that are moderate, not overly difficult or beyond the infant's grasp. Thus, the first solid foods have to be soft in consistency (the infant does not have teeth yet) and given on a spoon that is small enough to fit in the infant's mouth. Adults have to hold the spoon at just the right angle and move it in and out of the infant's mouth at the appropriate time.

Piaget's original work on infancy was based on observations of his own three children, Jacqueline, Laurent, and Lucienne, and he is known to have been empathically attuned to young children. His qualitative observations are unrivaled in their clarity, accuracy, detail, and theoretical import (see Qualitative Research, Chapter 1). Piaget's work is clearly distinguished from learning theories and from evolutionary theories. Piaget believed that development is not imposed on the infant from the outside, nor is it guided solely by genetically based maturational change. Adaptation suggests a more active, infant-centered perspective.

Piaget referred to emotional processes only very briefly, but he believed that emotional development

was parallel to the development of intelligence and should therefore follow his sequence of sensorimotor substages. The emotions of shame and pride, for example, do not appear in children until they have the cognitive ability to separate self from other and to recognize the existence of standards of behavior. Shame is the feeling of being exposed, and that means exposed in front of some other person. To be able to feel shame, we must realize that other people can see us as we see them. Similarly, pride is a sense of meeting or achieving some standard in the eyes of another person (see Chapter 7).

What Are the Problems with Piaget's Theory?

One problem with Piaget's theory is related to how Piaget decided to divide development into stages. As we discussed in the previous chapter, there is a certain arbitrariness in choosing a particular behavioral milestone to mark the beginning or end of a stage of development. Once you pick an indicator of a stage transition, then you do not expect to see that behavior appearing earlier or later in development. Unfortunately for stage theories, this often happens.

Research has shown, for example, that certain behaviors may appear earlier than Piaget's stages suggest that they should. A good example is imitation. Piaget (1962) claimed that infants younger than nine months could not imitate movements such as a facial expression that they could not see themselves make. Yet current evidence indicates that such imitation may be possible at birth (see Chapter 5).

Perhaps a more critical problem for Piaget's theory is that he failed to take account of the effects of adults on infants. Although he is given credit for helping us understand that infants are active learners, he did not attend to the facilitating and supportive environment that parents often provide and in which infants may exercise their curiosity. In order for infants to assimilate their eating to spoon feeding, for example, it requires an adult who can choose the right kind of food and spoon, an adult who is actively and constructively engaged with the infant. The role of adults is more explicit in systems theories, which offer the possibility for adult-infant co-construction, to be discussed later in this chapter.

INFORMATION-PROCESSING THEORIES OF COGNITIVE DEVELOPMENT

Imagine a toddler about two years old playing with her peers in a day care center. The toddler playroom is enclosed by glass windows that separate it from the entrance foyer of the day care building. Out of the corner of her eye, the toddler sees her mother come into the foyer. Her mother stops to speak with someone. The little girl gets up, walks to the door that opens onto the hall, walks down the hall, turns left, enters the foyer, and runs up to Mommy with arms outstretched. The child has solved a difficult problem in communication.

Piaget's explanation of this behavior, assuming this is not the first time it happened, would be simply "assimilation." Piaget might also place our toddler in the fifth or sixth sensorimotor substage, since she was able to see her mother

as a separate person, stop what she was doing, and walk around a barrier to reach her mother. A younger baby might recognize her mother but try to walk directly to her by going toward the glass wall.

Many developmentalists are dissatisfied with Piaget's explanation because it leaves unspecified the mental processes that may be involved. Let us think about what they might be. First of all, the child must be able to focus her *attention* on the person who walks in. Next, the jumble of colors, lines, and moving images must be organized into a coherent picture that has a meaning for the child; this is known as the *perceptual process*. The particular perception is organized according to specific categories using the processes of *recognition* and *recall memory*. The child interprets this perception as one that she has seen before, and she remembers what this perception means to her (Mommy!). At this point she can invoke thought processes to make some decisions. Should I go to see Mommy? How can I get there? Should I go through the door or wave at her through the window?

Information-processing theories attempt to specify the way in which the mind handles the information presented to it by the environment (see Figure 2.3). This type of cognitive theory does not run counter to Piagetian theory; it simply tries to provide a more specific picture of mental processes and their changes in the course of development. Research in information processing generally requires sophisticated technology to measure such things as visual fixation time, eye movement patterns, auditory sensitivities, and the like (see Chapter 1).

During the past thirty years, information-processing research has become the primary tool for studying infant cognition. Most of the research on perception and cognition reported in this book is based on an information-processing theory rather than on Piaget's theory of development. Piaget's work mapped the basic features of infant cognitive development. Information-processing research is now filling in the details.

Information-processing theory can be applied to the study of emotions. Changes in different

Figure 2.3   Components of Information Processing

components of the information-processing system may change the way emotions are expressed and experienced during infancy. Emotions become more complicated as different ones are combined (e.g., joy and anger mixed will become mischief). Emotional expressions can be modulated by cognitive processes such as remembering, thinking, and planning. These lead to emotion regulation and coping (e.g., biting the lower lip to hold back crying, finding appropriate versus inappropriate ways to express anger). Finally, emotional states become detached from direct emotional experience and associated with cognitive beliefs and expectations (e.g., trying to smile in a social situation even though one is feeling sad). This latter achievement, however, does not begin until after the infancy period.

One advantage of information-processing theory is that it can be applied to problems in early education and in the treatment of handicapped infants. In Piaget's view, infants pass through major stages in which all of their capacities are integrated and centered around a single stage. Information-processing views predict that infants may get off their cognitive developmental track if only one of their component processes is faulty. For example, an infant with poor perceptual skills may show signs of retardation even if everything else about the infant is intact and healthy. Without perception, however, nothing else can operate well. Simple interventions to improve hearing or eyesight, for example, may be all that is necessary to dramatically improve the developmental prognosis for some infants.

What Are the Problems with Information-Processing Theory?

One problem with information-processing theory is that it offers few clues about how each of the informational processing components develops. Each component—such as memory and perception—is presumed to change gradually, leading to overall improvements in cognition. Information processing is more a theory of how infants act and think than a theory of how action and thought develop.

Another problem is that there are many different approaches to information-processing theory and research and many thousands of research studies. Making sense of these different approaches is sometimes difficult, especially since there is no broader theoretical framework to use in interpreting the findings. So please beware. You should not expect the current knowledge on infant cognition to come neatly wrapped in nicely understandable packages.

SYSTEMS THEORIES

Systems theories share the view that all facets of the child and the environment are important, and that development is a complex process in which outcomes are determined through the active interaction of these facets. Rather than focusing on one element— emotion, cognition, or learning— systems theories attempt to understand developmental change in its entirety: the whole child in the whole environment.

A **system** is a set of interdependent components, each of which affects the others in reciprocal fashion. Systems theories recognize the mutual dependencies between the infant and the environment. The process by which systems components affect each other in a bidirectional and reciprocal way is known as **transaction** (Sameroff & MacKenzie, 2003). In the parent-infant interaction system, for example, the behavior of a parent is likely to depend on the sociability of the infant. Infants who smile more and cry less are likely to have parents who are more relaxed and socially attentive to the infant. This parental social attentiveness, in turn, will affect the infant's continued sociability.

Consider this parent-infant system during a transactional process. The infant's sociability affects the parents, which makes the parents more relaxed and which then affects the infant in ways that promote sociability. **Feedback** is a process by which components of a system have an effect on their own behavior during their transactions with other components. The behavior of the infant is fed back to the infant in terms of how the infant's behavior affected the parent's behavior.

Feedback transactions show how systems have the property of **self-organization**: the emergence of organized patterns due to the mutual influences of each component of the system on the others. Nothing from outside the system is required to maintain the transaction that enhances the infant's sociability; it is a product only of the system's transactions. The infant sociability transaction is an example of feedback that maintains the system over time. If the parent or infant has a bad day and is not so relaxed or socially attentive, it is likely that the sociability of one partner will help the other to calm down. Feedback that maintains a system's characteristics over time in spite of small deviations is called **deviation-correcting feedback** (or *negative feedback*).

In other cases, however, the deviation from the normal state of affairs is larger than the system can tolerate and still maintain itself. Suppose, for example, the infant becomes ill and fussy. Under normal conditions, the parent would remain cheerful and attentive. If the parent too is under stress, however, the infant's fussiness could lead to an increase in the parent's level of stress, which then leads to the infant's feeling even more distress and crying more, which leads to parental despair or anger. Feedback that drastically changes a system as a result of a small deviation is called **deviation-amplifying feedback** (or *positive feedback*).

Deviation-amplifying feedback generally works to change a system, while deviation-correcting feedback works to maintain it. Deviation amplification could also change a system for the better. The infant's sociability may, with the support of the parent's attentiveness, lead to the enhancement of the infant's social skills with peers and other partners and to the growth of a wider range of shared communication between parent and infant.

Another facet of systems is that they have multiple levels. A parent-child relationship system, for example, is embedded within a larger family system. In addition to the feedback between parent and child, a parent's relationship to the infant may also be affected by the parent's marital satisfaction, his or her relationship with other family members, the financial well-being of the family, his or her own job satisfaction, and even society's attitudes about the parenting role. Conversely, the successful functioning of society depends on the patterns of interaction and socialization within the family, where infants and children are initially prepared for their roles in that society.

Ecological Systems Theory

One of the first applications of systems theory to developmental psychology was the work of Urie Bronfenbrenner. He developed a conceptual framework for understanding the complex relationships between the infant, the family, and society. The **ecology of human development** is "the study of the progressive, mutual accommodation, throughout the life span, between a growing human organism and the changing immediate environments in which it lives, as the process is affected by relations obtaining within and between those immediate settings, as well as the larger social contexts … in which the settings are embedded" (Bronfenbrenner, 1979). Bronfenbrenner defined four levels of system functioning between persons:

Microsystem. The **microsystem** is made up of all the relationships between the person and his or her environment in a particular setting. For example, all of the transactions that take place between the child and the physical and social environment of the family form a microsystem. Other settings in which children are typically found are schools, camps, hospitals, play groups, and places of worship. Children are affected by many aspects of their immediate microsystem environment, including social interactions, housing, and nutrition (Melson, 1980). We shall deal with a number of these aspects in the course of this book.

Mesosystem. The **mesosystem** includes the relationships between the <u>major settings in which children are found</u>. An example would be the interaction between the family and the day care center. A child who is experiencing many difficulties in day care is likely to force the family to have more interactions with the center's teachers and administrators, and those family-school interactions should, in turn, have an effect on the child's functioning.

Exosystem. The **exosystem** extends the mesosystem to include other social systems that do not contain the developing child but have some effect on him or her. The world of work, neighborhood institutions, the media, the government, the economy, and transportation affect the functioning of the family, school, and other social settings in which children are found.

Macrosystem. The **macrosystem** contains all of the various subsystems that we have been discussing. It contains all of the general tenets, beliefs, and values of the culture or subculture and is made up of the written and unwritten principles that regulate everyone's behavior. These principles—whether legal, economic, political, religious, or educational—endow individual life with meaning and value and control the nature and scope of the interactions between the various levels of the total social system.

The idea of the macrosystem suggests that cultural values and practices have an effect on child-rearing practices and on the development of children. Throughout this book, we shall cite examples of cross-cultural studies showing how culture affects children's development. The relationships among these various subsystems are shown in Figure 2.4.

An example of ecological systems theory as applied to the family system suggests that infants may be influenced by and influence others either by **direct transactions** or by **mediated transactions**. A direct transaction occurs as part of a social relationship in which the child is an active participant: the infant-parent, infant-peer, or infant-sibling relationship. A mediated transaction occurs when the infant affects or is affected by people with whom the infant does not share an active relationship.

An example of a mediated transaction concerns the child's relationship with grandparents. Though children in North American society often spend little time with their grandparents, visiting perhaps only once or twice a year, they nevertheless seem to develop special relationships with them. This can be accounted for by parental mediation. Since the parent's relationship to his or her own parents is so important, this importance is transmitted to the child, who then comes to think of Grandma and Grandpa as special people (Lewis & Feiring, 1978; Lewis, 2005).

One model of the family system that incorporates these ideas is depicted in Figure 2.5 (Belsky, 1981). With mediated effects, the acts of one individual affect another, who then affects a third person. This model includes the effects of one individual (for example, the infant) on the relationship between the parents and, conversely, the effects of the marital relationship on the infant directly and indirectly as it affects each spouse's ability to parent. One other notable aspect of this model is that it includes feedback transactions. For example, the marriage may affect a spouse's ability to parent, which may affect the infant, whose subsequent behavior may affect the marital relationship. Each component is capable of affecting every other component in a mutually influential manner.

Ecological systems theory has contributed to research and applied work with infants. Since this theory's conception, a growing number of stud-

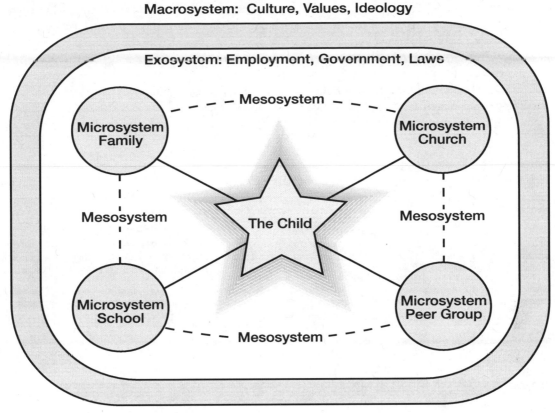

Figure 2.4 Ecological Systems Theory
The child is contained within a nested system of social relationships and institutions. Except in microsystems, children are not direct participants in any of the other social systems that may affect their lives.
Source: Adapted from A. Fogel and G. F. Melson, *Child Development*, 1988, p. 50. St. Paul, MN: West.

ies have examined the infant in the context of the family or day care. In addition, we are becoming more aware of the effects of the larger social and cultural ecosystem on infants. Nuclear radiation and environmental toxins affect prenatal development and mother's milk. The effect of having two parents working outside the home—on both the infant and the parents—is a complex family and social issue. We are becoming aware that child abuse and neglect are social ills related to poverty, discrimination, drug use, and stress.

What Are the Problems with Ecological Systems Theory?

A problem with ecological systems theory is that it does not specify the processes by which these effects might occur. For example, a disturbed parent-infant interaction may depend in part on the mother's drug use or the father's absence from the family. The precise transactional process by which the parent-infant interaction mediates these ecological factors is not explained by the theory. In addition, the theory does not provide any guidance concerning which of the many ecological factors are most likely to affect a family and under what circumstances the family is or is not affected. In other words, the richness of the conceptualization of multiple interacting effects is not supported by enough detail to guide research or practice. For that reason, most research based on ecological systems theory is descriptive of the processes that occur under a variety of social conditions.

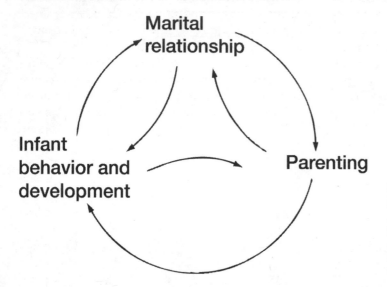

Figure 2.5 Model of Family System Functioning

Source: J. Belsky, Early human experience: A family perspective, 1981, p. 16. *Developmental Psychology, 17*, 3–23. Copyright © by the American Psychological Association. Adapted with permission.

Another problem with ecological systems theory is that it is not developmental. Although the theory points to factors that might affect infants of different ages, it is not a theory about how infants develop from one age to the next. Because adults are the primary mediators of ecological factors on infants, other versions of systems theory, which will be discussed next, focus on the infant-adult interaction in order to explain infant development. These theories deal with the process by which cultural skills, such as language, are transferred from parent to infant during social interaction.

Interactive Systems Theory

Up until the 1960s, the parent-infant relationship was viewed as a one-way process: parental behavior affects infant behavior. This was due to the general acceptance of learning theories, which view the parent as the primary socializer. In these theories, parents got all the credit for child-rearing success and all the blame for child-rearing failure. Cognitive theories had little to say about the role of the parent, assuming that cognitive development was the result of the individual's transactions with the physical environment.

In the early 1960s, an infant psychiatrist, Louis Sander, developed a theory of the early mother-infant relationship in which he explicitly recognized the reciprocal mutual transactions and feedback processes between mother and child (Sander, 1962). Sander's stages of development in the mother-infant interaction are given in Table 2.3. The importance of this theory is that it recognized that both parent and infant develop as a system in relationship to each other over time.

A large body of research since then has confirmed the transactional nature of the parent-infant interaction. The evidence is so persuasive that most developmentalists today accept the idea of transaction in the parent-infant system as fact. This change in theoretical orientation toward the parent-infant relationship contributed in part to a revival in the 1970s and 1980s of the nearly forgotten work of Lev Semanovich Vygotsky (1896–1934), a Soviet educator who worked with parents and founded a number of schools.

Vygotsky did most of his work in the early years after the Russian revolution. Following from the political theory of Marxism-Leninism, which viewed society as a complex system of mutual and cooperative influences, Vygotsky suggested that all individuals are defined by the social group, and that their knowledge is an active social construction. Vygotsky suggested that adults do not directly socialize the child into the culture but rather follow the child's own motivations to learn. By careful observation of what the infant wants to understand, adults can introduce forms of guidance that allow the infant to realize his or her goals.

The timing of parental guidance is crucial. According to Vygotsky, parents should wait for times when the infant appears to be trying to learn some new skill but has not yet mastered it (see Figure 2.6). Vygotsky referred to this phase of skill development as the **zone of proximal development**; that is, the time during which the proximal (next) achievement in skill is about to occur but has not occurred yet (Wertsch & Tulviste, 1992). Adults who tailor their guidance to fit the child's needs for support and information in the zone of proximal development will have the most lasting impact on learning.

Suppose, for example, the child is trying to express his or her desire for an object using grunts. If the adult suggests more culturally appropriate ways of requesting (speech, pointing, etc.), the child will pick up the cultural skills because those skills best serve the child's motivation at that par-

ticular moment. If the adult models appropriate forms of requesting when the child is not interested in requesting, the adult's model will not have an impact on the child.

The concept of the zone of proximal development, therefore, suggests that children will acquire culturally acceptable practices only if parents can adjust the timing and level of their actions to the ongoing motivational state of the children. Mutual, cooperative transaction is at the heart of Vygotsky's theory, which is why it is sometimes called *sociocultural theory*. Because Vygotsky became ill and died at the young age of thirty-eight, he was not able to elaborate his theory. Developmentalists today are taking over where he left off.

One of the theories derived from Vygotsky's work is that of Jerome Bruner (1983). Bruner suggested that language development arises out of earlier social-communicative routines between parents and infants. These routines must be ones in which the infant is an active participant. Bruner focused on simple parent-infant social games, such as peekaboo. The infant's participation in the game is part of his or her zone of proximal development because parents not only help to create the game's structure, they also make sure the game is a challenge for the infant that goes slightly beyond what

TABLE 2.3   Louis Sanders' Stages of the Development of Mother-Infant Reciprocity

Approximate Age (Months)	Description
0–3	The parent is concerned with helping the infant cope with the biological function and the establishment of regular patterns of sleeping, feeding, arousal and quieting. The infant begins to show differential responsiveness to the caregiver.
4–6	The beginnings of mutual play and reciprocal interactions can be seen. The parent and infant learn to anticipate signals from each other to coordinate feeding, playing, and caretaking activities.
7–9	The infant begins to take the initiative in social exchanges and shows preferences for certain kinds of social activities over others. The infant experiences feelings of success or frustration in meeting goals.
10–13	The infant makes directed demands on the mother and tries to test her availability. The parent is used as a secure base for exploration.
14–20	Infants take their own initiatives in a wider variety of settings. Infants learn to achieve success and pleasure autonomously (apart from the mother).

Source: Adapted from L. W. Sander. Issues in early mother-child interaction, 1962. *Journal of the American Academy of Child Psychiatry, 1*, 141–166.

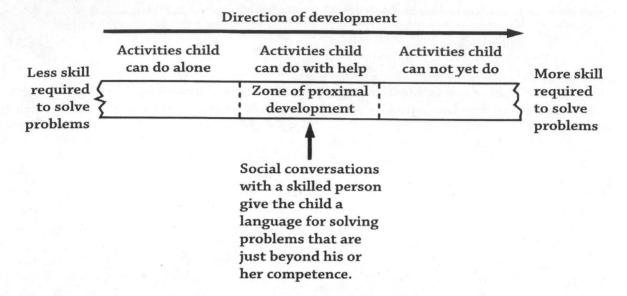

Figure 2.6   Vygotsky's Concept of the Zone of Proximal Development

the infant is capable of doing. Because the infant wants to play, he or she is more attuned to learning about the rules of the game and the behavior necessary to play. In Bruner's examples, the necessary behaviors are turn taking and language, which the child learns as part of enjoyable play routines in the company of an adult.

In many interactions, adult and infant are working on something together, but each has a different purpose. The adult is perhaps intent on instructing the child in the culturally appropriate uses of words and objects. The child may be more motivated by being a direct participant in the social world. The concept of **guided participation**, which is also based on Vygotsky's theory, reflects the active role that children play while observing and participating in the organized activities of the family and society in the company of adults (Rogoff, 1990). Although, from the adult's perspective, the child is merely "playing games" or "playing at" cooking or taking care of a doll, from the child's perspective, it feels like actually doing the task as an active participant.

Typically, in adult-child interactions, the children set the agenda for what they want to do and

for how much they want to be involved. The more skilled partner collaborates in the child's goals by giving the child responsibility for certain actions that are part of the larger task but within the range of the zone of proximal development; that is, so the child can assimilate the task. The adult must also constrain the child's participation for the sake of the child's, or of others', safety or rights. Eventually, the adult transfers responsibility for larger segments of the task to the child, in relation to the growth of the child's competence as assessed by the adult (Bruner, 1983; Heckhausen, 1988; Kaye, 1982; Lock, 1980; Rogoff, 1990). These points are summarized in Table 2.4.

There are cultural differences in styles of guided participation. In one study (Rogoff et al., 1989), mothers from the United States were compared with Mayan Indian mothers from Guatemala on how they helped their twenty-month-old children to use a set of nesting dolls. The U.S. mothers acted more like peers, wanting to take turns in combining dolls and commenting on the process. The Mayan mothers retained more of an adult-child status difference. They assumed the children would eventually learn the task. They

TABLE 2.4   Components of Guided Participation Between Adults and Young Children

Child sets the agenda according to interest and skill level

Adult adjusts level of child's participation according to child's skill

Adult constrains child's participation for the safety and rights of others

Adult transfers responsibility to child according to on-going assessment of child's abilities

Source: Adapted from B. Rogoff, *Apprenticship in thinking: Cognitive development in social context*, 1990. New York: Oxford University Press.

monitored the children's progress and gave verbal instructions, but they did not get very involved in the task.

One U.S. mother tried to play games with the dolls, then offered them to the child for "his turn." She gave instructions ("Put the lid on") and then cheered when the child did this ("Yeah! You're so smaaart!"). This mother tried to change the agenda when she judged that the baby's attention waned. She commented on all the child's actions and made requests for actions throughout the task.

A typical Mayan mother demonstrated how the dolls come apart and go back together, using a few words to encourage the child to look. The baby wanted to handle the doll, but soon after, the mother took it back and again demonstrated how to do the task. She pointed out the features of the task verbally as she performed the action. After that, she let the infant try for some time on his own while she watched but did not intervene. When he ran into trouble, the mother would say something to help ("Do this one first"). When the child made a successful move, the mother would simply say "Okay" or "I see" in a quiet tone. This study shows that the principles of guided participation work even in very different cultural situations and with different parental styles.

Interactive systems theories have had a major impact on research and on practice. Even during Vygotsky's era, these ideas influenced early childhood education. Teachers in day care centers and nursery schools have known for generations that education begins with the child's motivation, and that it is the teacher's job to adapt to the skill level of the infants. Many parents do this intuitively, and most current child-rearing advice books encour-

age this behavior. Teaching young parents how to pay attention to the inclinations of their babies is a major component of parent-education classes for parents who are having difficulty with their babies, such as teenage parents, single parents living in poverty, parents with clinical depression, and parents who have a handicapped infant (see Chapters 8 and 9).

Simple, one-directional parent-to-child socialization theories would not be acceptable in developmental research journals today. Research based on interactive systems theories has given detailed descriptive accounts of the ways in which parents and infants play games, come to understand each other, and develop over time.

What Are the Problems with Interactive Systems Theory?

One problem with interactive systems theory is that it focuses primarily on short-term developmental changes such as acquiring a new skill during guided participation with an adult. It does not provide a framework for understanding how these short-term changes contribute to the changes that move infants from one developmental stage to the next.

Another criticism of interactive systems theory is that it focuses on parent-infant relationships or small groups of co-participants, without taking account of the broader issues, such as those raised in ecological systems theories. Many interaction theorists study primarily the mother-infant interaction and fail to consider the family systems processes described earlier, including the roles of the father and siblings. Research inspired by

Vygotsky's work, on the other hand, does take explicit account of cultural factors and cultural differences in the developmental process.

Dynamic Systems Theory

Some of the pioneers in the study of human development—Darwin, Vygotsky, and Piaget—were interested in the problem of how new forms arise during development. At different times in evolutionary history, for example, new species emerge that have never been seen before. Similarly, during the life span of a person, new abilities, emotions, and experiences arise as stages unfold in time. The story of all living systems, in fact, is about the generation of novelty, the creation of something new that was not there before.

Until recently, however, the emergence of novelty could not be explained. Many developmentalists turned their attention to other topics, such as the age at which children acquired particular skills and the environmental conditions that facilitated the infant's development. The introduction of dynamic systems theory into developmental research, however, has given scientists the conceptual and methodological tools to return to the fundamental question that motivated Darwin, Vygotsky, and Piaget: the emergence of novelty in development (van Geert, 1998).

Dynamic systems theory takes its current form from the work of the physicist Ilya Prigogine (Prigogine & Stengers, 1984). Most of the matter in the universe slowly expends its energy and then burns out. But Prigogine was interested in phenomena that make their own energy, preserve themselves across time, and become increasingly complex by generating novel forms. This is the process that characterizes all living systems, from single-celled organisms to human beings. The ability of systems to maintain themselves and to develop new forms is called **self-organization**. The "self" in self-organization means that the maintenance and development of the system arises from the mutual transactions and feedback processes between the components of the system, rather than being imposed on the system by some preexisting plan.

Prigogine began his research by studying some nonliving physical systems that had the capacity to create their own energy and become more complex in form. One example is the weather, in which the forms—such as seasons or hurricanes—develop and maintain themselves over time. In spite of its dynamic complexity, the weather has patterns that repeat. Every year you can expect it to be cold in the winter and warm in the summer. Every winter is different from every previous winter in particular ways, however, and it is not possible to predict in advance what each new winter will be like.

Many dynamic systems display the following two properties:

1. They form predictable and stable patterns in their macroscopic behavior. The seasons in the weather system are one example; the stages of human development are another. All infants go through the same Piagetian substages in the same sequence, just as each year the earth goes through the same four seasons.

2. They are relatively unpredictable in their microscopic behavior. One may be able to predict the weather over the coming week or two within a range of possibilities depending upon the season, but the complexity of the weather system always leaves room for something novel to emerge. Similarly, we can describe what ten-month-old infants are likely to do in general, but their precise behavior on a given day and how they develop within the range of their possibilities cannot be predicted. Something novel happens every day that cannot be anticipated.

This microscopic unpredictability in the context of macroscopic stability is known as **chaos**. Chaos is a mathematical concept that expresses the property of complex systems to have some general structure that repeats over time but never in exactly the same way. The drawing in Figure 2.7 represents chaos. It is the trajectory of a mathematical equation that traces a path in three-dimensional space that is similar on each cycle, but is never exactly the same as any previous cycle. Each person's life course is similar in the transitions between developmental stages, but no two lives are exactly the same. The concept of chaos suggests that dynamic systems are partially determinate and partially indeterminate.

The concepts of chaos and indeterminism suggest how the application of dynamic systems theory to human development is different from all other developmental theories. All scientists will admit that with something as complex as human development, there is no way to predict precisely how a person will turn out. Most scientists believe, however, that if we could somehow measure all the relevant variables in the system, it would in fact be possible to predict a person's future. This idea of **determinism** suggests that all events have a cause, and the cause can be found with enough scientific work. In this view, we are unable to predict events in a person's life because we simply do not have sufficient data.

On the other hand, dynamic systems theory allows for the possibility of indeterminism. **Indeterminism** expresses the idea that not everything a person does, and not every turn in that person's development, can be predicted from known laws or principles. Indeterminism suggests that even if we could measure all the relevant variables in a system, we still could not completely predict its future behavior. This is because *self-organization spontaneously creates novelty*, something that did not exist prior to its creation and that could not have been predicted. Most living systems display a certain degree of indeterminism in their growth (Fogel, Lyra, & Valsiner, 1997; Prigogine & Stengers, 1984).

Scientists use the following example. Imagine a butterfly is flapping its wings somewhere in Asia. This movement is just enough to change the flow of a tiny bit of warm air. This tiny change in airflow may happen at just the right moment to

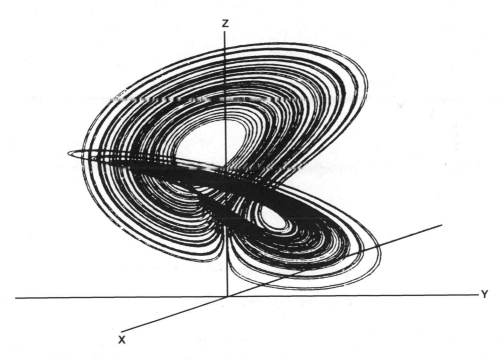

Figure 2.7 A Trajectory of Chaos
A mathematical equation generates a curve that repeats a similar shape in three-dimensional space. Each time the curve repeats the shape, however, it is in a slightly different place from where it has passed through before.
Source: F. Capra, *The web of life*, 1996, p. 135. New York: Anchor Books.

trigger a much larger change in airflow because of deviation-amplifying feedback, which then causes a change in the temperature distribution at higher elevations. At some point and without a specific cause, the conditions are created for a thunderstorm to emerge in the United States. Because of complex feedback processes and emergent novelty, it is impossible to trace the cause of the thunderstorm back to a single source (even the flight path of the butterfly depends in part on wind and weather conditions in that very moment!).

A **butterfly effect** occurs when a very small perturbation creates unpredictable novelty in a system, which then results in macroscopic developmental change in the system. Self-organization, chaos, and the butterfly effect have been used to explain why all snowflakes are similar but no two are exactly alike, the unpredictability of heart rhythms during a heart attack, and the development of differences and similarities between living cells (Capra, 1996; Hopkins & Butterworth, 1997).

Esther Thelen and I were among the first to apply dynamic systems theory to developmental psychology. We used it to explain infant locomotor development and infant socioemotional development (Fogel & Thelen, 1987; Thelen & Fogel, 1989). We proposed that infant development is not fixed to a genetic or maturational timetable, nor is it entirely predictable from adult guidance or infant learning. While these factors provide the context for development, new abilities emerge through the dynamic indeterminacy of self-organization.

Infants have all the necessary locomotor skills for walking as early as six months, but they do not walk until ten or twelve months. By six months, most infants can move their legs in a walking pattern, can support their own weight on their legs, and can take steps if held by an adult. They seem to have all the abilities but one: balancing themselves while upright. This balancing ability develops between six and ten months through a variety of experiences alone and with an adult. When the ability develops—and the exact age is unpredictable—infant walking self-organizes spontaneously. In just a few days from the first independent steps, the infant can walk across the room (Thelen, 1989;

Thelen & Smith 1994). This spontaneous and sudden developmental transition is one of the behavioral markers of a self-organizing process (Prigogine & Stengers, 1984): something novel emerges that was not present earlier.

Dynamic systems theory has the advantage of trying to explain development from the perspective of multiple possible causes and connections. Unlike most theories, dynamic systems gives credit to indeterministic factors in development, suggesting that there is a creativity and spontaneity in human development that goes beyond the inputs to produce unique effects: the special qualities of particular infant personalities and infants' remarkably inventive actions. Human development has many examples of butterfly effects; small and unexpected events that can change the course of a life (Fogel, 1990a; Thelen, 1990).

I have applied dynamic systems theory to the parent-infant communication system (Fogel, 1993; Fogel & Branco, 1997; Fogel, Garvey, Hsu & West-Stroming, 2006; Fogel & Lyra, 1997). Many forms of interpersonal communication are transactional, that is, they work by means of feedback between the participants. In my research, I discovered that this transaction has two important features:

- The continuous mutual adjustment of action
- Creativity

Unlike adults, whose conversations are in the form of speaking turns in which one person waits while the other talks, parents and infants communicate nonverbally in such a way that both participants are continuously active at all times. As a baby makes cooing vocalizations, for example, the parent is smiling at the infant, holding him, and moving him in rhythm with the vocal sounds. You can see this continuous mutual adjustment of actions in adult conversation if you take note of the facial expressions and body movements of the adults and not just their vocalizations. This continuous mutual adjustment also appears in all adult communication, including ordinary conversation, dancing, group singing, and team athletics.

The other feature of communication is creativity. During conversation, for example, people form their sentences and stories to express something they have in mind. There is never a perfect match between what someone wants to express and the way in which it is actually said. People have to make up their sentences as they speak, and no two sentences are ever exactly alike. In addition, as we hear the responses of others to our words, that feedback sometimes makes us work to clarify our meaning or even to change it according to the other's perspective. In this sense, communication is creatively self-organized because it emerges in the process of transaction. A participant's words and actions can have a butterfly effect, changing the direction of an interaction toward new topics and introducing a certain amount of indeterminism. We can call this type of communication "alive" (Fogel & Garvey, 2007).

Co-regulation is the continuous mutual adjustment and co-creativity that appears in spontaneous communication (Fogel, 1993; Fogel & Garvey, 2007). Co-regulation is a synonym for self-organization as applied to interpersonal communication. It accounts for why communication systems maintain repeating patterns of co-activity such as greetings, parent-infant games like peekaboo, or particular topics of conversation between a couple. Repeating patterns in a communication system, such as a topic of conversation, are called **frames**. Co-regulation also provides a way for novelty to enter into the system. Because communication is inherently creative, it contains the sources for its own change over time (Fogel, 1993).

Dynamic systems theory has been applied by an increasing number of infant researchers. The applications are in areas such as gene-environment interactions (Lickliter, 2008; Richardson, 2008), prenatal development (Messinger & Lester, 2008), motor development (Goldfield, 1993; Clark, Truly, & Phillips, 1993; Thelen & Smith, 1994), cognitive development (van Geert, 1993; Thelen & Smith, 1994), perceptual development (Bertenthal & Pinto, 1993; Butterworth, 1993), personality and temperament (Lewis, 1995, 2008), emotions (Camras, 1993; Fogel et al., 1992; Wolff, 1993), parent-infant mental health (Beebe & Jaffee, 2008; Downing, 2008; Greenspan, 2008), family-child

relationships (Fogel, 2008; Kerr, 2008), and peer play (Eckerman, 1993).

Consider the development of infant emotions. Infant self-soothing, to take one example, emerges quite suddenly when infants develop the ability to put their hands in their mouths, usually around the age of five months. This achievement reduces the intensity of crying and allows infants immediate control over the direction of their attention and action. Hand-mouth coordination would not normally be considered part of emotional development. When we look at the whole system, however, we can see that each component of the system may be affecting the others. In addition, a simple butterfly effect of the change of one small component can have big effects on the self-organization of the whole system. In addition to self-calming, infant laughter and sustained engagement in social and object play also occur around five months of age (Fogel, 1985; Fogel, Nwokah, & Karns, 1993; see also Chapter 7).

At each developmental period, dynamic systems theory suggests an important role for creativity in everyday action. When babies begin to acquire language, for example, they can create novel sentences never spoken before. These experiments with playful creativity provide the opportunities for novelty to enter the system and to enhance growth and development.

What Are the Problems with Dynamic Systems Theory?

Because dynamic systems theory is relatively new, its description of infant development is still rather general. Dynamic systems theory points to the inclusion of all the components of the system and the search for butterfly effects, but it does not have any specific guidelines for where to look for such things. It will take a great deal more research to fill in the blanks of the theory (as it took thirty years for information-processing theory to fill in the blanks of Piaget's more general theory of cognitive development). Research can be a slow process.

Because it came from physics, dynamic systems theory sometimes uses complicated mathematical models. Applying such models directly to human development is difficult because it is not easily reduced to measurable quantities such as velocity and acceleration. The mathematics of the theory has been most successfully applied in the study of motor development, because moving limbs can be measured according to displacement, velocity, and acceleration. We do not know whether socioemotional development fits the same mathematical principles as the physical systems on which the theory was originally based, or whether a very different mathematical approach will be needed to understand the more qualitative aspects of human experience. It is possible that there is a form of mathematics for the human psyche, but it has not been invented.

CLINICAL THEORIES

The infant's psychological experience of the world— what the infant knows, perceives, and feels—is not observable. Theories function to go beyond what is observed in order to explain what cannot be observed. Virtually all scientific theories of infant experience, such as Piaget's, are based upon direct observations of infants, creating a picture of infancy known as the **observed infant** (Stern, 1985).

An alternative source of evidence about infants' psychological experience comes from clinical work with older children and adults. During psychotherapy, for example, people sometimes appear to remember their experiences during childhood. Memories of particular incidents and events are called **conceptual memories**. Conceptual memories are composed of specific categories for type of event ("I was left alone"), time ("when I was five years old"), and place ("at the preschool"). Conceptual memory is recall about an event that is communicated in the form of a verbal narrative or story.

Memories of early infancy, however, are very different from conceptual memories of particular incidents. Memories of infancy are participatory memories. **Participatory memories** are non-

conceptual. They are not *about* a past experience; rather, they are felt as a *being with* or a *reliving of* past experiences. They are composed of emotions, desires, and a sense of familiarity, without any specific time or place (Bråten, 1998, 2003; Fogel, 2004; Heshusuis, 1994; Stern, 1985). A participatory memory, for example, is the re-creation of a feeling of what it was like to be cuddled and comforted, rather than a specific situation of being cuddled. An adult's participatory memory of feeling cuddled may include the adult's body curling into a fetal posture and the feeling of being very tiny and held by a much bigger person.

The **clinical infant** is the participatory memory of infancy in children and adults. The observed infant is constructed primarily from quantitative research methods. The clinical infant is based primarily on qualitative research methods and participant observations. Participatory memories of infancy and early childhood may occur during psychotherapy. Clinicians and their clients are participant observers and they typically report their "data"—clients' reexperiencing their own infancy during therapy—in terms of narrative descriptions of individual cases. The quantitative researcher relies primarily on conceptual analyses, describing and narrating about what has been observed. The qualitative researcher, on the other hand, uses a participatory method. The goal is *being with* the subject of the study, being a participant observer in the sense of *reliving* experiences, rather than standing outside those experiences (Heshusius, 1994).

Theory and qualitative research based on the clinical infant are often not accepted within the scientific community because of the belief that they cannot be proven. In part, this is due to a negative bias attached to qualitative and case study research methods by people who favor quantitative research as the only true scientific method. Also, it is very difficult to ascertain, for example, if an adult's participatory memory of his or her infant experience during psychotherapy is the "truth."

Because participatory memories are general rather than specific, focusing on feelings rather than events, they can never be located in partic-ular events. If, for example, in a psychotherapy session, a client has a participatory memory of trauma to her pelvic area, it may or may not be related to a history of sexual abuse. It could just as easily be related to toilet training difficulties or a forgotten injury. There is, in other words, no way to trace a participatory memory back to a specific source. Yet, as we shall see, children and adults can have very "realistic" feelings that have a sense of familiarity; that is, of a being a personal memory.

It is important to realize, on the other hand, that even scientific theories based on the observed infant cannot be proven. No matter what research method is used, *infants' psychological experience will always be unobservable by adults.* Adult scientists cannot get inside the skin of the infants being observed; they must use theory to fill the gap between what can be observed and what cannot.

Scientific theories are not "truth" but reason-able conclusions based on a systematic application of the assumptions of the theory and the meth-ods of research. There are many instances in the history of psychology in which theoretical conclu-sions about the infant's psychological experience have changed; witness the historical changes and controversies regarding ideas about infants during the twentieth century (Chapter 1) and the different views of infant experience that emerge from each of the scientific theories reviewed earlier in this chapter.

Each theory, then, is just one perspective on nature. No single theory can ever deal with the entire range of human developmental phenomena. Researchers, clinicians, parents, and educators can examine each of these theories and take what is most meaningful for any given application. These theories should be seen not as mutually exclusive but rather as complementary.

The purpose of this section on clinical theories is to describe several theories of infancy that are based on the clinical infant. In addition, I briefly explore the possible therapeutic effects on chil-dren and adults of the participatory remembering of infant experiences during clinical work.

Can Children and Adults Remember Their Infancy Experiences?

The clinical theories reviewed in this chapter assume that children and adults are shaped by their experiences during early infancy and the prenatal period. Is there any evidence that this is so? With regard to conceptual memory, people typically can recall only one or two specific incidents from early childhood, and not usually before the age of two or three years. Adults can have more detailed con-ceptual memories of events and situations begin-ning from when they were five or six years old. This is why it is commonly believed that we cannot remember our infancy, a phenomenon known as **infantile amnesia**.

As mentioned earlier, however, during thera-peutic and other emotionally salient situations, people have participatory experiences that appear to them to be memories of the prenatal and infancy periods that had been previously forgot-ten. Some therapeutic situations appear to allow people to recover the "unconscious," that part of the self that is not verbally remembered during ordinary waking states (Wade, 1996). Participatory memories are likely to be nonverbal ones because they occurred at a time when we did not have words to describe them or because they were in some way traumatic. We know this from research on three-year-olds remembering traumatic injuries that occurred when they were one or two years old (Peterson, 1999; Peterson & Bell, 1996; Peterson & Rideout, 1998).

While conceptual memories are primarily mental, participatory memories often involve the whole body. When particular patterns of move-ment, posture, and/or emotions occur repeatedly in particular situations, they are more likely to be remembered by the neuromotor system (Shore, 1994; Thelen & Smith, 1994). This is true, for example, in learning any skilled activity, such as music or athletics. Musicians may have conceptual memories of written music, but it is the participa-tory memory of moving their bodies that allows them to actually play or sing. Research on adults who experienced traumas as adults (such as assault, emotional trauma, war, or an automobile accident) also shows that their memories of the trauma are fragmentary (they do not have a particular time or place) and relived in the body. They may shake or break out in a cold sweat and experience a feeling of intense fear (Smyth & Pennebaker, 1999; Terr, 1994).

If an infant's needs are repeatedly ignored, for example, the infant develops feelings of distress and hopelessness. As the infant grows older, as a child or adult, similar situations will evoke similar participatory memories. If that person feels ignored, it is likely to lead to the experience of hopelessness (Gaensbauer, 2004). If that experience occurs repeatedly in life, it can lead to depression. The depression, therefore, may have its origins in a participatory memory from early infancy. There are also many ordinary, nontraumatic participatory memories. Movement patterns learned in infancy, such as kicking, reaching, crawling, and rolling over, underlie all later complex movements of older children and adults (Thelen & Smith, 1994). Patterns of emotional responses in infancy form the basis for many later adult emotions (Fogel, 2003; Stern, 1985).

Participatory memories are often transformed over time. The memory of being ignored in infancy, in the above example, may be changed into feelings of depression in the adult. The adult has a long developmental history, which may include other experiences of being ignored or of being recognized and loved. The early participatory memories, therefore, are filtered through this history of related experiences. These early memories may remain, or they may become lost or transformed.

Participatory memories are not verbal. For this reason, therapeutic methods that evoke these memories succeed by taking people away from their ordinary patterns of conceptual thinking and reasoning. The most common example of participatory memories in adults is dreams, which cannot be completely comprehended by verbal or logical means. Dreams are often used in therapeutic situations as a way to bring these participatory memories into conscious awareness. Although the

idea of participatory memories of infancy is theoretical, there is some evidence that they exist and can be reexperienced. This evidence comes from dreams and from experiences during therapeutic encounters (see Chapters 2 and 9).

In the remainder of this section, we review two different types of approach to the clinical infant: psychotherapeutic approaches and somatic awareness approaches. Psychotherapeutic theories use talking between client and therapist as the principal tool for enhancing awareness of participatory memory and how it affects the adults' psyche. Somatic refers to the individual's conscious awareness of the experiences of their bodies. **Somatic** awareness approaches use some combination of talk, movement, touch, and somatic awareness in order to access participatory memory. It is not the purpose of this section to review all types of clinical methods. We focus only on a few that have explicitly recognized the role of infant and other developmental experiences in the therapeutic process.

Psychotherapeutic Approaches

Sigmund Freud was a physician who noticed that his patients often came to him with physical symptoms that had no apparent medical cause. Freud saw that in some cases, people exhibited behavior that was thematically related to their physical symptom. A person with constipation, for example, might tend to be overly concerned with behavioral cleanliness, order, and punctuality. The mode of retention in the body organ corresponded with retaining tight behavioral control over one's life.

Freud speculated that these patterns of behavior might have their origins early in a person's life, around the time when infants are being toilet trained and becoming aware of the process of holding onto and letting go of the contents of their bowels. This occurs in children in Western cultures around the age of two years. Freud wanted to explore whether such people had any memory of a trauma that might have occurred around that age. He experimented with an early form of hypnosis and then later discovered a method that he called **free association**. He asked his clients to lie down and encouraged them to relax by providing a comfortable couch and a safe environment in which they could say anything without fear of retribution or judgment. As they talked about whatever came to mind, Freud helped them become aware of the possible participatory memories that were behind the behavioral symptoms, memories of which the client's conscious mind was unaware. The use of free association along with interpretation in psychotherapy is called **psychoanalysis**.

During free association, people who are over-controlled in their daily life may express participatory memories of fear, such as the fear of punishment or the fear of being controlled. This participatory memory is not of any specific toilet-training situation. These memories may be connected with nonverbal desires to lose control, to be uninhibited in their behavior, to let go of what they are carrying, and to release their pent-up feelings of frustration. This type of uninhibited behavior is what Freud (1903) referred to as the **id**. The id can be thought of as all of the person's needs and desires, but especially those desires that are irrational, overwhelmingly compelling, and not tolerant of any delay.

According to Freud, infants are dominated by the id and gradually learn to control some of these impulses. Their crying becomes less insistent, for example, and they develop the capacity to wait for gratification and to regulate their own needs. The **ego** is the ability to tolerate discomfort and frustration and to moderate the pursuit of pleasure. The ego, in psychoanalytic theory, refers to the regulatory functions of the person.

As the infant grows older, the ego relies increasingly on thought processes, mental representation, problem solving, and rational approaches to the world. Freud realized that thinking and reasoning about oneself are important for self-control and appropriate social behavior. These tools of the ego, however, are not useful in accessing the mostly nonverbal id memories, because the ego was developed specifically to repress the id. This is why Freud turned to free association: in order to get people temporarily out of the rational conceptual way in which they regulated their everyday life.

Based on what his adult clients revealed during free association, Freud theorized that the development from id to ego recurs during the life course, as new sources of id experiences mature. Id experiences relate to pleasurable or unpleasurable feelings of the body, and the location in the body of these feelings changes as the person grows older. He distinguished two major phases of id development during the first three years of life: the oral stage and the anal stage.

During the first year of life, the infant is particularly aware of sensations of pleasure and displeasure in the mouth region through activities such as sucking, chewing, biting, sound making, touching with the lips, and swallowing. This period is called the **oral stage**. During this stage, according to Freud's theory, the infant views the world from the point of view of consuming it. Freud felt that infants at this stage of development believe that they can incorporate everything and everyone—that the world is centered upon their own gratification—and trust in the inevitability of satisfaction.

The **anal stage** begins some time in the second year of life, when the primary sensitive zone becomes the anal region of the body. Freud recognized that children find pleasure in the distension of the bowel, the withholding of feces, and the elimination of feces. Gaining self-control over the bladder and bowel muscles is a major personal achievement, and the feelings associated with producing, owning, holding onto, and voluntarily giving up one's feces are thought to relate to the child's growing sense of self and personal autonomy.

The person with constipation, for example, may be holding onto things, according to Freud, because his anal id desires to let go and be messy either were not recognized or were punished by his family. He retains a participatory memory of his anal desires (to be messy), but that memory that have not been verbalized because the behavior was not tolerated or discussed when he was two years old.

These two stages and later developmental stages postulated by Freud are included in Table 2.5. A more detailed description of the later stages is beyond the scope of this book.

Erik Erikson (1950) accepted Freud's basic premise that changes in body sensitivity from oral to anal awareness form the core of the developing infant. He viewed each stage of development (eight stages in all across the entire life span) as a potential crisis of the personality leading to a new sense of individual identity. Individuals might continue their forward progress in development, or they might become sidetracked at any point. Erikson's developmental stages are also given in Table 2.5. Parents and parental behavior are a topic of this book as well, and parents are typically in Erikson's stage of generativity versus stagnation, the period of young adulthood and parental responsibility that follows the stage of identity versus role confusion shown in Table 2.5. **Generativity** means to create and to nurture.

Instead of emphasizing participatory memory of the body, as Freud did, Erikson focused on the way in which the infant's body related to the family and to society. The first conflict of the life cycle was related to the development of a sense of basic trust in the environment. This trust developed if the parent was able to recognize and gratify the infant's id needs in such a way that the baby came to expect the environment to be friendly and supportive. Mistrust occurred when the parent did not allow the infant to experience id feelings (mistrust in self) or when the infant came to expect that needs would not be met adequately (mistrust in others). In an adult, participatory memories of this period may be related to feelings of being ignored or supported by others.

In the second stage, the infant could develop either a sense of purpose and autonomy or else a sense of shame and doubt. This again depended upon the parent's ability to support the infant's desire to feel his or her own experiences of control and letting go, and to reward and to share in the infant's personal achievements. If the parent chastises the infant for being assertive or fails to delight in the infant's accomplishments, the infant may feel ashamed and develop a sense of doubt about his or her ability to be independent. In adults, participatory memories of this period may be felt as a fear of failure or a lack of self-confidence.

Both Freud and Erikson relied on observations of the clinical infant, the infant as experi-

TABLE 2.5 Psychoanalytic Stages of Development

Approximate Age (Years)	According to Freud	According to Erickson
0–1½	*Oral*: Focus on experiences of the mouth such as sucking, eating, crying, biting	*Trust vs. Mistrust*: Development of expectancy for either gratification or frustration
1½–3	*Anal*: Focus on experience in anal region such as elimination and retention	*Autonomy vs. Shame/doubt*: Self-assertiveness and self-control or uncertainty and shame
3–6	*Phallic or oedipal*: Foxus on genitals and desire to possess opposite-sex parent	*Initiative vs. Guilt*: Independent activity is approached with either a sense of purpose (initiative) or questioning (guilt)
6–11	*Latency*: Interest in learning new skills but no overt sexual desires	*Industry vs. Inferiority*: Interest in learning and skill development or a sense of inadequacy and loss of motivation
11–20	*Genital*: Adult sexual desires and the establishment of sexual relationships	*Identity vs. Role confusion*: Perception of self as a unique individual: development of personal values or confusion about identity and role in life

Source: A. Fogel & G. F. Melson, *Child Development*, 1988, p. 34. St. Paul, MN: West.

enced by adults during free association. Somewhat later, psychoanalysts began to rely on data from the observed infant. The issue of the growth of personal autonomy, for example, was studied by Margaret Mahler (1975). Mahler was a practicing psychoanalyst who devoted her clinical work to helping young children and their families. She believed that many psychopathologies could be prevented by intervention with families in the early years of the child's life.

Mahler's work and that of others led to the refinement of the field of **infant psychiatry**, the application of clinical psychology work directly to infants and their families (see the section on infant mental health in Chapter 9). Because of the psychoanalytic emphasis on the parent-infant bond, most clinical interventions in infancy involve a large component of parent education and enrichment. When infants have severe feeding, toilet-training, emotional regulation, or autonomy problems, clinicians will most often work with the mother-infant dyad.

Daniel Stern (1985) followed Mahler's approach of using data from both clinical and observed infants. Stern's theoretical emphasis is on self-awareness, and his theory is one of the most detailed regarding the types of infant experiences that correspond to later participatory memories of adults. He theorized that even from birth, infants have a sense of self. The early senses of self during the first three years of life remain with the person, even as new ways of knowing the self emerge in development.

Stern postulated that during the first two months, infants have a sense of an **emergent self** (see Chapter 5). They are aware of how the different movements, sensations, and feelings cohere into recognizable states. Between two and eight months, infants develop a sense of a **core self** (also called the *ecological self*; see Chapter 5). This is the experience of being an active agent that does things in the world, has feelings, and has a history of prior experiences. Between eight and fifteen months, infants discover that they have inner experiences that are different from others around them. This **subjective self** (see Chapter 5)

can choose to share feelings and experiences with others and is aware of its dependence upon and attachment to others. After fifteen months, the **verbal self** (which this book divides into the *categorical self* [Chapter 5] and the *conceptual self* [Chapter 5]) comes to use language to talk about inner states and to construct a coherent identity in the company of other people. The verbal self is the beginning of the individual's conceptual memory.

According to Stern, the ability to fully experience each of these senses of the infant self is fostered when parents recognize and support the infant in his or her endeavors to explore the self, its possibilities and boundaries. These senses of self are very vulnerable to being overwhelmed when parental action is not attuned to the infant's process of self-discovery. If parents are too controlling, infants may lose their sense of an emergent, core, or subjective self. They cannot feel any of their own control over their feelings and actions. Although this happens regularly to all babies and is part of the process of growing up, in some cases infants are chronically deprived of any ability to sense themselves.

Stern's theory suggests that adults may have both positive and negative participatory memories of the emergent, core, and subjective selves. In adults, the participatory memory of the emergent self is the feeling that things are "coming together," or, in contrast, that the events in one's life are chaotic or confusing. In adults, the participatory memory of the core self is the sense of having a lasting identity and the person's willingness to fully feel one's emotions. Alternatively, core self memories may be experienced as identity confusion, avoidance of emotions, loss of direction, and helplessness. In adults, the participatory memory of the subjective self is the presence or lack of sharing, security, and trust with which we relate our inner feelings to other people.

The work of Mahler and Stern led to a developmental approach to the treatment of children and adults who have lost touch with their infant selves. A developmental approach allows people to reexperience the core self—in a therapeutic context, for example—and then to use those experiences to recreate a more optimal sequence of self-development than they had in their own families.

The treatment method is similar to Freud's. Work with clients who may be suffering from a mistrust of others occurs in a setting that is conducive to relaxation and total acceptance of their feelings. Relaxation and acceptance are universally part of all therapeutic efforts—both psychotherapeutic and somatic awareness approaches—to relive one's infancy and to recreate a better developmental process. These are the basic conditions under which people can be made aware of their participatory memories of infancy.

The psychoanalytically oriented therapist also helps the client to focus attention on the threads of his or her early experience in order to explore the consequences for the self. This allows the client the freedom to weave these threads into a coherent pattern that promotes renewed developmental change. The basic elements of developmental therapeutic processes are given in Table 2.6. Working with young children, these goals can be accomplished using play therapy (Ryan & Wilson, 1995).

Somatic Awareness Approaches

The other branch of developmental clinical theory and practice that will be discussed here is grouped under the heading of **somatic awareness approaches**. In psychotherapeutic methods, therapists usually talk with their clients while they are seated or lying down. Somatic awareness approaches may also use talk, but they typically use body movement and touch as a way to access the participatory memories of early childhood. Since infants experience their world via movement and touch, for many somatic awareness practitioners, this seems to be a more direct route to an adult's infant experience than merely talking.

Somatic awareness approaches also use the three aspects of developmental therapy shown in Table 2.6: safety, exploration, and awareness. Safety is created in part by the physical environment. Some methods use soft music and low lighting. Safety is also created by an attitude on the part of the practitioner that permits openness and allows people to relax. If touch is used, clients are reassured that it will be for therapeutic and strictly nonsexual purposes. Exploration is created by letting the client direct the flow of the session. Awareness is enhanced as the practitioner helps clients to pay attention not only to their words, but to their body movements, emotions, and sensations. Because it is difficult for most adults to do this, access to participatory memory is aided by the creation of a deep state of relaxation that facilitates attention to the inner self.

One somatic awareness method that explicitly attempts to recreate an optimal infant experience is **Watsu**. In this technique, the practitioner floats the client in a pool of warm water. It was created by Harold Dull, who studied a Japanese massage method called zen shiatsu, in which the body is gently stretched in order to release tension. Dull found that the effects of zen shiatsu were enhanced in the water.

During a session, clients are moved freely in the water, stretched gently, and cradled in the practitioner's arms. In their parent's arms, fussy infants are comforted and touched, their tensions are eased, and they can return to focusing their relaxed attention on what they are doing and feeling. In this safe environment, they can really explore their bodies and continue to grow. A similar effect occurs in Watsu. "By being moved so freely through the water, by being stretched and repeatedly returned to a fetal position, the adult has the opportunity to heal in himself whatever pain or loss he may still carry from that time" (Dull, 1995, p. 65).

With the head and body in water, sound is muted, and clients can hear the rush of the water and the sound of their own heartbeat. They can also hear the practitioner's heartbeat and feel the contact of skin against skin. This is believed to evoke a preverbal experience, possibly even a prenatal experience, that provides a sense of wholeness (Brooke, 2001a; Sawyer, 1999). The method has been used to help adults recover from prenatal, birth, and early childhood trauma. It is also one of the more relaxing treatments for pregnant women, soothing both mother and fetus. Watsu

TABLE 2.6 Techniques of Developmental Therapies

Using these techniques, clinicians have found that clients are more likely to reexperience unconscious events from infancy and early childhood and to use that information to recreate a more optimal developmental process.

Technique	Description
Safety	The client is allowed to feel secure. This is done by creating a comfortable and stable physical setting and by the therapist's maintaining an open and accepting attitude.
Exploration	Clients and therapists are allowed to follow the leads of whatever comes up and to explore their consequences and meanings for the client. Clients should be allowed to feel their unconscious emotions and thoughts in this protected situation, which is more like pretend play than "for real." This defuses the power of the unconscious to control the clients' behavior.
Awareness	The therapist's role is to help the clients maintain their attention on the sources and consequences of the unconscious patterns. The therapists are not expected to heal the clients. Rather, the clients heal themselves as they develop a sense of competence and control over their own actions, which is a direct result of their expanded awareness of their previously unconscious processes.

is also believed to help both mothers and fathers connect with their fetus and infant.

In the **Rosen method**, clients lie on a padded table while the practitioner's open and relaxed hands make gentle contact with areas of the body that appear to hold muscular tension and restrict free breathing. By listening to the client's body with gentle touch and to the words they use to describe their experience, the practitioner can help the client to relax, relieve pain, and breathe easier. The Rosen method was developed by Marion Rosen, who began her studies of the body as a young woman in Germany in the 1930s. After working many years as a physical therapist, she began incorporating her own observations into her treatments. Following the client's natural breathing pattern with gentle touch resulted in deep relaxation. She listened as clients sometimes talked about how their injuries had occurred. Often the client would connect with the felt sense of an earlier experience that related to the injury. When this happened, the client's breath would deepen, relaxation would occur, and pain would often disappear (Rosen, 2003).

Rosen began to understand that the body tells its own story, shaped by our early life experiences, many of them forgotten and nonverbal. If we are born healthy, we come into the world breathing fully, with the full swing of our diaphragm moving every muscle in our body. We expect to have all our needs met and to be loved. But these expectations cannot be fully met even under the best of circumstances. As a result of either ordinary or traumatic events, we shape ourselves through muscular tension in whatever way that helps us to survive.

These situations are believed to be registered deeply in our bodies as participatory memories, which contribute to our characteristic patterns of muscular tensions, emotions, and postures. These emotions are held in abeyance by muscular tension until we feel big enough, strong enough, and safe enough to finally allow ourselves a felt sense of the old experience. Through the gentle touch of the Rosen method, as we deeply relax and breathe more easily, we begin to remember the experiences that we had learned to suppress and contain and through that knowledge we regain fuller movement, ease, and well-being (Wooten, 1995). You can experience the quality of Rosen Method "listening touch" by following the exercise based on Rosen Method in the Experiential Exercises section of Chapter 6.

Moshe Feldenkrais (1904–1984), originally a physicist and judo instructor, invented a system of body movement education—**the Feldenkrais method**—that reawakens, develops, and organizes capacities for kinesthetic (sensorimotor) learning. Whereas children before the age of three learn movements by relying on their sensorimotor experience, older children and adults in technological cultures often behave according to social expectations, distancing themselves from their bodily feelings. Feldenkrais also observed that very young children use all their senses and every part of their bodies, a process he called **organic learning**. Adults appear to involve less of themselves, unless they are fully absorbed in what they are doing.

Feldenkrais believed that such alienation from the body contributes to habitual, usually patterns of muscular tension and psychosomatic illnesses. Because the Feldenkrais method involves the emulation of how young children learn, its therapeutic value hinges on releasing capacities for learning that had been left behind in childhood (Reese, 1985).

To teach his methods, Feldenkrais invented thousands of "Awareness through Movement" lessons, many of which are based on the movements performed by babies as they first learn to roll, sit, crawl, walk, and explore their bodies in the environment. Students are asked to make small, slow movements, reduce their efforts, and sense how even simple movements are connected with every part of the body. This book contains some Awareness through Movement lessons, those written by Feldenkrais practitioner Mark Reese and found in the Experiential Exercises sections of Chapter 4. Doing these may help you enhance your self-awareness and possibly access your own participatory memories of infancy. Feldenkrais practitioners also use hands-on techniques called functional integration. In this work, students lie on a padded table as a practitioner gently touches and moves them, often in babylike ways, in order to promote deep relaxation, kinesthetic awareness, and openness to learning new ways to move.

Feldenkrais methods are used to increase physical coordination and integration and to bring greater enjoyment and satisfaction in life. They are also used for adults and children with muscular problems, cerebral palsy, Down's syndrome, and other developmental disabilities (Baniel, **www.anatbanielmethod.com**), and other developmental problems, and with adults who suffer from neurological or orthopedic problems.

Bodymind centering (BMC) is a method of body and movement awareness in which adults perform exercises based on the normal stages of infant sensorimotor development (Hartley, 1995). Bodymind centering was created by a dance teacher and physical therapist, Bonnie Bainbridge Cohen, during the 1960s and 1970s. Cohen discovered that she could help many of her clients by taking them step by step through the sensorimotor stages of prenatal and infant development. This is done by giving verbal directions and using touch to guide movement when necessary. In this way, clients can reconnect with a sense of self and self-discovery that may have been lost as they grew up.

Clients are first guided through the prenatal experience of feeling the pull of gravity, the movement of their breathing, and their heartbeat. Then they do exercises focused on feeling the sensations around the mouth, just as a newborn baby explores with mouth and sucking movements. The infant's first movements are generated through the torso and spine, and these are explored before movements that entail pushing and pulling with the arms and legs. "First we simply *feel* the new sensations, perceptions, and mobility in a very direct and immediate way, as does an infant or child. Conscious recognition of change may occur in the adult only after the movement has been fully experienced" (Hartley, 1995, p. 99). BMC has been used in the treatment of parent-infant relationships at risk (Frank, 2001) and working directly with infants who experience sensorimotor difficulties (Brook, 2001b). An Experiential Exercise, naval radiation, based on BMC can be found in Chapter 3.

Related to BMC is **Dance Movement Psychotherapy**, in which infants and children can be engaged using expressive dance-like movements to foster a more integrated sense of self in relation to other people. It has been successful for infants and children with autism, communication delays, sensory integration difficulties, hyperactivity, and trauma (Tortora, 2006). Infants and chil-

Clockwise from upper left: Watsu with infants; Feldenkrais Functional Integration; Dance movement therapy; Body Mind Centering, Bonnie Bainbridge Cohen.

Sources: www. massageandbodywork.com/Articles/FebMar2003/ Watsu.htm; www.anatbanielmethod.com; www.adta.org/resources/media.cfm, www.bodymindcentering.com

dren learn to sequence their movements in space and time in order to connect with others and achieve personal goals. One of the key concepts of this work is kinesthetic empathy, the ability to feel another person's feelings by moving like that other person. Dance movement psychotherapists use **kinesthetic empathy** with their clients, and children learn this by engaging with the therapist. You can better understand this approach by doing the Experiential Exercises in Chapter 7. Another related field is **somatic psychotherapy**, which focuses on felt sensations in the body, breathing, and movement on the pathway to psychological well-being (Aposhyan, 2003; Totten, 2005).

What Are the Problems with Clinical Theories?

Clinical theories have offered an alternative perspective for understanding infant development, the perspective of children and adults who are taught how to become aware of their participatory memories of being a baby. Although no theory can be proven, clinical theories have not been subjected to quantitative research tests of their predictions in the same way as the other theories reviewed in this chapter.

Clinical research is rooted in qualitative methods, which is a strength because they help us to understand how particular individuals have been shaped by their infant experience. On the other hand, more could be learned from clinical approaches by the systematic introduction of qualitative research and also by the complementary use of quantitative methods. Claims about increased relaxation and a renewed sense of well-being could be measured in treatment and no-treatment contrast groups.

It is difficult to substantiate whether the participatory memory of infancy revealed during a therapy session is the same as what that adult actually experienced as a baby. First of all, memories of early infancy are typically about feelings and body states, not about particular incidents. Second, the adult clients' middle-aged or elderly parents would find it difficult to remember whether a particular event happened, and even if they did, their experience of it as a parent would not be the same as the infant's experience. It may be that the acceptance of particular body feelings as belonging to a person's past, regardless of how they actually occurred, is of such significant therapeutic value that an exact verification is not necessary.

A problem with psychoanalytically oriented psychotherapeutic theories is that like learning theories, they tend to focus reward or blame for the child's behavior on the parents. Our earlier review of systems theories suggested, on the contrary, that children contribute to their own development by influencing parental behavior. It is easier to be sensitive and calm with a relaxed and happy baby than with one who cries much of the time.

All clinical approaches are limited in the effectiveness of their treatment. Most approaches work best for a particular range of child or adult concerns and problems. No one approach can treat all behavioral and psychological issues of children and adults. Clients should be informed about both the possibilities and the limitations of each approach. Newer approaches to parent-infant mental health will be reviewed in Chapter 9.

EXPERIENTIAL EXERCISE

Exploring the Clinical Infant

Because the infant's psychological experience is unobservable, one might conclude that understanding an infant is no different from understanding the psychological experience of a nonhuman animal. Adult humans, however, have all been human infants, and we have all had infant experiences. On scientific grounds, it would be pointless to ignore such a rich source of potential data on infancy as the *clinical infant*, the re-experiencing of infant-like movements, sensations, and states of being.

Many of the chapters in this book will have a section like this one, called Experiential Exercises. These sections will include simple exercises that allow an opportunity to experience the clinical infant for yourself. It is important to do these exercises in a quiet room where you can feel what is happening in your body. Many students feel self-conscious when first doing this. It is, after all, unusual for adults to act like babies! Almost all students, however, change their minds after actually doing the exercises for a while.

You can also enhance your learning about the clinical infant by finding opportunities to interact with infants (see the Co-Regulating with Baby sections in most chapters for ideas about this). You might want to keep a journal of your reactions to each of these exercises and encounters with babies. It is best to write in your journal immediately following the exercise. As a *participant observer*, note your physical and emotional reactions.

Doing these exercises, many students become aware of their own body in new ways, such as noticing unnecessary tension and effort in their movements. Students often report a sense of relaxation, peace, calm, and enhanced well-being, and they can see the similarities of doing these exercises to other kinds of movement and somatic awareness education in which they have participated, such as dance, yoga, massage, meditation, and athletics.

When students do the exercises and observe babies, they say things like, "Being an infant is not as easy as I used to think it was." As a result of this, students often change their approach from being an observer of infants to being someone who can really share the infant's feelings and experiences. This is a shift from a conceptual stance of *learning about* infants to a participatory stance of *being with* infants.

Another way to enhance your understanding of the clinical infant is to investigate your own infancy. Talk to your parents or guardians about what they remember about your infancy. Were you a healthy baby? Were you born prematurely? Did you experience trauma as an infant, or was your infancy reasonably happy? What was that time like for your mother and father?

Was their relationship supportive or difficult, intact or separated? Did either of your parents have a physical or mental illness? Did either of them leave or die when you were a baby? Did one or both of them work, and was that work satisfying or stressful? Was your family rich or poor? Did you spend a significant amount of time with someone other than your parents? What was life like for those individuals?

Try to match your spontaneous experiences of participation in the exercises with what you can find out from others about you, the family, and the environment that you lived in as a fetus and as an infant. Review the principles of qualitative research from Chapter 1 as well as the research on the observed infant presented in this book, and ask yourself: Does trying to re-create the *clinical infant* help me understand my own

infancy? Does it help me understand infants in general? Try the finger painting experiential exercise that follows and see what you think.

Finger Painting
(by Alan Fogel)

Finger painting is a wonderful and enjoyable way to begin to re-connect with participatory memories of your early childhood experience. It can be done individually or in groups. Just get the materials at any crafts or toy store, clear a space and time, and start painting. Notice the concrete feelings in yourself, such as emotions or sensations of color, temperature, texture. Notice if any memories come back to you. Are they pleasant or unpleasant? What does this experience tell you about yourself today? About yourself as a child?

SUMMARY

Biological Approaches

- Species and individual phenotypes evolve by natural selection.
- Behavior ecology theory is the study of a species' evolved behavior characteristics.
- Although certain survival functions are present across species, each species has a unique species-specific behavioral pattern.
- Critical periods are times in early development when the fetus or infant is particularly susceptible to environmental influence, and on which all later learning and development depend.
- Behavior genetics studies the probabilities of predicting individual differences between phenotypes using differences between either environments, genotypes, or both.

Learning Theories

- Classical conditioning is learning by association that occurs when unconditioned and conditioned stimuli are paired during training.
- Operant conditioning occurs when the frequency of behavior is controlled by its consequences: reinforcement, punishment, and extinction.
- Social learning theory suggests that learning occurs when the individual is motivated to attend to the consequences. Infants can also learn by observation and imitation.

Cognitive Theories

- Piagetian constructivist approaches suggest that infants develop intelligence by means of their own explorations in the world. Infant intelligence is of a sensorimotor rather than a verbal-symbolic form.

- Information processing theories break cognition down into a series of component processes, each of which can function independently of the others. Breakdowns in the cognitive system may occur if any of the components are not properly functioning.

Systems Theories

- A *system* is a set of interdependent components, each of which affects the others in reciprocal fashion. The process by which systems components affect each other is known as *transaction*.
- Ecological systems theory suggests that infant development is related in direct and indirect ways to the family and to society, and vice versa.
- Interactive systems theory focuses on the process of communication between parents and infants and the ways in which that communication leads to developmental change in the infant.
- Dynamic systems theory introduces elements of self-organization and indeterminacy into the process of development. Individual differences are not always predictable as a direct result of particular causes, but rather emerge creatively as part of the complex dynamics of action.

Clinical Theories

- Clinical theories use evidence from children and adults during therapeutic transactions to construct a view of infant experience and its meaning in later development.
- Children and adults remember their infancy in participatory ways via forms of body movement, muscular tension, and emotions.
- Psychoanalysis uses talking in the form of free association to evoke nonverbal participatory memories. It uses these memories to help adults understand sources of tension and emotion that were acquired during the oral and anal stages.
- Somatic awareness approaches use a combination of talk, movement, and touch to evoke nonverbal participatory memories, allowing people to remember the spontaneous capacities for organic learning and the full use of the senses and emotions that they experienced as an infant.

Chapter 3

Prenatal Development and Childbirth

CHAPTER OUTLINE AND OVERVIEW

Contraception and Fertility	*What is the process of fertilization? What causes infertility and how can it be treated? What are the most common methods of contraception? How is the birth rate controlled in different countries? Do cultural differences affect choices of contraceptive methods?*
Developmental Processes Before Birth	*What are the stages of prenatal development? What are the main behavioral, physical, and psychological characteristics of each stage?*
Genetic and Chromosomal Factors	*In what ways do fetuses differ? What are the major causes of these individual differences?*
The Childbirth Experience	*What is the process of labor and delivery? What are the common methods of childbirth?*
The Baby at Birth	*What are the physical features of the newborn? What are the typical complications of birth?*

Although many people think of birth as the beginning of life, it is now known that much of what takes place in the nine-month period before birth has important effects on subsequent development. During prenatal development, all of the major organ systems of the body, including the brain, undergo rapid development. It is just at the point of the most accelerated development that an organ is most susceptible to environmental influences.

As we shall see in this chapter and also in Chapter 9 which covers pre- and post-natal health, the womb—uterus and placenta—is not an impenetrable shield of nurture and security. The placenta functions as a communication link between mother and fetus. In some cases, the placenta becomes a wonderfully adept censor, keeping potentially harmful substances from crossing into the immature fetal circulatory system. Often, however, it does not. The womb is an environment, albeit a very special and uniquely suitable environment, to which the developing person must adapt during this phase of their lives. Variations of the prenatal environment contribute to individual differences between fetuses, some of which have long-term effects on the form of body structures, mental health, movement patterns, cognition, and sensory awareness.

This chapter will cover the development of the fetus from conception until the last month of pregnancy, followed by a discussion of birth and the newborn. In the first section, we discuss conception and fertility. The next section covers the stages of normal prenatal development, focusing in particular on behavioral development. This is followed by a section on genetic and chromosomal factors.

CONCEPTION AND FERTILITY

Conception

Human development begins with **conception**, the union of a female **ovum** and a male **spermatozoon**. Collectively, spermatozoa and ova are known as **gametes**. During sexual intercourse, many millions of sperm cells enter the vagina. These cells are propelled through the uterus and into the Fallopian tubes, partly by the pumping action of the vaginal and uterine muscles and partly by the swimming movements of the spermatozoa. Only a few hundred sperm cells will reach the Fallopian tubes, and even those will die if they do not encounter an ovum within 24 to 48 hours.

Ova are produced in the ovaries, usually one for each menstrual cycle. Adult females will have about 350 ovulations over approximately 30 years of fertility. The ovum is covered with small hairlike appendages that can be dissolved by an enzyme secreted by the spermatozoa, and it eventually decomposes if it does not encounter a sperm cell. For fertilization to take place, many spermatozoa must bind to the surface of the ovum, after which an opening is made at random for the entrance of a single sperm cell. Once that sperm cell enters the ovum, a chemical reaction occurs to prevent other sperm cells from entering. The fertilized ovum is called a **zygote**.

Fertility

The ability to contribute successfully to fertilization or conception is called **fertility**. Male fertility begins at puberty and, for most males, lasts their entire life. Female fertility begins at puberty and lasts until menopause, the cessation of menstrual cycling that occurs when the woman is about 50 years old.

All of a girl's ova are already formed in her ovary during prenatal development, but they remain immature until the girl reaches puberty and begins to menstruate. Near the end of each menstrual period, the time during the menstrual cycle when vaginal bleeding occurs, the pituitary gland secretes a hormone that allows one of the immature ova to ripen. This event leads to the secretion of estrogen, which stimulates the development of a lining in the uterus that will nourish a possible fertilized ovum. About 14 days after the onset of the menstrual period, the ovum is ready to be fertilized as it makes its way from the ovary to the Fallopian tubes. The zygote will journey to the uterus, where it becomes implanted in the newly formed uterine lining. If fertilization does not occur, the uterine lining and ovum are discharged through the vagina during the next menstrual period.

In some cases, more than one ovum ripens. If two ova are fertilized, two different zygotes, called fraternal or **dizygotic (DZ) twins**, develop. Identical or **monozygotic (MZ) twins** develop when the fertilized zygote divides and splits into two separate zygotes. Twinning happens in about 1 in 80 pregnancies. About three-fourths of the twins are MZ twins, and the rest are DZ twins. Since they split from the same zygote, MZ twins share identical sets of genetic material, while DZ twins are no more related than any two siblings from the same mother and father. Triplets occur in 1 out of 6,400 births, while quadruplets happen in 1 out of 512,000 births. Triplets and quadruplets can be either MZ or DZ or some combination.

Boys are not born with spermatozoa. Instead, the onset of puberty in the male triggers the production of hormones that stimulate the manufacture of about 2 million sperm cells per day for the rest of his life. Male fertility, therefore, is not cyclic like female fertility. During ejaculation, 2 to 4 million sperm cells are expelled through the penis in a liquid medium called seminal fluid or semen. The testes produce the sperm, and the prostate gland and seminal vesicles produce the semen.

Controlling Fertility: Contraception and Family Planning

At the end of 2009 the world has an estimated population of 6.8 billion people (U.S. Census Bureau, 2009. http://www.census.gov/main/www.popclock.html). This is more than double the number of people alive in 1960 and more than triple the world population in 1927. Although the rate of population growth is slowing, there are likely to be twice as many people alive in 2030 as there are today. Experts do not know how many people the earth can support, but all are concerned about the quality of life that will result. Although some of the growth is due to the fact that people are healthier and living longer than in the past, much of the population increase is due to high birthrates.

Family planning is the voluntary alteration of normal reproductive patterns using contraception methods. The type of family planning used, if it is used at all, depends on a complex network of social and cultural factors interacting with moral and interpersonal factors within the family. In wealthy countries, family planning is a matter of personal choice for middle- and upper-income families. Family planning becomes a critical issue when the population of a family or a whole country exceeds the ability of the available resources to provide for the health and welfare of the children that are newly born.

Contraception. One of the simplest and least expensive methods of contraception for family planning is called **natural family planning**. The same methods used to chart ovulation for the purpose of enhancing fertility can also tell a couple when to avoid intercourse if they wish not to conceive. If used properly and with the guidance of a physician or family planning counselor, natural family planning can be very successful but it is not foolproof.

A limited number of other options for contraception are also available. Methods that work prior to fertilization include male or female sterilization, which prevents the production or transport of gametes (used by 15% of couples); birth control pills, patches, implants, or injections, which prevent ovulation using hormones (used by 39%); condoms and diaphragms, which block the passage of sperm to the vagina (used by 25%); and spermicides (foams, sponges, and suppositories), which kill sperm before they can fertilize and are often used in combination with other methods (Forrest & Fordyce, 1993b). Several other methods are used, but with somewhat higher risk for conception. Breast feeding can suppress ovulation but typically only if the mother exclusively breast feeds, which is usually for no more than 6 months, and if menstruation has not yet resumed. Withdrawal of the penis prior to ejaculation is also used to prevent sperm from entering the vagina, but some sperm may be expelled prior to ejaculation. All these methods work better if couples carefully follow guidelines but most couples are more lax, increasing the risk of conception from under 5 in 100 in most cases to as much as 35 in 100 (www. engenderhealth.org/wh/fp/index.html).

Several methods that work after fertilization are also available. The intrauterine device (IUD) prevents the zygote from implanting in the uterine wall. Several "emergency" contraception procedures, also known as "morning after" pills, are available for women who engage in unprotected sexual intercourse. A drug known as RU-486 causes the uterine lining to be expelled, taking the embryo with it; the pill must be followed two days later by an additional drug that causes the uterus to contract and complete the expulsion process. There is also the Preven Kit, approved by the FDA in 1997. It is a series of birth control pills taken for up to 5 days within 72 hours after having unprotected sex. Each of these methods has advantages and disadvantages that depend upon one's religious beliefs, values, convenience, and medical conditions and risks.

On August 24, 2006, the United States Food and Drug Administration ruled that customers over the age of 18 should be able to buy these pills—currently marketed under the name of *Plan B*—without the need for a prescription. Some advocacy groups have worked to ensure access of *Plan B* to rape survivors, military women, and to a variety of pro-choice and family planning organizations. Other groups, based on religious values, seek to reverse the FDA ruling, and some pharmacies have declined to stock the item. Women and their partners should consult their doctors or family planning clinics for more specific advice and information.

Cultural perspectives on family planning. The World Health Organization reports that about one-quarter of pregnancies worldwide are unwanted, and about 50 million of them end in abortion each year. Curiously, relatively little research has been done on new contraceptive methods during the past 25 years. If there is a need for more contra-ception research, why is it not being done? The reason seems to be that most of the research on fertility and infertility is done in wealthier countries, where drug companies can make considerably more profit from infertility treatments than from contraception (see next section; R. F. Service, 1994). Individuals in advanced countries are not satisfied with existing contraception methods, however, and would like to see more research on new methods (Rosenfeld, Zahorik, Saint, & Murphy, 1993).

Those who live in poor countries therefore have fewer options. Countries can be divided into two groups based on whether they have low or high population growth rates. In countries with low growth rates, the population increases by about 1% each year. The United States falls into this group. In high-growth countries, the population may increase as much as 3% per year, doubling every 25 years or so. This high rate of growth increases the chances of pregnancy and birth complications, prematurity, maternal and infant mortality, and a continuation of the cycle of poverty.

India, for example, has one-third the area of the United States but three times the population. A significant proportion of the people are illiterate and live in rural areas below the poverty level. They have inadequate food, shelter, and clothing. There is active resistance to family planning, since these families depend for their livelihood on large numbers of children. In the 1970s, India passed a law requiring sterilization for all parents with two or more children who wanted to continue receiving welfare. Although the law was repealed in 1977, sterilization remains the most common form of birth control in India. The voluntary use of other contraception methods (see below) has increased, but not sufficiently to halt the population growth (Kumar, 1994).

China has been more successful in reducing its high birthrate. China has about the same area as the United States, but it has five times as many people. In the past 30 years, however, the Chinese have reduced their birthrate to 1% per year by allowing only one child per family (Feeney, 1994). The one-child policy is implemented by granting those who comply more vacation time and more welfare benefits. Elderly women in each village, called "granny police," are charged with counseling and disciplining women who wish to have a second child (Galvin, 1989; Associated Press, 1985).

One problem that has arisen in China is that rural families have a strong desire to have a male child who can help with the farmwork. This preference has resulted in increased loss of female infants, partly through surgical abortion once the infant's sex is determined by genetic counseling or by selective infanticide of female newborns. Currently the birthrate in China is 117 boys born for every 100 girls. Estimates are that by 2020, China will have 30 million more males than females, while India and Pakistan face similar male surpluses. Many of these males are now young men, and they are facing a shortage of eligible women to marry. There is also a reported increase in social violence and homosexuality (Hudson & den Boer, 2004). A change in government policy allows families whose first child is a female to have the opportunity for a second child (Coale & Banister, 1994). A recent change in the One Child Law is a provisions that couples who were both without siblings may have two children legally (Rosenberg, 2009; China's One Child Policy, http://geography.about.com/od/populationgeography/a/onechild.htm.)

Other Asian countries, such as Taiwan, Japan, and Korea, have also reduced their birthrates to 1% per year. In these countries, the change was due not to government policy, but rather to trends toward increased modernization over the past 30 years. With modernization, more people move to the cities, where they become better educated and have access to better health care. As a result, the infant mortality rate declines, and more children in the family survive and require financial support. Families therefore voluntarily limit the number of children they choose to have through various contraceptive procedures, including sterilization (Feeney, 1994; Thike, Wai, Oo, & Yi, 1993).

In many African countries, such as the Ivory Coast, where the population is growing at 4% per year, women have as many as seven children apiece, and as the infant mortality rate has declined, the population has increased drastically (Remez, 1996). Women use birth control to space births rather than to reduce the number of children. In some African countries, oral contraceptives are believed to be harmful, and in others, religious taboos against touching one's own genitals prevent the use of condoms and diaphragms. Some new birth control devices are proving highly effective, however. One device is a skin implant similar to birth control pills that prevents conception for 5 years and has been well accepted in cultures that use skin scarification as a beauty practice. Injections of birth control hormones work in areas where people have come to associate injections with good health. The use of female, but not male, sterilization is also becoming more accepted (C. Holden, 1988; Jack & Chao, 1992; Were & Karanja, 1994).

On the whole, it seems that culturally adapted interventions work the best, and that education of the people is a necessary ingredient in a successful family planning program. These cultural differences have an impact on the type of sex education offered to young people, a topic to which we now turn.

Risks of Teenage Pregnancies: Education and Contraception for Youth

The majority of infants with birth defects in the United States are born to teenage mothers. The rate of teenage births increased until the 1990s in the United States and has continued to decline gradually since that time for all racial and ethnic groups. The largest decline was for African American teenagers and for second births for teens who already have one child (National Vital Statistics Report, 2005; Ventura, Mathews, & Curtin 1998). In 2004, the birthrate for teens aged 15 through 19 was 38 in 1,000 for whites, 63 in 1,000 for African Americans, and 83 in 1,000 for Hispanic Americans. Thus, in spite of the declines, many teens are still giving birth, and the rate of teen pregnancy is almost twice as high for African Americans and Hispanic Americans as that of Caucasian Americans (Guyer et al., 1998). Teen pregnancy is still a major social problem because teenage mothers require great expense from society to cover their health care and financial support.

Teenage mothers tend to be at risk for all kinds of birth complications. The death rate for infants of teenage mothers by age one year is 3 to 4 times that for infants of older mothers, and the incidence of low-birthweight infants is much higher among infants born to teenagers. Are these problems associated solely with the age of the mother? The evidence suggests that there is nothing inherent in the age of the mother alone that would account for these problems. But teenage mothers seem to be at risk for childbearing because such a large proportion of teenage mothers come from poor socioeconomic conditions, with their attendant problems of poor nutrition, high stress, poor medical care, abuse and neglect, and poor family relationships (Coley & Chase-Lansdale, 1998; Phipps et al., 2002; Scaramella et al., 1998). Teenage mothers are seven times as likely to be poor before pregnancy as older mothers (Alan Guttmacher Institute, 1994). Teen parents, both mothers and fathers, are more likely to have low academic performance, be unpopular among their peers, and be poor (Xie et al., 2001).

Marriage and parenting also place increased stress on teenagers. The demands of child and spouse often conflict with the teen's own needs for development, education, and health, and of mature romantic and marital relationships (Coley & Chase-Lansdale, 1998). Teenage marriages often end in divorce, leaving many teenage mothers with the additional stress of being a single parent. In general, teenage mothers are less likely to be responsive to their young infants than older mothers are, and teenage mother-infant pairs experience less mutual affection and enjoyment compared to infants with older mothers (Barratt & Roach, 1995). Males and females between 30 and 55 years old, both African American and Caucasian American, who married as adolescents earned less income, completed fewer years of school, held lower-paying jobs, and engaged in more risky sexual behavior than those who married later (Hardy et al., 1998; Meade & Ickovics, 2005; Teti and Lamb, 1989).

Teenage fathers are similar to teenage mothers. They are more likely to be poor and to have come from troubled families. They work and earn more than non-parent peers, but because they obtain less education, their lifetime earning ability is considerably reduced. Because of high rates of divorce among teenage parents, only about 50% of teen fathers live with the mother and child sometime after the birth. Cohabitation rates are highest for whites, compared to African Americans and Hispanic Americans. By the time the child is of school age, fewer than 25% of teen fathers are still in contact with their children. This low rate of father involvement is related primarily to unstable or hostile relationships between mothers and fathers (Coley & Chase-Lansdale, 1998). To make matters even worse, when the children of teenage parents reach adolescence, they are more prone to delinquency, violence, and arrest than other teens, perpetuating an intergenerational cycle of disadvantage (Pogarsky et al., 2003). Much of this effect on the offspring can be accounted for by father absence during early childhood (Ellis et al., 2003).

The risks of adolescent pregnancy can best be understood from the perspective of social systems. These studies show how society has a direct impact on the developing infant and on the family. A family that is already stressed by economic factors is likely to view the pregnancy with apathy and resentment, leading to insufficient care during the prenatal months, and after the infant is born, family strife and long-term effects on the offspring.

Treatments for teenage pregnancy problems are complex. Teen pregnancy prevention programs should begin as early as the eighth grade for high-risk teens and involve the entire community and culture (Young et al., 2004; Coley & Chase-Lansdale, 1998). In general, teenagers are caught in a web of conflicting cultural standards. At home, they may receive the message that sex out of wedlock is prohibited; in school, there is peer pressure to engage in sexual behavior; and in the movies and on television, sexuality and sexual activity are glorified. Many movies and shows present macho and sexist themes in which men repress women. Girls from impoverished homes or those who have suffered physical and sexual abuse may see pregnancy as a way to leave home or establish their own identity. Programs should focus on internal locus of control, academic achievement, making effective life choices, and poverty alleviation (Young et al., 2004).

Once the teen is pregnant, other types of intervention should be used. Better pregnancy outcomes are associated with reduction of psychosocial stress, social support, prenatal care, more parental involvement with the infant, and a sense that these factors would continue through time (Boyce, Schaefer, & Uitti, 1985; Meade & Ickovics, 2005; Zaslow & Eldred, 1997). Intervention programs can provide information about prenatal health and nutrition and postnatal child-rearing methods and also provide teen parents contact with older parents who can serve as mentors, people to whom they can turn to for advice regarding child rearing, staying in school, and other concerns (Rhodes, 1993).

Research in the United States shows that the majority of teenagers do not have basic knowledge of sexuality, conception, and contraception (Ammerman et al., 1992). For this reason, sex education programs in junior and senior high school can significantly reduce the risk of teenage pregnancy and increase the incidence of sexual abstinence among adolescents. During the presidency of George W. Bush, the United States has had a policy of promoting premarital abstinence as the primary form of sex education. An alternative approach is to offer accurate and honest education about love, sexuality, ways to avoid unwanted sexual advances, conception and contraception, including making contraceptives readily available to sexually active youth. These programs have been consistently shown to be more effective than abstinence-only programs in preventing both sexual activity and pregnancy (Barth et al., 1992; Glazer, 1993a; Weed & Jensen, 1993). Abstinence-only programs are based on particular religious values that emphasize prohibition of premarital sex, so that, paradoxically, young people feel they cannot seek alternate methods of contraception if they in fact are sexually active. Teenagers, aware of such attitudes among adults, are often reluctant even to broach the subject of their sexuality with parents or counselors.

The fact is, however, that 50% of high school students report engaging in sexual activity, and this percentage has not changed significantly between 1990 and 2007. Of those who reported engaging in sexual intercourse, there has been an increase in the percentage reporting condom use, from 46% in 1991 to 62% in 2007 (childstats.gov/americas-children/tables.asp) due primarily to effective sex education. This still leaves many young people unprotected, and society needs to respond to this reality in ways that respect and protect these youths, their families, and their children within the bounds of constitutional protections of rights and privacies.

Infertility

For some families the problem is not reducing the number of births but increasing them. During a female's childbearing years, about one in six couples suffers from **infertility**: they are unable to conceive successfully for at least one year. Either the male or the female, or both, may be infertile. Female infertility is usually caused by a failure to ovulate (that is, the failure of the immature ova to ripen), or by some process that impedes the journey of the ripened ovum from the ovary to the Fallopian tubes. Failure to ovulate can be caused by factors such as excessive exercise or weight loss, obesity, some sexually transmitted diseases, excessive alcohol use, exposure to toxic chemicals, and hormonal imbalances, many of which are treatable (Ford, MacCormac, & Hiller, 1994; Grodstein, Goldman, & Cramer, 1994). Changes in diet, exercise, and hormonal treatments, called fertility drugs, can be used. In cases of blockage, both drugs and surgery have been tried. Fertility drugs sometimes lead to twinning and multiple births because they stimulate ovulation.

Causes of male infertility include using marijuana and cigarettes, wearing excessively tight underwear, taking hot baths or saunas, inability to maintain an erection, and premature ejaculation or failure to ejaculate (Howard, 1995). These can be treated with changes in behavior and sex therapies. Male infertility may also be caused by underdeveloped testes, prior injuries, and some childhood diseases. Some of these problems may not be treatable.

Enhancing Fertility

The chances of a successful conception can be improved by timing sexual intercourse to the period of the menstrual cycle when ovulation is taking place. Usually, this period lasts about 5 or 6 days before the day of ovulation (Wilcox, Weinberg, & Baird, 1995). Couples can monitor ovulation daily by recording the woman's body temperature, which rises about 1 degree Fahrenheit during ovulation. Ovulation can also be monitored by charting the changes in color, amount, and consistency of the cervical mucus. Kits are now sold in drugstores to monitor changes in hormone levels by testing urine samples.

Lovemaking and sexual intercourse should be a relaxed experience for the couple. Fertility is also enhanced if both partners are in good physical health, maintain appropriate body weight, eat nutritious diets, exercise regularly, and avoid excessive smoking and drinking. Males should avoid or reduce the use of hot tubs and saunas to prevent elevation of temperature around the testes.

If these natural methods fail and standard drug and surgical treatments for infertility are not successful, couples can choose several more expensive and higher-risk measures. The approach recommended by physicians is artificial insemination, in which sperm from the father or another male donor is transferred directly to the mother's Fallopian tubes (Velde & Cohlen, 1999).

If artificial insemination fails, another approach is **in vitro fertilization (IVF)**, sometimes referred to as assisted reproductive technology. In cases where healthy ova ripen but cannot pass to the Fallopian tubes, one of the mother's ova is surgically removed and joined with spermatozoa from the father in a sterile biological medium. After fertilization has taken place and the zygote has made a few cell divisions (it is now called an *embryo*; see below), it is surgically implanted into the mother's uterus.

Generally, in vitro fertilization is very expensive, ranging from $60,000 up to almost $1 million, depending on the problems and the number of unsuccessful cycles (Neumann, Gharib, & Weinstein, 1994). In 2009, the average cost for IVF was $12,000 in the U.S., but the range for one cycle of IVG was between $10,000 and $15,000 (Gurevich, 2009). The failure rate for IVF can be as high as 30%. Couples who choose these methods have a strong desire for children. One or more such failures can lead to depression and to doubt about themselves and their marriage. Because of the uncertainty of the procedure, many IVF couples delay their psychological preparation for parenthood (McMahon, Tennant, Ungerer, & Saunders, 1999; see Chapter 8). These couples require empathy and support (Osofsky, Rosenthal, & Butterbaugh, 1999).

On the other hand, if the fertilization procedure is successful, long-term pregnancy outcomes for embryos fertilized in vitro are similar to those of natural conceptions (Winston & Handyside, 1993). In the past, there was an increased incidence of multiple births because doctors would implant a number of embryos, hoping that at least one would survive. The number of multiple births has been declining, however, due to technical advances (Thurin et al., 2004). After birth, babies conceived in vitro are no more likely to have health problems than are normally conceived infants (Leslie, Gibson, McMahon, Tennant, & Saunders, 1998); they are also no more likely to suffer from parental acceptance and have similar levels of psychological well-being as those from normal births (MacCallum et al., 2007).

In some cases, many ova are removed from the mother are frozen, in a process called **embryo cryopreservation**. This method is still experimental because the data on long-term pregnancy outcomes are still insufficient (Winston & Handyside, 1993), although it can be useful when other approaches fail (Grover & Permezel, 1994). Reasons for doing this are that it may take many menstrual cycles for success using IVF, so that doing only one surgical removal is less stressful for the mother. If a woman needs radiation treatments for cancer that might damage her ova, or if she is approaching the end of her reproductive years and has not yet conceived, she may wish to have some of her ova removed for fertilization. Another variation on IVF is if sperm function too poorly to break down the lining of the ovum; they can be injected directly into the ovum using **sperm microinjection**, which has shown good success rates.

In other variations of IVF, gametes from a donor may be substituted for those of the parent who cannot produce his or her own. Donors can be family members, friends, or anonymous public donors (Winston & Handyside, 1993). An in vitro zygote from the mother and father can also be implanted into the uterus of another woman, called a **surrogate mother**, who carries the infant until birth and then gives the baby to the parents who contributed the zygote. This practice is more controversial, however, and is used less often.

What are the social issues related to in vitro fertilization methods? Advances in technology to treat infertility have raised new social issues about the nature of conception, birth, and parenthood. If the genetic parents contribute the embryo but a surrogate mother carries the baby to birth, whose child is it?

Although some states in the United States have laws regulating contracts between the genetic parents and the surrogate, courts have struggled with lawsuits from surrogate mothers who wanted to retain custody of the child (Hansen, 1993). In 1993 Florida passed a statute, the Florida Assisted Reproductive Technology Act, that grants parental rights under two conditions: parents are those who contribute the child's genetic inheritance and those who hold the original written intent to be the child's parents (Maun, Williams, Graber, & Myers, 1994). This law also applies to frozen embryos, which may be used later by the genetic parents or by others.

The underlying premise of this law and others like it is that parenting is a matter of choice rather than destiny. In the freedom-granting politics of the United States, people have come to believe that choosing to have or not to have a child is a right, even if factors such as disease, age, or infer-

tility conspire against it (R. Mead, 1999). As new methods for manipulating reproductive outcomes are invented, each individual and the society as a whole will have to struggle with the morality of such freedoms.

What if parents have fertilized zygotes frozen and then divorce? In one New York case, the mother wanted to use her eggs to get pregnant, but her ex-husband objected. New York courts ruled in the husband's favor, suggesting that parents who undergo this procedure should decide what happens to the zygotes in the event of a separation (Associated Press, May 8, 1998). In Los Angeles, a woman's husband, a 30-year-old man, died suddenly of an allergic reaction. Doctors extracted the sperm from his testicles after death, froze them, and used them to impregnate the wife 15 months later. She had a normal pregnancy and birth (Associated Press, March 28, 1999).

Some women cannot produce healthy ova. A lively business of egg donation has developed during the past few years. Donors are catalogued on the Internet or in private agencies in order to be matched to infertile couples. One recent newspaper ad read: "Egg donor needed. You must be at least 19 and have a 1400 SAT score." The couple was offering $50,000 for the donation. Such ads appeal to young women with financial needs, since most donors receive considerably less money. Donating eggs is a painful and risky procedure requiring the donor to be injected with large doses of hormones that substantially alter her body chemistry and functioning. The long-term effects on donors' health and fertility are currently unknown. In addition, egg and sperm donation raises the possibility that couples can introduce desired genetic traits into their family line, especially privileged, primarily Caucasian families, who can afford the high cost (R. Mead, 1999). On the other hand, behavior genetics research (see Chapter 2) shows that the effects of genes are probabilistic, meaning that the child may not have the same phenotype (body form or intelligence, for example) as the donating parents. Because of these ethical issues, some states in the United States ban donor and surrogacy agreements or they ban paid agreements.

We now have the technology to implant post-menopausal women with their own previously frozen embryos or the embryo of a donor couple. Medical evidence shows that women between the ages of 50 and 60 are just as capable of carrying a pregnancy to birth as younger women, although the risks of pregnancy to the mother are somewhat higher (Paulson et al., 2002). In a survey conducted in Australia, only 38% of respondents from a representative sample approved of the donation of embryos to postmenopausal women (Bowman & Saunders, 1994). Society will have to ponder the question of what happens to children in middle childhood and adolescence when their parents are of an advanced age and perhaps less capable of the physical demands of parenting (Winston & Handyside, 1993). On the other hand, as postmenopausal parents become more common, they may reveal forms of resilience in older adults that have never been observed.

Recall that during prenatal development, a lifetime supply of ova is formed inside the ovaries of female fetuses. Due to a shortage of donor ova for women needing transplants for in vitro fertilization, a fertility laboratory in Great Britain implanted ova from an aborted fetus into an infertile woman. On the one hand, this method could give new hope to infertile women and also in some ways replace the loss of the aborted fetus. On the other hand, it raises the possibility of "fetus farming," where women would conceive infants only to have an abortion and sell the fetus for profit.

Fears of fetus farming have also been raised regarding the production of **embryonic stem cells**, embryonic cells that can be transformed into many different types of tissue by implanting them into the bodies of adults whose tissues have been damaged by injury or disease. Stem cell research holds the promise of treating stroke and other brain damage, spinal cord injuries and paralysis, and diseases of the internal organs. Currently, the practice of stem cell research is limited in the United States because new stem cell lines can only be obtained by abortion of embryos. States like California and other countries, however, feel that the promise of stem cell treatments is worth the cost, especially if embryos are obtained by elective abortion and not for payment. Because of the risks of "embryos for sale," however, states and nations need to pass regulatory laws (Baird, 2002).

Some of the social, legal and ethical problems of these technologies might be eliminated if human cloning was available. **Cloning** is a method of creating a zygote by removing the donor mother's DNA from the ova and implanting the DNA from any cell in the body of another person—for example, the intended mother or father. This bypasses the need to use a particular person's ova or sperm. The cloned zygote is genetically identical to the adult DNA donor. Currently, cloning has been successful in a few animal species but is against the law for humans. If the techniques are perfected, cloning may be used simply to grow tissues or organs needed to implant in an ailing adult donor from whom the genetic material was harvested. Or it could be used to create babies with the particular characteristics of the DNA donor. Cloning may solve some problems, but it raises others. Society is only beginning to grasp the ethical issues related to these new technologies (see also the later section on ethical issues in genetic counseling).

DEVELOPMENTAL PROCESSES BEFORE BIRTH

How does a fully developed human emerge from its beginnings as a zygote? At the start of development, several processes are important in inducing developmental change. One process comes from inside the cells themselves, and another relates to the cells' interactions with the environment inside the mother's body. In this section, I review the stages of prenatal development that are common to all humans. In the next section, we discuss individual differences in prenatal development.

Prenatal Developmental Processes

Within the cell nucleus, the genotype or genetic material is in the form of a spiral-shaped molecule

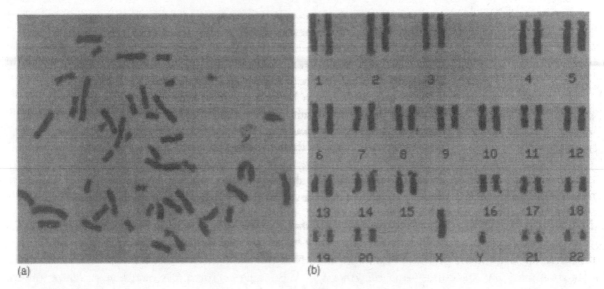

(a) (b)

Figure 3.1 Human Chromosome Pairs Before and After Karyotyping
Humans have 23 pairs of chromosomes, and in the karyotype, the pairs have been matched. One member of each pair is from the mother and one is from the father. The X chromosome of the 23rd pair is shown in the middle of the bottom row.
Source: Courtesy of Dr. J. Aznar.

called deoxyribonucleic acid (**DNA**). Inside this spiral are locations at which any one of a number of different types of smaller molecules called bases may be attached. The DNA is segmented into sections, each of which contains a different set of bases. Each segment is called a **gene**. The genes are arranged in long strings, much like beads on a necklace, into structures called **chromosomes**.

Chromosomes can be seen under a microscope, as shown in Figure 3.1. Most chromosomes look like the letter X. The X is made up of two strands that are joined near their middle. The genes can be seen in Figure 3.1 as alternating bands of light and dark. Chromosomes come in matched pairs, as shown in part (*b*) of Figure 3.1. This arrangement of chromosomes into pairs is achieved by cutting the photo in part (*a*) and placing the chromosomes in order. The rearranged photo is called a karyotype. Note that chromosomes come in different sizes and that a single Y-shaped chromosome on the 23rd pair contains the genetic code for a male.

Every cell in one's body, except for the gametes, contains 46 chromosomes, representing about 1 million bits of genetic information. Each

of the body's cells contains the same set of genes and chromosomes. Each gamete normally contains only 23 chromosomes. The 46 chromosomes in most body cells represent 23 pairs.

Individual cells develop by dividing into two identical daughter cells. During **mitosis**, each chromosome within the cell nucleus makes a copy of itself before cell division occurs. The original set of chromosomes and their identical copies do not get mixed up: each set pushes away from the other until they occupy opposite sides of the nucleus. The cell will divide into two only after this physical separation of the two identical sets of chromosomes occurs (McIntosh & Koonce, 1989).

Although every cell in an individual's body carries the same set of genes and chromosomes, every individual has a slightly different set. This genetic variability arises first during the creation of the gametes. In the special biological environment of the female ovaries and the male testicles, cells divide in the absence of the chromosome copying process that is characteristic of mitosis. In **meiosis**, each daughter cell contains only 23 chromosomes. When sperm and ovum unite during fertilization, the resulting zygote will have a unique combination of 46 chromosomes, half from the mother and half from the father. Since each individual gamete contains a slightly different set of chromosomes and genes and the particular pair that unite for fertilization is random, the number of genetically different individuals is enormous. This explains how siblings can be genetically different.

Every individual begins life as a zygote that progresses through the initial state of mitosis. As a result of mitosis, the number of cells in the developing organism grows rapidly, doubling every few hours. Because mitosis is an exact copying process, each of these cells has the same genetic material.

One of the great mysteries of early development is how, given identical genes in each cell, the different tissues and structures—muscles, blood, sensory receptors, and so on—can develop. The biologist Waddington expressed it thus:

> a simple lump of jelly… eventually turns into a recognizable small plant or worm or insect or some other type of organism. Nothing else that one can see puts on a performance which is both so apparently simple and spontaneous and yet, when you think about it, so mysterious. (Waddington, 1966, p. v)

To find some solutions to this mystery, we have to go outside the cell and examine its environment.

Research on nonhuman prenatal development has shown that in almost all species of animals, the cells of the zygote form a spherelike cluster (Sameroff, 1984). Because some of the cells are on the surface and some on the interior of the sphere, these different regions are in contact with different environments. The interior cells are next to other cells like themselves, while the exterior cells will have cells like themselves on one side, and be in contact with the cells of the uterine environment on the other side.

Each of these environments exposes the cell to different molecules that may be transported into the cell from the neighboring cells. In addition, physical forces on the cell will cause it to produce specific molecules in the cell's body. These molecules compose the **epigenome**, the set of biochemical markers that are responsive to the environment and that turn on or turn off the actions of particular genes within each cell. The epigentic molecules attach to certain regions of the DNA in order to activate some of the cell's genes and inhibit the action of others. When particular genes are activated, they begin to send specific chemical messages back out to the main cell body, changing the cell's structural characteristics. This is the beginning of the process of differentiation of the properties of the interior cells from those of the exterior cells.

As cell division proceeds, cells form groups in which distinct molecular processes occur and in which particular groups of genes are active. Boundaries form between the different groups that prevent the processes of one group from leaking into another (Trevarthen, 1973). Thus, the development of the phenotype—the cell's specific characteristic as, for example, neuron or muscle—is the result of a constant and dynamic interaction between the genotype, the epigenome, and the intra- and extracellular environment (Antonelli, 1985).

The effect of the cell's environment has been shown in a series of experiments on nonhuman embryos. Early in the process of the formation of different regions, cells can be removed from one region and placed in an entirely different one. After a few cell divisions, the transplanted cells resemble the region in which they were placed, not the region that they came from (Spemann, 1938; Ebert & Sussex, 1970). At this stage of development, the cells can literally shift shape to become like the other cells around them. These are the **embryonic stem cells** that may hold the promise of regenerating damaged or diseased tissues when transplanted from embryos into older children and adults who no longer have stem cells in their bodies.

The important point to remember is that even though every cell in the embryo has the same genes, because the epigenome is responsive to the local environment, different genes become active in different types of cells. As cells begin to differentiate into distinct regions, physical struc-

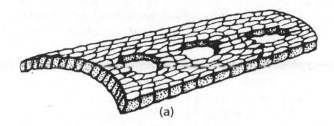

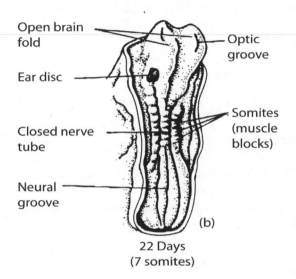

Open brain fold

Optic groove

Ear disc

Closed nerve tube

Somites (muscle blocks)

Neural groove

(b)

22 Days
(7 somites)

Figure 3.2 Creation of a Structure
(a) During the process of cell differentiation, some cells begin to create structures. The early formation of a tube with holes is shown. The cells become less elastic on one side and more elastic on the other, causing the sheet of cells to bend. Differential rigidity around the region of the holes can create spaces between cells. **(b)** In the 22-day-old embryo, such a tube structure will eventually become the spinal cord and spine.

Source: C. Trevarthen, Neurological development and the growth of the psychological functions, 1980. In J. Sants, *Developmental psychology and society*, 46–95. New York: St. Martin's Press. Copyright © by J. Sants. Reprinted by permission of St. Martin's Press, Inc.

tures begin to form. The most common type of embryonic structure is the formation of a tube. Figure 3.2 shows how this occurs. In (*a*), cells on the top of the sheet have been genetically activated to reproduce cells with the ability to stretch. Cells on the bottom of the sheet have been activated with a different set of genes to produce contraction. As cells divide and increased differential stretching and contracting occur, the sheet eventually curls into a tube. Tubes can also be formed when a ball of cells contracts in the center, eventually making a kind of doughnut shape. In all animals, the first tube formed is the gut. In vertebrate animals, one of the early-forming tubular structures is the spinal cord and spine (see Figure 3.2(*b*)).

It is usually assumed that prenatal development is a continuous series of acquisitions along the road to maturity. Prenatal development does show a number of aspects that are continuous, but there are also instances in which certain structures form only to disappear at a later point. The types

of developmental changes that occur all during prenatal development are as follows (Meredith, 1975):

Changes in kind.   One of the most noticeable prenatal changes is the gradual differentiation of multiple kinds of tissue from the relatively uniform zygote. Certain structures also emerge and disappear. For example, the pronephros, the precursor of the kidney, is only there for 2 weeks, fish-like gill arches are present for three weeks, an external tail appears and disappears between the second and fourth months, and finger pads are seen between the third and fifth months.

Changes in number.   Depending upon the particular structure or organ, cell numbers increase and decrease over time. Obviously, the overall number of cells continues to increase.

Changes in position.   The relative orientation and position of the organs in the fetus change.

When the heart is formed, for example, it lies near what will become the face. Over time it moves lower, more toward the back, and rotates and tilts. Other organs and limbs undertake their own particular paths of migration.

Changes in size. Changes in size vary with the time and location of the organ. During the second month, the head and neck regions grow faster (cephalocaudal development), there is more growth near the spine than in the front (dorsoventral development), and the growth rate is higher near the shoulders and hips than near the extremities (proximodistal development). As development proceeds, these trends reverse.

Changes in shape. Immediately after fertilization, the organism has an oval shape. Several weeks later, its shape is elongated and is mostly head. There are also changes in the shape of cells and organs.

What Are the Major Phases of Prenatal Development?

The prenatal period is usually divided into three parts: the zygote, the embryo, and the fetus. The period of the zygote begins at the time the ovum is fertilized and lasts about 2 weeks, or until the ovum is implanted in the uterine wall. The period of the **embryo** begins about 2 weeks after fertilization and extends until the end of the second month, at which time the embryo is designated a **fetus**. This designation is applied when the organism begins to resemble a human in its external features, and the bones begin to harden into a more rigid skeletal structure. In this book, the fetal period will be divided into three phases (7 to 16 weeks, 17 to 22 weeks, and 23 to 36 weeks). These divisions correspond to changes in structure and behavior that will be explained later. The period of human gestation lasts about 38 weeks, but this can vary from between 36 and 40 weeks for a full-term infant.

In the first half week, the zygote divides to about 20 cells, and at the end of the week, some differentiation can be noted. At the end of the second week, there is a clearly defined **embryonic disk** that lies between the **amniotic sac** and the **yolk sac**, which themselves have differentiated out of the original zygote. This organism is now called the **blastocyst**, and it implants itself in the lining of the uterus sometime during the third week. The blastocyst, still only 1/125 of an inch long, triggers the secretion of hormones that inhibit menstruation. As the concentration of these hormones, known as **human chorionic gonadotropin (HCG)**, increases, they can be detected in the urine; they are used in laboratory pregnancy tests (see Figure 3.3).

The Period of the Embryo

The blastocyst structure—the embryonic disk, the yolk sac, and the amniotic sac—will differentiate further. The embryonic disk differentiates into three layers. The **endoderm** eventually becomes part of the digestive, urinary, and respiratory systems. The **mesoderm** will become the muscles, bone, circulatory system, and reproductive system. The **ectoderm** will become the central nervous system and brain, the sense organs, and the skin, hair, nails, and teeth.

The yolk sac produces blood cells and becomes part of the liver, spleen, and bone marrow, all of which later produce blood cells. By the end of the embryonic period, the yolk sac has disappeared. The amniotic sac persists throughout gestation. It grows to cover the embryo and contains the amniotic fluid, which provides a cushion for the fetus against sudden movements of the mother's body.

Surrounding all of these developments is a membrane called the **chorion**. The placenta, which forms from the outer surface of the chorion, functions as a link between the bloodstreams of mother and embryo, which are not directly connected. The placenta passes nutrients and oxygen from the mother's blood to the fetus's through the umbilical cord and serves to eliminate the fetal wastes via the mother's bloodstream. The fetus is in the upright position throughout most of the pregnancy, so there is no danger of the

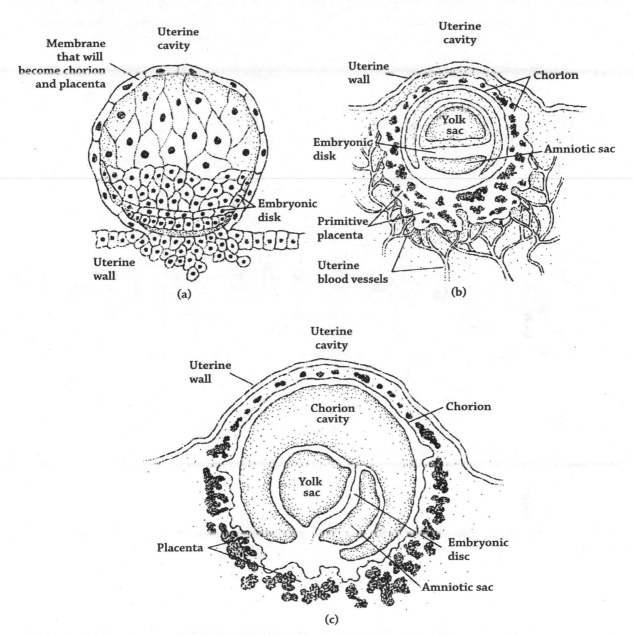

Figure 3.3 Early Stages of Prenatal Development
(a) *Blastocyst stage*: The fertilized egg (zygote) has made its way down the fallopian tube and has undergone repeated cell division and multiplication on the way. It attaches to the uterine lining and begins to grow into the uterine wall in search of nutrients. **(b)**, **(c)** Cell division and differentiation continue at a rapid pace, and specific structures begin to take shape. The developing organism is now a bulge on the uterine wall. **(d)**, **(e)** *Embryo stage*: Gradually, the form of the embryo takes shape. By the end of the first month, the head and the arm and leg buds are visible, a primitive heart has started to pump, and other organs are beginning to develop. At this stage, the human embryo closely resembles the embryos of most other animals.
Source: M. J. Gander & H. W. Gardiner, *Child and adolescent development*, 1981, p. 63. Boston: Little, Brown. Copyright © M. J. Gander & H. W. Gardiner. Reprinted by permission of the publisher.

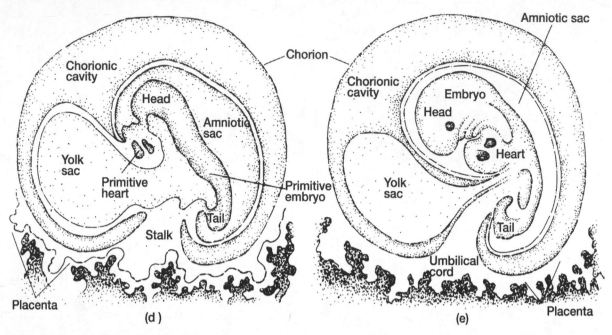

(d)

(e)

cord choking the fetus because of its location, the effect of gravity, and the relative inflexibility of the cord from the pressure of the blood circulating in it (like a hose with the water turned on). The risk of choking increases at birth because the fetus has changed position—head down for delivery—and the head may now come in contact with the cord.

By the third week, one can distinguish the head and primitive circulatory and skeletal systems. By the end of the first month, the heart is beating, and there are cavities for the ears, nose, and mouth (see Figure 3.4). The head is large relative to the rest of the body and has gill arches, and the body has upper limb buds and a small tail. At this point the embryo may be between 3 and 5 millimeters (1/6 inch) long.

Now development is occurring very rapidly. In the next 2 weeks, the beginnings of the eyes, nose, lungs, and liver grow, and bones begin to form. The gill structures are transformed into bones of the inner ear, the neck, and cartilage of the larynx, as well as the eustachian tubes, thyroid and thymus glands, and the trachea. By 6 weeks, the limbs are beginning to differentiate rapidly, and fingers and toes will appear shortly. The tail is still present and may comprise 15% of the embryo's total length

of 12 millimeters (1/2 inch). The total weight is about 2 grams (1/14 ounce). About half of the weight of an 8-week-old embryo is in its head. It has all of the major organs except genital organs. It has a skeleton, eyebrows, knees, fingers, toes, and buds for teeth. Its rapid growth during this period makes the embryo more vulnerable to environmental risks (see the Individual Differences in Prenatal Development section below).

The first evidence of prenatal behavior is seen during the embryonic period in the movements of the muscles of the heart. The movements are jerky and spontaneous at first but gradually become more rhythmic as they pump blood cells between the heart, yolk sac, and chorion. The origin of these rhythmic movements is unknown, since they occur before the embryo has developed its nervous system (Hofer, 1981).

By the 32nd day of life (4 ½ weeks), the human embryo has a rudimentary sensory system (see Figure 3.4), but these sense organs are not yet connected to any nerve fibers. The first nerve cells form between 4 and 5 weeks, and the first spontaneous movements of the body occur a week later. By 7 weeks, the embryo is responsive to touch in the mouth region and will turn its head to the side (Trevarthen, 1973).

32 days (5 mm)

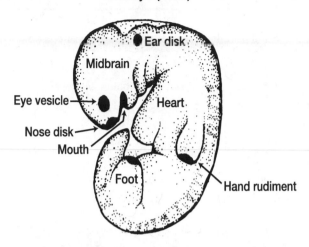

Figure 3.4 Sensory Surfaces of a Human Embryo at Four Weeks

Source: Adapted from C. Trevarthen, *Behavioral embryology*. In E. C. Carterette & M. P. Friedman, eds., *Handbook of Perception* (Vol. 3), 1973, p. 93. New York: Academic Press. Adapted by permission of the publisher and editor.

The Period of the Fetus I: Seven to Sixteen Weeks

During the early part of the fetal period, a large number of spontaneous behaviors emerge, including mouth and limb movements. The fetus can be stimulated to act by a number of occurrences. These include maternal muscle contractions, sounds, and changes in maternal glucose and oxygen levels. The whole body may shudder or jerk when a sensitive area like the mouth is touched. As the fetus develops during this period, movement responses become more localized to the stimulated area, and specific reflexes emerge. Areas of reflex activity spread out to the peripheries of the body, including hands and feet.

The behavior developments during this fetal period are listed in Table 3.1. Fetal behavior can be observed using several different methods. **Ultrasound** is a method in which high-frequency sound waves are bounced off the fetus's body to reveal the outline of the soft tissues. New ultrasound techniques produce 3D (3-dimensional) clear images of the whole body and details. Also available in some hospitals, 4D ultrasound adds the dimension of time to produce brief "movies" of the fetus over time (Avni et al., 2007). At the time of this writing, many 4D ultrasound movies are posted on YouTube and are available for viewing.

The purpose of these early fetal movements is not entirely clear. One experimental technique used with nonhuman embryos involves studying development after a fetal movement has been prevented from occurring, either through severing the nerve connections or by introducing a local anesthetic. Chick embryos that have been prevented from moving in this way were unable to move later. The muscles and nerves of these chicks developed normally, but their joints had become frozen into bone (Drachman & Coulombre, 1962). In another study with mice, inability to move the tongue embryonically resulted in deformation of the soft palate (Walker & Quarles, 1976). The relatively high incidence of cleft palate in infants of alcoholic mothers may be due to the anesthetic effects of alcohol on fetal mouth movements (Hofer, 1981). Other experiments have shown that movement in the fetus helps to induce the development of nerve endings in the sensory receptors.

About 90% of fetuses can be seen in ultrasound pictures to be sucking their right thumb, 10% their left thumb at 15 weeks after conception. A sample of 75 children in England were followed up at age 12 years. All 60 children who sucked their right thumb in utero used their right hand preferentially for most tasks (Hepper et al., 2005). It could be that a genetic influence caused the fetus to suck one or the other thumb, or it could be that

TABLE 3.1 Chronology of Fetal Behavior (First Period)

Age (Weeks)	Behavior
8½	Stroking the mouth region produces flexion of upper torso and neck and extension of arms at the shoulder.
9½	Some spontaneous movements. More of the whole body responds when the mouth is stroked.
10½	Stroking the palms of the hands leads to partial closing of the fingers. Hiccups. Cyclic movements begin.
11½	Other parts of face and arms become sensitive. Head rotation.
12½	Sensitive area spreads to upper chest. Hand-face contact.
13½	Specific reflexes appear: Lip closure, swallowing, Babinski (See Chapter 1), squinting, sucking.
14½	Entire body is sensitive, with more specific reflexes, such as rooting, grasping, finger closing. Body stretching.
15½	Can maintain closure of the fingers (grasp) with muscle tightening, muscle strengthening. Yawning.
16½	Frowning, grimacing.

Sources: D. Hooker, *The prenatal origin of behavior*, 1952. Lawrence: University of Kansas Press; T. R. B. Johnson, R. E. Besinger, & R. L. Thomas, The latest clues to fetal behavior and well-being, 1989. *Contemporary Pediatrics*, 66–84; C. D. Laughlin, Pre- and perinatal brain development and enculturation: A biogenetic structural approach, 1991. *Human Nature*, 2, 171–213; S. S. Robertson, Temporal organization in fetal and newborn movement, 1990. In H. Bloch & B. I. Bertenthal (Eds.), *Sensory-motor organizations and development in infancy and early childhood*. Netherlands: Kluwer Academic; C. Trevarthen, Behavioral embryology, 1973. In E. C. Carterette & M. P. Friedman (Eds.), *Handbook of perception: Vol. 3. Biology of perceptual systems*. New York: Academic Press.

the movement experience of hand preference in utero established the pattern of later handedness.

Fetal movements may also serve to help the fetus survive as an organism trying to adapt to its environment. As the mother moves about during her normal routine, her movements can shift the position of the fetus, and her activity may change the chemistry and composition of the amniotic fluid and blood supply. Fetal movements may have the effect of reorienting the fetus to the most comfortable position for itself and maximizing its chances of being protected and well nourished (Gandelman, 1992).

This is an example of a developmental systems transaction. As tissues and structures form, spontaneous movements are produced. The movements induce further development in those same tissues and structures, which by feedback strengthens the movement pattern, making it more responsive and predictable.

Aside from behavioral development, physical development is also occurring. The brain forms into two distinct hemispheres beginning around 9 weeks, and by 15 weeks there is an increased ability of the brain to communicate with the sense organs and muscles. Not only can the brain stimulate muscle movement by 15 weeks, but it can also begin to inhibit movement, allowing for the beginnings of motor control (Fifer et al., 2001).

By about 16 weeks, the fetus has become about 3 inches long and weighs about 1/2 ounce. During the period from 12 to 16 weeks, the external genitals form as a result of the interaction of the fetus's genes with the environment of the cells. The genetic determination of sex occurs at conception. Females have two X-shaped chromosomes in the 23rd pair, while males have one X- and one Y-shaped chromosome. All of the ova a woman produces have only X chromosomes. About half of the spermatozoa produced by men contain an X and the other half a Y chromosome in the 23rd place. The genetic sex of the zygote will thus depend on which of the father's spermatozoa actually fertilizes the ovum. For reasons not fully understood, more males are conceived than females, in the ratio of 105 to 100. Over the

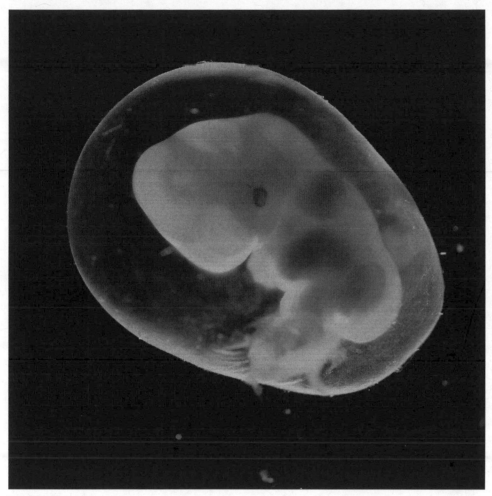

The 6-week-old embryo is less than an inch long. It has a heartbeat, eye patches, a rudimentary brain, and a stomach and liver. At this age there are no connections between the brain and the rest of the body.
Source: Photo originally appeared in *A Child is Born*, by Lennart Nilsson (New York: Dell Publishing Company).

course of the life span, an increasing number of females survive at every age, so that by age 60, the ratio of males to females is 70 to 100.

Up until the third month after conception, genetic males and genetic females have similar external structures in the genital area. During the second month, the hormone testosterone is secreted in male fetuses; it activates particular genes that induce the development of the internal ducts that will later connect to male genitals. The continued action of testosterone causes the development of the external male genitals at around three months. Female genitals do not require any

specific hormone to develop at this stage (Lamb & Bornstein, 1987).

This same fetal testosterone may also begin to make the male fetal brain different from that of the female. In one study, 4 year-old children were shown computer displays of objects moving toward and away from each other. When the children were asked what they thought was happening, those who had the most testosterone when they were fetuses were the least likely to attribute intentions (such as "wants to" or "trying to") to the objects. In other words, the girls—and the boys with the least fetal testosterone—described

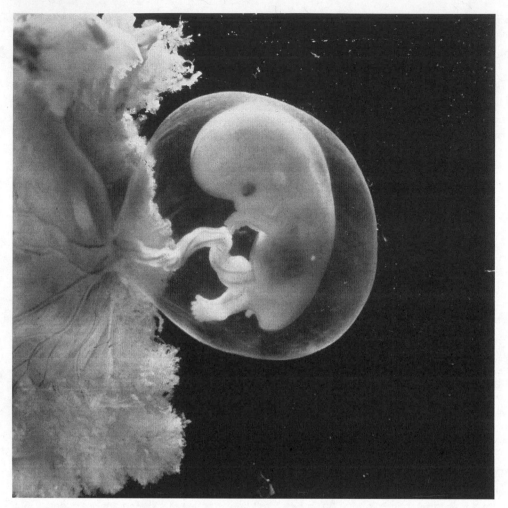

Just after three months, the fetus is about 2½ inches long and weighs ½ ounce. Most of the internal organs are formed, and fingers and toes can be seen. At this age, the fetus is capable of reflexive movements such as sucking, swallowing, grasping, and stretching.

Source: Photo originally appeared in *Behold Man*, by Lennart Nilsson (Boston: Little, Brown and Company).

the objects with social intentions. Because autistic children tend to lack "female" social skills and tend to have more "male" spatial skills, in may be the case that excessive fetal testosterone plays a role in autism (see Chapter 9; Ingudomnukul et al., 2007; Knickmeyer et al., 2006).

These early gender differences in the brain may impact late fetal development. During the third fetal period, male fetuses are more active than females (DiPietro Hodgson, Costigan, & Johnson, 1996). Male fetuses also appear to develop organized states of arousal earlier than females (DiPi-

etro et al., 1996). The findings on activity level suggest that boys are born with more motor experience. Since boys are more active postnatally, this suggests that early gender differences are not due entirely to postnatal environmental and parental influences (see Chapter 10).

The Period of the Fetus II: Seventeen to Twenty-Two Weeks

Up until the 16th week, the list of newly acquired spontaneous and stimulated fetal behavior continues to grow. Between 17 and 22 weeks, however, the fetus becomes quieter, after which activity begins again and lasts until birth. You might think that the development of the brain would induce more movement, rather than less. Up until this time, the brain stimulated large movements that involved the whole body, including arms and legs. These uninhibited movements originated in the brain stem regions. During the period between 17 and 22 weeks, the brain is beginning to develop subcortical and cortical cells and pathways to inhibit such uncontrolled, spasmlike movements (Fifer et al., 2001). The result is that after 22 weeks, the movements of the fetus will be more specialized and controlled (see Table 3.2). After this point, for example, specific facial expressions and coordinated hand movements begin to emerge.

This period of prenatal development, therefore, is characterized by rapid brain development. As shown in Figure 3.5, the brain's weight and volume increase by a factor of four during this period. Throughout fetal development, the major process of brain growth is cell division and inter-cell connections in the nervous system. After 22 weeks, new brain cells continue to be formed, but at a much slower rate. Following birth, the major processes of brain development are an increase in intercell connections and in cell specialization. Thus, during the early fetal period, when the brain is growing the most rapidly, it is the most susceptible to influences from the environment. More details about brain development will be given in Chapter 5.

During this period of development, the fetus is changing its physical characteristics. In the fourth month, fine, long hair, **lanugo**, grows over most of the body. Coarser hair appears on the head in the fifth month, and eyebrows and eyelashes grow in the sixth month. During this period, the skin glands secrete a waxy substance, the **vernix caseosa**, that serves to protect the delicate skin. This period is also marked by the formation of fingernails, toenails, and the adult tooth buds.

The inhibition of movement by the brain makes sense from the point of view of physical development. The rapid increase in fetal size

TABLE 3.2 Chronology of Fetal Behavior (Second and Third Periods)

Age (Weeks)	Behavior
19	Gag reflex. Early coordinated body movements in response to noxious stimulation (these are different from whole-body spasms of the early part of the first fetal period).
20	Audible crying.
21	As sensitive to touch as a 1-year-old. Beginnings of prenatal learning ability.
24	Hearing structures developed, listens to mother's heartbeat, can blink eyes. Sleep-wake pattern first appears.
25	Moves in rhythm to drumbeats.
26	Lungs can breathe on their own, can regulate body temperature, remembers sounds heard previously, reacts to differences in maternal emotions, can open eyelids, can survive if born prematurely.
32	Brain wave patterns show all primary brain areas functioning. REM sleep and mature sleep-wake pattern. Fetuses sleep about 75% of the time. First signs of visual attention.
34	Can habituate, active visual attention.
35	Evidence of visual recognition memory.

Source: J. A. DiPietro, D. M. Hodgson, K. A. Costigan, & T. R. B. Johnson, Fetal neurobehavioral development, 1996. *Child Development, 67* (5); R. Gandelman, *The psychobiology of behavioral development*, 1992. New York: Oxford University Press; C. D. Laughlin, Pre- and perinatal development and enculturation: A biogenetic structural approach, 1991. *Human Nature, 2.*

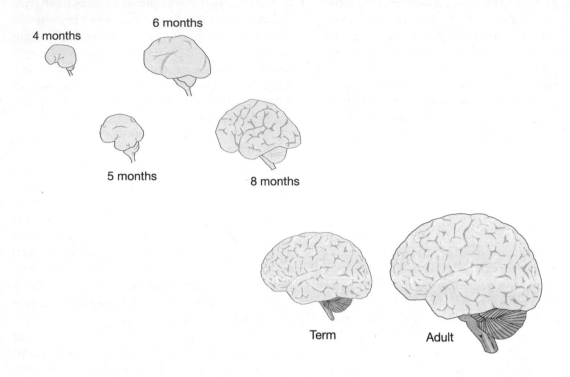

4 months

6 months

5 months

8 months

Term

Adult

Figure 3.5   Development of the Human Brain
Upper set: Human brains at the same scale of magnification.
Lower set: Development of the corpus collosum linking the hemispheres and of the cerebellum.

Source: C. Trevarthen, Neurological development and the growth of psychological functions, 1980. In J. Sants, *Developmental psychology and society*, 46–95. New York: St. Martin's Press. Copyright © J. Sants. Reprinted by permission of St. Martin's Press, Inc.

means that the fetus has less space in which to move around. At 6 months, the fetus weighs about 900 grams (2 pounds). Most babies born at this age do not survive, and if a baby is less than 600 grams or less than 24 weeks, the chances of survival are exceedingly slim.

The Period of the Fetus III: Twenty-Three to Thirty-Six Weeks

During this period, fetuses are active about 20% to 30% of the time. They move less often than during the first fetal period but with more vigor (DiPietro, Hodgson, Costigan, & Johnson, 1996). The beginning of this period is the time when mothers can first feel the fetus moving. By now, a doctor can detect the fetal heartbeat with a stethoscope. Data from infants born prematurely and also from ultrasound recordings of the fetus inside the womb provide evidence for a large number of new patterns of movement that begin during this period.

The fetus has been observed to cry, grunt, and yawn. By 28 weeks, the fetus has all the facial, arm, and chest movements of a newborn who is crying, down to a trembling chin (Gingras et al., 2005). Other related research shows that between 26 and 30 weeks, it is likely that the regions of the brain's cortex—the thalamus and its conections—are sufficiently developed for the fetus to feel pain (Lee at al., 2005; Slater et al., 2006). Although the fetus can make withdrawal and grimacing movements as early at the sixteenth week, this is not linked to any brain activity that could create the sensation of pain.

By the eighth month, the fetus can suck its thumb and open its eyes. Grasping and postural adjustment movements have also been observed. By this time, the fetus can see, hear, feel, and smell. Thus, by about the seventh month, most fetuses could survive if born, given appropriate intensive care (see Chapter 9).

One of the most remarkable achievements of the late fetal period is the development of clear-cut states of arousal (Hofer, 1981; T. R. B. Johnson et al., 1989). A **state of arousal** is an organized pattern of infant physical and physiological response that is related to the internal level of arousal or activation. States are alternating periods of activation and quiescence. During the fourth and fifth months, periods of activation and quiet in the fetus are irregular, and transitions from quiet to active are sudden and jerky. By the sixth month, a clear and regular alternation between activity and rest occurs about once every 40 minutes, based on data taken from sensors placed on the abdomens of sleeping women (Sterman & Hoppenbrouwers, 1971). This basic rhythm continues unchanged until after birth (S. S. Robertson, 1987).

These earlier periods of activity and rest become waking and sleeping states during this period. Fully developed sleep states appear in the fetus as early as 24 weeks (DiPietro et al., 1996). From its first appearance, sleep is divided into a period of quiet sleep and a period of active or REM sleep. **REM (rapid eye movement)** sleep is characterized by short, jerky, vertical eye movements, spontaneous body movements, and irregular respiration. The 32-week-old fetus spends about three-quarters of its time in REM sleep. The purpose of REM sleep is not fully understood. One hypothesis (Ruffwarg, Muzio, & Dement, 1966; Vertes, 1986) is that it is a form of self-stimulation similar to earlier body movements.

The last month of gestation is a period during which the fetus gains a considerable amount of weight. From 900 grams at 24 weeks, the fetus typically grows to about 3,500 grams at 36 weeks (about 7 pounds); most of this weight is subcutaneous fat tissues that will provide the newborn with insulation against the cold. Because of this weight gain, the fetus becomes too cramped to move its body. REM sleep may provide a less physically demanding source of movement stimulation to assist the development of the fetal brain and sensory organs.

Another remarkable achievement of the last few months of prenatal development is the emergence of the ability to learn. A number of people have speculated that fetuses may become imprinted to the heartbeat sounds of their mothers so that after birth, the sound of heartbeats is comforting to the infants. Indeed, it has been found that a majority of adults hold infants on the left side of the adult's body, closer to the heart (Harris, Spradlin, & Almerigi, 2007; Salk, 1973).

Using a response-contingent procedure (see Chapter 2), DeCasper and Sigafoos (1983) found that newborn infants will change their rate of sucking to imitate the sound of a heartbeat. Although these studies do not prove that newborns recognize the specific heartbeat of their mothers, they seem to suggest that a general preference for heartbeat sounds may have been learned. Holding the infant on the left side has another advantage, however: it frees up the right hand to do other things.

Because the late-term fetus can hear, a number of studies have attempted to see if the fetus can learn songs or speech, or recognize particular voices. Because of the uterine and abdominal walls, however, fetuses primarily hear lower frequencies of sounds coming from the outside, like the bass notes on the piano (Smith et al., 2003). In one study (Panneton & DeCasper, 1986), researchers asked pregnant women to sing "Mary Had a Little Lamb" frequently during the period 2 weeks prior to their due dates. After birth, the newborns' preference for "Mary Had a Little Lamb" over the song "Love Somebody" was tested using the conditioned sucking procedure (see Chapter 1). The newborns could clearly perceive the difference between the two songs, and in addition, they preferred to listen to the song that they had heard prenatally. DeCasper and Spence (1986) found postnatal preferences for stories read prenatally. Along these same lines, infants preferred hearing their mother's voice, compared to that of a stranger, when the voices were filtered for only the low-frequency components that the fetus might have heard through the insulating uterine wall. When higher-frequency whispered voices were used, newborns showed no preference (Spence & Freeman, 1996).

The studies reviewed so far have tested newborns for preferences related to their experiences before birth. Several studies have tested fetuses before birth and found an ability to learn in utero. One study examined whether fetuses 36 to 39 weeks old could distinguish between a male and a female voice (Lecanuet, Granier-Deferre, Jacquet, Capponi, & Ledru, 1993). One voice was presented until the fetal heart rate became habituated, and then the voice was changed. The criterion for fetal recognition of a change from one voice to the other was the dishabituation of the heart rate. Heart rate changes were significantly different when the voice was changed from male to female, or vice versa, and were significantly different from a control group for whom the voice was not changed. Fetal heart rate was also found to habituate to a vibroacoustic sound presented at intervals near the fetal head (Sandman, Wadhwa, Hetrick, Porto, & Peeke, 1997), and fetal heart rate changes when they hear their own mother speaking compared to the voice of another mother, both of which were played through a loudspeaker next to the mother's abdomen (Kisilevksy et al., 2003).

Prenatal learning has been convincingly demonstrated in other animals. Rat pups that had been exposed prenatally to a mint smell, after birth preferred to suck on mother's teats to which the same smell had been applied (Smotherman & Robinson, 1987). Other work with animal fetuses shows conditioning effects from stimulation due to sound, light, and chemicals (Gandelman, 1992). Human newborns also prefer familiar smells and tastes. They orient more to the odor of their mother's amniotic fluid than to formula milk or to amniotic fluid taken from another woman (Marlier, Schaal, & Soussignan, 1998a; Marlier, Schaal, & Soussignan, 1998b). Mothers who were randomly assigned to drink carrot juice had infants who, at six months, preferred carrot flavor more than infants whose mothers did not drink carrot juice (Menella et al., 2001).

What is the purpose of this learning ability in the fetus? It may be that it has no particular purpose for the fetus, and that its importance is for the development of learning ability that will be required after birth. On the other hand, this research demonstrates that prenatally learned associations become postnatal preferences. Fetuses exposed to prenatal maternal sounds and chemicals are more likely to recognize and prefer those same sounds and sensations after birth, and they are more likely to avoid sounds and smells that they found aversive prenatally. Thus, prenatal learning ability may serve as an early mechanism for mother-infant attachment and for the orientation of infants to the smells, tastes, and sounds of the environment into which they are born (Gandelman, 1992). It may also be that prenatal learning experiences, like prenatal movements, play a role in the development of connections between sensory, motor, and information processing areas of the brain before birth (Laughlin, 1991).

What Is It Like to Be a Late-Term Fetus?

Do late-term fetuses have psychological experiences of sensation and emotion? In order to have a psychological, as compared to a physiological, response the individual needs to be able to orient to the sensation, focus on it, and during that period of focused attention, show a recognizable response. From the data on learning reviewed in the previous section, this is very likely to be the case. The ability to self-regulate in order to pay attention may be firmly established in the final month of gestation, around 33 weeks (Kisilevsky et al., 2004). The onset of fetal crying and other organized states also suggests that they have rudimentary emotion-like experiences connected with distress and arousal. Their psychological world is probably similar to that of the newborn but not as richly textured with the opportunities for learning that occur after birth. As you do the Experiential Exercises of this chapter, try to follow your own awareness into different sensory, motor, and emotional experiences.

The vestibular system begins to develop after 22 weeks, probably providing an awareness of the orientation of the body with respect to gravity and an awareness of the movement of the whole body, as the mother moves and as the fetus turns inside the mother. In adults, this would be like the sensation of being a passenger in a moving vehicle, as it turns, stops, and starts. Of course, the fetus has no concept of moving and turning. The fetus is just aware of the feeling of being moved. The onset of REM sleep may also be a developmental continuation of an increasing awareness of internal processes. It is likely that the fetus becomes aware of rhythmical and cyclical movements during the late fetal period. Fetuses can probably sense the feelings of waking up and falling asleep. They may also be aware of the rhythms of their mother's heartbeat and breathing and of the sound of her voice.

Using 4D ultrasound, researchers in Japan observed late-term fetal arm movements (Masako-Yamakoshi & Takeshita, 2006). They found that more than half of these arm movements resulted in having the hand contact the mouth. When the hand did contact the mouth, two things were notable. First, there was a tendency to repeat the same movement, almost as if the fetus was consciously intending to do it again. Second, before the actual contact of the hand, the mouth could be observed opening, as if in anticipation of the hand coming closer. The researchers suggest that these observations indicate the beginnings of a bodily self-awareness in the fetal period, a kind of "knowing" how one part of the body relates to another part. This type of self-awareness is clearly observable after birth (see Chapter 5).

The fetus's awareness and the possibility that infants retain some participatory memories of this period suggest another question. Does enriched or impoverished experience during the last few months of pregnancy lead to positive or negative developmental pathways? We know that healthy prenatal environments lead to positive development for all periods of prenatal development. Perhaps a better question is whether specifically enriching the prenatal environment—playing classical music or massaging the fetus, for example—has any lasting effect.

Just because newborns can recognize sounds heard prenatally does not necessarily make them smarter or more talented for having heard them. Fetuses will move their bodies to loud or percussive music, but this does not mean they like it or that it will help them grow. Many books and Internet sites make strong cases for providing this kind of enrichment to the fetus. Beware when reading these materials, and examine the research they present very carefully to be sure about the limitations of their findings. In many cases, the goal is to get you to buy the book, tape, or equipment that is supposed to enhance fetal development.

Having said all that, singing to, talking to, and massaging the fetus can be a healthy and rewarding thing to do for both mother and fetus. These methods give the fetus a sense of familiarity after he or she is born. They are also natural and enjoyable for mother and father and their attachment to the fetus develops. Singing has all the important features of the human voice and language. Lullabies and other songs convey feelings of love and attachment that are essential for the mother to express and certainly cannot hurt the fetus. These things are free of charge, spontaneous, and can be done any time of the day or night, and they make parents feel good.

Do people have memories of their prenatal life, and if so, how would these be experienced by an older child or adult? My interpretation of current research (see also the concept of participatory memory in Chapter 2) is that there is no verifiable evidence for people having specific conceptual event memories for anything in their lives before the age of 2 or 3 years, not until language is acquired.

On the other hand, participatory memories of the prenatal period may exist in the form of preferential orientations for certain kinds of movement, posture, sound, taste, and touch. Examples are the infant's preference for carrot juice at 6 months, if this was consumed by their mothers during pregnancy, and the prevalence of right-handed 12-year-olds who had sucked their right thumb as a fetus.

Here are some suggestions about what you might observe in yourself as possible prenatal participatory memories. We know, for example, that lying in a fetal posture on a comfortable surface can be relaxing and soothing for children and adults. Infants and young children often curl into fetal postures and suck their thumbs, a behavior commonly found in later-term fetuses. Heartbeat-like sounds, such as drumming and other deep rhythms, can be either soothing or arousing in pleasurable ways. Do we like or dislike the kind of food that our mothers ate while they were pregnant with us? Are we more prone to depression or joyfulness because of our mother's experiences and the possible physiological effects on our fetally developed neurotransmitters?

Because emotional and behavioral development continues after birth, and few memories from early life are exact replicas of the early experience, they have been transformed and changed through later experience and interpreted in terms of the remembering person's self-understanding at that time. The impact of the prenatal period on behavioral and psychological development, therefore, is a complex systemic process that has yet to be fully understood.

Genetic and Chromosomal Influences on Development

In Chapter 2, we discussed how behavior geneticists view the origins of individual differences in the phenotype as being the result of individual differences in genotypes and/or environments. Individual variations in phenotypic characteristics that are closely correlated with individual characteristics in genotypes are less susceptible to variations in the environment. Physical characteristics, such as hair and eye color, baldness, and height, fall into this category, although all of these phenotypes can be influenced by the environment to

some extent. Let us examine some of these processes in more detail.

Genes rarely act alone in determining a phenotype. Most phenotypes are derived from **polygenic inheritance**; that is, they arise from the action of a combination of genes interacting with the environment. In most cases, at least two genes enter into the phenotype: one from the mother and one from the father. With a polygenic characteristic such as skin color, a number of genes from the mother combine with an equal number from the father, and the offspring's skin color is likely to be somewhere between the skin colors of the parents. Children in the same family may exhibit a range of skin colors.

Because chromosome pairs in an individual are made up of singles from each parent, genes that typically interact with each other to produce a phenotype are located at similar sites along the chromosome of each member of the pair. This is illustrated in Figure 3.6. Genes that act together to express a particular phenotype are called **alleles**.

In the past, it was believed that some phenotypic characteristics were inherited by a simple two-allele combination called **dominant-recessive inheritance**. Eye color is one example. The dominant allele (the one related to brown eyes) will always be expressed, even in the presence of a recessive mate (the allele for blue eyes). Thus, a person with brown eyes might actually carry a recessive allele for blue eyes, and two brown-eyed parents could produce a blue-eyed child if the zygote happens to contain two blue recessive alleles and no brown dominant allele. It takes two recessive genes for a trait to appear in the phenotype. The dominant trait appears in the phenotype, however, if only one dominant gene is present, either from the mother or from the father, or if both genes are dominant. Therefore, the dominant characteristic will appear in the phenotype 75% of the time.

It is rare for only one or two genes to determine a phenotype, however. Even characteristics that are strongly influenced by a pattern of dominant-recessive inheritance act along with other genes to produce the phenotype. Therefore, eye color, like skin color, comes in many different

Individual Genes

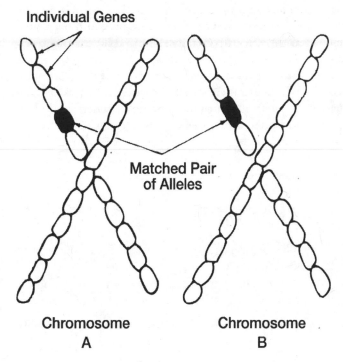

Matched Pair
of Alleles

Chromosome
A

Chromosome
B

Figure 3.6
The Relative Position of Two Alleles in a
Chromosome Pair
Source: A. Fogel & G. F. Melson, *Child develop-
ment*, 1988, p. 89. St. Paul, MN: West. Copyright
© West Publishing Company. Reprinted by permis-
sion. All rights reserved.

shades and variations—the typical signature of
polygenic inheritance.

Another pattern of inheritance relates to those
characteristics that are displayed differentially
between the sexes. **Sex-linked inheritance** relates
to phenotypes that are tied to genes that appear on
the 23rd chromosome. Recall that genetic males
have an X and a Y chromosome as their 23rd pair.
Not only is the Y chromosome missing one of its
arms compared to the X chromosome, but the Y is
also considerably smaller than the X. For this reason, one might think that women would have more
sex-linked characteristics than men, but this is not
the case. For females, the alleles on the X chromosome will express themselves in interaction with
their matched alleles on the other X chromosome
of the 23rd pair. For males, alleles on the X chromosome of the 23rd pair will express themselves
in the absence of an interaction with a matched
allele.

Sex-linked inheritance produces primary (genitals) and secondary (facial hair, body shape, etc.)
sexual characteristics in males and females. Other

sex-linked characteristics are baldness, color blindness, and a disorder of blood clotting processes
called hemophilia, all of which occur primarily in
males.

In most cases, these latter sex-linked characteristics are caused by a recessive allele on the X
chromosome. If the recessive allele is paired with
a dominant allele on another X chromosome, that
dominant allele will override the influence of the
recessive gene. Recall that it takes two recessive
genes to produce the characteristic in the phenotype. Females are thus less likely to display the
phenotype for baldness because they can inherit
both the dominant and recessive allele. A male
who inherits a recessive allele for baldness on his
X chromosome will not have the corresponding
dominant allele on his Y chromosome: there is no
site for it to occupy (see Figure 3.7).

Because the X chromosome in the male's 23rd
pair always comes from his mother (Y chromosomes are produced only by males), women are the
carriers of these sex-linked characteristics. A male
is more likely to have a hairline like his maternal

grandfather's than like his own father's (McClearn, 1970).

In some cases, however, a woman will inherit two recessive alleles for a characteristic such as baldness. Some of these women will be bald, while others will not. In addition, while most men who inherit a recessive baldness gene actually go bald, some of these men retain their hair. How can this happen?

Much like the formation of the external genitals in the third month of prenatal development, baldness is a characteristic that is expressed in the phenotype only when the genes for baldness are exposed in the adult male to the hormone testosterone. Testosterone triggers the production of an epigenetic marker that turns on the baldness gene. Because men typically have higher levels of circulating testosterone than females, their baldness gene will almost always be expressed. Men who do not become bald are either not genetically predisposed to baldness or are predisposed but have low levels of circulating testosterone. Simi-

larly, females who become bald carry two recessive genes, and they must also have higher than average testosterone levels. Female baldness can be treated with estrogen (a female hormone) supplements, but these have undesirable side effects, such as the prolongation of menstruation and the disruption of normal menopausal processes.

We will return to the topic of genetic and chromosomal influences in Chapter 9. The section on prenatal health reviews genetic and chromosomal disorders and in addition the effects of the prenatal environment on health and disease.

CHILDBIRTH

This section deals with the infant's transition from prenatal to postnatal life. During the pregnancy period, family members have been anticipating the moment of birth with both hope and concern, while the fetus is making movements that prepare for the next phase of its life. In normal circumstances, the pregnancy period ends with parents

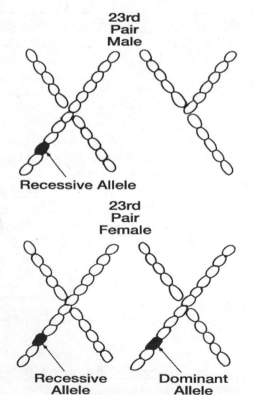

Figure 3.7
Sex-Linked Inheritance
The male Y chromosome is missing dominant alleles that are found on the lower left-hand branch of the female's X chromosome.

Source: A. Fogel & G. F. Melson, *Child development*, 1988, p. 89. St. Paul, MN: West. © West Publishing Company. Reprinted by permission. All rights reserved.

already being attached to their infants. The baby is born not only into a world of light and air, but also into a world of love.

After reviewing some data on birthrates, the process of birth will be covered. Birth complications that may affect the infant's development will be covered in Chapter 9 on health. The next section of this chapter provides a brief description of the physical features of the newborn infant.

Birthrates

How many babies are born each year? The **birthrate** is the average number of infants born for every 1,000 people. Birthrate data is usually kept by government agencies as part of a country's vital statistics. **Vital statistics** are numerical estimates in a population of events related to birth, death, and the incidence of illnesses and accidents. The birthrate for women in the United States between 1950 and 2004 is given in Table 3.3.

The birthrate has been cut almost in half in the United States since 1950. In 1950, women in the United States had an average of three children. This dropped to two children in 1980 and remains about the same today. Table 3.3 also shows the number of children per family in more and less developed nations. The lowest birthrates are in Western Europe and in Eastern Asia. Some countries, such as Italy and Japan, have an average of only one child per family today. This birthrate is not enough to maintain the present population of those countries, so their work force is increasingly being filled by immigrants. The effect of this is that the racial and cultural balance of these two countries, which traditionally have had a relatively homogenous population, changes. The highest birthrates in the world are in Eastern, Western, and Middle Africa with some contries having birthrates between 40 and 53 infants per 1,000 people (Population Reference Bureau, 2009).

The Stages of Labor

The birth process itself begins during the last several weeks of pregnancy. The muscles in the uterus begin to contract and expand at irregular intervals, sometimes days or weeks apart. These gentle muscle contractions, called **Braxton-Hicks contractions** or false labor, have two important effects. First, they help to widen (dilate) the cervix to a width of 1 to 2 centimeters. The **cervix** is the membrane at the opening between the uterus and the vagina. Normally closed during pregnancy, the cervix must dilate to a width of about 10 centimeters (5 inches) to enable the fetus to pass from the uterus into the vagina.

Second, the Braxton-Hicks contractions may help to move the fetus closer to the cervix in preparation for birth. In almost all cases, the fetus's head is oriented downward. About 4% of all births are **breech presentations** (with the buttocks first), and a small fraction are **transverse presentations** (the fetus is oriented on its side). These presentations are shown in Figure 3.8. Cesarean deliveries are usually recommended when there is a breech or transverse presentation, since the fetus cannot be turned once it has descended into its prebirth position.

Labor begins when contractions start to appear at regular intervals spaced about 10 to 20 minutes apart. Labor is usually divided into three stages (see Figure 3.9). The first stage lasts until the cervix is fully dilated to 10 centimeters and effaced (made thin). Contractions in this stage help to efface and open the cervix. This is the longest stage of labor and may vary in duration from a few minutes to

TABLE 3.3 Vital Statistics for Births

	1950	1980	2004	2009
Birthrate per 1,000 population in U.S.	24.1	15.9	14.0	14.0
More-developed nations			11.0	12.0
Less-developed nations			23.0	22.0

Source: Population Reference Bureau (2009): www.prb.org/pdf09/09wpds_eng.pdf

a few days (Guttmacher, 1973). The mean duration of the first stage is about 8 to 14 hours for **primiparous** mothers (mothers giving birth for the first time) and about 6 hours for **multiparous** mothers (Danforth, 1977; Parfitt, 1977).

During the first stage of labor, the pain of the contractions increases over time. During the early part of the first stage, contractions are regular and moderately intense. Women may be able to walk around, do household chores, watch television, nap, or take a bath. During the late part of the first stage is the time to go to the hospital or birthing center. Contractions last 40 to 60 seconds and are spaced at intervals of 3 to 4 minutes. The pain is especially intense in the final phase of the first stage, when the cervix must dilate between 8 and 10 centimeters. This is the time that a woman may elect to begin the use of pain control methods (see next section). Mothers can move around, change positions, or take a warm bath or shower.

In the second stage of labor, the infant passes through the cervix and vagina. For women who choose natural childbirth, the pain of this phase of labor may be accompanied by panic, anger, and confusion (Lesko & Leski, 1984). Some mothers begin to shake or feel nausea. Contractions last 60 to 90 seconds and come once every 2 or 3 minutes. Fortunately, this stage is not as long as the previous stage. As the infant begins to descend

into the vagina, contractions serve to push the baby out. In natural childbirth, mothers will feel an urge to push. If a local anesthetic is used, mothers feel pressure and will need coaching to determine when to push. The intensity of the pain and feelings of nausea or disorientation are balanced by the sense of relief that the end is near. Some women may begin to feel euphoria.

The final stage of labor is the birth of the placenta, often called the afterbirth. This stage takes less than 1 hour in most cases. By that time, the mother's attention and emotion are occupied with the newborn, and most women do not pay much attention to what is happening in the vaginal area. Contractions continue for several hours as the placenta is expelled and the uterus closes up to prevent bleeding. These contractions are not as intense as during the previous stages, but the woman may continue to experience some pain.

If you ever wondered where the name "labor" comes from, it is because difficult muscular work is involved. Although some fortunate women go through all three stages in a matter of several hours, other mothers may be in labor for 20 or 30 hours, during which time they have little chance to sleep or rest.

Babies are expected to be born 280 days from the first day of the mother's last menstrual period, but only about 4% of all births occur on their exact due date. Births occurring within 2 weeks

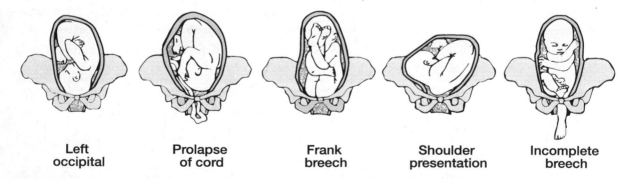

| Left occipital | Prolapse of cord | Frank breech | Shoulder presentation | Incomplete breech |

Figure 3.8   Various Deviations from the Most Optimal Vertex Presentation
The first drawing on the left shows a minor deviation in which the head is first but is turned to the side. The next shows a prolapsed cord. The more extreme presentations are shown in the three drawings on the right.
Source: Adapted from J. F. Rosenblith & J. E. Sims-Knight, *In the beginning: Development in the first two years*, 1985, p. 158. Belmont, CA: Brooks-Cole.

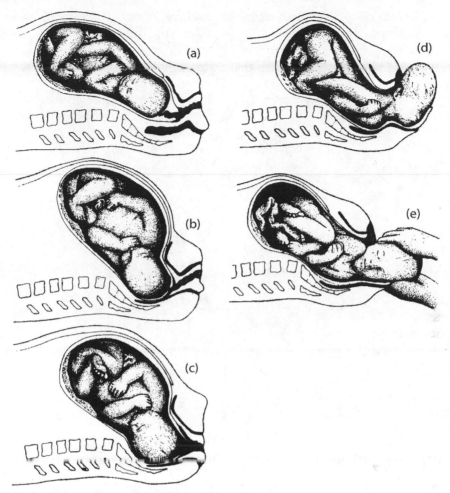

Figure 3.9   Birth Processes: Stage 1 and Part of Stage 2
(a) End of the first stage of labor; the baby's head is moving through the cervix. **(b)** Transition; the baby's head is moving through the birth canal, the vagina. **(c c)** The second stage of labor; the baby's head is moving through the opening of the vagina. **(c)** It emerges completely. **(d)** The head is then turned so that the rest of the body slides out **(e)**.

Source: A. Fogel & G. F. Melson, *Child development*, 1988, pp. 116-117. St. Paul, MN: West. Copyright © West Publishing Company. Reprinted by permission. All rights reserved.

before or after the due date are generally considered to be in the normal range.

The timing of birth is controlled by a protein called corticotropin-releasing hormone (CRH). Women with the highest levels of CRH in their blood during the fourth month of pregnancy were more likely to deliver their infants prematurely. Tests for the concentration of CRH are currently being developed. Given the risks of premature birth (see the section on prematurity in Chapter 9), it may be possible in the future to delay birth by regulating the production of CRH during pregnancy (R. Smith, 1999).

Technologies for Labor and Delivery

Advances in medical technology have led to the development of a variety of tools to assist childbirth. These include **fetal monitoring**, mechanical aids to speed delivery (forceps and vacuum extraction), cesarean section (a surgical rather than vaginal delivery), and drugs to reduce pain and speed labor.

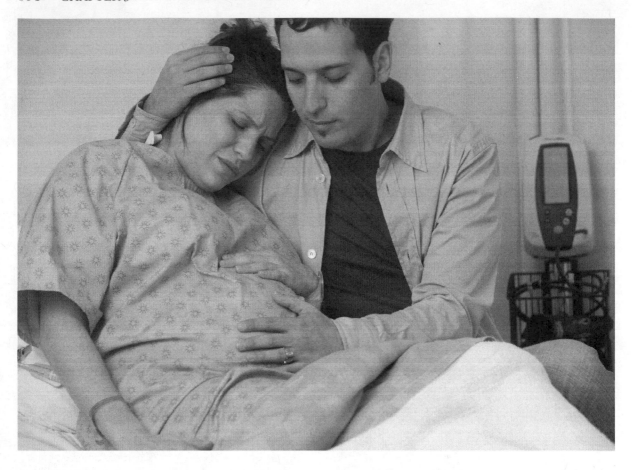

Childbirth can be an exceptionally moving experience for all members of the family. In many hospitals, fathers are encouraged to attend the childbirth, providing support for their mates and enhancing their own feelings of particpation.

Fetal monitoring is the use of electronic devices to detect and display the fetal signs (heart rate, respiration, blood gases, pH balance) during the delivery and birth process. In invasive fetal monitoring, electrodes are inserted through the vagina and cervix and attached to the fetus. This procedure deprives the mother of opportunity for movement. In a less invasive form, the mother may wear a belt around her abdomen. Invasive fetal monitoring is controversial because it restricts the mother, often requires additional drugs for pain control, and carries a risk of infection for both mother and baby. Experts suggest that fetal monitoring should only be used in high-risk deliveries (Freeman, 1990; Shy et al., 1990). The American College of Obstetrics and Gynecology does not consider fetal monitoring part of standard care for childbirth. Furthermore, research shows that fetal monitoring does not produce healthier infants with fewer complications (*Birth*, 1988). Ultrasound can also be used to determine the position and behavior of the fetus prior to birth.

Forceps are instruments, usually made of metal or plastic, that are shaped to fit around the newborn's head and used to pull the infant through the birth canal. The use of forceps is declining in favor of cesarean section and spontaneous vaginal delivery because they may cause brain and spinal cord injuries if used during early phases of labor (high forceps). The effect of forceps used at the very end of delivery (low forceps) has not been studied. It seems generally safe, although bruises may be left on the head in some cases. With **vacuum extraction**, a cup connected to a suction device is placed on the baby's head. Research shows that the risks of vacuum extraction are lower than with cesarean section or high forceps (Meyer et al., 1987; Nagan et al., 1990). These mechanical methods are used more frequently in the United States than in Europe (Korte & Scaer, 1990).

Vaginal deliveries occured in about 71% of all births in the United States in 2004; the remainder were done by cesarean section. In a **cesarean section**, an incision is made in the mother's abdomen and uterus while she is under a local or general anesthetic. Then the baby and placenta are both removed. Cesarean sections, also called C-sections, are used in the case of breech or transverse presentations. C-sections are also recommended in multiple births (twins, triplets, etc.), when the baby's head is too large for the mother's pelvis, when the fetus becomes dangerously entangled in the umbilical cord, and in the case of fetal distress. Some diseases that infect the mother's vagina, such as syphilis, herpes simplex, and AIDS, can be transmitted to the infant during delivery, and a C-section birth helps to prevent the transmission of this infection to the infant. A new drug, nevirapine, can reduce the risk of transmitting AIDS to the newborn. It is inexpensive and can be used in African countries where AIDS has reached epidemic levels.

Fetal distress is a sudden loss of oxygen or a change in the heart rate or respiration of the fetus, usually determined by fetal monitoring. Severe fetal distress can cause serious complications. For example, too much pressure on the fetal head during delivery can cause excess blood pressure and possibly bleeding inside the scalp, called *intraventricular* hemorrhage. Loss of oxygen, which sometimes occurs in long and difficult labors, can lead to fetal brain damage. Using a fetal monitor, a physician can decide if the risk to the infant requires an emergency C-section.

C-sections have saved the lives and health of many mothers and infants. They are not without risk to the mother, however. Because a C-section is a surgical procedure, the mother is at greater risk of infection and postoperative stress. In the past, it was thought that once a woman had a C-section, she could not have vaginal deliveries in the future. This belief is changing as an increasing number of C-section mothers are having vaginal deliveries of later-born children.

The number of C-sections performed in the United States has increased over the past 30 years, which is hard to account for since the proportion of breech and difficult labors has not changed. Between 1998 and 1999 the C-section delivery rate rose to a total of 22 per 100 births (Ventura, Martin, Curtin, menacker, & Hamilton, B., 2001). In some countries, C-sections are done in over 40% of births. Some people have complained that obstetricians are too quick to perform C-sections in an attempt to avoid lawsuits against them if the baby or mother suffers during a vaginal delivery or in an effort to make more money by doing surgery compared to a routine delivery. It is difficult to prove these claims, however. Other explanations for the increase in C-sections are better nutrition and therefore larger babies and more accurate fetal monitoring that allows a more sensitive and early detection of fetal distress. More recently, however, a growing number of mothers are choosing to have C-sections rather than vaginal births, perhaps because they can be planned in advance and seem easier for the mother.

There is little evidence that a C-section has any lasting negative side effects on mothers or on infants, even in long-term follow-up studies, although it is not associated with any benefits either (Entwisle & Alexander, 1987; Field & Widmayer, 1980; Hollenbeck, Gewirtz, Seloris, & Scanlon, 1984; Whyte et al., 2004). Fathers may be more involved with C-section infants because the mother receives more medication and takes longer to recover than with a vaginal delivery. In sum, although C-sections carry some increased risk for the mother due to complications of surgery, if the mother or infant is at risk, the health benefits justify the procedure. On the other hand, if there is no health risk, mothers should think twice. While it may seem more convenient and less painful, the fact is that it takes much longer for the mother to recover from major abdominal surgery than from vaginal childbirth. Even under ideal conditions, cesarean section surgery carries greater health risks to the mother and baby (Clarke & Taffel, 1995, McFarlan, 2004). Also, there is data indicating that C-section is a modest risk factor for ectopic pregnancy and an important risk factor for placental problems (Hemminki,E., & Meriläinen, J., 1996; McFarlan, 2004).

Drugs and delivery. In either a vaginal or a cesarean delivery, many mothers are given some type of medication to control pain and/or to regulate the course of labor. According to Judeo-Christian tradition, women are supposed to suffer during childbirth as punishment for Eve's sins: "In sorrow thou shall bring forth children" (Genesis 3:16). This belief persisted until 1847, when a Scottish obstetrician, James Young Simpson, gave ether to a delivering mother to ease her pain. In his fight to use pain relievers during childbirth, Simpson had to combat both medical practice and religious values. He argued that the Hebrew word previously translated as "sorrow" should have been translated as "work" or "labor." Furthermore, he cited the "deep sleep" that God imposed on Adam when Eve was "delivered" from one of his ribs. Painless childbirth rapidly became popular and was encouraged by the use of chloroform during two of Queen Victoria's childbirths (Brackbill, 1979).

Today, the science of drug use during labor and delivery is complex. Perhaps because obstetricians who delivered babies were less concerned with the infant than with the mother, the development of **anesthesia** (loss of sensation) and **analgesia** (pain relief) proceeded without much concern for the welfare of the infant, although this has recently been changing.

In most industrialized nations, the method most used for pain control is drugs. Although drugs are medically controlled and have been proved safe for the mother, it is now well established that most general anesthetics administered to the mother cross the placenta during labor and delivery. Unfortunately for the neonate, those organ systems that are the most susceptible to chemical insult (primarily the central nervous system) and those that would be the most effective for drug clearance (the liver and kidneys) are the least well developed. Other organs of the newborn, such as the heart and lungs, are better developed, but these systems have little or nothing to do with helping the system get rid of the drugs.

How long the drugs remain in the newborn's system depends on the type of drug, the time during labor at which it was given, and the dosage given to the mother (Golub, 1996). In general, newborns of women who took analgesia during childbirth were slower to respond to breast feeding, had higher temperatures, and cried more (Ransjö-Arvidson et al., 2001).

One should not conclude from this review that most drugs are without impact. Even though no effects can be shown overall, some infants and mothers may show extreme but short-term reactions. Some drugs may impair a mother's ability to participate in her delivery by paralyzing muscles normally used to push the baby out, while others may make her drowsy. Many women seem to suffer from gaps in their memories of the childbirth experience. In one study (Affonso, 1977), 86% of the women interviewed could not remember some of the events of their childbirth and wanted to know more. They asked the doctor and nurses; they had bad dreams and felt somewhat frustrated. Some mothers asked the same questions over and over. This problem seems to occur when labor is either extremely long or extremely short, in high-risk conditions, or when the level of medication is high.

Epidurals are a local anesthetic administered in the lower (lumbar) spine that block pain sensation in the pelvic area but allow the mother to remain awake and aware. Epidurals have been shown to cause fevers during childbirth in about 15% of women. Although there is no measurable effect on the newborn, some doctors may react to the maternal fever by preventive treatment of the newborn for infection (Lieberman et al., 1997). Epidurals also increase the risk for postpartum depression (see Chapter 8). Before electing them, women should discuss the use of epidurals with their doctors or midwives.

On the other hand, for some mothers anxiety and pain increase dramatically prior to and during labor and delivery (Westbrook, 1978). Research shows that women who choose epidurals, compared to natural childbirth, are more likely to be fearful of childbirth and to take a relatively passive role, preferring to turn over the management of the birth process to professionals (Heinze & Sleign, 2003). Drugs serve to calm these mothers and reduce their discomfort, making them better able to enjoy the birth of their infant (Field & Widmayer, 1980; Shnider, 1981). Prenatal preparation for childbirth is important in order for the doctor and the parents to understand all the different options available for pain control and to choose the one that is best for mother and infant. In the next section, we turn to different types of childbirth practices, including methods for the behavioral and psychological control of pain.

The Management of Childbirth

Most childbirths in North America and Northern Europe today take place in hospital settings. From a medical perspective, the hospital environment allows a large staff to assist in labor, delivery, and the care of the newborn. Hospitals also provide access to emergency medical care in the event of fetal distress or complications with labor.

At the beginning of the twentieth century, most childbirths took place in the home. Once it became accepted practice to give birth in the hospital, however, the experience of childbirth for women and their families changed. In the home, the mother could be surrounded by familiar sights and sounds and have the support of other family members. In the early days of hospital births, mothers were left in sparsely furnished rooms for labor, and birth took place in a sterile operating chamber. Family members were prohibited from accompanying the mother. The babies were separated from the mothers for several days, bottle feeding was encouraged, and hospitals stays could last up to a week for normal deliveries.

Birthing centers. Today, childbirth in hospitals has become more humane. There is a growing recognition of the need to treat childbirth less like a disease and more like a normal event. Birthing centers are alternatives to standard hospital deliveries. They are based on the idea that most births are natural and nonmedical and should take place in a comfortable, homelike environment. Birthing centers are typically located in hospitals, but they keep medical technology to a minimum and provide comfortable furnishings, quiet, and privacy. Thus, they combine the relative comfort and privacy of a home birth with the availability of medical assistance if it is required.

Parents find birthing centers very rewarding and enriching for their childbirth experience (Eakins, 1986; Waldenström, 1999); such centers are a safe and effective alternative to traditional hospital deliveries for low-risk pregnancies (Rooks et al., 1989). Birthing centers are especially effective for low-income mothers, who benefit from the additional social support and long-term care (Lubic, 1999). Low-income mothers who used a birthing center in New York City tell about the effectiveness of the birthing center in their own words:

> If you have given birth, you have given life, and if you have given life then you can do anything—you can get a job and you can go to school and you can do anything you want as long as you put your mind to it.

> That's the best thing about the birth center concept. It empowers women, and in turn, they empower their families, and families empower the community and it just grows and grows. (Lubic, 1999, p. 21)

In one study of 8,677 childbirths in the United Kingdom, compared to conventional hospital rooms, birthing centers reduced the need for medical interventions and increased maternal satisfaction. Women who gave birth in birthing centers required less analgesia and anesthesia, were more likely to have a vaginal compared to a caesarian birth, had fewer episiotomies (surgical cutting of the labia thought to prevent severe tearing during delivery), and were more likely to initiate breast feeding (Hodnett et al., 2005). Because of a new awareness about the psychological benefits of early mother-infant and father- infant contact, babies are separated from parents only in the case of a medical complication. Otherwise, early and frequent contact is desirable.

Every hospital has different practices, however. Parents who desire the presence of fathers during delivery, rooming in (allowing the newborn to sleep in the mother's room rather than in the hospital nursery), or natural childbirth need to consult their health care providers and inquire about hospital practices. It helps if the parents make their desires known and act assertively to get their personal needs met. Hospitals, like all large institutions, have rules of standard practice, but sometimes these can be tailored to fit the individual and family, if their needs are made known to the hospital staff.

Early discharge. In the case of normal deliveries, hospital stays can last from 1 to 3 days. Some hospitals allow discharge within 3 hours after the birth if the mother receives no analgesia or anesthesia and the infant is in good health. Under these conditions, there is no increased risk associated with early discharge (Mehl, Peterson, Sokolsky, & Whitt, 1976). More recently, early discharge has been allowed on demand in consultation with the physician. In 1998, an act of the U.S. Congress ensured that mothers and infants were not discharged before 48 hours after delivery without the mother's consent (Kanto, 2002).

Women who elect early discharge feel that the home is a better and more supportive environment for comfort, recovery, and early adaptation to their babies. Early-discharge mothers report more social support in the home (availability of relatives and friends) and are more confident in their ability to manage on their own (Lemmer, 1987). On the other hand, early discharge limits the ability of the hospital staff to provide parent education and to detect feeding problems and other abnormalities (Kiely, Drum, & Kessel, 1998). It may also deprive women of some needed rest to recover from the delivery. Women should try to evaluate their preferences and discuss them with staff.

Behavioral pain control and childbirth preparation. While drugs offer the advantages that they can be administered in controlled doses and are effective, a number of behavioral and psychological alternatives to speed labor and relieve pain are available. Many diverse kinds of pain-relieving methods have been used throughout human history. One common practice, used by the Laotians, the Navaho, and the Cuna of Panama, among others, is the use of music during labor. Among the Comanche and Tewa Indian tribes, heat is applied to the abdomen (M. Mead & Newton, 1967). Other alternative natural pain relief methods for labor may include massage, acupressure, hypnosis, herbs, and water births (Liebermann, 1992).

Some groups believe that pain and ease of delivery are functions of the mother's body position during labor and delivery. Many cultures encourage women to give birth in a sitting position, usually held from behind by another woman. The Taureg of the Sahara insist that the laboring mother walk up and down small hills to allow the infant to become properly placed to facilitate delivery. Taureg women usually deliver from a kneeling position. In fact, most obstetrics textbooks in the United States at the turn of the century advocated an upright position during labor (M. Mead & Newton, 1967).

For some peoples, prevention is the best cure. The Ainu of Japan believe that maternal exercise will make the fetus small and encourage a shorter labor. This belief is actually supported by recent research (see Chapter 9; Campbell & Mottola, 2001; Clapp et al., 2002) although lower birthweight may be a risk factor in some cases. The Japanese value smaller newborns and are not pleased with multiple births, which they consider too animal-like. In a number of other cultures, including the Hopi of the American Southwest, women are encouraged to exercise during pregnancy (M. Mead & Newton, 1967).

Nonchemical pain control during labor in developed Western countries today is sometimes achieved using the **Lamaze method**. Working in France, Frederick Lamaze developed a system of exercise, breathing, and massage that was based on a theory of pain during labor developed by Grantly Dick-Read in Great Britain (Dick-Read, 1933/1972). According to Dick-Read, women become afraid during childbirth due to the pain that develops when muscles are contracted. He suggested that if women were to employ some commonly known methods of relaxation, their experience of pain would be lessened. Female animals naturally fall into panting and breathing patterns. Using these observations and the work of Dick-Read, Lamaze based his method on the use of rhythmic breathing as a mental distraction from pain and on relaxation methods to prevent it (Karmel, 1959). The Lamaze method has been the most widely used approach to childbirth education in the U.S. (Leifer, 1999). Dick-Read believed that natural methods, those that had been used over many human generations, were the best choice for many women (Mascucci, 2003).

Mother's reports of higher pain during childbirth has also been associated with negative attitudes toward pregnancy and childbirth (Nettlebladt, Fagerstrom, & Udderberg, 1976) and with a lack of support from the husband. Mothers can perceive when fathers show inadequate involvement in childbirth an this contributes to the mother's feeling of dissatisfaction in the childbirth experience (Mackey, 1995). Parental involvement in childbirth is associated with the father's later involvement in caregiving (Parke, 1995). Women whose husbands were present during the labor and delivery, as well as those whose husbands stayed with them for longer periods, perceived childbirth as less painful (Davenport-Slack & Boylan, 1974; Nettlebladt et al., 1976). It could be, however, that women who were more likely to view childbirth as less painful were those who requested their husband's presence for longer periods during the delivery. In addition, people who choose such approaches are a self- selected group whose positive attitudes about labor and delivery might help them, even under adverse conditions.

There is some debate, though little concrete data, on how childbirth preparation affects women (Wideman & Singer, 1984). Some suggest that the effect is due to education and the ability to anticipate fearful events. Some think it is due to the relaxation techniques and/or the social support provided by the Lamaze approach, while others think the effect is related to positive images about the childbirth experience (Nichols & Humenick, 1988). Here are some examples of imagery techniques that have been used (C. Jones, 1987):

Imagine that you and your baby are breathing in harmony. Now imagine that you are inside the womb, face-to-face with your unborn child, who is comfortable and secure in a private sea of crystal-clear water. (p. 87)

Imagine yourself opening. Envision the baby's head against the cervix and the cervix widening to let it pass. At that time, mentally say yes to the contractions as they come and fade away. (p. 145)

Some research has shown, however, that relaxation techniques may be superior to this approach since these images tend to be transitory, whereas breathing and massage can be sustained for longer periods (Markman & Kadushin, 1986). Lamaze-trained mothers, especially if they are accompanied by the father and receive professional support during the delivery, require less pain medication and fewer episiotomies (Copstick, Taylor, Hayes, & Morris, 1986; Hodnett & Osborn, 1989).

The enhancement of relaxation to control pain is also at the heart of the somatic awareness methods reviewed under the clinical theories in Chapter 2. The Rosen method, the Feldenkrais method, Watsu, and bodymind centering all rely on helping clients to relax and easing chronic tension and stress. Although these methods are probably not useful during childbirth, they may be helpful in childbirth preparation and recovery. Acupuncture and acupressure, massage, hypnosis, relaxation techniques, yoga, warm baths, walking, and music have also been shown to help ease labor pain. Somatic education helps a mother to be more in touch with her body. This reduces anxiety and pain and gives mothers greater confidence in their decisions to use or not to use drugs during delivery. Home-like hospital rooms and relaxation contribute to maternal well-being, lower the need for drugs, and reduce episiotomies. The latter have been shown to lead to longer post-birth recovery times for the mother compared to the stitching of small tears that may occur naturally during vaginal childbirth (Fleming et al., 2003; Hartmann et al., 2005).

Upright postures. During traditional hospital labors and deliveries, women had been confined almost the entire time to a supine position. There is a growing recognition that upright postures may be beneficial to both mother and infant. Anatomically, when a mother is upright, her pelvis widens, access to the birth canal is easier for the fetus, and pushing is more effective because of the assistance of gravity. Upright postures also improve the blood circulation to the mother's abdominal muscles and increase the oxygen supply to the fetus, reduce the need for forceps, lower the rate of episiotomies, and reduce pain (Cottrell & Shannahan, 1987; de Jonge et al., 2004). Some studies find beneficial effects such as fewer birth complications, shortening of labor, less backache pain, and easier pushing (Gardosi, Hutson, & Lynch, 1989; Holland & Smith, 1989; Lupe & Gross, 1986). In a recent meta-analysis of 21 studies with a total of 3,706 women it has been found that the first stage of labor was approximately one hour shorter for women in upright positions compared to those who were lying down (Lawrence, Lewis, Hofmeyr, Dowswell, & Styles, 2009).

Upright postures can be achieved in a number of ways. During labor, some women find it helpful to get up and walk around, stand, or squat. Hospital beds can be tilted so that the mother is sitting. Some hospitals have birthing balls, large inflated exercise balls on which a mother can sit or lean. In other places a birthing bar is used. The bar is suspended about two feet above the bed. It allows the mother to pull herself upright any time during labor. Just changing positions sometimes relieves discomfort.

Midwives and doulas. A **midwife** is a practitioner who has been trained to assist women who are giving birth. Lay midwives receive informal and formal training, while nurse midwives are registered nurses who receive their training as part of their nursing education. Midwives often work alongside doctors and assist the mother as long as the labor is without complications. They are trained to recognize which complications require the attention of a physician. Midwives are usually less costly to parents than physicians, and they also provide both prenatal and postnatal care for the family. Midwives help families understand the various birthing options and the risks and benefits of drugs and surgical procedures, and they work with the family to enhance the healthy development of parents and baby. Midwives assist in the delivery of 80% of births worldwide.

Doula is an ancient Greek word meaning "an experienced woman who guides and assists a new mother in her infant-care tasks." A doula works alongside doctors or midwives to provide emotional support during labor and delivery. Doulas are trained to recognize birth as a key life experience that the mother will remember all her life. Doulas serve as advocates and supporters of the parents in preparing for and carrying out their plans for the birth. Doulas attend the birth, provide emotional support and physical comfort measures, and help the mother and her partner communicate with the hospital staff. Randomized clinical trials using low-income first-time mothers found that doula-assisted delivery shortened the labor, reduced the number of forceps and cesarian deliveries, and increased satisfaction with the childbirth experience. Doula-assisted mothers also were more likely to initiate and maintain breast-feeding (Glink, 1998).

Doulas can be used by any woman who would like support and advocacy at an important and sensitive time in her life. If women have a close relationship to their physician or midwife, and if they believe they can obtain the kind of delivery they desire, a doula may not be necessary. On the other hand, even in the best of circumstances, physicians and midwives will have relatively little time to spend with each individual patient. Doulas take the perspective of the mother and serve as her support and advocate. When the clinician is too busy with assisting the actual delivery, the doula remains by the mother's side, explains what is happening, ands helps her to make decisions if she becomes confused or disoriented. Finding the right doula can alleviate a lot of anxiety for the mother and father, who can then concentrate their energies on preparing themselves physically and emotionally for the birth.

Home births. An alternative to hospital delivery is the modern practice of birth at home. Home births are standard practice in some countries, such as the Netherlands and most of Scandinavia. These births are assisted by professional midwives, and the incidence of infant mortality is lower in these countries than in the United States. On closer examination, though, this effect is due not to home birth itself but to other factors. These countries have a relatively high level of education and a low incidence of poverty. In addition, women who are at risk are not allowed to have home births. These women include very young or very old mothers, unmarried women, low-income women, and those with medical risks (Rosenblith & Sims-Knight, 1985). With a trained professional in attendance, screening for risk, and a nearby hospital in case of emergency, home births in the United States are no more risky than hospital births (R. Cohen, 1981; Hazell, 1975; Howe, 1988; de Jonge, van der Goes, Ravelli, Amelink-Verburg, Mol, Nijhuis, Gravenhorst, & Buitendijk, 2009).

The Leboyer method: Birth without violence. Frederick Leboyer (1975) suggested that some of the hospital routines used in the 1970s were traumatic for the infant: holding the infant upside down in the cold air, placing the baby on a cold metal scale, putting silver nitrate in his or her eyes, separating the infant from the mother, putting the baby under bright lights, exposing him or her to loud sounds, and prematurely cutting the umbilical cord. With the **Leboyer method**, the delivery room is quiet and dimly lit, and the infant is placed on the mother's warm abdomen right after birth until the umbilical cord stops pulsing. After the cord is cut, the infant is placed in a warm-water bath. Leboyer reports that infants so treated tend to be more relaxed and alert than other infants. This method has many similarities to Watsu (see Chapter 2).

Leboyer's claims that such procedures increase the newborn's alertness have not been verified scientifically. Most studies reporting positive effects were biased by the observer's preference for the method and the lack of a control group (e.g., Rappoport, 1976). One well-controlled study (Nelson et al., 1980) found no difference in alertness between Leboyer and non-Leboyer babies, nor were there any differences in developmental test scores between the two groups at 8 months. Furthermore, half of the Leboyer babies reacted to the warm-water bath following birth with irritated crying. As with upright postures and childbirth preparation classes, it is difficult to establish a conclusive effect for these practices. On the positive side, most of the practices discussed here cannot be shown to have any harmful side effects, and they may be effective for many of the people who use them. LeBoyer's work, however, did have an effect on the formation of birthing centers, which reduce stress on both mother and newborn. The Leboyer method has not been widely used in the U.S. since research has not supported its effectiveness (Maziade, Boudreault, Cote, & Thivierge, 1986).

Regardless of whether a mother chooses a physician, midwife, or doula, it is a good idea to make a birth plan in which the mother, her partner, and her care provider discuss what they would like to happen during labor and delivery. Several Internet sites are also available to help mothers understand their options and to construct a birth plan that suits their needs. The next section covers the physical characteristics of the normal newborn infant as well as newborns who are at risk.

THE BABY AT BIRTH

The transition from an essentially aquatic existence to a world of air, light, and gravity is one of the most abrupt and remarkable developmental shifts in the human life span. Much of what we can observe in the human newborn is the result of making this adaptation to extrauterine life. Some of the souvenirs of their prior home will stay with the infants as they make this change.

As you might imagine, the newborn's lungs are filled with mucus and amniotic fluid, making its initial attempts at breathing difficult. As the mucus gradually drains over the first few weeks of life, the infant's breathing becomes more regular and quieter. Just about any kind of stimulation can induce respiration, even the mere exposure to air. Breathing can also be stimulated by a sneeze, cough, yawn, or cry. Some alternative birthing methods use massage or dip the infant into warm water as a stimulus to start breathing. Slapping the baby is not necessary.

Another major adaptation of the newborn to extrauterine existence is the loss of the umbilical connection to the mother. Immediately after birth, the infant's abdominal muscles surrounding the umbilical vessels contract to inhibit the circulation of blood in the cord. Once the cord has been cut, the navel opening usually heals within a week, and the dried remains of the cord fall off in another few days. The umbilical cord contains cells that assist in the manufacture of new blood cells, much as the cells in bone marrow do. For this reason, physicians have begun to collect umbilical cords for use in the treatment of blood and immune disorders, such as leukemia and AIDS, in children (C. Thompson, 1995).

Once the umbilical cord has been severed and respiration has begun, it takes about 30 hours for the oxygen level of the blood to reach nearly normal levels. The blood pH balance needs about 1 week to become established, and blood pressure takes about 10 days to reach normal levels.

Just after birth, infants are wet with amniotic fluid, and their skin may still be coated with the white, cheesy **vernix caseosa**. The color of the skin may be pale to pink, or it may be slightly yellowish due to **normal physiological jaundice**. Jaundice is caused by unbalanced liver function. It can be treated by placing the baby under special lamps.

Almost all babies are born with smoky blue eyes, which do not develop their true color until later in the first year. Even neonates from parents of color may have light skin and blue eyes for the first few days of life, since eye and skin pigments depend on white light for further development.

At birth, the newborn retains some of the physical characteristics of the fetus. The newborn's head is about one-fourth its total length, the legs about one-third. A newborn has virtually no voluntary control over his or her head, although if the head is cradled, the infant can turn it from side to side. The newborn has somewhat bowed legs, with the feet bent inward at the ankles so that the soles of the feet are almost parallel. The typical "baby face" includes a very short neck, no chin, and a flattened nose. Newborns' heads are often temporarily misshapen from the pressures of the birth process. This gradually disappears by the end of the second week of life. Some fetal hair may remain on the infant's head, eyebrows, and back (the **lanugo**). This hair usually is replaced by more permanent hair within the first few months.

Newborns have six soft spots on the top of their heads, called **fontanels**. These openings provide some room for the various bones of the skull to move during the birth process, called molding. The fontanels also allow for the growth of the brain during the first years of life. They do not fully close until about 18 months. The initial shifting of the fontanels after birth is shown in Figure 3.10. The time of fontanel closure is unrelated to infant sex, race, birth measurements, or later growth measurements; slowly closing fontanels are not a sign of abnormal development (Kataria, Frutiger, Lanford, & Swanson, 1988).

At birth, virtually all the nerve cells in the brain are present, but they have not developed very far. During the first year, the brain doubles in size (from 350 to 750 cubic centimeters), and it doubles again by the sixth year. Most of the postnatal brain growth is accounted for by the increase in **myelination**, the development of a protective sheath around the nerve pathways, as well as by an increase in the volume and den-

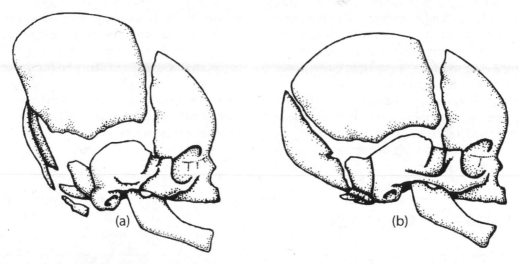

Figure 3.10   Skull of a Newborn
(a) Molding of the bones of the baby's head during passage through the birth canal. (b) By the 3rd day of life, the bones return to their normal position.

Source: A. Fogel & G. F. Melson, *Child development*, 1988, p. 126. St. Paul, MN: West. © by West Publishing Company. Reprinted by permission. All rights reserved.

sity of dendritic connections between the cells. **Dendrites** are the branchlike filaments that connect the nerve cells and transmit nerve impulses between the cells.

While these processes of brain development are occurring, the cells that receive fewer inputs and connections will eventually die. Thus, postnatal experience tends to actively select certain areas and cells in the brain for further development. Those areas and cells that are not used will eventually be lost (Greenough, Black, & Wallace, 1987). A more detailed discussion of brain development is in Chapter 5.

Other important changes are occurring in other parts of the newborn's body. At birth, the newborn's genitals appear large and prominent. Both sexes may have slightly enlarged breasts that may excrete a white, milk-like substance, and females may have a brief "menstrual flow." These phenomena are caused by the massive infusion of maternal hormones during the birth process, and the effects disappear quickly. Newborns may also look withered because they have very little body fat except in the cheeks, where it is needed for sucking. This withered look is even worse for pre-

mature infants, since the fat pads in their cheeks are underdeveloped.

Each baby's body has a characteristic muscle tone and response to tactile stimulation. Some babies are cuddly; they will mold into the arms of the caregiver and curl up when held. Others are tense and tight; some squirm and some sprawl. An adult can almost hold the entire infant in one hand.

Taking in food through the mouth is not an entirely new experience to a newborn, since babies suck amniotic fluid in the uterus. Nevertheless, one of the major prenatal-to-postnatal transitions involves the handling of nutrients. Before birth, nutrient intake and waste matter both pass through the umbilical cord. After birth, the newborn's digestive system must take over those functions. The intestines of the newborn are filled with a greenish-black substance called **meconium**, which consists of digested bits of mucus, amniotic fluid, shed skin, and hair that was ingested prenatally. Due to the excretion of meconium and also because the mother's milk does not develop before the first few days, the infant typically experiences weight loss during the first week, but the weight is rapidly regained. The fluid that is excreted by the mother's breasts in the first few days is called the **colostrum** (see the section on feeding in Chapter 9).

The process of keeping physiological signs at a steady level is known as **homeostasis**. At birth, temperature homeostasis is not fully functioning, and infants can easily become chilled if not wrapped. Infants can also become easily over-heated if they are too heavily clothed. Infants should not be overdressed; as a general rule, they should wear the same number of layers of clothing as the adults in the same room. Infants need to be exposed to cold as well as warmth to help them develop the capacity to regulate their body temperature. This capability will not fully develop until after 1 month of age, when the sweat glands become more fully functional.

EXPERIENTIAL EXERCISE

The prenatal environment is alien compared to life outside the womb. In the womb we are surrounded by liquid and largely free from the effects of gravity. Even though capable of many movements, we are restricted by our tight encapsulation in the womb. and we depend upon our umbilical cord for life support. Perhaps we can get a glimmer of what prenatal experience might be like by changing our relation to gravity, relearning some fetus-like movements, and altering how we use our senses. Here are some experiments you can try.

Awakening your Senses
by Alan Fogel

Blindfold yourself for a period of at least 3 hours, preferably up to 24 hours. Do this at home so that you are in a familiar environment. Try to go about your various activities to the extent that the blindfold allows. The longer you stay blindfolded, the more you will grow accustomed to relying on your hearing and sense of touch. For sighted people, the majority of information from the environ-ment comes from vision. The longer we interrupt our use of vision, the more we will depend on our other senses, and those senses will therefore become more acute. In the womb, our hearing and sense of touch developed before our visual sense. Despite the vast array of visual information we receive, the other senses may remain, in some way, more fundamental.

While you are blindfolded and going about your usual activities, spend some time noticing features of your environment that are external to you and spend some time turning your focus inward, noticing what is happening within you. After doing this exercise with the blindfold on, try over the next few days to notice some of the things that came up when you were wearing the blindfold, while now engaging in your typical activities without the blindfold. For instance, if you noticed the movement of the air on your skin while you were blindfolded, see if you can notice that at other times during the week. You can even put the blindfold back on for short periods and compare your experiences with and without the blindfold.

Navel Radiation Patterns Based on Body-Mind Centering Exercises
(See Chapter 2) Adapted from Hartley (1994).

1. Relax on the floor—preferably on your back—but if that hurts, choose a different position.

2. Feel your body touching the floor. Where does(n't) it touch?

3. Feel the ground spreading out below you. Feel how it supports your weight— imagine the foundations of the building reaching deep into the earth.

4. Now observe the movement of your breath flowing gently in and out, and notice where in your body you can feel the breath going. Where can you feel the rising and falling patterns of the breath moving through you?

5. Are there any places where you cannot feel the breath? Any places of tension? Just notice.

6. Can you feel the filling and emptying motion of the breath spreading through your whole body? Into the chest—abdomen—and down to your pelvic area? Can you imagine it going up

into your arms and legs—into your fingers and toes—and up into your face and head?

7. Imagine your breath entering through the navel, filling the middle of your body—front to back—side to side—and radiating from there to all parts of your body as you inhale. As you exhale and empty, imagine that the breath is flowing out through your navel.

8. Keep imagining this movement of the breath—into and out of your navel—until you can begin to feel the flow of energy carried by the breath through each limb—from the navel to the fingers— toes—top of the head— and tail of the spine, filling as you inhale, then returning back to the center again, emptying out as you exhale. If you feel a lack of con-nection between the center and any of your limbs, direct your breathing to this area.

9. Allow the breath to move you, in and out. Begin with small movements through each limb, extending out and compressing or folding back into the center with the flow and rhythm of the breath. Try to maintain the sense of connection between your limbs, through the center.

10. You can explore connections between two or more limbs simultaneously. Feel how they relate to each other and know each other through the navel. They are separate, yet connected. Through the center, a dialogue is taking place between the head and tail of the spine—between the two arms all the way to the fingertips—the two legs and feet—between the right arm and the right leg—the left arm and leg—the right arm and the left leg—the left arm and the right leg.

11. Let yourself enjoy the sensations of moving and being moved by the flow of your breath. Allow your breath and these internal connections to support your movement. This can feel as moving in water…

12. Gently explore these movements. You can make them a little more active. Allow your whole body to roll, stretch, curl up, wriggle, wind, and unwind with the rhythm of the breath.

13. Now just lie on the floor and rest. Slowly come back to the room, the sounds, the other people in the room, and open your eyes. When you're ready, slowly and gently come back to sitting up…

SUMMARY

Conception and Fertility

- Fertilization takes place when one spermatozoon enters the ovum, creating a zygote.
- Female ova are present but immature at birth. Males do not begin to produce spermatozoa until adolescence.
- The choice of family planning/contraceptive methods depends on personal and cultural values. Family planning is most needed in societies where the size of the population outstrips the ability of the economy and resources to provide for everyone's welfare.
- Male infertility is caused by different factors than female infertility. Fertility can often be enhanced by natural methods.
- When natural methods fail, surgery and/or in vitro fertilization may be required. In vitro fertilization is usually safe and effective.
- In vitro fertilization raises social and ethical issues that both parents and society need to consider carefully.
- Contraceptive practices vary between individuals. Most people can find a contraceptive method that suits their needs; however, more research needs to be done to find newer methods.

Developmental Processes Before Birth

- All cells in the body except the gametes have the same set of genes and chromosomes.
- Development of a cell depends as much on its location and chemical environment as on its genetic composition.
- The period of the embryo begins when the zygote implants in the uterine wall.
- Embryos display rudimentary behavior patterns, such as heartbeats, respiration, and whole-body jerky movements.
- The period of the embryo ends when most of the major internal organs are formed.
- During the period of the fetus, the major developments occur in the brain and nervous system. Later in fetal development, the beginnings of controlled movements, such as facial expressions and grasp-

ing take place. After 28 weeks, fetuses have states of arousal and REM sleep, and they can learn.
- Fetal behavior has two purposes: to prepare the child for establishing initial preferences after birth, and to stimulate growth and development of bones, muscles, and the central nervous system.
- Genetic influences can occur through polygenic inheritance, dominant-recessive inheritance, or sex-linked inheritance.

The Childbirth Experience

- The overall birthrate in first-world nations has been declining, but the rate of multiple births has been increasing.
- Labor occurs in three stages: the opening of the cervix, the passage of the infant through the vagina, and the birth of the placenta.
- Both risks and benefits are associated with medical technologies such as fetal monitoring, forceps, and vacuum extraction.

- About 16% of births are done by cesarean section. There seem to be no ill effects of C-sections compared to vaginal deliveries.
- Drugs are used to speed labor and ease pain. Drugs can be safe if used sparingly. Short-term effects are common, but few long-term effects can be demonstrated.
- Conventional hospital childbirth was compared with a number of alternatives, including early discharge, Lamaze childbirth, upright postures, midwives, birthing centers, home births, and the Leboyer technique. If implemented properly, these practices are all effective and safe for those who choose to use them.

The Baby at Birth

- The newborn has unique physical characteristics, most of which disappear after a few weeks of life. These characteristics are the remnants of prenatal life and the effects of the birth process.

Chapter 4

The Body:
Movement and Sensation

CHAPTER OUTLINE AND OVERVIEW

The First Two Months — *How is the newborn's behavior organized (sleeping, crying, and waking)? In what ways can the newborn act on the environment? What can newborns see, hear, taste, feel, and smell?*

Two to Five Months — *What are the features of physical growth during this period? What types of motor skills do infants have? What perceptual abilities develop during this period? Can infants perceive their own actions?*

Six to Nine Months — *What are the infant's motor skills at this age? Do infants have a preferred hand? How do motor skills develop? Can infants perceive object properties at this age? Can they appreciate pictures in books and on television?*

Ten to Twelve Months — *How do infants learn to walk? What are the developments in the infant's ability to explore?*

Twelve to Eighteen Months — *What kinds of motor skills can infants perform at this age?*

Eighteen to Twenty-Four Months — *When can babies be expected to use a toilet and sleep through the night? What do symbolic thought and pretend play contribute to the child's thinking? What are the effects of TV at this age?*

Twenty-Four to Thirty-Six Months — *In what way are verbs acquired? How does grammar develop? What are the conversational skills at this age? What changes occur in parent and peer relationships?*

This chapter covers the emergence of the infant's body sense: the ability to feel sensory impressions and to execute voluntary and goal-oriented movements. This ability remains with us throughout life. It is essential for humans to navigate in the world and to use our sense to avoid pain and seek sources of comfort.

Movement is fundamental to all forms of developmental change. The development of motor skills usually is correlated with changes in other areas. As infants make simple movements, such as turning their heads, the visual images on the retina change. These self-produced spontaneous movements allow the child to compare perceptual inputs and to begin constructing a clearer view of the solidity of objects and spatial patterns. Crawling and walking allow infants to access new parts of their world and enhance the awareness of the self as an independent agent. Infants often move just for the pleasure of it, like dancers exploring different possibilities for their bodies. Infant motor skills progress from simple acts, such as sucking and turning over, to locomotor skills, to fine motor coordination of objects and tools, such as toys and crayons.

Infants also develop their senses—vision, touch, hearing, smell, balance, and taste—and the way the these sensory modalities are used to acquire knowledge about the world. Perceptual skills are not fully developed at birth; in fact, the human infant has a relatively rudimentary perceptual system for the first months of life. Perception and sensation are central to the experience of being an infant. Unlike older children and adults, infants can spend several hours each day just watching, listening, and feeling. Their senses are alive and salient for them and unlike adults, infants are not thinking about anything. They are fully living in the present moment.

The First Two Months

At birth, the baby must adapt to the physical changes needed to breathe air, to obtain nutrients orally, and to self-regulate body temperature. Birth also introduces a vast array of lights, sounds, touches, tastes, and smells that challenge the newborn's senses. What must the first taste of milk be like, or the first look at a human face? Do these things have any meaning for the newborn infant?

From another perspective, birth is not a major developmental change for the infant. Studies of preterm infants (Chapter 9; and ultrasound studies of fetuses, Chapter 3, show that many of the motor and perceptual systems of the newborn are already developed by 36 weeks' gestational age. By this age or before, for instance, the fetus can suck. Furthermore, the amniotic fluid has tastes similar to the mother's milk, since both are flavored by what the mother eats. The mother's voice is already familiar to the infant. And even an infant who is raised by someone other than the mother is already familiar with movements like breathing and crying, has developed receptors and neural pathways for all the sensory systems, and has a distinct pattern of sleeping and waking states.

The abilities of the newborn infant have been the subject of a great many speculations and investigations by scholars. For thousands of years, philosophers have built theories of the human mind based on what they presumed was acquired by experience and what was already endowed at birth. In the last 150 years, the sciences have taken up the investigation of the newborn's abilities, as psychologists, biologists, physicians, and nurses have tried to answer questions related to their own areas of interest.

States of Rest and Activity

During the fetal period, distinct periods of rest and activity begin to emerge at about 26 to 28 weeks' gestational age. These primitive patterns of activity and quiescence change cyclically about once every 40 minutes. By 32 weeks, both rest and activity are more complex and are divided into distinct states. As defined in Chapter 3, a **state** is an organized pattern of physical and physiological responding that is related to the infant's level of activation or arousal. Once newborn infants enter a particular **state** (see Table 4.1), they are likely to

TABLE 4.1   Newborn States of Arousal

State Name	Description
Quiet Sleep (NREM)	Respiration is regular, eyes are closed and not moving, and the baby is relatively motionless.
Active Sleep (REM)	Muscles are more tense than in quiet sleep, the eyes may be still of display REMs, breathing is irregular, and spontaneous startles, sucks, and body movements occur in rhythmic bursts.
Drowsiness	Opening and closing of the eyes, increased activity, more rapid and regular breathing, and occasional smiling.
Quiet alert	Eyes are open and the environment is being scanned; the body is still, and respiration is more rapid than in sleep.
Active alert	Awake with body and limb movements, although infants are less likely to attend to external stimulation and focus their eyes less often than in the quiet alert state.
Crying	Elevated activity and respiration rate, cry vocalization, and facial expression of distress.

remain in that state for as little as 15 minutes or as long as several hours. It is not easy to soothe newborns who are crying, to induce sleep, or to arouse them once they are sleeping. This suggests that states are relatively stable behavioral processes that form the base from which all other actions of the newborn must be understood (Wolff, 1993; Zeskind & Marshall, 1991).

At least two sleep states are present at 32 weeks' gestational age: rapid eye movement sleep (called REM sleep or active sleep) and non-REM sleep (called NREM sleep or quiet sleep). By 38 weeks, or full-term gestational age, several other sleep states are present, including periodic sleep (a combination of REM and NREM sleep) and drowsiness (a transitional state between sleep and waking). These states are described in Table 4.1, along with the waking states of the normal full-term newborn infant. Researchers disagree about the number and type of infant states. Table 4.1 shows 6 levels of state, but some researchers have used as many as 11 different state distinctions (Zeskind & Marshall, 1991).

Sleep States

How much time a newborn spends sleeping and when during the day or night the baby sleeps are issues of great concern to parents. Newborns sleep an average of 16 to 17 hours per day,

although this can vary between 11 and 21 hours, with 50 percent of their sleep spent in active REM sleep (Parmelee, Schultz, & Disbrow, 1961; DeHart, Sroufe, & Cooper, 2000). By 2 weeks, the average sleep time is decreased to about 14 to 15 hours, again with large differences between infants (St. James-Roberts & Plewis, 1996). Unlike adult sleep, infant sleep does not occur as one continuous period. Sleep periods range from 2 to 10 hours. For the first few weeks after birth, these periods can occur almost any time during the 24-hour day, to the dismay of sleepless parents. By 3 or 4 months of age, infants regularly sleep more at night than during the day, but night wakings are common throughout infancy and early childhood (Anders, Goodlin-Jones, & Zelenko, 1998; Kleitman, 1963).

Some babies show a preference for night sleeping, while others are more likely to wake at night. Individual infants appear to be highly consistent. Their preference for sleeping through the night or for waking at night remains stable over many years. There is recent evidence that these preferences may appear during the late fetal period, affected in unknown ways by maternal patterns of activity during the day/night cycle and by daily fluctuations of maternal and infant hormones. The propensity to sleep through the night, then, may be partially acquired prenatally (Cofer et al., 1999; Colombo, Moss, & Horowitz, 1989; Zeskind & Marshall, 1991)

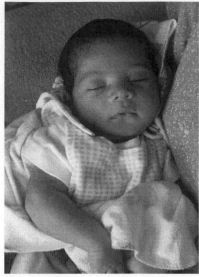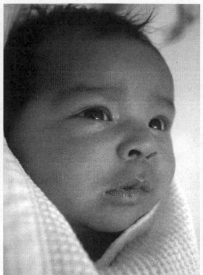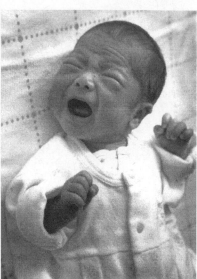

Three newborn states: Sleeping, alert inactivity, and crying.
Photos: Left: David Young-Wolff/PhotoEdit; Middle: Christine Kennedy/PhotoEdit; Right: Elizabeth Crews

but there are no consistent post-birth predictors of a child's sleeping patterns (Adams et al., 2004).

These individual differences affect the person's later interactions with others. Infants who are awake more at night are perceived as more difficult. During childhood, children who prefer being awake during the evening hours have a harder time getting up for school and do less well in school. It helps if parents are aware of whether their child is a morning person (goes to bed early and gets up early) or an evening person and adjust their expectations accordingly (Cofer et al., 1999).

Whether the child goes to bed early or late, some research shows that infants can be trained to sleep through the night during the first month of life. The procedure is based on reducing stimulation in the late afternoon, when infants naturally tend to become more fussy, and creating the habit of an early bedtime (Godfrey & Kilgore, 1998). The procedure is given in Table 4.2. After using this procedure for 3 to 4 weeks, parents report that their infant is more likely to sleep through the night and to avoid fussing during night wakings. If the time between night feedings is gradually increased, even breast-fed infants can learn to tolerate not getting a night feeding. If the infant does not get fussy until later in the evening, then parents can

adjust the times accordingly. On the other hand, it is difficult for parents to follow these routines because of the daily variability of newborn behavior, so there is not a high success rate (St James-Roberts et al., 2001). In addition, 30 minutes of gentle massage therapy for the infant provided by the mother helped infants to fall asleep earlier and to stay asleep longer (Ferber et al., 2002).

While the procedure in Table 4.2 may work for some families, training babies to sleep on their own is not necessarily desirable. In some families and some cultures, co-sleeping with parents is the norm. Although no research exists, co-sleeping advocates estimate that worldwide, 80% to 90% of parents co-sleep with their infants for as long as 1 to 4 years. In North America, co-sleeping goes against the white middle-class cultural norm of raising an independent child and is not recommended by many of the best-known infant care advice books. On the other hand, a large number of North American and Northern European parents from diverse ethnic and cultural backgrounds report co-sleeping with their babies at least occasionally, and many report long-term co-sleeping arrangements. The practice appears to be more common in non-white ethnic groups in these countries compared to white families (Willinger et al., 2003).

TABLE 4.2
For families who value independent sleeping, this method can be used to teach young infants to sleep through the night.

1st Month	Place the baby on back or side on a firm mattress. Do not let the baby sleep with breast, bottle, or pacifier in mouth, or while being held.
2nd Month	Reduce the amount of handling and stimulation after 4 p.m., or when evening fussiness begins. Bathe the baby in early evening, 6–7 p.m., follwed by a gental rubdown or massage, and dress the baby for the night. Feed the baby and then put the baby to bed around 7 p.m. Some fussing may persist for 3–5 days. If the baby cries loudly, enter the room every 5–10 minutes and then leave without turning on an overhead light. If feeding is necessary, keep it brief, do not turn on the light, and reduce the amount of stimulation. If this routine is interrupted due to travel or sickness, retraining is necessary.

Breast-feeding is cited most frequently as the reason for co-sleeping. Research shows that about 80% of breast-feeding infants spend some time in their parents' bed. Co-sleeping increases the rate of breast-feeding each day and also the number of months that the baby is breast-fed. Infant irritability and illness, as well as a parental desire to be close to the baby, are also frequently cited reasons to bed-share (Ball, 2002; McKenna & Volpe, 2007).

Independent sleeping is favored when there is a strong family and cultural value for independence. But does independent sleeping really promote independence later? Parents of preschoolers whose babies either co-slept or did not co-sleep were asked about independence in their children. Non-co-sleeping children were indeed more likely to fall asleep alone, sleep through the night, and be weaned earlier. On the other hand, co-sleepers as infants were more likely to enter quiet sleep states and stay in them longer, and as toddlers were more self-reliant (such as dressing themselves) and were more socially independent, for example, by making friends more easily (Hunsley & Thoman, 2002; Keller & Goldberg, 2004). In general, when children are followed up through the teen years, there seem to be no long-term risks or benefits to co-sleeping (Okami et al., 2002).

Some parents become concerned about a reduction in sexual activity if the baby sleeps in the same bed. In either case, parents can expect to experience some sleep deprivation during the first few months, until the family finds a mutually beneficial way of sleeping. On the other hand, once fathers adapt to co-sleeping, they feel it increases their intimacy with the infant and gets them involved more in the infant's nighttime care (Ball et al., 2000). Whether or not co-sleeping is practiced depends upon the social and cultural attitudes of the parents and their ability to agree with each other about them. Children with the most sleep problems come from homes in which the parents disagree about sleeping arrangements and in which there is consequently more marital disharmony (Germo et al., 2007).

If the average newborn sleeps 17 hours a day, what happens during the rest of the time? On average, about 3 hours are spent in quiet alert, 2 hours in active alert, and 2 to 3 hours in crying. Of course, some babies are awake more than 3 hours and some less. Some babies cry for as much as ten hours per day and others as little as one hour.

Waking States

Waking states are important for the processing of stimulation from the environment— processing that will lead to perceptual and cognitive development. Newborn infants have two basic modes of response to stimulation: orienting and defense. The **orienting response** is a heightened alertness on the part of the individual baby that includes behavioral localization toward the source of the stimulation (a head turn to the source of a sound). A **defensive response** is a behavioral action that involves withdrawal from the source of stimulation.

Stimulation that is moderate in intensity will elicit orienting responses: soft talking, moderate light levels, and holding and rocking can enhance alertness in the newborn (Arditi et al., 2005). Most adults—whether they are right or left-handed— prefer holding infants on the left side. At first, researchers thought this was because the baby was being held closer to the adult's heart but this was never confirmed. More recently, studies have shown that adults are better at perceiving emotions through the left eye and left ear, both of which are connected to the right (more emotional) brain. Thus, left-side holding is likely to enhance emotional communication between parent and infant, not through the heart, but through the senses (Turnbull & Bryson, 2001; Vauclair & Donnot, 2005).

Stimulation that is intense and sharp produces defensive reactions. A sudden change in light level, a loud noise, or a sudden change in body position will produce a blink or a startle response. If the intense stimulus continues, newborns will turn away, grimace, or cry. Low-intensity stimulation, such as gentle rocking or whispering, may not produce any reaction in the newborn. When newborns orient to a source of stimulation, they are relatively slow to respond compared with a 2-month-old, whose latency to respond is similar in speed to an adult's (Berg & Berg, 1987; Graham, Anthony, & Zeigler, 1984; Karrer, Monti, & Ackles, 1989).

As infants develop, they become able to orient to a wider range of both low- and high-intensity stimulation (Field, 1981b; Krafchuk, Tronick, & Clifton, 1983). It is as though the newborn were looking at the world through a very small window centered on the moderate range of stimulation. Developmental changes expand the size of the window to include both lower and higher intensities of stimulation so that the older infant is more sensitive to subtle cues and less sensitive to intensity (Berg, 1975).

Motor Coordinations: Reflexes

Aside from the waking and sleeping states discussed above, newborns possess a variety of semiautomatic patterns of behavior—such as grasping, head turning, and sucking—that actually began to function prenatally, during the final months of fetal development. This kind of semiautomatic behavior is called a **reflex**. Reflexes are triggered only by specific elicitors—such as the presence of fluid in the mouth (sucking) or an object in the palm (grasping)—and they look about the same every time they are triggered. Once triggered, a reflex must run its course without stopping.

The newborn infant is equipped with various primitive reflexes (Illingworth, 1991). Reflexes associated with different parts of the body are listed in Table 4.3. Some of these reflexes reflect primitive forms of orienting behavior, including rooting, sucking, and grasping. Other reflexes are primitive defensive reactions, including the Moro reflex and the reaction to a cloth on the face or the head placed face down. Other reflexes seem to contain the elementary coordinations needed for later adaptive and voluntary movements. These include the stepping, standing, crawling, and swimmer's reflexes. Other reflexes do not seem to have a clear function, such as the Babinski reflex; however, the lack of a Babinski response may indicate neurological disorder.

In spite of the semiautomatic structure of reflexes, there is a wide variability in their display. In the same infant tested on different occasions, a reflex might be present at one time and not later. Some reflexes become more prominent in the days following birth, having been absent immediately after birth due to birth recovery processes. Some reflexes are easier to elicit in sleep states and others in waking states. The strength and clarity of response also differ between infants. After their cheeks are stroked to elicit rooting, one baby may barely turn his or her head to that side, while another may make a strong head turn, open the mouth, and begin to suck. Other factors that affect the strength and quality of a reflex response are age, time since last feeding, and the number of repeated attempts to evoke the reflex (Kessen et al., 1970; Prechtl, 1977).

Each reflex has its own developmental course starting at different gestational ages. Some reflexes persist throughout life—such as startle and blinking—while others disappear in early infancy. Since

TABLE 4.3 Newborn Reflexes

Body Part	Name of Reflex	Description	Baby's Age at Reflex's Disappearance (Months)
Head and Face	Head turning	Place baby face down on a mattress. Baby will turn head to side to free breathing passages.	4
	Rooting	Stroke baby's cheek gently near the mouth. Baby will turn head to the side that is being stroked.	5
	Sucking	Place a nipple-sized object in baby's mouth. Baby will start sucking movements.	6
	Defensive reaction	Cover the baby's nose and mouth with a cloth. Baby will turn head and move arms in an attempt to free breathing passages.	4
Arms	Asymmetrical tonic neck reflex	Turn the baby's head to one side or the other. The baby's arm will extend in the direction in which the head is turned and the other arm will flex upward. This is also called the fencer's reflex.	4
	Moro	Drop the baby's head slightly but abruptly. The baby's arms and legs will spread open and make an embracing movement, as if to grasp hold of something. This is a kind of startle reaction.	6
Hands	Palmer	Lightly touch the baby's palm. The fingers will clamp into a fist.	4
Torso	Swimmer's reflex	While baby is lying on its stomach, gently tap the back along the side and above the waist.	3
	Crawling	Push against the soles of the baby's feet while the baby is lying on the stomach, and rudimentary crawling movements will result.	4
Legs	Standing	Hold the baby gently under the arms while the feet touch a table. As you release support slowly, the baby will begin to show some resistance to the weight by stretching the muscles of the legs.	3
	Stepping	Hold the baby under the arms with the baby's feet touching a table and move the baby forward, keeping contact between table and feet. The baby will take "steps."	3
Foot	Planter	Similar to the Palmer reflex. The toes will curl inward where the instep is lightly touched.	9
	Babinski	Gently stroke the outer side of the bottom of the baby's foot. The toes will curl outward like a fan.	12

the reflexes that disappear do so between 3 and 6 months of age, traditional explanations have assumed that the disappearance is the result of the development of the motor cortex of the brain (see Figure 5.3) that regulate voluntary movement (Fiorentino, 1981; Illingworth, 1966; Molnar, 1978; Peiper, 1963). When adults receive damage to the motor cortex, some of these primitive reflexes reappear (Paulson & Gottlieb, 1968).

This view of the centrality of the brain in regulating reflexes was challenged by several experiments. The stepping reflex is elicited in a newborn when the infant is held upright with the foot gently touching a flat surface. When the foot touches the surface, the newborn will pick up the foot by bending the leg at the knee in a kind of march-step movement. Remarkably, newborns do not pick up both legs at the same time; they alternate steps in the manner of later walking.

It turns out that stepping disappears earlier in infants who have the most rapid weight gain. Researchers studied 4-week-olds who could still step reflexively. To experimentally simulate weight gain, they added weights to the babies' legs in amounts predicted to reflect the possible weight gain of the legs in the next few weeks. These weights practically eliminated stepping. In another experiment, 4-week-olds were tested for stepping while their legs were submerged under water and then again on dry land. The step rate was much higher underwater, again suggesting that weight and gravity, rather than brain development alone, contribute to the disappearance of stepping (Thelen, Bradshaw, & Ward, 1981). The researchers also found that stepping movements could be seen in the form of alternate-leg kicking in any age infant when the infant was lying on his or her back.

In this experiment, the decline in stepping was not due to the effect of weight gain alone. Rather, stepping declines because fat grows faster than muscle after birth. This means that babies' legs simply became too heavy for them to lift on their own! In another study, stepping did not disappear in babies who were given stepping exercises every day. The workout program may have built their tiny muscles to be capable of lifting more

than those of the average baby of a particular age. Similar practice also helps babies to sit earlier (P. R. Zelazo, 1976; N. A. Zelazo, Zelazo, Cohen, & Zelazo, 1993).

In summary, newborn reflexes are extremely important for orienting the infant to the environment and for protecting the infant from harm. Although we do not know the purpose of all the reflexes, many of them—such as the defensive reaction—have obvious functions. The data also suggest that the actual movements related to reflexes are not simply discharges in the brain, but depend on muscle movement, weight, state, illness and many other factors. Like the spontaneous movements of the fetus (see Chapter 3), reflexes play a role in the active development of the muscles, leading to increased strength and coordination.

Asynchronous Growth

The finding that the newborn stepping reflex disappears when the infant's legs become too heavy is not meant to suggest that 1-month-olds should go on diets, exercise their legs, and do weight training. First of all, giving babies stepping exercises does not make the babies walk any sooner than if they receive no such training (P. R. Zelazo, 1976). Second, there is a good reason why babies of this age need to increase fat rapidly: to keep warm and protect their muscles against shocks. Fat is kept at a minimum prenatally to make birth easier and because most of the fetal energy resources go into brain development. Muscles get stronger later in the first year.

These findings show that infants do not grow "all at once." Different body regions grow faster at different times; this is called **asynchronous growth** and is shown in Figure 4.1 Because physical growth depends on the body's ability to metabolize nutrients to create energy to support the growth, the body invests its growth resources in at most a few domains at a time.

What makes some areas turn on their growth spurt and others turn off? This is difficult to determine, but it may be in part genetically controlled and in part related to opportunities in the

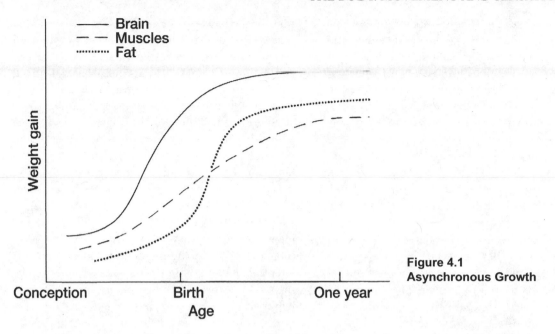

**Figure 4.1
Asynchronous Growth**

environment. Fetal resources are used primarily to develop the brain and perceptual systems. This is due partly to the fact that movement opportunities are limited for a fetus, and muscles do not develop without exercise. Because newborns rely on the care of adults, they do not need strong and able muscles early in life. Chimpanzees, on the contrary, have to be strong enough to cling to their moving and swinging mothers from the day of birth. Their survival depends more on physical strength and speed compared to human newborns.

A comparison of chimpanzee and human newborns' scores on selected items of the Brazelton newborn assessment test confirms this. Chimpanzees score about the same as human newborns on state control, alertness, and attention to social and nonsocial stimuli. Chimpanzees score higher on motor skills in the pull-to-sit task and on irritability (Bard, Platzman, Lester, & Suomi, 1992; Hallock, Worobey, & Self, 1989).

Sucking

One reflex that is of crucial importance to survival is sucking. Sucking is an example of a reflex that begins prenatally and does not disappear. This statement is a bit misleading, however, since suck-

ing becomes more voluntary and changes form and mode of expression in later infancy. Sucking is accomplished through the combined action of three sets of sucking pads: the lips, the gums, and the fat pads inside the cheeks. It is the gums—not the lips—that form a closed pressure seal around the nipple, while the cheek pads prevent the oral cavity from collapsing from the **negative pressure** created (Kessen et al., 1970).

As you may notice when practicing the Experiential Exercise on sucking in Chapter 9, sucking is a two-phase process. In the first phase, the lower jaw drops to create negative pressure in the mouth. This method works because the gums form a closed seal around the nipple, but it differs from that used by an adult, who creates negative pressure by breathing in. In the second phase of sucking, called **milk expression**, the newborn's tongue presses the nipple against the hard palate while moving from the front to the back of the mouth. Finally, the presence of fluid in the mouth triggers the swallowing reflex. Apparently, the newborn sucks and swallows in a single-action pattern in which the tongue moves in and out while the baby swallows. Did you discover this for yourself when you practiced the Experiential Exercise sucking lesson?

The action of the tongue in sucking explains why young infants have trouble eating solids and drinking from a cup: the pushing action of their tongues tends to expel more material from their mouths than they are able to successfully ingest. The ability to separate the expressing and swallowing movements does not occur until late in the first year.

Sucking, like crying, tends to occur in a rhythmic pattern. While the infant is actually sucking, there are usually about two sucks per second. Typically, infants suck in a **burst-pause pattern**: bursts of successive sucks separated by pauses. The bursts usually last from between 5 and 24 sucks. Like the other reflexes, the sucking rate depends primarily on the state of arousal rather than on factors related to hunger. The number of pauses is primarily determined by the milk flow. If the flow is too fast, pauses disappear, reappearing only when the flow is reduced (see Figure 4.2). Pauses do not appear to be associated with fatigue, since infants can suck without pausing for long periods under high milk-flow conditions (Kessen et al., 1970).

Earlier in this chapter, it was mentioned that nonnutritive sucking provides a source of pacification for the newborn infant. It would seem natural that infants under 2 months, who cry more than older infants, would use their own hands and fingers as sources of sucking stimulation. In fact, hand-to-mouth behavior is a relatively rare occurrence at this age, but it does happen under some conditions. For example, it occurs in newborns when the arms are flexed and the hands come near the mouth when the baby begins to cry (Hopkins, Janssen, Kardaun, & van der Schoot, 1988), if the infant is given sweetened water when upset (Blass, Fillion, Rochat, Hoffmeyer, & Metzger, 1989; Rochat, Blass, & Hoffmeyer, 1988), or if the infant's hand is held near the mouth by an adult (Fogel, 1985). Apparently, infants do not do this intentionally until about 4 months of age. Before then, the meeting of the hand and the mouth is a happy accident from which the infant can take temporary comfort (Fogel, 1985; Hopkins et al., 1988).

Giving the infant a mildly sweet solution to suck not only increases the frequency of hand-to-mouth contact, but has the additional effect of calming infants who are crying (Barr, Quek, Cousineau, Oberlander, Brian, & Young, 1994; Blass & Ciaramitaro, 1994; Buka & Lipsitt, 1991; Fernandez et al., 2003). Milk is sweet, which may

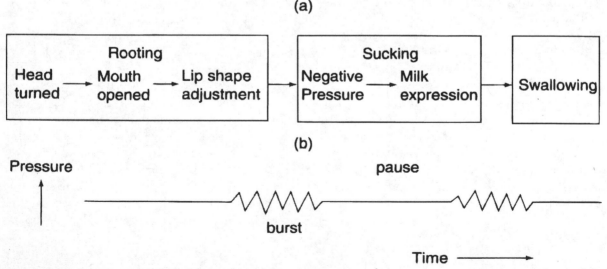

Figure 4.2 Organization of Sucking Behavior
(a) Sequence of acts comprising sucking behavior, from initial orientation to the nipple until swallowing has occurred.
(b) Changes in sucking pressure with time, showing the characteristic burst-pause pattern.

explain the added calming effects of nursing over and above that of nonnutritive sucking. The smell of milk, learned in the first weeks of life, can also contribute to the calming effects of nursing (Delaunay-El Allam et al., 2006).

On the other hand, newborns will actively search for a nipple with their mouths. If they feel a nipple with their cheek, they will move their head backward, open their mouth, and move their mouth toward the nipple in one smooth movement (Koepke & Bigelow, 1997). This pattern of action is called *rooting*. Although it is considered one of the basic reflexes, rooting varies according to the size, shape, and location of the nipple.

Newborn Hand and Arm Movements

The newborn's arms and hands are among the least controlled part of the body. By contrast, actions of the face—such as sucking and crying—are highly developed and can be used by the infant to meet specific needs. Nevertheless, newborn hand and arm activity is more controlled under certain conditions. In the previous section, for example, we saw that if infants are given a mild sucrose solution to suck, it increases the probability that they will bring their hand to the region of the mouth. Similarly, hand-to-mouth contact is more likely to occur just before feeding and is often accompanied by anticipatory mouth opening as the hand approaches the region of the mouth (Lew & Butterworth, 1995).

Newborn hand and arm movements may appear random in real time, but patterns are revealed when these movements are observed carefully in slow motion. In one study on hand and arm movements, newborns were presented with three conditions: a person facing them, a ball moving slowly in front of them, and a control condition with neither a person nor a ball. Results showed a higher frequency of finger movements and flexion of the hand in the social condition compared to the other two conditions. In the object condition, infants were more likely to extend the fingers of their hand (as if to anticipate a grasp), to move the thumb and index finger (as if to grasp), and to extend their arms forward (as if to reach) (Ronnqvist & Hofsten, 1994). In a related study, newborns resisted attempts at manipulation of their arms and were able to visually follow the movements of their arms if they could see them (Meer, Weel, & Lee, 1995). Finally, studies have found that newborns presented with an object in different locations direct more arm and hand movements in the direction of the object (Bloch, 1990).

These studies show that even though newborns cannot actually reach or grasp, they already have motor patterns that are adapted to particular kinds of social and object situations. This research also reveals a surprising amount of coordination in newborn activity that has never before been suspected. It is likely, however, that you could not observe these newborn responses with the naked eye. As explained in the section on research methods (Chapter 1), we can only detect some of these sophisticated infant abilities through the use of controlled experiments and detailed videorecording. These studies reveal that the parts of the brain responsible for voluntary movements are already beginning to develop in the first weeks of life.

Summary of Physical and Motor Development during the First Two Months

In many ways, the newborn infant is a highly organized individual. In a sense, people are more tightly organized and predictable as newborns than at any later time in life. Newborns cycle regularly through states of rest and activity. Although parents cannot predict exactly when a baby will wake up or fall asleep, they have a pretty good idea of how much their baby sleeps and how alert he or she can be and under what conditions.

Behavior ecology theories suggest that the regularities of the newborn's behavior—states, state changes, and reflexes—can be explained by genetic programming in which the sources of these behaviors lie in precise locations in the brain. The argument is that the newborn needs to suck, cry, calm, sleep, and self-stimulate in order to survive and develop.

Dynamic systems theory, on the other hand, suggests that all behavior is the result of a complex interaction among a large number of related factors including the brain. We saw in Chapter 3 that not even prenatal development is under the direct control of the genotype: a series of events in the environment of the cell and in the uterine environment of the mother must be present in order for a gene to express its message in the phenotype.

Postnatally, we observe even more complexity in developmental pathways. Whether we observe a strong or a weak reflex or no reflex at all, for example, is explained by a combination of factors, including whatever genetic codes exist for giving the newborn's body its particular structure, whether the baby has had time to unstretch its prenatally flexed arms, the rate of development of fat versus muscle, and whether or not the baby has something in its mouth at the moment. In addition, even reflexive movements are not rigidly programmed. They vary according to the infant's past experience and the contextual conditions under which they are elicited. As we will see in the next sections, perceptual and cognitive development show similar patterns of adaptability to current conditions and individual experiences.

Perceptual Development

The sensory systems of the body—sight, sound, taste, smell, and touch—provide the basic fabric of our psychological experiences. The senses form the basic ways in which we are connected to the environment. A baby "knows" the mother because she has a characteristic visual shape, auditory pattern in her voice, and quality of touch. She is permeated with fragrance from her body and clothing. Her milk tastes sweet and is flavored by the food she eats. These sensations fill up the baby's psychological experience of other persons and things. There is no overlay of thought or judgment, so common in adults.

This kind of experience that relies on direct perception through the senses is called **ecological perception** (J. J. Gibson, 1966). Ecological perception is available to people of all ages, but its purest form exists during early infancy. The infant is totally attuned to the play of light and color, the melodies of sound, and the pleasure of being touched. In some ways, the infant's psychological world is similar to that to which monks and meditators aspire: total awareness in the here-and-now, being fully present in the moment, feeling fully life's sorrows and joys. This kind of experience remains intense during childhood but gradually fades into the background as we devote more of our time to thinking, doing, achieving, and working, and less to simply being fully present to our sensory experience and how that experience connects us directly to the rhythms of the earth and to its inhabitants. Allowing ourselves as adults to be fully immersed in the baby's world can be refreshing and enlightening as we let go of our own everyday thoughts and worries and see the world through the infant's eyes and ears (Schafer, 2004). One of the goals of the body awareness clinical methods reviewed in Chapter 2 is to help children and adults reconnect with their senses. Practicing the Experiential Exercises sections in this book is also a means to reawaken your ecological perception.

The Visual World of the Newborn

The sensory world of the newborn infant is not as sharply focused or as discriminating as that of the adult. Nevertheless, newborns have the ability to see, hear, taste, smell, and feel. There has been a great deal of research on the topic of the newborn's perceptual abilities, especially in the areas of vision and audition.

Vision is one of the most powerful of the senses because it is so diverse. One sees shape, color, distance, texture, and the relative locations of objects in space. Compared to touch, which only takes in information that can be physically contacted by the hand or mouth, vision takes in the entire environment.

The visual world of the newborn, however, is focused primarily on the near environment. When people ask whether newborns can see, they usually are wondering about visual **acuity**. Visual acuity is a measure of the lens's ability to focus images on the retina, as well as the retina's ability to decode the light. A common measure of acuity is the Snellen chart, with the large letter E on the top and successively smaller letters below. An acuity rating of 20/20 is given to a person who can see a particular line on the chart clearly at 20 feet. A person with 20/50 vision is able to see at 20 feet with the same clarity as a person with 20/20 vision can see at 50 feet.

Newborns' visual acuity is tested by their ability to see stripes of decreasing thinness in comparison to an all-gray stimulus, using a pattern preference test (see Chapter 1). Although estimates vary between studies, a newborn's visual acuity is between 20/300 and 20/800, with an average of about 20/500 (Aslin, 1987). This low level of visual acuity in newborns is not related to an inability of the lens to focus. Rather, it seems to be the result of the immaturity of the dendrites and axons of the neurons in the retina and optic nerve and the relative lack of myelination (L. B. Cohen, DeLoache, & Strauss, 1979; Salapatek & Banks, 1978). By 6 months, as a result of experience-dependent brain development, visual acuity improves to nearly 20/20 in most infants.

This means that the visual world of the newborn is rather blurry, like an out-of-focus photo or film. On the other hand, newborns can see colors (Aslin, 1987). Thus, their visual world is probably filled with fuzzy regions of one color adjoining regions of other colors, each with different levels of brightness, forming an abstract mosaic of light. If you are, like me, sufficiently nearsighted, you will have no trouble replicating the newborn's visual world by simply removing your glasses or contacts. If not, try looking around when your eyes are bleary, when you are very sleepy, or just after waking up.

The eyes do a lot more than just focus their lenses. **Oculomotor skills** are the movements that the eye must make to bring objects into focus, follow moving objects, and adjust for objects at different distances. Newborns' tracking of moving objects is a bit jerky, and they are able to follow only relatively slowly moving objects. More

adult-like following begins between 6 and 8 weeks (Aslin, 1981; Kremenitzer, Vaughan, Kurtzberg, & Dowling, 1979).

Scanning occurs as the eye traces a path across a visual stimulus. Since the eye cannot see an entire image all at once, it must make small, rapid movements to move from one point of fixation to the next. One-month-olds tend to scan small, localized regions of a figure, usually around its edges, while by the age of 3 months, infants spend more time scanning finer details of a figure (see Figure 4.3). Adults scan like newborns when they look at large objects from a distance, like a city skyline or a mountain range.

Oculomotor control adjusts the eyes to see objects at different distances. The ability to judge the relative distances between two objects and determine whether objects are close or far is called *depth perception*. We have the sensation of depth because each of our eyes sees a slightly different view of the same object. To see for yourself, try looking at an object nearby with one eye and then the other. The ability to compare the two retinal images, and therefore to see distance, emerges slowly between 3 and 6 months. Thus, until about 2 to 3 months of age, infants have functional but limited oculomotor skills. However, in spite of these limitations, infants can use their vision in a variety of ways and may even be able to recognize visual patterns after repeated exposure.

Can newborns see patterns within the complex jumble of lines, depths, and colors that they can see? We know from a number of studies that newborns can detect differences between visual images and seem to prefer some images more than others. Newborns prefer to look at objects with clearly marked edges and outlines. They also prefer circular patterns to straight lines (Fantz, Fagan, & Miranda, 1975). Newborns like to look at the external contours of a figure, especially if the edges are sharp; their gaze tends to follow these lines, and once on a line, they rarely break out to scan other regions of a figure (Haith, 1980; Maurer & Salapatek, 1976; Milewski, 1976).

These pattern preferences in newborns seem to match their relatively poor visual acuity, while

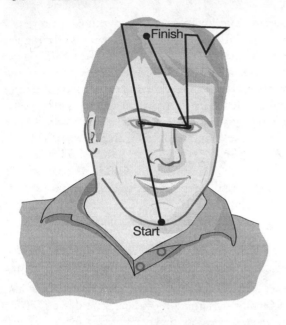

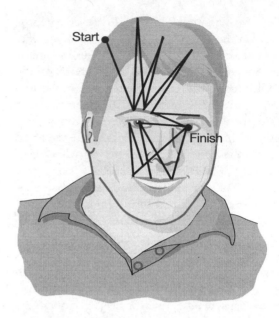

One-month-old

Two-month-old

Figure 4.3 Facial Scanning Patterns
The superimposed lines show where a baby will look at a face. One-month-olds look mostly around the outside, while older babies look at the inner details, espcially at the eyes.

Source: Adapted from A. Fogel & G. F. Melson, *Child development*, 1988, p. 158. St. Paul, MN: West. Copyright © by West Publishing Company. Reprinted by permission. All rights reserved.

allowing them to actively explore objects with their eyes. As we saw in the fetus, active sensory and motor exploration seems to be a form of self-stimulation that is necessary to maintain continued development of the brain and the associated motor skills. In this view, the patterns the newborn prefers are not necessarily meaningful: they merely serve to help the visual system develop by the age of 3 months to a point at which the infant can see the world more clearly and pick out enough details to make meaningful distinctions, such as between a familiar and an unfamiliar person.

This perspective suggests that infants need experience with the perceptual world before they can make sense of it. Starting with some simple preferences for physical features of a stimulus, the infant later comes to attach particular features with other sources of information. Thus, the sounds, smells, and touches that an infant has come to understand as "mother" will only match up with the visual recognition of her at 3 months.

This view is similar to that of Piaget, who held that infants gradually build up representations of the world by means of repeated encounters, each of which is compared with the others via assimilation and accommodation. The infant constructs perceptions by active engagement and experience.

Although infants have to build up a concept such as "mother" through repeated experiences over many months, they also have preferences at birth that guide them in their search for meaning. Newborns have visual preferences that seem to be attuned to social stimulation, orienting them to the most important figures in their environment—adults—who will help them survive. These early perceptual preferences are predicted by behavior ecology theory (J. J. Gibson, 1966). Newborns have inherited perceptual preferences that are most likely to bring them into contact with things that enhance their survival.

Infants are attracted to facelike stimuli and prefer faces over other objects (M. H. Johnson,

Dziurawiec, Ellis, & Morton, 1991). Even more remarkable is that infants only 1 day old will change their sucking response to see a picture of their mother's face rather than the face of an unfamiliar female. When the mother is shown wearing a scarf, however, the newborn does not distinguish the mother from a stranger. These findings show that the outline of the face, including the hairline, is an important recognition cue for infants at this age (Pascalis, de Schonen, Morton, Deruelle, & Fabre-Grenet, 1995; Turati at al., 2006; Walton, Bower, & Bower, 1992). Perhaps more remarkable is the finding that newborns prefer to look at faces judged by adults to be more attractive. The preference is found regardless of the age, gender, or race of the face (Slater et al., 1998). Newborns also prefer to look at faces in which the other person's gaze is directed toward the infant rather than averted (Farroni et al., 2004).

In summary, research has shown that infants as young as 1 month respond to their mother's face in a meaningful way and prefer attractive faces, supporting behavior ecology theory. Nevertheless, in accord with constructivist (Piagetian) theory, additional meanings will be built through active experience. Due to their relatively poor visual acuity and the slowness of their visual response, newborns' visual relationship to the world is relatively limited; the onset of more mature visual perception does not begin until at least 3 months of age (see below). On the other hand, it is not so bad to begin one's life bathed in the intense sensation of colors and pleasing shapes. In order to draw or to paint, visual artists must relearn this infant-like way of seeing the world in terms of color and shape, rather than in terms of objects. The infant has other senses in addition, and these are considerably more acute at birth than vision.

Auditory Perception

Auditory perception does not require the same motor components as vision. Thus, developments in the sensitivity of the ears are likely to depend on the maturation of the auditory nerve and the components of the ear's anatomy. These structures are more mature at birth than those associated with vision. The auditory nerve is almost completely myelinated, and the bones of the middle ear are almost adult size at birth. After birth, most development occurs in the expansion of the auditory canal and the eardrum and the articulation of the auditory cortex in the brain. These processes reach adult levels by about 1 year, which is the same time that speech begins (Eilers & Gavin, 1981).

Auditory sensitivity. Sensitivity to sounds involves two basic aspects: loudness and pitch. Loudness is usually measured in decibels (dB). Loud thunder is about 120 dB, 70 dB is a noisy street corner, 60 dB is a normal conversation, and 40 dB is a whisper. Pitch is the frequency of the sound wave and is usually measured in hertz (Hz). One Hz is one cycle per second. A high C on a piano is 3951.07 Hz, and the low C is 65.41 Hz. This range of notes also corresponds to the frequency range of the human voice.

How loud does a sound have to be before a baby can hear it? Sensitivity to sounds is measured by observing a change in heart rate, a blink response, or a head turn; by recording brain waves; or by using a conditioned head turning or conditioned sucking procedure (see Chapter 1). The softest sounds a newborn baby can hear are in the range of 40 dB to 60 dB (Berg & Berg, 1979), although sounds from 50 dB to 70 dB are necessary to awaken a sleeping infant (Wedenberg, 1956).

In general, the research shows that while most adults can hear sounds as low as 0 dB to 5 dB, the most sensitive newborn cannot hear below about 20 dB (Schulman-Galambos & Galambos, 1979), although this ability improves over the first year. Babies are more sensitive to sounds in the middle range of the piano's notes, although they tend to prefer higher to lower pitched sounds (Kessen et al., 1970). Finally, in experience-expectant fashion, babies prefer sounds made up of more than one note, of a wide band of frequencies (Eisenberg, 1976), and they prefer melodic sequences rather than a jumble of unrelated notes (Masataka, 2006; Ruusuvirta et al., 2003).

If we put together all the characteristics of sounds that are most easily heard, and in fact preferred, by newborns, the most common source of such sounds is an adult female voice either talking or singing. Newborns, in fact, prefer to listen to an adult singing infant- directed songs rather than adult-directed songs (Masataka, 1999). Although newborns are sensitive to a wide range of sounds and will orient to men who raise the pitch of their voice, researchers have speculated that prenatal experience with the sound of the mother's voice may have attuned infants to sounds of that level of loudness and mixture of pitches.

Recognition of mother's voice. We saw in Chapter 3 that newborns preferred to listen to a song or story that their mothers had sung or read aloud 2 weeks prior to birth compared to a song they had not heard, and that newborns seem to prefer heartbeat sounds similar to those they must have heard prenatally. Other research seems to support the view that infants can distinguish the voice of their own mother from the voices of other women. Thus, in addition to recognizing his or her mother visually, as we learned in the last section, a newborn can recognize her voice; as we shall see in the next section, newborns can also recognize their mother's smell. Prenatal and postnatal exposure to the mother thus set the infant on the path to developing a special tie to that particular person. The strong attachments to a particular person that develop later in the first year, therefore, are built upon early perceptual orienting preferences that begin in the last month of prenatal life.

Recognition of speech sounds. How, though, do newborns recognize their mother's voice and distinguish between different songs and stories that they have heard prenatally? They may detect overall patterns of rhythm and pitch that differentiate one person from another (Nazzi, Floccia, & Bertoncini, 1998; Rosen & Iverson, 2007; Sansavini, 1997; Sansavini, Bertoncini, & Giovanelli, 1997). In addition, infants may be able to hear differences among syllables that give them cues about a speaker's uniqueness.

One-month-olds can distinguish between two very closely related speech sounds: "p" having the sound "puh," and "b" having the sound "buh" (Eimas, Siqueland, Jusczyk, & Vigorito, 1971). By 2 months, babies can recognize not only consonant differences but also vowel differences in sounds (Kuhl, 1981; Swoboda, Kass, Morse, & Leavitt, 1978). Newborns can remember sounds to which they were exposed the day before, and they will change their sucking in order to hear recordings made in their native language rather than those in a foreign language (Bijeljac-Babic, Bertoncini, & Mehler, 1993; Moon, Cooper, & Fifer, 1993; Swain, Zelazo, & Clifton, 1993). Boyson-Bardies (1994) has found that by the end of the first year, infants select and prefer sounds from their own language.

It seems that newborns can not only recognize the broad category of speech compared to nonspeech and mother compared to nonmother, but they can also distinguish between some of the finer aspects of speech sounds. As discussed earlier with respect to vision, behavior ecology theory suggests that this match may be necessary to ensure the survival of the human newborn, who is totally dependent on adults. On the other hand, learning theory suggests that newborns construct a preference for human voices and a recognition of their native language and their mother's voice as a result of hearing these voices prenatally. This early exposure to sound enhances the development of the auditory components of the brain and auditory nerves and predisposes the infant to similar sounds in the future.

Taste, Smell, and Touch

Even before birth, infants can taste, with mature taste buds developing by 14 weeks gestation (Eliot, 1999). They even show a positive response toward sweet tastes before birth (Mennella & Beauchamp, 1993). Newborns appear to be able to distinguish the four basic tastes: sweet, salty, sour, and bitter. We saw earlier how a sweet solution helped to calm a crying baby. Infants will consume more of a sweeter solution than a less sweet one, although they will stop sucking if the solution gets too sweet (Crook, 1978; Desor, Miller, & Turner, 1973). Sweet fluids seem to relax infants, as shown by the sequence of facial actions in Figure 4.4. At

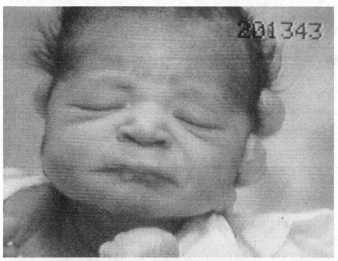

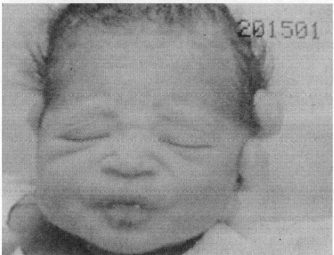

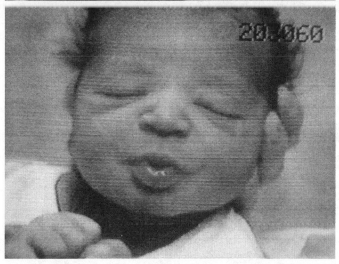

Figure 4.4
Facial Expressions Elicited by the Sweet Solution
Infant negative facial actions are followed by relaxation and sucking.

Source: D. Rosenstein & H. Oster, Differential facial responses to four basic tastes in newborns, 1988, p. 1561. *Child Development, 59*, 1555–1568. Copyright © The Society for Research in Child Development, Inc. Used with permission of the author and publisher.

first, babies show a negative expression, followed by relaxation and sucking (Blass, 1997; Rosenstein & Oster, 1988; Steiner, 1973).

In response to sour and bitter tastes, newborns show more consistently negative expressions, especially upper lip raising (as in disgust) and nose wrinkling. They also become more restless and stop sucking (Rosenstein & Oster, 1988; Steiner, 1973). Newborns do not like salty solutions (Crook, 1978); however, at around 4 months infants prefer salty tastes (Beauchamp, Cowart, mennella, & Marsh, 1994).

Some of the same facial expressions as those described above for tastes have been seen in response to smells (Steiner, 1977). In fact, it appears that the sense of smell is well developed prenatally. A study by Varendi, Porter, and Winberg (1997) indicates that newborns prefer a breast treated with amniotic fluid over an unwashed breast. Newborns can differentiate between such odors as vinegar, licorice, and alcohol. In response to unpleasant odors, newborns will make faces of disgust. They will turn away from unpleasant odors and turn toward pleasant ones (Lipsitt, Engen, & Kaye, 1963).

Odors may be another way, besides sounds, by which infants recognize their mothers. Infants older than 6 days tend to turn their heads more often to a pad containing their own mother's breast milk than to a pad containing the milk of another woman (MacFarlane, 1975). In a study using similar methodology, breast-fed infants were able to recognize pads containing their own mother's underarm odor compared to pads worn by unfamiliar women, although bottle-fed babies showed no evidence of recognition (Cernoch & Porter, 1985). Breast-fed infants can also distinguish their own mother's perfume from other perfume smells, and they show a clear olfactory preference for breast milk from any woman over other types of smells (Porter, Makin, Davis, & Christensen, 1992; Schleidt & Genzel, 1990). These differences between breast- and bottle-fed infants are probably due to the fact that breast-fed babies spend a longer time in direct contact with their mother's bare skin than bottle-fed babies do.

Interestingly, new mothers—whether their deliveries were vaginal or cesarean—were able to recognize their own infant's odors (Porter, Cernoch, & Perry, 1983; Russell, Mendelson, & Peeke, 1983). There seems to be a mutual olfactory (odor) sensitivity between infants and mothers. Thus, infants and mothers have a number of alternative and complementary channels of communication that ensure the beginnings of an emotional bond.

Olfactory and taste responses are probably not mediated by the cortex at this age. Both normal infants and deformed infants born without a cortex were able to detect odors and tastes (Steiner, 1977). This suggests that these perceptions are linked to the limbic and brain stem survival functions related to sucking and feeding.

Finally, newborn infants seem highly sensitive to tactile stimulation. The presence of the newborn reflexes bears witness to this fact because many of them are stimulated by touch. There are benefits of massage and nurturing touch for both preterm and full-term newborns (Chapter 9; Weiss et al., 2001). Researchers have found changes in behavior and heart rate when infants are stimulated with touch or with an air puff on various regions of the body (Bell & Costello, 1964; Rose, Schmidt, & Bridget, 1976). Infants' mouths and hands are especially sensitive, and even in the first few weeks of life, they make different kinds of hand and mouth movements when soft or hard objects are placed in their hands or mouths (Rochat, 1987). Newborns are also able to change their hand movements depending upon whether a surface is smooth or textured (Molina & Jouen, 1998). Newborns can visually recognize an object they had previously touched, but not the other way around, attesting to greater tactile compared to visual acuity (Sann & Steri, 2007).

Although it is possible that infants use touch to recognize their mothers, no studies have been done on this topic. Research has shown, however, that infants touch the mother's breast using massage-like hand motions during breast-feeding. These hand movements stop during a sucking pause and resume again during sucking. The purpose of these movements for the baby are not clear, but similar cyclical hand movements have been shown to serve the perception of texture in newborns (Molina & Jouen, 2004). On the other hand, infant massaging plus sucking stimulates the release of the hormone oxytocin from the mother's pituitary gland. Oxytocin facilitates nursing and the feeling of closeness to the infant (Matthiesen et al., 2001).

Newborns also feel pain. In response to normal medical procedures such as injections and circumcision, infants show increased distress and may exhibit disturbances of sleep for the next few days (Emde, Gaensbauer, & Harmon, 1976; Karns, 2000). Newborns during vaginal delivery show more pain-related facial expressions than those born by cesarian section (Delevati & Bergamasco, 1999). Although medical procedures on newborns have traditionally been done without anesthetics, recent findings on pain sensitivity in newborns are leading to the increased use of local anesthetics.

In summary, infants are able to perceive with all their senses, and their sensitivity improves rapidly over the first few weeks and months of life. Certainly, this improvement is due in part to changes in the brain. On the other hand, the changes in the brain depend closely on the kinds of experiences the infant has during this period. There is also evidence that newborns recognize many forms of perception as meaningful: they recognize their mothers, and they cry in response to pain. It is also true that many forms of stimulation have no particular meaning for the infant: a face may be perceived simply as a series of lines, a melody as a sequence of sounds. The process of making sense of sensation is one of the major developmental tasks of infancy and we should not expect infants to come into the world with an understanding of more than a few simple things. Those simple things, however, are ecological in the sense that the infant has a direct connection with the thing perceived. In the next section, we take up the issue of the newborn's ability to understand, learn, and feel.

Two to Five Months

Physical Development

In infancy and early childhood, physical development occurs as a natural accompaniment to psychological development. Physical development is usually measured in terms of height and weight. Additional indices include the circumference of the head, the fat-to-muscle ratio, the emergence of baby teeth, and bone growth. Standard charts for height and weight for boys and girls from birth to 36 months are available from the United States Center for Disease Control web site at (www.cdc.gov/nchs/about/major/nhanes/ growthcharts/ charts.htm).

At birth, most infants are 19 to 21 inches in length and weigh between 7 and 8 pounds. Boys are slightly longer and heavier than girls and remain so, on average, throughout life. The most rapid growth in both height and weight occurs in the first 6 months of life. By this age, height increases by a factor of 1.5, while weight increases by a factor of 2. This is a lot of growth in a short period. Imagine a teenager (the teenage years are the other period of life when rapid growth occurs) whose height increased by half again in 6 months—say, from 5 feet to 71/2 feet! Teens grow fast, but not that fast.

Individual differences in birth height and weight are relatively small, since they are limited by the need for the infant's body to fit through the mother's pelvis and vagina during birth. Individual differences become larger with age (the range of heights and weights is wider among 2-year-olds than among 1-year-olds). In addition, as the infants get older, their height becomes a better predictor of their adult height. Infant weight is not a very good predictor of adult weight, since weight is more variable than height and more dependent upon environmental factors. As we shall see in Chapter 9, weight gain in premature infants can be influenced not only by diet but also by age-appropriate stimulation. In Chapter 9, we return to the topic of infant nutrition and its effects on growth.

Also, keep in mind that growth is asynchronous. Different parts of the body grow at different rates, and growth spurts occur at different times in each body region. Before birth, the head grows faster than the rest of the body, while after birth, the body begins to grow faster. The process by which the head grows earlier than the body is called **cephalocaudal development**. Growth also proceeds outward, first centered on the torso of the body and later on the developing limbs in a process called **proximodistal development**. Because their limbs develop more slowly than the central part of the body, it takes almost a year for babies to begin standing and walking. These growth processes are illustrated in Figure 4.5. Infant sleep also changes during this period. By 3 months infants are still sleeping about the same amount as newborns, but they can sleep for longer periods before waking up and are more likely to sleep through the night. About half of their sleep time is in REM sleep. This percentage decreases gradually so that in adults, only 20% of sleep is REM sleep. The section of Chapter 9 about SIDS (Sudden Infant Death Syndrome) discusses sleep a bit more, since most of these deaths occur when the baby is sleeping.

Motor Development

At the same time that the body is growing physically, the infant is also becoming more skilled at a variety of motor movements. In the realm of motor development, we consider control over posture, locomotion, and the movements of the hands and arms.

Motor development was studied extensively in the early part of the twentieth century (Gesell, 1928; McGraw, 1935; Shirley, 1931). Because of this research, the infant's level of motor development can be assessed today using a variety of standardized testing situations. Some of the commonly used motor developmental assessment tests are listed in Table 4.4.

The ability to roll over, starting from lying on the back, begins around 2.5 to 3 months. It is not as easy as you think, as you can see from the Expe-

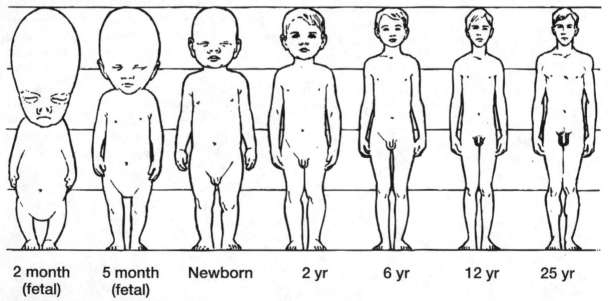

| 2 month (fetal) | 5 month (fetal) | Newborn | 2 yr | 6 yr | 12 yr | 25 yr |

Figure 4.5 Developmental Changes in Body Proportion
The way different proportions of body length accounted for by the head, trunk, and legs at different ages or stages of development. The disproportion is greatest in fetal life. The head decreases from 50% of total body length at 2 months postconception to only 25% at birth and 12% in adulthood.

Source: J. F. Rosenblith & J. E. Sims-Knight, *In the beginning: Development in the first two years*, 1985, p. 296. Belmont, CA: Brooks/Cole. Copyright © Wadsworth, Inc. Reprinted by permission.

TABLE 4.4 Commonly Used Infant Development Tests

Name of Test	Areas of Competency Assessed
Gesell Scales (Gesell, 1925)	Motor behavior, language behavior, adaptive behavior, and personal-social behavior.
Bayley Scales of Infant Development (Bayley, 1969)	Motor area (gross body coordination) and mental area (adaptability, learning, sensory acuity, and fine motor coordination).
Denver Developmental Screening Test (Frankenburg et al., 1975)	Personal-social behavior, fine motor-adaptive behavior, language behavior, and gross motor coordination.
Einstein Scales of Sensorimotor Development (Escalona & Corman, 1968)	Prehension, object permanence, and space (detour behavior and perspective taking).
Infant Psychological Development Scales (Uzgiris & Hunt, 1975)	Object permanence, development of means, development of imitation, development of causality, development of objects in space, and development of schemes for relating to objects.

Source: A. Fogel & G. F. Melson, *Child development*, 1988, p. 150. St. Paul, MN: West. Copyright © by West Publishing Company. Reprinted by permission. All rights reserved.

riential Exercise on rolling over in this chapter. This is because infants have to do this without the help of their arms and legs which do not have the muscle strength to push off from the ground.

Based on results from using these tests with many infants, both the average age of achievement of a skill and the range of ages seen in normal infants is usually reported. The age norms for the achievement of body postures and hand and arm control between 2 and 5 months of age are given in Table 4.5 using the standard scores from the Bayley test. Between 2 and 5 months of age, boy and girl infants do not differ, on average, in motor skills or amount of motor activity (Cossette, Malcuit, & Pomerleau, 1991).

These assessment procedures are useful for diagnosing retardation and motor deficits in infants, but they only work well under specific conditions. First, the test norms apply only to infants in a particular cultural and economic group. Second, the test is applicable only if it is administered in precisely the same manner for each infant. The ability to grasp a cube is supposed to be assessed when the infant is supported in a sitting position. What if, instead, you presented the cube while the baby was lying supine? How might such a postural change affect the infant's hand motor skills?

Physical exercise and environmental support for motor skills can enhance the infant's ability to achieve motor coordination. As a simple case, consider how an infant seat, a high chair, and an infant walker provide postural support so that babies can execute manual and locomotor movements that they would not be able to do while lying on their backs. Similarly, the positions in which adults hold infants also influence the range of motor skills that the infants can display. In general, the ability of a baby to perform a motor skill depends in part on two factors: the difficulty of the task and the supports and resources present in the environment in which the task is carried out.

Task difficulty. We saw earlier in this chapter that infants older than 2 months, when held upright with the feet placed on a surface, cannot execute stepping movements. When the same infant's legs are underwater or when the infant is lying supine, on the other hand, stepping becomes easier. In conditions in which the stepping task is less difficult, in other words, infants can do it (Thelen, Skala, & Kelso, 1987).

Similar effects of task difficulty have been shown for fine motor skills, such as manipulating objects. Between the ages of 2 and 5 months, infants have more difficulty handling objects like balls and cubes

TABLE 4.5   Norms for the Development of Motor Behavior Patterns in North America

Test Item	Average Age	Normal Age Range
A. Head and body control		
Holds head erect when upright	7 weeks	3 weeks–4 months
Holds head steady when upright	2.5 months	1 month–5 months
Elevates chest and head in prone position	2.2 months	3 weeks–5 months
Thrusts arms and legs in supine position	1 months	1 week–2 months
Turns from side to back	2 months	3 weeks–5 months
Turns from back to side	2.5 months	2 months–7 months
Sits with support	2.2 months	1 month–5 months
Sits with slight support	3.7 months	2 months–6 months
Sits alone momentarily	5.2 months	4 months–8 months
Pulls self to sitting position	5.7 months	4 months–8 months
B. Hand and arm control		
Holds onto large ring in supine position	1 month	3 weeks–4 months
Grasps 1-inch cube with palm	3.7 months	2 months–7 months
Grasps cube with partial use of thumb	5 months	4 months–8 months
Reaches with one hand	5.5 months	4 months–8 months

Source: Bayley Infant Development Tests, as reported in and adapted from J. F. Rosenblith & J. E. Sims-Knight, *In the beginning: Development in the first two years*, 1985, Tables 8.2 and 8.5. Reprinted by permission of Sage Publications.

than objects that have graspable appendages, such as a cube with holes into which the baby can insert his or her fingers or a ring (which is simply a ball with a hole in the middle). They are also better at grasping small versus larger objects.

At 3 months, grasping movements are relatively primitive. Babies will grasp an object and move it directly to their mouths without even looking at it. Beginning at about 4 months, however, babies will alternate putting the object in their mouths and looking at it, and they can hold the object in one hand while looking at it and finger the object with the other hand (Rochat, 1989). The older baby uses more motor actions and more perceptual systems in exploring the environment (Bushnell, 1982; Ruff, Saltarelli, Capozzoli, & Dubiner, 1992). Between 2 and 6 months of age, the movements of the arm and hand become more refined and more adapted to the size and shape of an object (Angulo-Kinzler & Horn, 2001; Bhat & Galloway, 2006; Rocha et al., 2006). Infants are also discovering what their hands do by feeling and watching them (see Experiential Exercises, this chapter).

The ability to make sophisticated movements toward objects also differs according to the baby's emotional state (Fogel, 1981; Hannan, 1987; H. Papousek & Papousek, 1977; Trevarthen, 1977). Figure 4.6 shows some of these state-related arm and hand movements. Infants 2 and 3 months of age were more likely to point if they were in an alert and attentive state. Typically, the pointing movements are not directed to the object of the infant's attention: pointing is more like an expression of interest than a direct communication about the object at this age (Fogel & Hannan, 1985; Thelen & Fogel, 1989) (see Figure 4.7).

In general, therefore, infants will perform better on easier motor skill tasks. This, of course, is no different at any age. Children can ride a bike with training wheels before they can ride without them. Adults can help infants by making appropriate adjustments when tasks are too difficult.

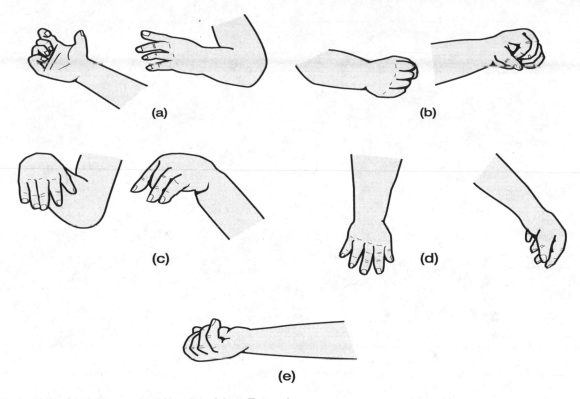

Figure 4.6   State-Dependent Hand and Arm Extensions
The position of hands in different behavioral states of infants: **(a)** alert waking state; **(b)** closed fists in uncomfortable or distressing situations; **(c)** passive waking state; **(d)** transitional states to sleep; **(e)** sleep.

Source: Adapted from H. Papousek, Mothering and the cognitive head start: Psychobiological considerations, 1977, p. 71. In H. R. Schaffer (Ed.), *Studies in mother-infant interaction*, 63–85. Copyright © Academic Press, Inc.

Supports and resources. As infants develop, they can perform tasks that were once too difficult for them. How do these changes come about? What is the cause of motor development? As explained in Chapter 5, brain development is experience-dependent; that is, the infant has to practice making movements with easy tasks for the brain to develop the connections needed to enhance motor skills (Lobo et al., 2004). Since human infants have a limited ability to move around in the environment or to think about how to make tasks easier, they need social partners to help them. Usually, the infant's caregiver creates supports and resources by which object manipulation and motor movements are made easier.

During simple social play with objects, adults help infants to practice their budding motor skills (Lyra & Ferreira, 1987; Lyra & Rossetti-Ferreira,

1995). At first, when infants are unable to reach, adults will show an object to the baby and demonstrate the object's properties (shaking a rattle or squeezing a soft toy). During this period, adults may also place the object in the infant's hands, allowing the infant to grasp and hold the object or bring the object to the mouth. After infants acquire the ability to reach for objects, adults stop showing and placing and begin to hold the objects steady and within reach of the babies, apparently to give the babies the opportunity to practice reaching. Once reaching is mastered, mothers begin to challenge the babies with more complex objects and with two objects at one time (Fogel, 1990b; Fogel, Garvey, Hsu, &West-Stroming, 2006).

Another way in which adults provide supports and resources for motor skills is by holding the

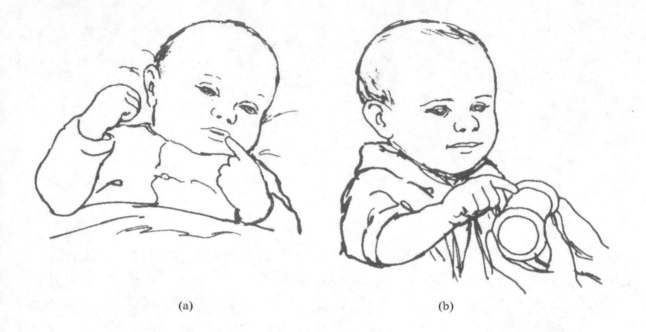

(a)   (b)

Figure 4.7   Development of Pointing
(a) Point at 2 months during face-to-face interaction with mother. Index finger extends while arms are flexed and does not indicate direction of gaze. **(b)** Point at 9 months during free play with mother. Both arm and finger are extended in the direction of the object of interest.

Source: E. Thelen & A. Fogel, Toward an action-based theory of infant development, 1989, p. 53. In J. Lockman & N. Hazen (eds.), *Action in a social context: Perspectives on early development*, 23–63. New York: Plenum Press.

infants in postures that are most conducive to the execution of those skills. For example, when infants are first learning to sit, they need to balance their bodies with one hand. This detracts from their ability to reach for things with two hands (Rochat, 1989). When adults hold the baby upright, it frees both of the infant's hands. Upright babies are more attentive to the physical environment, while supine babies are more likely to look at their mothers (Fogel, Dedo, & McEwen, 1992; Fogel, Nwokah, Hsu, Dedo, & Walker, 1993). Similarly, infants in upright rather than supine positions are more likely to reach for objects that are presented within their reach (Savelsbergh & Kamp, 1993).

The effect of adult support for motor development is also seen in some African cultures. One study done in Mali (Bril & Sabatier, 1986) found that mothers put babies through some active work-out routines. From birth, the babies were given postural control exercises, including training in sitting and standing. Mothers also stretched the babies' muscles and suspended the babies by their arms and legs (see Figure 4.8). Similar patterns have been found for West African families living in Paris (Rabain-Jamin & Wornham, 1993).

As a result of this practice, many African babies have advanced motor coordination compared to Caucasian babies. In addition, because the babies' limbs are exercised frequently, certain reflexes such as stepping do not disappear after 2 months, as found in North American infants (Super, 1976). On the opposite end of the spectrum are Navaho (from the southwestern United States) infants, who spend many hours strapped tightly onto cradle boards. Their motor development is slower than that of the other groups (Chisholm, 1983).

STRETCHING

(1) 1 month   (2) 1 month   (3) 1 month

SUSPENSION

(4) 1 month   (5) 1 month   (6) 1 month

(7) 2 months   (8) 1 month   (9) 2 months   (10) 5.5 months

Figure 4.8   Postural Manipulations by Adults

Source: B. Bril & C. Sabatier, The cultural context of motor development: Postural manipulations in the daily life of Bambara babies (Mail), 1986, p. 445. *International Journal of Behavior Development, 9*, 439–453

In summary, differences in task difficulty and in supports and resources for motor development seem to influence the age at which the motor skill is first acquired. Eventually, however, most healthy babies achieve the important motor milestones. These findings show that motor and physical development in the first half year is the result of a systems interaction between infants, adults, and the environment. Generally speaking, the ability of a person to perform a coordinated task is based on three systemic factors: task, environmental supports, and existing abilities. This is shown in Figure 4.9.

Whether a baby can reach for objects, for example, can be explained according to Figure 4.9 as follows: The task is to reach for an object. The environmental supports are whether the object is within reach or out of reach, whether it is held by an adult or not, and the size and shape of the object. The abilities are whether the infant has learned to reach (after 4 months, usually) and whether the infant can turn, sit upright, or move toward the object. Reaching will be coordinated and successful depending upon how these factors come together.

Perceptual Development

As we have seen, perceptual development is also influenced by the kinds of experiences the child encounters. Lack of exposure to sensory information can impede the experience-dependent articulation of brain pathways for sensory acuity and information processing. The period from 2 to 5 months includes a major shift in perceptual development. During the first 2 months, infants can see, hear, smell, taste, and feel. Newborns have clear preferences for certain types of perceptual experiences, such as looking at sharp and bold outlines of figures or listening to high-pitched voices. In some cases, infants under 2 months can recognize particular patterns that seem to have a meaning to them—looming objects, their mothers' voices and smells—but pattern detection is the exception rather than the rule. Between 2 and 4 months, infants begin to recognize and prefer meaningful patterned stimuli (a smiling face, for example) regardless of its level of intensity, complexity, or sharpness.

Visual Pattern Perception

The visual world comes to us in the form of line, shape, brightness and color. Adults do not perceive these simple features, however; they perceive whole objects. Newborn infants perceive the lines and colors but do not detect the patterns. Adults perceive like a newborn when they are trying to draw or paint an object and they need to break it down into its basic elements. Consider the following figure: 母. Does this mean anything to you? To a Chinese or Japanese speaker, this figure means "mother." To the rest of the world, it is just an interesting shape made by intersecting lines. Before 2 months, many of the things babies see may seem as if they are looking at Chinese without knowing the language.

The ability to perceive whole patterns, rather than lines and shapes, increases dramatically at about

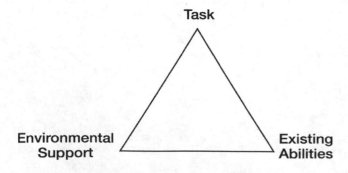

Figure 4.9 Systems Model of Task Difficulty
A task will be easy or difficult for an infant depending upon what the infant is being asked to do (the task), the help and resources the infant receives from others (environmental support), and the skills that the infant brings to the task (existing abilities).

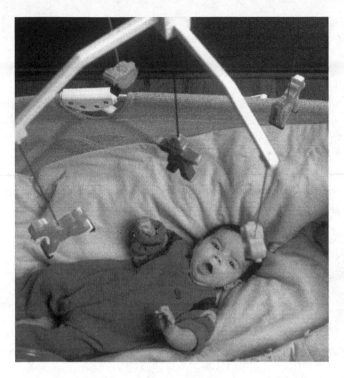

Visual perception develops by seeing the same object from a number of different perspectives. Colorful mobiles with varied shapes are particularly interesting. Research using mobiles has found that babies of this age can tell the difference between a familiar mobile and the same one with only a single piece removed.
Photo: Elizabeth Crews

3 months. To discover this, researchers show infants a picture of a figure— usually two-dimensional— during a familiarization period. Then, using habituation procedures, the familiar figure is replaced with either an unfamiliar one or the same figure rotated into different orientations or seen from different angles. Generally, by 3 months, infants will dishabituate when a totally novel figure is introduced, but not when a different view of the familiar figure is shown (Bornstein, Krinsky, & Benasich, 1986; McKenzie, Tootell, & Day, 1980). This means they see the different images as if they were different views of the same figure. If they were just seeing lines, the different orientations of the same figure would appear to the babies to be different figures.

Another procedure is to observe scanning movements made by infants looking at pictures of simple figures, such as circles and squares, drawn with dashed or dotted lines. Infants older than 3 months will scan these figures as if they were drawn with a solid line. If one of the dashed-line elements is drawn at an orientation that does not follow the outline of the figure, infants will scan this element more than the other elements that appear to them to be part of a pattern (Van Giffen & Haith, 1984). This means they expect visual patterns to form into a meaningful whole.

By 3 months, infants are able to visually differentiate familiar from unfamiliar faces from a variety of live and photographed faces of mothers compared to unfamiliar women (Barrera & Mauer, 1981; Kurzweil, 1988). However, infants at 3 months of age find it difficult to tell faces apart if a shower cap is placed around the face (Atkinson, 1995). They also prefer faces from their own ethnic-racial group over faces from a different group (Bar-Haim et al., 2006; Kelly et al., 2005). Infants of this age prefer looking at faces over nonface stimuli that have been carefully constructed to have exactly the same complexity, brightness, and black-and-white contrasts (Dannemiller & Stephens, 1988) (see Figure 4.10). Remarkably, both 3-month- olds and 6-month-olds prefer to look longer at faces that adults have judged as attractive than at faces adults judged as less attractive (Langlois et al., 1987).

Why should infants prefer faces over other types of visual stimuli? Faces do have clear out-

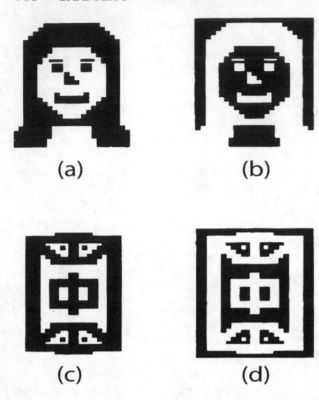

(a)   (b)

(c)   (d)

Figure 4.10   Stimuli Used in Face Preference Survey

Source: J. L. Dannemiller & B. R. Stephens, A critical test of infant patterns preference models, 1988, p. 212. *Child Development, 59*, 210–216. Copyright © The Society for Research in Child Development, Inc.

lines and moderate complexity. They are composed of closed circular shapes that babies like to look at. Babies seem to prefer shapes that are symmetrical (shapes in which one side is the mirror image of the other). Faces have vertical symmetry, and 3-month-olds prefer vertical symmetry to horizontal symmetry (Bornstein & Krinsky, 1985; Fisher, Ferdinandsen, & Bornstein, 1981). Newborns show this preference as early as 3 days after birth (Slater, von der Schulenberg, Brown, Badenoch, Parsons, & Samuels, 1998).

Is it a fortunate coincidence that faces happen to have just those elements that make them attractive to babies? Or is the visual system designed in such a way that its first preferences direct it toward social objects? It could be that both things are true. We share similar visual systems with other vertebrate species, and most vertebrates have symmetrical faces. Perhaps both faces and visual systems evolved together in relation to each other.

Preference for the face continues to develop throughout the first year of life (Maurer, 1985). Three-month-olds can perceive some facial expressions. They are best at recognizing a smile, particularly if it is a wide, open-mouth smile and if their mothers encourage attention to faces (Kuchuk, Vibbert, & Bornstein, 1986). Not until 6 months, however, do infants become competent at recognizing a variety of specific facial expressions and emotions.

Visual Perception of Moving Objects

One problem with the research presented so far is that most of the test stimuli are drawings or photographs—in other words, static two-dimensional representations. You might think that babies would be more familiar with moving three-dimensional objects and faces and thus might recognize differences between moving objects better than stationary ones.

This seems to be true. Infants at this age look longer at dynamic faces and moving patterns than at static ones (Kaufmann & Kaufmann, 1980; C. A. Samuels, 1985). By 3 or 4 months, infants perceive moving objects as whole units. By 5 months, infants will reach for small moving objects that appear to be in front of larger stationary objects, but do not reach for small moving objects that are behind the larger object (Van de Walle & Spelke, 1996; Von Hofsten & Spelke, 1985). In a study by Kellman and Spelke (1983), infants at 4 months were shown a moving rod partially hidden behind a block. The infants could only see the rod's top and bottom, and yet they perceived the rod as a unified object. Later studies indicate that infants as young as 3 months perceive the rod as a whole (S. Johnson, 1997).

By using movement cues, 4-month-old infants are also aware that objects are solid and that they take up their own space. In one study, a platform resembling a drawbridge was rotated back until it hit the top of an object projected on a screen; then the platform stopped. In another condition, the platform kept rotating as if it were passing directly through the solid object. Babies looked longer at the second event, suggesting that they were puzzled by this spatial impossibility (Baillargeon, 1987). In some studies, a moving object is made to disappear behind a small barrier and then re-emerge on the other side. Infants of this age will continue to track the presumed path of the object and "expect" to see it emerge on the other side of the barrier (Bremner et al., 2007; von Hofsten et al., 2007). It appears that infants become increasingly skilled at detecting moving objects and their trajectories over the first 6 months, and this depends upon their ongoing experience with objects (Johnson et al., 2003).

Finally, infants appear to detect complex patterns of motion. Using a "point-light display" technique (Figure 4.11), the movements of a human body walking can be represented by a series of moving lights on the joints. A computer can then invert this light display or move the lights to create displays that would not be biologically possible (joints in incorrect locations and body parts moving in opposite ways). Between 3 and 5 months, infants prefer to look at normal walkers or runners over inverted or biologically impossible ones (Bertenthal, Proffitt, & Cutting, 1984; Bertenthal, Proffitt, Kramer, & Spetner, 1987; Fox & McDaniels, 1982).

As with the infant's preference for faces, it appears that the perceptual system early in life is disposed to detect real-world information. Infants are able to see whole objects and not just patterns. They are better at detecting relevant information (such as whether the object can be reached and grasped or whether the object is familiar) if they are able to see the object from multiple perspectives and in motion.

Some have suggested that the perception "this is a whole object" is derived from detecting the object's invariant properties as seen from different perspectives (Ruff, 1978; 1985). **Invariance** refers to those aspects of an object that remain the same regardless of how the object is viewed. For example, a ball always has a round shape no matter how you look at it. A cube has sides of equal length and three sides that meet in right-angle corners regardless of which side of the object you are looking at or from what direction. Adults immediately detect the invariances of most simple objects without much thought. It is not clear whether babies do the same or have to puzzle over whether two views of something are indeed the same thing. We also do not know how infants detect invariance (do they compare angles, distances, overall shapes, or what?); but there is no doubt that infants like to seek out invariant properties of objects at a very early age. In other words, the infant is *able* to perceive meaningful wholes because human infants are predisposed to finding the similarities and differences between things; no one has to tell a baby to do this.

Auditory Perception

Infant auditory perception is rather good during the first 2 months of life. Infants recognize and prefer their mothers' voices at birth, for example. By 4 months, infants prefer human speech to nonspeech sounds (Fernald, 1985). Infants appear to be able to detect different emotions expressed in the voice earlier than they can see differences between facial expressions. Five-month-old infants listen longer to positive compared to negative vocalizations, and they smile more to voices

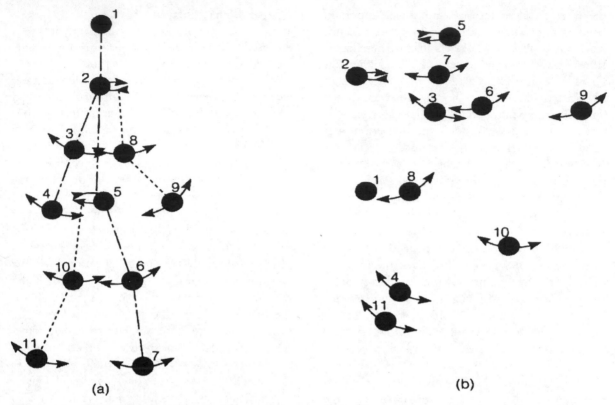

Figure 4.11 Motion Perception Stimuli

Panel **(a)** shows a display of eleven point-lights moving as if attached to the head and major joints of a person walking. The arrows drawn through the points represent the perceived motions of the display. Panel **(b)** depicts the scrambled walker display, which is identical to (a) except that the relative locations of the point-lights are scrambled. Correspondingly numbered points in the two displays undergo identical motions.

Source: B. I. Bertenthal, D. R. Proffitt, & J. E. Cutting, Infant sensitivity to figural coherence in biomechanical motions, 1984, p. 217. *Journal of Experimental Child Psychology, 37*, 213–230.

expressing approval and frown more to voices expressing disapproval (Fernald, 1993). Since the babies cannot understand the content of the speech, they must detect the emotional information from the auditory cues alone: pitch, timing, and intensity. The ability to detect emotion from speech improves if the infant can also see the adult's face making an expression that is related to the positivity or negativity of the sounds (Walker-Andrews & Lennon, 1991).

Infants at 4 months like music. When exposed to consonant (as opposed to dissonant) music, they look more in the direction of the sound and become less motorically active, apparently because they are listening more intently (Zentner & Kagan, 1998). Infants of this age show more sustained attention to maternal singing compared to motherese, and they can remember songs for at least a week without hearing them in between (Nakata & Trehub, 2004; Trainor et al., 2004). Infants like play songs ("Eensy Weensy Spider") and lullabies ("Rock-a-Bye, Baby") better if they are sung directly to them in a loving tone of voice, compared to prerecorded songs (Trainor, 1996; Trainor, Clark, Huntley, & Adams, 1997), suggesting that the song is less important to the infants than the way it is sung to them. Infants also direct more attention to their own bodies when being sung lullabies and more attention to the singer when being sung play songs (Rock, Trainor, & Addison, 1999). Perhaps these traditional melodies were developed over many centuries simply by watching how infants respond to the sounds.

Speed of auditory processing also improves. At birth, infants can recognize sounds and locate sound sources, but only if the sound is repeated many times or is heard for at least 20 seconds. By 3 to 4 months, sounds can be recognized after shorter exposures, and infants can localize the source of briefly heard sound at wider angles from the midline of the body than they could at birth (Aslin, 1987; Jusczyk, Kennedy, & Jusczyk, 1995; Morrongiello, Fenwick, & Chance, 1990). This means that infants at this age appear to process sounds at about the same speed as adults.

Cross-Modal Perception

Infants of this age have **cross-modal perception**, the ability to integrate information coming from at least two sensory modalities. After about 4 months, infants expect sights and sounds to "go together." Infants prefer, for example, to hear a film soundtrack where the visual object's movements and the sound are synchronized, rather than a soundtrack that has been altered (Bahrick, 1988), and they prefer to look at moving faces in which the lips are moving in synchrony with the vocalizations (Patterson & Werker, 1999). Babies prefer to look at visual objects that make a noise compared to silent objects (Lawson & Ruff, 1984). Sound localization is improved by 3 months if the infant has visual cues about the sound source, compared to a sound heard in the dark or made from behind a screen (Morrongiello & Rocca, 1987).

These studies show that by the time infants reach the age of 3 or 4 months, their world is not disjointed. Objects are perceived as coherent wholes. Infants expect the different properties of the same objects to go together, and they will respond by looking away more if things are presented to them in a disjointed form.

Six to Nine Months

Physical and Motor Development

By the age of 5 months, infants can sit supported, and they can reach and grasp objects. Between 6 and 9 months, improvements in posture lead to independent sitting and to supported standing. Muscle strength improvements allow babies to roll over and to move their bodies by creeping or by crawling (see Experiential Exercises, this chapter). By 9 months, infants can take a few steps while holding on to furniture or an adult hand. Their grasp becomes more precise, so that by 9 months, infants can pick up small objects such as peas or carrot slices using just the tips of the thumb and index finger. Some of these developments are listed in Table 4.6.

Hand Movements and Hand Preference

One of the distinguishing features of the human brain is that the left and right hemispheres serve different functions. Although researchers disagree about the precise allocation of functions to each side of the brain, the right hemisphere is believed to control spatial patterns and nonlinguistic (emotional) information processing, while the left hemisphere is more sensitive to sequential processing of the sort used in understanding language. These left-right brain differences are found in right-handed people; in left-handed people the hemisphere functions are reversed.

Because brain hemisphere specialization is linked to **handedness**, or the preference for the use of one hand over another, the emergence in infancy of a preferred hand is thought to be related to milestones in the development of the brain. If there is a hand-use preference in early infancy, it might suggest that the left and the right cortices of the infant's brain are already functioning differently.

At first glance, there seems to be good evidence for left-right differences. Infants begin to exhibit a hand preference at about 2 months of age, around the time when visually guided reaching begins.

TABLE 4.6 Norms for the Development of Motor Behavior Patterns in North America

Test Item	Average Age	Normal Age Range
A. Body Control		
Sits alone steadily	6.5 months	5–9 months
Pulls self to sitting	8.2 months	6–11 months
Pulls self to standing	8.5 months	6–12 months
B. Locomotion		
Stopping movements while standing	8.7 months	6–12 months
Walks with help	9.5 months	7–12 months
Sits down	9.5 months	7–14 months
C. Hand and arm control		
Can scoop small pellet	5.5 months	4–8 months
Finger-to-thumb grasp of cube	7 months	5–9 months
Finger-to-thumb grasp of pellet	9 months	7–10 months
Rotates wrist while holding cube	5.7 months	4–8 months
Combines objects at midline	8.5 months	6–10 months
Pat-a-cake at midline	9.7 months	7–15 months

Source: Bayley Infant Development Tests, as reported in and adapted from J. F. Rosenblith & J. R. Sims-Knight, *In the Beginning: Development in the first two years*, 1985, Tables 8.3, 8.4, and 8.5. Belmont, CA: Brooks/Cole. Copyright © Wadsworth, Inc. Reprinted by permission of Sage Publications

Like adults, more infants preferentially reach with their right than with their left hands. Furthermore, this hand preference is relatively stable in babies over the first year of life (McDonnell, Anderson, & Abraham, 1983; Young, Segalowitz, Misek, Alp, & Boulet, 1983). However, many infants show an irregular preference for handedness, going from left to right, or using both hands equally (Butterworth & Hopkins, 1993).

These left-right differences are not the same as those found in adults, however. About 90% of adults in all cultures are right handed. However, only about 30 to 50% of infants under 1 year show a preference for the right hand in reaching, while 10 to 30% have a left-hand preference. The remaining infants show no hand preference. In adults, hand preference is correlated with the hand preference of one's parents, but this is not true for infants (McCormick & Maurer, 1988). Thus, it seems that infants do have a right-side bias, but it is not nearly as strong nor as stable as adults'. More permanent adult-like hand preferences in infants do not emerge until the second year of life.

Why should we prefer to use one hand more than the other? Actually, handedness does not mean that we use one hand and not the other; it means that each of our hands may be doing different things. When a baby explores an object, the hand that is doing the grasping and manipulating is no less important than the hand that is holding the object steady. Perhaps handedness evolved in order to allow each hand to perform a different but complementary function (Fagard & Jacquet, 1989).

When infants first begin to reach for objects, they use two hands and reach symmetrically toward the midline of the body. More mature reaching, beginning at around 6 months, involves reaching with a single hand for the object. What happens to the non-reaching hand at this time? The babies, who by 6 months are just learning to sit without support, extend the non-reaching hand backward to balance their upper bodies as the reaching hand moves forward (Rochat & Senders, 1990). Single-handed reaches would be impossible for babies without the postural counterbalance provided by the other hand and arm. Two-handed reaches after

6 months are also more sophisticated because they typically occur with larger objects (like a big ball) and they can cross the midline of the body to retrieve objects off to one side (van Hof et al., 2002).

Crawling

Being able to extend one arm independently of the other is also believed to be important for the development of crawling. Observations of infants reveal that there are different types of crawling (see Table 4.7). As long as babies are still reaching with two hands at the same time (showing no hand preference), they either creep or rock. They begin to crawl as soon as they can reach with one hand, probably because crawling requires the extension of one hand and leg and then the other (Goldfield, 1989). The Experiential Exercises in this chapter may help you to understand how this works.

Not all infants go through the sequence of types of crawling shown in Table 4.7. Some infants creep before they crawl, while others skip the creeping phase and go directly to crawling. Infants who creep before they crawl, however, are better at crawling than those who do not creep. When they crawl, the creepers move faster and their movements are larger and more efficient, although the non-creepers become proficient crawlers after a couple of weeks (Adolph, Vereijken, & Denny, 1998). There is no evidence, therefore, of any permanent effects of the delay in crawling proficiency for the non-creepers. On the contrary, infants are creative in combining all of the types of movements related to crawling, each in their own unique way. Apparently, infants use whatever means are available to achieve their goals, rather than staying with the most advanced form of movement all the time (Goldfield, 1993).

How Motor Skills Develop

The research on crawling shows that even though infants can get up on their hands and knees in a crawling posture, they still cannot crawl because they lack one of crawling's necessary skill components: alternate extension of the arms and legs. When doing the Experiential Exercises in this chapter, you can see how difficult it is to achieve this skill. This is similar to the younger infants who could not step because their leg muscles lacked the strength to lift the legs. Dynamic systems theory predicts that new motor skills develop by adding additional components to existing skills.

TABLE 4.7   Operational Definitions of Locomotor Stages

Pivot	Arms alternatively flex and extend, one after the other, causing the trunk to pivot on the abdomen. Symmetrical leg extension is followed by forward flexion of one knee, in adduction. Head lifts.
Low creep	Both arms are flexed symmetrically or extended symmetrically, or one is flexed while the other is extended. Legs flex, one at a time. Face is lifted, but chest and abdomen contact supporting surface.
High creep	Both arms are extended, and both legs are flexed symmetrically. Knees are forward under trunk in adduction, lifting abdomen and chest from supporting surface. Head is well up from floor, and eyes look ahead.
Rocking	Arms extend symmetrically, and both legs are flexed symmetrically. Knees are forward under trunk, lifting abdomen and chest from supporting surface. Infant rocks back and forth, remaining in one location.
Crawling	Both arms extend downward from shoulder, then extend forward, alternately. Legs flex forward alternately. Arms and leg on opposite sides of the body move simultaneously.

Note: These definitions were modified from Gesell and Ames (1940).

Source: E. C. Goldfield, Transition from rocking to crawling: Postural constraints on infant movement, 1989, p. 916. *Developmental Psychology* 25, 913–919. Reprinted by permission.

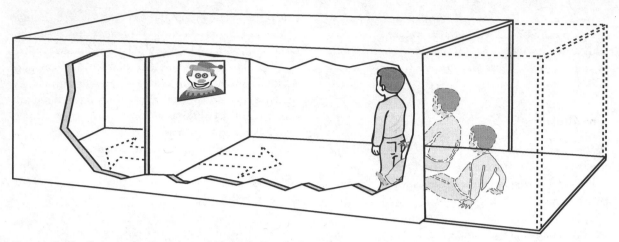

Figure 4.12 Schematic Drawing of Moving-Room Apparatus
Depicted inside the room is a child falling backward as a function of the room moving toward the child. This compensatory response would occur if the child perceived the optical flow produced by the room movement as specifying a forward sway rather than a movement of the walls.

Source: Adapted from B. I. Bertenthal & D. L. Bai, Infants' sensitivity to optical flow for controlling posture, 1989, p. 39. *Developmental Psychology, 25*, 936–945.

A similar analysis could be applied to the development of walking. In this age period, 6 to 9 months, infants can stand and take a few steps, but they cannot yet walk. Why not? Nine-month-old infants seem to possess the prerequisites of walking. They can pull themselves into a standing position, take steps while holding onto something, and alternate their leg movements. What they lack, however, is the ability to control balance. This was discovered in research using a "moving-room" technique (see Figure 4.12). A baby stands in a miniature room, the floor of which is stationary but whose walls and ceiling are moved either toward or away from the baby. Infants under 1 year will fall in the direction in which the wall appears to be moving. Infants older than 1 year may sway but are less likely to lose their balance (Bertenthal & Bai, 1989). The moving room recreates the visual experience of moving without asking the baby to take steps at the same time. It is this visual experience of the room seeming to flow past the eyes that appears to cause babies to lose their balance.

This research suggests that perception of one's own movement in space is a key ingredient in controlling the posture necessary for locomo-tor development. Creeping or crawling experience enhances the infants' self-awareness in relation to objects in space: their ability to understand the differences between close and distant objects, and their ability to remember novel events (Clearfield, 2004; Herbert et al., 2007).

Balance and posture also influence other motor developmental processes. The difference between a creep and a crawl (Table 4.7 and the Experiential Exercises section of this chapter), for example, is the ability to balance on the hands and knees while moving forward. Once balance is acquired in the crawl, infants' movements become more efficient and uniform (Adolph, Vereijken, Denny, Gill, & Lucero, 1995). Infants who had experience with creeping or crawling were observed in the moving room apparatus and compared with infants who had not yet begun to locomote themselves. Those infants who had already begun self-produced locomotion were better able to make postural adjustments to the moving room, showing that the balance needed for walking may come from earlier experiences of balance while trying to crawl (Higgins, Campos, & Kermoian, 1996).

Postural control while sitting is important for the development of skilled reaching. Before infants can sit upright steadily, they reach for objects with two hands at the same time. After they can sit steadily, they are able to reach with a single hand, allowing them to use their other hand for something else. Infants of this age also seem to know how far they can reach for an object based on how stable they are in a sitting posture. They reach out farther when they feel more stable and do not reach when they feel unstable (Pieraut-Lebonniec, 1990; Rochat, 1992; Rochat & Goubet, 1995; Rochat, Goubet, & Senders, 1999). Thus, not only is motor development a complex systems interaction of the different parts of the motor system (legs, trunk, and arms), but it also includes the perceptual system and the type of environment in which the child is moving.

Infants can execute walking movements, for example, if they are supported in their posture—by an infant walker or an adult—and allowed to move their legs cyclically (Thelen & Ulrich, 1991). The onset of walking is later in infants with fewer opportunities to exercise these movements. Infants in northern climates who are born in summer and fall will walk on their own an average of 3 weeks later than infants born in winter and spring. The reason for this is that babies born in winter and spring are more likely to be practicing walking skills in the summer or fall, and the warmer temperatures give them more opportunity for movement without the constriction of a lot of clothing (Benson, 1993).

Infant motor development is also facilitated by giving babies opportunities to move and explore on their own without equipment. In one study, infants were ranked according to how much they used equipment such as a jolly jumper, walker, exersaucer, playpen, or swing. Those infants who used such equipment more had higher scores on motor development assessments at 8 months of age (Abbott & Bartlett, 2001). It is recommended that moderate use of these devices may not be detrimental so long as infants are also exposed to free play experience on the floor with adults.

In the next section, we discuss perceptual development. Just as motor development involves a complex interplay of perception and environmental processes, perceptual development involves the motor system and its development. At this age, therefore, it is not really possible to divide the infant's development into distinct categories like motor skill, perception, and cognition. They are all part of a dynamic developing system.

Perceptual Development: New Developments in the Recognition of Objects and Depth

By 4 months, infants are able to recognize objects even though they may look different when seen from different orientations. By 4 months, infants perceive objects as being solid and will become puzzled if one solid object appears to pass through another. Infants of this age can also perceive differences in distances between objects and will reach preferentially to objects they perceive as nearer to them. For infants under 6 months, however, object recognition and depth perception are easier if the objects are moving and if real objects, rather than pictures of objects, are presented.

After 6 months, however, infants can infer object properties and depth merely from visual cues alone (Craton, 1996; Wilcox & Baillargeon, 1998). Another way to say this is that by 6 months, infants can "see" three dimensions when they are shown objects in two dimensions, as in a drawing or a photograph. Suppose two pictures of different sizes but of the same object, such as a car, are placed next to each other. Adults looking at the pictures with one eye (monocular vision) would assume that the smaller car is farther away. Looking with two eyes, adults can easily see that two cars are at the same distance but of different sizes. These perceptual conclusions must be based only on the relative sizes of the pictures and not on the movements of one car away from the other or the movements of the perceiver in a three-dimensional space.

By about 7 months of age, infants with a patch over one eye will reach toward the larger of two identical pictures of a face, apparently perceiving it as closer (Yonas, Pettersen, & Granrud, 1982). If a small and a large checkerboard are used, the infants do not reach more frequently for the larger one, since checkerboards have no standard size. If the infants are allowed to reach while looking with both eyes, they do not show a preference for the larger object, either the car or the checkerboard. Thus, by 7 months, infants use visual cues, such as size, to judge depth.

Also by 7 months, infants can use other visual cues to judge depth. If one object partially blocks the view of another, the blocked object is perceived as farther away (Granrud & Yonas, 1984). Relative shading in a drawing depicting a bump or a depression causes 7-month-olds, but not 5-month-olds, to reach for the object shaded like a bump (Granrud, Yonas, & Opland, 1985). Both 5- and 7-month-olds reach for actual bumps. Finally, by 7 months, when objects are presented in a perspective drawing, infants use the perspective information to reach for the object that is apparently nearer to them (Arterberry, Yonas, & Bensen, 1989). Infants' ability to recognize objects in two dimensions leads to increased interest in picture books and television at this age.

During this period, infants learn to perceive object properties through touch as well as through vision. Perception of the properties of an object using touch is called **haptic perception**. Through haptic perception, infants soon after birth can distinguish different properties of objects primarily by using their mouths. In the early months, the mouth is perhaps the most sensitive haptic organ. Between 4 and 6 months, infants begin examining objects by active exploration combining hand, mouth, and vision (Morange-Majoux, Cougnot, & Bloch, 1997; Oakes & Tellinghuisen, 1994; Ruff, 1986). After 6 months, infants develop specialized hand movements to detect information about specific object properties such as size, texture, and shape (Bourgeois et al., 2005; Bushnell & Boudreau, 1993). To perceive an object's relative size, for example, infants will enclose their hands around the outside of the object. Other perception-action correspondences are shown in Table 4.8. Through both haptics and vision, therefore, infants become increasingly sophisticated in their knowledge of object properties.

Other Perceptual Developments

Besides recognizing pictures in books, infants in this age period can recognize differences between simple melodies. Six-month-olds can discriminate between six-note melodies differing by only one note (Trehub, Bull, & Thorpe, 1984), and they can discriminate between melodies in which the pauses between notes are varied (Thorpe & Trehub, 1989). By this age, therefore, babies can recognize some nursery rhymes and simple melodies heard in songs.

Also by this age, babies show continuing evidence of cross-modal perception. Thus, infants are sensitive to distortions in the sound track of a film showing a rattle shaking at a particular rhythm. If the sound is faster or slower than the rattle's movements, the babies notice the difference (Bahrick, 1987). As the visual and auditory display becomes more complicated, however, infants preferentially process the sound but not the vision, reflecting the fact that even at 6 months, auditory perception is

TABLE 4.8 Haptic Perception-Action Correspondences for Infants

Object Property	Haptic Action
Size, volume	Enclosing external contours
Hardness	Applying pressure
Exact shape	Following the contour with fingers
Temperature	Static palm or finger contact
Texture	Side-to-side movements of palms or fingers

more advanced than visual perception (Lewkow-icz, 1988, 1996). This auditory dominance is also true for adults, as when light displays flashed to accompany music seem to move at the same beat as the music. If the visual displays are flashed in a regular manner that makes their rhythm salient, however, infants and adults will pay more attention to the visual compared to the auditory display (Lewkowicz, 1994). These findings are important because they show that cross-modal perception is becoming more controlled for infants: under certain conditions, they can distinguish between the separate attributes of each modality.

Infants older than 6 months can also use cross-modal perception to infer information about object properties. Infants of this age who are familiarized with an object only by touch can recognize the object by sight alone (Ruff & Kohler, 1978), and infants will alternatively look at and touch objects and put them into their mouths while exploring them (Ruff, 1984). Furthermore, if babies hear a sound in the dark, they will reach for an object in the direction of the sound. Infants can also distinguish whether the object is within or out of their reach based on hearing its sound in the dark (Clifton, Perris, & Bullinger, 1991; Perris & Clifton, 1988).

Finally, infants were given sweet and tart foods in cups of different colors. On subsequent color-choice trials, the infants consistently picked the color that had been paired with the sweet food (Reardon & Bushnell, 1988).

In summary, these studies of perception show that by the middle of the first year of life, infants can use subtle cues to infer regularities in their perceptual world. They can now learn from pictures in books and on television. They can pick up relationships between different senses in order to pay attention to aspects of their environment that most interest them, such as the color of the baby food jar that contains their favorite flavor. These perceptual abilities lead to clear preferences. Babies begin to take the initiative in expressing their desires for particular pictures, objects, and tastes. As infants learn to perceive the world, they also learn about themselves.

Ten to Twelve Months

By the age of 1 year, infant growth rates have leveled off (see the growth charts at the Center for Disease Control: www.cdc.gov/nchs/about/major/nhanes/growthcharts/charts.htm). Most year-old boys are between 28 1/4 inches (71.75 cm) and 32 inches (81.25 cm) in length, and girls are between 27 1/2 inches (69.85 cm) and 31 1/4 inches (79.38 cm). Both boys and girls will continue to grow at a rate of about 4 to 5 inches (10 to 13 cm) per year for the next several years. At 1 year, boys weigh between 18 1/2 and 26 1/2 pounds (8.4 to 12.0 kg), while girls weigh between 17 1/4 and 24 3/4 pounds (7.8 to 11.2 kg). By the twelfth month, most babies are eating a variety of solid foods, including table foods that are cut up for them. Most infants are holding their own spoons and can drink from a cup with both hands. By this time, almost all infants will have experienced teething pains and will have several teeth to help them chew their food.

With respect to motor development, 11 months is the average age at which infants can stand alone (the range is 9 to 16 months), and at 11 3/4 months, the average baby can walk alone (the range is 9 to 17 months). By 1 year, most infants can sit down from a standing position, and most can climb up and down stairs by crawling.

Infants between 3 and 15 months were observed every 3 weeks going up and down a moderate slope in a laboratory (Adolph, 1997). The methods used to go up and down depended upon whether the infant was a belly crawler (also called a creeper), a hands-and-knees crawler, or a walker (see Figure 4.13). Most of the infants adapted their locomotion by checking out the slope in relation to their abilities. The more experience they had with the slope, the more conservative they became in their method and the less need there was to rescue the infant from a possible fall. With experience, infants began to make "smart" locomotor decisions that required less adult guidance, and parents reported a similar progression at home.

Infants used four different strategies, depending upon their ability. There was the quick glance

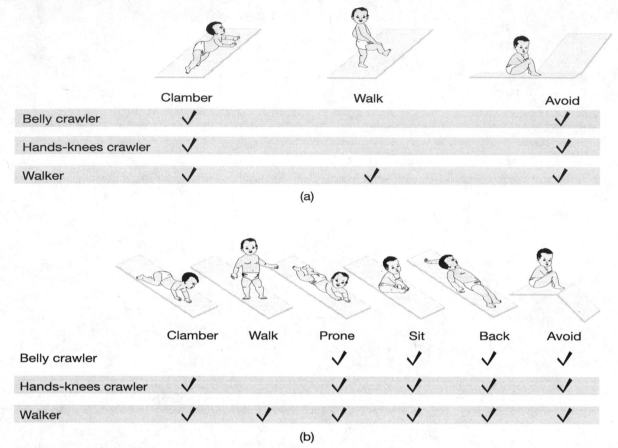

Figure 4.13 Possible locomotor methods for going up and down hills for belly crawlers, hands-and-knees crawlers, and walkers.
(a) 3 uphill, **(b)** downhill

Source: Adapted from K. E. Adolph, Learning in the development of infant locomotion, 1997, p. 51. *Monographs of the Society for Research in Child Development, 62*(3).

followed by a plunge, typically when infants felt the surface was safe enough to proceed. If the glance suggested some difficulty, the infants took a long look while swaying their bodies, then proceeded with their typical method of locomotion. If that did not work, infants took more time to look, and they also touched the slope to check the slant. This was sometimes followed by their typical means of locomotion and sometimes by an alternative means. If these techniques did not work, as a last resort, infants would hold onto the landing and try out different means of locomotion before proceeding. At this point, if they perceived the slope as too risky

they would await a rescue from the adult. If not, they typically chose a sliding method.

The first months of independent walking initiate what some refer to as the toddler period of infant development. The label "toddler" seems to derive from the characteristic gait of the child who has not fully mastered the skill of walking. The earliest forms of childhood bipedalism have a distinct resemblance to a duck out for a jog—a sight that never fails to produce humorous delight in most caregivers.

What accounts for this precarious-looking form of locomotion? When adults walk, both legs are moving at the same time: while one is moving forward, the other moves backward relative to the body. This kind of movement is called *symmetrical gait*. In the gait of toddlers, many steps are symmetrical, but many are also unsymmetrical. This happens because the toddlers often plant one foot and then seem to fall forward onto the other foot in a robot-like walk. Toddlers still have trouble balancing and they need to walk this way to keep from falling.

Thus, while adult walkers are smoothly making every step symmetrical, toddlers have much more variable steps. Smoothness of gait reaches nearly adult levels about 6 months after the infant begins walking, regardless of the age at which the infant started taking steps (J. E. Clark, Truly, & Phillips, 1993; J. E. Clark, Whitall, & Phillips, 1988). If infants are given support by an adult, their variability lessens, and they seem to be better-coordinated walkers. This suggests that balance, not the timing of the limb movements, is the limiting factor (Bril & Breniere, 1993; Clark, Whitall, & Phillips, 1988). Balance improves gradually over time with increases in muscle strength and experience walking (Roncesvalles et al., 2001).

Locomotion has benefits other than the ability to move from place to place. After beginning to walk, 10-month-old infants increase their frequency and duration of social contacts. This occurs whether the walking is supported or unsupported. It appears that an upright infant is more likely to be able to look, vocalize, and smile at adults (Gustafson, 1984).

Even more surprising is that locomotor experience enhances cognitive development. As we will see in Chapter 5, one of the tests typically used to assess cognitive knowledge is the ability to search for hidden objects. Infants with more locomotor experience, who are apparently more accustomed to moving around in the environment, are the most likely to persist in searches for hidden objects. The locomotor experience could be either crawling or assisted walking (Bai & Bertenthal, 1992; Bertenthal, Campos, & Barrett, 1984; Kermoian & Campos, 1988). The development of walking also facilitates the search for hidden objects by blind infants, even though blind infants walk later than sighted infants (Bigelow, 1992). Being able to move oneself through the environment is essential for understanding spatial arrangements and the locations of things in that space.

The motor skill of reaching continues to improve during this period. Between 6 and 8 months, infants discover that they can lean forward to get objects just outside their reach. By 10 months, infants understand the limits of how far they can reach both by leaning forward and by extending their arms. By 12 months, infants are able to use mechanical and social aids to get things out of their reach, such as using a long object to get another or asking an adult for help (McKenzie et al., 1993).

Fine motor development also is intimately linked to cognitive and perceptual development. In one research study (Ruff, 1984), infants at 6, 9, and 12 months were observed while playing with objects that differed in weight, shape, or texture. Infants were handed one object to explore and then given another differing only in one property (for example, two cubes of the same size and weight, one with a bumpy texture and the other with a smooth texture). Between 6 and 12 months, mouthing the objects decreased, while fingering increased. The 12-month-olds also used more actions that were specific to the properties of the object. If only the object's texture was changed, babies increased the amount of time they looked at and fingered the object. If only the shape was changed, looking at and fingering the object increased, but so did rotating the object and transferring it between both hands. Although infants do not finger or look at heavier objects differently than lighter objects, they do use a stronger grip for the heavier ones (Molina & Jouen, 2003).

Related research has shown that by 12 months, infants use touching, listening, watching, and mouthing as alternative sources of information gathering. This involves more than intersensory coordination; it is the coordination of different types of motor skills in the service of directed exploration of objects (Bushnell, 1982; Gottfried, Rose, & Bridger, 1977).

This research shows that by 12 months, infants are using specific actions that are adapted to the type of object they are holding. Motor skill improvements and improvements in the ability to relate information cross-modally (such as between vision and touch) are essential in fostering cognitive development because they put infants into direct contact with more aspects of their world.

Twelve to Eighteen Months

Walking Becomes More Skilled

As we saw, balance is the limiting factor in the emergence of stable walking. A complete sense of balance takes a long time to develop. Walking tends to smooth out and have less of an unstable toddler look about 6 months after the infant begins to walk (J. E. Clark, Whitall, & Phillips, 1988). Around this time, infants begin to show the ability to stand on one foot with help and to walk up and down stairs with help. These skills emerge at about 16 months for the average baby (a range of 12 to 23 months) (Rosenblith & Sims-Knight, 1985). By this age a baby's steps are longer, narrower (more under the hips), straighter, and more consistent (Adolph et al., 2003).

Balance is still an issue in more challenging tasks. Infants can use handrails, and are more likely to use a handrail in situations in which they perceive the need to support their ability to balance (Berger & Adolph, 2003). Babies still need to use crawling for going up and down stairs. When experimenters put a pack of 15% of the infant's weight on the front or the back of a 14-month-old baby, the baby had more difficulty maintaining balance (Garciaguirre et al., 2007).

Infants of this age period begin to adjust their behavior to the type of surface on which they walk. When jogging, for example, people run more slowly and step more carefully on a rocky surface than on a smooth one. They do not wait until they step onto the rocks to slow down. Instead, they use perceptual information about the surface to adjust their steps before they get to the rocks. Do walking infants have the same kind of link between their perception and action?

Several studies suggest that infants can perceive how different types of surface affect their locomotor actions. Infants prefer to walk on matte rather than shiny surfaces. If the matte surface looks like it is moving in waves (the researchers used a water bed), infants shift to crawling (Gibson et al., 1987). They also prefer to walk on rigid compared to deformable surfaces (Toselli et al., 2001). We saw how infants adjusted their locomotor behavior when encountering a sloping surface. Fourteen-month-old infants are able to regulate their locomotor behavior depending upon the steepness of the slope. If they perceived the slope as too steep for walking down, they sat and slid down (Adolph, Gibson, & Eppler, 1990).

These studies show that an awareness of the surface on which one is acting is an essential ingredient of advanced motor skills. As at earlier ages, these skills develop as a complex system between perception, action, and the difficulty of the task. You can experience the differences between your own and an infant's walk with the Experiential Exercises section of Chapter 7 on kinesthetic empathy.

Coordinated Actions with the Hands

The same holds true for fine motor skills. During explorations of different types of toys, year-old infants were placed at either a foam or a hard table. At the foam table, infants did more mouthing and held the object with both hands. At the hard table, infants used each hand differently (one for support and the other for object manipulation, or each hand held a different object), and they used the table to explore the objects by scooting and banging (Palmer, 1989). Babies of this age are beginning to discover what properties of the environment are best suited to support their motor actions. This matching of motor action with the type of surface is essential for operating safely and successfully.

As infants progress in their ability to adapt their skills to the properties of objects and surfaces, they are more able to use objects as means toward goals rather than as goals in themselves. Thus, at the beginning of the first year, we see the emergence of deliberate tool usage in infants. A practical tool infants in many cultures need to use is the spoon. One research team has charted the development of spoon use in the second year of life in detail (Connolly & Dalgleish, 1989). Their work has produced a fascinating story about the developmental unfolding of a skill. They classified different types of spoon grips, different heights at which the spoon was lifted between bowl and mouth, different paths the spoon takes between the bowl and the mouth, and different uses of the opposite hand.

In the first stage, infants take the spoon in and out of their mouths or in and out of their dishes, but these two repetitive cycles are not connected. No food actually makes it from the dish to the mouth. In the second stage, there emerges the outlines of the complete action sequence, but babies are not paying attention to how much food gets onto the spoon. Often the only taste the babies get is the food that manages to cling to the convex surface of the spoon. The movements from the dish to the mouth are jerky, and the spoon is not held in a grip that permits it to contain the food. During these two stages, caregivers need to help feed infants.

By the third stage, the action sequence of moving the spoon from the dish to the mouth now incorporates the function of moving the food. Although still not very efficient, at least the babies are getting somewhere. In this stage, not only is the action sequence functional, but it is correcting itself for errors. Thus, the babies will keep dipping the spoon into the dish until they are satisfied that it is holding enough food. They will also hold the dish steady. Similarly, the infants will continue to put the spoon into their mouths until it is clean. Infants at this stage can also alternate which hand holds the spoon and the type of grip (McCarty, Clifton, & Collard, 1999).

This study shows that spoon use can be a complicated motor challenge for a baby. These developments take 6 to 8 months from the onset of spoon use. The use of other grip tools that are directed toward the self—hair brushes for example—develops in similar ways. Grip tools that are directed toward objects—like a hammer—take longer to learn (McCarty et al., 2001). Successful tool use involves not only making all the right moves at the right time, but also the ability to adjust the movement to correct errors that occur in the process. In mature eating, few errors are made, and if they occur, they are adjusted very quickly.

Eighteen to Twenty-Four Months

Infants' locomotion is so stable that they now prefer to be independent walkers and may resist holding an adult's hand. They easily make the transition from walking to running, so by this age, most infants can run reasonably well (Forrester, Phillips, & Clark, 1993). More experience with self-propelled locomotion also increases the infant's awareness of and memory for spatial locations (Clearfield, 2004). It is not until the third year that infants living in cultures where there are homes with stairs can negotiate them on their own, however. Most 18-month-olds can feed themselves, and most prefer to manage their own food. Self-dressing is well under way by 18 months, and many infants will be able to put on their own coats, shoes, and socks by the time they are 2 years old.

One of the big advances, from a parent's perspective, that is likely to occur at this age is toilet learning. Based on findings from some African countries in which toilet learning begins in the first month of life (see Chapter 8), it is likely that infants have the potential to regulate their bowels and bladders well before they are trained in most Western countries. So why should people in Western cultures wait so long? The reason is that in these African societies, there is almost constant physical contact between the mother and infant, enabling mothers to detect the signs of impending elimination. In societies where physical contact is at a minimum, infants must signal their intentions across a distance. Typically, this means using words. So the trick in Western societies is to help the child associate the need to eliminate with a verbal communication about being taken to the toilet. Toilet learning in industrialized cultures is most likely to begin between 18 months and 3 years, although it may take up to a year to complete (although, see the "diaper- free" movement, www.diaperfreebaby.org).

Another aspect of physical development that concerns parents is the child's sleep patterns. Most infants of this age are still napping during the afternoon, and they can sleep through most of the night. It is not uncommon, however, for infants between the age of 1 and 3 years to wake occasionally at night (Richards, 1977). Out of 77 babies in one study, 29 were waking during the night at 1 year. The style in which parents handled the situation, such as how much the baby was encouraged to "cry it out," did not affect whether the baby woke at night. Families had tried different techniques to handle the problem: verbal battles with the babies; sleep deprivation by keeping the baby awake during the day; and, as a last resort, the modification of parental lifestyles so the parents could spend several hours awake with the baby at 3 a.m.

Since none of these parental methods seemed to change the babies, what accounts for night waking? Babies who woke at night at 1 year had been born after longer labors and were more wakeful—but more fussy—during the first 10 days of life. At 3 years, these same children slept through the night, but it was still difficult to get them to sleep (Blurton-Jones et al., 1978; Richards, 1977). The findings suggest that night waking may result from a biological predisposition. Some infants are night owls, probably from birth or even prenatally, and this pattern tends to persist for many years (Cofer et al., 1999). Although no documented method exists for changing sleep patterns, some methods are available (see above) to train children to sleep independently from parents. These methods, however, do not guarantee that the child will remain asleep throughout the night. It may help parents to know that they do not have the only baby who cannot sleep through the night and that

they are probably not the cause of the problem. Also, it is important to have infants' sleep patterns assessed if they begin to display irregular sleep cycles. This may provide information about the maturity of the nervous system and help to identify infants who are at risk for later disorders (Myers, Fifer, Grose-Fifer, Sahni, Stark, & Schulze, 1997).

Twenty-Four to Thirty-Six Months

From a motor perspective, the third year is an exciting developmental period. Table 4.9 lists some of the motor achievements that occur in the third year. Age norms are not available for all these items, so I list them according to whether they develop early or late in the third year. It is important to remember that there are wide individual differences in the age these skills are acquired, so some children will not be doing all of these things by the end of the third year.

Most infants have developed their adult hand preference by the age of 3 years, although for some infants a stable preference does not finally emerge until the age of 5 years (Hardyck & Petrinovich, 1977; Ramsay, 1980). There is no evidence that left- handed children (about 12% of the population) have cognitive and motor deficits, and it is unjustified on typical developmental grounds to try to encourage children to switch their hand preference (Tan, 1985). Indeed, there may be advantages to being left-handed as studies indicate that the prevalence of left-handed athletes in interactive sports is much higher than in the general population (Aggleton & Wood, 1990; Goldstein & Young, 1996).

Whether right- or left-handed, by age 3, children are drawing squiggles and making simple shapes on paper. Research shows that these early drawings are not usually mirrors of the child's emotional life but reflect the motor limitations of the arm and the hand (Freeman, 1980; Golomb, 1974). Once children begin to draw shapes, they prefer simple ones, such as circles and rectangles. Eventually, these shapes are combined into more

TABLE 4.9   Motor Achievements During the Third Year of Life

	Small Motor	Large Motor
First half of third year	Uses large crayons and pencils. Uses hand gestures and sign language.	Rides large-wheel toys. Walks up and down stairs with both feet on each step. Jumps with two-foot takeoff. Throws a ball 4 to 5 feet. Walks sideways and backward. Runs. Engages in free-ranging movement out of doors.
Second half of third year	Uses building toys with many possible shapes (blocks, Legos, etc.). Uses paints and clay. Hammers.	Walks up and down stairs by alternating each foot. Walks a line, heel-to-toe. Hops 2 or 3 times. Walks a short balance beam. Throws a ball 10 feet. Engages in rough-and-tumble play. Finds route in unfamiliar places.

complex pictures (Goodnow, 1977). The development of one child's ability to copy a square is shown in Figure 4.14. Note that even in the first drawings using spiral forms, there is a crude representation of a square. During the period when Matthew was using the spiral forms shown here, he was also representing human figures with spirals. After he was able to draw the square at 2 years, 9 months, and 13 days, his drawings of human figures began to look more realistic and include facial details. This research shows that children in the third year develop the ability to draw simple visual units (like circles and squares) from which they construct more complex images (Stiles, 1995). Children of this age, then, can make approximate drawings of physical objects. Children of this age can also identify, when asked, what they have drawn and can remember the "content" of their drawing for up to 6 months (Gross & Hayne, 1999). It takes at least another year for children to draw symbolic objects such as letters, words, and graphic symbols like smiley faces (T. C. Callaghan, 1999).

The drawings shown in Figure 4.14 were done when the child was asked to copy a particular figure. Not all the drawings that children produce during this period are meant to represent something in the world, and it is not always appropriate for adults to interpret the drawings as being real or representational. Rather, the child may be using the materials to explore the medium: to discover what kinds of shapes, lines, and colors can be made with this brush or that crayon.

Another aspect of motor development is physical play. During the first 2 years, physical play consists primarily of explorations of the body's abilities, primary and secondary circular reactions, and the child's efforts to acquire new motor skills such as sitting, standing, and walking. These types of physical play are similar to doing Experiential Exercises. During the second and third years, children develop what is called **exercise play**. Exercise play is playful locomotor movement that is physically vigorous, such as running, chasing, and climbing; it may or may not be social. It accounts for about 7 to 14% of behavior in day-care settings for 3-year-old children (Pellegrini & Smith, 1998). Boys tend to engage in exercise play more than girls, and boys of this age have a higher overall activity level than girls (Campbell & Eaton, 1999; Pellegrini & Smith, 1998).

Exercise play appears to have the same sorts of benefits for young children as for adults. It increases fitness, endurance, strength, and skill.

MODEL

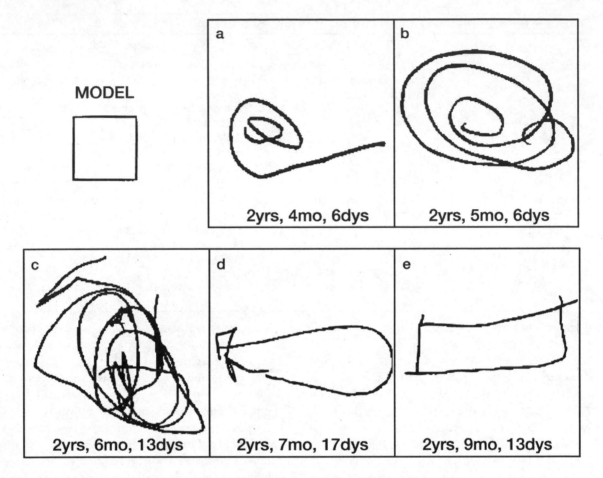

Figure 4.14 Squares Produced by Matthew When Asked to Copy the Square Model
Source: J. Stiles. The early use and development of graphic formulas: Two case study reports of graphic formula production by 2-to-3-year-old children, 1995, p. 132. *International Journal of Behavioral Development, 18*(1), 127–149. Reprinted by permission of the International Society for the Study of Behavioral Development.

There is some evidence that physical play in young children reduces fat and increases the ability of the body to regulate temperature (Thigpen, 2007). Some have suggested that exercise play enhances cognitive ability, but research has not been able to clearly distinguish the effects of exercise play from the effects of just having playground breaks during the more demanding cognitive tasks in day care and preschool. In any case, it is clear that both boys and girls need exercise play for the healthy development of both body and mind (Pellegrini & Smith, 1998).

By the end of the third year, most children have learned how to use the toilet. There are no differences in age of toilet learning depending upon whether a child attended child care outside the home, but girls tend to be trained earlier (on average, at about 35 months) compared to boys (at 39 months) (Schum et al., 2001). Children first acquire words for the potty, to show that they need to go. Flushing the toilet and washing hands were skills learned next. The final level of learning is using a regular toilet, wiping efficiently, and staying dry all night (Schum et al., 2002).

EXPERIENTIAL EXERCISE

Somatic Awareness of the Hands
by Alan Fogel

1. Find a comfortable way to sit in your chair. Close your eyes if you feel comfortable doing that.

2. Feel your body touching the chair. Where does(n't) it touch?

3. Become aware of your breathing, that in fact you are breathing. Now observe the movement of your breath flowing gently in and out, connecting your inner space with the surrounding space. Breath is the connection between inside and outside.

4. Notice where in your body you can feel the breath going. Where can you feel the rising and falling patterns of the breath moving through you?

5. Are there any places where you cannot feel the breath? Any places of tension?

6. Notice the parts of your skin that are clothed versus exposed to the air. Notice the differences in sensation. Which feels more comfortable? Adjust your posture if you need to do that.

7. Notice the sounds in the room and how they are affecting you.

8. Now pay attention to your feet. What position are they in? What part of your feet is contacting a surface? Are your feet relaxed? Can you move your feet so they feel more comfortable?

9. Now, notice your hands. Without moving them, notice the position they are in. Does it feel comfortable or uncomfortable? Does this position feel familiar or unfamiliar?

10. Slowly move your hands to a different position. Does it feel comfortable or uncomfortable? Does this position feel familiar or unfamiliar?

11. Separate your hands if you had them together. Slowly begin to curl and uncurl your right hand. Notice how that feels. Notice if you can feel anything in your arms or shoulders as you do this. Gradually reduce the effort. Compare your right side with your left side.

12. Do the same on your left side.

13. Experiment with using your hands to explore your body, clothing, or the chair. Pay attention to the different sensations. Rest.

14. Bring your hands up in front of your face with your eyes closed and let them explore each other through touch.

15. Open your eyes and look at your hands as if you've never seen them before. Relax your hands and close your eyes again.

16. Slowly come back to your breathing, the room, the sounds, the other people in the room, and open your eyes.

Comments

It takes a while for adults to get used to "dropping down" in a "babymind" state of somatic self-awareness. So, it helps to follow all these steps before focusing on the hands. The instructions are meant to bring your attention to very concrete parts of your awareness, and away from your usual patterns of thought.

Rolling Over
by Eileen Rojas, Modern Dancer

1. Lying on your back, place an object right above your head. Pick it up with your hand and, lying down, move your arm backward and place your object there.

2. Close your eyes and concentrate on your breathing.

3. Direct your internal focus to your abdominal area. Imagine the walls of your abdomen filling up with air like a balloon. You can put a hand on your belly to feel it go up and down with each breath. Feel the air reach all the way to your lower back and pelvis. Feel your back widen into the floor with each breath. Continue.

4. As you do this, think about how babies' movements are initiated from their core (abs, pelvis, stomach). Movements in the arms and legs result sequentially from core movements and a connection between the head and tail.

5. As you continue to breathe deeply, flex your abdominal muscles and then release them. What does it feel like to flex just your abs? Repeat. Do you feel any reactions in other parts of your body? Do you feel a connection between your head and tail because of your abdominal muscles? Rest.

6. Now, as you lie on your back, still breathing, turn your head

toward your right shoulder. Direct your gaze above your shoulder to the object you placed there earlier. Stare at your object for a moment. Babies often stare at the things they want, although they cannot reach them. Rest (30 sec.)

2. Again, shift your head to the right and look up at your item of desire, still breathing. This time as you stare at your item, engage your abdominal muscles. Flex and release them as you did earlier. See if this affects any other part of your body. Rest.

3. Try to imagine a little baby lying on his back looking at something so hard that it takes his head further and further reaching towards his toy making his back arch. Arch back.

4. Once again, shift your head to the right and look up at your object again. Let your focus reach further and further, so far that you can't help but arch your back and start turning to your side. You may feel your hands or your feet trying to assist you, but try to use just your abdominal/core muscles and your head and tail connection to get you to a balanced position on your side. Remember babies' arm and leg muscles are not as strong or developed as their core. Try to refrain as much as possible from using your arms to help you get to your side. What may help you get over?

5. Try to balance on your side as if your body were a seesaw and you want it to remain in the middle without either side touching the ground. Once you figure out how to balance there, release your abdominals and see if you fall forward or backward.

6. Try this a few times, continuing to breathe, reaching for the object, and using the core.

7. This time as you balance on your side, experiment with what may turn you on your belly. You might have gotten there already but this time try to feel the weight of the pelvis. Try to feel how gravity and momentum may affect you, and continue being aware of your core.

8. Once on your belly, rest, breathe, and take an inventory of your body. Take a look at your object.

9. You may notice that one of your arms is under the weight of your chest. Don't just move your arm. Remember, babies aren't that strong. Try to engage your abdominals as you lift your head to create a space under your chest to move your arm through. Again, imagine that arching image and the stretch between the head and the tail that can help lift your torso just enough to swipe your arm through.

10. You made it, you rolled over. Now look and see where that object is. Can you reach it? If you can, grab it. If you can't reach it, how does that make you feel?

Beginning to Crawl
by Mark Reese, Feldenkrais Practitioner

Position and Suggestions: Stand on your hands and knees. You may want to use extra padding under your knees if the pressure on the floor is too uncomfortable. Rest a while on your back after each variation before going on to the next one.

1. In slow motion begin to lift your right knee a millimeter (one-eighth inch) or two away from the floor and return it to the floor. Do not lift your foot, only the knee. Notice how your pelvis shifts over the left leg and then returns to the middle when your right knee returns to the floor. Each time you lift your knee, notice how the weight distribution changes on the two hands. Now, gently lift and lower your left knee just a small amount and return it to the floor. Notice how you shift your weight onto your right knee, and alter the weight on your hands in order to lift your knee. Do everything in slow motion and pause between movements so you can discover the nuances. Alternate lifting one knee and then the other. Which knee is easier to lift? Rest on your back.

2. Bring your knees and feet together to touch each other. Again, lift one knee and then the other just a small amount. Notice how easy it is to lift the knees when the legs are together. Your base of support is now more narrow, so that you are less stable but more movable. Rest on your back.

3. Move your knees very far apart. Again, alternate lifting one knee and then the other, and notice how much more difficult it is. Your base of support is now wider, so that you are more stable, but it is harder to move. Rest on your back.

4. Now experiment with different distances between your knees in order to find the optimum position. Where is the best balance between stability and instability? Rest on your back.

5. Repeat movements 1 to 4 with your hands. Discover how you need to shift your weight and determine the best distance for your hands to be apart. Rest on your back.

6. Now lift your right hand and foot just a small amount, and at the same time see if you can lift and lower them simultaneously.

Discover how you need to balance and shift your weight. Always pause after each movement. Now lift and lower your left hand and left foot. Alternate between lifting the right hand and foot and then the left hand and foot. Which side is easier to lift? Rest on your back.

7. Lift and lower your right hand together with your left knee. How do you need to shift your weight? Now do the other diagonal, lifting and lowering your left hand together with your right knee. Try to lift the knee and hand at exactly the same time. Which diagonal is easier to lift? Which is easier, lifting diagonals or lifting the hand and foot on the same side? Rest on your back.

8. Lift both hands off the floor and move in the direction of sitting on your heels. As you shift your weight back, begin to lift one hand before the other and see which hand you lift first. Rest on your back.

9. Rock back and forward on your hands and knees. Find a comfortable rhythm. Can you find a rhythm that feels connected to the movement of crawling? Do you feel like you are preparing yourself to advance forward? Look around. Does anything in the environment draw your attention?

10. Now begin to crawl forward several steps and then back. Notice the order you use in lifting the hands and knees. If you move the hand and knee on the same side, this is called homolateral crawling. If you move your hand on one side as you move your knee on the other side, this is called the contralateral crawling. As you crawl, experiment with both homolateral and contralateral crawling. Does it change from one to the other when you change direction to crawl either backward or forward? Is it easier to go backward or forward? Many babies go backward first. Can you feel why this is so? If you are confused, maybe you are not yet ready to crawl.

11. Return to the movements in step 1. Is it easier than it was at the beginning? After resting on your back, get up on your feet and walk. Has revisiting crawling improved the fluency of your walking?

SUMMARY

The First Two Months: Motor Development

- The fetal states of rest and activity develop into sleeping and waking states.
- Newborns sleep about 17 hours per day.
- Responsiveness to the environment is related to orienting and defensive responses. Newborns will orient to stimuli of moderate intensity and complexity.
- Reflexes are highly variable within and between infants. Many disappear by about 6 months, while others remain for life. Both brain and motor factors may contribute to the disappearance of reflexes.
- The infant does not grow all at once; different parts of the body grow at different rates and at different times.
- Sucking is a complex activity that can be adapted to the environment.
- Newborn arm and hand movements are directed to objects in different locations and differ between social and physical objects, although detailed videotape analysis is required to observe these patterns.

The First Two Months: Perceptual Development

- Newborn visual acuity and visual processing are poor but improve rapidly during the first 3 months.
- Infants can perceive some meaningful visual patterns, but in most cases, they do not attach meanings to their perceptions.
- Hearing, smell, and taste are more acute at birth than vision, perhaps due to prenatal experiences. Infants can recognize their mothers by sound and by smell.

Two to Five Months: Motor Development

- The most rapid period of physical growth in human life occurs between birth and 6 months.
- Some developmental disorders may be detected from standardized tests of infant motor skill.
- Motor performance depends on the level of brain development, on the complexity of the task, and on the types of supports and resources available in the environment, especially from adults.

Two to Five Months: Perceptual Development

- Acuity and speed of information processing improve in all perceptual modalities between 2 and 5 months.
- Infants can detect color differences and a wide variety of visual patterns. They can perceive the solidity of objects and can recognize them from different points of view and using different sense modalities.
- Infants have a strong preference for looking at faces and at moving objects and are better able to perceive differences between objects if the objects are moving.
- Infants show a preference for infant-directed speech and songs.
- Cross-modal perception is the ability to perceive that different sense modalities give complementary information on the same object.

Six to Nine Months: Motor Development

- During this period, infants learn to locomote by crawling; they can sit alone and pull themselves up to standing. Grasping and reaching are well coordinated.
- Infants have a preferred hand, but their hand preference may change during the first year of life. Hand preference leads to the development of different uses for each hand that are necessary for the acquisition of unimanual reaching and crawling.
- Walking develops after infants gain postural control.

Six to Nine Months: Perceptual Development

- Infants can now perceive objects from visual cues alone, allowing them to process information in pictures and on television.
- Haptic perception is also used to perceive object properties through action.

- Infants can recognize melodies and relate sound patterns to visual patterns.

Ten to Twelve Months

- During this period, infants begin to walk. Balance is the limiting factor in the stability and regularity of their steps.
- The onset of independent locomotion enhances both cognitive and social development.
- Infants' exploratory actions are more coordinated and adapted to the properties of objects.

Twelve to Eighteen Months

- At this age, infants can adjust their locomotor movements to the characteristics of the surface. They will not cross a wavy surface or downward-sloping surface while standing. They perform different actions on objects when the table is hard than when it is soft.
- Spoon use becomes more efficient during this period, including corrections for the amount of food on the spoon and entering the mouth.

Eighteen to Twenty-Four Months

- Motor advances include self-feeding, toilet training, and stable sleep patterns.
- The ability to think about actions without actually performing them develops. Infants can solve some problems mentally, without trial and error.

Twenty-Four to Twenty-Six Months

- Motor skills become more complex and adaptive during the third year, including running, jumping, constructing with blocks, and making art.
- Motor skills become integrated with language and cognition, as language regulates the execution of a motor skill and self-produced movement enhances cognition.

Chapter 5

Cognitive and Brain Development

CHAPTER OUTLINE AND OVERVIEW

Brain Development	*What are the structures and functions of the brain? How does the brain grow during fetal and infant development? How does stress and trauma affect the brain? What is optimal brain development?*
Cognitive Development	*Can newborns learn? Can they imitate? What types of things do infants remember? What type of intelligence do infants have? Are infants aware of objects when the objects are out of sight? What are the developments in conceptualization and categorization? What are some uses of and individual differences in pretend play?*
Development of Self-Awareness	*Fetuses and young infants can recognize ownership of body parts and movements. By the end of the first year, they can distinguish their own from other's intentions. By 18 months they can recognize their image in a mirror and by 36 months, they have a self-concept including a gender identity. How does this development occur and what does it mean for infants and adults?*

Cognitive developmental studies chart changes in the infant's capacity to make sense of the world in both intelligent action (like putting nesting cups together) and thought. For example, a major cognitive change occurs at about the age of six months, when infants begin to form conceptual categories. Infants of this age have been shown to distinguish males from females and adults from children. By nine months, infants are beginning to develop an awareness that objects exist independently from the self. It is only in the latter part of the second year that infants behave as if they are actually thinking, reasoning, and planning actions mentally. Up until this time, the infant could execute a plan of action but had to act out all of the trial and error of the attempt; the infant lacked the mental ability to preselect appropriate courses of action and eliminate others.

The crowning achievement of cognitive development in the first three years of life is the emergence of representational and symbolic thinking: the ability to grasp the idea that a sound or a picture (a spoken or a written word) can represent something entirely different. The written word for "dog" bears no visual similarity to a real canine, nor does the sound of the spoken word "dog." This achievement ushers in a rich new phase of children's development: pretend play and shared meaning with others through language.

The brain develops rapidly during infancy as a result of continual engagement with the world. As children learn new motor and cognitive skills, new neural connections are made that allow the brain to work more efficiently, solve increasingly complex problems, and allow the child to pay attention longer. The brain also grows a different way for each infant as a result of differences in social experiences (Chapters 6 and 8), emotion and attachment (Chapter 7), and whether or not the child is exposed to disease, abuse, poverty, or other trauma (Chapter 9).

This chapter begins with a review of the basics of brain development in infancy. The later chapters also refer back to this section on the brain. This is followed by a review of infant cognitive development and finally a section on the development of infant self-awareness.

BRAIN DEVELOPMENT DURING INFANCY

Brain development in the fetal and infancy periods is becoming one of the new frontiers of developmental research. This is partly due to the rise of new methods for monitoring brain activity (see Research Methods, Chapter 1) that have allowed clinicians to diagnose abnormal brain activity at younger ages and have given researchers a new window on the neural processes that underlie behavioral development. **Neuroscience** is the study of the brain and nervous system as it relates to psychological and behavioral functions such as moving, thinking, and feeling. In this section, the basic structures of the brain that are important during infancy will be covered. This is followed by a review of some of the developmental processes that explain why the fetus and infant are undergoing a critical period (see Chapter 2) for brain development. Finally, the impact of non-optimal infant care on the developing brain is discussed.

Brain Structures and Functions

The human brain can be divided into three basic regions: the brain stem, the limbic system, and the cortex. The **brain stem** at the lower back of the head includes the lower brain stem that connects to the spinal cord, the upper brain stem or medulla that connects to the rest of the brain, and the cerebellum (see Figure 5.1). This part of the brain contains areas responsible for autonomic activities, such as respiration, heart rate, sucking and other reflexes. The **limbic system** is located more or less in the very center of the head, between the ears, and includes structures such as the amygdala, the hippocampus, the hypothalamus, and the pituitary gland (see Figure 5.1). This part of the brain is related to processes such as attention, memory, the regulation of states like sleeping and waking,

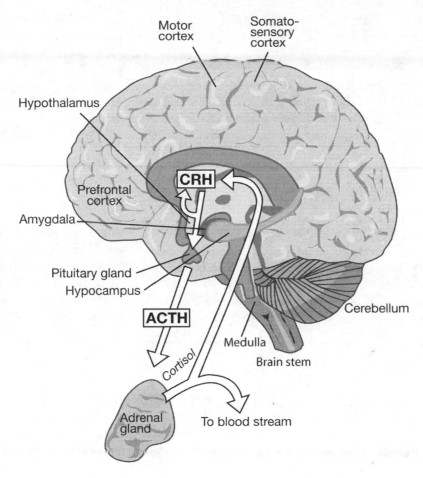

Figure 5.1
Brain Structures that Develop During Infancy

temperature regulation, urinary and bowel control, emotion, and responses to stress and trauma. These two areas are the most functional at birth. Finally, the **cortex** is the outer layer of the brain, the largest part of the human brain, that covers the limbic system and connects with it. The cortex is responsible for perception (the somatosensory cortex), movement (the motor cortex), language, cognition, self-awareness, and most important, the voluntary regulation of behavior and emotion. The **prefrontal cortex** is located roughly above and behind the eyes. It forms a link between the limbic system and the cortex and therefore plays an important role in how the infant learns to regulate states and emotions.

A number of structures within the limbic system are important for infant development. The **hippocampus** is a horseshoe-shaped structure (see Figure 5.1) that plays an important role in the formation of memories for events and sequences, known as **autobiographical memory**. Autobiographical memory is the ability to tell a story in words about oneself, and it does not begin until the third year of life. During the first three years, the immature hippocampus develops links with the language and cognition areas of the cortex. The **amygdala** is a small bulb at the front end of the hippocampus (see Figure 5.1; amygdala means almond in Latin). There are two, a right and a left. The amygdala plays a role in the formation of emotional memories, especially those around fear and safety, and is functional at birth.

Along with the hypothalamus and pituitary, the amygdala is very important in the development of responses to stress and trauma, as explained below. The **hypothalamus** is a small structure in the middle of the limbic system that links the brain to the endocrine (hormonal) system of the body via the pituitary gland. In response to stimulation coming from the body, the hypothalamus begins a cascade of hormones that activate the pituitary gland to release a variety of hormones into the blood stream. The hypothalamus can sense the level of those hormones in the blood and can add more or less stimulation to the pituitary in order to supply what the body needs. The hypothalamus regulates stress, body temperature, hunger, thirst, and day-night rhythms so it is very important in the development of state, feeding, and self-regulation in the newborn period. The **pituitary** is a hormone-producing endocrine gland. It is stimulated by the hypothalamus to produce hormones for stress regulation, maintenance of body state, sexual activity, milk production in nursing mothers, and cell growth throughout the body.

Although all the cells of the cortex have formed prenatally, their connections with the limbic and brain stem regions have only begun to develop. This explains why the infant has some basic emotions like distress, but these emotions are not well regulated. Similarly, the reflexes are semi-automatic and there is little voluntary control over movement at this age. Infants need adults to help them calm down, to obtain food and other objects, and to stimulate them. For this reason, adults and the way in which they interact with infants play a crucial role in how infants develop the connections between the cortex and the other areas. Adults, in other words, play a major part in infant brain development.

Finally, the brain is divided into two halves, or hemispheres. The **right hemisphere** controls movements on the left side of the body. It is also where the majority of social and emotional activity is processed. It undergoes major development during the first two years of life when infants are discovering how to regulate their emotions and form emotional attachments to the primary people in their lives. The **left hemisphere** controls movements on the right side of the body. It is more specialized for thinking and language and develops more rapidly after the first two years of life.

Fetal and Infant Brain Development: A Critical Period

The period from the fifth gestational month through the age of 3 to 4 years is now understood to be critical for the development of the human brain. What happens to the individual during this approximately 4-year period can determine whether the brain grows in a healthy and developmentally appropriate manner, or whether brain growth is compromised in some way. To understand how this process works, it is necessary to take a look at the structure of the neuron.

Neurons are the information storage and transfer cells of the nervous system. The anatomy of the neuron is shown in Figure 5.2. The cell body of the neurons code and transmit information in the form of electrochemical currents, called **action potentials**, that travel from the cell body along the axons to the axon terminals. The **axon** is a nerve fiber that conducts electrical activity away from the cell body. The electrical activity stimulates the production of neurochemicals at the cell junction, the synapse. The **synapse** connects the axon terminals of the transmitting cell to the dendrites of the receiving cell, as shown in Figure 5.2. These neurochemicals, called **neurotransmitters**, of which there are many varieties, such as serotonin and dopamine, signal from one neuron to another processes such as voluntary reflex movements, state regulation, memory, emotion, and pain. Finally, **dendrites** (from the Greek word *dendron*, or tree) are the branching structures that receive information at the synapse from other neurons and transmit it to the cell body.

All processes related to brain development are based in the basic structure of the nerve cells. The brain develops by four basic processes:

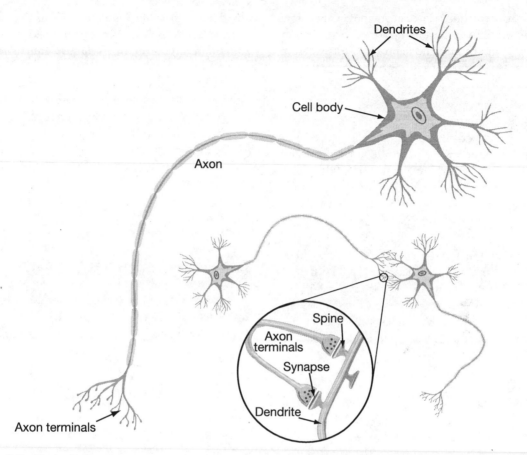

Figure 5.2   Brain Cells

Source: Adampted from Teyler & Chiaia, in *A child's brain* (ed. M. Frank). New York: Haworth Press, 1984.

1. New cells are created via mitosis. Virtually all of one's lifetime supply of brain cells is produced during the prenatal period of development. Although a small number of new neurons are produced by the brain during adult development, following the prenatal period, most of the brain's development occurs by making connections between cells and by "pruning," or selective death of unused neurons.

2. The axons lengthen and the cells migrate to form distinctly different regions of the brain that are connected to different parts of the body. Brain development occurs from the inside out, as cells destined to become part of the motor cortex, for example, send out axons and connections that eventually meet the nerves connected to the muscles that travel through the spinal cord (Greenough, Black, & Wallace, 1987). Neuronal growth and migration are guided by the glial cells, which are the structural cells in the brain that hold the neurons in their place. This process is usually completed by the seventh prenatal month. These first two processes of brain development take place primarily prenatally (Webb et al., 2001).

In addition to lengthening, the axons also become more efficient conductors by developing a kind of insulation called **myelin**. Myelination improves the speed of electrical conduction along the axon by a factor of about three. Myelination occurs most rapidly during the end of gestation and the first few postnatal months but continues throughout life. One-month-olds process information about three times faster than newborns.

3. The postnatal development of the brain involves processes by which the cells become more complex, growing more dendrites and axon terminals and making an increasing number of synaptic connections and neurotransmitters (Webb et al., 2001). This process is called **synaptogenesis**. By 1 year, the child's brain has 150% of the number of synapses as the adult's; this number begins to decline in the second year (M. H. Johnson, 2000, 2003). By the age of 2 years, a single neuron may have as many as 10,000 different connections to other cells (Adinolfi, 1971). These new connections are thought to be related to the rapid behavioral and cognitive developments that take place during the

infancy period. The rapid and differential rate of synaptogenesis in different areas of the brain during the first years of life is shown in Figure 5.3. Note, for example, that the auditory cortex develops earlier than the visual cortex (babies' hearing is better at birth than their vision; see section on sensory development below). These sensory systems develop earlier than the prefrontal cortex responsible for the regulation of emotion (waiting patiently for a meal instead of crying, for example). Note also that brain development continues all through life though at a slower pace than during infancy.

Neuromotor pathways and brain regions already developed at birth, those that prepare the infant for survival, are called **experience expectant** because the brain appears to be ready and waiting for a specific type of environmental input

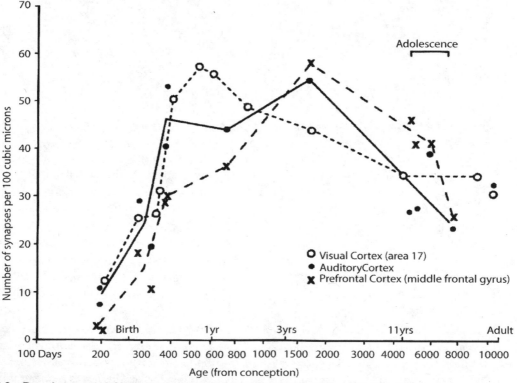

Figure 5.3   Developmental Changes in Synaptic Density of the Human Brain

Source: Adapted from P. Huttenlocher & A. Dabhoklar, Regional differences in synaptogenesis in human cerebral cortex, 1997. *Journal of Comparative Neurology* (4), 387.

(such as pain) for which a particular behavioral skill (such as crying) is best adapted. Many areas of the brain, on the other hand, do not have a specialized function at birth. Some cells and synapses have developed prenatally whose only purpose is to become ready to learn about a particular individual's experiences. These cells and connections are called **experience dependent**. As particular sensory and motor patterns are repeated in early development, specific experience-dependent synapses and cells are used more than others. The synapses that are used the most become strengthened, while those that are used the least eventually die (Greenough et al., 1987; Thelen & Smith, 1994).

In reality, all neurons and neural connections are experience dependent in the sense that they develop at some point in time with respect to the kind of environment to which the infant is exposed (M. H. Johnson, 2000). Cells and pathways that at birth are experience expectant were, at some time during prenatal development, made up of more general cells that were experience dependent. Recall that sucking, which is a well-established experience-expectant pathway at birth, develops out of the tactile and motor experiences of the fetus and requires stimulation and repetition during the fetal period for the neural pathways to become strengthened into an experience-expectant behavior at birth. All during development, as we acquire new actions, the neural pathways become more expectant of skill specific information, which increases the skillfulness of the action.

The developmental changes in numbers of synapses follow a similar course in each of the major areas of the cortex, the part of the brain that controls voluntary actions, including motor skills, perception, and emotion regulation. The number of synapses increases rapidly until birth and then decreases gradually, stabilizing at about the age of 3 years (Goldman-Rakic, 1987).

These changes in cell and synapse development show that the brain's development is highly dependent on the individual's experiences (M. H. Johnson, 2006; Westermann et al., 2007). The brain's construction tailors its development to the experiences of its owner. These neural develop-

mental processes help us to understand how birth defects occur. Alcohol that the mother ingests during pregnancy limits the production of new axons and dendrites (Dow & Reoppelli, 1985), while lead exposure destroys myelin (Lampert & Schochet, 1968). These conditions limit the number of experience-dependent connections and cause information processing to be slower, making for a less adaptive, less intelligent individual.

These results, and others like them, demonstrate the dynamic system of linkages between brain, experience, and behavior. And during the first few months after birth, infants experience stimuli of increasing intensity and complexity, and connections favoring those types of stimuli will be strengthened. By feedback from brain to behavior, the window of sustained attention will widen. As sustained attention allows the infant to inspect and explore specific stimuli, feedback to the brain will correspondingly create connections that make those specific events more easily recognized on subsequent occasions (K. W. Fischer, 1987; Goldman-Rakic, 1987; Hebb, 1949; Thelen & Smith, 1994).

Optimal and Non-Optimal Brain Development During Infancy

One way to interpret the discussion in the previous section is that the human brain is not pre-set at birth for all future experiences. On the contrary, what distinguishes humans from most other animals is the degree to which our brain has a talent for learning new skills and patterns from infancy to old age. **Neural plasticity** is the ability of the brain and nervous system to seek novelty, learn, and remember by continuing to alter the patterns of connections between neurons.

Consider an individual who is blind at birth and for the first few years of life, and then later has surgery to correct the problem. Even though this person now has visual signals traveling from the eye to the brain, he or she still cannot see the world as the rest of us see it. That's because the regions of the brain required to distinguish objects out of light and shadow develop during the first few years.

It is not until 10 months of age that infants can recognize and distinguish one object from another and view it as a separate and permanent entity (see below). Infants who are reared in orphanages with little adult attention, or those who are not exposed to appropriate language experience, will develop severe impairments in social and linguistic function along with brain abnormalities (Nelson, 2007; Paterson et al., 2006).

For most humans with an intact brain, that brain retains a certain amount of plasticity throughout life. Appropriate educational and therapeutic experiences (see Chapter 2) may be able to partially repair the effects of early deprivation. On the other hand, since the brain grows gradually, the older infantile patterns of connection are never lost and a person who "recovers" from early deprivation will never be the same as one who never suffered from that experience. The prognosis for treatment and recovery depends upon the severity of the deprivation.

One area in which we know a great deal about differences in brain development during infancy is the effects of stress and trauma. The evidence is consistent across both human and animal studies. Basically, *each baby in the first two years of life comes to assess the social world as either a safe or a threatening place.* This assessment is not made as a conscious choice, but rather a nonconscious evaluation that comes as a result of encountering and coping with difficult experiences in the company of adults. This nonconscious evaluation of safety or threat is called **neuroception**, meaning that the nervous system makes the decision and not the conscious mind (Porges, 2004).

The neuroception of safety versus threat in the social world creates two very different babies and two very different physiologies. One type of baby feels that the world is a safe place. When threatened, they trust that the threat will pass and that they can consistently rely on the adults in their environment for support, help, and comfort. The other type of baby feels unsafe much of the time. Even when a threat is not present, they show signs of "worry" or insecurity. They are less able to settle down and play alone or with others, and they feel that adult support is not consistent or trustworthy (see section on attachment, Chapter 7). There are three basic patterns of neuroception: immobility, mobility, and social engagement (see Table 5.1).

Neuroception is regulated in part by very rapid and nonconscious processing in the sympathetic and parasympathetic nervous system. The **sympathetic nervous system** prepares the body for action by elevating heart rate, increasing metabolism, and temporarily suppressing growth functions such as digestion. The **parasympathetic nervous system** allows the body to relax, slow down, rest, process information, engage socially with others, learn and grow. One of the nerves of the parasympathetic system, the vagus nerve, is the one most responsible for neuroception (Porges, 2004).

Neuroception is also regulated by the hormonal system via the brain, particularly by the links between the hypothalamus, pituitary gland, and adrenal gland (located on top of each kidney, near the middle of the back), called the HPA Axis. The **HPA Axis** is the system by which the neuroception of stress is translated into the release of

TABLE 5.1 Three Forms of Neuroception

Social World	Type of Neuroception	Characteristics
Threatening	Immobilization	Freezing, feigning death, behavioral shutdown, dissociation from the body
Threatening	Mobilization	Fight or flight behavior, increased heart rate, slowed digestion and growth
Safe	Social engagement	Relaxation, emotional engagement and regulation, appropriate challenges, growth

Source: Porges, S. W. (2004). Neuroconception: A subconscious system for detecting threats and safety. *Zero to Three,* 24(5), 19–24.

hormones from the hypothalamus to the pituitary (via corticotropin-releasing hormone CRH), from the pituitary to the adrenal gland (via adrenocorticotropin-releasing hormone ACTH), which results in the secretion of the hormone cortisol into the blood stream (see Figure 5.1).

Cortisol, like the sympathetic nervous system, prepares the body for action in response to stress. It increases blood sugar needed for action and, via the blood, feeds back into the limbic system, where it heightens the formation of memories related to the stressful event. On the other hand, prolonged activation of cortisol due to ongoing stress suppresses the immune system and physical growth. If stress is persistent, either prenatally or postnatally from maternal stress or depression, or postnatally from lack of consistent, loving, and appropriate care and disturbances in social interaction, cortisol is overproduced because the infant's well-being is threatened. In small amounts the body needs cortisol, and some cortisol is normally present during the waking day. In large amounts, cortisol is toxic to the brain, as shown in Table 5.2 (Eichenbaum & Cohen, 2001; Field et al., 2006; Gunnar & Cheatham, 2003; Herschkowitz et al., 1997; Keenan et al., 2003; Schore, 2003).

When cortisol returns to the hippocampus and amygdala via the bloodstream, it can alter their structure. Since these are the two areas where memory is formed, cortisol not only changes the neurotransmitters and receptors as well as the connections between the limbic system and the rest of the brain, cortisol also changes the way early experiences are remembered. Too much stress leads to a tendency to feel fear and threat in the future, even when the future situation is not necessarily fearful to an outside observer. It also leads to post-traumatic stress syndrome (PTSD), a decreasing ability of the individual to cope with the stress (mediated by the right prefrontal cortex) in appropriate ways, creating a person who is more likely to freeze (shut down and become unresponsive in severe cases), fight (tantrums, resistance, negativity), or flee (hide or withdraw) when they feel threatened. We will return to the topic of PTSD in later chapters, especially around the topics of infant attachment (Chapter 7) and infant mental health (Chapter 9).

In summary, the first three years of life is a critical period for brain development. When people think of brain development, they are most likely to think about cognitive development and the role of the cortex. Research shows, however, that infancy is not a critical period for cortical and left-brain processes like reading, math, thinking, or musical ability. These abilities develop after the age of 3 years and continue throughout life. Infancy is a critical period for the development of the limbic and prefrontal parts of the right brain—that regulate attention, emotion and attachement—all of which are fundamentally and crucially dependent upon the quality of love, emotional sharing, and social engagement received and perceived by the infant. Without a healthy right brain, it is difficult to develop a healthy left brain later. *It is considerably more important for infant brain development for parents and other adults to spend quality one-on-one and family time with a baby—playing together, sharing the baby's*

TABLE 5.2 Effects of Stress on the Developing Brain
The overproduction of cortisol due to stress changes how the brain develops

Amygdala	Hippocampus	Prefrontal Cortex
Increase in CORT receptors in amygdala lead to a bias to detect fear and anxiety, PTSD, health risks	Decreased receptors for CORT in the hippocampus lead to decreases in the ability to self-regulate responses to stress, overproduction of CORT, adrenal fatigue	Impaired cell growth decreases ability to self-regulate emotions and self-awareness, and impairs ability to form secure attachments

Sources: Eichenbaum, H. & Cohen, N. (2001). *Memory systems of the brain*. Oxford University Press; Gunnar, M. & Cheatham, C. L. (2003). Brain and behavior interface: Stress and the developing brain. *Infant Mental Health Journal, 24*, 195–211; Schore, A. (2003). *Affect dysregulation and disorders of the self*. New York: Norton.

delight in the world, doing normal caretaking, and providing a sense that the world is safe and secure when the baby feels distressed—than letting the baby play for long periods with expensive toys, or listen to Mozart, or watch baby TV programs, all of which are marketed to parents on the (false) presumption that they help the infant's brain to develop (see discussion of smart toys, below).

COGNITIVE DEVELOPMENT

The ability to think conceptually, using words or symbols, does not begin until the middle of the second year of life. Newborns and young infants, however, possess a number of ways to process information that are collectively referred to as cognition. These processes include learning and memory, orienting and habituation, and imitation. These functions are related to the development of the limbic and prefrontal areas as they are linked to sensory and motor cortices and a growing integration of function across the brain. In this part of the chapter, we review infant cognitive development as a function of ages: 0–2 months, 2–5 months, 6–9 months, 10–12 months, 12–24 months, and 24–36 months. Each of these developmental periods bring new cognitive skills.

The First Two Months: Can Newborns Learn?

The answer to this question is most certainly yes. We have already reported that in late pregnancy, fetuses are capable of learning certain sound patterns, such as songs, and can recognize their mother's voice. This means that fetuses not only learn to distinguish the sounds, but also remember the differences when they hear the sounds weeks later, after they are born, implying that they also have a memory of what they learn. Newborns have important limitations on their learning ability, however. Perhaps a better way to ask the question of whether newborns can learn is to ask under what conditions they are most likely to learn.

Newborns can learn by classical conditioning (see Chapter 2), at least under the specific circumstances of a certain type of research study.

Researchers used the unconditioned response of rooting and sucking to the unconditioned stimulus (UCS) of a sweet fluid in the mouth. The presentation of the sweet fluid was paired during training with a light stroking of the infant's head (the conditioned stimulus, or CS). After training, the infants rooted and sucked to the stroking stimulus in the absence of the sweet fluid. In addition, when the sweet fluid was removed entirely, the babies rooted and sucked to the stroking, but they also cried, showing that they had learned a connection between the stroking (CS) and the sweet taste (UCS) (Blass, Ganchrow, & Steiner, 1984). Classical conditioning may be possible when the UCS evokes a powerfully rewarding natural response, such as a sweet taste. This may explain the common observation that after a few days of feeding experience, newborns will root and suck at the sight of a nipple, even before they begin to taste the milk. If no milk comes out, they will cry or fuss.

Operant conditioning is much easier to demonstrate in the newborn. Recall that the conditioned sucking procedure (Chapter 1) involves the operant conditioning of infants to alter their sucking rate in the presence of particular sounds or pictures (DeCasper & Fifer, 1980) or syllables (Jusczyk, 1985). Head turning can also be conditioned successfully (H. Papousek, 1967). Once the infants learn the connection between their behavior and the reinforcement, they can signal their preferences with the "correct" sucking rate or head turn direction.

These studies of operant conditioning show that newborns can remember the link between their behavior and its consequence long enough to complete the experiment on that day. Suppose, however, that you trained a week-old infant to suck for the sound of her mother's voice by increasing her sucking rate. Now, if you bring the same baby back to the laboratory on the following day and put her in the experimental setting with no further training, will she remember the training and begin to suck at a faster rate?

This kind of procedure is the basis for most studies searching for infant memories. Do babies under 2 months of age remember what they learned 24 hours ago? It is very likely that they may remember under certain conditions, although not enough research has been done on this age group. Babies of this age seem to remember the sound of their mother's voice and some of her characteristic odors. When a group of mothers was asked to repeat the same word 60 times a day each day to their babies who were between 2 and 4 weeks of age, the infants recognized the word after delays of between 15 and 42 hours (Ungerer, Brody, & Zelazo, 1978). Perhaps the key to establishing a long-term memory in the newborn is a great deal of repetition, rather than a single exposure. Below, we will review research showing that by 3 months of age, infants can remember things, even from brief exposures, up to 2 weeks later.

If newborns respond to something as if it is familiar, this shows that they can remember it from previous encounters. Newborns are more attracted to familiarity rather than novelty. Unlike older infants, who seem to prefer novelty, newborns prefer the sound of their mother's voice, the smell of their mother's milk, and the sight of their mother's faces (Lock, 2000). They will also choose a familiar face from a set of faces and a familiar sound from a set of sounds (Barrile, Armstrong, & Bower, 1999).

Habituation in the First Two Months

Another form of infant learning and short-term memory is habituation. Like conditioned sucking, habituation is a reliable response that is used as the basis of a number of infant testing procedures (see Chapter 1). Recall that habituation is the gradual decline in the strength of a response following repeated presentations of the same stimulus. For example, if you live on a noisy street, you eventually habituate to the noise; that is, you no longer notice it on a regular basis. If some new element is added to the noise, for example, a siren or the screech of brakes, this is enough to renew your interest in the street noise. This renewal of interest is called *dishabituation* or *recovery*.

Researchers have found evidence of habituation in newborns' motor and heart rate responses

to auditory stimuli (P. R. Zelazo, Brody, & Chaikan, 1984), visual stimuli (Slater, Morison, & Rose, 1984), and tactile stimuli (Kisilevsky & Muir, 1984). In addition, habituation can be shown in premature newborns (Field, Dempsey, Hatch, Ting, & Clifton, 1979). In one study, infants born without a brain cortex (anencephalic) did not habituate to noise (Brackbill, 1971), while other studies have found heart rate response habituation to an auditory stimulus in such infants (Graham, Anthony, & Ziegler, 1978).

In summary, studies of learning and habituation in newborns show that some simple forms of learning take place between the late fetal period until about 2 months of age, after which the infant's ability to learn expands. These rudimentary learning abilities may be mediated by the cortex, but they also could be built into the brain stem structures of the brain as basic survival mechanisms or into the limbic system if they have emotional relevance (pleasure or distress). These simple learning and memory processes are fundamental to the survival of newborns. The recognition of maternal sounds and smells orients the newborns to their primary resource for survival. Learning how to orient themselves to and approach sources of food (sweet fluids and milk) and how to avoid noxious smells and tastes on future exposures seems so fundamental to survival that a brain stem mediation of such responses is quite plausible. More sophisticated forms of learning and cognition—complex associations, long-term memory, categorization, and inference—must await the further development of the brain's cortical connections and the enhanced acuity of the senses.

Imitation in the First Two Months

A final area of newborn cognition that we will discuss is imitation. Piaget believed that newborns lacked the cognitive skills to imitate. He thought this ability began only at 8 or 9 months of age. Studies have shown, however, that infants can indeed imitate under certain conditions. Researchers studied 12- to 21-day-old infants' abilities to

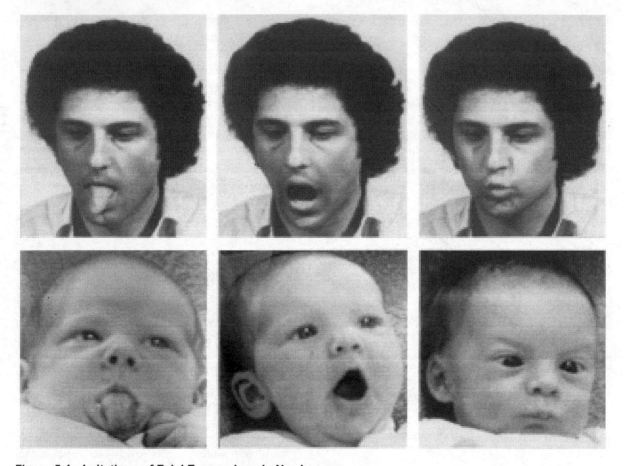

Figure 5.4   Imitations of Fcial Expressions in Newborns

Sample photographs from videotape recordings of 2-to-3-week-old infants imitating **(a)** tongue protrusion, **(b)** mouth opening, and **(c)** lip protrusion demonstrated by an adult experimenter.

Source: A. Meltzoff & W. Moore, Imitation of facial and manual gestures by human neonates, 1977, p. 77. *Science*, *198*, 75–78. Copyright © the American Association for the Advancement of Science. Reprinted by permission of the publisher and the author.

match tongue protrusion, lip protrusion, mouth opening, hand opening, and hand closing (A. Meltzoff & Moore, 1977). In this study, each infant was shown a series of gestures made by the same adult. If the infant could reliably produce the same gesture following the adult's display of that gesture, compared with following the adult's display of another gesture, imitation could be inferred. The researchers found that infants were much more likely to demonstrate a particular gesture following the modeling of that gesture than at any other time (see Figure 5.4).

A number of replications of this study have been successful in producing correct matching of gestures in very young infants. Another study found correct matching of tongue protrusion and hand-opening models, but it also found that other stimuli could evoke the same responses in the newborns. Moving a ballpoint pen toward and away from the infant's face in the same manner as a tongue might move in and out was also successful in eliciting tongue protrusion in infants. A dangling ring elicited hand opening and closing. It was concluded that the infants were not imitating a particular gesture as much as they were imitating a movement pattern or responding with some oral exploratory behavior (S. W. Jacobson, 1979; S. S. Jones, 1996).

Other work shows that infants do match expressions. During the demonstration of the surprise face, newborns showed more wide eyes and wide mouth opening. During the demonstration of the sad face, they had tight mouths, protruded lips, and furrowed brows. During the happy-face demonstration, infants had more wide-lip expressions. Matching was more likely to occur during the middle trials, suggesting that it is not due to the immediate arousal of the visual display nor is it a reflexive response. These possibilities could be true only if the infants imitated on the first few trials (Field, Woodson, Greenberg, & Cohen, 1982).

Other replications of this work have reported imitation of head movement (A. Meltzoff & Moore, 1989), lip widening and lip pursing with a sample of Nepalese newborns (Reissland, 1988), and tongue protrusion and mouth opening. Infants who imitated more at birth gazed away from their mothers less during social interaction at 3 months, suggesting that early imitation reflects a possible social receptivity (Heimann, 1989).

On the other hand, some teams of researchers have failed to replicate the findings (Koepke, Hamm, Legerstee, & Russell, 1983; B. McKenzie & Over, 1983). One view is that although there is a slightly elevated probability of the baby displaying the modeled gesture, in fact, all babies display a wide variety of gestures following the model; furthermore, there are wide individual differences between babies (Anisfeld, 1979). In another study, newborns showed wide, attentive eyes to both mouth opening and tongue protrusion but imitated only the tongue protrusion, suggesting to the authors that the effect was not imitation per se but rather heightened general arousal (Anisfeld, Turkewitz, Rose, Rosenberg, Sheiber, Couturier-Fagan, D., et al., 2001).

Thus, although the evidence is in favor of some form of newborn imitation, the response is fleeting and hard to detect. Its occurrence in any form reflects a rather remarkable capacity of the immature human brain and perceptual system to process information and reflect it back to the outside world. Like the simple abilities for learning and habituation, even occasional imitative responses are likely to orient the caregiver in a positive way toward the infant and enhance the probability of an early parent-infant attachment.

For newborns, imitation may be a way of relating to people by establishing a connection of similarity between the baby and another person. Even as adults, we are drawn to people that we perceive as being like us in some way. Imitation is a nonverbal way of establishing this social connection. In one study, not only did newborns imitate the adult's tongue protrusion model, the newborns initiated tongue protrusion as if to get a response back from the adult. The imitation response showed a different pattern of heart rate change compared to the initiation response, suggesting that each type of tongue protrusion felt different to the infants (Nagy & Molnar, 2004).

Six-week-old infants were exposed to an adult who modeled mouth opening and tongue protrusion, which the infants imitated. Then after a delay of 24 hours, the infants saw the same adult once again. Without the adult doing anything, the infants spontaneously produced the imitative response they had learned the day before (A. N. Meltzoff & Moore, 1994). Copying another person as a way of knowing and connecting with them can be seen in later behaviors such as taking another person's point of view, following another person's lead, and letting oneself be influenced by a role model (A. N. Meltzoff & Moore, 1997). It is remarkable that newborns have the rudimentary ability to connect with other people in this way.

Two to Five Months

In Chapter 2, the information processing view of cognition was discussed in terms of different steps: perceiving, habituating, learning, and remembering. A number of important developmental changes take place in these areas between the ages of 2 to 5 months. Another way to think about cognition is not as separate information-processing steps but as a unified approach to understanding and acting in the environment. This approach is more typical of Piaget's theory of cognitive development in infants (see Chapter 2). In this section, we first discuss the developments in habituation and memory as examples of information processing and then describe Piaget's views on infants of this age.

Habituation Between 2 and 5 Months

From the ages of 2 to 5 months, infants improve in their speed of information processing, due in part to rapid changes in myelination and the experience-dependent formation of synapses, and in part to an increasing ability to focus attention on familiar types of tasks. While a newborn could take as long as 5 or 10 minutes to habituate to a repeating stimulus, by 3 months of age, infants typically habituate within 1½ to 2 minutes. By 6 months, this time drops to half a minute (Bornstein, 1985). Like all cognitive and perceptual tasks, the speed of information processing also depends on the complexity and difficulty of the stimulus and on the infant's alertness at the time of testing.

There are individual differences in the speed of habituation. Infants who are fast habituators at 3 months are more likely to be fast habituators at 6 months (Colombo, Mitchell, O'Brien, & Horowitz, 1987; Mayes & Kessen, 1989). Infants who are faster habituators tend to have parents who stimulate their ability to focus visual attention (Bornstein & Benasich, 1986). Slower habituators are more likely to have perinatal risk factors: illness, malnutrition, and poor state control (Bornstein, 1985; Moss, Colombo, Mitchell, & Horowitz, 1988). Faster habituators are more efficient in their information processing (Colombo, Mitchell, Coldren, & Freeseman, 1991; Frick, Colombo & Saxon, 1999). Thus, speed of habituation may be used as an early index of cognitive differences. Although these individual differences seem to be fairly good predictors over a period of 4 or 5 months, they are not likely to predict long-term differences in cognitive development.

Long-Term Memory Between 2 and 5 months

We saw above that infants have short-term memories lasting several hours or days right from birth.

By 3 months, infants can remember situations for up to 2 weeks, as was shown using a contingent learning procedure (Sullivan, Rovee-Collier, & Tynes, 1979). Babies were placed supine in cribs with brightly colored mobiles suspended overhead. Experimenters decided beforehand that they would move the mobile if the baby kicked with either the right or the left foot (but not with both feet). The mobile was moved more the harder the infant kicked, thus increasing the speed of conditioning. On the initial training day, the babies were given about 15 to 20 minutes of training. Then the babies were brought back to the same laboratory a few days later and placed in cribs without any further training. Infants who were tested less than 2 weeks after training managed to repeat the same leg movements they learned during training, although the longer the delay between training and testing, the longer it took the infants to remember to kick in a particular way. After a delay of longer than 2 weeks, infants behaved as if they had never seen the mobile.

If infants are retrained at intervals shorter than 2 weeks, the memory can be reactivated for an indefinite period (Rovee-Collier, Enright, Lucas, Fagan, & Gekoski, 1981). In another study, infants were given a reminder by showing them a mobile 24 hours before 2 weeks had elapsed since their original training. If the mobile was moving, the infants remembered their earlier training when tested the next day, but if the mobile was stationary, the infants could not remember their initial training (Hayne & Rovee-Collier, 1995; Rovee-Collier, Evancio, & Earley, 1995). On the other hand, giving the infants a reminder by showing them a cloth of the same color that had draped the crib during training was just as effective as the moving mobile in helping them to remember the earlier procedure as much as 4 weeks after training (Hayne & Findlay, 1995). These studies suggest that infants can remember for an indefinite period, so long as they continue to receive nonverbal reminders of the early situation (Rovee-Collier & Barr, 2000).

Infant memory, however, is very specific to the situation in which the initial learning occurs. When babies are retested in different cribs, in the same cribs with different colored bumpers, or with different mobiles, they are less likely to remember the event (Butler & Rovee-Collier, 1989). When infants are retested with different odors in the room or with different music playing, they are also more likely to forget the training (J. Fagen et al., 1997; G. B. Rubin, Fagen, & Carroll, 1998). These findings suggest that familiar, routine environments may be important for infant memory at this age, as they begin to develop a sense of permanence and stability of the world and what to expect from it. The findings also show that infants pick up visual, auditory, and odor cues that become part of the memory for them.

On the other hand, lack of stability in the environment may have negative consequences for cognitive development. Crying and the negative emotion associated with it seem to create a kind of amnesia for experiences associated with the crying (J. W. Fagen, Ohr, Singer, & Klein, 1989). Using a similar mobile-kicking contingent procedure, during training the experimenters substituted a mobile with only 2 components for one with 10 components. Some of the infants cried as a result of this change; others did not. The infants who cried were not able to reactivate the kicking technique to the 10-component mobile even 1 week later. The infants who did not cry when the mobile was changed could easily reactivate the kicking.

Apparently, the emotion associated with a learning situation becomes part of the memory, as do the specific sights, sounds, and smells of the surrounding environment in which the training takes place. This suggests that infants remember whole situations, rather than specific events. These memories can last indefinitely with periodic reminders, but over time, novel aspects of a repeating situation may become integrated into the memory. These findings suggest that infants of this age have a sense of **self-history,** the experience that the past can be connected to the present by means of recreating one's own actions in similar situations.

These findings call for reevaluation of the common observation that people do not remember their experiences as infants, a phenomenon known as **infantile amnesia**. To remember specific infantile experiences, one would have to be in almost exactly the same situation and the same emotional state as during the original experience. Since older children and adults are unlikely to ever be in exactly the same kinds of situations as when they were infants (primarily because their perceptual, cognitive, emotional, and physical abilities have all changed), they are unlikely to be able to retrieve early memories for specific events (Hayne & Rovee-Collier, 1995).

On the other hand, people may in fact have memories of early infancy, but because it is difficult to replicate the exact context, they may be unable to locate the memories in a specific time and place (Rovee-Collier & Barr, 2000). In one study, children who were 2 ½ years old were retested in a procedure that had required them to reach for objects in the dark when they were 6 months of age. Compared to infants who did not have the experience at 6 months of reaching in the dark, the children who had the experience were better at the task at 2 ½ years, even though it is unlikely that these children remembered the actual experience of doing this when they were 6 months old (Perris, Myers, & Clifton, 1990). In a similar study, 2 ½ year olds who had experienced a "still face" experiment (when the adult stops interacting and just stares at the baby; see below) when they were 5 months old looked less at a photo of the person who had done the still-face compared to two other photos. Other 2 ½-year-olds who did not participate in the experiment at 5 months showed no preference between these faces (Bornstein et al., 2004).

These studies of infant memory provide support for the idea of *participatory memories* (see Chapter 2) of early infancy, reported by people during somatic awareness and psychotherapeutic encounters. It may be possible to reexperience a feeling, an odor, a body posture, or a pattern of movement without remembering a specific time or place when it first occurred. Even though the specific time and place cannot be remembered, these memories seem to come from a very early period in one's life. When older individuals have memories in which a sense of familiarity is coupled with amnesia for how, when, and where the memory was acquired, such memories may "feel" baby-like. You may feel something similar while doing the Experiential Exercises.

Piagetian Perspectives on Cognitive Development

The findings on the holistic and integrative way in which infants remember support the theories of Jean Piaget (refer to Chapter 2). Piaget viewed infant actions as adaptations to the environment that involve the whole infant; motor, cognitive, and emotional aspects are interconnected. During the newborn period, which Piaget called Sensorimotor Stage I, the majority of the infant's actions are in the form of semi-automatic reflexes. The infant uses reflexes (such as rooting, sucking, and grasping) to adapt to the environment, but reflexes are not rigid and mechanical. Even reflexes can be accommodated to a particular situation, as in sucking on different-shaped nipples or displaying stepping movements only when lying supine.

During the period from about 1 to about 5 months, which Piaget called Sensorimotor Stage II, infants begin to act more purposefully. They are able to recognize the connections between their behavior and events in the environment, as we saw in the research related to making mobiles move when kicking. We know from some studies that even newborns can recognize the connections

between their behavior and the environment. For example, infants can be trained using conditioned sucking techniques to suck in a particular way to hear their own mother's voice. However, it takes a long time to train newborns to do this and the training is not always successful.

By 2 to 3 months, the ability to recognize simple connections between behavior and its effect is very well established and can be seen in almost everything the baby does. Piaget noticed this in each of his own three children—Laurent, Lucienne, and Jacqueline. As they discovered the relationship between their behavior and its effects, they would repeat the same behavior many times and often with great delight. Observations 5.1 and 5.2, taken directly from Piaget's observation notes, describe how Laurent at 2 months and 21 days of age repeatedly bends his head back to look at his crib. At about the same age, Lucienne repeatedly coughs for the "fun" of it.

Piaget called these repetitive movements *circular reactions*. During Sensorimotor Stage II, the circular reactions described in the box are called **primary circular reactions**. Primary circular reactions are repetitive movements in which the infant focuses on his or her own actions. In some cases, the actions involve other objects (like kicking to get a mobile to move), and in other cases, they involve the infant's own body. The infants at this stage do not appear to be interested in the object for its own sake.

Observations

Stage II Behavior (Piaget, 1952, pp. 70, 79)

Observation 5.1

At 0;2(21), in the morning, Laurent spontaneously bends his head backward and surveys the end of the bassinet from this position. Then he smiles, returns to his normal position and then begins again. ...

Observation 5.2

In certain special cases the tendency to repeat, by circular reactions, sounds discovered by pure chance, may be observed. Thus at 0;2(12) Lucienne, after coughing, recommences several times for fun and smiles. Laurent puffs out his breath, producing an indefinite sound. At 0;2(26) he reproduces the peals of his voice which ordinarily accompany his laughter, but without laughing and out of pure phonetic interest. At 0;2(15) Lucienne uses her voice in similar circumstances.

According to Piaget, *the meaning of a particular object or person to the infant is the action and experience the child brings to it.* For example, a rattle means "graspable, seeable, suckable." During this stage of sensorimotor development, the rattle is not yet "an object to be grasped, seen, or sucked," for that kind of conceptualization of the rattle as object would require that the infant understand the object as if observing it from outside the self, which does not begin until 9 months of age. In Stage II, the "object" is "known" simply by the actions that can be performed on it. Infant actions are not intended to explore the object's properties, but rather to experience their own behavior and its effects. This suggests that infants during this period are developing a sense of **self-agency,** the feeling that they are a causal agent that can successfully affect their own bodies and the environment.

Later in Stage II, infants begin to combine different primary circular reaction schemes into more unified behavior patterns. An example of this is the development of visually guided reaching at about 4 months. Piaget viewed this as the integration of vision, arm, and hand actions: the baby somehow makes the connection between seen objects and his or her own actions. These observations are consistent with the finding that babies of this age have the ability for cross-modal perception, and that their memories are integrated wholes of sights, sounds, smells, and movements. This suggests that infants have a sense of **self-coherence,** the feeling that they and the objects around them are integrated wholes that have distinct boundaries.

One aspect of self-agency and self-coherence at this age is the experience of contingency (see Chapter 2). Two-month-olds are capable of discovering contingencies, and one study has shown that the babies enjoy it. In a study done by Watson (1973), the movements of a mobile were linked to infants' head presses on an automatic pillow. If the infants discovered that the mobile would move with respect to their head presses, they usually smiled and cooed. In contrast, if the pillow was "capricious" and inconsistently rewarded head presses, infants became frustrated and distressed. Other research shows that infants are more likely to display these emotions when people behave contingently than when objects behave contingently (Legerstee, 1997).

Once a contingency is discovered, infants come to expect or anticipate a similar pattern in the future. Infants of this age prefer to interact with strangers who have been trained to respond with the same kinds of contingencies as the infant's mother (A. E. Bigelow, 1998). Related research has shown that if infants are exposed to a visual series of repeating events, they can anticipate the likely next event in the sequence (Canfield & Haith, 1991; S. W. Jacobson et al., 1992; Wentworth & Haith, 1992).

These findings have implications for the kinds of experiences adults should provide for infants during Piaget's Stage II. If babies realize that their environment is controllable—that their own actions will produce predictable responses in the people and objects around them—they will show increasing positive involvement with the world. If the environment is capricious, infants will become distressed, angry, and withdrawn or simply uninterested (Watson, 1973). It is important, therefore, for adults to adapt their behavior to be responsive to infants so the infants will gain a sense of efficacy that will lead to further exploration. In early infancy, exploration, cognition, and motor behavior are all part of the same underlying developmental process.

The primary circular reactions create powerful motivations for babies to become engaged in the environment. They especially enjoy when adults create highly ritualized and repetitive situations as in feeding, playing, bathing, and diapering. A limitation of babies of this age is that they do not enjoy deviations from the routines, which makes it difficult for them to adapt quickly to new caregivers. Even though Piaget integrated motor, perceptual, cognitive, and emotional aspects of the infant, he failed to recognize the role of adults in supporting infant development. Even before infants can reach for and manipulate objects, adults bring objects into view, manipulate the objects in appropriate ways (like shaking a rattle and turning a ball around), and place them into the babies' hands (see the earlier discussion of supports and resources for motor development in this chapter). We return to these interactive systems processes in the chapter on social and language development (Chapter 6).

Six to Nine Months

Memory Between 6 and 9 Months

During the period from 6 to 9 months, the infant's brain continues to develop. Studies using kicking to make mobiles move have shown that infant memory during this period is similar to memory at 3 months. However, while 3-month-olds can remember how to produce mobile movements for up to 14 days, 7-month-olds can remember for as long as 21 days without a reminder (Hill, Borovsky, & Rovee-Collier, 1988). In the previous section, we saw how 3-month-olds required the exact duplication of the original learning situation in order to remember something. By 7 months, their memories are somewhat less context dependent, meaning that infants can remember a salient event that has been learned in several different but related situations. Infants of this age have more control over reactivating their own memories and do not have to rely entirely on contextual cues (Amabile & Rovee-Collier, 1991; Bhatt, Rovee-Collier, & Weiner, 1994). Infants also can remember longer sequences of events, like longer melodies or longer sequences of flashing colored lights on electronic toys (Bahrick et al., 2002; Ross-Sheehy et al., 2003).

Although the memory of infants of this age is improving, it is still limited and localized to the situation, at least compared to that of a preschool child or an adult. Nevertheless, one can begin to see the seeds of more lasting participatory memories. The fact that infants can remind themselves means that they are beginning to take a role in creating their own self-history that transcends particular situations. By 6 months, therefore, infants take a more active role in the processing of information.

Increasing Use of Concepts to Organize and Process Information Between 6 and 9 Months

This increasingly active information processing means that infants in this age period are able to group different stimuli into higher-order conceptual categories. Using a habituation procedure, researchers showed babies a series of pictures of the same face in different poses. During the test trial, the infants dishabituated to an unfamiliar face but not to the same face in a different pose. This shows that the babies had organized all the different poses they saw into a higher-order concept of a particular face. Seven-month-olds, but not 5-month-olds, were able to do this (L. B. Cohen & Strauss, 1979). In a similar type of study, 7-month-old infants were habituated to different faces having the same facial expression (a smile). They dishabituated to a different face with a non-smile expression but not to a different face with a smile expression (R. F. Caron, Caron, & Myers, 1982).

In an interesting variant of this procedure, infants were familiarized with somewhat distorted versions of a prototype figure (Younger & Gotlieb, 1988). A **prototype** figure is one that is the clearest example of the form being represented. If infants are actively organizing the images of the distorted figures into a category, then they should prefer to look at a related prototype compared to an unrelated prototype, in a test trial in which both are available to look at. Infants who were familiarized with the "plus sign" distortions preferred the "plus sign" prototype at ages 3, 5, and 7 months. Only 7-month-olds could recognize the prototype from the distorted versions.

Because of their ability to perceive objects as whole entities, infants of this age are beginning to relate objects together into higher-order classifications. Seven-month-olds, for example, can distinguish horses from some other four-legged mammals such as cats, zebras, and giraffes (Eimas & Quinn, 1994). Infants develop motor categorizations for objects, grouping them into things shakable, drinkable, squeezable, and so on (Baldwin, Markman, & Melartin, 1993; Bushnell &

Boudreau, 1993; Catherwood, 1993). By 9 months, infants can distinguish these object properties visually as well as haptically (Coldren & Colombo, 1994).

Infants of this age are able to judge whether objects are too big to fit into containers, when shown objects and containers of various sizes (Aguiar & Baillargeon, 1998). They understand that moving objects should follow along their prior path of movement and that larger objects can support smaller objects (Baillargeon & De Vos, 1991; Baillargeon, Needham, & De Vos, 1992; Sitskoorn & Smitsman, 1995). Infants will respond differentially when the same object is placed above as opposed to below another object, showing that they have a category for these kinds of spatial relationships (Quinn, Cummins, Kase, Martin, & Weissman, 1996).

Infants of this age may even have a concept of number or quantity of objects. Infants were habituated to a puppet jumping in the air either two or three times. They dishabituated when the number of jumps changed, from two to three or from three to two (Wynn, 1998). Piaget discovered that his children had a sense of quantity at 11 months of age when he tried to get them to imitate sounds (Piaget, 1952, p. 241). If Piaget said "papa," Laurent replied with "papa." If Piaget said "pa," so did Laurent. By adding more "pa" syllables, Piaget discovered that Laurent had trouble with more than three. Saying "papapa-papapa" only got a "papapapa" in return. Other research found that 10- to 12-month-olds could easily discriminate visual arrays that differed only in number, particularly for one versus two objects, one versus three objects, and two versus three objects. They had a harder time with four versus three objects, and no luck at all discriminating four from five objects (M. Strauss & Curtis, 1981; Wood & Spelke, 2005). Studies like these show that infants of this age have a concept of quantity—more versus less—but they do not prove that infants of this age know numbers and can do math problems. That ability begins in the third year (Brannon et al., 2006; Mix, Levine, & Huttenlocher, 1997; Xu et al., 2005). All of the infant's rudimentary categorical abilities will develop rapidly after 9 months.

Piaget's Third Sensorimotor Stage: Secondary Circular Reactions

The infant's growing abilities to perceive and conceptualize the properties of objects were also noticed by Piaget. Beginning at about 4 months and continuing until about 8 or 9 months, infants pass through Piaget's third stage of sensorimotor development: the stage of **secondary circular reactions**. This stage is a natural extension of the preceding one. Instead of only repeating actions that they discover by chance on their own bodies (the primary circular reaction), infants soon begin to repeat actions that, by chance, produce some effect on the objects and people in the environment. The idea of *chance*—the fortuitous discovery of some interesting result—is what distinguishes this stage from the ones that follow. Once the chance discovery is made, however, infants make deliberate, intentional attempts to repeat that action.

In a primary circular reaction, babies repeat a movement of their own bodies but do not make the connection between that movement and its effect. The movement creates a good feeling (a sound or a sight), but the babies seem focused on the efforts of their own bodies. In secondary circular reactions, babies are focused more on the objects in the environment. They not only repeat actions that produce effects on objects; they also vary the actions in order to explore changes in the effect. Piaget (1952) suggested that infants are trying to "make interesting sights last."

Babies between 6 and 9 months will drop objects off the edge of their high chairs, perhaps listening for different sounds or looking at different movements when the objects hit the floor. They shake objects in different ways to notice the effect or repeatedly dump things (such as their food) out of containers.

Infants in this period tend to apply the movements they use for particular objects as a way of representing or referring to the object (see Obser-

Observations

Stage III Behavior (Piaget, 1952, pp. 187, 195)

Observation 5.3

Laurent: at 0;4(21) has an object in his hands when, in order to distract him, I shake the hanging rattles which he is in the habit of striking. He then looks at the rattles without relinquising his toy and outlines with his right hand the movement of "striking."

Observation 5.4

At 0;7(10): Laurent cries in the morning as soon as he hears his mother's bed creak. Until then, although awake, he did not show his hunger. But, at the slightest creak, he moans and thus demands his bottle.

vation 5.3). When Piaget shakes his son's rattles, Laurent at 4½ months is too busily engaged in playing with the toy he is holding to actually strike his rattle. He seems to indicate the potential action by making a striking movement in the air. Instead of saying verbally, "Those are my rattles," Laurent expresses himself through a motor movement that has the exact form of his previous interactions with that object.

At the same time, repeated occurrences in the environment take on meaning for the baby (see Observation 5.4). By 7 months, Laurent knew that he would be fed shortly after he heard his mother's bed creak. Earlier in his life, he would cry with hunger as soon as he woke up. Now he cries in relation to certain environmental events that have come to have a meaning for him. Like the act of "pretend" striking, the cry is a motor way of saying, "That's the sound of my food!"

These observations suggest that infants are becoming more intentional and goal directed, and also that they can perceive the intentional behavior of other people. Nine-month-old infants were shown an actor grasping first one toy and then another. They were also shown an actor touching one toy with the back of her hand and then touching another toy the same way. The infants looked longer when the grasping hand contacted the second toy than they did when the actor touched the second toy with the back of her hand (Woodward, 1999). This suggests that infants are more interested in actions of other people that seem to have a clear goal.

Out of Sight, Out of Mind?

Another aspect of conceptualizing objects is whether infants believe that objects have a permanent existence. **Object permanence** is the ability to remain aware of an object even after it has gone out of sight. Piaget (1952) showed that infants will not actively search for an object that has been hidden until after the age of 9 months, during Stage IV. Can infants at a younger age keep track of a visually hidden object in a setting that does not require the use of the motor skills that Stage III infants do not have?

Given what we know about the memory of infants under 9 months, it seems quite likely that they should be able to remember objects when they can no longer see them. In one study, infants aged 7 to 8 months saw an object sitting on one of two red placemats that were 8.5 inches (21.5 centimeters) apart. Next, two purple screens big enough to hide the object were slid in front of the placemats (see Figure 5.5). A hand then reached behind the screen and reappeared holding the object in either a possible situation or an impossible situation (Figure 5.5). Infants looked longer at the hand following the impossible situation compared to the possible one, showing that they remembered the object's location and were surprised when the object appeared from behind the screen opposite that behind which they had seen it placed (Baillargeon & Graber, 1988). In a similar study with infants of the same age, this time with their parents present in the room, the infants

Possible event

Impossible event

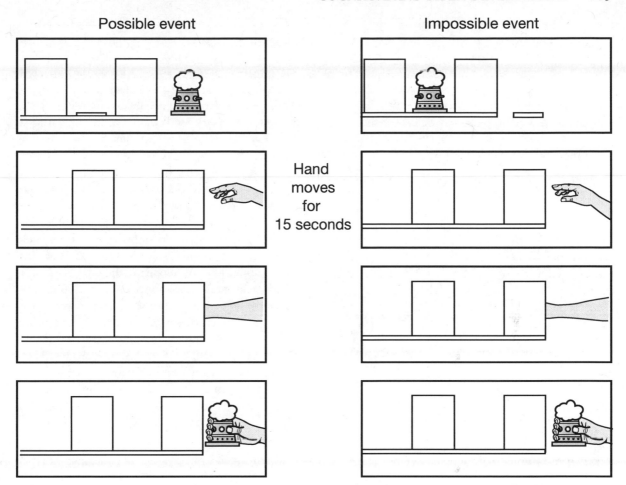

Hand moves for 15 seconds

Figure 5.5   Sequence of Events Used in an Object-Permanence Task

Source: Adapted from R. Baillargeon & M. Graber, Evidence of location memory in 8-month-old infants in a nonsearch AB task, 1988, p. 505. *Developmental Psychology, 24*, 502–511. Copyright © American Psychological Association. Reprinted with permission.

not only looked longer at the impossible situation; they also looked more at their parents as if to share their puzzlement (Walden et al., 2007).

This type of research has been repeated for different kinds of visual events in which objects appear and disappear in possible and impossible ways. Infants between 3 and 7 months come to understand that objects seen in the light will still be in the same place when the lights are turned off (Clifton et al., 1991; Clifton et al., 1994). In one study, infants were shown an object falling and making a noise on impact, after which they were allowed to reach for the fallen object. Next, the lights were turned off. When the infants heard the

sound of the impact, they reached for the object in the dark at the same location (Goubet & Clifton, 1998; McCall & Clifton, 1999). Generally speaking, if infants have prior exposure to the situation in which the object is to be located, their memory abilities at this age allow them to search for the object in the correct location (Bojczyk & Corbetta, 2004; Marcovitch et al., 2002).

In summary, infants between 6 and 9 months are becoming aware of objects and people and whole entities. They can appreciate that objects have features and boundaries, that they occupy unique locations in space, and that they do not disappear when out of sight. The same is also true for infant's conceptions of people. People, however, are understood by infants as having intentions. The ability to perceive another's intentions corresponds with the infant's awareness of their own intentions, their ability to have an effect on the environment. We will return to this topic in the section below on the sense of self at this age.

Ten to Twelve Months

Conceptualizing Relationships Between Objects and Events

By the age of 7 months, infants are just beginning to understand that objects exist as whole entities, and they are starting to categorize objects on the basis of their similarity to a prototype. By 10 months, infants are beginning to discover the relationships between objects, between people and objects, and between people. This can be seen, for example, in the development of **relational play**. Relational play is action that demonstrates a knowledge of the relationships between two objects, for example, putting lids on pots, cups on saucers, or spoons in cups (Fenson, Kagan, Kearsley, & Zelazo, 1976). The more perceptually distinct the two objects, the more likely it is that babies will combine them correctly (Bates, Carlson-Luden, & Bretherton, 1980). For example, if a box and its lid are different colors, infants will be more likely to see how they go together. Also, if the adult places the lid of the box on a table positioned near the top of the box, rather than near the bottom, babies are more likely to put the lid on the box in an appropriate manner. Year-old infants can tell the difference between a visual display of a block that enters an opening of a box and one that rests precariously on the rim of the opening (Sitskoorn & Smitsman, 1997). These studies suggest that infants understand how different objects may be related to each other. A block is supposed to go inside the opening rather than rest on the rim. Infants of this age are also able to perceive the relationship between a tool and its use. Infants first saw a toy sitting on the far end of a long piece of cloth. The near end of the cloth was pulled by an experimenter, moving the toy closer to the experimenter. Next they saw the toy sitting next to the cloth. In one instance the cloth was pulled and the toy did not move closer (as expected) and in another instance the cloth was pulled and the toy moved closer (an impossible event). The infants were surprised when seeing the impossible event, suggesting that they understood the relationship between the cloth tool and the object being retrieved (Schlesinger & Langer, 1999; Sommerville & Woodward, 2005). In another variant of this procedure, infants watched one puppet (the giver) give a flower to another puppet (the receiver). When the two puppets' positions were reversed, the infants still expected the original giver puppet to continue being the giver regardless of physical location (Schöppner et al., 2006).

Forming relationships between objects can also be seen in studies in which infants were placed in front of a tray containing different groups of identical objects, for example, four identical human figures, four balls of the same color, and four identical toy cars. Six-month-olds pick up the objects in random sequence, even though they can visually distinguish the different types of objects in a standard habituation procedure. By 12 months, infants will pick up three or four identical objects in a row before going on to pick up other objects. About 40% of 12-month olds will take those identical objects and place them in a new pile by themselves (Starkey, 1981). By 10 months, infants are able to classify pictures of animals (dogs versus cats), male versus female faces, and plants versus kitchen utensils (Furrer & Younger, 2005; G. Levy & Haaf, 1994; Mandler & McDonough, 1998; B. A. Younger & Fearing, 1999). The ability of infants of this age to categorize objects is related to their familiarity with those objects rather than to some abstract ability to categorize objects (McDonough & Mandler, 1998; Oakes, Coppage, & Dingel, 1997).

Infants of this age are also able to perceive the relationship between a prior event and a subsequent event, that is, between a cause and an effect. Infants can understand that when one toy car hits another toy car, the second one should move as a result of the collision (L. B. Cohen & Oakes, 1993). They also understand the relationships between faces and voices, that a male voice belongs with a male face and a female voice belongs with a female face, or that a toy when squeezed should make a sound (Perone & Oakes, 2006; Poulin-Dubois et al., 1994).

The Emergence of Infant Intentional Action between 10 and 12 months

In these studies, infants are acting as if their object play has particular goals, such as combining objects in a meaningful way. This deliberate combination of different actions into a unified pattern of behavior suggests that infants are intending to act in this way. This is different from what occurred in earlier periods, when infants first discovered actions by chance and then repeated those actions as primary or secondary circular reactions. This intentional and deliberate form of action is what Piaget (1952) called the *coordination of secondary circular reactions*. In Observations 5.5 and 5.6, Jacqueline's pushing away of her parent's hand shows how the infant can combine different actions with each hand to achieve a goal.

Notice that to perform these deliberate actions, the infant must relate two simpler secondary circular reactions, such as holding the toy in one hand and pushing the adult away with the other. Infants are also relating two actions when they search for hidden objects. In order to find an object that they see being hidden behind a barrier or a cover, infants have to move the barrier with one hand and grasp the uncovered object with the

other hand. Younger infants remember the hidden object's location, although they do not reach for the object once it is out of sight. Piaget found that by 10 months, infants will readily search for the hidden object and seem delighted to find it under the cover.

Now suppose you have two identical handkerchief-sized pieces of colored cloth on a table at which you are sitting opposite the infant. You engage the infant with an attractive toy, such as a set of colored keys, and then you hide the keys under one of the pieces of cloth. Infants 10 months and older, but not younger, will lift the cloth to retrieve the keys. Now suppose you take the keys back from the baby and hide them under the other piece of cloth. Infants younger than about 15 months typically will look under the first piece of cloth and will not persist in looking under the second piece of cloth to find the object even though it was hidden in their plain view! This is easy to demonstrate with a year-old infant, if you want to convince yourself that babies could actually make such an obvious error.

This mistaken search for the missing object is called the **A-not-B error** by infancy researchers. The infants who find the object at location A, the first location, cannot find the object at location B, the second location. This error has aroused the curiosity of many infant researchers. Why does it happen? It seems as if infants lose the intention to find the object after more than one hiding.

According to Piaget, the infants act as if part of their definition of the object includes its location. In other words, infants do not yet conceive

---

Observations

Stage IV Behavior (Piaget, 1954, p. 219)

Observation 5.5

At 0;8(8) Jacqueline tries to grasp her celluloid duck but I also grasp it at the same time she does. Then she firmly holds the toy in her right hand and pushes my hand away with her left.

Observation 5.6

At 0;8(17) after taking the first spoonful of medicine, she pushes away her mother's hand which extends to her a second one.

When an object is hidden, young infants often act as if it does not exist anymore.
Photo by Elizabeth Crews.

of a whole independent object as you and I might. Rather, infants define the object as the "keys-under-the-cloth," or the "ball-under-the-chair." This sort of thing also happens to adults. Most of us have had the experience of meeting someone briefly, say, at a party, and then failing to recognize the same person in another location, such as the grocery store. If we encountered that person at another party at the same place, we would have no trouble recognizing the individual.

Following Piaget's elegant first experiments and his contextual explanation, there have been a number of seemingly contradictory results. First of all, it should be noted that by 9 months, infants are almost 100% correct in reaching for hidden objects at the A location (Wellman, Cross, & Bartsch, 1986). Second, if objects are displaced at several different locations without being hidden or if objects are hidden under transparent covers, so long as the infants are first familiarized with the covers and objects, they are almost 100% correct in reaching for the object in either location, A or B (Butterworth, 1977; Yates & Bremner, 1988). The only case in which this is not true is if the object or the infant is moved along complex paths with

many twists and turns (B. Landau & Spelke, 1988). This suggests that following the path of a moving object in space is not limiting the infant's search when the objects are hidden.

Memory of the hidden object cannot be a problem for 9-month-olds, as shown by the studies of Baillargeon, in which 8-month-old infants remembered an object's location so long as they did not have to act on it. It appears, then, that infants of this age already have a concept of objects as existing when out of sight, and they do not appear to associate objects with particular locations, since they will directly search for the object in multiple locations so long as they can see the object.

The A-not-B error is made most frequently when the object is out of sight, but even then, infants succeed under certain conditions:

1. If there is no delay between the hiding and the opportunity to search for the object, they can find it. Errors are increased if infants are restrained for at least 3 seconds after the object is hidden at location B (Diamond, 1988; Diamond & Doar, 1989).

2. If the infants are shown the object being hid-

den in the A location multiple times, they are more likely to search in the B location (Marcovitch & Zelazo, 1999).

3. If the infants are allowed to lean their bodies in the direction of the hidden object, they can sometimes find it even after a delay by following the direction of their lean (Diamond & Doar, 1989).

4. If the objects are hidden under covers that are perceptually very different, it is easier for the infants than if the objects are hidden under identical covers (Bremner, 1978).

5. It also helps if the infants are familiar with the objects or if the objects are interesting to them (Munakata, 1997). They will search more readily for their hidden mothers than for an unfamiliar person or a large object (Bigelow, MacDonald, & MacDonald, 1995).

The A-not-B error is not a serious deficit for infants, and they overcome it within a few months or if the objects are presented in ways that facilitate their search, as described above. The importance of the A-not-B error lies in questions it raises for understanding human development. Development offers many examples in which the emergence of a new skill (like searching for hidden objects) is accompanied by a curious but not serious deficit (like being unable to search in more than one hiding place). When we discuss language development in Chapter 6, we will encounter another example, called *overgeneralization*, which occurs when children begin to make grammatical errors after they have seemingly acquired the correct rule. Developmental researchers would like to better understand why these patterns occur.

Imitation Between 10 and 12 Months

Imitation is another skill that requires making a conceptual relationship between two actions, in this case, between another person's actions and one's own. The imitations of newborns occur only for acts that they can already do. Observing an adult doing the same types of acts increases the probability of the newborn's selecting a similar act. However, newborn imitation is slow and does not happen for all infants. Six-month-olds can imitate actions that they have not done before, but only if you give them many demonstrations and allow them plenty of time to process the information (Kaye & Marcus, 1978). Between 10 and 12 months, infants become more proficient at imitating actions that they see for the first time or have not done before.

Typically, babies are better at imitating actions that are close to what they can already do. Nine-month-old infants can imitate simple actions on objects such as opening a box, shaking a toy rattle, and pushing a button. In addition, when the same babies were shown the objects 24 hours later, they reproduced the actions that had been modeled previously (A. Meltzoff, 1988). Imitation that occurs following a delay from the time the action is observed is called **deferred imitation**. Deferred imitation also shows that infants can remember the relationships they learn, at least for a short time. If infants are allowed to imitate the action immediately, they can remember and imitate after longer delays compared to infants who were only allowed to watch and not imitate the action (Lukowski et al., 2005).

Individual Differences in Cognition and Attention Between 10 and 12 Months

The basic trends in cognitive development discussed in this chapter have been found to occur at about the same ages in different cultures around the world (Agiobu-Kemmer, 1986). On the other hand, within any group there are individual differences in the age of attainment of cognitive milestones and in the quality of cognitive abilities.

One important component of cognition is the ability to attend to objects for a long enough time to remember their locations, watch their paths of movement, or learn about their properties during exploratory play. Individual differences in the duration of sustained attention to objects have been found at the age of 1 year (Power, Chapieski, & McGrath, 1985). Infants who can sustain attention for longer periods engage in higher levels of exploratory play (Caruso, 1993; L. Fenson, Sapper, & Minner, 1974) and score higher on developmental tests of mental and motor abilities (Kopp & Vaughn, 1982; Ruff, Lawson, Parrinello, & Weissberg, 1990).

What factors account for individual differences in attention? To some extent, these differences may be related to differential development of the brain and may be partly constitutional (Rothbart & Posner, 1985). We will return to evaluate this explanation in Chapter 10. On the other hand, differences in the caregiving environment have been shown to influence the quality of infant attention.

When mothers are trained to enhance their object-related behaviors during social play with infants—by demonstrating object properties, pointing to and naming objects, and questioning—the complexity of the infants' exploratory play is enhanced (Belsky, Goode, & Most, 1980; Tamis-LeMonda et al., 1992; Tomasello, 1995). Actually, this effect works best for infants who have short attention spans. Their duration of attention increases following an intervention in which adults work to point out object properties and refocus the infants after a loss of attention, while the duration of attention for high-attending infants does not change following the intervention (Lawson, Parrinello, & Ruff, 1992; Parrinello & Ruff, 1988).

Another approach to the study of individual differences in cognitive ability is to assess the infant's mastery motivation. **Mastery motivation** is an inherent motivation to be competent in a particular situation, and its measurement involves persistence in solving problems. At 12 months of age, persistent goal-directed actions on objects are typically followed by the expression of smiling or laughter by infants (McTurk, McCarthy, Vietze, & Yarrow, 1987), suggesting that persistence is in fact motivated by a goal and that the achievement of the goal results in positive feelings of efficacy.

Like adults' effects on infant attention, adult object-related behavior increased the level of mastery motivation only for 12-month-olds who were rated as being temperamentally low in activity. For infants who were highly active, parental intervention had no effect or an interfering effect on the

infants' mastery (Wachs, 1987). Thus, more active infants are less in need of adult encouragement and intervention in their play than less active infants.

These studies suggest that adults can play important roles in the cognitive development of infants, particularly if their actions are designed to enhance the infants' attention to objects and their properties. The adults need not so much teach or reinforce as support the infants' own initiatives and help the infants to regulate their limited attention spans. A similar pattern of parental support also enhances word and language learning. These results also suggest that adult behavior needs to be adapted to the individual infant. Babies who are less active and poor attenders may need a more involved adult to help organize their play. Babies who are more active and attentive may have different needs for adults, perhaps needing them to be an appreciative audience to whom the infants can show off their self-directed achievements.

In summary, infants of this age are making the discovery that objects and events are related to each other. They can combine objects according to their function (lids on pots), their category (trucks versus cars), or how they need to be combined to achieve a goal (using a fork to get food). As we shall see, this ability to form mental relationships between things is related to important developments in emotion, communication, and the sense of self.

Twelve to Twenty-Four Months

The period between 12 and 24 months encompasses Piaget's Stages V and VI of sensorimotor development. As Observations 5.7 and 5.8 show, infants in Piaget's Stage V are not merely using familiar means to achieve their goals: they are creatively inventing new ways of doing things. This is the stage that Piaget called **tertiary circular reactions**, the beginnings of active experimentation and the search for novelty. In the previous stages, infants were most comfortable in familiar settings and were most likely to use the means they had discovered—largely by chance—to handle situations that arose. In Stage V, children become able to adapt to brand-new situations, both by using tried and true methods and by seeking out and discovering new methods of acting upon the environment. Stage V is sometimes called the stage of trial-and-error behavior, since infants attempt new combinations of action schemes until they find the one that will solve the problem.

A characteristic behavior of infants at this age is experimenting to discover new ways of doing things. It is almost as if they are aware of themselves as a persistent part of the series of actions in the experiment, a manifestation of their growing subjective self. Infants discover that a distant object can be retrieved by pulling the blanket on which the object sits, or they find new ways to open containers. They try to figure out which objects best fit into particular containers. Unlike the previous stage, in which infants tried out new means to reach a single goal, babies in this stage seem to have multiple goals, and they examine the techniques available to determine which are best suited to the particular goal they have in mind at the moment and which are better suited to other goals.

In the previous stage, the infant was able to find a hidden object if the adult showed the baby where the object was being hidden. The baby often was fooled, however, if the adult moved the object in plain view to a new location. The Stage V infant is no longer so easily tricked. So long as the object can be seen moving from one place to another, the baby can follow the path of the object and find its hiding place, even after a long series of moves or after a 24-hour delay (Moore & Meltzoff, 2004). This accomplishment implies that the infant has an increased awareness of space and an increased cognitive ability to comprehend longer periods of time.

In the area of imitation, the infant is able to model acts that are completely different from those seen before. This flexibility allows the toddler to become a very good copycat. The baby will try to imitate complicated actions done by an older sibling or a peer without having much understanding of the reason for those actions. These are the origins of role play and dramatic play, both of which will take on increased significance after 18 months, when the infant will begin to understand what it means to play a role and get vicarious experience by so doing. Babies between 12 and 18 months are simply having fun copying. Often babies will copy to get a laugh out of the person being copied rather than to try on a role for size (see the later discussion of this behavior).

Imitation has been used as a way to study infants' understanding of the world and their memory skills. Before the age of 1 year, infants are beginning to understand that other people have intentions. In one study, 14 to 18 month olds watched adults operate simple tools, such as one in which a party favor appears after pressing a lever. Sometimes the adult said "There!" (intentional action) after pressing the level and other times "Whoops!" (accidental action). Infants

---

Observations

Stage V Behavior (Piaget, 1952, pp. 269, 285)

Observation 5.7

At 0;10(11) Laurent grasps in succession a celluloid swan, a box, etc., stretches out his arm and lets them fall. He distinctly varies the position of the fall. Sometimes he stretches out his arm vertically, sometimes he holds it obliquely, in front of or behind his eyes, etc. When the object falls in a new position (for example on his pillow), he lets it fall two or three more times in the same place, as though to study the spatial relation; then he modifies the situation.

Observation 5.8

At 0;10(27) seated on her bed Lucienne tries to grasp a distant toy when, having by chance moved the folded sheet she saw the object sway slightly. She at once grasped the sheet, noticed the object shake again and pulled the whole thing toward her.

were twice as likely to imitate if the action was intentional, showing that they use intention to make sense of adult behavior. They are not, in other words, simply reproducing a mechanical action but acting for a purpose, the same purpose observed in the adults (Bellagamba & Tomasello, 1999; Carpenter, Ahktar, & Tomasello, 1998; Carpenter, Call & Tomasello, 2005; Sodian et al., 2007). In other studies, 12-month-olds were more interested in a toy the experimenter reached for inside of a transparent box than in the box, also showing that the infants seemed to understand the purpose of the adult's reaching (Woodward & Sommerville, 2000).

Imitation has also been used to demonstrate how infants of this age remember. During the first year, memory is nonverbal and participatory. Infants under 1 year can remember how to kick to make a mobile move, remembering the task in action. Can infants older than a year remember a task they observed but did not actually perform? Researchers have found that infants as young as 13 months can do this, but the infants' "descriptions" of what they saw are given by means of imitation.

An infant of this age period is shown a teddy bear, a blanket, and a book, and the experimenter enacts a scene of putting the teddy bear to bed. A week later, given the same materials, the child will reenact the sequence of pretend events (Bauer, 1996; Chen, Sanchez, & Campbell, 1997; Hanna & Meltzoff, 1993; A. Meltzoff, 1988). Infants will remember for longer if they are given multiple demonstrations and if they can imitate the demonstration immediately. In addition, children of this age will spontaneously use words as they are reenacting the original event, commenting on their own actions in a way that suggests that verbal memories are beginning to form around the nonverbal participatory memories (Bauer, 1996).

These memory studies once again reveal that under the appropriate conditions, we do not observe infantile amnesia. When infants are tested using familiar objects and events, when they are allowed multiple exposures, when they can enact the sequence in action rather than in words, and

when there are reminders, they can recall events for long periods of time. This age period is also a transitional period for infant memory. In the next period, infants begin to have verbal-conceptual memories. It is difficult for the older infant and child, however, to translate the earlier participatory memories into conceptual memories. Thus it may seem that most people "forget" their infant experiences.

Finally, infants develop more advanced categorization skills during this period. Recall that in the first year, infants could understand the relationships of particular examples to a simple category, such as faces, birds, or geometric figures of a certain prototypical shape. A simple categorization task is to recognize different sizes and shapes of birds as belonging to the category "bird." A higher-order task is to be able to group birds, fish, lions, cats, and dogs into an "animal" category. Experiments have shown that by 15 months, infants can correctly form higher-order categories for familiar objects. They can classify animals together, but they will not include cars with the animals (Oakes, Plumert, Lansink, & Merryman, 1996; Roberts & Cuff, 1989).

Symbolic Play Between Twelve and Twenty-Four Months

Somewhere in the middle of the second year, infants begin their transition from Piaget's Stage V to Stage VI. Piaget has referred to the sixth and final stage of infant sensorimotor development as *the invention of new means through mental combinations.* In the previous stage, the infant could experiment with new ways of making things happen. However, all this trial and error happened in the sphere of real action. The child had to actually do all the alternatives to get to the goal.

All this changes in Stage VI, because children no longer have to physically carry out the actions: they can think about the possible paths to a goal, eliminate the most improbable ones, and only then act. According to Piaget (1952), the child's first thoughts are internalized action sequences. Babies now can find objects after any number of visible

Exploring objects that are challenging to understand leads to a sense of mastery and personal competence. Exploratory play also contributes to cognitive development. At this age, play becomes more symbolic and includes pretending.
Photo by Nancy Sheehan/PhotoEdit.

or invisible displacements; they can go around a detour to get at something.

At the heart of all forms of human thought is the **symbol**, a representation of a thing or event that is conventionally shared among the members of a community. A road sign is a symbol of what lies ahead, such as a curve or a steep hill or an intersection. A word is a symbol for the object it represents. A plastic bowl can be used for eating, or it can be used symbolically when a child pretends that the bowl is a hat or a boat. By 18 or 20 months, infants understand that the symbolic object (the bowl) is not the same thing as the thing it represents (the hat or the boat), or that a pretend snack is not the same as a real snack (Lilliard & Witherington, 2004; Younger & Johnson, 2004).

Symbols appear only gradually in children's repertoires. At first, children represent objects by performing some action related to the objects and physically similar to the represented objects, like moving one's open hand through the air to represent an airplane or a bird (Ungerer et al., 1981). Later, symbols become arbitrary, in the sense that the form of the symbol bears no physical resem-blance to the thing it represents. The word "airplane," for example, neither looks nor sounds like an airplane. Words as verbal symbols are arbitrary in this sense, but they are also a form of **conventional communication**: how and when they are used in communication is not arbitrary but bound by the rules of meaning and grammar of the linguistic community. See the descriptions of verbal symbol usage that Piaget made of his own children in Observations 5.9 and 5.10.

In Stage VI, the symbol becomes detached from its original context of meaning and becomes something that, like objects, can be manipulated and explored. Several researchers have developed systems for classifying different levels of symbolic play (see Tables 5.3 and 5.4). Although there is no clear-cut age at which infants begin to display a particular level of play, by 18 months most babies are entering some of the early stages of pretend play. By the age of 2 years, most children can execute complex sequences of play requiring multiple symbols and advance planning, such as pretending to cook a whole meal using blocks and pegs to substitute for food and utensils (Belsky & Most, 1981; Nicolich, 1977; Ungerer et al., 1981).

Observations

Stage VI Behavior (Piaget, 1962, pp. 121, 124)

Observation 5.9

At 1;6(30) Jacqueline said cry, cry to her dog and herself imitated the sound of crying. On the following days she made her bear, a duck, etc., cry. At 1;7(1) she made her hat cry.

Observation 5.10

At 1;8(30) Jacqueline stroked her mother's hair, saying pussy, pussy. At 1;9(0) she saw a shell and said cup. The next day, seeing the same shell she said glass, then cup, then hat and finally boat in the water.

Development of the Ability to Categorize Objects Between 12 and 24 Months

Even during the first year of life, infants begin to organize the information they see and hear into meaningful groups of items or events. At first, this is done at the level of simple categories: faces, birds, cars, and the like. Next, infants group items into higher-level categories, such as animals and vehicles. By 18 months, another important principle of categorization emerges: categorization by sequential order, or by cause and effect. Infants at this age remember items and events better if they are organized into a sequence. For example, in a bath sequence with a teddy bear, the bear's shirt is removed, the bear is put into the tub, the bear is washed, and then it is dried. Infants can remember exact sequences up to 2 weeks later whether they are familiar sequences, such as the bath, or unfamiliar, such as events related to a train ride. Some evidence suggests that even when events are not related naturally, infants will remember them by the sequence in which the events were observed (Bauer & Dow, 1994).

When concepts and memories are organized in terms of how the events are related to each other in time, this kind of conceptual organization is called a **script** (K. Nelson, 1978). Scripts become increasingly important as ways of representing complex aspects of reality, such as remembering to get dressed, eat, get in the car, get out of the car, walk inside the day care center, take off one's coat, and go to one's assigned area. All of the separate events required to get from bed to the day care center would be difficult to remember if they were not organized into expectable sequences of events. Thus, although 2-year-olds cannot memorize long lists of new words or concepts, they can execute complex sequences of related actions.

Square Pegs in Round Holes

What are the best toys for children of a particular age? In general, toys are age-appropriate if they match a child's cognitive level and if they provide a modest degree of challenge to the child. Between 18 and 24 months, for example, children love pegboards in which they can fit objects of different shapes in the corresponding holes. The challenge of pegboards is to try to match the object and its slot mentally. By 22 months, most infants can look at an object and mentally match it to the correct hole: they do not need to use trial-and-error to see what fits (Örnkloo & van Hofsten, 2007). The more practice that children have with this and other challenging toys, they better they become and the more they can use their memory to find the correct match (Hayne, Barr, & Herbert, 2003).

Containers are another favorite toy for children this age. Children love to put things into containers, and they also enjoy nesting-cup toys, in which smaller cups are placed inside successively larger cups. By the age of 18 months, infants understand the concept of containment, as shown by the following experiment. Infants were shown videotapes of sand being poured into cups and tubes. In some cases, the sand poured right through the container and came out the other side (violation condition). In other cases, the sand did not go through the

TABLE 5.3   Level of Symbolic Play

1. Presymbolic acts, such as combing one's own hair

2. Self-symbolic acts, such as pretending to be sleeping

3. Object-centered symbolic games, such as feeding a doll

4. Object-combination symbolic games, such as taking a baby doll and a teddy bear for a walk.

5. Planned symbolic games, such as saying "let's cook dinner," before actually doing it.

Source: L. M. Nicolich, Beyond sensorimotor intelligence: Assessment of symbolic maturity through analysis of pretend play, 1977. *Merrill-Palmer Quarterly, 23*, 89–100.

TABLE 5.4   Levels of Exploratory and Pretend Play

1. *Mouthing*: Indiscriminate mouthing of materials.

2. *Simple manipulation*: Visually guided manipulation (excluding indiscriminate banging and shaking) at least 5 seconds in duration that cannot be coded in any other category (e.g., turn over an object, touch and look at an object).

3. *Functional*: Visually guided manipulation that is particularly appropriate for a certain object and involves the intentional extraction of some unique piece of information (e.g., turn dial on toy phone, squeeze piece of foam rubber, flip antenna of Buzy Bee toy, spin wheels on cart, roll cart on wheels).

4. *Relational*: Bringing together and integrating two or more materials in an inappropriate manner, that is, in a manner not initially intended by the manufacturer (e.g., set cradle on phone, touch spoon to stick).

5. *Functional-relational*: Bringing together and integrating two objects in an appropriate manner, that is, in a manner intended by the manufacturer (e.g., set cup on saucer, place peg in hole of pegboard, mount spool on shaft of cart).

6. *Enactive naming*: Approximate pretense activity but without confirming evidence of actual pretense behavior (e.g., touch cup to lip without making drinking sounds, tilting head back, or tipping cup; raise phone receiver in proximity of ear without making talking sounds; touch brush to doll's hair without making combing motions)

7. *Pretend self*: Pretense behavior directed toward self in which pretense is apparent (e.g., raise cup to lip; tip cup, make drinking sounds, or tilt head; stroke own hair with miniature brush; raise phone receiver to ear and vocalize).

8. *Pretend other*: Pretense behavior directed away from child toward other (e.g., feed doll with spoon, bottle, or cup; brush doll's hair; push car on floor and make car noise).

9. *Substitution*: Using a "meaningless" object in a creative or imaginative manner (e.g., drink from seashell; feed baby with stick as "bottle") or using an object in a pretense, act in a way that differs from how it has previously been used by the child (e.g., use hairbrush to brush teeth after already using it as a hairbrush on self or other).

10. *Sequence pretend*: Repetition of a single pretense act with minor variation (e.g., drink from bottle, give doll drink; pour into cup, pour into plate) or linking together different pretense schemes (e.g., stir in cup, then drink; put doll in cradle, then kiss good night).

11. *Sequence pretend substitution*: Same as sequence pretend except using an object substitution within sequence (e.g., put doll in cradle, cover with green felt piece as "blanket"; feed self with spoon, then with stick).

12. *Double substitution*: Pretense play in which two materials are transformed, within a single act, into something they are not in reality (e.g., treat peg as doll and a piece of green felt as a blanket and cover peg with felt and say "night-night"; treat stick as person and seashell as cup and give stick a drink).

Source: J. Belsky & K. Most, From exploration to play: A cross-sectional study of infant free play behavior, 1981, p. 635. *Developmental Psychology, 17*, 630–639. Copyright © 1981 by the American Psychological Association. Reprinted with permission.

container but filled it up to the rim (nonviolation condition). Only infants older than 18 months looked longer at the violation condition, suggesting that they found it unusual (A. J. Caron, Caron, & Antell, 1988).

On the other hand, when actually presented with a set of nesting cups, children of this age period had trouble stacking them without errors. The infants might combine one or two cups correctly. Then they take a small cup and place it at the large end of their stack. Typically, infants under 24 months of age try to force the cup to fit, perhaps because they see that it might fit if the bottom cup were not in the way. At this point, most infants of this age will actually take the cups apart and start all over again or else just give up; they do not attempt alternative solutions, such as simply moving the cup to the other end of the stack (DeLoache, Sugarman, & Brown, 1985).

These studies show that even though infants recognize what is necessary for containment, they have trouble organizing their actions when a series of containers is present, which is why such toys are challenging at this age. This is similar to the A-not-B error in Stage IV, in which infants understand that objects exist when out of sight but persist in searching for them where they were last seen. If they fail, they give up the search. It is not until about 2 ½ years that infants are able to understand that two objects could have multiple relationships with each other: a cup that will not fit when placed on top of another might fit when placed under it. When younger infants place one cup on top of another, they fail to realize that the order of placement of the same two cups could be reversed.

Smart Toys, TV, and the Internet: Do They Make Babies Smarter?

Increasingly, parents who can afford it are buying so-called "smart toys." These are typically high-tech gadgets such as robots, digital images that move on a screen, buttons that "speak" or play music when pressed. There is also a line of "Baby Einstein" products from the Disney Corporation that include DVDs and CDs with lullabies and images, hand signs, and baby "movies." Television stations also broadcast shows aimed at children under the age of three years such as *Teletubbies*. Four brightly colored characters—Tinky Winky, Dipsy, Laa-Laa, and Po—live in Tubbyland. They resemble chubby children in blanket sleepers with television screens on their stomachs and television antennae on their heads. Tubbyland has green hills with artificial flowers and a sun in the sky with a baby face in the center. The tubbies' homes have slides, a living vacuum named Noo Noo, and a machine for making "tubby custard." There is a lot of repetition of simple actions. The tubbies speak motherese in a high-pitched voice using mispronounced words. Sometimes there are video clips on the tummy television screens, like a child washing a car, watching rabbits, or packing for a trip.

During the period between 18 and 24 months, infants begin to be more interested in television (Barr & Hayne, 1999; Valkenburg & Vroone, 2004). Infants also appear to be interested in most age-appropriate smart toys. Surveys show that by 3 months of age, about 40% of children in the United States regularly watched TV, DVDs, or videos. Children younger than a year were exposed to an average of 1 hour per day and by 2 years to an average of 1.5 hours per day. About 75% of parents report that their children under age 2 watch TV, and 1 in 5 of these children watch at least 2 hours per day (Cardinal & Lumeng, 2007). Parents' reasons for using these media were listed as entertainment, baby-sitting, and education (Zimmerman et al., 2007).

But do smart toys and videos really make a baby smarter? Or perhaps a better question is do they make a baby smarter than low-tech toys like pegboards, nesting cups, and blocks? Many parents and child advocates are strongly against using smart toys. They claim that smart toys and TV put infants in a passive role instead of actively exploring their world. The critics think smart toys will create television addicts and sedentary children. In North America, excessive television watching by children takes up time that could be used for other activities and for social interaction. Websites accuse the Teletubbies of everything from communism to devil worship. Those who market the show insist that it can be effective in language acquisition and making children comfortable with technology. They think the show creates a happy fantasy that can be a respite from the frustration of being a toddler. PBS, which airs the show in the United States, recommends that children watch it with an adult.

One study shows that smart toys are neither beneficial nor harmful (Plowman, 2004). That makes sense if we think of infants as capable of engaging with the world at their own level, then it makes little difference what kind of toy is available so long as it is interesting to the children. That means that parents can encourage cognitive and brain development with inexpensive low-tech toys just as easily as with expensive ones.

TV, DVD, and video viewing, on the other hand, have recently been shown to have *harmful effects on cognition and brain development for children under the age of 3 years*, just the opposite of the marketing pitches about these products. Children who watched more hours of TV, DVD or video at ages 1 and 3 were more likely to have problems with aggression by age 4, and attention and hyperactivity at age 7, regardless of gender, health, prenatal exposure to tobacco or alcohol, maternal depression, or ethnicity (Christakis et al., 2004; Ostrov, Gentile, & Crick, 2006). Watching TV and baby DVDs and videos under the age of three significantly impairs communication and language. For every hour of TV watched per day, 2-year-olds knew 6 to 8 fewer vocabulary words at age 2 years (Zimmerman et al., 2007). Finally, infants do not learn as well from watching adults on TV as opposed to watching live adults (Schmitt & Anderson, 2002).

These studies suggest that TV before the age of 3 years can actually impair normal brain development and slow cognitive development, even if infants view TV with an adult. These products actually make infants less smart rather than smarter. It is not clear why. It could be that they put the infant in a passive role. We know from research cited above that infants learn best by acting and not by simply observing. Before the age

of 2 years, in Piaget's stages I to V, the mental life of infants is in doing rather than in thinking. One reason for the language impairment could be that the videos, while visually interesting, show scenes that cannot be easily verbalized. In the language development section below, note that infants learn words better in the company of a live adult who refers to concrete objects in an action context that has direct meaning for the infant (Do you want some juice?).

Children under the age of 3 certainly should not be left alone in front of the television. If parents choose to let their child watch with them, it may be an enjoyable learning experience but exposure times should be low, probably 15 to 30 minutes per day or less. Most child development experts advocate that parents should carefully monitor children's television viewing at any age and limit the amount of time children are allowed to watch. The bottom line is that pots and pans will make a baby of this age just as smart as a toy that costs a lot of money, and TV, DVD, and video have demonstrated harmful effects.

These conclusions apply to children under 3 years of age. Preschool children, however, can get more out of smart toys, TV, and the Internet because of their more advanced cognitive and social skills. One study found that children who watched more of *Sesame Street* at age 5 had higher scores in high school on English, math, and science, spent more time reading books outside of school, perceived themselves as more competent, and were less aggressive than children who watched less (Huston et al., 2001).

On the other hand, these results could be explained by parental influence. Those parents who encourage *Sesame Street* viewing as opposed to commercial TV, may be more concerned with educational rather than entertainment values. In general, there is a growing tendency in Western countries to replace active engagement in the environment with vicarious electronic media; playing video games about outdoor adventures, for example, rather than just playing outside. Outdoor play and other nature experiences have been shown to lower depression, improve attention and concentration, and increase self-discipline, yet children in the United States spend an average of only 30 minutes of unstructured outdoor time per week (Thigpen, 2007; Zaradic & Pergams, 2007).

Twenty-Four to Thirty-Six Months

The Emergence of Thinking Grounded in Action

During the third year, children increase their ability to perform complicated sequences of action, as demonstrated by the following investigation (Bullock & Lutkenhaus, 1988). Researchers gave children three tasks. The first was to build a house from blocks in a particular fashion modeled by the experimenter. The next was to clean a blackboard, and the last was to dress a doll so that it would not be cold. After age 2, but not before, the children were able to perform all the actions in the sequence given by the experimenter (the constructed house, the clean blackboard, and the dressed doll).

When the younger children made an error in putting the blocks together to build the house, they simply stopped or went on to another activity. The older children were able to correct the error and persist until the task was completed to a reasonable approximation of the standard. This ability to combine a series of actions together in a flexible way and to persist until a standard or conventional goal is reached is a major cognitive achievement. This achievement is reflected in a variety of areas, including object play, pretend play, social play, peer play, self-control, and language (Bauer, Schwade, Wewerka, & Delaney, 1999; Brownell, 1988; Jennings, 2004; Messer, Rachford, McCarthy, & Yarrow, 1987). Self-control is seen in the ability to wait as requested by an adult (Vaughn et al., 1986). In the realm of language, for example, children at this age are beginning to use grammatical syntax in which a number of words are combined according to conventional usage into a flexible sequence.

What causes these changes to occur? Since attention span also increases around the same age, you might think that an increase in some kind of cognitive capacity allows the infant to process a longer series of actions. Some researchers believe, on the contrary, that longer attention is the result of more skilled action sequences that require the child to spend more time following through with the details of completing a task (Ruff & Lawson, 1990).

In related studies, it has been found that the more children comprehend of television programs, such as *Sesame Street*, the longer they will watch, and that television watching increases markedly at 30 months, about the same time these other changes are happening (Anderson & Levin, 1976; Anderson & Lorch, 1983). This kind of more focused attention to television is different from what was observed during the previous age period.

Self-produced action does appear to affect cognition. In one study, 3-year-olds were taken into a children's area in a natural history museum (Hazen, 1982). Some of the children were allowed to explore the area on their own, while others were led through it by an adult. Those who went on their own had a more accurate spatial cognition of the layout of the area than those who were led. This study shows that self-produced action involves active cognitive processing, and that by their action, children are increasing their knowledge of the environment.

Language Aids both Thought and Action

If attention increases as a result of more articulated action, that still leaves open the question of what causes action to develop. According to Piaget (1952, 1962), development of both action and language is caused by developmental increases in cognitive abilities such as logical thinking. Piaget also concluded that errors committed by children older than 2 years were errors of logical thinking: he assumed the primacy of cognition over action after age 2 years. He gave children problems such as the following: "Bill is older than Tom. Tom is older than Steve. Who is older, Bill or Steve?" A typical 3-year-old, according to Piaget, will not be able to answer because of an inability to understand the logical chain of comparisons.

An alternative to the logical-error hypothesis is that children have a difficult time comprehending the language used in such problems. Children often have difficulty understanding differences between similar words with different endings, such as the difference between *old* and *older*. Some research has shown that what children actually comprehend is something like this: "Bill is old; Tom is not old. Tom is old; Steve is not old." This seems like contradictory information. How can Tom be old and not old at the same time? Thus, the error may be due to a linguistic problem, rather than to a deficit in cognitive ability (Bryant & Trabasso, 1971; Riley & Trabasso, 1974).

Let us return to the original question; that is, what accounts for the development of complex action sequences? In the last section, we reviewed research showing that younger infants appear more skilled in pretend play when in the company of adults. They are also more advanced linguistically with adults than with peers. The adult guidance and the adult language seem to regulate the infant's actions, providing a kind of external support system that the infant cannot maintain alone or with a peer. After 30 months, it seems, infants have begun to internalize this social-linguistic regulatory system as thought, carrying it over into their activities in the absence of adults.

How do we know this? Beginning at 30 months, children begin to use language to regulate their behavior. For example, in one study, children were given a peg-and-hammer toy and told to hammer the pegs into the board in a particular order according to the color of the peg. If the children were allowed to say out loud the given order while hammering, they were more accurate than if told not to speak (Balamore & Wozniak, 1984).

At around 30 months, children begin, literally, to talk to themselves. **Private speech** is the use of language to regulate one's own behavior without the intention of a social communication. Private speech is different from the child's speech play seen in the first year (such as saying "mmmmm" while eating) because private speech uses both conventional words and conventional syntax. Private speech reflects the transition from social regulation to individual self-regulation.

Research has shown that private speech occurs in the following situations: the child talks about an intended action ("I put that there"), describes ongoing action ("Banging it"), makes a statement to an inanimate object ("Get out of my way, chair!"), or asks a question and then answers it ("Why are you crying, dolly? Because I'm sad"). In all cases, these words are said without looking at anyone else or seeking social confirmation (Berk, 1986; Furrow, 1984).

In summary, according to Piaget's theory, the development of more complex action sequences is the result of developments in the cognitive realm: the ability to hold more events in mind and link them logically. The alternative perspective, derived from the work of Vygotsky (1978; see Chapter 2), sees language and social experience as the primary cause of the development of action sequences. Since private speech is an internalized version of what earlier occurred socially during the regulation of the infant's action by means of caregiver speech, the development of complex action sequences has its origins in earlier social interaction. In a sense, babies turn social dialogue into private monologue and language into thought, and the result is the self-regulation of action (Vygotsky, 1978).

The Development of Pretending and the World of Make-Believe

Because they say out loud (private speech) most of what they are thinking, children of this age are delightful to watch. Pretend play, discussed in the last section, is a kind of private speech that allows children to construct their own version of reality. At the beginning of the third year, children develop more complex forms of pretending. The child begins to reconstruct whole scenes and experiences in play:

At 2;1(9) Jacqueline put her doll's head through the balcony railing with its face turned toward the street and began to tell it what she saw: "You see the lake and the trees. You see a carriage, a horse," etc. The same day she seated her doll on the sofa and told it what she herself had seen in the garden. (Piaget, 1962, p. 127)

In the previous example, the child tried to faithfully reproduce reality. In the following example, the child makes some attempt to change or correct reality to make it more to her own liking. These games are the beginning of **imaginative pretend play**, in which the child is able to invent whole new situations in make-believe:

At 2;4(8) Jacqueline, not being allowed to play with the water being used for washing, took an empty cup, went and stood by the forbidden tub and went through the actions, saying: "I'm pouring out the water." (Piaget, 1962, p. 131)

The final type of pretend play that occurs during the third year of life is what Piaget called **liquidating pretend play**. This usually happens after the child experiences something unpleasant or threatening. Later, the child will try to relive the difficult situation in play as a way of coping with it. By removing it from its original unpleasantness, the child is better able to understand and assimilate what went on:

At 2;7(2) Jacqueline had fallen down and cut her lip. She consoled herself by projecting it all on to "Cousin Andree," who took the form of a doll: "Oh! It's Cousin Andree. They're washing her because she fell down and hurt her lip. She made a little hole in it. She cried."

At 2;7(15) a friend of her mother went for a walk with them. Jacqueline, who did not care for the presence of the third person, expressed frankly what she felt: "She's naughty … she can't talk … I don't like people to laugh." Then, as soon as the walk was over, Jacqueline accepted her, put her beside her in the bath, then in her bed, talked to her,

and went for the walk again with her (all in imagination). (Piaget, 1962, p. 133)

These kinds of games allow the self to emerge victorious in the face of failure or to save face in the case of embarrassment. Children of this age also develop **pretend role play**, in which they act out the roles of mother, father, or other important figures in their lives, typically in the company of adults or peers.

During this same period in which children are developing their pretending skills, they can also understand when adults refer to pretend situations. In one study, adults pretended that a cup contained tea. The adults also did things like "pouring" or "spilling" the tea. After 28 months (2 years, 4 months), children can participate in these pretend episodes. They will "drink" from the cup and help "clean up" the "spilled" tea. The children also use language that makes clear they understand the situation is make-believe and not real (P. L. Harris & Kavanaugh, 1993; Rokoczy, Tomasello, & Striano, 2004).

Pretending is also manifested as dreaming, which children of this age can talk about for the first time. Dreams often concern experiences the child has had, physical changes such as toileting, and strong emotions.

At 2;2(23) X. woke up crying: "Poupette has come back." Poupette was a little girl she had met the day before and who had obviously worried her by unceremoniously taking possession of all her toys. At 2;8(11) X. woke with a loud scream: "It was all dark, and I saw a lady over there (pointing to her bed). That's why I screamed." Then she explained that it was a horrid lady who stood with her legs apart and played with her feces. (Piaget, 1962, p. 177)

These dreams are examples of some of the things reported by 2-year-old children upon awakening. These dreams are classic nightmares, or dreams about fears that are still so frightening that the dream is unable to resolve them or make them better. In one case the child fears her toys will be stolen, and in another she fears her own feces. The latter is a common problem in 2- and 3-year-old children who are becoming aware that their own bodies can manufacture these products. Children of this age are both fascinated by their feces and repelled and confused by them at the same time (see the discussion of psychoanalytic theory in Chapter 2 and Erikson, 1950). Some children feel possessive about these products and may refuse toilet learning for fear of losing part of themselves. Other children may show more curiosity and playfulness about their stools and urine than most parents are able to tolerate, and still others do not seem to be at all concerned with these matters.

Another common dream in very young children is the "transposition of an organic stimulus" (Piaget, 1962). A good example is when children dream about a watering can at just the moment when they feel like (or are in the process of) urinating. Dreams other than nightmares may fulfill a wish, or they may take a painful event and finish it off with a happy ending. According to Freud (1900/1953), dreams are the "guardians" of sleep. Without dreams to transform and soothe our minds, we might keep waking up with painful or troublesome thoughts.

Because of these new abilities, children no longer have to be content with what actually happens. They can make up a better outcome as they play with dolls, siblings, and peers. We all do this when we imagine becoming famous, getting out of our difficulties and achieving success, or taking revenge on someone who has wronged us. The only problem for 3-year-olds is that they are never sure about the limits of this newfound ability to make up a more congenial world. If they could make things up so easily, why is everything not just pretend? Children may think they can make their parents disappear by wishing it. A boy might believe that he will change into a girl if he talks in a high voice for a long time. If the real can be imaginary, then the imaginary could be real.

Children fear their own imaginary monsters, get shaken awake by nightmares, and worry that they will lose themselves when their feces get sucked down the toilet drain. These fears are very real for children of this age, and they often do not have a sufficient command of language to fully express themselves.

Do adults have such experiences? Recall a period after which you first entered into a completely different social and cultural situation. This might be going to a new school or college for the first time, going to a foreign country for the first time, moving to a new city or neighborhood where you do not know anyone, or signing up for a class about which you know nothing at all.

During the first few days or weeks of being in a completely new situation, you may have the feeling that there is something unreal about it. This may seem like a pretend world in which the language and customs are totally arbitrary. From the newcomer's perspective, this world seems to have been suddenly made up, so it could suddenly go away. On the other hand, there is often a fear of not being in control, of there being things out there that could sneak up on you and hurt you. Your conversations are limited to a few words, usually when people are asking you questions or when you need help. You do not always understand what people are saying to you.

These feelings usually pass after a while, when you can see that the people in this strange world are similar to the ones you knew before. They just dress and speak differently. As you begin to develop a theory of mind for those people, you can see their world is not just made up but has its own meaning and value. As you get acculturated, your fears of the unknown lessen, and you begin to interact in a more adult way.

THE DEVELOPMENT OF INFANT SELF-AWARENESS

Self-awareness is a relatively recent topic in infant studies. It was once thought that infants were not aware of themselves at all until the age at which they could recognize themselves in a mirror, around 18-20 months. We now know that even the fetus is aware of itself, as shown in the study, reviewed in Chapter 3, that late-term fetuses will open their mouth in anticipation of meeting their own hand as it moves toward the mouth. This is a form of self-awareness that does not involve a self-concept. In fetal self-awareness, one part of the body seems to know the location and movements of another part of the body. This could not happen unless the fetus was somehow aware of its own movements and senses, at least in this limited domain of hand-to-mouth coordination. As we shall see in this section, there are a series of increasingly complex forms of infant self-awareness—of the body, of the emotions, and of the infant in relationship to others—that develop in the 18 months prior to mirror self-recognition and continue to grow after that.

Newborn Self-Awareness: The Emergent Self

When a newborn imitates mouth opening or tongue protrusion, it is necessary for them to match a facial expression of their own with that of the adult. This is surprising because newborns have never seen their own face in a mirror, yet somehow, out of all the possible facial expressions, they can pick one of their own that fits with the one they see. This may mean that newborns can distinguish the movements of their own bodies from the movements of others, an early form of self-awareness (A. N. Meltzoff & Moore, 1997).

Some research suggests that newborns can tell the difference between being touched on their cheeks by another person and touching themselves on the cheek. They are more likely to show the rooting reflex (see Table 4.3 on page 123) when being touched by another person than when touching themselves (Rochat & Hespos, 1997). Newborns also cry more and suck less when they hear the cries of another infant played on a tape recorder compared to when they hear their own cries played on the tape recorder (Dondi, Simion, & Caltran, 1999). This is related to the fact that late-term fetuses show a similar familiarity with their own movements when they open their mouths as their hand approaches the mouth.

It is possible that these studies merely show that newborns can tell the difference between familiarity and unfamiliarity. On the other hand, the familiarity in these examples comes from their own bodies. It may be that rudimentary self-awareness emerges from the repeated familiarity of living in the same body and experiencing the same sounds and feelings many times. This sense of sameness and familiarity is also enhanced by the parents, who tend to respond to the infant's repeating actions in similar ways each time they occur. Thus, the infant's growing awareness of self-familiarity is enhanced by the parent's consistent form of responding (Kaye, 1982).

This early form of self-awareness that appears during the late fetal period and continues through the first 2 months of life has been called the **emergent self**, the perception of self-sameness over time in behavior, feelings, and states of arousal (Stern, 1985; see Chapter 2). The emergent self is the sense of familiar experience of the body and of the familiarity in the way others respond to those experiences.

The newborn's sense of self-sameness is fleeting. Because newborns spend a lot of time sleeping, eating, or crying, the times that they are in alert states are relatively brief. Imagine being very busy, on the move, unsettled, or seriously ill. People in these situations are so preoccupied that they have little time for feeling themselves. Their sleep and waking patterns may change day to day, and they find it difficult to know when or if they are hungry. Some things, however, emerge as islands of permanence and familiarity: the feeling of falling asleep, a warm shower, a familiar voice, or a predictable routine. One of the remarkable abilities of the newborn is to be able to detect that stability, within the flow of change. It seems, therefore, that the human mind from its earliest beginnings needs to locate the self and its familiar feelings against the background of change.

Self-Awareness Between 2 and 5 Months: The Sense of an Ecological Self

We know that infants of this age are beginning to perceive objects and people as coherent wholes. They perceive familiar patterns of interaction—frames—as coherent wholes, and they get upset when those patterns are altered (see Chapter 6). We also learned that infants of this age practice a form of self-exploration, the primary circular reactions by which they feel themselves move and act. Given these abilities, can young infants perceive themselves as a coherent entity?

The traditional test of self-recognition is done by secretly putting a spot of red makeup (rouge) on the infant's forehead and placing the infant in front of a mirror. Touching the red spot while looking in the mirror is taken as evidence that the infant recognizes his or her own image in the mirror. Infants do not pass this rouge test of mirror self-recognition until 18 months.

Many infancy researchers now believe that infants between 2 and 5 months can also recognize themselves as separate and whole individuals, but not by their image in a mirror. How is this possible? Infants under 6 months of age have what is called an ecological self. This conclusion is based on some of the research already reviewed on infant perception and cognition. The ecological self has four basic features (Kaye, 1982; Neisser, 1991; Stern, 1985):

1. *Self-agency* is the sense that one is capable of generating one's own actions and expecting that these self-generated actions will have consequences, such as the sense that it gets dark when the eyes are closed or the arm moves when one wants it to move.

2. *Self-coherence* is the sense of being a whole physical entity with boundaries and limitations, such as sensing the difference between touching someone or something and being touched by someone.

3. *Self-affectivity* is the sense of having inner emotional feelings that routinely go together with specific experiences, such as feeling happy when one's mother approaches and sad when she leaves.

4. *Self-history* is the sense of enduring, of having a past, of going on even through changes, as when one acts and feels in similar ways with familiar people or in familiar situations.

Each of these four aspects of the ecological self is experienced *in relation to* something else. One senses self-coherence, for example, by feeling where one's own body ends and where the environment begins. According to ecological systems theory (Chapter 2), an ecology is a system of relationships, as in the ecosystem of plants and animals. Plants and animals cannot live without each other. They exchange oxygen and carbon dioxide. Animals eat plants and plants depend upon animals (worms and insects) to decompose their remains to create soils in which the plants can grow. So, while plants and animals are mutually interdependent, they each have their boundaries and can be identified one from the other.

Infants (and adults) can see some part of their own bodies—their nose, at a minimum—at all times in their field of vision. You can check this by closing one eye and looking straight ahead: you will see your nose in your peripheral vision. This means that at the same time you are seeing things in the environment, you are also seeing part of yourself. Thus, your perception of the environment is also a perception of yourself in relation to the environment (Fogel, 1993; J. J. Gibson, 1966). This is why this early sense of self is called the ecological self, the self sensed as being situated in relation to the environment. **Self-agency** is the sense of the relationship of one's action and its effect on the environment. **Self-affectivity** is the sense of one's emotions as experienced in the company of another feeling person. **Self-history** is a sense of the relationship with one's past (Fogel, 2000; Trevarthen & Aitken, 2001).

Cross-modal perception, the relationship between the different senses, is one source of the ecological self. By 3 1/2 months, infants begin to watch their hands moving in front of them. Because they can also feel their arms and hands making these movements, it is likely that this cross-modal experience gives the infants a sense of self-recognition through self-coherence. Babies recognize their hands as their own because the hands are the same ones the babies have been feeling for months (Neisser, 1991; Stern, 1995). In a similar way, infants can recognize their own sounds because their different forms of vocalization (contented or distressed) will be cross-modally associated with different internal feelings (Gustafson, Green, & Kalinowski, 1995).

Young infants also explore their own bodies, feeling the relationship between the touching hand and the part of their bodies that is being touched. In the first few hours of life, newborns touch their own head in an ordered sequence beginning with the mouth, then moving to the face, head, ear, nose, and eyes. This process occurs only when the infant is awake (Kravitz et al., 1978, as reported in Butterworth, 1990). As described in Chapter 3, just prior to hand-to-mouth contact, late-term fetuses and newborns will open their mouth in anticipation. Once infants can reach, around the fourth month, they self-explore by touching different parts of the body, beginning with the fingers and ending months later with the toes (Kravitz et al., 1978, as reported in Butterworth, 1990).

In one experiment, 3-to-5-month-old infants were shown videotaped images of their own legs. The video cameras were suspended above the infants to photograph the legs. The infants could see the video image of their legs, but they could not see their own legs directly. The infants were wearing striped leg-length socks to make their legs visually salient. Using this method, the researchers could manipulate the video image to show the infant's legs either as the infant would see them normally or in mirror image, with the right leg on the left side and vice versa. Infants gazed longer and kicked more to the reversed mirror image of their legs, suggesting that they could recognize the normal configuration of their own bodies and were curious about the unusual-looking reversed legs. The increased kicking also suggests that the

infants were trying to figure out if the video legs were indeed their own (Rochat & Morgan, 1995). Similar experiments have been done using infant arm movements (Schmuckler, 1996).

Another unique experiment was done with conjoined twins who were born connected at their lower abdomens, facing each other. A week before they were surgically separated at 4 months, researchers noticed that the twins sometimes sucked on their own hands and sometimes on their sister's hands.

> When twin A (Alice) was sucking on her own fingers, one of us placed one hand on her head and the other hand on the arm that she was sucking. We gently pulled the sucking arm away from her mouth and registered (in our own hands) whether her arm put up resistance to being moved from her mouth and/or whether her head strained forward to go after the retreating hand. In this situation, Alice's arm registered the interruption of sucking, but she did not give evidence of straining forward with her head. The same procedure was followed when Alice was sucking on her sister Betty's fingers rather than her own. When Betty's hand was gently pulled from Alice's mouth, Alice's arms showed no resistance, but Alice's head did strain forward. Alice seemed, in this case, to have no confusion as to whose fingers belonged to whom and which motor plan would best reestablish sucking. (Stern, 1985, pp. 78–79).

This suggests that the ecological self is experienced in relation not only to the physical environment but also to the social environment. As one interacts with another person, it is possible to feel the part of the interaction that comes from the self in comparison to that part contributed by the other. This is illustrated in Figure 5.6. Even during a continuous movement, such as when the mother takes the infant's arms and pulls the infant into a sitting position, there is a co-regulated dialogue in which the effort of the mother and baby changes

For a baby of this age, the act of touching the toes is not automatic. It takes a while for the baby to focus on the task of discovering (self-agency) where to find the toes with the hands (self-coherence), to remember how to do it each time (self-history), and the discovery is usually accompanied by enjoyment at the achievement (self-affectivity).
Photo by Elizabeth Crews.

but remains in balance. Sometimes the baby pulls a bit harder than the mother, feeling himself or herself as an agent in the co-regulation. Sometimes the baby does not have the strength to pull so the mother pulls harder, allowing the infant to feel the mother's side of the co-regulated dialogue. The baby can feel his or her effort as less than, more than, or the same as the mother's. As with the example of seeing the nose in the visual field, the experience of the ecological self is always an experience of a self in relation to the environment (Fogel, 1993). This kind of participatory co-regulated relationship with another person also gives the infant information about the other person in relation to the self, a sense of **intersubjectivity** (Bråten, 1998; Trevarthen, 1998; Trevarthen & Aitken, 2001).

In summary, the ecological self is a sense of one's body in the environment and the ability to recognize one's own movements. This sense of self comes from the infant's experiences relating to other people, the environment, and their own bodies. You can better appreciate the infant's and your own ecological self by doing the Experiential Exercises at the end of each chapter. Participating in active communication with an infant is a way to sense your own compared to the infant's contribution to the dialogue. Infants of this age do not have a cognitive concept of themselves or of their mothers as whole people with different feelings, ideas, and motivations. The emergence of self-concepts begins during the third year of life. Thus, when doing the exercises, try to focus your attention on the movements and sensations of your body. To the extent that you can do this in a *participatory* way—without thought, judgment, evaluation, or conceptualization—you will be connecting with your ecological self, that part of your-

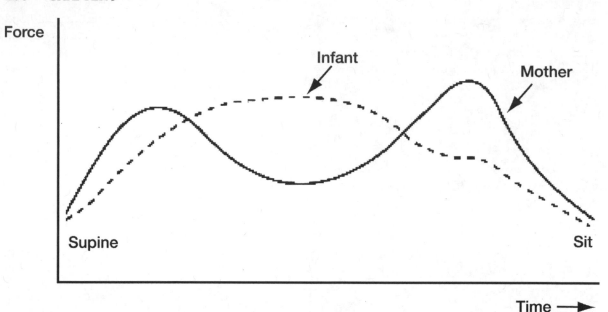

Figure 5.6 Self and Other Experiences During Co-Regulation
The diagram shows the amount of effort exerted by mother and infant when the infant is pulled by the mother from a supine to a sitting position. The dashed curve shows the infant's effort, while the solid curve shows how the mother exerts more or less force depending upon the co-regulated dialogue. Infants feel themselves when they are exerting more force than the mother, and they feel their mothers when the mother's force is more dominant.

Source: A. Fogel, *Developing through relationships*, 1993, p. 18. Chicago: University of Chicago Press. Reprinted with permission from the University of Chicago Press.

self that began when you were between 2 and 5 months old.

Self-Awareness between 6 and 9 Months: The Sense of a Differentiated Ecological Self

In the previous stage, infants developed a sense of an ecological self but it is rather rudimentary. Infants between 3 and 5 months old may feel as if there is a coherence between moving their hand to touch their own face and the sensation felt in the face. They know that this feels different from other kinds of contact with their face, say, from their blanket or another person's touch. Infants of that age, however, do not know that there is a self and another person who are different centers of subjective experience. All they know is that some touches feel different from others, and that there is a special significance to touches that are accom-

panied by a sense of their own movements (that is, self-touches). Babies between 3 and 5 months cannot put labels on these different kinds of touches. They have a sense of agency, but only for these simple actions on their own body. They do not know they can affect the world beyond their body. They experience the world receptively and unquestioningly.

A 3-month-old baby is aware of the environment in the same way that a fish is aware of water. A fish "knows" that to propel its body it must exert a certain force, and that the force is different at different times (we as outside observers would be able to observe that these different times are changes in the speed and direction of the water currents). The fish, however, does not know water as a separate entity, different from itself. The fish has an ecological self. It knows what to do and how to move, has a memory of past experiences, and can adapt to changes, but it cannot separate itself from the ecology. It is unified with the ecology.

Between 6 and 9 months, we see the first evidence that babies are becoming aware of a world "out there" in relation to the self. They are still part of the ecology of relationships with things and people (indeed, so are all of us), but now they are starting to see that the ecology has local regions, each of which has different properties and each of which has an existence in relation to the self. As they begin to differentiate objects as whole entities having an existence even when out of sight, they also begin to see themselves as being different from but related to those objects.

Infants of this age call attention to themselves in a number of ways that did not exist in the previous stage. These features make up a sense of a **differentiated ecological self**.

1. *Asking for help*. If their needs are not met, infants are beginning to find ways to let others know. Asking for help suggests that the infant believes the source of help comes from outside their own bodies.

2. *Taking the initiative*. Infants will start games, like covering their face as if to ask to play peekaboo. It is as if they are "waking up" to the fact that they are not completely helpless. If they do or do not like something, they can actually do something to make it happen or to change what is already happening.

3. *Clowning and showing off*. Infants begin to do things to get an emotional reaction from others. They act clever or silly, violate social rules to get a laugh from others, make odd facial expressions, put their pajamas on their head, and blow "raspberries" (Reddy, 2000). This suggests that the infant has a sense of other people as different from the self, at least insofar as being an audience.

4. *Demanding*. The quality of crying changes as infants become angry at others and persist in their demands until something changes.

5. *Hiding and escaping*. Infants like to play peekaboo, tickle, and chase games that involve a temporary separation from the other followed by a reunion. This suggests that they have a growing ability to differentiate themselves from other people and objects, and that they have a sense of permanence (a person or an object can reappear after hiding).

Another indication of a differentiated ecological self is the emergence of gender and temperamental differences at this age. Infants begin to seem as if they have their own personalities. Their emotions are becoming more complex, and they are beginning to take events into their own hands. Infants of this age, however, do not yet have a sense of subjectivity. They have feelings—getting angry or happy—but cannot yet stand apart from those feelings. They do not have a sense of an "I" that feels, and, consequently, they do not have a sense that other people are separate subjects with their own feelings. Other people are still being treated partially as extensions of the infant's own needs—as an audience for the infant's jokes or as a satisfier of the infant's demands—and are not seen in their own right as separate individuals.

The differentiated ecological self is more advanced than the fish in water. The infant now senses that the "water" is different but believes that the water is there only for the self. Can you think of times that you were demanding without regard for another person's feelings? Or when you needed an audience or confirmation, without thinking about the emotional state of your partner? If so, you were behaving like a 9-month-old!

The sense of a **subjective self** begins after the age of 10 months. After 10 months of age, infants begin to point at objects in the company of others, as if to say they have a sense of having a perspective on the world that truly differs from that of other people. This means that by 10 months, infants begin to have a sense of being a subject, an "I" who can perceive or feel and who can share those feelings with other people. The subjective self seems to have an understanding that other people can feel similar or different types of emotions as the self. Between 6 and 9 months, the infant's positive and negative emotions become more complex, and each has some interpersonal significance (see Chapter 7). Anger is typically directed toward another person. It highlights the concerns of the self that may have been violated. The enjoyment of escape during tickle and chase games is a feeling of trying to get away from someone else. So, while infants of this age are not yet aware of others as separate subjects, they are beginning to experience others as a meaningful part of their own emotional life.

Self-Awareness Between 10 and 12 Months: The Sense of a Subjective Self

As we shall see in Chapter 6, the fact that infants begin to gesture and use words suggests that they make a deliberate attempt to share what is on their mind with others. Behaviors like clowning and showing off at this age, different from similar behavior in the previous period of the differentiated ecological self, reveal that there is an "I" that wants to be recognized.

This sense of "I" is the **subjective self** (Stern, 1985). The subjective self is a participatory (see Chapter 2), rather than a conceptual, sense of "I." When infants of this age show off, they act as if they are saying, "Look at me." The infants are not, however, actually saying "look at me." Babies of this age do not use the word "I," nor do they have a language to describe themselves or a concept of "self." These will take almost another year to develop. This is the crucial difference between the subjective self and the conceptual self, which emerges around the child's second birthday. On the other hand, intentional communicative actions like showing off, pointing and requesting, and social referencing (looking to another person's emotions to evaluate a situation, Chapter 6) are also fundamentally different from the fish-in-water sense of the ecological self or from the self-centered use of others in the differentiated ecological self.

How can an infant have a sense of "I" but no word or concept for it? Imagine looking into someone's eyes in a way that says "I love you" or "I'm afraid of you." You do not need any words to express this. It is clear, however, that there is

an "I" that feels love or fear, and also that this "I" comes into awareness in the act of trying to communicate nonverbally, in a participatory way, with another person. Teenagers will sometimes show off and act silly when around members of the opposite sex. Perhaps all people do this when they are falling in love! These behaviors call attention to the self in a way that says "look at me" without actually saying it. In many cases, the person who is doing the showing off is not even conceptually aware of it. Their behavior is a participatory form of self-consciousness in communication.

The development of attachment (see Chapter 7) during this age period is another way in which infants reveal the sense of a subjective self. They begin to look at other people in a participatory way that says "I love you" or "I'm afraid." The infant's showing off at this age means "look at me," and also "I know you will look at me because we love each other." They communicate their sense of affection, fear, or loneliness by making deliberate attempts at approaching or avoiding, by signaling their desire to be with particular people, and by asking for comfort and assistance. Because the subjective self is participatory, babies do not think about whether or not to do these things; they just engage in the actions and experience the consequences.

The emergence of the subjective self is the beginning of a uniquely human consciousness, a consciousness that is aware of itself thinking, feeling, and doing. Why is it a developmental achievement to acquire an "I"? Imagine the experience of an intense emotion, such as losing your temper at someone. During the experience there is no sense of "I" or "you." There is just the anger that is directed outward. This is the experience of the differentiated ecological self. Later, however, you can say, "I completely lost myself," or "I didn't know what I was doing." At the time such statements are made, one is subjectively aware of oneself as *having had an experience of anger*. One is also conceptually aware of the differences between self and other, so that, hopefully, apologies and restitutions can be made.

Now imagine teenagers or adults who are strong enough to really inflict harm on others or the self but who do not have a sense of a subjective or conceptual self. These people would be a danger to themselves and to other people, and a number of psychopathological conditions stem from not progressing emotionally beyond the differentiated ecological sense of self. Some of these disturbances of the mature sense of self have their origins during this early period of infancy (see the section on clinical theories, Chapter 2, and Chapter 9).

According to psychoanalytic theories, for example, when the infant's intentional communicative actions are not recognized by the family system to help the infant appreciate what acts lead to what consequences, then the inner experience will not be felt as the infant's own (Sander, 1962). The capricious and confusing messages given by their parents may fail to create a sense of "I" for the infant. If these conditions persist until they become teenagers, these children suffer from **dissociation**, or the inability to connect themselves with their experiences. They hurt themselves and others as if there were no self to feel the hurt.

People can also lose their sense of "I" when they become depressed or alienated. In these conditions, one feels helpless to change circumstances, as if the "I" is not an effective, intentional being. Infants who experience their world as excessively controlling or intrusive develop a similar inability to develop subjectivity. So, the sense of a subjective self is crucial to mental health. We need to know who we are in relation to other people, what we need and how to ask appropriately for it, and how to communicate about those things with other people.

At this age, babies begin to develop some of the human frailties of the self that plague us all: vulnerability to loss and separation from loved ones, irrational fears, and insatiable curiosity. There are some limits to this. Babies of this age do not suffer from self-doubt or pride. These peculiarly human vulnerabilities need at least another year before they begin to flower.

The wonderful news is that the vast majority of infants at this age develop a healthy sense of a subjective self with at least one person, and that this sense of self arises naturally and spontaneously during frames for coordinated joint attention (Chapter 6). Infants simply need to be able to express themselves though gestures, to have someone respond appropriately, and to take pleasure in creating playful and satisfying communicative routines. It is not necessary to teach babies about themselves. You only have to be aware of the signs of their budding self-awareness and be available when infants need your assistance, when they look to you for guidance, and when they want you to share in their discoveries.

Self-Awareness between 12 and 18 Months: The Sense of an Elaborated Subjective Self

During the period from 9 to 12 months, the subjective self emerges. At this age, the infant has a sense of being a subject who can feel and experience and who is different from other subjects. The subjective self is shown by such behaviors as showing off, intentional communication, and social referencing. These same behaviors continue during the period between 12 and 18 months, and other similar behaviors are added. In the realm of showing off, for example, infants at this age will exaggerate their facial expressions and other social actions as if they are exploring their own subjectivity in relation to another person. In the realm of intentional communication, 12-to-18-month-olds will not only gesture or use a word, they will persist when their attempts are not understood. They lean toward the adult, whine, use additional gestures, or pull on the adult's arm.

In the realm of social referencing, infants of this age still rely on adults for emotional guidance, but they also discover that they have some emotion regulation skills of their own (Chapter 7). They attempt to control their own distress by biting their lip or hugging themselves. When with another person, babies will look toward that person for confirmation of an achievement, but they will also smile, jump, or wave their arms to recognize the achievement for themselves.

One gets the sense that the subjective self in this age period is becoming more elaborated, that the infant is filling in the blanks of self-experience and trying out the possibilities and limitations of it. It is interesting that all of this self-exploration and self-knowing goes on for at least 9 months before the infant acquires the word "I," which begins during the next developmental period. In the period between 12 and 18 months, the infant is still a participatory subjective self, a lived self rather than a conceived self.

During the period between 12 and 18 months, participatory subjectivity becomes more active. Infants not only become more persistent in expressing themselves, they begin to imitate complex sequences of adult action, almost as if trying the activity on for size. They may, for example, pick up a toy telephone and try to talk "like Mommy," imitating the mother's actual telephone conversation. Or they may want to type on the computer or stir the pot. Without any understanding of what the computer is used for, and without an "I" that wants to take control, what could these actions possibly mean for the baby? It is also notable that infants imitate not just any adult action, but intentional adult action. This means that infants are understanding the action subjectively, that is, as actions done by a person for a purpose. By copying these actions, the infants are coming to feel themselves as purposeful, feeling subjects.

This kind of behavior happens in older children and adults. Imagine listening to a song on the radio. You do not understand all the words, you do not want to be a rock star, you just like the way the song sounds and want to try singing it yourself. Maybe you can reproduce some of the words of the song. If not, you either hum or make up some of the words. It is all playful and enjoyable. You do not think about it as "I am singing this song," but you nevertheless feel yourself singing it and it feels good, or silly, or funny, or whatever. You are aware that there is an "I" singing; it is not the performer on the radio singing, for sure. If you liked doing it, maybe you will try another song.

People do this type of participatory, subjective imitation most frequently when developing new skills, such as taking lessons in music, dance, or athletics, or taking a math or science class. The step of participatory involvement is a prelude to the emergence of a self who possesses a particular skill. When you can say, "I'm a dancer," "I studied algebra," or "I like to play tennis," you have moved on to a different kind of experience of self with respect to that skilled activity.

These examples reveal why infants of this age seem to be having so much fun. It is as if they are always experimenting with new things and feeling themselves doing it. On the other hand, they have not yet gotten to the point where they have formed a sense of self that has possessions, goals, or plans. So, while they are full of energy and love to feel themselves, they are not burdened by expectations for success or failure, they are not troubled by meeting a particular schedule, and they do not feel ashamed of themselves if they make a mistake. They do not even have a concept of a mistake. If we adults could reserve part of each week for this kind of carefree joyfulness, we would probably be a lot happier with ourselves, both with our successes and our failures.

Self-Awareness between 18 and 24 Months: The Sense of an Existential Self

From early in the first year, infants can differentiate their own feelings and movements from those of others, and they can distinguish their own acts relative to the environment. This is called the **ecological self**. Beginning at 9 months, infants have a sense of their own subjectivity, the **subjective self**, but they do not yet have a concept of "I."

With the advent of script-based memory (see above), infants are now able to categorize and remember sequences of events that are most familiar to them. Among such sequences are the actions performed and the feelings experienced by the children themselves. Because of script-based memory, the infant at 18 months is beginning to put all of these self-experiences together into a whole picture of himself or herself as someone who can be recognized and distinguished, as a whole person, from other people. This ability, marked by self-recognition in a mirror, is called the **existential self**. Beginning at 18 months, the infants can say things like "I cry" or "I tired," (see Chapter 6) indicating that not only does the child have the subjective sense of one who gets tired, but he or she can also combine that with a pronoun indicating a person who has or possesses that feeling. The growth of the prefrontal cortex, associated with self-monitoring and self-regulation, may underlie these developments (Frith & Frith, 2001).

Children's earliest linguistic references to the self during this age period are with the personal pronoun I rather than words like *me*, *mine*, or *my*. When using *I*, children express their intended actions ("I do it," "I hold it"), make requests or proposals ("I wanna play with that one"), or state a proposition ("I have the crayon"). They rarely use the word *you* (Imbens-Bailey & Pan, 1998). Typically, use of personal pronouns begins around the same time or a little bit after mirror self-recognition (Courage, Edison, & Howe, 2004; Lewis & Ramsay, 2004).

One method that has been developed to study the emergence of the existential self is to observe infants' reactions to their own mirror images (M. Lewis & Brooks-Gunn, 1979). Initially, infants are put in front of the mirror for a few minutes. Even young infants will show interest in the mirror image, touching the mirror or parts of themselves, smiling and showing other emotions. After this period of free play with the mirror, the experimenter removes the infants and pretends to wipe their faces with a cloth. In actuality, the experimenter dabs a bit of red rouge on the infants' noses without the babies realizing it. Then, the babies are returned to the mirror. If the infants recognize that the mirror image is of themselves, they will touch their own noses, but not the mirror image nose. By 24 months, the majority of children will touch their own noses after seeing the red spot. Table 5.6 describes the steps in the infant's development of self-recognition.

Recall that babies during the first year are able to form simple mental categories: they can recognize male versus female faces, and infants compared to older children and adults. In the next section, we discuss the development of the **categorical self**, or self-concept, which emerges when children can identify their own membership in one or more

By 18 months, most babies can recognize their own image in a mirror.
Photo by Elizabeth Crews.

TABLE 5.6   Stages in the Development of the Existential Self, the Ability to Recognize the Physical Features of the Self

Behaviors	Approximage Age in Months	Interpretation
Emergence of Self as Subject, as Active, Independent, Causal Agent		
I. Interest in mirror image; regards, approaches, touches, smiles, vocalizes. Does not differentially respond to self versus Other in mirror, videotape, or pictorial representation.	5–8	No evidence that self is perceived as a causal agent, independent of others. No featural differentiation between self and other.
II. Understands nature of reflective surface; contingency play, imitation, rhythmic movements, bounding, waving; can locate objects in space, attached to body. Differentiates between contingent and noncontingent videotape representations of self.	9–12	Active agent in space emerges, awareness of cause-effect relationship between own body movements and moving visual image.
III. Uses mirror to locate people/objects in space. Reaches toward person, not image, and reaches toward object not attached to body. Distinguishes between self-movement and movement of others on videotape.	12–15	Self-other differentiation with regard to agency. Appreciates self as an active, independent agent separate from others, who can also cause his or her own movements in space.
Emergence of Self as an Object of One's Knowledge		
IV. In mirror and videotape, demonstrates mark-directed behavior. Sees image and touches rouge on nose. Points to self. Distinguishes between self and other in pictorial representation and videotape.	15–18	Featural recognition of self; internal schema for own face that can be compared to external visual image.
V. Verbal labeling: infant can state name, attach appropriate personal pronoun to own image in mirror. Can distinguish self from same-gender infant in pictures and can label self.	18–24	Appreciation that one has unique featural attributes that can be verbally labeled as the self.

Source: S. Harter, Developmental perspectives on the self-system, 1983, p. 283. In E. M. Hetherington (Ed.), *Handbook of child psychology: Socialization, personality, and social development* (Vol. 4), pp. 265–290. New York: Wiley. Reprinted by permission of John Wiley & Sons, Inc.

conceptual categories, such as "I am a boy," "I am a brother," and "I am not a baby" (Harter, 1983). Curiously, it takes until the third year for this conceptual skill to be applied to the self. One research study on the application of such concepts to self and to mother gives some insight into why it takes babies so long to discover themselves.

In this study (Pipp, Fischer, & Jennings, 1987), infants were given the standard rouge test on themselves and also on their mothers. A number of different self and other recognition tasks were given to the children as well (see Table 5.7) (As an aside, these tasks are great fun to do with babies of this age). In addition to these recognition tasks, infants were asked to perform actions either on a doll, on themselves, or on their mothers. An example would be pretend feeding the doll or self or pretend feeding the mother.

The results show that before 18 months, infants are able to correctly recognize their moth-

TABLE 5.7   Self- and Other Physical Feature Recognition Tasks

Infant Version	Mother Version
Infant touches own nose with rouge after seeing self in mirror.	Infant touches mother's nose with rouge after seeing mother in mirror.
"Where's [child's name]?"	"Where's Mommy?"
"Who's that?" (said while pointing to child).	"Who's that?" (said while pointing to mother).
"Whose shoe is that?" (said while pointing to child's shoe).	"Whose shoe is that?" (said while pointing to mother's shoe).
"Are you a boy or a girl?"	"Is Mommy a boy or a girl?"

Source: S. Pipp, K. W. Fischer, & S. Jennings., Acquisition of self- and mother knowledge in infancy, 1986, p. 90. *Developmental Psychology, 23*, 86–96.

ers and respond correctly to questions about mother at earlier ages than those at which they can recognize and respond to questions about themselves. This is consistent with studies of concept development done in the first year: infants are able to recognize the common features of objects and group them into categories. Before 18 months, on the other hand, infants are more successful at *performing actions* on themselves or the doll than on the mother. After 18 months, infants were equally adept at verbally describing self and mother.

Other research finds that children's awareness of their bodies with regard to the environment also changes at this age. Children aged 15, 18, and 21 months were asked to do things like put on clothing that was too small, pass through openings that were too narrow, or pick up a mat on which they were sitting or standing. The older children were better at judging their own size and weight and did not try to do the tasks that did not fit their body size (Brownell, Zerwas, & Ramani, 2007; Moore et al., 2007).

In the previous age period, infants preferred to imitate intentional rather than mechanical actions of adults. After 18 months, infants are also beginning to reason about other people's desires. In one study, 14- and 18-month-old infants watched while adults ate either crackers or broccoli. For some babies at each age, the adult said "Mmm," making a happy expression, when eating the crackers, and "Eeew," making a disgusted expression, when eating the broccoli. For other infants, the adult acted as if she liked the broccoli but not the crackers.

The adult then asked the infants to offer her one or the other type of food. Fourteen-month-olds offered the adult only crackers, assuming that the adult would like what the child liked, regardless of the adult's expressed preferences. The 18-month-olds, on the other hand, offered whichever food the adult seemed to prefer. This means the older infants were beginning to be aware of the psychological desires of the adult and respond appropriately (Repacholi & Gopnik, 1997). These older babies realized that their own preferences were not necessarily the same as the adult's, a major advance in distinguishing between the internal experiences of self and other.

Infants differ in their level of self and other understanding, however. Some infants are better at the task of self and other recognition. These infants notice more details and can respond with more complex answers to the questions in Table 5.7. These more self- and other-aware infants are more securely attached to their mothers and fathers, show more concern for other's distress, can coordinate mirror image imitation, and are more competent in peer play (Asendorpf & Baudonniere, 1993; Asendorph, Warkentin, & Baudonniere, 1996; Pipp, Easterbrooks, & Brown, 1993; Pipp, Easterbrooks, & Harmon, 1992; Zahn-Waxler, Radke-Yarrow, Wagner, & Chapman, 1992). These studies suggest that positive social relationships are likely to enhance one's understanding of oneself and one's relationships to others.

Other research shows that children who reacted with greater distress to inoculations and who had higher levels of the stress hormone cortisol during the first year of life were more likely to be able to recognize themselves in the mirror at 18 months than infants with who reacted with less distress during the first year. This finding suggests that infants who are more sensitive to their internal experiences are more likely to be aware of themselves at this age (M. Lewis & Ramsey, 1997). Interestingly, insecurely attached children, who are also more likely to have higher cortisol responses, use different language to describe themselves compared to securely attached children. The insecure children at this age are more likely to talk about their own negative, as compared to positive, feelings (Lemche et al., 2007).

Symbols are conventionally shared among the members of a linguistic community. When children use the word "dog," they not only represent dogs symbolically, they partake of a socially shared way of representing dogs. At the end of the first year, the child's first words are an example of **idiosyncratic communication**: they represent things but not in a way that can be shared by more than the people who are closest to the child. When the children use the word "dog," they are referring to that particular animal and they are accepting the rights and responsibilities of being a member of a community of people who have agreed to use that word. To be a member of a community is to comply with its rules (the animal we know as a dog is to be called by the word "dog") and also to be consciously aware of abiding by the rules.

The awareness that *communication takes place in a community* is also part of the existential self, which begins to develop after the age of 18 months. Babies of this age become aware that they are being watched. This must be a rather startling discovery for a baby, as the following example may illustrate. Think of some ways that you express yourself privately, ways you have not shown to anyone or even talked about with anyone, like singing in the shower, writing poetry, or drawing pictures. You are probably perfectly happy doing these things alone and you can feel yourself, your mind and body, as you do them. This is your subjective self coming out.

Now imagine that someone overhears you, or finds your poems and reads them, or sees your drawings. Your privacy has been invaded and you would most likely be embarrassed. This is the voice of your existential self waking up to the fact that you can be exposed when you least expect it. Depending on your style of emotional regulation and on the person who discovered you and their way of behaving with you about this discovery, you might be defiantly angry and feel violated, or you might be relieved and proud that someone likes your work.

Whatever way you feel about it, your world has been changed. You cannot operate in total isolation any more. You have to do something about your new awareness that you are living in a household community. One thing you might do is negotiate the boundaries of your privacy with the other person, coming to an agreement about what is yours alone and what you are willing to share. Alternatively, you could slam the door to your room and scream at the other person. Or you could welcome the other person into your world and open that world to shared experiences. No one of these strategies is better than another. Each depends upon you and the situation.

What they have in common, however, is that you are being compelled to recognize your membership in a community. The more of yourself that you open up to that community, the more of an opportunity you have to share, but the more you must comply with the standards and rules of the community. If you are willing to comply, it may lead to increased skills and self-awareness, such as when one takes singing, writing, or drawing lessons, for example. These activities provide access to community standards and practices and the symbols with which members of those communities communicate about their work.

The developmental challenge for infants of this age, then, is to open up to the pleasures (pride, mastery, sharing) and pains (shame, defiance, having to comply) of being an active member of a community. This is not easy to do, and in fact, it is a lifelong issue that only begins at 18 months. How much of your willingness to comply in particular situations is related to an nonverbal participatory memory of your style of compliance as a toddler? Perhaps you can ask the people who knew you as a baby about your style of compliance back then and compare it to your style of compliance today.

The other major developmental lesson of this age period is opening up to new dimensions of psychological experience. Up to this point in their development, children's awareness has been participatory. Now they can put linguistic labels on their experiences and attach those labels to a subject ("I," "you"). When children say "I'm tired," they can identify their experience with a word and at the same time bring it into the community for guidance and assistance. "I'm tired" is a way of saying "pick me up" or "put me to bed."

Imagine feeling as though you are low in energy but not knowing why. You have a conversation with a friend, and somehow you realize that this feeling is because you have been working really hard or faced some new or difficult challenges. Because you were so caught up in what you had to do (subjective self), you did not have an opportunity to find a name for your feeling and recognize that it was part of you (existential self). After the conversation, you can say, "Oh, yes, I'm really tired," which may give you permission to take it easy or to treat yourself nicely for a while. You deserve it!

The clinical theories reviewed in Chapter 2, both the psychotherapeutic and somatic approaches, suggest that this developmental change comes from the coupling of psychological and body awareness with words or gestures shared with another person in the context of a therapeutic relationship. Research and clinical practice have shown that simply communicating—verbally or nonverbally—with another person in a therapeutic situation about those areas of your mind and body that were hurting, confused, or in the darkness of anxiety is often sufficient to change them for the better (Feldenkrais, 1981; C. Ginsburg, 1999; Hartley, 1995; Hunt, 1995; Smyth & Pennebaker, 1999; Varela, Thompson, & Rosch, 1995; Wooten, 1995).

Self-Awareness in the Third Year: The Emergence of the Categorical Self

By the third year, children can talk to themselves using private speech (Chapter 6) and talk to others about the self. These abilities are related to having a **categorical self**, or a self-concept, which emerges during this period. The categorical self is the ability of people to identify their own membership in one or more conceptual categories, such as "I am a boy," "I am a brother," and "I am not a baby"; it begins around the child's third birthday. Given a set of pictures of people of different sexes and ages, children of this age are quite accurate in labeling both age and sex differences in other people (Edwards, 1984; Keller, Ford, & Meacham, 1978). Thus, by the end of the second year, you might hear a child say, "I'm not a baby anymore!"

Autobiographical Memory. As we saw in the previous section, by age 2, infants are beginning to organize their memories according to scripts or sequences of events. They can often remember complex sequences, and in some cases, they can remember sequences that happened some time ago, so long as there is some kind of nonverbal reminder and the child is allowed to demonstrate the memory nonverbally by imitation.

The ability to remember experiences *verbally* is called **autobiographical memory**. Autobiographical memory serves to create a sense of one's life history. It is constructed in conversations with others beginning in the third year of life. Children whose autobiographical memory is more detailed have mothers who are more likely to elaborate on children's recall by filling in the details of the past event and asking questions of children to clarify their stories about themselves; in other words, when there is a joint conversation about current and past events in which both mother and child take part (Fivush, 1994; Haden et al., 2001; Harley & Reese, 1999; Wang, 2006). Children with more advanced verbal skills are better at autobiographical remembering (Simcock & Hayne, 2003) and children who use more mental state words like "thinking," "knowing," and "remembering" are better at producing autobiographical details (Cherney, 2003).

By the beginning of the third year of life, the ability to verbally narrate a past situation depends, on whether or not they had verbal skills at the time of the event they are trying to remember. Researchers in Canada studied children who had a traumatic injury that brought them to the hospital emergency room some time during their first two years of life (C. Peterson, 1999; C. Peterson & Bell, 1996; C. Peterson & Rideout, 1998). If the injury occurred around the age of 2 years, children could recall the situation verbally up to two years later. One such child had burned his hand on a lawn-mower exhaust when he was just under 2 years old. A year and a half later, he could state that he burned his hand, who was there, why it happened, and that he saw a doctor.

Children who were injured before 18 months are interesting from the perspective of the transition from **participatory memory** to verbal auto-biographical memory. At 16 months, a child fell and cut his forehead. His emergency room visit was traumatic for him, since he had to be tightly wrapped in a blanket to keep him from moving during the stitching. For the next few months, he showed sleep disturbances and fear of strangers, did not want to leave the house, and became hysterical when blankets were put on him. He was interviewed by the researchers when he was 22 months old. At that time he still did not have verbal skills sufficient to describe the situation, but when he heard the word "hospital," he pointed to the place on his forehead where he had received the stitches. He was shown several pictures, one of which was of his doctor. He picked up the doctor's picture and showed it to his father, saying, "Doc, doc." When interviewed 18 months after the accident (at 34 months of age), he still had no verbal memory of it, but his parents said he still refused to be wrapped in a smock when getting his hair cut.

These studies show that if an incident, especially a traumatic one, occurs earlier than age 2, participatory memories remain nonverbal (not wanting to be covered with a smock) but not verbally. Individuals may have participatory memories

of their early infancy that persist for long periods in the form of nonverbal patterns of action. Infantile amnesia, therefore, is primarily a verbal amnesia.

People with adult amnesia due to brain injury are more likely to have participatory memories than verbal memories. They may look and act like "themselves," using their somatic participatory memories even though they do not remember autobiographically who they are when asked questions about themselves (Baddeley, 1994; Hirst, 1994). Interestingly, many cases of adult amnesia are related to damage to the **hippocampus**, that part of the limbic system that is responsible for the organization of sequences of events in memory. The hippocampus does not develop as quickly as other parts of the limbic system, and is not fully mature until 3 to 4 years of age, helping to explain why it takes that long for autobiographical memory to develop.

In addition, as we saw in Chapter 2, adult trauma victims are more likely to have participatory memories than verbal memories of their trauma. They may have recurring dreams or behavior patterns, or they may have fragmentary flashbacks in which they relive some part of the trauma, such as being suddenly intensely afraid and breaking into a cold sweat for no apparent reason (Smyth & Pennebaker, 1999; Terr, 1994). The hippocampus may be implicated here also, since one of the features of trauma is that events unfold too quickly for the hippocampus to process. In an automobile accident or a physical assault, for example, rapid **neuroception** via the **amygdala**, **sympathetic nervous system**, and **HPA axis** are the primary neural processes. Conscious, autobiographical memory formation via the hippocampus is bypassed.

This suggests that traumatic memories from infancy (or anytime in life) may be particularly likely to persist in the form of nonverbal participatory memories. The child may not verbally "know" why he is afraid of being wrapped up in a blanket because he is unable to verbally articulate and understand why, but the memory persists somatically. Likewise, adult victims of violence cannot consciously link their cold sweats, nightmares, or phobias to an autobiographical memory of the violent event. Participatory somatic memories will continue if the conditions that created the memories—or similar conditions—persist and continue to be reenacted (Hudson & Sheffield, 1998). This is because the amygdala alters its cellular structure with trauma, leaving the person vulnerable to perceive fear even in relatively benign situations.

This research is consistent with other studies of infant nonverbal memory reviewed in this chapter. These findings support the testimony of clinicians, especially those who work with somatic therapies such as play therapies with children and with adults, using the Rosen method and body-mind centering, who report that infantile participatory memories and traumatic memories are often experienced during therapeutic encounters (see Chapter 2).

One child in play therapy at 4 ½ years had witnessed her mother being blown up by a bomb when she was 12 months old. During play therapy, the child thrashed about on the floor, made loud explosion-like noises, and scattered the toys around the room, all in relation to a doll that represented the "mother" (Gaensbauer, 2004). Therapeutic interventions that allow traumas to be relived safely, and then transformed into verbal memories by writing or talking, diffuse the trauma and lead to increases in mental and physical health (Smyth & Pennebaker, 1999).

More research is needed, however, to better understand why some participatory memories remain and others do not. We also need to better understand the circumstances in which these memories can best be revealed. Are children and adults more likely to retain participatory memories of traumatic events that occurred before the age of 2 years than of everyday events that occurred during infancy? Or are infantile traumatic experiences less likely to be transformed into verbal memories in the absence of the emotional safety of a therapeutic situation? Finally, there is controversy over whether such memories can be falsely implanted in a child by therapists and investigators who seek to verify that child abuse may have occurred (Theirry & Spence, 2002). We will return

to some of these topics when we discuss the traumatic effects of child maltreatment during the infancy period in Chapter 9.

Gender identity and gender roles. In addition to autobiographical memory, another aspect of the categorical self is identification with being either a boy or a girl. By the beginning of the third year, children are beginning to notice sex differences in behavior and appearance, and to show early signs of sexual behavior. Although there are cultural differences in the frequency of sexual behavior, normally developing children (not sexually abused) of both genders become interested in watching other people undress and in seeing their genitals. They begin to hug non-family members, like to walk around naked and expose their genitals, try to touch other children's genitals, and stimulate their own genitals with their hands (Larsson & Svedin, 2002). This interest in sexuality appears to be a normal form of curiosity about their own and other's bodies and part of the development of **gender identity**: the affiliation with being either male or female.

Not all children identify with members of their biological gender. In some cases, this is because the child has a birth defect in which the genitals do not completely form or in which they have characteristics of both males and females or internal characteristics of one gender and external characteristics of the other gender (called **intersex**, but an older term is hermaphroditism). Some of these cases are caused by genetic and chromosomal abnormalities (Berenbaum & Bailey, 2003; Zucker, 1999), and others are caused by too high or too low levels of maternal testosterone during the period of prenatal development when the genitals are forming (see Chapters 3 and 9). Even when the genitals are normal, some individuals may develop an identity with the "opposite" gender, in some cases for a few years and in other cases for a lifetime (as in homosexuality and transvestitism). Little is known about the causes of these nontraditional forms of gender identity, although some evidence suggests genetic and/or prenatal testosterone abnormalities (Hines et al., 2002; Reiner & Gearhart, 2004).

As a result of curiosity about one's own gender identity, children of this age develop **gender labeling**, when the child can identify self or other verbally as male or female. This begins at about 18 months (G. Levy, 2000; Poulin-Dubois, Serbin, & Derbyshire, 1998). Up until the age of 3 years, however, children do not understand that these labels reflect enduring characteristics of people. Two-year-olds will say correctly that they are a boy or a girl and will even engage in gender-stereotyped toy play, but they do not understand that a boy will always grow up to be a man. Children believe that gender might be changed by changing one's appearance or dress, which might explain why they are fairly rigid in their adoption of gender-role stereotypes ("Ladies can't wear pants"; "Boys don't play with dolls"). Children may actively discourage each other from playing with opposite gender–typed toys or even with members of the opposite sex (Gelman, Collman, & Maccoby, 1986; Slaby & Frey, 1975). They will also look longer at gender inappropriate behavior (such as a man putting on lipstick), suggesting that they already have a sense of what males and females are likely to do ordinarily (Serbin, Poulin-Dubois, & Eichstedt, 2002).

Interestingly, 2-to-3-year-old children who are more advanced in gender labeling (those who give the correct gender response to the question, "Who are you?") and who score higher on verbal intelligence tests are also more explicit about gender-role behaviors. That is, they will classify tasks and tools as male (car repair, shovels) or as female (cooking, irons). These children will also more readily adopt same-sex playmates in peer groups. Additionally, a number of studies have found that boys begin gender labeling and gender stereotyping somewhat earlier than girls. Girls, for example, are more likely to play with opposite-sex toys than are boys (Bauer, 1993; Fagot & Leinbach, 1989; Fagot, Leinbach, & Hagan, 1990; McGuire, 1988; O'Brien & Huston, 1985; Weinraub et al., 1984).

These studies of gender understanding suggest that cognitive and linguistic factors play some role, because children who are more linguistically and cognitively advanced are also more stereotypic in their gender-role concepts. However, it may be that children who are more articulate about gender roles have parents who talk more about such issues, so we cannot rule out a possible social influence in such factors.

One area that has been studied a great deal is parental influence over the child's choice of toys—specifically, parental reactions to traditional masculine toys (trucks, hammers, guns) and feminine toys (dolls, kitchen utensils) for their boys and girls. This is a difficult area in which to do research because reactions to a child's behavior regarding gender roles are highly culture specific. Interpreting this research is complicated because different studies use different measures (observations, questionnaires, parental reports) and because most of the research is done in middle-class Caucasian American families. However, with these qualifications, the following conclusions can be reached.

Few parents explicitly instruct their children in the gender-appropriate choice or use of toys. Gender-role stereotypes are communicated to children by the parents' emotional reactions to the children's choice of toys. First of all, when children are between 18 and 24 months, parents have more emotional reactions, both positive and negative and not necessarily gender stereotyped, to any kind of gender-related toy. At this age, parents react less to toy choices that are not gender related (such as blocks and nesting cups). Children who begin gender labeling early have parents who evince more emotional reactions to gender-typed toys during this early period (Fagot & Leinbach, 1989).

During the second year, as the children's toy choices become more gender typed, some parents begin to discourage gender-inappropriate toys and encourage gender-appropriate toys, again through emotional reactions rather than instruction (Caldera, Huston, & O'Brien, 1989; Fagot & Leinbach, 1989; Weinraub et al., 1984). Parents also contribute to gender-role identity by discouraging aggression and encouraging prosocial behavior in girls and by encouraging responsibility in boys. In addition, most parents dress and cut their children's hair in gender-appropriate ways in order to avoid other people's incorrect identification of the children's gender (McGuire, 1988; Power & Parke,

1986). In addition, parents talk in general about gender and gender roles, and it is nearly impossible to talk about a person without mentioning personal pronouns such as "he" and "she" (Gelman, Taylor, & Nguyen, 2004).

Few studies have found differences between mothers and fathers in the encouragement of gender-appropriate behavior. Mothers and fathers typically agree on the kinds of gender roles they want for their children (Fagot & Hagan, 1991; Fagot & Leinbach, 1989). In one study, the types of speech, length of utterances, and number of questions and directives were the same for mothers and fathers when each interacted individually with the infant (Golinkoff and Ames, 1979). A study of verbal and nonverbal behavior of mothers and fathers found no parental sex differences in responsiveness to the infant, use of stimulation, affection, or effectiveness (A. Clarke-Stewart, 1978).

Even though mothers and fathers are using similar behavior toward the children, the early onset of gender labeling and the frequency of gender-typed toy play in children are predicted by personality characteristics of the father rather than of the mother. Early labelers, both boys and girls, have fathers who have more traditional gender-role orientations and who engage in more traditionally masculine tasks (car washing, lawn mowing, carpentry) than feminine tasks (laundry, cooking, dishwashing) at home. Additionally, in homes where mothers work outside the home or where fathers are absent (single-parent mother-headed homes), children have less traditional gender-role stereotypes (Fagot & Leinbach, 1989; Fagot, Leinbach, & O'Boyle, 1992; McGuire, 1988; Stevenson & Black, 1988; Weinraub et al., 1984).

This research is difficult to sort out. Why should gender-role development of children be correlated with the father's personality or absence, even though the mother and father in the same family encourage gender-role behavior in a similar way? Could it be that fathers are influencing the mothers' actions? Or could it be that these women married men who had similar beliefs? Finally, it could be that both parents are being affected by the child's behavior. Although a parent-to-child socialization effect is the most plausible explanation, it is difficult to get unambiguous evidence in support of this position.

There is really too little evidence and too much variability between studies and between families to draw firm conclusions about parent-infant sex differences and their effects on development. More evidence exists for older children whose gender-role behavior is more obvious and salient. The most we can say about gender-role development in the third year is that it is a topic of interest for both parents and children, and that children are using information available in the environment, as well as their own thinking about self-concept, to form ideas about gender roles.

EXPERIENTIAL EXERCISE

The Ecological Self
by Ise de Koeyer

As humans, we can see part of our bodies in our field of vision at all times. You can try this by closing one eye and looking straight ahead: you will see your own nose. Thus, whenever you perceive your environment, you perceive yourself— parts of your body, its boundaries, and the quality and aliveness of your own movements. Perceiving the environment is co-perceiving yourself. The ecological self is the sense of self as situated in the environment. Starting at least around 2 months and probably from birth, young babies already have a sense of themselves in this way. This sense of self is still present in adults, but much more in the background of experience. You can explore your ecological sense of self during everyday activities.

1. Self-agency: the sense that your own actions will have consequences (closing your eyes and it gets dark; moving your arm when

it wants to move). You may notice this most when your movements are blocked or thwarted.

2. Self-coherence: the sense of being a whole physical entity with boundaries and limitations (sensing the difference between touching and being touched; moving your hands and seeing them move at the exact same time). An example of this in adulthood is when you move something and at the very same time something falls behind you. You may wonder "Was that me?"

3. Self-affectivity: the sense of having emotional feelings that routinely go together with certain experiences (seeing mom and feeling happy; feeling sad when she leaves). Do you get a warm feeling when you see a loved one, or some other feeling? Do you have a sense of security when you get home, or some other feeling?

4. Self-history: the sense of the relationship with your past, the sense of familiarity with certain people or situations you find yourself in. This characteristic is part of the 3 others. For example, your body knows exactly how to sit down on a chair or how to get into the car. Or you may feel a sense of familiarity when you come home or see a loved one.

The ecological self extends to the use of tools or other objects. For example, when you use a pair of scissors, they become an extension of yourself. A good example is driving. As you move around in your car, it is as if it becomes part of you. You may notice a lack of agency, for instance, when you try to start your car and it doesn't

respond. Also, you may find that your sense of your ecological self feels different when you walk, ride on your bike, or drive. In all of these situations, your body moves around in different ways, and this may make you see and notice different aspects of the environment. Experiment with moving around in different ways (fast, slow, careful, large or small movements, etc.) and experience the differences in how you perceive yourself in the world.

Mirror Self-Recognition
by Alan Fogel

The purpose of this exercise is to evoke the experience of seeing oneself in a mirror for the very first time, and thus to re-create some of the feelings of a toddler finding the "existential self" during the "rouge" test: the sense of otherness or foreignness of the mirror image, sense of shame or pride, etc. Because we adults all have extensive experience with mirrors, the exercise relies on using a mirror to observe one's own face in unusual ways and with more scrutiny than is typical for most people.

Students should bring to class a small hand-held mirror. Students sit comfortably with a mirror and something on which to write. Notes are made following each step of the exercise. A brief relaxation exercise may be done before starting.

1. Please look at your face in the mirror. Take as much time as you need. Look especially at parts of your face that you don't typically notice or see. As you study your

face, remain aware of your sensations and emotions. Possible emotions may be curiosity, disgust, embarrassment, a sense of unfamiliarity, or enjoyment. Also remain aware of your body sensations as you do this. Notice the parts of your face that you like and the parts that you do not like. Write down your experience and then close your eyes and rest. (2–3 minutes)

2. Sometimes each eye has its own point of view. With your eyes closed notice whether there are differences in how each eye feels. Open your eyes and this time, cover one of your eyes with a piece of folded paper. Again, examine your face and notice your feelings and sensations. Ask yourself: Who is this person? Do I know this person? Do I like this person? Write down your experience, and then close your eyes and rest. (2–3 minutes)

3. With your eyes closed, consider the possibility that the other eye may see yourself differently than the one you just looked through. Cover your other eye. Repeat the looking with the same questions as for the first eye. Take a minute to compare the views of yourself with each eye. Write, rest. (2–3 minutes)

4. It has been said that the eyes are the windows to the soul. This time look directly into one of your eyes and examine it and your feelings about that eye. Finally, look directly into the other eye and repeat what you just did. Compare your views of each eye. Write down your experience, and then close your eyes and rest. (2–3 minutes).

SUMMARY

Brain Development

- The major areas of the brain are the brain stem, limbic system, and cortex.
- The brain stem areas control autonomic functions such as breathing and heart rate.
- The limbic system processes emotions and memories as well as some body functions. Within the limbic system, the important structures during infancy are the hippocampus, amygdala, hypothalamus, and pituitary.
- The prefrontal cortex connects limbic and cortical areas and is responsible for social and emotional regulation. The cortex involves thinking, reasoning, and judging.
- The brain is divided into two hemispheres, the right more emotional and the left more cognitive and linguistic.
- Brain development depends on experience with the environment. Part of the brain is experience expectant, while other parts are experience dependent. Brain growth involves cell loss as well as increases in connections.
- The HPA axis responds to and regulates the effects of stress and trauma.

Newborn Cognition

- Newborns are susceptible to both operant conditioning and classical conditioning.
- Habituation and conditioning reflect rudimentary memory processes as infants need to compare current with past experiences. Most newborn memories seem to last no more than a few hours, unless the stimulus is repeated often.
- Newborns appear to be able to imitate simple gestures they themselves can make. Imitation is irregular and not especially salient to a casual observer.

Two to Five Months

- The time taken for habituation decreases, and the infant's attention span increases.
- Infants have participatory memories for up to 2 weeks, but reminders make the memories longer. Memory is dependent upon emotional and contextual cues present at the time of the learning.

- Infantile amnesia may be due to the fact that infant memory is so closely related to the situation in which the infant was first exposed to the stimulus. Since the exact situation rarely recurs later, people seem to forget what happened to them as infants. People do, however, have participatory memories of feelings and sensations from infancy, even though they cannot locate the exact time, place, or situation.
- The main form of adaptation is primary circular reactions, in which the infants are exploring the effects of their own body movements and vocalizations.

Six to Nine Months

- Infant memory improves in duration, and infants can process information faster than in the previous stage.
- Infants now try to form concepts out of their perceptual experiences. Concept formation appears to be organized around prototypes.
- Using secondary circular reactions, infants discover relationships between their actions and the environment, and they vary their actions to observe the effects.
- Infants of this age can remember object locations, so long as they do not have to act on the objects.

Ten to Twelve Months

- Infants can perceive and act on relationships between objects, such as between cups and saucers, between causes and effects, between objects and their hiding places, and between the actions of others and their own actions.
- Infants act in deliberate and intentional ways, persisting until a goal is achieved.
- Although infants can find hidden objects in some circumstances, they are still puzzled by complicated paths of movement and multiple hiding places.
- Infants can now imitate actions that they have never performed before and can reproduce acts even after a 24-hour delay.
- Individual differences in cognition result from an interaction between infant temperament and attentional skills and adult intervention.

Twelve to Eighteen Months

- Infants are experimenting to find new ways to cause similar effects, such as trying alternate strategies to reach goals through trial-and-error exploration.

- Infants can now conceive of higher-order categories, such as "animals" and "vehicles."

Eighteen to Twenty-Four Months

- Symbolic play develops by the combination of different types of symbols into complex event sequences. Infants still do not understand all the connections between their own actions on objects.
- Script-based memories allow for categorization of events according to the sequences in which they typically occur.
- Children of this age become interested in simple television programs, but it helps if adults watch along with them.

Twenty-Four to Thirty-Six Months

- Children are now able to execute complex sequences of action, work toward an adult standard, and correct their own errors. This leads to increases in attention span.
- Language becomes internalized as private speech, such that prior forms of social regulation now become self-regulatory.
- Make-believe and pretend become complex and creative.

Development of Self-Awareness

- Newborns appear to have a rudimentary sense of self, experienced as a feeling of the familiarity of their own bodies, feelings, and behaviors.
- Infants can perceive an ecological self, the sense that they have agency, coherence, location in the environment, and feelings that belong to them. This is extended up until 10 months with the emergence of an awareness that other people exist.
- The subjective self begins around 10 months as infants learn to communication intentionally, check in with others about their emotions, and share emotions and interests with others.
- An existential sense of self emerges when children can recognize themselves in the mirror and when they begin to use the word "I."
- A sense of categorical self emerges, including age and gender self-labeling.
- The acquisition of gender-role stereotypes is a complex developmental process involving cognitive understanding of gender and family role relationships and the development of autobiographical memory.

Chapter 6

Social and Communicative Development

CHAPTER OUTLINE AND OVERVIEW

Infants begin to learn social skills long before they ever acquire their first words. Some of the social skills that infants need to learn are so basic to human life as we know it that it is hard to believe that there was a time in our lives when we did not possess such capabilities. One of these very basic social skills is the ability to take turns in a conversation. Although infants seem to be born with naturally occurring bursts and pauses in their behavior, any semblance of taking turns is apparently created by the adult partner, who learns to insert smiles, coos, and words into the natural silences left by the infant. Although the infant does not initially intend to leave these spaces, the experience of having them filled by the adult eventually leads to the child's growing awareness that he or she is indeed a partner, one who can initiate, pause, speak, or act in concert with another. This ability usually does not appear before the age of five or six months.

Learning a first language built upon these early communicative skills is an educational accomplishment of such magnitude that it would be hard to duplicate it at any later point in life. There is more to language than just learning the meanings of words. It is also necessary to learn how words are used, when to speak and when to listen, and how to understand what others are saying. Language in this sense is really only one form of a broader intention to communicate, to share information, and to learn more about the world. Language, if we look at how it is used in everyday situations, is just as much a social skill as a cognitive skill. This chapter covers both social and linguistic development in the first three years.

The First Two Months

Adults and infants have sensitivities and responses that make a good mutual fit. Newborn sucking responses are perfectly suited to obtain milk from the breast; the newborn's appearance, sound, and smell are powerful attractors of adult attention and care; and the newborn is primed to recognize the primary caregiver by smell, sound, and possibly touch.

According to behavior ecology theory, especially that of John Bowlby (1969), in the early weeks and months of life, we share a common heritage with most other mammals who nurse and show a good deal of solicitude toward their young. Not every order of animals behaves this way. Reptiles give birth to eggs and usually leave the young to fend for themselves after hatching. Bird species do not nurse their young, nor do they give birth to live infants; however, they do show parental caregiving behavior.

After the domestic cat gives birth, the mother lies on her side to expose her nipples. She licks the kittens, which are blind at birth, and the licking helps them orient to her body, nuzzle into her fur, and begin to search for the nipple. After only a few days, each kitten has a preferred nipple, and there is rapid improvement in the speed with which a kitten can find its nipple (Rosenblatt, 1972).

The example of the domestic cat illustrates the idea that a complex series of communicative co-actions occurs between mother and infant by which each learns to adjust to the other. Over time, the initial trial-and-error response is reduced, and nursing and other forms of interpersonal interaction become more efficient. In this case the mother, no less than the infant, is subject to the tug of powerful evolutionary forces that ensure the survival of the young. In one study, human mothers of newborns were blindfolded and then guided to touch the hand and cheek of three newborns, their own and two other infants. Two-thirds of the mothers were able to identify their own infant from touching the infant's hands, while half identified their infant from touching the face (Kaitz, Meirov, & Landman, 1993). This study shows that mothers have a nonverbal and nonvisual sensitivity toward their own babies that matches the infants' recognition of their own mothers by auditory, taste, and tactile cues.

People use the word "bonding" to signify this initial communicative coordination between infant and parent, speaking of a relationship as either "bonded" or "not bonded." Bonding also has been used to refer to the events that take place during the first few hours after birth, when mother and infant are placed alone together and in skin-to-skin contact. The concept of bonding grew out of the pioneering work of Marshall Klaus and John Kennell of Case Western Reserve University. Their first reports detailed an apparently universal pattern of behavior seen in mothers presented with their naked newborns immediately after birth. The mothers in their study first began to touch the neonates' fingers and toes. This phase usually lasted between 4 and 8 minutes. After this, the mothers began to move inward, touching the infants' limbs, and ended their exploration by an encompassing palm contact with the infant's abdomen, accompanied by massaging movements (Klaus, Kennell, Plumb, & Zeuhlke, 1970). The same study found that mothers of premature infants progressed through the same phases but spent more time in each one.

Since then, the pattern of maternal behavior at first contact with the neonate has been replicated on many occasions and in a wide variety of settings. It has been shown that fathers, when given the same opportunity to lie next to their newborn children, progress through the same sequence of phases (D. McDonald, 1978; Rodholm & Larsson, 1979). Remarkably, this same pattern of exploration of the newborn has been observed in chimpanzee mothers with their newborn infants (Bard, 1994). The adult response to the first contact with the newborn is similar to adult responses to the cry, the smile, and the facial configuration of the neonate, a part of the species survival characteristics considered by behavior ecology theory.

The research initiated by Klaus, Kennell, and colleagues led the way for more humane treatment of newborns and mothers, making the hospital experience more emotionally meaningful for both parents and infants. The majority of hospitals in the United States allow for skin-to-skin contact between parents and infants immediately following birth. There is, however, no conclusive evidence linking these first few minutes of contact with later attachment security or insecurity or later communicative ability. In cases of prematurity, adoption, and risk, parents may not have an opportunity for this immediate post-birth physical contact. They can, however, form lasting relationships with their infants in a relatively short period of time when they are finally able to reconnect.

In addition to the physical aspects of communication, there is also a social-psychological component that may form the basis of later interpersonal communication between adult and infant. Mothers and infants were observed on the day after birth and again at 2 weeks of age during breast- or bottle-feeding while the mother jiggled the infant (Kaye, 1977; Kaye & Wells, 1980). Jiggles were anything the mother did to stimulate sucking, such as shaking the infant or gently moving the nipple in and out of the mouth. Jiggles rarely occurred, but when they did, they tended to occur during pauses in sucking, and mothers claimed they were using the jiggling to get the infant to start sucking again. To test whether the jiggling was effective, the duration of the pauses without jiggles was measured in relation to the duration of the pauses containing a jiggle. When the mother jiggled during a pause, the jiggling actually *lengthened* the pause. The mother's intervention tended to delay the onset of the next burst of sucks by about 2 seconds. This pattern held true so long as the mother continued to jiggle the infant.

If, however, the mother jiggled momentarily and then stopped, the infant was more likely to begin a burst of sucks than in either the no-jiggle or the continuous-jiggle condition. The pattern that developed—suck-pause, jiggle-stop, suck-pause, jiggle-stop, and so on—is the precursor to later forms of social discourse. The pattern looks very much like a dialogue in which there is an exchange of turns: baby, mother, baby, mother.

This turn-taking situation is still rather one-sided. Although the infant can adjust the timing of the onset of the burst of sucking within a limited range, he or she cannot change the pattern altogether. The mother, on the other hand, is quite capable of changing her behavior to fit the situation. She is able to choose what to do and when to do it. It is almost as if the pauses in sucking serve as "slots" or "spaces" into which the mother can insert her interventions. Although the whole thing has the appearance of turn taking, that seems to be an illusion created mostly by the mother's ability to adapt to the infant.

Newborns require an adult to make them complete, to fill in the missing pieces of their ability, and to give their world psychological coherence. This takes a lot of patience, because newborn expressions and movements are subtle and sometimes confusing.

Bringing coherence to the newborn's awake states is difficult for these reasons and also because the newborn is awake and alert relatively infrequently, and alertness is a rather fragile and easily disrupted state. On the other hand, just as jiggling prolongs sucking pauses, animated adult faces and brightly colored objects prolong periods of alertness (Sander, Stechler, Burns, & Lee, 1979; Wolff, 1987). As a result of repeated attempts to engage, taking advantage of initially brief periods of alertness, the duration of parent-infant face-to-face play and infant attention gradually increases over the first 2 months of life (Lavelli & Fogel, 2002; Thoman, Acebo, Dreyer, Becker, & Freese, 1979). This increase is clearly a product of the dynamically changing parent-infant communication system.

Two to Five Months

This simply sucking and touching dialogue in the first month is quickly replaced by more complex forms of parent-infant communication as each partner develops increasing sensitivities to the other's behavior. By the age of 2 months, infants make distinctly different actions toward adults compared to other animate stimuli. For example, infants are more likely to smile, vocalize, and make relaxed arm movements with responsive adults than with peers (Fogel, 1979), inanimate faces (Field, 1979a), or animate or inanimate toys (Ellsworth, Muir, & Hains, 1993; Legerstee, 1991, 1992; Legerstee, Pomerleau, Malcuit, & Feider, 1987). Duirng the period between 2 and 5 months, we first examine the effects of infants on adult behavior and some cultural differences in adult behavior. Then, we discuss how adult behavior affects infants.

The Effect of Infants on Adult Behavior

Exaggeration. With young infants, adults tend to exaggerate particular aspects of their speech and body movement. Facial expressions are made larger than usual, as in mock surprise and mock sadness. Adults shake and nod their heads in deliberate movements. When speaking, adults raise the pitch of their voices and have wider variations in pitch than when speaking to other adults. This has been found in a large number of different cultures (Fernald & Kuhl, 1987; Fernald & Simon, 1984; J. L. Jacobson, Boersma, Fields, & Olson, 1983; M. Papousek, Papousek, & Bornstein, 1985; Stern, Spieker, Barnett, & MacKain, 1983). Even in languages in which the pitch of a syllable conveys linguistic meaning—tonal languages such as Mandarin Chinese—researchers have found overall increases of pitch when adults talk to babies compared to other adults (Grieser & Kuhl, 1988).

Slowing down and simplification. A second aspect of adult behavior with young infants is the tendency to slow down and simplify behavior. Each action, such as a head nod or a facial expression, is held for a longer period with an infant than with another adult. In addition, when talking to infants, adults leave longer pauses between their individual actions (Fernald & Simon, 1984; M. Papouseket al., 1985; C. E. Snow, 1977; Stern, 1977). Adults prolong particular syllables and speak more slowly overall, giving their speech a melodic or singsong quality (M. Papousek & Papousek, 1981). Similarly, adults reduce the complexity of their behavior and their speech when talking to infants, using single words instead of sentences or simple actions, such as a single head nod and a wide smile.

Rhythm and repetition. Adults also use highly repetitive and rhythmic activities. They may say the same word or phrase many times with minor variations or make a series of exaggerated head nods punctuated with a clap or a vocalization. Different rhythms are used depending upon the purpose of the behavior (soothing versus attention getting) and the baby's responsiveness to the adult (Fogel, 1977; H. Papousek & Papousek, 1987).

Parental speech to infants contains characteristic melodies that are related to ordinary tasks of parent-infant communication. For example, adults use different melodic contours to prohibit, elicit attention, encourage infant participation, encourage imitation, approve, and soothe. Furthermore, these melodies are similar in many different languages, including tonal languages such as Chinese (M. Papousek, 1994; M. Papousek, Papousek, & Symmes, 1991).

. When applied to speech, exaggeration, slowing down, rhythm, and melody make up a package that investigators have called **infant-directed (ID) speech** or more commonly, **motherese**. Infant-directed speech has a higher pitch and more exaggerated contrasts between high- and low-pitched sounds and is more melodic than speech directed toward adults. Not only does it appear to occur in many different languages, but motherese also appears in monkeys (Maestripieri & Whitham, 2007). This is most likely because these speech characteristics fit the kinds of listening preferences of infants after the age of 4 months (Colombo, Frick, Ryther, Coldren, & Mitchell, 1995; Cooper, Abraham, Berman, & Staska, 1997; Cooper & Aslin, 1989; 1994; M. Papousek, Bornstein, Nuzzo, Papousek, & Symmes, 1990).

The features of motherese even appear in deaf mothers using signed languages. One study found that a mother's signs to an infant, compared to signing to another adult, are significantly slower in tempo, are repeated more frequently, and use exaggerated movements related to each sign (Masataka, 1992). Mothers of deaf infants exaggerate their nonverbal and facial behaviors when with their infants, although they also exaggerate their directiveness and control over the infants and they touch their babies more than with hearing infants (Koester, 1994; Koester et al., 2000). Researchers have identified a nonverbal form of motherese, dubbed "motionese." When interacting with or demonstrating objects to young infants compared to interacting with an adult, adults' movements are higher in enthusiasm, range of motion, repetitiveness, and simplicity (Brand et al., 2002; Brand et al., 2007).

Similar patterns of motherese appear in lullabies. When lullaby melodies from different areas of the world were played without words to adults who were unfamiliar with those particular lullabies, the adults could differentiate them from songs not meant to be sung to infants (Trehub, Unyk, & Trainor, 1993). There are only a few cultures, such as the Quiche Maya in Guatemala, where motherese has not been observed in adult speech (Pye, 1986).

Unlike other rhythmic vocalizations, maternal laughter occurs at times when mothers are particularly enjoying their babies and thus may reflect a deep sense of appreciation for specific aspects of infant behavior. As Table 6.1 shows, mothers especially enjoy it when the infant discovers something new or masters a skill, smiles or laughs, or plays a game with her, or when the mother perceives her own behavior as funny or enjoyable (Nwokah & Fogel, 1993).

Matching and attunement. A large share of adult behavior is aimed at matching or imitating the infant's behavior. Although infants can imitate adults, adults imitate babies much more. This imitation may involve matching infant vocal sounds, pitches, rhythms, facial expressions, body movements, and so on (Malatesta & Haviland, 1982; Moran, Krupka, Tutton, & Symons, 1987; H. Papousek & Papousek, 1987). A concept related to matching is **attunement** (Stern, 1985), in which the adult's behavior is similar to the infant's but not an exact copy. For example, the infant may shake his or her arm up and down in a rhythmical motion. The parent may respond in a different modality, such as vocalizing "yea-yea-yea-yea" in exactly the same rhythm as the baby's arm movements.

Turn taking. Adults also engage in turn-taking behavior with babies. In the early months, infants do not yet have a concept of turn taking. As in the sucking dialogue, adults fill in the natural pauses of the infant's actions with their own actions, creating the appearance of turn taking (Brazelton, Koslowski, & Main, 1974; J. Cohn & Tronick, 1988; Fogel, 1977; Trevarthen, 1977). This adult-

TABLE 6.1 Summarized Descriptions of Probable Causes of Maternal Laughter

1. *Onset of infant behavior or facial expression*. Child produces a change in bodily posture, movement, or facial expression (smiling, banging a toy, or tilting the head).

2. *Onset of infant vocalization*. Child produces a sound, string of sounds, words, or phrase, excluding those related to bodily functions such as a sneeze or cough.

3. *Onset of infant laughter*. Child laughs aloud with a long or short laugh and accompanying active smile facial expression.

4. *Premastery*. Child strives to achieve a goal, such as standing up, holding a large object, or holding two objects at a time, but does not succeed.

5. *Social games*. A game is a playful social interaction in which a behavior is repeated more than twice. Games are characterized by repetition, nonliterality, mutual involvement, and usually turn alternation. At an early age, mutual involvement may be only attentiveness, and turn alternation may be minimal. There is almost always a lack of negative affect.

6. *Maternal interaction*. The mother engages in any playful social activity, such as shaking a toy near the infant or tickling him or her, that is not repeated more than twice.

7. *Other*. Includes mastery achievement such as walking for the first time, no apparent cause, reaction to a continued infant state such as sleeping, and mother laughing at her own joke or comment.

Source: E. Nwokah & A. Fogel, 1993.

controlled pattern of turn taking has been called **protoconversation** (M. C. Bateson, 1975; Trevarthen, 1977). During this early period, adults often overlap their vocalizations and actions with those of the infant, creating a sense of shared emotion, as when adults vocalize at the same time the baby is cooing (G. P. Ginsburg & Kilbourne, 1988; Stern, Jaffe, Beebe, & Bennett, 1975).

Between 4 and 6 months, infants begin to shift to a more interactive mode of behavior: they learn to wait until the adult pauses before beginning their own actions. Infants appear to take the initiative more often by looking in the mother's direction and waiting until she responds before smiling or vocalizing (J. Cohn & Tronick, 1988; Kaye & Fogel, 1980). By about 5 months, then, infants are beginning to become true social partners, rather than merely appreciative audiences for the display of motherese.

These developmental changes in infants coupled with the special features of infant-directed adult behavior, create regularly recurring communication routines called **frames** (Fogel, 1993). Some of the frames that emerge during this period are social games like face-to-face play, tickle and other tactile games, peekaboo, and frames for playing with toy objects. There are also frames for caregiving, such as bedtime, bathing, and feeding routines. Frames are the natural result of everyday communication. While some frames are similar between families, parents and infants often develop frames that are unique to their relationship and give it a special meaning and sense of familiarity for the participants.

The effects of individual differences between infants on adults. Just as infants prefer to listen to adults making infant-directed speech, adults prefer infant vocalizations that are relaxed and resonant and have greater pitch contours. These types of sounds are considered more speech-like (K. Bloom, D'Odorico, & Beaumont, 1993; K. Bloom & Lo, 1990).

Adults are drawn to facial features that have baby-like characteristics, such as large eyes, a round face, thin eyebrows, and a small nose bridge (Zebrowitz & Montepare, 1992). Individual differences in infant facial attractiveness affect maternal behavior. In a study of newborns and 3-month-olds, mothers were more affectionate and playful if their infants were judged by adult raters to be attractive. Mothers with less attractive infants were more attentive to other people besides the infant and were more likely to spend time in caretaking routines rather than affectionate behavior. These differences were not as strong at 3 months as they were at birth. In a related study, mothers of 6-month-olds expected less attractive infants to be more developmentally advanced (Langlois, Ritter, Casey, & Sawin, 1995; Ritter, Casey, & Langlois, 1991). Mothers of infants with cleft lip and cleft palate are less sensitive and more directive with their infants compared to mothers of normal infants (Koomen & Hoeksma, 1992).

Gender differences between infants also affect adult behavior, at least in middle-class white North American and Northern European families. When talking to girls, both mothers and fathers are more likely to comment on the present situation and the infant's current state. Comments about absent or future events are more common when parents talk with boys. Parents use first names more when talking to boys compared to girls (Pecheux, Labrell, & Pistorio, 1993). Mothers of male infants stimulate them more in general, while mothers of girls are more likely to stroke and caress their infants (Grant, 1994). Apparently gender-typical socialization can begin very early in life.

Even at birth, babies differ from each other in expressive behavior. Some babies have highly expressive facial and body movements, and others are relatively poker-faced or inexpressive (Field, Greenberg, Woodson, Cohen, & Garcia, 1984; N. A. Fox, 1985; Lipsitt, 1981). Such differences can be found throughout the first year of life (Stifter, Fox, & Porges, 1989). These expressive differences are related to infant temperament, discussed in more detail in Chapter 7.

It is clear that babies make some contribution to how others respond to them. A baby who is easily aroused is likely to withdraw from social interaction rather quickly. Adults often overreact to this withdrawal by trying even more aggressively to get the baby's attention, which in turn causes the baby to withdraw even more (Field, 1987; Gianino & Tronick, 1988). Under most circumstances, adults are highly attuned to the baby's responses. Most adults, regardless of age or parenting experience, are able to correctly identify an infant's state just by hearing the sounds the baby makes in each state

(M. Papousek, 1989). On the other hand, if infants are persistently difficult to handle, mothers rate their own self-efficacy as parents lower than mothers whose infants are not so difficult (Teti & Gelfand, 1991). When communicating with infants, it is important for adults to be aware of their own emotions and the effects of those emotions on their behavior.

In summary, adult behavior is consistently different toward boys and girls, toward attractive and unattractive infants regardless of gender, and toward infants differing in expressiveness. These findings are not surprising if one thinks about Western culture, which encourages independence, values different attributes in boys and girls, and promotes an abstract ideal of beauty in its products and practices (just look at the infants in any advertisement for baby products or, for that matter, at any adult models used in commercial advertisements). Perhaps the surprising point is that these cultural ideals begin to be instilled as early as the first months of life.

The Effects of Adult Behaviors on Infants

We do not know to what extent parents' use of motherese and related verbal and nonverbal baby-directed communication actually contributes to infant social and emotional development. A large number of studies have documented correlations between mother behavior during social interaction and infant behavior at the same age and also at later ages. Unfortunately, it is impossible to determine whether these correlations result from the effects of the parents on the infants or from differences between infants that may affect the way the parents behave.

Some research, however, asks mothers to modify their normal behavior with their infants so that the effect of such changes on the infants can be assessed. These studies reveal that beginning at 2 months of age, babies seem highly sensitive to how others interact with them.

The effect of adult contingent responsiveness. Contingency refers to the responsiveness of the adult to the infant's behaviors. A contingent response is an appropriate one that immediately follows some infant action, like a maternal smile following an infant's smile. When responses are contingent, infants tend to smile, coo, and look more at the adults. When responses are noncontingent, infants are more likely to fuss, cry, or look away (Bigelow & Rochat, 2006; Legerstee, 1997; Legerstee & Varghese, 2001; Striano et al., 2005; Yale et al., 2003). Infants also look and smile more when adults are producing the kinds of exaggerated behavior described earlier, such as motherese (Cooper, Abram, Berman, & Staska, 1997).

Experimental disturbances of play frames. The infant's reaction to contingent responsiveness can also be assessed by experimentally perturbing interaction sequences during normal play frames. In one type of study, infants and mothers play face-to-face games with each other, but instead of actually being face-to-face, they are each viewing a videotaped image of the other. Under these conditions, the infants respond normally. The researchers then show the infant a videotape of the mother playing with the infant that was made on an earlier occasion. In this condition, the mother's behavior is more or less the same, but she is no longer responding contingently to the infant. When this occurs, infants decrease the amount of smiling and gazing at the television monitor compared to when they were interacting "live" (Hains & Muir, 1996; L. Murray & Trevarthen, 1985; Nadel, Carchon, Kervella, Marcelli, & Plantey-Reserbat, 1999).

In another type of study, peekaboo games are played with infants, some in the normal way and other times in a disorganized way, such as by saying "peekaboo" before covering the face or not uncovering the face at the expected time. Once again, infants smile and gaze more when the frame is organized in the expected way compared to the disorganized play (Fogel et al., 2006; Rochat, Querido, & Striano, 1999).

In another type of study procedure used with babies between 2 and 5 months, the mother is asked to play with and talk to her baby as she might do at home. After several minutes of positively toned play, the experimenter asks the mother to perturb her behavior by ceasing to talk and holding her face in a neutral, nonexpressive pose. This is called the **still-face** procedure.

What do babies do when confronted with this unexpectedly unresponsive mother? Some babies continue to smile and look at the mother for a few seconds; then they stop smiling and look away from the mother for increasingly longer periods of time. If the distorted mother behavior goes on for more than a few minutes, the baby becomes increasingly distressed and withdrawn. When mothers are asked to resume their normal interactions, most of the infants begin to cry if they have not cried already, perhaps with the intent to communicate the prior distress (J. F. Cohn & Elmore, 1988; J. F. Cohn & Tronick, 1983; Toda & Fogel, 1989; Tronick, Als, Adamson, Weise, & Brazelton, 1978). The same effects are observed in different cultures (Kisilevsky et al., 1998) and with both mothers and fathers (Braungart-Rieker, Garwood, Powers, & Notaro, 1998; Kisilevsky et al., 1998).

At the age of 3 to 4 months, infants are more distressed at the still face than at separation from the mother (Field, Vega-Lahr, Scafidi, & Goldstein, 1986). Babies get equally upset if the still face is posed by the live mother or an image of the mother over closed-circuit television, but there is no change in the infants' behavior if the television mother continues to be expressive while the sound is turned off (Gusella, Muir, & Tronick, 1988). Apparently, it is the sight of the unresponsive mother, rather than the absence of the mother, that is upsetting to the babies (Striano, 2004). In addition, the still-face suppresses the parasympathetic (relaxation) nervous system (the vagus nerve pathway) and increases the level of cortisol, both signs of biological stress response (see Chapter 5; Haley & Stansbury, 2003; Moore & Calkins, 2004).

In another variant of the procedure, mothers are allowed to touch their infants while maintaining the still face. In this case, the effect of the still face on the infant is significantly less noticeable. When being touched during the still face, infants continue to smile and gaze at both the mothers' hands and face (Stack & Arnold, 1998; Stack & LePage, 1996; Stack & Muir, 1992). Therefore, touching can compensate for the sight of an unresponsive mother. Touching that is affectionate and soothing can help infants regulate emotions even under normal circumstances (Hertenstein, 2002; Moreno et al., 2006). If both of the infant's parents are present and the parent with whom the infant is interacting is asked to perform a still-face, the infant turns to the other parent and begins to interact normally (Fivaz-Depeursinge & Corboz-Warnery, 1999).

Finally, if mothers are more contingently responsive during the normal play episodes, infants recover more quickly following the still-face episode and these infants show less physiological suppression of the parasympathetic and cortisol systems (Haley & Stansbury, 2003; Kogan & Carter, 1996; Moore & Calkins, 2004). It could also be the case, however, that infants who have poor physiological regulation are less responsive to maternal contingencies and more highly reactive to interactive disturbances, since physiological reactivity in the newborn period predicts the infant's responsiveness to the mother at 3 months (Feldman, 2006).

These studies reveal that infants are certainly sensitive to changes in contingency and breaks in communication frames. In addition, infants also seem to be able to recover from such breaks by simple interventions such as having access to touch or to another adult. More serious effects on the infants are seen when parental unresponsiveness goes on for a long period of time and there is no one else to whom the infant can turn.

The effects of maternal depression and stress on infants. Even though the still-face is a very brief intervention, it produces both behavioral and physiological effects. These effects are relatively short term as the infant calms down following the experiment. One might expect that long-lasting maternal nonresponsiveness, such as with maternal depression, may have serious consequences for infants. Compared to normal psychological states and to other

psychological problems, depression has the strongest effect on infants, since its main symptom is a lack of emotionality and responsivity. Depressed people are not merely sad; rather, they are characterized by a flat emotional tone and preoccupation with themselves. These factors make depressed mothers less responsive as parents, which can be a major problem, since severe depression occurs in 10 to 13% of women following childbirth (Field, 1987; Josefsson et al., 2001).

Depressed mothers with infants under 6 months of age do not use the exaggerated and positive actions typical of normal mothers (Bettes, 1988; Campbell, Cohn, & Meyers, 1995; Kaplan, Bachorowski, & Zarlengo-Strouse, 1999); they are less affectionate and show more negative forms of touch, such as poking and pulling (Fleming, Ruble, Flett, & Saul, 1988; Malphurs, Raag, Field, Pickens, & Pelaez-Nogueras, 1996); they are not often contingently responsive to their babies (Bettes, 1988; Donovan, Leavitt, & Walsh, 1998; Field et al., 1985; Zlochower & Cohn, 1996); they rate their infant's behavior more negatively than non-depressed mothers (Field, Morrow, & Adelstein, 1993; Field, Grizzle, Scafidi, & Schanberg, 1996; C. R. Fox & Gelfand, 1994); or they alternate between disengagement and intrusiveness (J. F. Cohn, Matias, Tronick, Lyons- Ruth, & Connell, 1986).

Depressed mothers have trouble tracking the activities of their infants and may fail to protect them from potential dangers by letting the babies fall off their laps, for example, or letting them get into electrical equipment. Compared to nondepressed mothers, depressed mothers report having more parenting stress, more daily hassles, less marital satisfaction, and less social support (C. R. Fox & Gelfand, 1994; Gelfand & Teti, 1990; Gelfand, Teti, & Fox, 1992; Simons, Lorenz, Wu, & Conger, 1993).

Infants of depressed mothers are more likely to be fussy, to show more negative facial expressions, to have low levels of physical activity, and to be withdrawn. They orient less to their mothers and gaze less at them compared to infants of nondepressed mothers. Infants of depressed mothers also have higher levels of circulating cortisol as well as asymmetries in brain activity indicative of a withdrawn mood state. These patterns can be seen even when these infants interact with nondepressed adults (J. F. Cohn et al., 1986; J. F. Cohn, Campbell, Matias, & Hopkins, 1990; Dawson et al., 1999; Field et al., 1985; Field et al., 1988; Field, Healy, & LeBlanc, 1989; S. Hart, Field, Letourneau, & Del Valle, 1998; N. A. Jones et al., 1997; Pickens & Field, 1995).

There is some controversy, however, about the consequences of maternal mental illness for the infant. Most of the studies showing infant depression when interacting with nondepressed adults have used adults who are unfamiliar to the infant, which could account for the less than positive behavior of the infants. When infants of depressed mothers are observed interacting with their nondepressed fathers or with familiar nursery school teachers, these infants do not show signs of depression (Hossain et al., 1994; Kaplan et al., 2004; Pelaez-Nogueras et al., 1994). A large-scale demographic study of 262 families found no significant effects of maternal mental illness on infant behavior at 4 and 12 months (Seifer, Sameroff, Anagnostopolou, & Elias, 1992). Effects on infants are more likely to show up if their mothers remain depressed over many years and if the infants have few opportunities to interact regularly with nondepressed adults.

Maternal stress is another factor that contributes to poor mother-infant communication. Both depression and stress during pregnancy can affect the fetus (see Chapter 9). Mothers who are stressed after birth often over-, rather than under-arouse their babies. These mothers do not recognize infant cues to slow down or to change behavior. When the infant looks away, rather that waiting patiently for the infant to self-regulate and look back, these mothers "go after" the infant, trying desperately to get the infant's attention because the mother takes the infant's behavior as a rejection. Her behavior creates stress and physiological arousal for the baby, who begins the neuroception patterns of flight or freeze (see Chapter 5). This in turn makes the mother more anxious and more insistent, creating a mutually escalating spiral of "chase-and-dodge" and physiological and emotions dysregulation (Beebe, 2004). Left untreated, these dyads go on to develop an insecure attachment relationship (see Chapters 7 and 9).

In summary, during play frames, parents modify their behavior in a way that infants can most readily appreciate, and infants' smiling and gazing encourage the parents to continue. During everyday communication, the mutual influence is coregulated and dynamic. The effects of one partner on the other can only be determined by looking at individual differences between infants (such as infants who are difficult) or between parents (such as maternal depression) or during experimental perturbations of adult behavior.

Six to Nine Months

Social-Object Frames

Because of the newly developed motor, perceptual, and cognitive abilities for acting upon objects (Chapters 4 and 5), a good deal of parent-infant communication at this age is focused on objects. In the previous developmental period, much of the parent-infant communication involved mutual gazing and frames for face-to-face play in the absence of objects. While infants smiled and cooed, their parents made exaggerated facial expressions and vocalizations. These types of frames are very satisfying to both participants. As infants become increasingly interested in objects, between 4 and 6 months of age, and the earlier face-to-face frames give way to social-object play frames, parents sometimes feel a sense of disappointment. For the infant's part, the developmental task is to integrate interest in objects with the desire to remain socially and emotionally connected to the parents.

In the first part of this developmental period, infants are primarily focused on the objects themselves. It is up to the parents to provide frames for mutual communication about objects. Typically, this is done by holding objects within the infant's reach, making objects attractive to infants, helping the infants steady the object in order to explore it,

TABLE 6.2   Attention-Directing Strategies of Parents

Act-ons	Moving the infant through some activity, such as pulling the infant up and saying "up."
Shows	Moving an object across the infant's line of sight, or moving the object toward and away from the infant.
Demonstrations	Using a particular action on an object, such as how to comb a doll's hair or how to shake a rattle.
Points	Using a gesture to direct the infant's attention to a particular feature of an object or to a specific location in space, such as *over there*.

Source: Adapted from P. Zukow-Goldring. A social ecological realist approach to the emergence of the lexicon: Educating attention to amodal invariants in gesture and speech, 1997. In C. Dent-Read & P. Zukow-Goldring (eds.), *Evolving explanations of development: Ecological approaches to organism-environment systems*, pp. 199–250. Washington, D.C.: American Psychological Association.

and sometimes just sitting nearby and commenting while the infant manipulates or sucks on a toy (Fogel et al., 2006). The types of actions performed by parents at this age are shown in Table 6.2.

When using the actions shown in Table 6.2, parents employ strategies with toys similar to those they used earlier with their own faces, taking advantage of simple changes in rhythm, timing, and exaggeration to help infants attend to particular objects or to particular properties of objects. Parents will animate a toy dog, for example, by making it jump and matching the intensity of the jumping to the changes in the infant's delight (Stern, 1985). When trying to get the infant's attention to a jar of vitamins, a mother shook it rhythmically, saying, "shakey, sha … key, SHA … KEY!," increasing the volume and changing the timing of pauses between syllables (Zukow-Goldring, 1997).

The infant's ability to coordinate his or her attention to people and to objects is enhanced if parents regularly create frames in which these kinds of object-directed actions occur. The more attentive and animated the parents are with respect to the infant's attention to objects, the more likely it is that the infant will learn to co-regulate attention with others (Brighi, 1997). This is important, because infants who are more attentive to what adults do and say are more likely to learn language and come to learn, by 3 or 4 years of age, to share the mental perspectives of other people (Moore, Angelopoulos, & Bennett, 1997; Morales, Mundy, & Rojas, 1998; Striano & Rochat, 1999).

By the end of this developmental period, infants begin to be more aware of the adult and of the connection between the object, the self, and the adult. By around 9 months, infants become aware that other people have intentions, that they are agents, the subjective self (Chapter 5). This change is also seen in the infant's growing ability to appreciate and to make "jokes," clowning with adults. Prior to 9 months, the infant might bang a ball on the table. If the parent discourages the activity, the infant may stop momentarily and begin again or else ignore the parent. By about 9 months, the infant may bang the ball on the table, look at the parent, and grin mischievously (Lock, 2000; Reddy, 2000).

At 6 months, infants appear to be in a receptive mode, ready to participate in the frames created by the parents. By 8 or 9 months, infants are beginning to take initiatives in social frames. In one experiment, mothers were asked to see if infants would take the initiative in asking for help. During ordinary play with objects, mothers were asked either to hold a toy out of the infant's reach, stop demonstrating a toy, or delay giving help even if the child seemed to need immediate assistance. One-third of the 6-month-olds and two-thirds of the 9-month-olds showed evidence of asking the mother for help by gazing at her, making a demanding vocalization, or making a gesture (such as pulling on her arm) that indicated a help request (Mosier & Rogoff, 1994). By 8 months, infants "ask" to be picked up by making sad facial expressions or raising their hands above their heads, especially if adults indicate a willingness to pick them up (Service, Lock, & Chandler, 1989). Finally, the frequency with which infants make demands of mothers increases markedly once the infants begin to walk (Biringen et al., 1995).

Another aspect of initiative taking is that infants during this period are becoming more selective with respect to adults than during the previous period. By 8 or 9 months, infants will smile and laugh more toward familiar and trusted adults than toward unfamiliar ones. They may show some wariness in response to unfamiliar persons, but this has not yet blossomed into the more severe fearful reactions to strangers seen in some infants after the age of 10 months (Chapter 7).

Babbling: A Prerequisite for Later Vocal Communication

From the beginning of life, infants communicate vocally as well as behaviorally with the cry. In the period between 2 and 5 months, cooing or speech-like vocalization emerges. These are primarily vowel-like sounds such as "oooo" and "aaaah." At birth and up until 4 to 6 months, the infant's tongue fills most of the oral cavity, and it can only execute some primitive thrusting movements designed to help in sucking and swallowing (see Chapter 4). The young infant's epiglottis, a small fold of tissue behind the tongue, is in contact with the soft palate at the back of the roof of the mouth. This configuration covers the air tube from the lungs (the larynx) and helps prevent choking and inhaling of food particles. Beginning at 4 months, the oral cavity and vocal tract widen and lengthen, and the epiglottis begins to move away from the soft palate. The net effect is to allow air to be taken in and pushed out through the infant's mouth more readily, with the epiglottis moving up and down to stop the flow of air (Kent, 1981).

Before the age of 4 months, infants cannot breathe well through their mouths. This is why it is important to keep the very young baby's nasal passages clear of mucus. After 4 months, oral breathing allows the infant a much greater latitude for making new types of sounds. After 6 months, infants begin to explore sound production by using their ability to vary the direction of air flow, the pitch of the sound, and its loudness by abruptly stopping the air flow with the epiglottis (Zlatin, 1973). We can compare the oral and laryngeal manipulation of airflow to the manual manipulation of objects. The "goo"s and "gah"s that result, or **babbling**, sound almost as though the babies are talking to themselves as they roll off a string of related vowel and consonant sounds to accompany their eating or playing.

Many parents report that babbling sounds like speech. Although infants of this age are not imitating the words of speech, there is evidence that babbling has the intonation contours (the rising and falling pitches) of sentences (Nakazima, 1972). Indeed, in a study done in French-, Chinese-, and Arabic-speaking homes, the intonation contours of babbling match quite well the intonation contours of the speech spoken in the infant's home (DeBoysson-Bardies, Sagant, & Durand, 1984).

In one experimental study, some mothers were asked to respond contingently to infant babbling by smiling or talking or touching the baby for a 10-minute period. Another group of mothers were asked not to respond to the babbling also for 10 minutes. Following this, the infant's babbling was studied for the following 10 minutes. Infants whose mothers were contingent produced more "mature" babbles that had more recognizable syllables, strong contrasts between consonants and vowels, and a more fully voiced sound (Goldstein et al., 2003). This suggests that babbling may be speech-like because it occurs during parent-infant contingent vocal interaction.

The relationship of babbling to future speech is further supported by research showing that right-handed reaching and rhythmical banging with the hands increases in frequency at the same age infants begin to babble (Locke, 1993). The right hand is controlled by the left brain, and the left brain is known to be the primary location of speech processing. This means that the infant's vocalizations at this age come increasingly under the control of the left brain, setting the stage for linking vocalization and cognition necessary for the development of speech. Another study carefully tracked the way babies opened their mouths when smiling compared to babbling. When babbling, there was a slightly wider mouth opening on the right side; when smiling, the mouth opened more on the left side (Holowka & Petitto, 2002). This study confirms that the right brain is more emotional while the left brain more linguistic, a difference that appears in the second half-year of life.

A final link between babbling and future speech is that babbling typically occurs along with rhythmic arm and hand movements. Babies of this age are more likely to move their hands and arms, rather than their legs, while babbling, and specifically there is a preference to move the right arm. This work suggests that pre-speech babbling is linking to a kind of pre-gesture rhythmic movement of the hands (Iverson & Fagan, 2004).

Early observations suggested that even deaf babies babble in ways similar to hearing babies up until about 9 months of age (Lenneberg, 1969). Other research suggests that this is not the case, as shown in a careful descriptive analysis of babbling in deaf infants (Oller & Eilers, 1988). First of all, the onset of babbling in deaf infants is substantially delayed, in some cases occurring between 6 and 18 months later than in hearing infants. Second, the deaf infants produce considerably fewer well-formed consonant-vowel syllables. Although this study does not show that hearing infants copy the speech sounds of adults at this age, it does show that the ability to hear oneself vocalize contributes to the development of vocalization.

Speech Perception

Indeed, the development of auditory perception seems to parallel the development of sound production in hearing infants. Before the age of 6 months, infants are universal language perceivers. They can distinguish important sound contrasts from many different languages. Infants between 6 and 9 months are beginning to organize the sounds they hear, especially speech sounds, into conceptual categories. Recall that in research on visual perception, after being familiarized with a set of somewhat distorted figures, infants preferred to look at the prototype figure that best fit the series of distorted figures seen before. A similar study done with distorted versions of speech syllable prototypes yielded very similar results (Grieser & Kuhl, 1989). The auditory stimuli were syllables in which the vowel sound was subtly altered in pitch using a computer simulation.

This means that infants of this age hear the variations of the sound as the "same" as the prototype sound. Since the prototype sounds for most babies are those most commonly heard in their linguistic environment, it means that infants will be less likely to hear a wide diversity of sounds and more likely to hear sounds that "sound like" those occurring in the native language (Kuhl, 1998).

A developmental study (Werker & Tees, 1984) looked at infants between 4 and 6 months and between 10 and 12 months from three different language groups: English, Salish (a Native Canadian language), and Hindi. Babies from each group were tested with syllable contrasts from each language. Syllables were chosen in such a way that a native speaker could hear the differences between them, but a non-native speaker could not. An example of this is the contrast in English between /ra/ and /la/. Japanese speakers cannot distinguish perceptually between these two syllables and often get them mixed up when they speak English. English speakers have a similarly difficult time distinguishing between the Japanese syllables /ki/ and /kii/, as in *kite* (come) and *kiite* (listen). In the second syllable, the /ii/ sound (pronounced like the "e" in "be") is held just slightly longer than the /i/ sound in the first syllable; otherwise, the two sounds are identical.

The results of the study showed that the younger infants could distinguish the syllable contrasts from all the languages, but the older infants could only distinguish between the contrasts of the language heard in the home. A later study replicated these findings using computer-simulated sound contrasts similar to those found in English and in Hindi (Werker & Lalonde, 1988). Thus, between the ages of 6 and 9 months, infants lose a perceptual sensitivity that they had at an earlier age.

The loss of perceptual sensitivity may be related to the selective processes of brain development discussed in Chapter 5. At first, synapses are overproduced, and later some (those that are responsive to the sounds heard in the environment) are selected and strengthened, while synapses for sounds that are not frequently heard disappear. In the auditory cortex, the overproduction occurs during the first 6 months; by 10 months, the number of synapses has started to drop (Goldman-Rakic, 1987).

Infants of this age can distinguish between a wide variety of speech sounds in their native language but are less sensitive than adults (Aslin, 1987). Their ability to distinguish between sounds improves when the test sounds are embedded in a series of familiar speech sounds (Karzon, 1985) or in sentences in which adults are speaking motherese (Fernald, 1985).

Infants can apparently distinguish between the intonation patterns of different languages. Some infants from monolingual English-speaking homes and some from bilingual English- and Spanish-speaking homes were familiarized with a video display of a woman reciting a passage in either English or Spanish. In the test condition, infants dishabituated to the woman reciting a passage in the language they had not heard during familiarization but not to a different passage read in the language with which they had been familiarized (Bahrick & Pickens, 1988). In American English, the majority of two-syllable words are stressed on the initial syllable (strong-weak pattern of stress). By 9 months, American infants preferred to listen to words having a strong-weak stress pattern, compared to a weak-strong stress pattern. Six-month-olds showed no such preference (Jusczyk, Cutler, & Redanz, 1993).

Overall, these results show that by the second half of the first year of life, even though infants would not be considered to be speaking or understanding language, they are beginning to recognize and produce some of the characteristics of language as a system of sounds. Babbling infants may sound to adults as if they are trying to talk, but it is more appropriate to view them as exploring how to make familiar sounds, those heard in the home environment, rather than as trying to communicate with sounds. Nevertheless, this is a remarkable ability. The intonation patterns of language are complex and rich.

It seems as if babies first learn the music and later they learn the words. This music is learned in the context of parent-infant frames, including social games. And, speaking of music, infants older than 9 months are better at discriminating differences between the rhythmic structure of songs from their own culture (the ones the hear frequently) compared to songs from another culture (Hannon & Trehub, 2005). By this age, it appears, we are better at tapping our feet to familiar compared to unfamiliar music.

Parent-Infant Games

By 8 months, the infant is much more likely to take the initiative in play situations rather than simply respond to the caregiver (Gustafson, Green, & West, 1979; Kaye & Fogel, 1980). Social play is more frequent and more spirited, with laughter and squealing in the sound track.

A large variety of new social frames emerges in the parent-infant relationship at this age. Table 6.3 describes the typical playful frames found in parent-infant play during the second half-year of life. Figure 6.1 shows the relative frequency of each game at 6, 8, and 12 months of age. As infants get older, they learn to play an increasing number of new social games, such as "point and name" and "give and take" at 12 months. In playing those games that are played at every age—such as ball, vocal games, and peekaboo—infants take an increasingly active role as they get older. Games like "gonna get you" and "horsie," in which the 6-month-old played a relatively passive role, occur only rarely at 12 months (Gustafson et al., 1979; Rome-Flanders et al., 1995).

Note that these games are typical of white middle-class North American populations and do

TABLE 6.3 Descriptions of Conventional Games

Gonna get you: Mother repeatedly tickles, grabs, jostles, or provides other tactual/kinesthetic stimulation to the infant. Often includes a repeated vocalizaton such as "I'm gonna get you" or "Ahhhhh-boom!" that terminates just as physical contact is made. (Active participation by an infant could include fleeing when approached or attempting to "get" the mother.)

Pat-a-cake: Primary components are the mother's saying "pat-a-cake" and clapping or banging performed by either the mother or the infant. (Active participation by the infant would include beginning to clap only after the mother said "pat-a-cake" or patting the mother's hands.)

Horsie: Primary component is the mother's bouncing the infant, who is sitting on her knees or foot. The mother's verbalizations include "Want to play horsie?" or "Ride the horsie." (Active participation by the infant involves initiating the game or trying to prolong it by continuing to bounce after the mother has stopped.)

Peekaboo: One member of the dyad is hidden and reappears. Hiding is typically accompanied by the mother's calling to the child (if the mother is hidden) or by her asking "Where's [child's name]?" (if the child is hidden). Reappearance is typically accompanied by verbalizataions such as "Peekaboo," "Peepeye," or "There he/she is!" (Mother may control all the hiding and uncovering, or the infant may actively perform some of these activities.

Ball: Involves the infant's repeatedly receiving and losing the ball. (Mother may hold up both ends of the game by tossing the ball to the infant and then taking it away, or the infant may actively participate by presenting or returning the ball to the mother.)

Vocal game: Minimal requirement is that the mother be attempting to elicit a word or vocalization from the infant. In expanded form, these interactions are verbal or vocal-verbal "conversations."

Build tower–knock down: One member of the dyad builds a tower of blocks, and the other knocks the tower over. The sequence may be repeated many times. (Active participation by the infant is typically limited to knocking the tower down.)

Give and take: Involves a repeated giving and receiving of objects. Receiving by the mother is often accompanied by a carefully articulated "Thank you." Typically, the infant gives and the mother receives, although the mother often returns the object to the infant.

Point and name: One member of the dyad (usually the infant) repeatedly points to objects, each time waiting for a vocalization by the other (usually the mother, in the form of naming the object), before pointing to the next object. Pointing is sometimes accompanied by a questioning vocalization or by the query, "What's this?"

Miscellaneous: Any traditional infant game that occurs very infrequently at a particular age. Included are the game "Overboard," in which the mother repeatedly turns the infant upside down and says "Little girl overboard," and the game "So Big," in which the mother says, "How big are you?" and the infant stretches his or her arms out while the mother says, "So big." Also included are sequences with a toy telephone in which the receiver is put to the infant's ear and the mother says "Hello," and interactions in which one or both members of the pair wave or say, "Bye-bye."

Source: G. E. Gustafson, J. A. Green, & M. J. West, The infant's changing role in mother-infant games: The growth of social skills, 1979, p. 304, *Infant Behavior and Development, 2*, 301–308. Reprinted by permission of Ablex Publishing Company.

not necessarily represent what parents and infants do in other cultures. Furthermore, even in this particular population, games were observed in only about 10% of all social interaction episodes. The rest of the time is taken up with frames for caregiving (such as feeding, calming, bathing and bedtime rituals) and for infant solitary play with objects, which increases at this age.

Ten to Twelve Months

Coordinated Joint Attention

During this age, period infants seem to become less obsessive in their attention to objects and more likely to share their interest in objects with adults. It is as if the infant realizes, for the first

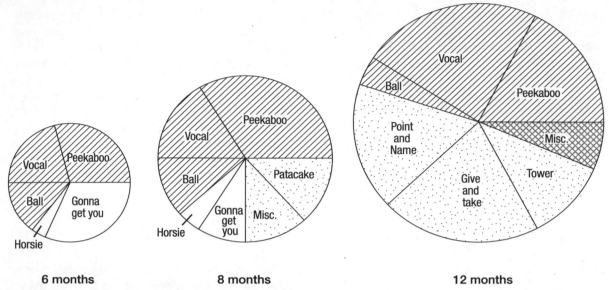

Figure 6.1   Relative Frequency of Parent-Infant Games
Dotted areas represent games in which the infant's role is explicitly active; blank areas represent games in which the infant's role is typically passive. Hatched areas represent games played at all ages. Cross-hatched areas represent both active and passive games.

Source: G. E. Gustafson, J. A. Green, & M. J. West, The infant's changing role in mother-infant games: The growth of social skills, 1979, p. 304, *Infant Behavior and Development, 2*, 301–308. Reprinted by permission of Ablex Publishing Company.

time, that others have different intentions, and that the infant must act in a way that helps to coordinate intentions between self and other (Lock, 2000). This ability is called **intersubjectivity** (Trevarthen & Hubley, 1978) and a part of this involves **coordinated joint attention** (Adamson, 1995), sharing a focus of attention on a single object with another person.

In addition to looking at the adult in order to share information about objects on which they are acting, infants of this age begin to follow the adult's line of gaze or pointing in order to detect something about what the adult is looking at. This aspect of coordinated joint attention is called **joint visual attention** (Butterworth, 2000; Corkum & Moore, 1995). Infants are especially likely to follow the gaze of people, or of objects that behave in some intentional way (S. Johnson, Slaughter, & Carey, 1998), and for that reason, they are more likely to follow the direction of an adult's head turning when the adult has open rather than closed eyes (Brooks & Meltzoff,

2005). This means that gaze following is genuinely a way to coordinate and communicate with another mind, not simply a mechanical act of following a moving object.

The Emergence of Intentional Gestures

Developmentally, infants first become involved in frames for coordinated joint attention between 9 and 10 months. Next, they begin to produce simple gestures, like pointing and requesting, at around 10 months. Finally, at 11 months, infants begin to follow the direction of the adult's gaze or pointing gesture. These developments are followed during the next few months by increasing gesture and word use. In fact, the more coordinated joint attention shared by mother and infant during this age period, the more rapidly infants will develop skills for complex play involving linguistic and gestural communication in the second year (Bigelow et al., 2004; Brooks & Meltzoff, 2005; Carpenter, Nagell, & Tomasello, 1998).

At 3 to 5 months, pointing is a spontaneous display of attention or interest (Fogel & Hannan, 1985); after 5 months, pointing is used instrumentally to touch or tap objects while exploring (Bates, O'Connell, & Shore, 1987; Fogel & Thelen, 1987), but it is not until about 10 months that infants use pointing in intentionally communicative ways (see Figure 6.2). We can say that infants use pointing and other gestures to intentionally communicate if they look between the adult and the object alternately—coordinated joint attention—and if they keep trying to communicate when the initial attempt does not succeed (Bates et al., 1987; Lock, 1980; see Figure 6.3). Infants will point to interesting objects the adult is not looking at (as if wanting to direct the adult's attention there) and they will point to objects the adult shows interest in (as if wanting to share that interest), again suggesting that points at this age are part of intentional communication (Liszkowski et al., 2007; Tomasello et al., 2007)

In addition to pointing during this age period, infants begin to use gestures such as showing, offering, giving, and requesting (Camaioni, 2000). In research done in my laboratory (D. S. Messinger & Fogel, 1998; Reinecke & Fogel, 1994), we examined the development of infant offering of objects. Before 10 months, infants hand objects to their mothers in the course of exploratory play with the objects. When this happens, the infants never take their eyes off the object. They look at the object as their mothers take it and then hand it back. If mothers playfully keep the object, the infants become frustrated. Beginning at 10 months, infants alternate their gaze between mother and object during the offering, especially if the infant initiates the object exchange. When the mother requests an object, the infant does not look at her during the offer. Finally, and importantly, when infants initiate offers and alternate gaze, they are likely to smile or laugh when the offer is completed. Although com-

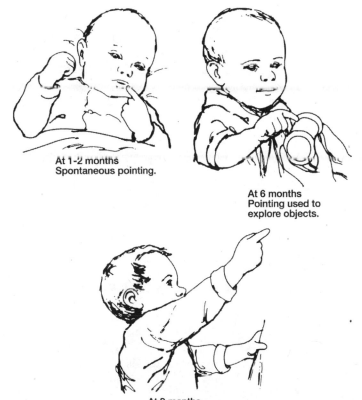

At 1-2 months
Spontaneous pointing.

At 6 months
Pointing used to
explore objects.

At 9 months
Pointing intentionally
used as a gesture.

Figure 6.2   Infant Pointing Pattern

Source: A. Fogel & G. F. Melson, *Child development*, 1988, p. 175. St. Paul, MN: West. Copyright © by West Publishing Company. Reprinted by permission. All rights reserved.

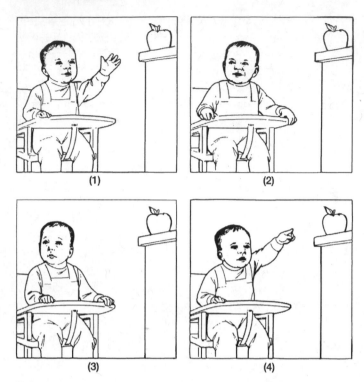

Figure 6.3   Gestural Communication at One Year

Source: A. Lock, *The guided reinvention of language*, 1980, p. 98. London: Academic Press.

municative offering continues to be part of the infant's repertoire, the smile and laugh during offering lasts only a few weeks. It suggests that infants are pleased with the discovery of a new communicative ability and that positive emotion may help to consolidate the developmental achievement.

Adults can use the infant's ability for joint visual attention to direct his or her attention to an object ("Look, there's a doggie"), a person ("Where's Daddy?"), a picture in a book, or even a particular feature of an object ("Where's Mommy's nose?"), thus creating a host of new opportunities for learning and communication (Zukow-Goldring, 1997). The infant's attention to the adult's gestures means that the infant wants to be included in what the adult is doing. If the adult turns away to talk to another person, the infant may try to engage also with the other person (Nadel & Tremblay-Leveau, 1999), or may show signs of jealousy, as discussed earlier.

Adults typically respond to infant gestures by interpreting what the infant wants. This includes coordinating their activities using objects with those of the infant, such as playing an object manipulation game by building with blocks or feeding a baby doll. In addition, caregivers are using words more deliberately as part of their actions on objects. An example would be describing in words what the baby is doing, requesting objects, offering objects, and saying, "Here's the baby's bottle" (Bakeman & Adamson, 1984; Hodapp, Goldfield, & Boyatzis, 1984; F. T. Hunter, McCarthy, MacTurk, & Vietze, 1987). In the next sections, we discuss the infant's first use of words and the infant's understanding of the parent's words.

Speech Production by Infants: First Words

Between 9 and 12 months, in the context of frames for coordinated joint attention, infants begin to make a variety of sounds that attentive caregivers recognize as words or word-like utterances (Camaioni, Aureli, Bellagamba, & Fogel, 1999). As in the development of babbling, these new sounds are made possible by further anatomical developments of the vocal tract. The sounds are used repeatedly in similar situations and not in other situations. Table 6.4 lists the first seven "words" in one child's vocabulary, recorded in one of the early studies of language development. Some research suggests that the child's first words of this sort have sound patterns similar to the favorite sounds the child makes when babbling. Since the babbling sounds are also similar to those heard in the linguistic environment of the home, these early words will begin to sound intelligible to adults (DeBoysson-Bardies, 1990).

Researchers disagree over whether these sounds are true words or true names for things, since they are arbitrary and idiosyncratic, rather than conventional. Instead, they seem like accompaniments to action, like saying "brrroom" when moving a toy car or grunting when exerting physical effort (Bates et al., 1987; McCune, 1989).

The meaning of such sounds, as well as of many of the infant's gestures, still depends on the interpretive activity of the caregiver, who recognizes a relationship between the sound or gesture and the situation in which the child uses it (Adamson, Bakeman, Smith, & Walters, 1987; Lock, 1980). Observations 6.1, 6.2, and 6.3 provide some examples of caregiver interpretations of infant acts, both verbal and nonverbal, at this age.

This combination of communication and emotion that we saw with gestures has also been discovered in relation to the use of first words. When infants actually utter a word for the first time, they tend to have a neutral facial expression. Immediately following the word, their expression changes, typically to a positive expression (Bloom & Beckwith, 1989). Once the infants begin to use the words more regularly, they no longer smile after saying them. The smiling is related to the infant's achievement of making their very first words.

Developments in Infant Perception of Adult Speech

Before the age of about 10 months, infants are capable of perceiving differences in intonation patterns, which allows them to recognize differences between melodies and passages of speech. In speaking to year-old children, adults continue to raise the overall pitch and to exaggerate the intonation contours of sentences. In one study, adults were recorded while talking to 1-year-olds and to other adults about attention getting, approval, prohibition, comfort, and play. Then the tapes were synthetically modified to remove all speech content while preserving the intonation. These modified tapes were played to other adults who were asked to judge the content of the speech. The judges were significantly likely to be more correct about the original content of the speech (whether the speech was about approval or prohibition) when they heard the modified speech to babies rather than the modified speech to adults

TABLE 6.4   The First Seven "Words" in One Child's Vocabulary

Utterance	Age (Months)	Meaning
eh	8	Said to people, distant objects, and toys.
Dididi	9	Disapproval (loud) or comfort (soft).
Mama	10	Refers to food; also means tastes good, and hungry.
Nnene	10	Scolding.
tt!	10	Used to call squirrels.
Piti	10	Always used with a gesture and always whispered; meaning that's interesting.
Duh	10	Used with same gesture as for piti; seems to be a comment on ongoing action.

Source: W. Leopold, *Speech development of a bilingual child*, 1949. Chicago: Northwestern University Press, 1949. Copyright © Northwestern University Press. Also in A. Fogel & G. Melson, *Child development*, 1988, p. 177. St. Paul, MN: West. Copyright © West Publishing Company. Reprinted by permission. All rights reserved.

Observations

Coordinated Joint Engagement

Observation 6.1 (Trevarthen & Hubley, 1978, p. 200)

At 40 weeks, Tracey's mother became an acknowledged participant in actions. Tracey repeatedly looked up at her mother's face when receiving an object, pausing as if to acknowlege receipt. She also looked up to her mother at breaks in her play, giving an indication of willingness to share experiences as she had never done before.

Observations

Communicative Behavior (Lock, 1980)

Observation 6.2

Mary, age 12(20): (1) Mary turns around in her chair and tries to pick up an apple from behind her. (2) She fails and turns back to her mother, who has been watching her, and cries. (3) Mother: "What do you want?" (4) Mary gesturally reaches toward the apple. Mother then gives it to her.

Mary, age 11(5): Mary is sitting in her high chair with mother next to her. She has finished eating. Some of her toys are on the table in front of her. Mother picks up a squeaky duck and shows it to Mary.

Mother: "Who's this?" (squeak, squeak) "Who is it? Is it the duck? What does the duck say?"

Mary: "ugh."
Mother: "He doesn't say 'ugh.' He says 'quack, quack, quack, quack' ... 'quack, quack, quack, quack' Ooh, and *who's* this? It's the doggie, isn't it? And what does the doggie say? What does the doggie say? Mary? Oh, he doesn't yawn? What does the doggie say? 'Woof, woof, woof, woof, woof,' 'Woof, woof, woof, woof, woof.' Don't you want the doggie? Oh, you say it, 'woof, woof, woof, woof, woof.'" Mary say it. 'Woof, woof, woof, woof, woof.' And who's this? Who's this? It's Teddy, isn't it? And Teddy says 'aah.' It's Teddy, isn't it? Aah, love Teddy. Ah, is it Teddy? Aah."
Mary picks up the dog.
Mother: "Oh, is that your doggie? What does the doggie say? What does the doggie say? What does the doggie say? 'Woof, woof, woof, woof, woof.' 'Woof, woof, woof, woof, woof.' Doesn't he?"

(Fernald, 1989). This means that there are more cues to speech content in intonation patterns when adults are speaking to babies than in speech to other adults.

In related work, speech to year-old infants was sampled in France, Italy, Germany, Japan, Britain, and the United States. In all cases, the speech had similar exaggerated intonation contours, although the American mothers did the most exaggeration (Fernald et al., 1989). Thus, the capacity to recognize meaningfully different speech intonation patterns is well established by the age of 1 year (Ferland & Mendelson, 1989; Trehub, Thorpe, & Morrongiello, 1987). Futhermore, mothers who speak more clearly by emphasizing sound contrasts within and between words have infants who are better able to perceive differences in intonation patterns (Liu et al., 2003).

There is some evidence that adults actually make their speech more exaggerated and simpler for year-old infants than they did earlier in the first year. When the baby was 3 months old, the parents mostly were content to comment on the baby's condition or state or make some general inferences about their relationship to the baby. By the time the baby is 8 months old, parents tend to use more commanding and directive language in relation to specific aspects of their baby's behavior. Compared with parents' speech to 4-month-olds, their speech to 8-month-olds is more related to what the child is doing; it is somewhat simpler in structure, almost as if the parents are simplifying their sentences because they think the infant is capable of understanding now (Davis, 1978; Sherrod et al., 1977; Sherrod et al., 1978).

By the end of the first year, parents begin to make specific verbal responses in commenting about infant activity, such as saying, "Put the toy over here," which enhances the infant's ability to make connections between action and speech. Parents not only name objects, but they name small details of the objects, such as color, texture, response properties, and the infant's familiarity with the object. They also make the object more real, such as making a toy cow moo or a stuffed dog bark. In some cultures, infants are treated to pop quizzes: "What does the cow say?" The mother corrects the baby's pronunciation and gives little compliments when things are done correctly. She instructs the child on how to play with a toy or how to behave, and she uses polite expressions, such as "please" and "thank you" (West & Rheingold, 1978).

Parents often do not correct infants, and they seem to enjoy the verbal mistakes infants make. The Marquesas Islanders enjoy their infants' incomplete development. They try to get the babies to perform their incomplete movements or to make verbal mistakes. These are humorous and enjoyable moments for the family (Martini & Kirkpatrick, 1981).

In addition to becoming perceptually attuned to the speech spoken in the home, infants are beginning to grasp the meanings of some words and gestures. For example, around 9 months, infants will make the appropriate action when parents say things like "play pat-a-cake" or "wave bye-bye to Daddy." Soon parents begin spelling out words like "bottle" or "candy" when speaking to each other in the baby's presence, so as not to get the baby interested at that moment (Bates, O'Connell, & Shore, 1987).

How does a baby of this age know that different words might refer to distinct objects? One reason is their developing skills at category learning, discussed earlier. Babies appear to be understanding that there are differences between one and another objects, just as there are differences

between the self and another person. If infants take a greater role in coordinating joint attention—such as by looking frequently between the adult speaker and the object—they learn words more easily (Gogate et al., 2006). Infants who show great attention to the intentions of adults at this age have more advanced language skills in the second year (Baldwin & Moses, 2001; Newman et al., 2006). Another reason infants learn that objects and words are connected is the way adults alter their speech patterns, intonation, questions, and gestures in the presence of different objects. Because infants are now more aware of the adult's perspective, and if the adults use different sounds and gestures for different objects, then the infant picks up on this (Dewar & Xu, 2007; Gogate et al., 2001; Pruden et al., 2006).

Twelve to Eighteen Months

At the end of the first year, infants are just beginning to use word-like sounds and gestures to communicate intentionally. Language development proper, however, begins in the second year. Since this age period is of primary importance in the development of language, and since we already have hinted at the importance of spoken language for human behavior and development, this section will introduce some of the basic concepts of language development.

What Are the Basic Properties of Languages?

Hundreds of languages, as well as countless dialects, are spoken around the world today. Some other languages, such as American Sign Language, are not spoken at all. All human languages—no matter where or how they are used (spoken, signed, or written)—share important properties that distinguish them from other kinds of communication systems, such as those found among other animals or those used for specific purposes, such as computer languages.

Human language has three basic properties (Brown, 1973). The first, **semanticity**, is the capacity of a language to carry meaning for both speaker and listener. Human adults are geared to find meaning in words and in all forms of social behavior. It is not unusual for an adult to try to interpret a gesture or a phrase made by someone else, whether that person intended it as meaningful or not. Adults, for example, try to find meaning in the more or less automatic behavioral expressions of very young infants. Not until the last quarter of the first year do infants begin to use words and gestures in meaningful ways, however.

Productivity refers to the ability of a speaker to express many different meanings with a relatively small number of words simply by rearranging them into novel combinations following the rules of grammar. Infants during the one-word stage of this age period cannot be productive in their language use, but when they begin to combine words into sentences, after 18 months, language becomes productive.

Displacement is the property of language that enables speakers to describe distant or absent objects and communicate abstract notions such as peace and justice, and it allows speakers to discuss the past, present, and future. Displacement is based on the fact that words bear an arbitrary relationship to the things they represent. The English word "cat" does not look or sound like a cat, but English speakers can understand what it means. Arbitrary words must be used when describing abstract concepts, since there is no concrete physical image to which a concept like justice corresponds. Infants of this age do not understand abstract concepts, but they are beginning to use words that have an arbitrary relationship to the objects they represent.

Aside from these three properties, language has a characteristic structure and function that sets it apart from other systems of communication. The structure of language, called grammar or **syntax**, refers to the fact that out of all possible combinations of word order, only a small number are meaningful to the native speaker. The function of language everywhere is to communicate. The study of a language's social and communicative function is called **pragmatics**. Pragmatics is more concerned with why people say something than with how they say it.

What Are the Theories of Language Acquisition?

Learning theory. Some developmental psychologists and developmental psycholinguists of the last century first viewed language development in behavioral terms. Like any other behavior, speech can be conditioned and imitated. Although children must use imitation to acquire the speech patterns of their own linguistic community, developmentalists differ over the extent to which imitation and reinforcement alone can account for how children acquire a language's syntax and how they come to use language productively. Learning theorists explain these accomplishments with concepts like "delayed imitation" and "generalization" of learned responses (Bandura, 1977; Bijou & Baer, 1965; Whitehurst & Vasta, 1975).

Nevertheless, learning theory cannot fully account for the fact that sentences have a very similar structure all over the world (subject, verb, and object—though not necessarily in that order). Imitation and reinforcement may help explain the learning of specific words and phrases but not the presence of linguistic universals of syntax. Another problem with the learning theory perspective is that it cannot explain why language is acquired at the particular time in the infant's life that it is. Why does it happen right at the end of the first year and coincident with Piaget's Stages IV and V (see Chapter 5)? If learning were the only mechanism available, we might expect to see a much wider range of ages for language acquisition than we now see.

Behavior ecology theory. Theories based more on biological factors arose to try to explain these two problems with learning theory. As for the observation that all language has essentially the same structure, Noam Chomsky (1975) reasoned that each infant is born with a rudimentary notion of syntactic structure—an innate universal grammar. According to Chomsky, this is the only way to explain how infants, especially after 18 months, can take sounds and organize them into meaningful sentences. Careful scrutiny of children's one-word productions and the incipient word order found in early two- and three-word utterances led to an attempt to write down grammatical rules for infant speech (McNeill, 1970).

The problem is that infant speech could not be easily fitted into these simple rules: there were too many exceptions. Martin Braine (1976) has concluded that rather than expressing some underlying universal grammar, the child's "first productive structures are formulae of limited scope for realizing specific kinds of meanings" (p. 4). Language acquisition, according to Braine, is better understood from the point of view of pragmatics—what the child is trying to say and why—than from a syntactic, or structural, perspective.

Functional theory. As a response to the deficiencies in both learning and biological theories, functional theories of language acquisition have attempted to study language development in its natural context: the parent-infant interaction. The functional theory of language acquisition is one type of *interactive systems theory* (see Chapter 2). In contrast to purely psychological, or individual-oriented, theories, the functional approach attempts to study language development in relation to the social system in which it naturally occurs. As we will see, the key milestones of the functional theory of language acquisition are not individual achievements (such as babbling, single-word utterances, and multiword sentences) but achievements of the parent-infant dyad, such as taking turns, paying **coordinated joint attention** to an external object (both parent and infant direct their attention to the same thing), and sharing meaning of particular gestures, words, and phrases (Camaioni, 2001).

Coordinated Joint Attention as a Frame for Language Development

We have seen how parents and infants create frames for coordinated joint attention. From a functionalist perspective, these frames are essential prerequisites for the emergence of language. Once a joint focus of attention is created, it is relatively easy for infants to begin to associate objects and events with words. Studies in which words are introduced when the infant is looking at an object, compared to when the infant is looking elsewhere, show that infants are more likely to acquire the correct object word if they are looking at the object being named (P. J. Dunham, Dunham, & Curwin, 1993; Woodward & Hoyne, 1999). In addition, infants who are more skilled in establishing joint attention to an object acquire language at an earlier age than children who are less able to jointly attend (Mundy & Gomes, 1998).

During frames for coordinated joint attention, the adult's level of language use, the specific instruction regarding objects and their uses and names, has a great impact on the child's language development (Broerse & Elias, 1994; McCune, 1995; Tamis-LeMonda & Bornstein, 1990; Tamis-LeMonda et al., 1996). Play with peers involves much less language and gesture than play with adult caregivers. With mother, compared to with peers or being alone, infants use significantly more words and gestures, and their play is more symbolic and relational (Turkheimer, Bakeman, & Adamson, 1989; Zukow, 1986). A similar finding has been reported comparing parent-infant and older sibling-infant interactions (Teti, Bond, & Gibbs, 1988).

Once the infant's attention is on the object, adults can use combinations of pointing, showing, and words to highlight specific features of the object. The more mothers do this, the more advanced the child's language skills (Baldwin, 1995; Zukow, 1990; Zukow-Goldring, 1996). Some mothers are more likely to emphasize single words in their speech. They do this either by saying only one word in an utterance ("dog"), by repeating the same word in a subsequent utterance ("That's a dog; look at the dog"), or by changing a word in a repeating sentence frame ("That's a cat; that's a dog"). Mothers who were more likely to do this had children who, as their language skills improved, were more likely to speak clearly and not run their words together (Pine, Lieven, & Rowland, 1997). The child's participation in frames for shared book reading at 14 months predicted

Once coordinated joint attention is established, infants can acquire gestures and words more easily.

Photo by Elizabeth Crews.

language skills 4 months later (Laakso, Poikkeus, & Lyytinen, 1999), and infants who were better at joining in frames for joint attention at 15 months were more socially competent at 30 months (van Hecke et al., 2007). These studies all show that participation in frames for coordinated joint attention significantly enhances language acquisition, providing support for the functionalist theory.

The adult's role in creating frames for coordinated joint attention is also matched by the infant's ability to participate in these frames and pay attention to objects and words. Earlier than 12 months, when adults point at an object, infants are more likely to look at the adult's hand than at the object. Around 15 months this changes, and infants are more likely to pay attention to an object or a feature of an object when adults point (Desrochers, Morissette, & Ricard, 1995). At the beginning of the second year, infants begin to take the initiative in creating joint frames of reference. They develop the ability to follow their mothers' line of vision (Butterworth & Cochran, 1980; Collis & Schaffer, 1975; Scaife & Bruner, 1975); they begin to use pointing to direct their mothers' interest to something they want (Leung & Rheingold, 1981; Murphy, 1978); and they begin to imitate their parent's words more consistently (Masur & Rodemaker, 1999).

The ability to search for new means to reach goals (Piaget's Stage V) imparts this persistence to the infant's communicative attempts. If infants do not get what they want by pointing or reaching for it, they are likely to look at their mothers, pull on them, point or reach for something, and look back at their mothers until they get what is needed (Blake, McConnell, Horton, & Benson, 1992; Harding & Golinkoff, 1979; Lock, 1980; Mayes, Carter, & Stubbe, 1993). If the mother is asked not to respond to the infant's requests or pretends not to understand the infant, the infant will repeat the request using more exaggerated movements, like leaning or whining, or will change the form of the request such as by replacing a gesture with a word or vice versa (Marcos & Chanu, 1992). These studies suggest that a good deal of language acquisition is infant-initiated. The infant has something to say or wants to know a word and approaches the adult for assistance (L. Bloom, Margulis, Tinker, & Fujita, 1996). These observations are consistent with Piaget's descriptions of an active and persistent infant during this stage.

In the last age period, we saw the emergence of simple intentional gestures, such as pointing and offering. The child persists until a desired result is obtained but tends to repeat the same gesture. After 12 months, infants begin to use gestures in combinations to communicate more complex meanings (Lock, 1980), as shown in Observation 6.4. In this example, the child first cries intentionally, and then, after the mother arrives, the child points.

Intersubjectivity, the ability to act cooperatively and to incorporate others as meaningful agents in one's actions, also expands at this age. During the previous age period, infants became aware of how their communicative actions affected others. Between 12 and 18 months, infants become more aware of the relationship between self and other. **Metacommunicative events** are communicative acts that refer to the communication in the relationship itself, in contrast to ordinary communicative events, which refer to the world outside the relationship, such as gesturing toward or talking about objects and other people. When infants persist in trying to get an adult's attention or assistance, they are using metacommunication by referring—implicitly or explicitly—to a failure of communication within the relationship.

We have studied metacommunication in infants during this age period during mother-infant play with a pair of toy telephones (Fogel & Branco, 1997; Reinecke & Fogel, 1994). When infants are less than 1 year old, they treat the telephone as a physical object, something to push and bang. When mothers try to get the infants to pretend that the toy phone is a real phone, that is, to pretend to talk to someone, the infants resist. The infants' metacommunication consists of pushing the phone away if the mother tries to hold it

to their ear, making disgusted facial expressions, shaking their heads, and grabbing the phone away from the mother.

Metacommunication changes as the relationship changes. One infant who could pretend play with a toy phone put it to her ear and said, "Dada?" The mother, talking on the other phone, said, "No, it's Grandma." The infant responded with "Dada," and this exchange continued for five rounds, with mutual smiling. In the last round, however, the baby's tone of voice became more serious. The mother interpreted this as a metacommunication and said, "Should we put the phone away?" The baby held the phone and without looking at the mother said (in a robotlike tone), "Da-da-da-da-da." The mother took the phone away saying, "OK," showing that she understood the infant's metacommunica- tion meant not wanting to pretend talk to grandma. After the phone was taken away, the baby continued, "Da-da, da-da, da-da," almost squealing the sounds and smiling at the mother. This type of behavior is different from clowning, seen during the previous age period, because the infant seems to be commenting on the mother-infant relationship rather than simply being a participant.

The Emergence of Conventional Gestures and Words

During the previous age period, infants used a variety of gestures and words. Their gestures were simple acts of directing another person's attention, such as pointing and requesting. Prior to 1

Observations

Communicative Behavior (Lock, 1980)

Observation 6.4

Paul; age 13 months (27 days): Paul is playing with his football, which becomes stuck among chair legs. He tries to free it but is unable to. He starts crying while on his hands and knees, then moves to a sitting position and continues wailing. Mother comes in.

Mother. "What's the matter? What's the matter?" Paul continues crying but also points in the direction of the chair.
Mother. "Oh, have you got it stuck again? I think you do it on purpose some times," and she gives him the ball.

Paul continues crying but less and less vigorously, until he stops.

year, infant words are most likely to mimic sounds that accompany an action, like saying "vrooom" when playing with a toy car. After 1 year, gestures and words become conventional. **Conventional actions** are those that represent an action or object using some type of ritualized manner of expression (Acredolo & Goodwyn, 1985; Camaioni et al., 2003; Camaioni, 2001; McCune-Nicolich, 1981). For example, a child who wants her hair combed will hold a comb and pretend to comb her hair. Pretending to drink from a cup might signal the need for a drink. Waving "bye-bye" is another conventional gesture. Such gestures may refer to the past or the future and to objects that are out of sight. Thus, they have the character of words that are used to name objects and events. There is some evidence, however, that gestures may be easier to learn for infants than words (Goodwyn & Acredolo, 1993). The developmental sequence of conventional gestures are given in Table 6.5.

Some time between 10 and 16 months, most infants begin to use words to communicate some intention. One manifestation of this developmental change is the onset of naming. Naming is the intentional use of a gesture or a word to refer to a specific object or event. Carlotta, one of the infants whose speech development has been reported in the literature (E. Bates, Camaioni, & Volterra, 1975; E. Bates, O'Connell, & Shore, 1987), used the sound "bam" when knocking over a tower of blocks. Several weeks later, Carlotta was sitting silently among her toys. She stopped, looked up, and said "bam," and then she turned and started to bang on her toy piano. What has changed here? The word "bam" has been removed from its original context as an accompaniment to action and is now being said in advance of the action to stand symbolically for the action that is about to occur. Another example of naming is given in Observation 6.5.

Around the same time, Carlotta began to do other naming procedures. When asked during the reading of a book, "How does the doggie go?" Carlotta consistently replied, "Woowoo." She also said "woowoo" when she saw a dog in real life or

heard a dog barking. At the same age, she was rapidly developing names for toys, foods, and clothing.

Children first acquire words for objects (*car, shoes, teddy, cup*), for social interaction (*hello, no, yes, bye-bye*), and for some simple concepts (*gone, more, there*). Infants of this age acquire only about one to three words per month (Adamson, 1995; Camaioni, 2001). Once they begin to use words, infants seem to prefer objects and events for which they already have a word or name (Schafer, Plunkett, & Harris, 1999). During picture-book reading, for example, infants will spend more time on pictures for which they already know a name.

Babies can be taught conventional gestures, a kind of sign language, to understand and express their feelings prior to having acquired the words. There are a number of websites and books that give parents helpful advice about what kinds of signs work best with babies and how to teach a baby to understand and use the signs (www.mybaby-cantalk.com, www.signingbaby.com). Fingers to the mouth, for example, might mean "hungry" or "eat." Tilting the head to the side and resting it on a hand might mean "sleepy" or "tired." Parents report that infants can learn the signs easily and appear to enjoy using them.

These early words tend to be used like conventional gestures in the sense that they are like the conventionally used adult word and that they are used consistently in similar situations. These words lack an important property that is discovered by infants only after 18 months: words are symbols. Symbols, as we will see in the next age period, stand for or represent something else. A word is not the real thing; it is an arbitrary pattern of sound that represents that thing. Between 12 and 18 months, infants seem to use the words and gestures as if they are part of the real thing, and they use those words only when the real thing is present or nearby. Infants of this age are aware of semanticity but not of displacement.

When children first acquire a word or first make one up, a considerable period of time passes before they use that word in the same way adults use it. Infants make many errors in the application of words. In one type of error,

TABLE 6.5 Developmental Order of Emergence of Conventional Gestures

Gesture	Average Age (in months) of first appearance
Waving	8.4
Clapping	8.9
Dancing to music	10.2
Giving	11.9
Hugging	12.7
Shaking head no	13.3
Lip smacking	15.3
Blowing kisses	15.6
Nodding head yes	15.9
Fingers to lips (shhh)	16.8
Shrugging shoulders	16.9

Source: Crais, Douglas, & Campbell (2004)

called **overextension**, the child uses the word for instances not included in the adult's definition. For example, a child might use the word "car" for a wide range of vehicles, including motorcycles, bicycles, trucks, and planes. Does this mean the child does not really understand the true meaning of the word "car"? Or does it mean that the child has a faulty concept of cars and believes that all vehicles are cars?

Children's overextending while naming an object reflects their active attempt to try to categorize objects. By naming all vehicles "cars," children "elaborate for themselves the similarities among things" (K. Nelson, Rescorla, Gruendel, & Benedict, 1978, p. 964). Bowerman (1978) reported that her daughter Eva first used the word "moon" to describe the real thing and then extended the word's use to such things as grapefruit sections, lemon slices, and steer horns—anything she saw with a crescent shape. In such cases, the child does not appear to be saying that "a car is a plane" or "a lemon slice is a moon." Instead, the child may be saying that "a car is like a plane" or "a lemon slice is like a moon," much as an older child might say, "It looks like a car," or "Look, it's crescent shaped."

Generally, adults have three choices when infants overextend their word use. They can accept the child's own version of the word; they can say that the child is not correct; or they can provide the correct label for the object (Gruendel, 1977). However, even when the adult says something like

---

Observations

Communicative Behavior (Lock, 1980)

Observation 6.5

Peter, age 13 months (13 days):
(a) Mother is putting Peter's slippers on. Peter reaches upwards, laughs and shrieks "Lieee."
Mother: "Yes, it's the light"
Peter: "Dieee."
Mother: "That's right, light, light."

(b) I am talking to Mother. Peter comes up to me and touches my wrist.
Peter: "Dik do."
Andy: "Yes, it's a tick tock."

I continue talking to mother, the above occurring without intruding into our conversation.

"That's not a cookie" in response to the child's overextension of the word "cookie" to refer to a hamburger, the child may not understand or hear the negation. Failure to understand the word "not" may lead the child to interpret the adult's response to mean "It's okay to call that a cookie. Mommy said it, too" (Gruendel, 1977). As soon as the adult stops referring to the object with the child's overextension and uses only the adult word for it, the child soon picks up the correct name.

Relationship of Production to Comprehension

The same child who used the word "car" to describe many different vehicles was able to readily point out the correct vehicle when asked a question like "Where's the truck?" In another case, a child could correctly point out strawberries when asked but insisted on calling them "apple." Research has shown that 13-month-olds can understand about 50 words, but they cannot speak 50 words until they are about 19 months of age. Thus, infants can comprehend a word considerably earlier than they can produce it.

The earliest instances of word comprehension have been found at the age of 10 months for objects that are both salient and very familiar. At that age, however, it takes great effort to teach infants to understand a word, and they may rely more on the adult's pattern of intonation and gesture in identifying the correct object. By 17 months, however, infants can acquire word meanings easily—sometimes after a single exposure—and it may be from overheard conversation and not necessarily speech directed to the infant (Floor & Akhtar, 2006; Masur, 1993; Oviatt, 1978; Woodward, Markman, & Fitzsimmons, 1994).

Not all children have such noticeable lags between comprehension and production; in fact, some children can understand far more than they produce, while for others production is much more closely related to comprehension. How can this be? Some children who produce little but understand a great deal may suffer from a speech or hearing disorder, but this accounts for only a small percentage. Some children may be overly cautious about speaking out until they are certain that they understand how to use the word, which may be related to a temperamental propensity to shyness (E. Bates, Thal, Whitesell, Fenson, & Oakes, 1989). Lags in production may also be related to the amount of explicit naming done by caregivers (Vibbert & Bornstein, 1989). Currently, there is no complete explanation of what accounts for these individual differences.

On the other hand, those children who have high linguistic comprehension show high levels of gestural production. Thus, even though they hesitate to communicate with words, they have articulated a rich array of symbolic gestures (E. Bates et al., 1987). This can be seen clearly in deaf children, who develop a large number of gestural signs that signify objects and actions at ages similar to when hearing children develop linguistic names (Petitto, 1985; Reilly, McIntire, & Bellugi, 1985). Thus, virtually all children at this age try to make themselves understood in one way or another.

The lag between comprehension and production suggests that children in the second year know more than their verbal behavior would indicate, and that their efforts to speak are not crude groupings reflecting incomplete understanding but active efforts to make sense out of a complex world of objects and people. The young child's speech may be an important part of the process of concept formation, rather than a mere comment on a concept the child already has attained. At least one study has shown that after adults label novel objects for infants, the infants pay closer attention to those objects (Baldwin & Markman, 1989). Thus, in complex ways, the acquisition of language may place the infant on a fast track toward conceptual and cognitive development.

Eighteen to Twenty-Four Months

The period between 18 and 24 months is marked by a number of important changes in communication and language, due in part to the child's more conceptual and symbolic forms of cognition as discussed in Chapter 5. First, there is a dramatic increase in the size of children's vocabulary, and second, children begin to use multiword sentences.

The Vocabulary Spurt

Between 12 and 18 months, new words are acquired slowly, a few per week. Sometime around 18 months, there is typically a rapid increase in vocabulary in which children begin to acquire five or more words per week. This growth of vocabulary consists primarily of object names. It is as if children discover that objects have names and become obsessed with naming things and asking for the names of things, in what has been called the *naming insight* (McShane, 1980). They may repeatedly ask "What-da?" to request object names and point to many different objects, wanting to hear the name (Camaioni, 2000).

When learning words, infants of this age seem to be helped by their growing ability to categorize objects into groups. If children are given a pile of different objects, by about 18 months they can sort them into similar groups: all the pencils in one group, for example, even though each pencil has a different shape and color. This seems to make it easier for children to learn the word "pencil." On the other hand, if 20-month-old children are given a set of unfamiliar objects and the experimenter gives each object a name, they are likely to sort together those objects with the same name. This means that language and cognition are related to each other, each one facilitating the development of the other (Booth, Waxman, & Huang, 2005; Gopnik & Nazzi, 2003; Samuelson & Smith, 2005). Word learning is also helped if the child can direct attention to the object being named by the adult (Fernald, Perfors, & Marchman, 2006).

By 18 months, children have an active vocabulary of about 90 words, but by 24 months this has expanded to 320 words. A typical 6-year-old knows 14,000 words, and a high school graduate knows about 60,000. People learn nine or ten words per day between the ages of 2 and 18 years (Adamson, 1995). This means that most language is actually acquired after the infancy period!

Although nouns predominate in all languages that have been studied (Bornstein et al., 2004), children in this age period also acquire some verbs (*play*, *kiss*), adjectives (*hot*, *yucky*), and adverbs (*up*, *more*). They can use words to make comments on objects (*gone*, *dirty*) and on their own actions and feelings (*uh-oh*, *tired*) (E. Bates, O'Connell, & Shore, 1987). When children use a verb or an adjective, it suggests that they are referring not simply to the word itself, but to several words or things. Saying "gone," for example, implies that some object is no longer present; "hot" refers to an object that is at a high temperature.

When children under 18 months say "shoe," they may be referring to the shoe in the form of simply naming. After 18 months, they may point to the shoe and say "dirty" or "Mommy." This type of behavior could be interpreted as "the shoe is dirty" or "this is Mommy's shoe." It seems, therefore, that just before the acquisition of multiword speech, infants begin to use single words in more complex ways that suggest a subject and a predicate (E. Bates et al., 1987; Greenfield & Smith, 1976; Lock, 1980). Nevertheless, their language is still limited in what can be expressed. The additional discovery of combining words increases what a child of this age can say, but it is not until the third year that children become able to speak in fluent sentences (Adamson, 1995).

Multiword Speech

The main advance in language in this age period is the emergence of the sentence. Correlational studies show that sentences emerge at about the same age (on the average, about 20 months) when children begin to pursue objects after multiple hidings, use tools in deliberate ways, and engage in symbolic play (Chapter 5). This is also the age at which they can combine symbolic objects and gestures in novel ways, classify objects by sorting, and solve complex problems mentally without trial-and-error behavior (E. Bates et al., 1987; McCune-Nicolich, 1981; Piaget, 1962; Shore, 1986; Sugarman, 1982; Zachry, 1978). Again, we can see how cognitive abilities guide language learning.

The onset of sentences with a series of words parallels the emergence of the use of a series of related gestures, or a combination of words and gestures, to communicate meaning (Acredolo & Goodwyn, 1988; Lock, 1980; Mayer & Musatti, 1992; McCune-Nicolich, 1981). An example would be pulling on the mother's skirt, lifting the arms up, looking distressed, and perhaps saying, "Mommy up." The pragmatic view of language development, discussed above, suggests that language serves one main purpose for young children: to communicate their intentions. As children develop cognitively, they discover better ways to get their point across to others. During the previous stage, children relied on the context or situation, intonation patterns, and interpreting adults to communicate their meanings with single words.

Prior to using two-word sentences, the child may combine a gesture and a word to achieve a similar meaning. Thus, seeing a sleeping bird, the child might point at the bird and say "nap." A month later, the child can say "bird nap" to mean the same thing: the bird is taking a nap (Iverson & Goldin-Meadow, 2005).

In this phase, children discover they can create new meanings simply by changing *the order in which several words are spoken together*. When gestures and words first are used in intentional communication, they are a direct extension of some sensorimotor act of the child. These **idiosyncratic communication** gestures only gradually develop into **conventional communication** signs. We see a parallel development in the realm of grammar or syntax: the first two-word combinations are idiosyncratic usages that only later become conventionalized in the form of adult syntax (see Table 6.6).

The child's first multiword utterances are not as sophisticated as adult grammar. Apparently, children first use word order to express meanings with a fairly limited set of speech patterns. These speech patterns are better thought of as **formulas** than as sentences: children seem to use a particular kind of word sequencing in which they can "fill in the blanks" to vary the meaning of the phrase. Table 6.7 gives these early formulas, along with their meanings and some examples.

Formulas similar to those found in Table 6.7 have been reported for children from six different language groups. For example, "more milk" is found in Germany as "mehr Milch," in Russia as "yesche moloka," and in Finland as "lisaa kakkua" (Slobin, 1970). Similar patterns can be seen in the first word combinations of deaf children acquiring sign language. One study found hand signs that could be interpreted as "Daddy work" (Daddy is at work) and "Barry train" (referring to a brother's train) in a language-learning deaf child (Dale, 1976).

The speech examples in Table 6.7 are called **telegraphic speech**, because they tend to leave out small words such as prepositions and word endings such as *-ing, -s* sounds, and *-ed*, which add additional refinements to the meaning of words and sentences. Usually, simpler endings such as *-ing*, the plural *-s*, and the possessive *-'s* are acquired first, followed by the more difficult use of the verb "to be" with all its tenses, auxiliaries, and contractions (deVilliers & deVilliers, 1973).

Individual Differences: Two Types of Speech Style

While these syntactic refinements are taking place, children continue to develop a vocabulary. This

TABLE 6.6   Development of Conventionalized Semantics and Syntax

Age	Semantics	Syntax
9–12 months	Sensorimotor gestures	
12–18 months	Idiosyncratic words (symbols)	
19–24 months	Conventional words (signs)	
Over 24 months		Idiosyncratic word order
		Conventional word order

TABLE 6.7 Early Two-Word Combinations

Function	Formula	Example
Drawing attention to something	see + X here + X	see car here milk
Object's properties	big/little + X hot + X old + X	big house hot pipe old cookie
Possession	X + Y	doggy hold pig tail Kendall birthday
Plurality	number + X	two book
Recurrence	more + X other + X	more raisins other hand
Disappearance	all gone + X all done + X	all gone airplane all done juice
Negation	no + X not + X	no water no eat
Actor-action relations		sits doll sleeps baby Kendall break Mommy hit Kendall
Location	X + preposition	rock outside milk in there milk in cup
Request	want + X	want dessert want get down

Source. M. D. S. Braine, Children's first word combinations, 1976, p. 57. *Monographs of the Society for Research in Child Development, 164*, 56–57

entails increasing the number of conventional words they know how to use and refining the meanings of the words that have been overextended or used incorrectly in the past. Young children show two distinct styles of vocabulary acquisition: **referential speech** and **expressive speech**. Differences between referential and expressive word use are summed up in Table 6.8.

Some examples of expressive language are "I don't want it," "Don't do it," "I'll get it," and "I don't know where it is." These phrases have the characteristics of being spoken as a single word, since the individual words are poorly articulated. There is no evidence that the use of either of these styles of language acquisition relates to later behavior in any way. Indeed, most children use them both in different contexts; for example, in referential versus interpersonal situations (Camaioni, 2000; K. Nelson, 1981). Some studies have shown that as children get older, they tend to favor one style over another—a more social-oriented versus object-oriented approach—although the evidence is based almost entirely on a few case studies.

Children's use of one or the other style may reflect the speech spoken to them. If a caregiver responds to questions by clearly labeling objects, the child may focus more on individual words. If the caregiver uses social control language like "D'ya wanna go out" or "I dunno where it is," the child is likely to hear these as whole phrases rather than as a series of single words.

Relationship Between Language Development and the Social Environment

It is extremely rare for adults to correct children's language errors directly. What do adults actually say and do that might be conducive to the development of speech? One major trend is an increasing reliance on verbal suggestions and commands, as compared to nonverbal gestures, in the last half of the second year. When this happens, mothers tend to emphasize two basic verbal forms: requests and comments. Requests may include asking for information through "what" and "where" questions ("What's this?" "Where's the doggie?"). Mothers also request that the children speak about something ("Talk to Daddy on the telephone"; "Tell me what you saw in the park"). Comments are responses to the children's utterances or attempts to initiate a conversation ("Yes, that's an apple"; "The duck is swimming"; "This is the same car we saw the other day") (Stella-Prorok, 1983).

Similar patterns were found in a study of picture book reading (Ninio, 1983). Mothers referred to pictures using simple labeling, "what" questions ("What's that?" "What does the doggie say?"), and "where" questions ("Where's the kitty?") that elicited pointing by the children. Mothers also imitated their infants' utterances. Imitation was most likely to occur when the child made an error of pronun-

ciation. Rather than correct the child's speech, the mother simply repeated the correct pronunciation (Bohannon & Stanowicz, 1988).

Research that measures the total amount of maternal speech provides only indirect evidence that these methods actually promote speech development, although generally mothers who talk more to their infants have infants who are more advanced linguistically (Sigman et al., 1988; Tomasello, Mannle, & Kruger, 1986). More to the point, if mothers time their verbal inputs to instances when the infants are looking at them or at an object, the infants develop higher language production scores compared to situations in which the mothers first attract the children's attention to an object and then comment on it (M. Harris, Jones, & Grant, 1985; F. F. Schachter, 1979; Tomasello & Farrar, 1986; Whitehurst et al., 1988). It also helps if mothers verbally direct their infants' attention to an object before saying something about it (Flom & Pick, 2003). Clear speech to the child also helps. Children of this age seem to notice the differences between well-pronoucned and mispronounced words, and between grammatical and nongrammatical speech, and will pay more attention to the former (Kedar, Casasola, & Lust, 2006; Soderstrom & Morgan, 2007; Swingley, 2007).

In general, the child develops greater linguistic competence when the adult uses speech that

TABLE 6.8   Two Styles of Word Use in Infancy

Attribute	Referential Speech	Expressive Speech
Word Type	Object names	Social routines
Part of Speech	Nouns	Pronouns
Syntax	Single Words	Phrases
Size of Vocabulary	Large	Small
Content	Substantive	Relational
Production	Original	Imitative
Articulation	Clear	Mumbled
Situational	Referential	Interpersonal
Context	As in reading books	As in free social play

Source: K. Nelson, Individual differences in language development: Implications for development and language, 1981, p. 182. *Developmental Psychology, 17*, 170–187. Adapted with permission of Katherine Nelson.

Picture-book reading is a particularly good setting for guided participation in language development.

Photo by SW Productions.

is more responsive to the child's focus of interest and uses the child's interest to achieve a joint focus of attention before talking (Aureli, 1994; Baldwin, 1993; Hoff-Ginsberg, 1986; Hoff-Ginsberg & Shatz, 1982; Olson, Bates, & Bayles, 1984; M. Papousek, Papousek, & Bornstein, 1985; Snow, 1984). To the extent that maternal speech around the world shares some of the characteristics mentioned above, then it is likely to be the particular style of speaking to the child, rather than simply the amount of child-directed speech, that is the important factor.

The use of requests and comments as the primary mode of maternal speech may also be understood from the results of a study on infant imitation of adult actions during the period from 18 to 24 months (Hay, Murray, Cecire, & Nash, 1985). Infants were shown how to use a party hat as a horn or a shoe and how to use a string of beads as a telephone or a comb. The infants showed a much greater tendency to imitate adults' novel actions using these objects if the adults explained in words what they were doing ("I think you need a new shoe. Here's a pretty new shoe!"). Thus, verbal requests for action, when embedded in an action sequence, are more likely to be acted on by the child, providing more opportunities for language to be coupled with action. Children are also more likely to learn words if the adult is actually pointing to the object or looking at the object when saying the word (Baldwin et al., 1996). These studies show that children play a role in what words they choose to try out, opting for words that appear to be connected to intentional adult action. They also suggest that adults adapt their speech style to that of the children.

Guided Participation between Infants and Adults

These studies on linguistic interaction reflect some more general patterns of adult-infant communication that emerge around this age. In most interactions, adult and infant are working on something together, but each has a different purpose. The adult may be intent on instructing the child in the culturally appropriate uses of words and of objects. The child may be more motivated by being a direct participant in the social world. The concept of **guided participation** reflects the active role that children take in observing and participating in the organized activities of the family and society in the company of adults (Rogoff, 1990). Although from the adult's perspective, the child is merely "playing games" or "playing at" cooking or taking care of a doll, from the child's perspective, the child is actually doing the task as an active participant.

Typically, in adult-child interactions, the children set the agenda for what they want to do and how much they want to be involved. The more skilled partner collaborates in the child's goals by giving the child responsibility for certain actions that are part of the larger task but within the range of the child's competence. In this first phase, the task is to establish coordinated joint attention beginning from the child's initiatives.

The adult must also constrain the child's participation for the sake of the child's or others' safety or rights. Eventually, the adult transfers responsibility for larger segments of the task to the child, in relation to the growth of the child's competence as assessed by the adult (Bodle, Zhou, Shore, & Dixon, 1996; Bruner, 1983; Heckhausen, 1988; Kaye, 1982; Lock, 1980; Raver, 1996; Rogoff, 1990). These points are summarized in Table 6.9.

There are cultural differences in styles of guided participation. In one study (Rogoff, Mosier, Mistry, & Goncu, 1989; Rogoff, Mistry, Goncu, & Mosier, 1993), mothers from the United States were compared with Maya Indian mothers from Guatemala on how they helped their 20-month-old children use a set of nesting dolls. The U.S. mothers acted more like peers, wanting to take turns in combining dolls and commenting on the process. These mothers took seriously their role as teacher. The Maya mothers retained more of an adult-child status differential. They assumed the children would eventually acquire the ability to do the task. They monitored the children's progress and gave verbal instructions, but they did not get very involved in the task.

One U.S. mother tried to play games with the dolls, then offered them to the child for "his turn." She gave instructions ("Put the lid on") and then cheered when the child did this ("Yeah! You're so smaaart!"). This mother tried to change the agenda when she judged that the baby's attention waned. She commented on all the child's actions and made requests for actions throughout the task.

A typical Maya mother demonstrated how the dolls come apart and go back together, using a few words to encourage the child to look. The baby wanted to handle the doll, but soon after, the mother took it back and again demonstrated how to do it. She pointed out the features of the task verbally as she performed the action. After that, she let the infant try for some time on his own, while she watched but did not intervene. When he ran into trouble, the mother would say something to help ("Do this one first"). When the child made a successful move, the mother would simply say "Okay" or "I see" in a quiet tone.

Both of these cases illustrate the general principles of guided participation listed in Table 6.9, but they differ markedly from each other. Similar differences in levels of involvement have been observed between American and North African mothers with infants of this age (Guillain et al., 1998). American mothers were more actively involved than those in North Africa, but both practiced guided participation.

It is generally true that when adults become collaborators or participants in what children spontaneously seem interested in doing, children can achieve higher levels of language play and cognitive development compared to when adults do not become involved. (O'Connell & Bretherton, 1984; Slade, 1987a; Zukow, 1980). Particular types of adult involvement, however, are more effective in promoting higher cognitive levels in the development of symbolic play. The establishment of coor-

TABLE 6.9 Components of Guided Participation Between Adults and Young Children

Child sets the agenda according to interest and skill level.

Adult adjusts level of child's participation according to child's skill.

Adult constrains child's participation for the safety and rights of the child and others.

Adult transfers responsibility to child according to on-going assessment of child's abilities.

Source: B. Rogoff, *Apprenticeship in thinking: Cognitive development in social context*, 1990. New York: Oxford University Press.

dinated joint attention with children of this age is less likely to occur if mothers are depressed or have a low sense of self-efficacy (D. F. Goldsmith & Rogoff, 1997; Teti, O'Connell, & Reiner, 1996). Parents who understand the relationship between play and development and who engage the child in higher levels of symbolic play are more likely to encourage the child's participation at a higher level of performance (Bornstein et al., 1999; Damast, Tamis-LeMonda, & Bornstein, 1996). Children develop higher levels of symbolic play when their mothers give more options that stimulate the child's creativity. If a child tries to put a doll into a toy cup, an options-limiting maternal response might be, "No, dolls don't go like that. We play with dolls in the dollhouse." An options-promoting reply might be, "Is the doll going swimming in the cup? Maybe she would like to have some lemonade in the dollhouse when she's done?"

Remarkably, the same process of guided participation that helps human infants acquire language also occurs when baby chimpanzees and baby bonobos are taught to use signs in the company of human adults. Chimpanzees and bonobos, along with gorillas, are great apes and our closest primate relatives. Compared to animals who are raised by their own mothers, chimpanzees and bonobos who are raised with human adults acquire signs in way similar to that in which human infants acquire verbal language, at least up until the age of 2 years (Savage-Rumbaugh et al., 1993; Tomasello, Savage-Rumbaugh, & Kruger, 1993). There is no evidence that nonhumans can acquire grammar, outside of a few simple formulas.

In addition to attesting to the power of guided participation in the development of language, these studies also tell us about the evolution of language. That chimpanzees and bonobos can acquire some linguistic signs when taught by humans clearly shows that they have the cognitive ability for forming symbols to represent objects and events. This means that symbolic ability probably evolved before the evolution of speech. The likely evolutionary scenario is that as humans evolved upright, bipedal locomotion, the vocal organs in the throat were reoriented, permitting the closure

of the soft palate. Recall that when this closure happens developmentally in infants at around 5 months, it allows the infants to create consonant sounds and produce syllable-like utterances that sound like words. In this way, humans evolved the ability to create meaningful speech using that part of the cognitive system that is common to both apes and humans (Savage- Rumbaugh et al., 1993).

Aside from cultural differences in guided participation and development, there are also individual differences. More explicit instructions (compared to sharing and mutuality) are given to children who are temperamentally difficult or who show attachment problems; such instructions are also more likely to be used by fathers than by mothers (Fagot & Kavanagh, 1993; Marcos, 1995). Sharing and mutuality also vary depending upon the task or situation.

In particular, instances of parent-infant pretend play evoke relatively more sharing than instances in which the child is trying to or is expected to learn something (Nishida & Lillard, 2007). Pretending can be used just for fun as parent and child together create pretend scenarios, such as going for a ride in the car (using the couch as the car), playing house (using a cardboard box as the house), or reversing roles (the mother becomes the child and vice versa). Pretending can also be used to metacommunicate about more serious conflicts or disagreements. Mothers may engage in pretend play to give the child something to do, to redirect an otherwise undesirable activity, or to make light of a negative emotion (Farver & Howes, 1993; Haight, Masiello, Dickson, Huckeby, & Black, 1994; Haight & Miller, 1992). Pretend play is more likely to be used for guidance, such as teaching proper conduct, in Taiwanese than in North American families. The North American families were more likely to use pretend play for fun and fantasy games (Haight, Wang, Fung, Williams, & Mintz, 1999).

The Development of Discipline and Compliance

As it turns out, these basic principles of guided participation and collaboration in infants' activities are the foundation for effective discipline of children at this age. These principles include adjusting one's actions to the child's agenda and providing clarity about adult guidelines and standards (T. Gordon, 1988; Rocissano, Slade, & Lynch, 1987).

Research suggests that in Western cultures the most effective forms of parental discipline combine empathy and firmness (Baumrind, 1973). Caregivers should be sensitive to the reasons for the child's behavior and to the natural negative reactions children are likely to have when restrictions are imposed. The most successful discipliners make firm demands and are appropriately expressive of their own angry or distressed reactions to the child's behavior. These parents did not use power as a means of controlling the child. These kinds of parents, whose style Baumrind called **authoritative parenting**, have children who show purposive, independent behavior, are cooperative with adults, show friendliness to peers, and are more likely to imitate their mothers; they are also more likely to become upset when they have violated standards of conduct (Kochanska, Forman, & Coy, 1999; Spinrad et al., 2007; also see the Emotional Development, Chapter 7). The key, therefore, seems to be a combination of love and control.

By this age, it appears that the father begins to play a substantial role in family processes. Fathers who are rated as more sensitive and involved with their children have children who are more socially competent and less defiant in both Caucasian American and African American families with toddlers (M. M. Black & Krishnakumar, 1998; Kelley, Smith, Green, Berndt, & Rogers, 1998).

To get more specific details about ways to obtain compliance, mothers were asked to try to get their babies to play with all the toys that were set out in a laboratory free-play situation (Schaffer & Crook, 1979, 1980). Researchers distinguished three types of compliance. *Orientation compliance* refers to getting infants to look where the adult wants them to. Mothers succeeded in this about 50% of the time on the first try. It helped if they used a nonverbal gesture. Almost all the mothers succeeded in getting orientation compliance if they persisted long enough. *Contact compliance* refers to getting children to touch a designated toy. First-time success rates ran at 33%. In this case, success was more likely if the children were already looking at the toy, either because of their own interest or as a result of orientation compliance. *Task compliance* is shown when an infant manipulates a toy in an appropriate manner. It occurred only one-fourth of the time, and as you might expect, the likelihood of task compliance was higher if the infant was already looking at and touching the toy.

What conclusions can we draw about compliance from this research? First, it is important to get the child's attention; second, it helps if the child is already starting to do what is wanted. In other words, the mothers made their children look more compliant than they actually were by timing their requests for compliance to coincide with a behavior of the child that was most likely to lead to the desired response.

If a baby is playing, for example, and you want to do something else, such as go out, give her a bath, or feed her dinner, one approach is to sit down on the floor next to the baby and start playing with her. The parent should become part of the baby's play for only a few minutes to maneuver the game to a logical conclusion. For example, the parent might pick up the ball the baby is playing with, roll it back and forth with the baby a few times, tap it playfully on her stomach and nose, and then pick up the baby with a tickle and carry her to the dinner table or bathtub. In this way a parent can skillfully change the baby's goals without causing a confrontation (Spock, 1957).

The importance of these recommendations was confirmed in a study by G. W. Holden (1983). Unobtrusive observations were made of 24 middle-class mothers and their 2-year-old infants in the supermarket. What were mothers' strategies in dealing with undesired behavior, such as asking for food, reaching for things, standing in the cart, and ignoring the mothers' requests? One group of mothers used *contingent responses*; that is, they scolded or reprimanded the infant after the transgression had occurred. The other group of mothers used *preventive responses*, such as talking to the child while shopping and giving the child something to eat. The children of the mothers who used preventive measures showed fewer instances of undesired behavior. When it comes to discipline and compliance in the second year, prevention is the best cure.

Preventive measures fall under the heading of **parental proactive behavior**, including any action that has the goal of a positive outcome for the child. Table 6.10 lists some examples of proactive behavior used by adults. This approach to discipline suggests that one may avoid potential problems by proactively controlling or regulating access to the environment. In a healthy, safe, and developmentally appropriate environment, infants have fewer opportunities to get into danger or out of control.

Finally, it is worth noting that even though infants of this age want to try things out for themselves and often resist parental requests that directly interfere with their own actions, the infants also have a strong desire to be part of the social group and to join in with whatever adults might be doing. Infants are attracted to objects that adults are handling and want to do the same, and they seem to think that most household tasks the adult is doing are fun and want to join in (Hay, Murray, Cecire, & Nash, 1985; Rheingold, 1982; Rheingold, Cook, & Kolowitz, 1987). Rather than ignoring or complaining about the children being nuisances for interfering, adults can encourage the

children's collaboration by giving them small tasks. This requires the adults to slow down and think about how to best include the children's efforts (Rogoff, 1990).

It is clear, however, that infants of this age are capable of developing self-control. In one study, an experimenter placed an attractive toy on the table while talking with a child. The experimenter then told the child that she (the experimenter) had to go out of the room to get something and asked the child to please wait and not to touch the toy. By age 2 years, children could wait on average for a full minute before being tempted to touch the toy, a long time for a 2-year-old (Vaughn, Kopp, & Krakow, 1984).

Compliance is more easily assured if it is clear to the infants that the expected behavior affects how they relate to others, and if they are shown how their behavior affects others. For this to happen, verbal skills are necessary, and indeed, compliance with requests is correlated with verbal development (Kaler & Kopp, 1990; McLaughlin, 1983; Schneider-Rosen & Wenz-Gross, 1990; Vaughn, Kopp, & Krakow, 1984).

Some parents, however, use more coercive and controlling disciplinary techniques. One research study examined 69 families with their firstborn sons when they were 15 and 21 months old. Some of the families at each age were identified as "troubled." These families used control as the pri-

TABLE 6.10 Examples of Parental Proactive Behavior

Type	Short Term	Long Term
Direct	Occupy with activities. Divert attention. Engage child in game. Prepare verbally for upcoming situations. Set limits in advance. Monitor child's action when danger is present.	Take child on an outing. Train child to be wary of dangers. Organize peer groups. Select a day care center.
Indirect	Place child in car seat. Dress child appropriately for weather. Use night light. Serve appropriate foods.	Buy a home in a neighborhood conducive to child's development. Build a fence to keep child from danger. Keep poisons locked up. Purchase safe toys and furniture.

Source: G. W. Holden, How parents create a social environment via proactive behavior, 1985, p. 130. In T. Garling & J. Valsiner (Eds.), *Children within environments: Towards a psychology of accident prevention*, 116–142. New York: Plenum Press

Effective discipline requires a balance of firmness and affection.
Photo by Joe Heider.

mary disciplinary method and were unlikely to use guided participation; the children in these families showed the most defiance and the most negative emotion. More troubled families included men who showed more negative attitudes and were less social and less friendly than men in nontroubled families. Both mothers and fathers in these families, however, were more likely to use control techniques in place of guidance and authoritative approaches (Belsky, Woodworth, & Crnic, 1996). Teenage mothers are more coercive and tend to infer more anger and defiance in emotion expressions of infants (Strassberg & Treboux, 2000). As predicted by a dynamic systems model (Chapter 2), a vicious cycle can develop so that harsh parenting creates defiance and negativity, which in turn sparks harsh parenting (Scaramella & Leve, 2004).

One form of coercive parental behavior is **corporal punishment**, such as spanking, defined as using physical force that causes pain to the child but not injury. One investigation on corporal punishment summarized the results of 88 different studies with a total of 36,309 children. Children who had experienced corporal punishment in the early years were more likely to show poor self-control, have a poor relationship with their parents throughout childhood, show more criminal or antisocial behavior, and abuse their own children or spouse in adulthood (Gershoff, 2002).

These results, although powerful, do not say that all children who experience corporal punishment will turn out this way. Some parents and psychologists suggest that occasional spanking may be used in serious offenses, such as running out into the street, especially if the spanking is later accompanied by explanations, recognition of the child's feelings, and expressions of love. In Caucasian American families, children who were spanked were at 5 times greater risk for later behavior problems but for African American and Hispanic American families, there was no relationship to parenting (Slade & Wissow, 2004). In the latter two ethnic groups, spanking is viewed as a normal parental behavior and is rarely done impulsively or in anger. In general, parents are encouraged to focus on praise for good behavior, proactive parenting, respect for the child's own point of view, and use of milder sanctions, such as time out, when possible.

Another thing to consider is that toddler defiance is not necessarily a bad thing. It is often a way for children to express their feelings, to assert their budding self-awareness, and to experiment with taking initiative and taking charge. These are all important developmental achievements (Dix et al.,

2007). On the other hand, defiance that is aggressive or violent is typically a sign of an emerging vicious cycle implication of parental coercion and aggression (Brook et al., 2001; Calkins, 2002).

Twenty-Four to Thirty-Six Months

Near the end of the second year, a vocabulary spurt occurs, as discussed above. Some time during the third year, or later for some children, there is a spurt in the **mean length of utterance (MLU)**. The MLU is the average number of morphemes in each utterance spoken by the child. A *morpheme* is a meaningful unit of language; it is usually a word, but it can also be a word ending, such as *-ed*, *-s*, or *-ing*. The word "walking," for example, has two morphemes: *walk | ing*. Increases in MLU for three children are shown in Figure 6.4. Notice the wide range of individual variation. Eve has reached a peak in MLU development before Adam and Sarah have even begun to use more than one or two morphemes in an utterance (R. Brown, 1973).

These utterances are becoming less formulaic and more like a flexible and productive standard grammar for the language spoken in the home (Bates, O'Connell, & Shore, 1987). Speaking in a sentence requires at least two basic components: a subject and a verb. In a grammatical sentence, the components must agree with one another in number (and gender in gender-based languages, such as Spanish and French). Sentences do not truly emerge until children begin to use verbs in a systematic manner—near the end of the second year of life.

In most cases, children acquire verbs more slowly than nouns. The time between when the first noun is acquired (about 10 months) and the first verb is acquired (about 20 months of age) is about the same as the time between birth and the first nouns acquired. While English is a noun-based language, other languages such as Korean and Mandarin Chinese are more likely to organize their sentences around verbs. In these languages, verbs occur at the ends of sentences and can occur alone. Verbs, therefore, are more salient to both

children and adults using these languages. Children acquiring these languages have more verbs in their early vocabularies than those speaking English, but in all languages, nouns predominate over verbs during the second and third years (Tardif, 1996; Tardif, Gelman, & Xu, 1999).

Nouns and verbs are fundamentally different. Nouns represent the descriptions of things or objects; they serve a referential function. Nouns refer to concrete things the child can see, touch, or feel. Verbs, in contrast, tell us about the relationship between things—between the subject and the object, for example. Verbs are relational rather than referential. The ability to understand relationships between things and to express these in words begins during the second year (Gentner, 1978; S. S. Jones, Smith, & Landau, 1991; Waxman & Senghas, 1992).

Because verbs are relational, they can express nontangible things. When you say "The ball rolls across the floor," the verb represents a transient action—one that relates the ball and the floor. The words *ball* and *floor*, in contrast, make fewer intellectual demands on the listener; these objects are there for all to see whenever they wish to. Verbs can also represent abstract properties that are difficult for a young child to appreciate, for example, to *think* and to *feel*.

When children first start to express action words, they often combine the action and its result in the same word. The word *up* can be used for a variety of situations, such as being lifted, being put down, asking to be picked up or to climb on someone's lap, climbing up or down stairs, or even requesting out-of-reach objects (Clark, 1978). *Off*, *on*, *out*, and *open* can be used in similarly extended ways.

The next step in the development of action expression is the use of simple verbs, such as *do* and *make*. The initial meaning of these words is not always clear to the listener, because the child uses them in many different ways. Thus, it is important to see the child speaking in the context of the ongoing activity (Table 6.11).

A final way children express actions is by using an object word to talk about the action (E. V. Clark, 1978). Some examples include "The man is keying the door" (opening the door with a key); "I'm

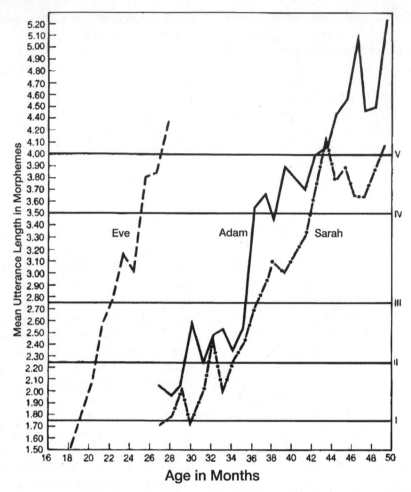

Figure 6.4   Average Length of Utterance in Morphemes at Different Ages for Three Children

Source: From Brown, Cazden, & Bellugi-Klima, The child's grammar from I to III, 1969, p. 29. In J. P. Hill (Ed.), *Minnesota Symposium on Child Psychology* (Vol. 2) Copyright © The University of Minnesota Press. Reprinted by permission. Also in A. Fogel & G. F. Melson, *Child development*, 1988, p. 286. St. Paul, MN: West. Copyright © by West Publishing Company. Reprinted by permission. All rights reserved.

souping" (eating soup); or "Pillow me!" (throw a pillow at me).

Children of this age also make errors in the use of verbs similar to the overextension of nouns. Some examples are given in Table 6.12. Such errors usually happen after the children understand the similarity in meaning between verbs that they accidentally substitute for each other (Bowerman, 1978). *Put* and *give*, for example, are both words that a person uses to make an object move from one place to another. The substitution "errors" shown in Table 6.12 require that the child under-

stand the basic relationship between *put* and *give*, since children rarely substitute words that have no semantic relationship to each other.

If you think about the order of events in an action sequence (rolling a ball from me back to you), some words represent the source of the action (*from, out, off, away*), some represent the path of the action (*back, up, down, across, through*), and some represent the goal or end point of the action (*to, in, at, there*). Children acquire these words in the same order: source-path-goal (Stockman & Vaughn-Cooke, 1992). Source words are acquired at the end of the first year ("Get this *out* her mouth [said taking a thermometer out of a doll's mouth]"; "Go *away* [telling a cat to leave the play area]"). Path words are acquired in the middle of the second year ("He climb *up* a tree [looking at a picture of a boy in a tree]"; "Make the man go *around* [placing a toy figure on a merry-go-round]"). Finally, goal words are acquired at the end of the second year ("All of 'em go *to* here [putting items in a purse]"; "I blow *at* Coty [aiming soap bubbles at Coty]").

These results show that language development is influenced by the temporal relations between elements in a sequence (Naigles & Kako, 1993; Stockman & Vaughn-Cooke, 1992). Children are better able to acquire new nouns when they occur in sentences with a familiar verb. If there are a number of foods on the table and the adult says, "rutabaga," the child may have difficulty picking out the right object and may not pay attention to the word. If the adult says, "Daddy is *eating* the rutabaga," it gives the child a clue about the object to which the word *rutabaga* refers (Goodman, McDonough, & Brown, 1998). This may help explain the vocabulary spurt that began during the previous age period. As children begin to acquire verbs it also helps them to understand more nouns.

Adding the Proper Endings

Children still have more to know about verbs in the preschool years, in particular about verb meaning and tense. One interesting phenomenon is that just after children acquire the past tense of regular verbs (such as *looked* for *look* or *helped* for *help*), they apply the *-ed* rule to all verbs, including irregular verbs. So, instead of saying *went*, the child says *goed*. Instead of saying *made*, the child says *maked*. This pattern of grammatical error is called **overregularization**. Overregularization errors are relatively rare, happening only 2.5% of the time the child intends to use an irregular past tense. They occur from the age of 2 years up through the elementary school years. These errors probably reflect minor memory slips and are not symptomatic of poor language development (Kuczaj, 1978; Marcus, Pinker, Ullman, & Hollander, 1992). In fact, they

actually reflect progress in learning the underlying grammatical rules.

Similar processes occur in acquiring the plural forms of nouns. The way children acquire plurals is very similar to the way they acquire verb tenses. Children first acquire some irregular forms such as *men* and *children* almost without realizing that they are plurals of *man* and *child*. Once they acquire the general rule of adding an s, they apply that rule to anything, even the words they previously had acquired in the irregular plural forms: *mans* and *childs* (Berko, 1958).

Another type of meaningful word ending is negation. Although younger infants express negation by saying *no* or *not*, children of this age use contractions, such as *can't* and *don't* (H. H. Clark & Clark, 1977). Although the ability to put the proper endings on words is slow to be acquired, apparently by the age of 2 years children can understand the difference between words with different endings (Gerken, Landau, & Remez, 1990).

When Do Children Begin to Ask Questions?

After children master the subject-verb-object composition of sentences, they usually move quickly beyond simple declarative sentences to form questions. Questions usually begin with *wh*- words, and a definite developmental sequence in the order of acquisition of these words has been found (see Table 6.13). The ages listed in Table 6.13 are approximations, and we can expect individual differences in the age of acquisition.

The reason for this developmental sequence is that the *wh* questions differ in their complexity. *What*, *where*, and *who* all ask for single-word responses that usually are simply extracted from a situation: "What did Bobby make?" "A tower." *Why*, *how*, and *when* require a more extended response giving a reason, process, or time.

The initial use of questions by 2-year-olds also reflects a rudimentary ability to use the questions in a fully expressive manner. Most of the questions addressed by children of this age are not dependent upon the previous topic of discussion. Thus,

TABLE 6.11 Uses of Do, Go, and Make in the Third Year*

Verb	Utterance	Context
Do	I do it again.	Said as knocks over blocks.
	You …do …doing that.	Said as watches O build blocks into a tower.
	You do do it. OK?	Asking O to unroll some computer tape, after trying unsuccessfully to do it himself.
	You do that!	Indicating which toy O should take out of a box.
	Uh oh. I did.	Said as he turned off the tape recorder by pushing a knob.
	The clown do!	Adking O to make the toy clown do what clowns do.
Make	Make name!	Telling O to write his name.
	I make a little doggie.	Said as cut a dog shape out of Play-Doh.
	Make a dog.	Telling O what to draw next.
	Make it go in there.	Asking O to get a crayon back into its box.
	Make that.	Said as pointed to the hand moving on a clock; seemed to be request for O to move the hand down.
Go	It go there.	Talking about a block lying on the floor.
	Red went Boom.	Talking about a red block that fell on the floor.
	They go in the car.	Talking about two storybook characters.
	'N turn go up.	Said as turned a puzzle piece the right way up.
	'N go like that.	Said as dropped puzzle pieces on the floor.

*Examples cited come from the first month of recordings from S, a child taped at weekly intervals for 1 year from age 2 years. The utterances cited occurred without any immediately preceding use of the particular general purpose verb by either the observer (O) or the parents.
Source: E. Clark, Strategies for communicating, 1978, p. 957. *Child Development, 49*, 953–959. Copyright © The Society for Research in Child Development. Reprinted by permission of the Publisher and the author.

TABLE 6.12 Verb Substitution Errors

A. *Put* substituted for *give*.

E (2–2): I go *put* it to Christy. (Starting off with a rubber band, then gives it to C.)

E (2–4): Can I go *put* it to her? (Then takes juice and gives it to C.)

E (2–4): M: It's all gone. (Re: C's juice.) E: Then *put* her some more.

E (2–4): How come you're *putting* me that kind of juice? (As M prepares to give unfamiliar juice to E.)

E (2–4): Were *putting* our things to you. (To D after M has told children that it's time to give him their Father's Day presents.

B. *Give* substituted for *put*.

E (2–7): *Give* some ice in here, Mommy. *Put* some ice in here, Mommy. (Pointing to ice crusher.)

E (2–9): *Give* those crayons right here (Indicated to M spot on table near where she is sitting.)

E (2–10): I'm gonna *give* your glasses right here. (M: Huh?) I'm gonna *put* your glasses right here.

E (2–10): Don't *give* those next to me. (As C dumps things on couch near E's seat.)

*C = Christy, E = Eva, M = Mother, D = Daddy.
Source: M. Bowerman, Systematizing semantic knowledge: Changes over time in the child's optimization of word meaning, 1978, pp. 984–985. *Child Development, 49*, 977–987. Copyright © The Society for Research in Child Development. Reprinted by permission of the publisher and the author.

children use questions to start a conversation rather than to continue one. The only exceptions to this rule are why questions (L. Bloom, Rocissano, & Hood, 1976; L. Bloom, Merkin, & Wootten, 1982). Although some parents get annoyed with the constant "why"s of their young children, the ability to ask *why* reflects a growing linguistic sophistication that presages a more complex use of verbs and other *wh-* questions over the next few years.

In general, however, children definitely want information when they ask a question. They are not just trying to get the adult's attention (Chouinard, 2007). Because they want information, they will typically stop asking questions when they get an answer that satisfies the intention of their question or that gives a fuller explanation of what an object can do rather than just giving the name of the object (Kemler Nelson & O'Neil, 2005; Kemler Nelson, Egan, & Holt, 2004).

Children's question asking tells us that they have become aware of the importance of language for communication. When children ask *why* questions, they are not only requesting information but making a kind of statement as well. They are saying, "I know you know the answer," "I know I can use language to get a response or an explanation from you," and possibly even "I have the right, duty, and privilege to ask you this question." These unstated forms of linguistic awareness, or awareness about the function of language and of the implicit relationship between speakers, are known as **metalinguistic knowledge** (Kaye, 1982; P. J. Dunham & Dunham, 1996; Y. Levy, 1999). Metalinguistic means "above" or "outside of" language itself.

In What Ways Is the Two-Year-Old's Language Limited?

In spite of the major accomplishments in the linguistic realm taking place during the third year of life, children still have a great deal more to learn about language. They still make errors in pronunciation, fail to comprehend certain words and sentences, and have only rudimentary conversational skills.

Young children acquiring English have an endearing tendency to confuse r and l and to make them both sound like *w*. Sound spectrographs of children who said *gwass* for both *glass* and *grass* could detect differences between the child's pronunciation of the two words, however, even though the human ear could not (Kornfeld, 1971).

Another study examined a similar group of children who confused *r* with *w*. They all said *wake* to refer to the garden tool used to gather leaves. About two-thirds of the group, however, were able to tell the difference between an adult's pronunciation of *wake* and *rake*. Children become annoyed when adults try to mimic their mispronunciations (Locke, 1979; W. R. Miller, 1964).

The evidence suggests that comprehension continues to be ahead of production. Even though children can hear the difference, and even though they apparently are attempting to pronounce the words correctly, they are still unable to do this perfectly. This error tends to persist in the speech of some children until school age, whereas other children never have problems with the *r-l* distinction. All children, however, need a good deal of time to get the correct pronunciations of most of the words they routinely use.

Some researchers have collected tape-recorded samples of children's private speech with a microphone hidden in their cribs. During these monologues, children have been heard to practice their pronunciation. One child practiced the *r* in *story* as follows: "Stoly/Stoly here/want a stoly/Dave, stoly/story, story/story's de hat/story's de big hat/store's a hat" (R. H. Weir, 1966).

Some children, however, continue to have difficulty with pronunciation even during preschool. Such children show more delay in learning other features of language, such as MLU, grammar, and vocabulary (Carson et al., 2003). They are also more likely to have difficulty learning to read (McBride-Chang & Kail, 2002). Continuing pronunciation difficulties into the fourth and fifth year, therefore, may be a reason to have a child assessed for possible language intervention.

Finally, children of this age have trouble comprehending unusual grammatical sequences. If you

TABLE 6.13   Order of Acquisition of *wh-* Questions

Age (Months)	Question
26	Where and What
28	Who
33	How
35	Why
36	Which, Whose, and When (occured rarely at this age)

Source: L. Bloom, S. Merkin, & J. Wootten, Wh-questions: Linguistic factors that contribute to the sequence of acquisition, 1982, p. 1089. *Child Development, 53*, 1084–1092.

were told that the robin is being kissed by the blue-jay, how would you answer the questions "Who did the kissing?" and "Who was the kisser?" You are probably wishing all your test questions were this easy. However, 2-year-olds could not get the right answer. Half the time they said the robin was the kisser, and half the time they said the bluejay (Bever, 1970).

They all got the right answer when they were told "The bluejay kisses the robin" or "It's the robin that the bluejay kisses." The first sentence—the one that confused the children—is a passive construction. Evidently, whenever the children hear a noun followed by a verb, they assume the noun represents the actor. Not until children are in elementary school can they understand sentences such as "Donald Duck was liked by Goofy" (Maratsos, Kuczaj, Fox, & Chalkley, 1979).

How Well Can a Two-Year-Old Carry on a Conversation?

The mother and child in Table 6.14 were reading a Richard Scarry picture-book together. In the same study from which this conversation was taken, mothers and children also played with a set of toy teacups and plates, as well as with a Fischer-Price play family with a table, chairs, a dog, and a car, among other things (Kaye, 1982). The children were videotaped at 26 months and again at 30 months doing these things with their mothers (28 children in all).

What is the difference between this conversation and one you might hear between two adults?

When adults talk to each other, the conversation is likely to continue because both partners are used to taking initiatives and starting new thoughts. In Table 6.14, the parent was more likely to get a response from the child if she asked the child a question or created a situation that required a response from the child. Thus, the parent needs to keep prompting the child to continue the conversation. At this age, the child does not have a mature ability to carry on dialogue, even though the child may have mastered the words and phrases of the language. As an apprentice conversationalist, the child can respond to the adult, who makes the child look more capable than he or she really is (Kaye, 1982; Shatz, 1978; C. E. Snow, 1977).

Aside from using prompts and questions in conversations, adults have other skills designed to make the infant a more active participant. Adults use a greater number of hand gestures and gestures of a more complex variety with their preschoolers than they do with their toddlers (Gutman & Turnure, 1979). These gestures are of three major types. From the beginning of the second year, parents use such gestures as pointing or otherwise specifying the location of something. As children acquire meanings and become symbol users, parents employ gestures that copy or imitate the attributes of an object or situation (as in "Eensy Weensy Spider"). Finally, parents use gestures that add emphasis to speech, much as they would when talking to another adult.

No doubt these gestures help the child understand more complex sentences, much as gestures helped the prelinguistic child to interpret the parent's meaning. Gestures function the same as the mother's speech in Table 6.14, in that they help children maintain an active participation in a conversation that might otherwise be beyond their comprehension and production capacities.

Research has shown that by age 2, social class differences in linguistically based parent-child communication emerge. One study in the United States found that middle-income dyads spend twice as much time in mutual play as lower-income dyads. Mothers in lower-income groups spend more time reading to themselves, and their children are observed more often in independent play (Farran & Haskins, 1980). Even within middle-income groups, there seem to be individual differences. Parents with professional backgrounds—especially teachers—are more likely to read to and interact with their children than parents with blue- or white-collar jobs (Feiring & Lewis, 1981).

Lower- versus middle-income comparisons in Israel showed similar differences. Lower-income mothers thought infants were slower to acquire cognitive skills than did middle-income mothers. The tendency to see the infant as precocious, and therefore to create the "pseudodialogues" previously described, was found for middle-income parents only (Ninio, 1979). In observations of parents reading picture-books to their children, Ninio (1980) found that middle-income Israeli mothers asked more questions, talked more during the reading session, and modeled more new words than the low-income mothers. The final chapter will discuss whether these differences in parental behavior have any lasting impact on the child's social and intellectual development. In general,

middle-income children have more advanced language development and larger vocabularies than lower-income children (Hoff, 2003).

Discipline and Compliance in Parent-Child Relationships

During the third year of life, children widen the scope of their activities and language, not all of which fits into their parents' ideas about appropriate behavior. Parents need to provide continued discipline to orient the child toward acceptable and competent patterns of action. Parents introduce a wide variety of controls over toddler behavior. Children of this age are told when to do things ("Tie your shoe") and when not to do things ("Don't yell"), and they are asked to control their future actions ("Be good while I'm gone"). Parents ask children to perform actions requiring a high level of competence ("Take care of your brother"; "Put the crayons away"; "Say thank you"; "Don't write on the wall"; "Go play in the other room"). Children can either comply or resist. Resistance can be passive or it can involve direct defiance, with the child exploring all the different ways of using the word *no* (Kuczynski & Kochanska, 1995).

The findings on parental discipline and child compliance at this age are similar to those reported during the previous age period. Research shows that authoritative patterns of parental discipline (combining firmness, respect for the child, and warmth) are associated with cooperative and compliant children. On the other hand, oppositional children have parents who attempt to control the child's social behavior. Oppositional children

TABLE 6.14 A Conversation

Mother	Child (30 Months)
1. (Points to picture) What is that one?	2. Kitty cat.
3. Well what is it?	4. Kitty cat.
5. Well, I know there's a kitty.	6. Huh?
7. What's he riding in?	8. Airplane.
9. Right.	10. (turns page)

Source: K.Kaye, *The mental and social life of babies*, 1982, p. 100. Chicago: University of Chicago Press. Copyright © The Society for Research in Child Development, Inc. Reprinted by permission of the publisher and the author.

receive fewer demands for performing competent behavior and fewer requests to control their future actions.

It is not clear whether this style of parenting causes oppositional children, or whether the parents adapt their style to a less compliant child by making fewer demands on the child. Most likely, this is a relational pattern that emerges during the history of their prior communications. In any case, the parent and child enter into a cycle in which the parents avoid confronting the child, and the child is deprived of opportunities to become more competent. In other cases, a cycle of mutual conflict and parental nagging results (Achermann, Dinneen, & Stevenson-Hinde, 1991; Kuczynski & Kochanska, 1995; Leonard, 1993).

It is difficult to break these cycles, and they may persist for a year or more (Aber, Belsky, Slade, & Crnic, 1999). Intervention from a third party, another adult family member or a family therapist, may be needed if they persist and lead to breakdowns in parent-child communication. Intervention is helpful since these negative cycles often lead to behavior problems of the child with peers and in child-care settings.

The good news is that during the third year, the frequency of defiance and refusals to cooperate gradually diminishes. It is replaced by children's use of negotiation strategies. Instead of simply saying "no" or "I don't want to," when asked to clean up their toys for example, by 30 months or so children may begin to say things like "Let me play a little longer and then I'll clean up," "You clean some and I'll clean some," or "Don't leave and I'll clean up" (Klimes-Dougan & Kopp, 1999). This type of child behavior is more likely to occur if parents were less confrontational during conflicts and more likely to hear the child's perspective and negotiate (Laible & Thompson, 2002).

EXPERIENTIAL EXERCISE

Receiving and Giving Touch
by Alan Fogel, based on Rosen Method Bodywork (see Chapter 2)

This exercise is about creating the type of touch that parents use with young infants. This is a listening touch that is accepting and receptive but not demanding. It is also the type of touch used in Rosen Method Bodywork, as explained in Chapter 2. Choose a partner and find one chair. Introduce yourselves and talk for a few minutes. One person sits and the other stands behind. The following instruction is provided.

1. Everyone please close your eyes. Notice your breathing. Notice your contact with the chair and/or the floor. Notice comfort levels and emotions. Notice sounds in the room.

2. Those of you who are sitting, please keep your eyes closed and monitor your ongoing experience. Those of you who are standing, please open your eyes and look at the person sitting in front of you. Ask yourself: Who is this person? Let your gaze be soft and curious but uncritical.

3. Place your hands gently on your partner's shoulders, not too softly and not too firmly, but in a way that lets that person know you are there and present. Notice your feelings as you are doing this. Without doing anything, and without moving your hands, use your hands and your eyes to notice the person. Do they feel relaxed or tense? Can you feel the movement of their breath? Can you feel a change as a result of your touching? (at least 2 minutes).

4. Get a sense of a part of your partner's shoulders, upper back, or neck that calls to you to be touched, and gently move your hands there. Once your find the spot, settle in with a contact that meets the person and let your hands be soft and receptive. Notice changes in yourself and your partner: breathing, temperature, color (2 minutes).

5. In that same place or a different one, let your grip go very loose, so that you are making only superficial contact. What do you notice? Now make your grip more intense, like you really want to take hold of the person (but without inflicting pain). What do you notice?

Now return to the middle ground, the place where you feel you can meet and notice the other person (they know you are there, but you are just being present and not demanding).

6. Use your hands in a way that says "goodbye" to your partner, and then place your hands at your sides and close your eyes. Again, notice how you feel.

7. Change roles silently and repeat.

8. Discuss in pairs.

Mutual Gazing
by Alan Fogel

This exercise is about the parental role and the infant experience during face- to-face interaction and during movements of the infant

toward and away from the parent using either gaze. The class is divided up into pairs who do not know each other very well. Once a partner is chosen, pairs sit on the floor or in chairs facing each other.

1. Explain that now students will play the role of either the parent or the child, after which the roles will be changed. Speaking to the parents: your responsibility is to witness the child with a steady gaze. "Parents" should continue to feel their own emotions and arousal, but it is important to keep those feelings inside and just observe them. Their job is to be there for the child. As adults, they should be able to control their emotions. Speaking to the children: you can do anything you

want while sitting there. You can feel free to look at your parent or look away as much as you need or want to. Allow about 2 minutes.

2. Repeat the same process with the same roles, only this time the adult, instead of being attentive, acts distracted by something in the room.

3. Repeat the same process with the same roles, only this time the adult, instead of being attentive, acts intrusive, trying to get the "baby's" attention.

4. Then change roles, repeating the instructions to the parents and then to the children.

5. Sit in pairs and discuss the experience with each other.

SUMMARY

Two to Five Months

- Adults display characteristic patterns of behavior with infants that include motherese- type vocalizations and actions.
- Some aspects of motherese are universal, but cultures differ in the amount and type of verbal versus nonverbal behavior that is directed toward infants.
- Research shows that adults are affected by their infants' behavior, and infants are affected by adult behavior, making the origins of individual differences hard to determine in most cases.
- Infants are at risk when mothers have emotional disorders such as depression.

Six to Nine Months

- Infants can communicate nonverbally through action; however, they do not fully understand the meaning of their own behavior. Adults are required to interpret the infant's meaning, which ultimately contributes to the infant's understanding of communication.

- Infant social play becomes oriented toward objects, and parents can play a role in directing the infant's attention to objects and their properties.
- Parent-infant games are elaborated during this period. There are cultural differences in the amount of play versus caregiving that are related in part to ecological factors.
- Babbling mimics the intonation patterns of speech and develops in conjunction with auditory perception of speech sounds. However, infants are not using babbling to express themselves in a meaningful, linguistic manner.
- In specializing in their perception of the language spoken in the home, infants lose their sensitivity to sound contrasts that are not made in that language.

Ten to Twelve Months

- Infants and parents develop frames for coordinated joint attention and joint visual attention.
- Infants become more selective in their perception of speech, losing their ability to recognize sound contrasts in languages other than the one heard in the home.

- Intentional communication begins at this age, more with gestures than with words. Most gestures are related to infants' interactions with objects.
- At this age, genuine turn-taking exchanges with peers begin. Infant-peer relationships evolve around different themes from those that define infant-adult relationships.

Twelve to Eighteen Months

- Languages have properties that distinguish them from other forms of communication.
- Functional theories of language are discussed at length, and most of the recent research is on how infants use language to communicate.
- At this age, infants develop both linguistic and gestural referential communication, naming, gestural combinations, and the ability to coordinate their communications with those of the adult.
- Infants typically comprehend more than they can produce, although the gap between comprehension and production is much larger for some infants than for others.
- Particular forms of adult response seem more conducive to infant language development than others.
- Infants are able to metacommunicate; that is, to communicate about their relationships with others and change the way in which the communication occurs.
- Linguistic communication is more likely in certain situations, and gestural communication is more likely in others.

Eighteen to Twenty-Four Months

- A vocabulary spurt begins at this age, corresponding with the insight that things have names.

- Symbolic play and tool use correlate with the onset of multiword speech and the vocabulary spurt at around 20 months.
- Infants combine words in flexible formulas that allow different meanings to be constructed but are not as rigid as grammar.
- Individual differences in style and amount of speech emerge at this age.
- A linguistic environment conducive to infant language development is one in which adults are responsive to the infant's speech initiative by commenting and asking questions.
- Apes appear to have language abilities similar to those of human infants, and with human adult guidance, they can acquire signed languages.
- Guided participation is a general principle that applies to language, play, and discipline interactions.
- Discipline can be achieved by guided participation and by proactively regulating the environment.

Twenty-Four to Thirty-Six Months

- Grammar emerges with the use of verbs and the ability to add the appropriate endings to words for tense and number.
- Complex question asking emerges.
- Limitations of language include pronunciation problems, inability to appreciate complex grammar, and lack of skill in maintaining conversations.
- Toddlers who are more compliant have parents with more authoritative child-rearing styles.

Chapter 7

Emotion and Attachment

CHAPTER OUTLINE AND OVERVIEW

Emotional Development

What types of emotions can infants feel at different ages? What are their capacities for emotion regulation? What are the negative emotions? What are the positive emotions? Can infants recognize the facial expressions of other people? Do infants have lasting temperamental characteristics? How does the infant use speech and gesture to express emotions? How do symbolic thought and the sense of self affect the infant's emotions? How do children cope with stress? How do they deal with separations from parents? How do children talk about their emotions? Can infants understand the emotions of other people?

Attachment

What are the main theories of attachment? How are individual differences in attachment assessed? What are the disorders of attachment? What are the predictors of secure attachment? Can infants form attachments to people other than the mother? Can infants become attached to adoptive parents? Are there cultural differences in attachment?

An important part of the infant's development is the ability to experience emotional states, as well as to express what is felt. The research on infant emotional development indicates that the kinds of emotions infants can feel change with age. It is generally agreed that infants do not know the feeling of fear before about eight months, and that they cannot experience the "social emotions," such as guilt, pride, or shame, until they are almost three years old. Even though most of the basic emotional expressions can be observed in newborns, infants develop the capacity to express mixed emotions and subtle shades of feeling as they mature. They also develop the ability to control the kinds of emotions they wish to express, but this usually does not happen until the second and third years of life.

Along with the development of these emotions, infants also develop self-regulatory skills to cope with the stresses of everyday life. The hallmarks of successful self-regulation are sleeping through the night, waiting patiently while a meal is being prepared, handling the fear and distress of separation from parents, and fighting assertively to retrieve a toy from a meddling sibling. All of these milestones, and many others that occur during the first three years of life, represent the growing autonomy of the child's functioning and therefore lead to a greater sense of freedom for the parents or caregivers. Common to all these events is the ability to continue to function in the face of high levels of emotional arousal. We shall see in this chapter that not only do infants need to cope with high levels of negative arousal, but they must also learn to deal with high levels of positive arousal in situations where excitement and enjoyment threaten to become overwhelmingly intense.

EMOTIONAL DEVELOPMENT

The First Two Months: Crying State

One of the earliest forms of infant emotional expression is the cry. Newborns have different kinds of cries that seem to be associated with different kinds of distress. Cries have four phases: expiratory (exhaling; the actual creation of the crying sound), a rest period, an inspiratory period (inhaling), and another rest period. As Table 7.1 shows, the different types of infant cries can be distinguished on the basis of the length of these phases.

One feature of the neonatal pain cry, for example, is an exceptionally long rest phase, which gives the listener the feeling that the baby has stopped breathing. This long silence no doubt accounts for the salience of this cry to an adult. The pain cry also has a long expiration phase, much like the cry evoked when the infant is teased by having a pacifier pulled out of his or her mouth repeatedly. The expiration of the teased cry, however, is not followed by a long rest. These cry patterns repeat themselves over and over to form a crying bout.

Crying also involves a pattern of body movement including facial expressions of distress, movement of the arms and legs, changes in muscle tone and skin color, and alterations in breathing patterns. The intensity of pain or distress changes not only the acoustic features of the cry but also the body expressions (J. A. Green, Gustafson,

TABLE 7.1   Properties of Neonatal Cries*

Cry Phase	Basic Cry	Angry Cry	Pain Cry	Being-Teased Cry
Expiratory	0.62	0.69	3.83	2.67
Rest	0.08	0.20	3.99	0.07
Inspiratory	0.04	0.05	0.18	0.13
Rest	0.20	0.11	0.16	0.13

* All values are time in seconds.

Source: P. H. Wolff, The causes, controls, and organization of behavior in the neonate, 1966. *Psychological Issues 5*, 202–204

Irwin, Kalinowski, & Wood, 1995; Lock, 2000). The different responses of the whole body and the cry sound between the different cries suggests that newborn crying is a meaningful "language" that expresses the newborn's internal state (Clarici et al., 2002).

Neonatal crying is symptomatic of a range of "normal" internal states, but it may also reflect a number of abnormal conditions. A series of studies has examined variations in neonatal cry patterns under various conditions of mild to severe abnormalities. Cries were elicited by snapping a rubber band against the sole of the infant's foot. The cry sounds were recorded on a sound spectrograph. In general, infants with more complications required higher levels of stimulation to initiate the cry, took a longer time before they started to cry, had a shorter first cry expiration, cried for a shorter total time, and had cries of a higher pitch than infants with few or no complications. Higher infant arousal also changes the pattern of cry acoustics (Boom & Gravenhorst, 1995; J. A. Green, Gustafson, & McGhie, 1998; Zeskind & Lester, 1981).

These studies have several implications. Parents and caregivers can use crying to "read" an infant's internal state, and health professionals can use it to diagnose potential abnormalities. An abnormal cry, however, is not always associated with a serious or permanent underlying abnormality. Such a cry may merely indicate that the infant was born under conditions of stress or that the infant is highly responsive to external stimulation (St James-Roberts et al., 2003). Many birth complications have no lasting effects, and the infant's cries eventually return to normal. Crying, then, just as your grandmother could have told you, is a fairly reliable indicator of a newborn's degree of discomfort, pain, or stress.

Differences Between Infants: Quiet and Colic

Among normally developing newborns with no health complications, there is an increase in the frequency of crying between birth and 2 months of age, particularly during the late afternoon and early evening hours (Anders et al., 1998). After that time, the amount of crying begins a decrease that continues over the first year of life. This developmental phenomenon is similar for infants in many different cultures having different patterns of infant care and response to crying (Barr, 1990). Nevertheless, during this 2-month period of the most intense crying, infants differ with respect to how long they cry during the day. And although there are striking differences within cultures, there are even bigger ones between cultures.

Hunter-gatherer societies are composed of small bands of humans who sustain themselves by hunting game and gathering wild roots and plants to eat. Although hunter-gatherer societies are believed to have been the only form of human society before the invention of agriculture some 10,000 years ago, relatively few such societies survive today. Research on their child-care practices provides an important comparison for understanding child development in non-Western societies.

In hunter-gatherer societies in Africa, for example, infants cry as frequently as in Western countries. The hunter-gatherer infants, however, sustain their cries for only brief periods and less intensely, while Western babies typically cry for much longer and with more intensity. This difference seems to be due to the fact that in hunter-gatherer societies the infant is in almost constant contact with a caregiver, who carries the infant in a sling or pouch at all times. The infant is never left alone, and the caregiver responds immediately to any fussiness (Barr, 1990; Barr et al., 1991).

Western infants are not tended so closely. They are typically carried only for brief periods and are kept physically separate from the caregiver. Even when parents sensitively respond to the infant cry, the physical separation requires a longer response time than in hunter-gatherer societies. Infants have more time to build the pitch and volume of their cries, and they cry for longer periods until they are tended. In some cases their crying continues even after they are picked up. Research in Germany has shown that when parents are generally slower to respond to infants, the infants cry more (H. Keller et al., 1996; M. Papousek & von Hofacker, 1995).

Of particular concern is a group of infants in Western countries who cry excessively. **Colic** is crying in which: (1) the infant cries at least 3 hours per day, on at least 3 days per week, and for at least 3 successive weeks; (2) the parents judge the crying to be very intense; (3) the infant is otherwise normal; and (4) the infant is relatively unresponsive to soothing and feeding (Barr et al., 1992).

What causes colic? Research has shown that infants with colic, compared to noncolicky infants, are more likely to cry following feeding, to have more distress- related facial expressions, to have more turbulence in the cry sound, and to be rated as more difficult and negative by their parents. This merely reflects the differences in their cries and not the cause of it. No differences have been found, however, between colicky and noncolicky infants in the amount of stomach swelling after feeding, vomiting, hiccuping, or bowel movements (Barr et al., 1992; Lester et al.,1992; Zeskind & Barr, 1997). Thus, digestive problems, as is commonly believed, is not the cause of colic. There are also no overall differences between colicky and noncolicky infants in the level of sympathetic nervous system (arousal), activity, or in the daily levels of cortisol, a stress hormone (see section on the brain below) (Kirjavainen et al., 2001; White et al., 2000).

Some Western parents are attempting to replicate the hunter-gatherer pattern of close physical contact. They advocate "evolutionary parenting" or "attachment parenting," in which they hold infants closely, nurse often, and immediately respond to crying (Kestenberg-Amighi, 2004). Hunter-gatherer peoples also do not use diapers. Since the baby is constantly in contact with the mother's body, she can feel the baby getting ready to urinate or defecate and will hold the baby away from her over an appropriate location. A "diaper free" movement in Western countries attempts to teach parents the body language and vocalizations—called "elimination communication"—the babies use to express that they are ready to eliminate. The parents then hold the infant over the toilet (www.diaper- freebaby.org).

Comparisons of babies raised with attachment parenting and those in traditional Western infant care show that the attachment parenting infants cried 50% less overall. On the other hand, there were no differences between the groups in the amount of unsoothable crying and colic (St. James-Roberts et al., 2006). Even in hunter-gatherer and other societies in which there is almost continual close physical contact with infants, there are individual differences between infants, with some babies crying more than others. Even though the extremely fussy hunter-gatherer infants are less fussy than the extremely fussy Western infants, it suggests that colic or some form of it may be universal for some percentage of infants and may even be considered "normal" at least for some infants (Barr, 1998; Barr et al., 1991).

On the other hand, some data suggest that mothers who experienced high levels of stress during pregnancy were three times as likely to have a colicky infant (Søndergaard et al., 2003). Infants with colic sleep less than others, and they have more difficulty establishing a normal daynight rhythm of sleeping and waking (White et al., 2000). Along these lines, colicky infants have more difficulty feeding, including less rhythmic sucking and less ability to adapt to the feeding situation (Miller-Loncar et al., 2004). Finally, in follow-up studies at 3 and 8 years, children who were colicky as infants were more likely to be inattentive, emotionally reactive, and to show heightened sensitivity to touch, food, and other stimulation (Desantis et al., 2004).

These data suggest that colic is not benign, even though all infants end their colicky period around 5 to 6 months of age. Sensory sensitivity and poor emotion regulation could be the cause of colic, but they could also be the result of colic. If we consider the parent- infant relationship as a dynamic system, small factors in early infancy may lead to excessive crying by means of deviation-amplifying feedback. If the infant has some sensitivities to stimulation, if the parents are under stress or uncertain about themselves, it may take only a short time for infant crying to increase to levels that are difficult to regulate (Cuisinier, Janssen, de Graauw, & Hoogduin, 1998; M. Papousek & von Hofacker, 1995). For some infants who cry a great deal during the newborn period, higher levels of crying and fussiness will continue to be characteristic of their behavior during the first year of life and perhaps later (St. James-Roberts, Conroy, & Wilsher, 1998; St. James- Roberts & Plewis, 1998).

Colic also has a negative effect on parents. Both mothers and fathers of excessively fussy babies respond to them less and are less warm with them than parents with normally fussy babies. These very fussy babies also tend to decrease marital satisfaction and marital communication (Räihä et al., 2002; Stifter et al., 2003). Almost 50% of mothers of colicky babies report symptoms of moderate to severe depression, with more severe depression associated with lower self-esteem, more parenting stress, and a more difficult infant (Maxted et al., 2005).

What can parents do if their infants have colic? Perhaps nothing but wait for it to end in 2 or 3 months. One strategy, however, is to find ways to reduce parental stress, which comes partly from prenatal factors and partly from having an unconsolable infant. Some parents may feel that they have to hold their babies all the time, day and night, even if they baby does not calm down. This can be emotionally and physically draining. Parents need to get rest and sleep. Once they are certain that the infant is not wet or hungry or sick, it may be important for the parent to leave the infant on its own for short periods. This gives the parents a break and may also promote self-regulatory skills in the infant. In addition, if there is a chance the infant may have sensory sensitivities, steps can be taken to keep noise and lighting levels low, use gentle touch and soft clothing, and in general keep stimulation to a minimum (Desantis et al., 2004; Lester, 2005).

The Effects of Crying on Adults

Even when infants do not have colic, their crying affects adults in important ways. Adult women can perceive differences between basic cries and pain cries, whether they are mothers or not (Gustafson & Harris, 1990). These same women, however, when observed with an infant mannequin that emitted either a pain or a basic cry, showed no differences in their responses to each type of cry. Regardless of the type of cry, the women rocked, talked to, touched, held, distracted, and checked the diaper of the mannequin when asked to pretend to take care of it. They first tried actions to soothe the infant (such as holding and rocking) and later attempted to relieve the source of distress (by diapering or feeding). Crying, therefore, is heard as a general index of infant distress, and adults then try to figure out the source of that distress.

Particular aspects of the cry are more likely to affect how adults perceive the cry. Adults rate cries of high pitch and of long duration as urgent and irritable, while cries of variable pitch are rated as signs of infant sickness (Gustafson & Green, 1989; Zeskind, Klein, & Marshall, 1992; Zeifman, 2004; Zeskind & Marshall, 1988). Experimental modifications of infant cry sounds show that adults perceive cries with extremely short pauses as more arousing, aversive, and rough (Zeskind, Wilhite, & Marshall, 1993).

Nonparents appear to be about as responsive to crying as parents (Zeskind, 1980), and generally equal levels of physiological arousal and responsiveness to crying have been found for men and women (Frodi, Lamb, Leavitt, & Donovan, 1978). On the other hand, child abusers have greater physiological arousal and express more annoyance at cries than nonabusers (Frodi & Lamb, 1980).

You might think, therefore, that infants who cry a great deal or who have especially irritating cries are more at risk for insensitive or abusive parental treatment. This seems to be the case only when irritable crying is also associated with abnormal behavioral tendencies typical of infants with mental and motor perinatal defects and prematurity (Field, Widmayer, Stringer, & Ignatoff, 1980) or when mothers have a preexisting negative attitude toward their infants that in part contributes to the high levels of infant distress (Crockenberg & Acredolo, 1983; Crockenberg & Smith, 1982). For normally developing infants, crying brings adults closer to them. More-irritable infants are held more in the newborn period, and parents spend more time in social play with them at 2 months (Lowinger, 1999).

Infants who are rated by their parents as having a **difficult temperament** in early infancy (see below), based on their irritability and responsiveness to adults, can remain difficult for periods up to several years, although the majority of infants rated as difficult early in life do not remain difficult for more than a few months (Boom & Hoeksma, 1994; C. Lee & Bates, 1985; Swets-Gronert, 1984). Difficultness has few consistent effects on normal parent-infant relationships and is not related to measures of maternal warmth or responsiveness (J. E. Bates, Olson, Pettit, & Bayles, 1982; Daniels, Plomin, & Greenhalgh, 1984; Olson, Bates, & Bayles, 1984; Wachs & Gandour, 1983). Some studies have actually found increased maternal attention directed to infants rated as difficult (J. E. Bates et al., 1982; Pettit & Bates, 1984).

In summary, most adults find crying to be arousing, and they can reliably perceive differences between types of crying. Adults also respond to crying infants in an attempt to soothe the cry and relieve the source of the discomfort. Since most adults use similar means of trying to relieve infant distress, it is important to examine what research has shown about the effectiveness of these soothing techniques.

What Are the Best Ways to Soothe a Crying Baby?

Many calming techniques have been used historically: sucking, swaddling, rocking, and singing. Do they really work? Under what conditions does one technique work and not another?

Sucking on a pacifier. Whether sucking pacifiers is harmful or beneficial is a question of practical concern to parents. Sucking on a pacifier, or nonnutritive sucking (NNS), occurs in many forms throughout the infancy period. If we count any incidence of NNS—on pacifiers, toys, fingers, thumbs, and adults' fingers—about 60 to 90% of all infants will do it. NNS usually stops at the end of the first year of life. It may continue to occur, however, when a child is hungry, tired, or unhappy, until the child reaches 4 to 7 years of age. A small proportion of children suck their thumbs until adolescence. In infants, thumb sucking after the age of 4 months appears primarily during sleep (Kessen, Haith, & Salapatek, 1970).

It would appear from these statistics that NNS is not an unusual occurrence in infancy and early childhood. It may even serve some important functions for the infant. Pacification is one reason infants suck. Sucking is an activity that immediately induces a state of calm in the infant, whether it is associated with nutritive intake or not. Another reason for NNS is that it feels good. This could come about because sucking is genetically associated with pleasure or because the infant develops a conditioned association between the sucking response and the pleasurable intake of nutrient. Sucking could also have an inhibitory effect on other states or behavior.

Regardless of the particular reason, NNS appears to be a spontaneous behavior that has some important benefits to the newborn and the older infant. One study (R. G. Campos, 1989) examined the effects of pacifiers on calming infants at 2 weeks and 2 months of age during routine medical exams. At 2 weeks, the infants received a heel prick to draw blood, and at 2 months, they received an injection. Pacifiers were immediately effective in reducing crying and heart rate acceleration in response to the pain at both ages. NNS also reduces infant blood pressure (Cohen et al., 2002).

Long-term pacifier and thumb sucking may, however, affect the development of the teeth and mouth. Children who sucked pacifiers more than two years, or their thumbs more than three years had upper front teeth that protruded too far over the lower front teeth, so that the teeth did not meet when the jaw was closed. Depending upon the severity, these problems may require orthodontic correction later (Warren & Bishara, 2002).

Swaddling. Swaddling, or wrapping the infant in a blanket, tends to reduce motor movement and spontaneous startles. Swaddling is less effective than the pacifier in reducing pain-elicited distress in 2-week-olds, although it lowers their heart rate (R. G. Campos, 1989). When a pacifier falls out of an infant's mouth, she or he will begin to cry again. Once swaddled, on the other hand, infants remain calm for long periods.

Swaddling is practiced among many traditional cultures such as the Quechua Indians living at high altitude in the Peruvian Andean Mountains. The Quechua swaddle infants in a pouch. The temperature inside the pouch is higher and more stable than in the outside atmosphere, and the humidity is higher. The pouch protects the infant against environmental stress due to cold temperatures and dryness. On the other hand, in the closed environment of the pouch, the infant gets less oxygen and less stimulation than it would without the pouch. Since the Quechua live in unheated surroundings and spend a great deal of time out of doors, the benefits of the pouch seem to outweigh the potential risks (E. Z. Tronick, Thomas, & Daltabuit, 1994).

Massage. Massage is a technique related to swaddling in that the whole body is stimulated and the infant's movements are controlled. Massage has been shown to increase weight gain and responsiveness in preterm infants (see Chapter 9). In normal full-term infants, regular massage for 15 minutes each day has been shown to enhance alertness when awake, deepen sleep, reduce stress, modulate emotions, increase growth rate and weight gain, and lower the amount of crying (Field, 1998; Field et al., 2004). Massage may also have calming effects on adults. Grandparents were assigned either to receive massages for 1 month or to give massages to their grandchildren. Giving massages had more positive effects than receiving them. Those who gave massages had lower depression scores, increased self-esteem, and enhanced health behaviors (Field, 1998). Parents who take relaxation and massage baths with their babies have higher levels of marital satisfaction and self-esteem and lower levels of postpartum depression (Stack, 2000).

Massage is used regularly in a variety of cultures, for example, in India and Guatemala. Touching and massage are known to reduce stress in animals, adults, and infants. Touch stimulation reduces hormones related to stress and increases hormones related to growth (Stack, 2000). Gentle massage has no negative effects, and it can be a rewarding and relaxing experience for both infant and adult, even if not used directly in response to crying. A book on infant massage techniques for caregivers and parents is available (McClure, 1989).

Rocking. The effects of rocking were studied in a group of 36 crying infants who were offered either vertical (on the adult's shoulder) or horizontal (supine) rocking to calm them. In general, rocking in any form helped calm the infants. The best form of rocking to calm a distressed infant turned out to be rocking intermittently (rather than continuously) in the vertical plane. The best form of rocking for putting the infant to sleep was continuous rocking in the horizontal plane (Bryne & Horowitz, 1979).

Sound. Sound, too, has a calming effect on the baby, but apparently not all types of sound work. Intermittent sound increases infant arousal, whereas continuous sound is calming. The calming effect of continuous sound is enhanced when the sound is moderately loud and in the low frequencies of the vocal range (Brackbill, 1971; Friedman & Jacobs, 1981; Hazelwood, 1977). Humming and singing lullabies have these features. Singing has been shown to lower stress among pre-term infants (Coleman, Pratt, Stoddard, Gerstmann, & Abel, 1997). High-pitched vocal sounds can be used to alert infants or attract their attention.

The soothing effects of continuous stimulation are not limited to sound: any stimulus that is continuous can work. Sucking, rocking, swaddling, and humming are all forms of continuous stimulation. Using more than one method has a cumulative effect. Individual infants also show a wide range of differences. Some infants are better soothed by one method than another, and some infants appear to be more easily consoled than others, regardless of the particular method used.

Developmental changes also affect what best soothes the baby. While any kind of continuous auditory stimulation soothes in the infant's first 2 months, the mother's voice is more effective by 3 months (Kopp, 1982). Visual stimulation becomes increasingly effective by 3 months, as does stimulation from objects to touch and hold (Kopp, 1982; Wolff, 1966).

First Emotions

Do newborns have the ability to experience emotions? If they can see, hear, taste, smell, learn, and remember, it makes sense to conclude that they also have feelings. In the past, however, many hospital staff assumed that newborns could not feel pain, and medical procedures were administered without anesthetic. Fortunately, this practice is changing, along with the outdated belief that newborns cannot feel.

The scientific recognition of newborn feelings was the result of an accidental discovery. A group of researchers at Brown University were studying the newborn's ability to learn and also exploring the range of newborn sensitivity to taste and smell (see Chapter 4). While investigating newborn preferences for sweet fluids, Lipsitt (1979b) and Crook (1978) found that the babies sucked in longer bursts, with shorter pauses between bursts. Within a sucking burst, the interval between sucks is higher for sweetened water than for plain water, and the newborn's heart rate increases while he or she is sucking the sweet water. Thus, the babies were sucking for longer periods and holding the sweet liquid longer in their mouths before swallowing. The researchers concluded that the babies were "savoring" the pleasurable sensation of the sweet taste. In addition, when plain water was given following the sweet water, the babies showed aversive reactions.

All researchers today agree that newborns can feel. The current debate is about the range and depth of the newborn's emotional experience. Newborns, for example, do not feel many of the emotions that are experienced by older infants

and children. They show no signs of fear (which begins about 9 months), anger (which begins about 6 months), or shame (which begins about 18 months).

How do we know what newborns might feel if we can't ask the m to describe their inner state? One way is if an expression occurs in a situation that would generally elicit a particular emotion in an adult. One example is the newborn's disgust expressions in response to tastes and smells (see Figure 4.4 on page 133). Crying generally occurs in situations in which one presumes the newborn might feel some distress or pain. In addition to facial expressions, newborns can convey emotion with other parts of their bodies. During distress, for example, there may be reddening of the entire body, kicking and thrashing, contorted arm movements, and stiffening of the body. These whole body responses reflect the activation of the sympathetic nervous system and hormonal secretions that activate changes in behavior and physiology and that are consistent with emotional responses.

In addition to disgust and distress, newborns appear to experience the emotions of interest and surprise (Dondi, 1999; Lavelli & Fogel, 2005). These expressions occur during waking states and are keyed to the infant's attention to faces, social interaction, and moving objects. Newborn attention may shift between states of simple attention (simply observing), concentrated attention (when there appears to be an effort made to recognize or to take in the object of attention), and excited attention (when the infant seems momentarily startled but still attentive). These expressions are shown in Figure 7.1.

On the other hand, some expressions do not occur with any clear link to the situation. Newborns smiles are more likely to occur during sleep and drowsy states and less frequently when awake (Dondi et al., 2007). Newborn smiling may be related to some kind of simple contentment or relaxation rather than to the feeling of joy that we begin to see more clearly around 2 to 3 months of age. In addition, newborns have a wide variety of facial movements that do not fall neatly into

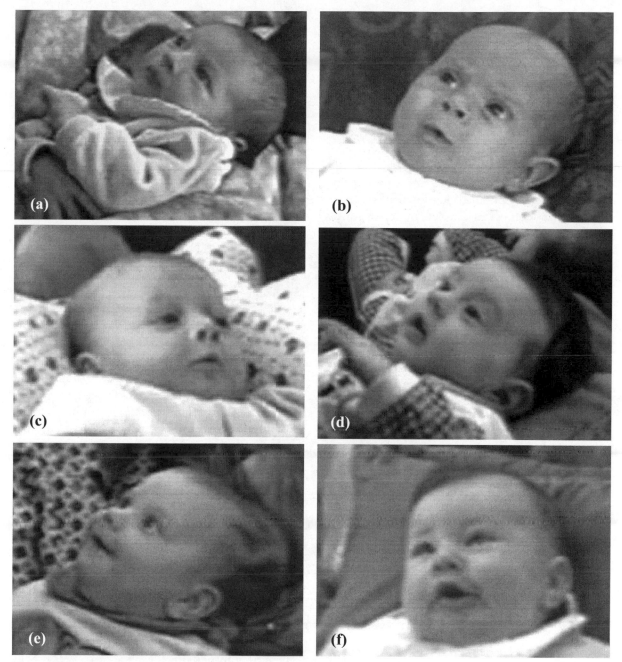

Figure 7.1 Interest and Enjoyment Expressions
(a) Simple attention: Visual fixation in a quiet alert state.
(b) Concentrated attention: Visual fixation with effortful movements of brow and mouth.
(c) Excited attention: Visual fixation with active motor movement of arms, legs, and/or mouth.
(d) Astonished attention: Fascinated and motionless visual fixation.
(e) Smile: Relaxed visual fixation with smiling.
(f) Cooing: Visual fixation, with mouth making the shape of a vocalization, either with or without actual vocalizing.
Source: Manuela Lavelli, University of Verona, Italy.

one of the usual emotion categories: odd- seem- ing twists and turns of facial muscles. Only after 2 months of age do these movements begin to coalesce into organized and recognizable patterns of facial expression that are more clearly linked to specific emotions.

The full range of human emotions—like perceptions and cognitions—are not experience expectant at birth. They develop over many years in experience dependent fashion, which partly accounts for individual differences in emotionality. The process of emotional development depends in part on how these incomplete newborn forms of expression are interpreted by adults. Even when adults do not know what the infant wants, feels, or needs, they are quick to attribute meaning to the infant's behavior and respond according to this attribution. In these cases, the adult responds "as if" the baby had a fully developed emotion (Adamson, 1995; Kaye, 1982). Adults observe a contraction of the infant's lip corners, assume the baby is happy, and make happy expressions and sounds to the baby. Or, an infant may cry in such a way as to make the adult think the baby is hungry or tired or angry.

After many repetitions of adult interpretive responses to incomplete infant expressions, those expressions begin to consolidate into recogniz- able patterns. According to a dynamic systems perspective, particular emotions emerge from the interaction of the infant's relatively unformed facial displays and the social environment in which particular patterns of facial display are interpreted by adults as being communicative (Dondi, 1999; Fogel, Nwokah, et al., 1992; Fogel, Dickson, et al., 1997). This transaction process consolidates the diffuse expressions and experiences of the child into socially recognizable emotional expressions and feeling states. The resulting infant emotion is not made up by or shaped by the adult. Rather, emotions emerge in their relationship as a process of development.

It seems wise for caregivers to make the assumption that infants of all ages have feelings, since it helps us to understand their needs. The interventions we make that are consonant with our interpretations of infant emotions often seem to have the intended effect. We pick up a crying baby to soothe what we believe to be the child's pain or discomfort as much as to stop the crying, and the subsequent relaxation of the infant confirms our belief about his or her feelings.

Two to Five Months

As the infant develops, emotions become more elaborated and defined. In this section, we take a closer look at emotional development in terms of three related topics: emotion expression, emotion experience, and emotion regulation. The develop- ment of emotional expression involves the study of the behavioral manifestations of emotional experience, the inner world of feelings. Self-control over emotions is called **emotion regulation**.

These three areas—expression, experience, and self-regulation— are part of ongoing develop- ment. Many other areas of interest also fall under the general heading of emotional development. These include people's verbal expression of their emotions, their ability to conceptualize their emo- tions, and their ability to perceive another person's emotions. These abilities mostly apply to the older infant and young child, and the later sections of this chapter will touch on them.

Emotional Expression and Experience

Distress, anger, and wariness. Infants were once thought to have all the basic emotional expres- sions at birth (Peiper, 1963), but these are reflex- ive movements that disappear after several weeks. A 1-month-old infant has only a relatively small number of functional expressions, and these are primarily related to the emotion of distress. The expression involves frowning (knitted brows with the mouth turned down at the corners). It usually is accompanied by crying, generally with the eyes closed. Younger infants often exhibit a trembling of the lips during crying, as well as a reddening of the face if the cry is intense enough. Recall the different auditory characteristics of the types of crying seen in young infants. Adults have a difficult time categorizing the distress expressions of infants under 4 months into recognizable adult emotions, which suggests that infants do not have a fully differentiated set of adult-like emotions (Matias & Cohn, 1993; Oster, Hegley, & Nagel, 1992).

The duration of distress significantly decreases during the first 3 months. In spite of this, adults rate the cries of 6-month-olds as more intense than the cries of younger infants, primarily because the older infants' cries, while shorter in duration, are louder and more energetic (Leger, Thompson, Merritt, & Benz, 1996). After 3 months, infants develop a brief negative-sounding vocalization, usually called *fussing* as distinguished from crying, that accompanies a distress facial expression. Fussing babies usually vocalize for a brief period, then become silent or coo for a while, and then return to fussing (Hopkins & von Wulfften Palthe, 1987). Even though crying lessens in almost all infants over the course of the first year, infants who cried more during the first 3 months, such as those with colic, are likely to cry more on average for the rest of the first year of life (McGlaughlin & Grayson, 1999).

By 4 to 5 months, infants may still exhibit intense distress cries, but now they often cry with their eyes open and looking at their parent in particular, an expression that has been interpreted as the first signs of anger, which develops more fully in the next age period. In fact, the longer infants look, the longer they cry, suggesting that the attention may play a feedback role to increase or lessen the anger (Axia, Bonichini, & Benini, 1999; Moscardino & Axia, 2006; M. D. Lewis, Lamey, & Douglas, 1999). Crying may also be accompanied by directed actions such as kicking, pulling, or pushing, and it may involve few or no tears.

Fear, another expression related to distress, does not appear until later in the first year, but infants at 4 months can show "wary" or hesitant expressions. Infants of this age are capable of turning their heads or looking away from an unpleasant or confusing situation. Their wary or ambivalent expressions consist of an increased rate of gazing away from and looking back at the situation, com-

bined with a reduction of expressions of positive affect (Bronson, 1972; Sroufe, 1979).

Attention and enjoyment. During waking states, infants of 1 month may exhibit a range of expression between alertness and drowsiness. When infants are alert, their eyes are wide and bright, and their brows and mouth may alternate between movement and stillness. Infants of this age have difficulty switching their attention from one thing to another and may stare motionless for long periods. They often fade into brief periods of "dulling." Their eyes, although open and fixed, take on a glazed or dull quality. Smiles usually are not seen during alert states until about 6 to 8 weeks of age.

Around the age of 2 months, a significant change can be seen in infants' facial expressions. They are more complex and animated and better coordinated with events in the environment around them (Sroufe, 1995). When smiling, infants learn cognitive tasks more slowly than when showing an attentive expression without smiling. This shows that smiling corresponds to a non-analytical emotional experience (Rose, Futterweit, & Jankowski, 1999). Attention also changes. Infants look for longer periods and they can more easily shift their gaze from one thing to another, apparently due to experience-dependent brain development in the part of the limbic system and motor cortex that regulates attention and movement (Robertson et al., 2001).

After 2 months, babies also develop new facial expressions of attention and enjoyment, shown in Figure 7.1. In the first two months of life, infants show primarily simple and concentrated attention. After 2 months, more complex attention expressions, as well as smiling and cooing expressions, appear (Lavelli & Fogel, 2005). These developments in the expression of attention suggest that the infant is also developing different attention-related emotional experiences such as concentration, excitement, and astonishment.

Smiling during face-to-face interaction also develops between 2 and 5 months. Beginning at 3 months, smiling occurs in clusters during social interactions. Infants smile four or five times in

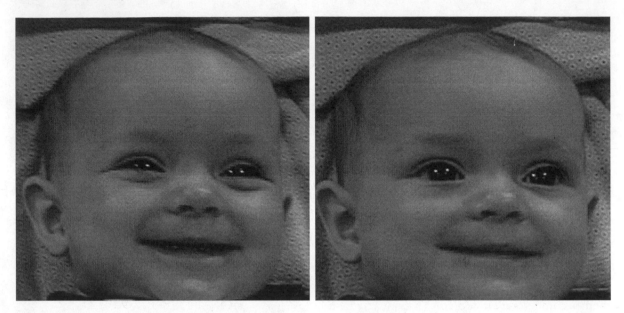

Figure 7.2 Duchenne and Non-Duchenne Smiles
An infant's non-Duchenne smile (on the left) followed approximately 2 seconds later by a Duchenne smile (on the right) in which the cheeks are raised more prominently.
Source: Daniel S. Messinger, University of Miami.

rapid succession, followed by a relative pause of 20 or 30 seconds, after which a new bout of smiles begins (Fogel, 1982a). By this age, infants show multiple types of smiles that communicate different types of positive emotional experience. A smile involving the raising of the cheeks and some wrinkling around the eyes (called a Duchenne smile) is observed in the context of mother-infant face-to-face play when the infant is held upright and is able to see the mother smiling and talking (see Figure 7.2). A smile that involves an extremely wide-open mouth and dropping of the jaw (play smile) is observed when infants are held closer to the mother, kissed, or tickled (Messinger, Fogel, & Dickson, 1998). Duchenne smiles appear to be related to visually and cognitively pleasurable events (peek-a-boo games, for example), while play smiles are related more to tactile and physically arousing events (like tickling games).

In the period between 2 and 5 months, all types of smiles may occur interchangeably during social play, suggesting that the infant is beginning to experience a complex range of positive feelings (Fogel et al., 2000, 2006; Messinger, Fogel, &

Dickson, 2001). In addition, about 15% of smiling is followed immediately by looking away from the social partner, which some researchers have interpreted as an early manifestation of "coyness," an emotion that may indicate an awareness of self in the interaction (Reddy, 2000).

After 2 months of age, infants also begin to express positive emotions through vocalizations. During the first 2 months of life, infants' vocalizations are of three sorts: cry, discomfort, and "vegetative" (Stark, Rose, & McLagen, 1975). The cry is used to express acute distress, whereas discomfort sounds are associated with distress that is not as severe; they are more like fussing or complaining than crying. The infant's vegetative repertoire includes a series of biological noises, such as the cough, burp, sneeze, hiccup, suck, snort, grunt, and sigh. These sounds are all so basic to the biological necessities of the infant organism that there is very little individual variation across infants, nor do they change much in sound characteristics over time.

Somewhere between 5 and 8 weeks, most infants begin to "coo." As distinguished from the other sounds already in the infant's repertoire, cooing is primarily an expression of comfort. If all the infant's sounds are analyzed with sophisticated sound recording and frequency amplitude–resolving equipment, all the auditory properties of cooing can be found in the more primitive forms of sound making. According to Stark (1978), these findings suggest that infants are beginning to take the sounds they made reflexively and recombine them in the form of exploratory vocal activity. Recalling Lucienne's coughing for fun (see Observation 5.2), we see that infants begin to use their voicing in repetitive ways reminiscent of other circular reactions.

Two kinds of infant non-distress vocalizations appear after 2 months: speech-like and non-speech-like. Speech-like sounds are produced in the front of the mouth and have a more resonant quality. Non-speech-like sounds are produced in the back of the mouth, lack projection, and have a more nasal quality. Speech-like sounds—of which cooing is one—increase between 2 and 5 months, while non-speech-like sounds decline (Hsu, Fogel, & Cooper, 2000). Mothers also respond differentially to these two types of vocalization, and the speech-like vocalizations often occur when the baby is smiling, suggesting that speech-like sounds are expressions of positive emotion (Hsu & Fogel, 2001; Hsu, Fogel, & Messenger, 2001)

According to a dynamic systems theory of emotion (see Chapter 2), emotion is closely related to the social communication system (Chapter 6). So, different communicative tasks—different types of play (social-visual versus social-tactile), for example—will require different forms of facial communication and will be accompanied by different types of internal feelings (J. J. Campos, Campos, & Barrett, 1989; Fogel et al., 1992). Just as the infant's cognition is integrated across different perceptual modalities, infants have organized patterns of expressive movements that are integrated across the face, vocalization and body movement that occur in specific types of communicative situations (Hsu & Fogel, 2003; Lavelli & Fogel, 2005; Weinberg & Tronick, 1994; Yale, Messinger, Cobo-Lewis, Oller, & Eilers, 1999).

Examples of organized patterns of emotion are positive engagement (positive facial expressions and vocalizations, looking at adult or objects, mouthing parts of own body); attentive engagement (facial expressions of attention, looking at adult or objects, mouthing objects); passive withdrawal (facial expressions of sadness, fussy vocalizations); and active protest (facial expressions of anger, fussy and cry vocalizations, pickup requests, and escape movements). These organized patterns are flexible, dynamic, and tied into the communication system. These patterns also show that infants have some control over the type of social and emotional processes in which they participate; that is, they are developing emotion regulation skills.

Development of Emotion Regulation

Emotion regulation, the ability to control one's internal state and outward expression, gradually emerges over the first years of life. During the first 4 months, increases in emotion regulation are shown by several transitions: a decrease in the overall amount of crying, an ability to easily shift gaze from one thing to another, and the mastery of continuous and repeated bouts of smiling.

If emotion regulation works well, it allows the individual to control the intense or overwhelming aspects of a situation without losing touch with it. A baby may look away momentarily from a positive interaction with an adult in order to cope with the high level of arousal. Emotion regulation is shown not merely by looking away, but by the overall pattern of looking away and then back in a repeated fashion.

A second important emotion regulation skill that develops in the infant's third month is the smile itself. Studies on the relationship between heart rate changes and the occurrence of smiling have shown that smiles occur neither when the heart rate is increasing nor when it is at its peak, but rather when the heart rate is on the decline (Sroufe & Waters, 1976). Smiling is a relaxation response, and it seems to be a way of reducing arousal without looking away from the situation. On the other hand, after particularly intense smiles, 5-month-olds may need to look away from the situation, an indication that with intense positive emotion, multiple emotion regulation strategies may be required (Stifter & Moyer, 1991).

While infants are developing new ways to maintain attention during periods of emotional arousal, they also are widening the range of arousal levels they can tolerate. At the upper end of arousal, the 1-month-old is able to tolerate stimulation only if it is gentle and slowly changing, whereas the 3-month-old can handle a wider variety of stimulation with more abrupt changes, such as a highly animated, talking adult.

Another contribution to emotion regulation is the baby's developing sensorimotor skills. During this period, the ability of infants to regulate their own distress improves as they can reach for objects and hold them without dropping them (Kopp, 1989). In relation to hand-to-mouth activity, discussed above, infants can calm themselves down after 4 months, when they can reliably get the hand to the mouth and keep it there while engaged in other activities (Thelen & Fogel, 1989; Toda & Fogel, 1989). During experimental perturbations of the mothers' behavior (see the Experimental Disturbances of Play Frames section below), 6-month-olds, but not 3-month-olds, were able to retain their composure by putting their hands in their mouths or focusing their visual attention on what their hands were doing (usually exploring their clothing or the infant seat) (Toda & Fogel, 1993).

Researchers are gradually beginning to recognize that young infants use their whole bodies in emotion expressions and emotion regulations. Emotion regulation derives from the use of some nonemotional action patterns (like reaching for objects) to help the baby calm down when upset (J. J. Campos, Campos, & Barrett, 1989; Kopp, 1989). On the other hand, reaching for objects and other sensorimotor skills brings the infant into contact with situations never before encountered. The ability to reach generates new pleasures and also new sources of frustration. In this sense, emotion and emotion regulation are not mere responses to the situation, but also represent the baby's goals in the situation (J. J. Campos, Campos, & Barrett, 1989).

A final contribution to emotion regulation is the infant's adult partner. Often caregivers can provide just the right support that, when combined with the infant's own abilities, results in a spontaneous relaxation. Not surprisingly, when a baby cries the parent is likely to pick up, hold, rock, touch, feed, talk to, and/or sing to the baby. Parents who did this more frequently and consistently in response to crying at 2 months had babies who cried for a shorter period at 6 months (Jahromi & Stifter, 2007). There is a correspondence between the amount of parental soothing behavior and infant crying duration, with less of both at 6 compared to 2 months (Jahromi, Putnam, & Stifter, 2004).

A small percentage of infants fall into the category of having a regulatory disorder. These infants have disturbances of sleep, feeding, state control, sensory and perceptual processing, and self-calming. In some cases, these infants may be later diagnosed with autism or other developmental disorders (see Chapter 9). In one study (DeGangi et al., 1996) regulatory disordered infants given a 12-week intervention during the first 6 months were compared between 7 months and 3 years with regulatory disordered infants who did not receive treatment. The treatment consisted of training parents to be more responsive to their infant's needs, following the infant's lead, and learning what the infant may want (Greenspan & Weider, 1997). Although all of the regulatory disordered children still had regulatory difficulties at the age of 3 years, the untreated children showed more emotional and social problems, such as depression and aggression.

From a dynamic systems view, emotion regulation is the result of both infant and adult contributions and the unfolding of the parent-infant relationship around regulatory issues.

Six to Nine Months

The Development of Negative Emotions

Until the beginning of Piaget's Stage III (Chapter 5; around 5 months), babies have basically one response to a negative experience: they cry. With the onset of secondary circular reactions, infants become more "aware" that they can cause things to happen in the environment. This sense of themselves as a causal agent—part of the ecological self—accounts in part for the reduction in the amount of crying that occurs between 3 and 5 months. When infants cannot succeed at being an effective causal agent—when they cannot get a toy they want, for example—a new source of negative experience enters their lives: *anger*.

Anger in infants is a direct result of their having their motives disrupted. Although both anger and distress are accompanied by crying, the facial expression during anger is different from that of distress, as is the baby's underlying feeling (Izard, 1981; Sroufe, 1979). In one study, infants' reactions to inoculations were observed at 2, 4, and 7 months. At 2 and 4 months, infants reacted with physical distress, a direct response to pain. Distress is expressed by crying with tightly shut eyes. By 7 months, the babies responded with more angry expressions, crying with open, vigilant eyes (Izard, 1981; Izard, Hembree, & Huebner, 1987).

It is almost as if the quality of the gaze signals that the infant is angry at the person being watched. If you have an opportunity to experience this with a baby, you can feel what it is like when an upset baby looks at you in this particular way. Anger can be expressed in many different ways as infants get older, such as by kicking, biting, sulking, yelling, pouting, or temper tantrums (Barrett & Campos, 1987; Campos & Barrett, 1984).

Separation from the mother is another situation that causes negative emotions. Before the age of 6 months, infants cry with distress, particularly if their mothers leave, act depressed, or perform a still face in the middle of a feeding or play session. The distress arises from the cessation of the pleasurable interaction. After 6 months, infants respond to parental separation with some anger, especially if the parent happens to be a part of the infant's activity—such as during play or feeding—when he or she leaves (Izard, 1981). Expressions of anger are also seen in 7-month-olds when

a teething biscuit is removed from their mouths or when their arms are restrained (Stenberg, Campos, & Emde, 1983).

Another negatively toned emotion seen at this age is **wariness**. Infants may become quiet and stare at a stranger or a strange situation, knit their brows, become momentarily sober, and look away (Bronson, 1972). Because wariness allows the infant to observe what is happening, it is a considerably more adaptive reaction to strange situations than is the withdrawal of infantile fussing and crying of previous ages (Emde, Gaensbauer, & Harmon, 1976; Malatesta et al., 1986).

Aside from these general trends, there are also individual differences. Infants of this age were taught to pull a string attached to their wrist in order to activate a slide projection of an infant's face accompanied by the *Sesame Street* theme song. After they learned this procedure, the experimenters stopped turning on the slide projector and music when the infant pulled the string. Most of the infants reacted to this contingency failure with anger, although some showed expressions of sadness. When the contingency was renewed, the infants who expressed anger immediately became interested again in the task, while those who showed sadness reacted to the renewal of the contingency with less enjoyment (Lewis et al., 1992). This shows that anger is an adaptive and useful response for some babies, who perceive the renewal of the contingency as under their control. The babies who were saddened, however, may perceive themselves as helpless to change the course of events.

At this age, then, the helpless fussing of earlier ages gives way to demanding crying, anger, and wariness. Each of these forms of negative emotional expression is considerably more adaptive from the infant's point of view, and these developments reflect some significant advances in the infant's ability to cope with negative situations. Wariness, for example, allows for even more prolonged inspection of the potentially worrisome stimulus rather than a simple rejection of it. We might say that the end result of this increasing sophistication in the realm of negative responding is to bring the infant back into a positive engagement with the environment.

The Development of Positive Emotions

The positive emotions also become more complex during this age period. In one study, mothers and infants were observed playing peekaboo and tickle games. Different types of smiles had different emotional meanings depending upon whether the infant was attending to the mother or not (Fogel, Nelson-Goens, Hsu, & Shapiro, 2000; Fogel, Hsu, Shapiro, Nelson-Goens, & Secrist, 2006). Simple smiling (lip corner retraction without cheek raising) accompanied by gazing at the mother during peekaboo represents *an enjoyment of recognition* or perhaps an *enjoyment of readiness to engage in play.* The feeling may be similar to an adult's experience of being delighted to be with a familiar person and to engage in enjoyable things together. Simple smiles occurring without gazing at mother after a previous tickle are often accompanied by gasping for air and sighing. The feeling associated with these smiles may be *an enjoyment of relief* or perhaps *an enjoyment of relaxation,* similar to pauses between laughter episodes in playful conversations of children and adults.

Duchenne smiles (lip corner retraction with cheek raising) occur with gazing at the mother primarily when she uncovers her face during peekaboo. These smiles may reflect *an enjoyment of agency,* sensing oneself as an active rather than passive participant in the game (Holt, Fogel, & Wood, 1998; Stern, 1985). This may mean that the pleasure of peekaboo is in the experience of active visual searching for when and how the mother will reappear after hiding. Duchenne smiles without gazing at the mother occur most frequently during a tickle, often as infants turn their whole bodies away as if trying to hide or to protect themselves. These Duchenne smiles may reflect *an enjoyment of hiding* or perhaps *an enjoyment of escape,* as during hiding and chasing games in older infants and children.

These findings reveal that infants of this age are showing the beginnings of adult-like emotional experiences. When co-regulating with an infant of this age, one gets the impression that babies are aware of their feelings and of some of the effects of those feelings on others. Beginning around 8 months of age, infants who smile when looking at an object will spontaneously turn to smile at a nearby adult (Venezia et al., 2004). Taken together with the gazing at the adult that occurs in anger expressions, there is a growing ability in infants of this age to communicate with others about emotions.

The first laughs could be seen in the previous stage, primarily as a result of tickling and other vigorous stimulation. By the age of 6 months, babies will laugh at your jokes. They will laugh when you play tug with them, when they see you suck on their pacifiers or bottles, and when they try to pull the bottles out of your mouth (Fogel, Nwokah, & Karns, 1993; Nwokah et al., 1993; Sroufe, 1979).

Babies also laugh at very abrupt and highly arousing stimuli. They may laugh at things that once made them cry, such as a loud noise or a loss of balance. The laugh will sometimes follow a very serious or wary expression, almost as if the babies were trying to make up their minds about whether to get upset or enjoy the situation. In one study, 8-month-old babies watched while someone wearing a scary mask approached them. When the mask was worn by a stranger, the babies cried. When it was worn by their mothers, the babies laughed (Sroufe & Wunsch, 1977).

Emotion Regulation

This experiment suggests that by this age, the infant is beginning to use cognition to *decide what to feel*, a process known as **appraisal**. This means that there is a growing relationship between infant emotion and attention to the events and processes related to that emotion. Seven-month-old infants were familiarized with a computerized drawing of a face and asked to choose between the familiar face and an unfamiliar one using a paired preference procedure. If infants studied the familiar faces with a neutral facial expression, they looked at the pair of faces for a shorter time and were better able to distinguish the familiar from the unfamiliar faces. If the infants were smiling, they looked longer at the familiar faces and were less efficient in their discrimination during the paired preference test. This means that positive emotions are related to a less analytical style of attending and most likely reflect right-brain processing (Rose, Futterweit, & Jankowski, 1999).

Different patterns of communication between mothers and their male and female infants are related to gender differences in emotion regulation. Six-month-old boys and girls were observed during face-to-face play, followed by maternal still-face (see Chapter 6). During the still-face condition, boys were more likely than girls to show expressions of anger, to fuss, to gesture to be picked up, or to try to get out of the infant seat. Boys also were more likely to try to get the mother's attention by smiling and vocalizing to her. Girls, on the other hand, spent more time gazing at objects and showing expressions of interest. The boys also had a more positive interaction with the mother during the normal face-to-face period (Weinberg, Tronick, Cohn, & Olson, 1999).

You might think these findings are counterintuitive. Under the assumption that girls may be more social, shouldn't girls be more positive with their mothers and more upset during the still face because of an apparent break in the mother-infant communication? This study, however, does not reveal that boys are more social than girls but, rather, that boys are less able to regulate their emotions under stressful conditions. The girls were able to manage their emotions during the still face by becoming more observant of the objects in the environment. The more positive interaction between mothers and sons during the normal condition may reflect a necessity to achieve co-regulated communication because boys are more upset when there are breakdowns in communication (Weinberg et al., 1999).

In summary, the findings on emotion regulation show that infants of both genders are highly tuned into their emotional communication with others. They are able to experience subtle differences of emotion as a function of how their atten-tion is directed and whether the communication is co-regulated or disrupted. The result is that in older children and adults, males and females, emotions are related to their early experiences in interpersonal communication.

Recognition of Emotional Expressions

Research shows that infants' ability to recognize and discriminate among different emotional expressions increases between 6 and 9 months. Babies seem more capable of recognizing smiles than other expressions (Bornstein & Arterberry, 2003). Infants were familiarized with pictures of faces with smiles of different intensities. Later, they dishabituated to non-smile expressions but not to smiles differing in intensity (Ludemann, 1991; Ludemann & Nelson, 1988). Their ability at this age to distinguish between other expressions, such as fear and anger, is relatively poor (Nelson, 1987). Curiously, 7-month-old infants whose mothers are high in their display of positive emotions are more likely to respond to negative facial expressions, perhaps because of their relative novelty (de Haan et al., 2004).

On the other hand, infants recognize emotion in the voice earlier than emotion in the face. When facial expressions of emotions are combined with voices expressing those emotions, 7-month-olds improve considerably in their ability to distinguish between emotions (Caron, Caron, & McLean, 1988; Phillips et al., 1990; Soken & Pick, 1992). When faces are presented dynamically, that is, by videorecordings rather than still pictures, 7-month-old infants' ability to distinguish different types of expression also improves (Soken & Pick, 1999). Infants also more readily recognize emotional differences if the facial expression is paired with a matching (compared to a mismatched) intonation pattern, as when an angry expression is matched with an angry versus happy tone of voice (Grossman et al., 2006).

Except for a happy expression, to which infants will respond with a smile, there is little evidence that infants of this age view facial expressions alone as meaningful emotion signals (Nelson,

1987). The ability to extract meaning from viewing another person's face is extremely slow to develop, but we will see the beginnings of this skill in the next stage. It is not clear why infants have a concept for smiles earlier than they do concepts for other facial expressions. It makes sense, however, that the infant would be particularly attuned to facial expressions related to happiness, which probably increase the infant's sense of connection to the other person.

Infants of this age prefer to look at faces judged by adults to be attractive, regardless of the race or gender of the faces they are looking at (Langlois et al., 1991). Apparently, attractiveness, like recognition of particular people, can be inferred from more global features of the face that do not involve specific expressions (Rubenstein, Kalakanis, & Langlois, 1999). Infants can also distinguish between the faces of children and adults (Bahrick, Netto, & Hernandez-Reif, 1998). In summary, infants of this age have a rudimentary ability to perceive information from the face, and this ability will continue to improve in the coming months.

The Formation of an Infant's Temperament

Some research has shown that the infants who are less expressive are actually more aroused by stimulation than the more expressive infants. The low-expressive infants tend to have higher overall heart rates, higher cortisol (see Chapter 5; a hormone related to arousal), and higher muscle tension (Field, 1987; N. A. Fox & Davidson, 1988; Kagan, Reznick, & Snidman, 1987). These children have been referred to as inhibited, because they are physiologically predisposed to be highly responsive to stimulation but tend to withdraw from stimulation rather than express signs of engagement or enjoyment. Very similar patterns of individual differences have been observed in infant monkeys (Suomi, 1987).

Another question related to infant emotional development is whether there are lasting patterns of emotional responding and regulation in infants. We know that at any age different infants exhibit differing amounts of difficulty, fussiness, or happiness. The question is whether these differences persist over time. Is the same infant who is difficult at 3 months also difficult at 6 or 12 months? **Temperament** is a persistent pattern of emotion and emotion regulation in the infant's relationship to people and things in the environment.

Researchers have identified a number of expressive and responsive dimensions along which infants vary. One list of temperamental dimensions is given in Table 7.2. On each dimension, some children are especially high or especially low, and such extreme cases have been referred to as "easy" or as "difficult" (see Table 7.2; Thomas & Chess, 1977). Considerably shorter lists of temperamental dimensions have been developed by other groups of researchers and are shown in Tables 7.3 and 7.4.

In addition to proposing different definitions of temperament, each research team has a slightly different view of the origins of stable temperaments. According to Thomas and Chess, temperament is a style of approach to the environment and may be affected by the situation. For Plomin (Buss & Plomin, 1984; Plomin & Saudino, 1994), temperament is stable because it is an inherited personality trait that appears early in life. While some traits are acquired, the three dimensions shown in Table 7.3 are believed to have some inherited basis (Goldsmith et al., 1987; Goldsmith, Buss, & Lemery, 1997; Goldsmith et al., 1999).

Research done using twin studies and behavior genetics methods (see the section on behavior ecology theory in Chapter 2) has found that some aspects of temperament are partly inherited (Emde & Hewitt, 2001). Inhibition to the unfamiliar (see Table 7.4), as observed in the laboratory, and infant negative emotions, as rated by parents, both have some genetic influence (Emde et al., 1992). Negativity and inhibition both appear early in life and are persistent characteristics in 5 to 10% of all infants up until at least the ages of 5 to 7 years. In addition, similar proportions of persistently inhibited children are found in different countries and even in infant monkeys, which further suggests some genetic contribution (Gar-

TABLE 7.2   Temperamental Characteristics Crucial in Classifying Children as Easy or Difficult

Temperamental Quality	Two months	Two Years
Activity Level	Does not move when being dressed or during sleep.	Enjoys quiet play with puzzles. Can listen to records for hours.
	Moves often in sleep. Wriggles when diaper is changed.	*Climbs furniture. Explores. Gets in and out of bed while being put to sleep.*
Rhythmicity	Has been on 4-hour feeding schedule since birth. Regular bowel movement.	Eats a big lunch every day. Always has a snack before bedtime.
	Awakes at different time each morning. Size of feeding varies.	*Nap time changes from day to day. Toilet training is difficult because bowel movement is unpredictable.*
Approach/ Withdrawal	Smiles and licks washcloth. Has always liked bottle.	Slept well the first time he stayed overnight at grandparents' house.
	Rejected cereal the first time. Cries when strangers appear.	*Avoids strange children in the playground. Whimpers first time at beach. Will not get into water.*
Adaptability	Was passive during first bath, now enjoys bathing. Smiles at nurse.	Obeys quickly. Stayed contentedly with grandparents for a week.
	Still startled by sudden, sharp noises. Resists diapering.	*Cries and screams each time hair is cut. Disobeys persistently.*
Intensity of Reaction	Does not cry when diapers are wet. Whimpers instead of crying when hungry.	When another child hit her, she looked surprised, did not hit back.
	Cries when diapers are wet. Rejects food vigorously when satisfied.	*Yells if he feels excitement or delight. Cries loudly if a toy is taken away.*
Quality of Mood	Smacks lips when first tasting new food. Smiles at parents.	Plays with sister; laughs and giggles. Smiles when he succeeds in putting shoes on.
	Fusses after nursing. Cries when carriage is rocked.	*Cries and squirms when given a haircut. Cries when mother leaves.*

* Temperamental ratings and behaviors for difficult children are in italic type; those for easy children are in regular type.

Source: From Thomas, Chess, & Birch, 1970. In A. Fogel & G. F. Melson, *Child development*, 1988, p. 209. St. Paul, MN: West. Copyright © by West Publishing Company: All rights reserved.

cia-Coll, Kagan, & Reznick, 1984; Kagan, 1997; Kagan & Reznick, 1984; Kagan et al., 1988; Kagan et al., 1994; Lewis, 1993; Mullen, Snidman, & Kagan, 1993; Reznick et al., 1986; Shwalb, Shwalb, & Shoji, 1994; Worobey & Lewis, 1989).

One long-term study found that infants who were the most inhibited at 4 months were more likely to be subdued in unfamiliar situations, to have a dour mood, to report more anxiety, and to have an overactive sympathetic nervous system response when they were teenagers (arousal, see Chapter 5) (Kagan et al., 2007). Another study

found that adults who were inhibited as infants showed a higher activation in the amygdala (the part of the limbic system responsive to fear) when viewing pictures of unfamiliar faces than adults who were not inhibited as infants. This fear of new faces reflects the persistence of social anxiety in inhibited individuals (Schwartz et al., 2003).

According to both Rothbart (Rothbart & Derryberry, 1981; Rothbart, Derryberry, & Posner, 1994) and Kagan (1987), temperament is rooted in biological processes but not necessarily inherited. For these researchers, behavioral characteristics

TABLE 7.3   Dimensions of Infant Temperament (Buss and Plomin, 1984)

Temperamental Quality	Description
Emotionality	Emotional infants have strong fear, anger, or distress responses, as shown by high ANS activity. Emotional infants may also respond more to minimal aversive events and may be less easy to calm or to appease. Emotional infants tend to "specialize" in one emotion, showing, for example, strong anger but not strong fear or distress.
Activity	Active infants tend to be busy or energetic. They move around a lot and prefer more active forms of play.
Sociability	Sociable infants tend to spend more time in the company of others. This concept refers more to frequent initiation of contact with a wide range of individuals than to intimate contact with attachment figures. Sociable infants prefer being with people rather than alone and seem genuinely pleased by social contact.

Source: Information from A. H. Buss & R. Plomin, *Temperament: Early developing personality traits*, 1984. Hillsdale, NJ: Erlbaum. Used with permission.

TABLE 7.4   Temperamental Dimensions of Reactivity (Rothbart & Derryberry, 1981) and Inhibition (Kagan, 1987)

Reactivity	Includes brain activation, ANS processes, and hormonal processes. High reactivity includes both a rapid response and a high-intensity response, and it may also include a slow recovery from the response.
Inhibition	Inhibited children are restrained, watchful, and gentle. They tend to experience uncertainty about how to respond or how to think about a situation. Inhibition can also be characterized by particular brain, ANS, and hormonal processes.

called temperamental must be associated with specific central nervous system (CNS) and autonomic nervous system (ANS: sympathetic-arousal and parasympathetic-relaxation) activity (S. D. Calkins, Fox, & Marshall, 1996; Kagan, Reznick & Snidman, 1987; Rothbart, 1986). In this view, temperament is a somatic pattern, involving both mind and body. Infants and children who have difficulties with attention and emotion regulation—those rated as highly reactive, emotional, inattentive, or inhibited—have different patterns of activity in the prefrontal cortex compared to well-regulated infants (Rothbart, Sheese, & Posner, 2007). The prefrontal cortex is that part of the brain associated with self-regulation (see Chapter 5).

For example, inhibition (see Table 7.4) is related to brain-wave and heart-rate patterns as well as to stress responses to frustration. Physiological stress responses to frustration, such as heart-rate acceleration, cortisol secretion, and sympathetic nervous system activation, are present at an early age for some inhibited infants and may persist for periods of up to 1 year (S. Calkins & Fox, 1994; N. A. Fox, 1989; M. Gunnar, 1994; M. Gunnar, Mangelsdorf, Larson, & Hertsgaard, 1989; Healy, 1989; Huffman et al., 1998; M. Lewis & Ramsay, 1995; C. A. Nelson, 1994).

Some research has shown that infant temperament and its associated physiological features, are correlated with parental personality. Infants who are more inhibited, for example, are more likely to have parents who are introverted, shy, and anxious (Kochanska et al., 2004; Pauli-Pott et al., 2004; Rickman & Davidson, 1994). Also, persistent infant inhibition and high levels of negativity are related to lower scores on maternal adaptation to pregnancy, maternal sensitivity to the infant after birth, and maternal self-esteem (Crockenberg & Leerkes, 2004; Fish, Stifter, & Belsky, 1991; Martin, Noyes, Wisenbaker, & Huttunen, 1999). Mothers who rate infant cries as more aversive are more likely to rate their infants as difficult (Pedersen & Moran, 1996). These findings, while they suggest that parents play a role in the development of infant temperament, do not necessarily rule out a partial genetic explanation for inhibition, since parents and infants could both share similar genetic make-ups.

Another finding that may call the genetic explanation into question is that children do not necessarily exhibit continuity of temperament. Inhibited children may, with appropriately sensitive child rearing, eventually lose their extreme sensitivity. Normal children may become more inhibited in extremely stressful environments. While extreme fussiness at birth predicts later emotionality in full-term infants (Worobey & Blajda, 1989), fussiness at birth is not related to later behavior in premature infants (Riese, 1987). The stress of premature birth may have made it impossible to assess the infant's temperament at the time of birth. If there is a biological predisposition toward inhibition or other temperamental factors, such as emotionality, it does not operate in the absence of environmental influences (Kagan, 1987; Wachs, 1988).

While some temperamental characteristics in infancy, such as inhibition (see above) predict long-term personality characteristics or behavior disorders, not all of the person's behavior is related to early temperament. Temperament may have short-term influences on cognitive information processing, as when an inhibited infant is unlikely to approach a novel stimulus, but there is less evidence that temperament contributes to longer-term cognitive deficit or enhancement (J. E. Bates, 1987; Kagan, 1987; M. D. Lewis, 1993). One reason may be that parents adjust their short-term behavior to the child's reactivity. If parents respond cautiously to inhibited children or work to desensitize them, and if they reduce the intensity of stimulation for highly active children, the parental behavior may attenuate the long-term effects of the early temperamental characteristic (Gandour, 1989; Kagan, 1987; Kagan, Snidman, & Arcus, 1998; S. Park, Belsky, Putnam, & Crnic, 1997).

Aside from parental factors, factors in the infant may contribute to the stability of temperament. Inhibited children who showed more positive emotion were less likely to be inhibited at age 3 than inhibited children who tended to be more negative (S. Park et al., 1997). It seems that both

parental and child factors can interact to influence the stability of temperament over time.

Temperament assessed at the end of the infancy period, between 2 and 4 years of age, tends to show long-term stability (Lemery, Goldsmith, Klinnert, & Mrazek, 1999). Two-year-olds who were rated as more difficult had more attention problems and aggressive behavior at 12 years (Guerin, Gottfried, & Thomas, 1997). Three-year-olds who were rated low on self-control had more adjustment problems and interpersonal conflicts as adults (Newman, Caspi, Moffitt, & Silva, 1997).

In summary, temperamental characteristics such as inhibition and negativity clearly exist in infants and may persist over many years. Less clear is the origin of these temperamental characteristics. The evidence suggests that they have multiple and complex causes related to inheritance, physiology, environment, and parent-child relationships. Temperament is apparently best explained by some type of systems theory. In the next section, we turn to the problem of how temperament is measured.

The Measurement of Temperament

One of the problems in studying temperament is that it must be observed over a long period of time. Temperament is by *definition* those aspects of infants that are consistent over some period of time. A child who is sociable on a particular day is not necessarily temperamentally sociable unless there is a consistent pattern of such behavior over a weeks or months. For this reason, the study of temperament is more difficult than other areas of research because the investigator has to identify what stays the same when other things are changing. Because infants change in so many ways, it is difficult to capture their essence (J. E. Bates, 1987; J. E. Bates, Wachs, & Emde, 1994; Kagan, 1987; Wachs & Bates, 2000).

Another problem is that of language. Even though we might have some strong intuition about the consistent temperament of a baby we know, it is hard to describe that consistency in words. Once a word such as "inhibited" is chosen, it cannot describe exactly what the temperamental quality is, and the word itself often distorts what is unique about the baby (Kagan, 1987). To call a baby "inhibited" does not do justice to the fact that the child may play, walk, and talk like most other children. Under certain circumstances, however, such as in the presence of an unfamiliar person, this child may be especially shy.

Given the difficulties in identifying a common-sense concept of temperament, it should come as no surprise that researchers have found temperament to be a difficult construct to measure in a reliable and valid manner. Some have attempted to observe children's responses to particular situations over a long period, such as their reactions to distress and separation, or to examine their overall activity level. More typically, parents are asked to rate their children's temperaments under the assumption that the parents have the most complete, long-term experiences with the children and can better assess any stable characteristics (J. E. Bates, 1987).

On the other hand, what is probably the best source of information about the child's temperament is not always reliable. When mothers and fathers are asked to rate the same child, their reports agree only about half the time (J. E. Bates & Bayles, 1984; H. H. Goldsmith & Gottesman, 1981; Hubert, Wachs, Peters-Martin, & Gandour, 1982). Similarly, there is only a moderate amount of agreement between mothers and outside observers (J. E. Bates, 1980), although there is more overall agreement about the difficulty of an infant than about any other dimension of temperament.

Some evidence also suggests that temperament is related to other measures of the infant's behavior. Infants rated as "distractable" by their parents at 2 weeks, for example, had lower scores on the Brazelton Neonatal Assessment Scale at 1 week and lower scores on the Bayley infant assessment test at 10 weeks (Sostek & Anders, 1977). Infants who were rated as "difficult" had cries that were independently rated as more irritating and had longer pauses between cry sounds, as revealed by sound spectrograph analysis, giving their cries a greater sense of urgency (Huffman et al., 1994; Lounsbury & Bates, 1982). Mothers' ratings of infant temperamental fussiness correlated with direct observations of crying behavior at 3 months (Crockenberg & Acredolo, 1983). Infant fear and pleasure responses as measured in a laboratory setting correlated with similar dimensions of parent-rated infant temperament (H. H. Goldsmith & Campos, 1990). The correlation between parental reports and actual behavior is improved if infants are selected only from the extreme ends of the behavioral scale. Infants who were either extremely inhibited or extremely uninhibited in a laboratory situation had parents who also rated them in this manner (Garcia-Coll et al., 1984). These findings suggest that although there is some correspondence between parental reports and actual behavior, in many cases, correspondence is lacking.

It could be that each parent and each observer have different experiences with the child and thus have different "databases" from which to draw conclusions. Also, the child may actually behave differently across situations and in the company of different observers. It could also be that the questions asked on rating forms (ranging from general questions about the overall difficulty of the child to specific questions about the child's reaction to strangers) are not sufficiently sensitive to capture the individuality of the child.

Another possibility is that the parental reports reflect the parents' personalities more than the child's (Matheny, Wilson, & Thoben, 1987; Miebert, 1991; Vaughn, Bradley, Joffe, Seifer, & Barglow, 1987) or reveal something about the current psychological state of the parents. Mothers who were multiparous and extroverted were more likely to rate their infants as easy than other mothers (J. E. Bates, Freeland, & Lounsbury, 1979). Other studies found that mothers from low-income groups who were African American, had a history of mental illness, or scored high on tests of anxiety rated their infants' temperament as more difficult than mothers who did not fall into any of these groups (Sameroff, Seifer, & Elias, 1982; Vaughn, Taraldson, Crichton, & Egeland, 1981).

Another way to test the validity of temperament measures is to study their consistency over repeated testings. On the whole, parental reports and observational measures are only moderately stable over the infancy period. In other words, children who are rated as "fearful," "inhibited," or "sociable" at 1 year are not necessarily rated the same way at 3 years (J. E. Bates, 1987; Seifer, Sameroff, Barrett, & Krafchuk, 1994). This could be because the infants themselves changed or the parents changed in the way they perceived the infants.

In summary, parents' ratings of infant temperament have some usefulness, but they must be interpreted with caution. Some ratings reflect the parents' own personalities or current levels of stress and may be inconsistent over time. It is not surprising that parents' interpretations of their infant's temperament are colored by their own experiences. No less is true of adults' interpretations of the behavior and personality of other adults. The best research strategy is to use a combination of parental reports, direct observations, and physiological measures (such as cortisol and sympathetic nervous system activity) made at repeated intervals in the child's life.

Ten to Twelve Months

As the earlier chapters on motor, cognitive and social development suggest, the infant's life at the end of the first year is becoming increasingly integrated into patterns of intentions and relationships. Motor skills create the tools with which the infant can operate on the environment to achieve goals, and goals increasingly structure the way in which the infant behaves. During the previous age period, infants became upset when someone caused them pain or when some expected event did not happen. Between the ages of 10 and 12 months, infants become upset when their goals are blocked and are pleased when they achieve an intended goal. They also develop new emotions regarding their relationships with other people.

The Development of Anger

Anger is the emotion most frequently elicited in year-old infants when their goals have been disrupted. An angry expression has distinct charac-

teristics. By the end of the first year, the anger expression is more defined. The mouth is open with a squarish shape that is angled downward toward the back of the mouth. The brows are lowered, and the eyes are opened and intense (see Figure 7.4). In the expression of distress, the mouth is similar, but the eyes are usually closed or partially closed (Figure 7.4). Anger typically involves a bracing of the jaw.

When the infant is crying and making the anger expression at the same time, the state of emotion is more intense. When anger expressions were observed without crying, EEG recordings from the infants' scalps showed heightened activity in the left frontal region. When the infants were angry and crying, there was more activity in the right frontal region. The right frontal area is believed to be associated with more-intense states of negative emotions. These results suggest that low levels of anger, without crying, are probably more cognitively based (left brain) and maintain the infant's orientation toward the environment (N. A. Fox & Davidson, 1988).

The emotion of anger began in the previous stage as a more vigilant and intense form of distress. Between 10 and 12 months, anger becomes more purposeful and directed. Infants do such things as stomp their feet, hit away objects or interfering hands, or slap and kick (Sroufe, 1979). These expressions have the quality of outbursts, and they coincide with the development of goal-directed behavior seen in other realms of infant functioning during this period.

The Development of Fear

Around the age of 6 months, infants develop a wary look, which may involve a raised brow furrowing above the nose and a relatively relaxed mouth. Wariness is related to the emotion of fear, since both involve an inhibition of action and may reflect a tendency for the individual to withdraw from the situation. The expression of fear includes the raised and furrowed brow of wariness while the mouth corners are retracted straight back (Figure 7.4).

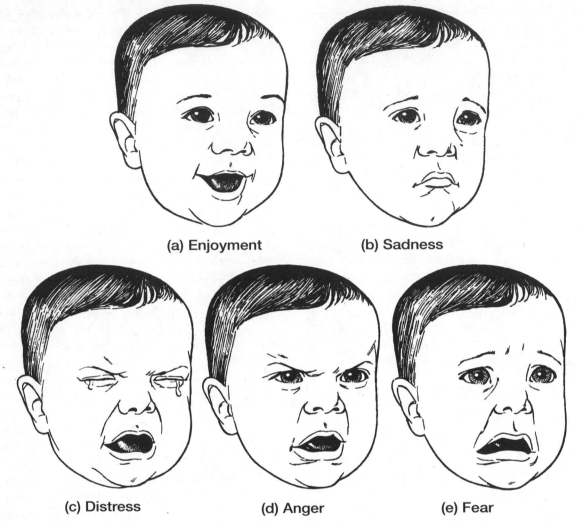

(a) Enjoyment   **(b) Sadness**

(c) Distress   **(d) Anger**   **(e) Fear**

Figure 7.4   Infant Expressions

Source: C. Izard, *The maximally discriminative facial movement coding system*, 1983 (January), p. 97. Instructional Resources Center, University of Delaware, Newark, DE, pp. 93, 95–98.

True fear expressions are rare in infancy, but they first appear around the age of 10 months (Camras et al., 2007; Demos, 1982). Fear expressions may appear briefly and then change to anger or sadness (see Figure 7.4). Fear is more likely to be expressed by behavioral inhibition in the absence of a facial expression. Infants may stop their movements or actively avoid approaching the source of the fear. Infants feel fear when unexpected or threatening events occur. Below are some of the situations that may arouse fear in year-old infants.

Heights. Fear of heights has been assessed using the **visual cliff** situation. A piece of hard, clear plastic is extended over a box with a shallow side and a deep side. Beginning at 9 months of age, infants show fear in approaching the deep side of the cliff (see Chapter 1; E. J. Gibson & Walk, 1960; A. Schwartz, Campos, & Baisel, 1973).

Unpredictable objects and movements. Infants will show fear responses to any objects—either people or inanimate moving objects—that loom unexpectedly in front of them (Bronson, 1972; Cicchetti &

Mans, 1976). Surprising events, like a jack-in-the-box popping up, may also cause fear (Ricciuti & Poresky, 1972). Unpredictable, noisy mechanical toys can cause fear. However, in one study, infants were given control over the movements of such toys. When the infants were in control, the toys were significantly less fearsome (Gunnar, Leighton, & Peleaux, 1984).

Acquired fears. Infants may become fearful of an otherwise benign situation because it reminds them of something they found stressful, fearful, or painful in the past. These fears can be said to arise from a conditioned association. They are different from fears of such things as heights or looming objects, which may be universal. Acquired fears are learned. Examples are fear of particular people, of doctor's offices, or of certain kinds of sounds, such as a dog's bark (Bronson, 1972; see Observation 7.1).

Strangers. Fear of strangers takes two forms. One is an acquired fear of particular people or people wearing a particular kind of clothing or hairstyle. The other is a general wariness of the unfamiliar that appears in most infants in every culture beginning about 8 months of age. Infants show less fear if the stranger approaches them slowly and keeps an appropriate distance (Kaltenbach, Weinraub, & Fullard, 1980; Ricard & Decarie, 1993; Trause, 1977); if their mothers are present when the stranger approaches (Eckerman & Whatley, 1975; Ricciuti, 1974; Trause, 1977); if they are with familiar caregivers, such as baby-sitters or child-care providers (N. A. Fox, 1977; Ricciuti, 1974); if the stranger is a little person or a child (Bigelow, MacLean, Wood, & Smith, 1990;

Brooks & Lewis, 1976); if the stranger does not tower over them (Weinraub & Putney, 1978); if the stranger is sensitive to the infants' signals and allows the approach to be regulated by the infants (Mangelsdorf, 1992); and if the infants are in an unfamiliar setting, such as a laboratory, compared to a home (Brookhart & Hock, 1976; Skarin, 1977).

You might expect a baby to be less fearful at home than in a strange place, but this is not the case. In strange places, infants seem to expect to see unusual or unfamiliar things. When the stranger intrudes on the familiar and predictable setting of the home, however, the infant gets disturbed. In fact, mothers take their babies many places, such as doctors' offices and grocery stores, and the babies are rarely upset by the many unfamiliar people they meet in those situations. A number of studies have shown that babies can engage in positive and rewarding social interaction soon after meeting a new person. If the stranger proves acceptable to the baby, the baby often will spend more time playing with this interesting visitor than with his or her own mother (Klein & Durfee, 1976; Ross & Goldman, 1977b).

If you want to make friends with a baby of this age, the rules are much the same as with anyone else: go slowly, be sensitive to signs of withdrawal or wariness, let the baby get to know you on his or her own terms, and make sure the baby is properly chaperoned by his or her mother or caregiver before you make any serious proposals. Finally, do not forget that year old babies develop acquired fears. If the baby screams in terror at the mere sight of you, it could be that you remind the baby of a negative encounter. Even though it is hard to keep from feeling downright insulted, it is probably not your fault. It may take some extra sensitiv-

---

Observations

Stage IV Behavior (Piaget, 1952, p. 249)

Observation 7.1

At 1;1(10) she [Jacqueline] has a slight scratch which is disinfected with alcohol. She cries, chiefly

from fear. Subsequently, as soon as she again sees the bottle of alcohol she recommences to cry, knowing what is in store for her. Two days later, same reaction, as soon as she sees the bottle and even before it is opened.

Infants of this age are naturally wary of new situations. They find great comfort in the company of familiar caregivers.

Photo: Robert Brenner/PhotoEdit.

ity on your part to help the baby learn to like you for yourself.

The Development of Sadness

The emotion of sadness has a different expression than anger and fear. During sadness, the brows are raised at the center and drop at the sides, and the mouth corners are drawn back and down (see Figure 7.4). As we reported for anger, sadness without crying is less intense, showing left-frontal brain activity. With crying, sadness is accompanied by right-brain activation. In the earlier months, sadness accompanies disappointment when an expected event fails to happen, for example, when the baby expects to receive a treat or a hug and does not get it. By 9 or 10 months, sadness accompanies a feeling of loss. Because infants can now connect their memory of absent objects with some concrete action on the objects, the infants may become sad if an object disappears and they cannot find it after a search.

In some cases, but not all, sadness accompanies separation from caregivers. This emotion is sometimes called *separation distress*. Research has shown, however, that if mothers leave their babies behind in the company of the regular caregiver (the grandmother, baby-sitter, father, and so on), there is little or no separation distress (Ricciuti, 1974; Stayton, Ainsworth, & Main, 1973; Suwalsky & Klein, 1980). Infants respond more positively to separation from their mothers if they are left with any other person, particularly a familiar one; if they are left with toys of any kind; if they can see or hear their mothers in an adjoining room (Corter, 1977); and if they are left with their own pacifiers (Halonen & Passman, 1978; Hong & Townes, 1976). The mothers' saying "bye-bye" or making some other parting gestures before they left had no effect on 1-year-olds (Corter, 1977). These parting gestures do seem to help older infants, however. In general, the longer parents take to say good-bye, the harder it is for the babies to initially adjust to the new situation (Field, Gewirtz, et al.,

1984; Weinraub & Lewis, 1977). Babies who go to a new preschool or day care center, or who must be hospitalized, show less distress if accompanied by peer friends or by siblings (Field, Vega-Lahr, & Jagadish, 1984; Heinicke & Westheimer, 1966; J. Robertson & Robertson, 1971).

There are cultural differences in infant response to separation, as shown by a study of brief (30-second) mother-infant separations in Japan (Hoshi & Chen, 1998). About half of the Japanese infants showed distress, even at this brief separation, perhaps because of the close contact between Japanese mothers and their infants and because separation is relatively rare. In addition, about one-third of the mothers apologized to the infant during the reunion. Their apologies were done in an intonation pattern that matched the infant's crying, such as saying *Hai, hai, gomen nei, gomen nei, oh, oh* (yes, yes, oh, I'm so sorry, so sorry, well, well). The mothers seemed to endorse the infant's feelings as if to join in their misery and seek their forgiveness, a pattern of emotional sharing commonly seen in Japanese adults. Whether Western mothers do the same is unknown, but such behavior has never been reported in the thousands of studies on separation in Western countries.

If infants are separated from parents for long periods and are not provided with adequate substitute caregivers, more serious depression and withdrawal can result, including both behavior and physiological changes (Reite, Kaemingk, & Boccia, 1989; Tizard & Tizard, 1971). These effects can be ameliorated to some extent once the infants are restored to stable adult care, either with their biological parents or with adoptive parents (Reite et al., 1989; Suomi & Harlow, 1972; Tizard & Tizard, 1971). The effect on infants of substitute care by nonparental caregivers is an important topic to which we will return in Chapter 8.

The Development of Enjoyment and Affection

In the earlier months, infants showed positive responses to their caregivers. The smile of recognition appears at 2 months, and laughter of enjoyment during social play appears at 5 months. At 10 months, the infant has a deeper and more lasting type of positive feeling that has been called affection (Sroufe, 1979). *Affection* has a characteristic expression that is similar to a simple smile in the mouth region accompanied by a widening of the eyes (see Figure 7.4). Such smiles occur at the approach of familiar caregivers and are accompanied by right-brain activation. Infants' smiles at strangers usually lack the wide-eye component; such smiles activate the left side of the brain (N. A. Fox & Davidson, 1988).

After a brief separation, infants often feel genuinely happy to see the caregiver. This is a positive emotion that goes beyond the particular situation and expresses a lasting bond. Infants express these feelings not only to caregivers but also to favorite toys and to siblings. Infants of this age smile more in the presence of people, especially familiar people, and their favorite objects (S. S. Jones, Collins, & Hong, 1991). As we saw earlier in this chapter, smiling is related partly to emotion and partly to communication with others. Smiling is a reflection of a socially shared emotion.

Differential responsiveness to people on reunion is probably one of the earliest and most reliable ways of telling who the most important people in a baby's life are (Stayton, Ainsworth, & Main, 1973). In a stressful situation, if both the mother and another caregiver are present, infants will approach the mother (Klein & Durfee, 1976). Even when infants spend more hours of the day in the company of caregivers, as on an Israeli kibbutz, they show more positive responses when reunited with their mothers after a brief separation than when reunited with their **metapelets**, or caregivers (N. A. Fox, 1977). These findings suggest that babies have a growing awareness of the specialness of certain people and respond to them in ways that communicate the depth of their feelings.

The Development of Mixed Emotions

Before leaving the topic of emotions, it is necessary to touch on the subject of mixed emotional expressions. In one study, a stranger presented dolls and teddy bears to infants of this age. The babies alternatively reached out toward the objects and pulled their arms back (Ricciuti & Poresky, 1972). Lest we think this sort of ambivalence was merely an artifact of testing infants in an unfamiliar laboratory setting, we should note that another study found evidence for mixed emotions by naturalistic observation in the infants' homes. This study found that pure expressions of joy, anger, distress, excitement, or fear occur only about half the time. The other half of the time the infant's face expresses more than one emotion (Demos, 1982).

Enjoyment, for example, often is expressed with elements of excitement or surprise, as when a smile is combined with a "jaw-drop," producing a wide-open, smiling mouth. This is called a *play smile*. In my research, play smiles in 12-month-olds occur during games involving some physical activity or touch combined with an element of excitement. These are games like tickle, chase, and tossing the baby in the air. Play smiles are more likely to occur in physical games and thus appear more during father-infant play than in mother-infant play (L. Dickson, Fogel, & Messinger, 1997). Smiles have also been observed to occur with nose wrinkles, blinks, blows, and waves; each combination reflects a slight variation in the meaning of the enjoyment. Try each one out and see if you can figure out what it might mean.

In an effort to regulate emotion, distress will sometimes be combined with biting or stiffening the lip, showing that the baby is trying to control the crying. One-year-old babies often alternate between distress and enjoyment, showing that they are able to maintain interest in a toy or in social interaction even though they may be tired or frustrated. One-year-olds will sometimes look directly at the caregiver when crying, or they may pull at the caregiver, gesture to be picked up, or

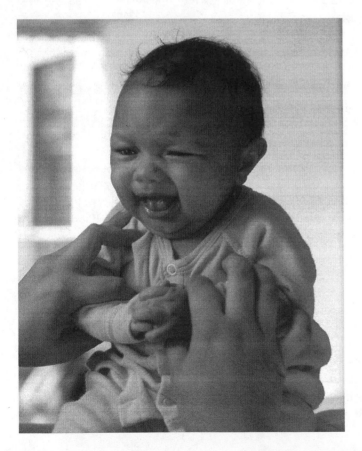

This baby is experiencing a mixed emotion. If you cover the eyes and look only at the mouth, what would you say the baby feels? Now cover the mouth, looking only at the eyes, and guess the baby's feelings. Putting the two parts together gives a mixed emotion.
Photo by Mary Kate Denny/PhotoEdit.

point to the offending object or event (Gustafson & Green, 1991). Relaxed touching and holding by the caregiver can provide encouragement for the infant's efforts to gain control over frustration, teaching the baby the capacity to persist (Hertenstein & Campos, 2001). The baby can learn that feeling distressed and frustrated does not necessarily mean the end of the game—that these "negative" affects are both tolerable and manageable (Demos, 1982).

Another example of a mixed emotion appearing at this age is jealousy. Year-old infants were observed while their mothers and a strange adult female played with a picture book or a child-sized doll. Infants showed more protest and negative vocalization and their play was more inhibited primarily in the mother-with-doll condition (Hart, Field, Letourneau, & Del Valle, 1998). These responses were interpreted as jealousy because the infant was not upset about the mother with a book, nor about the stranger's behavior. Jealousy is an example of wanting to approach the mother but avoiding her at the same time.

Because of the emergence of mixed emotions, new forms of parent-child play develop as a way to help infants understand and cope with emotional changes. Teasing games are especially important in this regard. A tease takes something that has a serious emotional tone and alters it into a more positive tone. Between 9 and 12 months, infants learn the art of teasing and also become able to appreciate the teases of others (see Observations 7.2, 7.3, and 7.4). The contradictory messages in these games provide important opportunities for infants to learn how to regulate their emotions, how to affect other people, and also how to have fun (Nakano, 1995; Reddy, 1991; Reddy, 2000). Teasing is relatively more frequent in father-infant than in mother-infant play (Labrell, 1994).

In summary, these findings show that infants are becoming emotionally complex. Not only are they aware of the relationships between objects and between events, they are also aware of the relationships between their different feelings. They may not always be able to resolve these relationships but at a minimum, their emotional life is becoming more diverse. In Chapter 6, we saw that infants are also becoming more aware of interpersonal relationships. Indeed, findings show that jealousy and teasing are clearly emotions that take account of different kinds of interpersonal relationships.

Observations

Teasing Games (Nakano, 1995; Reddy, 1991)

Observation 7.2

Rebecca (8.5 months) "accidentally" discovers her impact on others of going in front of the television in her walker while someone is watching. After that, each time the television is turned on, Rebecca scoots, stands in front of it and giggles. Mother makes getting Rebecca away from the television into a game by playing "I'm gonna get you," while grabbing her away.

Observation 7.3

Stephanie (7 months) developed a shrill shriek that she used when she was not getting enough attention. In the supermarket, her mother heard the shriek, turned toward Stephanie quickly and with alarm, to find Stephanie sitting in her stroller grinning at her mother.

Observation 7.4

Mother claps her hands rhythmically to get her 10-month-old's attention. When the infant looks at her hands, the mother says, "my hands are stuck together and I can't pull them apart." She shrieks with an exasperated tone and asks the baby for help getting her hands apart. At the moment when the baby reaches out to help, the mother startles the baby by pulling her hands apart, saying "Bang!" at the same time. The mother answers the baby's surprised look with a smile and laugh and then the baby smiles joyfully.

Individual Differences in Emotion Regulation

As we saw in the previous age period, infants of this age are learning emotion regulation to maintain some self-control in the face of highly arousing (either exciting or distressing) situations. Between 10 and 12 months, infants show differences in how they use people or objects to regulate emotions.

Heart-rate measures have shown that even when infants do not cry during maternal separation, they do get aroused. We may observe an extended glance at the door, perhaps a sad expression, and then a concerted effort to become involved with the toys. It is almost as if the babies were using the toys to prevent feeling sad and lonely. Conversely, other infants who may ignore their mother when she returns from a separation also show elevated heart rates. These babies are coping with their ambivalent feelings about their mother in relation to the feeling of loss they must have experienced when she was out of the room. The manner in which the infants cope with these feelings is not necessarily adaptive, since it effectively removes them from the only source of comfort they might receive: their mothers (Sroufe, 1979).

Some infants are temperamentally more fearful and withdrawn, and they are more likely to become fearful or sad in stressful situations, such as during separations and in the presence of strangers or unusual situations (Blackford & Walden, 1998; Bohlin & Hagekull, 1993; K. A. Buss & Goldsmith, 1998; J. J. Campos et al., 1975; Connell, 1985; Kagan, 1989; R. A. Thompson, Connell, & Bridges, 1988). These differences in emotionality are associated with individual differences in brain asymmetry. That is, infants who become easily distressed to the point of crying by a maternal separation have more marked differences between left- and right-brain activity in the frontal area (N. A. Fox & Davidson, 1987). These findings show that the infant's ability to remain attentive to the situation, rather than to withdraw, may be in part responsible for higher levels of regulation of fear (Kochanska et al., 1998; M. D. Lewis et al., 1997).

This suggests that there is a relationship between cognition (attention) and emotion regulation. Sustained attention to tasks is related to exploratory play, are also relevant here. Some infants are more focused, attentive, and not easily upset, while others seem more emotional and require more support from adults in challenging situations. We do not know about the long-term consequences of these differences. Most likely, they are simply normal temperamental differences that need to be taken into account when co-regulating with a baby.

Developments in the Infant's Ability to Perceive Emotion and Intention Expressed by Other People

By 6 or 7 months, infants are capable of perceiving a few simple facial expressions. By 9 or 10 months, however, infants can distinguish more expressions, and they are beginning to use the emotional information displayed by others in a meaningful manner. These developments in the perception of emotions in other people are one of the ways in which the infant is becoming increasingly aware of relationships. Even more important, infants at this age are beginning to get the idea that other people have emotions that differ from their own. This is shown by some of the following processes.

Affective sharing occurs when infants wish to communicate their feelings to another person or to confirm their feelings with another person. An example would be when a baby discovers an interesting relationship (such as how a lid goes onto a pot), smiles, and then looks to the caregiver. In this case, the infant is expecting a smile in return, as a way of confirming their own feeling of accomplishment.

Social referencing occurs when infants face an uncertain situation. In this case, they look to another person's emotional expressions to help them decide what to do in this situation. When infants are presented with a noisy, unpredictable toy, they may look around to see how adults are responding to the toy. Positive responses from the adults may encourage the infants to approach the toy. Try the social referencing exercise in the Experiential Exercises section of this chapter.

Underlying both affective sharing and social referencing is the development of the ability to delay an immediate emotional reaction to a situation and to evaluate how one is going to feel about the situation. **Appraisal** is the ability to use cognitive comparisons of alternate interpretations to regulate one's emotions. The appraisal at this age, however, differs from the appraisal seen during the period between 6 and 9 months. In that earlier period, infants are often observed to show a slight delay in their emotional reactions, as if deciding what to feel in a particular situation. After 10 months, however, the infant looks to *another person* to decide what to feel.

Between 9 and 12 months of age, affective sharing is the most common response in social situations, and it tends almost always to involve positive emotions (Hornick & Gunnar, 1988; Klinnert, 1984; Walden & Ogan, 1988). When infants in this age range are given novel toys or shown a rabbit in a cage, for example, they tend to focus mostly on the objects and look at the caregiver for confirmation, primarily the display of a positive expression by the caregiver (Hagekull, Stenberg, & Bohlin, 1993).

Between 10 and 12 months, infants begin to use social referencing systematically, although social referencing does not occur as frequently as affective sharing in naturalistic situations (Hornick & Gunnar, 1988; C. A. Nelson, 1985). By 10 months, if mothers display a negative expression, some infants will avoid crossing a visual cliff, avoid playing with toys or avoid approaching a rabbit in a cage, and they will show more aversive responses to strangers to whom the mothers show negative expressions. Opposite patterns of behavior can be seen if the mothers display positive expressions in these situations, although negative expressions seem to have a more powerful effect on regulating infant behavior at this age (Feiring, Lewis, & Starr, 1984; M. R. Gunnar & Stone, 1984; Hornick, Risenhoover, & Gunnar, 1987; Sorce, Emde,

Campos, & Klinnert, 1985; Zarbatany & Lamb, 1985). Infants will reference almost any available adult and show equal responsiveness to mothers, fathers, and strangers; and they can use both adult facial expression and adult voices in the absence of facial expressions (Dickstein & Parke, 1988; Klinnert et al., 1986; Mumme, Fernald, & Herrera, 1996; Vaish & Striano, 2004).

Female infants are more likely to regulate their distance from fearful objects as a result of maternal referencing than are males (Blackford & Walden, 1998; W. D. Rosen, Adamson, & Bakeman, 1992). These findings are consistent with the gender differences reported earlier, in which females were observed to be more effective at regulating their emotions at still-face condition than males. By 10 months, when emotional regulation becomes more social for both boys and girls, girls begin to use other people more effectively to regulate themselves than boys. A study of 9-month-olds in Sweden found that mother-daughter dyads spent more time in close proximity than did mother-son dyads, once again suggesting that girls begin to use their mothers as emotional guides more than boys do at this age (Lindahl & Heimann, 1997).

In addition to this directed referencing in uncertain situations, infants are influenced by adults' emotions and attention. During a play period, mothers were instructed to use facial and vocal expressions of either joy or sadness. In the joy condition, infants expressed more joy and looked more at their mothers while engaging in higher-level play behavior. In the sadness condition, infants expressed more negative emotions, looked less at their mothers, and played less (Barna & Legerstee, 2005; Stenberg & Hagekull, 1997; Termine & Izard, 1988).

In addition to perceiving and using adult emotion, infants—who are themselves becoming intentional in their actions—begin at this age to perceive the intentions of adults. Infants preferentially reference adults who are looking at the infants over adults who are looking away from the infants, suggesting that infants are aware of the adult as another person who has the intention to communicate with the infants or not to communicate (Stenberg, 2003; Striano & Rochat, 2000). Infants of this age will also look more at adults whose actions seem intentionally directed toward an object compared to adults whose actions appear unrelated to that object (Falck-Ytter et al., 2006; Johnson et al., 2007). Infants will also act more frustrated if an adult teases them with a toy than when the adult tries to give the toy to the child (Behne et al., 2005).

In summary, these studies show that by the second half of the first year of life, emotion is no longer a private experience. Perhaps without intending to do so, infants nevertheless begin to alter their own emotions according to what others are expressing. It would not be correct to infer that infants understand the feelings of others at this age or even that infants can differentiate their own feelings from those of others. These developments begin almost a year later. They are simply aware that feelings can be shared and that they "have" feelings. Coupled with new perceptual and cognitive skills, infants probably discover that particular types of facial expression are related to actions that either enhance or interrupt their own activities. Thus, by the end of the first year, those facial expressions of adults have become part of the means by which infants regulate their own actions. From the adult's perspective, the infants are becoming more socially responsive and are entering into more meaningful social communications.

Twelve to Eighteen Months

In the previous stage, infants were able to use the adults around them to regulate their own level of arousal. Social referencing enabled the infant to determine the appropriate way to react to a situation simply by watching a nearby adult. Infants also approached an adult caregiver when they needed comfort, and they used the caregiver as a secure base from which to explore the environment. After 12 months infants still seek help from adults in regulating their emotions, but now we can see the beginnings of an attempt to control their own positive and negative emotions.

Positive Emotion

In the previous stages, infants might smile at their caregivers or laugh at a "joke," but these emotions were direct responses to the environmental events that provoked the emotion. Now infants can remain happy over a long period without the continuation of the stimulating event. This prolonged feeling of enjoyment has been called *elation* (Sroufe, 1979). Infants also play an active role in creating situations in which happiness is produced and maintained. During the previous age period, babies would show off to provoke repeated laughs from the caregiver. During the period between 12 and 18 months, babies will self-consciously exaggerate facial expressions, making funny faces or sticking out their tongues for an especially receptive audience (Demos, 1982). This exaggeration of actual routines in play can also be seen during co-regulated communication frames. By 18 or 20 months, babies and mothers play emotion games in which the children slap their mothers lightly, for example, the mothers pretend to cry, and then the children comfort them (Bretherton, Fritz, Zahn-Waxler, & Ridgeway, 1986).

Finally, infants show delight in their own achievements (Sroufe, 1979). Because they are becoming aware of their own abilities to act on the environment, to create new means, and to experiment, they appreciate the sense of accomplishment that mastery over a new task brings. It is another indication of an expanding sense of a subjective self, a person who persists and achieves. The babies' obvious delight when they take their first steps or find a toy they have been searching for is an example of this new sense of self-appreciation.

Babies continue to show their affection for the special people in their lives. These expressions may change from physical contact to expressions from a distance, such as a smile and a wave. In one study of infants' behavior upon reunion with their mothers after a brief separation, 11-month-olds approached their mothers and sought physical contact immediately. Fourteen-month-olds, in contrast, were less likely to approach the mothers upon their return and more likely to use some form of signaling from a distance: crying, whining, or raising their arms as if to ask to be picked up. By 19 months, the babies rarely even used this form of signaling. When their mothers returned, the babies were content merely to look at them before resuming their play (Serifica, 1978).

Negative Emotion

In the previous stages, situations of stress tended to evoke fear or distress from the infant almost immediately. During an episode of separation from the mother, for example, infants were likely to cry or approach another friendly adult for comfort. After 12 months, infants visibly fight back tears and use other self-comforting behaviors such as stroking and hugging themselves and redirecting their attention to a toy (Bridges, Grolnick, & Connell, 1997; Parritz, 1996; Sroufe, 1979). Since these babies are not overwhelmed with the distress, they search more for their mothers (Serifica, 1978). When their mothers are out of the room, infants often alternate between pouting and frowning (Sroufe, 1979) or biting their lower lips to control distress (Demos, 1982). As previously mentioned, the baby who so successfully fought back tears during separation almost certainly will burst into tears upon the mother's return. Studies done in the United States and in the Gusii agricultural society in Kenya have shown a relative reduction of attachment behavior during the period between 12 and 18 months; that is, fewer approaches to the mother and fewer bids for attention and support (Reed & Leiderman, 1981).

As infants get older, parents are more willing to expose them to potentially stressful events. Parents are less likely to intervene when the infant has an everyday problem—such as an argument with a sibling, waking up at night, a nonserious fall, or needing attention. Parents are also more likely to leave the infant with a baby-sitter or in child care, and they are more likely to take trips without the infant. This is partly because infants are beginning to cope with these events (Hildebrandt, Lake, & Parry, 1994). There are individual differences in the infant's ability to cope. Infants who are temperamentally inhibited and who have insecure attachments (see below) are more likely to show distress at even minor stresses (Nachmias et al., 1996).

When the mother takes a short (2- or 3-day) trip, leaving the infant in the company of the father or another caregiver, infants of this age experience relatively few sleep or behavior problems and can maintain their typical level of positive smiling and verbal interaction with adults. For longer separations, such as when the mother is in the hospital for a prolonged period, infants are likely to show more severe disturbances in their routines and less positive engagement, both while the mother is away and for some weeks after she returns. Infants with more difficult and withdrawn temperaments take these separations harder than others (Field, 1994). These findings suggest that infants of this age can cope with a wide range of stresses, but they need adult support and encouragement. After the parents return, they should also expect to spend extra time reestablishing the infant's routines and providing emotional reassurance.

Eighteen to Twenty-Four Months

More complex event memories and concepts and the ability to think symbolically account for some of the changes in emotional development during this period of infancy. The infants' emotional expressions continue to become more complex and more closely related to communicative situations. They are less likely to show full-face expressions typical of earlier ages (see Figure 7.4). Now, their facial expressions can be more subtle, involving fewer facial muscles, to reveal more complex feelings and a greater ability to regulate emotions. Supporting this view, 18-month-olds who showed more full-face expressions were more likely to be rated as having a difficult temperament (Izard & Abe, 2004).

During the second year, the infants' predominant emotional expressions are smiling and laughter (Malatesta et al., 1989). Prior to this period, smiles occur when infants accomplish a task such as the successful completion of an offering or a request gesture (Messinger & Fogel,

1997). After 18 months, infants are more likely to smile when both they and their mothers establish joint activity and attention, and when they experience periods of affective sharing, rather than just at their own achievements (S. S. Jones, Raag, & Collins, 1990; Mundy, Kasari, & Sigman, 1992). Infants of this age are also increasingly likely to initiate positive emotions in their communications with the parent, acting like a more emotionally autonomous individual (Grolnick, Cosgrove, & Bridges, 1996).

Our studies on infant laughter have revealed significant changes between the first and second year of life (Nwokah, Hsu, Dobrowolska, & Fogel, 1994). During the first year, most infant laughter occurs while the mother is smiling or laughing. In the second year, infant laughter takes on a specific meaning within the mother-infant communication system. A solitary infant laugh might mean "this is fun," an infant laugh following the mother's laugh might mean "if you think this is funny, so do I," and infant laughter while the mother is not displaying positive emotion, especially during teasing situations, might mean "I enjoy it when you look shocked so long as you are not really angry." Laughter also serves as an attention-getting device. A laugh can reestablish visual attention or direct the mother's attention back to the infant, who may laugh at his or her own antics.

We also found that mother-infant dyads developed their own styles of laughing together. For example, a mother would frame an opportunity for infant laughter by providing all the facial features of a laugh, such as a wide open mouth, and wait until the infant provided the actual laugh before she laughed in unison. In another couple, mother and infant would stare silently, smiling at each other, and then burst out laughing almost simultaneously.

How Does Symbolic Thought Affect the Child's Emotional Experiences?

The ability to form mental images and create symbols increases the range of the infant's emotional experiences. In the previous stage, fear, for example, could be triggered by a concrete event that might remind the infant of a related and unpleasant past event. Seeing someone in a white coat might remind the infant of a doctor and cause the infant to become frightened and cry.

After 18 months, fear can be evoked by a symbolic mental image, such as a monster or the thought of being sucked down the drain of a sink. Starting at this age, children develop fears of the dark and of things that might lurk behind doors, refrigerators, and other unseen places (Sroufe, 1979). Dreams, which at this age begin to take on representational forms that can be remembered and talked about, also can be a source of fears, although nightmares do not appear until after the second birthday (Piaget, 1962). Piaget reported observing instances of dreaming in one child as young as 21 months; she called out the names of several of her friends in the middle of the night, and on one occasion said, "Kitty's hiding."

Symbolic skills also increase the probability that infants will talk about their emotions. Indeed, by 20 months, about one-third of all children will talk about one or more of the following states: sleep/fatigue ("tired"), pain ("ouch"), distress ("sad"), disgust ("yuck"), affection ("love Mommy"), and value ("good," "bad") (Bretherton et al., 1986; Ridgeway, Waters, & Kuczaj, 1985). By the age of 24 months, infants engage in conversations about their feelings, talk about the causes of their feelings, and play games with siblings in which they pretend to have certain kinds of feelings (J. Dunn, Bretherton, & Munn, 1987). These types of conversations are illustrated in Observations 7.5 and 7.6. Aside from the connection between emotions and symbols, this kind of talk also shows that the child is becoming increasingly aware of internal experience. The verbal expression of that internal experience is one of the major characteristics of the existential self compared to the subjective self of earlier ages (see Chapter 5).

Self-Conscious Emotions

At this age, children can recognize themselves in a mirror, the sign of an existential self (see

Observations

Communicative Behavior Between Siblings
(J. Dunn, Bretheron, & Munn, 1987)

Observation 7.5

Family M., child 24 months: Baby sibling is crying after child knocked him (accidentally). Mother comes into room.

Child: Poor Thomas.
Mother: What?
Child: I banged his head.
Mother: You banged it?
Child: Yes.
Mother: Are you going to kiss it?
Child: Yes
Mother: Kiss his head.

Observation 7.6

Family Th., child 24 months: Older sibling has been showing a child a book with pictures of monsters. Child leaves sibling and goes to Mother.

Child: Mummy, Mummy. (whines)
Mother: What's wrong?
Child: Frighten.
Mother: The book?
Child: Yes.
Mother: It's not frightening you!
Child: Yes!
Mother: It did, did it?
Child: Yes.

Chapter 5). The primary emotion that they experience when they first recognize themselves is embarrassment. In one study, infants' reactions to the mirror were compared with infants' reactions to an unfamiliar adult. To the adult, the predominant expression was wariness, defined as an attentive look, a sober facial expression, and a cessation of ongoing action or vocalization, followed by a gaze aversion. To the mirror, infants were embarrassed, as shown by a turning to the nearest adult with a smiling facial expression, followed by a gaze aversion and movement to touch the hair, hands, or face in a self-conscious manner (M. Lewis et al., 1989).

Embarrassment, or *shame*, is fundamentally different from the other emotions that infants had experienced up to this point in their lives. Shame is a **self-conscious emotion**, that is, it requires an awareness that the self can be seen by another. Shame is always felt in the eyes of someone else. In order to feel shame, one has to realize that others are different from the self, and that the self is exposed, separate, and likely to be evaluated by others (M. Lewis, 1995). Other self-conscious emotions are guilt, jealousy, and pride (K. C. Barrett & Nelson-Goens, 1997). Self-conscious emotions begin to emerge around the child's second birthday.

Pride occurs when infants see themselves as effective and competent individuals in the eyes of another person, able to achieve and to have an impact on others. In previous stages, children expressed enjoyment at being a cause, at being contingent, and at having an effect on others. In this stage, the feeling of pride is the result of meeting their own standards, as well as the awareness of having accomplished a personal goal in the eyes of another person.

Children observed an experimenter rolling a ball to knock down a bowling pin, and later the children were asked to do it themselves. Children smiled when the pin fell in both conditions, but they only looked at the experimenter when they had done the task themselves. This look seems to be one indication of a sense of pride. Similarly, children of this age period are more likely to show pride reactions when achieving goals they determine for themselves rather than those set for them by their mothers (Stipek, 1995). Some behavioral characteristics of pride and shame are shown in Table 7.7.

Both pride and shame are developed in the context of communicating about success or failure in meeting socially accepted standards, rules, and achievements (K. C. Barrett & Nelson-Goens, 1997). Children at this age become aware of standards, such as completing an entire puzzle or finishing one's food. Rules include cleaning up after playing with toys or not touching electrical outlets. Achievements occur when children reach a level of new mastery after putting in some effort, such as putting on their own shirt.

The parent's responses to these everyday events play a role in the development of the toddler's emotions. Children whose parents respond most positively to the child's achievements and to when the child follows everyday social rules are more likely to show guilt reactions when a doll they are playing with during an experimental situation breaks. In one study, the doll had been designed by the experimenter to come apart easily. When it appears they have broken the doll, these children are more likely to point out the problem to the experimenter and try to repair the doll. Children whose parents were more negative in response to children's failure during everyday social situations were more likely to pretend that the doll did not break and to avoid mentioning the problem to the experimenter. Children whose parents respond positively when they are successful at something are more likely to react negatively when they are unsuccessful (K. C. Barrett & Nelson-Goens, 1997).

It is possible that the parents of these children react more positively because they can see the child is

very sensitive to failure. It is also possible that when parents are highly supportive and positive, children develop high standards for themselves. Most likely, there is a co-regulation between parents and children, such that their styles of emotional communication become more similar over time, with each influencing the other (K. C. Barrett & Nelson-Goens, 1997; Dunsmore & Halberstadt, 1997).

In the realm of *anger*, a growing sense of independence and a feeling that the self is separate from others leads to feelings of *defiance, negativism*, and *aggression* (Sroufe, 1979). These feelings, which arise out of earlier feelings of anger provoked by frustration or the immediate situation, are due more to the *mental idea* that the self is and should be independent. Defiance of parents is one way infants experience themselves—one way they make a declaration of self-sufficiency and explore the boundaries of the existential self.

Thus, in Stage VI (Chapter 5), anger is no longer a private response to an unyielding situation; it becomes a communication tool used willfully to affect other people. It is, therefore, one of the first signs of the child's sense of personal autonomy and signals the first break in the cycle of initial dependency. These patterns of emotion as related to the development of the self have been nicely described by Erikson's theory of development (see

TABLE 7.7 Characteristics of Pride and Shame

	Price	*Shame*
Situation	Success at achieving standard	Failure to achieve standard
Behavior	Approach others, show/tell, stand erect, smile broadly	Increase distance from others, reduce exposure, hide face
Social	Self as dominant, achiever	Self as submissive, small
Self	Maintenance of good feelings about self	Maintentance of others' respect
Other	"Everyone thinks I am good"	"Everyone is looking at me"
Vocalization	Wide, full voice	Narrow, thin voice
Physiology	High heart rate, flushed face	Low heart rate, blushing

Sources: K. C. Barrett, A functionalist approach to shame and guilt, 1995, p. 42. In J. P. Tangney & K. W. Fischer (Eds.), *Self-conscious emotions: The psychology of shame, guilt, embarrassment, and pride*, 25–63. New York: Guilford Press; M. Lewis, S. M. Alessandri, & M. W. Sullivan, Differences in shame and pride as a function of children's gender and task difficulty, 1992, p. 633. *Child Development, 63*, 630–638; M. F. Mascolo & K. W. Fisher, Developmental transformations in appraisals for pride, shame, and guilt, 1995, p. 100. In J. P. Tangney & K. W Fischer (Eds.), *Self-conscious emotions: The psychology of shame, guilt, embarrassment, and pride*, 62–113. New York: Guilford Press.

Defiance is one way infants come to know themselves in relation to other people.
Photo by Michael Newman/PhotoEdit.

Chapter 2). He referred to autonomy (pride, defiance) and shame (doubt, disappointment) as two emotional poles of this developmental phase. We will discuss more about the emotion of defiance in a later section on discipline and compliance.

How Do Infants of This Age Cope with Stress?

At this age, children come to rely on their teddy bears and favorite blankets to comfort themselves in stressful situations and when their parents are not around. Children can become attached to these objects in the sense that they desire constant proximity with the objects and show signs of anxiety and distress when separated from the objects. Studies compared the behavior of children who were attached to a blanket with others who were not (Passman, 1977; Passman & Weisberg, 1975). The children, who ranged in age from 20 to 40 months, were observed individually in a novel play situation with either their mother, their blanket, a favorite toy, or no available objects. There were no differences in exploratory behavior or in the amount of distress between children with their mothers present and blanket-attached children with their blankets. Children in these two situa-

tions performed considerably better (had more exploratory play and less distress) than either non-blanket-attached children with their blankets, all children with only a favorite toy, or children without any objects.

It seems that a 2-year-old may attach himself or herself to a blanket as an effective substitute for the mother, at least for brief periods. There are a number of reasons why this might be true. Blankets are soft and cuddly, and they carry plenty of familiar smells that may remind the child of the comforts of home and impart an increased sense of security.

Children's reliance on blankets as sources of comfort comes at a time when they are becoming aware of their physical and psychological separateness from the caregiver. Although this sense of self as an independent individual does not fully take hold until the third year of life, when the conceptual self emerges (see Chapter 5), the development of the existential self (Chapter 5) at the end of the second year can be thought of as an important transitional phase in the growth of independence. The blanket and other such attachment objects, therefore, have been called **transitional objects** (Mahler, Pine, & Bergman, 1975; Winnicott, 1971), because they seem to serve as an intermediate bridge between a child's total reliance and dependence on the mother and the development of individuation.

Not all children develop blanket attachments. In countries where there is relatively more physical contact between infants and caregivers, a blanket attachment is less likely to develop (Super, 1981). In a study of Italian children, only 4.9% of rural children had transitional object attachments, whereas 31.1% of urban children in Rome had them (Gaddini, 1970). Korean infants used transitional objects less than a matched sample of U.S. infants, and there was less sucking on fingers and pacifiers among the relatively more indulged (compared with North American) Japanese infants (Caudill & Weinstein, 1969; Hong & Townes, 1976). Only 38% of Japanese infants had an object attachment compared to 62% of U.S. infants. While the U.S. infants used their objects when distressed or when sleeping, the Japanese infants were more likely to use the object only at bedtime (Hobara, 2003). It seems that in societies where children have continued access to physical contact with other people, there is little need for transitional objects. On the other hand, in cultures where there is less close physical contact, transitional objects can be effective and adaptive for some children.

There are individual differences in infants' reactions to stressful or frustrating situations. In one study, infants were exposed to a variety of frustrating situations—for instance, a desirable object was placed in a Plexiglas container so the child could not get it, or food was placed nearby but the child could not eat it, or the child was asked to sit for 5 minutes in a highchair. Some children screamed loudly when frustrated, while others showed little or no distress. Those who were more distressed were more likely to act out by hitting, kicking, or banging. These more distressed children were less able to use self-comforting strategies, such as finding something to distract themselves, seeking the mother, or making a constructive attempt to get the toy or the food (S. D. Calkins & Johnson, 1998; Raver, 1996).

The mothers of the more distressed children were also more likely to do things to help the children, rather than letting the children solve the problem themselves. This may be because the mothers know the children will have negative reactions and want to avoid the distress. Or it may be because the mothers never let the children do things on their own, so the children never acquire their own coping skills (S. D. Calkins et al., 1998; S. D. Calkins & Johnson, 1998). On the other hand, if mothers have a history of talking to their infants about their feelings, thereby giving children more of a sense of their own emotional state, the children are better regulated (Taumoepeau & Ruffman, 2006). These findings suggest that the parent plays a crucial role in the development of emotion-regulation skills.

Some evidence suggests that infants of this age who are less able to regulate their negative emotions may have deficits in neurological development that began at an earlier age. Children whose mothers smoked prenatally (see Chapter 9), for example, are more disruptive and less able to self-calm than other infants (Wakschlag et al., 2006). Infants who were less able to establish joint attention with their parents in the first year are more likely to show emotion- regulation difficulties by the end of the second year.

Generally speaking, children of this age adopt the emotion-regulation styles found in their families (Dunsmore & Halberstadt, 1997). In one study of 2-year-olds in a preschool setting, children tended to seek comfort and assistance from caregivers who reported a family history similar to that of the children's mothers. If the mothers had a positive relationship with their own parents in the past and present, their children sought out caregivers who also had a positive relationship with their own parents. Similarly, if the children's parents were conflicted or ambivalent about their own parents, so were the caregivers that the children approached (Shulman, Becker, & Sroufe, 1999).

This finding is rather surprising. One might expect that children whose mothers were more conflicted would turn to more secure adults when given the opportunity. On the other hand, adults typically choose partners who have similar family histories and attachment styles, even when their partners show negative behaviors toward them similar to those that their parents displayed (P. A. Frazier et al., 1996). This work supports the idea that children develop internal working models with expectations for particular kinds of attachment styles and continue to replicate those styles, even when it is not in their best interests. Breaking out of the cycle of difficult interpersonal relationships often requires individual, couple, or family psychotherapy.

These findings show the importance of the parent-infant relationship and the active role of adults in emotion regulation at this age. A transitional object is useful but cannot replace an adult. Children of this age are better able to cope on their own with distress and frustration when an adult is nearby. They typically have limited ability to do this, such as finding alternative objects to play with when the one they want cannot be obtained, as shown in the study just reviewed and in other related research (Grolnick, Bridges, & Connell, 1996). Children of this age do not have the ability to comfort themselves verbally, which appears during the next age period. Even at this age, when children are beginning to acquire language, most of their emotion regulation is accomplished nonverbally. The participatory memories (Chapter 5) of these adult-child regulatory processes may help explain why they have a lasting effect on the formation of later interpersonal relationships.

What Happens to Children During Separations from Their Primary Caregivers?

We already know that when even very young infants are left in the company of familiar substitute caregivers, few problems are seen. Infants quickly adapt to the new situation, and they are able to use the familiar substitute as a secure base for exploration, as well as a source of support and comfort. This is true even though infants almost always prefer their mothers when given the choice.

By the end of the second year, because of cognitive advances related to understanding scripts and sequences, infants can understand that their parents will return after a separation, so they begin to take their own initiatives in separating from the parents. Infants of this age observed with their parents in a public park were not afraid to wander some distance from the parents. Although males left the parents' side more often than females, there were no significant sex differences in how far the children went or how much total time they spent at a distance (Ley & Koepke, 1982).

The situation is different, however, when the parents initiate a separation. This could happen for many reasons. The parents may want to go out in the evening, or they may need to travel away from the child for several days. This is often the age when mothers go into the hospital to have a second child. Other separation occasions include a parent's business trips and even brief hospitalizations for a child who is ill or needs an operation.

Research suggests that separation episodes are more tolerable to the infant if the parent prepares the child for them beforehand. In one study (Weinraub & Lewis, 1977), children were least upset during the separation if the mother explained that she would be leaving and gave the child instructions on what to do in her absence. This was especially true for children who were more developmentally advanced and could better understand the mother's instructions. It also seemed to help the child during the separation if the mother spent more time at a distance, and less time in close physical contact with the infant, in the 3 minutes just prior to the departure.

A somewhat contradictory finding was reported in another study. The longer a mother spent in preparing a child for separation (70 seconds versus 10 seconds), the less content the child remained during the separation (Adams and Passman, 1981). It could be, however, that mothers in this study who were assigned to the 70-second preparation condition also spent more time in close contact with the infant before departure.

In a related study (Lollis, 1990), mothers were instructed to be extremely brief in separating from their infants. They were told to say only, "I'm going to leave for a little while. You stay here and play until I come back." These departures took only about 20 seconds. Another group of mothers were asked to take leave of the infants quickly, but no instructions were given about what the mothers should say. These uninstructed mothers took a bit longer but prepared the infants for the separation more thoroughly. The infants who were prepared more thoroughly fared better during the separation. This suggests that it is not the duration of leavetaking but rather how well the infant is prepared by the parent during this time that is the important factor.

Several other related findings are of interest here. Infants are more predisposed to separate from parents if they are dropped off at a familiar day care setting or preschool, due primarily to the presence of peers already in the setting (Gunnar, Senior, & Hartup, 1984). This suggests that the environment in which the child is left is an important factor in regulating separation protest. Other research has found that infants left at the preschool or day care setting show more protest when dropped off by their mothers than by their fathers. The mothers took longer to leave the children than did the fathers (Field, Gewirtz, et al., 1984).

The best way for parents to prepare their 2-year-olds for a brief separation is to avoid close contact just before they leave, give the children some concrete suggestions about what they might do while the parents are gone, and try to tailor speech to the comprehension level of the infants. Even given this advice, and knowing that children of this age do quite well in brief separations, parents still find it difficult to leave their babies alone in a strange place with a new baby-sitter or to go out on their own for the first time.

No matter how hard parents try to prepare themselves and their children, the children almost inevitably get upset as soon as they understand that their parents are *actually* leaving. Little in the annals of parenthood is more emotionally wrenching than the painful wails of a child being left behind. This phenomenon is called parental separation anxiety. **Parental separation anxiety** afflicts many working mothers and mothers who leave their children behind in day care (Hock & DeMeis, 1990; Jarvis & Creasey, 1991). Both mothers and fathers can experience parental separation anxiety.

One additional finding should provide at least a small measure of comfort to parents or prospective parents. Researchers discovered that the infant's immediate response to the parent's departure was not correlated with anything the parent said or did. Only after this initial response, when the infant finally calmed down, did the baby's behavior begin to reflect the efforts of the parent's work at preparation (Weinraub & Lewis, 1977). Indeed, it seems common for babies of this age to protest loudly during the actual departure of the parent. As soon as it is clear that these protests are ineffective, the 2-year-old generally is capable of quieting down and even enjoying the substitute caregiver.

Perhaps the most striking demonstration of this was offered in a study of children left by their parents in a British residential nursery for several days. The children were provided with a warm and affectionate substitute caregiver. Some of the younger children showed almost no signs of distress or despair, and they gradually became attached to the substitute. Some of the older children in their study—the 4-year-olds—started off their stay with some sadness and a lowered tolerance for frustration, but they were able to use the foster parent to sustain their feelings, and their intimacy with her increased over time. All the children in the study greeted their parents warmly upon their return. It was not the separation per se that caused the problems but the psychosocial environment of the situation in which the child was left. Similar findings have been reported for infants institutionalized over the long term and infants in foster-care situations. The lack of social interaction in the institution was the most important factor accounting for the delayed or disturbed development of some institutionalized infants (Robertson & Robertson, 1971; B. Tizard & Rees, 1974; J. Tizard & Tizard, 1971).

Twenty-Four to Thirty-Six Months

Talking About Emotions

The major feature of emotional development in the third year is that children are more consistently talking about their feelings and labeling emotional and physiological states accurately (Denham, 1986; M. Lewis & Michalson, 1983), they can talk about future and past emotions, and they can discuss the causes and consequences of emotions (Bretherton, Fritz, Zahn-Waxler, & Ridgeway, 1986; Reissland & Harris, 1991). By 28 months, most children have extensive emotion vocabularies for positive emotions (*happy, fun, good time, funny, like, love, feel better, proud*) and negative ones (*sad, scared, mad, yucky, messy, feel bad*). Children from different cultural groups also acquire emotion words around this age (Tardif & Wellman, 2000). Also common across different cultural groups is that children talk about their own and other people's emotions first, and then, about 6 months to 1 year later, begin to talk about their own and others' thoughts (know, think) (Tardif & Wellman, 2000).

Sex differences in emotional communication occur outside the context of which toys are used. Girls talk more spontaneously and earlier in development about their emotions compared to boys (Cervantes & Callanan, 1998; Farver & Wimbarti, 1995). Research suggests that this may also be due partly to differences in parent-child emotional communication. Parents are more likely to respond to their daughters with a similar emotion, creating a shared emotional state (Robinson, Little, & Biringen, 1993). In talking about emotions with daughters, parents are more likely to provide a way to resolve their emotions with another person. With sons, parents more typically encourage the child to resolve the situation on their own. With anger, for example, parents encourage daughters to make up with their friend who took a toy by approaching or playing with the friend. Parents are more likely to encourage sons to retaliate. A daughter's expressed desire to retaliate is discouraged, while a son's desire to retaliate is typically encouraged (Fivush, 1994). Girls are being social-

ized to resolve their emotions within the boundaries of their ongoing relationships. Boys, on the other hand, are expected to be autonomous and to stand up for themselves.

Understanding Other People and Their Emotions

As we saw in Chapter 5, the development of self-understanding and self-concept develops in parallel with the development of understanding others. Children of this age are developing categories for other people, describing others' emotions, and understanding that other people have emotions and states of mind. These findings raise the question of whether infants of this age have a **theory of mind**, an understanding that other people have psychological states, and that those states may be different from their own.

In addition to labeling their own emotions, 2-year-olds can talk about the emotions of other people (Bretherton et al., 1986; Hoffman, 1975; Radke-Yarrow & Zahn-Waxler, 1984). Types of emotion talk about self and others are shown in Table 7.8.

Children of this age also appear to have a sense of empathy toward others. Two-year-olds are visibly affected by the emotions of others. In an experimental situation, children observed an experimenter having either an angry or a pleasant conversation with their mother. In the angry situation, the children expressed concern for their mother, sought her reassurance, and tried to comfort her (Cummings, Pellegrini, Notarius, & Cummings, 1989). Children of this age also show "concerned attention" toward others who are in distress, combined with helpful initiatives toward the other person and attempts to elicit help from bystanders (R. A. Thompson, 1998).

In general, girls show more caring and concern for the distress of others than boys do. In play sessions with peers, boys show slightly more anger than girls, but the differences are not strong (Malatesta-Magai et al., 1994). Children of mothers with severe depression show more caring behavior than children of nondepressed mothers,

TABLE 7.8   Statements of Emotion Made by Two-Year-Olds

Positive	I give a hug. Baby be happy.
	I laugh at funny man.
	I not cry now. I happy.
	Mommy exercise. Mommy having a good time.
Negative	Me fall down. Me cry.
	It's dark. I'm scared.
	No cry, Mama. It will be all right.
	I feel bad. My tummy hurts.
	Mommy, you went away. I was sad.
	He's sad. He'll be happy when his daddy comes home.
	I'm mad at you, Daddy. I'm going away, good-bye.
	If you go on vacation again, I'll cry.

Source: I. Bretherton, J. Fritz, C. Zahn-Waxler, & D. Ridgeway, Learning to talk about emotions: A functionalist perspective, 1988. *Child Development, 57*, 529–548.

perhaps because the children have had to prematurely attend to the emotional states of others in order to get attention in return (Radke-Yarrow, Zahn-Waxler, Richardson, Susman, & Martinez, 1994). It is not uncommon for children of this age to blame themselves for their mother's depressed feelings (thinking that their mother's feeling is the result of something the child did) (R. A. Thompson, 1998). Observations with peers suggests that children show more empathy with a peer's distress if it was the child himself or herself that caused the distress (Demetriou & Hay, 2004).

In one experiment, children of this age were given a doll that would break as soon as they began to play with it. Most of the children reacted to the planned mishap with frustration, shame, anger, or sadness, and they attempted to correct the problem by putting the doll back together. On the other hand, children of depressed mothers were more likely to suppress their frustrations by showing more solicitude toward their depressed parent. It seems that children of depressed mothers may become disconnected from their own feelings in an attempt to protect their parent from undue emotional arousal (Cole, Barrett, & Zahn-Waxler, 1992).

On the other hand, children who score high on tests of understanding others' emotions are more likely to come from families in which there is frequent talk about feelings and the causes of feelings, in which children have an opportunity to observe parents talking with siblings about their feelings and behavior, in which children are encouraged to cooperate with their siblings during coordinated play, and in which there is a secure attachment with the mother (J. Dunn, 1998; Garner, 2003; McElwain & Volling, 2004; Ruffman, Slade & Crowe, 2002; Watson, Painter, & Bornstein, 2001). It seems that emotional understanding of others not related to guilt is facilitated in families in which emotional discourse occurs between all the members.

Some research suggests that children who are temperamentally inhibited or overly uninhibited are less likely to show understanding of others' feelings (Carlson, Mandell, & Williams, 2004; Chasiotis et al., 2006; S. K. Young, Fox, & Zahn-Waxler, 1999), but it is not clear how much of this inhibition can be explained by the family processes mentioned above. Children who are either inhibited or overly active may be less susceptible to observing the nuances of family emotional dialogues. They may require a more directive style of parental teaching in order to understand others' emotions (Zahn-Waxler & Robinson, 1995).

These findings suggest that children's concept of self and emotional states of self are associated with their relationships to other people. Children of this age are aware of multiple forms of self-other relationships (P. J. Miller et al., 1992). They can talk about sharing activity with others ("We went down by the pool"), distinguish themselves as part of a relationship ("No one was holding my hand"; "You were far away"), and **metacommu-nicate** about their interpersonal relationships with others ("I hate Leslie"; "He wanted to play with me"). This suggests that the categorical self forms as part of a network of interpersonal relationships such that individuality is always defined in terms of one's connections, relations, similarities, and differences (Fogel, 1993).

Other findings also support this view that children can understand some aspects of others' mental states. Three-year-olds—both boys and girls—can modify their speech in the form of motherese when talking to a baby (J. Dunn & Kendrick, 1981; Shatz & Gelman, 1973). Children as young as 3 years are able to describe the kinds of things you might do to take care of a baby (Melson, Fogel, & Toda, 1986). When asked to show a picture to another person, 3-year-olds turned the picture around to face that person (Lempers, Flavell, & Flavell, 1977). Children of this age were more likely to gesture toward a "lost" object when they knew that the parent was unaware of the object's location than when the parent was aware of the location (O'Neill, 1996; Tomasello, Call, & Gluckman, 1997), suggesting that children of this age not only recognize but understand the intentions of other people.

These studies show that children have an understanding of some of the needs of other people that go beyond other's emotions and may include their mental state or level, but they do not demonstrate conclusively that 3-year-olds have a theory of mind. A child can copy the parent's speech to a baby brother or sister or just describe what others do for a baby. Attempts to comfort a hurt adult have to be looked at with respect not only to what the child says (Table 7.8) but also to what the child actually does. Two-year-olds often try to comfort adults with blankets, bottles, and pacifiers, suggesting that the children may be trying to calm their own upset by stopping the crying of the adult (Hoffman, 1975). The use of emotion language could perhaps refer to facial expressions and actions of other people that the children have come to label in a particular way without realizing that others have feelings like themselves.

You do not have to presume that the child understands that other people have minds or feelings, and some scholars suggest that genuine empathy for others does not begin to develop until 4 or 5 years of age (Hoffman, 1975; Selman, 1980). Adults, for example, can operate computers just by following instructions without having any notion at all of what makes computers work. Similarly, 2-year-olds who are exposed to robot toys that respond to them and talk to them will enter into conversations with the robots, apparently without thinking about how the robots work or what the robots might be feeling (P. J. Dunham, Dunham, Tran, & Akhtar, 1991).

On the other hand, evidence in favor of a rudimentary theory of mind comes from studies of the development of the ability to deceive others. Three-year-old children were left alone in a room with what they were told was a surprise toy. They were asked not to peek while the experimenter left the room. Observed from behind a one-way mirror, almost all of the children peeked, but when the experimenter returned and asked, "Did you peek?" only 38% of those who peeked admitted that they had done so. The ones who confessed showed little change in facial expression. The ones who actually peeked but said they had not peeked showed an increase in smiling, while those who peeked but refused to answer the question showed an increase in nervous self-touching (Lewis, Stanger, & Sullivan, 1989).

Do these differences in facial expression suggest that children may be aware of what adults are thinking; that is, do the children assume that the adult believes they peeked and therefore try to change the adult's beliefs? In a related study (Chandler, Fritz, & Hala, 1989; Hala, Chandler, & Fritz, 1991), children were asked to hide a treasure from an experimenter. They could do this in a number of ways: by covering up the trail to the treasure, by creating false leads about where the treasure was hidden if the experimenter asked for help, and by lying. Children as young as 2 ½ years used all three strategies, suggesting that they were acting to create a false belief in the adult. To create a false belief, you have to have a theory of mind; that is, you have to assume that others are capable of holding some beliefs. According to the authors, the children "not only slyly lied and disingenuously misled, but they did so with what often amounted to disarming delight in leading others astray" (Chandler et al., 1989, p. 1275).

Nevertheless, even though a case can be made that children of this age have a theory of mind, it is likely to be a rather simple theory, something like: "Adults will believe what I want them to believe, and they can't really tell that I'm trying to deceive them." In other words, children of this age probably believe that adults are in some ways extensions of themselves and entirely in tune with their wishes.

According to P. L. Harris (1989), children need the following abilities in order to have a genuine theory of mind: self-awareness, the capacity for pretending, and the ability to distinguish reality from pretending. We know that by the beginning of the third year, most children have both self-awareness and the ability to pretend. These factors are necessary because, as Harris suggests, a theory of mind requires one to imagine that others have feelings like one's own. Because we have no direct confirmation of another's feelings, we have to imagine what someone might feel under certain circumstances.

What 3-year-olds lack, however, is the ability to separate pretend from reality (R. P. Hobson, 1991; Woolley & Cox, 2007). Until children can do this, they will see others as mere extensions of their own desires. How do we know children of this age cannot always separate reality from fantasy? One study found that when adults entered into a child's pretend game, the child became confused about the difference. A mother pretended to hold up an umbrella and suggested to her 30-month-old son that he hold out his hand to feel the rain. He did this and then very soberly looked at the palms of his hands to see if they were wet (DeLoache & Plaetzer, 1985). Another child, while playing at cooking, turned to a peer and said, "This is pretend, right?" (Slade, 1986). Another was pretending to be a monster by making growling noises.

She became afraid of the noises she herself made and began to cry (DiLalla & Watson, 1988).

Of course, children in the third year can sometimes make the fantasy-reality distinction, but it would be more accurate to say that they are never really sure which is which. A greater feeling of certainty does not emerge until the age of 4 years, and therefore, it is not until this age that children solidify a theory of mind, an appreciation of the feelings and desires of others as independent from their own (P. L. Harris, 1989, 1998). In language, children before the fourth year do not produce words representing conditional or temporary states, such as *could* and *would* as opposed to *can* and *will* (Kuczaj & Maratsos, 1983). By the age of 4 years, a child might say to a younger sibling, "You don't get it. It's just pretend. I could have fooled you!" On the other hand, at the beginning of the third year, it is fair to say that children begin to catch glimmers of the differences between self and other as part of their ongoing social interactions.

Positive Emotion: Laughter

During the third year of life, toddlers become more active and child-like when participating in social relationships with others. One way this occurs is by an increasingly sophisticated repertory of emotional forms of communication. The research I have done with my colleagues shows this pattern with respect to the development of laughter in the third year (Nwokah, Davies, Islam, Hsu, & Fogel, 1993). Recall that infants can produce different types of smiles (Duchenne, or cheek-raise, smiles, and play, or jaw-drop, smiles). We found that these different types of smiles are associated with specific types of social communicative situations during the first year of life. Duchenne smiles are more likely with peekaboo games, for example, and play smiles with tickling games. A similar pattern occurs with laughter. Three-year-old children have different types of laughs—called comment, chuckle, rhythmical, and squeal—and each laugh is associated with a specific type of communicative situation (Nwokah et al., 1993).

A *comment laugh* is brief and sounds like an exclamation; typically, it follows a funny action on the part of the mother. Here is an example of a communicative situation for a comment laugh:

Mother and Betsy are playing with a toy picnic set. Betsy starts to open a bag of plastic potato chips. Mother makes a pretend, sad face and says quietly and wistfully, "Are you gonna share the chips with me?" Betsy replies, "Yeah." Mother opens her mouth, smiles, and says, "Okay," as she throws her head back and laughs. Betsy watches, smiles, and gives a short comment laugh while turning to peek into the chip bag.

A *chuckle laugh* is soft with a low tone and reflects mild amusement. Chuckles occur in situations involving more excitement than the situations that evoke comment laughs. The following is an example from our data:

Betsy is standing and puts a toy doll's feeding bottle into her own mouth. Mother says, "Yukk!" and attempts to grab the bottle from Betsy's mouth. Betsy quickly pulls backward and sits down so mother misses. As Betsy sits down she emits a chuckle laugh with a wide grin, but keeps the bottle in her mouth, continuing to look at mother.

A *rhythmical laugh* is the longest type of laughter; it consists of a series of regularly spaced syllables (ha-ha-ha). Rhythmical laughs occur in a wide variety of highly arousing situations, usually when both partners are laughing:

Mother has a Daffy Duck puppet on her hand. Betsy is lying on her back on the floor and mother makes the puppet talk. Betsy says, "Shut up, Daffy Duck!" Mother then tickles Betsy's leg with the puppet. Betsy makes a rhythmical laugh as she tries to roll away, her eyes half closed and her mouth wide open.

Finally, a *squeal laugh* is a long, high, shrill sound. The following example illustrates its occurrence:

Betsy is holding a puppet while lying on her stomach. Mother, while smiling, moves her hand slowly to the puppet to get hold of it. Betsy gives a squeal laugh as mother touches the puppet. Betsy's head is raised with a wide open mouth smile.

As this research shows, children use laughter and other facial expressions and body movements, along with words, to express their positive feelings. These findings also show an increasing awareness of the emotions of self and other.

Negative Emotions: Anger, Shame, and Sadness

By the third year, children are becoming increasingly skilled at regulating their emotion expression depending upon the situation. Children of this age are more likely to show negative emotions when with their parents, and more likely to show sadness when they have their parent's attention (Buss & Kiel, 2004). Children are also more likely to show their bad feelings with their parents if they have a history of successfully talking about and sharing those feelings with that parent (Spinrad et al., 2004).

One study compared emotion regulation in two different cultural groups from Nepal. The Tamang group expects their children to be socially graceful and never angry. The Brahman group expects their children to show a sense of pride and superior bearing as reflects their high social caste. Findings show that Tamang children who are angry are rebuked, while if they show shame the parents are more likely to yield to their demands and reason with the child. The Brahman parents, however, yield to and reason with the angry child but ignore the child's shame (Cole, Tamang, & Shrestha, 2006). These findings show that children's emotion is increasingly shaped by the social environment, so that children are learning what they can express, when, and to whom.

One form of anger is physical aggression, such as hitting, kicking, and biting. The rate of normal physical aggression is higher between the ages of 24 and 36 months than at any other time in the life course. Children show individual differences in aggression that remain stable over several years, with some children showing more and others less or no aggression. Boys show more aggression overall (Alink et al., 2006; Persson, 2005). These differences may be the result of social regulatory processes such as those discussed above, particularly since parents, and especially fathers, engage in more physical play with boys (Lindsey & Mize, 2001).

Finally, by this age, children are beginning to show longer-lasting mood states. The first signs of depression appear at this age. Depressed 3-year-olds are sadder, grouchier, more whiney, have poorer appetites, more sleep problems, and more trouble concentrating than non-depressed peers. The depressed children expressed the feeling that nothing was "fun" (Luby et al., 2003). These symptoms are similar to those of depressed older children and adults. It is one of the downsides of having a categorical self and autobiographical memory (Chapter 5) that children can begin to identity with their own negative feelings and realize that they have a long-lasting negative mood state.

In summary, emotion becomes increasingly social as it is subject to labeling and explicit regulation by others. The ways adults respond to happy expressions versus temper tantrums ultimately affect the child's own emotional understanding. In general, research suggests that adults should accept children's emotions as genuine expressions of feeling, while working toward changing the manner in which the emotion is expressed or talked about ("I can see that you're angry, but I don't permit throwing things in the house"). The general principles for dealing with emotions are the same as those discussed in the previous chapter for guided participation: accept the child's initiative (even if this is negative) and then find ways to encourage the child into culturally and socially acceptable forms of expression (Demos, 1982; Lewis & Michalson, 1983; Rogoff, 1990). As children understand more about their own and other's emotions, it enhances the development of the categorical self.

THE DEVELOPMENT OF ATTACHMENT

Attachment Theory

Attachment refers to a lasting emotional tie between people such that the individual strives to maintain closeness to the object of attachment and acts to ensure that the relationship continues. The process by which infants develop lasting, affectionate emotional ties to adults over the first few years of life has been the subject of a great deal of scientific research. Before reviewing the findings of these studies, let us first look at some of the theoretical perspectives on how attachment develops.

Psychoanalytic theory suggests that attachment is the normal resolution of the oral stage of development (see Chapter 2). If the id's oral urges are gratified regularly during the first few months of life, the baby will develop the expectation that needs can be met and that distress will not continue for long without some relief.

After the baby is 2 or 3 months old, parents begin to notice that the baby's cry is a little less urgent when the baby is hungry or tired. At this time, psychoanalytic theory prescribes that the parents should wait a short time before responding to the baby. If the baby calms down, the parents have allowed the baby to meet this small crisis with his or her own resources. Not only do these minor frustrations lead the baby toward self-control, but they also make the baby aware of the person who is responsible for satisfying the oral needs. This awareness gradually expands into a dependency on that particular person and later into affection, attachment, and trust.

Learning theory has focused not on the feelings or concepts of the infant, but on the behaviors observed when caregivers and infants are together. Caregivers seek positive reinforcements from their

An attachment relationship is one in which each partner seeks to maintain physical and emotional closeness to the other.
Photo by Elizabeth Crews.

infants. For example, when parents pick up a baby, they expect the baby to become calm or to smile. When parents feed the baby, they expect the baby to coo and gurgle. When these positive reinforcements occur, the frequency of the same parental actions is increased on future occasions, which in turn reinforces the calming down, smiling, cooing, and gurgling of the baby. Learning theory, therefore, predicts that attachment behaviors develop by a complex process of mutual reinforcements (Cairns, 1979; Gewirtz, 1972).

Behavior ecology theory suggests that adults have inherited some kinds of caregiving responses that are triggered in the presence of infants and young children and that infants are innately drawn to particular aspects of the caregiver. In a classic study of the maternal-infant feedback system in infant monkeys (Harlow & Harlow, 1965), the babies were provided one "mother" made of wire mesh with a milk bottle attached and another "mother" of the same size made of wire covered with a soft cloth. The monkeys took food from the wire mother but spent almost all of the rest of the time with the softer mother substitute. In fearful situations, the monkeys clung to the soft mother and, when they got older, were even seen to carry the cloth mother around as a security object.

For monkeys, contrary to the predictions of psychoanalytic theory, physical contact with the mother is more important than food in the formation of attachments. Contrary to the predictions of learning theory, infant monkeys became attached to the soft object (an innate preference) and not to the object that gave positive reinforcement—the food-giving wire mother.

Studies of human infants (Schaffer & Emerson, 1964) have shown that they are most attached to the people who play and interact with them. Some babies who live in extended families with many siblings and who have mothers who concentrated primarily on caretaking tasks such as feeding and diapering are less attached to the mother than to any aunt, uncle, or older sibling who spent the most time playing with the baby. This suggests that attachment in humans is based more on social interaction and communication than on feeding or physical contact as predicted by psychoanalytic theory.

Dissatisfaction with the psychoanalytic and learning theory accounts of attachment led John Bowlby (1969) to develop a behavior ecology theory of attachment in humans. Bowlby suggested that mutual responsiveness and attraction between adults and infants resulted not because of mutual reinforcements but because the physical appearance and behavior of both the adult and the infant innately attract the other. Table 7.5 shows the stages in the development of attachment as proposed by Bowlby.

The newborn and small infant's physical appearance, called *babyishness*, elicits protective responses from adults. Babies also have a host of behaviors, such as crying, sucking, smiling, looking at the caregiver preferentially, following the adult around, and becoming distressed when the adult leaves, that have the net effect of orienting the caregiver to the infant and increasing the time that the infant spends in proximity to the caregiver. Because of the universality of this mutual attraction and its importance for survival, attachment can be thought of neurologically as experience-expectant (see Chapter 5) because neurological processes exist at birth that require the presence of an adult (Barnett, Butler, & Vondra, 1999; Schore, 2003). The way attachment forms over the first years of life—whether it is secure or insecure, and to whom—is experience-dependent affecting both brain and behavior (Schore, 2003).

Bowlby suggests that as the infant develops cognitively, attachment shifts from relying on innate responses to any adult to identifying and recognizing a particular adult and seeking that adult in an intentional, goal-oriented manner. This facet of attachment is neurologically experience-dependent because the child's developmental history plays a role in the nature of his or her attachment to the parent (Barnett et al., 1999). The baby establishes a goal of maintaining proximity to the parent and uses information about the parent's present and past movements, as well as his or her own locomotor skills and current needs, to keep the parent within view or to seek contact when needed.

By 8 or 9 months of age, because of the developments in goal-oriented action and emotion reviewed earlier in this chapter, infants begin to develop some of the same kinds of emotional feelings of closeness to the parents that the parents had felt for the infant since before the birth. We know this because infants of this age begin

TABLE 7.9 Stages in the Development of Attachment (Bowlby, 1969)

Approximate Age (Months)	Stage	Description
0–2 and over	Orientation to signals without discrimination of a figure	The infant shows orientation to social stimuli—grasping, reaching, smiling, and babbling. The baby will cease to cry when picked up or when he or she sees a face. These behaviors increase when the baby is in proximity to a companion, although the baby cannot distinguish one person from another.
1–6 and over	Orientation to signals directed toward one or more discriminated figures	Orientation behaviors similar to those in Stage I appear, but they are markedly directed toward the primary caregiver. Evidence of discrimination begins at 1 month for auditory and at 2½ months for visual stimuli.
6–30 and over	Maintenance of proximity to a discriminated figure by means of locomotion as well as signals	The repertoire of responses to people increases to include following a departed mother, greeting her on return, and using her as a base for exploration. Strangers are treated with caution and may evoke alarm and withdrawal; others may be selected as additional attachment figures (e.g., fathers).
24–28 and over	Formation of a goal-corrected partnership	The child begins to acquire insight into the mother's feelings and goals, which leads to cooperative interaction and partnership.

Source: Adapted from J. Bowlby, *Attachment and loss: Vol. 1. Attachment*, 1969. New York: Basic Books.

to display affectionate responses to the parents. During reunions after brief separations, 1-year-olds feel genuinely happy to see the parent and may approach briefly for a hug or kiss (Sroufe, 1979). Infants will follow the parent and may be distressed at separation.

Bowlby's theory has been refined and expanded by others. Mary Ainsworth, who studied attachment in Uganda and North America (Ainsworth, 1979), suggests that there is a distinction between the **attachment system** (the network of feelings and cognitions related to the object of attachment) and **attachment behavior** (the overt signals such as crying and following that bring the parent and child into close proximity). She points out that each child's attachment system may be expressed through behavior in a unique way. For example, if a baby does not get upset when his or her mother leaves, it does not indicate a lack of attachment. Rather, it may indicate the infant's relative feelings of security to carry on temporarily without the mother present.

Assessment of Attachment

Ainsworth believed that virtually all infants are attached to their parents but differ in the sense of security they feel in relation to the adult. The ease with which a distressed infant feels comforted by a caregiver is called the *quality of attachment* and has four basic patterns: securely attached, insecurely attached-resistant, insecurely attached-avoidant, and disorganized-disoriented (Ainsworth, Bell, & Stayton, 1971, Ainsworth et al., 1978; Main & Solomon, 1986).

Attachment quality is assessed in the Ainsworth Strange Situation Test (ASST), in which infants are observed with their caregivers in an unfamiliar playroom (Ainsworth & Bell, 1970). The test consists of eight episodes:

1. Parent and infant are brought to the observation room by the observer.
2. Parent and infant play together for several minutes.
3. Parent and infant play with an unfamiliar adult.
4. The mother leaves the baby with the stranger for 3 minutes.
5. The stranger leaves, and the mother returns.
6. The mother leaves the baby alone.
7. The stranger returns without the mother.
8. The stranger leaves, and the mother is reunited with her baby.

The ASST and the four types of attachment quality by which infants can be classified have been shown to be highly reliable and valid. Test-retest reliability has been found in middle-class North American samples (Waters, 1983). This means that a baby who is classified as securely attached at one age will typically remain so at later ages—but not always.

An infant who demonstrates **secure attachment** will seek comfort from the caregiver during the reunion (episode 8) and, once comforted, will return to independent play. Securely attached infants show interest in objects and in the stranger and will get acquainted with the unfamiliar setting by making brief forays, always returning to the adult's side, using the caregiver as a secure base from which to explore. Such infants will feel comfortable and secure in most situations.

There are two types of insecure attachments. Infants who demonstrate **insecure-resistant** attachment have a more difficult time feeling comfortable in a strange situation. They will vacillate between mother and an interesting object, but once near the object, they will not explore as freely as will the securely attached infants. The resistant infant is more wary of strangers and tends to get more upset when the mother leaves the room. During the reunion, such infants show ambivalent responses to the mother, first approaching her and then pushing her away. Insecure-resistant infants (also called insecure-ambivalent) tend to be temperamentally vulnerable to stress, have limited coping skills, have mothers who are inconsistently available, and have limited skills at independent exploratory behavior (Cassidy, 1994; Cassidy & Berlin, 1994).

Infants who display **insecure-avoidant attachment** tend not to be upset when left with an unfamiliar person or in a strange setting. During the reunion episode, they may avoid approaching caregivers for comfort and may actively resist any attempts to be comforted by turning away and squirming to get down if picked up. Insecurely attached–avoidant infants seem neutral in their emotions regarding the mother. However, this apparent calm may be superficial. These infants show a pattern of physiological arousal indicative of masked anger (Cassidy, 1994; Spangler & Grossman, 1993).

The first three types of attachment, both secure and insecure, are considered to be within the normal range of functioning. You can begin to get a sense of your own attachment style by doing the Experiential Exercises of this chapter. You can also use the criteria for each of the three attachment styles above as a guide to think about the attachment patterns in your current relationships with parents or romantic partners.

Disorders of Attachment

In some cases, attachment patterns are so severely disturbed that they will typically require the intervention of a Parent-Infant Mental Health specialist (see Chapter 9) because the problems are too difficult for the family to handle alone. One type of disturbed attachment can be assessed in the ASST at the final reunion with the parent. Infants who exhibit **disorganized-disoriented attachment** display contradictory behavior during the ASST. The infant may give a broad smile and then abruptly turn away from the mother. Or the infant may approach the mother by crawling backward toward her with gaze averted from her. Other infants may have frozen postures during reunion, sitting and staring at a wall or sucking their thumbs. Although this pattern of attachment occurs considerably less often than the first three, it is very disturbing to watch these infants.

Almost all infants who show this type of attachment come from families with a history of child abuse, maltreatment, maternal psychopathology, infant malnutrition, and/or alcoholism. Characteristics of parents whose infants display disorganized-disoriented attachment include giving contradictory signals to the infant, being frightening to the infants, being frightened by the infant, intrusive or abuse behavior toward the infant, seductive or sexual behavior toward the infant, or acting emotionally distant from the infant (Carlson et al., 1989; Forbes et al., 2007; Madigan et al., 2006; Main & Solomon, 1985; O'Conner, Sigman, & Brill, 1987; Pipp-Siegel, Seigel, & Dean, 1999; Valenzuela, 1990).

Because parental behavior in this type of attachment relationship is so disturbed, it is not surprising that infants develop severe and disturbed reactions. These infants tend to show hostile, aggressive, and other maladaptive behaviors when they enter preschool, and they are at risk for developing psychopathology when they get older (Forbes et al., 2007; van Ijzendoorn et al., 1992; Lyons-Ruth, Alpern, & Repacholi, 1993).

Two other types of attachment disturbance are assessed outside the ASST, typically by a Mental Health Specialist to whom the child is referred. **Reactive attachment disorder (RAD)** is a standard psychiatric diagnosis (DSM-IV 313.89). It begins before age 5 and is marked by one of two types of patterns: (1) *Inhibitions*. The child is excessively inhibited, hypervigilant, or ambivalent and contradictory. The child may, for example, respond to caregivers with frozen vigilance, mixed approach-avoidance, and resistance to comforting. This type of RAD is similar to disorganized-disoriented attachment. (2) *Disinhibitions*. The child shows indiscriminate sociability with inability to form appropriate selective attachments. The child may, for example, be overly familiar with strangers, show seductive or manipulative or other inappropriate behavior, or lack the ability to become attached to any particular attachment figure.

This disorder is always associated with disturbances in parental care, such as failure to meet the child's physical or emotional needs, abuse and neglect, and changes in caregivers—such as going from one foster home to another—so that no stable attachment can form. Children with RAD can be disturbing to be with. They can be unpredictable and they don't respond to social overtures. They can appear to "look right through you," as if they do not have an awareness of other people's emotions. As they get older, they can become violent with caregivers, animals, or other children. They are prone to lying and stealing and may show sexually inappropriate behavior. Treatment is difficult and there are relatively few centers that are equipped to handle RAD cases (see www.radkid. org for more information).

Separation anxiety disorder (DSM-IV 309.21) is one of a number of psychiatric anxiety disorders. It is much more severe than the typical separation anxiety felt by most infants. A child diagnosed with this disorder refuses to be separated from the parent, even to go to bed, and has excessive distress when not at home with parents. The behavior must be intense, last at least 1 month, and be inappropriate for the child's age in order to meet the criteria for diagnosis. It is more prevalent in children who can voice their concerns verbally. This disorder is more likely if the child is temperamentally inhibited or if one parent or close relative has panic disorder or another form of severe anxiety.

Separation anxiety disorder must be diagnosed by a Mental Health Specialist, but even some normally functioning infants become anxious at separation. Whether the child is diagnosed with this disorder or not, parents and caregivers can ease the anxiety over separation using some of the simple strategies shown in Table 7.6.

Brain development in infancy is especially experience-dependent upon relationships with caregivers. Because infants are relatively helpless to get their needs met, according to Bowlby's theory, they require another person on whom to rely for basic soothing, protection, and love. The infant brain is primarily a social, rather than a cognitive, organ, designed to seek out faces and voices at birth in experience-expectant ways, and also designed to develop feelings and behaviors that orient them toward safety and security in an experience-dependent fashion.

Disturbances of attachment lead to experience-dependent pathologies in infant brain development, particularly in the right limbic and prefrontal areas responsible for emotion regulation and feelings of safety. Inconsistent or frightening parenting creates patterns of neuroception of mobilization (fight or flight) or immobilization (freezing). The result is that the hypothalamus generates stress homones through the HPA axis that lead to an overproduction of cortisol, which then leads to changes in receptors for stress and fear in the right hippocampus and amygdala that become hypersensitive to fearfulness. Finally, the right prefrontal cortex becomes damaged so that normal pathways of emotion regulation, such as by seeking assistance and care from other people, are not available (see Chapter 5; Schore, 2003).

Maladaptive strategies for emotion regulation, such as those described in the behavior patterns of disorganized and RAD infants, become predominant. There is also an impairment of self-awareness and a failure to develop *subjective self-awareness* (discussed earlier). Because the pathologies of attachment are not only behavioral, but also physiologically based in neuron-hormonal cellular structures and pathways, they take a long time and special efforts to treat. Early intervention is much more successful at dealing with attachment problems (see Chapter 9) than waiting until later in life

Antecedents of Attachment

What are the possible causes of secure and insecure attachments at 1 year of age? There are three possible explanations: variations in the parent's ability to create a warm and sensitive relationship with the baby during the first year, temperamental factors in the child that no parental response can change, and issues that arise in the relationship between parent and infant that cannot be attributed directly to either one of them.

Because Bowlby's theory focuses on the mother-infant relationship as the source of attachment, Ainsworth and others have predicted that sensitive maternal behavior toward the infant will be one of the main causes of secure attachment. Many studies have shown that the more responsive

TABLE 7.8   Ways to Help an Infant With Separation Anxiety

Have baby-sitters come before the child develops stranger anxiety. If you leave your baby with a sitter for short periods when they respond well to any caring person, they'll become accustomed to being with different people.

Schedule separations after naps or feedings. Babies are more susceptible to separation anxiety when they're tired or hungry.

Have a consistent primary caregiver. If you hire a caregiver, try to keep him or her on the job from the baby's infancy into toddlerhood.

Practice separation for brief periods and short distances, increasing as the child can tolerate it. Praise the child for managing well. If your baby initiates separation by going into another (babyproofed) room, wait a few minutes before going after him; this will enhance his sense of independence.

Make new surroundings familiar. Let your child become comfortable with new surroundings with you present. The first time you leave a child with a relative, for example, shouldn't be the first time you and the child have visited that relative's house. Allow your child to bring a favorite object of hers or yours.

Develop a "goodbye" ritual. Rituals are reassuring and can be as simple as a special wave through the window or a special kiss.

Have a calm, positive attitude. Babies and toddlers are sensitive to your moods and will pick up any tension in your voice, face, touch, or gestures. And don't give in to the child's tears, which are a ploy to get you to stay. If you keep running back when your baby fusses at being without you, that just reinforces the anxious behavior.

Tell your child when you go that you are leaving and that you will return. Then go. Don't stall or repeat goodbyes; that will just make your child more anxious and clingy. Tell the child where youre going and when you'll be back in terms he can understand. Conversely, don't sneak away without saying goodbye; that will undermine the child's sense that she can rely on you.

the mother is to the infant's needs at 3 months, such as during face-to-face play or in responding relatively soon to the infant's cries, the more likely the baby is to be securely attached at 1 year (Ainsworth, Bell, & Stayton, 1971; Belsky, Rovine, & Taylor, 1984; Blehar, Lieberman, & Ainsworth, 1977; Carmen et al., 1993; De Wolff & van Ijzendoorn, 1997; Grossman et al., 1985; Pedersen & Moran, 1996; Posada et al., 2004; Tomlinson et al., 2005). Related research has revealed similar maternal factors during the first year that are associated with attachment at 12 months. For example, there is a relationship between secure attachment and maternal tender style, including a moderate tempo of speech, expressions of quiet pleasure, few directives, no impatience, even attentiveness, prompt soothing, and general responsiveness to all types of infant behavior. Reciprocal and mutually rewarding social interactions are also associated with secure attachment. Infants and mothers who show coordinated joint attention are more likely to

be securely attached. These links between maternal sensitive and infant attachment appear to be similar across different cultural and ethnic groups (Bakermans-Kranenburg et al., 2004; Grossman et al., 1985; Isabella, 1993; 1998; Isabella & Belsky, 1989; Isabella & Belsky, 1991; Schölmerich et al., 1995; Schölmerich et al., 1997; Vereijken, Riksen-Walraven, & Kondo-Ikemura, 1997).

Behavior ecology theory does not expect all mothers to be equally sensitive. According to this theory, the parent's investment in time and effort toward the child must be balanced by an investment in the parent's own survival. In cases where the mother is under stress, living in poverty, is depressed, or has limited physical or emotional resources, behavior ecology theory predicts that the infant will adapt by displaying more demanding and dependent behavior. Insecure patterns of attachment, therefore, are just as adaptive from the perspective of survival as secure attachment patterns (Thompson, 1995). This means that the "causes" of security or insecurity are not "in" the mother's handling of the infant but rather "in" the relationship between the mother and her ecological context: her family of origin, her relationship with her husband, economic status, job, neighborhood, and other mesosystem, exosytem, and macrosystem factors (Belsky, 1995; Hrdy, 1999; Thompson, 1995). This perspective takes the blame away from the mother and leads one to examine the larger systems in which the mother lives.

This systems perspective is supported by a number of findings. First of all, factors in the mother's family affect attachment. Mothers who perceive themselves as having little control over their children's behavior and who suffer from depressed moods are more likely to have insecurely attached infants. These maternal behaviors are the result of family history factors (Donovan & Leavitt, 1989; Isabella, 1998; Izard et al., 1991; Smith & Pederson, 1988; Teti et al., 1995). The disturbed behavior of mothers of disorganized- disoriented infants can also be explained by trauma, harsh punishment, and/or sexual abuse in the mother's early history (Lyons-Ruth, Bronfman, & Parsons, 1999). Finally, the mother's ability to be insightful about her infant's state of mind, her "reflective function," predicts infant attachment security versus insecurity on the one hand, and is predicted by the mother's own attachment to her parents and early history of trauma on the other (Bernier & Dozier, 2003; Fonagy & Target, 2005).

In such cases, one can clearly see a pattern of intergenerational transmission of psychopathology. The parent's attachment to his or her own parents can be assessed using the Adult Attachment Interview. The parent's rating of security or insecurity with regard to his or her own parents is moderately associated with the child's attachment to them, as assessed in the ASST at 12 months (Steele, Steele, & Fonagy, 1996).

Contributing to the systems perspective, infant behavior can also affect the mother's behavior, and hence attachment. Infant temperament as well as colic and feeding problems may mediate the mother's responsiveness. It is possible that a mother who has a fussy baby might respond to the baby less often simply because she has learned that her interventions are not always effective. Lack of security of attachment may therefore reflect primarily an inborn inability on the part of the baby to regulate distress and a heightened feeling of anxiety or wariness, and only secondarily an effect of the mother's behavior (Chatoor et al., 1998; Goldsmith & Alansky, 1987; Isabella, 1993; Lamb et al., 1984; Rosen & Rothbaum, 1993).

Some studies suggest that infant temperament is a direct predictor of attachment (Seifer et al., 1996). For example, temperamental fearfulness is related to resistant behavior in the strange situation (Thompson, Connell, & Bridges, 1988). Children who at 3 months were less sociable and preferred playing with toys to playing with people were more likely to be scored as avoidant at 12 months, and vice versa; infants who were more likely to attend to their mothers and who were better co-regulated with them at 3 months were more likely to be secure at 12 months (Beebe et al., Lewis & Feiring, 1989; Völker, 2007). Infant negative emotionality is also associated with insecure attachment (Seifer et al., 2004; Vaughn et al., 1992). Some scholars have suggested that whether the child is secure or insecure is related primarily to maternal sensitivity, while different types of insecurity may be more related to the infant's temperament (Susman-Stillman et al., 1996). On the other hand, infants rated as secure are more likely to show affective sharing and to enjoy being touched, and less likely to be difficult (Pedersen & Moran, 1996).

It is unlikely, however, that either the mother or the infant is the sole determiner of attachment quality. A 3-month-old may cry more because the mother is not responsive to his or her needs, thus setting up a negative cycle of infant fussiness countered by maternal insensitivity that leads to a lack of security of attachment at 1 year (Belsky, Rovine, & Taylor, 1984; van Ijzendoorn & Baker-mans-Kranenburg, 2004). In an even more complex pattern of findings, highly active and intense young infants became securely attached so long as their mothers did not try to pick them up and cuddle them often. On the other hand, active and intense infants became avoidant in the strange situation if they had mothers who insisted on a great deal of physical contact (Bohlin et al., 1989).

Another set of findings supporting the systems theory perspective on attachment is that concurrent social support for the family is a predictor of the infant's attachment. Support can alleviate situations in which the infant or the parent is at risk. Take the example of difficult infant temperament. Insecure attachments at 12 months were predicted by newborn fussiness, but only for those mothers who were not responsive to the infant's cries at 3 months and who had few opportunities for social support outside the home (Crockenberg, 1981). In addition, parents who are at risk for failures of attachment—teenage mothers, adoptive mothers, or single parents—can often inspire babies toward secure attachments. It is only when these parental risk factors are compounded by a lack of support networks, poverty, or a history of psychiatric disorders that insecure attachments develop (Allen et al., 1984; Belsky, 1995; Brooks-Gunn & Furstenberg, 1986; Huth-Bocks et al., 2004; Jacobson & Frye, 1991; Sameroff & Seifer, 1983; Singer et al., 1985; Zeanah et al., 2005;).

During the first year of the infant's life, mothers who were at risk for attachment problems (due to low income, poor social support, and anxiety or depression) were allowed to participate in a program that provided social support, education for infant care, and psychotherapy. Compared to control families of the same group who did not receive the intervention, there was a higher percentage of securely attached infants in the intervention groups (Boom, 1994; Lieberman, Weston, & Pawl, 1991).

These findings suggest that neither parent nor infant is solely responsible for the attachment outcome. Bowlby's concept of attachment suggests that it does not evolve from one or another person's sole influence, but rather has more to do with the way the parent and infant have developed their relationship to maintain proximity in times of stress (Sroufe, 1995). This idea is supported by evidence showing that infants can form different types of attachments in different relationships. Mothers and fathers form unique attachments to infants and make unique contributions to their development (see below), and infants also can form independent attachment relationships with professional caregivers (Cox et al., 1992; Easterbrooks & Goldberg, 1984; Goossens & van Ijzendoorn, 1990; Oppenheim, Sagi, & Lamb, 1988; Schaffer & Emerson, 1964; Volling & Belsky, 1992).

Each relationship has a unique character and develops through its own life history, in much the same way that each person has a unique temperament and developmental course (Fogel, 1993). The types of attachment security represent ways parents and infants have developed to communicate about their feelings and needs in a stressful situation. As in any interpersonal relationship (think of your own relationships with friends or romantic partners, for example), some couples can easily communicate their feelings and support each other in times of stress. Other couples tend to become anxious and hesitant under stress (insecure resistant/ambivalent), while still others resolve the problem by avoiding difficult topics of discussion (insecure avoidant).

Are Infants More Attached to Mothers or to Fathers?

On the whole, there are few differences between attachment to mother and to father (Bridges & Connell, 1991; N. A. Fox, Kimmerly, & Schafer, 1991). This does not mean that infants have the same kind of relationship with each, but only that they can be adequately comforted in a stressful situation by either parent. Some research has shown that if their mother and father are both present in a stressful situation, infants will choose the mother (Bridges, Connell, & Belsky, 1988; L. J. Cohen & Campos, 1974). Other work shows that infants would much rather be with one of their parents than with a stranger (Lamb, 1977).

There are, however, differences between families. In a sample of 41 maritally intact families in the United States, 78% of the infants had the same type of attachment security with both parents (Rosen & Burke, 1999). The remaining 22% of the sample were more attached to one than the other (not necessarily the mothers). In general, the more time the father spends with the infant, the more extroverted the father, and the greater the father's marital and work satisfaction, the more likely it is the father and infant will share a secure attachment and mutual communication (Belsky, 1996; Cox, Owen, Henderson, & Margand, 1992; Pedersen, Suwalsky, Cain, & Zaslow, 1987; Volling & Belsky, 1992). Failure to become securely attached to one person does not preclude becoming attached to another. In a small percentage of families, however, infants will be insecurely attached to both parents (Lamb, 1978b; Main & Weston, 1981). If an infant becomes securely attached to either the mother or the father, the baby will be significantly less wary of strangers than an infant who is not securely attached to either parent (Main and Weston, 1981).

Attachment Between Adoptive Parents and Their Infants

The transition to parenthood (see Chapter 8) for adoptive parents is rather different than for biological parents. Adoptive parents are already in a special category because typically many of them cannot have children of their own. They may have a history of infertility and may have made many attempts to treat it (see Chapter 3). They are also people with a very great desire to have children. If adoptive parents are not infertile, then they probably have a strong desire to rear children who would otherwise be disadvantaged. Thus, it is not surprising that adoptive parents enter parenthood with much higher expectations for success than biological parents.

Adoptive parents also experience more stress, at least initially. The "delivery" of their infants is often sudden and may follow a period of several years of waiting. They are thrust into the parenting role without the prior stage of pregnancy during which most new parents adjust to that role. Also, they may worry about how their own parents will feel about having a grandchild who is not their kin. Adoptive couples want to be seen as "real" parents by family, friends, and the workplace (Levy-Shiff, Goldschmidt, & Har-Even, 1991; Shahmoon-Shanok, 1999).

Research on the outcomes of parent-child attachment and marital relationships during the infancy period shows that there are few differences between adoptive and nonadoptive families in spite of the differences in the transition to parenthood (Humphrey & Kirkwood, 1982; Levy-Shiff et al., 1991; Singer et al., 1985). Even when adoptive infants come from at-risk groups, attachment can be facilitated with simple interventions that prepare the parents for the task at hand (Juffer et al., 1997). There is about the same percentage of secure infants (about 70%) in nonadoptive samples as in domestic adoptions within the same racial group, transracial adoptions, and adoptions of infants from other countries (Juffer & van Ijzendoorn, 2005; Juffer & Rosenboom, 1997; Marcovitch et al., 1997).

This pattern also holds for infants adopted from Romanian orphanages, in which infants are known to have suffered deprivations of care, although the longer time spent in the orphanage has a negative effect on adoptive parent-infant attachment (K. Chisholm, 1998; Marcovitch et al., 1997). Infants adopted from orphanages often suffer from PTSD (see Chapter 5) and have higher levels of cortisol (stress hormone) and lower levels of oxytocin (affiliation hormone), even after several years living with adoptive parents compared to infants reared by their biological parents (Fries et al., 2005).

One reason for this may be that adoptive parents are older or have higher incomes and take a more mature approach to the adjustments required to help the infant adapt (Palacios & Sánchez-Sandoval, 2006). Adoptive parents are more likely to name their children after family members (parents and other relatives) than are nonadoptive parents, perhaps as a way to integrate the child into the family (J. L. Johnson, McAndrew, & Harris, 1991). These findings may also reflect the resilience of infants and their ability to respond to loving care when it is provided.

On the other hand, research on adults who were adoptees shows that they are more likely to rate their parents as more critical and less fair minded than nonadoptees (Silverman, Dickens, Eals, & Fine, 1993). There is an apparent contradiction between the studies of adoptees as infants and adoptees as adults. One explanation for the differences is that the adopted adults come from an older generation when treatment of and attitudes about adopted children may have been less tolerant than today. When these adults were infants, there were no treatments for infertility and no such thing as surrogate parents. Another explanation is that differences between adopted and nonadopted children may not emerge until later childhood and adulthood. A final explanation is that the findings on adults are from their own report of their adoptive parents. These reports may be influenced by a feeling of loss about not being raised by their birth parents rather than by the quality of the adoptive parent-child relationship. This is compounded when adoptive children come from different racial or ethnic groups, or even from different countries than their adoptive parents. We are unlikely ever to know which of these explanations is correct.

The results suggest that adoption is a viable alternative for infertile parents and can provide a nurturing environment for infants who have been given up by their own parents. Even so, adoptive parent-child relationships are always going to be different from those in nonadoptive families. If the child has had significant trauma prior to adoption, there is the risk of an attachment disorder (see section on Development of Attachment, this chapter). With the rise of international adoptions, there is also the potential for the child's sense of loss of the home culture and language. In cases of potential risk, parents may want to consult an infant mental health specialist (see Chapter 10; Rochat & Richter, 2007). Adoption can be a reflection of the human capacity for multiple and unique forms of love that transcend biological ties, and there are a growing number of services for adoptive families to smooth the transition (see www.nlm.nih.gov/medlineplus/adoption).

Cultural Differences in Attachment

According to the systems theory of attachment, cultural differences in the macrosystem should also contribute to differences in attachment, independent of maternal and infant behavior. Cross-cultural research has generally found this to be the case. While all cultures that have been studied have about the same percentage of secure infants (Posada et al., 1995; Tomlinson et al., 2005), they differ according to the types of insecurity found. In general, avoidant classifications are more frequent in North America and Northern Europe, while resistant classifications are more frequent in Japan, Indonesia, and Israel (Grossman et al., 1985; Miyake, Chen, & Campos, 1985; Sagi et al., 1985; Thompson, 1995; Van Ijzendoorn & Kroonenberg, 1988; Zevalkink, Riksen-Walraven, & van Lieshout, 1999).

A number of explanations have been offered for these differences. The Strange Situation Test may be too stressful for Japanese infants, who are rarely separated from their mothers or exposed to strangers during their first years of life (Takahashi, 1986). The higher percentage of resistant infants in the Japanese sample may be the result of the infants' becoming overly stressed during the testing situation, and thus resisting attempts by the mother at comforting. We saw earlier that Japanese infants became rather upset at even a 30-second separation, and the separation period in the ASST is longer and repeated frequently. A similar pattern of closeness and rapid response to infant distress may be observed in Indonesia (Zevalkink et al., 1999).

The resistant attachments in Israeli infants come primarily from infants who are reared in a communal setting called a *kibbutz*. These infants spend most of their time with peers and caregivers and see their parents relatively infrequently (Sagi et al., 1994). These infants may prefer to be comforted by people other than their parents, especially in the context of the ASST. In partial confirmation of this hypothesis, the parent's security on the Adult Attachment Interview was less strongly related to the infant's security of attachment in Israeli kibbutz samples in which the infant slept at home with the parents than in kibbutz samples in which infants co-slept communally with other infants.

The home-sleeping samples were more similar to those found in North America and Northern Europe (Aveizer et al., 1999; Sagi et al., 1997). It is thought that the higher percentages of avoidant infants in North America and northern Europe may be due to higher demands for infant independence in those countries. As infants are encouraged to play independently and to occupy themselves at a distance from the mothers, they may be less likely to approach the mother for comfort.

A related issue concerns the security of attachment of infants who from an early age spend a good deal of time in day care. Although the results are mixed, with many studies finding no differences in attachment between day care and home care infants, some studies find that day care infants are more avoidant than home care infants (see Chapter 8 for a fuller discussion). This is consistent with the pattern of more avoidant infants in countries that encourage independence at an early age.

Researchers disagree about how to interpret these findings on cultural differences. On the one hand, they are clearly consistent with the ecological systems theory. Certain factors in the cultural norms and expectations may make mothers more or less protective or more or less encouraging of independence. These factors, in turn, unwittingly affect the mother's relationship with the infant.

On the other hand, these findings may also reflect a potential limitation of the ASST. It may be too stressful for Japanese infants, for example, who are not used to such separations from their mothers. On the contrary, infants who are used to daily separations from mother may not be disturbed by the series of separations and strangers in the ASST, and they may appear avoidant when their mothers return. At a minimum, the findings on cross-cultural differences reflect the need to interpret the results of the ASST with some sensitivity to the cultural and contextual factors of the infant and family.

Does Attachment Security in Infancy Predict Later Behavior?

One of the successes of the ASST is its ability to predict child behavior many years into the future. Securely attached children at 1 year, for example, were found during later infancy and early childhood to be more sociable with peers (Arend, Gove, & Sroufe, 1979; Fagot, 1997; Park & Waters, 1989; Slade, 1987b) and unfamiliar adults (Main & Weston, 1981; Thompson & Lamb, 1982), to be more aware of their emotions (Steele et al., 1999), and to be more securely attached to their mothers at 6 years of age (Main & Cassidy, 1988; Teti et al., 1991). Securely attached infants are also more likely to be better problem solvers in preschool and kindergarten, to be more persistent and enthusiastic, to be more socially competent and less lonely, and to have fewer behavioral problems (Bates, Maslin, & Frankel, 1985; Berlin, Cassidy, & Belsky, 1995; Block & Block, 1980; Erickson, Sroufe, & Egeland, 1985; Meins, 1998; Sroufe, 1983; Wartner et al., 1994).

Children who were maltreated in infancy and were scored as having a disorganized attachment at 1 year continue to be disorganized during early childhood (Barnett, Ganiban, & Cicchetti, 1999). Disorganized children are more likely to display evidence of child behavior problems (disobedience, fighting, withdrawal) and adolescent psychopathology, in particular *dissociation* (mental confusion, lack of *subjective self-awareness*, out- of-body experiences, accident proneness, and self-harm or suicide proneness) (Carlson, 1998; Lyons-Ruth, Easterbrooks, & Cibelli, 1997). Clearly, disorganized attachment in infancy is a serious developmental problem and should be cause for concern and possible intervention at an early age.

Because insecure attachment activates the HPA axis to overproduce cortisol, it may create long-term physiological imbalances in the body and brain that predispose the adult to some forms of mental illness, particularly depression (Beatson & Taryan, 2003). Insecurity in infancy is also related to childhood peer rejection and behavior problems (McCartney et al., 2004; Wood et al., 2004).

We are still left with the question of how early attachment patterns are maintained over time and are translated into a variety of behavioral competencies or disfunctions. Bowlby (1969, 1980) proposed that attachment has long-term effects because of an **internal working model**. An internal working model is a sense of self and of other people that allows one to anticipate future behavior, react to new situations in a competent manner, and appraise the likelihood of success for action. For example, based on past experiences with the mother, the infant constructs a model of her as the person from whom particular types of support are likely to be received. As the infant's internal working model becomes solidified through experiences with the mother, actual behavioral monitoring of the mother becomes less necessary, and the infant is able to tolerate separations and react favorably to reunions.

Thus, the internal working model is relatively stable and is updated gradually. The model is determined in part by interactive experiences but eventually comes to affect interactions. Thus, a baby who has been disappointed by the mother many times in the past is not likely to accept changes in the mother's behavior if at a later time she desires more closeness to the baby (Bretherton, 1985). The notion of an internal working model is related to a number of cognitive and emotional theories that postulate the existence of a generalized representation of the individual's history of interpersonal experiences between self and other (Bretherton, 1987; Stern, 1985). It is also supported by the neurophysiological differences between secure and insecure infants, reviewed earlier.

These ideas may have potential for explaining some of the long-term correlations of child behavior with earlier attachment classification,

especially if we consider that caregivers also have internal working models of themselves and their infants. The long-term stability of interaction patterns between mothers and infants may be maintained by stable internal working models in both mother and infant, which may enhance or inhibit interpersonal closeness over a long period of time (Main, Kaplan, & Cassidy, 1985).

Of interest in this regard is a study on adolescents who had been evaluated in the ASST with their mothers when they were 12 months old. No relationship was found between their 1-year attachment classification and their behavior and emotional adjustment during adolescence. Their behavior was related to their views on the supportiveness and emotional availability of their parents, information obtained from the Adult Attachment Interview when the adolescents were 10 years old. This research suggests that relationships between parents and children can change over time and that the most recent pattern of emotional communication between them—the most updated internal working model—best predicts child behavior. As we have seen, some parents may not be able to be emotionally available to their infants. This research shows that parent-child relationships can improve—or worsen—leading to corresponding changes in the child's well-being (Sameroff & Emde, 1989; Sroufe, 1989; Zimmermann et al., 1995).

In summary, parent-child attachment has been the subject of a great deal of research. Although there are different theoretical interpretations of the findings, one thing is clear. The early development of the parent-infant relationship is crucial for the continuing social and emotional development of the infant. On the other hand, attachment can change as relationships improve or worsen, and infants can derive benefits from a secure attachment to any person. The results speak not only to the negative effects of inconsistent, unavailable, and abusive parents, but also to the resiliency of relationships and their ability to change for the better under optimal conditions of social and cultural support.

EXPERIENTIAL EXERCISE

Social Referencing
by Ilse de Koeyer

1. Spread out across the room toys (different shapes, colors, things that can make sound) and "scary" objects or things that can break (such as remote controls, scissors, medicine bottles).

2. Start to walk around the room in any direction your feet are taking you. You can move in circles, squares, or lines, however you wish. Now, find yourself a partner. See if you can do that without using words. Also, find yourselves a place to sit down on the floor.

3. Sit opposite from each other on the floor. One of you will play the baby; the other will be an adult. Please divide roles now. We will change roles later.

4. If you are in the role of baby, imagine that you are here for the first time and you are full of wonderment. You could imagine you were in a strange country. You feel like you want to explore and learn more, but you also want to make sure that it is safe to do that. To find out, you will look at your "guide," your "parent."

5. After observing your "parent's" reaction, look back at the object you were looking at before. How do you feel about it now? Do you still want to explore it? Would you like to approach it? Avoid it? Would you like to move further away from it?

6. If you are in the role of parent, you may also imagine that you are in this strange country. You, as the adult, may not know this particular situation either. But based on your previous experiences, you may have a better sense of this place and the objects in it. During the exercise, your child will be looking at you to figure out how to feel about a particular object he or she is looking at. You need to show him or her how you feel, as clearly as possible, in a nonverbal way. Improvise your reaction, so the child won't know beforehand which emotion you will be showing.

7. Maybe you would like him or her to explore and play with the object. You may very much enjoy watching your child, and feel happy being in this room with him or her. You could show that by giving him or her a big smile or nodding your head. Maybe you think this thing is dangerous and you are concerned about your child. Maybe you feel annoyed because you've told your toddler 100 times NOT to play with it…. now she wants to grab it again. Whatever feeling you choose, go into that feeling 100% and express it to your child in a nonverbal way, with your face and body.

8. Do this multiple times, with different objects.

9. Then change roles and do the same thing.

10. Discuss together in pairs.

Attachment Styles
by Alan Fogel

This exercise is about the parental role and the infant experience related to approaching and avoiding. It is similar to the "Mutual Gazing" exercise in Chapter 6, except that the emphasis here is on seeking or avoiding proximity. The goal is to experience, through the exercise, your own attachment style: secure, resistant, avoidant, or disorganized. The class is divided up into pairs who do not know each other very well. With pair members facing each other, half of the group will stand along one wall of the room and the other half of the group along the opposite wall.

1. As in the gazing exercise, students will play the role of either the parent or the child, after which the roles will be reversed. Speaking to the parents: Your responsibility is to witness the child with a steady gaze. "Parents" should continue to feel their own emotions and arousal but it is important to keep those feelings inside and just observe them. Your job is to be there for the child. As adults, parents should be able to control their emotions.

2. Speaking to the children: Come about half way across the room and stop, looking at your parent. Take a few moments to feel this. Now close the space between you and your parent again by half and feel the difference. Finally, approach the parent no closer than arm's length and without touching. Parents and children should feel the differences in the different distances. Finally, children return to the opposite side of the room.

3. Again, speaking to the children: Now, you can move anywhere you want in the room, either close to or far away from your parent. You can do anything you like (explore, play with the other children, stay by yourself). Let youself go and do what you really feel like doing (no touching others!), but remember where your parent is located. You can feel free to look at your parent or look away as much as you need or want to. Allow about 2 minutes.

4. Repeat the same process with the same roles, only this time the adult, instead of being attentive, acts distracted by something in the room.

5. Repeat the same process with the same roles, only this time the adult, instead of being attentive, acts intrusive, trying to get the "baby's" attention.

6. Then change roles, repeating the instructions to the parents and then to the children.

7. Sit in pairs and discuss the experience with each other.

Kinesthetic Empathy
by Alan Fogel, using concepts from Dance Movement Therapy (Tortora, 2004)

Part I:
This exercise focuses on the movement of walking. In this part, the leader talks about how psychological states may be communicated in posture and movement. Begin with a few stretches of upper arms with deep breaths. The leader then demonstrates each of the following movement dimensions, and students are asked to stand and do their own versions.

Body inter-relationships: (1) move only one part of body, keeping other parts still, such as upper or lower, arms only, one leg, etc; (2) Coordinate different parts with each other such as right arm and left leg shake; (3) Have the left leg shake and the right arm rotate, etc.

Use of space: Taking up a lot of space with arms and legs extended versus contracted and small.

Sequencing: Try different walking sequences, such as extending arm and leg on same side of body versus opposite side.

Shape: Rounded, straight, snake-like.

These patterns are combined when making any ordinary movement and can communicate to others about one's psychological state using kinesthetic empathy, the ability to feel another's experience simply by watching his or her movements. The leader demonstrates some common states (sadness, haste, anger) with his or her body by walking in front of the class while the students guess the feeling being demonstrated. Attempts should be made to focus on body movement and not on facial expression. Then, the students are asked to try this for themselves using some of the following prompts. The leader gives only the first word (for example, "proud") and the students try it and describe what they did.

Proud: Chest out, shoulders back and down, head high, regular steps.

Dejected: Chest caved in, shoulders hunched, head down, slow and small steps.

Determination: Straight arms and legs, head forward of body, forceful steps.

I'm cool: Shoulders and hips relaxed and swaying, head loose.

Vigilant: Closed posture, small rapid steps, rapid shifts of head direction.

Toddler: Hip rotations, heavy legs, little knee bend, no leg swing (A video of a toddler walking can be used to illustrate this, and students can then try it out). It helps to switch between adult and toddler walking to compare the differences.

Talk about what each of these movements felt like, especially trying to walk like a toddler. What is the difference between adult and toddler walking, especially in the balancing and leg swing?

Part II:
In this part, the class divides itself up into triads. There are three roles: witness, walker, and follower. The walker walks around a more or less normal way, and the follower tries to match the walk while the witness observes. This is done silently. Everyone is asked to notice his or her own experience. The roles change until everyone has played each role with each of the partners. Using kinesthetic empathy, students discuss the experience of following and being followed in their triads sharing with each other about what it was like to "be" the other person, and using the concepts from Part I. A general discussion can focus on how parents use these skills with their babies, and how this method can be used in treating infants and young children with difficulties. Also, it can lead into a discussion of how babies take on the walk or movement patterns of their parents: this is more than copying but involves feeling a connection and empathy.

SUMMARY

The First Two Months

- Crying is an organized rhythmic activity that has reliable effects on adults. Infants who cry a great deal are not necessarily at risk for problems in parent-infant attachment.
- Colic is a pattern of excessive crying with no known cause. It does not seem to have lasting effects on parents or infants.
- Each method of soothing infants has advantages and disadvantages.
- Newborns have a large repertoire of facial expressions and body movements, some of which are related to emotion expression.
- Newborns can feel distress, contentment, disgust, interest, and surprise.

Two to Five Months

- A distinction can be made between emotion expression, emotion experience, and emotional regulation.
- The infant's emotional expression becomes more complex and varied. Infants can use their whole bodies for emotional expression.
- Negative emotions decrease over time, while positive emotions increase.
- Improvements in emotional regulation occur, but new challenges create new sources of frustration for babies.

Six to Nine Months

- Anger and wariness are two new negative emotions seen during this period.
- Laughter emerges as a new positive emotion, and other positive emotions develop at this age.
- Infants can recognize positive facial expression better than negative expression; however, they do not seem to attribute meaning to those expressions.
- Infants have stable temperamental characteristics, although the origins of these patterns are not understood.
- Measuring temperament is difficult because it requires understanding how the infant changes or remains the same over long periods of time.

Ten to Twelve Months

- New forms of expression of anger, fear, sadness, and joy all develop at this age.
- Infants can now express mixed emotions and ambivalence.
- Affective sharing and social referencing both enhance infants' ability to use information about other people's emotional expressions, although infants do not yet understand that others have emotions.
- Teasing games are opportunities for infants to experience mixed emotions and develop their skills at emotion regulation.

Twelve to Eighteen Months

- Infants are getting better at making good feelings last and controlling negative feelings.
- Infants know how to tease adults by varying the patterns of normal routines or stopping just short of misbehavior and laughing.

Eighteen to Twenty-Four Months

- Fears originate in mental and symbolic images, and some dreaming begins. Infants develop new emotions, such as defiance, embarrassment, and pride.
- Transitional objects serve to comfort infants when adults are unavailable.
- Smiling and laughter develop as important forms of communication about positive emotion.
- Pride and shame develop as emotions related to the existential self.
- Separations are easier for children if parents explain what will happen and when they will return, if the environment is one in which the infants feel comfortable, and if the infants have experience with separations.

Twenty-Four to Thirty-Six Months

- Descriptions of emotional states of the self and others become elaborate.
- Three-year-olds can act by taking the behavior of others into account, but they do not yet behave as if they have a clear theory of the other's mind.
- Children of this age lack the ability to differentiate reality from make-believe in most cases.
- New developments emerge in both positive and negative emotion expression.

- There are individual differences in children's willingness to express negative feelings or to show aggression.

Development of Attachment

- Specific attachments develop. The quality of attachment can be assessed using the Ainsworth Strange Situation Test (ASST).

- The ASST has both advantages and disadvantages. The results for a particular infant may reflect the infant as much as the infant-caregiver relationship and the ecological system.

- Disorders of attachment are both behavioral and neurophysiological.

Chapter 8

Family, Society, and Culture

CHAPTER OUTLINE AND OVERVIEW

Transition to Parenthood   *What are the physical and psychological aspects of the mother's adaptation to being pregnant? How do fathers and siblings adapt to the pregnancy? What are the mother's psychological reactions to childbirth? What are the developmental tasks of adults in the transition to parenthood? Are there differences in parenting between men and women? What are the effects of maternal employment on infants and families? What is the effect of non-parental child care on infants and their families? How does public policy affect the types of child care available to infants and their families?*

Cultural Differences   *What are some cultural differences in childbirth and infant care practices? How does the culture of poverty affect infant development? What are the causes and preventions of poverty? What kinds of support and intervention programs are available for families with infants? What is the impact of these programs?*

Peer Relationships   *How do relationships with same-age infants change over time? What is the function of peer relationships in infancy?*

Sibling Relationships   *How does age affect sibling relationships? What is the function of sibling relationships? How are older and younger siblings different? What are some family and cultural differences in sibling relationships?*

This chapter covers the social systems in which infants are raised. According to systems theories (Chapter 2), we connect understand infant development in the absence of the links and networks in which infants are embedded. This includes the family, the parent's employment, the availability and use of non-parental childcare, family income and other resources. In addition, the culture of the society and family—whether the infant grows up in rural India or New York City—will alter all of these societal and family relationships.

THE TRANSITION TO PARENTHOOD

Parents, no less than their infants, develop and change with experience. New parenthood is a major life transition in adult development. It is a phase of life, not unlike infancy or adolescence, that requires a good deal of adaptation. Like most other important developmental phases, parenthood has its own pleasures and sorrows, rewards and misgivings, and memories both fond and painful. For most people, the first step in becoming a parent is pregnancy. The first issue that new parents must deal with is the physical changes that a woman's body undergoes during that 9-month period.

What Are the Physical Changes Associated with Pregnancy?

As can be seen from our discussion of health and risk factors during pregnancy (Chapters 3 and 9), maternal and fetal health is extremely important in maintaining fetal development on a normal course. In this section, the factors and behaviors that promote health during pregnancy will be reviewed, including checkups, diet, and exercise.

What are the first signs of pregnancy? The failure to menstruate is usually considered to be the most reliable indicator, but it is not foolproof. A woman may menstruate for 2 or three months after she has conceived, and failure to menstruate may occur for other reasons, such as age, illness, or emotional upset. Breast changes may also be symptomatic of pregnancy. These may occur in the form of fullness, tingling, or hypersensitivity. About half of all women experience some nausea, usually in the morning, but this typically passes after 8 weeks. Some believe "morning sickness" is related to biochemical changes in the body, while others think it is an adaptive mechanism that functions to provide a reason for the mother to get more sleep and rest or to enhance the development of the placenta and embryo. During the first 3 months of pregnancy, women are more likely to feel a sense of disgust around some food and body products, suggesting that morning sickness may be adaptive in making mothers more selective of what they eat, thus reducing the possibility of consuming teratogenic agents (Fessler et al., 2005). Morning sickness may be controlled naturally by changes in diet and rest patterns. Other demonstrated sources of relief, at least for some women, include vitamin B6 supplements, ginger, and acupuncture. In extreme cases, some physician-prescribed antihistamines are effective and have no known teratogenic effects (Knight et al., 2001; Niebyl & Goodwin, 2002; Seto, Einarson, & Koren, 1997; Vutyavanich et al., 2001; Werntoft & Dykes, 2001).

Other symptoms of pregnancy are fatigue and frequency of urination. Conclusive diagnosis can only be obtained through laboratory tests, however. Pregnancy test kits are currently available for use at home, but they are not reliable in all cases.

During pregnancy, the uterus grows from about 2 ounces to 2 pounds, and the mother's abdominal muscle fibers grow to about 10 times their original length. Maternal uterine muscles are extremely important for a number of reasons. They will open the cervix at birth to provide a passage for the baby, contract to push the infant out, and continue to contract after birth to restrict the continued flow of blood to the uterus. The latter function is essential to avoid a major blood loss. The vaginal muscles also change during pregnancy. The vagina increases in length and capacity, and more blood is supplied to the area. In addition, vaginal secretions increase in quantity and in bacteriological action.

Because of these secretions, sexual intercourse during pregnancy may be more satisfying to some women than it was before. On the other hand, many women report a lowering of libido, especially during late pregnancy (Hamela-Olkowska et al., 2003). In general, sexual intercourse during pregnancy is not harmful. Consultation with one's physician is suggested since each woman is different, and intercourse during late pregnancy may not be advisable.

Physicians who care for the health of the mother and fetus during pregnancy and who deliver babies are called **obstetrician/gynecologists**. Midwives (see Chapter 3) also provide prenatal care and support. Those who care for the baby immediately after birth and during childhood are called **pediatricians**. Women should be encouraged to discuss all aspects of their pregnancy and delivery with their obstetricians. Obstetricians differ in their willingness to answer questions and to allow a mother to make decisions about the course of her labor and delivery. To the extent possible, women should select an obstetrician whose beliefs and practices accord with their own. Most midwives and obstetrician/ gynecologists recommend regular prenatal checkups. The frequency of these checkups and what is done depend upon the mother's health status and risk factors.

Proper health care during pregnancy has been shown to prevent many environmentally caused birth defects, reduce the rate of premature births, and reduce prenatal mortality and health risks for both mother and fetus. Due to poverty, fear, or unwanted or teen pregnancy, as many as 20% of women in the United States do not receive prenatal care during the first trimester of pregnancy. Government and health care officials are working to reduce this percentage (Fischer & Rozenberg, 1999; Klerman & Goldenberg, 1999).

As pregnancy proceeds, the placenta forms within the uterus and secretes hormones that nurture the fetus and also prepare the mother's body for birth. The placenta is constructed to enhance the exchange of nutrients and other substances between the mother's and the fetus's blood supply (see Figure 8.1). The placenta filters some things and allows others to pass through.

In reality, because the fetus has genes from the father as well as the mother, it exists within her as a foreign body. Under most circumstances, such foreign cells would be attacked by a person's immune system. Why does this not happen to the fetus? Apparently, the cells in the uterus near the placenta are responsible for blocking the local production of the immune response system. Studies of how the uterus does this may have applications in can-

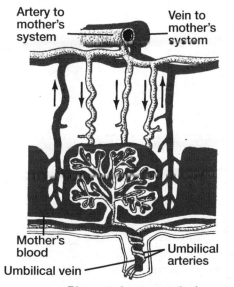

Figure 8.1 Changes in Maternal Circulatory System During Pregnancy
A detailed cross-section of the placenta is shown here. Note that the placenta has two portions—the embryo's portion and the mother's and that they are interwoven. Those parts of the drawing that belong to the embryo are shown in light gray; those of the mother are in a darker gray. The gray umbilical vein and arteries carry the embryo's blood, exchanging nutrients, wastes, and the like with the mother's blood, but the two blood supplies do not come in direct contact.

Source: A. Fogel & G. F. Melson, *Child development*, 1988, p. 108. St. Paul, MN: West. Copyright © West Publishing Company. Reprinted by permission. All rights reserved.

cer research (because cancerous tumors may block the immune system) and in organ transplants, where doctors would like to stop the normal process of rejection (Silberner, 1986).

The placental hormones also induce changes in the breasts as they become ready for lactation. They increase in size as fat is replaced by mammary gland tissue and more blood supply. A clear, yellowish liquid called **colostrum**, high in protein and antibodies, may be secreted by the fourth month of pregnancy. Colostrum is the first food of the breast-fed infant. It is gradually replaced by milk during the first few days after birth.

In general, the mother's body adapts itself to work harder. The mother's digestive and eliminative systems (kidneys, intestines, and sweat glands) must begin to take on the requirements of the developing fetus. These extra requirements are often accompanied by discomfort. Typical complaints of pregnant women include leg cramps, varicose veins, temporary changes in skin pigmentation, stretch marks on the abdomen, shortness of breath, lethargy, indigestion, constipation, and moodiness. The quality of sleep also changes. Women wake up more frequently during the night and sleep less deeply (Brunner et al., 1994). The severity of these symptoms depends upon the woman's body structure, nutritional status, fatigue, and psychological sense of well-being.

All of these facts show how the mother and fetus comprise a unique biological system in which feedback between them accounts for their mutual development. As the fetus changes, the mother's body changes in response, and continued changes in her body and its functioning provide the nourishment and biological support necessary for fetal growth and development. Both mother and fetus act as a system in their exchange of materials with the outside environment.

How Do Mothers Adapt Psychologically to Pregnancy?

In writing about this phase of adult development, Alice Rossi (1968) coined the term "transition to parenthood." According to Rossi, parenthood, and not marriage, is the major transition into adult life. Erik Erikson referred to parenting as generativity, the giving of one's time and energy to the next generation (see Chapter 2). The birth of an infant is both a physical and a psychological point of no return. Unlike marriage, birth and parenthood are irreversible processes.

One of the reasons that pregnancy and childbirth are psychologically important is that, to some extent, they constitute a break from one's own childhood. Once people have a child of their own, they lose the "innocence" of being only a child of their parents. The new mother moves away from her previous sense of dependency on her mother and toward a greater sense of identification with her mother. Meanwhile, the new mother's parents may be encouraged to renew or readjust their feelings about their daughter by attempting to reestablish bonds that were strained or broken during adolescence or young adulthood.

Pregnancy is not entirely free of difficulties. The stress of carrying the child and adapting to the physiological changes of one's body, and the psychological conflicts attached to the awareness of inevitable, impending parenthood, contribute to the difficulty of the adaptation (Grimm, 1967). In general, adaptation to pregnancy involves coping with these unexpected emotions and with the physical changes of one's body.

During the later stages of pregnancy, many women in North America become preoccupied with their weight gain. In this culture, a high value is placed on a slender and attractive female body. Even though some women enjoy the sense of being pregnant, most worry about their appearance in some way. Many women feel as though they are losing control over their own bodies; they feel conspicuous or embarrassed at times. In the last months, women begin to feel awkward and sexually less attractive, and some worry about losing their husbands to more attractive women. Mothers who were ambivalent about their pregnancies and who were concerned about their appearance and behavior, however, eventually adapted to the parenting role (M. Leifer, 1980).

Although some women report a decline in cognitive abilities during pregnancy, research shows that this is not the case. Pregnant women outperform other women on recognition and recall of pregnancy-related words (Christensen et al., 1999). In the later months of pregnancy, however, women report an increase in daily hassles and a decrease in events that are uplifting (L. M. Thompson et al., 1997). Research shows that knowledge of pregnancy and childbirth helps a woman adapt successfully to the changes she experiences during pregnancy. Thus, prenatal education programs are particularly helpful for mothers (Rautava et al., 1992).

Other factors that are related to women's successful adaptation to pregnancy include the presence of the father, marital satisfaction, low levels of family stress, social support from family and friends, ability to remain active, and emotional well-being (Dragonas, Petrogiannis, & Adam, 1997; Klinnert et al., 1992; H. Taylor et al., 1997; K. J. Thorpe, Dragonas, & Golding, 1992). Regarding the protective factor of remaining active, some studies have reported that women adapt better if they continue to work at their jobs during pregnancy, while others have not found this effect. It may be that working is helpful if the mother wants to work and has low family stress (H. Taylor et al., 1997). Mothers who are more conscientious in their prenatal health care appear to be more psychologically involved with their fetus (Fares & Adler, 1998). As one would expect, women's reported feelings of attachment to their fetus increased over the course of pregnancy (Sjögren, 2004).

One study found that women who worried the least about the pregnancies were the most committed to becoming a parent and had the most involved husbands (M. Leifer, 1980). On average, there appears to be a slight decline in reports of marital satisfaction during the first few years of parenthood. Parents who were more likely to report that their marriages were satisfying, however, were less likely to experience a decline in feelings of tenderness and less likely to quarrel. Their infants were more securely attached at 12 months (Gloger-Tippelt & Huerkamp, 1998).

What Is the Father's Adaptation to Pregnancy Like?

The firstborn child is a major source of excitement for the entire family. Aside from the mother, the father is the most closely involved with this process, and the evidence suggests that he, too, undergoes some important developmental changes as well as some specific changes in mood and behavior during this period.

For the male, pregnancy may be seen as a sign of his masculine potency, but it may also be interpreted as a sign of bondage—an end to his fantasy of a life of adventure and freedom. Pregnancy can seem, at least initially, either welcoming or threatening.

Many expectant fathers do not see themselves in merely a supportive role. They have a sense that they, like their mates, are experiencing an important development in their lives. Some cultures have traditions, called **couvade**, that encourage expectant fathers to identify with their mates and to act out the female role in a culturally approved manner. Cross-cultural studies have shown that couvade occurs primarily in societies where females are salient and valued in their roles (B. Whiting, 1974).

How is couvade expressed in other societies? Fathers in the Ifugao tribe of the Philippines are not permitted to cut wood during their wives' pregnancy, as a form of identification with the changes in lifestyle associated with being pregnant. In the Easter Islands of the Pacific, the wife leans against the husband during labor and delivery. Among the Lepcha, both parents undergo a ceremonial cleansing in the fifth month of pregnancy (M. Mead & Newton, 1967).

It may be that the increased involvement of fathers in the childbirth process in our own culture reflects our increasing recognition of the importance of women's contributions to the family and to society. For a father to take time off from work, spend that time going to prenatal classes, discuss feelings openly, attend the delivery, and actively share in the "woman's" world of childbearing is an open expression of the value and worth of that world. In industrialized countries, fathers connect with the experience of being pregnant via "body-mediated moments." These include touching the mother's belly, feeling fetal movements and listening for the heartbeat, becoming involved in pregnancy testing, ultrasounds, morning sickness, nutrition, and of course, labor and delivery. These methods reduce the father's feelings of being "distant" from the process (Draper, 2002).

Many men do not share these feelings; they see the work of childbearing as less important or too threatening. The temptation to engage in extramarital sex increases during pregnancy, and some men report feeling emotionally distant from their wives during pregnancy and childbirth (Gelles, 1978; K. J. Thorpe et al., 1992). Unfortunately, physical abuse by men of their pregnant partners is not uncommon, affecting about one in six adult women in the United States. Risk of abuse increases with factors such as teenage pregnancy, low social support, low income, unmarried status, unplanned pregnancy, drug and alcohol abuse, and poor prenatal care. Abuse during pregnancy is a significant predictor of continued abuse after the child is born. Domestic violence during pregnancy also lowers a mother's attachment to her fetus and increases negative representations of themselves and the fetus (Gielen et al., 1994; Huth-Bocks et al., 2004; Martin et al., 2004; Parker et al., 1994; D. E. Stewart, 1994; Webster, Sweett, & Stolz, 1994).

Fortunately, most fathers develop a positive psychological attachment to the fetus. Mothers' and fathers' attachment to the fetus was assessed in a sample of 218 women and 147 of their mates. The sample was randomly distributed among income, ethnic, and racial groups, and the pregnancies were developing normally. The parents rated their attachment to the fetus and other feelings, as shown in Table 8.1. Both mothers and fathers were similar in their ratings, although fathers were more likely than mothers to be anticipating the birth, while mothers were somewhat more likely to express overt feelings of love for the fetus (Mercer et al., 1988).

Some of the same factors predict a smooth adaptation to pregnancy for both fathers and mothers; they include knowledge of pregnancy and childbirth, social support, marital satisfaction, low levels of family stress, and emotional well-being. Research shows that no single factor is more important than any other, that a successful transition to fatherhood depends on many different processes, and that men may differ with respect to what helps them the most (Hyssala et al., 1993; Klinnert et al., 1992). Many hospitals offer a variety of prenatal education and childbirth preparation classes. These can be very beneficial for maximizing the chances for a healthy and happy pregnancy and childbirth experience.

What Are the Attitudes and Emotions of Women and Men Following Childbirth?

Childbirth is unique in the life course. It is a major developmental transition for the family as the pregnancy ends and a new person is born. Parents, especially first-time parents, must learn new roles and take on important new demands and pleasures. Perhaps the transition is not as crucial for the infant. Although the baby must learn to

TABLE 8.1   Maternal and Paternal Responses to Feelings About the Unborn Baby

Response	Percentage of Women	Percentage of Men
Worry, anxiety, concern	8	4
Pleased, hopeful, positive	14	11
Talks to, loves, attached	18	8
Ambivalent, negative	13	12
Anticipating birth, curious	48	66

Source: R. T. Mercer et al., Further exploration of maternal and paternal fetal attachment, 1988, p. 92. *Research in Nursing and Health, 11*, 83–95.

breathe and live in an atmospheric as opposed to an aquatic environment, the ability to breathe, feel, suck, hear, and move had already been established in the last months of gestation.

Childbirth itself is an event full of powerful human emotions. Parents are filled with excitement and fear when the baby first appears. These emotions can turn suddenly into overwhelming joy with a normal baby or crushing despair and sadness if the baby has birth defects or suffers from a perinatal trauma or prematurity. With the exception of parents whose own poor health, malnutrition, drug addiction, or mental illness keeps them from appreciating the full impact of childbirth, the emotions of childbirth can be life-changing events that fix the experience indelibly within the person.

As with every other major event in life, we would expect childbirth to have a lasting impact on the individual and to be the source of a good deal of psychological adjustment in the days and weeks that follow. Westbrook (1978) asked women to remember their feelings during pregnancy, labor, and the hospital stay and upon returning home. Of the 200 women interviewed in Sydney, Australia, most reported high levels of positive feelings all the way through. In discussing their anxieties and worries, however, they noted changes depending on the stage the woman was at in the process. For example, women experienced the highest levels of total anxiety, fears of death, and fears of mutilation during pregnancy and labor. Most of these severe anxieties declined right after the birth.

One emotional change that can occur after birth is *postpartum blues*, which seem to occur in some form in about two-thirds of all women after childbirth (O'Hara, Schlechte, Lewis, & Varner, 1991; Yalom, 1968). These "blues" usually take the form of brief episodes of crying, mood swings, confusion, or mild depression that seems to begin and end suddenly and without warning. Postpartum blues lasts only a few hours or a few days. During this period, mothers may seem withdrawn and provide less affectionate care for their newborns (Ferber, 2004). The "blues" are probably part of the normal psychological and physiological recovery from pregnancy and childbirth.

Postpartum blues should be distinguished from the more serious occurrence of clinical postpartum depression. **Postpartum depression** is characterized by dysphoric mood, disturbances of sleep or appetite, fatigue, feelings of guilt, and suicidal thoughts. It occurs in between 8% and 15% of women following childbirth (O'Hara, 1997). One mother reported:

> Although I've got a routine with the kids, I've lost my own routine. … It's a terrible thing to admit but I went for two days without even washing. I sat down and had a good cry and I said to Mark "This just isn't on because I'm really going to go down if I'm not careful." And you think at the back of your mind "Oh God, am I suffering from depression?" (S. E. Lewis & Nicolson, 1998, p. 189)

Postpartum depression has been linked with prenatal factors such as life stresses, a perceived lack of social and financial support, poor marital adjustment, depressed mood, and a history of psychiatric illness (Berthiaume, David, Saucier, & Borgeat, 1998; J. M. Green, 1998; Loh & Vostanis, 2004; O'Hara et al., 1991; Seimyr et al., 2004; Whiffen, 1988). Following childbirth, women with postpartum depression report having the need for greater emotional support from their partners and lower levels of marital satisfaction compared to nondepressed women (Mauthner, 1998; O'Brian, Asay, & McCluskey- Fawcett, 1999; Stuchbery, Matthey, & Barnett, 1998). A small percentage of men also show symptoms of postpartum depression, especially if they are stepfathers or if their wives are depressed (Areias, Kumar, Barros, & Figueiredo, 1996).

Between 2 and 10% of mothers may experience childbirth as traumatic and suffer from **post-traumatic stress disorder (PTSD)**, characterized by intrusive thoughts, fears, nightmares, and heightened arousal (White et al., 2006). The causes of PTSD are different from those of postpartum depression. They include feelings of loss of control, fear of harm to self or infant during labor and delivery, having an induced labor, and having epidural anesthesia (S. Allen, 1998; Lyons, 1998). Other research has shown, however, that these effects are similar to those of any traumatic surgical event and are not specific to childbirth (Mandy, Gard, Ross, & Valentine, 1998). In most cases, women recover from these feelings after several weeks, but if they are in unsupportive or stressful environments, symptoms may continue for a year or more (White et al., 2006).

If there is a predisposition to other forms of mental illness, such symptoms may appear in the post-partum period, especially for first-time mothers who are at greater risk for being hospitalized for schizophrenia, bipolar disorder, and depression. The greatest risk is between 10 and 19 days after birth. Hospitalization for mental illness during this particularly important period of the mother-infant relationship can have consequences not only for mother and baby, but also for the rest of the family, who must step in to provide interim care (Munk-Olsen et al., 2006).

In general, the moods of men and women after childbirth are relatively stable and positive (Murai, Murai, & Takahashi, 1978; O'Hara, 1998). In a sample of 129 women in Australia, only 16 were severely depressed, and only 15 showed no mood changes following childbirth. The rest of the sample experienced one or more brief episodes of crying (Meares, Grimwalde, & Wood, 1976). Most fathers maintain positive attitudes and show a desire to be involved in the nurture of the newborn. Just thinking about their babies or looking at pictures of their own compared to other babies increases maternal positive mood. Seeing their baby's picture compared to pictures of other babies also activates the prefrontal cortex (see Chapter 5), the part of the brain that regulates emotions (Nitschke et al., 2004).

In many cases, due to fetal ultrasound (see Chapter 3), parents typically know if their baby is a boy or a girl long before birth. In North America, does it matter to parents whether they have a boy or a girl? One would think and hope that every baby is welcome regardless of gender. One would also think that sex-role socialization, the training of boys and girls about behavior

and manners appropriate to their gender, does not begin until the age of 2 or 3 years. In a study done in Canada, researchers examined 386 birth announcements published in newspapers between 2002 and 2004. Announcements for males more often used the words "pride" and "proud," while those for females were more likely to use words expressing "happiness" Gonzales & Koestner, 2005). This study suggests that subtle differences in parents' attitudes about boys or girls may alter their responses to each individual child regardless of that child's actual behavior or preferences.

What Is the Father's Role with Newborns?

Are fathers important to their newborns? Some studies have found that fathers spend very little time interacting with their newborns; others have found that fathers would like to spend more time with their babies; and still others have shown that when fathers actually do spend time with newborns, they can be just as competent as mothers in administering care and affection. In reality, these studies are not contradictory; they merely represent different aspects of the fathering role.

Studies of large-scale national samples of parents and infants show that fathers spend between 20 and 35% as much time as mothers in direct participation in infant care. Mothers appear to take the primary responsibility, while fathers take the role of helpers and baby-sitters (Lamb, Pleck, Charnov, & Levine, 1987; Pleck, 1983). Fathers have a strong desire to share in the experience of parenting but need a good deal of support to do so. Men's ability to participate in parenting tasks depends on the amount of social support they receive, particularly from their partners, and the more involved they are, the more involved they become (Fein, 1976; Leerkes & Burney, 2007).

Father-infant and mother-infant interaction can be enhanced by specific interventions to orient fathers to their newborns. In one program, fathers were given instruction in baby massage and bathing methods when the infants were 4 weeks old. When the infants were 12 weeks old, the fathers

Both fathers and mothers can become attached to their newborns.
Photo by Michael Newman/Photoedit.

who had received the instruction reported more marital satisfaction and less depression, compared to a control group of fathers who were not trained. In addition, 12-week-old infants in the massage and bathing group were more likely to maintain eye contact, smile, and vocalize with their fathers, and the fathers were more likely to be involved with their infants (Samuels, Scholz, & Edmundson, 1992; Scholz & Samuels, 1992). Parents who were given information about newborn responsiveness and behavior when the infant was 2 days old were more likely to interact synchronously with their infants (Wendland-Carro, Piccinini, & Millar, 1999).

Men who adjust better to parenthood have more knowledge about children and better relationships with their wives than men who have trouble adjusting to being fathers. This is in contrast to the factors predicting parental adjustment in women, which include self-esteem, identification with the mothering role, and adaptation to the pregnancy experience (Entwisle & Doering, 1981; Feldman & Nash, 1986; Leerkes & Burney, 2007; Wente & Crockenberg, 1976).

In a series of studies (Parke & Sawin, 1980; Parke & Tinsley, 1981; Sawin & Parke, 1979), infants were observed with mothers and fathers in a maternity ward of a hospital. During feeding and other caretaking tasks, fathers were at least as active as mothers and showed similar levels of sensitivity and affection. New fathers' heart rates and blood pressures were elevated while holding their newborns compared to when they were not holding the babies, suggesting heightened arousal (L. C. Jones & Thomas, 1989). On the whole, however, mothers spend more time caretaking during this period than the fathers.

On the other hand, the involvement of the father in caregiving affects the mother-infant relationship. Working mothers who left their newborn infants with fathers compared to other infant-care providers reported less anger, depression, and anxiety (Vandell, Hyde, Plant, & Essex, 1997). From the perspective of family systems theory, families in which the fathers are more involved have wives who show more interest and affection toward the neonate (Sawin and Parke, 1979). Of course, this result could be explained the other way around: interested, affectionate mothers may be more adept at encouraging fathers to take part in the care of the infant. Fathers do play an important role, even in the newborn period. They may not do as much as mothers overall, but with some encouragement and training, they are able to become competent caregivers.

Do Firstborns Have Different Interactions with Their Mothers than Laterborns?

Another factor influencing the family system at this period of time is whether the parents have had prior experience with an infant. As a general rule, newborns who are firstborn receive more caregiving interaction (Keller & Zach, 2002; Kilbride, Johnson, & Streissguth, 1977). Perhaps because of the novelty of the experience, parents devote more time and energy to the care of the firstborn than to infants born later. One study examined family photo albums and found considerably more photographs of firstborn children than of children born later (Titus, 1976).

One of the possible reasons for the differences in parental behavior toward first- versus laterborn children is that primiparous mothers (women who have given birth for the first time) receive more obstetrical medication than multiparous mothers (mothers who have given birth more than once), which may result in an infant who is somewhat slower to respond to stimulation. Not only do mothers spend more time with their firstborns, but firstborns are more passive and nonresponsive than babies born later. Could it be that mothers have to spend more time simply to get the infant sufficiently aroused to feed (Brown et al., 1975)?

Another explanation of the difference is that the mothers of firstborns are less skilled as caregivers. Do they spend more time because they are less efficient at getting the normal caregiving tasks accomplished? Primiparous mothers spend more time in nonfeeding activity during a feeding session. They are more likely to change activity frequently, such as shifting the infant's posture, providing more stimulation, and talking more to the newborn. Their infants spend less time on the nipple and do less sucking when attached than infants born later. These mothers could be spending more time because they are more uncertain about how to handle their infant or because they are more excited by the infant and wish to touch, explore, and talk to the infant. The number of changes of activity decreased over the first 3 days for primiparous mothers, suggesting that it does not take them very long to get down to the business of feeding during the feeding period (E. Thoman, Barnett, & Leiderman, 1971; E. Thoman, Leiderman, & Olson, 1972).

Another explanation is that first-time mothers are simply more anxious than other mothers. An anxious mood is likely to be caused by lack of security in the child-rearing role, and it may be enhanced by such factors as separation from the infant due to prematurity and illness. Anxiety in first-time mothers at birth is correlated with anxiety at 1 month but not at later follow-up observations (Fleming & Orpen, 1986; Fleming, Ruble, Flett, & Van Wagner, 1990), suggesting that most early insecurities that might influence behavior are reduced after a few months' experience.

In summary, adults and infants seem ready to interact with each other and have feelings and behaviors that mutually complement. Under the right conditions, any adult can interact successfully with a newborn and with enough exposure to the baby can develop a lasting attachment. The emotional tie between adults and infants does not seem to depend on a particular experience or a particular starting time. Rather, emotional bonds develop slowly and in a variety of ways. Many senses and behaviors can be involved, and if one pathway is absent (the parents do not have the opportunity for early contact, for example), other pathways are available to enhance the adult-infant communication process.

Developmental Tasks of Early Parenthood

Chapter 2 reviewed some of the current theories about the nature of family interaction. Family systems theory suggests that each member of the family is part of a feedback system with every other family member. In addition, when families have three or more members, the relationship between two of them can affect the third and vice versa. From this perspective, we might predict that the birth of a baby would bring major changes for a family. If it is a first birth, the married couple must adjust to becoming a three-person system. In a three-person family, a new baby creates disequilibrium and necessitates an adjustment by each of the other family members. In addition, developmental changes occur in all members of a family, including the adults and older siblings. In this section, we consider how adults develop through the transition to parenthood that occurs after the birth of the baby.

After a child is born, parents must learn to cope with a variety of new conditions, including a total alteration of lifestyle, lack of sleep, and the adjustment of the marital relationship to include new family members. In general, new parents must address four types of problems (Sollie & Miller, 1980).

First, there are the energy demands associated with infant care, such as loss of sleep and extra work, resulting in fatigue. Mothers, if they are the primary caregivers, must continue with the ordinary household tasks while trying to keep up with the baby. Fathers in the United States spend about half the time that mothers do in caregiving, and there are no differences across Caucasian, Hispanic, and African American groups (Hossain, Field, Pickens, Malphurs, & Del Valle, 1997) and no differences across groups differing in income level (Roopnarine et al., 2005). This suggests that there are few ethnic differences in the amount of father involvement, contrary to cultural stereotypes.

Women who are employed before the birth of the child must decide whether or not to continue working after the child is born. Theoretically, men should make the same decision, but in the vast majority of cases, it is the woman who decides whether or not to return to work. In general, women who are most concerned about the potential conflicts between family and work are the most likely to remain home with the infant. The type of work done by the mother outside the home does not predict whether she will stay home or go back to work (Symons & McLeod, 1994). On the other hand, if the mother chooses to work, some work environments are more consistent with the maintenance of positive parenting. In particular, parenting is enhanced if the mother works in an environment that is challenging, includes a complex variety of different people, and is stimulating (Greenberger, O'Neil, & Nagel, 1994; see below for a complete discussion of maternal employment).

Second, new parenthood places stress on the marital relationship. Problems may include less time spent together and perhaps jealousy of the baby for taking time away from the marriage. It may take many months for sexual relationships to become mutually gratifying and still more time before the couple is free to go out alone. Parents generally perceive a decline in marital satisfaction over the first year of the infant's life (Gloger-Tippelt & Huerkamp, 1998), especially if their infant is particularly fussy or has colic (Meijer et al., 2007). Interpersonal conflicts increase over the first year, and parents report less marital cohesion, less partner support, and less ability to cope. In general, couples with more conflicts felt less mutual support and found it more difficult to cope. These findings suggest that, while not a crisis that ends marriages, the first year of parenthood may be a difficult adjustment period for some couples (Frosch, Mangelsdorf, & McHale, 1998; Levy-Shiff, Dimitrovsky, Shulman, & Har-Even, 1998; Wicki, 1999).

Third, parents begin to feel the responsibility of caring for and rearing a child. No matter how psychologically prepared one is before the birth, the reality of the child's presence makes clear the lifelong commitment of parenthood. Parents may have doubts about whether they can manage this responsibility and be good parents for their child.

Finally, parents must cope with the additional costs of raising a child, in the form of food, clothing, and education. Just going to see a movie may cost double what it did before the child was born, after the cost of a baby-sitter is included. Whatever income a working mother might earn will be lessened by the cost of the child's daytime care. In addition, parents worry about day-to-day problems, such as infant health and sickness, crying, nutrition, and how to resolve conflicts (McKim, 1987; Wilkie & Ames, 1986).

Predictors of Success in the Transition to Parenthood

In general, the degree to which parents will adopt the parenting role depends on both developmental factors in the life of the adult and concurrent factors inside and outside the family system. Developmental factors include the adults' relationships with their own parents, their prior experience with child care, their self-esteem and belief in their own self-efficacy as a parent, and their readiness to have children. Concurrent factors include the marital relationship, other family members, the amount of social support available to the parents, and nonfamily factors, such as income and job satisfaction.

One of the key issues in the transition to parenthood is the effect of the infant on the marriage. Having a baby does not seem to alter existing marital relationships. Couples who have the most conflicts prenatally also have the most postnatally (Cowan & Cowan, 1981). The equality versus inequality of role relationships before childbirth tends to predict the amount of marital satisfaction after birth. In general, couples who are more likely to share responsibilities report higher marital satisfaction after childbirth than more traditional couples (Cowan & Cowan, 1981; Wicki, 1999). Other factors found to increase marital satisfaction following childbirth are a positive and warm relationship with one's own parents (Belsky & Isabella, 1985) and a postbirth experience that is not more difficult than anticipated (Belsky, Ward, & Rovine, 1986). The latter difficulty affects women more than men, since women, even in nontraditional marriages, are more likely to have most of the burden of care in addition to the fatigue following childbirth.

Marital quality itself is strongly associated with both men's and women's involvement in the parenting role. For mothers, a high level of marital satisfaction is related to warmth and sensitivity toward infants, and the amount of father involvement in the marriage plays a major role in the long-term ability of mothers to cope with child rearing. For fathers, marital satisfaction is associated with more positive attitudes toward the parenting role and with more time spent with the infant (Cox, Owen, Lewis, & Henderson, 1989; S. S. Feldman & Nash, 1986; Heinicke, 1984; Vandell, Hyde, Plant, & Essex, 1997).

Personality factors also affect adaptation to parenthood. Men who have had a good relationship with their own fathers and who have some personality traits traditionally associated with femininity (affiliation, warmth, nurturance) make better parents. Fathers who are more invested in their careers and who are in midlife are less likely to show warmth toward infants, although they are more involved in the practical and financial aspects of child care, since they make more money than younger fathers (S. S. Feldman & Nash, 1986; Levy-Shiff, 1994; R. D. Parke & Tinsley, 1987).

Interestingly, a very different set of personality factors is associated with parenting for women. Women who have higher self-esteem and a less egocentric orientation, that is, away from their own needs and toward the needs of others, show more nurturance toward their children. Unlike men, women who have children later in life show higher caregiving responsibility and more satisfaction with parenthood. Older primiparous mothers are more confident of their skills and may interact more successfully with their babies than younger primiparous mothers (S. S. Feldman & Nash, 1986; Heinicke & Guthrie, 1992; R. D. Parke & Tinsley, 1987; Ragozin, Bashan, Crnic, Greenberg, & Robinson, 1982).

While men's involvement in infant care depends primarily on social factors, such as marriage, job, and the social acceptability of parenting, women are more likely to be involved parents without such social supports. On the other hand, women's parenting suffers most when their self-esteem is low or when they experience depressed moods (Belsky, 1984; S. S. Feldman & Nash, 1986; Fleming et al., 1988). In an earlier section, we discussed the serious nature of maternal depression for infants.

Maternal Employment: Its Effects on Infants and Parents

One aspect of the transition to parenthood is the decision to return, or not, to adult work roles. According to ecological systems theory (Chapter 2), the world of work is in the exosystem. Even though infants may never enter the workplace, work will have a mediated effect on them through their parents.

The number of working mothers with children under the age of 6 years in the United States has been steadily increasing for the past 50 years. In 2001, 64% of these women were in the work force. For mothers with children between 6 and 17 years of age, 78% were working in 2001. Among other things, this increase in the number of working mothers raises the problem of how to provide adequate care for their infants, an issue to which we will return later in this chapter.

This section covers the impact the maternal work role has had on the American family and especially how it has affected both parents and infants. It should be noted that our discussion focuses on paid work, either inside or outside the home. Mothers do a substantial amount of unpaid work—child care, cooking, cleaning, gardening, and chauffeuring—which is estimated to be worth about $27,000 per woman per year. Much of this work goes unrecognized (Eyer, 1996).

First of all, how does maternal employment affect the mother's relationship with her infant and the infant's development? In general, infant-mother attachment is not seriously altered by maternal employment (Easterbrooks & Goldberg, 1985; Vaughn, Grove, & Egeland, 1980; Youngblut, Loveland-Cherry, & Horan, 1993). On the other hand, if attachment is going to be affected, it is most likely to decline between employed mothers and their infant sons rather

A working mother must learn to balance multiple demands of work and family, even if she does not take her baby to work with her.
Photo courtesy of Corbis.

than their daughters (Chase-Lansdale & Owen, 1987).

Why are boys more affected? It may be that boys are perceived as more independent and as requiring less parental nurture and attention than girls, who are seen as more vulnerable (Parke & Sawin, 1980). Thus, when mothers are under extra stress and time pressures from their jobs, they may spend less time with their sons than with their daughters. Other research suggests that there is a correlation between a son's insecure attachment and a mother's perceived level of stress. Mothers who felt more stressed by their jobs and the demands of family life had less securely attached sons (Benn, 1986). The effects of stress are compounded for low-income mothers, for whom not just employment but also the stresses of living in poverty may affect attachment in both sons and daughters (Barglow, 1987a).

These results suggest that the impact of maternal work on infant-mother attachment is mediated by the mother's adjustment to the work role. Better psychological adjustment will lead to more sensitive infant care. Thus, researchers have asked what factors promote maternal adjustment to employment. A number of studies find that the important variable is the mother's desire to work, not the mere fact of working. Mothers who are doing what they prefer—either working or staying at home with their children—tend to be well adjusted. On the other hand, there are adverse effects on adjustment if the mother does not want to work but has to for economic reasons, or if the mother would like to return to work but feels she should stay home with her children (Alvarez, 1985; DeMeis, Hock, & McBride, 1986; Pistrang, 1984; Stifter, Coulehan, & Fish, 1993). In addition, if mothers perceive that their children are suffering because of their absence from the home, they are more likely to feel stress and conflict between work and family roles (Lee et al., 2003).

On the other hand, staying home with the baby is also stressful for some mothers. Research has shown that problems with coping, dissatisfaction with life, depression, and loneliness are significantly higher in young mothers who do not work outside the home than in those who do, and that there are higher levels of functioning in families in which the mothers are employed (Sogaard, Kritz-Silverstein, & Wingard, 1994; Vandell & Ramanan, 1992).

Whether mothers work by choice or because of necessity, they typically end the day fatigued because of a phenomenon called **role overload**. Role overload occurs when the demands of a role are more than an individual can easily cope with, or when the same person is required to perform too many roles. After a full day at work, many women come home to traditional conceptions of the roles of both wife and mother. Women often continue to do most of the infant care and most of the housework, compared to men, even if they are working as many hours outside the home as the men (L. C. Jones & Hermann, 1992; Scarr, 1984). Role overload is inevitable for single parents.

Role overload and its consequences for the mother increase if the child has a difficult temperament at age 1 year or a hostile aggressive temperament at age 3. In this case, mothers are more likely to perceive themselves as less competent in both the parenting and work roles, and are more likely to feel depressed (Hyde et al., 2004). A mother who is already under pressure from both home and work, therefore, is likely to reach a breaking point if she feels she cannot handle her own child.

Even though fathers with working wives do more infant care and housework than husbands of women who are not employed outside the home, men with working wives increase their contribution to family work by only an average of 15 minutes per day (Crouter, Perry-Jenkins, Huston, & McHale, 1987; Pleck & Rustad, 1980). This general difference between mens' and womens' contribution to infant care, however, may depend in part on the fact that fathers are more likely to do more work outside the home. Fathers may spend relatively little time with their infants during weekdays, but then spend most of the weekend days with the family (Yeung et al., 2001).

Research also shows that men do proportionately more work at home if their wives have a less traditional attitude toward the male role. Thus, it may be the mother's own perception of her central family role and her failure to strongly encourage the husband's participation in the family that leads to low levels of father involvement. Women may be trying too hard to be "supermoms" (R. C. Barnett & Baruch, 1987; Palkovitz, 1984; Scarr, 1984) and in the process may be contributing inadvertently to role overload.

When women work, however, there are more pressures on fathers, and they too can experience a form of role overload. When women remain at home, fathers can choose when and how to become involved with their infants. These fathers show more positive emotion toward their infants and are more attuned to the infants' needs, especially if the infants are boys (Manlove & Vernon-Feagans, 2002). In contrast, fathers whose wives work experience more tension and frustration with being called upon to take more child-care responsibility. During the first year, such fathers show more negative behavior with their infants. After the first year, however, they are just as sensitive to their infants as the husbands of mothers who do not work outside the home (Grych & Clark, 1999). These are general patterns, however, so each family may be different in the balance of mother and father roles.

Parental Leave Policies

Unfortunately, the amount of work a person does outside the home is only partially defined by the individual. Much has to do with cultural and economic demands placed on workers by society and by employers. Most work situations in the United States take little account of a person's obligations to family. An inflexible daily work schedule leaves little time or opportunity for parents to be involved in the day-to-day life of the family. Corporations often have a policy of moving their employees from city to city as part of a training and advancement program.

This is especially the case for women. Even when mothers are paid, they earn only 71 cents for every dollar earned by a man in the same position. They are often relegated to low-paying jobs such as secretary (98% are women), child-care provid-

ers (98%), nurses (93%), and bank tellers (91%). Even highly educated women face job and salary discrimination, especially if they get pregnant or are raising a child (Eyer, 1996). These sources of discrimination in the ecological system make working especially burdensome for women and increase their level of guilt.

Some alternatives exist, but they are not widespread. More flexible work schedules (flextime) began to be instituted in Europe in the early 1960s. Workers can have time off to take a child to the doctor, watch their child participate in sports, or do whatever they desire. After a child is born, Swedish workers, for example, are legally entitled to maternity and paternity leaves. Some Swedish employers allow husbands and wives to share the same jobs. That way both can work and spend time at home. Swedish women earn about 90% the wages men do for similar jobs, and 86% of women with young children are in the work force (Eyer, 1996).

The opportunity to take infant care leave of some type, without suffering loss of income or profession, is mandated by law in at least 75 nations, including all the industrial societies in the world. In 1993, the U.S. Congress enacted the Family and Medical Leave Act of 1993 (FMLA, Public Law 103–3), which established a family leave policy. This law provides unpaid leave from employment for up to 12 weeks without loss of rank or position in the workplace in businesses with more than 50 employees. The leave applies to both mothers and fathers as well as to non-pregnancy-related illnesses. Unfortunately, 95% of businesses are exempt from the FMLA because they have fewer than 50 employees. In addition, most parents cannot afford to take unpaid leaves (Eyer, 1996).

Although mothers are more likely to take a parental leave (on average, about 3 months), research done in the United States in 1993 found that almost all fathers took at least a few days of leave. The average length of leave for fathers was 6.5 days, with 71% of fathers taking 5 or fewer days (Hyde, Essex, & Horton, 1993). Research shows that mothers who take shorter leaves are more likely to feel stress and symptoms of depression, show negative emotions toward their infants and spouses, and have less interest in their infants. Fathers who took shorter leaves worked for employers who did not have a positive reaction to the employee's fatherhood were less involved with their infants and had less communication with their spouse about the infant (R. Clark et al., 1997; Feldman et al., 2004). This means that even with the FMLA, too few parents are able to take advantage of parental leave, with negative consequences for themselves and their children.

Better pay and benefits for part-time work could also be helpful for young parents. Many employers provide medical insurance, unemployment compensation, and other benefits only to full-time employees. A parent who would like to spend more time at home is caught between the demands of the family and the very real needs to be covered by those benefits. Employer-sponsored day care, a topic to which we return later in this chapter, is also helping working parents.

The end result is that the current state of parental leave policies in the United States does not meet the needs of most families. With little opportunity to take time off from work, for example, young mothers cannot breast-feed for as long as recommended by the American Academy of Pediatrics (see Chapter 9). Mothers may choose drug-assisted childbirth or C-sections, even if they would have preferred a natural birth, in order to get themselves back on their feet sooner and back to work (Galtry & Callister, 2005). Compared to other industrialized countries, the United States is not a nation that fully supports children and families.

Some advocacy groups in the United States are working to promote the adoption of European-style parental leave policies at the state and national level (Gornick & Meyers, 2003; Secret & Sprang, 2001). In addition, some progressive private companies have realized that supporting working mothers is one way to preserve talent and loyalty. They have taken the lead responding to their female workers' child-rearing needs by providing flexible schedules and leaves, part-time employment with full benefits, and paid personal time beyond the 12 weeks of paid leave mandated by FLMA. These are companies such as Bayer, Chrysler, Ford, Johnson & Johnson, Microsoft, and Verizon. A complete list of the 100 best companies for working mothers compiled by *Working Mother* magazine is available at www.workingmother.com/?service=vpage/109.

The Effects of Nonparental Child Care on Infants and Parents

If both parents choose to return to work, then alternative childcare becomes an issue, not just for the infants but for the lives of the parents as well. In the first edition of this book, published in 1984, I reviewed research on the effects of out-of-home care for infants. There were relatively few studies, and most showed no harmful effects, so long as the infants were left in high-quality care. Since 1984, there has been an explosion of new research, new findings, and, especially, new public interest in the question of child care.

One of the most significant contributions to this important research issue has been the National Institute of Child Health and Human Development (NICHD) study of early child care. Child care in this case means care given by any person other than the child's mother. A total of 1,364 children took part in the study, which began in 1991. The composition of this nationwide sample was 76% Caucasian Americans, 13% African Americans, 6% Hispanic Americans, and the remainder were other minorities. The study sample came from a wide range of income and education levels, using a wide variety of types of child care, including center child care, child care homes, and in-home care from relatives or nannies. The researchers assessed multiple variables, including the child's experience in child care, quality of child care, family income, parental psychological adjustment, quality of the mother-child interaction, and the home environment.

The statistics from this representative sample show the importance of child care for infants and their families in the United States. The children in this sample received an average of 33 hours of

TABLE 8.2 Primary Child Care Arrangements Used by Working Mothers with Children Under the Age of Three Years

	Percentage
Parent Care	27
Relative Care	27
Center-based Care	22
Family Child Care	17
Nanny/Baby Sitter	7

Source: Capizzano et al., 2000

nonmaternal care per week. Hispanic infants used nonmaternal care the least, while black infants used it the most. Most of the infants were placed into some type of care prior to 4 months of age. When they first entered care, half of the infants were with the father or grandparent, 20% were in child care homes, and only 8% were in a child care center. Mothers with higher incomes and those who had an economic need to work were most likely to place their children in child care. After the first year, there are an increasing number of children in center care (see Table 8.2). The findings from this and other child care research will be reported in the remainder of this section.

After 20 years of research, we can now conclude with more certainty that the effects of child care on children still depend on the quality of that care. We know that high-quality child care is correlated with successful outcomes for children. Children in high-quality care receive better caregiving from staff, are more securely attached to their caregivers, and are more competent with their peers and with adults than are children in low-quality care. Children in high-quality care score better on school readiness and on cognitive and linguistic abilities, have fewer behavior problems, and are more securely attached to both their mothers and their care providers (Burchinal, Bryant, Lee, & Ramey, 1996; de Schipper et al., 2006; Howes, 1997; Howes, Galinsky, & Kontos, 1998; Howes, Phillips, & Whitebook, 1992; Love et al., 2003; NICHD Early Child Care Research Network, 1997a; 1998a; 2002; 2003). We also know what is necessary to create high-quality care (NICHD Early Child Care Research Network, 1996; see Table 8.3) .

In addition to the quality of child care, research also shows that the quality of the family environment is one of the most important predictors of child outcomes for children who attend child care. In one large-scale study in Sweden, children who were in high-quality child care under the age of 1 year performed better in school at 8 and 13 years of age than other children (Andersson, 1992). Part of this result may be accounted for by the fact that children who entered child care early in this study had two professional parents. It is well known that parents with higher levels of education and income have children who achieve better in school. A similar study in Israel found that the social competence and communicative skill of children in preschool were more related to parental positive interaction with the children than to early child care experience (N. K. Rosenthal, 1991).

The NICHD study confirmed these findings. If mothers were depressed and/or not contingently responsive to the children, their children in child care had lower scores on social and cognitive tests and had more behavior and attachment problems (NICHD Early Child Care Research Network, 1998a,b). These studies show that the quality of child care and the social and economic abilities of parents can buffer children against any adverse effects of early child care. Put another way, for children who come from supportive and loving families, placement in high-quality child care does not adversely affect development and may even enhance it.

Most researchers agree that child care after the age of 12 months is not harmful and might even be beneficial to the child. Compared to home-reared

TABLE 8.3   Accepted Standards of High-Quality Child Care*

Group size	Caregiver-child ratio between 1:4 and 1:10 over 3 years of age; between 1:4 and 1:8 over 2 and under 3 years; between 1:3 and 1:6 over 1 and under 2 years; and 1:3 under 1 year.
Caregivers	Trained in specialized, formal teacher-training programs that emphasize early childhood education and experienced in working in child care settings. Caregivers should be nurturant, supportive, and responsive to children's cues; they should talk to, hug, and smile at children and enjoy their company. Also, they should be willing to firmly and appropriately enforce guidelines for behaviors that affect the rights and safety of others, as well as have respect for parents' points of view and concerns.
Staffing	Low staff turnover, staff support, and low burnout; only one or two caregivers should be responsible for the same child.
Curriculum	Planned in advance, emphasis on development. Age-appropriate and safe toys, flexible program with special events and outside trips. Curriculum adapted to needs of the individual child. Opportunities for diverse activities and movement.
Parents	Should be informed daily about child's day and any special problems or special achievements; should be encouraged to visit at any time and to participate if desired.
Faculty	Clean, bright, safe, lots of room for toddlers to move about. Nap times and quiet areas, access to a fenced outside play area. Emergency essentials available. Food safe and nutritious.

* Applicable to child care centers and family child care.
Source: K. Magid & C. A. McKelvey, *High risk: Children without a conscience*, 1987, p. 170. New York: Bantam; S. Provence, Infant day care: Relationships between theory and practice, 1982, p. 34, in E. F. Zigler & E. W. Gordon (Eds.), *Day care: Scientific and social policy issues*, 33–35. Boston: Auburn House; S. Scarr, *Mother care/other care*, 1984, p. 212. New York: Basic Books; K. S. Weintraub & L. N. Furman, Child care: Quality, regulation, and research, 1987, p. 333. *Social Policy Report: Society for Research in Child Development, 2*, 317–342.

infants, child care infants are more cognitively and socially advanced and are more likely to show independence in compliance to rules (Caldwell, 1986; Clarke-Stewart, 1984; Schuetze, Lewis, & DiMartino, 1999; Siegal & Storey, 1985; Volling & Feagans, 1995). Infants older than 12 months are able to adjust to repeated separations from their mothers during ordinary child care attendance. The separation reactions of infants on their first day of child care are considerably greater than after 1 or 2 weeks, including higher levels of cortisol in the first hour after the parent leaves (Ahnert et al., 2004; Field, 1991). Infants, even those who are insecurely attached to their mothers, are able to use caregivers and teachers as attachment figures and secure bases (Howes & Smith, 1995). Insecurely attached infants, however, had higher cortisol responses following separation and may therefore need more help adapting to the transition to child care (Ahnert et al., 2004).

In contrast to these findings, a number of research studies have reported that the proportion of infants with insecure attachments increases if the infants have been in child care for at least 4 months beginning before the first birthday and for more than 20 hours per week; that is, children whose mothers are employed more than half time (Barglow, 1987a; Belsky & Rovine, 1988; Caldera & Hart, 2004; P. Schwartz, 1983; Vaughn, Grove, & Egeland, 1980). In samples of infants in the United States whose mothers do not work outside the home, the proportion of secure attachments is about 65 to 75%. In these samples of early child care infants, the proportion of secure attachments across all studies is 57% (Belsky & Rovine, 1988). The difference in security between early child care and home care infants is small but statistically significant. In these studies, the dependent measure is attachment security as assessed by the Ainsworth Strange Situation Test.

What accounts for those infants who develop insecure attachments? The infants most at risk for insecure attachments tend to be boys who are rated as difficult and/or fussy, who are insecure-avoidant, and who have mothers who have strong career orientations, work full time, and express less anxiety about being separated from their infants. Generally speaking, the quality of the mother-infant relationship is a stronger predictor of insecure attachments than the child care situation is. Insensitive mothering coupled with low-quality child care accounts for most of the reported insecurity of attachment (Barglow, 1987a; Belsky & Braungart, 1991; Belsky & Rovine, 1988; Chase-Lansdale & Owen, 1987; NICHD Early Child Care Research Network, 1997b). If the quality of care is high and mothers are sensitive, there appear to be few adverse effects of the early child care experience on infant-mother attachment, either at 1 year or later (Burchinal, Bryant, Lee, & Ramey, 1992; Lamb, Sternberg, & Prodromidis, 1992; NICHD Early Child Care Research Network, 1997b; Roggman, Langlois, Hubbs-Tait, & Rieser-Danner, 1994).

In cases where the mother is insensitive, a high-quality child care experience can be beneficial. Research shows that the security of the early child care infant's attachment to mother does not pre-dict social and emotional competence in preschool; rather, the security of attachment to the substitute caregiver and/or the quality of the early care setting is the best predictor of social and emotional competence in preschool (Howes, 1988; Howes & Stewart, 1987; Oppenheim, Sagi, & Lamb, 1988; Phillips, McCartney, & Scarr, 1987; Schindler, Moely, & Frank, 1987; Vaughn, Deane, & Waters, 1985). These relationships were found for infants in the United States in child care centers or family child care homes and on Israeli kibbutzim in which the child's primary attachment is with the metapelet. As we saw in Chapter 7, for infants primarily reared at home, it is the child's attachment to the mother that is the best predictor of preschool social behavior (Egeland & Hiester, 1995).

The data suggest that substitute care for infants under the age of 1 year is indeed a different experience for the infants than if they are placed in such care after the age of 1 year. Under the age of 1 year, infants appear to be more sensitive to the effects of child care quality and to the availability of nonparental attachment figures within the child care setting. These factors are less important for infants older than 1 year, who have already formed a strong attachment to one or both parents. In addition to attachment issues, more hours spent in child care under the age of 1 year is related to

The effects of nonparental child care on infants depend on the conditions of the child care setting, the infant's age, and the parent-infant relationship. Only a small percentage of infants in the United States are able to attend a high-quality child care facility.

Photo by Elizabeth Crews.

lower school readiness scores at age 5, while hours in child care after the age of 1 year are related to higher school readiness at age 5 (NICHD Early Child Care Research Network, 2004).

Does this mean that one should not place children under the age of 1 year in child care for more than a few hours a week, and that mothers or fathers should plan to stay home with infants for at least 1 year? Some observers make a strong case for this position on the following grounds: First, this early experience outside the home somewhat reduces the importance of the parental role. Second, and more important, it may not be possible in the United States today to guarantee high-quality child care for more than a handful of children. If this is true, one may be justified in supporting home care for infants under a year (Barglow, 1987b; Belsky & Rovine, 1988; Magid & McKelvey, 1987). In addition, some mothers want to stay at home with their children if they can afford it financially.

On the other hand, some parents may not be disturbed by a change in their parental role. The findings do not mean that parents are unimportant, only that they have a different type of relationship and provide different sorts of needs for their children than parents who choose to stay at home. In many countries, such as Israel, China, and the former Soviet Union, extensive out-of-home child care is an accepted part of the culture. Advocates of child care in the United States argue that if child care were made more of a national priority, we could guarantee high-quality care for all infants. In the meantime, these advocates provide guidelines for parents to use in evaluating the quality of care in order to assure a good setting for their infants (Howes, 1988; Phillips, McCartney, & Scarr, 1987; Scarr, 1984).

Child Care Policy and Practice

In 1987, Congress began to draft new federal child care legislation in collaboration with a number of child advocacy groups, including the Children's Defense Fund, the Society for Research in Child Development, the American Psychological Association, the American Academy of Pediatrics, and the American Federation of Teachers. Called the ABC bill (Act for Better Child-care), it was designed to provide child care for low-to-moderate- income families and to provide incentives for states to improve the quality of care in centers and in family child care. The ABC bill was finally enacted in late 1990.

The ABC bill, however, met the needs of only a small percentage of children and families. Although we are one of the world's wealthiest nations, we are subsidizing child care for less than 10% of our children under 6 years, compared to 100% in Sweden, 90% in France, and 50% in Israel and Hungary. More than half of young children in the United States are in second-rate child care situations, with substandard facilities, poor staff training, and high staff turnover, in spite of the overwhelming evidence showing the importance of high-quality child care. Three million children in the United States under the age of 14 years are in programs guided by no national standards that reflect current knowledge obtained by research in child development. Licensed child care facilities currently account for only 25% of out-of-home care for children. The rest of the children are in nonlicensed, family-run child care homes.

Although more employers are providing child care at work, these employers still represent less than .1% of the nation's employers. Only 2% of the 1.2 million companies with more than 10 employees have child care on site (Sancier & Mapp, 1992). The private sector is not stepping in and picking up the responsibility. The generally poor care available to many children and the even worse care available to children from low-income and minority groups (B. P. Klein, 1985; Magid & McKelvey, 1987; Kontos, Howes, Shinn, & Galinsky, 1997; J. R. Nelson, 1982; Ruopp & Travers, 1982; Slaughter, 1980; Weintraub & Furman, 1987) testify to the large gap between children's needs and the willingness of our leaders to provide adequately for them.

Slaughter (1980) gives several reasons for the lack of effective child care policies. The first is the myth that the modern family can be independent and self-sufficient. In spite of growing evidence to the contrary, people tend to think they are the masters of their own destiny. Hence, there is a strong resistance to the idea of social policy and social legislation (Bennett, 1987). Studies on the ecology of child development (Bronfenbrenner, 1979; Belsky, 1981) have shown that what happens to the child and the family depends, to a large measure, on the exosystem, mesosystem, and macrosystem of the surrounding society (see Chapter 2). Although a parent may believe that child care services should be found close to or in the home, the reality is that many parents leave their children in situations that are often inadequate and unregulated by state and federal laws.

A second reason given by Slaughter is the fragmentation of social services that exists for families, especially for high-risk families with low incomes. Support services are scattered among many different agencies, making it difficult for parents to obtain necessary services and nearly impossible for the government to exert reasonably efficient regulatory controls. Efforts to unify and streamline these services typically meet with strong political opposition, since many of them fall under the authority of different branches and departments of government (Weintraub & Furman, 1987).

Cultural differences in child care have received relatively little attention. In some societies, nonmaternal care is the norm rather than the exception. In these cultures, the mother is not believed to be the sole contributor to the child's development. This is the case, for example, in African American culture. For most of the research on child care, outcome measures reflected the child's independent competence and ability, such as social and intellectual competence. In other societies, children are not expected to become autonomous but rather to focus on group sharing and cooperation. In such cultures, outcome measures should relate to group orientations rather than to individuals. The cultural diversity of child care philosophies, both for type of care and desired outcomes, have not been sufficiently studied (Friedman, Randolph, & Kochanoff, 2000; Leach, 1997; M. K. Rosenthal, 1999).

In summary, while a great deal of research and practice has been done with respect to child care,

we have a long way to go in the United States. The recent federally funded research on the NICHD child care study is an important step in creating a database that encompasses a wider range of children from diverse settings. More work needs to be done to study how to improve child care quality, how to address cultural differences, and how to implement these findings into workable public policies.

Age and Sex Differences in Nurturance Toward Infants

At what age do people develop an interest in infants, and in being a parent? Are the gender differences? As the results of research on maternal employment suggest, infant care is thought to be part of women's work. Implicit in this belief is that nurturance is part of the female biological heritage, and that women should be able to do this under any circumstances and without support. In actuality, these beliefs are simply not true. Research has shown that the interest and ability to care for babies is present in both males and females early in life and will continue in both genders if fostered by the social environment. In the following sections, we review age and sex differences in responses to infants.

Preschool Age

Are there differences between boys and girls in their responses toward infants? One study that used a single female infant placed in a playpen in a nursery school found that girls approached the baby more than did boys. Once the children were near the baby, however, both boys and girls spoke to, reached out for, and touched the baby equally (Berman, Monda, & Merscough, 1977). Another study used both male and female infants in a waiting-room situation. Preschool children were asked to wait in a laboratory room with a baby and mother for 10 minutes. In this rather unusual situation, many children did not approach the baby. When they did, boys and girls approached in equal numbers, and there were no differences in the types of interaction attempted by male and female children. They usually sat down on the floor, handed the baby toys, or showed the baby his image in a mirror (Melson & Fogel, 1982).

These children almost never talked to the baby. If they wanted to find something out or make a comment, they would talk to the baby's mother about the baby. In addition, there was a same-sex effect for these unfamiliar infant-preschooler pairs similar to that found for sibling pairs (Dunn & Kendrick, 1982). At the ages of 2 and 3 years, boys were more likely to approach male babies, and girls were more likely to approach female babies (Melson & Fogel, 1982).

One interesting twist in this study was that by the time children were 4 to 5 years old, there were still no overall sex differences in the amount of time males and females interacted with the baby. However, both the males and the females preferred to interact with female babies. Perhaps the older boys no longer identify with the babies. By the time the boys were 5 years old, being a boy and being a baby were no longer compatible.

If adults encourage children to become involved with unfamiliar infants, both boys and girls increase their amount of interaction with the babies, and both boys and girls ask the adults questions about the babies (Fogel, Melson, Toda, & Mistry, 1987). Interviews with children in kindergarten and second grade reveal equal interest and equal knowledge about infant care on the part of boys and girls (Melson, Fogel, & Toda, 1986). In general, the research suggests that few sex differences are found among children in their attitudes, knowledge about, and behavior toward infants if they are exposed to infants with adult guidance (Melson & Fogel, 1988). For most children, this exposure occurs in the context of the family, with baby brothers or sisters.

Siblings

Similar types of sex differences have been observed among siblings; that is, same-sex dyads tend to be more positive in their interactions than mixed-sex dyads (Dunn & Kendrick, 1982; Lamb, 1978b). On the other hand, when preschool-age children talk to their infant brothers and sisters, both boys and girls modify their speech to make it sound more like motherese (Dunn & Kendrick, 1982; Sachs & Devin, 1976; Shatz & Gelman, 1973).

The children's speech includes simple utterances, repetition, and high pitch, as in the following example taken from a 4-year-old talking to her younger brother: "Harry! Harry! Have my camera! Have my camera! Naughty boy. You . . . aah! Aah! No!" (Dunn & Kendrick, 1982, p. 124). In some cases, the preschoolers used repetition twice as often as their mothers when talking to babies. About 25% of the preschool-age children were observed to use endearing terms toward the baby and to ask soliciting questions (Are you hungry? Are you getting frustrated?). On the other hand, the majority of the preschoolers rarely asked questions of the baby, whereas question asking is a major form of adult speech to infants (Dunn & Kendrick, 1982).

Later Childhood

Among children aged 8 to 14 years, girls interact more with babies and ignore them less than do boys. Interestingly, however, there are no sex differences in blood pressure, skin conductance, and heart rate: both boys and girls are equally aroused or unaroused by the sight of an infant. Girls, it would seem, make the choice to interact, whereas boys do not (Frodi & Lamb, 1978). A similar study of African American children also found that girls are more likely to look at the babies than boys (Berman, Goodman, Sloan, & Fernandez, 1978).

These differences in male versus female interest in babies continue through high school (Feldman & Nash, 1979a) but they seem to vanish for college students and for young adults (Feldman and Nash, 1978, 1979a; Frodi, Lamb, Leavitt, & Donovan, 1978). Some studies with adults have compared the responses of parents to babies with those of nonparents. The most responsive group is usually new mothers. Men's child-rearing status does not affect their responsiveness to babies (Feldman & Nash, 1978; Sagi, 1981). Mothers tend to be more accurate in their identification of the type of cry (pain, distress, and so on) than fathers, but both mothers and fathers can distinguish their own infant's cry from cries of unfamiliar infants (Wiesenfeld, Malatesta, & DeLoach, 1981).

Parenthood: Mothers versus Fathers

In most comparisons of fathers' and mothers' styles of interaction with infants, fathers are found to be more physical and active with infants than mothers. Fathers are reported to be less contingently responsive with infants and have a style of play and interaction that is more directive and characterized by abrupt changes of activity. By contrast, mothers' games are quieter and more likely to depend on the pace set by the infant. Mothers also engage in proportionately more caregiving than fathers (Lamb et al., 1982; Parke & Sawin, 1980; Pedersen, Suwalsky, Cain, & Zaslow, 1987; Ricks, 1985; Sagi, 1981). These differences are considered important for infants. While contingent responsiveness fosters infants' understanding of the connections between their own actions and those of others, the more directive and unexpected style of father-infant play may lead infants to develop adaptive responses to challenges as they strive to keep up with the father's expectations.

We observed mother-infant and father-infant play in 60 middle-class families (K. L. Dickson, Walker, & Fogel, 1997). Unlike previous studies done as much as 15 or 20 years earlier, our observations of North American, primarily Caucasian fathers in the 1990s found virtually no differences in play style or contingent responsiveness with their 1-year-old infants. It is quite likely that cultural changes have made middle-class fathers more involved and sensitive parents. In another study, mothers and fathers in England were videotaped interacting with their infants with an observer present and later without the observer present. There were fewer mother-father differences when the observer was absent. This suggests that fathers may be somewhat more self-conscious when observed and therefore may appear to be less sensitive (C. Lewis et al., 1996).

There are large cultural differences in the amount of father involvement. In most Asian countries, mothers are expected to play a more traditional role and devote most of their time to the

Fathers and mothers play different types of games with their babies. Both paternal and maternal styles of play are important to infant development.

Photo by Yancey Hughes.

infant while the father works outside the home. In one study done in Taiwan, for example, mothers held, smiled, talked to, and played with infants more than fathers, but both parents displayed similar amounts of soothing and affection toward their infants (Sun & Roopnarine, 1996).

Anthropologists studied primate species that differed in the amount of father involvement. Orangutans and chimps are species in which mothers do virtually all the infant care. Siamangs and gorillas have about as much father care as humans. Owl monkeys and titi monkeys are species in which the fathers do more of the care than mothers. There was a direct correspondence between the amount of infant care and the average life span. Generally speaking, doing more child care is correlated with living longer. Females outlive males in those species where there is more female care, and vice versa (Allman, Rosin, Kumar, & Hasenstaub, 1998). Although this study does not prove that individuals who do more child care will live longer, it certainly suggests that there may be important health benefits, for both men and women, to being involved in child care. Other related research shows that people who give up their own time to help or care for others, at any age, are more likely to live longer and be healthier. Giving, more than receiving, has health benefits (Post, Neimark, & Moss, 2007).

Grandparents

The next phase of caring for infants, following parenting, is becoming a grandparent. Investigators studied the responsiveness to babies of 30 parents of adolescents, 28 parents whose grown children had left home, and 26 grandparents of infants. As you might have guessed, grandparents were more responsive to babies than the other two groups. Grandmothers were more responsive than grandfathers, but grandfathers were more responsive than men at other ages, who tended to be less responsive to babies than their wives (Feldman & Nash, 1979b).

There are very few empirical studies of grandparents and grandchildren and only a handful on grandparent-infant relationships. With the decline of the extended family living under one roof, developmentalists have not taken much interest in grandparents as a source of influence on infants. In many cases, grandparents do not live near their children, and the once-a-year contact with the family is hardly enough to make much of an impression on an infant.

The degree to which grandparents become involved in infant care varies considerably. In some families, grandparents have daily contact with the infants and participate in caregiving as well as play. In others, there may be little or no contact. One reason for this difference may be that adults can become grandparents as young as 30 years of age or as old as 90. Younger grandparents are still employed and have little time for infant care and very old grandparents may not have the strength or health to be involved (Bales, 2002; Cohler & Grunebaum, 1981; Kornhaber & Woodward, 1981; Tinsley & Parke, 1984). Some grandparents also report little interest in being involved with their grandchildren, regardless of how close they live or how much free time they have (Mueller et al., 2002).

A few studies have been done on grandmother-infant attachment (see Chapter 7) at 1 year. The subjects were white, primarily middle-class families in which the grandmother lived nearby and had relatively frequent contact with the infant. This research shows that mothers and grandmothers are nearly interchangeable as attachment figures: infants approach both in times of stress. The more time a grandmother spends with the baby, the more secure the attachment relationship (Myers, Jarvis, & Creasey, 1987; Schaffer & Emerson, 1964).

Spending time with the infant also means spending time with their own daughters or daughters-in-law. This allows for more communication about differences of opinion and belief about child rearing, which improves the mother-grandmother relationship and also the grandmother-infant attachment. In the 1990s, mothers and grandmothers were generally in agreement over beliefs. Mothers, however, were more accepting on the whole than grandmothers of table messiness and

In all cultures, grandparents and infants share a special relationship.
Photo by David Hiser.

nudity indoors, more relaxed about when to begin toilet training, and less rigid in differentiating sex roles in child play. This sample did not, however, differ in their basic beliefs about moral domains; the disagreements were more about personal and social behaviors (Honig & Deters, 1996).

Some studies have shown that grandmothers in African American families are considerably more involved with their infant grandchildren than in Caucasian American families. The grandparents tend to live close by their grown children and devote much of their free time to their children's infants (Cherlin & Furstenberg, 1986; Pearson, Hunter, Ensminger, & Kellam, 1990; Wilson, 1986). Compared to Caucasian parents, African American parents of infants have more frequent contact with kin—including grandmothers—and respect the advice of relatives, showing concern for what the relative thinks is important (Wilson, 1986).

This strong network of ties between relatives was carried to the Americas from traditional African societies. Research has shown that the extended family system is important in the reduction of family stress, especially for low-income, teenage, and single mothers. Typically, the grandmothers are warmer and more patient with the infants than are the infants' teenage mothers. In addition to providing a buffer against the effects of mothers who

have too many of their own problems to cope with their babies, the grandmothers serve as valuable sources of advice and instruction about parenthood for their own daughters. With the support of their mothers, many of these adolescent and at-risk parents are able to continue in their education and eventually become economically self-supporting and caring parents (Colletta & Lee, 1983; Furstenberg, Brooks-Gunn, & Morgan, 1987; Spieker & Bensley, 1994; Stevens, 1984; Wakschlag, Chase-Lansdale, & Brooks-Gunn, 1996).

These studies suggest that involvement between infants and grandparents is dependent on ecological systems factors, including ethnicity, culture, life history factors, and patterns of residence (Mueller & Elder, 2003). These factors also determine the amount of mutual reliance and mutual trust between family members, both of which affect the quality of the social network of kinship in which the child develops. Social support networks are discussed more thoroughly later in this chapter.

In summary, it seems that the biggest differences in male versus female responsiveness to infants appear in middle childhood and adolescence. Preschool boys, men of child-rearing age, and grandfathers are about equally responsive to babies as their female counterparts. These studies suggest that sex differences in interest in babies may be related to society's expectations of how males and females should behave rather than to some underlying biological predisposition favoring females. Males' interest in babies corresponds to the times in the life cycle when men are exposed to babies and are expected to take an interest in them. Women are more likely to be expected to be interested in babies all through their lives.

CULTURAL DIFFERENCES IN INFANT CARE PRACTICES

As mentioned earlier, culture has a major impact over all phases of infant and childcare, both within and outside the family. Cultural beliefs are passed down between generations and dictate practice. There is, however, a surprising amount of within-culture variability in every society. Some parents are more conservative and some more liberal in interpreting the cultural beliefs and putting them into practice.

Childbirth

How childbirth is experienced is dictated in large measure by the cultural beliefs of the society. Not all societies greet the event of birth in the same way. Some peoples consider it an illness or an abnormality, whereas others view it as part of the fabric of everyday affairs. The Cuna of Panama consider birth to be a secret event. In the United States, birth is considered a private affair, with only medical personnel and a few family members in attendance. Some cultures on the extreme end of the privacy dimension consider birth to be defiling and insist that women give birth in a separate area, which often is reserved for such things as childbirth, menstruation, and excrement (M. Mead & Newton, 1967).

At the other extreme, the Jahara of South America give birth under a shelter in full view of everyone in the village—even small children. A number of Pacific Island communities also regard the birth of a child as an event of interest to the entire community.

To illustrate the cultural influences on childbirth and child-care practices in the newborn period, a portrait of three cultures from widely different parts of the globe will be presented: Zinancantecan Indians from Mexico, originally of Mayan descent; villagers from the south of Italy; and the Japanese.

No drugs are used during labor among the Zinancantecans. The mother is supported and encouraged by an ever-present midwife. After birth, the newborn is placed naked before a fire. The midwife, who is still in attendance, begins to say prayers asking the gods to look kindly upon this child. A long skirt made of heavy fabric is brought out and put on the infant. Extending beyond the feet, the skirt is worn by both males and females throughout the first year of life. For fear of losing parts of the soul, the newborn is wrapped snugly in several layers of blankets; even the face is covered, except during feedings. This practice is believed to ward off evil spirits and illnesses during the first few months of life (Brazelton, 1977).

On the other side of the Atlantic, birth in a small village in southern Italy usually takes place in a hospital, attended by a midwife. Just after the birth, as in Mexico, the newborn is dressed in clothing and ceremonial linens the family has provided. When the infant is dressed, usually within about 10 minutes of the birth, the midwife goes into the hall, where the mother's entire immediate and extended family has been waiting. They all accompany the midwife back to the mother's room, where everyone takes a turn congratulating, kissing, and fondling both the mother and the baby.

The family then provides a party of pastries and liqueurs to share with one another and with those who attended the birth. During the labor, the mother was never left alone, and she will continue to be supported by rituals like this one. The mother will be visited by many of her friends and relatives for some time after the birth. These visits have the effect of recognizing the contribution the mother has made to the community. This social support system is embodied in the role of the mother-in-law. From a few days before until about 1 month after the birth, she feeds the mother rit-

Each culture has different rituals for childbirth and newborn care. In most places, newborns are immediately integrated into family life. This family is from Morocco.
Photo by Owen Franken.

ual foods of broth, marsala, and fresh cheeses. All mothers breast-feed their infants, and the infant usually sleeps in the same bed as the mother or in a nearby cradle (Schreiber, 1977).

Finally, in traditional Japanese society, interdependent relationships between people are viewed as extremely important. Children are valued and loved, and their development is celebrated by a number of community rituals. These rituals start during the fifth month of pregnancy, when the woman begins to wear a special belt (called an iwata-obi) around her abdomen under the kimono. This ritual is believed to establish the child's first tie to the community. After birth, the umbilical cord is dried and saved in an ornamental box, reminding the mother and child of their once-close physical bond. From birth until late childhood, children sleep with their parents, since it is believed that sleeping alone breaks the family psychological bonds.

On the day of the birth and on the third and seventh day of the infant's life, elaborate feasts are celebrated among all the relatives. Since these early days are thought to be critical to the infant's survival, the feasts ensure health for the baby. A special naming ceremony is performed on the seventh day, and at 1 month, the baby is taken to the Shinto shrine for blessing. At the age of 100 days, the infant is given a grain of rice as its first token solid food (Kojima, 1986). Although some of these traditional practices are changing due to the urbanization of Japan, the basic commitment to the infant's value remain.

Cultural Differences in Adult Behavior Toward Young Infants

We have already mentioned that some aspects of motherese may be universally seen in all cultures

(Chapter 6). In general, because babies are similar around the world, we can expect them to elicit similar sorts of behavior from adults. On the other hand, there are some notable cultural differences in adult-infant communication.

We have already seen how some African mothers interact with their babies using a large variety of postural manipulation and motor exercise. In a study of infant development in Nigeria, Elauma infants were compared to a group of infants in Oxford, England (Whiten & Milner, 1986). The Elauma are hunter-gatherers. At 3 months of age, Elauma infants spend almost all their time, whether awake or asleep, in physical contact with an adult or within three feet of the adult. When the Elauma infants cry, they are responded to more often and more quickly than are the English babies, and the response from the adult is more likely to be physical than verbal. The Elauma infant is more a part of the mother's everyday life. She carries the baby around with her, and babies often ride on the mothers' backs or sit in their laps while the mothers go about their daily chores. The babies sleep next to their mothers.

The pattern of close physical contact and rapid response to crying (called attachment parenting; see Chapter 7) is common among hunting and gathering cultures worldwide (Konner, 1977). Hunter-gatherer groups move camps several times a year. They are egalitarian with respect to age and gender differences and have little political hierarchy. In one study, a hunter-gatherer group (the Aka) was compared with a neighboring agricultural group (the Ngandu) in Central Africa. The Ngandu are sedentary farmers with strong chiefs and clear inequalities in age and gender roles. In the Aka, men and women contribute equally to infant care and other tasks. Roles are divided along traditional lines in the Ngandu. The Ngandu have more infant-care devices, the infants wear more clothing, and are more likely to be physically separate from their mothers compared to the Aka. The Ngandu mothers are more likely to let their infants fuss or cry. Like mothers in the urban cultures, they tend to use more distal play and object play with their babies (Hewlett,

Lamb, Shannon, Leyendecker, & Schölmerich, 1998). This study shows that differences in infant care are not due simply to urban versus rural factors, or Western versus non-Western, but rather to differences in lifestyle. The more egalitarian society, used to equality and sharing of resources, seems to promote closer and more lasting contact with the infant.

Japanese mothers also react in different ways to their babies than North American mothers. Japanese mothers spend less time in physical contact with their babies than American mothers when the babies are awake, although Japanese babies sleep with their mothers at night. American mothers hold, rock, bounce, touch, and kiss their babies considerably more than Japanese mothers, and when interacting with babies, American mothers hold their faces closer to the babies (Caudill & Weinstein, 1969; Fogel, Toda, & Kawai, 1988; Otaki, Durrett, Richards, Nyquist, & Pennebaker, 1986; Shand & Kosawa, 1985).

When they verbalize to babies, Japanese and American mothers are quite different. Over the course of an entire day, Japanese mothers tend to use more negative vocalizations, such as prohibitions and expressions of negative feelings. When actually engaged in a playful interaction with their babies, Japanese mothers use more nonsense sounds and more baby talk, as shown in Table 8.4, while American mothers use more complete sentences and more recognizable adult words. When an American mother might use vocalizations to get her baby's attention, a Japanese mother either uses vocal noises or makes noise with her hands, like clapping and finger snapping (Bornstein, Tal, et al., 1992; Fogel, Toda, & Kawai, 1988; Toda, Fogel, & Kawai, 1990). American mothers are more likely to label objects, while Japanese mothers are more likely to talk about how to incorporate objects into social play (Fernald & Morikawa, 1993).

Navajo mothers rarely talk to infants, although they are responsive to babies' cries and touch the babies a great deal. Traditional Navajo keep babies more physically distant from their mothers with the use of cradle boards (Callaghan, 1981; J. S. Chisholm, 1983). Similar patterns of behavior

TABLE 8.4   Examples of Baby Talk Used by Japanese Mothers

English Equivalent	Adult Speech	Baby Talk	Explanation
Are you hungry?	Onaka suita?	Onaka shuita	Phonological change
Let's play	Asobimashee	Achobimachoo	Phonological change
Please	Doozo	Doojo	Phonological change
Eye	Me	Meme	Duplication
It hurts	Itai	Itai-tai	Duplication
Get up	Okiru	Okki	Shortening
Hiccup	Shakkuri	Hikku hikku	Mimic sound of action
Lamp	Denki	Denki-san	Use of honorific
Dirty	Katanai	Batchii	Entirely new word

Source: S. Today, A. Fogel, & M. Kawai, Maternal speech to three-month-old infants in the United States and Japan, 1990, p. 287. *Journal of Child Language, 17*, 279–294.

have been observed among the Maya Indians of Mexico (Brazelton, 1977).

In the Japanese and Native American cultures, adults believe, as did the seventeenth- century European romantics, that infants are precious and innocent beings who are close to God, and that they should generally be kept quiet and not influenced by adults until they begin to make some of their own initiatives, around the age of 6 months. This "hands-off" respect for the infant's autonomy and individuality is not found in the West. Influenced by John Locke's seventeenth-century idea of empiricism, we try to affect sleeping, feeding, and interactive social behavior from an early age. We want our babies to be scheduled, to smile at us, and not to cry (Fogel, Stevenson, & Messinger, 1992). American and European adults especially like to encourage independence through didactic (teaching) behaviors leading to infant socialization (Bornstein, Tamis-LeMonda, et al., 1992).

The East Asian (Indian) philosophy of child rearing is summed up in the elaborate rituals performed for infants in Hindu culture in India (see Table 8.5). Indian families tend to keep the babies quiet and introduce them very gradually to the world. This introduction does not begin in earnest until 6 to 9 months, when early childhood is considered to begin. Indian mothers talk to and touch their babies more than the Japanese do. Infant massage is commonly practiced in India, and even the mothers receive regular massage from their female relatives.

Some of the recent interest in somatic awareness and touch therapies in North America and Europe has been adapted from ancient Indian somatic practices such as Yoga, Buddhist meditation, and massage. Chinese and Japanese somatic awareness methods such as tai chi, judo, kendo, and zen also have their origins in ancient Indian culture.

There are wide differences between cultures in the amount of time mothers spend with babies, in parental beliefs about infant care, and in the types of activities they perform when with the babies. Climate is one factor that accounts for cultural differences in child-rearing patterns. In warm countries, infants tend to be carried by their caregivers, to remain in close physical contact throughout most of the day and night, and to be breast-fed longer than infants reared in cold climates. Infants in cold climates are more likely to be separated from their mothers at an earlier age. They sleep in cradles, are carried in strollers and buggies, and are kept at a distance from the parents through the use of infant seats and playpens (Agiobu-Kemmer, 1986; Keller et al., 2004; Whiten & Milner, 1986; J. Whiting, 1981).

These differences are believed to be due to the need to wrap babies in cold climates against the cold (see Figure 8.2). Since both the adult and

TABLE 8.5   Hindu Beliefs About the Stages of Infancy and Childhood

Stage	Mode of Relationship	Ritual Performed at the End of the Stage
Garbha (fetus)	Symbolic	Jatakama: Birthing ritual
Ksheerda (infancy)	Dyad intimiacy (0–1 month)	Namakarana: Naming ceremony; the child meets the father and siblings for the first time
	Dyad in family (1–4 months)	Nishakarmana: First outing, first look at the sun and moon
	Dyad in world (4–8 months)	Annaprasana: Introduction to solid foods, weaning from the breast
Ksheerannada		Chudakarana: First ritual cutting of (early childhood) hair

Source: P. Sharan, One view of the cultural context for the study of childrearing in India, 1988, p. 8. *Newsletter of the International Society for the Study of Behavioral Development, 13*, 1–8.

infant must wear many layers of protective clothing, parent-infant skin contact is very difficult. Over many centuries, child-rearing practices have evolved to adapt to this fundamental ecological constraint (J. Whiting, 1981).

There are also cultural differences in parental beliefs about emotion regulation and parent-infant communication about emotions that emerge in the second half year (Harkness et al., 2007). In North America, for example, parents are most frequently concerned about providing sufficient stimulation for the baby's brain and overall development. This means that parents want infants to learn how to handle a variety of toys, books, and adults without getting upset. At the same time, North American parents want their infants to know they are loved by giving explicit reassurances. One mother said of her infant:

Right now, at his age, I try to hold him as much as I can, and I have Michael hold him as much as he can, and I have Tony give him kisses because I feel that even at this age we're instilling love in him, and he knows we love him, and I don't want him to ever think that he's not loved. (Harkness et al., 2007, p. 20)

Korean mothers are like the North Americans in their interest in providing books, reading, music and other stimulation to foster the infant's development. The Koreans do not expose the infant to a variety of people outside the immediate family. The baby is seen as vulnerable, in need of protection, and that it is up to the parents to follow the baby's lead and adapt. According to one Korean mother:

Being a mom is a very happy event but at the same time I feel a heavy responsibility… I think I have to be flexible. If I push him too much then it will be too stressful for the baby and for me too. So I have to learn and study about parenting. And I need to plan ahead. (Harkness et al., 2007, p. 31)

Another Korean mother said, "I am willing to hold him whenever he wants to be held even though it might be physically hard on me" (p. 31), a theme of parental co-dependence on the infant that does not appear salient in North American and Northern European cultures.

Mothers from Italy, a more southern culture in a warmer climate, had similar feelings about expressing love and feeling emotional closeness with the baby as the North American mothers but the Italians were not as focused on cognitive stimulation and brain development. Instead, Italian mothers made attempts to expose the infant to social and family groups, and they judged their infants not on whether they felt love or had

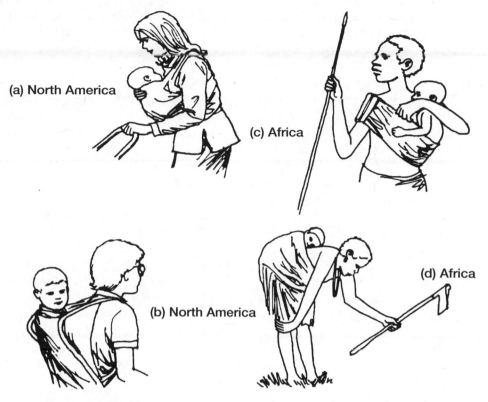

Figure 8.2 Infant-Carrying Practices
In warm climates, infants spend more time in skin-to-skin contact with adults. Infants in cold climates must wear protective clothing, making them more difficult to carry for long periods.
Source: A. Fogel & G. F. Melson, *Child development*, 1988, p. 187. St. Paul, MN: West. Copyright © West Publishing Company. Reprinted by permission. All rights reserved.

enough stimulation but rather on whether they liked the company of other people, whether they were socially alive and engaged (*vivace*).

Research on Latin American cultures reveals similar patterns. Franco, Fogel, Messinger, & Frazier (1996) did a study of mother-infant physical contact during play between 26 Hispanic American and 26 Anglo-American mothers and their 9-month-old infants. Although the overall amount of touching and physical contact did not differ between groups, Hispanic mothers touched, kissed, hugged, and held their infants physically closer than Anglo mothers. On questionnaires, the Hispanic mothers reported placing a higher value on touch and affection than Anglo mothers. These cultural differences were the same in all income levels in the sample.

As a general rule, the cultures of southern Europe and Central and South America have close patterns of touching, physical contact, kissing, and hugging even between adults. It seems that these behaviors are seen as expressions of close social ties between people at all ages. Puerto Rican mothers, for example, are more likely than Anglo mothers to physically direct the child's body and behavior during play and feeding situations. The Anglo mothers are more likely to use praise and suggestions, focusing on verbal means of communication (Harwood et al., 1999).

In more technical and industrial societies, mother-infant play is embedded in a matrix of communication and warmth. In these societies—including, for example, Japan, Korea, Europe, and North America, and urban families everywhere—

the parent will begin to *interpret the infant's intentions.* Assuming that the parent has made a correct interpretation, the next step is usually to *help the infant carry out the intended act.* In addition, parents often *create new intentions* that were not there in the first place. Instead of simply helping infants get objects they see, parents may hold out an object to get the baby interested or make sounds or movements to try to get the baby to imitate them (Adamson, 1995; Kaye, 1982; Lock, 1980; Rogoff, 1990).

The situation is much like the study of music or language, for example, in which teachers require that their pupils learn simple exercises. The student has little notion of the purpose of learning scales, arpeggios, the parts of speech, or conjugations. Nevertheless, the instructor understands the relationship of the exercises to the final skilled performance. Some examples of these kinds of instructional interactions involving a 7-month-old baby are given in Observations 8.1 and 8.2.

By contrast, in nontechnical agricultural and hunter-gatherer communities, adults are more directive and ritualistic in their interactions with infants (Whiten & Milner, 1986). Among the Gusii, an agricultural community in Kenya, when mothers taught children to do a task, they used a lot of repetition, provided direct demonstration of the whole task (they did not break it into simpler components), and pulled on the infants' hands to encourage participation. The mothers used very little vocalization and little praise or reinforcement (Dixon, LeVine, Richman, & Brazelton, 1984). Chomorro mothers, from a fishing community on the Pacific island of Guam, were highly directive when interacting with infants; they talked quickly, dominated the interactions, were highly repetitive, and abruptly shifted activities in a manner more suited to their own pace than to the infants' (Carlile & Holstrum, 1989).

It is not necessarily the case that one style of play and teaching is better than another. Each style has evolved to fit the needs of the particular culture. Problems may arise, however, when cultures are forced to interact. Cultural-minority families from traditional backgrounds are often at a disadvantage when they enter urban envi-

---

Observations

Early Communicative Interactions Rely on Adult Interpretations (Lock, 1980)

Observation 8.1

Mary: age 7(10): A spoonful of food has just been placed in Mary's mouth when the telephone rings. Mother takes Mary's left hand and wraps it round the spoon handle, which is sticking from Mary's mouth.
Mother: "You take it while Mummy answers the phone."
Mary: pulls the spoon from her mouth and while eating waves it about. While still holding the spoon, she pushes her hand around in her dinner and then starts licking her hand. While she is doing this mother returns.
Mother: "There's a clever girl, are you feeding yourself? Here, let's wipe you, you're ever so mucky."
She takes the spoon from Mary to wipe her.

Mary cries and struggles, then reaches out toward the spoon.
Mother: "All right, here you are. Let me show you."
She gives Mary the spoon and then guiding her hand, places it into the dish and then to Mary's mouth.
Mother: "Oh, aren't we clever! Aren't we clever!"

Observation 8.2

Mary: age 7(27): Mary is in her chair, having finished her afternoon meal.
Mother comes through the door with a packet of biscuits in her hand. The door is behind Mary and out of her view. As mother comes in, Mary coos and smiles, turning around to see her mother.
Mother: "Yes, you heard me coming, didn't you?"
She enters Mary's field of view, and Mary reaches out towards her mother's hand; her whole body straining in the chair.
Mother: "Yes, they're your favourites, aren't they?"

ronments. Their styles of interaction are not well suited to the urban lifestyle and the demands of school-based learning. Hispanic Americans, as a minority culture in the United States, often feel self-conscious about their cultural styles of raising infants. They report feeling self-conscious in the company of their Anglo-American neighbors and think of themselves as "too affectionate" with their infants (Franco et al., 1996). These patterns of cultural tension reveal how difficult it is for some parents to maintain the traditional values and practices of their minority culture. In support of this observation, research shows that as Latin American families acculturate to North American society—learning English, becoming educated in North American schools, and adopting Northern cultural values— they are less likely to preserve the language and cultural values of the home country (Cabrera et al., 2006).

According to ecological systems theory, this is a conflict between the microsystem of the family and the macrosystem of the culture, especially when the family values are different from those of the dominant culture. The research reviewed in this section shows that cultural differences become important in early development, well before the child enters school.

THE CULTURE OF POVERTY AND ITS IMPACT ON INFANTS

It has been widely recognized that families with widely different income levels, even within the same country or region, constitute different cultural environments. The infant care practices and beliefs of the poor differ dramatically from those of the middle class, and the middle class from the very wealthy. Each of these groups has different access to resources and each adapts their childrearing styles to the conditions in which they live. Of particular concern, however, is the effect of poverty and its culture on developing children.

In 1960, one-quarter of all children under 5 years old in the United States were living in poverty. By 1980, this figure had fallen to 17%; by 1994, it had risen again to 25% of all children, but by 2005 it had fallen to 18%. An increasing proportion of these poor children live in female-headed single families, which today constitute the fastest growing poverty group in the United States. These figures are shocking. When we compare them to statistics for other wealthy nations, they become a matter of national shame. When our childhood poverty rate was the lowest, in 1980 at 17%, the childhood poverty rate was 10% in Canada, 8% in West Germany, 5% in Sweden, and 11% in the United Kingdom. Child poverty rates have continued to decline in these other countries (Bane & Ellwood, 1989; Hernandez, 1997; Huston, 1994; McLoyd, 1998; Smeeding & Torrey, 1988).

On a worldwide scale, there are 2.2 billion children in the world, of which 1 billion are living in poverty. Most of these children have little or no access to adequate health care, shelter, clean water, or education. The United Nations estimates that 30,000 children in the world die *every day* from the consequences of poverty.

What Are Some of the Causes of These Poverty Rates and National Differences?

Single parenthood. In all countries, as you might expect, single-parent families are poorer than two-parent families because of the reduced earning power of a single adult. In addition, due to the structure of most welfare systems, it is not advantageous for many single mothers to work outside the home because of the added costs and risks of child care.

For example, an unemployed single mother with two children in the United States in 1986 could collect $6,284 in welfare and food stamps. If she worked full-time in a minimum wage job, she would earn a salary of $6,700 and could still collect $2,744 in welfare. By the time she paid for child care (about $3,000) and taxes ($373), her resulting income would be $6,817, only $533 more than if she were unemployed and stayed home with her children (Bane & Ellwood, 1989).

Twenty years later, in 2006, the situation would be no different.

Diverse populations. In the United States, poverty level varies considerably as a function of race and ethnicity. The percentage of African American children living in poverty (the number of poor African American children divided by the total number of African American children) is three times as high as for Caucasian children, and the rate for Hispanic children is twice as high as for Caucasian children. Even so, the poverty rate of Caucasian children alone is higher than in most other wealthy nations. Obviously, not all poverty occurs in minority groups.

Lack of public support for families. In the United States, welfare and other public benefits are given to individuals, not to families. One of the problems is that children do not have their own rights to such benefits. While the poverty rate among the elderly has dropped in recent years due to increased medical and Social Security benefits to individuals, the poverty rate for children has increased. At least 25% of families with children living below the poverty level in the United States receive no welfare or other forms of support. In contrast, almost 100% of poor families receive benefits in Canada, Germany, Sweden, and the United Kingdom (Smeeding & Torrey, 1988). Contrary to popular belief, one or both parents work in over three- quarters of the poor families with children in the United States. Of the remaining 25% of families, 15% have parents who do not work because of illness or disability or because they are past retirement age (Bane & Ellwood, 1989). Thus, the welfare system cannot be blamed for keeping families in poverty. Most parents work if they are able to.

The economic system. Since none of the above factors by itself—single parenthood, race and ethnicity, and welfare—can explain why so many families are poor, what does? The best explanation seems to be the economy as a whole. If the economy slows down, middle- and upper-income families fare better than those at the bottom.

Lower-income families suffer more from the lack of an annual raise or the loss of a job, since they have no other resources on which to depend. In addition, the number of blue-collar jobs is steadily declining in favor of jobs requiring more technical training, such as working with computers.

Analysts suggest some alternatives to welfare that might help these poor families. These alternatives include better tax credits for lower-income families (in the United States, higher-income families receive the most tax credits), a higher minimum wage, better child care alternatives that are not based on how much money you can afford to pay, and better medical care to alleviate the chronic health problems associated with poverty. Nonwelfare options may also contribute to a better life for such families. These include enforcing child support payments from absent fathers, parent education and job training, and community support and intervention services (Bane & Ellwood, 1989; Huston, 1994). In fact, the children of low-income working mothers who also receive some welfare assistance have better cognitive and mental health outcomes than for mothers who did not work. Apparently, working gives access to social support, better coping strategies, and more stimulating home learning environments, while supplementary welfare payments reduce financial stress (Brooks- Gunn et al., 2001).

How Are Children Affected By Living in Poor Families?

Poverty breeds mental and health risks due to an increased and continuous stream of stressful life events, including job loss, worry about bills, eviction, illness, alcoholism and drug dependency, marital discord, assault, arrest, and imprisonment. In addition, poor children receive lower-quality prenatal care, lower-quality day care, and lower access to informal and formal support systems (McLoyd, 1998; NICHD Early Child Care Research Network, 1997; Roach et al., 2005). These factors feed off each other, leading to increasingly dismal cycles of loss, stress, and despair. When these factors are then compounded with racial and social-class prejudice, the risk to mental health is enormous (McLoyd, 1990; McLoyd, 1998).

Due to these stresses, poor parents have been shown to be less emotionally available for their children, less affectionate, harsher in their disciplinary styles, and more likely to respond punitively to relatively minor forms of child misbehavior. Fathers seem particularly affected; they grow more harsh, and many leave the family entirely. On the positive side, however, some families report greater parent-child closeness following job loss, as well as more family solidarity. Evidence from a variety of sources—including the effects of the Great Depression in the 1930s, the experience of inner-city families, and the results of job losses due to farm foreclosures and plant closings in middle-class America—reveals a surprising pattern of individual variation in family response to poverty, ranging from renewed parent-child closeness to child abuse and neglect (Coles, 1971; Davis & Mantler, 2004; Elder, Nguyen, & Caspi, 1985; Ispa et al., 2004; McLoyd, 1990; 1997; Perrucci & Targ, 1988; G. Peterson & Peters, 1985; Portes, Dunham, & Williams, 1986). Some research even suggests that harsher parental discipline may better prepare children for the hardships they will face growing up in poverty (Sameroff & Seifer, 1983). In general, however, poverty has more negative than positive effects on parent-child relationships.

Children from poor families suffer more from depression, poor peer relations, social withdrawal, low self-esteem, deviant behavior patterns, aggressiveness (particularly in boys), and lowered aspirations (especially for girls). In addition, these children often contract more infectious diseases, are less skilled verbally and interpersonally, and do less well in school and on other indices of cognitive development (Bronfenbrenner, 1986; McLoyd, 1990; McLoyd & Wilson, 1991; Patterson, Kupersmidt, & Vaden, 1990; Ramey & Campbell, 1991).

Conclusions

Children under the age of 3 years are disproportionately represented in poverty rates. Because of their relative helplessness and vulnerability, infants may suffer more from the effects of poverty than older children do (Bronfenbrenner, 1986). Consider the following chain of events: A teenage girl or young woman has grown up in an inner-city culture of poverty. She has suffered from parental neglect and malnutrition. Even if she is lucky enough to have escaped physical or sexual abuse, she has been hardened against her own feelings and those of others. She gets sick often, takes alcohol and drugs to excess, eats mostly junk food, and gets no exercise or fresh air. She is likely to become pregnant before her twentieth birthday and is likely to bear and keep the child. She may not detect that she is pregnant until the second or third month, may not see a doctor until near the end of her pregnancy, and is unlikely to change any of her risky health behaviors. What would you predict is likely to happen to her child, based on what you know about the needs of a typically developing fetus?

It is statistically likely (see Chapter 9) that her baby will be born prematurely, and in addition, may suffer from a variety of prenatal and perinatal disorders, many of which will have lasting effects on the future development of the brain and body. The long-term follow-up data suggest that high-risk newborns who are raised in high-risk families are likely to develop mental and physical health problems, behavior disorders, and intellectual deficits (see Chapter 10). When this child becomes a teenager, will she fare better than her mother? The conditions of poverty, acting through generational developmental cycles, perpetuate the suffering and widen the gap between rich and poor.

The U.S. government does not place the welfare of families and children high on the national agenda. The attitude of the government seems to be that the community will take care of itself, and that private business, if given enough tax credits, will share the burden. This has not happened. Indeed, corporations and businesses spend millions of dollars to lobby against federal legislation for day care, parental leave, and a higher minimum wage. This is because these programs cost money, which would take a share of the business profits. Businesses that support the family, in the community and for their own employees, make up a very small minority of all businesses.

THE CULTURE OF COMMUNITY SUPPORT SYSTEMS FOR FAMILIES WITH INFANTS

Even small amounts of community support can have lasting positive effects on families and children living in poverty. On the other hand, without intervention, some of the effects of early malnutrition, disease, abuse, and neglect may be irreversible. This raises a broader question about the ways families with infants interface with their communities. Even well-functioning, middle-income families require support and intervention from their families and communities. In cases of poverty and other risks to parenting, community support is essential and makes a difference in the outcomes for both parents and children. We discuss both informal and formal supports for families with infants.

Informal Support Systems

Informal support systems are social networks that include friends, relatives, neighbors, co-workers, and other acquaintances, as well as community organizations that are not run by government agencies, such as churches, YWCAs, and community centers (Parke & Tinsley, 1987). One of the primary informal support systems is the marriage and extended family.

Research has shown that in two-parent families, the spouse is the most used and effective member of the social network. Spouses can provide relief from child care and consultation about child-rearing issues and can mediate when stresses on the partner predispose the partner toward impatience and harshness toward the children. Spouses can also provide needed encouragement and emotional support to each other (Levitt, Weber, & Clark, 1986; Parke & Tinsley, 1987; Weinraub & Wolf, 1983).

Typically, the infant's maternal grandmother is the next most frequent source of support; this is true for both two-parent and single-parent families. As discussed earlier and in Chapter 7, grandparents who live nearby and spend time with the infants share secure attachments with the infants and provide similar types of support for the parents as a spouse does. The special value of spouses and grandparents is that they are embedded in the family and are willing to intervene directly in the parent-child relationship. This may take the form of explaining child-rearing principles and mediating between the parent and the infant (Levitt, Weber, & Clark, 1986; McLoyd, 1990; J. H. Stevens, 1988). Teenage single mothers, both African American and Caucasian, are less punitive to their infants if the grandmother is involved (see the section on adolescent mothers in Chapter 3). The teens say things like "I would hit him more if it weren't for my parents" and "My parents won't let me spank him as often as I think he should be spanked" (McLoyd, 1990, p. 335).

As a general rule, emotional support is correlated with better parenting outcomes, regardless of where the support comes from. Parents, particularly mothers, who receive more support are less likely to be punitive in their child rearing (Colletta, 1981), more likely to play and be affectionate with their infants (Cotterell, 1986), respond more quickly to the babies' cries, have more secure attachments (Crockenberg, 1987; Crockenberg & McCluskey, 1986), are more nurturant, have more positive attitudes about child rearing (Weinraub & Wolf, 1983), and abuse their infants less (Garbarino, 1976). Having a larger and more complex support network is related to better-quality support and to parental competence in child rearing (Ball & Pianta, 1993; Melson, Hsu, & Ladd, 1993).

Factors Mediating the Impact of Informal Support Systems

Social attitudes. Unfortunately, however, not all families benefit from social support systems. In some cases, this is due to social attitudes associated with certain types of families and children. For example, studies comparing social support for families with preterm and special-needs infants with families of typically developing infants find that the latter receive more social support. Well-functioning, middle-class families with preterm infants report receiving fewer offers of support and gifts, such as clothing and furniture, than similar families with full-term infants (Feiring et al.,1987).

Even when friends and family provide support to parents of preterm infants, the quality of that support may be diminished. With a preterm birth, network members may not know how to respond appropriately, and their attempts to help result in ambiguous or stressful communications, leading to a lessening of the impact of their support on the family (Zarling, Hirsch, & Landry, 1988). In general, social networks are more supportive when the psychological stress of the parents is relatively low, when the family is experiencing an expected or understandable life transition (such as a temporary job loss or a death in the family), and when the source of stress is a single event rather than a long-term problem (Crnic & Greenberg, 1987; Crockenberg, 1987; Dressler, 1985).

Parental personality. A number of studies have shown that abusive parents have small social networks and an overall poorer quality of support. This may be due in part to the fact that the personality of the abusive parent keeps the child and the social network at a distance. These parents may actively discourage those who seek to help (Crittenden, 1985; Trickett & Susman, 1988). Some parents may have poor interpersonal skills that lead to an inability to seek help and maintain supportive social ties (Parke & Tinsley, 1987). On the other hand, seeking help from family and friends entails some cost in the form of obligations for friendly behavior and doing favors in return. Some parents may prefer isolation to the burden of these obligations (McLoyd, 1990).

Cultural attitudes about seeking help. Finally, the effects of informal support networks may be lessened if parents distrust the sources of support. African American and Caucasian mothers find different types of supports most useful. For example,

African American mothers tend to rely more on the extended family for support. They view professionals as unsympathetic and cannot reconcile professional advice with family norms and values. Caucasian mothers are more likely to rely on professional sources of support (Colletta, 1981; Crockenberg, 1987; J. H. Stevens, 1988). These differences may be explained by the fact that most professionals are Caucasian and may not appreciate the differences in values between their culture and the minority family culture.

Formal Support Systems

Formal support systems are structured programs designed to meet the special needs of parents and infants. Some programs are specifically focused on parent-infant mental health (see Chapter 9) while others take a broader focus including health care, education, counseling services, Internet-based services, social services, housing, welfare, and recreational facilities. Other services may include childbirth education (see Chapter 3), well- baby care, parent training programs, and early childhood education for disadvantaged toddlers. The variety of services available and their effects will not be discussed here for reasons of space (see Berlin, O'Neal, & Brooks-Gunn, 1998; Greenspan & Wieder, 1997; Parke & Tinsley, 1987; D. R. Powell, 2001 for a more complete review).

Generally, educational interventions for parents, even in small doses, can be enormously effective, especially when combined with health care and income support. Short classes, films, Internet sites, and books can enrich the parenting experiences in well-functioning families and give parents needed confidence. Young fathers, who typically would be less likely to join a group outside the home, find that Internet support groups—such as www.fathersnetwork.org and www.fathers.net— enhance parenting self-efficacy and satisfaction (Hudson et al., 2003). For families at risk, a more comprehensive effort is most effective. Some of the more successful programs combine preschool education for the infants, a nurse-home visitor for home-based parent education, and an effort to link parents up with other formal and informal community supports (education, job training and placement, recreational facilities, etc.).

One example of a family support intervention program included a home visitor who served as a counselor and liaison with other agencies, pediatric care, day care, and developmental testing that the parents were able to observe. The families who participated were from a low-income inner-city area, the infants had no birth complications and were firstborns, and the mothers had no history of serious psychological illness. A follow-up study of the children 10 years after their participation in the program compared the children who were in the program to a matched sample of children who did not attend. The children in the intervention program had better school attendance and required less welfare and special education programming. The mothers were more likely to be economically independent, had completed more years of school, and had fewer children than the control mothers (Field et al., 1983; Seitz, Rosenbaum, & Apfel, 1985).

Other multisite, multimethod intervention programs have been shown to decrease reliance on welfare, reduce parental substance abuse, and lower the incidence of criminal acts when the infants become adolescents (Honig, 2004; A. J. Reynolds, 1998). Generally speaking, the most successful programs are those that provide high-quality educational child care for the infant coupled with home- and center-based support services for the parents and families. Neither parent education alone nor child care alone is as effective as the two are in combination (M. M. Black & Krishnakumar, 1998; D. R. Powell, 2000; C. T. Ramey & Ramey, 1998; Yoshikawa, 1999).

Head Start is a federally funded national preschool (3 to 6 years) education program with goals similar to the projects mentioned above. Since it was started by President Lyndon Johnson in 1965, Head Start has enjoyed bipartisan support in Congress, but it has received funding for only 40% of all eligible children. In the 30 years between 1965 and 1995, Head Start served more than 14 million poor (83% had family incomes below

$12,000) preschool children: one-third were Caucasian, one-third were African American, and the rest were Hispanic and Native American. In 1994, 740,493 children were enrolled at a annual cost of $4,343 per child.

Recent long-term follow-up research comparing Head Start children with those who attended other day care or had no support show that Head Start children were more advanced educationally and cognitively; however, the differences between the Head Start and the other groups diminished with increasing age (V. E. Lee, Brooks-Gunn, & Schnur, 1988; V. E. Lee, Brooks-Gunn, Schnur, & Liaw, 1990). Although the cognitive gains are not impressive, other research shows that 15 years after Head Start the participating children had fewer teen pregnancies and a higher high school graduation rate, and they were more likely to be employed and less likely to have been arrested (Berrueta-Clement et al., 1984; Ludwig & Phillips, 2007; Schweinhart & Weikart, 1979). Other research shows gains for Head Start similar to those found for the family intervention program described above (Lazar & Darlington, 1982). The problem is that these gains may obtain only for the highest quality Head Start programs in which the research is done. On the other hand, everyone agrees that Head Start children have a more enriched early childhood experience and do better in preschool and elementary school than controls. This, it can be argued, is sufficient reason to continue the program (S. L. Ramey, 1999).

Head Start continues to add new experimental programs. Currently, it is undertaking an initiative to include children under the age of 3 years. Other experimental programs include family service centers (to provide job training and education for parents), transition to elementary school programs (to provide training for elementary school teachers who will teach the Head Start graduates), comprehensive child developmental centers (to provide training in prenatal nutrition and parent skills), and family child-care projects (to allow single parents to work full time while supporting the child and family). These efforts combine services for the developing child with attempts to lift the family from poverty (D. L. Cohen, 1993; Glazer, 1993b).

PEER RELATIONSHIPS

Peers constitute a part of most infant's social networks. Peers are encountered in informal play groups arranged by parents, in public parks and recreation areas, and in childcare settings. Just as the infant's ability to relate to adults becomes more sophisticated over the first three years, the same is true for peer relationships. Unlike adults, however, peers do not have the ability to structure the relationship. When peers are first encountered in the first year, therefore, not much interaction can be seen.

The First Year

At the beginning of the first year of life, infants make different responses to peers than to their parents. At 3 months of age, infants are more likely to look at a peer for long periods and to make abrupt, jerky movements of the body while watching the peer. Their behavior toward their mothers is much smoother, with more smiling and vocalizing (Fogel, 1979).

From 6 to 12 months, peer play is more likely in the absence of objects (Eckerman & Whatley, 1977; J. L. Jacobson, 1981; Vandell, Wilson, & Buchanan, 1980). When babies get together, they explore each other with mutual touches, smile and gesture at each other, and imitate each other. By the age of 1 year, peer play in the absence of

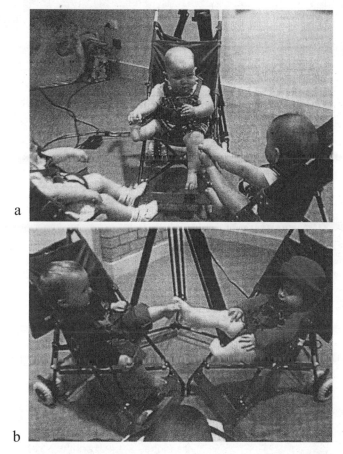

a

b

(a) Paula, in center of the picture, and Esther toe-holding together. (b) Ann, at right; and Joe play footsie.
Source: Selby & Bradley, 2003.

objects begins to take on the quality of a dialogue, with mutual exchanges of tickling, touching, and laughing at each other (Ross & Goldman, 1977a). In one study of 9-month-old infants playing together, the infants imitated each other by touching their own feet with their own hands, which was then followed by the infants touching their feet together (see photos). These tactile games were embedded in a long sequence of mutual gaze, vocalization, self and other touching (Selby & Bradley, 2003).

By 12 months, toys are becoming more important to the maintenance of the social interaction (J. L. Jacobson, 1981; Vandell et al., 1980). Games with toys have the same reciprocal quality as purely social games. There is mutual giving and taking of objects, offering and receiving, rolling and throwing balls back and forth, and so on. By this age, taking turns is such an essential part of peer play that interactions usually are disrupted if one child fails to take his or her turn (Ross & Goldman, 1977a). In comparison, infants at 12 months express a wider range of emotions in their interactions with their mothers and take more turns with them, perhaps due to the mothers' attempts to create dialogues through active structuring of the interaction (Adamson & Bakeman, 1985; Vandell & Wilson, 1987).

Twelve to Eighteen Months

Peer relationships are one way to observe the growing link between language and social development. Peers increasingly attempt to show contingent responses to one another (Mueller & Lucas, 1975), for example, in sharing behavior, which begins in this stage (Rheingold, Hay, & West, 1976). In response to a verbal request or a visual regard on the part of one infant, a peer will show or give an object to the infant who requests it. Although this does not happen all the time, peers tend increasingly to focus their attention jointly on the same object of interest (Eckerman, Whatley, & Kutz, 1975). In general, however, joint attention occurs much less at this age during peer play, compared to adult play (Turkheimer, 1989). At this age, about 77% of peer play is parallel play (see Table 1.1, Chapter 1); that is, peers play alongside each other but independently (Howes & Matheson, 1992).

Between peers, toys have a different role from the one they have between adults and infants. With adults, toys can be objects of a request or an offer, or the subject of naming and labeling routines. Toys are just part of a more complex interaction involving many levels of meaning. On the other hand, with peers, toys become the major focus of attention and serve as vehicles for the initiation

Toddler friendships are genuine and important. Sharing and contingent responses are just beginning at this age.

Photo by Elizabeth Crews.

and maintenance of social interactions. If someone else in the room is touching or manipulating a toy, the infant is likely to approach that person and make contact with the toy. Intentional communication—unlike a single-minded interest in the toy itself—requires that the infant not only touch the toy but also look at the other person and verbalize to that person about the object. Babies 11 to 13 months of age were likely to smile, vocalize, and gesture to an adult just before and just after making contact with the toy the adult was touching, but this happens less often between peers (Eckerman, Whatley, & McGehee, 1979; Turkheimer et al., 1989). In one study of infants during this age period, a novel toy was introduced into play between adults and infants and between infant peers (Marcos & Verba, 1990). In the infant-adult interaction, the infant pointed to the toy and looked at the mother, requesting the toy's name and wanting to use it. When the same toy was introduced between two peers, they just looked at each other and laughed.

Does the Mother's Presence Affect the Way an Infant Plays with Peers?

Because of the infant's newfound awareness of persons as potential communicators, we might expect the parent's presence to affect peer interaction. Infants still approach peers for different reasons than they approach parents. In general, given the simultaneous presence of both mother and peer, a child is more likely to initiate play with a peer (Vandell, 1979). With their mothers, children are more likely to seek physical contact and show negative emotions like distress and anger.

To answer the question posed at the beginning of this section, however, we need to compare the infant's behavior toward peers when the mother is present with that when she is absent. In a familiar setting—a parent co-op nursery school—10- and 14-month-olds were found to be more social and less negative to peers when their mothers were out of the room (Field, 1979). The main difference between the mothers' presence and their absence was that more conflict, toy snatching, and crying occurred when the mothers were present, even when the infants were playing with peers. These behaviors may serve as signals to the mother of the infant's relative discontent about something.

What Other Situational Constraints Affect Peer Relationships?

The mother's presence during a peer interaction is referred to as a **situational constraint**—an aspect of the environment that affects the nature of the peer relationship. We saw in Chapter 2 how factors outside a social system can affect the functioning of that system. The presence of a third person is one such constraint. Others include the infant's familiarity with the peer and each infant's level of peer experience.

Familiarity has been shown to affect how 1-year-olds play together. When children are asked to identify which other children are their friends, friends are more likely to interact together than nonfriends, even under controlled laboratory situations in which friend and nonfriend pairs are formed artificially and allowed to play by themselves for a short period of time (Becker, 1977; Young & Lewis, 1979). Friends are more likely than nonfriends to touch and lean on each other, more likely to initiate interactions with each other, and more likely to show positive affect with each other (M. Lewis, Young, Brooks, & Michalson, 1975).

Apparently, then, friendship can be shown to exist as early as 12 months of age. Although it is not clear from these studies whether infants at this age have the same kind of attachment to their friends as older children and adults do, infants are more comfortable and expressive in the company of familiars.

The amount of experience an infant has had with peers is not as strong a situational constraint as peer familiarity. Some evidence suggests that experienced toddlers are more active in peer encounters than relatively inexperienced toddlers, and that the experienced toddlers are more likely to show more complex social behaviors such as mutual imitation and cooperative play (Mueller & Brenner, 1977; Vandell, 1979). Nevertheless, infants seem to need little prior exposure to other infants to act competently in their company, and infants seem to understand the ins and outs of peer play very quickly.

Eighteen to Twenty-Four Months

There is a major change in the child's relationship to peers at this age. When given a choice of whom to play with, infants almost always choose a peer—familiar or unfamiliar—over their mothers. They spend more time with the peer and make fewer bids for their mother's attention when a peer is present (Rubenstein, Howes, & Pedersen, 1982). A similar pattern can be seen in a day care setting: 2-year-olds spend more time with one another than with teachers (Finkelstein, Dent, Gallacher, & Ramey, 1978).

When the tables are turned and the adult is with an adult peer while the child is not, the child increases the number of bids for attention and close contact. In fact, the child is more demanding of the mother's attention when she is with a friend than when the mother and child are home alone (Rubenstein et al., 1982). This finding should come as no surprise to any parent who has tried to carry on a conversation with a friend while the baby is around. It is probably best not to ignore the child's need for attention and wish to be included. At the same time, children have to understand that they cannot necessarily be a part of everything that the parent does. Some balance between the parent's and the child's needs should be struck.

We saw earlier that toddler-peer play is different in quality from toddler-parent play. Studies of 19-month-olds show that this trend continues with age. Toddlers are more likely to play with, imitate, offer toys to, and talk to peers than to their mothers, although they touch peers and mothers about the same amount of time (Rubenstein & Howes, 1976). When they play with their mothers, toddlers are more likely to have longer periods of sustained attention to single objects (N. L. Cohen & Tomlinson-Keasey, 1980).

Some time between 18 and 24 months, peer play begins to take on a more gamelike quality. Children take simple turns involving complementary roles, such as offering and accepting, throwing and catching, or simple verbal exchange ("You're a sissy"; "No, I'm not"). Words are used in such games, but not at the same level of elaboration as in adult-infant games. At this age also, there are few instances of actual cooperation and collabo-

By this age, children can cooperate in a common activity and develop sophisticated social pretend games.

Photo by Elizabeth Crews.

ration on a task, as may be found during adult-infant interaction, although cooperation with peers becomes more pronounced after 24 months (Brownell, 1986; Brownell, Ramani, & Zerwas, 2006; Eckerman, Davis, & Didow, 1989; Howes & Matheson, 1992; Warneken & Tomasello, 2007). Cooperation and complex verbal exchanges and pretend play with peers will be discussed in the next section.

Children of this age are just beginning to form lasting relationships with peers. A **relationship** is a continuing pattern of communication between two or more people in which past encounters provide a historical background for future encounters. In the parent- infant relationship, for example, a relational perspective (Fogel, 1993) suggests that the history of their communication patterns during the first year leads to differences between dyads in their security of attachment at 1 year. It is not until the end of the second year of life that children can form lasting relationships with other children.

Children preferentially direct positive or negative behavior to particular others. Some children (compatible friends) direct mostly positive behaviors toward each other and refrain from conflicts. Other children (enemies, or fighting friends) tend to engage in conflicts most of the time they get together. Other children tend not to interact with each other (ignoring), either positively or negatively. It could be said that even these ignoring pairs have a relationship, since the same children tend to ignore each other day after day (Ross et al., 1992).

Finally, the types of toys used in peer play influence the types of interactions between the children. Eighteen-month-old infants were observed playing in pairs in four different play settings: a typical play setting, one with no play materials, one with only small portable toys, and one with only large nonportable play equipment (DeStefano & Mueller, 1982).

The researchers found more sophisticated social interaction and a greater expression of positive emotion in the setting with the large play equipment (ladders, slides, and boxes). With the small portable toys, more conflict and more negative emotion was expressed. This is understandable,

since children tend to fight over the possession of small toys. With only large toys, children tend to treat the environment as a space to be shared and enjoyed together.

Surprisingly, the children were most creative in the no-toy situation: they actually invented their own toys! The radiator became a "base," they took off articles of clothing to be used as play objects, and they even used each other as if they were toys. When playing with infants, adults tend to introduce toys and other play materials to keep the pace of play up or keep the toddlers out of their way. Perhaps peer interaction provides time for the child to be more inventive and develop independent initiatives.

When conflicts over small toys do arise, children of this age are more likely to share than children older than 2 years. This may be because the older children have a more consolidated sense of a conceptual self that includes possessions (see Chapter 5), and also because the younger child would prefer to avoid serious conflicts (Caplan, Vespo, Pedersen, & Hay, 1991; Hay, Caplan, Castle, & Stimson, 1991). Although it is relatively rare at this age, a third child may come over to intervene in the toy conflict between two other children (Ross et al., 1992).

Twenty-Four to Thirty-Six Months

By the third year of life, children are capable of engaging in social interaction and of adapting to the messages and demands of the listener (Wellman & Lempers, 1977). Between 22 and 30 months, infants increase their rates of verbalizations to peers, watch each other more, and increase their overall rates of social interaction (Mueller et al., 1977). Children also show a greater tendency to engage in mutual social play, and a decreasing amount of parallel play is seen near the end of the third year (Bakeman & Brownlee, 1980).

The kinds of interactions taking place, as well as the content of the interactions, are also undergoing important changes. Children gradually incorporate their symbolic play into peer interactions. No longer content to construct elaborate pretend sequences on their own, preschool children work together to elaborate a pretend game. At first, children simply copy or echo their partners in their peer exchanges. Later, they provide complementary responses, and finally, they elaborate and embellish the other's responses (Camaioni, Baumgartner, & Perucchini, 1991; Garvey, 1974; Gunnar, Senior, & Hartup, 1984).

Table 8.6 shows some of the social processes that account for this development in the ability of peers to achieve and maintain coordinated action (Eckerman & Didow, 1989). One important change is that peers begin to imitate each other, first nonverbally and later verbally. Based on both naturalistic observations and observations in which adults acted like peers and imitated children, research shows that the experience of being imitated is a powerful motivator of social behavior. Being imitated by someone gives one immediate and recognizable feedback of one's effect on the other person and inspires one to imitate him or her in return (Eckerman, 1993; Eckerman, Davis, & Didow, 1989; Eckerman & Stein, 1990). Some examples of imitation that are

specific to peer relationships in the third year are given in Table 8.7.

A second component of increasing peer coordination, also shown in Table 8.7, is the emergence of complementary roles and alternative responses. In this case, the child makes a different but appropriate response to the partner's overture. This might even occur as a slight variation in the context of imitation: one child might throw a ball and the other a beanbag. A third developmental change is the growing use of language as part of a coordinated interaction. Instead of overt actions, the child begins to use words as directives, requests, or comments and responses.

Imitation, therefore, seems to serve as a social bridge between the simple kinds of uncoordinated peer play seen in the second year and the complex coordinated interactions seen later in the third year. One of the social functions of imitation is that it increases a feeling of closeness between two people (Nadel & Fontaine, 1989; Uzgiris, 1983). Thus, we might expect similar feelings of interpersonal closeness to emerge between 2-year-old peers.

TABLE 8.6 Development of Emerging Skills in Achieving Coordinated Action

Age Period	Behavior Skills	Characteristic Interaction
Younger than 16 months	Assume and maintain complementary role in familiar, ritualized games.	Sustained ritualized games, little coordinated action in other contexts.
16–18 months	Imitation of nonverbal acts as general strategy for coordinated action in nonritualized contexts; repeated imitation across turns of action.	Widespread imitation of other's acts, resulting in imitation games and games with both imitative and complementary roles.
28–32 months	Verbalizations coordinated to another's actions begin to occur with appreciable frequency; increasingly accompany nonverbal forms of coordinated action with verbal regulations, descriptions, and imiitations. Increasingly respond to another's overtures with alternative overtures composed of words and nonverbal actions or words alone.	Words coordinated to partner's actions increasingly occur in context of games structured largely by nonverbal imitation; words begin to serve as turns in games. Games intermixed with periods of negotiation of topic for interactions
Older than 32 months	Use of overtures thematically related to ongoing activities to vary or elaborate on the ongoing coordinated action.	Games less repetitive across turns; coordinated action sustained for longer periods of time, with changes in topic occurring during the bout.

Source: C. O. Eckerman & S. M. Didow, Toddler's social coordinations: Changing responses to another's invitation to play, 1989, p. 803. *Developmental Psychology, 25*, pp. 794–804

TABLE 8.7 Types of Imitative and Complementary Actions Seen in Peer Interactions During the Third Year

Type of Act	Example
Imitative	Exchanging an object; playing catch, peekaboo; hitting each other; both running, copying sounds, laughing, screaming; faking laugh or cry; clapping; sticking out tongues; singing; jumping.
Complementary	Finding a hidden peer; playing leader and follower; giving/following directives ("Go jump"; "Come here"); answering question.

Source: C. O. Eckerman, C. C. Davis, & S. M. Didow, Toddler's emerging ways of achieving social coordination with a peer, 1989, p. 448. *Child Development, 60*, pp. 440–453; L. Kuczynski, C. Zahn-Waxler, & M. Radke-Yarrow, Development and content of imitation in the second and third years of life: A socialization perspective, 1987, p. 280. *Developmental Psychology, 23*, pp. 276–282.

Peers use both language and nonverbal action for metacommunication about their relationship. Children can engage in pretend fighting by metacommunicating (such as smiling or saying "This is pretend"). Or a child can deflect a real attack by making it into a game with a teasing expression. Often children play in a very intense way and pretend to scream as if in pain. If one child accidentally gets hurt, a change in that child's intonation or posture can metacommunicate to the other children the more serious nature of the scream (Fogel & Branco, 1997).

Do Two-Year-Olds Behave the Same No Matter Whom They Are With?

The answer to this question is no. Children of this age can adapt their behavior to the characteristics of the other child and the type of relationship they have with that child. One dimension of relationship difference is friendship. Apparently, 2-year-olds can make friends. Research shows that there is a difference in social interaction between children who call themselves friends and those who do not (Ross & Lossis, 1987). In one study, children were left in an unfamiliar room either with a familiar peer, with an unfamiliar peer, or by themselves. The children with the familiar peer were the most comfortable, and the children left alone were the most upset (Ispa, 1981).

In another study, children were asked to rank all their nursery school playmates according to how much they liked being with each person. The children were paired off and taken to an unfamiliar place, where they played together. Half the pairs were made up of children who rated each other as preferred playmates, and half were made up of children who did not rate each other as preferred. At the end of 10 minutes of play in the new setting, an experimenter took one of the children off to play a special game, leaving the other in the room alone. Children whose friends left them behind were more likely to be disturbed during the separation than children left behind by nonfriends. Thus, there is some indication that peer friendships show an attachment-like quality—that children are fond of their friends and like to be with them (Melson & Cohen, 1981).

Another dimension of relationship difference is dominance. Beginning at this age, children's play groups form **dominance hierarchies**. A dominance hierachy is a pattern of social relationships in which the members of a group are ranked according to their relative power or lack of power over others. A child who is with a more dominant peer will do more observing and take a less assertive and active role in exploring the environment. The same child with a subordinate peer will take more of a leadership role and have more initiative in the play (P. H. Hawley & Little, 1999).

Do Family Factors Affect Peer Relationships?

Family factors do affect peer relationships. One study found that children without siblings were more sociable with unfamiliar peers than were firstborns with siblings, and firstborns were more sociable than children born later. Children without siblings were the most outgoing of all. This could be because the children born later had the most nonpeers to play with or because they expected from peers the same kinds of aggressive rivalry they received from their siblings, making them more wary of peers (M. E. Snow, Jacklin, & Maccoby, 1981). The child's relationship to the parents also matters. Children who are more securely attached to their mothers and who demonstrate better self-control in frustrating situations also are more likely to show competence in peer encounters (Calkins, Gill, Johnson, & Smith, 1999; Leiberman, 1977; Matas, Arend, & Sroufe, 1978). Children who have an insecure-avoidant relationship with their mothers are more likely to show hostile-aggressive behavior with their peers, while children with an insecure-resistant attachment show less self-assertion and are less able to concentrate on pretending and exploring (McElwain et al., 2003).

Do Sociocultural Factors Affect Peer Relationships?

Sociocultural factors also affect peer relationships. For example, Israeli children who were brought up in kibbutzim (farm cooperatives) showed more cooperative play with one another than Israeli children reared in an urban environment (Shapira & Madsen, 1969). The more a society is family oriented rather than peer-group oriented, the less the children will be encouraged to play in peer groups. This has been found in Mexico (Madsen & Shapira, 1970) and Switzerland (Boehm, 1977).

In smaller, agrarian societies, such as some African tribal societies, children have relatively few age-mates living in the same village. Children in these settings tend to play in mixed-age groups rather than peer groups (Konner, 1975). Mixed-age groupings are rare in modern, urbanized settings. They typically occur between siblings in the same family. Even preschools tend to be age segregated in Western countries. Although there is little research on the topic, we might suspect that some of the same benefits that exist in sibling relationships—such as the ability to lead and follow, to imitate and serve as a role model, to learn and teach—would exist in mixed-age groupings of children outside the family. For example, when socially isolated preschool children were asked to interact with children younger than themselves, the older child became more sociable over time (Furman, Rahe, and Hartup, 1979).

Societies differ in the amount adults supervise peer groups. In urban settings, young children are

Societies differ in how much structure they provide for peer relationships. In Japan, young children wear uniforms, and their activities are coordinated by an adult.
Photo by Alan Oddie/PhotoEdit.

always under the watchful eyes of a caregiver, for obvious ecological reasons. In rural societies and smaller societies, children are relatively less supervised, even at a young age. The Foré people of New Guinea allow infants total freedom of movement as soon as they can walk (Sorenson, 1979). In the Marquesas Islands, starting at 2 years of age, children spend most of the day in unsupervised peer groups ranging in size from three to six children. They are allowed to play near the sea, in boathouses, on bridges, and near streams (Martini & Kirkpatrick, 1981). Neither Sorensen nor Martini and Kirkpatrick ever observed children becoming lost or injured, but how the children avoided accidents is not clear. These examples suggest that 2-year-olds are indeed autonomous individuals, as well as that the social and physical ecology of the setting determines the manner in which that autonomy is expressed.

SIBLING RELATIONSHIPS

A final part of the infant social network that we will discuss is the relationship to siblings. Although there are some similarities between siblings and peers, the age difference between siblings as well as the more or less continual exposure to each other during the day, make for very different types of interactions.

How Do Siblings Adapt to the Pregnancy?

The older siblings' relationship to the younger ones begins, like the parents, during pregnancy. Advice books for parents tend to recommend that the first child be prepared for the arrival of the baby, although there are differences of opinion about how much to say. An early study (Sewall, 1930) found that differences in preparation of the first child during pregnancy did not relate to the severity of the jealousy reactions of the child following the birth of the baby. Other studies (J. Dunn & Kendrick, 1982; Trause et al., 1978) have also found no relationship between prena-

tal preparation and the later quality of the sibling relationship.

It seems that the first child, typically only 2 to 4 years old, is unlikely to understand the meaning of the mother's attempts at preparation. Even if the child does understand, he or she is unlikely to anticipate the emotional experience that occurs when the new baby arrives. In families in which there is a high level of confrontation between the mother and the first child and in which the mother used prohibition and restraint, the first child was more likely to behave in an interfering or irritating manner toward the new baby (J. Dunn & Kendrick, 1982).

Types of Sibling Interactions During Infancy

All sibling pairs share both positive and negative interactions. Furthermore, no matter what the interaction is, the children get something specific from their siblings that they do not receive in other relationships.

If the 2-year-old is a younger sibling, he or she will spend a lot of time paying attention to the older sibling and following him or her around. Younger siblings have been observed to imitate older siblings more often than they are imitated by older siblings; younger siblings are more likely to follow older siblings' directions and suggestions, and they are more compliant in taking designated roles in games. Futhermore, infants with older siblings are more likely to imitate other people in general, suggesting that they have come to see themselves in the role of follower rather than a leader (Abramovitch, Corter, Pepler, & Stanhope, 1986; Barr & Hayne, 2003; Brody, Stoneman, & MacKinnon, 1982; Lamb, 1978b; Stoneman, Brody, & MacKinnon, 1984).

In one study, 23-month-old children were observed both with and without their older siblings (H. R. Samuels, 1980). When they were with the siblings, the toddlers went farther from their mothers, left their mothers sooner, stayed away longer, and showed more independent exploratory behavior than did toddlers whose siblings were not

---

Observations

Speech to Younger Siblings by Three-Year-Olds

Observation 8.3 (England)

The younger sister, Robin, has just picked up a piece of candy from the floor and is licking it. The older brother, Duncan, tells Robin that the dog, Scottie, will eat it. When Robin doesn't listen, Duncan pushes her gently through the door.

Duncan: "No, don't you eat it. Scottie will eat it. Scottie will eat it. No, not you. Scottie will eat it. Not you. Scottie. Not you. Shall we go in door? Right, come on. Come on. In door, Robin. In door." (J. Dunn & Kendrick, 1982, p. 126).

Observation 8.4 (Mexico)

Older sister Victoria and younger sister Lucha play in their courtyard with a small rabbit. Lucha is having some trouble keeping the rabbit in one place and is trying to do so by holding its ears.

Victoria: "Mira tuno sabes!" (Look, you don't know how!) Victoria then demonstrates how to hold the rabbit correctly (Zukow, 1990, p. 30).

---

present. The increased boldness seems to be due almost entirely to their following the older siblings around and imitating their behavior. In this way, younger children have the advantage of an older guide as they begin to explore the environment. This study does not suggest that the older sibling intentionally chooses to lead the way and teach the younger one, only that the younger one will follow what the older one does. Parents often remark that the laterborns seems to do things at a younger age than the firstborn; such imitative behavior may partially explain this observation.

On the other hand, older siblings are more likely to give directives, to orient the attention of the younger children, to command and prohibit, to support, and to tease. Older siblings address infants in a form of motherese, except they rarely ask questions of the babies (J. Dunn & Kendrick, 1982; Ellis & Rogoff, 1982; C. P. Jones & Adamson, 1987; R. A. Stewart, 1983). Older siblings who had experienced more discussion of internal states and emotions with their mothers were more likely to be sensitive to the emotional states of their younger siblings and the younger siblings in turn were more likely to be comforted by and learn from their older brothers or sisters, perhaps because the older siblings were more advanced in empathy and theory of mind (see above) (Howe & Rinaldi, 2004; Klein, Feldman, & Zarur, 2002). Observations 8.3 and 8.4 show representative directives of 2-to-3-year-old siblings to their baby sisters.

The evidence suggests that after the birth of a new baby, older children become somewhat more dependent compared with firstborns of the same age without siblings. They tend to seek help more, seek proximity to their mothers more, and cry more. Research shows that the older child has good reason for behaving this way. The mother's behavior to the older child changes somewhat when the new baby is around: confrontation increases and positive involvement with the firstborn decreases. Even when the mother is not occupied with the baby, she tends to spend less time with the older child (Kendrick & Dunn, 1980; R. A. Stewart, Mobley, Van Tuyl, & Salvador, 1987). The increase in confrontations between mother and firstborn is due primarily to an increase in "deliberate naughtiness" on the part of the older child. It seems that the older child's feelings of being displaced are met by the mother's increased workload as she cares for two young children instead of only one (Kendrick & Dunn, 1980).

On the other hand, 2-year-olds are becoming more sensitive to the dynamics of the family environment. They are really very skilled at knowing just how to annoy the younger sibling (teasing, making disparaging remarks, showing a toy spider to a sibling who does not like spiders), on the one hand, and enlisting the support of the mother during sibling conflicts (J. Dunn & Munn, 1985), on the other. Tattling occurs between siblings of this age in the majority of families. Sometimes children

TABLE 8.8   A Conversation

Mother	Child (30 Months)
1. (Points to a picture) What is that one?	2. Kitty cat.
3. Well what is it?	4. Kitty cat.
5. Well, I know there's a kitty.	6. Huh?
7. What's he riding in?	8. Airplane;
9. Right.	10. (turns page)

Source: K. Kaye, *The mental and social life of babies*, 1982, p. 100. Chicago: University of Chicago Press. Copyright © The Society for Research in Child Development, Inc. Reprinted by permission of the publisher and the author.

tattle to get the mother on their side during a conflict. Other times, tattling is used just to inform the parent about the sibling's misbehavior. Children do not tattle about just anything. They tattle primarily about physical aggression and about property damage and disputes (den Bak & Ross, 1996).

The older siblings also become adept at making eloquent justifications to the mother for their disputes with the sibling. For example, after taking a toy away from a younger brother, the older child might say to mother, "He took it first!" or "But I needed that" (J. Dunn & Munn, 1987). They also become able to steer the direction of a mother-baby interaction toward their own needs or concerns (J. Dunn & Shatz, 1989).

Although older siblings do not shy away from causing conflict with the younger ones, when the conflict is between the mother and the younger sibling, the older sibling might be the first to come to the rescue of the baby. Some of the strategies used by the older child to diffuse the conflict between mother and younger sibling include repeating the sibling's action that the mother did not like (drawing the mother's attention away from the younger one), giving the younger child a similar object to the one the mother had just taken away, prohibiting or scolding the mother for her punishment of the sibling, and comforting the sibling.

Although some conflict is inevitable in family relationships, sibling relationships have many positive aspects. In conversations between siblings when the mother is present, for example, infants are able to join in the talk between mother and older sibling at a much higher level than when they are with the mother alone. This is because the older child does not always have the ability to reply as a full conversational partner (see Table 8.8), which leaves room for the young sibling to enter into the conversation (Barton & Tomasello, 1991).

There is also evidence that siblings have a special relationship that is different from the parent-child relationship. In particular, siblings like to talk more about their emotions with each other than with parents. Older siblings verbally label the younger sibling's emotional reactions ("You don't like that, do you? I don't want it!"). Siblings like to share jokes about "yucky" bugs or gender categories ("You like Barbie dolls!"). They also express feelings of liking and disliking ("I'm really proud of you [accompanied by kissing]!" "Ginny, you drive me mad!") (J. R. Brown & Dunn, 1992; N. Howe, 1991). There is also evidence that siblings form attachments to each other and would rather be together than with an unfamiliar peer (Kier & Lewis, 1993).

In some societies, it is common for older siblings, even those as young as 3 years, to have some responsibilities for taking care of babies (with adult supervision). Sibling caretakers for infants typically are found in societies that are relatively less complex and more traditional (Whiting & Whiting, 1975). If the division of labor in the family is such that the mother cannot stay at home to take care of the infant, siblings are likely to take over this function. In non-technological societies, all family members are called upon to do extra work. The children have more chores around the house than children in technological societies, and infant care is one of these tasks.

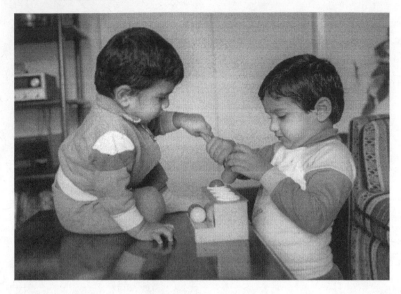

Older children can be important as models and teachers for their younger siblings. The younger child seems to enjoy the company of the older, even if the younger one does not always understand what is going on.
Photo by Elizabeth Crews.

In Taira, a village in Okinawa, preschool girls patted, bounced, and talked to infants to calm them. If this did not work, the girls returned them to mothers or grandmothers. Girls in Taira never bathed or fed infants, nor did they put them to bed. In Tarong, on the island of Luzon in the Philippines, child "nurses" were trained at age 3 to entertain, rock, and hold the baby, but adults continued to supervise them.

Among the Gusii living in Nyansongo, Kenya, child nurses were somewhat older (5 to 8 years), and they were given more responsibility. They were assigned the total care of an infant beginning when the infant was around 2 months of age. They fed, bathed, and cared for the infants while the mothers worked in nearby fields (Whiting & Whiting, 1975). In the Marquesas Islands, 2-year-olds are important as companions, instructors, and comforters of their infant siblings. The adults hold these children in high esteem and often ask them to show off the baby. Children are relied upon to calm an infant if an adult fails (Martini & Kirkpatrick, 1981).

In summary, these studies reveal that siblings are important to each other's development. Younger siblings benefit from the guidance and protection of a role model, and they also acquire self-protective social skills and learn how to resolve conflicts. Older siblings benefit from being tutors and caregivers by focusing their attention on the needs of others. When they are scolded for annoying the younger child, the older children understand the nature of codes of conduct and some complex social and emotional regulatory skills.

Interfamily Differences in the Types of Sibling Interactions

Why do some siblings fight more than others? What should parents do to help their children get along better with each other? A number of family and child factors have been associated with a higher incidence of both mother–older child and older child– younger child confrontations. We discuss the evidence for some of the factors in this section.

Each sibling's relationship with the mother. Research shows that each sibling's attachment to the mother affects the quality of the sibling relationship. When the mother is present with the children, securely attached 2-year-old younger siblings are less likely to be aggressive to the mother or to the older sibling when the mother plays exclusively with the older sibling. Older siblings who are securely attached are more likely to respond to the needs and distress of the younger sibling in the mother's absence; older siblings who are not securely attached are less likely to do so (Teti & Ablard,

1989). A similar result has been found for twins (Vandell, Owen, Wilson, & Henderson, 1988). It is typical for both children in the same family to have similar attachment classifications (Ward, Vaughn, & Robb, 1988).

The older sibling's prior relationships outside the family. Research shows that higher-quality sibling relationships are associated with the older sibling's relationships with peers outside the family. Children who are more positive with their siblings show more positive peer play, fewer peer conflicts, more extended pretend play with peers, and more lasting peer friendships (Kramer & Gottman, 1992). Children with more knowledge of emotion and role-taking skills are more positive with their younger siblings (Garner, Jones, & Palmer, 1994).

Both sibling interaction and social competence with peers are related to the child's security of attachment, so you might think that the relationship between positive peer play and positive sibling interaction is simply the result of a more secure attachment to the mother. The research shows that while the parent-child relationship is important for developing the child's ability to care for the younger sibling, the child's experience with peers makes its own independent contribution (Kramer & Gottman, 1992). With peers, children are exposed to some basic rules of respect and responsibility for others that carry over into relationships at home, especially if the child's socially responsive behavior is supported by the parents.

Sex and age differences between siblings. Another factor that may play a role in the incidence of positive versus negative sibling relationships is the sex composition of the sibling pair. Although there is a great deal of variability across families, same-sex pairs tend to have fewer instances of aggression than mixed-sex pairs, and parents are more likely to treat children in same-sex pairs equally than children in mixed-sex pairs (Corter, Abramovitch, & Pepler, 1983; R. A. Stewart et al., 1987). Firstborn females are somewhat more prosocial, whereas firstborn males are somewhat more aggressive; however, these differences do not appear across all studies. Finally, the number of years between siblings does not seem to have any measurable effect on the amount of prosocial or aggressive behavior exchanged between them (Abramovitch, Corter, & Landau, 1979; Lamb, 1978c).

Temperamental differences between siblings. Because the findings on age and sex differences between the siblings do not strongly predict the level of conflict between the siblings, some researchers have suggested that temperamental factors might be more important. Indeed, research shows that temperament is a better predictor. If one of the siblings is rated as having a generally negative mood and as being temperamentally nonadaptable, the siblings are less likely to engage in joint play. A mismatch in the temperament of the siblings is related to higher levels of conflict (Munn & Dunn, 1989).

One interpretation of these results is that the temperamental characteristics of the children affect the way that they relate to each other. Another interpretation is possible, however. One of the issues related to the measurement of infant temperament is that a parental rating of infant temperament is generally used (see Chapter 7). This introduces a possible bias in the parent's perception of the child, independent of the child's actual behavior.

The alternative interpretation related to differences in temperament between siblings is that these differences are created in part by the parents, who attempt to differentiate between siblings by viewing them as different individuals in a process called **sibling de-identification**. In this regard, research has shown that parents tend to rate the first two children in the family as having different temperaments, while temperaments for later-born children are rated more alike (F. S. Schachter & Stone, 1985) In a longitudinal study in which observers studied mother-infant interaction for the first two children in the family when each was 24 months old, the researchers found that mothers expressed similar levels of affection and verbal responsiveness to both children but the amount of parental control of the children differed. Control was measured by the amount of direct interventions in the child's actions in the form of commands, rejections, and disciplinary actions (J. Dunn, Plomin, & Daniels, 1986).

In summary, many factors are likely to play a role in how well siblings get along with each other. From a family systems perspective, it is difficult to say with certainty that a single factor taken in isolation is the cause of sibling aggression. Temperament, although strongly related to sibling conflict, could be multiply determined by parent-child and child-child interactions over the course of the first years of life. Is the child really difficult, or has the child come to be labeled as difficult? Or is difficult temperament a stance one takes in the face of a sibling who is constantly rejecting or ignoring? It may be some time before we can sort out the answers to these questions.

Parent intervention in sibling disputes. Parents can choose whether or not to intervene in sibling disputes. The effects of their actions depend upon the age of the siblings. When the older child is under 3, parental non-involvement in sibling disputes tends to predispose the siblings to continued conflict. Parents of children of this age tend to intervene primarily in the most serious fights. Before the intervention, children are most likely to use aggression and coercion in disputes. Immediately following the intervention, children are more likely to use negotiation strategies to resolve their conflicts, suggesting that parents can indeed play a role in helping children to negotiate. On the other hand, non-involvement is a more effective strategy for older siblings who are less close and less involved with each other if the parent intervenes in their disputes in any way. This means that over time, siblings develop new ways to negotiate their disputes on their own. Self-interested justifications decrease and cooperative discourse increases (J. Dunn, Kreps, & Brown, 1996; Kramer, Perozynski, & Chung, 1999; Perlman & Ross, 1997).

At least in middle-class Caucasian North American families, when parents intervene, it is typically as third-party mediators. Parents tend to favor younger siblings in such disputes and to discipline the older sibling. When fathers in particular disciplined the older sibling primarily and mothers disciplined both siblings equally, these families were rated as more harmonious, both in the marital relationship and in the sibling relationships. If both parents pick on the older sibling, that child is more likely to show behavior problems in preschool (Volling & Elins, 1998). Better developmental outcomes are likely, therefore, when parents expect the older sibling to be the more responsible person and when the younger sibling is sometimedsisciplined by at least one parent. This not only helps the older sibling become more responsible, but also helps prevent his or her feeling that the parents favor the younger sibling.

When parents intervene, they are not likely to get involved in children's claims of ownership ("It's mine") or possession ("I had it first"). Parents in general are more interested in getting children to share their activities rather than fight over who owns something, and they act to prevent property damage. Parents want children to resolve their differences, to play together harmoniously, and to end the dispute as quickly as possible (Ross, 1996). In summary, parental involvement in sibling disputes decreases over age as children develop, primarily from their parents, new ways to negotiate peaceful settlements. There are, however, between-family differences in these patterns.

SUMMARY

Transition to Parenthood

- Mothers must learn to cope psychologically with the physical changes in their bodies that occur during pregnancy.
- Fathers often identify with their mates' changes and act in supportive roles, depending upon their personality and cultural expectations.
- Most women adjust to the birth of their children rapidly and without long-term psychological effects. A small percentage of women suffer from postpartum depression.
- Each society has its own unique way of welcoming newborns into the world. This involves a variety of

rituals that ensure the health of the newborn and mother and carry a blessing for a happy life.

- Parents must adapt to a number of new challenges during the transition to parenthood.
- Different factors predict the success of adaptation to parenthood for men and women.
- Typically, maternal employment does not affect the attachment between mothers and infants. The important factor is whether the mother desires to return to work, in which case her adjustment is more successful.
- Parental leave policy helps the family's initial adjustment to a new baby, but few parents can take advantage of it.
- At all ages, boys and girls are equally responsive to and knowledgeable about babies. Differences arise in social situations in which individuals are encouraged toward or away from nurturing roles.
- Preschool-age siblings are capable of adapting their speech and behavior to the needs of the baby.
- Fathers often have a more directing and challenging style than mothers, but in most cases, their behavior with infants is similar.
- Child care has different effects on infants and families, depending on the age of the child upon entering child care, the parent's feelings about child care and returning to work, and the quality of care.

Cultural Factors in Infant Development

- Cultural beliefs affect almost every aspect of infant care.
- Poverty is a different culture from middle class and wealthy families with adverse effects on infant development.
- All families rely on both formal and informal sources of support during infancy.
- Factors mediating the effectiveness of support include social attitudes about different types of

infants, parental personality and its effect on support sources, and cultural attitudes about seeking help.

- Early childhood intervention for disadvantaged families shows gains for infants in some areas but not in others.

Peer Relationships

- In the first year, peer interaction is more focused on direct actions on objects, while adult-infant interaction has more referential communication about objects.
- Peers are more likely to get along better when one of the parents is not around.
- By the second year, peers begin to play more reciprocal games. They also begin to form lasting relationships.
- By the third year, peer interaction shows evidence of coordinated actions, imitative and complementary turn taking, and the emergence of friendships.

Sibling Relationships

- Preparing a first child for the birth of the second child does not seem to affect the amount of later sibling rivalry.
- Older and younger siblings derive different benefits from their mutual interactions. Younger siblings benefit from the guidance and protection of the older sibling and develop self-protection skills. Older siblings pay attention to the needs of others and develop skills in a leadership role.
- Interfamily differences in sibling conflict may depend on the children's prior relationships and attachments to parents and to their peers, on the sex similarity of the pair, on the temperament of the children, and on sibling de-identification by the parents.

Chapter 9

Health and Risk

CHAPTER OUTLINE AND OVERVIEW

Prenatal Health	*What are causes—genetic, chromosomal, and environmental—and preventions of birth defects? What is the effect of maternal stress and depression on the fetus?*
Newborn Health	*How is newborn health assessed? What are typical complications of birth? What is premature birth, what are its effects, and what are the most effective interventions to help premature infants? What is euthanasia?*
Infant Mortality	*What is the difference between spontaneous and elective abortion? Under what conditions is elective euthanasia applied to newborns? How many babies and mothers die during the perinatal period and why? How do families respond to infant death? What is SIDS? How is it caused? Can it be prevented?*
Infant Safety	*What are the main threats to infant health and safety? What are some methods of responding to emergencies? What kinds of immunizations are recommended for infants?*
Infant with Special Needs	*What are some ways of helping infants with special needs? How do infants with special needs affect the family and society?*
Infantile Autism	*What is early childhood autism, and how does it affect the self at this age? Can autism be diagnosed and treated during the first two years of life?*
Infant and Child Maltreatment	*What are the causes and effects of child maltreatment? What are the limitations of research on child maltreatment?*

This chapter covers the broad field of infant and parent health, both physical and mental. Health considerations begin in the prenatal period as the things the mother eats and the environmental factors to which she is exposed may have an impact on fetal development. Thos chapter also covers topics such as nutrition, safety, immunizations, infant death, birth complications and prematurity, infant maltreatment, infants with special needs, autism, and parent-infant mental health.

PRENATAL HEALTH

Problems may arise in prenatal development from factors intrinsic to the fetus, including genetic and chromosomal influences. Additionally, the outside environment may impair fetal development, most of which are preventable through diet and behavior on the part of the parents. Refer to Chapter 3 on prenatal development to review concepts and terms used here.

Genetically Based Disorders

Certain types of disorders can be carried by the genes from one generation to the next. These genetically based disorders are not totally deterministic of a particular phenotype (see Chapter 2). Rather, if an individual carries a particular gene, the probability of acquiring its related disorder is increased.

In some cases, genetic disorders are so severe that the fetus will die and be expelled from the mother's body. This is called spontaneous abortion. It has been estimated that two out of every three conceptions are spontaneously aborted in the early months of pregnancy. In a large majority of these cases, the embryo has genetic or chromosomal abnormalities. In addition, over 80% of newborn deaths can be accounted for by neural tube defects (15%) and chromosomal and genetic abnormalities (67%) (Strobino & Pantel- Silverman, 1987; Tharapel, Bannerman, & Tharapel, 1985; I. D. Young, Clarke, & Rickett, 1986). On the other hand, environmental factors play a role.

Women who consume more than 5 alcoholic drinks per week during the first trimester were 5 times more prone to spontaneous abortion than other women (see Fetal Alcohol Syndrome, below; Kesmodel et al., 2002). Thus, spontaneous abortion and mortality of malformed fetuses seem to be natural biological functions to eliminate malformations. In other cases, infants stricken with a serious genetic disorder can live for several years or even longer, depending on available treatments.

Most of the evidence for genetic disorders is derived from genealogical studies in which the path of a disorder can be traced through a family tree. For example, manic- depressive disease occurs in a high incidence in the Old Order Amish community in Lancaster, Pennsylvania. Because the entire population of this Amish community is descended from fewer than one hundred people who settled there before 1750, and because the community kept excellent genealogical, disease, and death records, researchers were able to study the chromosomes of hundreds of afflicted individuals. When this is done, the specific gene that causes the disorder can be detected because it is the only one that is identical in all cases. However, other characteristics also occur along with this gene, making it difficult to say what the gene actually causes. In the general population, some forms of manic-depressive disorder (also called bipolar disorder) may be related to multiple genes, while other forms may not be genetically related.

When a specific gene can be isolated, it gives hope for the early detection and possibly the treatment of the disorder. Treatment takes many forms, but one of the most effective is to prevent exposure of the individual to the types of environments that might trigger the formation of epigenetic markers by which the phenotype is most likely to emerge, or conversely, to provide environments that are conducive to health. Environmental treatments have been effective for physical disorders, such as PKU (see below). They may also be useful as behavior genetic researchers discover the genetic and epigenetic bases for behavioral disorders such as particular types of psychopathologies (Plomin & Rutter, 1998).

Genes cannot be changed, so treatments must focus on changing the environment and thus changing the epigenome (Chapter 3) to regulate the expression of the harmful gene. Research shows that the epigenome is responsive not only to therapeutic drugs and other chemicals, but also to the behavior of other people, such as the type of maternal behavior toward the infant (Dolinoy, Weidman, & Jirtle, 2007; Szyf, 2007; Weaver et al., 2004). A relatively recent innovation, epigenetic therapy, is being used to reverse the formation of cancer cells in adults (Feinberg, 2007).

Of the 3,000 known genetic disorders, researchers have isolated the genes for only about 30 of them. This kind of work is extremely difficult to do. First, one needs good family genealogies, and second, it takes years to find the single gene or genes out of the many thousands of genes carried by humans.

Consistent sex differences are also used as clues to the genetic origins of certain disorders. Sex-linked inheritance accounts for color blindness and hemophilia in males. Hemophilia is known as the "disease of royalty," because the female descendants of England's Queen Victoria were carriers of the disease, and many of the males in the family inherited it. Hemophilia can be treated today with various medications that aid in blood clotting. Other sex-linked disorders are color blindness and some forms of muscular dystrophy.

Fragile X syndrome, another sex-linked disorder, is caused by an abnormal gene on the bottom end of the X chromosome. It is the most common inherited cause of mental retardation. Males affected with the disorder have autistic-like symptoms (see below) such as hand flapping, self-injurious behavior such as biting the hands, poor eye contact, shyness, repetitive behaviors, and mild to moderate mental retardation. Fragile X males are different from autistic males, however, because the former will begin to interact socially in familiar settings. They may also have deficits in attention and information processing. Girls who are carriers show only mild cognitive deficits. These children tend to have long faces and prominent ears (Burack et al., 1999; Einfeld, 2005; Hagerman, 1996).

Several other single-gene disorders are also related to mental retardation and difficulties with social interaction. **Prader-Willi syndrome** is associated with low muscle tone, obesity, short stature, small hands and feet, and lowered intelligence, especially in short-term memory and mathematical skills. These individuals have poor emotion control such as temper tantrums, self-biting, and mood swings (Bertella et al., 2005; Einfeld, 2005). **Williams syndrome** individuals have short stature, heart defects, and intellectual deficits, especially in spatial abilities. Compared to the other syndromes mentioned here, Williams syndrome individuals are highly social, and in some cases indiscriminately social, seemingly willing and able to talk to anyone about anything (Einfeld, 2005; Gray et al., 2006).

In some cases, a single recessive gene can have multiple effects. **Marfan's syndrome** is one example. This disorder is associated with a weakened heart, mild bone structure deformities, long fingers, and eye lens problems. It is believed that Abraham Lincoln suffered from this disease. **Phenylketonuria (PKU)** is a recessive disorder in which the person cannot properly metabolize phenylalanine, an essential amino acid found in most forms of protein. If detected early, the level of phenylalanine-containing foods in the child's diet can be lowered, thus reducing the chances that mental and nervous deficits will develop. Even with appropriate treatment, however, preschool children with PKU showed less ability for planning and search behaviors, although their memory skills were similar, compared to matched control children who did not have PKU (Welsh, Pennington, Ozonoff, Rouse, & McCabe, 1990). These effects are related to the concentration of phenylalanine in the child's blood, suggesting that additional dietary and drug treatment may provide hope for treatment (Diamond, Prevor, Callender, & Druin, 1997). PKU occurs in 1 in 25,000 births. It can be tested for at birth, and parents can be counseled about their baby's diet (H. L. Levy, Karolkewicz, Houghton, & MacCready, 1970).

Another recessive disorder is **cystic fibrosis**, which affects 1 in 2,500 births. It is the most common genetic disorder among people with a northern European ancestry. The disorder is characterized by the clogging of the lungs with mucus, which leads to infection and death in young adulthood. It can be detected prenatally, and many countries routinely screen newborns for the disease.

Some disorders afflict particular racial or ethnic groups whose members are likely to intermarry, increasing the chances of having a child inherit two recessive genes. Jewish couples in which both members can trace their origins to European ancestry (Ashkenazic Jews) have a 1 in 3,600 chance of producing a baby with **Tay-Sachs disease**, an enzyme deficiency that brings about a steady deterioration of mental and physical abilities. Infants may become blind or deaf, have paralysis, and lose the ability to swallow. Few live past the age of 5 (Silver, 1985).

Black infants have a 1 in 400 chance of inheriting **sickle-cell anemia**, a disorder of the red blood cells in which they tend to clot and block off blood vessels. People afflicted with sickle-cell anemia may become mildly retarded or have heart and kidney problems. Unlike Tay-Sachs disease, sickle-cell anemia can be partially treated, and its victims can live normal lives. The sickle-cell gene is also associated with a positive side effect: those who have the disease as well as those who are merely carriers of the gene are partially immunized against the deadly disease of malaria. People with sickle-cell genes are not good hosts for the malarial parasite, which spends part of its life cycle in the blood. Malarial protection is probably the reason why the sickle-cell gene was maintained in the population.

Huntington's disease is a particularly poignant genetic disorder. It is caused by a dominant gene, so half of the children of a parent with the disease will also acquire it. The problem is that the symptoms do not appear until the age of 35 or 40, well after those children have begun to have children of their own. The symptoms include depression, loss of memory and motor control, and other problems caused by the death of brain cells. It occurs in 1 out of 18,000 births, and there is no treatment. A recently developed test can determine whether an individual carries the gene for Huntington's disease. While such a test may be useful for counseling these individuals about whether or not to have children, it also tells them whether they will acquire the disease themselves. Because many people do not want to learn that they might have an incurable disease, relatively few individuals at risk for this disease come to a clinic for genetic screening (S. D. Taylor, 1994). Another dominant disorder is **familial Alzheimer's disease**, which is also associated with brain deterioration and loss of social and cognitive control.

Other genetic disorders are polygenic. Because these disorders require a combination of factors in order to occur, their incidence is less than that of the single-gene sex-linked and recessive disorders. Polygenic disorders include cleft lip and cleft palate, spina bifida (exposed spinal cord), some forms of diabetes, and some forms of heart defects. Genetic causes may also be implicated in some forms of schizophrenia, autism, alcoholism, and homosexuality, although less is known about the genetic basis of these conditions. Considerably more research is required to investigate these and other genetic causes.

Chromosomal Disorders

During the process of meiosis, errors sometimes occur as chromosomes split and recombine. One gamete may wind up with too many chromosomes, another with too few. A **monosomy** is an abnormality of the 23rd pair, the sex chromosomes. Monosomies occur when one member of the pair is missing. In **Turner's syndrome**, a female has only one X chromosome. This is associated with a lack of complete sex determination, other physical deformities, and mental retardation. Approximately 1 in 2000 infants are born with genitals that are neither male nor female, sometimes called intersexuals. As in all forms of sexual development, the incidence and severity of the genital deformations depend partly on the chromosomes and partly on the availability of specific sex hormones. Hormonal treatments are increasingly common in these conditions (Robboy & Jaubert, 2007)

A **trisomy** is a chromosome pair that has an extra chromosome accidentally attached to it. Trisomies can occur on the sex chromosomes, resulting, for example, in **Kleinfelter's syndrome** (XXY) in which the male has female behavioral characteristics and may be mentally retarded, although normal in appearance. The best-known of the trisomies is trisomy 21, in which an extra chromosome is attached to the twenty-first pair. The resulting disorder, which in the past was sometimes called "mongolism" but is now known as **Down's syndrome**, is characterized by short stature, flabbiness, cardiac and glandular abnormalities, small mouth, mental retardation, and folds of skin over the eyes.

It is known that Down's syndrome and other genetic and chromosomal errors are more prevalent in infants born to mothers nearing the end of their fertility and for older fathers over the age of 40. For this reason, most parents over the age of 35 are counseled to have amniocentesis (see below) to test for the presence of chromosomal abnormalities during pregnancy. It has been hypothesized that estrogen levels in the mother may explain Down's syndrome. Since estrogen production is highest between the ages of 20 and 35, women older than this may be more likely to have a Down's baby than are women between those ages. Estrogen may enhance the process of meiotic cell division, and its lack may cause incomplete cell division (Crowley, Gulati, Hayden, Lopez, & Dyer, 1979).

Furthermore, the risk of Down's syndrome and other disorders increases when fathers are older than 40 years; errors in the meiosis of sperm cells may account for as much as one-fourth of all Down's cases (Arehart-Treichel, 1979; Zhu et al., 2005). Women are also more at risk for miscarriage when the father is over the age of 40 (Slama et al., 2005). Since older mothers typically have older male partners, there is no way to determine in a particular couple whether the risk of Down's syndrome is caused by maternal or paternal factors.

Aside from the genetic and chromosomal risks, older couples seem just as capable of bearing children as younger couples. In several studies of first-time mothers over 35 years of age, the rate of complications of pregnancy and birth was no different than for younger first-time mothers (Porreco et al., 2005; Prysak, Lorenz, & Kisly, 1995). Nevertheless, due to the social and psychological issues surrounding childbearing for older women (see the earlier section on infertility), they can be helped by prenatal counseling and genetic screening of their fetus (O'Reilly-Green & Cohen, 1993).

Environmental Influence on Prenatal Development

In this section, environmental influences on the development of individual differences are covered. Little is known about how variations in the prenatal environment are related to normal individual differences that develop postnatally. We are, however, learning a great deal about more serious variations in the prenatal environment, those that lead to birth defects and complications of pregnancy. Many kinds of hazardous substances can penetrate the otherwise peaceful world of the fetus. For a pregnant woman and her family, therefore, this section is extremely important. It is reasonably easy to avoid many of the things that may cause harm to an unborn baby if you are aware of them. The purpose of this section is not only to report the current research findings on this topic, but also to keep you informed about the ways to achieve a healthy pregnancy.

The study of birth defects is known as **teratology**, from the Greek word *tera*, meaning monster—hardly a pleasant association. Teratology, however, is an extremely valuable area of investigation because it attempts to find the causes of birth defects so that they may be avoided in the future. Up until this century, birth defects were mysterious. They were often attributed to magical, spiritual, or supernatural causes, or else they were read as omens or signs. The ancient Babylonians considered birth defects to be omens because that is how they viewed any "unnatural" occurrence.

Many primitive societies today have some theories of the causes of birth defects, but these are mostly superstitious beliefs, such as the admonition that eating twisted or deformed plants may lead to birth deformities (M. Mead & Newton, 1967).

If the birth defect arises because of some environmental cause rather than a chromosomal or genetic abnormality, then the agent responsible for the defect is known as a **teratogen**. Teratogens come in many different forms, from viruses to chemicals to nuclear radiation, and their existence testifies to the importance of environmental-infant interactions even before birth.

The general public was made aware of the devastating effects of toxic agents on fetal development through two drugs that were once widely prescribed for pregnant women: thalidomide and DES. Thalidomide was a mild tranquilizer that was available in Europe in the 1950s. Pregnant women took it in the early months of pregnancy to help control nausea and insomnia. It was discovered to be teratogenic after a number of physicians traced the presence of heart defects and deformed or missing limbs to the mother's use of the drug during pregnancy. It was found that the time in pregnancy at which the mother had taken the drug determined the particular deformity. If she took it just at the time when the arms were forming, for example, then the arms suffered the most deformity.

Another way in which teratogenic agents may operate is illustrated by the case of the drug diethylstilbestrol (DES), a hormone given to pregnant women between 1948 and 1969 to help prevent miscarriage and to enhance reproductive health. Between 500,000 and 2 million women are believed to have taken this drug. In this case, however, the effects did not show up at birth, but rather when the offspring of these women had reached adolescence. A rise in the number of cases of vaginal cancer in teenage girls and of sterility and other genital abnormalities in teenage boys was eventually traced back to DES. The good news is that continued follow-up into childbearing years of these girls who had genital abnormalities showed that none of their daughters had abnormalities (Kaufman & Adam, 2002; Titus-Ernstoff et al., 2006).

The effects of these drugs and the other toxic agents reviewed in this section can be attributed to changes in the epigenome of the fetus. As a result of exposure to a toxin, particular types of epigenetic markers form that shut down the expression of genes that would otherwise be normal during development. As we saw earlier, all of the female's ova are formed prenatally. Thus, exposure to DES alters the epigenome of the gametes of these females, suggesting that some forms of the epigenome can be inherited, much like the inheritance of the genome itself (Whitelaw & Whitelaw, 2006).

As a general rule, the effects of toxic agents on the fetus will depend upon a number of factors. Among them is the point in pregnancy at which the exposure occurs. Since two-thirds of all birth defects occur in the first trimester, the first 3 months of pregnancy, the earlier in pregnancy one is exposed to a toxic agent, the greater the risk (see Figure 9.1). In reality, the first few days and weeks of fetal life allow for a minimum of susceptibility. The effect of the teratogenic agents increases and peaks during the period of the rapid differentiation of the organs and limbs and then declines again. If the exposure occurs during the time when organs are growing at a rapid rate, the result will likely be a structural defect. If it occurs after organ growth is mostly completed, the result will more likely be growth retardation or a behavioral abnormality (Kopp & Parmelee, 1979; Fifer et al., 2001). Other factors include the size of the dosage and the length of exposure, with longer, larger doses creating the greatest risk. A **dose-response relationship** occurs when levels of the drug consumed are directly correlated with the strength of the outcome effect (Bookstein, Sampson, Streissguth, & Barr, 1996; Vorhees & Mollnow, 1987).

As more research has been done, the list of teratogenic agents has increased. Some of these are given in Table 9.1. For some of these agents, the effects are well established in both animal and human studies. Effects that are listed as suspected may have been confirmed in animals but not in humans. One problem with isolating the effects of particular agents is that more than one factor may occur at the same time. For example, it is difficult

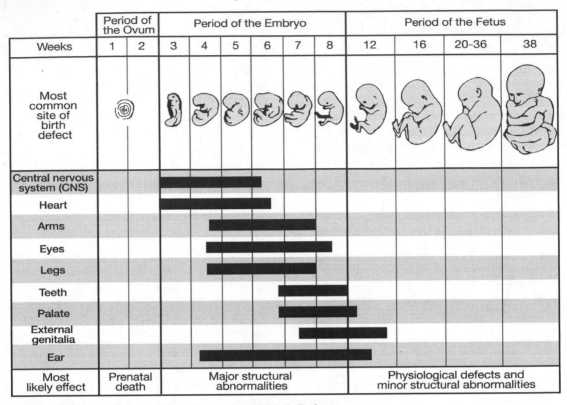

	Period of the Ovum		Period of the Embryo						Period of the Fetus			
Weeks	1	2	3	4	5	6	7	8	12	16	20-36	38
Most common site of birth defect												
Central nervous system (CNS)												
Heart												
Arms												
Eyes												
Legs												
Teeth												
Palate												
External genitalia												
Ear												
Most likely effect	Prenatal death		Major structural abnormalities						Physiological defects and minor structural abnormalities			

Figure 9.1   Stages of Prenatal Development and Birth Defects

Source: A. Fogel & G. F. Melson, *Child Development*, 1988, p. 89. St. Paul, MN: West. Copyright © West Publishing Company. Reprinted by permission. All rights reserved.

These five-month-old fraternal twin girls have some of the characteristics of fetal alcohol syndrome: narrow heads, widely spaced eyes, underdeveloped jaws, and growth retardation.

Photo by George Steinmetz.

TABLE 9.1   Common Teratogenic Agents and Their Effects

Agent	Known or Suspected Effects
Drugs	
Alcohol	Growth retardation, heart problems, mental retardation
Analgesics (for pain)	Respiratory problems at birth
Antibiotics	Streptomycin can cause hearing loss; tetracycline can stain teeth and inhibit bone growth
Arsenic (in water)	Suspected growth retardation and malformation
Aspirin	In large amounts, suspected respiratory problems and bleeding at birth for mother and infant
Barbituates (sedatives)	No long-term effects, but newborns may experience withdrawal and respiratory problems
Caffeine	No known long-term effects for moderate use, but increased activity, heart rate, and arousal in fetus during periods of maternal consumption; also, caffeine may enhance the negative effect of other drugs, such as tobacco and alcohol.
Cocaine	See text
Diethystilbestrol (DES)	Genetic abnormalities; genital cancer in female infants
Heroin, morphine	Respiratory problems, growth retardation, increased risk for mortality, sleep disturbances; newborns experience withdrawal
Hydantoins, dilantin, valproic acid (anticonvulsants)	Can cause heart defects, cleft lip and palate, limb reduction, and mental retardation, but some of the effects may be caused by maternal epilepsy
Lithium (for depression)	Cardiovascular disorders (suspected)
Marijuana	See text
Methamphetamine (stimulant)	Brain growth retardation and cognitive deficits
Prozac (and related antidepressants)	No known effects
Sex hormones (for birth control, fertility, and prevention of miscarriage)	Suspected cardiovascular disorders; no known effects in humans
Thalidomide	Limb deformities, hearing loss, higher risk of mortality
Tobacco	Higher risk for newborn mortality, low birthweight, neurological changes, postnatal growth retardation, cleft lip and palate, sudden infant death
Tranquilizers	No known long-term effects, but newborns may experience withdrawal
Vitamins	Large doses of vitamin A (used to treat acne) cause defects in heart, head, neck and brain, and other deformities; large doses of other vitamins are suspected of causing defects
Diseases (sexually transmitted)	
AIDS	See text
Chlamydia	Eye infection and risk of pneumonia in newborn

TABLE 9.1 Common Teratogenic Agents and Their Effects

Gonorrhea	Prematurity and eye infection in newborns, higher risk of newborn mortality
Hepatitus B	Prematurity, low birthweight, higher risk of newborn mortality
Herpes simplex	Mental retardation, eye damage, higher risk of newborn mortality (can be prevented by cesarean section)
Syphilis	Mental retardation, blindness, deafness, higher risk of mortality
Diseases (others)	
Anemia (iron deficiency)	Higher risk of stillbirth, newborn mortality, brain damage
Diabetes	Can cause malformations and higher risk of mortality
Hypertension	Higher risk of mortality and miscarriage
Influenza	Cardiovascular and central nervous system defects, spontaneous abortion
Mumps	Higher risk of spontaneous abortion and stillbirth
Rh incompatibility	Higher risk of stillbirth, miscarriage, heart defects, and mental retardation
Rubella	Deafness, cataracts, heart disease, mental retardation, higher risk of spontaneous abortion and stillbirth
Other viruses	In particular, sytomegalovirus and chicken pox increase the risk of skin and muscle defects, deafness, blindness, mental retardation, and infant mortality
Environmental hazards	
Lead	Anemia, hemorrhage, increase risk of miscarriage
Radiation	Small head size, growth retardation, leukemia, cataracts, higher risk of miscarriage and stillbirth
Methylmercury (in contaminated fish)	Cerebral palsy, neurological disorders
Pesticides, PCB	Higher risk of stillbirth, low birthweight, mental delays
Cleaning agents, solvents	Possible effects of low birthweight and some defects (suspected)
Air pollution	Cardiac defects and chromosomal abnormalities (suspected)
Maternal conditions	
Stress	Pregnancy complications, increased risk of Down's syndrome, attentional and motor defects
Malnutrition	Prematurity, low birthweight, growth retardation, mental retardation
Age	Older women have higher rates of Down's syndrome in their fetuses
Depression	Infant depressed behavior and higher stress hormones (cortisol) at birth but no birth defects

Sources: Alwan et al., 2007; B. A. Buehler et al., 1994; D. Bukatko & Daehler, 1995; Chang et al., 2004; R. E. Dahl et al., 1995; Field et al., 2006; R. Gandelman, 1992; M. S. Golub et al., 1998; S. W. Jacobson et al., 1985; D. Kennedy & Koren, 1998; Kulin et al., 1998; B. M. Lester & Dreher, 1998; Lundy et al., 1999; Martinez-Frias et al., 1998; Nehlig & Debry, 1994; Perera et al., 2005; Ritz et al., 2002; Rizzo et al., 1997; Roy et al., 1998; Schneider et al., 1999; Schuetze & Zeskind et al., 1997; Vorhees & Mollnow, 1987; Vreugdenhil et al., 2002; Whyatt et al., 2004.

to determine the effect of an antinausea drug apart from the condition that caused the severe nausea in the first place (Vorhees & Mollnow, 1987).

Substance Abuse. Perhaps the area of teratology that has attracted the most research is the effects of maternal alcohol consumption. **Fetal alcohol syndrome (FAS)**, which was discovered in 1973, is associated with some forms of mental retardation, facial abnormalities such as small narrow heads with widely spaced eyes and an underdeveloped jaw, hyperactivity, growth retardation, more premature births and miscarriages, lower birthweight, and heart defects. FAS occurs at an incidence of 1 to 3 per 1,000 births in the United States (Fifth Special Report to the U.S. Congress on Alcohol and Health, 1984). The heaviest drinkers, those who consume more than five drinks per day on the average, have a 30% higher risk of having an FAS child (Landesman-Dwyer, 1981; Rosett, 1980).

Infants born to moderate drinkers, those who consume one or two drinks per day, are not likely to have physical deformities. Follow-up studies show that by age 4, however, these children have mild to severe learning disabilities and slightly retarded physical growth. This pattern of outcomes has been called *fetal alcohol effects (FAE)* (Abel, Randall, & Riley, 1983). Long-term follow-up studies have shown continuing effects in children in a dose-response relationship as late as 14 years of age, including problems with attention (including Attention Deficit Hyperactivity Disorder, ADHD), speed of information processing, motor coordination, and learning problems (Biederman, 2002; Lee et al., 2004; Roebuck-Spencer et al., 2004; Streissguth et al., 1994). The effects are relatively small for children whose mothers had one drink per day but increase rapidly with higher rates of consumption.

The evidence is not strong that low levels of alcohol consumption during pregnancy will have an effect, but there may be unmeasured consequences. Some research shows that occasional *binge drinking* during pregnancy—having multiple alcoholic drinks in one day—may be more harmful than steady low-level consumption. This is because the high and rapid intake of alcohol can damage fetal nerve cells (Jacobson & Jacobson, 2001). Pregnant women are best advised to eliminate all alcohol consumption until after their babies have been born. On the other hand, if you are currently pregnant and have been a light or occasional drinker since conception, the chances of this having an effect on your baby are relatively small. Nevertheless, you should terminate further alcohol consumption until after the birth of the baby.

Prenatal smoking of both tobacco and marijuana has been shown to cause respiratory problems, birth complications, growth retardation, antisocial behavior, and learning disabilities in early childhood, although unlike alcohol, smoking does not generally lower IQ scores (Fried, 2002; Hurd et al., 2005; Lester & Dreher, 1989; Wakschlag et al., 2002; Wang et al., 2004). Maternal cigarette smoking has also been associated with a greater risk for infantile excitability, colic and gastrointestinal symptoms, and childhood obesity, asthma and other respiratory disorders, and conduct problems (Gilliland et al., 2001; Law et al., 2003; Maughan et al., 2004; Kries et al., 2002; Søndergaard, et al., 2001). Maternal prenatal cigarette smoking also lowers their son's sperm count and testes size when these boys reach adolescence and predisposes teens of both sexes to nicotine addiction (Abreu-Villaça et al., 2004; Jensen, 2005; Ramlau-Hansen et al., 2007).

Remarkably, the effect of cigarette smoking on reducing the birthweight of the fetus is the same whether it is the mother or the father who smokes, and if both smoke, the effect is doubled. As in related studies of older children and adults, passive smoking has effects just as severe as those of direct smoking and causes respiratory problems in those exposed (D. H. Rubin, Krasilnikoff, Leventhal, Weile, & Berget, 1986). Both parents should refrain from smoking during the mother's pregnancy. Programs to prevent smoking in pregnancy have had only limited success, partly because smoking is sustained within the context of a particular culture and nation. Even if a program succeeds in limiting smoking during pregnancy, most parents will begin to smoke again with a year of their child's birth (Cnattingius, 2004; Ershoff, 2004).

With cocaine and intravenous drug use on the rise, there is an increasing incidence of cocaine-addicted pregnant women, as well as women infected with the AIDS virus. Cocaine use by mothers reduces birthweight and creates circulatory, respiratory, and urinary problems. It also increases the risk of Sudden Infant Death Syndrome (see below), attentional difficulties, withdrawal, language delay, and lags in motor development. Although cocaine-exposed infants often fall within the normal range, they have slight deficits in attention and emotional responding compared to nonexposed infants. Also, as with other teratogenic effects related to drug and alcohol abuse, mothers who abuse substances may have other health risks, such as poor diet and poor prenatal care, and these other risks, rather than the drug itself, may be the cause of problems in the newborn. The long-term effects of cocaine on the infant may also be confounded with behavioral factors associated with drug abuse, such as poverty, maternal depression, family disruption, child abuse, and neglect. Alleviation of these contextual factors can in most cases eliminate the effects of the prenatal cocaine exposure (Arendt, Singer, Angelopoulos, Bass-Busdiecker, & Mascia, 1998; Bendersky & Lewis, 1998; Espy, Riese, & Francis, 1997; B. A. Lewis et al., 2004; Mayes et al., 1997; Mitra, Ganesh, & Apuzzio, 1994; Morrow et al., 2003; L. T. Singer et al., 2004; Tronick et al., 2005).

One of the problems that occurs with infants born to substance-abusing mothers is that professionals who come in contact with the infant, such as nursing staff, may inadvertently provide less adequate care. This is due to the popular belief by professionals that cocaine and other recreational and illegal drugs have strong and lasting effects on the infant, even though the research evidence suggests that there is considerable controversy about whether such effects actually occur. The lower quality of care by professionals may also be due to stereotypes that stigmatize drug abusers. It is recommended that professionals maintain a neutral and unbiased demeanor toward such infants, who certainly have had no choice in their own fates and may be just as healthy at birth as nonexposed infants (Messinger & Lester, 2008; Meyers & Kaltenbach, 1992).

It is also important to treat both the mother and the infant for the effects of drug withdrawal and to help the family recover from drug abuse. Extra support services are needed to help the family become economically and emotionally stabilized. Comforting an infant who is experiencing withdrawal symptoms is also difficult. It is recommended that the infant be kept quiet in a room with dim lights and low noise levels. Play soft music, hold and rock the baby gently and frequently, speak softly and calmly, and give gentle massages (Pawl, 1992; White, 1992).

Maternal Depression. The effects on the fetus of prenatal maternal depression has received particular attention from researchers. The lifetime incidence of depression in women is between 10% and 25%, and it is estimated that 9% to 14% of women show signs of depression during pregnancy. Other estimates show that up to 35% of women take psychotropic medication during pregnancy, primarily drugs that are called selective serotonin reuptake inhibitors (SSRIs) including the brand names of Paxil, Prozac, Celexa, and Zoloft, among others. It is difficult to separate the effects of these medications on the fetus compared with the effects of depression alone. In general, neither depression nor SSRIs cause birth defects. There is some evidence that newborn behavior is somewhat depressed in infants of these women (lower activity level, more sleeping, longer latency to respond to stimulation), but the effects generally decline over the next month after birth. Since chronic depression itself is a risk factor for maternal well-being, maternal care, and infant socioemotional development (see Chapter 6), physicians recommend that mothers continue taking SSRIs during their pregnancies and after as prescribed (Einarson et al., 2001; Field et al., 2006; Zeskind & Stephens, 2004).

Maternal anxiety and stress. Compared to depression, maternal stress and anxiety during pregnancy appear to have more toxic effects on prenatal and postnatal development. Fetuses of stressed mothers have a higher activity level than for non-stressed mothers. Infants exposed to prenatal maternal stress cried and fussed more and had difficulties with emotion regulation and social behavior. As children, they are more likely to show symptoms of ADHD and anxiety, lower attention ability, and socioemotional problems. As adolescents, they continue to show problems with ADHD and anxiety and have lower IQ scores compared to children of non-anxious mothers. As adults, these individuals are more susceptible to mental illness, including schizophrenia, depression, and anxiety. When an individual is anxious or feels stressed, there is an increased activation of the hypothalamic-pituitary-adrenal (HPA) axis by which a central nervous system (hypothalamus and pituitary) perception of stress leads to the secretion of the stress hormone cortisol into the blood by the adrenal glands (located above the kidneys). Continued elevation of cortisol in the blood then affects the hypothalamus by causing it to be overactive, sending messages of stress even when there may be none present. This mechanism is believed to account for feelings of chronic anxiety.

Elevated cortisol levels are found in anxious mothers. Since cortisol can cross the placenta, it likely affects the development of the fetal brain and HPA axis, making it more susceptible even to mild stresses later in life. It is more difficult to control anxiety, compared to depression, using medication, and the effects of these drugs on the fetus have not been studied. Behavioral stress reduction, including meditation and hypnosis, have been shown to be effective in pregnant women. So has eating chocolate (!), which appears to have a calming effect on some women (DiPietro et al., 2002; Guse et al., 2006; Huizink et al., 2004; O'Connor et al., 2005; Räikkönen et al., 2004; Rieger et al., 2005; van den Bergh et al., 2004; Wurmser et al., 2006).

AIDS. Another area of recent research work is the transmission of acquired immune deficiency syndrome (AIDS) from the pregnant woman to the fetus. AIDS has become a global epidemic, affecting more than 6 million people worldwide. More than 20 million are infected with HIV-1, the virus that causes AIDS. In the United States, AIDS is the leading cause of death among younger men and the fourth leading cause of death among younger women (T. C. Quinn, 1995). The proportion of infants who contract AIDS prenatally varies across studies, but reported percentages range from 15% (Europe and North America) to 30% (Africa).

AIDS may contribute to low birthweight, although it is difficult to separate its effects from the effects of other risk factors like drug abuse (drug abusers may have contracted the AIDS virus from unclean needles). The biggest risk comes after birth, when infants begin to show signs of the disease. These infants are susceptible to infections that may lead to mental or motor deficits. It is not entirely clear how infants become infected with the AIDS virus. Some may get it prenatally. As with other sexually transmitted diseases (see Table 9.1), there may be a risk of infection by the virus as the infant comes into contact with the mother's body fluids during its passage through the birth canal. In some, but not all, cases, the risk may be reduced by as much as half by cesarean birth (A. Blank, Mofenson, Willoughby, & Yaffe, 1994; Paiva, Hutto, Antunes, & Scott, 1994; Spinillo et al., 1994; Touraine, Sanhadji, & Firouzi, 1994; Towers, Deveikis, Asrat, Nageotte, & Freeman, 1993). In addition, the risk of perinatal HIV has been found to be reduced by 30 to 50 percent if the mother takes a medication called Zidovudine during pregnancy (Fiscus, Adimora, Schoenbach, Lim. McKinney, Rupar, Kenny, Woods, & Wilfert, 1996; Parks, 1996; Wortley, Lindegren, & Fleming, 2001). There is a concern, however, that this medication may increase the risk of cancer in childhood in those infants exposed to it prenatally (Health Watch, 1997). A third possible route of transmission is through breast milk after birth (see below).

Other toxins. One problem with understanding teratology is that so much of our modern environment is made up of potentially harmful chemicals, pollutants, and radiation (see Table 9.1). Some are harmful to people of all ages, causing cancer and other diseases. In some cases, the fetus may be more susceptible than older children and adults. Another problem in establishing the effects of a teratogenic agent is that these effects are not always seen immediately. Some effects may take 20 or 30 years to develop, if, for example, they affect the functioning of the adult (Karcew, 1994). Teratogens may not always operate through the mother, although there is relatively little evidence at the current time that the father's exposure to drugs and other agents causes birth defects either through the sperm or by contact with the mother during pregnancy (Little & Vainio, 1994).

The findings on the epigenetic transmission of toxic effects to the fetus means that exposure to environmental toxins via maternal behavior during pregnancy has the potential to influence not only the fetus but possibly the fetus' children and grandchildren! Young parents-to-be, therefore, have a responsibility to all their heirs to take care of their physical and mental health during pregnancy and after.

Experts advise that pregnant women should take no drugs unless explicitly advised by a physician. Even a seemingly harmless drug like aspirin, especially when taken late in pregnancy, can cause problems with labor and delivery, although there is no evidence that aspirin causes birth defects (Kozer et al., 2002). With all prescription drugs, it is wise for the mother to question the physician about the availability of research on the drug's teratogenic effects. Women are counseled to avoid alcohol, cigarettes, X-rays, microwaves, food containing preservatives, colorings and other artificial additives, and contact with people who have viral diseases and other infections. Consult with a physician before taking vitamins or using caffeine (note that many cola drinks contain caffeine). Use sodium bicarbonate (baking soda) as an antacid and natural fiber foods as a laxative. Literature on making pregnancy safe for the baby and mother is available from the March of Dimes Birth Defects Foundation, www.marchofdimes.com.

Can Birth Defects Be Prevented?

The prevention of all forms of birth defects involves two aspects: diagnosis and treatment. If parents suspect that they may be at risk for having children with genetic, chromosomal, or teratogenic disorders, they should consult with their physician. Usually, parents are referred for **genetic counseling**, a service that can help investigate family histories and prescribe certain kinds of diagnostic approaches.

Most chromosomal abnormalities and many genetic disorders can be detected in fetuses as young as 16 weeks by **amniocentesis**. During this procedure, a small amount of amniotic fluid is withdrawn from the mother's uterus through a long hollow needle inserted into the mother's abdomen. The fetal cells present in the fluid can be tested for the presence of more than 100 genetic or chromosomal abnormalities. The sex of the fetus can also be determined.

Usually, amniocentesis is done only in circumstances where some problem is suspected—for example, if the mother or father is over the age of 35 or if there is a history of genetic disorders in the family—because some risk is associated with the procedure. One or 2 out of every 200 women will have a spontaneous abortion after the procedure, and 4 to 6 fetuses may receive minor injuries due to puncture wounds. In addition, the cost of the procedure increases depending upon the number of laboratory tests that are needed to analyze the amniotic fluid. On the positive side, a long-term follow-up study of children aged 7 to 18 whose mothers had amniocentesis, compared to a group of children whose mothers did not undergo the procedure, found no significant differences in the two groups on learning skills and motor and physical development (Baird, Yee, & Sadovnick, 1994).

Another procedure for diagnosing genetic abnormalities is ultrasound. Ultrasound carries less risk than amniocentesis, but it is less able to detect genetic and chromosomal problems: only abnormalities visible on the exterior of the body can be seen and detected using this procedure. Ultrasound has also been used during amniocentesis to help locate the position of the fetus's body before the needle is inserted. Ultrasound can detect the presence of multiple fetuses and the placement of the fetus (Barss, Benacerraf, & Frigoletto, 1985).

One problem with these methods is that they cannot be done until relatively late in the pregnancy, usually at the beginning of the second trimester. By that time, the parents' anxiety levels are likely to be high, and the decision to abort a malformed fetus is more difficult because of the mother's growing emotional attachment to it and because an abortion will require more complex surgical techniques.

In **chorionic villus sampling (CVS)**, a bit of the chorion is sampled. CVS has the advantage of diagnosing a wider range of disorders, and it can be done during the first trimester. It does not require that the physician puncture the amnion, and it is relatively painless since the uterus is entered through the vagina rather than through the abdomen. Ultrasound may be used to guide the sampling procedure. CVS causes only minor discomfort to the mother and has a 100% diagnostic success rate. Some mothers experience spotting following the CVS procedure, but other problems are rare (D'Alton, 1994). The data on the safety of CVS for the fetus are mixed. Some research reports no increased risk from the use of the procedure (J. E. Green et al., 1988; Smidt-Jensen & Hahnemann, 1988). On the other hand, several studies have found that CVS produces a higher percentage of both spontaneous abortions and limb defects. The incidence of limb deformities may depend on the timing of the test, so more research is needed (Hsieh et al., 1995; Palo, Piiroinen, Honkonen, Lakkala, & Aula, 1994). On the other hand, the actual percentage of problems resulting from these procedures is extremely low from 0.5 to 2.0% of all the tested pregnancies. Families need to weigh the benefits and risks of the procedure against their reasons for seeking genetic counseling (Boss, 1994; Cutillo et al., 1994).

Unfortunately, many types of disorders cannot be detected with any of these diagnostic procedures. In addition, each disorder requires a specific test, and each test can be quite costly. Thus, genetic counseling must be selective and done only with a thorough knowledge of the family history.

In actuality, very few of the causes of birth defects and prenatal disorders are clearly understood, and when defects or disorders are discovered, parents are often upset and confused. Research shows that it is better for parents to consult professional genetic counselors rather than their primary care physicians. Many physicians do not know the field of genetic research and may not understand the options available for parents when a prenatal disorder is detected (Geller et al., 1993; Wright, 1994).

Several disorders, including spina bifida (exposed spine) and anencephaly (exposed brain), can be detected by testing the mother's blood between the fifteenth and eighteenth weeks of pregnancy. The test is for **maternal serum alpha-fetoprotein (MSAFP)**, and it is safe for both mother and fetus. Researchers are developing experimental methods for testing the fertilized zygote before it is implanted. Called **preimplantation genetic diagnosis (PGD)**, the test may provide significant information without spontaneous abortion of an already implanted embryo, which may be an unacceptable risk for some families who would otherwise choose CVS (Verlinsky & Kuliev, 1994). PGD requires procedures similar to those used during in vitro fertilization: the zygote would be removed from the mother for testing and then implanted if it proves healthy.

After such tests are made and a prenatal disorder is discovered, what can be done to treat the problem? Currently, three avenues of treatment are available: the fetus can be treated medically while inside the uterus, the doctor and family can make concrete plans for treatment following the birth, or the family can choose to abort the fetus.

Fetal medicine is one of the fastest-growing fields of medicine. Doctors have had success treating certain disorders by giving specific vitamins to the mother. In other cases, tubes have been inserted into the fetus to draw blood or to drain harmful buildups of fluids from the head or the bladder. Some malformations, such as intestinal openings or blockages and respiratory and neural disorders, can be repaired surgically. Ultrasound can be used to monitor the progress of the disease, the intervention, and the treatment. Fetal medicine can pose risks to both mother and fetus, however, and these need to be carefully evaluated by future research. Among the problems of doing surgery on a fetus are how to move it into the desired position for the intervention, how to make the fetus relax during the procedure, and how to administer anesthetics, all without undue risk to the mother (Collins, 1994; Forestier, Kaplan, & Cox, 1988; Frigoletto, Greene, Benacerraf, Barss, & Saltzman, 1986). A growing number of advanced post-childbirth surgical and drug treatments are becoming available for such disorders as heart defects, facial deformities (cleft palate, for instance), and PKU. Information on genetic counseling is also available from the March of Dimes Birth Defects Foundation.

What Are Some Ethical Issues Raised by Genetic Counseling?

Like in vitro fertilization, genetic counseling and screening for prenatal disorders raise significant ethical questions. If a serious disorder is discovered, few treatments are available, and abortion is often the only option for a family that does not want to bring a child into the world who is likely to be severely handicapped (see the next section). Another side of the picture is the use of prenatal screening to enable parents to choose to carry or abort a child who does not meet their specifications but is otherwise healthy. Already parents can use CVS to determine the embryo's sex and choose to carry to term only a boy or a girl, depending upon their preference.

It is possible that these procedures may produce a higher percentage of wanted compared to unwanted infants. Research in Sweden shows that better parent-child relationships, even over a long-term follow-up lasting 25 years, result from raising children who fit the parents' prenatal sex preference (Stattin & Klackenberg-Larsson, 1991). However, this does not mean that selecting one sex and

aborting another will automatically lead to better parent-child relationships.

Consider the following futuristic possibility. Using in vitro fertilization methods, one cell is removed from the developing embryo. In the relatively near future, we will be able to analyze the entire genetic code of this embryo, and we may have some knowledge of how the entire genotype transforms into the phenotype of the whole individual. According to one scientist,

> All of this information could be transferred to a supercomputer, together with information about the environment—including likely nutrition, environmental toxins, sunlight, and so forth. The output will be a color movie in which the embryo develops into a fetus, is born, and then grows into an adult, explicitly depicting body size and shape and hair, skin, and eye color... speech and musical ability; the mother will be able to hear the embryo—as an adult—speak or sing. (Lodish, 1995, p. 1609)

Could medical technology make this happen? That depends upon your theoretical point of view (see Chapter 2)—in particular, on whether you believe that the development of the individual is completely determined by the genes, the environment, or their links. One theory reviewed in Chapter 2, *dynamic systems theory*, suggests that we will never be able to predict the outcome of human development, even if we know everything about the genetic code. Development involves a certain amount of indeterminism—butterfly effects—that could easily change the course of a person's development and for which no direct causes could be found.

Perhaps future computers will be so sophisticated that they will be able to introduce a few butterfly effects, such as a kind word said by a teacher or a chance meeting that leads to a career choice, and thus generate a lot of possible future adults from a single embryo. Would parents then be permitted to abort an embryo if they did not like any of these simulated adults? Or could parents, with this knowledge, know when and how to expose their children to particular butterfly events, thereby controlling the children's entire lives so as to sculpt them into the kind of persons the parents imagine? Would children become mere puppets in the hands of such godlike parents and scientists? Are these ideas any more than fantasy and science fiction? Only the future will tell us.

NEWBORN HEALTH

Assessing the Infant's Status at Birth

Once a baby is born, a series of assessments may be done to determine whether there are any complications or whether the infant is in need of special attention. Assessments are divided into three basic groups. **Screening assessments** give an indication of the newborn's ability to survive and whether there are any immediate medical needs. **Neurological assessments** test for problems in the newborn's central and peripheral nervous system, such as major brain, spinal cord, or sensory damage. **Behavioral assessments** are used to rate the presence and strength of behavioral responses to stimulation and spontaneous activity. Some of the more common newborn assessment procedures are listed in Table 9.2.

One of the most widely used newborn screening tests was developed by Virginia Apgar (1953)

and is known as the **Apgar score**. The test is relatively easy to do and takes only a few seconds. The rating usually is made at 1 minute and again at 5 minutes after birth. Table 9.3 shows the categories of the Apgar rating and the possible score an infant may receive in each of five areas: respiration, heart rate, muscle tone, color, and reflex irritability. The infant's total score is summed over each of the five areas. A total score of 7 or greater usually indicates that the infant is in no immediate danger, whereas a rating of less than 7 indicates some kind of severe risk to life. If the rating is less than 4, the infant is in critical condition.

The reason for making two ratings is to encourage hospital staff to continue to monitor the newborn over several minutes. Often staff members are distracted by other events and may miss the possible deterioration of the infant's condition. In addition to the Apgar, the infant can be screened on the basis of its physical appearance, color, and the presence of any obvious deformities (Judd, 1985; Olds, London, & Ladewig, 1984; Sardana, 1985).

Apgar scores have been found to relate to a variety of prenatal and birth complications. The scores are less likely to predict later outcomes of the infant, however, probably because low scores indicate the need for immediate treatment that may alleviate the problem (Francis, Self, & Horowitz, 1987). On the other hand, low Apgar scores are

TABLE 9.2 Newborn Assessment Tests

Type of Test	Name of Test	Description of Test
Screening	Apgar	Heart rate, respiration, and other vital signs
Neurological	Dubowitz assessment of gestational age	Differentiation of small-for-date infants from infants with appropriate weight for gestational age
	Neurological examination of Prechtl & Belnema	Tests of reflexes, posture, and motor development
Behavioral	Graham-Rosenblith tests	Responses to physical objects, strength of grasp, and response to covering the nose and mouth
	Brazelton neonatal assessment	Reflexes, responses to social and physical stimuli, response to covering nose and mouth, time spent in different states, and number of changes between states

Source: A. Fogel & G. F. Melson, *Child Development*, 1988, p. 135. St. Paul, MN: West. Copyright © West Publishing Company. Reprinted by permission. All rights reserved.

TABLE 9.3 The Apgar Rating Scale

Sign	Scale		
	0	1	2
A—appearance (color)	blue, pale	body pink (extremities blue)	completely pink
P—pulse	absent	below 100	over 100
G—grimace (reflex irritability, response to stimulation of sole of foot by a slap)	no response	grimace	cry
A—activity (muscle tone)	limp	slow, flexion of extremities	active motion
R—respiratory effort	absent	slow, irregular	good, strong cry

Source: J. Butterfield and M. Covey (1962). Practical epigram of the Apgar Score. *Journal of the American Medical Association, 181*, 353. Copyright 1962, American Medical Association.

strongly correlated with infant mortality, especially if the scores decrease between the two testings.

Although the Apgar score is useful for determining the infant's viability, it is a relatively crude assessment scale. It tells us little about actual complications the infant may have. Accordingly, pediatricians and developmentalists require an assessment procedure that aids early identification of childhood behavioral and functional disorders. If such problems can be detected in the newborn, medicine and psychology could more effectively concentrate their efforts on prevention, rather than simply treating problems after they appear. A number of neurological and behavioral examinations of the newborn infant can be used for specific diagnoses (see Table 9.2). Each of these examinations has its specific limitations and range of usefulness (Self & Horowitz, 1979).

Among the neurological tests, the Dubowitz scale tests for the **gestational age** of the infant at birth. The gestational age is the number of weeks since conception. (Gestation is another word for pregnancy.) To check the gestational age, raters use the infant's muscular control, physical size measurements, skin texture and color, amount of lanugo, and the size and development of the ears, breasts, and genitals. The Dubowitz scale can predict the gestational age to within a few days (Dubowitz, Dubowitz, & Goldberg, 1970; Jaroszewicz & Boyd, 1973). The neurological test of Prechtl and Beintema examines all of the newborn's basic reflexes.

It is related to the short-term status of the newborn, but like the Apgar, it is less clearly related to long-term outcomes (Francis et al., 1987).

The Graham-Rosenblith test and the Brazelton behavioral assessments use similar types of procedures. For example, the infant's head is placed face down on a mattress. Most normal infants will turn their heads to one side to free the nasal passages. In a similar test, a cloth is placed gently over the face. In another test, the infant is pulled by the arms into a sitting position to check for head control and muscle tone. A flashlight and a bell are moved from side to side to see if the infant can localize the stimulus by turning his or her head. Faces and voices are also used in the Brazelton test. In addition, observations are made about the infant's ability to control distress and maintain an awake state.

Because the Brazelton test involves a larger range of newborn behavior, it is the most frequently used. The Brazelton test has been studied extensively. It relates well to other newborn tests, such as the Prechtl and Beintema test. The test finds reliable individual differences between normal infants and can also be used to diagnose the behavioral difficulties of high-risk infants (Brazelton, Nugent, & Lester, 1987; Francis et al., 1987).

Another use of the Brazelton test is as an intervention. Research has found that mothers and fathers increased their knowledge of and responsivity to the baby if they observed their baby while it was undergoing the Brazelton test, especially if the examiner explained the test and responded to the parents' questions (Liptak, Keller, Feldman, & Chamberlain, 1983; Myers, 1982; Worobey & Belsky, 1982).

The field of newborn assessment is rapidly improving as researchers determine the most reliable indicators of long-term problems. Improved scoring procedures and statistics and a large number of longitudinal follow-up studies have also contributed to the development of better assessments. The hope of predicting many childhood disorders from newborn assessments, however, has not been realized. In the last chapter of this book, the findings on the possible long-term persistence into childhood and adulthood of individual differences between infants will be discussed.

Birth Complications

The infant's early history is usually divided into three main phases: the prenatal, the **perinatal** (the period from 1 month before birth to about 1 month after), and the **neonatal** (the newborn until the age of 4 to 6 weeks). Although the leading cause of severe impairment stems from prenatal problems (Kopp & Parmelee, 1979), most of these problems do not show up until the perinatal period. In addition, a number of complications of the perinatal period are due to the birth process itself. Between 3 and 5 children in 1,000 show severe developmental problems before entering school, and about 85% of these problems can be attributed to prenatal and perinatal causes. Compared with the effect of prenatal and perinatal causes on later development, the contribution of neonatal problems—illness, disease, and accidents—is relatively small (Kopp & Parmelee, 1979).

Perinatal problems usually derive from disorders of delivery, perinatal infections, asphyxia, hypoglycemia (low blood sugar levels), prematurity, and cardiac and respiratory difficulties. Several of these problems appear to be caused by prenatal factors, many of which we discussed in the last chapter. There is considerable evidence that a number of the complications of the perinatal period can be overcome if the infant is exposed to a supportive social and physical environment. Infants who are raised in inadequate social and economic conditions are more likely to develop permanent deficits as a result of a perinatal complication (Kopp & Parmelee, 1979; Sameroff & Chandler, 1975). We will discuss the developmental outcomes of early deficits in Chapter 10.

One birth complication, prematurity, has received a good deal of attention from psychologists, parents, and physicians. Much of this interest has to do with modern improvements in neonatal intensive care that have permitted more premature infants to survive.

TABLE 9.4   Forms of Prematurity

Classification Factor	Premature Category
Birthweight:	
Less than 1,000 grams (2 lbs. 3 oz.)	Extremely low birthweight (ELBW)
Between 1,000 and 1,500 grams (2 lbs. 3 oz. and 3 lbs. 5 oz.)	Very low birthweight (VLBW)
Between 1,500 and 2,000 grams (3 lbs. 5 oz. and 4 lbs. 6.5 oz.)	Low birthweight (LBW)
More than 2,500 grams (5 lbs. 8 oz.)	Normal birthweight
Gestational age:	
Less than 37 weeks	Premature birth
More than 37 weeks	Full-term birth
Weight less than expected for gestational age	Intrauterine growth retardation
Weight appropriate for gestational age	See weight and term classifications above

What Is Prematurity?

Some confusion surrounds the labeling of various classes of premature infants. In general, a number of factors can vary in the determination of an infant's status. These are the birthweight, the gestational age, and the relationship between the two. Table 9.4 lists some of these classifications.

Earlier in this chapter, we looked at a variety of genetic, chromosomal, and teratogenic agents that may lead to premature birth. Although they are not the only causes, lower birthweight often results from such factors as smoking and alcohol use and poor maternal health or nutrition. Indeed, cigarette smoking during pregnancy is the largest single preventable cause of low birthweight, accounting for 20 to 30% of low- birthweight cases (Ogunyemi, Hullett, Leeper, & Risk, 1998). Exceptional stress and persistent family discord during the pregnancy period have also been associated with low birthweight (Chomitz, Cheung, & Lieberman, 1995; Ramsey, Abell, & Baker, 1986; Reeb, Graham, Zyzanski, & Kitson, 1987; A. Stein, Campbell, Day, McPherson, & Cooper, 1987). Infertility treatments that produce multiple births and low maternal weight gain also contribute to the incidence of low birthweight (Ogunyemi et al., 1998). A small percentage of infants are low birthweight even if the pregnancy had no risk factors.

The incidence of low birthweight and infant mortality varies by ethnicity (see Table 9.5). There is also a strong correlation between low birthweight and mortality. Note, however, that the mortality rates are only one-tenth as high as the rates of low birthweight. Typically, low birthweight and mortality increase as the availability of good prenatal health care and nutrition declines. It is there-fore curious that the rates of mortality and low birthweight for African Americans exceed those of all other groups in industrialized countries. On the average, African American mothers have less education, are less likely to be married, are more likely to give birth during their teenage years, and have more general health problems than do other ethnic groups in the United States. These differences, however, are not enough to account for the fact that rates of low birthweight and mortality in African Americans are nearly double those in other ethnic groups, so more research is needed (Chomitz et al., 1995). One thing is clear: poor, young, African American women are at special risk for birth complications and should be the focus of national efforts to prevent low birthweight (see below).

Problems and Prospects for Premature and Low-Birthweight Babies and Their Families

In 1975, about 40% of premature infants developed serious intellectual and neurological deficits. Due to improvements in medical technology and knowledge about the premature infant, the percentage of later deficits continues to decrease. Infants who would have been severely handicapped a generation ago, had they even survived, have a better prognosis for developing normally.

The youngest and smallest babies still run the most risk of complications and death. Babies under 1,000 grams (extremely low birthweight, or ELBW) or of less than 32 weeks' gestational age are currently considered to be at the most risk. Although more of these babies are saved each year, it increases the chances that babies with handicaps will survive from this group (Hack, Klein, & Tay-

TABLE 9.5 Percentage of Low-Birthweight Babies and Infant Mortality by Ethnicity in the United States (1997)

Group	Very-Low-Birthweight Babies < 1,500 grams (2 lbs. 3 oz.)	Low-Birthweight Babies < 2,500 grams (5 lbs.. 8 oz)	Mortality Under 1 year
Caucasian American	1.1	6.5	0.6
African-American	3.0	13.0	1.4

Source: United States Center for Disease Control: http://www.cdc.gov/mmwr/preview/mmwrhtml/mm5127z1.htm

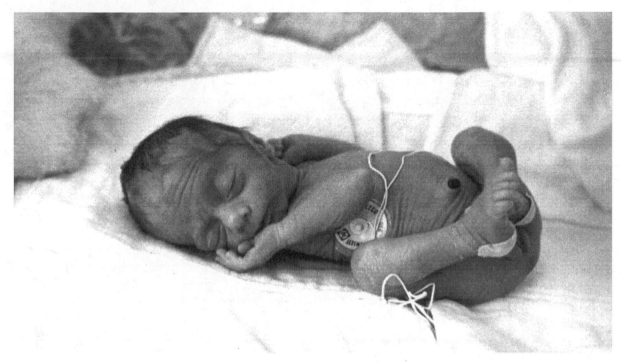

Premature infants often spend weeks in intensive care units. With appropriately gentle medical intervention and sensitive handling, most of these infants will develop normally into adulthood.
Photo by Elizabeth Crews.

lor, 1995). Infants under 1,000 grams (ELBW) show the least improvements in outcomes.

Recent research shows that a large proportion of infants born prematurely, regardless of weight, may have more health, motor, and intellectual problems than full-term infants, both in the short term and in the long term. The short- and long-term consequences of premature birth will now be covered, followed by a review of the research on improvements in neonatal intensive care.

Short-term effects. Because of their early birth and/or low birthweight, prematures are often at a disadvantage in getting a good start on adaptation to the real world. They suffer more from a lack of oxygen during the birth process (respiratory distress), they are more likely to have jaundice and to suffer physical and mental impairments as a result of the birth process, and many of them will die, depending upon the severity of their complications and birthweight. Two-thirds of premies under 1,000 grams were likely to die in 2000; about 15% of those between 1,000 and 1,500 grams died, but less than 5% died if they weighed between 1,500 and 2,500 grams (Matthews et al., 2002).

Generalizing about the abilities of premature infants is difficult because they vary widely in weight and gestational age, because prematurity has many different causes, and because the quality of neonatal care is highly variable. Researchers today categorize infants into experimental groups on the basis of weight, gestational age, and whether they have medical complications in addition to the prematurity. In follow-up studies of the effects of prematurity, researchers compare normal infants with premature infants of the same gestational age, rather than comparing infants of the same natal age. For example, a 3-month-old normal infant might be compared with a 4-month-old premature infant, both of whom were conceived about the same time.

Using gestational age rather than birth age is based on the ideas of Gesell (see Chapter 1), who charted the ages at which the average infant reached developmental milestones. In many cases, gestational age is the best indicator of developmental status. Many premature infants cannot suck from a bottle successfully until they have reached a gestational age of 35 weeks, about the age of a full-term newborn (Brake, Fifer, Alfasi, & Fleischman, 1988). Typical patterns of sleep and waking displayed by full-term babies do not begin until 34 weeks' gestational age; until then, premature infants spend considerably more time sleeping than waking (Korner et al., 1988). Thirty-four weeks appears to be the age at which premature infants show a marked increase in their ability to respond appropriately to external stimulation. Before that age, it takes a considerable effort on the part of an adult to keep the baby still and alert in the presence of a new tactile, auditory, or visual stimulus (Als, Duffy, & McAnulty, 1988). The problem with using gestational age is that it is based on averages and thus may not fit the developmental abilities of any particular infant.

Long-term effects. The long-term effects of any particular event or risk factor in early infancy are particularly difficult to assess. In Chapter 10, we return to the general problem of how to determine the effects of early experiences. For now, you should keep in mind that the effects of prematurity independent of other factors cannot be completely determined. This is because many premature infants have other complications, and we cannot assign infants randomly to experimental groups based on prematurity and health status. In addition, many premature and sick infants receive a variety of short-term and long-term interventions—including special attention from their families—that may alleviate their conditions. It would be unethical to withhold intervention or family support just so we can observe how a baby would develop without these resources.

Individuals who were born prematurely are shorter and smaller on average than people who were full term at birth. The difference is greatest during the first 2 years of life, during which babies who are small at birth often show some catch-up growth if they receive appropriate care and nutri-

tion (Peña, Teburg, & Hoppenbrouwers, 1987). **Catch-up growth** refers to a more rapid growth rate than for normal infants early in life and a more normal growth rate once the infant reaches a weight that is appropriate for his or her gestational age. For most prematures, catch-up growth is the most rapid during the first year of life (Peña et al., 1987). Catch-up growth may occur at any point in childhood if the individual suffers a deprivation, accident, or illness and is later restored to normal functioning (Barrett, Radke-Yarrow, & Klein, 1982; Tanner, 1970). Catch-up growth does not mean that the individual will eventually enter the normal range, but rather that he or she will grow faster than normal following the trauma.

The effects of prematurity on intelligence, motor skills, perceptual skills, and emotion are often compounded by heath factors. In one study, a group of premature infants was classified according to health status at birth: high-, moderate-, and low-risk groups were formed according to respiratory problems in the hospital. At 12 and 18 months of age, the high-risk premature infants had considerably more difficulty coping with stressful situations, and once they became distressed, they were more difficult to soothe (Stiefel, Plunket, & Meisels, 1987). This study shows that health risk, when added to prematurity, has a significantly greater impact on emotional regulation than prematurity alone.

In another study, infants who experienced intraventricular hemorrhage (IVH) were assessed on motor and behavioral measures at 1 and 2 years (Sostek, Smith, Katz, & Grant, 1987). The infants were grouped according to severity of IVH and birthweight. Birthweight and IVH had a minor correlation with outcome at 1 year and no relationship at age 2. More recent research, on the other hand, finds that IVH is one of the most important predictors of long-term motor and health deficits (Messinger, Dolcourt, King, Bodnar, & Beck, 1996). Many, but not all, infants who have IVH will suffer from deficits. Those who have a difficult temperament and who come from low-income single-parent families with high parenting stress were more likely to show long-term deficits in social skills (Miller et al., 2001; Saylor et al., 2003). Many IVH children who are not otherwise at risk are able to recover although it may take several years. This pattern of recovery is called **self-righting** and is comparable to catch-up growth.

For factors related to the parent-infant relationship, we find in some cases no differences between full-term and very-low-birthweight infants (less than 1,500 grams) in mother- and father-infant attachment at 1 year when the comparison is made at equivalent gestational ages (Easterbrooks, 1989). Other research shows that parents of premature infants are more active and stimulating than parents of full-term babies, at least during the first year. Premature infants receive more holding, vocalizing, and caretaking during the first year, even though these infants are less attentive and less likely to play and vocalize than full-term babies. These compensatory parenting behaviors contribute directly to self-righting in the more healthy premature infants (Weiss et al., 2004). As the more healthy prematures catch up with the full terms, their parents also show more normal levels of behavior toward them (Barratt, Roach, & Leavitt, 1996; Branchfeld, Goldberg, & Sloman, 1980; Crawford, 1982). It may be that these additional parental actions are used to compensate for a less active infant, and they may actually help the infant to recover.

For some parents, however, dealing with a premature infant can have short-term effects and may lead to lasting difficulties in the relationship. Parents experience additional stress, depression, and emotional trauma just by the fact of having their baby in a hospital for a long period of time (Conner & Nelson, 1999; Cronin, Shapiro, Casiro, & Cheang, 1995; Hughes, McCollum, Sheftel, & Sanchez, 1994; Nagata et al., 2004; L. T Singer, Salvator, Guo, Collin, Lilien, & Baley, 1999). In early infancy, prematures become easily overwhelmed with stimulation, smiling less and fussing more, and parents may experience them as unrewarding (Eckerman, Hsu, Molitor, Leung, & Goldstein, 1999). Some parents experience burnout in their role (Barnard, Bee, & Hammond, 1984), and there is a higher than expected percentage of premature infants among children who are later abused or neglected (R. S. Hunter, Kilstrom, Kraybill, & Loda, 1978), some studies reporting that 40 percent of abused and neglected children are either premature or low birthweight babies (Yampolskaya, Greenbaum, & Berson, 2009). In general, the quality of the home and school environments can have an effect on alleviating long-term effects of prematurity (Dittrichová et al., 1996; Kalmar, 1996; Sansavini, Rizzardi, Alessandroni, & Giovanelli, 1996).

Many prematures, especially those who were very low birthweight (VLBW), have deficits that last until middle childhood and adolescence and perhaps even longer. These deficits are in such areas as attention, behavior problems and emotional maturity, language skill, memory, intelligence and educational performance, perceptual and motor function, serious illnesses, and mental retardation (Blackman, Lindgren, Hein, & Harper, 1987; Botting, Powls, Cooke, & Marlow, 1998; Grigoroiu-Serbanescu, 1981; Hack et al., 1995; Lefebvre, Bard, Veilleux, & Martel, 1988; Miller et al., 2001; Rieck, Arad, & Netzer, 1996; Robson & Cline, 1998; Vicari et al., 2004). In general, researchers have discovered long-term effects of perinatal risk only for the most extreme cases of illness or very low birthweight or for families who suffer the most stress (such as low income and lack of education). More subtle and as yet unmeasured effects of prematurity may last a lifetime.

Remember also that even when there are few differences between premature and full-term infants in later life, it does not mean that life has been normal or easy for the prematures and their families. Their improved status in later life may have been the result of persistent, difficult, and costly interventions on the part of parents and professionals (Lewit, Baker, Corman, & Shiono, 1995). In the next section, early intervention procedures will be covered.

Interventions for Premature Infants

Improvements in neonatal intensive care have saved many lives and improved the health of many premature babies (Battin, Ling, Whitfield, MacKinnon, & Effer, 1998; Richardson et al., 1998). Better ways have been found to manage the hospital care for these infants, and new methods have been developed to help parents once the infants have come home. Only about 5% of newborns require intensive care; most of these are due to low birthweight. Most infants in intensive care will require between 15 and 50 days (Hack et al., 1995).

Medical procedures in the hospital. In a modern neonatal intensive care unit (NICU), an increasing number of procedures are adapted to the special needs of premature infants. The smallest infants need high levels of oxygen, warm temperatures, bedding that does not bruise their thin and delicate skin, and nutrients. In the past, providing these needs produced more complications for the infants, who were exposed to dangerously high levels of noise and light inside incubator boxes, bruised from touch, and scarred from needle pricks. Blindness resulted from too much oxygen and deafness from too much noise.

Research has demonstrated that late-term fetuses, premature infants, and full-term newborns feel pain. Repeated experience of untreated pain has the effect of making infants hypervigilant during social interaction and causing them to exhibit increased tension in response to tactile stimulation. In addition, preemies may suffer from the stress of separation from their mothers and long-term isolation due to hospitalization (Karns, 2000).

Today, premature infants are on open beds in a nursery that has higher concentrations of oxygen in the air. They are warmed with low-intensity lights, and their bedding is extremely soft. Some hospitals use sheepskins or water beds. The babies are touched gently and as little as possible, sound and light are kept at moderate levels, and the oxygen content of the blood is monitored continuously by a probe attached to the skin surface, reducing the need for blood sampling. Pain control is managed by drugs, pacifier sucking, giving sucrose, and providing soothing sounds (Furdon, Pfeil, & Snow, 1998; Kawakami, Takai-Kawakami, Kurihara, Shimizu, & Yanaihara, 1996; Korner,

1987; Sell, Hill-Mangan, & Holberg, 1992; Stevens et al., 1999).

Behavioral procedures in the hospital. A variety of approaches have been used either to compensate for missing intrauterine experiences or to try to enhance catch-up growth. One important form of stimulation that a premature lacks is whole-body movement, called **vestibular-proprioceptive stimulation**. Premature infants have received rocking stimulation from adults, in hammocks, from a breathing teddy bear, and from oscillating waterbeds. This rhythmic stimulation has been designed to be similar to the kinds of movements and breathing rhythms that a full-term infant would feel inside the mother during the last weeks of pregnancy. If these natural rhythms are attuned to the needs of individual infants so as not to overstimulate them, the infants increase weight gain, improve sleeping and other physiological indicators, and can be discharged earlier from the hospital (Gatts, Wallace, Glasscock, McKee, & Cohen, 1994; Ingersoll & Thoman, 1994; Korner, 1987; E. B. Thoman, 1993).

Although prematures, especially the smallest ones, cannot ingest fluids, they can suck readily on a pacifier; this is called **nonnutritive sucking (NNS)**. Fetuses of the same gestational age inside the uterus also suck regularly. In several studies, premature infants who were provided with pacifiers on a regular basis required fewer tube feedings, started bottle feeding earlier, slept better, gained more weight, and were discharged earlier from the hospital (G. C. Anderson, Burroughs, & Measel, 1983; T. Field et al., 1982; Woodson, Drinkwin, & Hamilton, 1985). NNS reduces the infant's average heart rate, thus allowing the infant the opportunity to use its energy resources for growth instead of life maintenance (Woodson & Hamilton, 1988).

Another form of behavioral intervention is stroking and handling. It appears that for very-low-birthweight infants (less than 1,500 grams), stroking can actually be detrimental due to the extreme sensitivity of the infant's skin. In studies of this group of infants, talking helped to bring the infants into an attentive state, while talking plus touching caused the infant to withdraw (Eckerman, Oehler, Medvin, & Hannan, 1994; Oehler & Eckerman, 1988; Weiss, 2005).

For babies between 1,500 and 2,500 grams, stroking in the form of back massage, neck rubbing, and movement of arms and legs had remarkable effects. Massage for 15 minutes per day over 10 to 15 days can increase weight 31 to 47% compared to prematures who did not receive stroking and also reduce birth complications (Field, 2001). Studies of animal infants have shown that touch stimulates hormones that regulate the action and development of the brain and body function, including decreases in cortisol and increases in growth hormone and oxytocin. The latter hormone is associated with feelings of well-being and interpersonal attraction (Dieter et al., 2003; Field, 2001; Schanberg, Bartolome, & Kuhn, 1987). These studies clearly show that the overall amount of stimulation is not important. Rather, some specific forms of stimulation work better than others, and the most effective stimulation will depend on the infant's gestational age and weight. Music in the form of male and female singing voices, for example, leads to earlier discharge, improved respiration, and more weight gain (Cassidy & Standley, 1995; Coleman et al., 1997; Weiss, 2005).

Another approach that emphasizes touch and handling is known as **kangaroo care**. In kangaroo care, the infant, wearing only a diaper, is placed on the parent's chest. The infant's head is turned to the side so the baby's ear is against the parent's heart. Any tubes or wires are taped to the parent's clothing. Kangaroo care originated in Bogotá, Colombia, in 1983 because electrical power often failed and expensive equipment did not often work. Infant mortality was reduced significantly. Since then, many studies have been conducted showing positive effects on preterm infants and their families. Preterms who get kangaroo care cry less, sleep for longer periods, gain more weight, have more coordinated breathing and heartbeat patterns, are more attentive and interact better with their parents, have lower cortisol levels, and need less supplemental oxygen. Both mothers and fathers also feel closer to their babies and to each other, experience less stress and less depression, and increase in their confidence that they can take care of the babies at home (G. C. Anderson, 1999; Feldman, Eidelman, Sirota, & Weller, 2002; Feldman, Weller, Sirota, & Eidelman, 2002; Feldman et al., 2003; Gitau et al., 2002; Ludington-Hoe, Ferreira, & Goldsten, 1998; Ludington-Hoe & Swinth, 1996; Messmer et al., 1999; Tallandini & Scalembra, 2006). Kangaroo care's close skin-to-skin contact is probably a good way to handle all babies. Because babies live in a world of touch and warmth, they respond best when these ingredients are provided. A behavior ecology theorist would not be surprised to hear about kangaroo care; it has been around for millions of years.

Finally, interventions can be made with the parents to educate them about the special needs of the premature infant. Parental visitation to the NICU gives the infant more opportunities for stimulation and aids in the parents' positive perceptions of their infant. Both mothers and fathers benefit from frequent visitations (Levy-Shiff, Sharir, & Mogilner, 1989), and infants who are visited more frequently by parents are released sooner from the hospital (Zeskind & Iacino, 1984). Since many mothers of prematures are low-income teenagers, educational interventions directed at making mothers more aware of their responsibilities and setting more realistic goals are effective in improving the outcomes for their babies (Field, Widmayer, Stringer, & Ignatoff, 1980; Pridham, 1998; Zeskind & Iacino, 1987).

Parents may have difficulty communicating with a premature infant because they fear that the child may be vulnerable, and indeed premature infants are more passive and slower to respond to adult social contacts. Premature infants often show a pattern of having either rigid or floppy body posture, and their facial expressions and crying may be different from those of normal babies. Parents need to understand that these differences are normal and will eventually disappear with sensitive handling (van Beek & Samson, 1994).

Preterm birth is a serious health problem that costs the nation more than $26 billion annually,

TABLE 9.6   Uses of Neonatal Stimulation in Hospitals in the United States

Type of stimulation	Percentage of Hospitals in the United States
Doulas during childbirth	30
Maternal massage during childbirth	30
Mother-baby skin-to-skin contact following birth	83
Music in the NICU	72
Rocking in the NICU	85
Kangaroo care in the NICU	98
Nonnutritive sucking in the NICU	96
Breast-feeding in the NICU	98
Infant massage in the NICU	38

Source: Field, T., Hernandez-Reif, M., Feijo, L., & Freedman, J. (2006). Prenatal, perinatal and neonatal stimulation: A survey of neonatal nurseries. *Infant Behavior & Development, 29*(1), 24–31.

according to a report from the Institute of Medicine. Nearly 543,000 babies—one out of every eight—are born too soon each year in the United States and the rate has risen more than 36 percent since the early 1980s. Preterm birth is a leading cause of newborn death, and babies who do survive face the risk of lifelong health conditions (March of Dimes, 2009). In 2005 the average cost of a normal vaginal birth in a hospital with no complications was $6,973 (National Association of Childbearing Centers, 2004; U.S. Agency for Healthcare Research and Quality, 2010). The medical costs for one premature baby could cover the cost of a dozen healthy births (March of Dimes, 2009). The average medical cost for healthy full-term babies from birth through their first birthday was $4,551 in 2007 dollars, of which more than $3,800 is paid for by health plans, according to the March of Dimes data. For premature and/or low birthweight babies (less than 37 completed weeks gestation and/or less than 2500 grams), the average cost was nearly $50,000, of which more than $46,000 was borne by the health plan.

"Preventing preterm birth is one way we can begin to reign in our nation's skyrocketing health care costs and help businesses protect their bottom line," says Dr. Jennifer L. Howse, president of the March of Dimes. "The best prevention of prematurity is good maternity care." (March of Dimes, 2009).

Because many of the families who have low-birthweight children are poor, these costs are borne by government assistance programs such as Medicaid and by increased health insurance premiums for everyone. In addition, prematurity may lead to other long-term costs, such as the prosecution and incarceration of persons who exhibit criminal and delinquent behavior that may result from early brain damage and later deprivation. Thus, it is essential that governments devote funding to study the causes and preventions of prematurity (Lewit et al., 1995).

Prevention costs considerably less. Good prenatal care for low-income women could reduce prematurity and complications radically and cost less than $1,000 per child. Simple hospital interventions such as those described here also have long-term benefits to society. The percentage of hospitals using the various techniques mentioned in this section are shown in Table 9.6. Unfortunately, low-income women find it difficult to obtain good prenatal care, Medicaid places limits on the number of allowable prenatal visits, and it takes a long time to process claims. Ultimately, the prevention of birth defects will require radical changes in our society, including the elimination of poverty and prejudice (Alexander & Korenbrot, 1995).

What Can We Learn about Fetal Psychology from Premature Infants?

Infants born prematurely are the same age as late-term fetuses and have the same behavioral, sensory, and neurological abilities. Because premies have experienced the birth process, and because they had to adapt to life outside the uterus, they may have acquired abilities that the fetus does not possess. On the other hand, the NICU behavioral interventions that are most successful seem to offer clues to the characteristics of the prenatal environment that are most conducive to fetal psychological development.

In Chapter 3, we learned that in the third fetal period, the fetus was responsive to movement, touch, and sound, and that it could suck. Because of the success of interventions involving these modalities with premies, it is reasonable to conclude that fetuses require vestibular-proprioceptive, tactile, and auditory stimulation, as well as opportunities for sucking. The prenatal environment is uniquely suited to provide these requirements for growth. Vestibular-proprioceptive stimulation comes from maternal movements. Tactile stimulation is provided in terms of the soft feeling, warm temperature, and constant flow of the amniotic fluid over the fetus's body. Auditory stimulation is provided by the mother's heartbeat and voice.

These forms of stimulation are apparently necessary to sustain normal fetal development. They probably are related to feelings of pleasure, comfort, and security. It is also possible that the fetus has a sense of an emergent self (see Chapters 2 and 5), as these various sensory modalities are experienced in an integrated way that provides a sense of completeness.

INFANT MORTALITY

Fetuses and infants may die from a variety of causes. Although the rate of infant mortality has steadily fallen in first world nations, pregnancy, childbirth, and early post-natal life present risks that must be managed in the best interests of the child and family.

Prenatal Mortality

Prenatal mortality, or pregnancy loss, is rather common. Spontaneous abortion (the rejection of the zygote or embryo by the mother's body) is believed to occur in 40 to 60% of pregnancies (Little, 1988). In many cases, women may not even be aware that they were pregnant. Many spontaneous abortions occur due to genetic and chromosomal abnormalities of the embryo. The term "spontaneous abortion" typically applies to an embryo, while "miscarriage" is used with respect to a fetus. Miscarriage during the fetal period is caused by genetic and chromosomal abnormalities, by some teratogens, and by diseases of the maternal reproductive system. Finally, stillbirth is the loss of a full-term infant who dies just before or during delivery. Stillbirth may be caused by some of the same factors as miscarriage and also by poor prenatal care and poverty (Kapoor, Amand, & Kumar, 1994; Katz & Kuller, 1994).

Following miscarriage and stillbirth, both mothers and fathers (Puddifoot & Johnson, 1999) suffer from grief due to the loss. Often they feel self-blame and anger (Madden, 1994; Wheeler, 1994). It helps parents to enter a support program that empathizes with their situation and helps them work through their strong emotions (A. F. Hartmann, Radin, & McConnell, 1992; Speraw, 1994). Non-Western and ancient cultures have developed a variety of healing rituals to help parents resolve their grief and even to attempt to prevent the loss. These practices include ritual purification, special prayers, and herbal medicines. The rituals emphasize the depth of feeling both men and women have for the loss of their child (Kuller & Katz, 1994). In the next section, we examine the effects of pregnancy on the family.

Elective Abortion

There are many reasons why parents might make the choice to end a pregnancy by means of induced or elective abortion: to prevent birth defects, to protect the life or health of the mother, in cases of rape or incest, because of poverty, and as a means of birth control. The last two reasons— low income and birth control—account for most abortions and in theory are totally preventable with adequate knowledge and access to contraceptive methods.

On an international level, the worldwide trend is toward the liberalization of abortion laws (Henshaw, 1994). Abortion is currently legal in the United States. The Constitution of the United States includes the right to privacy, and that right pertains especially to personal decisions made in the context of the home and the family. In their 1973 decision in *Roe v. Wade*, the justices of the U.S. Supreme Court concluded that the decision to terminate a pregnancy is part of a woman's right to privacy guaranteed by the Constitution. The Court's decision divided pregnancy into three equal periods. In the first period (conception to 12 weeks), the decision to abort was up to the mother and her physician. In the second period (13 to 24 weeks), because abortion is more complicated, the health and safety of the mother was the main deciding factor. No limitations were placed on the reasons for abortion during these two periods. After 25 weeks, abortions were not permitted, except when the mother's life or health was in extreme danger. In 1992, in *Planned Parenthood v. Casey*, the Court made clear that states may not criminalize abortion prior to 24 weeks nor prevent any woman from exercising her choice to terminate her pregnancy (Kolbert & Miller, 1994).

In 2003, the U.S. Congress passed the Partial Birth Abortion Ban Act, which prohibits so-called "partial birth abortions," also known as "intact dilation and extraction." Partial birth abortions are used in the second period and are controversial because of the procedure used. Labor is induced, the cervix dilated (see Chapter 3), and the fetus pulled out by the feet, leaving the head undelivered. The fetal brain is then extracted before delivering the head. The procedure is used relatively rarely and primarily in cases where the mother's life is in danger. In 2007, the U.S. Supreme court ruled that the Partial Birth Abortion Ban Act does not violate a woman's constitutional right to an abortion guaranteed by *Roe v. Wade*, since the law limits a particular procedure and not abortion per se. Opponents of the ban say that this method is often the only available means to save the mother's life.

A central issue in *Roe v. Wade* was the question of fetal viability. **Viability** refers to the ability of the fetus to survive on its own, without dependence on the mother. Medically speaking, a fetus is viable if after birth it can be sustained on life-support systems in a neonatal intensive care unit (see below). Viability begins between 24 and 30 weeks (Grobstein, 1988). These medical findings are consistent with the Roe decision.

An entirely different issue is, "When does human life begin?" According to Lewis Thomas of the Memorial Sloan-Kettering Cancer Center in New York City, the question of when human life begins can be resolved "only in the domain of metaphysics. It can be argued by philosophers and theologians, but it lies beyond the reach of science." Taking the opposite view, Charles A. Gardner states:

> There will always be arguments based on spiritual or ethical beliefs to convince an individual of the rightness or wrongness of abortion, but each person should first understand the biology to which those beliefs refer. (Gardner, 1989, pp. 557–559)

With regard to biological development, it is often argued that the zygote at conception is human because it contains all of the necessary genetic instructions to make an individual human being. As we saw Chapter 3, however, the zygote can develop only by a complex process of interaction with the prenatal environment. The location and biochemical environment of a cell, not just its genetic code, are what determines the phenotype. There is no preformed person residing in the zygote or even in the embryo; the person is a complex gene-environment interaction that takes a long time and the proper nutrients to grow.

Abortion foes suggest that one way to decrease the number of abortions used for family planning is simply to encourage more contraception. This idea has both merits and drawbacks. Another alternative to abortion is carrying the infant to term and placing the infant for adoption. However, because most abortions are performed on young women living in poverty who may suffer from drug and alcohol abuse and poor prenatal care, removing abortion rights from these women increases the chances of teratogenic effects, ranging from preterm birth at one extreme and retardation and deformity on the other. The costs to society (who will take care of these children, and who will pay for their care?) and the ultimate quality of life of the children (related to their particular ailments and to the fact that handicapped children in foster care have a high probability of being subjected to child abuse) must be taken into account in formulating public policies on adoption versus abortion.

Another argument used by abortion opponents is that the fetus feels pain prior to 24 weeks. As we saw earlier, it is anatomically impossible for the fetus to feel pain before about 30 weeks. Anything even closely resembling a human brain does not form until the twentieth week, and brain electrical activity (EEG) resembling that of adults does not begin until between 26 and 30 weeks. This age corresponds with other measures of viability, suggesting that a brain that is capable of feeling pain and behaving intentionally develops only late in fetal life.

Should these scientifically based observations take precedence over moral and ethical considerations? Certainly not. The decision to seek an abortion is a personal one based on social, scientific, medical, and moral considerations and made in consultation with genetic counselors, physicians, family members, or religious leaders.

Abortion rates can be reduced by providing individuals with more education and access to family planning methods. In the Netherlands, abortion rates have declined steadily due to a reduction in unwanted pregnancies. The Dutch have achieved this decline through their success in preventing teenage pregnancies (by means of sex education, open discussion of sexuality in the mass media, educational campaigns, and family planning services that are available to everyone) and also through the growing acceptance of sterilization as a contraceptive practice (Ketting & Visser, 1994).

Elective Euthanasia: The Case of Baby Doe

On April 9, 1982, a baby was born in Bloomington, Indiana, who was given little chance to survive. The baby had Down's syndrome and multiple complications, including a blocked esophagus and an enlarged heart. In this case, the physicians agreed that surgery would not be worthwhile because it had a limited chance of success and would only prolong the infant's life for a few weeks, increasing the suffering of both the infant and family.

The medical decision, to which the parents agreed, was to withhold treatment for the infant. Because of the infant's state of health, this decision was an act of euthanasia: keeping the infant comfortable and well fed while waiting for an inevitable death.

This baby continued to live longer than the doctors expected, and the case caught the attention of the county prosecutor, who charged the parents and physicians with criminal neglect. Two county judges agreed with the parents' decision, but the prosecutor eventually asked the Indiana Supreme Court to issue an order to provide treatment for the infant, who later became known as Baby Doe.

The issues in the Baby Doe case are similar to the issues in the abortion debate. On the one side are those who feel that newborns should have a constitutional right to treatment even without the consent of their parents, and on the other side are those who argue for the newborn's right to die peacefully in cases where the low quality of life is considered to outweigh the need to preserve life.

Because of Baby Doe and other similar cases, in 1984 the U.S. Senate amended the 1974 Child Abuse and Prevention Act. The amendment states that "withholding of medically indicated treatment from disabled infants with life-threatening conditions" could be considered a form of child abuse and neglect. However, the amendment lists three exceptions to this rule, which specify when euthanasia is permitted:

1. The infant is chronically ill and irreversibly comatose.

2. The provision of such treatment would merely prolong dying and would not be effective in ameliorating or correcting the infant's life-threatening condition.

3. The provision of such treatment would be virtually futile in terms of the survival of the infant, and the treatment under such circumstances would be inhumane.

While many accepted this legislation, the American Medical Association did not endorse it because the amendment does not mention issues related to the quality of life. Suppose, for example, that the infant would survive with an appropriate medical intervention. The law clearly states that such an intervention must be provided. But what if the infants who survive are so deformed, sick, or handicapped that their lives would involve constant pain, discomfort, and severe restriction of movement? It is this quality-of-life issue that doctors would like to have the freedom to consider in making recommendations to parents.

The Baby Doe case raises important questions about how society is to decide what is in the best interests of children. Is life worth preserving at any cost? Is the best intervention in some cases not to intervene? How should quality of life and stress—emotional and financial—on the family be weighed in decisions about the rights of children? As our technology advances, we can do extraordinary things, such as save the life of an extremely fragile or extremely low birthweight newborn. Unfortunately, individuals and governments are not able to cope with the complex ethical and legal issues that this technology raises.

Some examples illustrate the strong emotions and conflicting values involved in such cases. In 1994, Gregory Messenger of Michigan removed his extremely low birthweight (ELBW) son from life support and was later charged with manslaughter. In 1989, Rudy Linares of Illinois unhooked a respirator from his 15-month-old son while holding a gun on the hospital staff. The child had been comatose for 9 months after swallowing a balloon. Linares was not charged with a crime. A mother in Virginia, on the other hand, fought a hospital's decision to end life support for her 2-year-old, who was born without most of her brain. Meanwhile,

TABLE 9.7 Rates of Infant Mortality by Country per 1,000 Live Births (2006)

Country	Rate
Japan	2.8
Sweden	2.4
France	3.6
Denmark	4.4
Australia	4.9
Italy	4.1
Canada	5.3
USA	6.7
Mexico	21.0
Less-developed countries	57.0

Source: Population Reference Bureau: www.prb.org/pdf06/06worlddatasheet.pdf

the number of parents—often poor, on drugs, or mentally ill—who abandon their infants in the hospital is increasing. Nationally, the number of abandoned babies in the hospital rose by 43% from 21,600 in 1991 to 30,800 in 1998 (National AIA Resource Center, 2005).

Who should take care of these babies, and what is to be done if they are at risk for major disorders?

To help resolve these difficult problems, professionals in the field of medical ethics are beginning to create a philosophical standard to guide doctors, nurses, parents, lawyers, and hospital administrators. Many hospitals today employ medical ethicists as consultants.

Perinatal Mortality

Like prematurity and health risk, infant mortality is greatest in groups who have low incomes and inadequate health care. Most of the causes of perinatal death can be found in poor prenatal care, ill health, or malnutrition of the mother during pregnancy. Current statistics for infant mortality are shown in Table 9.7. Although infants are more likely to die than mothers, those countries and ethnicities that have high infant mortality also have high maternal mortality (United Nations Department of Economic and Social Affairs, 1986). The causes of maternal mortality are very different from the causes of infant mortality, however. The leading causes of maternal death in the United States are pregnancy-induced high blood pressure, hemorrhage (excessive bleeding following childbirth), and respiratory failure (Grimes, 1994).

Apparently, a trend over time toward decreasing mortality has been going on since records began to be kept in 1750. Balog (1976) traced the changes in mortality over the last 200 years in the United States and found no obvious dips in the rate after major medical advances, such as drugs and sterilization procedures. He concluded that changes in mortality rates reflect trends in general economic growth, a higher standard of living, and better education—in short, social and economic factors.

The one place in the world where maternal mortality has been increasing over the past 30 years is sub-Saharan Africa. There are several explanations for this extraordinarily high incidence of maternal deaths in Africa. The deteriorating economic, political, and social conditions that lead to starvation and deprivation for all people are a factor. Another is the high rate of sexism and violence against women. Women are expected to have as many children as possible, even in the worst of circumstances. Many of these countries also practice female genital mutilation, a widespread procedure in which a young girl's clitoris is removed to prevent her from experiencing sexual pleasure. Thus, the African situation is complicated by cultural factors over and above the usual social and economic factors that cause maternal death (WIN News, 1992).

In the United States, even though mortality has fallen for all ethnic groups, African American infants are still twice as likely to die as Caucasian Americans. This difference has existed for at least half a century. What could be the cause? Homicides, birth injuries, and congenital abnormalities are nearly the same in all ethnic groups in the United States, so these are not factors. Hispanic infants are also less likely to die than African American infants. In general, infant mortality comes from a combination of factors including poverty, poor prenatal nutrition and care, teen pregnancy, family stress, obesity, and prematurity.

Research shows that for African American mothers, the stress of racism adds to these other factors to increase infant mortality. Black women describe the lasting effects of their own childhood experiences of racism from teachers and others, and as adults from employers and the community. Poor black women have to make stressful choices about what to eat (e.g., nutritionally poor fast food that is cheap) and where to live (in neighborhoods with high crime rates and poor schools). Because we know that stress impacts fetal development, the newborns of these mothers are starting life with compromises to their physical functioning (Lu & Lu, 2007).

The most common causes of neonatal mortality among the poor in the United States and in developing nations are respiratory problems and diarrhea. They derive from the immature system's inability to cope with normal bacterial infections and physical insults and stem largely from deficits—like stress from the mother—acquired prenatally. Studies have shown, for example, that adequate nutritional supplementation during pregnancy can cut the infant death rate by as much as half (Werner, 1979). In the United States, only a very small percentage of infant or maternal deaths can be attributed to ineffective hospital care during and after birth (Escobar et al., 1998).

Apparently, malnutrition, poverty, racism, and ill health act as a system: one condition feeds upon another to worsen or maintain high death and disease rates. In many countries, people who cannot make a living on farms move into the cities to join the growing poor population in the inner city. Forced to live in slums with poor sanitation, they have little food and no money. Urban employment places special burdens on mothers who must travel away from home, and there are seldom adequate child-care facilities. Lack of energy from malnutrition contributes to the inability to cope with these enormous problems.

The prevention and elimination of these problems depend on intervention in the cycle of poverty, racism, and ill health. Community-based clinics providing medical care during pregnancy, simple disease-screening procedures, immunizations, nutrition education, fertility advice, upgrading of parental competence, improved sanitation, and the effective management of diarrhea already are being implemented in many less developed countries (Puffer & Serrano, 1973; WIN News, 1992; World Health Organization, 1976).

Supplemental nutrition given to mothers has a greater effect on infant mortality than on infant birthweight. In a study done in Bogotá, Colombia, supplemental food for malnourished mothers increased birthweight by only 77 grams but decreased the neonatal death rate from 42 to 23 per 1,000 births. Food availability for pregnant mothers in developing countries can be increased by larger contributions from rich nations. This assistance will reduce pressures to use land for cash crops (such as coffee and cocoa) and allow local farmers to grow their own food. Supporting local health care and breast-feeding will also help to reduce infant mortality (Falkner, 1985).

The United Nations has developed and tested a successful health education program called GOBI, which stands for Growth charts, Oral rehydration, Breast-feeding, and Immunization (Werner, 1986). By comparing their own infant's development to standard growth charts, parents can detect growth retardation and conditions such as failure-to-thrive. **Failure-to-thrive** is a condition in which infants fail to respond to the environment and continue to deteriorate even when intervention is available and even when parents do everything possible. Failure-to-thrive has unknown causes, but intervention can help in some cases even though failure-to-thrive children may permanently lag behind others in language, intelligence, and emotional maturity.

Oral rehydration—providing fluids—is the primary treatment for infantile diarrhea. Breast-feeding provides adequate and sanitary nourishment as well as natural immunization (see the section on breast-feeding in this chapter). Immunization protects children from many infectious diseases.

An alternative explanation for the reduction in infant mortality is that it may be associated with the decrease in the number of pregnancies a woman will have. In the 1700s, a woman might expect to carry 10 to 15 conceptions to term, which would mean an increased probability of mortality for each infant. The age of the mother, the spacing between pregnancies, and the number of pregnancies all account for a portion of the risk of infant death.

Age and sex are also important factors in determining the probability of infant death. The highest probability of death is when an infant is less than 24 hours old. In fact, if a baby survives beyond the first day, the odds of mortality are extremely low, about 1 per 1,000 or less. With regard to sex, males tend to have a higher death rate all through their life spans. More males are conceived, but more are miscarried or spontaneously aborted.

These raw statistics are sobering, but they do little to make us aware that each time an infant dies, the family feels a major loss. The next section will try to give you insight into the human element behind the mortality tables.

How Does the Family Respond to the Death of an Infant?

The loss parents feel when a newborn dies may not be the same feeling as when an older child or some other close relative dies, but neonatal death can deeply affect parents (Helmrath & Steinitz, 1978). If parents are encouraged to mourn the loss and deal successfully with the painful feelings and memories, the bereavement process may lead to more adaptive parenting with later children. Social supports, hospice services, and religious traditions for dealing with death and loss can be extremely comforting for parents. Older children in the family also need support and counseling to understand the loss and their parent's grief (Drotar & Irvin, 1979; Hass & Walter, 2006–2007; Hesse & van Ijzendoorn, 1998; O'Leary, 2007).

The normal sequence of emotions parents experience after neonatal death is similar to other kinds of grief reactions. Upon hearing the news that their baby has died or will soon die, parents experience shock and denial. They think a mistake has been made and wonder if it can be corrected. The next phase is feelings of sadness and loss mixed with anger. This anger may be directed at others, such as the obstetrician, or it may be directed at themselves in the form of self-blame. Gradually, parents come to accept the death and readjust the reality to their lives. This can often take several years. Having healthy children later on helps this process, but parents continue to fear that something will go wrong with the next child and wonder what their lost child might have been like (Abboud & Liamputtong, 2005).

A number of practitioners have argued that the loss of the newborn should be treated like any other death in the family. Some hospitals simply dispose of the body without allowing the parents any option to view it. Parents often are concerned about the actual disposition of the infant's body. They may have painful and frightening fantasies: perhaps the infant did not die naturally but was used for some strange experiment; perhaps the child's body is on display in a jar for medical students to look at; was the infant cremated or just thrown away? As unlikely as these fantasies are, they are quite common among such parents (L. Cohen, Zilkha, Middleton, & O'Donnohue, 1978).

In one program (L. Cohen et al., 1978), parents are offered the option of viewing the body. If they elect to do this, a nurse brings the infant wrapped in a blanket. The blanket is tucked to hide any abnormalities. At the sight of the deceased infant, mothers are less afraid than expected. In all cases in this program, infants are given appropriate religious services and burials. In the United Kingdom, hospitals follow the "Sands Guidelines" that follow the parents' needs and wishes about whether or not to view the body, to have an autopsy, and to have a burial or cremation (Schott & Henley, 2007).

Some hospitals take photographs of sick infants at birth. Because parents are distressed to hear that their infant is ill and may die, the hospital photo may be the only one that is taken. Many states now have support groups for parents following perinatal death. Similar grief reactions are seen in cases of miscarriage, especially in instances of repeated miscarriage, and in sudden infant death syndrome, in which death occurs unexpectedly between 1 and 6 months of age (see next section). In all cases, factual and frank discussions with medical personnel, the availability of the autopsy report, and a funeral service may help the parents cope (Dyregrov & Matthiesen, 1987; Kotch & Cohen, 1986).

Between life and death, there are some gray areas. Infants may be born viable but suffer from gross deformities or other conditions that would impair later functioning. The issues faced by parents and doctors in these situations are not unlike those faced by the families of persons in comas or with terminal and painful diseases or by those close to the elderly and infirm. **Euthanasia** is the act of causing a painless death or of letting someone die naturally without trying to prolong life with "heroic" medical procedures. As you can imagine, the idea of euthanasia involves some serious and difficult religious, ethical, legal, medical, and personal issues that are not easily resolved. With the advent of sophisticated neonatal intensive care, parents and pediatricians are facing these issues more and more.

UNEXPECTED DEATH IN INFANCY

What Are Some Causes of Unexpected Death in Infancy?

Earlier in this chapter, we discussed some of the causes of infant death during the newborn period. We saw then that the vast majority of infant deaths occur during the first few days of life. After the first month, the primary causes of infant death may be labeled "unexpected," since in most industrial societies, fatal infant diseases have been all but eliminated through the use of vaccines and preventive care.

Accidents are one of the major causes of unexpected death in the first year of life. These may be traffic accidents or home accidents, such as suffocation, burns, poisoning, and drowning (see section on safety, below). Another major cause of unexpected death is homicide, including maltreatment, infanticide, sexual offenses, kidnapping, and killing accompanied by parental suicide (Hartmann & Molz, 1979). The most frequent cause of unexpected death in the first year of life is **Sudden Infant Death Syndrome (SIDS)**, also called *crib death*. SIDS claims the life of 1 infant in every 1,000 (Karns, 2000).

What Causes SIDS?

One of the problems in diagnosing and preventing SIDS is that no single disorder accounts for all the cases. The only thing they have in common is the manner of death. The SIDS diagnosis is applied if parents discover that their baby has died, perhaps at night or during a nap, and there is no apparent cause

of death. Sometimes an investigation will reveal a non-SIDS cause of death. Some other causes of death appear to be SIDS-related but are not; they include accidental asphyxiation, overheating, and infant abuse (Bass, Kravath, & Glass, 1986).

In the past, a case of SIDS might have brought the parents under suspicion of murder by suffocation. The threat of this insinuation, plus the shock, grief, and guilt brought on by the loss of the baby, placed an unusually heavy burden on the parents, many of whom wondered if they indeed had been the cause of death.

The fact that many SIDS cases seemed to be associated with colds or some mild respiratory problem led some researchers to study the relationship between respiration and SIDS. Very young infants often cease breathing for brief periods, a condition known as **apnea**. These pauses in breathing, or apneic pauses, almost always occur during sleep. Since most crib deaths occur during sleep, researchers have attempted to establish some connection between apnea and SIDS.

What Are Some Other Possible Causes of SIDS?

A number of possible causes have been associated with SIDS. Heat is one suspected cause of SIDS, and SIDS victims have symptoms similar to those of heat stroke. Some victims of SIDS were found to be excessively covered or dressed at the time of death (Stanton, Scott, & Downhan, 1980).

Since all infants have apneic episodes, these cannot be considered causes of SIDS. On the other hand, SIDS may be related to some sensorimotor and neurological deficit that prevents the infant from making the correct movements and heart rate changes that will assist in recovery from the apnea (Lipsitt, 1979a; Lipsitt, Sturges, & Burke, 1979). Some of the sensorimotor deficits that may prevent recovery from apnea during the first year may have been caused by loss of oxygen during the perinatal period or by genetic factors associated with low motor control over breathing (Black, Steinschneider, & Sheehe, 1979; Lipsitt, 1979a; Naeye, 1980; Schiffman, Westlake, Santiago, & Edelman, 1980). Slower myelination of

TABLE 9.8: How To Prevent SIDS

DO:	DON'T:
Place the baby on back (supine) or side when sleeping.	Overheat the baby with excessive clothing or bedding.
Use a firm mattress and bedding materials.	Smoke near the baby.
Remove soft objects and loose bedding materials.	Place the baby on stomach (prone) to sleep.
Breast-feed if possible.	
Obtain adequate prenatal care.	

the nerves in the brain stem related to the control of breathing has also been found in SIDS infants (Cruz-Sanchez et al., 1997; Morgan et al., 2002). The inability to cope with relatively mild stresses, such as heat, apnea, or even mild toxicity, may result from some other systemic weakness.

Respiratory infection has been studied as a possible cause of SIDS. In some cases, the infection may be acquired prenatally, but it is more likely to have environmental causes. Higher rates of SIDS have been found during outbreaks of influenza (Moreno, Ardanaz, Olivera, Castilla, & de Pedro, 1994). A more consistent link has been found for cigarette smoking in the home, which accounts for 28% of SIDS cases (Blackwell et al., 1994; Hilder, 1994; Lindsay, Johnson, Wallace, & Soos, 1994; Peduto, Musu, Gatto, & Ghilli, 1994). The effects of smoking may have their origin in pregnancy, since smoking, as well as alcohol and drug addiction during pregnancy increase the risk for SIDS (Friend et al., 2004; Guffanti et al., 2004; Morgan et al., 2002).

Although no one symptom can predict SIDS in all cases, SIDS infants have some of the following: difficulty in waking, shrill crying, few movements during sleep, poor oxygenation of the blood, pneumonia, and repeated hospitalization (Einspieler, Widder, Holzer, & Kenner, 1988; Golding & Peters, 1985).

Can SIDS Be Prevented?

There is currently no foolproof method of preventing SIDS. Some infants may be identified at birth as being at risk. Infants who are from deprived socioeconomic settings, who have suffered oxygen deprivation, who have a high apnea rate, whose mothers smoked, or who have siblings who died or nearly died of SIDS are all at risk for SIDS.

Since the causes of SIDS are related to respiratory, feeding, and state-control problems, some simple procedures are recommended for use with all infants (see Table 9.8). Of these recommendations, perhaps the most important is to avoid a prone sleeping position. A supine position (on the back) makes it easier for the infant to breathe. Controlled studies have shown a significant reduction—up to 50%—in the SIDS death rate when parents are told to place their infants in the supine position (Goldman, 1994; Helweg-Larsen, Lundemose, & Bille, 1994; Wigfield, Gilbert, & Fleming, 1994).

A parent can also use a home apnea monitor, which emits an alarm if the infant stops breathing during sleep. This system has both advantages and disadvantages for use in the home. Monitor use can cause extreme anxiety for the first month and lead to a restricted social life for the parents. Once they get over their initial anxiety, however, parents feel that home monitoring is beneficial; it causes few marital problems, and few parents resent the extra burden involved. Fans as well, may reduce the risk of SIDS, or sudden infant death syndrome, a new study shows. Babies who slept in a room with a fan were 72% less likely to die from SIDS, according to a study from Archives of Pediatrics & Adolescent Medicine. The study included interviews with the mothers of 185 infants who died from SIDS and the mothers of 312 other babies (Coleman-Phox, K., Odouli, & Li, 2008). Also, research shows that monitoring for only 24 hours can determine if the infant is at risk for SIDS (Cain, Kelly, & Shannon, 1980; l'Hoir et al., 1994; Rebuffat, Groswasser, Kelmanson, Sottiaux, & Kahn, 1994).

If SIDS is caused by a basic impairment in sensorimotor development, it may be possible to train infants to exert more effective control over breathing failures. One possibility is to encourage parents to let their babies sleep with them until the risk period for SIDS is past. If a baby is likely to make errors in respiratory control, exposure to parental breathing can have a significant effect on the regularity of the infant's breathing by creating a rhythmic cue to which the infant can become entrained. It is extremely unlikely that parents would suffocate an infant by rolling over on the infant while sleeping, since they are mutually attuned to one another's position even when sleeping (McKenna, 1987; McKenna & Mosko, 1994; McKenna et al., 1994).

How Can the SIDS Victim's Parents and Family Be Helped?

Bereavement over SIDS victims shows a similar pattern over time as that for neonatal death: negativism, anger, shock, disbelief, and guilt (Mandell, McAnulty, & Reece, 1980; Smialek, 1978). Following the death of the infant, wives may become more dependent on their husbands for support. This, combined with the possibility that a husband may secretly resent or blame his wife for the death, may cause marital discord (Gruen, 1987). Siblings in the family may also be affected, both because of a sense of loss and because parental preoccupation may detract from the parents' relationship with the older children. Siblings may also suffer from grief reactions similar to those of the parents (McConkie-Rosell & Iafolla, 1993; M. Powell, 1991). In some cases, even professionals, such as nursing staff who come in contact with the family, may also be affected by the death (McCalin & Mandell, 1994).

The more knowledgeable the parents' community, friends, relatives, and physicians are, the easier it will be for the parents to cope with the loss. Perhaps the best source of possible comfort and assistance is the family's pediatrician. Often, however, the pediatrician is either unwilling or, because of ignorance, unable to help. In such cases, parents may contact one of several national groups that have been organized by parents of SIDS victims, such as the American SIDS Institute (www.sids.org) or the National SIDS/Infant Death Resource Center (www.sidscenter.org). These groups are dedicated to medical research, providing support for survivors, public education, and informing the parents of their right to an autopsy. Autopsy is considered an essential element in relieving parents' guilt (Terjesen & Wilkins, 1979), although there are often delays and difficulties in dealing with local coroners and medical committees (Bluglass & Hassall, 1979).

For these reasons, parents of SIDS victims would benefit from contact with such groups and other knowledgeable individuals in the community, particularly other families of SIDS victims. Legal, social, and psychological assistance is part of a complete intervention package to help parents recover fully. Parents should also treat the death as meaningful and rely on the same religious and spiritual rituals that would help them in the event of death for any family member (Fabrena & Nutini, 1994).

NUTRITION

Proper nutrition is important throughout life. We are now learning that diets with high contents of fat, sugar, and carbohydrates can increase the risk of obesity in children and adults. Lack of sufficient exercise is also a concern. Obesity increases the risk for a wide variety of health problems. On the other side of the equation are vast number of poor people in the world who do not get adequate nutrition and suffer other types of health consequences. Nutrition, therefore, is an essential factor to consider in the healthy development of the fetus and infant.

Nutritional and Exercise Requirements During Pregnancy

The purpose of good prenatal nutrition is to avoid depletion of maternal stores of nutrients, to allow the mother to produce sufficient milk for breast-feeding, and to provide sufficient nutrients for the fetus. Malnutrition during pregnancy does more than simply deplete the mother's nutritional supplies; physical and brain development can be severely hampered in an infant born to a malnourished mother. Because the number of neuronal brain cells does not substantially increase after 20 weeks' gestational age, the early months of pregnancy are a critical period for brain development, and the nutrition that the fetus receives from the mother will determine how many cells are produced.

The recommended diet during pregnancy is shown in Table 9.9. Mothers are advised to eat a diet of balanced foods. A high protein, low carbohydrate diet, recommended in many weight loss programs, is not appropriate since it elevates cortisol levels in both mother and fetus. Balanced maternal diets also promote fetal growth and contribute to the reduction of chronic diseases in adulthood (Herrick et al., 2003; Wu et al., 2004).

Micronutrients, vitamins and minerals found in foods and in dietary supplements, are also important during pregnancy. Particular micronutrients are essential to a healthy pregnancy. These include folic acid, vitamin B9 (deficiencies limit blood supply to the fetus and cause some birth defects and delivery complications), zinc (lack causes some birth complications, physical, immunological, and neurological growth retardation),

iodine (lack contributes to miscarriage, some birth defects, and preterm birth). Other vitamins and minerals are also important (Black, 2001). Taking vitamin and mineral supplements should be done only in consultation with one's doctor. They may not be necessary with normal diets, and some vitamins may harm the fetus if taken in large quantities. On the other hand, in situations where there is a risk of malnutrition (as in developing countries and in cases of poverty) or for other medical reasons, appropriate supplement- ation may be useful (Shah & Sachdev, 2004; Vahratian et al., 2004).

The question of whether pregnant mothers should eat fish or take fish oil supplements containing omega-3 fatty acids has been somewhat controversial. For adults in general, omega-3 fatty acids, found in oily fishes, promote neurological development and reduce cardiac and other inflammatory diseases. There are, however, no long-term follow-up studies on the effects of this substance on the children of mothers who eat more fish or take more omega-3 fatty acid supplements during pregnancy. Some studies suggest that these supplements lower the risk of preterm birth and improve placental blood flow. One well-controlled study of 2,109 pregnant women from Massachusetts, however, found a slight *reduction* in fetal growth for women who took the most of these supplements. It is unknown whether this affects later develop-

TABLE 9.9 Nutritional Recommendations For a Balanced Diet During Pregnancy

Grain Products (5–12 Servings)
Examples of 1 serving = 1 slice of bread; 30g of cold cereal; 175 mL (3/4 cup) of hot cereal
Examples of 2 servings = 1 bagel, pita or bun; 250 mL (1 cup) of pasta or rice

Vegetables (3–5 servings) and Fruit (2–5 servings)
Examples of 1 serving = 1 medium-size fruit or vegetable; 125 mL (1/2 cup) fresh, frozen or canned vegetables or fruit; 250 mL (1 cup) of salad; 125 mL (1/2 cup) of juice

Milk Products (3–4 servings)
Examples of 1 serving = 250 mL (1 cup) of milk; 50g or 2 slices of cheese; 175 mL (3/4 cup) of yogurt

Protein and Alternatives (2–3 servings, 6–9 ounces per day)
Examples of 1 serving = 50–100 g of meat, poultry or fish; 1–2 eggs; 125–250 mL (1/2–1 cup) of canned beans; 100 g (1/3 cup) of tofu; 30 mL or 2 tablespoons of peanut butter

Other Foods
Taste and enjoyment can also come from other foods and beverages that are not part of the 4 food groups. Some of these foods are higher in fat or calories, so use these foods in moderation.

Source: www.babies.sutterhealth.org/during/preg_nutrition.html

ment or whether this slight risk outweighs other possible benefits. Mothers should check with their doctors about the latest information (Oken et al., 2004; Olsen & Secher, 2003; Saldeen & Saldeen, 2004). Pregnant teens require even more careful attention to nutritional needs than adults because their bodies are still growing.

The average weight gain for women in pregnancy is about 24 pounds, although it can be as high as 50 pounds or more, depending upon the size of the infant and the mother's constitution. Severe restriction of calories during pregnancy is not recommended and may even be harmful. With the rise in the rate of obesity in industrialized countries, however, overeating creates an increased risk of affecting not only the mother's but the infant's health. Too little weight gain is associated with low-birthweight infants, while excessive weight gain is associated with overly high birthweights and with later childhood obesity (Cogswell, Serdula, Hungerford, & Yip, 1995; Oken et al., 2007; Surkan et al., 2004). In addition to contributing to childhood obesity, maternal obesity during pregnancy is associated with birth complications, gestational diabetes, hypertension, and urinary tract infections in the mother (Kumari, 2001; Sebire et al., 2001). The best means for controlling weight gain without compromising the fetus should be discussed with the mother's doctor.

Mothers may continue to exercise during pregnancy and will derive benefits of cardiovascular fitness similar to those they experience when they are not pregnant. Intense exercise is helpful for fetal development but only during the first trimester of pregnancy. After that, too much exercise reduces birthweight, which is a risk factor for later disorders (Campbell & Mottola, 2001; Clapp et al., 2002). Since exercise contributes to the mother's sense of well-being, light-to-moderate exercise in late pregnancy is recommended. Mothers should check with their physicians to determine the right level of exercise in relation to the condition of their pregnancy (Technical Bulletin no. 189, 1994).

Aside from nutrients, the mother receives information from the social environment, and the feedback processes that govern this exchange may ultimately affect the health and development of the baby. One of the most important sources of interchange for the mother is her relationship with her family and her own psychological adjustment to the state of becoming a parent. Although the effect is most apparent in first-time parents, each new baby brings with it a continuing psychological adaptation within the mother and within each of the other family members.

Newborn Feeding Practices

In the United States, breast-feeding was the general practice until the beginning of the twentieth century. In 1900, only 38% of mothers breast-fed, and this percentage declined until only 18% were breast-feeding in 1966. The number of women breast-feeding took a major turn upward in the 1970s, so that by 1976, about half of all mothers were breast-feeding at the time of discharge from the hospital. The incidence of breast-feeding in the United States varies with class and education. The rate of breast-feeding in the United States is highest among higher-income, college-educated women who are more than 30 years old and live in the Mountain and Pacific regions of the country. In 2003, more than 72% of mothers in the United States reported breast-feeding their infants at birth, with the rate declining to 52%, 38%, and 16% at 3, 6, and 12 months, respectively (Singh et al., 2007). This is a significant increase from 61% of mothers who initiated breast-feeding at birth in 1996 (American Academy of Pediatrics, 1997).

Because breast-feeding is being encouraged as a way to prevent infant death in developing countries, the reduced quantity of milk from malnourished mothers presents a dilemma for the mother who is undernourished. The World Health Organization recommends teaching mothers when and how to supplement the diets of breast-fed babies with foods prepared from locally available products (World Health Organization, 1985).

The evidence suggests that mothers automatically produce milk after birth. Milk will be produced even under conditions of maternal malnutrition. In such cases, the milk will be made in less quantity, but it will have the same nutrient quality as that of well-nourished mothers (Guthrie, 1979; Kloeblen-Tarver et al., 2002; Rempel & Rempel, 2004). This quality is usually maintained at the expense of the mother's reserve stores of nutrients.

Some women can even breast-feed without having given birth, as reports from around the world show. In one study of mothers who nursed adopted babies, the sample consisted of 18 women who had never been pregnant, 7 who had been pregnant but had never lactated, and 40 who had previously lactated. All were able to nurse their adopted infants. Their success seemed to depend on factors such as the support of the husband and family, preparation by either hand-pumping the breast or nursing another infant at least 1 month in advance, having an infant as young as possible, and nursing a great deal at first. Apparently, sucking stimulation is more effective than hormone treatments in inducing lactation (Hormann, 1977).

Sucking stimulation can maintain the supply of breast milk even if the infant is feeding only once a day. This kind of minimal breast-feeding is often used by mothers who work outside the home, who are weaning a baby from the breast, or who

are using breast-feeding for "comfort" nursing for older infants. It is not necessary to mechanically express milk to maintain the supply during periods of minimal breast-feeding (Michaelson et al., 1988).

The nutritive demands of the lactating mother are far in excess of the demands made during prenatal life because of the accelerated weight gain of the infant just after birth. The milk secreted in just 1 month represents more calories than the net energy cost of pregnancy (Guthrie, 1979). The mother can meet this increased nutrient need by eating the equivalent of an additional meal of 500 kilocalories each day.

The composition of human milk not only differs from cow's milk-based infant formulas, but breast milk composition changes over time and according to the infant's nutritional needs (see Table 9.10). *Colostrum*, the clear, yellowish liquid that is secreted from the breast in the first few days, is relatively high in protein. It also has enzymes that inhibit the growth of bacteria, microorganisms (*Lactobacillus bifidus*) that depress the growth of pathogens, and large "eating" cells (microphages) that enhance the immune system against

Breast-feeding can be a great source of pleasure for the mother and infant, especially in quiet family times. For some mothers, breast-feeding is inconvenient and difficult. Although breast-feeding is recommended, each family should choose the feeding option that best suits their lifestyle.
Photo by Felicia Martinez/PhotoEdit.

TABLE 9.10 Components of Breast Milk Compared with Formula

Nutrient Factor	Breast Milk Contains	Formula Contains
Fats	Omega 3 fatty acids	Low in omega 3s
	Automatically adjusts to infant's needs; levels decline as baby gets older	Doesn't adjust to infant's needs
	Rich in cholesterol	No cholesterol
	Nearly completely absorbed	Not completely absorbed
	Contains fat-digesting enzyme, lipase	No lipase
Protein	Soft, easily-digestible whey	Harder-to-digest casein curds
	Lysozyme, an antimicrobial	No lysozyme
	Rich in protein components	Deficient or low in some proteins
	Rich in growth factors	Deficient in growth factors
	Contains sleep-inducing proteins	Does not contain as many sleep-inducing proteins
	Infants aren't allergic to human milk protein	May cause allergies
Immune Boosters	Rich in living white blood cells, millions per feeding	No live white blood cells—or any other cells. Dead food has less immunological benefit.
	Rich in immunoglobulins	Few immunoglobulins and most are the wrong kind
Enzymes and Hormones	Rich in digestive enzymes, such as lipase and amylase	Processing kills digestive enzymes
	Rich in many hormones; thyroid, prolactin, oxytocin, and more than fifteen others	Processing kills hormones, which are not human to begin with
	Varies with mother's diet	Always tastes the same

Source: www.askdrsears.com/html/2/t021600.asp; © Copyright 2006 AskDrSears.com. All rights reserved.

bacteria and some viruses (American Academy of Pediatrics, 1997; Bocci et al., 1993; Guthrie, 1979).

To make cow's milk used for most commercial infant formulas more similar in composition to human milk, it is usually modified. The protein content is lowered, and the milk is treated to make it more easily digested (the whey protein of human milk is easier to digest than that of cow's milk). Vitamins A, D, and C, and sometimes iron are added to fortify the formula as well as fatty acids that are known to stimulate brain development. But all the necessary nutrients for brain and body development are the most balanced in breast milk. Formulas can also be tailored to infants with special needs, such as soy formulas for infants with allergies. Today, formula and breast milk have similar nutrient values, but human milk is more nutritionally matched to infants, changes over time to match the infant's needs, and contains other important substances that promote immunization.

Human milk has a sweet taste. It also takes on some of the flavors found in the maternal diet. Amniotic fluid is also flavored with the mother's foods, suggesting that there is an acculturation toward local foods that begins prenatally (Mennella, 1997). Human milk is also low in sodium, and breast-fed infants have less of a preference for salt than bottle-fed infants (Karns, 2000).

The Effects of Breast- and Bottle-Feeding on Mother and Infant

Breast-feeding has important health benefits for both the mother and the infant. One advantage of breast-feeding is that it serves as a natural way to help mothers recover from childbirth. The sucking stimulation from the infant triggers the release of several maternal hormones, in particular oxytocin and prolactin. Oxytocin, as you may recall from Chapter 3, is used as a drug to speed up contractions during labor. It is essential following the third stage of labor, since continued uterine contractions are necessary to shrink the uterus to normal size and prevent uterine hemorrhage. The oxytocin released by sucking does this naturally. If mothers do not breast-feed, they must be given oxytocin. Oxytocin also stimulates the breast to deliver milk only when sucking occurs and not otherwise. Prolactin stimulates the mammary glands to produce more milk.

There is some evidence that breast-feeding has a long-term effect on mothers's health, in particular, the partial prevention of ovarian and breast cancer. Women who breast-fed their first-born infants longer than 1 month had a significantly lower risk of developing breast cancer, at least during the period before the onset of menopause (American Academy of Pediatrics, 1997; Byers, Grahm, & Rzepka, 1985; Siskind, Schofield, Rice, & Bain, 1989). Breast-feeding also helps women return faster to their pre-pregnancy weight. These two factors—prevention of breast cancer and weight control—were cited as the primary reasons why women chose to breast-feed their babies (Charrol et al., 2004). Breast-feeding also lowers the risk of hip fractures in the postmenopausal period, helps women retain minerals in their bones, and lowers the risk of arthritis especially if women breast-feed for over 15 months (Karlson et al., 2004).

There are also health benefits to the infant. Mother's milk contains immunizing agents that protect against a variety of infections, such as respiratory infection, asthma, ear infection, bacterial meningitis, and urinary tract infection. Breast feeding may also reduce the risk of sudden infant death syndrome (SIDS), diabetes, allergic diseases, and digestive diseases. Finally, there is some evidence that breast-feeding may enhance motor development and state regulation during infancy, and reduce the risk of obesity in later life (American Academy of Pediatrics, 1997, 2005; Feldman & Eidelman, 2002; Hart et al., 2003; Jelliffe & Jelliffe, 1988; Stettler et al., 2005). Some claims have been made that breast-feeding also enhances cognitive development, but more research is needed to sufficiently justify such claims (Soliday, 2007).

Breast-feeding for more than 6 months significantly reduces the risk of developing childhood cancer, especially lymphomas. Non-breast-fed children are five times more likely to get lymphoma, a form of cancer that is higher in children with immune deficiencies (American Academy of Pediatrics, 1997; Smigel, 1988).

The immunologic effect of human milk derives from the protein called *secretory IgA*, or SIgA. This protein coats the inner lining of the baby's intestines, acting to trap and kill harmful bacteria. SIgA also enters the lungs and breathing passages whenever the infant gurgles and blows milk bubbles and thus may protect against respiratory diseases. If a mother has a bacterial infection, her milk contains higher levels of SIgA, which helps to further protect the infant from catching the mother's infection (Pollitt, Garza, & Leib, 1984).

If breast milk protects the infant against disorders of the immune system, what happens if the mother has an immune system disorder such as AIDS? There is some controversy about whether infants can acquire AIDS from their mothers by breast-feeding. If a mother is infected with AIDS, HIV is typically present in her breast milk. The chance of an infant's acquiring AIDS from its mother is about 15%, but part of this transmission may occur either prenatally or during the birth process. It is difficult to determine which of these routes is most likely to infect the infant.

Medical agencies have come up with conflicting recommendations about whether an AIDS-infected mother should breast-feed. It is thought that SIgA may neutralize the AIDS virus and that the risk of an infant acquiring other diseases because of a lack of breast milk SIgA may be just as high as the risk of getting AIDS from breast milk, especially in poor countries where the incidence of AIDS and other diseases is high. Others believe that the chance of acquiring AIDS from breast milk is not worth the risk of spreading the disease and therefore recommend against breast-feeding. Infected women should consult their physician before making the choice to breast-feed (American Academy of Pediatrics, 1997; D. T. Dunn, Newell, Ades, & Peckham, 1992; Goldfarb, 1993; Kennedy et al., 1990; Peckham, 1993; Porcher, 1992; Van de Perre et al., 1993). Breast-feeding is also not recommended if the mother uses illegal drugs or is receiving chemotherapy for cancer.

Behavioral differences between breast- and bottle-fed infants have been found. A study of 100 healthy, full-term, vaginally delivered newborns found that breast-fed infants are more irritably fussy than bottle-fed infants (DiPietro, Larson, & Porges, 1987). This irritability, however, was associated with a more optimal physiological functioning, such as a slower heart rate, compared to bottle-fed infants. The physiological functioning of breast-fed infants is more energy-efficient, as judged by differences in the patterns of heart rate, breathing, and sleeping of bottle- and breast-fed infants (Zeskind, Marshall, & Goff, 1992). The higher irritability of breast-fed infants is not due to a less optimal mother-infant interaction. Some research has shown, on the contrary, that breast-fed infants get talked to, smiled at, touched, looked at, and rocked more by their mothers (J. Dunn, 1975; Lavelli & Poli, 1998) during feeding, although no long-term behavioral differences have been found. Nor is the effect due to the fact that breast-fed babies get hungrier than bottle-fed infants (DiPietro et al., 1987).

Rather, DiPietro and associates (1987) propose that "the irritability of breast-fed neonates be regarded as the norm of neonatal behavior. Formula may have a depressant effect on behavior" (p. 472). This may be due to the differences in the specific types of proteins and sugars that constitute the two types of milk. If more irritability is the norm, these authors argue that it serves two purposes. First, it enhances physiological functioning by giving the infant experience with varying degrees of arousal. Second, crying may serve to stimulate more mother-infant interaction and pro-

vide more opportunities for feeding (Hunziker & Barr, 1986).

Taken together, the benefits of breast-feeding appear to be immunological, physiological, behavioral, and psychological. Because of the growing number of research studies supporting the superiority of breast milk and breast-feeding for both mother and infant, the American Academy of Pediatrics (AAP), the Canadian Paediatric Society, and the American Dietetic Association all strongly encourage breast-feeding (American Academy of Pediatrics, 1997; 2005; Karns, 2000). The AAP recommends:

Exclusive breast-feeding is ideal nutrition and sufficient to support optimal growth and development for approximately the first 6 months after birth. Infants weaned before 12 months of age should not receive cow's milk feedings but should receive iron-fortified infant formula. Gradual introduction of iron-enriched solid foods in the second half of the first year should complement the breast milk diet. It is recommended that breast feeding continue for at least 12 months, and thereafter for as long as mutually desired. (American Academy of Pediatrics, 1997, p. 4)

Although breast-feeding is recommended, personal preferences, illness, family and social support, and cultural norms may influence the choice of feeding method. Most mothers in the United States either stop breast-feeding altogether before 6 months, or they begin supplementing with formula too early (Li et al., 2003). The major factor for predicting success in breast-feeding is the desire of the mother to do so and the support of her partner. Some fathers have feelings of jealousy, uselessness, and sexual frustration associated with their mate's breast-feeding. Some men may also experience feelings of ambivalence about the breast: Who does it "belong" to? Who and what is it for? Research shows that these feelings can be alleviated somewhat by enhancing the father's participation in the birth experience and by improving father-mother communication on such issues as infant care and sexual fulfillment (Karns, 2000; Teitler, 2001; Waletzky, 1979).

An effort is being made in the United States to encourage health-care professionals to promote breast-feeding. Mothers can also receive information and support from local hospitals, clinics, and breast-feeding advocacy groups. These supports are necessary to counteract the effects of cultural beliefs against breast-feeding, embarrassment, lack of self-confidence, and family attitudes (Karns, 2000).

Introduction of Solid Foods

Coincidences are common in human development. For example, the depletion of fetal supplies of iron coincides with the beginning of the teething period, the ability to make fine motor movements with the hands to grasp and pick up objects, and the decline of the extrusion reflex of the tongue, in which most things placed in the mouth are pushed out just at the time when the infant's body is beginning to need a supplementation of nutrients (mother's milk has little iron). In other words, the baby begins to develop the ability to handle food, chew it, and swallow it. Is this more than a chance coincidence? We will probably never really know, but it all works out nicely for the baby, who develops the skill to consume solid foods just at the time when he or she needs them.

The American Academy of Pediatrics maintains that infants do not need supplementary foods besides milk until 6 months (American Academy of Pediatrics, 2003). By 6 months, the baby has certain abilities that will help in processing solid foods. These include enzymes to digest carbohydrates, chewing and swallowing skills, and the ability to express satiety by head shaking (R. A. Stewart, 1981). Data indicate no relationship between the early introduction of solid foods or the amount of food the baby eats and whether the baby will sleep through the night. Thus, no clear benefits can be gained from the early introduction of solid foods (Chubet, 1988; Grunwaldt, Bates, & Guthrie, 1960).

Can the Early Introduction of Solid Foods Do Any Harm?

Some hazards are associated with the early introduction of solid foods. The best source of nutrition for infants under 6 months is milk—preferably human. Any solid food is inferior nutritionally, so proportionately more is required to satisfy nutritional needs. This will lead to less consumption of milk and to a tendency to distend or overtax the stomach, resulting in the short term in gastrointestinal upset and in the long term in possible obesity. Early feeding of solids also has been associated with the development of food allergies, kidney malfunction, iron deficiency, and an increased likelihood of developing strong food dislikes (Committee on Nutrition, 1998; Guthrie, 1979; Pipes, 1985; C. H. Robinson, 1978; Weir & Feldman, 1975).

How Should Solids Be Introduced?

By the age of 5 months, the digestive systems of most babies develop the enzymes to digest most proteins, and saliva production increases to lubricate swallowing. Drooling begins about this time, because the production of saliva exceeds the baby's ability to keep it under control. Furthermore, chewing, swallowing, and teeth pushing up under the gums all make it easier to handle the demands of eating solids (Guthrie, 1979; Pipes, 1985; Sheppard & Mysak, 1984).

The first teeth typically do not erupt through the gums until about 8 months, although individual infants may vary from the average dates of tooth eruption by as much as 6 months before or after (Lunt & Law, 1974; R. McDonald & Avery, 1983). In response to teething, some babies become fussy, while others do not seem to notice, although most babies like to bite semisoft objects as their teeth are coming in. Infants under a year may be given cookies to chew on, and babies older than 1 year may be given large carrot sticks.

Weaning is the process by which children reduce their intake of milk and become accustomed to the foods eaten by adults. General guidelines on how to introduce solid foods are available from a number of sources. Because of the possibility of food allergies, most experts recommend introducing one food at a time—for at least a week or two—before trying another. New foods should be offered in small amounts at first, and caregivers should never force infants to take a food they do not like.

Even in the first six months, infants develop taste preferences. They prefer formulas that they are used to, even if those formulas are rated as bland or even bitter by adults (Mennella et al., 2004). Thus, solid food should be seasoned lightly or not at all. Salts and sugars are not harmful in small quantities, but there is no need for them, and infants will eat what they are used to eating; they seem to be more important for the feeder than for the baby (Guthrie, 1979; C. H. Robinson, 1978). Some commercially available baby foods contain added sugars and salts, but one can buy foods without these substances, and organic baby foods with no additives are also available. Since infants and young children typically eat some between-meal snacks, it is important to provide both meals and snacks that are high in nutrition and low in calories (Skinner et al., 2004).

Solid foods are usually introduced to babies in the following order: cereals (one at a time), strained fruit or juice (except orange), vegetables, proteins (meat and cheese), egg yolk (not until 8 months), and egg white (not until 10 to 12 months) (Guthrie 1979; C. H. Robinson, 1978). This order is related to a number of developmental factors, such as production of digestive enzymes, the consistency of the food and the ability to chew, and the possibility of an allergic reaction (egg whites are one of the biggest troublemakers in this regard). Fruit juice should be limited to less than 8–10 ounces per day, and should not be given in a bottle (Committee on Nutrition, 1998). Because cow's milk should not be used for the first year, dry cereals should be mixed with breast milk or formula. Rice cereals are the most easily tolerated in the first year, and rice or soy milk formulas can also be found (Karns, 2000). It is estimated that between 15 and 25% of parents do not follow these guidelines, risking food refusal and allergies (Briefel et al., 2004).

Infants can eat a vegetarian diet with certain precautions (Karns, 2000). Vegetarian diets are high in bulk, and infants need denser foods such as nuts, olives, dates, and avocados. Macrobiotic diets present the greatest risk, but infants who eat milk and/or eggs have normal growth patterns. Infants need to ingest dietary fat for a number of reasons: it is a source of energy; it is a carrier of fat-soluble vitamins such as A, D, E, and K; and infants need certain essential fatty acids.

Up until 1 year, food should be mashed or chopped until it is fine enough not to cause choking. Foods most likely to cause choking are hot dogs, grapes, raw vegetables, popcorn, nuts, and hard candy (Karns, 2000). Finger foods are good for 6-month-olds, and by 9 to 12 months, infants can begin to feed themselves with a spoon. Until about 18 months, spilling and messing food is quite common. Why should babies not explore food just as they do everything else? A good recommendation is for the feeder to come armed with a towel, a sponge, and a sense of humor.

If infants persist in spilling food as part of a game or to get the caregiver's attention, caregivers can remove the food temporarily, while firmly stating that food is for eating. It is usually not necessary to coax infants to eat: they will eventually eat to satisfy their hunger. Thus, intake in any one meal is not so important. Caregivers may wish to insist on proper mealtime behavior (considering the limits of the infant's motor abilities and allowing for a little bit of fun), but insisting that the infant eat particular foods and particular amounts of foods is generally not recommended. Babies may avoid food because of its taste or because they are not hungry.

At the end of the first year, babies who are teething like to chew on carrots or dry toast but tend to mangle these foods more than consume them. Babies often go on food jags, refusing to eat more than one or two different kinds of foods. They can be erratic in their appetites and seem to have strong ideas about when and what to eat (Pipes, 1985). Picky eaters have been reported at all infant ages, for both sexes, all ethnicities, and all ranges of household incomes. Parents may need to

Self-feeding requires more coordination than most infants can manage. Parents need to give infants foods that are easily handled.
Photo by Mark Richards/PhotoEdit.

introduce a new food up to 15 times before a picky eater may be willing to taste it (Carruth et al., 2004).

How to eat is also a big concern for most babies. They may eat something only if it is presented in a ritualized way—cut or arranged a certain way or served on a certain dish. There is not too much the caregiver can do except live with these idiosyncrasies, accepting them with good humor and the recognition that preferences are part of being human. Some people like their hamburgers with catsup and others like mustard; some people like grits with their breakfast and others eat bagels.

For a baby, a meal is more than food intake; it is an occasion for play, learning, and socializing. Mealtimes are an important part of the infant's social, cognitive, and emotional development, not just a refueling for physical growth. Parents should try not to rush meals and should cut down on stimulation, such as the television, that might compete with the social aspects of feeding the baby.

Mealtimes contain complex sequences of co-regulated social interaction. Issues of control arise often. The baby wants to hold the spoon, for example, but is doing more banging than eating. The mother takes the spoon and begins to feed the baby, who starts to protest and refuses to eat. Mother eventually returns the spoon to the baby. The best solution is to allow the baby as much time as needed to complete the meal. When this is not possible, caregivers do need to model more appropriate eating habits, but without undue domination. In eating, as in other aspects of development, infants will never learn independent behavior unless they are allowed to develop their own sense of control and achievement in this realm. Patience and praise are the best teaching tools.

INFANT SAFETY

What Are the Main Threats to Infant Safety?

Each year, about 3,500 children under the age of 4 years die in the United States from unintentional injuries. This accounts for about 35% of all deaths in this age group, making injuries the leading cause of death (Karns, 2001). Many more injuries occur that do not result in death. For every death, there are 1,120 emergency room visits and an unknown number of untreated injuries or injuries treated at home. Infant mortality due to unintentional injuries can be categorized as follows: motor vehicle collisions (32%), fire (19%), drowning (18%), choking (7%), falls (3%), poisoning (2%), and other causes (19%) (Lewit & Baker, 1995). In this section, we discuss each of these different causes of injury.

Collisions and falls. Automobile accidents are the leading cause of injury and death among infants. In the United States, about 1,100 children under 4 years of age die every year in such accidents, and 7,000 infants per year suffer injuries. The tragedy is that most of these could be prevented by the use of well-designed car seats and seat belts, since most injuries occur when infants are riding in the front seat of a car on someone's lap. Even though every state has a safety restraint law for infants, less than half of all infants are safely strapped in. Safety restraints are highly effective, and the number of deaths per year has been dropping under the new safety belt laws (D. Davis, 1985; National Safety Council, 1987). In 2007 the percent of infants ages 0–3 years using seat belts/restraints in the front or back seat, was 97 %, up 9% percent from 88% in 1994 (U.S. Department of Transportation, National Highway Traffic Safety Administration. http://www-nrd.nhtsa.dot.gov/pdf/nrd-30/NCSA/RNotes/2007/809845.pdf).

Buy an infant car seat that is easy to install correctly. The seat should be in the center of the back seat. Be firm with the baby and do not let him or her out of the seat even if the child fusses. Do not let the child eat lollipops or hold sharp or pointed objects while the car is moving, and do not put loose items like groceries in the back seat (Chubet, 1988).

At home, falls and collisions can be prevented by taking simple precautions. Never leave a baby unattended on a table or a bed. Block off access to stairs, and keep the baby's highchair away from a table or wall that could be used as leverage to push the chair over. Even though babies at this age have developed a wariness of the deep side of a visual cliff (see Chapter 7), most infants do not have sufficient control over their locomotor skills at this age to prevent a fall.

All infants suffer minor tumbles and shocks as they try to expand their motor skills. These are generally not serious unless there is some suspicion of a broken bone or a severe head injury. A number of excellent books are available for parents and other caregivers on the diagnosis of medical problems in infants and children. Be sure to read about the signs of concussion and know what to do if you see one. Severe head injury trauma can occur even from short falls onto hard surfaces (Prange et al., 2003).

Infants can also fall from cribs, high- chairs, walkers, windows, and grocery carts. Cribs should be checked for sturdiness and should have a mattress that can be lowered as the baby grows. The posts or slats should be no more than 2 3/8 inches apart to prevent infants from getting their heads stuck. Be sure that mobiles are securely fastened and will not fall if the baby grabs them. Do not use plastic bags to cover the mattress, and do not allow any strings within reach of the baby. Do not tie pacifiers to strings, as the baby can easily become entangled or choke (Chubet, 1988).

Highchairs should not have sharp edges, springs that can catch the baby's skin, or straps in which the baby can become entangled. The seat should not be so slippery that it causes the baby to slide down. It should be extremely easy to remove the tray without hurting the baby. Walkers are safe if the wheelbase is wider than the seat and grip area and if they are not used near stairs or near furniture with sharp edges. Always strap infants into grocery carts, and never allow children to stand in a cart. For highchairs, walkers, jumpers, grocery carts, and changing tables, the most important rule is that *under no circumstances are you to leave the baby unattended.* If the phone rings, either ignore it or take the baby with you to answer it.

Finally, if you live in a building with more than one story, do not trust screens to keep an active toddler from falling out a window. Windows can be blocked so that they can open only enough for ventilation but not wide enough for a baby to fit through. Safety gates are recommended near stairs or to block off rooms that hold dangers for the baby. Buy gates that will not pinch a baby and that are easy for adults to open and close; otherwise they will stay open.

Poisoning. Modern households are filled with lethal poisons, and most of them are kept within easy reach of an inquisitive infant. The cabinets under the kitchen and bathroom sinks are the most likely repositories of poisonous substances in the house: soaps, detergents, cleaning fluids, cosmetics, insecticides, and other toxic substances. It is wise to keep all such substances completely out of the infant's reach, since parental discipline is often not effective at this age in totally keeping the infant away from these dangers. Cabinets should be locked or childproofed or the toxic substances moved well out of the infant's reach. Even if most things have childproof caps, the caps and outer surfaces of the containers may contain enough toxin to make the infants ill if they should put them in their mouths. Child-care providers and parents should learn some of the common poisons and their antidotes. A poison antidote chart is available from most hospitals and pediatricians and should be posted in the kitchen or bathroom, where it can be readily consulted in an emergency.

Other potential sources of poisonous material include the leaves and flowers of houseplants and lead and lead-based paints. Never allow babies to be in rooms where there are paint flakes and plaster dust. Like plaster dust, baby powders can be toxic and are so fine that they can easily clog immature lung passages. Breathing can also be obstructed by plastic bags, and uninflated or broken balloon pieces are especially dangerous (although inflated balloons are not).

Finally, infants—like fetuses—are affected by passive smoking; for infants, the danger lies in inhaling the smoke from burning cigarettes or the exhalations of smokers. Infants exposed to passive smoking had more sympathetic (stress and arousal) and less parasympathetic (calming and relaxing) nervous system arousal and higher heart rates compared to infants not exposed to smoke (Schuetze & Eiden, 2006).

Swallowing small objects. If a small object becomes lodged in an infant's throat, it can disrupt breathing or cause choking. As with poisons, any object that can easily fit into an infant's mouth should be removed from the child's reach. The most common cause of suffocation at this age is latex balloons. Mylar and paper balloons are better, but all balloons can explode, which may cause pieces to become lodged in the baby's throat.

Beads, coins, uncooked grains, paper clips, and so on are candidates for chokers. Be sure the button eyes of stuffed toys are sewn on securely and that rattles (with beads inside) are not cracked. As the infant learns to stand while holding onto furniture, small objects on the tops of tables and desks are vulnerable to the infant's reach. Make sure they are on high shelves or in childproofed drawers. Foods that are cut too small can also be dangerous for babies who cannot yet chew effectively. Hot dogs, peanuts, and other hard foods are not recommended. Parents may want to be trained in the Heimlich maneuver and other methods for helping a choking infant.

Burns and drowning. Infants suffer more from home fires and smoke inhalation than do older children and adults. They are less mature and have more sensitive skin and lungs. They are also less able to escape on their own. Many burns also occur from overly hot bathwater, stove tops, splashing grease, and radiators. Be sure the child knows the meaning of the word "hot." Keep the infant away from sources of heat, and always test the bathwater before putting the baby in.

Baths also present the danger of the child's slipping and/or drowning. Be sure to use nonslip pads in the bottom of the sink or tub. You can also buy a molded sponge in which the baby can sit. Keep infants away from pools, and keep toilet seats down. Never leave a baby unattended near or in water. Parental attention is imperative at all times when a baby is near water; bathtub seats and molded sponges are no substitute for an adult's vigilance.

Other dangers. Sharp and pointed objects are another common source of danger. Pencils, pens, and screwdrivers should never be given to infants of this age. If they want to scribble, let them use a nontoxic crayon (not a felt-tipped marker). Heavy objects, especially those infants can pull down on top of themselves, are also potential dangers. Keep the baby away from ropes or cords (such as venetian blind pulls), electrical outlets, and avoid clothing that ties around the neck. The best way to prevent many dangers is to crawl around and look at the house from the point of view of someone who is 2 feet tall, curious, and clumsy. Sun exposure can damage infant skin more readily than for adults. Infants should have sunblock, appropriate clothing, and a hat when out of doors for more than a few minutes at a time.

Finally, toys are potentially dangerous. They should have no small parts, such as buttons, that are detachable. Small objects, such as marbles, should not be used. Toys should have no sharp edges, small holes, or openings that can cut, trap, or pinch fingers or tongues. Toys should be sturdy. Plastic is always better than glass, which can break or shatter. Toys should not contain any strings, elastic bands, or ropes longer than 10 or 12 inches. Stuffed toys should not be so soft that the baby can suffocate, and they should be easy to wash.

Emergency Procedures

Even with the best attempts at prevention, infants will sometimes face life-threatening accidents or injuries. It is recommended that parents and caregivers be familiar with the basics of first aid and cardiopulmonary resuscitation (CPR). A number of excellent infant health books and websites are available, and first aid classes can be found through local health organizations. CPR is useful in cases of shock or drowning to help the infant resume breathing and provide heart massage. Simple but specific techniques should be learned to control bleeding, treat burns, stop choking, stop electrical shock, and treat poisoning (Chubet, 1988).

What Are Some Important Health Considerations?

Most of the serious diseases of infancy and early childhood have been eliminated by immunization procedures. Babies should be given a series of inoculations during the first 2 years of life. These are shown in Table 9.11. It is generally recommended that children not receive immunizations later than scheduled to avoid unnecessary exposure.

Most of the common diseases of infancy involve gastrointestinal or respiratory problems.

Symptoms of the former include vomiting, stomach pains, diarrhea, and constipation. Signs of respiratory problems are a runny nose, sore throat, coughing or wheezing, and trouble breathing. A fever is also a sign of illness. Consult medical care manuals. They generally give advice about which conditions can be treated at home and which require a doctor's attention.

Although some illnesses are caused by viral or bacterial infections, repeated occurrences of particular symptoms should be taken as warning signs. The infant may be expsed to infectious or unsanitary conditions, or the illness may be a symptom of an allergic reaction. In the latter case, the physician should work with the family to isolate the possible source of the allergy.

A study done in 1998 in Great Britain by Wakefield and colleagues indicated a link between the MMR vaccine and autism (Wakefield, Murch, Anthony, Linnell, Casson, Malik, Berelowitz, Dhillon, Thomson, Valentine, Davies, Walker-Smith, 1998). This study made the headline news, however it was later discredited due to the study's many limitations, including a very small sample of 12 children, having been based on parental reports that were subjective, and most of the authors subsequently retracting the findings. In addition, further studies showed no correlation, and certainly no causation between the MMR vaccine and childhood autism (The Economist, 2008; Gerber & Offit, 2009). There was a dip in infant vaccinations in the years following the Wakefield et al. study, however the rebuttals appear to have sufficiently quieted the hysteria, and vaccination levels have returned to their former levels, although some continue to labor under the misinformation from this 21st century scare.

INFANTS WITH SPECIAL NEEDS

When an infant has a long-term or permanent challenge—a disability, deformity, or special need—a systems approach predicts that this infant will affect the entire family and that the family's response to the infant will affect the

TABLE 9.11   Recommended Immunization Schedule (Birth—6 years) (2001)

Vaccine	Age for Administration
Hepatitis B (HiB)	Birth–3 months (first); 1–4 months (second); 6–18 months (third)
Diptheria Tetanus Pertussus (DTP)	2 months (first); 4 months (second); 6 months (third); 15–18 months (fourth); 4–6 years (fifth)
Heamophilius influenza Type b (Hib)	2 months (first); 4 months (second) 6 months (third); 12–15 months (fourth)
Inactivated Polio (IPV)	2 months (first); 4 months (second); 6–18 months (third); 4–6 years (fourth)
Pneumococcal Conjugate (PCV)	2 months (first); 4 months (second); 6 months (third)
Measles, Mumps, Rubella (MMR)	12–15 months (first); 4–6 years (second)
Varicella	12–18 months
Hepatitis A	24 months (in selected areas)

Source: Centers for Disease Control and Prevention (2001). Recommended childhood immunization schedule—United States, 2001. *Morbibity and Mortality Weekly Report, 50*(1), 10.

infant's own development. This section will explore these possibilities. You might want to go back and read the sections in this chapter on teratology and euthanasia for neonates with birth defects and with birth complications. Because the infant will affect every member of the family for a long time, the issues discussed in this section should be a part of any decision regarding life, death, or institutionalization for these infants at the time of birth.

How Does an Infant with Special Needs Affect the Family?

Infants with special needs constitute an important population of babies. Such infants may have suffered from a birth defect that affects the brain or body, or they may have acquired a disability following birth. This population of infants is referred to in many ways: special needs, developmentally challenged, developmentally disabled, handicapped, or developmentally delayed. One problem with some of these terms is that they have a negative connotation. Although the babies to whom the terms refer have some deficit with respect to the population of typically developing infants, a great deal can be done to improve their developmental outcomes. To help parents and professionals realize the enormous potential for growth in these babies,

we refer to them as **infants with special needs**. Infants with special needs create some degree of emotional trauma for most families.

Effects on Individuals

Parents, siblings, and other relatives go through a series of difficult feelings. They almost always experience chronic sorrow or depression—a feeling that the child will never fit into their lives or dreams. Individuals around the infant with special needs may feel an emotional rejection of the infant that may result, in part, from a lack of knowledge about the infant's condition. Family members also experience difficulty adapting—even to everyday demands—and they find most of their interpersonal relationships strained (Blake, Stewart, & Turcan, 1975; Brooks-Gunn & Lewis, 1982; Heiman, 2002; Preisler, 1997; Rapoport, Rapoport, & Strelitz, 1977).

Parents may be in a state of high emotional arousal much of the time. The shame and guilt they feel at being the "cause" of the problem are coupled with the extra difficulties of caring for the child. These may include extra visits to doctors and hospitals, special difficulties (such as soiling and wetting), special housing or equipment needs, financial difficulties, special care arrangements, special clothing, and special transportation (Rapo-

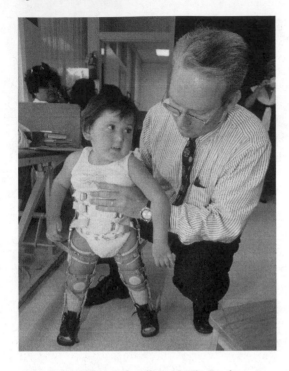

Many infants with special needs are capable of social relationships. Some require regular medical interventions. All such infants demand special care and attention from their families.

Photo courtesy of Corbis.

port, Rapoport, & Strelitz, 1977). In the course of all this, a parent may swing between the extreme attitudes of either wanting to abandon the child or trying to overprotect the child. One parent, after hearing the diagnosis of her infant, said, "I cried a lot, a lot of terrible thoughts came into my mind. I was covered with a cold sweat, and my heart beat very fast. I was afraid I'd have a heart attack" (Heiman, 2002, p. 164).

Siblings have unique individual responses to the situation. They may have trouble with peer relationships, become restless and disobedient, display temper tantrums, or live in a state of emotional misery. Part of the difficulty for siblings is that the added stress on the parents reduces the amount of parental time and emotional energy available to give them. Parents also worry about these potential effects on the siblings (Heiman, 2002).

Infants with special needs even affect their grandparents. In one study (D. Davis, 1967), maternal grandmothers were less supportive of their daughters if the daughters had infants with special needs rather than typically developing infants. The feedback a mother receives from her own mother may make her feel less supported and

therefore affect her ability to care for the baby. If the grandmother senses that her daughter is not doing her job, the grandmother may withdraw even further. These mutual feedback effects show how the family system can work against the benefit of the infant. However, mutually supportive feedback can lead to a strengthening of the family to the ultimate benefit of the infant.

Effect on the Marital Relationship

Most of the research on the effect of a child with special needs on marital discord has shown that there is little or no effect. Couples who separated or divorced after having a child with special needs did so because of some problem in the marriage that existed before the child was born (Howard, 1978). Marital discord that could be directly traced to the child amounted to only 4% of the cases studied in a sample of 243 children with a rubella-related birth defect (Korn, Chess, & Fernandez, 1978). Indeed, for almost two-thirds of families, having a child with special needs brings the couple closer together because the parents collaborate more on child-rearing issues than do parents in families without an infant with special needs. As one parent said, "Communication between us is better now than before" (Becker, Houser, Engelhardt, & Steinmann, 1993; Heiman, 2002, p. 166).

Effects on the Family

In contrast, the child with special needs has a definite impact on family interaction patterns. Effects may include changes in family routines, lack of vacations and other out-of-home visits, a limited social life, and parents' neglect of other children. These problems only occurred in about one-fourth of a sample of 243 children with a rubella-related defect (Korn et al., 1978), but some of these families had experienced similar disruptions even before the infants' births. In general, the more serious disabilities requiring more care and adaptive equipment result in the biggest impacts on parental and family life (Kelly & Booth, 2002).

In general, most families who are provided with adequate social, economic, and psychological support come to an effective resolution of these issues, although it may take a long time. A resolution usually means a realistic assessment of the child's abilities and limitations, continued feelings of sadness—but about the child rather than about the effect on the parents—and recovery of the parents' self-esteem. Most (75%) of parents report the growth of feelings of love, joy and acceptance over time (Heiman, 2002; Mintzer, Als, Tronick, & Brazelton, 1985; Shonkoff, Hauser-Cram, Krauss, & Upshur, 1992).

How Do Disabilities Affect the Parent-Infant Interaction?

Most evidence suggests that interactions are adversely affected by a child's disabilities. The amount of disruption of the parent-infant interaction depends on the severity of the disability (Landry, Chapieski, & Schmidt, 1986). Perhaps the mildest effects are seen in premature infants, many of whom would not be classified as disabled.

Mothers of these infants are often overindulgent and overstimulating during the first year (Field, 1981a). Disturbances in mother-infant communication depend upon the severity of the deficits due to prematurity, some of which may last for many years. Premature infants who were delayed in smiling, for example, were smiled at less by their mothers (Field, 1982; Malatesta, Grigoryev, Lamb, Albin, & Culver, 1986).

Many but not all of these differences tend to disappear after the first year, perhaps because the preterm infants gradually catch up with full-term infants (Branchfeld, Goldberg, & Sloman, 1980; Crawford, 1982). Even though preterm infants showed less vocalization, play, and attentive behavior than full-term infants in interaction with their mothers at 6, 8, and 10 months, most of these differences were no longer significant at 12 months. In addition, the extra holding and caretaking that preterm infants received during the first year, compared with full-term infants, was no longer apparent at 12 months (Crawford, 1982). Even though the differences between preterm and full-term groups were lessened by 1 year for these behavioral indicators, other studies have shown that more subtle effects of prematurity may persist until early and middle childhood in such areas as emotional maturity, language skills, and perceptual-motor functioning (Grigoroiu-Serbanescu, 1981; Taub, Goldstein, & Caputo, 1977).

In general, however, by the time the children reach the age of 3 years, differences between preterm and full-term groups are typically absent. In preterm groups, as for full-terms, individual differences are best predicted by security of attachment at 1 year (Plunkett, Klein, & Meisels, 1988), by the severity of birth complications independent of prematurity (Landry et al., 1986), and by the infant's history of illness during the first years of life (Jarvis, Myers, & Creasey, 1989). Thus, the factors that complicate preterm birth have a longer-lasting impact than the prematurity itself.

Another example of a less severe developmental disability is infants with an unattractive craniofacial deformity. Here we see a pattern similar to that observed for premature infants. Mothers of these infants appear to be less nurturant than parents of typically developing children during the early part of the first year (Barden, Ford, Jensen, Rogers- Salyer, & Salyer, 1989). By the end of the first year, however, there are no differences in attachment security between these infants and typically developing infants (Speltz, Endriga, Fisher, & Mason, 1997).

Lasting interactive deficits are seen in more serious disorders (Hauser-Cram, 1996). One study of 110 infants with special needs (with Down's syndrome, cerebral palsy, and developmental delay) found that the infants with special needs smiled and vocalized less than the matched sample of typically developing infants (Brooks-Gunn & Lewis, 1982). In fact, one-third of the infants with special needs never smiled in the first two years of life, although by age 3, 80% had smiled. These babies cried more at older ages than the controls. Children with cerebral palsy are likely to receive less maternal warmth if they are not walking by 3 years of age than if they walk earlier (Korn et al., 1978). In the second year, parents of infants with any kind of physical disability are both more reinforcing of what the child actually can do and more likely to ignore the larger number of difficulties the child experiences than are parents of typically developing infants (Wasserman, Allen, & Solomon, 1985).

Down's syndrome babies tend to be slower to develop than typical infants. Parents tend to interrupt their Down's syndrome infants' vocalizations more than their typically developing infants', even though the Down's infants vocalize less (Berger & Cunning- ham, 1983). Although most 4-month-old infants, when presented with a maternal "still face" during social interaction (see Chapter 6), will cease smiling and gaze away, Down's infants actually gaze longer and may even smile (Legerstee & Bowman, 1989). This suggests that Down's babies may be overstimulated by social interaction and find it easier to express themselves when mothers are relatively quiet. Other research has shown that maternal attention-directing strategies during object play are usually less successful with Down's babies, and coordinated joint attention episodes are less frequent (Cielinski, Vaughn, Seifer, & Con-

treras, 1995; Landry & Chapieski, 1989; Legerstee & Weintraub, 1997). In response to these actions, mothers of Down's babies are likely to respond less and to attempt new interactions less than mothers of typically developing infants (Brooks-Gunn & Lewis, 1982; O. Jones, 1977). The prognosis for Down's syndrome infants is better when there is high family cohesion and a sensitive mother-infant relationship (Hauser-Cram et al., 1999).

Down's syndrome infants are also less likely to be securely attached than are typically developing infants, although this may be due in part to their cognitive deficits and inability to understand the strange situation (Atkinson et al., 1999). In general, infants with neurological disorders are more likely to be insecurely attached than other special needs infants. If there are no neurological problems, there are few or no differences between special needs and normally developing infants (Clements & Barnett, 2002; Tessier et al., 2002).

Blind and deaf infants are a special case because they have sensory but not cognitive or motor deficits. Parents of blind infants feel less attached and are likely to interact less with their infants (Fraiberg, 1974). Blind children, for example, are delayed by up to 1 year in the communicative skills discussed in Chapter 6. During the second year, they do not use gestures like pointing, showing, or giving, they do not seem to be oriented to external objects, they show few intentional behaviors, and they do not, of course, look at the parent for social referencing. Blind infants do not engage in pretend play or use spoken language until their third year or later. They also do not imitate adults (Preisler, 1997).

These deficits make it very difficult for parents to establish frames for coordinated joint attention (see Chapter 6), a cornerstone of development of the self and of communication. This means that parents must work hard to observe subtle signs of attention in the infant. They tend to overcompensate, which further delays the emergence of initiative taking in the child. Once language begins to be acquired in the third year, blind children become more socially oriented. Even so, they require an environment in which others remain visually attentive to them and can pick up their sometimes subtle cues (Preisler, 1997; Recchia, 1997).

Deaf children in general fare better developmentally than blind children. Most of the forms of establishing coordinated joint attention are visual, and the deaf child can observe parents, imitate, gesture, and produce typical facial expressions. Even with gesture and sign language, deaf children may be somewhat delayed compared to hearing children (Bornstein, Haynes, Pascual, Painter, & Galperin, 1999). Interestingly, deaf mothers of deaf infants and hearing mothers of hearing infants are both rated as more sensitive than unmatched dyads in which either mother or infant is deaf. The matched dyads also spend more time in episodes of coordinated joint attention. These findings suggest that the more attuned the mother is to the infant's communicative actions, the more the dyad is co-regulated (Meadow-Orlans & Spencer, 1996).

Some research has shown that the developmental prognosis is better for infants with special needs whose social interactions with their mothers are more like those of typically developing infants. The frequency of social interaction in the early part of the first year of life predicted a child's competence at age 2 on the Gesell Developmental Schedule, the Bayley Scales of Infant Development, and a language development scale (S. E. Cohen & Beckwith, 1979). This suggests that the more parents treat their infants as if they were typically developing children with special problems rather than as abnormal or problem children, the better off the children are in the long run. Several studies have shown that if maternal question asking, which is found at high frequency for typically developing infants, is maintained at a high level for special needs and language-disordered infants, it can have a marked effect on their social and communicative development (J. S. Leifer & Lewis, 1983; Yoder, 1989).

One problem is that often parents may not understand the nature of their child's disorder. Another is that parents have trouble being happy and playing with a baby that is less responsive. Even when the baby makes an occasional response, the parent often is unprepared and is not able to anticipate an appropriate answer (Fogel, 1982b; Koester, 1994).

What Can Be Done to Help Parents Help Their Children with Special Needs?

Intervention programs designed to educate parents about their children's disabilities, to provide emotional support and the supportive network of a system of peers (other parents with similar problems), and to teach parents how to respond to and anticipate the needs of their individual children have a significant success rate. Mothers in such intervention programs enjoy and respond more to their infants (Bromwich & Parmalee, 1979; Calhoun, Rose, Hanft, & Sturkey, 1991; Field, 1981a; Fraiberg, 1974; Glidden, 2002; Kellyi & Booth, 2002). Parents who are more positive about improving the family communication are more likely to participate in such programs (Gavidia-Payne & Stoneman, 1997).

In addition, local and state governments provide support services for children with special needs through child care and school systems, as well as through hospital programs. Federal funds are available through such programs as Developmental Disabilities, Early Periodic Screening Diagnosis and Treatment, Head Start, Education of the Handicapped (PL 94–142), Title XX Social Services, and the National Institute for Mental Health. Most of these programs make funds available through community and state education and welfare agencies (McPherson, 1983).

Another federal law (PL 99–457) provides for family-centered, rather than child-centered, services. This law encourages the states to implement comprehensive, multidisciplinary, and interagency services for early intervention with families and children who have special needs. The program focuses on identifying family strengths, goals, and needs while developing an intervention plan to meet those needs (Rounds, 1991).

On the other hand, is it sometimes difficult for parents to obtain the services they need. Free services vary in availability and quality according to school districts and income levels. A government funded program may not suit the needs of a particular child or family, who then need to obtain private services at their own expense. The more serious the disorder, the more it costs to support it, and many families who do not have access to services or who cannot afford them are left without support (Diamond & Kontos, 2004; Glidden, 2002).

John D. McKee, who was born in 1919 with cerebral palsy, writes articles and books about what it is like to grow up as a special needs individual. In his autobiography, he writes eloquently about his life and family (McKee, 1974). His works express ideas that modern scientific research is only beginning to discover: that knowledge burns brighter than ignorance, that all children need love and a chance to make it on their own, and that a sense of humor is one of the best shields against depression and guilt. McKee wrote:

> At home with my family, I was perfectly relaxed. If I spilled something at the table, it was only as if one of my brothers spilled his milk or dropped his bread butter-side-down on the floor. Once in a while, if I was having a particularly tough time and was spreading my food around the dining room with a lavish hand, Mother would say, "Why don't you sit on the floor, Jack? Anything that falls up, we'll hand down to you." In the laugh that followed, the tension was broken, and I could usually finish my meal with a minimum of spilling. (McKee, 1974, p. 201)

INFANTILE AUTISM: A DISTURBANCE OF SELF AND RELATIONSHIPS

Autism is a developmental psychopathology with symptoms that include impaired ability to interact socially, speech and language deficits, and unusual movements of the body. About two to four times as many males as females are diagnosed with *autism spectrum disorders* (ASD). This range of disorers related to autism has increased in its incidence in the past ten years. Recent statistics about autism compiled from sources including the National Institutes of Health, the Centers for Disease Control and Prevention, the U.S. Department of Education, and the Autism Society of America (NECC, 2010) show that it affects 1 in 250 births and 1 to 1.5 million Americans. It is the fastest-growing developmental disability, and the increase from the 1990's is 172%. The annual cost of services for autism is currently $90 billion and 90% of the costs are in adult services. The cost of lifelong care can be reduced by 2/3 with early diagnosis and intervention.. This increase is not due solely to better diagnoses (Baird et al., 2006; Newschaffer et al., 2007; Rutter, 2005).

Autistic children have a difficult time establishing coordinated joint attention with others, and therefore they are not able to enter into early forms of intersubjectivity by which typically developing infants acquire an understanding about relationships, self, and others (Chapters 6 and 7). Autistic infants do not use social referencing or affective sharing, do not respond appropriately to the desires or distress of others, are less distressed at separation from mothers, are less likely to imitate others, do not pretend, and are unlikely to initiate social interaction. When they talk, it is typically in monologues, and they have a difficult time letting others contribute to the conversation.

By the time typically developing infants are 18 months old, they have established a sense of an existential self and existential other (Chapter 5). It is quite likely that many autistic children never develop this ability. Children diagnosed with autism do not show embarrassment in front of a mirror or when getting a photo taken, and they do not seem to have a sense of guilt, suggesting that they cannot see themselves in the eyes of others. Autistic children are less likely to use personal pronouns or to refer to themselves in conversations (Carpenter, Tomasello, & Striano, 2005; Charman et al., 1997; Hobson, 1990; 1993; Hobson & Mayer, 2005; Hobson et al., 2006; Ozonoff & South, 2001; Sigman & Kasari, 1995; Sigman & Ruskin, 1999; Tanguay, 1990; Trevarthen, Aitken, Papoudi, & Robarts, 1998).

On the other hand, autistic children can develop secure attachments with their mothers (Ozonoff & South, 2001), although autistic children are more likely to show disorganized patterns of attachment even with parents rated as sensitive (van Ijsendoorn et al., 2007). They can use pointing and requesting gestures to ask for what they want, even though they may have a difficult time in establishing coordinated joint attention (Camaioni, Perucchini, Muratori, & Milone, 1997). They can also be more advanced in some perceptual and object-related skills. They can imitate object-related tasks better than typically developing children but have a difficult time imitating facial expressions, vocalizations, and social movements.

Research has shown that autistic children differ from both typically developing children and children with other developmental disorders. Compared to children who are either hearing impaired, language impaired, or mentally retarded, or who have no disorders, 3-to-6-year-old autistic children are less likely to be able to perform motor imitation—such as imitating stirring a cup with a spoon, talking on a toy telephone, giving a drink to a toy animal, touching their nose, or raising an arm. Autistic children's play is less likely to be symbolic and more likely to be aggressive or self-stimulatory, and they are less likely to approach peers to initiate social play. Finally, autistic children are more likely to use toys in ways different from their appropriate functions, such as banging a toy telephone rather than pretending to talk (Heimann, Ullstadius, Dahlgren, & Gillberg, 1992; Sigman & Ruskin, 1999; W. L. Stone, Lemanek, Fishel, Fernandez, & Altemeier, 1990). On the other hand, they can acquire pretend play when adults use guided participation strategies (see the Chapter 6).

One of the more unusual features of a small number of autistic children is that they may be exceptional in one specific area. Some autistic children can solve remarkably complicated mathematical calculations in their heads much faster than someone with a calculator can do it. Some are gifted artists but draw only one subject, such as public buildings and monuments. Some have specialized knowledge in an odd area such as plumbing fixtures or animal classifications. The popular 1988 movie *Rain Man* starred Dustin Hoffman as an autistic adult who had exceptional abilities in arithmetic and baseball statistics but was unable to relate in ordinary ways to other people. It is important to remember, however, that autism covers a wide spectrum of symptoms, and only a few autistic individuals will behave like Rain Man.

Autism is very difficult to treat. In the most severe cases, individuals may remain institutionalized all their life (as in *Rain Man*). Others, known as high-functioning autistics, have been able to hold jobs and create a life for themselves. One autistic adult, Temple Grandin, has become a well-known agricultural engineer and has written her autobiography as well as a book about the feelings and experiences of animals based on her experiences as an autistic person (Grandin, 2005; Grandin & Scariano, 1986). Another autistic adult, Donna Williams, has also written a series of books about her life (Williams, 1999), which was marked with abuse and neglect in addition to autism. The prognosis for most autistic children, however, is that they will change little and acquire only minimal social skills (limited receptiveness to others, socialization to rules) and self-care (Harty, 1990; Lelorde, Barthelemy, Martineau, & Bruneau, 1991).

Since treatments for autism occur in later childhood, they are beyond the scope of this book. A wide variety of treatments are available, however, with wide differences in their claims for success. Some people think autism can be cured, while others believe that treatment can only improve the quality of life for autistic individuals and help their families to understand the unique characteristics and contributions of people with autism (Trevarthen et al., 1998).

Autism is believed to have its origins in early infancy and possibly prenatal development. It is known to be associated with some genetic and chromosomal abnormalities and may result from brain and other physiological problems that emerge during early development. These include abnormalities in the limbic system, the auditory region of the brain stem, and myelin pathologies. Children with autism have impairments in the limbic areas of the brain—the amygdala—responsible for regulating fear (see Chapter 5), suggesting that some of their behavior may be withdrawal from an environment perceived as threatening. Some evidence suggests that the genes responsible for regulating the growth rate of the brain may be impaired, resulting in too rapid brain cell growth, followed by insufficient pruning of unused cells (Courchesne, 2004; Dawson et al., 2004; Herault, Martineau, Petit, & Perrot, 1994; Kemper & Bauman, 1993; Singh, Warren, Odell, Warren, & Cole, 1993; Trevarthen et al., 1998; Wong & Wong, 1991).

Even though autism originates in early infancy, it typically is not diagnosed until children are between 4 and 5 years of age. One reason for this is the low incidence of the disorder (1 per 250 children; NECC, 2010). In addition, the symptoms change with age and may overlap with other problems, such as hearing and speech disorders. If autism could be diagnosed earlier, preventive and more successful treatments might be possible. Recently, some breakthroughs in the early diagnosis of autism have occurred.

The methodology used by the researchers involves comparing autistic children, diagnosed at age 4 or 5 years, with nonautistic children. The researchers search for records of these children's development before the age at which they were diagnosed. Past medical records, parent interviews and reports, home videos of children's first-year birthday parties, and various other records have all been searched for data. Although these data sources are not always reliable, a consistent pattern of findings is beginning to emerge.

By the age of 18 months, there are clear signs of difference between typically developing and autistic children. One study discovered four behaviors that, if they occurred together in the same 1-year-old child, led to a correct classification

of these children as later diagnosed with autism. These behaviors were lack of pointing, of showing objects, of looking at others, and of orienting to their name. Another study found that children with two or more of the following symptoms at 18 months were most likely to be diagnosed as autistic at 30 months: lack of pretend play, lack of pointing, lack of interest in social relationships, absence of social play, and inability to establish joint attention with the caregiver. Specialists recommend that an 18-month-old who shows this combination of symptoms be referred to a specialist in autistic assessment for possible diagnosis and treatment (Adrien et al., 1993; Baron-Cohen, Allen, & Gillberg, 1992; Osterling & Dawson, 1994; Rogers & DiLalla, 1990). There is now a website for parents showing video clips of normal and autistic infants of this age, which is intended to help parents decide whether their child should be referred for diagnosis: (www.autismspeaks.org).

Many of these signs of early autism are based on small sample research and anecdotal evidence. An alternative method is to sample a large randomly chosen population of infants at 18 months, assess them on a few chosen criteria, and then determine whether they later develop autism. A study of 16,000 children was done in England. At 18 months, all the children were assessed for ability to point, to engage in social communication, and to pretend play. Twelve out of the 16,000 children failed all three of these tests, and of these, ten were diagnosed as autistic at 3 ½ years of age. Of the children who failed one or two of the items, none was later diagnosed as autistic. In spite of the small numbers of autistic children that appeared in the sample, the three factors were highly predictive of autistic symptoms in early childhood (Baron-Cohen et al., 1996).

This large population study illustrates the difficulty of doing research on the early screening of autism. Autistic children make up a small percentage of the population, so many thousands of children have to be tested. This is extremely costly and time consuming. However, large population research and small sample studies together are yielding a converging pattern of social and symbolic deficits that characterize autism as a developmental disorder.

One of the implications of all this research is that autism is a disorder of the brain and of cognition that makes it difficult for these children to comprehend the features of social interaction and to process emotions that will lead to the development of a sense of self and other. Another possibility is that autism is related to a deficit in sensory and motor patterns that, from an early age, prevents these infants from engaging with the environment in such a way that their brains and minds can understand what is needed.

One recent research study has discovered abnormal movement patterns between 4 and 6 months of age that are presumed to distinguish autistic from typically developing infants (Teitelbaum et al., 1998). The authors studied the home videos of 17 infants who had been diagnosed with autism when they were 3 years old and compared them with home videos of typically developing 4-to-6-month-old infants. When rolling over, for example, typically developing infants turn their pelvis to one side, followed by the trunk, and then the head. Later they lead with the head, followed by the trunk and pelvis. Three of the babies later diagnosed with autism turned over by lying on their sides and, while lifting their heads and legs at the same time, flopped their body in a single movement either onto their backs or onto their stomachs. Some of the autistic infants fell from sitting positions easily, showing no compensatory actions, so that they appeared to topple like a cut tree. When learning to crawl, some of the autistic infants had a hard time adjusting their base of support, leaned on their elbows instead of their hands, and had a difficult time distributing their weight evenly because of asymmetries between right and left sides.

Although this study provides some possible new directions for the study of the causes of autism, it must be read with caution. First of all, the authors were not consistent in reporting the numbers of children with such deficits. They typically discussed only one or two infants or used words like "some infants [showed the deficit]." Thus, we do not know if any of the autistic children were more typical, or if any of the typically developing children had some of these similar deficits. Finally, the coders of the infant's movement patterns were not blind to whether the child was autistic or typically developing.

It is well known that autistic children and adults have motor asymmetries and sometimes walk unsteadily. They often have an aversion to touch, eye contact, and other forms of sensory overstimulation. Autistic children's difficulty in imitating another person is believed to be due to neuromotor deficits, the failure to clearly link perception and action (Ozonoff & South, 2001). Both Donna Williams and Temple Grandin describe the difficulties they have with being touched, for example, and the lengthy process by which they discovered means to safely touch and be touched. It is plausible, therefore, that movement and sensory deficits may play some role in autism. If an infant has to struggle with something simple like turning over, their participatory experiences of everyday life may be extremely difficult, creating disturbances in the sense of an ecological self. In later development, one can imagine that these early disturbances of the ecological self may become transformed, through social and cognitive development, into later pathologies of the existential self.

In summary, diagnosis of autism in the second year involves deficits in the very behaviors and skills that are acquired by typically developing 18-month-old infants: social intersubjectivity, a sense of an existential self, and, as we shall see in the next section, a wide repertoire of self-conscious emotions. Diagnosis in the first year points to sensorimotor deficits. Most treatment approaches for young autistic children focus on improving the child's ability to engage with another person and to develop coordinated joint attention. The studies of sensorimotor deficits may lead to new ways of treating infants for movement and sensory disorders that might possibly affect the development of the brain and improve the chances for later cognitive and emotional development. There is always the hope that treatments begun early enough may have a more lasting effect than treatments begun after 4 or 5 years of age.

INFANT AND CHILD MALTREATMENT

Child abuse and neglect are two forms of child maltreatment that should concern anyone who cares about the welfare of children. These problems can take a number of forms that vary in relative severity. *Abuse* typically refers to cases in which a child sustains a non-accidental injury from a parent or other caregiver. *Neglect* is a pattern of ignoring the basic developmental needs of the child for physical and psychological support and nourishment which are typically the responsibility of the caregiver to provide (Strauss & Kantor, 2005).

Estimates of the incidence of child abuse and neglect are not very accurate due to deficiencies in reporting procedures. Approximately 5 million cases of suspected child abuse were reported to Child Protective Service agencies in the United States in 2000. Although not all of these cases are confirmed, the number of children abused may actually be higher because not all cases are reported. It is estimated that 3 to 5 children die every day as a result of abuse, with children under one year accounting for almost half of the deaths, and 18,000 children per year receive permanent disabilities from abuse. Abuse occurs equally in all ethnic and income groups and for both boys and girls, but girls are 4 times more likely to be sexually abused. At least 20% of American women and 5 to 15% of men are likely to have been sexually abused as children (Lambie, 2005).

What Are the Causes and Effects of Child Maltreatment?

No one knows for sure what causes child maltreatment, although certain factors have been implicated. The four most important are: (1) child characteristics, (2) parental personality, (3) the history of the parent-child interaction, and (4) the

relative level of social stress on the family (Belsky, 1980; Lamb, 1978b).

Some infants and children, by virtue of being endowed with undesirable characteristics, are more likely to be maltreated. Infants who are handicapped, slow to develop, or relatively unresponsive, or who are judged to have a difficult temperament place demands upon their caregivers that typically developing infants do not. Research suggests that premature infants and infants with special needs, Down's syndrome, and other illnesses are over- represented in the maltreated population (Bugental & Happaney, 2004; Sherrod et al., 1984; Sidebotham & Heron, 2003; Wu et al., 2004). These babies are often expensive to care for and thus contribute to family stress. They require more effort and are more fussy and demanding than other infants. In addition, they show less positive emotion and therefore provide fewer reinforcements for the caregiver.

Parental factors play an important role in child abuse. Abusive parents show fewer positive emotions, interact with their babies less, are more likely to use control strategies and physical punishment with their infants, and talk less to their babies than do non-abusive parents (Boddy & Skuse, 1994; Burgess and Conger, 1978; Straus, 1994). Abusive parents are less adept at verbal skills in general, score lower in abstract reasoning, and show a reduced capacity for planning and control over impulses. Abusing fathers, in particular, are lower in parental warmth and interpersonal relationships, and they are more introverted than non-abusive fathers (Hyman & Mitchell, 1977; Wu et al., 2004). Child abusers have been found to be hypersensitive to their infants. Instead of adaptively tuning out a loud or piercing cry, the abusers are likely to become annoyed and aroused by the crying (Frodi & Lamb, 1980).

Abusers are less able to correctly identify emotion signals, and in some cases, they interpret negative emotion as positive (Kropp & Haynes, 1987). Compared to non-abusing parents, child abusers view child rearing as less satisfactory and more difficult, and they and their children tend to live more isolated lives (Hutcheson, Black, & Starr,

1993; Trickett & Susman, 1988). Some evidence suggests that parents who abuse their children were themselves abused as children (R. Parke & Collmer, 1975; Weston, Coolton, Halsey, & Covington, 1993).

Parents who neglect their children but do not abuse them seem to be somewhat different. The overall picture of the abusing parent is of a hypersensitive and non-empathic person. The neglectful parent, in contrast, seems to be more apathetic and depressed (Polansky, 1976). Fortunately, none of these factors conclusively predicts that parents actually are going to abuse or neglect their children. Many parents who suffer from these problems in their personality or personal histories never show signs of maltreating a child.

Another important factor in child maltreatment is family stress. Higher rates of child maltreatment have been recorded in lower social classes (Bugental & Happaney, 2004; Burgess, 1979; Garbarino, 1976; Garbarino & Crouter, 1978; Gil, 1970). The stress in lower-income families may be caused by a number of factors. Low income is one factor, but economic stress alone is not a major factor (Berger, 2004; Garbarino, 1976). More important ones seem to be the availability of social support systems and the stability and continuity of day-to-day existence. Families whose size, composition, and location are constantly changing are more at risk for maltreatment than others. Higher welfare benefits and more social support reduce the likelihood of abuse (Berger, 2004; Huebner, 2002; Lyons, Henly, & Schuerman, 2005).

Maltreated children do not fare as well as children who have not been maltreated. At 2 years, maltreated children show more anger, frustration, and opposition, as well as a relative slowdown in developmental progress over the first year (Egeland & Sroufe, 1981; Éthier, Lemelin, & Lacharité, 2004). They are less likely to show pride in succeeding on a task and also less likely to show shame when they fail than are typically developing children, suggesting that they have deficits in their formation of a sense of an existential self (Alessandri & Lewis, 1996). In a day care setting, maltreated children are less likely to seek comfort from adult caregivers, more likely to avoid contact with caregivers and peers, and more likely to be aggressive (George & Main, 1979).

Several studies have found that the attachment patterns of maltreated children do not fit into the three typical categories used in the Ainsworth Strange Situation Test. Resistant infants alternate between clinging and pulling away, while avoidant infants tend to ignore the presence of the mother and reject her advances. Maltreated infants' response to the Strange Situation has been described as disorganized/disoriented, comprised of a strong proximity seeking of the mother on reunion, followed immediately by a strong avoidance of her or gaze aversion while approaching her (Carlson, Cicchetti, Barnett, & Braunwald, 1989; Lamb, Gaensbauer, Malkin, & Schultz, 1985; Main & Solomon, 1986). This pattern may be the result of fear of the mother mixed with normal attachment motivations, creating a conflict between approach and withdrawal (see Chapter 7).

These effects may all have a common source in disturbances of the neurohormonal systems responsible for the emotion regulation, responsiveness to fear and stress, and **post traumatic stress disorder** or PTSD (see Chapter 5). Maltreated infants and children have dysregulated **HPA axis** and **cortisol** levels, higher **sympathetic nervous system** activation, are more likely to show symptoms of PTSD, such as perceiving danger even when it is not present and inability to cope with normal life stresses (Bugental, Martorell, & Barraza, 2003; Pollak et al., 2005; Shea et al., 2004).

Other negative effects of maltreatment on infants include a lack of concern for the distress of peers and an often inappropriate response to distress, such as physical aggression (Main & George, 1985). Compared to non-maltreated ones, maltreated infants have shorter MLU (mean length of utterance), less speech related to their own emotional states, and less speech that is relevant to the ongoing topic of conversation (Coster, Gersten, Beeghly, & Cicchetti, 1989).

Since the children in these studies are under the age of 3 years, the conclusions are very disturbing. They suggest that abusing parents can disrupt the usual developmental process by which infants come to seek help, comfort, and information from people around them. In other words, maltreated children as young as 2 years old show behavior that is non-adaptive to the extent of avoiding those who might offer and extend support and encouragement.

These findings also suggest that maltreated children have already developed serious distortions in their sense of self. They do not seem to take an interest in their own achievements, do not share an appreciation of community standards, and do not have a well-developed theory of mind. If maltreatment occurs under the age of 3 years, children may retain participatory memories of the maltreatment that never become translated into verbal forms of knowing (see Chapter 5). This means that their autobiographical memories lack a means of understanding their nonverbal behavior. Therapeutic interventions—both psychotherapies and somatic therapies (see Chapter 2)—that address the participatory memories are likely to be most helpful.

What Are the Limitations of the Research on Child Maltreatment?

All the factors previously mentioned are probably interrelated in their impact on child maltreatment. For example, mothers of a lower social class have higher rates of special needs and premature infants. However, it is possible that the reporting rates are higher for lower-class children than for middle-class children. A more difficult problem is that the causes of child maltreatment are likely to be specific to the situation: some factors are more likely to operate with certain people than with others (Garbarino, 1982). Research designs that do not take into account the complex interactions among different types of people, circumstances, and infant characteristics will find few systematic effects.

Another problem with research on child maltreatment is that studies almost always begin with a sample of maltreated infants and maltreating parents. The search for causes of child maltreatment then is limited to only those people who actually demonstrate the symptom. Usually, researchers try to trace the maltreating adult's or the maltreated infant's history back in time. Findings such as "child maltreaters were maltreated as children" and "special-needs infants are more likely to be maltreated" are typical conclusions from this kind of research.

When a target sample's history is traced backward through time, the study is known as a *retrospective study*. While it may be the case that most abusing parents have been maltreated as children, it is not true that a person who was maltreated as a child will become an abusive parent. If we looked at the data prospectively, we would have to sample all children in a generation, follow them until they became parents themselves, and then see which of them maltreat their children. Obviously, such a *prospective study* cannot be done. If it were, however, we would probably find that only a very small percentage of adults who were maltreated as children actually end up maltreating their own children.

What can be concluded from this evidence? A history of maltreatment in the family of origin is one factor that may contribute to a person's becoming a maltreating parent, but other factors must operate on maltreated children to make them into maltreating parents. We do not know what these factors are at present because of the difficulty of doing this kind of research. Social and cultural influences are major factors likely to affect the outcomes of parents with a history of maltreatment. We live in a society in which violence is accepted. It occurs in the streets, and we are inundated with mass media violence. Physical punishment is widespread, occurring in at least 35% of infants, and is often considered to be an accepted cultural practice in many communities (Garbarino, 1993; Gil, 1970; Holden, Thompson, Zambarano, & Marshall, 1997; Straus, 1994; Straus & Stewart, 1999).

Do these factors cause child maltreatment? It is hard to say, and still harder to do research that might establish a conclusive link between social values, physical punishent, and the incidence of abuse and neglect. We might think of doing a cross-cultural study in which we would select different cultural groups that place different amounts of value on violence and physical punishment and then look to see if this dimension correlates with child abuse or neglect. The problem is that these cultures are likely to differ on factors other than the value of violence, and we could not say whether violence alone, violence in combination with other factors, or those other factors alone were most responsible for the observed amount of child abuse.

It would not be totally unwarranted at this time, however, to say that abuse and neglect are social and family problems—not merely the result of individual factors in the parent. If this is true, it suggests that we can act to prevent child maltreatment by strengthening community and neighborhood support systems for parents, providing human services for families as a whole rather than for single individuals, and taking preventive measures to strengthen community support systems when the child is born (Berger, 2004; Huebner, 2002; Lyons, Henly, & Schuerman, 2005). Since the incidence of physical punishment for infants is much higher than even advocates for this disciplinary strategy would endorse, a stronger stand against its use and education about more authoritative parenting styles would also be helpful. The birth of a child invariably brings parents into contact with community institutions. Action at this time is essential, since some parents may not contact other community institutions until the child is in school, and by then it may be too late (Garbarino, 1982; Hamilton, 1989; Strauss & Stewart, 1999; Wiehe, 1989).

INFANT-PARENT MENTAL HEALTH

Infant development becomes at risk because of poverty (see Chapter 8) and maltreatment. It may also be the case that well-meaning and otherwise competent parents require help if their infants have special needs or are diagnoses with autism or an attachment disorder (see Chapter 7). Fortunately, there is a growing body of clinical practice and research on Infant-Parent Mental Health (IPMH) interventions that focus on the relationship between the parent as primary provider and the infant.

Basic Principles of IPM
by Mark Ludwig, LCSW, Associate Professor, Department of Somatic Psychology, California Institute of Integral Studies

Infant-Parent Mental Health is an emerging multidisciplinary specialization focusing on the relational context of the total development of young children with a deep commitment to transdisciplinary integration and to the treatment of developmental, relational, and emotional distress from a whole-child-in-relationship perspective. Mounting research evidence over the past 3 decades (Fogel, 1993; Stern, 1985; Tronick, 2007) has thrust the developmental and relational experience of infants into the foreground of clinical interest and mental health practice. Extensive professional and public interest in the significance of these early experiences for later child, adolescent and adult functioning has spurred even greater efforts to unravel the complexities of early psychophysical, neurological, and emotional development (Fonagy et al., 2004; Perry, 2005; Porges et al., 1999; Schore, 2003; Siegel, 2001) This research points toward the overarching and predominant developmental importance of the quality of the early caregiver-infant relationship (see Chapter 10).

Basic concepts of IPMH. The core of IPMH is a dynamic systems model of human development (see Chapter 2). Because of their extended gestation, human children require a prolonged period of needs management by caregivers. The child's needs system is therefore functionally inseparable from an intimate relationship with a caregiver and from the wider context of co-existing family, social, and cultural systems. We might think, for example, about the children's growing ability to participate in their own feeding by gesturing to communicate hunger, setting the pace of the feeding, and moving toward self-feeding. On the other hand, across the whole early feeding process, there is an interdependent need to rely on the caregiver to provide the nutritional elements and respond appropriately to the child's signals.

As children develop, their self-regulatory capacities grow to supplant this early interdependence with co-regulatory processes. As this happens, caregivers can help less with tasks the children can perform themselves, but continue to stand by in an attuned fashion to provide containment, support, and perspective. IPMH practitioners understand that humans "swim in a human sea," in a lifelong matrix of essential and sustaining mutual "holdings." A variety of research reviewed in this book indicates that the adult's capacity for forming and maintaining mature relationships is predicated on and predicted by the nature of the successes and shortcomings of early childhood relational experience (Fonagy et al., 2004; Sroufe et al., 2005).

In addition to dynamic systems thinking, attachment (Bowlby's theory; see Chapter 7) and psychoanalytic theories (see Chapter 2) are frequently blended to help understand the developmental impact of early child-parent interaction in IPMH. From Bowlby, the study of interactional behavior patterns and of the process by which children develop **internal working models** (see Chapter 7) of their caregivers and themselves have created a rich and sustaining framework for clinical intervention.

Donald Winnicott, the English pediatrician and psychoanalyst, was one of the first to emphasize a dyadic focus of this approach with his assertion that "there is no baby without a mother" (Winnicott, 1971). A similar perspective was described by Margaret Mahler and Louis Sander (Mahler et al., 1975; Sander, 1962), who proposed developmental stages during the first three years that involved changes in the infant-caregiver system (see Chapter 2). Renee Spitz extensively researched the massive developmental failures visited on institutionalized children who were not provided with regular intimate interaction with a stable caregiver (Spitz, 1965; see topic of deprivation in Chapters 2 and 10). Finally, Selma Fraiberg, a psychoanalytically oriented clinical social worker, opened the door to the problem of transgenerational transmission of

developmental psychopathology when she introduced the notion of "ghosts in the nursery" (Fraiberg, Adelson, & Shapiro, 1975). The "ghosts' in question were the unconscious maternal thoughts and feelings about herself, her baby, and herself as a baby with her own caregivers—thoughts that had an impact on how she raised her own children.

Clinical practice in IPMH. In IPMH practice, the caregiver-child relationship is the "client" rather than the parent or the child individually. The unique constitutional elements of each member of the dyad as well as the particular qualities of the way in which they interact are relevant in this matter. Since it is often the case that parents who have unconscious ghosts were themselves maltreated, intervention with such parents can break the cycle of intergenerational transmission of pathology. Working with traumatized parents in relation to their infants has been called a search for "angels in the nursery," allowing such parents to tap into their own strengths and desires to be a better parent to provide the child with a sense of being understood, feeling accepted, and creating a sense of security (Lieberman et al., 2005).

Angels in the nursery may also be another adult in the family who does not cause the child stress. Here is one example of an adult remembering her childhood during a psychotherapy session. Note how the description is very sensory and feeling-based, suggesting the importance of pre-verbal experience.

> My aunt... she was just always a very gentle, very loving... she'd brush my hair very gently and never pulled my hair, like my mom did. My mom was always in a hurry to get the hair brushed... get it over and done with, and my aunt would just take her time, and be so gentle... She was like a warm blanket, she was just wonderful. (Lieberman et al., 2005, p. 509)

A good example of effective relationship-based IPMH practice is portrayed in the PBS Frontline documentary "When the Bough Breaks." Three middle-class families struggle with problems between parents and infants—sleeping and eating issues in this case— which they initially think are "in" their children. As the story unfolds, they and the viewers come to understand how the caregivers' attitudes and behaviors are an essential part of the story (view this online at www.frontline.org). The next section of this chapter, on the work of IPMH consultants, provides another example.

In the past, parents—and particularly mothers—were often blamed for "causing" the infant's problems. IPMH has a refreshing new take on this situation, using strength-based and collaborative models of caregiver facilitation. Caregiver curiosity regarding children and their internal world is actively supported. As a field that accepts the fact of transgenerational transmission of relational patterns, there has been a healthy reduction in caregiver scapegoating. IPMH is ultimately a preventative approach, responding to difficulties in the infant-parent relationship before they become major problems. Interventions are designed to make contact with the dyad in multiple ways, such as those shown in Table 9.12 (Weatherston, 2000).

Assessment and Diagnosis. A growing number of assessment tools can be used by IPMH consultants to look at the qualities of the infant-parent relationship, such as temperament, dyadic "fit,"

rhythms, gaze coordination, and mutual arousal profiles (Barnard, 1985; Zeanah et al., 2005; Slade, 2005). Three decades ago there was a paucity of diagnostic classifications for disturbances of childhood and no relationship-based diagnostic systems of any kind. The DC: 0–3R (2005) is a diagnostic manual specifically for disorders of children under the age of 3 years. In addition to having categories for problems with separation, sleeping, feeding, anxiety, depression, and PTSD, the DC: 0–3R also has categories for different types of parent-infant relationships that may be problematic. Categories in the relationship dimension include disruptions in parental behavior serious enough to cause symptoms in the child, such as parents who are under-involved or over-involved having infants who are anxious or tense in response, or parents who are abusive or neglectful (DC: 0–3R, 2005).

Focus on Multiply Stressed Dyads. While IPMH treatment models are effective with a range of populations including "normal" families, the focus of treatment has typically been on multiply stressed infants and caregivers: premies, foster care, Child Protective Service cases, early Head Start referrals, drug and alcohol exposed infants. Two programs with a national scope are particularly relevant here. A Home Within is a pro bono

TABLE 9.12 Intervention Practices in Infant-Parent Mental Health

Explicate and encourage normal developmental processes

Educate the caregiver about being responsive to the child's needs

Stabilize and support the caregiver-child "fit"

Elucidate with the caregiver the unique qualities of this baby

Help support the caregiver's tracking, cueing and response processes

Support mutual attunement and make experiences shareable

Support the ability of the caregiver to self-reflect on own actions

Point out mutually reinforcing negative interaction patterns

Help parents to find pleasure in their relationship with the infant

Attend to the parent's own history of trauma and unresolved loss from childhood

Target punitive parenting practices and dysregulating caregiver and child behaviors within a context of cultural sensitivity

Support contingent communication and face-to-face exchanges especially those featuring mutually pleasurable transactions

Support the "something new" that can emerge in open dyadic interaction network of therapists and supervisors committed to guaranteeing long-term support for foster care children (Heineman & Ehrensaft, 2006). The Circle of Security (Marvin et al., 2002) model is an attachment-based, 20-week intervention that uses video clips of caregiver-child interactions in small caregiver-therapist groups. The focus is on education in attachment dynamics and supporting the healthy interaction patterns of each dyad. The original treatment methods were developed with families referred through the Spokane, Washington Early Head Start program.

Video Based Interventions. Frame-by-frame video microanalysis is an important technology for studying infant-caregiver interactions (see Chapter 1). Now, video-based interventions are also increasingly common in IPMH programs (Downing, 2005). Watching interactions together with the therapist provides the caregiver with an opportunity to jointly consider caregiving decisions and to reflect on internal states of self and child without the pressure of live interactions. In particular, video seems to facilitate caregiver attunement to the child's experience.

Since infants and children of mothers who suffer from depression or stress are at increased risk for social and emotional difficulties, these mothers should be under some form of psychological or psychiatric treatment. A number of intervention programs have become available. One type of program teaches mothers to focus on childcare tasks, to pay attention to the needs of their infants, and to use touch in addition to facial and vocal behavior (Field et al., 1985; Gelfand & Teti, 1990; Leitch, 1999; Pelaez-Nogueras, Field, Hossain, & Pickens, 1996). In one such program, the therapist makes a videotape of the mother and infant interacting. While watching the video with the mother, the therapist can point out times when the baby withdraws and teach the mother to regulate her own behavior while helping the baby (Beebe, 2004). Another type of intervention program focuses on increasing positive moods in the mothers and infants. This can be accomplished either by giving infants and/or their mothers daily massages or by

using music therapy (Field, 1998; Field, Grizzle, Scafidi, F., & Schanberg, 1996). Sensitive touch, apparently, can partially alleviate the effects of negative mood for mothers and for infants during periods of maternal unavailability.

Home Visits. Since the generative work of Selma Freiberg in the 1960s, home visits have been a staple of infant-caregiver work. IPMH-trained postnatal visiting nurses and mental health professionals have a uniquely potent point of contact. By and large, parents of young children, regardless of their opportunities and circumstances, are very invested in being good parents. Since the IPMH model is primarily a model of prevention, these early contacts provide important opportunities for support, education, referral, and information.

Infant-Parent Mental Health Consultants
by Dr. LaDonna Atkins, Associate Professor, Department of Family and Child Studies, University of Central Oklahoma

Elayna screams when other children get near her. At 17 months of age, she is very irritable, often throwing intense tantrums, especially when she is tired. Elayna has been attending an infant and child care center for about five months. The staff at the facility have become increasingly concerned about Elayna's behavior.

Elayna's mother is 21, single, and she was 19 when Elayna was born. Recently, overwhelmed with the stress of working to support herself and her child, she moved back in with her family to gain needed support for herself and her infant daughter. Not long after she moved back home, Elayna's mother and grandmother both expressed concerns for Elayna to the center staff. They described how the staff at the previous center Elayna attended would often call her mother, asking her to pick Elayna up because her incessant crying would keep the other infants awake.

After visiting with Elayna's family, the staff at the center decided to make an appointment with an infant-parent mental health (IPMH) consultant (see section on IPMH, this chapter). The staff hoped this consultation would assist with developing strategies to help them and Elayna's family provide a more healthful environment for Elayna and the other children at the center.

IPMH consultants can develop programs to help prevent future problems such as school failure, child abuse, sickness, and teen/adult mental illness. IPMH is an interdisciplinary field that is rapidly growing as a result of research identifying behavioral and mental health problems in infants and toddlers. As defined by the national professional advocacy organization, Zero to Three, IPMH includes "the young child's capacity to experience, regulate, and express emotions, form close and secure relationships, and explore the environment and learn. All of these capacities will be best accomplished within the context of the caregiving environment that includes family, community, and cultural expectations for young children" (Zeanah et al., 2005, p.4).

As described in the section on IPMH in this chapter, the field of IPMH focuses on relationship-based interaction, with the understanding that relationships are central to healthy development, and that an infant is best understood within the context of the important adults in his or her life. Infants learn about the world through relationships with their parents, family members, and care providers. Infants who feel secure and loved have better social and emotional skills. Research reviewed in this book has shown that early experiences impact a child's brain development, physical health, and life-long mental health (see, for example, Gunnar & Barr, 1998). Even an infant can display stress, as evidenced by problems with attachment, behavior, or digestion. Today, infants and toddlers face significant time away from their families, often, and unfortunately, placed in inconsistent and/or poor quality child care. Societal problems such as substance abuse, poverty, and maltreatment also contribute to IPMH problems.

Based on recent research indicating IPMH consultations can improve aspects of child-care programs, Elayna's child-care staff requests a referral, stating that Elayna is a child with challenging behaviors (Alkon, Ramler, and MacLennan, 2003). Carolyn Morris, a local IPMH consultant, agrees to the engagement. Carolyn observes Elayna in her child-care classroom, talks with her teachers, mother, and grandmother. As an IPMH specialist, Carolyn's goal is to develop an understanding of each family's challenges by occupying the role of keen observer and listener. Carolyn's role as an IPMH consultant is not to impose her own agenda, but instead, to listen to the experiences and desires of the family and care providers. For Carolyn, developing a sense of trust and respect for cultural and individual uniqueness is essential. Carolyn will gather information, self-reflect, and may suggest further assessments or strategies for improvement. Carolyn may work with the family on her own or as part of a team. When the fact gathering is complete, Carolyn will create a plan for the family and center, while still continuing to observe, discuss, and support the family as they care for Elayna's individual circumstances.

In Elayna's case, Carolyn recommended positive play activities to strengthen the bond between Elayna, her caregivers, and her family. Carolyn suggested the staff follow Elayna's lead but also encourage Elayna to engage in parallel type play so she can slowly get used to other children. Carolyn also encouraged the staff to evaluate their environment. She suggested the environment have several private spaces where Elayna could be off by herself. Carolyn encouraged Elayna's family to establish a predictable schedule. She also talked to the family about reading Elayna's cues so they could learn to use distraction techniques such as singing or reading a book before Elayna's tantrums started. Carolyn also made the decision to conduct additional observations of Elayna's attachment and her use of communication skills. She understands that her suggestions are only the first steps and eventually more assessments and/or therapeutic strategies may be recommended.

Child-care centers offer a unique setting for mental health consultants. Child care in America today serves a significant number of children.

The opportunity and need for educating caregiving staff and families is unlimited. IPMH specialists may also be found working in hospitals, home visitation programs, and community agencies. The increasing interest in IPMH has led many states and communities to adopt plans for varying levels of services for the under- three age group.

A growing need for more education in the infant and family field has spawned new training programs, and endorsement and certification programs are being implemented around the world. The first of the IPMH academic programs was the Infant Parent Mental Health Training Program at the University of Michigan. The Fielding Graduate University in Santa Barbara, California, now has a psychology doctoral program with an IPMH specialization. Other professional training opportunities in IPMH are: Zero to Three: a national program supporting early intervention; Interdisciplinary Council on

Developmental and Learning Disorders, Maryland; The Infant-Parent Institute, Champaign, Illinois; Infant-Parent Training Institute at the Jewish Family and Child Services, Boston, Massachusetts; Napa Infant-Parent Mental Health Fellowship Program, Napa, California; and the Erikson Institute, Chicago, Illinois. For more information, see www.zerotothree.org and The World Association for Infant Mental Health, at waimh.org.

Being an IPMH consultant is one of many careers in which it is possible to work with infants. Other careers are listed in Table 9.13. Careers vary considerably in the amount of training required (such as medical schools, nursing schools, business schools, massage schools, psychology or social work programs) and in the salaries of workers. More information about each career is available by searching the Internet.

TABLE 9.13 Careers in the Field of Infancy

Health Related Careers

Pediatrics
Pediatrician
Neonatologist
Neonatal intensive care unit worker
Nursing and Women's Health
Women's health nursing
Pediatric nursing
Neonatal intensive care unit nursing
Neonatal nursing
Obstetrician/gynecologist
Midwife
Doula

Technical
Biomedical Engineer
Neonatal intensive care unit technician
Designer/marketer of health and safety equipment

Nutritional
Nutritionist
Dietitian
Baby food salesperson

Early Intervention Programs
Infant-Parent Mental health consultant
Infant stimulation specialist
Rehabilitation/special education worker
Early intervention specialist, and program designer and assessor
Placement and adoption/foster care worker
Social worker/child protection worker
Audiologist/speech therapist
Child life specialist
Physical therapist
Child life specialist
Physical therapist
Massage therapist for infants and mothers
Feldenkrais, Bodymind Centering, Rosen methods, or Watsu practitioner
Pediatric Psychology
Developmental tester
Follow-up assessor and researcher
Psychosomatic disorders specialist

TABLE 9.13   Careers in the Field of Infancy (cont.)

Education-Related Careers

Infant Care
Child-care teacher, supervisor, or administrator
Infant/toddler nursery program teacher, supervisor, or administrator

Parent Education
Parent educator
Family life educator
Parent-chld programmer
Counselor for teenage parents
Psychotherapist or psychiatrist
Marriage and family counselor

College Teaching and Research
Researcher
College teacher
Administrator of college programs in early childhood and child development

Other Careers with Infants

Baby product salesperson, designer, or manufacturer
Toy salesperson, designer, or manufacturer
Baby clothing salesperson, designer, or manufacturer
Environmental and furniture designer for nurseries and child care centers
Journalist

Writer/producer of books and other media for young children
Legislative aide
Policy analyst
Child advocate
Web site designere
Media specialist

EXPERIENTIAL EXERCISE

Sucking
by Mark Reese, Feldenkrais Practitioner

Position: Lie on your right side in a fetal position. In other words, curl into a ball with your knees and arms bent, and place your hands not far from your mouth.

1. With your mouth slightly open, gently protrude your lips and tongue and then relax them. As you protrude your lips, allow them to turn slightly inside out. Keep your lips full, soft, and moist. Experiment with slower and faster rhythms. Try protruding your mouth sometimes a little to the left, sometimes to the right (rooting movements), and feel the difference in ease between the two directions due to the pull of gravity.

2. With your lips and tongue slightly protruded, begin to make soft sucking movements with your jaw and mouth. Note that this is very different from the ways you squeeze your lips when you suck through a straw. Try to sense how your head, neck, and the rest of your body become involved in the sucking movement. Rest often, and continue sucking. You will probably find that the longer you suck, the more you will feel how the movement involves your entire body. There is a tendency for the head to move a little forward and tilt slightly back, as if to help the movement of opening the mouth and reaching with it. This gentle movement of the mouth, jaw, and head tends to produce a soothing, wavelike movement down the entire spine, all the way to the pelvis and legs. Rest.

3. In order to help relax your mouth, use your fingers to gently pull your lower lip forward, softly coaxing it to turn inside out. Relax your mouth in order to make your lip more elastic. Rest, and notice the differences in sensation between your upper and lower lips.

4. Repeat the same movements with your upper lip.

5. Return to the sucking movements performed in step 2 and feel the difference. Is it easier? Is your mouth softer and more elastic? Begin to experiment with the length of the sucking bouts, making fewer or greater rhythmical

sucking movements before pausing. Rest.

6. If you want to continue the experiment, repeat movements 1 to 5 while lying on your left side and also on your back. Feel how the subtle effects of gravity are different in each position. After birth, the infant must suck differently due to the new needs to coordinate breathing and swallow milk. This is more complex than it might sound. Notice the timing of when you swallow in relation to sucking and how you move your mouth while you swallow. How does sucking influence your breathing just before and just after the swallowing takes place?

Comments

Sucking is one of many movements that we learn to do while still a fetus. Throughout our lifetimes, and especially during our fetal development, our movements help shape the form of our bodies. Just as later in infancy, weight bearing will alter the curvature of our legs and spine, sucking helps to form our palate. Babies who do not suck normally do not form the high palate that other children have. Also, how infants suck affects the development of their teeth and future patterns of swallowing and speech.

Sucking is the first mouth movement that we master. Later we build on our infant sucking ability as we learn to control thousands of other movements of our mouth and face, including chewing, expressing our emotions, speaking, and singing. Many people experience a deep relaxation of the facial muscles after doing the sucking movements in this lesson. What was your experience?

Feeling Helpless
by Alan Fogel

What would it be like to be a helpless newborn infant, someone who does not know anything about the world and who needs someone else to provide for all needs? Also, you don't have any words to communicate your needs, and you lack the basic skills necessary for making gestures. About all you've got are some facial expressions, body movements, and vocalizations like crying, fussing, burping, and grunting. It is actually very difficult for adults to simulate a newborn's experience, but you can try the following exercise.

Find a friend or relative with a good sense of humor and ask them to feed you with a spoon and give you a drink from a cup or glass. The food can be anything soft or liquid that you like. Of course, newborns don't eat or drink this way, but you can try out your repertoire of nonverbal and nongestural communication skills (fuss, cry, make faces, wiggle, turn toward or away) in order to communicate to your partner what you want or don't want, or like or do not like, about the way he or she is feeding you.

SUMMARY

Prenatal Health

- The action of the genes, as well as the occurrence of genetic disorders, depends on the interaction of the genes with their environments.
- Chromosomal disorders involve additions and deletions of chromosomes.
- Teratogenic effects occur when the maternal environment transmits harmful substances to the fetus. Alcohol, drugs, and diseases are among the common teratogens that produce birth defects of varying severity.
- The higher incidence of birth defects and premature births among teenage mothers can be attributed to the effects of poverty and poor prenatal care, rather than to the age of the mother alone.

- Many birth defects can be diagnosed prenatally through genetic counseling. Treatments include fetal medicine, postnatal intensive care, and abortion.

Newborn Health

- The art of newborn assessment is rapidly improving. Reliable and valid tests exist for determining the newborn's risk in terms of survival, neurological problems, gestational age, and behavioral status.
- Perinatal problems account for a large proportion of later deficits.
- Prematurity is the largest single category of birth complication and seems to be caused by a variety of prenatal factors.
- Premature infants are likely to be smaller and sicker and to lag behaviorally, compared to full-term infants.

- The most severe long-term deficits occur primarily for very-low-birthweight infants, under 1,500 grams. Most infants between 1,500 and 2,500 grams tend to recover eventually and lead normal lives, but many will show mild to severe effects of prematurity.
- The type of intervention that improves the long-term outcome for premature infants depends on the infant's gestational age and health. Medical interventions are improving and becoming less invasive. Behavioral procedures are extremely effective in improving health and weight gain at low cost. Parent education is also an effective strategy.
- The research on preterm infants suggests that late-term fetuses require movement, touch, sound, and sucking in order to continue their development, all forms of stimulation uniquely found in the prenatal environment.

Infant Mortality

- Abortion is a controversial issue in the United States, especially if it is done because of low income or for family planning. The rights of a woman to privacy conflict with the possible rights of the fetus in most legal decisions. It is difficult to establish when human life begins, but scientific research can add important information to the debate.
- Euthanasia for newborns is practiced under conditions in which the infant is likely to die or in which the treatment would unnecessarily prolong suffering.
- Parents and physicians need to consider a number of ethical issues in making decisions about euthanasia for newborns, including quality of life in the future for the child and family.
- Poverty and disease are the biggest causes of infant mortality worldwide.
- Supplemental maternal and infant nutrition, breast-feeding, growth monitoring, rehydration, and immunization can prevent many perinatal deaths.
- Parents who lose an infant can be expected to grieve in the usual manner and thus should be helped through this process by medical personnel and family.
- Euthanasia for newborns is a controversial topic that involves social, psychological, legal, and moral issues.
- SIDS does not have a known cause but is believed to be linked to sensorimotor difficulties of respiration.
- Several preventive steps can be taken with infants at risk for SIDS, but none is foolproof.
- Parents who lose a baby to SIDS need special counseling and understanding from relatives and their community.

Nutrition

- Proper diet and exercise is essential for maternal and fetal health during pregnancy
- Breast milk is superior to other forms of infant feeding. Infants should be breast-fed until twelve months and for as long after as mutually convenient for mother, infant, and family. Solid foods should be supplemented after 6 months.
- The age at which solid foods are started coincides with changes in the infant's physical and motor development that make eating solids possible.
- Foods should be introduced one at a time to allow babies to express possible allergies.
- Younger babies need food that is ground or mashed.
- Eating is a social experience, and parents should allow plenty of time for meals

Infant Health and Safety

- Caregivers need to be aware of the common sources of danger and accidents for infants.
- Caregivers should learn emergency treatment techniques to handle a variety of potential hazards.
- Health care and immunization is essential for normal development.

Infants With Special Needs

- Family members face a difficult period of adapting to an infant with special needs.
- The effect of a disability on the parent-infant interaction depends on the severity of the disability and how long it persists. In general, parents tend to adapt their behavior to suit the needs of the infant with special needs.
- Families are encouraged to seek support services to help with coping and education.

Infantile Autism

- A pathology of self and relationships, can be diagnosed as early as 18 months, which may lead to the development of new treatments.

Infant and Child Maltreatment

- Factors contributing to child maltreatment include child, parent, and societal influences. Child maltreatment is multicausal, and treatment approaches should recognize this.

- Research on child maltreatment is problematic because of the way the data are gathered and interpreted.

Infant-Parent Mental Health

- IPMH is an emerging field that focuses on the therapeutic and educational treatment of families at risk.

- IPMH consultants work in a variety of settings including child care centers, hospitals, and homes.
- There are a growing number of training programs in IPMH.
- A wide variety of careers involving infants are available. They vary in training requirements, working conditions, and salaries.

Chapter 10

The Effects of the Infancy Period on the Formation of Individual Differences

CHAPTER OUTLINE AND OVERVIEW

Development as a Complex Dynamic Process	*What is the importance of infancy? How does one's experience as an infant affect one's life?*
Research on Continuity	*What are the ways in which experiences during infancy can be related to later outcomes?*
Perinatal Factors	*What are the long-term consequences of premature birth and of prenatal and genetic influences?*
Motor Development	*Do advances or lags in infant motor development affect later motor skills?*
Parental Contributions	*What are the effects of having a working mother or being in child care? Do parents make a difference in children's later behavior and development?*
Risk and Disadvantage	*What are the conditions under which infants can recover from early risk factors?*
Culture	*How do cultural differences affect developmental outcomes?*
Gender	*Does infant experience affect boys and girls differently?*
Intellectual Development	*Is intelligence predicted by the amount or type of stimulation an infant receives?*
Temperament	*Do temperamental characteristics persist for long periods?*
Developmental Systems of Multiple Interacting Factors	*Can any single event, trauma, or factor that occurs during infancy have lasting consequences in a person's life? Can the effects of early trauma be alleviated?*

Is what happens to a person during infancy important or critical for later development? Do traumatic experiences in infancy, such as extreme poverty or maternal depression, affect later cognitive or social functioning? Can we predict whether a child will be bright, average, or dull from scores on assessment tests done in early infancy? Can later developmental dysfunctions be diagnosed from early infant testing? What is the importance of infancy in the human life cycle?

These questions have been reserved for the last chapter of this book for several reasons. First, answering them requires an examination of individual continuity and change across the entire age span of infancy and from infancy to later childhood and adulthood. Second, answering these questions requires an examination of the concepts and methods used in longitudinal research. Although we have discussed findings of longitudinal studies—such as the relationships between attachment at 12 months and peer competence in the preschool—we have not addressed the potentials and problems unique to the interpretation of such studies.

The questions raised in the first paragraph do not have simple answers. For some questions, we have no answers at all, aside from theoretical speculation. An appreciation of the research difficulties requires some familiarity with the way in which research in this area is carried out and the implicit and explicit theories that guide the work.

DEVELOPMENT AS A COMPLEX DYNAMIC PROCESS

Before getting into research and theory, it might help to put the questions raised in the first paragraph in a broader perspective. What do the answers to those questions mean to children, their families, and society? How, for example, should we interpret strong evidence predicting later outcomes from something that occurred during infancy? We might be pleased to find an early marker for some later disorder or an early sign of intelligence or social adjustment. If we are able to

predict with certainty how a person will turn out based on some early factor, does that mean there is little hope for people who suffer some kind of deficit or trauma during infancy? Does it mean that people are marked for life by things that happened to them before they could walk or talk?

Perhaps, what researchers hope is that evidence of strong prediction will lead us to discover ways to break down the grip of early experiences on negative outcomes by discovering new treatments or interventions. Advocates for early intervention and early enrichment programs look to evidence of strong prediction to make a case for their work. This logic, however, is somewhat contradictory, since strong prediction implies a lack of change. Does it make sense that the justification for a program intended to induce change is research showing that people do not change? Medical research operates on this principle. Once a link between a gene or a virus and some disease is found, researchers can then seek out treatments that deal with the root cause of the disease.

Now, consider the opposite: research that shows a lack of ability to predict later from early factors. Should we take this research as saying that infancy has no value, in the sense that early experiences or predispositions are unimportant for later outcomes? People who are against investing money on early childhood education and intervention programs, who would prefer to see public and private funds invested in helping older children succeed at school or preventing crime, take this kind of research as an argument for their position (Bruer, 1999).

Development Is a Complex Process Involving Many Factors

The research on long-term outcomes, reviewed in this chapter, does not fit either of these extreme possibilities. No single early factor—such as the prenatal environment, parental sensitivity, or infant temperament—predicts later outcomes 100% of the time. Most of the factors that we have studied in this book turn out to be both necessary and influential for later outcomes, but only some of the time, and only for some people and not others. The answers to the questions raised in the first paragraph, therefore, are not simple. Early development is a complex process, and we need to take the time to understand that complexity if we are to do justice to the important issues facing infants, families, and society.

The phases of an individual's life are never completely unconnected; there is always some influence of the earlier phases on later ones. Perhaps the most salient example of apparent developmental disconnection is the life cycle of moths and butterflies. Here we have stages of development that are so radically different—larva, cocoon, and adult—that it seems almost certain that the experiences of the larva, for example, could not impact on the adult. And yet there are such influences. The olfactory (smell) experiences of the larva have been shown to influence the food choices of the adult (Klopfer, 1988).

In humans, developmental processes of the infant are embedded in social dyadic and family systems, and families are embedded in the multiple and interconnecting systems of the larger society and culture. Several features of such complex systems are worth mentioning again here (see Chapter 2) in the context of this discussion of the effects of infancy on later development.

First, in complex systems, changes in one factor are likely to affect other factors in such a way that the system as a whole adapts to the change in any single part. We have seen countless examples of this kind of system effect in this book, as infants and parents, siblings and peers, and families and cultures affect each other in a variety of ways. Developmental outcomes are typically the result of a large number of factors acting in combination.

In the first paragraph of this chapter, we asked whether early factors have an impact on later outcomes. Perhaps a more systems-oriented way to ask the question is: *Under what circumstances, in what combinations, and for which types of individual do early factors impact later outcomes?* What are those combinations, and do they lead to positive or negative outcomes? Another way to say this is: *What is the developmental process by which desirable and undesirable outcomes are formed?* If a child exhibits a desirable tendency early in life, we would like to find ways to preserve it, and if he or she suffers an unfortunate circumstance early, we would wish to bring the individual back to a closer approximation of typical development and behavior.

Second, when systems are perturbed by some risk factor, the response of the whole system is not necessarily a change for the worse. Often, in fact, the system achieves a kind of dynamic balancing act in which it returns to a stable mode of functioning (Fogel, 1993; Fogel & Thelen, 1987; Sroufe et al., 2005; Thelen & Smith, 1994). A good example is the development of some premature infants. Due to the compensatory actions of the parents to provide extra support and stimulation for their infant at risk, the developmental course of the infant may approach that of fullterm infants, and the family system may return to a stable mode of functioning following an earlier period of stress and uncertainty. Alternatively, system dynamics may progressively move a child and family off the typical developmental course. An example of a continuing spiral of negative effects that amplify each other is the cycle of persistent poverty, ill health, infant disadvantage, and maladaptive parental behavior.

An explanation for why some family systems achieve stable states of positive functioning, becoming self righting after a trauma, and others become unstable must lie in the dynamic interactions between family members and between the family and society. The overwhelming body of research on the development of all species of animals suggests that the more complex the system and the more alternatives available (formal and informal supports, economic resources), the more likely it is that these multiple facets of the system will eventually absorb and defuse the negative effects of the initial trauma.

The more the continued trauma depletes the system of resources, the more likely that the child will develop some type of developmental difficulty (Brauth, Hall, & Dooling, 1991; Klopfer, 1988; Sroufe et al., 2005). Lack of resources constrains development and forces individuals into the limitations of their heredity and their early experiences. Availability of resources (home, family, nutrition, support, etc.) opens development up to a wider range of possibilities. In the research reviewed in this chapter, we will see examples in which early predispositions and risk factors were essentially eliminated as causal factors for later development, and in which later outcomes are a product of a complex set of events that are unique to each individual.

No Two Individuals Respond in the Same Way to the Same Situation

Individuals vary in how they are affected by any single factor in infancy that contributes to later developmental outcome (Wachs, 2000). In Chapter 9, for example, we found that suffering abuse as an infant does not guarantee that individuals will go on to abuse their own infant. Only a small proportion of abused children become child abusers. The IQ range of children who were prenatally exposed to alcohol can range from retarded to having normal intelligence. There is a range of severe to mild retardation even in the case of major genetic disorders, such as fragile X syndrome (Chapter 9). There is a wide range of outcomes, therefore, even when individuals have some things in common at an earlier point in time.

A number of theories of development suggest that such variability and complexity of outcome is the rule rather than the exception. Behavior ecology theory, for example, suggests that species evolve because each individual is different. If everyone were the same, there would be no opportunity for natural selection to guarantee survival. Species evolve because those individuals who are best able to survive live long enough to reproduce.

Dynamic systems theories suggest that very small perturbations—butterfly effects—may have unpredictable consequences for the growth of the system. Suppose you were able to chart the developmental histories of many individual infants, recording all the relevant family and environmen-

tal factors that may affect their development. This cannot be done, of course, because of the complexity of human individuals and their social systems. But if it could be done, do you think you could find, ultimately, a reasonable explanation for everything that individual does, and for how the individual develops over time? Many developmental researchers would say yes, given all the important data, they could predict in all cases the developmental outcomes of the person. As one such scientist puts it this way:

All scientists are determinists. It is difficult to imagine what not being a determinist could mean ... There is no magical force ... that shapes development, apart from genetic/biological systems that propel and guide development and environments that are necessary and provide opportunities for its expression. (Scarr, 1993, pp. 1342–1343)

Determinism is the view that all natural phenomena are the result of some specifiable cause or a series of interlocking causes (see Chapter 2). An alternative scientific perspective—based on dynamic systems theory—suggests that there is indeterminism in development:

Webs and chains of historical events are so intricate, so imbued with random and chaotic elements, so unrepeatable in encompassing such a multitude of unique (and uniquely interacting) objects, that standard models of simple prediction and replication do not apply. (Gould, 1994, p. 85)

Indeterminism is the idea that not all natural phenomena can be predicted from known laws or principles. In Chapter 2, we talked about the weather as a complex system in which chaotic or indeterministic factors play a role. Another example of an indeter- ministic process is the history of society. Many natural processes are **historical processes** in the sense that they are not simple accumulations of past events. Rather, they are uniquely emergent creations that can never be

What makes children different from each other? The formation of individual differences is a complicated field of study about which we understand very little. These children are all supposed to be doing the same thing, but each has interpreted it differently.
Photo by Felicia Martinez/PhotoEdit.

exactly repeated. Indeterminism, "magic," and butterfly effects are just as much a part of human development as determinism and logic (see Chapter 2; Fogel, Lyra, & Valsiner, 1997; Prigogine & Stengers, 1984).

Although some aspects of developmental change are determined by specifiable sequences of events, many outcomes are indeterminate (Fogel, 1993; Fogel & Thelen, 1987). Individuals are continually open to opportunities that they do not plan and cannot predict. A baby may discover an important contingency between his or her own behavior and something in the environment merely by chance, because the baby happened to turn his or her head to see something and was ready to follow up the opportunity without fully understanding where this direction might ultimately lead. Sometimes the infant is able to make sense of this foray into the unknown and sometimes not. Sometimes the meaning of the infant's attempt is clarified by an adult, who "explains" to the child what he or she just did.

One could argue that this "discovery" by the child is nothing more than a potentially knowable combination of genes and environments that predispose the child to make such a discovery. But is the fact that the child makes the discovery there and then, at that particular moment in his or her life, explainable? The child decides, in the emotion of the moment, to take the risk of jumping into something new and unknown or to stay within the safety of what is already understood. Is this decision determined in any logical way? And could the flowering into the social world of a previously shy or withdrawn child have been predicted even by the people most intimately connected with the child? Or could they have predicted that such a change would occur quite suddenly at a particular point in the child's developmental history?

In summary, there are two basic principles for developmental change. One is that *development is a complex multifactor process.* The other is that *no two individuals respond in the same way to the same factor—variability and the opportunity to capitalize on chance outcomes is inherent to the developmental process* (Fogel, 1993; Thelen & Smith, 1994; Wachs, 2000). In the next section of this chapter, we review some of the findings on the relationship between early infancy factors and later developmental outcomes.

Research on Continuity between Early and Later Development

Developmentalists generally talk about lasting individual differences in terms of the concept of developmental continuity. **Continuity** is the extent to which aspects of the individual are preserved from one age to another. The existence of developmental continuity means that a particular sensitivity or ability acquired in infancy is likely to affect the functioning of the individual in some way at later ages. There are many forms of continuity, some of which are listed in Table 10.1.

Continuity has been investigated in many different areas, all of which cannot be covered in this chapter. In this book, we have already reviewed a considerable amount of research related to continuity, although it has not been labeled as continuity research. We begin with a brief review of these topics, including perinatal factors; motor development; parental contributions; risk and disadvantage; culture; gender; intellectual development;

and temperament. The reader is encouraged to go back to the relevant sections from earlier in the book to re-examine them from the perspective of continuity.

PERINATAL FACTORS

The long-term effects of heredity on later behavior were discussed in Chapters 2 and 3. The data suggest that the effects of one's heredity are non-deterministic. That is, not everyone with the same types of genes or chromosomes will inherit the phenotypic characteristic typically associated with those genes or chromosomes. Even among those who show the phenotypic features, there will be a great deal of variation between individuals (Wachs, 2000). Some genetic structures have a higher probability of being expressed in the phenotype, and these structures are typically associated with severe disorders. The genetic contributions to behavior, cognition, emotion, and personality

TABLE 10.1   Forms of Developmental Continuity

Type of Continuity	Example
Absolute consistency	A lack of change during development. Once an ability is acquired, such as the ability to form attachments or to think symbolically, it is never lost or altered.
Consistent pattern of change	A particular ability has a predictable and invariant developmental course. For example, cooing, babbling, and single words precede the onset of language.
Consistent pattern of behavior	A predominant mode of behaving in spite of minor fluctuations. An infant who generally is withdrawn may show some instances of openness, but more usually, a pattern of withdrawal can be inferred across a variety of circumstances.
Consistent relation to the group	Even though developmental change occurs, individuals maintain their relative ranking within a group. For example, an infant grows taller but may always be short compared to other infants of the same age.
Consistency in process	Behavior is not consistent, but the underlying process may not be different across time. For example, a sensitive and warm social partner may be necessary at all ages, but the type of relationship will not be the same at each age (infant-mother, infant-teacher, infant-peer).
Consistency between early and later factors	Events and experiences early in infancy have an impact on some later outcome. For example, the security of early attachments predicts other social and cognitive abilities during the preschool years.

Source: M. Rutter, Continuities and discontinuities from infancy, 1987, p. 82. In J. D. Osofsky (Ed.), *Handbook of infant development*, 2nd ed., pp. 67–86. New York: Wiley.

have a much lower probability of being expressed universally in the phenotype because many genes are involved and because they require a specific set of environmental contingencies in order to be expressed.

Hereditary influence is an example of continuity in which there is a consistency between early and later factors (Table 12.1); that is, an early factor (the genes) is consistently related to a later outcome (for example, PKU or temperament). Our earlier discussion of heredity shows that strict continuity is observed only in some cases. It is more typical for environmental mediating factors to influence the way those genes are expressed or not expressed in the individual.

As we saw in Chapter 2, however, some researchers differ with this view. One behavior geneticist has claimed that the influence of the genes in explaining individual differences in outcomes is so strong that family influences "make few differences in children's personality and intellectual development" (Scarr, 1992, p. 3) unless the family is abusive or outside the typical range. More than 60 years ago, one of the pioneers of infant behavior research, Mary Shirley, reached a similar conclusion. She wrote that "although the personalities of the babies are undoubtedly influenced by training and treatment, strong characteristics are not ironed out by training" (Shirley, 1933, p. 207). The most recent research evidence suggests, on the contrary, that these statements are true for only a very small percentage of individuals. Most people are susceptible to a wide variety of influences—from family and society—that can limit or expand their genetic potentials (Plomin & Rutter, 1998; Wachs, 2000).

Another topic we have already discussed is premature birth and other perinatal factors (see Chapters 3 and 9). Newborns are susceptible to a wide range of perinatal problems ranging from oxygen deprivation to low birthweight. For all infants, the period immediately following birth is a time of adjustment from intrauterine to extrauterine life. An infant who suffers from one or more risk factors in the perinatal period may be unable to cope with the typical stresses of the first months of life

and therefore may fall behind in developmental progress.

In general, research has found that many perinatal problems can be at least partially alleviated by a supportive environment. In a multiracial, multiclass sample of 670 infants born on the Hawaiian island of Kauai, all groups of children—regardless of race, social class, or age of mother—had about the same proportion of perinatal complications. In this sample, 13% suffered moderate complications, and 3% had severe complications. However, group membership predicted how well the infant recovered from the complication. Children born into lower-income families were less likely to recover fully by age 2. By age 10, the effects of perinatal problems had all but disappeared for all the groups, but children from lower-income groups had lower scores on intelligence tests and were doing worse in school than children from middle-income groups (Werner, Bierman, & French, 1971). This research shows that between-individual variability is multidetermined in part by perinatal factors and in part by later environmental factors.

Other research in this area has supported these conclusions. In general, the more stressful the environment and the fewer economic and social support systems the parents have, the more likely it is that infants will not recover quickly from perinatal risk factors. The continuity with negative outcomes tends to be related to the total number of risk factors and/or traumas, which have an additive effect (Baker & Mednick, 1984; Bradley et al., 1994; Breitmayer & Ramey, 1986; Crockenberg, 1981; H. Johnson, Glassman, Fiks, Rosen, 1987; Rutter, 1987; Sameroff & Chandler, 1975; Sigman, Cohen, Beckwith, & Parmelee, 1981; Waters, Vaughn, & Egeland, 1980). In addition, even the same traumatic situation, if it continues over a long period of time, can also have cumulative effects. Short periods of harsh discipline, malnutrition, stress, or family instability have far less serious developmental outcomes than if those factors persist over many years (Wachs, 2000).

However, if there are adequate economic resources, if the parents are not under psychosocial stress, and if the perinatal complications are not too severe, the effects are usually not continuous over the long term. Continuity arises because of consistency in the environments to which the infant is exposed—environments that either alleviate or exacerbate the early risk factor.

In some cases, preterm infants may even be at some advantage with respect to full-term babies. At equivalent gestational ages (the time since conception), preterms have had more experience outside the uterus than full terms. Preterms begin to babble at earlier ages than full terms, presumably because they have had more exposure to auditory stimulation at the same gestational age (Eilers et al., 1993).

Another general proposition to emerge from this research is that the more severe the perinatal disorder, the more likely that long-term effects will be continuous. Infants who have very low birthweight (VLBW, less than 1,500 grams), for example, do less well in sensorimotor development during the first half year than other preterms (Gerner, 1999). Healthy preterms weighing more than 3,000 grams, on the other hand, do as well on sensorimotor tests as full terms (Bonin, Pomerleau, & Malcuit, 1998). By the gestational age of 2 years, when most preterms have caught up with full terms, VLBW infants are more passive, less attentive, and less securely attached to their mothers than full terms of the same gestational age. Some VLBW infants have continuing motor, social, cognitive, and attentional deficits at preschool and school age (Barrera, Rosenbaum, & Cunningham, 1987; Bracewell & Marlow, 2002; Kanazawa, Shimizu, Kamada, Tanabe, & Itoigawa, 1997; Landry, 1995; Langkamp & Harris, 1992; Mangelsdorf et al., 1996; Tessier, Nadeau, Boivin, & Tremblay, 1997; Vohr & Coll, 1985).

Other extreme factors, such as auditory neurological deficits measured at birth that relate later to impaired auditory sensitivity (A. D. Murray, 1988) and other forms of severe brain damage at birth have also been found to be related to later cognitive and sensory impairment (A. Stewart, 1983). Early visual impairment is associated with slower development in all domains during the preschool period (Hatton, Bailey, Burchinal, & Ferrell, 1997). Finally, particular types of early-onset teratogens, especially those that occur during the periods of rapid growth of the limbs, organs, and brain, are generally continuous with later disorders, such as fetal alcohol syndrome and later learning disabilities (B. A. Lewis et al., 2004; Metosky & Vondra, 1995). Some recent research suggests that there is a continuity between exposure to particular types of teratogens, such as excessive maternal cigarette smoking, and violence in adulthood, especially for males (Brennan, Grekin, & Mednick, 1999; Karr-Morse & Wiley, 1997).

Nevertheless, it is important to remember that even in the worst cases of risk, there is variability in outcome between individuals (Wachs, 2000). Down's syndrome infants, for example, are better at daily living skills and communication if they come from cohesive families with sensitive parents (Hauser-Cram et al., 1999). On the other hand, findings from continuity studies suggest important ways to reduce the risk of serious disorders by means of simple interventions in the prenatal and perinatal periods.

We saw in Chapters 3 and 9 that maternal stress during pregnancy has the potential to affect fetal and infant development. One research project examined two-year-old children's behavior in relation to maternal stress due to a natural disaster—a destructive ice storm— during pregnancy. Mothers who reported more objective stress—such as damage to the home, personal injuries, loss of power and water, exposure to falling power lines and branches during that time—had children whose play was less mature and less creative, and whose motor development was delayed at age 2 years. Furthermore, the effects were greater if the storm occurred during the first two trimesters of pregnancy, and the effects of the objective stress were more predictive of toddler behavior than the mother's self-reported subjective feelings of stress (Laplante et al., 2007).

One might think that the subjective feelings of stress would be a better predictor than objective stress, since prenatally, maternal stress hormones from the HPA axis would cross the placenta and affect the infant (see Chapter 9). Why would objective stress (the damages and injuries) be a stronger predictor? This is mostly likely the case since the objective stressors were ongoing: rebuilding a damaged house or recovering from an injury, for example, takes time and money and drains family resources. The stress, in other words, is ongoing. Similar to the effects of poverty, which is also ongoing, the outcomes are not the result of a single prenatal factor, but rather a combination of ongoing factors that affect parent and child well-being.

The findings discussed in this section represent many of the types of continuity shown in Table 12.1. For example, the deformation of a limb or a disorder of auditory neurology reflects absolute consistencies in which the affected organ reaches a final state during early life and does not change later. The effects of very low birthweight could be part of an absolute consistency associated with brain damage, or they could reflect a general retardation of developmental progress and thus be an example of consistency in relation to the group; that is, these babies continue to score lower than full terms even after many years.

If infants are not at risk, their behavior in the perinatal period seems not to predict any later aspects of infant functioning. One study (Bell, Weller, and Waldrop, 1971) found virtually no perinatal behavior that predicted the behavior of children in the preschool years. The success (or lack of success) with which the mother and infant adjusted to each other during early feedings does not predict later mother-infant interaction patterns (J. Dunn, 1975).

These studies on both typically developing and at-risk infants speak to the newborn's **buffering** against difficulties of early adjustment. Infants have a **self-righting** ability; given an appropriately responsive environment, the more mild perinatal complications may not create any lasting organismic deficits (Sameroff & Chandler, 1975). Perhaps if mothers are not under stress and are predisposed to providing competent care, the infant at risk evokes more maternal attention and solici-tude than typically developing infants (Bakeman & Brown, 1980; Beckwith & Cohen, 1978; Beckwith, Rodning, & Cohen, 1992; Crawford, 1982; Eizirik, Bohlin, & Hagekull, 1994; Landry et al., 1996; Liaw & Brooks-Gunn, 1993; Wijnroks, 1998). This increased solicitude may be a factor in alleviating the early deficits over the first year or two of life, even for infants who have severe deficits such as VLBW or teratogen-exposed infants (Knickmeyer et al., 2005; Landry, Smith, Miller-Loncar, & Swank, 1997; Landry, Smith, Miller-Loncar, & Swank, 1998).

This hypothesis is further supported by an intervention study to train mothers of preterms in responsiveness, which showed that infants with VLBW were most likely to improve (Landry, Smith, & Swank, 2006). Thus, in certain circumstances, the environment can provide **compensation** for individual variation in perinatal factors.

On the other hand, it could be that while the child's development normalizes, there may be subtle and hard-to-detect factors by which the effects of early experience persist, at least in some individuals. Nineteen-year-olds who had been born preterm, for example, while otherwise no different from full-term peers at their age, were more emotionally vulnerable to separations from parents and significant others (Tideman et al., 2002). This may possibly be an unconscious participatory memory of the early separation during hospitalization.

MOTOR DEVELOPMENT

Environmental influence on typical motor development was discussed in Chapter 4. As a general rule, environmental stimulation of particular motor systems does advance the infant receiving that stimulation in the short term, compared to other infants. We reviewed in particular the case of infant motor development in Africa, where infants are given a rigorous program of exercises and stretches, leading to an earlier onset of sitting, standing, and walking than in Europe and North America. We also discussed the research on attempts to give babies practice in standing and walking.

In general, however, these differences in environmental stimulation do not lead to long-term differences. Even though the exercised babies may sometimes achieve a motor milestone earlier, it does not mean that as preschoolers they will be superior in motor development to babies who achieved their milestone at a later date. At least as far as the evidence gleaned from typical variations of infant development shows, there does not seem to be any continuity between early motor practice, physical stature and weight, and later developmental outcomes (Gorman & Pollitt, 1993; Largo, 1993). As mentioned earlier, however, relatively little research has been done in the area of long-term effects of enhancing early infant motor development, so drawing any general conclusions at this time would be unwarranted.

In infants at risk, however, physical and motor stimulation can have an important remedial effect leading to catch-up growth. This is especially the case if infants have moderate to severe disorders of self-regulation, such as poor motor coordination, difficulties with state regulation (such as sleeping or feeding problems), sensory deficits (such as blindness or deafness), or impaired emotion regulation (difficulty self-calming or regulating arousal), or pervasive sensorimotor problems such as autism. Unless these conditions are treated with some type of intervention program, they are likely to remain stable and continuous into the preschool years and later (Aylward, 2004; Degangi et al., 1993; Degangi et al., 2000; Mayberry, Lock, & Kazmi, 2002).

Consider sleeping as one example. For most infants, nighttime sleep duration increases and the number of night wakings decreases over the first three years. Sleep duration and night waking during the first year does not predict these factors in the third year: there is no developmental continuity. On the other hand, a small percentage of children in the first year had difficulty getting to sleep and settling back to sleep when they awoke at night. These children were more likely to have sleep and self-regulation problems at 3 ½ years of age (Scher, Epstein, & Tirosh, 2004; Scher, Zuckerman, & Epstein, 2005).

The general conclusion that extra motor stimulation in the first two or three years of life does not contribute to lasting individual differences unless the infant is at risk, however, does not apply for older children. In the preschool and later years, practice with a motor skill does have a definite effect on later ability, as when children are taught sports, art, dance, gymnastics, and music. Training and guidance during this period does in fact lead to later excellence in those areas and may be a critical period for their development (Sternberg & Davidson, 1985; Wallach, 1985). It is more difficult to achieve high levels of expertise in athletics and the arts unless training begins before adolescence.

Some preschool children may have a particular facility and desire for one area of endeavor or another, but this has not been shown to be related to hearing Mozart in the womb or being given aerobic workouts during the first few years of life (see Chapter 3). If the child does not exhibit early desire and facility, however, early intensive skill testing and training are not advisable for the majority of children under the age of 3 years. A preschool education program that is responsive to the needs of the individual child and has the resources to challenge each child at his or her level of interest seems to be the most useful approach (Johnson, 1983).

PARENTAL CONTRIBUTIONS

Maternal Employment and Child Care

We discussed the effects of maternal employment and the effects of child care in Chapter 8. There does not appear to be a direct continuity between maternal employment or child care and later child developmental outcomes. Instead, the long-term effects are mediated by other factors, such as maternal sensitivity and number of hours working per week (Brooks-Gunn, Han, & Waldfogel, 2002; Chin-Quee & Scarr, 1994). One of the major risks related to maternal employment is for the mother herself, especially if she has an economic need to work but would prefer to stay at home, or if she is highly career motivated and suffers from role overload (Stifter, Coulehan, & Fish, 1993). In some but not all cases, these mothers may have some difficulty establishing a secure relationship with their infants. We know little, however, about the long-term effects of maternal employment during infancy on later child development, and the issue is clouded by methodological problems in the research (Burchinal & Clarke-Stewart, 2007).

The risks in child care lie primarily in the quality of care available and the age at which the child attends. The risks are highest for infants under one year who do not have supportive family environments and who are in poor-quality care. These children may fare worse than their peers in preschool and kindergarten. The research, however, is difficult to interpret because of methodological problems and differences across studies. It is important to remember, once again, that the severity and duration of these effects vary greatly across infants. Some infants who are reared in low-quality child care show no deficits, while others do.

Attachment

Research on attachment has found consistency between early and later factors (Table 12.1); for example, in the relationship between parental sensitivity in the first year and later security of attachment, and between security of attachment at age 1 year and later social and intellectual competence in preschool. Consistency of process is shown by similarity of attachment security between the ages of 1 year and 6 years, even though the specific types of attachment behavior differ at each age (see Chapter 7; Gloger-Tippelt et al., 2002). Consistency between early and later factors occurs as insecure children are more likely to have emotion regulation problems (fearfulness, anxiety) and psychosomatic complaints (headache, stomach ache) during middle childhood (Hagekull & Bohlin, 2004).

In addition, long-term longitudinal studies show continuity of attachment into adulthood, and in some cases, into the next generation. Corresponding to the Ainsworth Strange Situation Test (ASST) for infants, there is an Adult Attachment Interview (AAI) that assesses the security of attachment of adults to their own parents and to their romantic partners. There is evidence in some studies for moderate continuity between childhood ASST and AAI done during adolescence and adulthood (Fraley, 2002) and no relationship between the ASST (except for disorganized attachment; see below) and the AAI in other studies (Sroufe et al., 2005). Maternal security on the AAI is related to the child's attachment security on the ASST (Gloger-Tippelt et al., 2002). Mothers who remember being accepted when they were children by their own mothers were more likely to be sensitive to their own infants (Kretchmar & Jacobvitz, 2002). Teens who are rated as "dismissive" on the AAI (denying and devaluing attachments) are more likely to have had less sensitive mothers during infancy than teens who rated their adult attachments as more secure, but the effects of infant experiences are mediated by other life events during childhood, such as parental divorce (Beckwith, Cohen, & Hamilton, 1999). Finally, there is a moderate predictability between attachment security in infancy and ability to resolve conflicts and shared emotions in romantic relationships in early adulthood (Sroufe et al., 2005).

Disorganized attachment in infancy also shows consistency between early and later factors. Children with disorganized attachments are more likely to show behavior problems at all later school ages and more likely to develop psychopathologies in childhood and adolescence (separation anxiety disorder, oppositional disorder, depression, phobias, and dissociation). Even here, however, there is variability in the severity of the outcomes across individuals (Carlson, 1998; Madigan et al., 2004; Sroufe et al., 2005; Weinfield, Whaley, & Egeland, 2004).

The current explanation for these types of continuity is the concept of the internal working model of attachment, which suggests that individuals acquire particular expectations from their early social relationships that carry over into other relationships. Because internal working models are relatively stable and are changed only very slowly, they may account for the long-term consistencies in attachment across time. On the other hand, there is variability across families. While most attachments remain stable, some infants will change their attachment security, becoming either more or less secure over time (see Chapter 7).

Caregiving and Disciplinary Styles

In Chapter 6, we discussed guided participation in parent-infant interaction. Guided participation is based on following up the child's spontaneous interests and actions, structuring those actions in ways that enhance the child's competence and sense of participation, and then allowing the child to take increasing responsibility. Parents who use more guided participation with their children are more likely to have children with more advanced language and cognitive skills.

Guided participation is also related to authoritative parenting styles that combine respect for the child's interests and points of view with parental firmness in the enforcement of rules. Such child outcomes as independence, cooperativeness, and social competence have been associated with authoritative parenting. We also saw that parental proactive behavior—preparing the environment or the child for anticipated positive outcomes—is part of guidance and authoritative disciplinary styles. Infant compliance is more readily assured if parents use proactive planning and guidance strategies, rather than confrontational approaches.

Social competence, intelligence, attentional control, emotion regulation, and language ability during early childhood are correlated with maternal vocalization, contingent responsiveness, mother-infant synchrony, and parenting involvement during the first two years, and in the third year with parental proactive behavior, such as providing opportunities to interact with other people and to explore the environment (Bradley & Caldwell, 1995; Carew, 1980; Feiring & Lewis, 1981; Feldman, Greenbaum, & Yurmiya, 1999; Olson, Bates, & Kaskie, 1992; Vyt, 1993; Wachs, 1993; Wachs & Gruen, 1982). Lack of maternal responsiveness during infancy also predicts disruptive behavior problems (aggression, defiance, antisocial behavior) during early and middle childhood and the effect is consistent across cultural groups (Bor et al., 2003; Ispa et al., 2004; Symonds, 2001; Wakschlag & Hans, 1999). Maternal depression during early infancy predicts infant cognitive development at 18 months and preschool language, cooperation with peers, and behavior problems (Leadbeater, Bishop, & Raver, 1996; Murray, Fiori-Cowley, Hooper, & Cooper, 1996; NICHD Early Child Care Research Network, 1999).

The research in this area is not entirely conclusive. Global measures of parenting often are not sensitive to variations in disciplinary style that depend on the nature of the infraction and the responsiveness of the child to adult interventions. Furthermore, there are cross-family and cross-cultural differences in caregiving that are difficult to compare on any absolute scale of parental effectiveness or sensitivity. Finally, all of the findings in this area are based on correlations, which have two implications; first, the parent's style could be shaped by the child's behavior, at least in part; second, the correlations are typically positive but small, meaning that while a general association exists between caregiving and child behavior, there is wide variability between families. Simply put, while many children who experience maternal insensitivity during infancy will have behavior problems or attachment difficulties, there are others who do not have such difficulties.

The important question is not whether sensitive parenting matters. It does matter. Parental figures are a necessary and irreplaceable part of infant development. Rather, we need to know whether the continuity between caregiving and later outcome for the child is sustained by factors inherent in the child over time, by the consistency of adult care over time, or by an ongoing transaction between the adult and the child in which the interaction promotes consistent behaviors in both participants. Consistency, or a lack thereof, could also derive from the influence of mediating factors on the parent-infant dyad, such as the effect of social supports and economic advantage and disadvantage (Chapter 8).

RISK AND DISADVANTAGE

Poverty. As we saw in Chapter 8, poverty is a clear case where consistency of negative outcomes can be maintained over long periods in the absence of other mediating factors. Children and parents from poor families suffer more from depression, poor peer relationships, social withdrawal, and low self-esteem (Middlemiss, 2003; Mistry et al., 2004; Pike et al., 2006). Children are more likely to have physical ailments, school problems, aggressiveness, deviant behavior, and language and cognitive deficits. In Chapter 9, we explored some of the cyclical processes that tend to maintain these negative outcomes over time. Stress, nutrition, health, and behavior interact to create increasingly negative patterns. On the other hand, some poor children can thrive depending upon circumstances. Children who come from homes that focus on promoting child development, that value education, and that provide support and protection from the stresses of poverty do better than those children not provided with these buffers (Mackner, Black, & Starr, 2003). Even in the case of poverty, therefore, some children show resilience that allows them to transcend their circumstances.

Stress. Another major risk factor in early development is severe stress on the infant and the family. Stress may be due to economic deprivation, disease, hospitalizations and other extended separations, family changes due to relocation or parental or sibling death, extreme conditions of social unrest, such as those created by war, persecution, natural disaster, or famine, and migration or flight as refugees. The research is complicated, detailed in some areas and not in others, and often dependent on personal recollections. Nevertheless, after extensive review of this literature, it can be concluded that a single stressful incident in early infancy has negligible long-term effects. However, multiple or long-term stresses create cyclical patterns of increasing risk and deprivation and are more likely to be associated with long-term emotional or behavioral disorders in later childhood (Rutter, 1979; Wachs, 2000).

Research on the neurophysiological processes related to stress, such as elevated levels of cortisol from overactivation of the HPA axis (Chapter 5), shows that ongoing parental stress in early infancy is correlated with elevated cortisol in their 4 ½-year-olds (Essex et al., 2002). Relationship stress and insecure attachment can also overactivate the HPA axis, leading to long-term susceptibility to even minor stress and a predisposition to depression (Beatson & Taryan, 2003).

Even with multiple or long-term stressors, however, some children show remarkable resilience and adaptability (Wachs, 2000). In some cases, an early stressor can prepare an individual to adapt to a similar stressor later in development, as when children who are repeatedly separated from parents in child care become less susceptible to the effects of routine separation from parents. On the other hand, some stressors can make people hypersensitive to repeated exposures, as in the example of the 3-year-old boy who did not like to be wrapped up in a cloth when getting a haircut because doctors had wrapped him in a blanket while stitching up an injury he had received when he was a baby (see Chapter 5). There is a great deal of variability in how a stressor will affect someone and how long the effect will be felt. Once again, there are no simple answers.

Parental psychopathology. Do parental anxiety disorder, depression, and other forms of mental illness affect the chances that the child will develop some form of mental illness or other deficit in later years? As you might suspect from what has been said in this chapter so far, the answer depends on the whether other risk and/or protective factors are present in the child's life. In general, there is only a small correlation, or none at all, between maternal psychopathology and later child outcome. The chances of the child being affected are increased if there is a familial genetic predisposition, if the child is temperamentally inhibited or aggressive, if there are a series of environmental and familial stressors, and if the attachment relationship is insecure. On the other hand, the chances are reduced if there is a sensitive non-pathological parent available, if the child has good self-regulatory control, and if the child perceives the environment to be secure and supportive (Hay et al., 2001; Henriksson & McNeil, 2004; Mezulis, Hyde, & Clark, 2004; Muris, 2006; Spence et al., 2002).

Child abuse and neglect. A similar set of conclusions can be made about the long-term effects of parental child maltreatment, as suggested in Chapter 9. Not all parents who were abused as children will go on to abuse their own children. Not all children who had been abused will show negative outcomes. On the other hand, long-term effects of child abuse—including violence and aggression, school problems, problems maintaining intimate relationships, suicide, depression, panic and anxiety disorders, and abuse of their own children—are more likely if the adult has low self-esteem, has a history of mental illness, or depression or violence, or is a teen parent (Coleman & Widom, 2004; Dixon et al., 2005; Evans, Hawton, & Rodham, 2005; Goodwin, Fergusson, & Horwood, 2005; Hildyard & Wolfe, 2002;).

Deprivation of normal parental care. Total deprivation of parental care, such as in the studies by Harry Harlow of monkeys who were raised without parents (see Chapter 2) is rare in humans. The closest analogies are infants reared in institutional settings such as orphanages. Orphanages are almost nonexistent in North America and Western Europe, where it is the practice to place abandoned children in foster or adoptive care. Institutionalization is more common in Eastern Europe, Russia, and China, and many international adoptions to the United States are from these countries.

The worst cases of institutional deprivation—lack of adequate nutrition, stimulation, and affection—have come from Romania, where children, as well as everyone else in that country, suffered for many years under a repressive dictator. After he was murdered by a mob in 1989, the country was opened to outsiders, and many of the children were placed into adoptive care. A team of researchers from Great Britain has been studying these Romanian children and their developmental

outcomes. Many of these children suffered from language and cognitive delays, brain abnormalities especially in the limbic and prefrontal areas that develop most rapidly in infancy and are responsible for basic functions and self-regulation (see Chapter 5), social and emotional problems, attention deficits and hyperactivity (Nelson, 2007).

On the other hand, some children's deficits were more severe than others. The more severe cases were institutionalized for longer than 6 months. If the children were placed in an adoptive family, their risk decreased except for a small minority who appeared to have sustained some type of brain damage that was resistant to the experience-dependent development possible in the adoptive family environment (Rutter et al., 2004; Rutter et al., 2007; Wilson, 2003).

Interventions for at-risk infants. In Chapter 8, we looked at the effects of early intervention programs such as Head Start and other parent-infant programs. Although research on the long-term effectiveness of these programs is difficult to do, there is some evidence that such interventions do make a difference, especially for children and parents from lower-income groups or from dysfunctional families, and especially when the intervention contains some parent-educational component either in the home or at the program center (Burchinal, Lee, & Ramey, 1989; Caughy, DiPietro, & Strobino, 1994; Lyons-Ruth, Connell, Grunebaum, & Botein, 1990; Roggman et al., 2004; Scarr & Eisenberg, 1993; Spitz, 1992; Wasik, Ramey, Bryant, & Sparling, 1990). High-quality educational child care, when combined with responsive care at home, can boost cognitive performance for poor children during the preschool period (Burchinal, Campbell, Bryant, Wasik, & Ramey, 1997; Raikes et al., 2006).

Malnutrition can have severe short- and long-term effects on reducing infant energy, emotional responsiveness, attention, and play (Lozoff et al., 1998; M. A. McDonald, Sigman, Espinosa, & Neumann, 1994; Pollitt et al., 1996; Wachs, 2000). Interventions involving nutritional supplementation are generally successful if they are accompanied by parent-child behavior interventions to enhance maternal sensitivity (See Chapters 9; Cravioto & Arrieta, 1983; Pollitt et al., 1996; Z. Stein & Susser, 1985; Valenzuela, 1997; Winick, Knarig, & Harris, 1975). In a study done in Colombia, malnutrition was treated in one group with only food supplementation for the entire family and in another group with food supplementation plus parent education during home visits. The children in the group that received supplementation plus parent education were taller and heavier at the age of 6 years, and there were fewer cases of mental retardation than in the food-only group (Super, Herrera, & Mora, 1990).

Interventions designed for premature infants have also shown signs of success. The most successful interventions combine long-term pediatric care with parent education and family support. These programs enhance children's cognitive and behavioral development and also increase the competence and enthusiasm of the parents (Achenbach, Phares, Howell, Rauh, & Nurcombe, 1990; Brooks-Gunn, Klebanov, Liaw, & Spiker, 1993; Rauh, Achenbach, Nurcombe, Howell, & Teti, 1988; Spiker, Ferguson, & Brooks-Gunn, 1993).

One problem with intervention research is that the populations of children served vary enormously between locations. In addition, even clearly outlined interventions will vary in their application according to location, staff training and interpretation, and the reactions of the children and their families. The Mother-Child Home Program, which has been found to work well with disadvantaged children in the United States, for example, was relatively ineffective in a broader-based population of children in Bermuda (Scarr & McCartney, 1988).

Thus, the best statement that can be made at the current time is that some programs work some of the time for some groups and that, overall, intervention programs provide an important source of enrichment and encouragement for parents who are under social and economic stress. In this perspective, short-term relief from stress may be as valuable as any long-term developmental benefit. It could be that the long-term effects are present

but that researchers have not been able to develop measures to assess them. Virtually all researchers and practitioners agree that early intervention is important and should continue for many years into the future.

CULTURE

We reviewed many examples of the effects of culture in this book. In particular, we have seen many cultural differences in child-rearing styles. Cultures differ, broadly speaking, according to whether they focus on individual development and achievement or on the family and the group. We saw, for example, that in some cultures older children are expected to provide child care for their younger siblings. In these collectivistic cultures, children are socialized from an early age to respect authority, to give their time to support the family, and to avoid standing apart from the group. Many Asian, African, Latin/Hispanic, Native American, and other indigenous cultures are collectivistic. Infants reared in collectivistic cultures achieve self-recognition in the mirror (the existential self) later than children reared in individualistic cultures (Keller et al., 2004).

These cultural influences can have a great deal of impact on social and emotional processes such as sharing, empathy, and self-disclosure. They can also affect gender-specific behavior, depending upon cultural attitudes toward traditional or nontraditional sex-role orientations.

Even though culture has a major impact on later outcomes, there is also a great deal of variability within cultures (Killen & Wainryb, 2000). Not all people raised in the North American culture of individuality are self-seeking and achievement oriented. Similarly, many people from collectivistic cultures are focused on getting ahead at the expense of others. In addition, culture interacts with all the other factors mentioned in this chapter. The cultural interpretation of poverty in North America may not be the same in South America, where a greater proportion of people are poor. Poverty may affect development differently in these two hemispheres. This suggests that sensitivity to the differences between ethnic and cultural minorities in a nation is likely to facilitate child development (Johnson et al., 2003).

GENDER

We saw in Chapter 5 that by 3 years of age, children are beginning to express a gender identity and to adopt gender role appropriate behavior. What has been difficult to establish is the extent to which individual differences in the gender-role orientations (from traditional to egalitarian) of children are consistent with any factors in their prior history. So far, research has not yielded any strong conclusions. Individual differences in gender- role orientations exist from a young age, but these differences do not possess a high degree of any form of continuity over time. The continuity of gender-role orientation may not emerge until later childhood or young adulthood. For example, the gender-role socialization behavior of the parents (selecting gender role–appropriate toys for children), especially that of the father, is strongly related to the father's prior history and beliefs about gender roles.

Sex differences during infancy have been related to factors other than gender-role socialization. For example, males seem to be more vulnerable to the effects of environmental stress. When they grow up in homes that are overcrowded, noisy, or confusing, males show deficits in their cognitive development, while females growing up in similar environments do not. Environmental opportunities to explore large areas in the home are more beneficial for the long-term cognitive development of males than females. Females, but not males, who are provided with a great deal of stimulus variety (different colors, shapes, and textures in the home) show higher levels of cognitive development (Rutter, 1979; Wachs & Gruen, 1982). Finally, higher levels of androgens (hormones associated with masculinity) at birth are correlated with lower scores on spatial ability for girls at 6 years, but variations in androgen level have no effect on variability of spatial ability in boys (Jacklin, Wilcox, & Maccoby, 1988). One also

has to remember that there are individual differences among boys and among girls such that the general pattern does not hold for everyone.

Although the reasons for these long-term continuities are not entirely clear, it may be that boys and girls process information differently, or that they require different types of environmental inputs in order to maintain their levels of cognitive growth. This has been called the environmental specificity of long-term effects (Wachs, 1982). **Environmental specificity** occurs when certain aspects of the environment are more effective in promoting specific types of competencies than others, or when certain aspects of the environment are effective in promoting development in some children but not in others.

INTELLECTUAL DEVELOPMENT

Environmental-specificity effects have been found in long-term continuity studies of factors in early infancy that promote cognitive and intellectual development. For example, early exposure in the first year to an enriched home environment with a variety of inanimate objects and to contingently responsive inanimate objects leads to greater skill in problem solving and exploratory play in the second year (Molfese, DiLalla, & Bunce, 1997; Saltaris et al., 2004; Yarrow, Rubenstein, & Pedersen, 1975). The provision of age-appropriate play materials during the first two years strongly predicts a child's Stanford-Binet IQ score at 4 1/2 years (Bradley & Caldwell, 1976), as well as elementary school achievement test scores between 5 and 9 years of age (VanDoorninck, Caldwell, Wright, & Frankenburg, 1981).

The development of spatial relations and perspective taking can best be predicted by avoidance of noise, confusion, and environmental overcrowding during the first two years. In contrast, exploratory play skills in the second and third year are best enhanced by caregivers providing objects that respond when the child moves them—such as mobiles and rattles—and a variety of objects in the first year. These factors, plus a well-organized

Many complex factors must combine to ensure healthy development during the infancy period. Adults have an important responsibility to provide the best possible environments and care that bring out the highest potential of each child.
Photo by Michael Weisbrot.

environment and the use of age-appropriate play materials, are the best predictors of a child's ability to invent new means and plan effective strategies (Wachs, 1982; Wachs & Gruen, 1982; Widmayer et al., 1990).

The variability of the efficiency of information processing in the first six months predicts cognitive developmental outcomes. In a habituation task, for example, some infants habituate rather quickly and require less looking time overall to process the visual stimulus. These efficient information-processing strategies in early infancy are correlated with higher childhood standardized cognitive and language development test scores. Infants who at 4 months continued to fixate on an unchanging stimulus had lower intelligence test scores in middle childhood (Bornstein & Sigman, 1986; Dougherty & Haith, 1997; Rose & Feldman, 1997; Rose, Feldman, & Wallace, 1988; Rose, Feldman, Wallace, & McCarton, 1989; Sigman et al., 1986; Tamis-LeMonda & Bornstein, 1989). Efficient information processing, especially when combined with a maternal style focusing on directing the infant's attention to tasks, leads to more advanced cognitive and language outcomes (Kavšek, 2004; Lewis, Alessandri, & Sullivan, 1992; McCall & Carriger, 1993; Rose et al., 1989; Tamis-LeMonda & Bornstein, 1989, 1993; Thompson, Fagan, & Fulker, 1991).

More specific measures of language behavior and its antecedents have also revealed strong predictive patterns. Verbal interaction with the child in the early years of life, not surprisingly, is one of the strongest and most distinctive predictors of later language competence in toddlers and preschoolers (Hart & Risley, 1992; Huttenlocher, Haight, Bryk, Seltzer, & Lyons, 1991; Sokolov, 1993; Wachs et al., 1993). Interventions for children at risk for poor language acquisition have been successful by training parents to talk with and read to infants. Children who stutter are helped when parents talk more slowly, giving the children time to take their turn in the conversation at their own pace (Ramig, 1993; Swan, 1993; Valdez-Menchaca & Whitehurst, 1992; Winslow & Guitar, 1994). These effects compound over time, so that children who talk early and competently also read earlier and are more advanced conceptually; thus, they have a head start on the literacy skills required for schooling (Crain-Thoreson & Dale, 1992; P. J. Dunham & Dunham, 1995).

In play tasks, some 1-year-old infants are more focused on a particular toy and persist in exploring many of the toy's properties, while others show more variable attention spans. They will move rapidly from one toy to the next without spending much time investigating the individual properties of each. These babies seem to move restlessly between things without fully appreciating the properties of any one item. Babies who are inattentive at 1 year also tend to be inattentive at age 3 and later score lower on intelligence tests (Heinicke, Diskin, Ramsey-Klee, & Oates, 1986; Heinicke & Lampl, 1988; Raine et al., 2002; Ruff, Lawson, Parrinello, & Weissberg, 1990; Wenckstern, Weizmann, & Leenaars, 1984).

In summary, the child's environment and information-processing abilities during infancy play some role in the prediction of later intelligence. These factors interact, however, and no one factor can account for all the variability. In addition, as we have mentioned earlier, children who suffer from poor information processing during the first six months will vary in their outcomes, some scoring lower and some scoring higher on IQ tests during later childhood. It is possible to enhance cognitive development for some children by talking with and reading to them. There is no evidence, however, that extra cognitive stimulation during infancy can create a genius.

TEMPERAMENT

Our review of **temperament** in Chapter 7 showed that there is limited evidence for continuity in infant temperament. Most of the research in this domain focuses on continuity with respect to group ranking, which is also called **stability**. Only when children fall into extreme groups on irritability, emotionality, reactivity, or inhibition can long-term stability be observed. We also found that stability in infant temperamental characteristics is more likely to be seen in the short term—six months to a year—rather than over several years. At older ages, stability can be seen for several years or more, but transformation and change are the rule just as often as stability (Caspi & Silva, 1995; Hagekull & Bohlin, 2003; Pedlow, Sanson, Prior, & Oberklaid, 1993).

Many of the factors that account for short-term continuity of temperament are likely to change over the long run. For example, infant irritability is one important temperamental dimension. Irritability is associated with a number of prenatal and perinatal risk factors, such as prematurity. As the effects of prematurity attenuate over time (see the earlier section on risk in this chapter), the early forms of irritability that may persist over the first year disappear or change in the second year (Coll et al., 1992). New factors, such as developmental challenges of autonomy and parent-child attachment, begin to account for individual differences in irritability and other temperamental factors in the second year. For a few children, first-year irritability persists into the second year, but most lose their infantile irritability. Some children transform it into more age-appropriate patterns of negativity such as anger and defiance.

While lack of continuity is the rule in temperament studies, the fact that development is marked by variability in outcome means that some children, under certain conditions, will show long-term continuity of temperament. This can occur when the parents have a temperamental pattern similar to that of the infant, and especially when both parent and infant show temperamental inhibition and shyness, which suggests that when parent and child share an attribute, their mutual interaction enhances the possibility that their genetically based inhibition will continue to be manifested in the phenotype (P. Cohen, Kasen, Brook, & Hartmark, 1998; Schmitz et al., 1999).

In summary, as we have seen in other sections of this chapter, research that shows statistical significance in long-term continuity does not mean that all children remain the same over time. We are still a long way from understanding the genetic, environmental, age, and context-specific conditions that promote continuity and change in temperament. Like intelligence and gender effects, temperament is continuous for some children under some conditions. In other cases, temperament may have some short-term continuity, but after several years, the child does not persist with the same characteristics. The study of temperament is confounded by inconsistencies in the definition of temperament and by the difficulty of obtaining reliable and valid measures (see Chapter

7). In the next section, I discuss the complexity of the findings reviewed in this chapter.

DEVELOPMENTAL SYSTEMS OF MULTIPLE INTERACTING FACTORS

The research reviewed in this chapter shows that many factors in early infancy have significant effects on outcomes in childhood and adulthood. The prenatal and perinatal environment, genetics, parental sensitivity, culture, gender, and temperament, among many other things, play a role in creating the individual person. Throughout this chapter, two major principles have been discussed: that no one of these factors can work in isolation (development is multifactorial and complex), and that no two individuals are affected in the same way by any one factor or any set of factors acting in combination (there is an inherent difference between-individual variability in developmental process and outcome).

These two principles are not independent from each other. This can be illustrated by the results of a study in which infants were tested on the Bayley Mental Scale at 4, 8, 12, and 18 months, and their performance later assessed on the Reynell Developmental Language Scales at 2, 3, and 4 years. The quality of the infants' home environments were also studied in this longitudinal study involving 148 infants (L. S. Siegal, 1981).

If we look at the early Bayley scores as predictive of the later language scores at 2 years, there was no relationship. Infants who scored low on the Bayley test could be developing typically at 2 years in the areas of language, or they could be slower than average. The same two outcomes were possible for children who had more typical scores on the Bayley test in the first year (see Figure 10.1). Of the four groups of 2-year-olds shown in Figure 10.1, two of them fit a single factor pattern. In group I, low Bayley scores led to low language scores; in group IV, more-typical Bayley scores led to high language scores. Groups II and III do not fit the single-factor pattern. In each of these cases,

another factor—the home environment—played a significant role (L. S. Siegal, 1981).

Infants in group II, who had low Bayley scores in the first year but scored high on language at age 2, had home environments that were significantly more enriched and stimulating than the home environments of group I babies. Infants in group III, who had low language scores even though they were developing typically in the first year, had a less enriched environment than infants in group IV (L. S. Siegal, 1981; Ungerer & Sigman, 1984).

Notice how the two different factors interact in complex ways. The home environment is more important for some infants (those in groups II and III), and the early psychomotor abilities, as measured by the Bayley score, are more important for the others. Another aspect of these findings, not shown in Figure 10.1, is that there is variability in outcome *within* each of the groups. In group I, for example, some infants with low Bayley scores had higher language scores than others within the group, even though the whole group was in the low range.

Multifactor processes with between-individual variability have been found for virtually every research study in which more than one factor is measured on the same group of infants (Wachs, 2000). Consider some of the following results from research.

Maternal smoking during pregnancy has known effects on neurological development of the fetus, with long-lasting effects on the child. Pregnant women who smoke, however, are more likely both to be depressed and to be poor (Leftwich & Collins, 1994). Depression and poverty affect the mother's behavior during pregnancy, which creates neurological deficits and an infant who is then more likely to succumb to the combined effects of maternal depression and poverty after birth. Children who are malnourished are more likely to be living in a home with low stimulation value and low parental responsiveness (Lozoff, 1998). Parental negligence is probably affected by poverty and stress, which compounds the effects on an already weak child. In these examples, one factor amplifies the effects of other factors. If fewer risk factors are present, such as maternal depression in

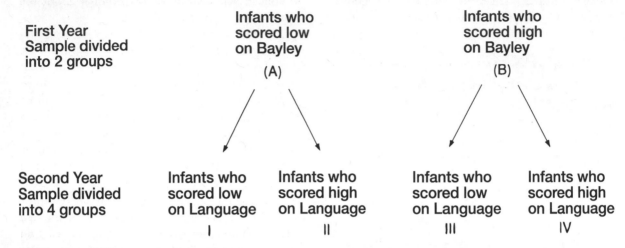

First Year Sample divided into 2 groups

Infants who scored low on Bayley
(A)

Infants who scored high on Bayley
(B)

Second Year Sample divided into 4 groups

Infants who scored low on Language
I

Infants who scored high on Language
II

Infants who scored low on Language
III

Infants who scored high on Language
IV

Figure 10.1   Relationship between Early Bayley and Later Language Development Scores

the absence of prenatal smoking and poverty, the effects will be different and specific to the particular combination of factors.

The age of exposure to a particular factor is also an important interacting factor in determining outcome (Bronfenbrenner & Evans, 2000; Wachs, 2000). We have seen this in prenatal development, when teratogens have a much more serious effect if the exposure occurs at critical periods in the formation of an organ system. Non-parental child care has different effects on younger and older infants. Another aspect of the multifactor process is that children may be affected in one domain of functioning and not in another. Maternal alcohol consumption during pregnancy, for example, affects neurological development but not physical development. Attachment disorganization affects psychosocial functioning but not intelligence.

In summary, one should distrust any claims that a single factor from early infancy has lasting outcomes for all infants exposed to it. Traumas can be serious in the short term, but they do not always have lasting effects. On the other hand, products and interventions that promise to make a child into a genius by exposing the infant to Mozart prenatally or providing extra cognitive stimulation during the first year of life also do

not have consistent outcomes. Some children may benefit, but many will not. Development is a complex dynamic system that resists simple explanations. Each baby's life is as rich and complex as an adult's in the sense that there are no easy answers, only more questions.

To return to the questions posed at the beginning of this chapter: Does this mean that infancy is not important? Does it mean that we should not provide the best parental care, nutrition, enriched environments, health practices, and love to infants? The answer to these questions is clearly *no*. Babies—indeed, people of all ages—should be afforded healthy, safe, enriched, and loving opportunities. These factors promote development without question. We do not need research to convince us that every human being is entitled to good prenatal care, a warm and loving home, quality education, and economic security. It is just the right thing to do. Research clearly shows that people are more likely to become healthy, happy, productive, and intelligent if they have these things.

Parents, educators, practitioners, and policy makers need to understand, however, that while infants benefit from having these opportunities, we cannot predict with certainty that a particular event or program will have particular outcomes.

We can only say that, in general, intelligence, social skills, and emotional control are promoted in healthy, safe, and loving environments. We can only say that, in general, these abilities are more likely to be deficient in impoverished and insensitive rearing conditions. We can say with certainty that *infancy is important* and that each person will get something different from their early years, both potentials and limitations.

FINAL THOUGHTS

One of the problems with research on long-term developmental outcomes is that the factors presumed to have an influence—such as genes, environments, parents, attachments, and the like—are conceptualized in terms of reliable and valid measurements. The very process of measurement as a tool for quantitative research requires that the measures be relatively insensitive to the daily life of the individual child. What good is a measurement of attachment security, for example, if the results change between morning and afternoon, or if the test is done on a day when the mother and baby are feeling good about each other instead of a day of frustration and anger?

There is an inherent opposition between the demands for standardized measurement in quantitative research and the basic principles of development showing that each person is special, unique, and individual. Suppose you participated in a quantitative study of the academic development of college students. In the study, you were interviewed as a freshman and your course grades that year were recorded. A similar interview was conducted when you were a senior, and your senior-year grades were noted. Perhaps the grade point averages of all the students in the study did not change much. While you were a solid B student as a freshman and also as a senior, another classmate was consistently an A student (which demonstrates stability, or consistency of ranking). The researcher concludes that you did not change much. This study does not give credit to the wealth of experiences you had

in college and tells us almost nothing about the processes in your life.

Unfortunately, this is the type of continuity study that is most frequently done on infants. Few studies observe the process of development within individuals to determine how they solved daily problems and did or did not maintain their equilibrium to stay on course. Research that looks at developmental processes rather than just the outcomes would be based on case study qualitative methods (Chapter 1). Until there are more such studies, our conclusions about how to foster desirable development and how to remedy early risk factors are going to be oversimplified. We know that multiple factors are involved, of course, but we do not know how they might operate for a particular person. This type of research is difficult to do, and relatively few researchers are doing it. The problem is how to get sufficient detail about an individual's life and still have the time to study many individuals in order to make more general conclusions.

Development is a continuously unfolding process of change. Every day in one's life presents new opportunities and new challenges. Infants, like people of all ages, are remarkably adaptable and uniquely individual. Little by little, many influences, actions, feelings, and thoughts transform us as we live from day to day. Day-to-day change is subtle, sometimes regressing rather than going forward, like babies who first crawl backward when they are really trying to move ahead. At some point we look back in time and realize that we have changed, that we are not the same any more. No single factor caused this, no single day—nothing we can define clearly.

And what about indeterministic factors in development, those chance occurrences and serendipitous events that happen without planning or premeditation? These are things we cannot explain, that do not seem logical. But human development and relationships, without a bit of magic and uncertainty, are dry and inhospitable. Creativity, surprise, and the excitement of the unknown keep pulling us forward as much as our genes and environments push us from behind. An individual whose developmental fate is determined by a predictable set of causes and effects could not also be open to the opportunity for discovery, exploration, risk taking, and personal growth in the absence of predictable guarantees.

Aside from this, infancy is a particularly magical time because much of what the infant does is not logical, deliberate, or scientific. Infants are grounded in their own ecological experiences. They accept what is. It is not until late in the second year that infants begin to seek control over external events, defy or try to change their world, and reason according to a set of community standards.

As we have seen from research presented in this book, events that occurred during infancy do in fact have some impact on later life, even if we cannot trace that impact to a specific event for specific people. Whether or not we can consciously remember our infancy, patterns of movement, thought, and feeling from infancy persist in our minds and bodies and contribute to the person we are today. It is not necessary to consciously or conceptually remember something, from any age period in your life, for it to have an influence over you. Conversely, just because you remember something does not mean that it had a major influence on who you are today. The point is that we are historical beings: who we are is partly the result of who we were. The specific links between our past and present, however, are unlikely to ever be fully sorted out. We are always transforming the past as we make it into the present, and there are indeterministic factors that enter into this transformation (Fogel et al., 2006; Sroufe et al., 2005).

Does indeterminism actually occur in human development? Science cannot answer this question. You should trust yourself and your own life experiences to provide an answer. As you encounter infants and young children in personal and professional roles, and as you enter into the infant's world through the lessons and exercises in this book, you will have to piece together the general principles from current research with your own personal experiences. It will be up to you to bridge the gap between the abstract and the specific. In doing so, you will be rewarded with a deepening understanding of human life and human development, with all its richness and surprises.

SUMMARY

Development as a Complex Dynamic Process

- Research should focus on the process by which desirable and undesirable developmental outcomes are formed.
- Developmental outcomes are determined by multiple factors.
- Human development in complex family and social systems is regulated by both deterministic and nondeterministic factors. Research has fewer ways to capture the nondeterministic effects.
- Variability is inherent in developmental processes, so that the same experience affects each person differently.

Research on Continuity between Early and Later Development

- Continuity is the extent to which aspects of the individual are preserved from one age to another.
- There are many forms of continuity, as shown in Table 10.1.

Perinatal Factors

- Outcomes for perinatal factors depend on the quality of the environment and on the severity of the initial disorder.

Motor Development

- In early infancy, motor skills can be enhanced in the short term, but there seems to be little long-term benefit.
- Motor skill enrichment programs show more lasting effects when they begin after the age of 2 years.

Parental Contributions

- Little is known about the long-term effects of maternal employment; however, few short- term effects have been found.
- Different considerations must be applied to the effects of child care for children under 6 months of age than for older children.

- Attachment shows strong continuity with early mother-infant relationships and with later social and emotional competence.
- The concept of the internal working model may best explain this continuity.
- Guided participation and authoritative and proactive caregiving styles are associated with long-term patterns of child cognitive, social, and emotional competence.
- Problems in the research make it difficult to determine whether the continuity is due to the parent, the child, or external mediating factors.

Risk and Disadvantage

- Economic disadvantage has long-term effects on development, usually due to the increased stress on the family. Other stress-producing factors also create the opportunity for negative outcomes.
- Intervention is typically helpful in alleviating the effects of risk and disadvantage if it includes both a child and a parent education component and, where necessary, nutrition and health care.

Culture

- Cultures differ according to whether they focus on individual achievement or on the family and group, and this affects the development of empathy, sharing, and cooperation.
- It is important to take account of variability within cultures, which may sometimes be as great as that between cultures.

Gender

- Few long-term influences on sex-role behavior can be found during infancy.
- Gender may mediate a child's response to the environment and the caregiver's response to the child, creating the possibility of differential outcomes.

Intellectual Development

- Specific aspects of the physical and social environment are linked to specific long-term cognitive developmental outcomes and only for specific groups of children.
- Some information-processing factors, including habituation and attention, may show unmediated long-term consistency.

Temperament

- There are many different definitions of temperament.
- Temperament is difficult to measure and shows consistency for some but not all infants.

Developmental Systems of Multiple Interacting Factors

- Development is composed of multiple interacting factors in a dynamic system.
- Each person is a unique individual and will have his or her own pathway of change through time.

Glossary

Accommodation A change in individual functioning and skill in order to meet new environmental demands.

Action potentials Electrochemical currents that transmit information in neurons. These currents travel from the cell body along the axons to the axon terminals.

Acuity The ability of a perceptual system to resolve incoming information into sharp focus.

Adaptation The process of becoming better suited to survive and succeed in a particular environment.

Affective sharing Occurs when the child seeks confirmation from others for his or her own felt emotion.

Allele A gene whose action depends upon at least one other gene, its allelic counterpart, to produce the phenotype. Usually, alleles are at the same location on each chromosome of a pair.

Amniocentesis Sampling a small amount of amniotic fluid for the purpose of determining the genetic and chromosomal make-up of the fetus.

Amniotic sac A membrane that encloses the embryo and fetus and contains amniotic fluid in which the fetus floats, providing a natural cushion.

Amygdala A small bulb at the front end of the hippocampus (amygdala means almond in Latin). There are two, a right and a left. The amygdala plays a role in the formation of emotional memories, especially those around fear and safety, and is functional at birth.

Anal stage A period that begins some time in the second year of life when the primary sensitive zone becomes the anal region of the body.

Analgesia Pain-relieving drugs.

Anesthesia Drugs used to mask the sensation of pain.

A-not-B error An error in finding hidden objects that occurs when an object is hidden first in one place (A) and then in another place (B). The child finds the object at A but not at B.

Apgar score A screening test used to rate the infant's current health status and likelihood of crisis, rated at 1 and 5 minutes after birth.

Apnea Short cessation of respiratory movements.

Appraisal The ability to evaluate a situation and its circumstances before making an emotional response.

Appraisal The process by which an individual uses cognitive judgments to regulate emotional experiences.

Assimilation The adaptive utilization of those aspects of the environment that are within the limits of our skills and biological processing capacities.

Association The psychological linkage between a stimulus and a response that occurs in the environment at about the same time.

Asynchronous growth Refers to the fact that growth occurs in different regions of the body at different times and different rates.

Attachment The maintenance of close proximity between infant and caregiver as part of an enduring relationship.

Attachment behavior The overt set of signals, such as smiling, crying, and following that bring parent and infant into close proximity.

Attachment system The network of feelings and cognitions related to the object of attachment.

Attrition The loss of subjects over time in longitudinal research studies.

Attunement Cross-modal matching of infant behavior by an adult or vice versa.

Authoritative parenting A style of parenting that combines warmth and firmness.

Autism A developmental disorder whose symptoms include impaired ability to interact socially, speech and language deficits, and unusual movements of the body.

Autobiographical memory The ability to remember experiences as events and sequences expressed verbally as a story about oneself.

Axon A nerve fiber that conducts electrical activity away from the cell body of the neuron.

Babbling Vocal behavior that includes reduplication (repetition) of consonant-vowel syllables.

Baby biography A detailed written observation of the day-to-day changes in the behavior of a single infant; one of the first forms of scientific observations of infant behavior.

Behavior genetics The study of between-individual variability in phenotypes as a result of variability in environments or in genotypes.

Behavioral assessments Tests used to measure the newborn's behavioral status, including reflexes, orientation to external stimuli, and state control.

Birthrate The average number of infants born for every 1,000 women of childbearing age.

Blastocyst A fertilized ovum during the first 2 weeks of prenatal development, before implantation in the uterus.

Blindness The provision of limited information about the goals and conditions of a research study in order to prevent bias from subjects or observers.

Bodymind centering A somatic awareness technique in which verbal directions and touch are used to guide people step by step through the reexperiencing of the sensorimotor stages of prenatal and infant development.

Bonding The feelings of attachment the caregiver derives from close contact with the baby.

Brain stem A structure located at the lower back of the head that includes the lower brain stem that connects to the spinal cord, the upper brain stem or medulla, and is connected to the cerebellum. This part of the brain contains areas responsible for autonomic activities, such as respiration, heart rate, body temperature, sucking, and other reflexes.

Braxton-Hicks contractions Contractions that serve to move the fetus into its prebirth position; also called false labor.

Breech presentation A presentation in which the fetus is aligned buttocks first against the cervix.

Buffering The ability of the environment to maintain infant development on a typical course in spite of deviations caused by early infant risk factors.

Burst-pause pattern The pattern of sucking behavior in which the baby sucks for a few minutes, stops, and resumes sucking.

Butterfly effect The idea that small effects can have major consequences as they are amplified in a dynamic system, with the implication that it is impossible to trace the system backward in time to isolate single causes for later changes in the system.

Case study The focus on a single individual, or a single interacting group such as a family or classroom, in order to follow changes in them over time.

Catch-up growth The higher rate of physical development seen in some cases of early deprivation or birth complications, compared to the normal growth rate.

Categorical self The ability of people to identify their own membership in one or more conceptual categories, such as "I am a boy," "I am a brother," and "I am not a baby."

Cephalocaudal development Growth that proceeds from the top of the body to the bottom.

Cervix The opening between the uterus and the vagina.

Cesarean section Delivery of the fetus through an incision in the mother's abdomen and uterus.

Chaos A mathematical concept that expresses the property of complex systems of having some general structure that repeats over time but never in exactly the same way.

Chorion The inner lining of the placenta separating it from the amniotic sac.

Chorionic villus sampling (CVS) A test for birth defects in which a small amount of the chorion is sampled. It can be done earlier in pregnancy than amniocentesis.

Chromosome An arrangement of about 20,000 genes, aligned in a long string. Each cell in the body contains 46 chromosomes, except for the gametes, which contain 23 chromosomes.

Classical conditioning Learning by association; the linking together of a stimulus and a response occurring at the same time.

Clinical infant The view of infant experience that emerges from the re-experiencing by children and adults of infant-like movements, sensations, and states of being.

Cloning A method of creating a zygote by removing the donor mother's DNA from the ova and implanting the DNA from any cell in the body of another person.

Co-construction The process by which what one knows depends upon how one acts on the environment and how the environment responds to those actions.

Coding The process by which observers record the presence or absence of predefined behavioral categories as they are watching an individual or a group.

Colic A complaint of excessive crying (at least 3 hours per day, for a least 3 days per week, for at least 3 weeks) in an otherwise normal infant.

Colostrum A clear, yellowish, high-protein liquid secreted by the breasts beginning in the fourth month of pregnancy and continuing until several days after birth.

Compensation The provision of additional environmental support for infants who suffer from early deficits.

Conception The fertilization of an ovum.

Conceptual memories Memories of specific categories for type of event ("I was left alone"), time ("when I was five years old"), and place ("at the preschool"); recall about an event that is communicated in the form of a verbal narrative or story.

Constant comparative method The process of revising the researcher's interpretations of the data upon repeated reviews of it until there are no further changes in interpretation.

Constructivist theory A theory in which knowledge is built up by the child's own action rather than being imposed on the child from the outside.

Continuity The preservation of individual characteristics across ages.

Contrast group A group used in experimental studies that receives a different manipulation or intervention from the experimental group.

Control group A group used in experimental studies that does not experience the intervention or manipulation received by the experimental group; allows a test of the effects of the manipulation compared with no manipulation.

Conventional actions Actions that represent another action or an object using some type of ritualized manner of expression, such as waving or saying "bye-bye."

Conventional communication A communicative act, such as a word, that is used by all members of the same speaking community.

Coordinated joint attention The process by which people co-regulate intentions with other people by attending to the same things at the same time (also called *intersubjectivity*).

Core self The experience of being an active agent that does things in the world, has feelings, and has a history of prior experiences.

Co-regulation The continuous mutual adjustment and co-creativity that appears in spontaneous communication. It is a form of self-organization as applied to interpersonal communication.

Corporal punishment Using physical force for the purpose of discipline that causes pain to the child but not injury.

Cortex The outer layer of the brain, and the largest part of the human brain, that covers the limbic system and connects with it. The cortex is responsible for perception, movement, cognition, and most important, the voluntary regulation of behavior and emotion.

Cortisol, like the sympathetic nervous system, prepares the body for action in response to stress. It increases blood sugar needed for action and, via the blood, feeds back into the limbic system, where it heightens the formation of memories related to the stressful event. On the other hand, prolonged activation of cortisol due to ongoing stress suppresses the immune system and physical growth.

Couvade A father's attempt to experience the mother's feelings during pregnancy and delivery, seen in the form of culturally accepted rituals.

Credibility A form of validity in qualitative research based on the skill, experience, and rigor of the observer.

Critical period A relatively short, well-defined period in the life cycle when the individual is particularly receptive to certain kinds of environmental stimulation; if that stimulation is not received, the individual is not likely to profit from later exposure to similar stimuli, and other normal developmental processes may be disrupted.

Cross-modal perception Integration of information across more than one perceptual modality.

Cross-sectional study A research study in which age differences are studied using different infants at each age.

Cystic fibrosis A genetic disorder that causes clogging of the lungs with mucus.

Dance Movement Psychotherapy A somatic awareness practice in which infants and children can be engaged using expressive dance-like movements to foster a more integrated sense of self in relation to other people.

Defensive response Avoidance or aversive response to noxious or potentially threatening stimuli.

Deferred imitation Imitation that occurs following a delay from the time the action is seen modeled.

Dendrites The branching structures on the neuron that receive information at the synapse from other neurons and transmit it to the cell body.

Dependent variable Measurable outcome behavior observed in response to changes in an independent variable; the presumed effect of a causal independent variable in an experimental study.

Determinism The view that all natural phenomena are the result of some specifiable set of causes.

Developmental change Change that is nonreversible, not temporary, and not haphazard.

Developmental stage A stable and persistent pattern of behavior, thought, and feeling that continues over a long period of time (months or years).

Deviation-amplifying feedback Feedback that drastically changes a system as a result of a small deviation.

Deviation-correcting feedback Feedback that maintains a system's characteristics over time in spite of small deviations.

Differentiated ecological self The awareness that the ecology has localized entities, such as self and other or self and object, shown by the different ways in which infants call attention to themselves, such as asking for help, taking the initiative, clowning and showing off, demanding, and hiding and escaping.

Difficult temperament A parental judgment regarding the relative non-responsiveness of the infant to parental interventions.

Direct transaction A transaction that occurs as part of a social relationship in which the child is an active participant: the infant-parent, infant-peer, or infant-sibling relationship.

Disequilibrium The infant's experience during failures at adaptation; the motivational force that leads the infant to adapt by means of assimilation and accommodation.

Disorganized-disoriented attachment The infant shows confused behavior in the Strange Situation Test, such as approaching the mother and then suddenly withdrawing.

Displacement The property of language to express concrete and abstract ideas and describe objects that are not physically in the speaker's presence.

Dissociation The inability to connect with one's own body or with one's own emotional experiences. May include the following symptoms: mental confusion, lack of subjective self-awareness, out-of-body experiences, accident proneness, and self-harm or suicide proneness

Dizygotic twins Twins formed when two ova are fertilized at the same time.

DNA (Deoxyribonucleic acid) A molecule that contains a biochemical code for the production of body tissues. Genes are sections of DNA that control the development of specific characteristics and functions of the individual.

Dominance hierarchy A pattern of social relationships in which the members of a group are ranked according to their relative power or lack of power over others.

Dominant-recessive inheritance A two-gene inheritance pattern in which the recessive gene appears in the phenotype only if no dominant gene is present.

Dorsoventral development Growth that begins at the spine and moves toward the front of the body.

Dose-response relationship A relationship between a drug's dosage and its effects in which increasing dosages lead to stronger effects.

Down's syndrome A chromosomal disorder that causes short stature, cardiac abnormalities, flabbiness, small mouth, and mental retardation.

Dramatists Children who classify objects based on a script or story in which the objects are embedded.

Ecological perception The kind of experience that relies on direct perception through the senses, not mediated by thought or judgment.

Ecological self The ability to experience the body and its senses, feelings, and movements in relation to the environment.

Ecological self The ability to recognize the body and its senses, feelings, and movements.

Ecology of human development The physical and social environments in which children develop.

Ectoderm One of the cell layers in the embryonic disk that will become the central nervous system, brain, sense organs, skin, hair, nails, and teeth (see also endoderm and mesoderm).

Ego The sum total of the person's regulatory functions, which includes coping, information processing, and emotions; the ego mediates between the person's needs and the demands of the environment.

Embryo The period of prenatal development beginning in the second week after conception and extending until the third month of pregnancy.

Embryo cryopreservation Freezing fertilized embryos for later implantation into the uterus.

Embryonic disk A layer of cells in the blastocyst that will eventually become the embryo's body.

Embryonic stem cells Embryonic cells that can be transformed into many different types of tissue by implanting them into the bodies of adults whose tissues have been damaged by injury or disease.

Emergent self The perception of sameness over time in behavior, feelings, and states of arousal; the sense of familiarity of the body that persists even when objects and people come and go.

Emotion regulation The ability to control the form and timing of one's emotional expression and feeling state.

Empiricism An eighteenth-century philosophical idea that knowledge is derived from direct observation and that human problems can be solved with logical reasoning.

Endoderm A layer of cells in the embryonic disk that will become the digestive, respiratory, and urinary systems (see also ectoderm and mesoderm).

Environmental specificity Continuities between the environment and the individual's development are found only for specific facets of the individual with specific features of the environment. Specific individuals are better able to profit from some environments than from others.

Epidurals are a local anesthetic administered in the lower (lumbar) spine that blocks pain sensation in the pelvic area but allows the mother to remain awake and aware.

Epigenome A set of biochemical markers that are responsive to the environment and that turn on or turn off the actions of particular genes within each cell.

Euthanasia Letting an individual die naturally without medical intervention, except to relieve pain.

Event-related potentials The detection and computation of electrical current on the surface of the scalp to map regions of brain activity.

Exercise play Playful locomotor movement that is physically vigorous, such as running, chasing, and climbing.

Existential self The ability to recognize one's own features as different from someone else's. It involves an awareness of the self as someone who can be recognized and can be distinguished as a whole person from other people.

Exosystem Includes systems that do not contain the developing child but that do affect the child's well-being, such as the parent's work, the government, and the economy.

Experience dependent Brain regions and pathways that are not fully formed and must await environmental input for their development.

Experience expectant Brain regions and pathways that are more or less fully developed at birth, allowing the infant to adapt to particular types of environmental stimuli related to basic survival.

Experiment A research strategy in which some factors are manipulated by the experimenter, while others are controlled or held constant across groups.

Expressive speech Speech that is socially oriented and uses more, but less well articulated, words per utterance.

Extinction The elimination of learned behavior by ceasing to reinforce the behavior.

Failure-to-thrive The slow deterioration of an infant's condition and lack of responsiveness to intervention; seen in cases of malnutrition and disease.

Familial Alzheimer's disease A genetic disorder that causes deterioration of the central nervous system, leading to lack of mental and motor control.

Family planning The voluntary alteration of normal reproductive patterns using contraception methods.

Feedback A process by which components of a system have an effect on their own behavior during their transactions with other components.

Feldenkrais method A system of somatic awareness and movement education that reawakens, develops, and organizes capacities for kinesthetic (sensorimotor) learning.

Fertility The ability to achieve fertilization and become pregnant.

Fetal alcohol syndrome (FAS) A teratogenic disorder caused by excessive alcohol consumption by a pregnant mother. Effects include physical malformations and attentional disorders.

Fetal distress A sudden loss of oxygen to the fetal brain caused by respiratory or heart problems or a restriction of the blood supply through the umbilical cord.

Fetal monitoring The use of electronic equipment to detect fetal heart rate, breathing, and other physiological signs during the birth process.

Fetus The period from the third month of prenatal life until delivery of the newborn.

Flextime A policy allowing flexible work schedules for working parents.

Fontanels Spaces between the bones of the newborn's skull, which can be felt as soft spots on the scalp.

Forceps An instrument that clamps around the infant's head to pull it through the birth canal.

Formal support systems Community programs that are specifically designed to serve the needs of parents and infants; usually funded by the government.

Formulas Flexible word orders that make up the first sentences of infants; not the same as mature grammar.

Fragile X syndrome A sex-linked genetic disorder that is the most common inherited cause of mental retardation.

Frames Repeating patterns of co-activity such as greetings, parent-infant games like peekaboo, or particular topics of conversation between a couple.

Free association A method of recovering unconscious memories by having clients lie down and encouraging them to relax in an environment safe enough to say anything without fear of retribution or judgment.

Gametes Spermatozoa or ova: reproductive cells having 23 chromosomes each.

Gender identity The affiliation with being either male or female based on a curiosity about children's own and other's bodies.

Gender labeling The ability to identify self or other verbally as male or female.

Gene A section of the DNA molecule that comprises the smallest unit of the codes for inherited characteristics.

Generalizability The ability of the results of a study to be correct for people other than those who were part of the study sample.

Generativity The life stage in Erik Erikson's clinical theory in which people focus on the nurture and support of others, typically shown in parental behavior.

Genetic counseling Assessing the parents' likelihood of producing a child with genetic or chromosomal abnormalities.

Genotype The set of chemical messages within the DNA that direct the formation of protein within a cell nucleus; an individual's genetic inheritance.

Gestational age The age of the infant starting from the date of conception.

Guided participation Collaboration of a responsive adult on a task the infant is already doing, allowing the infant to take small, culturally appropriate roles.

Gynecologist A physician who specializes in women's reproductive health (see also obstetrician).

Habituation The gradual decrease in looking or listening time across repeated presentations of the same visual or auditory stimulus.

Handedness The preferential use of one hand over the other; also refers to the use of each hand to do different things.

Haptic perception The perception of the properties of an object using touch.

HCG (human chorionic gonadotropin) A hormone whose presence signals the onset of pregnancy.

Head Start · A federally funded program for enriched early childhood education and parent education for disadvantaged families.

Heritability The proportion of individual variability in a group that can be explained as owing primarily to individual differences in genetic make-up.

Hippocampus A horseshoe-shaped structure in the limbic system that plays an important role in the formation of memories for events and sequences, what is known as autobiographical memory.

Historical processes Developmental processes that are not simple accumulations of past events but are uniquely emergent creations that can never be exactly repeated.

Homeostasis The maintenance of biological functions within normal levels; for example, the regulation of body temperature.

HPA Axis The system by which the neuroception of stress is translated into the release of hormones from the hypothalamus to the pituitary (via corticotropin-releasing hormone, CRH), from the pituitary to the adrenal gland (via adrenocorticotropic hormone, ACTH), which results in the secretion of the hormone cortisol into the blood stream

Huntington's disease A genetic disorder that causes progressive brain damage and death.

Hypothalamus is a small structure in the middle of the limbic system that links the brain to the endocrine (hormones) systems of the body via the pituitary gland. It regulates stress, body temperature, hunger, thirst, and day-night rhythms.

Id The uninhibited expression of the individual's basic needs; during infancy, these needs are centered primarily around the oral and anal zones.

Idiosyncratic communication A form of communication that the individual makes up. It requires a familiar adult to interpret its meaning.

Imaginative pretend play Play in which the child invents make-believe situations.

Imprinting A process in which the young of some animal species become attached to an object or person by means of a brief exposure to that object or person.

In vitro fertilization Fertilization achieved in a laboratory, outside the mother's body, by surgically removing ova and uniting them with spermatozoa.

Independent variable The variable controlled or manipulated by the experimenter; the presumed cause of the effects measured by the dependent variables in experimental research.

Indeterminism The idea that not all natural phenomena can be predicted from known laws or principles.

Infant psychiatry The application of clinical psychology to work with infants and their families.

Infant-directed (ID) speech A style of speech that includes exaggerated pitch, loudness, marked rhythms, and clear melodies (see also *motherese*).

Infanticide The deliberate killing of newborn infants as a means to limit family size.

Infantile amnesia The lack of adult conceptual memory of one's life before the age of two years.

Infant-Parent Mental Health (IPMH) An emerging multidisciplinary specialization focusing on the relational context of the total development of young children with a deep commitment to transdisciplinary integration and to the treatment of developmental, relational, and emotional distress from a whole-child-in-relationship perspective.

Infants with special needs Infants who suffer from prenatal and postnatal deficits, deformities, and developmental delays that create additional challenges for them and their families.

Infertility Failure to achieve fertilization.

Informal support system A family's social network of relatives, friends, and community resources.

Informed consent The voluntary consent by human research subjects, based on a complete description of the procedures, risks, and benefits of the research; a fundamental ethical principle of human research.

Insecure-avoidant attachment The infant does not approach the mother during the reunion episode of the Strange Situation Test and makes active efforts to get away if the mother tries to comfort the infant.

Insecure-resistant attachment An ambivalent pattern of responding in the Strange Situation Test such that the infant cannot feel comfortable with either the mother or the toys. Not as extreme or as abrupt as the disorganized-disoriented pattern.

Internal working model A set of mental representations and expectations one has about attachment figures.

Intersex A birth defect in which the genitals do not completely form or in which infants have characteristics of both males and females or internal characteristics of one gender and external characteristics of the other gender

Intersubjectivity The experience of another person in relation to the actions of the self. During participatory co-regulated dialogue, the infant can feel how her or his agency affects the other person and how the other's agency affects the infant's own.

Invariance Detection of what is similar about an object in spite of variations in the conditions under which it is perceived; the basis of recognizing the same object from different perspectives.

Joint visual attention The ability of partners to follow the direction of the other's gaze or pointing gesture.

Kangaroo care A method of communication with premature infants in which the infant, wearing only a diaper, is placed on the parent's chest. The infant's head is turned to the side so that the baby's ear is against the parent's heart.

Karyotype An arrangement of chromosome pairs for easy examination; made by photographing a micrograph of a set of chromosomes and then cutting the photograph and placing the chromosome pairs in order.

Kinesthetic empathy The ability to feel another person's feelings by moving like that other person, based on dance movement psychotherapy.

Kleinfelter's syndrome A chromosomal disorder that causes female-like males and mental retardation.

Labor Muscle contractions leading to the birth of the fetus and placenta.

Lamaze method Pain relief during labor that uses breathing and relaxation techniques.

Lanugo Fine hair that grows over most of the fetus's body, beginning in the fourth month.

Leboyer method An approach to delivery in which the newborn is kept warm in a water bath and subjected to low levels of sound and light.

Left hemisphere The left half of the brain that controls movements on the right side of the body. It is specialized for thinking and language and develops more rapidly after the first two years of life.

Limbic system A brain area that is located more or less in the very center of the head, between the ears, and includes structures such as the amygdala, the hippocampus, the hypothalamus, and the pituitary gland. This part of the brain is related to processes; such as attention, states like sleeping and waking, urinary and bowel control, emotion and responses to stress and trauma, and memory.

Liquidating pretend play Play in which the child's make-believe situation alters reality to better suit the child's desires.

Longitudinal study A research study that follows developmental changes in the same individual over time.

Macroanalysis The focus on overall patterns of behavior and summary variables rather than on events and sequences.

Macrosystem The system of beliefs, values, and rules of the society and culture.

Marfan's syndrome A genetic disorder associated with a weakened heart, mild bone structure deformities, long fingers, and eye lens problems.

Mastery motivation The desire to become competent at a particular goal.

Maternal serum alpha-fetoprotein (MSAFP) A prenatal test for spina bifida (exposed spine) and anencephaly (exposed brain) using the mother's blood; performed between the 15th and 18th week of pregnancy.

Maturation Developmental change that is controlled by hereditary timing mechanisms.

Mean length of utterance (MLU) The average number of morphemes across all the utterances of a child.

Meconium The contents of the newborn's intestines; a greenish-black substance containing digested amniotic fluid and particles of hair and skin.

Mediated transaction A transaction that occurs when the infant affects or is affected by people with whom the infant does not share an active relationship.

Meiosis The process of cell division that produces gametes, resulting in only half the usual number of chromosomes.

Mesoderm A layer of cells in the embryonic disk that leads to the development of muscles, bones, and the circulatory and reproductive systems (see also ectoderm and endoderm).

Mesosystem The system of relationships between the settings in which children live, such as between the home and the school setting.

Metacommunicative events Communicative acts that refer to the relationship between partners rather than to the world outside the relationship.

Metalinguistic knowledge An understanding of the uses and functions of language, independent of knowledge of semantics and syntax.

Metapelet A substitute caregiver on an Israeli kibbutz.

Microanalysis The focus on the occurrences and changes of specific events and event sequences.

Micronutrients Vitamins and minerals found in foods and in dietary supplements.

Microsystem The system of interpersonal relationships between the child and other people.

Midwife A professional trained to assist women during childbirth.

Milk expression The second phase of sucking, in which the infant presses the nipple against the roof of the mouth with the tongue to force milk out.

Mitosis The cell-division process by which each chromosome makes a copy of itself before cell division takes place.

Monosomy An abnormality of the 23rd chromosome in which one member of the pair is missing.

Monozygotic twins Twins formed by the splitting of the same zygote.

Motherese Changes in speech patterns involving exaggeration of pitch, higher pitch, use of rhythm and melody, slowing down, and simplification.

Multiparous A mother who has given birth more than once.

Myelin A protective coating over nerve cells that aids in the conduction of action potentials.

Myelination The development of a protective coating over nerve conduction pathways that improves transmission of information.

Natural family planning Limiting or enhancing the possibility of conception by using a method for determining the days of ovulation.

Natural selection The theory of the evolution of species, proposed by Charles Darwin, in which genetic changes are explained by different survival rates of offspring that have characteristics that are better or less well-suited to the environment.

Nature Refers to the belief that behavior and development are controlled primarily by hereditary influences.

Negative feedback Feedback that maintains a system's characteristics over time in spite of small deviations.

Negative pressure The first phase of sucking, in which the gums create a seal around the nipple and the jaw drops to create suction inside the mouth.

Negative reinforcer The absence of a consequence of an action that increases the frequency of that action.

Neonatal The period immediately following birth.

Neural plasticity is the ability of the brain and nervous system to seek novelty, learn, and remember by continuing to alter the patterns of connections between neurons.

Neuroimaging The use of different types of radiation to detect electrical and chemical changes in specific regions of the brain; includes PET and fMRI methods.

Neurological assessment Testing of newborn reflexes and postures to determine the intactness of the brain and nervous system.

Neuron A conductive cell in the central nervous system.

Neuroscience The study of the brain and nervous system as it relates to psychological and behavioral functions such as moving, thinking, and feeling.

Neurotransmitters Neurochemicals, of which there a many varieties such as serotonin and dopamine, signal from one neuron to another processes such as voluntary reflex movements, state regulation, memory, emotion, and pain.

Nonnutritive sucking (NNS) Sucking in the absence of fluids, including spontaneous sucking and sucking on a pacifier.

Normal physiological jaundice A slight yellowing of the skin caused by immature functioning of the liver.

Nurture Refers to the belief that behavior and development are controlled primarily by environmental influences.

Object permanence The ability to remember the location of objects that are out of sight.

Observational learning Learning without reinforcement or association by watching how others perform in certain situations.

Observational research A research strategy in which the experimenter does not manipulate the subjects but takes advantage of natural variations in the environment.

Observed infant A view of infant experience that derives from scientific observations of infant behavior.

Obstetrician A physician who specializes in prenatal care, delivery, and reproductive health (see also gynecologist).

Oculomotor skills The movements of the eye, including lens focusing, convergence and divergence, scanning, and tracking.

Operant conditioning An increase in the likelihood that a particular response will occur following a reinforcement of that response.

Oral stage The period during the first eighteen months of life when the infant is particularly aware of sensations of pleasure and displeasure in the mouth region through activities such as sucking, chewing, biting, and swallowing.

Organic learning The use of all one's senses and every part of the body in the process of learning new movements.

Orienting response The direction of attention and action toward an attractive stimulus.

Outcome variable The presumed effect of a cause represented by a predictor variable in observational research; analogous to the dependent variable in experimental research.

Overextension Applying a single word to refer to more objects and situations than it normally refers to in adult speech.

Overregularization The extension of regular verb endings for the past tense to irregular verbs.

Ovum Female gamete; plural *ova*.

Paired-preference procedure A research technique that relies on differences in infant looking time to assess perceptual preference.

Parasympathetic nervous system Allows the body to relax, slow down, rest, process information, engage socially with others, learn and grow.

Parens patriae The legal concept that children are possessions of their parents.

Parental proactive behavior An approach to discipline in which the adult controls the child's environment by anticipating future problems.

Parental separation anxiety A parent's feelings of loss or distress when he or she is separated from the child.

Partial birth abortion An elective abortion procedure for larger fetuses in which labor is induced, the cervix dilated, and the fetus pulled out by the feet, leaving the head undelivered until the fetal brain has been extracted.

Participant observer A form of qualitative research in which the observer is explicitly part of the process of observation and takes account of his or her effect on the subjects.

Participatory memories Memories that are in the form of feeling or sensation rather than being conceptualized as a specific incident; composed of emotions, desires, and a sense of familiarity, but without any specific time or place.

Patterners Children who classify objects based on similarities in their forms or functions.

Pediatrician A physician who specializes in the care of infants and children.

Perinatal The period from about 1 month before to about 1 month after birth.

Phenotype The functioning organism; everything other than the DNA.

Phenylketonuria (PKU) A genetic disorder that causes central nervous system damage if not treated by dietary control.

Pituitary A hormone-producing endocrine gland. It is stimulated by the hypothalamus to produce hormones for stress regulation, maintenance of body state, sexual activity, milk production in nursing mothers, and growth.

Polygenic inheritance When multiple genes are responsible for a single phenotypic characteristic.

Positive feedback Feedback that drastically alters a system as a result of a small deviation.

Positive reinforcer A consequence of an action that increases the probability of that action in the future.

Post traumatic stress syndrome (PTSD) The result of prolonged exposure to stress and threat resulting in a decreased ability of the individual to cope with stress (in the prefrontal cortex) in appropriate ways, creating people who are more likely to freeze, fight, or flee when they feel threatened.

Postpartum depression Sudden, transitory episodes of sadness or emotional lows; not related to pathological depression.

Prader-Willi syndrome A genetic disorder associated with low muscle tone, obesity, short stature, small hands and feet, and lowered intelligence.

Pragmatics The study of the functional uses of language, as opposed to the structural (grammatical) properties of language.

Predictor variable The presumed cause of an effect measured by an outcome variable in observational research; analogous to the independent variable in experimental research.

Prefrontal cortex Located roughly above the eyes, it forms a link between the limbic system and the cortex and therefore plays an important role in how the infant learns to regulate states and emotions.

Preimplantation genetic diagnosis (PGD) A method of testing cells from the zygote for genetic and chromosomal disorders before it they become implanted in the uterus.

Pretend role play A form of pretend play in which children act out the roles of their mother, their father, or other important figures in their lives.

Primary circular reactions Repetitive movements of the infant's body that are discovered by chance and repeated for fun.

Primiparous A woman who is giving birth for the first time.

Private speech An internalized dialogue with the self in which children describe their thoughts and actions out loud.

Probabilistic Refers to the nondeterministic influence of the genotype over the phenotype. A particular genotype will not lead to a specific phenotype for all individuals.

Productivity The ability of language to express multiple meanings using a small number of words simply by rearranging the word order in novel ways.

Prospective study A longitudinal research study in which data are gathered from subjects at periodic intervals, so that the subjects' current behavior and ideas are being observed.

Protoconversation An initial form of turn taking in adult-infant interaction in which the parent fills in the natural pauses in the infant's behavior, but the infant does not take any social initiatives.

Prototype The clearest example of a particular form or sound. Prototypes also represent the average of all exemplars across all relevant dimensions.

Proximodistal development Parts of the body closer to the trunk develop faster than the extremities.

Psychoanalysis The use of free association in psychotherapy leading to the interpretation of unconscious and participatory memories from the perspective of early childhood experiences.

Punishment A consequence that decreases the frequency of the behavior that it follows.

Qualitative research Research that focuses on the meaning of behavior for the participants.

Quantitative research Research that focuses on representing behavior using numerical variables.

Random assignment A procedure in which subjects are placed into experimental and control groups by the flip of a coin or some other nonbiased method.

Rapid eye movement (REM) sleep Sleep in which rapid vertical eye movements are accompanied by irregular body and respiration movements.

Rating scale A summary judgment about behavior, expressed as a numerical value along an ordinal scale.

Reactive attachment disorder (RAD) Begins before age 5 and is marked by one of two types of patterns: (1) *Inhibitions.* The child is excessively inhibited, hypervigilant, or ambivalent and contradictory. (2) *Disinhibitions.* The child shows indiscriminate sociability with inability to form appropriate selective attachments.

Recovery An increase in infant looking time in response to a change in the stimulus during a habituation procedure.

Referential speech Speech that is object oriented and contains a few, but clearly articulated, words per utterance.

Reflex A semiautomatic response to a specific stimulus that, once elicited, must run its course.

Reinforcer An environmental stimulus that, when it appears following a specific individual response, increases the likelihood that the response will occur again.

Relational play The ability to combine two or more objects appropriately according to their function.

Relationship A lasting pattern of communication between two or more people in which past encounters provide a historical background for future encounters.

Reliability The extent to which multiple observers agree about the coding of ongoing behavior.

Representative research A study in which the results from the group of infants who are observed can be generalized to a wider range of infants from different cultures and socioeconomic groups.

Response-contingent procedure A research technique in which different stimuli are made contingent upon different infant actions. Display of one or the other action by the infant usually means a preference for the contingently related stimulus.

Retrospective study A research study in which the subject recollects his or her past or the experimenter traces the subject's records backward in time.

Right hemisphere The right half of the brain that controls movements on the left side of the body. It is also where the majority of social and emotional activity is processed. It undergoes major development during the first two years of life when infants are discovering how to regulate their emotions and form attachments to the primary people in their lives.

Roe v. Wade A 1973 ruling by the justices of the U.S. Supreme Court concluding that the decision to terminate a pregnancy is part of a woman's right to privacy guaranteed by the Constitution.

Role overload Refers to one person trying to fill too many roles or facing excessive demands from a single role.

Romanticism An eighteenth-century philosophical idea that children are inherently good and have the ability to develop successfully with minimal guidance.

Rosen method A somatic awareness approach that uses listening to the client's body with gentle touch and to the words they use to describe their experience, allowing the client to relax, relieve pain, and breathe more easily.

Schemes The currently available set of skills and knowledge that a person has.

Scientific theory A system of concepts that explains the observable world with structures, processes, or mechanisms that are presumed to exist but that cannot be observed directly.

Screening assessment Tests of newborn functioning used to predict the need for medical interventions.

Script A form of conceptual organization in which events are remembered according to the sequences in which they usually occur.

Secondary circular reaction Deliberate repetition of an association between an action and its effect. In this case, each repetition is a slight variation of the one before in which the infant is exploring different ways to create effects.

Secure attachment The infant returns to independent play following comfort seeking from the mother during the Strange Situation Test.

Self-affectivity People's sense of having inner emotional feelings that routinely go together with specific experiences.

Self-agency People's feeling that they are causal agents that can successfully affect their own bodies and the environment.

Self-coherence People's feeling that they and the objects around them are integrated wholes that have distinct boundaries.

Self-conscious emotion An emotion that requires an awareness of an existential self in relation to an existential other; examples are shame, embarrassment, guilt, and pride.

Self-history People's feeling that the past can be connected to the present by means of recreating one's own actions in similar situations; a sense of self-similarity.

Self-organization The emergence of organized patterns that create their own structure and maintain their own source of energy due to the mutual influences of each element of the system on the others.

Self-righting The ability of the infant organism to assimilate those aspects of the environment that serve to return development to a more typical pathway.

Semanticity The ability of language to carry meaning for both speaker and listener.

Sensorimotor substage According to Piaget, the first two years of life, in which the child "understands" the world through action and sensation rather than through concepts and ideas.

Separation anxiety disorder A child who refuses to be separated from the parent, even to go to bed, and has excessive distress when not at home with parents. The behavior must be intense, last at least 1 month, and be inappropriate for the child's age to meet the criteria for diagnosis.

Sex-linked inheritance Refers to those characteristics that are carried in the genes of the sex chromosomes.

Shared environment That part of the family environment that contributes in the same way to the development of more than one sibling.

Sibling de-identification The process by which parents differentiate between siblings.

Sickle-cell anemia A genetic disorder that causes blood clots to form.

SIDS Sudden Infant Death Syndrome; a cause of death of unknown origins believed to be associated with errors in respiratory regulation, especially during sleep.

Situational constraints Elements of the context of a stimulus or event that determine a child's response to that event. In interactions with other children, for example, the peer's age, sex, and familiarity to the infant, the infant's experience interacting with other children, and the caregiver's location are all situational constraints that may determine the quality of the peer-infant interaction.

Social referencing A form of appraisal in which infants use the emotional expressions of others to regulate their own emotional reactions.

Somatic Individuals' conscious awareness of the experiences of their bodies.

Somatic awareness approaches Clinical approaches that use talk, body movement, and touch as a way to access the participatory memories of early childhood.

Somatic psychotherapy focuses on felt sensations in the body, breathing, and movement on the pathway to psychological well-being.

Species-specific behavior Behavior patterns that occur only in one species and are the result of evolution by natural selection.

Sperm microinjection Injection of sperm directly into a ripe ovum.

Spermatozoon Male gamete; plural *spermatazoa*.

Stability Continuity with respect to group ranking, when individuals preserve their ranking with respect to the same reference group over age.

State An organized pattern of physical and physiological responding that is related to the infant's level of activation and arousal.

State of arousal An organized system of physical and physiological responding that is related to the internal level of arousal, from sleep to waking.

Stereopsis The ability to compare the different images coming from each eye.

Still-face An experimental manipulation in which mothers are asked to hold their faces in a neutral pose and cease talking to or otherwise interacting with their infants.

Subjective self A sense of self that involves an awareness of the feelings and experiences of others and also of the self's dependence upon and attachment to others, in addition to a nonverbal sense of "I."

Surrogate mother A woman who carries the fertilized embryo of another woman and brings the embryo through pregnancy to birth.

Symbol A representation of a thing or event that is conventionally shared among the members of a community.

Sympathetic nervous system Prepares the body for action by elevating heart rate, increasing metabolism, and temporarily suppressing growth functions such as digestion.

Synapse The connection between axons and dendrites by which action potentials are transmitted between neurons.

Synaptogenesis The process by which neurons become more complex, growing more dendrites and axon terminals and making an increasing number of synaptic connections between cells.

Syntax The structure or grammar of a language; the rules that determine word order.

System A set of interrelated components that are governed by feedback processes and that exchange information and material between themselves and between the environment and themselves.

Tay-Sachs disease A genetic disorder that causes mental retardation, physical disabilities, and early death.

Telegraphic speech Speech having two or more words per utterance but with endings and connecting words left out.

Temperament A persistent pattern of emotion and emotion regulation in the infant's relationship to people and things in the environment.

Teratogen An agent that causes birth defects.

Teratology The study of birth defects.

Tertiary circular reactions Refers to the fact that new means are invented to achieve goals by trial-and-error experimentation.

Theory of mind The awareness that other people have independent beliefs and feelings.

Transaction The process by which systems components affect each other.

Transitional object An object to which the infant develops an attachment; it may be used for comfort in the absence of the caregiver.

Transverse presentations A presentation in which the fetus is oriented on its side.

Trisomy A chromosome pair with an extra chromosome attached to it.

Turner's syndrome A chromosomal disorder that causes incomplete sexual determination and mental retardation.

Ultrasound Obtaining an outline of the fetus by means of high-frequency sound wave reflections.

Unconscious That part of the self that is not remembered during ordinary waking states.

Vacuum extraction The use of a suction device attached to the head to extract the infant from the birth canal.

Validity The extent to which an assessment procedure accurately measures the concept or goal of the experimenter.

Verbal self That part of the self that uses language to talk about inner states and to construct a coherent identity in the company of other people.

Vernix caseosa A white, cheesy coating that protects the fetal skin.

Vestibular-proprioceptive stimulation The movement of the infant's body, usually accomplished by carrying and rocking.

Viability The ability of the fetus to maintain its own life outside the uterus.

Visual cliff An experimental apparatus used to determine the nature of an infant's fear of heights.

Vital statistics Numerical estimates of events in a population related to birth, death, and the incidence of illnesses and accidents.

Wariness A quieting or sobering of an infant, usually in response to a novel situation. Wariness is believed to be a precursor to fear.

Watsu A somatic awareness technique in which the practitioner floats the client in a pool of warm water, using stretching and water resistance to create a state of relaxation.

Williams syndrome A genetic disorder in which individuals have short stature, heart defects, are indiscriminately social, and have intellectual deficits, especially in spatial abilities.

Yolk sac A region of cells in the blastocyst that will eventually become the embryonic blood supply and internal organs.

Zone of proximal development Those infant skills that are in the process of developing and are the most uncertain.

Zygote A fertilized ovum.

References

Abboud, L., & Liamputtong, P. (2005). When pregnancy fails: Coping strategies, support networks and experiences with health care of ethnic women and their partners. *Journal of Reproductive and Infant Psychology, 23*(1), 3–18.

Abbott, A., & Bartlett, D. J. (2001). Infant motor development and equipment use in the home. *Child: Care, Health and Development, 27*(3), 295–306.

Abel, E. L., Randall, C. L., & Riley, E. P. (1983). Alcohol consumption and prenatal development. In B. Tabakoff, P. B. Sutker, & C. L. Randall (Eds.), *Medical and social aspects of alcohol abuse.* New York: Plenum Press.

Aber, J. L., Belsky, J., Slade, A., & Crnic, K. (1999). Stability and change in mothers' representations of their relationship with their toddlers. *Developmental Psychology, 35*(4), 1038–1047.

Abramovitch, R., Corter, C., & Landau, B. (1979). Sibling interaction in the home. *Child Development, 50,* 997–1003.

Abramovitch, R., Corter, C., Pepler, D. J., & Stanhope, L. (1986). Sibling and peer interaction: A final follow-up and a comparison. *Child Development, 57,* 217–229.

Abreu-Villaça, Y., Seidler, F. J., & Slotkin, T. A. (2004). Does prenatal nicotine exposure sensitize the brain to nicotine-induced neurotoxicity in adolescence? *Neuropsychopharmacology, 29,* 1440–1450.

Achenbach, T. M., Phares, V., Howell, C. T., Rauh, V. A., & Nurcombe, B. (1990). Seven-year outcome of the Vermont intervention program for low-birthweight infants. *Child Development, 61,* 1672–1681.

Achermann, J., Dinneen, E., & Stevenson-Hinde, J. (1991). Clearing up at 2.5 years. *British Journal of Developmental Psychology, 9,* 365–376.

Acredolo, L., & Goodwyn, S. (1985). Symbolic gesturing in language development. *Human Development, 28,* 40–49.

Acredolo, L., & Goodwyn, S. (1988). Symbolic gesturing in normal infants. *Child Development, 59,* 450–466.

Adams, R. J., & Passman, R. H. (1981). The effects of preparing two-year-olds for brief separations from their mothers. *Child Development, 52,* 1068–1070.

Adams, S. M., Jones, D. R., Esmail, A., & Mitchell, E. A. (2004). What affects the age of first sleeping through the night? *J Paediatr Child Health, 40*(3), 96–101.

Adamson, L. B. (1995). *Communication development during infancy.* Dubuque, IA: WCB Brown & Benchmark.

Adamson, L. B., & Bakeman, R. (1985). Affect and attention: Infants observed with mothers and peers. *Child Development, 56,* 582–593.

Adamson, L. B., Bakeman, R., Smith, C. B., & Walters, A. S. (1987). Adults' interpretation of infants' acts *Developmental Psychology, 23,* 383–387.

Adinolfi, A. M. (1971). The postnatal development of synaptic contacts in the cerebral cortex. In M. B. Sterman, D. J. McGinty, & A. M. Adinolfi (Eds.), *Brain development and behavior* (pp. 182–196). New York: Academic Press.

Adolph, K. E. (1997). Learning in the development of infant locomotion. *Monographs of the Society for Research in Child Development, 62*(3), 1–140.

Adolph, K. E., Gibson, E. J., & Eppler, M. A. (1990). *Perceiving affordances of slopes: The ups and downs of toddler's locomotion.* Report of Emory Cognition Project. Atlanta, GA: Emory University.

Adolph, K. E., Vereijken, B., & Denny, M. A. (1998). Learning to crawl. *Child Development, 69*(5), 1299–1312.

Adolph, K. E., Vereijken, B., Denny, M. A., Gill, V. S., & Lucero, A. (1995, June). *Increased balance requirements constrain variability in infant crawling.* Poster presented at the American Psychological Society, New York.

Adolph, K. E., Vereijken, B., & Shrout, P. E. (2003). What changes in infant walking and why. *Child Development, 74*(2), 475–497.

Adrien, J. L., Lenoir, P., Martineau, J., Perrot, A., Hameury, L., Larmande, C., & Sauvage, D. (1993). Blind ratings of early symptoms of autism based upon family home movies. *Journal of the American Academy of Child Adolescent Psychiatry, 32,* 617–626.

Affonso, D. (1977). "Missing pieces": A study of postpartum feelings. *Birth and the Family Journal, 4,* 159–164.

Aggleton, J. P., & Wood, C. J. (1990). Is there a left-handed advantage in "ballistic" sports? *International Journal of Sport Psychology, 21,* 46–57.

Agiobu-Kemmer, I. (1986). Cognitive and affective aspects of infant development. In H. V. Curran (Ed.), *Nigerian children: Developmental perspectives* (pp. 42–67). London: Routledge & Kegan Paul.

Aguiar, A., & Baillargeon, R. (1998). Eight-and-a-half-month-old infants' reasoning about containment events. *Child Development, 69*(3), 636–653.

Ahnert, L., Gunnar, M. R., Lamb, M. E., & Barthel, M. (2004). Transition to Child Care: Associations With Infant-Mother Attachment, Infant Negative Emotion, and Cortisol Elevations. *Child Development, 75*(3), 639–650.

Ainsworth, M. (1979). Attachment as related to mother-infant interaction. In R. Hinde & J. Rosenblatt (Eds.), *Advances in the study of behavior* (pp. 115–148). New York: Academic Press.

Ainsworth, M., & Bell, S. (1970). Attachment, exploration, and separation: Illustrated by the behavior of one-year-olds in a strange situation. *Child Development, 41,* 49–67.

Ainsworth, M., Bell, S., & Stayton, D. (1971). Individual differences in strange situation behavior of one-year-olds. In H. R. Schaffer (Ed.), *The origins of human and social relations* (pp. 240–262). London: Academic Press.

Ainsworth, M., Blehar, M. C., Waters, E., & Wall, S. (1978). *Patterns of attachment.* Hillsdale, NJ: Erlbaum.

Akhtar, N. (2005). The robustness of learning through over-hearing. *Developmental Science, 8*(2), 199–209.

Alan Guttmacher Institute. (1994). *Sex and America's teenagers.* New York, New York: Author.

Alessandri, S. M., & Lewis, M. (1996). Differences in pride and shame in maltreated and nonmaltreated preschoolers. *Child Development, 67*(4), 1857–1869.

Alexander, G. R., & Korenbrot, C. C. (1995). The role of prenatal care in preventing low birth weight. *The Future of Children, 5,* 103–120.

Alkon, A, Ramler, M., and MacLennan, K. "Evaluation of Mental Health Consultation in Child Care Centers." *Early Childhood Education Journal* 31(2) (2003): 91–99.

Alink, L. R. A., Mesman, J., van Zeijl, J., Stolk, M. N., Juffer, F., Koot, H. M., et al. (2006). The Early Childhood Aggression Curve: Development of Physical Aggression in 10– to 50–Month-Old Children. *Child Development, 77*(4), 954–966.

Allen, D. A., Affleck, G., McGrade, B. J., & McQueeney, M. (1984). Effects of single-parent status on mothers and their high-risk infants. *Infant Behavior and Development, 7,* 347–359.

Allen, S. (1998). A qualitative analysis of the process, mediating variables and impact of traumatic childbirth. *Reproductive and Infant Psychology, 16,* 107–131.

Allman, J., Rosin, A., Kumar, R., & Hasenstaub, A. (1998). Parenting and survival in anthropoid primates: Caretakers live longer. *Proceedings of the National Academy of Sciences of the United States of America, 95,* 6866–6869.

Als, H., Duffy, F. H., & McAnulty, G. B. (1988). Behavioral differences between preterm and full-term newborns as measured with the APIB system scores: I. *Infant Behavior and Development, 11,* 305–318.

Alvarez, W. F. (1985). The meaning of maternal employment for mothers and their perceptions of their three-year-old children. *Child Development, 56,* 350–360.

Alwan, S., Reefhuis, J., Rasmussen, S., Olney, R., & Friedman, J. (2007). Use of selective serotonin-reuptake inhibitors in pregnancy and the risk of birth defects. *New England Journal of Medicine, 356*(26), 2684–2692.

Angulo-Kinzler, R. M., & Horn, C. L. (2001). Selection and memory of a lower limb motor-perceptual task in 3–month-old infants. *Infant Behavior & Development, 24*(3), 239–257.

Amabile, T. A., & Rovee-Collier, C. (1991). Contextual variation and memory retrieval at six months. *Child Development, 62,* 1155–1166.

American Academy of Pediatrics. (1997). Breastfeeding and the use of human milk: Policy statement. *Pediatrics, 100*(6), 1035–1039.

American Academy of Pediatrics. (2003). *Pediatric nutrition handbook, 5th Edition.* American Academy of Pediatrics

Ammerman, S. D., Perelli, E., Adler, N., & Irwin, C. E. (1992). Do adolescents understand what physicians say about sexuality and health? *Clinical Pediatrics, 31,* 590–595.

Anders, T. F., Goodlin-Jones, B. L., & Zelenko, M. (1998). Infant regulation and sleep-wake state development. *Zero to Three 19*(2), 5–8.

Anderson, D. R., & Levin, S. R. (1976). Young children's attention to "Sesame Street." *Child Development, 47,* 806–811.

Anderson, D. R., & Lorch, E. P. (1983). Looking at television: Action or reaction? In J. Bryant & D. R. Anderson (Eds.), *Children's understanding of television: Research on attention and comprehension* (pp. 1–33). New York: Academic Press.

Anderson, G. C. (1999). Kangaroo care of the premature infant. In E. Goldstein & A. Sostek (Eds.), *Nurturing the premature infant: Developmental intervention in the neonatal intensive care nursery* (pp. 351–366). Oxford, England: Oxford University Press.

Anderson, G. C., Burroughs, A. K., & Measel, C. P. (1983). Non-nutritive sucking opportunities: A safe and effective treatment for preterm neonates. In T. Field & A. Sostek (Eds.), *Infants born at risk* (pp. 215–245). New York: Grune & Stratton.

Andersson, B. E. (1992). Effects of day-care on cognitive and socioemotional competence of thirteen-year-old Swedish schoolchildren. *Child Development, 63,* 20–36.

Anisfeld, M. (1979). Interpreting "imitative" responses in early infancy. *Science, 205,* 214–215.

Anisfeld, M., Turkewitz, G., Rose, S., Rosenberg, F., Sheiber, F., Couturier-Fagan, D., et al. (2001). No compelling evidence that newborns imitate oral gestures. *Infancy, 2*(1), 111–122.

Antonelli, P. L. (1985). *Mathematical essays on growth and the emergence of form.* Edmonton, Canada: University of Alberta Press.

Apgar, V. (1953). A proposal for a new method of evaluation in the newborn infant. *Current Research in Anesthesia and Analgesia, 32,* 260.

Aposhyan, S. (2003). *Body-mind psychotherapy.* NY: Norton.

Arehart-Treichel, J. (1979, December 1). Down's syndrome: The father's role. *Science News,* 381–382.

Areias, M. E., Kumar, R., Barros, H., & Figueiredo, E. (1996). Correlates of postnatal depression in mothers and fathers. *British Journal of Psychiatry, 169*(1), 36–41.

Arend, R., Gove, F. L., & Sroufe, L. A. (1979). Continuity of individual adaptation from infancy to kindergarten: A predictive study of ego-resiliency and curiosity in pre-schoolers. *Child Development, 50,* 950–959.

Arendt, R., Singer, L., Angelopoulos, J., Bass-Busdiecker, O., & Mascia, J. (1998). Sensorimotor development in cocaine-exposed infants. *Infant Behavior and Development, 21*(4), 627–640.

Arterberry, M., Yonas, A., & Bensen, A. S. (1989). Self-produced locomotion and the development of responsiveness to linear perspective and texture gradients. *Developmental Psychology, 25*(6), 976–982.

Asendorpf, J. B., & Baudonniere, P. M. (1993). Self awareness and other-awareness: Mirror self-recognition and synchronic imitation among unfamiliar peers. *Developmental Psychology, 29,* 88–95.

Asendorpf, J. B., Warkentin, V., & Baudonniere, P. (1996). Self-awareness and other-awareness II: Mirror self-recognition, social contingency awareness, and synchronic imitation. *Developmental Psychology, 32*(2), 313–321.

Aslin, R. N. (1981). Development of smooth pursuit in human infants. In D. F. Fisher, R. A. Monty, & J. W. Sanders (Eds.), *Eye movements: Cognition and visual perception* (pp. 540–557). Hillsdale, NJ: Erlbaum.

Aslin, R. N. (1987). Visual and auditory development in infancy. In J. D. Osofsky (Ed.), *Handbook of infant development* (2nd ed., pp. 146–169). New York: Wiley.

Atkinson, J. (1995). Through the eyes of an infant. In R. Gregory, J. Harris, P. Heard, & D. Rose (Eds.), *The artful eye* (pp. 141-156). New York: Oxford University Press.

Atkinson, L., Chisholm, V. C., Scott, B., Goldberg, S., Vaughn, B. E., Blackwell, J., Dickens, S., & Tam, F. (1999). Maternal sensitivity, child functional level, and attachment in Down syndrome. *Monographs of the Society for Research in Child Development, 64*(3), 46–66.

Aureli, T. (1994). Shared focus in mother-child joint activity in the second year of life. *Early Development & Parenting, 3,* 145–152.

Aureli, T. (1997). *L'osservazione del comportamento del bambino.* Bologna, Italy: Società editrice il Mulino.

Aviezer, O., Sagi, A., Joels, T., & Ziv, Y. (1999). Emotional availability and attachment representations in Kibbutz infants and their mothers. *Developmental Psychology, 35*(3), 811–821.

Avni, F., Cos, T., Cassart, M., Massez, A., Donner, C., Ismaili, K., et al. (2007). Evolution of fetal ultrasonography. *European Radiology, 17*(2), 419–431.

Axia, G., Bonichini, S., & Benini, F. (1999). Attention and reaction to distress in infancy: A longitudinal study. *Developmental Psychology, 35*(2), 500–504.

Aylward, G. P. (2004). Presidential Address. Prediction of Function from Infancy to Early Childhood: Implications for Pediatric Psychology. *Journal of Pediatric Psychology, 29*(7), 555–564.

Baddeley, A. (1994). The remembered self and the enacted self. In U. Neisser & R. Fivush (Eds.), *The remembering self: Construction and accuracy in the self-narrative* (pp. 236–242). Cambridge, England: Cambridge University Press.

Bahrick, L. E. (1987). Infants' intermodal perception of two levels of temporal structure in natural events. *Infant Behavior and Development, 10,* 387–416.

Bahrick, L. E. (1988). Intermodal learning in infancy: Learning on the basis of two kinds of invariant relations in audible and visible events. *Child Development, 59,* 197–209.

Bahrick, L. E., Gogate, L. J., & Ruiz, I. (2002). Attention and memory for faces and actions in infancy: The salience of actions over faces in dynamic events. *Child Development, 73*(6), 1629–1643.

Bahrick, L. E., Netto, D., & Hernandez-Reif, M. (1998). Intermodal perception of adult and child faces and voices by infants. *Child Development, 69*(5), 1263–1275.

Bahrick, L. E., & Pickens, J. N. (1988). Classification of bimodal English and Spanish language passages by infants. *Infant Behavior and Development, 11,* 277–296.

Bai, D. L., & Bertenthal, B. I. (1992). Locomotor status and the development of spatial search skills. *Child Development, 63,* 215–226.

Baillargeon, R. (1987). Object permanence in 3 1/2– and 4 1/2–month-old infants. *Developmental Psychology, 23,* 655–664.

Baillargeon, R., & DeVos, J. (1991). Object permanence in young infants: Further evidence. *Child Development, 62,* 1227–1246.

Baillargeon, R., & Graber, M. (1988). Evidence of location memory in 8–month-old infants in a nonsearch AB task. *Developmental Psychology, 24,* 502–511.

Baillargeon, R., Needham, A., & DeVos, J. (1992). The development of young infants' intuitions about support. *Early Development & Parenting, 1,* 69–78.

Baird, P. A. (2002). Overseeing embryo research: what is needed? *Clin Invest Med, 25*(1–2), 19–20.

Baird, P. A., & Sadovnick, A. D. (1987). Life expectancy in Down's syndrome. *Journal of Pediatrics, 110,* 849–854.

Baird, P. A., Yee, I. M., & Sadovnick, A. D. (1994). Population-based study of long-term outcomes after amniocentesis. *Lancet, 344* (8930), 1134–1136.

Bakeman, R., & Adamson, L. B. (1984). Coordinating attention to people and objects in mother-infant and peer-infant interaction. *Child Development, 55,* 1278–1289.

Bakeman, R., & Brown, J. (1980). Analyzing behavioral sequences: Differences between preterm and full-term infant-mother dyads during the first months of life. In D. Sawin (Ed.), *Psychosocial risks in infant-environment transactions* (pp. 390–415). New York: Brunner-Mazel.

Bakeman, R., & Brownlee, J. (1980). The strategic use of parallel play: A sequential analysis. *Child Development, 51,* 873–878.

Baker, R. L., & Mednick, B. R. (1984). *Influence on human development: A longitudinal perspective.* The Hague: Kluwer-Nijhoff.

Bakermans-Kranenburg, M. J., van Ijzendoorn, M. H., & Kroonenberg, P. M. (2004). Differences in attachment security between African-American and white children: Ethnicity or socio-economic status? *Infant Behavior & Development, 27*(3), 417–433.

Balamore, U., & Wozniak, R. H. (1984). Speech-action coordination in young children. *Developmental Psychology, 20,* 850–858.

Baldwin, D. A. (1993). Early referential understanding: Infants' ability to recognize referential acts for what they are. *Developmental Psychology, 29,* 832–843.

Baldwin, D. A. (1995). Understanding the link between joint attention and language. In C. Moore & P. J. Dunham (Eds.), *Joint attention: Its origins and role in development* (pp. 131–158). Hillsdale, NJ: Erlbaum.

Baldwin, D. A., & Markman, E. M. (1989). Establishing word-object relations: A first step. *Child Development, 60,* 381–398.

Baldwin, D. A., Markman, E. M., Bill, B., Desjardins, R. N., Irwin, J. M., & Tidball, G. (1996). Infants' reliance on a social criterion for establishing word-object relations. *Child Development, 67,* 3135–3153.

Baldwin, D. A., Markman, E. M., & Melartin, R. L. (1993). Infants' ability to draw inferences about nonobvious object properties: Evidence from exploratory play. *Child Development, 64,* 711–728.

Ball, H. L. (2002). Reasons to bed-share: Why parents sleep with their infants. *Journal of Reproductive and Infant Psychology, 20*(4), 207–221.

Ball, H. L., Hooker, E., & Kelly, P. J. (2000). Parent-infant co-sleeping: Fathers' roles and perspectives. *Infant and Child Development, 9*(2), 67–74.

Ball, R. M., & Pianta, R. C. (1993). Relations between maternal network size and maternal behaviour with five-year-olds across levels of maternal background and child ability. *Early Development & Parenting, 2,* 209–216.

Balog, J. (1976). A new look at our infant mortality. *Birth and the Family Journal, 3,* 15–23.

Bandura, A. (1977). *Social learning theory.* Englewood Cliffs, NJ: Prentice-Hall.

Bandura, A. (1989). Human agency in social cognitive theory. *American Psychologist, 44*(9), 1175–1184.

Bandura, A. (1996). *Social foundations of thought and action: A social cognitive theory.* Englewood Cliffs, NJ: Prentice-Hall.

Bane, M. J., & Ellwood, D. T. (1989). One fifth of the nation's children: Why are they poor? *Science, 245,* 1047–1053.

Bard, K. A. (1994). Evolutionary roots of intuitive parenting: Maternal competence in chimpanzees. *Early Development and Parenting, 3,* 19–28.

Bard, K. A., Platzman, K. A., Lester, B. M., & Suomi, S. J. (1992). Orientation to social and nonsocial stimuli in neonatal chimpanzees and humans. *Infant Behavior and Development, 15,* 43–56.

Barden, R. C., Ford, M. E., Jensen, A. G., Rogers-Salyer, M., & Salyer, K. E. (1989). Effects of craniofacial deformity in infancy on the quality of mother-infant interactions. *Child Development, 60,* 819–824.

Barglow, P. (1987a). Effect of maternal absence due to employment on the quality of infant-mother attachment in a low-risk sample. *Child Development, 58,* 945–954.

Barglow, P. (1987b). Some further comments about infant day-care research. *Zero to Three, 8,* 26–28.

Bar-Haim, Y., Ziv, T., Lamy, D., & Hodes, R. M. (2006). Nature and Nurture in Own-Race Face Processing. *Psychological Science, 17*(2), 159–163.

Barnard, K. (1985) *Nursing Child Assessment Satellite Training (NCAST), Feeding and Teaching Scale.* Parent-Child Interaction (PCI) Program: University of Washington.

Barnard, K. E., Bee, H. L., & Hammond, M. A. (1984). Developmental changes in maternal interactions with term and preterm infants. *Infant Behavior and Development, 7,* 101–113.

Barnett, D., Ganiban, J., & Ciccheti, D. (1999). Maltreatment, negative expressivity, and the development of type D attachments from 12 to 24 months of age. *Monographs of the Society for Research in Child Development, 64*(3), 97–118.

Barnett, R. C., & Baruch, G. K. (1987). Determinants of fathers' participation in family work. *Journal of Marriage and the Family,* 29–40.

Baron-Cohen, S., Allen, J., & Gillberg, C. (1992). Can autism be detected at 18 months? *British Journal of Psychiatry, 161,* 839–843.

Baron-Cohen, S., Cox, A., Baird, G., Sweettenham, J., & Nightingale, N. (1996). Psychological markers in the detection of autism in infancy in a large population. *British Journal of Psychiatry, 168*(2), 158–163.

Barr, R., & Hayne, H. (2003). It's not what you know, it's who you know: Older siblings facilitate imitation during infancy. *International Journal of Early Years Education, 11*(1), 7–21.

Barr, R. G. (1990). The early crying paradox: A modest proposal. *Human Nature, 1,* 355–389.

Barr, R. G., & Hayne, H. (1999). Developmental changes in imitation from television during infancy. *Child Development, 70*(5), 1067–1081.

Barr, R. G., Quek, V. S. H., Cousineau, D., Oberlander, T. F., Brian, J. A., & Young, S. N. (1994). Effects of intraoral sucrose on crying, mouthing, and hand-mouth contact in newborn and six-week-old infants. *Developmental Medicine Child Neurology, 36,* 608–618.

Barr, R. G., Rotman, A., Yaremko, J., Leduc, D., & Francoeur, T. E. (1992). The crying of infants with colic: A controlled empirical description. *Pediatrics, 90,* 14–21.

Barratt, M. S., & Roach, M. A. (1995). Early interactive processes: Parenting by adolescent and adult single mothers. *Infant Behavior and Development, 18,* 97–109.

Barratt, M. S., Roach, M. A., & Leavitt, L. A. (1996). The impact of low-risk prematurity on maternal behavior and toddler outcomes. *International Journal of Behavioral Development, 19*(2), 581–602.

Barrera, M. E., & Maurer, D. (1981). Discrimination of strangers by the three-month-old. *Child Development, 52,* 558–563.

Barrera, M. E., Rosenbaum, P. L., & Cunningham, C. E. (1987). Corrected and uncorrected Bayley scores. Longitudinal developmental patterns in low and high birth weight preterm infants. *Infant Behavior and Development, 10,* 337–346.

Barrett, D. E., Radke-Yarrow, M., & Klein, R. E. (1982). Chronic malnutrition and child behavior: Effects of early caloric supplementation on social and emotional functioning at school age. *Developmental Psychology, 18,* 541–556.

Barrett, K. C. (1995). A functionalist approach to shame and guilt. In J. P. Tangney & K. W. Fischer (Eds.), *Self-conscious emotions: The psychology of shame, guilt, embarrassment, and pride* (pp. 25–63). New York: Guilford Press.

Barrett, K. C., & Campos, J. J. (1987). Perspectives on emotional development II: A functionalist approach to emotions. In J. D. Osofsky (Ed.), *Handbook of infant development* (2nd ed., pp. 555–578). New York: Wiley.

Barrett, K. C., & Nelson-Goens, G. C. (1997). Emotion communication and the development of the social emotions.

In K. C. Barrett (Ed.), *New directions in child development: The communication of emotion: Current research from diverse perspectives, 77* (pp. 69–88). San Francisco: Jossey-Bass.

Barrile, M., Armstrong, E. S., & Bower, T. G. R. (1999). Novelty and frequency as determinants of newborn preference. *Developmental Science, 2*(1), 47–52.

Barss, V. A., Benacerraf, B. R., & Frigoletto, F. D. (1985). Ultrasonographic determination of chorion type in twin gestation. *Obstetrics and Gynecology, 66,* 779–783.

Barth, R. P., Fetro, J. V., Leland, N., & Volkan, K. (1992). Preventing adolescent pregnancy with social and cognitive skills. *Journal of Adolescent Research, 7,* 208–232.

Barton, M. E., & Tomasello, M. (1991). Joint attention and conversation in mother-infant-sibling triads. *Child Development, 62,* 517–529.

Bass, M., Kravath, R. E., & Glass, L. (1986). Death scene investigation in sudden infant death. *New England Journal of Medicine, 315,* 100–105.

Bates, E., Camaioni, L., & Volterra, V. (1975). The acquisition of performatives prior to speech. *Merrill-Palmer Quarterly, 21,* 205–226.

Bates, E., O'Connell, B., & Shore, C. (1987). Language and communication in infancy. In J. D. Osofsky (Ed.), *Handbook of infant development* (2nd ed., pp. 149–203). New York: Wiley.

Bates, E., Thal, D., Whitesell, K., Fenson, L., & Oakes, L. (1989). Integrating language and gesture in infancy. *Developmental Psychology, 25,* 1104–1119.

Bates, J. E. (1980). The concept of difficult temperament. *Merrill-Palmer Quarterly, 26,* 299–319.

Bates, J. E. (1987). Temperament in infancy. In J. D. Osofsky (Ed.), *Handbook of infant development* (2nd ed., pp. 35–69). New York: Wiley.

Bates, J. E., & Bayles, K. (1984). Objective and subjective components in mothers' perceptions of their children from age 6 months to 3 years. *Merrill-Palmer Quarterly, 30,* 111–130.

Bates, E., Carlson-Luden, V., & Bretherton, I. (1980). Perceptual aspects of tool using in infancy. *Infant Behavior and Development, 3,* 127–140.

Bates, J. E., Freeland, C. A., & Lounsbury, M. L. (1979). Measurement of infant difficultness. *Child Development, 50,* 794–803.

Bates, J. E., Maslin, C. A., & Frankel, K. A. (1985). Attachment security, mother-child interaction, and temperament as predictors of behavior-problem ratings at age three years. *Monographs of the Society for Research in Child Development, 50* (Serial No. 209), 167–193.

Bates, E., O'Connell, B., & Shore, C. (1987). Language and communication in infancy. In J. D. Osofsky (Ed.), *Handbook of infant development* (2nd ed., pp. 149–203). New York: Wiley.

Bates, J. E., Olson, S. L., Pettit, G. S., & Bayles, K. (1982). Dimensions of individuality in the mother-infant relationship at 6 months of age. *Child Development, 53,* 446–461.

Bates, J. E., Wachs, T. D., & Emde, R. N. (1994). Toward practical uses for biological concepts of temperament. In J. E. Bates & T. D. Wachs (Eds.), *Temperament: Individual differences at the interface of biology and behavior* (pp. 275–306). Washington, DC: American Psychological Association.

Bateson, M. C. (1975). Mother-infant exchanges: The epigenesis of conversation interaction. *Annals of the New York Academy of Science, 263,* 101–113.

Bateson, P. P. G. (1966). The characteristics and context of imprinting. *Biological Review, 41,* 177–220.

Battin, M., Ling, E. W., Whitfield, M. F., Mackinnon, M., & Effer, S. B. (1998). Has the outcome for extremely low gestational age (ELGA) infants improved following recent advances in neonatal intensive care? *American Journal of Perinatology, 15*(8), 469–477.

Bauer, P. J. (1993). Memory for gender-consistent and gender-inconsistent event sequences by twenty-five-month-old children. *Child Development, 64,* 285–297.

Bauer, P. J. (1996). What do infants recall of their lives? Memory for specific events by one- to two-year-olds. *American Psychologist, 51*(1), 29–41.

Bauer, P. J., & Dow, G. A. (1994). Episodic memory in 16– and 20–month-old children: Specifics are generalized but not forgotten. *Developmental Psychology, 30,* 403–417.

Bauer, P. J., Schwade, J. A., Wewerka, S. S., & Delaney, D. (1999). Planning ahead: Goal-directed problem solving by 2–year-olds. *Developmental Psychology, 35*(8), 1321–1337.

Baumrind, D. (1973). The development of instrumental competence through socialization. In A. Pick (Ed.), *Minnesota symposium on child development, 11,* 1112–1132. Minneapolis: University of Minnesota Press.

Baumrind, D. (1993). The average expectable environment is not good enough: A response to Scarr. *Child Development, 64,* 1299–1317.

Bayley, N. (1969). *The Bayley scale of infant development.* (Manual). Stanford, CA: Psychological Corporation.

Beatson, J., & Taryan, S. (2003). Predisposition to depression: the role of attachment. *Aust N Z J Psychiatry, 37*(2), 219–225.

Beauchamp, G., Cowart, B., Mennella, J., & Marsh, R. (1994). Infant salt taste: Developmental, methodological, and contextual factors. *Developmental Psychobiology; 27,* 353–365.

Beck, R. A., Kambiss, S., & Bass, J. W. (1993). The retreat of Hemophilus influenzae type B invasive disease: Analysis of and immunization program and implications for OTO-HNS. *Otolaryngological Head and Neck Surgery, 109,* 712–721.

Becker, J. (1977). A learning analysis of the development of peer oriented behavior in nine-month-old infants. *Developmental psychology, 13,* 481–491.

Becker, P. T., Houser, B. J., Engelhardt, K. F., & Steinmann, M. J. (1993). Father and mother contributions to family functioning when the child has a mental delay. *Early Development and Parenting, 2,* 145–155.

Beckwith, L., & Cohen, S. E. (1978). Preterm birth: Hazardous obstetrical and postnatal events as related to caregiver-infant behavior. *Infant Behavior and Development, 1,* 403–412.

Beckwith, L., Cohen, S. E., & Hamilton, C. E. (1999). Maternal sensitivity during infancy and subsequent life events relate to attachment representation at early adulthood. *Developmental Psychology, 35*(3), 693–700.

Beckwith, L., Rodning, C., & Cohen, S. (1992). Preterm children at early adolescence and continuity and discontinuity in maternal responsiveness from infancy. *Child Development, 63,* 1198–1208.

Beebe, B. (2004). Co-constructing mother-infant distress in face-to-face interactions: Contributions of microanalysis. *Zero to Three, 24*(5), 40–48.

Beebe, B. & Jaffee, J. (2008). Dyadic microanalysis of mother-infant communication informs practice. In A. Fogel, B. J. King, & S. Shanker (Eds.). *Human development in the 21st century: Visionary policy ideas from systems scientists.* Cambridge, UK: Cambridge University Press.

Bell, R., Weller, G., & Waldrop, M. (1971). Newborn and preschooler: Organization of behavior and relations between periods. *Monographs of the Society for Research in Child Development, 36* (Serial No. 142), 1–130.

Bell, R. Q., & Costello, N. S. (1964). Three tests for sex differences in tactile sensitivity in the newborn. *Biologia Neonatorum, 7,* 335–347.

Bellagamba, F., & Tomasello, M. (1999). Re-enacting intended acts: Comparing 12– and 18–month-olds. *Infant Behavior and Development, 22*(2), 277–282.

Belsky, J. (1980). Child maltreatment: An ecological integration. *American Psychologist, 35,* 320–335.

Belsky, J. (1981). Early human experience: A family perspective. *Developmental Psychology, 17,* 3–23.

Belsky, J. (1984). The determinants of parenting: A process model. *Child Development, 55,* 83–96.

Belsky, J. (1995). Expanding the ecology of human development: An evolutionary perspective. In P. Moen & G. H. Elder (Eds.), *Examining lives in context: Perspectives on the ecology of human development* (pp. 545–561). Washington, DC: American Psychological Association.

Belsky, J. (1996). Parent, infant, and social-contextual antecedents of father-son attachment security. *Developmental Psychology, 32*(5), 905–913.

Belsky, J., & Braungart, J. M. (1991). Are insecure-avoidant infants with extensive day-care experience less stressed by and more independent in the strange situation? *Child Development, 62,* 567–671.

Belsky, J., Goode, M. K., & Most, R. K. (1980). Maternal simulation and infant exploratory competence; Cross-sectional, correlational, and experimental analyses. *Child Development, 51,* 1168–1178.

Belsky, J., & Isabella, R. A. (1985). Marital and parent-child relationships in family of origin and marital change following the birth of a baby: A retrospective analysis. *Child Development, 56,* 342–349.

Belsky, J., & Most, R. K. (1981). From exploration to play: A cross-sectional study of infant free play behavior. *Developmental Psychology, 17,* 630–639.

Belsky, J., & Rovine, M. J. (1988). Nonmaternal care in the first year of life and the security of infant-parent attachment. *Child Development, 59,* 157–167.

Belsky, J., Rovine, M. J., & Taylor, D. G. (1984). The Pennsylvania infant and family development project III: The origins of individual differences in infant-mother attachment: Maternal and infant contributions. *Child Development, 55,* 718–728.

Belsky, J., Ward, M. J., & Rovine, M. (1986). Prenatal expectations, postnatal experiences, and the transition to parenthood. In R. D. Ashmore & D. M. Brodzinsky (Eds.), *Thinking about the family: Views of parents and children* (pp. 15–38). Hillsdale, NJ: Erlbaum.

Belsky, J., Woodworth, S., & Crnic, K. (1996). Trouble in the second year: Three questions about family interaction. *Child Development, 67,* 556–578.

Bendersky, M., & Lewis, M. (1998). Arousal modulation in cocaine-exposed infants. *Developmental Psychology, 34*(3), 555–564.

Benn, R. K. (1986). Factors promoting secure attachment relationships between employed mothers and their sons. *Child Development, 57,* 1224–1231.

Bennett, W. J. (1987). The role of the family in the nurture and protection of the young. *American Psychologist, 42,* 246–250.

Benson, J. B. (1993). Season of birth and onset of locomotion: Theoretical and methodological implications. *Infant Behavior and Development, 16,* 69–81.

Berenbaum, S. A., & Bailey, J. M. (2003). Effects on gender identity of prenatal androgens and genital appearance: evidence from girls with congenital adrenal hyperplasia. *J Clin Endocrinol Metab, 88*(3), 1102–1106.

Berg, W. K. (1975). Cardiac components of defense responses in infants. *Psychophysiology, 12,* 224.

Berg, W. K., & Berg, K. M. (1979). Psychophysiological development in infancy: State, sensory function, and attention. In J. D. Osofsky (Ed.), *Handbook of infant development* (pp. 283–343). New York: Wiley.

Berg, W. K., & Berg, K. M. (1987). Psychophysiological development in infancy: State, startle, and attention. In J. D. Osofsky (Ed.), *Handbook of infant development* (2nd ed., pp. 121–145). New York: Wiley.

Berger, J., & Cunningham, C. C. (1983). Development of early vocal behaviors & interactions in Down's syndrome and non-handicapped infant-mother pairs. *Developmental Psychology, 19,* 322–331.

Berger, L. M. (2004). Income, family structure, and child maltreatment risk. *Children and Youth Services Review, 26*(8), 725–748.

Berger, S. E., & Adolph, K. E. (2003). Infants use handrails as tools in a locomotor task. *Developmental Psychology, 39*(3), 594–605.

Berk, L. E. (1986). Development of private speech among preschool children. *Early Child Development and Care, 24,* 113–136.

Berko, J. (1958). The child's learning of English morphology. *Word, 14,* 150–177.

Berlin, L. J., Cassidy, J., & Belsky, J. (1995). Loneliness in young children and infant-mother attachment: A longitudinal study. *Merrill-Palmer Quarterly, 41,* 91–103.

Berlin, L. J., O'Neal, C., & Brooks-Gunn, J. (1998). What makes early intervention programs work? The program, its participants, and their interactions. *Zero to Three, 18*(4), 4–15.

Berman, P. W., Goodman, V., Sloan, V. L., & Fernandez, L. (1978). Preference for infants among black and white children: Sex and age differences. *Child Development, 49,* 917–919.

Berman, P. W., Monda, C. C., & Merscough, R. P. (1977). Sex differences in young children's responses to an infant: An observation within a day-care setting. *Child Development, 48,* 711–715.

Bernier, A., & Dozier M. (2003). Bridging the attachment transmission gap: The role of maternal mind-mindedness. *International Journal of Behavioral Development, 27*(4), 355–365.

Berrueta-Clement, J. R., Schweinhart, L. J., Barnett, W. S., Epstein, A. S., & Weikart, D. P. (1984). *Changed lives: The effects of the Perry Preschool Program on youths through age 19 (Monograph No. 8).* Ypsilanti, MI: High Scope/Educational Research Foundation.

Bertella, L., Girelli, L., Grugni, G., Marchi, S., Molinari, E., & Semenza, C. (2005). Mathematical skills in Prader-Willi Syndrome. *Journal of Intellectual Disability Research, 49*(2), 159–169.

Bertenthal, B. I., & Bai, D. L. (1989). Infants' sensitivity to optical flow for controlling posture. *Developmental Psychology, 25,* 936–945.

Bertenthal, B. I., Campos, J. J., & Barrett, K. C. (1984). Self-produced locomotion: An organizer of emotional, cognitive, and social development in infancy. In R. N. Emde & R. J. Harmon (Eds.), *Continuities and discontinuities in development* (pp. 175–210). New York: Plenum Press.

Bertenthal, B. I., & Pinto, J. (1993). Complementary processes in the perception and production of human movements. In L. B. Smith & E. Thelen (Eds.), *A dynamic systems approach to development: Applications* (pp. 209–239). Cambridge, MA: MIT Press.

Bertenthal, B. I., Proffitt, D. R., & Cutting, J. E. (1984). Infant sensitivity to figural coherence in biomechanical motions. *Journal of Experimental Child Psychology, 37,* 213–230.

Bertenthal, B. I., Proffitt, D. R., Kramer, S. J., & Spetner, N. B. (1987). Infants' encoding of kinetic displays varying in relative coherence. *Developmental Psychology, 23*(2), 171–178.

Berthiaume, M., David, J., Saucier, J. F., & Borgeat, F. (1998). Correlates of pre-partum depressive symptomatology: A multivariate analysis. *Reproductive and Infant Psychology, 16,* 45–56.

Bettes, B. A. (1988). Maternal depression and motherese: Temporal and intonational features. *Child Development, 59,* 1089–1096.

Bever, T. G. (1970). The cognitive basis for linguistic structures. In J. R. Haynes (Ed.), *Cognition and the development of language* (pp. 40–72). New York: Wiley.

Bhat, A. N., & Galloway, J. C. (2006). Toy-oriented changes during early arm movements: Hand kinematics. *Infant Behavior & Development, 29*(3), 358–372.

Bhatt, R. S., Rovee-Collier, C., & Weiner, S. (1994). Developmental changes in the interface between perception and memory retrieval. *Developmental Psychology, 30,* 151–162.

Bigelow, A., MacLean, J., Wood, C., & Smith, J. (1990). Infants' responses to child and adult strangers: An investigation of height and facial configuration variables. *Infant Behavior and Development, 13,* 21–32.

Bigelow, A. E. (1992). Locomotion and search behavior in blind infants. *Infant Behavior and Development, 15,* 179–189.

Bigelow, A. E. (1998). Infants' sensitivity to familiar imperfect contingencies in social interaction. *Infant Behavior and Development, 21*(1), 149–162.

Bigelow, A. E., MacDonald, D., & MacDonald, L. (1995). The development of infants' search for their mothers, unfamiliar people, and objects. *Merrill-Palmer Quarterly, 41,* 191–205.

Bigelow, A. E., & Rochat, P. (2006). Two-Month-Old Infants' Sensitivity to Social Contingency in Mother-Infant and Stranger-Infant Interaction. *Infancy, 9*(3), 313–325.

Bijeljac-Babic, R., Bertoncini, J., & Mehler, J. (1993). How do 4–day-old infants categorize multisyllabic utterances? *Developmental Psychology, 29,* 711–721.

Bijou, S. W., & Baer, D. M. (1965). *Child development: Vol. 2. Universal stage of infancy.* New York: Appleton-Century-Crofts.

Biringen, Z., Emde, R. N., Campos, J. J., & Appelbaum, M. I. (1995). Affective reorganization in the infant, the mother, and the dyad: The role of upright locomotion and its timing. *Child Development, 66,* 499–514.

Birth (June 1988). Report for American College of Obstetricians and Gynecologists. *Birth, 15,* 113.

Black, L., Steinschneider, A., & Sheehe, P. R. (1979). Neonatal respiratory instability and infant development. *Child Development, 50,* 561–564.

Black, M. M., & Krishnakumar, A. (1998). Children in low-income, urban settings: Interventions to promote mental health and well-being. *American Psychologist, 53*(6), 635–646.

Black, R. E. (2001). Micronutrients in pregnancy. *Br J Nutr, 85 Suppl 2,* S193–197.

Blackford, J. U., & Walden, T. A. (1998). Individual differences in social referencing. *Infant Behavior and Development, 21*(1), 89–102.

Blackman, J. A., Lindgren, S. D., Hein, H. A., & Harper, D. C. (1987). Long-term surveillance of high-risk children. *American Journal of Diseases of Children, 141,* 1293–1299.

Blackwell, C. C., Weir, D. M., Busuttil, A., Saadi, A. T., Essery, S. D., Raza, M. W., James, V. S., & MacKenzie, D. A. (1994). The role of infectious agents in sudden infant death syndrome. *FEMS Immunological Medicine and Microbiology, 9,* 91–100.

Blake, A., Stewart, A., & Turcan, D. (1975). Parents of babies of very low birth weight: Long-term follow-up. In Ciba Foundation Symposium (Ed.), *Parent-infant interaction* (pp. 150–177). New York: Elsevier.

Blake, J., McConnell, S., Horton, G., & Benson, N. (1992). The gestural repertoire and its evolution over the second year. *Early Development and Parenting, 1,* 127–136.

Blank, A., Mofenson, L. M., Willoughby, A., & Yaffe, S. J. (1994). Maternal and pediatric AIDS in the United States: The current situation and future research directions. *Acta-Paediatrica-Supplement, 400,* 106–110.

Blank, M., & Klig, S. (1982). The child and the school experience. In C. B. Kopp & J. B. Krakow (Eds.), *The child: Development in social context* (pp. 456–513). Reading, MA: Addison-Wesley.

Blass, E. M. (1997). Changing influences of sucrose and visual engagement in 2– to 12–week-old human infants: Implications for maternal face recognition. *Infant Behavior and Development, 20*(4), 423–434.

Blass, E. M., & Ciaramitaro, V. (1994). A new look at some old mechanisms in human newborns: Taste and tactile determinants of state, affect, and action. *Monographs of the Society for Research in Child Development, 59,* 1–102.

Blass, E. M., Fillion, T. J., Rochat, P., Hoffmeyer, L. B., & Metzger, M. A. (1989). Sensorimotor and motivational determinants of hand-mouth coordination in 1– to 3–day-old human infants. *Developmental Psychology, 25,* 963–975.

Blass, E. M., Ganchrow, J. R., & Steiner, J. E. (1984). Classical conditioning in newborn humans 2 to 48 hours of age. *Infant Behavior and Development, 7,* 223–235.

Blehar, M. C., Lieberman, A., & Ainsworth, M. (1977). Early face-to-face interaction and its relation to later mother-infant attachment. *Child Development, 48,* 182–194.

Bloch, H. (1990). Status and function of early sensory-motor coordination. In H. Bloch & B. I. Bertenthal (Eds.), *Sensory-motor organizations and development in infancy and early childhood* (pp. 163–178). The Netherlands: Kluwer Academic.

Block, J. A., & Block, J. (1980). The role of ego-control and ego-resiliency in the organization of behavior. In W. A. Collins (Ed.), *Minnesota symposia on child psychology* (Vol. 13, pp. 1550–1574). Hillsdale, NJ: Erlbaum.

Bloom, K., D'Odorico, L., & Beaumont, S. (1993). Adult preferences for syllabic vocalizations: Generalizations to parity and native language. *Infant Behavior and Development, 16,* 109–120.

Bloom, K., & Lo, E. (1990). Adult perceptions of vocalizing infants. *Infant Behavior and Development, 13,* 209–219.

Bloom, L., & Beckwith, R. (1989). Talking with feeling: Integrating affective and linguistic expression in early language development. *Cognition and Emotion, 3*(4), 313–342.

Bloom, L., Margulis, C., Tinker, E., & Fujita, N. (1996). Early conversations and word learning: Contributions from child and adult. *Child Development, 67,* 3154–3175.

Bloom, L., Merkin, S., & Wootten, J. (1982). Wh-questions: Linguistic factors that contribute to the sequence of acquisition. *Child Development, 53,* 1084–1092.

Bloom, L., Rocissano, L., & Hood, L. (1976). Adult-child discourse: Developmental interaction between information processing and linguistic knowledge. *Cognitive Psychology, 8,* 521–552.

Bluglass, K., & Hassall, C. (1979). Alternative forms of community support after sudden infant death. *Medicine, Science and the Law, 19,* 240–245.

Blurton-Jones, N., Ferreira, C., Brown, M., & MacDonald, L. (1978). The association between perinatal factors and later night waking. *Developmental Medicine and Child Neurology, 20,* 427–434.

Bocci, V., von Brenmen, K., Corradeschi, F., Franchi, F., Luzzi, E., & Paulesu, L. (1993). Presence of interferon-gamma and interleukin-6 in colostrum of normal women. *Lymphokine-Cytokine Research, 12,* 21–24.

Boddy, J. M., & Skuse, D. H. (1994). The process of parenting in failure to thrive. *Journal of Child Psychology and Psychiatry and Allied Disciplines, 35,* 401–424.

Bodle, J. H., Zhou, L. Y., Shore, C. M., & Dixon, W. E. (1996). Transfer by responsibility in parent-child play during the second year. *Early Development and Parenting, 5*(4), 185–194.

Boehm, L. (1977). The development of independence: A comparative study. *Child Development, 28,* 85–92.

Bohannon, J. N., III, & Stanowicz, L. (1988). The issue of negative evidence: Adult responses to children's language errors. *Developmental Psychology, 24,* 684–689.

Bohlin, G., & Hagekull, B. (1993). Stranger wariness and sociability in the early years. *Infant Behavior and Development, 16,* 53–67.

Bohlin, G., Hagekull, B., Germer, M., Anderson, K., & Lindberg, L. (1989). Avoidant and resistant reunion behaviors as predicted by maternal interactive behavior and infant temperament. *Infant Behavior and Development, 12,* 105–117.

Bohlin, G., Hagekull, B., & Lindberg, L. (1994). Infantile colic and parental experiences. *Early Development and Parenting, 3,* 63–69.

Bojczyk, K. E., & Corbetta, D. (2004). Object Retrieval in the 1st Year of Life: Learning Effects of Task Exposure and Box Transparency. *Developmental Psychology, 40*(1), 54–66.

Bonin, M., Pomerleau, A., & Malcuit, G. (1998). A longitudinal study of visual attention and psychomotor development in preterm and full-term infants during the first six months of life. *Infant Behavior and Development, 21*(1), 103–118.

Bookstein, F. L., Sampson, P. D., Streissguth, A. P., & Barr, H. M. (1996). Exploiting redundant measurement of dose and developmental outcome: New methods from the behavioral teratology of alcohol. *Developmental Psychology, 32*(3), 404–415.

Boom, D. C. van den (1994). The influence of temperament and mothering on attachment and exploration: An experimental manipulation of sensitive responsiveness among lower-class mothers with irritable infants. *Child Development, 65,* 1457–1477.

Boom, D. C. van den, & Gravenhorst, J. B. (1995). Prenatal and perinatal correlates of neonatal irritability. *Infant Behavior and Development, 18,* 117–121.

Boom, D. C. van den, & Hoeksma, J. B. (1994a). The effect of infant irritability on mother-infant interaction: A growth-curve analysis. *Developmental Psychology, 30*(4), 581–590.

Boom, D. C. van den, & Hoeksma, J. B. (1994b). How is development conceptualized in mother-child interaction? In W. Koops, J. Hoeksma, & D. C. van den Boom (Eds.), *Early mother-child interaction and attachment: Old and new approaches.* Amsterdam: Elsevier.

Booth, A. E., Waxman, S. R., & Huang, Y. T. (2005). Conceptual Information Permeates Word Learning in Infancy. *Developmental Psychology, 41*(3), 491–505.

Bor, W., Brennan, P. A., Williams, G. M., Najman, J. M., & O'Callaghan, M. (2003). A mother's attitude towards her infant and child behaviour five years later. *Aust N Z J Psychiatry, 37*(6), 748–755.

Bornstein, M. H. (1985). Habituation of attention as a measure of visual information processing in human infants: Summary, systematization, and synthesis. In G. Gottlieb & N. A. Krasnegor (Eds.), *Measurement of audition and vision in the first year of postnatal life: A methodological overview* (pp. 260–281). Norwood, NJ: Ablex.

Bornstein, M. H., & Arterberry, M. E. (2003). Recognition, discrimination and categorization of smiling by 5–month-old infants. *Developmental Science, 6*(5), 585–599.

Bornstein, M. H., Arterberry, M. E., & Mash, C. (2004). Long-Term Memory for an Emotional Interpersonal Interaction Occurring at 5 Months of Age. *Infancy, 6*(3), 407–416.

Bornstein, M. H., & Benasich, A. A. (1986). Infant habituation: Assessments of short-term reliability and individual differences at five months. *Child Development, 57,* 87–99.

Bornstein, M. H., Cote, L. R., Maital, S., Painter, K., Park, S.-Y., Pascual, L., et al. (2004). Cross-Linguistic Analysis of Vocabulary in Young Children: Spanish, Dutch, French, Hebrew, Italian, Korean, and American English. *Child Development, 75*(4), 1115–1139.

Bornstein, M. H., Haynes, O. M., Pascual, L., Painter, K., & Galperin, C. (1999). Play in two societies: Pervasiveness of process, specificity of structure. *Child Development, 70*(2), 317–331.

Bornstein, M. H., & Krinsky, S. J. (1985). Perception of symmetry in infancy: The salience of vertical symmetry and the perception of pattern wholes. *Journal of Experimental Child Psychology, 39,* 1–19.

Bornstein, M. H., Krinsky, S. J., & Benasich, A. A. (1986). Fine orientation discrimination and shape constancy in infants. *Journal of Experimental Child Psychology, 41,* 49–60.

Bornstein, M. H., & Sigman, M. D. (1986). Continuity in mental development from infancy. *Child Development, 57,* 251–274.

Bornstein, M. H., Tal, J., Rahn, C., Galperin, C. Z., Pecheux, M., Lamour, M., Toda, S., Azuma, H., Ogino, M., & Tamis-LeMonda, C. S. (1992). Functional analysis of the contents of maternal speech to infants of 5 and 13 months in four cultures: Argentina, France, Japan, and the United States. *Developmental Psychology, 28,* 593–603.

Bornstein, M. H., & Tamis-LeMonda, C. S. (1995). Parent-child symbolic play: Three theories in search of an effect. *Developmental Review, 15,* 382–400.

Bornstein, M. H., Tamis-LeMonda, C. S., Tal, J., Ludemann, P., Toda, S., Rahn, C. W., Pecheux, M. G., Azuma, H., & Vardi, D. (1992). Maternal responsiveness to infants in three societies: The United States, France, and Japan. *Child Development, 63,* 808–821.

Boss, J. A. (1994). First trimester prenatal diagnosis: Earlier is not necessarily better. *Journal of Medical Ethics, 20,* 146–151.

Botting, N., Powls, A., Cooke, R. W., & Marlow, N. (1998). Cognitive and educational outcome of very-low-birthweight children in early adolescence. *Developmental Medicine and Child Neurology, 40*(10), 652–660.

Bourgeois, K. S., Khawar, A. W., Neal, S. A., & Lockman, J. J. (2005). Infant manual exploration of objects, surfaces, and their interrelations. *Infancy, 8*(3), 233–252.

Bowerman, M. (1978). Systematizing semantic knowledge: Changes over time in the child's organization of word meaning. *Child Development, 49,* 977–987.

Bowlby, J. (1969). *Attachment and loss: Vol. 1. Attachment.* New York: Basic Books.

Bowlby, J. (1980). *Attachment and loss: Vol. 3. Loss, sadness and depression.* New York: Basic Books.

Bowman, M. C., & Saunders, D. M. (1994). Community attitudes to maternal age and pregnancy after assisted reproductive technology: Too old at 50 years? *Human Reproduction, 9,* 167–171.

Boyce, W. T., Schaefer, C., & Uitti, C. (1985). Permanence and change: Psychosocial factors in the outcome of adolescent pregnancy. *Social Science Medicine, 21*(11), 1279–1287.

Boyson-Bardies, B. (1994). Speech development: Contributions from cross-linguistic studies. In A. Vyt, H. Block, & M. Bornstein (Eds.), *Early child development in the French tradition: Contributions from current research* (pp. 191–206). Hillsdale, NJ: Erlbaum.

Bracewell, M., & Marlow, N. (2002). Patterns of motor disability in very preterm children. *Mental Retardation and Developmental Disabilities Research Reviews, 8*(4), 241–248.

Brackbill, Y. (1971). Cumulative effects of continuous stimulation on arousal level in infants. *Child Development, 42,* 17–26.

Brackbill, Y. (1979). Obstetrical medication and infant behavior. In J. Osofsky (Ed.), *Handbook of infant development* (pp. 380–402). New York: Wiley.

Bradley, R. H., & Caldwell, B. M. (1976). The relation of infants' home environment to mental test performance at fifty-four months: A follow-up study. *Child Development, 47,* 1172–1173.

Bradley, R. H., & Caldwell, B. M. (1995). Caregiving and the regulation of childgrowth and development: Describing proximal aspects of caregiving systems. *Developmental Review, 15,* 38–85.

Bradley, R. H., Whiteside, L., Mundfrom, D. J., Casey, P. H., Kelleher, K. J., & Pope, S. K. (1994). Early indications of resilience and their relation to experiences in the home environments of low birthweight, premature children living in poverty. *Child Development, 65,* 346–360.

Braine, M. D. S. (1976). Children's first word combinations. *Monographs of the Society for Research in Child Development, 164* (Serial No. 164), pp. 1–104.

Brake, S. C., Fifer, W. P., Alfasi, G., & Fleischman, A. (1988). The first nutritive sucking response of premature newborns. *Infant Behavior and Development, 11,* 1–19.

Branchfeld, S., Goldberg, S., & Sloman, J. (1980). Parent-infant interaction in free play at 8 and 12 months: Effects of prematurity and immaturity. *Infant Behavior and Development, 3,* 289–306.

Brand, R. J., Baldwin, D. A., & Ashburn, L. A. (2002). Evidence for 'motionese': Modifications in mothers' infant-directed action. *Developmental Science, 5*(1), 72–83.

Brand, R. J., Shallcross, W. L., Sabatos, M. G., & Massie, K. P. (2007). Fine-grained analysis of motionese: Eye gaze, object exchanges, and action units in infant-versus adult-directed action. *Infancy, 11*(2), 203–214.

Brannon, E. M., Lutz, D., & Cordes, S. (2006). The development of area discrimination and its implications for number representation in infancy. *Developmental Science, 9*(6), F59–F64.

Bråten, S. (1998). Infant learning by altercentric participation: The reverse of egocentric observation in autism. In S. Br;araten (Ed.), *Intersubjective communication and emotion in early ontogeny. Studies in emotion and social interaction, 2nd series* (pp. 105–124). New York: Cambridge University Press.

Bråten, S. (2003). Participant Perception of Others' Acts: Virtual Otherness in Infants and Adults. *Culture & Psychology, 9*(3), 261–276.

Braungart-Rieker, J., Garwood, M. M., Powers, B. P., & Notaro, P. C. (1998). Infant affect and affect regulation during the still-face paradigm with mothers and fathers: The role of infant characteristics and parental sensitivity. *Developmental Psychology, 34*(6), 1428–1437.

Brauth, S. E., Hall, W. S., & Dooling, R. J. (Eds.) (1991). *Plasticity of development.* Cambridge, MA: MIT Press.

Brazelton, T. B. (1977). Implications of infant development among the Mayan Indians of Mexico. In P. H. Liederman, S. R. Tulkin, & A. Rosenfeld (Eds.), *Culture and infancy* (pp. 336–352). New York: Academic Press.

Brazelton, T. B., Koslowski, B., & Main, M. (1974). The origins of reciprocity. In M. Lewis & L. Rosenblum (Eds.), *The effect of the infant on its caregiver* (pp. 150–185). New York: Wiley.

Brazelton, T. B., Nugent, J. K., & Lester, B. M. (1987). Neonatal behavioral assessment scale. In J. D. Osofsky (Ed.), *Handbook of infant development* (2nd ed., pp. 92–120). New York: Wiley.

Breitmayer, B. J., & Ramey, C. T. (1986). Biological nonoptimality and quality of postnatal environment as codeterminants of intellectual development. *Child Development, 57,* 1151–1165.

Bremmer, J. (1978). Egocentric vs. allocentric spatial coding in nine-month-old infants: Factors influencing choice of code. *Developmental Psychology, 14,* 346–355.

Bremner, J. G., Johnson, S. P., Slater, A., Mason, U., Cheshire, A., & Spring, J. (2007). Conditions for young infants' failure to perceive trajectory continuity. *Developmental Science, 10*(5), 613–624.

Bremner, G., & Slater, A. (Eds.). (2004). *Theories of infant development.* Malden, MA: Blackwell Publishing, Ltd.

Brennan, P. A., Grekin, E. R., & Mednick, S. A. (1999). Maternal smoking during pregnancy and adult male criminal outcomes. *Archives of General Psychiatry, 56,* 215–219.

Bretherton, I. (1985). Attachment theory: Retrospect and prospect. *Monographs of the Society for Research in Child Development, 50* (Serial No. 209), 3–35.

Bretherton, I. (1987). New perspectives on attachment relations: Security, communication, and internal working models. In J. D. Osofsky (Ed.), *Handbook of infant development* (2nd ed., pp. 1061–1100). New York: Wiley.

Bretherton, I., Fritz, J., Zahn-Waxler, C., & Ridgeway, D. (1986). Learning to talk about emotions: A functionalist perspective. *Child Development, 57,* 529–548.

Bridges, L. J., & Connell, J. P. (1991). Consistency and inconsistency in infant emotional and social interactive behavior across contexts and caregivers. *Infant Behavior and Development, 14,* 471–487.

Bridges, L. J., Connell, J. P., & Belsky, J. (1988). Similarities and differences in infant-mother and infant-father interaction in the strange situation: A component process analysis. *Developmental Psychology, 24,* 92–100.

Bridges, L. J., Grolnick, W. S., & Connell, J. P. (1997). Infant emotion regulation with mothers and fathers. *Infant Behavior and Development, 20,* 47–57.

Brighi, A. (1997). Patterns of mother-infant interaction and contingency learning in full-term infants. *Early Development and Parenting, 6*(1), 37–45.

Bril, B., & Breniere, Y. (1993). Posture and independent locomotion in early childhood: Learning to walk or learning dynamic postural control? In G. J. P. Savelsbergh (Ed.), *The development of coordination in infancy* (pp. 337–358). Amsterdam: Elsevier.

Bril, B., & Sabatier, C. (1986). The cultural context of motor development: Postural manipulations in the daily life of Bambara babies (Mali). *International Journal of Behavioral Development, 9,* 439–453.

Brody, G. H., Stoneman, Z., & MacKinnon, C. (1982). Role asymmetries among school-age children, their younger siblings, and their friends. *Child Development, 53,* 1364–1370.

Broerse, J., & Elias, G. (1994). Changes in the content and timing of mothers' talk to infants. *British Journal of Developmental Psychology, 12,* 131–145.

Bromwich, R., & Parmalee, A. (1979). An intervention program for pre-term infants. In T. Field, A. Sostek, S. Goldberg, & H. Shuman (Eds.), *Infants born at risk:*

Behavior and development (pp. 66–79). New York: Springer Medical and Scientific Books.

Bronfenbrenner, U. (1979). *The ecology of human development: Experiments by nature and design.* Cambridge, MA: Harvard University Press.

Bronfenbrenner, U. (1986). Ecology of the family as a context for human development: Research perspectives. *Developmental Psychology, 22*(6), 723–742.

Bronfenbrenner, U., & Evans, G. W. (2000). Developmental science in the 21st century: Emerging questions, theoretical models, research designs and empirical findings. *Social Development, 9*(1), 115–125.

Bronson, G. W. (1972). Infants' reactions to unfamiliar persons and novel objects. *Monographs of the Society for Research in Child Development, 47* (Serial No. 148), 1–46.

Brook, A. (2001a). *Water-based methods of healing.* www.anniebrook.com.

Brook, A. (2001b). *From conception to crawling: Foundations for developmental movement.* www.anniebrook.com.

Brook, J. S., Zheng, L., Whiteman, M., & Brook, D. W. (2001). Aggression in toddlers: Associations with parenting and marital relations. *Journal of Genetic Psychology, 162*(2), 228–241.

Brookhart, J., & Hock, E. (1976). The effects of experimental context and experiential background on infants' behavior toward their mothers and a stranger. *Child Development, 47,* 333–340.

Brooks, J., & Lewis, M. (1976). Infants' responses to strangers: Midget, adult, and child. *Child Development, 47,* 323–332.

Brooks-Gunn, J., & Furstenberg, F. (1986). Antecedents and consequences of parenting: The case of adolescent motherhood. In A. Fogel & G. F. Melson (Eds.), *Origins of nurturance: Developmental, biological, and cultural perspectives on caregiving* (pp. 166–185). Hillsdale, NJ: Erlbaum.

Brooks-Gunn, J., Han, W.-J., & Waldfogel, J. (2002). Maternal employment and child cognitive outcomes in the first three years of life: The NICHD study of early child care. *Child Development, 73*(4), 1052–1072.

Brooks-Gunn, J., Klebanov, P., Smith, J. R., & Lee, K. (2001). Effects of combining public assistance and employment on mothers and their young children. *Women & Health, 32*(3), 179–210.

Brooks-Gunn, J., Klebanov, P. K., Liaw, F., & Spiker, D. (1993). Enhancing the development of low-birthweight, premature infants: Changes in cognition and behavior over the first three years. *Child Development, 64,* 736–753.

Brooks-Gunn, J., & Lewis, M. (1982). Affective exchanges between normal and handicapped infants and their mothers. In T. Field & A. Fogel (Eds.), *Emotion and early interaction* (pp. 17–41). Hillsdale, NJ: Erlbaum.

Brown, J., Bakeman, R., Snyder, P., Frederickson, W., Morgan, S., & Helper, R. (1975). Interactions of black inner-city mothers with their newborn infants. *Child Development, 46,* 677–686.

Brown, J. R., & Dunn, J. (1992). Talk with your mother or your sibling? Developmental changes in early family conversations about feelings. *Child Development, 63,* 336–349.

Brown, R. (1973). *A first language: The early stages.* Cambridge, MA: Harvard University Press.

Brown, R., Cazden, C., & Bellugi-Klima, V. (1969). The child's grammar from I to III. In J. P. Hill (Ed.), *Minnesota Symposium of Child Psychology* (Vol. 2). St. Paul: University of Minnesota Press.

Brownell, C. A. (1986). Convergent developments: Cognitive-developmental correlates of growth in infant/toddler peer skills. *Child Development, 57,* 275–286.

Brownell, C. A. (1988). Combinatorial skills: Converging developments over the second year. *Child Development, 59,* 675–685.

Brownell, C. A., Ramani, G. B., & Zerwas, S. (2006). Becoming a Social Partner With Peers: Cooperation and Social Understanding in One- and Two-Year-Olds. *Child Development, 77*(4), 803–821.

Brownell, C. A., Zerwas, S., & Ramani, G. B. (2007). 'So big': The development of body self-awareness in toddlers. *Child Development, 78*(5), 1426–1440.

Bruer, J. (1999). *The myth of the first three years.* New York: Free Press.

Bruner, J. (1983). *Child's talk: Learning to use language.* New York: Norton.

Brunner, D. P., Munch, M., Biedermann, K., Huch, R., Huch, A., & Borbely, A. A. (1994). Changes in sleep and sleep electroencephalogram during pregnancy. *Sleep, 17,* 576–582.

Bryant, P. E., & Trabasso, T. (1971). Transitive inferences and memory in young children. *Nature, 232,* 456–458.

Bryne, J. M., & Horowitz, F. D. (1979). Rocking as a soothing intervention: The influence of direction and type of movement. *Infant Behavior and Development, 2,* 209–214.

Buehler, B. A., Rao, V., & Finnell, R. H. (1994). Biochemical and molecular teratology of fetal hydantoin syndrome. *Neurological Clinics, 12,* 741–748.

Bugental, D. B., & Happaney, K. (2004). Predicting Infant Maltreatment in Low-Income Families: The Interactive Effects of Maternal Attributions and Child Status at Birth. *Developmental Psychology, 40*(2), 234–243.

Bugental, D. B., Martorell, G. A., & Barraza, V. (2003). The hormonal costs of subtle forms of infant maltreatment. *Horm Behav, 43*(1), 237–244.

Buka, S. L., & Lipsitt, L. P. (1991). Newborn sucking behavior and its relation to grasping. *Infant Behavior and Development, 14,* 59–67.

Bukatko, D., & Daehler, M. W. (1995). *Child development: A thematic approach* (2nd ed.). Boston: Houghton Mifflin.

Bullock, M., & Lutkenhaus, P. (1988). The development of volitional behavior in the toddler years. *Child Development, 59,* 664–674.

Burack, J. A., Shulman, C., Katzir, E., Schaap, T., Brennan, J. M., Iarocci, G., Wilansky, P., & Amir, N. (1999). Cognitive and behavioral development of Israeli males with fragile X and Down syndrome. *International Journal of Behavioral Development, 23*(2), 519–531.

Burchinal, M. R., Bryant, D. M., Lee, M. W., & Ramey, C. T. (1992). Early day care, infant-mother attachment, and maternal responsivenss in the infant's first year. *Early Childhood Research Quarterly, 7,* 383–396.

Burchinal, M. R., Campbell, F. A., Bryant, D. M., Wasik, B. H., & Ramey, C. T. (1997). Early intervention and mediating processes in cognitive performance children of low-income African American families. *Child Development, 68*(5), 935–954.

Burchinal, M. R., & Clarke-Stewart, K. A. (2007). Maternal employment and child cognitive outcomes: The importance of analytic approach. *Developmental Psychology, 43*(5), 1140–1155.

Burchinal, M. R., Lee, M., & Ramey, C. (1989). Type of day-care and preschool intellectual development in disadvantaged children. *Child Development, 60,* 128–137.

Burchinal, M. R., Roberts, J. E., Nabors, L. A., & Bryant, D. M. (1996). Quality of center child care and infant cognitive language development. *Child Development, 67,* 606–620.

Burgess, R. L., & Conger, R. D. (1978). Family interaction in abusive, neglectful and normal families. *Child Development, 49,* 1163–1173.

Bushnell, E. W. (1982). Visual tactual knowledge in 8– and 91/2– and 11–month old infants. *Infant Behavior and Development, 5,* 63–75.

Bushnell, E. W., & Boudreau, J. P. (1993). Motor development and the mind: The potential role of motor abilities as a determinant of aspects of perceptual development. *Child Development, 64,* 1005–1021.

Buss, A. H., & Plomin, R. (1984). *Temperament: Early developing personality traits.* Hillsdale, NJ: Erlbaum.

Buss, K. A., & Goldsmith, H. H. (1998). Fear and anger regulation in infancy: Effects on the temporal dynamics of affective expression. *Child Development, 69*(2), 359–374.

Buss, K. A., & Kiel, E. J. (2004). Comparison of Sadness, Anger, and Fear Facial Expressions When Toddlers Look at Their Mothers. *Child Development, 75*(6), 1761–1773.

Butler, J., & Rovee-Collier, C. (1989). Contextual gating of memory retrieval. *Developmental Psychobiology, 22,* 533–552.

Butterfield, J., & Covey, M. (1962). Letter to the Editor: Practical epigram of the Apgar Score. *Journal of the American Medical Association, 181,* 353.

Butterworth, G. (1977). Object disappearance and error in Piaget's stage IV task. *Journal of Experimental Child Psychology, 23,* 391–401.

Butterworth, G. (1990). Self-perception in infancy. In D. Cicchetti & M. Beeghly (Eds.), *The self in transition: Infancy to childhood* (pp. 119–137). Chicago: University of Chicago Press.

Butterworth, G. (1993). Dynamic approaches to infant perception and action: Old and new theories about the origins of knowledge. In L. B. Smith & E. Thelen (Eds.), *A dynamic systems approach to development: Applications. MIT Press/Bradford Books series in cognitive psychology* (pp. 171–187). Cambridge, MA: MIT Press.

Butterworth, G. (2000). Joint visual attention in infancy. In J. G. Bremner & A. Fogel (Eds.), *Handbook of infancy research* (pp. 221–239). Oxford, England: Blackwell.

Butterworth, G., & Cochran, E. (1980). Towards a mechanism of joint visual attention in human infancy. *International Journal of Behavioral Development, 3,* 253–272.

Butterworth, G. & Hopkins, B. (1993). Origins of handedness. *Developmental Medicine and Child Neurology, 35,* 177–184.

Byers, T., Grahm, S., & Rzepka, T. (1985). Lactation and breast cancer: Evidence for a negative association in premenopausal women. *American Journal of Epidemiology, 121,* 664–674.

Cabrera, N. J., Shannon, J. D., West, J., & Brooks-Gunn, J. (2006). Parental Interactions With Latino Infants: Variation by Country of Origin and English Proficiency. *Child Development, 77*(5), 1190–1207.

Cain, L. P., Kelly, D. H., & Shannon, D. C. (1980). Parents' perceptions of the psychological and social impact of home monitoring. *Pediatrics, 66,* 37–41.

Cairns, R. (1979). *Social development: The origins and plasticity of interchanges.* San Francisco: W. H. Freeman.

Caldera, Y. M., & Hart, S. (2004). Exposure to Child Care, Parenting Style and Attachment Security. *Infant and Child Development, 13*(1), 21–33.

Caldera, Y. M., Huston, A. C., & O'Brien, M. (1989). Social interactions and play patterns of parents and toddlers with feminine, masculine, and neutral toys. *Child Development, 60,* 70–76.

Caldwell, B. M. (1986). Day care and early environmental adequacy. In W. Fowler (Ed.), Early experience and the development of competence. *New Directions for Child Development, 32,* 11–30.

Calhoun, M. L., Rose, T. L., Hanft, B., & Sturkey, C. (1991). Social reciprocity interventions: Implications for developmental therapists. Physical and Occupational Therapy in *Pediatrics, 11,* 45–56.

Calkins, S., & Fox, N. A. (1994). Individual differences in the biological aspects of temperament. In J. E. Bates & T. D. Wachs (Eds.), *Temperament: Individual differences at the interface of biology and behavior* (pp. 199–217). Washington, DC: American Psychological Association.

Calkins, S. D. (2002). Does aversive behavior during toddlerhood matter?: The effects of difficult temperament on maternal perceptions and behavior. *Infant Mental Health Journal, 23*(4), 381–402.

Calkins, S. D., Fox, N. A., & Marshall, T. R. (1996). Behavioral and physiological antecedents of inhibited and uninhibited behavior. *Child Development, 67,* 523–540.

Calkins, S. D., Gill, K. L., Johnson, M. C., & Smith, C. L. (1999). Emotional reactivity and emotional regulation strategies as predictors of social behavior with peers during toddlerhood. *Social Development, 8*(3), 310–334.

Calkins, S. D., & Johnson, M. C. (1998). Toddler regulation of distress to frustrating events: Temperamental and maternal correlates. *Infant Behavior and Development, 21*(3), 379–395.

Calkins, S. D., Smith, C. L., Gill, K. L., & Johnson, M. C. (1998). Maternal interactive style across contexts: Relations to emotional, behavioral, and physiological regulation during toddlerhood. *Social Development, 7*(3), 350–369.

Callaghan, J. W. (1981). A comparison of Anglo, Hopi, and Navajo mothers and infants. In T. M. Field, A. M. Sostek, P. Vietze, & P. H. Leiderman (Eds.), *Culture and early interactions* (pp. 503–536). Hillsdale, NJ: Erlbaum.

Callaghan, T. C. (1999). Early understanding and production of graphic symbols. *Child Development, 70*(6), 1314–1324.

Camaioni, L. (200). Early language. In J. G. Bremner & A. Fogel (Eds.), *Handbook of infant development* (pp. 605–635). Oxford, England: Blackwell.

Camaioni, L., Aureli, T., Bellagamba, F., & Fogel, A. (1999). *The transition from conventional to symbolic shared reference in mother-infant communication.* Paper presented at the 9th European Conference on Developmental Psychology.

Camaioni, L., Aureli, T., Bellagamba, F., & Fogel, A. (2003). A longitudinal examination of the transition to symbolic communication in the second year of life. *Infant and Child Development, 12*(1), 1–26.

Camaioni, L., Baumgartner, E., & Perucchini, P. (1991). Content and structure in toddlers' social competence with peers from 12 to 36 months of age. *Early Child Development and Care, 67,* 17–27.

Camaioni, L., Perucchini, P., Muratori, F. & Milone, A. (1997). A longitudinal examination of the communicative gestures deficit in young children with autism. *Journal of Autism and Developmental Disorders, 27,* 715–725.

Campbell, D. W., & Eaton, W. O. (1999). Sex differences in the activity level of infants. *Infant and Child Development, 8*(1), 1–17.

Campbell, M. K., & Mottola, M. F. (2001). Recreational exercise and occupational activity during pregnancy and birth weight: a case-control study. *Am J Obstet Gynecol, 184*(3), 403–408.

Campbell, S. B., Cohn, J. F., & Meyers, T. (1995). Depression in first-time mothers: Mother-infant interaction and depression chronicity. *Developmental Psychology, 31,* 349–357.

Campos, J. J. (1976). Heart rate: A sensitive tool for the study of emotional development in the infant. In L. P. Lipsitt (Ed.), *Developmental psychobiology: The significance of infancy* (pp. 405–426). Hillsdale, NJ: Erlbaum.

Campos, J. J., & Barrett, K. C. (1984). Toward a new understanding of emotions and their development. In C. E. Izard, J. Kagan, & R. B. Zajonc (Eds.), *Emotions, cognition, and behavior* (pp. 229–263). New York: Cambridge University Press.

Campos, J. J., Campos, R., & Barrett, K. (1989). Emergent themes in the study of emotional development and emotion regulation. *Developmental Psychology, 25*(3), 394–402.

Campos, J. J., Emde, R. N., Gaensbauer, T., & Henderson, C. (1975). Cardiac and behavioral interrelationships in the reactions of infants to strangers. *Developmental Psychology, 11,* 589–601.

Campos, J. J., Langer, A., & Krowitz, A. (1970). Cardiac responses on the visual cliff in prelocomotor human infants. *Science, 170,* 196–197.

Campos, R. G. (1989). Soothing pain-elicited distress in infants with swaddling and pacifiers. *Child Development, 60,* 781–792.

Camras, L. A. (1993). A dynamic systems perspective on expressive development. In K. Strongman (Ed.), *International review of studies on emotion* (pp. 210–224). New York: Wiley.

Canfield, R. L., & Haith, M. M. (1991). Young infants' visual expectations for symmetric and asymmetric stimulus sequences. *Developmental Psychology, 27,* 198–208.

Caplan, M., Vespo, J., Pedersen, J., & Hay, D. F. (1991). Conflict and its resolution in small groups of one- and two-year-olds. *Child Development, 62,* 1513–1524.

Capra, F. (1996). *The web of life.* New York: Anchor Books.

Cardinal, T. M., & Lumeng, J. C. (2007). Too much tube time? Television viewing and childhood obesity. *Zero to Three, 28*(1), 31–36.

Carew, J. V. (1980). Experience and the development of intelligence in young children at home and in day care. *Monographs of the Society for Research in Child Development, 45* (6–sup-7), 1–115.

Carlile, K. S., & Holstrum, W. J. (1989). Parental involvement behaviors: A comparison of Chamorro and Caucasian parents. *Infant Behavior and Development, 12,* 479–494.

Carlson, E. A. (1998). A prospective longitudinal study of attachment disorganization/disorientation. *Child Development, 69*(4), 1107–1128.

Carlson, S. M., Mandell, D. J., & Williams, L. (2004). Executive Function and Theory of Mind: Stability and Prediction

From Ages 2 to 3. *Developmental Psychology, 40*(6), 1105–1122.

Carlson, V., Cicchetti, D., Barnett, D., & Braunwald, K. (1989). Disorganized/disoriented attachment relationships in maltreated infants. *Developmental Psychology, 25,* 525–531.

Carmen, R. del, Pedersen, F. A., Huffman, L. C., & Bryan, Y. E. (1993). Dyadic distress management predicts subsequent security of attachment. *Infant Behavior and Development, 16,* 131–147.

Caron, A. J., Caron, R. F., & Antell, S. E. (1988). Infant understanding of containment: An affordance perceived or a relationship conceived? *Developmental Psychology, 24,* 620–627.

Caron, A. J., Caron, R. F., & MacLean, D. J. (1988). Infant discrimination of naturalistic emotional expressions: The role of face and voice. *Child Development, 59,* 604–616.

Caron, R. F., Caron, A. J., & Myers, R. S. (1982). Abstraction of invariant face expressions in infancy. *Child Development, 53,* 1008–1015.

Carpenter, M., Akhtar, N., & Tomasello, M. (1998). Fourteen-through 18–month-old infants differentially imitate intentional and accidental actions. *Infant Behavior and Development, 21*(2), 315–330.

Carpenter, M., Call, J., & Tomasello, M. (2005). Twelve-and 18–month-olds copy actions in terms of goals. *Developmental Science, 8*(1), F13–F20.

Carpenter, M., Nagell, K., & Tomasello, M. (1998). Social cognition, joint attention, and communicative competence from 9 to 15 months of age. *Monographs of the Society for Research in Child Development, 63*(4), 1–176.

Carpenter, M., Tomasello, M., & Striano, T. (2005). Role reversal imitation and language in typically developing infants and children with autism. *Infancy, 8*(3), 253–278.

Carson, C. P., Klee, T., Carson, D. K., & Hime, L. K. (2003). Phonological profiles of 2–year-olds with delayed language development: predicting clinical outcomes at age 3. *Am J Speech Lang Pathol, 12*(1), 28–39.

Caruso, D. A. (1993). Dimensions of quality in infants' exploratory behavior: Relationships to problem-solving ability. *Infant Behavior and Development, 16,* 441–454.

Caspi, A., & Silva, P. A. (1995). Temperamental qualities at age three predict personality traits in young adulthood: Longitudinal evidence from birth cohort. *Child Development, 66,* 486–498.

Cassidy, J. (1994). Emotion regulation: Influences of attachment relationships. *Monographs of the Society for Research in Child Development, 59,* 228–249.

Cassidy, J., & Berlin, L. J. (1994). The insecure/ambivalent pattern of attachment: Theory and research. *Child Development, 65,* 971–991.

Cassidy, J. W., & Standley, J. M. (1995). The effect of music listening on physiological responses of premature infants in the NICU. *Journal of Music Therapy, 32*(4), 208–227.

Catherwood, D. (1993). The robustness of infant haptic memory: Testing its capacity to withstand delay and haptic interference. *Child Development, 64,* 702–710.

Caudill, W., & Weinstein, H. (1969). Maternal care and infant behavior in Japan and America. *Psychiatry, 32,* 12–43.

Caughy, M. O., DiPietro, J. A., & Strobino, D. M. (1994). Daycare participation as a protective factor in the cognitive development of low-income children. *Child Development, 65,* 457–471.

Centers for Disease Control (1995, June). Recommended childhood immunization schedule—United States, 1995. *Morbidity and Mortality Weekly Report, 44, no. RR-5,* 1–8.

Centers for Disease Control and Prevention (CDC), (2001, January 12). Recommended childhood immunization schedule – United States, 2001. *Morbidity and Mortality Weekly Report, 50*(01). 7–10, 19.

Cernoch, J. M., & Porter, R. H. (1985). Recognition of maternal axillary odors by infants. *Child Development, 56,* 1593–1598.

Cervantes, C. A., & Callanan, M. A. (1998). Labels and explanations in mother-child emotion talk: Age and gender differentation. *Developmental Psychology, 34*(1), 88–98.

Chabrol, H., Walburg, V., Teissedre, F., Armitage, J., & Santrisse, K. (2004). Influence of mother's perceptions on the choice to breastfeed or bottle-feed: Perceptions and feeding choice. *Journal of Reproductive and Infant Psychology, 22*(3), 189–198.

Chandler, M., Fritz, A. S., & Hala, S. (1989). Small-scale deceit: Deception as a marker of two-, three-, and four-year-olds' early theories of mind. *Child Development, 60,* 1263–1277.

Chang, L., Smith, L. M., LoPresti, C., Yonekura, M. L., Kuo, J., Walot, I., et al. (2004). Smaller subcortical volumes and cognitive deficits in children with prenatal methamphetamine exposure. *Psychiatry Research: Neuroimaging, 132*(2), 95–106.

Charman, T., Swettenham, J., Baron-Cohen, S., Cox, A., Baird, G., & Drew, A. (1997). Infants with autism: An investigation of empathy, pretend play, joint attention, and imitation. *Developmental Psychology, 33*(5), 781–789.

Chase-Lansdale, P. L., & Owen, M. T. (1987). Maternal employment in a family context: Effects on infant-mother and infant-father attachments. *Child Development, 58,* 1505–1512.

Charis: s, A., Kiessling, F., Winter, V., & Hofer, J (2006) Sensory motor inhibition as a prerequisite for theory-of-mind: A comparison of clinical and normal preschoolers differing in sensory motor abilities. *International Journal of Behavioral Development, 30*(2), 178–190.

Chatoor, I., Ganiban, J., Colin, V., Plummer, N., & Harmon, R. J. (1998). Attachment and feeding problems: a reexamination of nonorganic failure to thrive and attachment insecurity. *J Am Acad Child Adolesc Psychiatry, 37*(11), 1217–1224.

Chen, Z., & Sanchez, R. P., & Campbell, T. (1997). From beyond to within their grasp: The rudiments of analogical problem solving in 10– to 13–month-olds. *Developmental Psychology, 33*(5), 790–801.

Cherlin, A. J., & Furstenberg, F. F., Jr. (1986). *The new American grandparent.* New York: Basic Books.

Cherney, I. D. (2003). Young children's spontaneous utterances of mental terms and the accuracy of their memory behaviors: A different methodological approach. *Infant and Child Development, 12*(1), 89–105.

Chin-Quee, D. S., & Scarr, S. (1994). Lack of early child care effects on school-age children's social competence and academic achievement. *Early Development and Parenting, 3,* 103–112.

Chisholm, J. S. (1983). *Navajo infancy: An ethological study of child development.* New York: Aldine.

Chisholm, K. (1998). A three year follow-up of attachment and indiscriminate friendliness in children adopted from Romanian orphanages. *Child Development, 69*(4), 1092–1106.

Chomitz, V. R., Cheung, L. W. Y., & Liebermann, E. (1995). The role of lifestyle in preventing low birth weight. *The Future of Children, 5,* 121–138.

Chomsky, N. (1975). *Reflections on language.* New York: Pantheon.

Chouinard, M. M. (2007). Children's questions: A mechanism for cognitive development. *Monographs of the Society for Research in Child Development, 72*(1, Serial No. 286).

Christakis, D. A., Zimmerman, F. J., DiGiuseppe, D. L., & McCarty, C. A. (2004). Early television exposure and subsequent attentional problems in children. *Pediatrics, 113*(4), 708–713.

Christensen, H., Poyser, C., Pollitt, P., & Cubis, J. (1999). Pregnancy may confer a selective cognitive advantage. *Journal of Reproductive and Infant Psychology, 17*(1), 7–25.

Chubet, C. T. (1988). *Feeding your baby: Breast, bottle, and baby foods.* Stamford, CT: Longmeadow Press.

Cicchetti, D., & Mans, L. (1976, September). *Down's syndrome and normal infants' responses to impending collision.* Paper presented at the meeting of the American Psychological Association, Washington, DC.

Cielinski, K. L., Vaughn, B. E., Seifer, R., & Contreras, J. (1995). Relations among sustained engagement during play, quality of play, and mother-child interaction in samples of children with Down syndrome and normally developing toddlers. *Infant Behavior and Development, 18*(2), 163–176.

Clapp, J. F., 3rd, Kim, H., Burciu, B., Schmidt, S., Petry, K., & Lopez, B. (2002). Continuing regular exercise during pregnancy: effect of exercise volume on fetoplacental growth. *Am J Obstet Gynecol, 186*(1), 142–147.

Clarici, A., Clarici, A., Travan, L., Accardo, A., De Vonderweid, U., & Bava, A. (2002). Crying of a newborn child: Alarm signal or protocommunication? *Perceptual and Motor Skills, 95*(3, Pt 1), 752–754.

Clark, E. V. (1978). Strategies for communicating. *Child Development, 49,* 953–959.

Clark, H. H., & Clark, E. V. (1977). *Psychology and language: An introduction to psycholinguistics.* New York: Harcourt Brace Jovanovich.

Clark, J. E., Truly, T. L., & Phillips, S. J. (1993). On the development of walking as a limit-cycle system. In L. B. Smith & E. Thelen (Eds.),*A dynamic systems approach to development: Applications* (pp. 71–93). Cambridge, MA: MIT Press.

Clark, J. E., Whitall, J., & Phillips, S. J. (1988). Human interlimb coordination: The first 6 months of independent walking. *Developmental Psychobiology, 21,* 445–456.

Clark, R., Hyde, J. S., Essex, M. J., & Klein, M. H. (1997). Length of maternity leave and quality of mother-infant interactions. *Child Development, 68*(2), 364–383.

Clarke, S. & Taffel, S. (1995). Changes in cesarean delivery in the United States, 1988 and 1993. *Birth, 22,* 63–67.

Clarke-Stewart, A. (1978). And daddy makes three: The father's impact on mother and young child. *Child Development, 44,* 466–478.

Clarke-Stewart, A. (1984). Day care: A new context for research and development. In M. Perlmutter (Ed.), *Minnesota symposia on child psychology* (Vol. 17, pp. 1015–1034). Hillsdale, NJ: Erlbaum.

Clarke-Stewart, K. A. (1998). Historical shifts and underlying themes in ideas about rearing young children in the United States: Where have we been? Where are we going? *Early Development and Parenting, 7,* 101–117.

Clearfield, M. W. (2004). The role of crawling and walking experience in infant spatial memory. *Journal of Experimental Child Psychology, 89*(3), 214–241.

Clements, M., & Barnett, D. (2002). Parenting and attachment among toddlers with congenital anomalies: Examining the strange situation and attachment Q-sort. *Infant Mental Health Journal, 23*(6), 625–642.

Clifton, R. K., Perris, E., & Bullinger, A. (1991). Infants' perception of auditory space. *Developmental Psychology, 27,* 187–197.

Clifton, R. K., Rochat, P., Litovsky, R. Y., & Perris, E. E. (1991). Object representation guides infants' reaching in the dark. *Journal of Experimental Psychology: Human Perception and Performance, 17,* 323–329.

Clifton, R. K., Rochat, P., Robin, D. J., & Berthier, N. E. (1994). Multimodal perception in the control of infant reaching. *Journal of Experimental Psychology: Human Perception and Performance, 20,* 876–886.

Cnattingius, S. (2004). The epidemiology of smoking during pregnancy: Smoking prevalence, maternal characteristics, and pregnancy outcomes. *Nicotine & Tobacco Research, 6*(2) S125–S140.

Coale, A. J., & Banister, J. (1994). Five decades of missing females in China. *Demography, 31,* 459–479.

Cofer, L. F. (2008). Dynamic views of education. In A. Fogel, B. J. King, & S. Shanker (Eds.). *Human development in the 21st century: Visionary policy ideas from systems scientists.* Cambridge, UK: Cambridge University Press.

Cofer, L. F., Grice, J. W., Sethre-Hofstad, L., Radi, C. J., Zimmerman, L. K., Palmer-Seal, D., & Santa-Maria, G. (1999). Developmental perspectives on morningness-eveningness and social interactions. *Human Development, 42,* 169–198.

Cogswell, M. E., Serdula, M. K., Hungerford, D. W., & Yip, R. (1995). Gestational weight gain among average-weight and overweight women: What is excessive? *American Journal of Obstetrics and Gynecology, 172,* 705–712.

Cohen, D. L. (1993). Stress Head Start quality, but spotlight 0–3. *Education Week, 12,* 10–20.

Cohen, L., Zilkha, S., Middleton, J., & O'Donnohue, N. (1978). Perinatal mortality: Assisting parental affirmation. *American Journal of Orthopsychiatry, 48,* 727–731.

Cohen, L. B., DeLoache, J. S., & Strauss, M. S. (1979). Infant visual perception. In J. Osofsky (Ed.), *Handbook of infant development* (pp. 419–435). New York: Wiley.

Cohen, L. B., & Oakes, L. M. (1993). How infants perceive a simple causal event. *Developmental Psychology, 29,* 421–433.

Cohen, L. B., & Strauss, M. S. (1979). Concept acquisition in the human infant. *Child Development, 50,* 419–424.

Cohen, L. J., & Campos, J. J. (1974). Father, mother and stranger as elicitors of attachment behaviors in infancy. *Developmental Psychology, 10,* 146–154.

Cohen, M., Brown, D. R., & Myers, M. M. (2001). Cardiovascular responses to pacifier experience and feeding in newborn infants. *Developmental Psychobiology, 39*(1), 34–39.

Cohen, N. L., & Tomlinson-Keasey, C. (1980). The effects of peers and mothers on toddlers' play. *Child Development, 51,* 921–924.

Cohen, P., Kasen, S., Brook, J. S., & Hartmark, C. (1998). Behavior patterns of young children and their offspring: A two-generation study. *Developmental Psychology, 34*(6), 1202–1208.

Cohen, R. (1981). Factors influencing maternal choice of childbirth alternatives. *Journal of the American Academy of Child Psychiatry, 20,* 1–15.

Cohen, S. E., & Beckwith, L. (1979). Preterm infant intervention with the caregiver in the first year of life and competence at age two. *Child Development, 50,* 767–776.

Cohler, B. J., & Grunebaum, H. V. (1981). *Mothers, grandmothers, and daughters: Personality and childcare in three-generation families.* New York: Wiley.

Cohn, J. F., Campbell, S. B., Matias, R., & Hopkins, J. (1990). Face-to-face interactions of postpartum depressed and nondepressed mother-infant pairs at 2 months. *Developmental Psychology, 26*(1), 15–23.

Cohn, J. F., & Elmore, M. (1988). Effect of contingent changes in mothers' affective expression on the organization of behavior in 3–month-old infants. *Infant Behavior and Development, 11,* 493–505.

Cohn, J. F., Matias, R., Tronick, E. Z., Lyons-Ruth, K., & Connell, D. (1986). Face-to-face interactions, spontaneous and structured, of mothers with depressive symptoms. In T. Field & E. Z. Tronick (Eds.), *Maternal depression and child development, New directions for child development* (pp. 31–46). San Francisco: Jossey-Bass.

Cohn, J. F., & Tronick, E. Z. (1983). Three-month-old infants' reaction to simulated maternal depression. *Child Development, 54,* 185–193.

Cohn, J. F., & Tronick, E. Z. (1988). Mother-infant face-to-face interaction: Influence in bidirectional and unrelated to periodic cycles in either partner's behavior. *Developmental Psychology, 24*(3), 386–392.

Coldren, J. T., & Colombo, J. (1994). The nature and processes of preverbal learning: Implications from nine-month-old infants' discrimination problem solving. *Monographs of the Society for Research in Child Development, 59,* 1–94.

Cole, P. M., Barrett, K. C., & Zahn-Waxler, C. (1992). Emotion displays in two-year-olds during mishaps. *Child Development, 63,* 314–324.

Cole, P. M., Tamang, B. L., & Shrestha, S. (2006). Cultural Variations in the Socialization of Young Children's Anger and Shame. *Child Development, 77*(5), 1237–1251.

Coleman, J. M., Pratt, R. R., Stoddard, R. A., Gerstmann, D. R., & Abel, H. H. (1997). The effects of the male and female singing and speaking voices on selected physiological and behavioral measures of premature infants in the intensive care unit. *International Journal of Arts Medicine, 5*(2), 4–11.

Coleman-Phox, K., Odouli, R., ; Li, D., (2008). Use of a Fan During Sleep and the Risk of Sudden Infant Death Syndrome, *Arch Pediatr Adolesc Med., 162*(10):963–968.

Colman, R. A., & Widom, C. S. (2004). Childhood abuse and neglect and adult intimate relationships: A prospective study. *Child Abuse & Neglect, 28*(11), 1133–1151.

Coles, R. (1971). *The South goes north.* Boston: Little, Brown.

Coley, R. L., & Chase-Lansdale, P. L. (1998). Adolescent pregnancy and parenthood: Recent evidence and future directions. *American Psychologist, 53*(2), 152–166.

Coll, C. T. G., Halpern, L. F., Vohr, B. R., Seifer, R., & Oh, W. (1992). Stability and correlates of change of early temperament in preterm and full-term infants. *Infant Behavior and Development, 15,* 137–153.

Colletta, N. D. (1981). Social support and the risk of maternal rejection by adolescent mothers. *Journal of Psychology, 109,* 191–197.

Colletta, N. D., & Lee, D. (1983). The impact of support for black adolescent mothers. *Journal of Family Issues, 4,* 127–143.

Collins, J. E. (1994). Fetal surgery: Changing the outcome before birth. *Journal of Obstetrics, Gynecology & Neonatal Nursing, 23,* 166–169.

Collis, G. M., & Schaffer, H. R. (1975). Synchronization of visual attention in mother-infant pairs. *Journal of Child Psychology and Psychiatry, 16,* 315–320.

Colombo, J., Frick, J. E., Ryther, J. S., Coldren, J. T., & Mitchell, D. W. (1995). *Merrill-Palmer Quarterly, 41,* 104–113.

Colombo, J., Mitchell, D. W., Coldren, J. T., & Freeseman, L. J. (1991). Individual differences in infant visual attention: Are short lookers faster processors or feature processors? *Child Development, 62,* 1247–1257.

Colombo, J., Mitchell, D. W., O'Brien, M., & Horowitz, F. D. (1987). The stability of visual habituation during the first year of life. *Child Development, 58,* 474–487.

Colombo, J., Moss, M., & Horowitz, F. D. (1989). Neonatal state profiles: Reliability and short-term prediction of neurobehavioral status. *Child Development, 60,* 1102–1110.

Committee on Nutrition, American Academy of Pediatrics. (1998). *Pediatric nutrition handbook* (4th ed.). Elk Grove Vilage, IL: American Academy of Pediatrics.

Connell, J. P. (1985). A component process approach to the study of individual differences and developmental change in attachment system functioning. In M. E. Lamb, R. A. Thompson, W. Gardner, & E. L. Charnov, (Eds.), *Infant-mother attachment* (pp. 223–247). Hillsdale, NJ: Erlbaum.

Conner, J. M., & Nelson, E. C. (1999). Neonatal intensive care: Satisfaction measured from a parent's perspective. *Pediatrics, 103,* 336–349.

Connolly, K., & Dalgleish, M. (1989). The emergence of a tool-using skill in infancy. *Developmental Psychology, 25,* 894–912.

Conrad, R. (1998). Darwin's baby and baby's Darwin: Mutual recognition in observational research. *Human Development, 41*(1), 47–64.

Conrad, R. (2004). '[A]s if she defied the world in her joyousness': Rereading Darwin on emotion and emotional development. *Human Development, 47*(1), 40–65.

Cooper, R. P., Abraham, J., Berman, S., & Staska, M. (1997). The development of infants' preference for motherese. *Infant Behavior and Development, 20*(4), 477–488.

Cooper, R. P., & Aslin, R. N. (1989). The language environment of the young infant: Implications for early perceptual development. *Canadian Journal of Psychology, 43,* 247–265.

Cooper, R. P., & Aslin, R. N. (1994). Developmental differences in infant attention to the spectral properties of infant-directed speech. *Child Development, 65,* 1663–1677.

Copstick, S., Taylor, K., Hayes, R., & Morris, N. (1986). The relation of time of day to childbirth. *Journal of Reproductive and Infant Psychology, 4*(1–2), 13–22.

Corkum, V., & Moore, C. (1995). Development of joint visual attention in infants. In C. Moore & P. J. Dunham (Eds.), *Joint attention: Its origins and role in development* (pp. 61–83). Hillsdale, NJ: Erlbaum.

Corter, C. (1977). Brief separation and communication between infant and mother. In T. Alloway, P. Pliner, & L. Krames (Eds.), *Attachment behavior* (pp. 143–168). New York: Plenum Press.

Corter, C., Abramovitch, R., & Pepler, D. J. (1983). The role of the mother in sibling interaction. *Child Development, 54,* 1599–1605.

Cossette, L., Malcuit, G., & Pomerleau, A. (1991). Sex differences in motor activity during early infancy. *Infant Behavior and Development, 14,* 175–186.

Coster, W. J., Gersten, M. S., Beeghly, M., & Cicchetti, D. (1989). Communicative functioning in maltreated toddlers. *Developmental Psychology, 25*(6), 1020–1029.

Cotterell, J. L. (1986). Work and community influences on the quality of child rearing. *Child Development, 57,* 362–374.

Cottrell, B. H., & Shannahan, M. K. (1987). A comparison of fetal outcome in birth chair and delivery table births. *Research in Nursing and Health, 10,* 239–243.

Courage, M. L., Edison, S. C., & Howe, M. L. (2004). Variability in the early development of visual self-recognition. *Infant Behavior & Development, 27*(4), 509–532.

Courchesne, E. (2004). Brain development in autism: Early overgrowth followed by premature arrest of growth. *Mental Retardation and Developmental Disabilities Research Reviews, 10*(2), 106–111.

Cowan, C. P., & Cowan, P. A. (1981). *Couple role arrangements and satisfaction during family formation.* Boston: Society for Research in Child Development.

Cox, M. C., Owen, M. T., Henderson, V. K., & Margand, N. A. (1992). Prediction of infant-father and infant-mother attachment. *Developmental Psychology, 28,* 474–483.

Cox, M. C., Owen, M. T., Lewis, J. M., & Henderson, V. K. (1989). Marriage, adult adjustment, and early parenting. *Child Development, 60,* 1015–1024.

Crain-Thoreson, C., & Dale, P. (1992). Do early talkers become early readers? Linguistic precocity, preschool language, and emergent literacy. *Developmental Psychology, 28,* 421–429.

Crais, E., Douglas, D. D., & Campbell, C. C. (2004). The intersection of the development of gestures and intentionality. *J Speech Lang Hear Res, 47*(3), 678–694.

Craton, L. G. (1996). The development of perceptual completion abilities: Infants' perception of stationary, partially occluded objects. *Child Development, 67*(3), 890–904.

Cravioto, J., & Arrieta, R. (1983). Malnutrition in childhood. In M. Rutter (Ed.), *Developmental neuropsychiatry* (pp. 515–538). New York: Guilford Press.

Crawford, J. W. (1982). Mother-infant interaction in premature and full-term infants. *Child Development, 53,* 957–962.

Crittenden, P. M. (1985). Social networks, quality of child rearing, and child development. *Child Development, 56,* 1299–1313.

Crnic, K., & Greenberg, M. (1987). Maternal stress, social support, and coping: Influences on the early mother-child relationship. In C. Boukydis (Ed.), *Research on support for parents and infants in the postnatal period* (pp. 25–40). Norwood, NJ: Ablex.

Crockenberg, S. B. (1981). Infant irritability, mother responsiveness, and social support influences on the security of infant-mother attachment. *Child Development, 52,* 857–865.

Crockenberg, S. B. (1987). Support for adolescent mothers during the postnatal period: Theory and research. In C. Boukydis (Ed.), *Research on support for parents and infants in the postnatal period* (pp. 3–24). Norwood, NJ: Ablex.

Crockenberg, S. B., & Acredolo, C. (1983). Infant temperament ratings: A function of infants, of mothers, or both? *Infant Behavior and Development, 6,* 61–72.

Crockenberg, S. B., & McCluskey, K. (1986). Change in maternal behavior during the baby's first year of life. *Child Development, 57,* 746–753.

Crockenberg, S. B., & Smith, P. (1982). Antecedents of mother-infant interaction and infant irritability in the first three months of life. *Infant Behavior and Development, 6,* 61–72.

Crockenberg, S. C., & Leerkes, E. M. (2004). Infant and Maternal Behaviors Regulate Infant Reactivity to Novelty at 6 Months. *Developmental Psychology, 40*(6), 1123–1132.

Cronin, C. M. G., Shapiro, C. R., Casiro, O. G., & Cheang, M. S. (1995). The impact of very low-birth-weight infants on the family is long lasting. *Archives of the Pediatric and Adolescent Medicine, 149,* 151–158.

Crook, C. K. (1978). Taste perception in the newborn infant. *Infant Behavior and Development, 1,* 52–69.

Crouter, A. C., Perry-Jenkins, M., Huston, T. L., & McHale, S. M. (1987). Processes underlying father involvement in dual-earner and single-earner families. *Developmental Psychology, 23,* 431–440.

Crowley, P. H., Gulati, D. K., Hayden, T. L., Lopez, P., & Dyer, R. A. (1979). A chiasma-hormonal hypothesis relating Down's syndrome and maternal age. *Nature, 280,* 417–419.

Cruz-Sanchez, F. F., Lucena, J., Ascaso, C., Tolosa, E., Quinto, L., & Rossi, M. L. (1997). Cerebellar cortex delayed maturation in sudden infant death syndrome. *Journal of Neuropathology and Experimental Neurology, 56*(4), 340–346.

Cuisinier, M., Janssen, H., de Graauw, D., & Hoogduin, K. (1998). Predictors of maternal reactions to excessive crying of newborns. Findings from a prospective study in a naturalistic situation. *Early Development and Parenting, 7,* 41–49.

Cummings, J. S., Pellegrini, D. S., Notarius, C. I., & Cummings, E. M. (1989). Children's responses to angry adult behavior as a function of marital distress and history of interparent hostility. *Child Development, 60,* 1035–1043.

Cutillo, D. M., Hammond, E. A., Reeser, S. L., Kershner, M. A., Lukin, B., Godmilow, L., & Donnenfeld, A. E. (1994). Chorionic villus sampling utilization following reports of a possible association with fetal limb defects. *Prenatal Diagnosis, 14,* 327–332.

Dahl, R. E., Scher, M. S., Williamson, D. E., Robles, N., & Day, N. (1995). A longitudinal study of prenatal marijuana use: Effects of sleep and arousal at age 3 years. *Archives of Pediatric and Adolescent Medicine, 149,* 145–150.

Dale, P. S. (1976). *Language development: Structure and function* (2nd ed.). New York: Holt, Rinehart and Winston.

D'Alton (1994). Prenatal diagnostic procedures. *Seminars in Perinatology, 18,* 140–162.

Damast, A. M., Tamis-LeMonda, C. S., & Bornstein, M. H. (1996). Mother-child play: Sequential interactions and the relation between maternal beliefs and behaviors. *Child Development, 67*(4), 1752–1766.

Danforth, D. N. (Ed.) (1977). *Obstetrics and gynecology* (3rd ed.). New York: Harper & Row.

Daniels, D., Plomin, R., & Greenhalgh, J. (1984). Correlates of difficult temperament in infancy. *Child Development, 55,* 1184–1194.

Dannemiller, J. L., & Stephens, B. R. (1988). A critical test of infant pattern preference models. *Child Development, 59,* 210–216.

Darj, E., & Nordstrom, M. L. (1999). The Misgav Ladach method for ceasarean section compared to the Pfanenstiel method. *Acta Obstetrica et Gynecologica Scandinavica, 78,* 37–41.

Darwin, C. R. (1859). *The origin of species.* New York: Modern Library.

Davenport-Slack, B., & Boylan, C. H. (1974). Psychological correlates of childbirth pain. *Psychosomatic Medicine, 36,* 215–223.

Davis, C. G., & Mantler, J. (2004). *The consequences of financial stress for individuals, families, and society.* Ottawa, ON, Canada: Carleton University, Centre for Research on Stress, Coping, and Well-being, Department of Psychology.

Davis, D. (1967). Family process in mental retardation. *American Journal of Psychiatry, 124,* 340–350.

Davis, D. (1985). Infant car safety: The role of perinatal caregivers. *Birth, 12*(Supplement), 21–27.

Davis, H. (1978). A description of aspects of mother-infant vocal interaction. *Journal of Child Psychology and Psychiatry, 19,* 379–386.

Dawson, G., Frey, K., Panagiotides, H., Yamada, E., Hessl, D., & Osterling, J. (1999). Infants of depressed mothers exhibit atypical frontal electrical brain activity during interactions with mother and with a familiar, nondepressed adult. *Child Development, 70*(5), 1058–1066.

Dawson, G., Webb, S. J., Carver, L., Panagiotides, H., & McPartland, J. (2004). Young children with autism show atypical brain responses to fearful versus neutral facial expressions of emotion. *Developmental Science, 7*(3), 340–359.

DC: 0–3R. (2005). *Diagnostic Classification of Mental Health and Developmental Disorders Of Infancy and Early Childhood.* NY: Zero to Three Press.

DeBoysson-Bardies, B. (1990). Some reflexions on sensory-motor organization of speech during the first year of life. In H. Bloch & B. I. Bertenthal (Eds.), *Sensory-motor organizations and development in infancy and early childhood* (pp. 457–466). The Netherlands: Kluwer Academic.

DeBoysson-Bardies, B., Sagant, L., & Durand, C. (1984). Discernible differences in the babbling of infants according to target language. *Journal of Child Language, 11,* 1–15.

DeCasper, A. J., & Fifer, W. P. (1980). Of human bonding: Newborns prefer their mothers' voices. *Science, 208,* 1174–1176.

DeCasper, A. J., & Sigafoos, A. D. (1983). The intrauterine heartbeat: A potent reinforcer for newborns. *Infant Behavior and Development, 6,* 19–26.

DeCasper, A. J., & Spence, M. J. (1986). Prenatal maternal speech influences newborns' perception of speech sounds. *Infant Behavior and Development, 9,* 133–150.

DeChateau, P. (1987). Parent-infant socialization in several western European countries. In J. D. Osofsky (Ed.), *Handbook of infant development* (2nd ed., pp. 642–668). New York: Wiley.

de Haan, M., Belsky, J., Reid, V., Volein, A., & Johnson, M. H. (2004). Maternal personality and infants' neural and visual responsivity to facial expressions of emotion. *Journal of Child Psychology and Psychiatry, 45*(7), 1209–1218.

Degangi, G. A., Breinbauer, C., Doussard Roosevelt, J., Porges, S., & Greenspan, S. (2000). Prediction of childhood problems at three years in children experiencing disorders of regulation during infancy. *Infant Mental Health Journal, 21*(3), 156–175.

DeGangi, G. A., Porges, S. W., Sickel, R. Z., & Greenspan, S. I. (1993). Four-year follow-up of a sample of regulatory disordered infants. *Infant Mental Health Journal, 14*(4), 330–343.

DeGangi, G. A., Sickel, R. Z., Wiener, A. S., & Kaplan, E. P. (1996). Fussy babies: To treat or not to treat? *British Journal of Occupational Therapy, 59*(10), 457–464.

DeHart, G., Sroufe, L., & Cooper, R. (2000). *Child Development: Its nature and course* (4th ed.). Boston: McGraw-Hill.

De Jonge, A., Teunissen, T. A., & Lagro-Janssen, A. L. (2004). Supine position compared to other positions during the second stage of labor: a meta-analytic review. *J Psychosom Obstet Gynaecol, 25*(1), 35–45.

De Jonge, A., van der Goes, B., Ravelli, A., Amelink-Verburg, M., Mol, B., Nijhuis, J., Gravenhorst, J., Buitendijk, S., 2009). *BJOG—An International Journal of Obstetrics and Gynaecology, 116,* 9: 1177–1184.

Delevati, N. M., & Bergamasco, N. H. P. (1999). Pain in the neonate: An analysis of facial movements and crying in response to nociceptive stimuli. *Infant Behavior and Development, 22*(1), 137–143.

DeLoache, J. S., & Plaetzer, B. (1985, April). *Tea for two: Joint mother-child symbolic play.* Presented at the meeting of the Society for Research in Child Development, Toronto, Canada.

DeLoache, J. S., Sugarman, S., & Brown, A. L. (1985). The development of error correction strategies in young children's manipulative play. *Child Development, 56,* 928–939.

DeMeis, D. K., Hock, E., & McBride, S. L. (1986). The balance of employment and motherhood: Longitudinal study of mothers' feelings about separation from their first-born infants. *Developmental Psychology, 22,* 627–632.

Demetriou, H., & Hay, D. F. (2004). Toddlers' reactions to the distress of familiar peers: The importance of context. *Infancy, 6*(2), 299–318.

Demos, V. E. (1982). Facial expressions of infants and toddlers: A descriptive analysis. In T. Field & A. Fogel (Eds.), *Emotion and early interaction* (pp. 188–209). Hillsdale, NJ: Erlbaum.

den Bak, I. M., & Ross, H. S. (1996). I'm telling: The content, context, and consequences of children's tattling on their siblings. *Social Development, 5*(3), 292–309.

Denham, S. (1986). Social cognition, prosocial behavior and emotion in preschoolers: Contextual validation. *Child Development, 57,* 194–201.

Denzin, N. K. & Lincoln, Y. S. (1994). *Handbook of qualitative research.* Thousand Oaks, CA: Sage Publications.

de Schipper, E. J., Riksen-Walraven, J. M., & Geurts, S. A. E. (2006). Effects of Child-Caregiver Ratio on the Interactions Between Caregivers and Children in Child-Care Centers: An Experimental Study. *Child Development, 77*(4), 861–874.

Desor, J. A., Miller, O., & Turner, R. (1973). Taste in acceptance of sugars by human infants. *Journal of Comparative and Physiological Psychology, 85,* 496–501.

Desrochers, S., Morissette, P., & Ricard, M. (1995). Two perspectives on pointing in infancy. In C. Moore & P. J.

Dunham (Eds.), *Joint attention: Its origins and role in development* (pp. 85–101). Hillsdale, NJ: Erlbaum.

DeStefano, C. T., & Mueller, E. (1982). Environmental determinants of peer social activity in 18-month-old males. *Infant Behavior and Development, 5,* 175–183.

deVilliers, J. C., & deVilliers, P. A. (1973). A cross-sectional study of the acquisition of grammatical morphemes in child speech. *Journal of Pyscholinguistic Research, 2,* 267–278.

De Wolff, M. S., & van Ijzendoorn, M. H. (1997). Sensitivity and attachment: A meta-analysis on parental antecedents of infant attachment. *Child Development, 68*(4), 571–591.

Diamond, A. (1988). Abilities and neural mechanisms underlying AB performance. *Child Development, 59,* 523–527.

Diamond, A., & Doar, B. (1989). The performance of human infants on a measure of frontal cortex function, the delayed response task. *Developmental Psychobiology, 22*(3), 271–294.

Diamond, A., Prevor, M. B., Callender, G., & Druin, D. P. (1997). Prefrontal cortex cognitive deficits in children treated early and continuously for PKU. *Monographs of the Society for Research in Child Development, 62*(4), 1–205.

Diamond, K. E., & Kontos, S. (2004). Families' resources and accommodations: Toddlers with Down syndrome, cerebral palsy, and developmental delay. *Journal of Early Intervention, 26*(4), 253–265.

Dick-Read, G. (1972). *Childbirth without fear: The original approach to natural childbirth* (Rev. ed.). H. Wessel & H. Ellis (Eds.). New York: Harper & Row. (Original work published 1933)

Dickson, K. L., Fogel, A., & Messinger, D. (1997). The social context of smiling and laughter in infants. In M. Mascolo & S. Griffen (Eds.), *The development of emotion* (pp. 253–273). New York: Plenum Press.

Dickson, K. L., Walker, H., & Fogel, A. (1997). The relationship between smile-type and play-type during parent-infant play. *Developmental Psychology, 33,* 925–933.

Dickstein, S., & Parke, R. D. (1988). Social referencing in infancy: A glance at fathers and marriage. *Child Development, 59,* 506–511.

DiLalla, L. F., & Watson, M. W. (1988). Differentiation of fantasy and reality: Preschoolers' reactions to interruptions in their play. *Developmental Psychology, 24,* 286–291.

DiPietro, J. A., Hilton, S. C., Hawkins, M., Costigan, K. A., & Pressman, E. K. (2002). Maternal stress and affect influence fetal neurobehavioral development. *Developmental Psychology, 38*(5), 659–668.

DiPietro, J. A., Hodgson, D. M., Costigan, K. A., & Johnson, T. R. B. (1996). Fetal neurobehavioral development. *Child Development, 67* (5), 2553–2567.

DiPietro, J. A., Larson, S. K., & Porges, S. W. (1987). Behavioral and heart rate pattern differences between breast-fed and bottle-fed neonates. *Developmental Psychology, 23*(4), 467–474.

Dittrichová, J., Brichacek, V., Mandys, F., Paul, K., Sobotkova, D., Tautermannova, M., Vondracek, J., & Zezulakova, J. (1996). Relationship of early behavior to later developmental outcome for preterm children. *International Journal of Behavioral Development, 19*(3), 517–532.

Dix, T., Stewart, A. D., Gershoff, E. T., & Day, W. H. (2007). Autonomy and children's reactions to being controlled: Evidence that both compliance and defiance may be positive markers in early development. *Child Development, 78*(4), 1204–1221.

Dixon, L., Hamilton-Giachritsis, C., & Browne, K. (2005). Attributions and behaviours of parents abused as children: a mediational analysis of the intergenerational continuity of child maltreatment (Part II). *Journal of Child Psychology and Psychiatry, 46*(1), 58–68.

Dixon, S. D., LeVine, R. A., Richman, A., & Brazelton, T. B. (1984). Mother-child interaction around a teaching task: An African-American comparison. *Child Development, 55,* 1252–1264.

Dolinoy, D. C., Weidman, J. R., & Jirtle, R. L. (2007). Epigenetic gene regulation: linking early developmental environment to adult disease. *Reprod Toxicol, 23*(3), 297–307.

Dondi, M. (1999). Maturità e specificità del comportamento facciale nelle più precoci fasi dello sviluppo. *Giornale Italiano di Psicologia, 26*(1), 23–53.

Dondi, M., Messinger, M., Colle, M., Tabasso, A., Simeon, F., Barba, B., Fogel, A. (2007). A new perspective on neonatal smiling: Differences between expert coders and naive observers. Infancy.

Dondi, M., Simion, F., & Caltran, G. (1999). Can newborns discriminate between their own cry and the cry of another newborn infant? *Developmental Psychology, 35*(2), 418–426.

Donovan, W. L., & Leavitt, L. A. (1989). Maternal self-efficacy and infant attachment: Integrating physiology, perceptions, and behavior. *Child Development, 60,* 460–472.

Donovan, W. L., Leavitt, L. A., & Walsh, R. O. (1998). Conflict and depression predict maternal sensitivity to infant cries. *Infant Behavior and Development, 21*(3), 505–517.

Dougherty, T. M., & Haith, M. M. (1997). Infant expectations and reaction time as predictors of childhood speed of processing and IQ. *Developmental Psychology, 33*(1), 146–155.

Dow, K. E., & Reopelli, R. J. (1985). Ethanol neurotoxicity: Effects on neurite formation and neutrotrophic factor production in vitro. *Science, 228,* 591–593.

Downing, G. (2005). Emotion, body, and parent-infant interaction. In J. Nadel and D. Muir (Eds.), *Emotional Development,* pp. 429–450. Oxford, UK: Oxford University Press.

Downing, G. (2008). A different way to help. . In A. Fogel, B. J. King, & S. Shanker (Eds.). *Human development in the 21st century: Visionary policy ideas from systems scientists.* Cambridge, UK: Cambridge University Press.

Drachman, D. B., & Coulombre, A. J. (1962). Experimental clubfoot and arthorogryposis multiplex congenita. *Lancet, 2,* 523–536.

Dragonas, R., Petrogiannis, K., & Adam, H. (1997). Working women, their emotional well-being and pregnancy in Greece. *Journal of Reproductive and Infant Psychology, 15,* 239–256.

Draper, J. (2002). It's the first scientific evidence': Men's experience of pregnancy confirmation. *Journal of Advanced Nursing, 39*(6), 563–570.

Dressler, W. (1985). Extended family relationships, social support, and mental health in a southern black community. *Journal of Health and Social Behavior, 26,* 39–48.

Drotar, D., & Irvin, N. (1979). Disturbed maternal bereavement following infant death. *Child Care, Health and Development, 5,* 239–247.

Dubowitz, L. M. S., Dubowitz, V., & Goldberg, C. (1970). Clinical assessment of gestational age in the newborn infant. *Journal of Pediatrics, 77,* 1–10.

Dull, H. (1997). *Watsu: Freeing the body in water* (2nd ed.). Harbin, CA: Harbin Springs.

Duncan, G. J. (2003). Modeling the Impacts of Child Care Quality on Children's Preschool Cognitive Development. *Child Development, 74*(5), 1454–1475.

Dunham, P. J., & Dunham, F. (1995). Developmental antecedents of taxonomic and thematic strategies. *Developmental Psychology, 31,* 483–493.

Dunham, P. J., & Dunham, F. (1996). The semantically reciprocating robot: Adult influences on children's early conversational skills. *Social Development, 5*(3), 261–274.

Dunham, P. J., Dunham, F., & Curwin, A. (1993). Joint-attentional states and lexical acquisition at 18 months. *Developmental Psychology, 29,* 827–831.

Dunham, P. J., Dunham, F., Tran, S., & Akhtar, N. (1991). The nonreciprocating robot: Effects on verbal discourse, social play, and social referencing at two years of age. *Child Development, 62,* 1489–1502.

Dunn, D. T., Newell, M. L., Ades, A. E., & Peckham, C. S. (1992). Risk of human immunodeficiency virus type 1 transmission through breastfeeding. *Lancet, 340,* 585–588.

Dunn, J. (1975). Consistency and change in styles of mothering. In Ciba Foundation Symposium (Ed.), *Parent-infant interaction* (pp. 108–135). New York: Elsevier.

Dunn, J. (1998). Siblings, emotion, and the development of understanding. In S. Br;araten (Ed.), *Intersubjective communication and emotion in early ontogeny. Studies in emotion and social interaction, 2nd series* (pp. 158–168). Cambridge, England: Cambridge University Press.

Dunn, J., Bretherton, I., & Munn, P. (1987). Conversations about feeling states between mothers and their young children. *Developmental Psychology, 23,* 132–139.

Dunn, J., & Kendrick, C. (1980). Interactions between young siblings in the context of family relationships. In M. Lewis & L. Rosenblum (Eds.), *The child and its family* (pp. 334–369). New York: Plenum Press.

Dunn, J., & Kendrick, C. (1981). Social behavior of young siblings in the family context: Differences between same-sex and different-sex dyads. *Child Development, 52,* 1265–1273.

Dunn, J., & Kendrick, C. (1982). *Siblings: love, envy, and understanding.* Cambridge, MA: Harvard University Press.

Dunn, J., Kreps, C., & Brown, J. (1996). Children's family relationships between two and five: Developmental changes and individual differences. *Social Development, 5*(3), 230–250.

Dunn, J., & Munn, P. (1985). Becoming a family member: Family conflict and the development of social understanding in the second year. *Child Development, 56,* 480–492.

Dunn, J., & Munn, P. (1987). Development of justification in disputes with mother and sibling. *Developmental Psychology, 23,* 791–798.

Dunn, J., Plomin, R., & Daniels, D. (1986). Consistency and change in mothers' behavior toward young siblings. *Child Development, 57,* 348–356.

Dunn, J., & Shatz, M. (1989). Becoming a conversationalist despite (or because of) having an older sibling. *Child Development, 60,* 399–410.

Dunsmore, J. C., & Halberstadt, A. G. (1997). How does family emotional expressiveness affect children's schemas? In K. C. Barrett (Ed.), *New directions in child development: The communication of emotion: Current research from diverse perspectives, 77* (pp. 45–68). San Francisco: Jossey-Bass.

Dupont, F. (1989). *Daily life in ancient Rome* (C. Woodall, Trans.). Oxford, England: Blackwell.

Dworetzky, J. P., & Davis, N. J. (1989). *Human development: A life span approach.* St. Paul, MN: West.

Dyer, A. B., Lickliter, R., & Gottlieb, G. (1989). Maternal and peer imprinting in mallard ducklings under experimentally simulated natural social conditions. *Developmental Psychobiology, 22,* 463–475.

Dyregrov, A., & Matthiesen, S. B. (1987). Stillbirth, neonatal death, and sudden infant death (SIDS): Parental reactions. *Scandinavian Journal of Psychology, 28,* 104–114.

Eakins, P. S. (Ed.). (1986). *The American way of birth.* Philadelphia: Temple University Press.

Easterbrooks, M. A. (1989). Quality of attachment to mother and to father: Effects of perinatal risk status. *Child Development, 60,* 825–830.

Easterbrooks, M. A., & Goldberg, W. (1984). Toddler development in the family: Impact of father involvement and parenting characteristics. *Child Development, 55,* 740–752.

Easterbrooks, M. A., & Goldberg, W. (1985). Effects of early maternal employment on toddlers, mothers, and fathers. *Developmental Psychology, 21,* 774–783.

Ebert, J. D., & Sussex, I. M. (1970). *Interacting systems in development* (2nd ed.). New York: Holt, Rinehart and Winston.

Eckerman, C. O. (1993). Toddler's achievement of coordinated action with conspecifics: A dynamic systems perspective. In L. B. Smith & E. Thelen (Eds.), *A dynamic systems approach to development: Applications* (pp. 333–357). Cambridge, MA: MIT Press.

Eckerman, C. O., & Whatley, J. L. (1977). Toys and social interaction between infant peers. *Child Development, 48,* 1645–1656.

Eckerman, C. O., Davis, C. C., & Didow, S. M. (1989). Toddlers' emerging ways of achieving social coordinations with a peer. *Child Development, 60,* 440–453.

Eckerman, C. O., & Didow, S. M. (1989). Toddlers' social coordinations: Changing responses to another's invitation to play. *Developmental Psychology, 25,* 794–804.

Eckerman, C. O., Hsu, H., Molitor, A., Leung, E. H. L., & Goldstein, R. F. (1999). Infant arousal in an en-face exchange with a new partner: Effects of prematurity and perinatal biological risk. *Developmental Psychology, 35*(1), 282–293.

Eckerman, C. O., Oehler, J. M., Medvin, M. B., & Hannan, T. E. (1994). Premature newborns as social partners before term age. *Infant Behavior and Development, 17,* 55–70.

Eckerman, C. O., & Stein, M. R. (1990). How imitation begets imitation and toddlers' generation of games. *Developmental Psychology, 26,* 370–378.

Eckerman, C. O., & Whatley, J. L. (1975). Infants' reactions to unfamiliar adults varying in novelty. *Developmental Psychology, 11,* 562–566.

Eckerman, C. O., Whatley, J. L., & Kutz, S. (1975). Growth of social play with peers during the second year of life. *Developmental Psychology, 11,* 42–49.

Eckerman, C. O., Whatley, J. L., & McGehee, L. J. (1979). Approaching and contacting the object another manipulates: A social skill of the one-year-old. *Developmental Psychology, 15,* 585–593.

The Economist (2008). Measles and MMR make their encore. http://www.econo-mist.com/world/britain/display-story.cfm?story_id=12725316

Edwards, C. P. (1984). The age group labels and categories of preschool children. *Child Development, 55,* 440–452.

Egeland, B., & Hiester, M. (1995). The long-term consequences of infant day-care and mother-infant attachment. *Child Development, 66,* 474–485.

Egeland, B., & Sroufe, L. A. (1981). Developmental sequelae of maltreatment in infancy. *New Directions for Child Development, 11,* 77–92.

Eichenbaum, H. & Cohen, N. (2001). *Memory systems of the brain.* Oxford University Press

Eilers, R. E., & Gavin, W. J. (1981). The evaluation of infant speech perception skills: Statistical techniques and theory development. In R. Stark (Ed.), *Language behavior in infancy and early childhood* (pp. 219–243). New York: Elsevier.

Eilers, R. E., Oller, D. K., Levine, S., Basinger, D., Lynch, M. P., & Urbano, R. (1993). The role of prematurity and socioeconomic status in the onset of canonical babbling in infants. *Infant Behavior and Development, 16,* 297–315.

Eimas, P. D., & Quinn, P. C. (1994). Studies on the formation of perceptually based basic-level categories in young infants. *Child Development, 65,* 903–917.

Eimas, P. D., Siqueland, E. R., Jusczyk, P., & Vigorito, J. (1971). Speech perception in infants. *Science, 171,* 303–306.

Einarson, A., Selby, P., & Koren, G. (2001). Abrupt discontinuation of psychotropic drugs during pregnancy: Fear of teratogenic risk and impact of counselling. *Journal of Psychiatry & Neuroscience, 26*(1), 44–48.

Einfeld, S. L. (2005). Behaviour Problems in Children with Genetic Disorders Causing Intellectual Disability. *Educational Psychology, 25*(2–3), 341–346.

Einspieler, C., Widder, J., Holzer, A., & Kenner, T. (1988). The predictive value of behavioral risk factors for sudden infant death. *Early Human Development, 18,* 101–109.

Eisenberg, R. B. (1976). *Auditory competence in early life.* Baltimore: University Park Press.

Eizirik, L. S., Bohlin, G., & Hagekull, B. (1994). Interaction between mother and pre-term infant at 34 weeks postconceptional age. *Early Development and Parenting, 3,* 171–180.

Elder, G., Nguyen, T., & Caspi, A. (1985). Linking family hardship to children's lives. *Child Development, 56,* 361–375.

Ellis, B. J., Bates, J. E., Dodge, K. A., Fergusson, D. M., Horwood, L. J., Pettit, G. S., et al. (2003). Does father absence place daughters at special risk for early sexual activity and teenage pregnancy? *Child Development, 74*(3), 801–821.

Ellis, S., & Rogoff, B. (1982). The strategies and efficacy of child versus adult teachers. *Child Development, 53,* 730–735.

Ellsworth, C. P., Muir, D. W., & Hains, S. M. J. (1993). Social competence and person-object differentiation: An analysis of the still-face effect. *Developmental Psychology, 29*(1), 63–73.

Emde, R. N., Gaensbauer, T. J., & Harmon, R. J. (1976) Emotional expression in infancy. *Psychological Issues, 10*(1).

Emde, R. N., & Hewitt, J. K. (2001). Infancy to early childhood: Genetic and environmental influences on developmental change. New York: Oxford University Press.

Emde, R. N., Plomin, R., Robinson, J., Corley, R., DeFries, J., Fulker, D. W., Reznick, J. S., Campos, J., Kagan, J., & Zahn-Waxler, C. (1992). Temperament, emotion, and cognition at fourteen months: The MacArthur longitudinal twin study. *Child Development, 63,* 1437–1455.

Entwisle, D. R., & Alexander, K. L. (1987). Long-term effects of cesarean delivery on parents' beliefs and children's schooling. *Developmental Psychology, 23,* 676–682.

Entwisle, D. R., & Doering, S. (1981). *The first birth: A turning point.* Baltimore: John Hopkins University Press.

Erickson, M. F., Sroufe, L. A., & Egeland, B. (1985). Relationship between quality of attachment and behavior problems in preschool in a high-risk sample. In I. Bretherton & E. Waters (Eds.), *Growing points of attachment theory and research. Monographs of the Society for Research in Child Development, 50* (Serial No. 209), 147–166.

Erikson, E. (1950). *Childhood and society.* New York: Norton.

Ershoff, D. H., Ashford, T. H., & Goldenberg, R. L. (2004). Helping pregnant women quit smoking: An overview. *Nicotine & Tobacco Research, 6,*(2) S101–S105.

Escalona, S. K., & Corman, H. H. (1968). *Albert Einstein scales of sensorimotor development.* Unpublished manuscript.

Escobar, G. J., Yanover, M., Gardner, M. N., Goembeski, D., Armstrong, M. A., Shum, F., & Kipnis P. (1998). Structured review of neonatal deaths in a managed care organization. *Pediatric Perinatal Epidemiology, 12*(4), 422–436.

Espy, K. A., Riese, M. L., & Francis, D. J. (1997). Neurobehavior in preterm neonates exposed to cocaine, alcohol, and tobacco. *Infant Behavior and Development, 20*(3), 297–309.

Essex, M. J., Klein, M. H., Cho, E., & Kalin, N. H. (2002). Maternal stress beginning in infancy may sensitize children to later stress exposure: effects on cortisol and behavior. *Biol Psychiatry, 52*(8), 776–784.

Éthier, L. S., Lemelin, J.-P., & Lacharité, C. (2004). A longitudinal study of the effects of chronic maltreatment on children's behavioral and emotional problems. *Child Abuse & Neglect, 28*(12), 1265–1278.

Evans, E., Hawton, K., & Rodham, K. (2005). Suicidal phenomena and abuse in adolescents: A review of epidemiological studies. *Child Abuse & Neglect, 29*(1), 45–58.

Eyer, D. (1996). *Motherguilt: How our culture blames mothers for what's wrong with society.* New York: Random House.

Fabrena, H., Jr., & Nutini, H. (1994). Sudden infant and child death as a cultural phenomenon: A Tlaxcalan case study. *Psychiatry, 57,* 225–243.

Fagard, J., & Jacquet, A. (1989). Onset of bimanual coordination and symmetry versus asymmetry of movement. *Infant Behavior and Development, 12,* 229–235.

Fagen, J. W., Ohr, P. S., Singer, J. M., & Klein, S. J. (1989). Crying and retrograde amnesia in young infants. *Infant Behavior and Development, 12,* 13–24.

Fagen, J. W., Prigot, J., Carroll, M., Pioli, L., Stein, A., & Franco, A. (1997). Auditory context and memory retrieval in young infants. *Child Development, 68*(6), 1057–1066.

Fagot, B. I. (1997). Attachment, parenting, and peer interactions of toddler children. *Developmental Psychology, 33*(3), 489–499.

Fagot, B. I., & Hagan, R. (1991). Observations of parent reactions to sex-stereotyped behaviors: Age and sex effects. *Child Development, 62,* 617–628.

Fagot, B. I., & Kavanagh, K. (1993). Parenting during the second year: Effects of children's age, sex, and attachment classification. *Child Development, 64,* 258–271.

Fagot, B. I., & Leinbach, M. D. (1989). The young child's gender schema: Environmental input, internal organization, *Child Development, 60,* 663–672.

Fagot, B. I., & Leinbach, M. D., & Hagan, R. (1990). Gender labeling and the adoption of sex-typed behaviors. *Developmental Psychology, 22,* 440–443.

Fagot, B. I., Leinbach, M. D., & O'Boyle, C. (1992). Gender labeling, gender stereotyping, and parenting behaviors. *Developmental Psychology, 28,* 225–230.

Falkner, F. (Ed.) (1985). *Prevention of infant mortality and morbidity.* Basel, Switzerland: Karger.

Fantz, R. L. (1961). The origin of form perception. *Scientific American, 204,* 66–72.

Fantz, R. L., Fagan, J. F., & Miranda, S. B. (1975). Early visual selection. In L. B. Cohen & P. Salapatek (Eds.), *Infant perception: From sensation to cognition* (Vol. 1, pp. 130–155). New York: Academic Press.

Fares, S. L., & Adler, N. E. (1998). "Top-of-the-head" descriptions of baby and self: Links to reported health behaviors and social context in early pregnancy. *Journal of Social and Personal Relationships, 15*(4), 555–564.

Farran, D. C., & Haskins, R. (1980). Reciprocal influence in the social interactions of mothers and three-month-old children from different socioeconomic backgrounds. *Child Development, 51,* 780–791.

Farver, J. M., & Howes, C. (1993). Cultural differences in American and Mexican mother-child pretend play. *Merrill-Palmer Quarterly, 39,* 344–358.

Farver, J. M., & Wimbarti, S. (1995). Paternal participation in toddlers' pretend play. *Social Development, 4,* 17–29.

Feeney, G. (1994). Fertility decline in East Asia. *Science, 266,* 1518–1523.

Fein, R. (1976). The first weeks of fathering: The importance of choices and supports for new parents. *Birth and the Family Journal, 3,* 53–58.

Feinberg, A. P. (2007). Phenotypic plasticity and the epigenetics of human disease. *Nature, 447*(7143), 433–440.

Feiring, C., Fox, N. A., Jaskir, J., & Lewis, M. (1987). The relation between social support, infant risk status and mother-infant interaction. *Developmental Psychology, 23,* 400–405.

Feiring, C., & Lewis, M. (1981). Middle class differences in cognitive development. In T. M. Field, A. M., Sostek, P.

Vietze, & P. H. Leiderman (Eds.), *Culture and early interactions* (pp. 73–97). Hillsdale, NJ: Erlbaum.

Feiring, C. Lewis, M., & Starr, M. D. (1984). Indirect effects and infants' reactions to strangers. *Developmental Psychology, 20,* 485–491.

Feldenkrais, M. (1981). *The elusive obvious.* Cupertino, CA: Meta Publications.

Feldman, R. (2006). From biological rhythms to social rhythms: Physiological precursors of mother-infant synchrony. *Developmental Psychology, 42*(1), 175–188.

Feldman, R., & Eidelman, A. I. (2003). Direct and indirect effects of breast milk on neurobehavioral and cognitive development of premature infants. *Developmental Psychobiology, 43*(2), 109–119.

Feldman, R., Greenbaum, C. W., & Yirmiya, N. (1999). Mother-infant affect synchrony as an antecedent of the emergence of self-control. *Developmental Psychology, 35*(1), 223–231.

Feldman, R., Sussman, A. L., & Zigler, E. (2004). Parental leave and work adaptation at the transition to parenthood: Individual, marital, and social correlates. *Journal of Applied Developmental Psychology, 25*(4), 459–479.

Feldman, S. S., & Nash, S. C. (1978). Interest in babies during young adulthood. *Child Development, 49,* 617–622.

Feldman, S. S., & Nash, S. C. (1979a). Changes in responsiveness to babies during adolescence. *Child Development, 50,* 942–949.

Feldman, S. S., & Nash, S. C. (1979b). Sex differences in responsiveness to babies among mature adults. *Developmental Psychology, 15,* 430–436.

Feldman, S. S., & Nash, S. C. (1986). Antecedents of early parenting. In A. Fogel & G. F. Melson (Eds.), *Origins of nurturance: Developmental, biological, and cultural perspectives on caregiving* (pp. 128–136). Hillsdale, NJ: Erlbaum.

Fenson, L., Dale, P., Reznick, S., Bates, E., Thal, D., & Pethick, S. (1994). Variability in early communicative development. *Monographs of the Society for Research in Child Development, 59* (5, Serial No. 242).

Fenson, C., Kagan, J., Kearsley, R. B., & Zelazo, P. R. (1976). The developmental progression of manipulative play in the first two years. *Child Development, 47,* 232–236.

Fenson, L., Sapper, V., & Minner, D. G. (1974). Attention and manipulative play in the one-year-old child. *Child Development, 45,* 757–764.

Ferber, S. G. (2004). The nature of touch in mothers experiencing maternity blues: The contribution of parity. *Early Human Development, 79*(1), 65–75.

Ferber, S. G., Laudon, M., Kuint, J., Weller, A., & Zisapel, N. (2002). Massage therapy by mothers enhances the adjustment of circadian rhythms to the nocturnal period in full-term infants. *J Dev Behav Pediatr, 23*(6), 410–415.

Ferland, M. B., & Mendelson, M. J. (1989). Infants' categorization of melodic contour. *Infant Behavior and Development, 12,* 341–355.

Fernald, A. (1985). Four month old infants prefer to listen to motherese. *Infant Behavior and Development, 8,* 181–195.

Fernald, A. (1989). Intonation and communicative intent in mothers' speech to infants: Is the melody the message? *Child Development, 60,* 1497–1510.

Fernald, A. (1993). Approval and disapproval: Infant responsiveness to vocal affect in familiar and unfamiliar languages. *Child Development, 64,* 657–674.

Fernald, A., & Kuhl, P. (1987). Acoustic determinants of infant preference for motherese speech. *Infant Behavior and Development, 10,* 279–293.

Fernald, A., & Morikawa, H. (1993). Common themes and cultural variations in Japanese and American mothers' speech to infants. *Child Development, 64,* 637–656.

Fernald, A., Perfors, A., & Marchman, V. A. (2006). Picking up speed in understanding: Speech processing efficiency and vocabulary growth across the 2nd year. *Developmental Psychology, 42*(1), 98–116.

Fernald, A., & Simon, T. (1984). Expanded intonation contours in mothers' speech to newborns. *Developmental Psychology, 20,* 104–113.

Fernald, A., Taeschner, T., Dunn, J., Papousek, M., DeBoysson-Bardies, B., & Fukui, I. (1989). A cross-language study of prosodic modifications in mothers' and fathers' speech to preverbal infants, *Journal of Child Language, 16,* 477–501.

Fessler, D. M. T., Eng, S. J., & Navarrete, C. D. (2005). Elevated disgust sensitivity in the first trimester of pregnancy: Evidence supporting the compensatory prophylaxis hypothesis. *Evolution and Human Behavior, 26,* 344–351.

Field, T. (1979). Differential behavioral and cardiac responses of 3–month-old infants to mirror and peer. *Infant Behavior and Development, 2,* 179–04.

Field, T. (1981a). Interaction coaching for high-risk infants and their parents. In H. Moss (Ed.), *Prevention and human sciences* (pp. 316–333). New York: Haworth Press.

Field, T. (1981b). Infant arousal, attention and affect during early interactions. In L. P. Lipsitt & C. Rovee-Collier (Eds.), *Advances in infancy research* (Vol. 1, pp. 121–144). Norwood, NJ: Ablex.

Field, T. (1982). Affective and physiological changes during manipulated interactions of high risk infants. In T. Field & A. Fogel (Eds.), *Emotion and early interaction* (pp. 480–501). Hillsdale, NJ: Erlbaum.

Field, T. (1987). Affective and interactive disturbances in infants. In J. D. Osofsky (Ed.), *Handbook of infant development* (2nd ed., pp. 70–91). New York: Wiley.

Field, T. (1991). Young children's adaptations to repeated separations from their mothers. *Child Development, 61,* 539–547.

Field, T. (1994). The effects of mother's physical and emotional unavailability on emotion regulation. *Monographs of the Society for Research in Child Development, 59,* 208–227.

Field, T. (1998). Maternal depression effects on infants and early interventions. *Preventive Medicine, 27,* 200–203.

Field, T. (1998). Touch therapy effects on development. *International Journal of Behavioral Development, 22*(4), 779–797.

Field, T., Dempsey, J. R., Hatch, J., Ting, G., & Clifton, R. K. (1979). Cardiac and behavioral responses to repeated tactile and auditory stimulation by preterm and term neonates. *Developmental Psychology, 15,* 406–416.

Field, T., Diego, M., & Hernandez-Reif, M. (2006). Prenatal depression effects on the fetus and newborn: A review. *Infant Behavior & Development, 29*(3), 445–455.

Field, T., Gewirtz, J. L., Cohen, D., Garcia, R., Greenberg, R., & Collins, K. (1984). Leave-takings and reunions of infants, toddlers, preschoolers, and their parents. *Child Development, 55,* 628–635.

Field, T., Greenberg, R., Woodson, R., Cohen, D., & Garcia, R. (1984). A descriptive study on the facial expressions of infants during Brazelton neonatal assessments. *Infant Mental Health Journal, 5,* 61–71.

Field, T., Grizzle, N., Scafidi, F., Abrams, S., Richardson, S., Kuhn, C., & Schanberg, S. (1996). Massage therapy for infants of depressed mothers. *Infant Behavior and Development, 19,* 107–112.

Field, T., Grizzle, N., Scafidi, F., & Schanberg, S. (1996). Massage and relaxation therapies' effects on depressed adolescent mothers. *Adolescence, 31,* 903–911.

Field, T., Healy, B., Goldstein, S., Perry, S., Bendell, D., Schanberg, S., Zimmerman, E. A., & Kuhn, C. (1988). Infants of depressed mothers show "depressed" behavior even with nondepressed adults. *Child Development, 59,* 1569–1579.

Field, T., Healy, B., & LeBlanc, W. G. (1989). Sharing and synchrony of behavior states and heart rate in nondepressed versus depressed mother-infant interactions. *Infant Behavior and Development, 12,* 357–376.

Field, T., Hernandez-Reif, M., Diego, M., Feijo, L., Vera, Y., & Gil, K. (2004). Massage therapy by parents improves early growth and development. *Infant Behavior & Development, 27,* 435–442.

Field, T., Hernandez-Reif, M., Feijo, L., & Freedman, J. (2006). Prenatal, perinatal and neonatal stimulation: A survey of neonatal nurseries. *Infant Behavior & Development, 29*(1), 24–31.

Field, T., Ignatoff, E., Stringer, S., Brennan, J., Greenberg, R., Widmayer, S., & Anderson, G. (1982). Non-nutritive sucking during tube feedings: Effects on preterm neonates in an intensive care unit. *Pediatrics, 70,* 381–384.

Field, T., Morrow, C., & Adlestein, D. (1993). Depressed mothers' perceptions of infant behavior. *Infant Behavior and Development, 16,* 99–108.

Field, T., Sandberg, D., Garcia, R., Vega-Lahr, N., Goldstein, S., & Guy, L. (1985). Pregnancy problems, postpartum depression, and early mother-infant interactions. *Developmental Psychology, 21,* 1152–1156.

Field, T. & Sostek, A. (1983). *Infants born at risk: Physiological, perceptual and cognitive processes.* New York: Grune & Stratton.

Field, T., Vega-Lahr, N., & Jagadish, S. (1984). Separation stress of nursery school infants and toddlers graduating to new classes. *Infant Behavior and Development, 7,* 277–284.

Field, T., Vega-Lahr, N., Scafidi, F., & Goldstein, S. (1986). Effects of maternal unavailability on mother-infant interactions. *Infant Behavior and Development, 9,* 473–478.

Field, T., & Widmayer, S. M. (1980). Developmental follow-up on infants delivered by caesarean section and general anesthesia. *Infant Behavior and Development, 3,* 253–264.

Field, T., Widmayer, S. M., Stringer, S., & Ignatoff, E. (1980). Teenage, lower class, black mothers and their preterm infants: An intervention and developmental follow-up. *Child Development, 51,* 426–436.

Field, T., Woodson, R., Greenberg, R., & Cohen, D. (1982). *Discrimination and imitation of facial expressions by neonates.* Paper presented at the International Conference on Infant Studies, Austin, TX.

Fifth Special Report to the U.S. Congress on Alcohol and Health (1984). *Alcohol Health and Research World, 9,* 1–72.

Finkelstein, N., Dent, C., Gallacher, K., & Ramey, C. (1978). Social behavior of infants and toddlers in a day-care environment. *Developmental Psychology, 14,* 257–262.

Fiorentino, M. R. (1981). *A basis for sensorimotor development—normal and abnormal: The influence of primitive, postural reflexes on the development and distribution of tone.* Springfield, IL: Charles C. Thomas.

Fischer, J., & Rozenberg, C. (1999). The maternity care coalition: Strategy for survival in the context of managed care and welfare reform. *Zero to Three, 19*(4), 14–19.

Fischer, K. W. (1987). Relations between brain and cognitive development. *Child Development, 58,* 623–632.

Fish, M., Stifter, C. A., & Belsky, J. (1991). Conditions of continuity and discontinuity in infant negative emotionality: Newborn to five months. *Child Development, 62,* 1525–1537.

Fisher, C. B., Ferdinandsen K., & Bornstein, M. H. (1981). The role of symmetry in infant form perception. *Child Development, 52,* 457–462.

Fiscus, S., Adimora, A., Schoenbach, V., Lim. W., McKinney, R., Rupar, D., Kenny, J., Woods, C., & Wilfert, C. (1996). Perinatal HIV infection and the effect of Zidovudine therapy on transmission in rural and urban counties. *Journal of the American Medical Association, 275,* 1483–1488.

Fivaz-Depeursinge, E., & Corboz-Warnery, A. (1999). *The primary triangle: A developmental systems view of mother, fathers, and infants.* New York: Basic Books.

Fivush, R. (1994). Constructing narrative, emotion, and self in parent-child conversations about the past. In U. Neisser & R. Fivush (Eds.), *The remembering self: Construction and accuracy in the self-narrative* (pp. 205–232). Cambridge, England: Cambridge University Press.

Fleming, A. S., & Orpen, G. (1986). Psychobiology of maternal behavior in rats, selected other species and humans. In A. Fogel & G. F. Melson (Eds.), *Origins of nurturance: Developmental, biological, and cultural perspectives on caregiving* (pp. 184–208). Hillsdale, NJ: Erlbaum.

Fleming, A. S., Ruble, D. N., Flett, G. L., & Shaul, D. L. (1988). Postpartum adjustment in first-time mothers: Relations between mood, maternal attitudes, and mother-infant interactions. *Developmental Psychology, 24,* 71–81.

Fleming, A. S., Ruble, D. N., Flett, G. L., & Van Wagner, V. (1990). Adjustment in first-time mothers: Changes in mood and mood content during the early postpartum months. *Developmental Psychology, 26,* 137–143.

Fleming, N., Newton, E. R., & Roberts, J. (2003). Changes in postpartum perineal muscle function in women with and without episiotomies. *J Midwifery Womens Health, 48*(1), 53–59.

Flom, R., & Pick, A. D. (2003). Verbal encouragement and joint attention in 18–month-old infants. *Infant Behavior & Development, 26*(2), 121–134.

Floor, P., & Akhtar, N. (2006). Can 18–Month-Old Infants Learn Words by Listening In on Conversations? *Infancy, 9*(3), 327–339.

Fogel, A. (1977). Temporal organization in mother-infant face-to-face interaction. In H. R. Schaffer (Ed.), *Studies in mother-infant interaction* (pp. 119–152). New York: Academic Press.

Fogel, A. (1979). Peer vs. mother directed behavior in 1– to 3–month-old infants. *Infant Behavior and Development, 2,* 215–226.

Fogel, A. (1981). The ontogeny of gestural communication: The first six months. In R. Stark (Ed.), *Language behavior in infancy and early childhood* (pp. 17–44). New York: Elsevier.

Fogel, A. (1982a). Affect dynamics in early infancy: Affective tolerance. In T. Field & A. Fogel (Eds.), *Emotion and early interaction* (pp. 15–56). Hillsdale, NJ: Erlbaum.

Fogel, A. (1982b). Early adult-infant face-to-face interaction: Expectable sequences of behavior. *Journal of Pediatric Psychology, 7,* 1–22.

Fogel, A. (1985). Coordinative structures in the development of expressive behavior in early infancy. In G. Zivin (Ed.), *The development of expressive behavior: Biology-environment interactions* (pp. 249–267). New York: Academic Press.

Fogel, A. (1990a). The process of developmental change in infant communicative action: Using dynamic systems theory to study individual ontogenies. In J. Colombo & J. Fagen (Eds.), *Individual differences in infancy: Reliability, stability, and prediction* (pp. 177–201). Hillsdale, NJ: Erlbaum.

Fogel, A. (1990b). Sensorimotor factors in communicative development. In H. Bloch & B. Bertenthal (Eds.), *Sensorimotor organization and development in infancy and early childhood. NATO ASI Series* (pp. 54–80). The Netherlands: Kluwer Academic.

Fogel, A. (1993). *Developing through relationships.* Chicago: University of Chicago Press.

Fogel, A. (2000). A relational perspective on the development of self and emotion. In J. A. Bosma & E. S. Kunnen (Eds.), *Identity and emotions: A self-organizational perspective.* Cambridge, England: Cambridge University Press.

Fogel, A. (2004). Remembering infancy: Accessing our earliest experiences. In G. Bremner & A. Slater (Eds.), Theories of infant development. Blackwell Publishers.

Fogel, A. (2008). Relationships that support human development. . In A. Fogel, B. J. King, & S. Shanker (Eds.). *Human development in the 21st century: Visionary policy ideas from systems scientists.*. Cambridge, UK: Cambridge University Press.

Fogel, A., & Branco, A. U. (1997). Meta-communication as a source of indeterminism in relationship development. In A. Fogel, M. Lyra, & J. Valsiner (Eds.), *Dynamics and indeterminism in developmental and social processes* (pp. 138–155). Hillsdale, NJ: Erlbaum.

Fogel, A., Dedo, J. Y., & McEwen, I. (1992). Effect of postural position and reaching on gaze during mother-infant face-to-face interaction. *Infant Behavior and Development, 15,* 231–244.

Fogel, A., Dickson, K. L., Hsu, H., Messinger, D., Nelson-Goens, G. C., & Nwokah, E. (1997). Communicative dynamics of emotion. In K. C. Barrett (Ed.), *New directions in child development: The communication of emotion: Current research from diverse perspectives, 77* (pp. 5–24). San Francisco: Jossey-Bass.

Fogel, A. & Garvey, A. (2007). Alive communication. *Infant Behavior and Development, 30,* 251–257.

Fogel, A., Garvey, A., Hsu, H., & West-Stroming, D. (2006). *Change processes in relationships: A relational – historical research approach.* Cambridge, UK: Cambridge University Press.

Fogel, A., & Hannan, T. E. (1985). Manual actions of 2– to 3–month-old human infants during social interaction. *Child Development, 56,* 1271–1279.

Fogel, A., Hsu, H., Shapiro, A. F., Nelson-Goens, G. C., & Secrist, C. (2006). Effects of normal and perturbed social play on the duration and amplitude of different types of infant smiles. Developmental Psychology, 42, 459–473.

Fogel, A., & Lyra, M. (1997). Dynamics of development in relationships. In F. Masterpasqua & P. Perna (Eds.), *The psychological meaning of chaos: Self-organization in human development and psychotherapy* (pp. 75–94). Washington, DC: American Psychological Association.

Fogel, A., Lyra, M. C., & Valsiner, J. (Eds.). (1997). *Dynamics and indeterminism in developmental and social processes.* Hillsdale, NJ: Erlbaum.

Fogel, A., Melson, G. F., Toda, S., & Mistry, J. (1987). Young children's responses to unfamiliar infants: The effects of adult involvement. *International Journal of Behavioral Development, 10,* 37–50.

Fogel, A., & Melson, G. F. (1988). *Child development.* St. Paul, MN: West.

Fogel, A., Nelson-Goens, G. C., Hsu, H. C., & Shapiro, A. F. (2000). Do different infant smiles reflect different positive emotions? Social Development, 9 (4), 497–520.

Fogel, A., Nwokah, E., Dedo, J., Messinger, D., Dickson, K. L., Matusov, E., & Holt, S. A. (1992). Social process theory of emotion: A dynamic systems perspective. *Social Development, 1,* 122–142.

Fogel, A., Nwokah, E., Hsu, H. C., Dedo, J. Y., & Walker, H. (1993). Posture and communication in mother-infant interaction. In G. J. P. Savelsbergh (Ed.), *The development of coordination in infancy* (pp. 395–422). Amsterdam: Elsevier.

Fogel, A., Nwokah, E., & Karns, J. (1993). Parent-infant games as dynamic social systems. In K. B. MacDonald (Ed.), *Parents and children playing* (pp. 391–417). Albany, NY: SUNY Press.

Fogel, A., Stevenson, M. B., & Messinger, D. (1992). A comparison of the parent-child relationship in Japan and the United States. In J. L. Roopnarine & D. B. Carter (Eds.), *Parent-child relations in diverse cultural settings* (pp. 205–230). Norwood, NJ: Ablex.

Fogel, A., & Thelen, E. (1987). Development of early expressive and communicative action: Reinterpreting the evidence from a dynamic systems perspective. *Developmental Psychology, 23,* 747–761.

Fogel, A., Toda, S., & Kawai, M. (1988). Mother-infant face-to-face interaction in Japan and the United States: A laboratory comparison using 3–month-old infants. *Developmental Psychology, 24,* 398–406.

Fonagy, P., Gergely G., Jurist, E. & Target, M. (2004). *Affect Regulation, Mentalization, and the Development of the Self.* London: Karnac Books.

Fonagy, P., & Target, M. (2005). Commentary: Bridging the transmission gap: An end to an important mystery of attachment research? *Attachment & Human Development, 7*(3), 333–343.

Forbes, L. M., Evans, E. M., Moran, G., & Pederson, D. R. (2007). Change in Atypical Maternal Behavior Predicts Change in Attachment Disorganization From 12 to 24 Months in a High-Risk Sample. *Child Development, 78*(3), 955–971.

Ford, J. H., MacCormac, L., & Hiller, J. (1994). Pregnancy and lifestyle study: Association between occupational and environmental exposure to chemicals and reproductive outcome. *Mutation Research, 313,* 153–164.

Forestier, D. F., Kaplan, C., & Cox, W. (1988). Prenatal diagnosis and management of bleeding disorders with fetal blood sampling. *American Journal of Obstetrics and Gynecology, 158,* 939–946.

Forrest, J. D., & Fordyce, R. R. (1993). Women's contraceptive attitudes and use in 1992. *Family Planning Perspectives, 25,* 175–179.

Forrest, J. D., & Fordyce, R. R. (1993b). Locomotor coordination in infancy: The transition from walking to running. In G. J. P. Savelsbergh (Ed.), *The development of coordination in infancy* (pp. 359–393). Amsterdam: Elsevier.

Forrester, L. W., Phillips, S. J., & Clark, J. E. (1993). Locomotor coordination in infancy: The transition from walking to running. In G. J. P. Savelsbergh (Ed.), *The development of coordination in infancy* (pp. 359–393). Amsterdam: Elsevier.

Fox, C. R., & Gelfand, D. M. (1994). Maternal depressed mood and stress as related to vigilance, self-efficacy, and mother-child interactions. *Early Development and Parenting, 3,* 233–243.

Fox, N. A. (1977). Attachment of kibbutz infants to mother and metapelet. *Child Development, 48,* 1228–1239.

Fox, N. A. (1985). Sweet/sour—interest/disgust: The role of approach-withdrawal in the development of emotions. In T. Field & N. Fox (Eds.), *Social perception in infancy* (pp. 165–181). Norwood, NJ: Ablex.

Fox, N. A. (1989). Psychophysiological correlates of emotional reactivity during the first year of life. *Developmental Psychology, 25,* 364–372.

Fox, N. A., & Davidson, R. J. (1988). Patterns of brain electrical activity during the expression of discrete emotions in ten-month-old infants. *Developmental Psychology, 24,* 230–236.

Fox, N. A., Kimmerly, N. L., & Schafer, W. D. (1991). Attachment to mother/attachment to father: A meta-analysis. *Child Development, 62,* 210–225.

Fox, R., & McDaniels, C. (1982). The perception of biological motion by human infants. *Science, 218,* 486–487.

Fraiberg, S. (1974). Gross motor development in infants blind from birth. *Child Development, 45,* 114–126.

Fraiberg, S., Adelson,E., & Shapiro,V., (1975). Ghosts in the nursery: A psychoanalytic approach to the problem of impaired mother-infant relationships. *Journal of the American Academy of Child Psychiatry, 14,* 387–421.

Fraley, R. C. (2002). Attachment stability from infancy to adulthood: Meta-analysis and dynamic modeling of developmental mechanisms. *Personality and Social Psychology Review, 6*(2), 123–151.

Francis, P. L., Self, P. A., & Horowitz, F. D. (1987). The behavioral assessment of the neonate: An overview. In J. D. Osofsky (Ed.), *Handbook of infant development* (2nd ed., pp. 170–208). New York: Wiley.

Franco, F., Fogel, A., Messinger, D., & Frazier, C. (1996). Cultural differences in physical contact between Hispanic and Anglo mother-infant dyads living in the United States. *Early Development and Parenting, 5,* 119–127.

Frank, R. (2001). Body of awareness: A somatic and developmental approach to psychotherapy. New Jersey: The Analytic Press.

Frankenburg, W. K., Dodd, J. B., Fandal, A. W., Kuzuk, E., & Cohrs, M. (1975). *DDST: Reference manual* (Rev. ed.). Denver: Ladoka Project and Publication Foundation.

Frazier, P. A., Byer, A. L., Fischer, A. R., Wright, D. M., & DeBord, K. A. (1996). Adult attachment style and partner choice: Correlational and experimental findings. *Personal Relationships, 3*(2), 117–136.

Freeman, N. H. (1980). *Strategies of representation in young children: Analysis of spatial skill and drawing processes.* London: Academic Press.

Freeman, R. (1990). Intrapartum fetal monitoring—A disappointing story (editorial; comment). *New England Journal of Medicine, 322*(9), 624–626.

French, V. (2002). *History of parenting: The ancient Mediterranean world.* Mahwah, NJ, US: Lawrence Erlbaum Associates Publishers.

Freud, A. (1965). *Normality and pathology in childhood.* New York: International Universities Press.

Freud, S. (1900/1953). [*The interpretation of dreams.*] In J. Strachey (Ed. and Trans.), *The standard edition of the complete works of Sigmund Freud* (Vol. 3, pp. 485–699). London: Hogarth Press. (Original work published 1900)

Freud, S. (1903/1953). [*Three essays on the theory of sexuality.*] In J. Strachey (Ed. and Trans.), *The standard edition of the complete works of Sigmund Freud* (Vol. 7, pp. 1550–1669). London: Hogarth Press. (Original work published 1903)

Fries, A. B., Ziegler, T. E., Kurian, J. R., Jacoris, S., & Pollak, S. D. (2005). Early experience in humans is associated with changes in neuropeptides critical for regulating social behavior. *Proc Natl Acad Sci U S A, 102*(47), 17237–17240.

Frymer-Kensky, T. (1995). Motherprayer: The pregnant woman's spiritual companion. New York: Riverhead Books.

Frick, J. E., Colombo, J., & Saxon, T. F. (1999). Individual and developmental differences in disengagement of fixation in early infancy. *Child Development, 70*(3), 537–548.

Fried, P. A. (2002). Conceptual issues in behavioral teratology and their application in determining long-term sequelae of prenatal marihuana exposure. *Journal of Child Psychology and Psychiatry, 43*(1), 81–102.

Friedman, S. L., & Jacobs, B. S. (1981). Sex differences in neonates' behavioral responsiveness to repeated auditory stimulation. *Infant Behavior and Development, 4,* 175–183.

Friedman, S. L., Randolph, S., & Kochanoff, A. (2000). Child care research at the dawn of a new millennium: Taking stock of what we know. In J. G. Bremner & A. Fogel (Eds.), *Handbook of infancy research* (pp. 415–437). Oxford, England: Blackwell.

Friedrich-Cofer, L. K. (1986). Body, mind, and morals in the framing of social policy. In L. K. Friedrich-Cofer (Ed.), *Human nature of public policy: Scientific views of women, children and families* (pp. 97–173). New York: Praeger.

Friend, K. B., Goodwin, M. S., & Lipsitt, L. P. (2004). Alcohol use and sudden infant death syndrome. *Developmental Review, 24*(3), 235–251.

Frigoletto, F. D., Greene, M. F., Benacerraf, B. R., Barss, V. A., & Saltzman, D. H. (1986). Ultrasonographic fetal surveillance in the management of the isoimmunized pregnancy. *New England Journal of Medicine, 315,* 430–432.

Frith, U., & Frith, C. (2001). The biological basis of social interaction. *Current Directions in Psychological Science, 10*(5), 151–155.

Frodi, A. M., & Lamb, M. E. (1978). Sex differences in responsiveness to infants: A developmental study of psychophysiological and behavioral responses. *Child Development, 49,* 1182–1188.

Frodi, A. M., & Lamb, M. E. (1980). Child abuser's response to infant smiles and cries. *Child Development, 51,* 238–241.

Frodi, A. M., Lamb, M. E., Leavitt, L. A., & Donovan, W. L. (1978). Father's and mother's responses to infant smiles and cries. *Infant Behavior and Development, 1,* 187–198.

Frosch, C. A., Mangelsdorf, S. C., & McHale, J. L. (1998). Correlates of marital behavior at 6 months postpartum. *Developmental Psychology, 34*(6), 1438–1449.

Furdon, S. A., Pfeil, V. C., & Snow, K. (1998). Operationalizing Donna Wong's principle of atraumatic care. Pain management in the NICU. *Pediatric Nursing, 24*(4), 336–342.

Furman, W., Rahe, D. F., & Hartup, W. W. (1979). Rehabilitation of socially withdrawn preschool children through mixed-age and same-age socialization. *Child Development, 50,* 915–922.

Furrow, D. (1984). Social and private speech at two years. *Child Development, 55,* 355–362.

Furstenberg, F. F., Jr., Brooks-Gunn, J., & Morgan, P. (1987). *Adolescent mothers in later life.* New York: Cambridge University Press.

Gaddini, R. (1970). Transitional objects and the process of individuation. *Journal of the American Academy of Child Psychiatry, 9,* 347–365.

Gaensbauer, T. J. (2004). Telling their stories: Representation and reenactment of traumatic experiences occurring in the first year of life. *Zero to Three, 24*(5), 25–31.

Galtry, J., & Callister, P. (2005). Assessing the Optimal Length of Parental Leave for Child and Parental Well-Being: How Can Research Inform Policy? *Journal of Family Issues, 26*(2), 219–246.

Galvin, E. S. (1989). Children and child care in China: Some observations. *Children Today, 19*–23.

Gandelman, R. (1992). *The psychobiology of behavioral development.* New York: Oxford University Press.

Gandour, M. J. (1989). Activity level as a dimension of temperament in toddlers: Its relevance for the organismic specificity hypothesis. *Child Development, 60,* 1092–1098.

Garbarino, J. A. (1976). A preliminary study of some ecological correlates of child abuse: The impact of socioeconomic stress on mothers. *Child Development, 47,* 178–185.

Garbarino, J. A. (1982). Sociocultural risk: Dangers to competence. In C. Kopp & J. B. Krakow (Eds.), *The child: Development in a social context* (pp. 246–268). Reading, MA: Addison-Wesley.

Garbarino, J. A. (1992). The meaning of poverty in the world of children. *American Behavioral Scientist, 35,* 220–237.

Garbarino, J. A. (1993). Children's response to community violence: What do we know? *Infant Mental Health Journal, 14,* 103–115.

Garbarino, J. A., & Crouter, A. (1978). Defining the community context for parent-child relations: The correlates of child maltreatment. *Child Development, 49,* 604–616.

Garcia-Coll, C., Kagan, J., & Reznick, J. S. (1984). Behavioral inhibition in young children. *Child Development, 55,* 1005–1019.

Garciaguirre, J. S., Adolph, K. E., & Shrout, P. E. (2007). Baby carriage: Infants walking with loads. *Child Development, 78*(2), 664–680.

Gardner, C. A. (1989). Is an embryo a person? *Nation,* 557–559.

Gardosi, J., Hutson, N., & Lynch, C. (1989). Randomized, controlled trial of squatting in the second stage of labor. *Lancet, 2,* 74–77.

Garner, P. W. (2003). Child and Family Correlates of Toddlers' Emotional and Behavioral Responses to a Mishap. *Infant Mental Health Journal, 24*(6), 580–596.

Garner, P. W., Jones, D. C., & Palmer, D. J. (1994). Social cognitive correlates of preschool children's sibling caregiving behavior. *Developmental Psychology, 30,* 905–911.

Gartner, L. M., Morton, J., Lawrence, R. A., Naylor, A. J., O'Hare, D., Schanler, R. J., et al. (2005). Breastfeeding and the use of human milk. *Pediatrics, 115*(2), 496–506.

Garvey, C. (1974). Some properties of social play. *Merrill-Palmer Quarterly, 20,* 163–180.

Gatts, J. D., Wallace, D. H., Glasscock, G. F., McKee, E., & Cohen, R. S. (1994). A modified newborn intensive care unit environment may shorten hospital stay. *Journal of Perinatology, 14,* 422–427.

Gavidia-Payne, S., & Stoneman, Z. (1997). Family predictors of maternal and paternal involvement in programs for young children with disabilities. *Child Development, 68*(4), 701–717.

Gelfand, D. M. (2000). Infant mental health in a changing society. In J. G. Bremner & A. Fogel (Eds.), *Handbook of infancy research* (pp. 362–385). Oxford, England: Blackwell.

Gelfand, D. M., & Teti, D. M. (1990). The effects of maternal depression on children. *Clinical Psychology Review, 10,* 329–353.

Gelfand, D. M., Teti, D. M., & Fox, C. E. R. (1992). Sources of parenting stress for depressed and nondepressed mothers of infants. *Journal of Clinical Child Psychology, 21,* 262–272.

Geller, G., Tambor, E. S., Chase, G. A., Hofman, K. J., Faden, R. R., & Holtzman, N. A. (1993). Incorporation of genetic counselling in primary care practice. *Archives of Family Medicine, 2,* 1119–1125.

Gelles, R. (1978). Violence toward children in the United States. *American Journal of Orthopsychiatry, 48,* 580–592.

Gelman, S. A., Collman, P., & Maccoby, E. E. (1986). Inferring properties from categories vs. inferring categories from properties: The case of gender. *Child Development, 57,* 396–404.

Gelman, S. A., Taylor, M. G., & Nguyen, S. P. (2004). Mother-child conversations about gender. *Monographs of the Society for Research in Child Development, 69*(1, Serial No. 275).

Gentner, D. (1978). On relational meaning: The acquisition of verb meaning. *Child Development, 49,* 988–998.

George, C., & Main, M. (1979). Social interactions in young abused children: Approach, avoidance, and aggression. *Child Development, 50,* 306–318.

Gerken, L., Landau, B., & Remez, R. E. (1990). Function morphemes in young children's speech perception and production. *Developmental Psychology, 26,* 204–216.

Germo, G. R., Chang, E. S., Keller, M. A., & Goldberg, W. A. (2007). Child sleep arrangements and family life: perspectives from mothers and fathers. *Infant and Child Development, 16*(4), 433–456.

Gerner, E. M. (1999). Emotional interaction in a group of preterm infants at 3 and 6 months of corrected age. *Infant and Child Development, 8,* 117–128.

Gershoff, E. T. (2002). Corporal punishment by parents and associated child behaviors and experiences: A meta-analytic and theoretical review. *Psychological Bulletin, 128*(4), 539–579.

Gesell, A. (1925). *The mental growth of the preschool child.* New York: Macmillan.

Gesell, A. (1928). *Infancy and human growth.* New York: Macmillan.

Gewirtz, J. L. (1972). *Attachment and dependency.* New York: Halsted Press.

Gianino, A., & Tronick, E. Z. (1988). The mutual regulation model: The infant's self and interactive regulation and coping and defensive capacities. In T. M. Field, P. M. McCabe, & N. Schneiderman (Eds.), *Stress and coping across development* (pp. 300–323). Hillsdale, NJ: Erlbaum.

Gibson, E. J., Riccio, G., Schmuckler, M. A., Stoffregen, T. A., Rosenberg, D., & Taormina, J. (1987). Detection of the traversability of surfaces by crawling and walking infants. *Journal of Experimental Psychology: Human Perception and Performance, 13,* 533–544.

Gibson, E. J., & Walk, R. D. (1960). The "visual cliff." *Scientific American, 202,* 64–71.

Gibson, J. J. (1966). *The senses considered as perceptual systems.* Boston, MA: Houghton Mifflin.

Gielen, A. C., O'Campo, P. J., Faden, R. R., Kass, N. E., & Xue, X. (1994). Interpersonal conflict and physical violence during the childbearing years. *Social Science and Medicine, 39,* 781–787.

Gies, F., & Gies, J. (1987). *Marriage and the family in the Middle Ages.* New York: Harper & Row.

Gil, D. G. (1970). *Violence against children: Physical child abuse in the United States.* Cambridge, MA: Harvard University Press.

Gilliland, F. D., Li, Y. F., & Peters, J. M. (2001). Effects of maternal smoking during pregnancy and environmental tobacco smoke on asthma and wheezing in children. *Am J Respir Crit Care Med, 163*(2), 429–436.

Gingras, J., Mitchell, E., & Grattan, K. (2005). Fetal homologue of infant crying. *Archives of Disease in Childhood -- Fetal & Neonatal Edition, 90*(5), F415–F418.

Ginsburg, C. (1999). Body-image, movement, and consciousness: Examples from a somatic practice in the Feldenkrais method. *Journal of Consciousness Studies 6*(2–3), 79–91.

Ginsburg, G. P., & Kilbourne, B. K. (1988). Emergence of vocal alternation in mother-infant interchanges. *Journal of Child Language, 15,* 221–235.

Glazer, S. (1993a). Outlook, testing theories. *C. Q. Researcher, 3,* 304–306.

Glazer, S. (1993b). Preventing teen pregnancy. *C. Q. Researcher, 3,* 409–431.

Glidden, L. M. (2002). Parenting children with developmental disabilities: A ladder of influence. In J. G. Borkowski, S. L. Ramey, & M. Bristol-Power (Eds.), *Parenting and the child's world: Influences on academic, intellectual, and social-emotional development* (pp. 329–344). Mahwah, NJ: Lawrence Erlbaum Associates, Inc.

Glink, P. (1998). A collaborative effort in perinatal support for birthing teens. *Zero to Three, 18*(5), 44–50.

Gloger-Tippelt, G., Gomille, B., Koenig, L., & Vetter, J. (2002). Attachment representations in 6–year-olds: Related longitudinally to the quality of attachment in infancy and mothers' attachment representations. *Attachment & Human Development, 4*(3), 318–339.

Gloger-Tippelt, G. S., & Huerkamp, M. (1998). Relationship change at the transition to parenthood and security of infant-mother attachment. *International Journal of Behavioral Development, 22*(3), 633–655.

Godfrey, A. B., & Kilgore, A. (1998). An approach to help very young infants sleep through the night. *Zero to Three, 19*(2), 15–21.

Goldfarb, J. (1993). Breastfeeding, AIDS, and other infectious diseases. *Clinical Perinatology,* 20, 225–243.

Goldfield, E. C. (1989). Transition from rocking to crawling: Postural constraints on infant movement. *Developmental Psychology, 25,* 913–919.

Goldfield, E. C. (1993). Dynamic systems in development: Action systems. In L. B. Smith & E. Thelen (Eds.), *A dynamic systems approach to development: Applications* (pp. 51–70). Cambridge, MA: MIT Press.

Golding, J., & Peters, T. J. (1985). What else do SIDS risk prediction scores predict? *Early Human Development, 12,* 247–260.

Goldman, M. B. (1994). Sudden infant death syndrome: Back to sleep campaign. *Caring, 13,* 52–55.

Goldman-Rakic, P. S. (1987). Development of cortical circuitry and cognitive function. *Child Development, 58,* 601–622.

Goldsmith, D. F., & Rogoff, B. (1997). Mothers' and toddlers' coordinated joint focus of attention: Variations with maternal dysphoric symptoms. *Developmental Psychology, 33*(1), 113–119.

Goldsmith, H. H., & Alansky, J. (1987). Maternal and infant temperamental predictors of attachment: A meta-analytic review. *Journal of Consulting and Clinical Psychology, 55,* 805–816.

Goldsmith, H. H., Buss, K. A., & Lemery, K. S. (1997). Toddler and childhood temperament: Expanded content, stronger genetic evidence, new evidence for the importance of environment. *Developmental Psychology, 33*(6), 891–905.

Goldsmith, H. H., Buss, A. H., Plomin, R., Rothbart, M. K., Thoman, A., Chess, S., Hinde, R. A., & McCall, R. B. (1987). Roundtable: What is temperament? Four approaches. *Child Development, 58,* 505–529.

Goldsmith, H. H., & Campos, J. J. (1990). The structure of temperamental fear and pleasure in infants: A psychometric perspective. *Child Development, 61,* 1944–1964.

Goldsmith, H. H., & Gottesman, I. I. (1981). Origins of variation in behavioral style: A longitudinal study of temperament in young twins. *Child Development, 52,* 91–103.

Goldsmith, H. H., Lemery, K. S., Buss, K. A., & Campos, J. J. (1999). Genetic analyses of focal aspects of infant temperament. *Developmental Psychology, 35*(4), 972–985.

Goldstein, M. H., King, A. P., & West, M. J. (2003). Social interaction shapes babbling: testing parallels between birdsong and speech. *Proc Natl Acad Sci U S A, 100*(13), 8030–8035.

Goldstein, S. R., & Young, C. A. (1996). "Evolutionary" stable strategy of handedness in major league baseball. *Journal of Comparative Psychology,* 110, 164–169.

Golinkoff, R. M., & Ames, G. J. (1979). A comparison of fathers' and mothers' speech with their young children. *Child Development, 50,* 28–32.

Golomb, C. (1974). *Young children's sculpture and drawing: A study in representation development.* Cambridge, MA: Harvard University Press.

Golub, M. S. (1996). Labor analgesia and infant brain development. *Pharmacology of Biochemical Behavior, 55*(4), 619–628.

Golub, M. S., Macintosh, M. S., & Baumrind, N. (1998). Developmental and reproductive toxicity of inorganic arsenic: Animal studies and human concerns. *Journal of Toxicology and Environmental Health, 1*(3), 199–241.

Goodman, J. C., McDonough, L., & Brown, N. B. (1998). The role of semantic context and memory in the acquisition of novel nouns. *Child Development, 69*(5), 1330–1344.

Goodnow, J. (1977). *Children drawing.* Cambridge, MA: Harvard University Press.

Goodwin, R. D., Fergusson, D. M., & Horwood, L. J. (2005). Childhood abuse and familial violence and the risk of panic attacks and panic disorder in young adulthood. *Psychol Med, 35*(6), 881–890.

Goodwyn, S. W., & Acredolo, L. P. (1993). Symbolic gesture versus word: Is there a modality advantage for onset of symbol use? *Child Development, 64,* 688–701.

Goossens, F. A., & van Ijzendoorn, M. H. (1990). Quality of infants' attachments to professional caregivers: Relation to infant-parent attachment and day-care characteristics. *Child Development, 61,* 832–837.

Gopnik, A., & Nazzi, T. (2003). Words, kinds, and causal powers: A theory theory perspective on early naming and categorization. In D. H. Rakison (Ed.), *Early category and concept development: Making sense of the blooming, buzzing confusion.* (pp. 303–329). London: Oxford University Press.

Gordon, T. (1988). The case against disciplining children at home or in school. *Person-Centered Review, 3,* 59–85.

Gorman, K. S., & Pollitt, E. (1992). Relationship between weight and body proportionality at birth, growth during the first year of life, and cognitive development at 36, 48, and 60 months. *Infant Behavior and Development, 15,* 279–296.

Gornick, J. C., & Meyers, M. K. (2003). *Families that work: Policies for reconciling parenthood and employment.* New York: Russell Sage Foundation.

Gottfried, A. W., Rose, S. A., & Bridger, W. H. (1977). Cross-modal transfer in human infants. *Child Development, 48,* 118–123.

Gottlieb, G. (1991a). Experiential canalization of behavioral development: Theory. *Developmental Psychology, 27,* 4–13.

Gottlieb, G. (1991b). Experiential canalization of behavioral development: Results. *Developmental Psychology, 27,* 35–39.

Gottlieb, G. (1995). Some conceptual deficiencies in "developmental" behavior genetics. *Human Development, 38*(3), 131–141.

Goubet, N., & Clifton, R. K. (1998). Object and event representation in 61/2–month-old infants. *Developmental Psychology, 34*(1), 63–76.

Gould, S. J. (1994). The evolution of life on earth. *Scientific American,* 85–91.

Graham, F. K., Anthony, B. J., & Zeigler, B. L. (1984). The orienting response and developmental processes. In D. Siddle (Ed.), *Orienting and habituation: Perspectives in human research* (pp. 166–183). New York: Wiley.

Graham, F. K., Leavitt, L., Strock, B., & Brown, H. (1978). Precocious cardiac orienting in a human anencephalic infant. *Science, 199,* 322–324.

Grandin, T. (2005). *Animals in translation: Using the mysteries of autism to decode animal behavior.* New York: Simon & Shuster.

Grandin, T., & Scariano, M. (1986). *Emergence: Labeled autistic.* Novato, CA: Arena Press.

Granrud, C. E., & Yonas, A. (1984). Infants' perception of pictorially specified interposition. *Journal of Experimental Child Psychology, 37,* 500–511.

Granrud, C. E., Yonas, A., & Opland, E. A. (1985). Infants' sensitivity to the depth cue of shading. *Perception and Psychophysics, 37,* 415–419.

Grant, V. J. (1994). Sex of infant differences in mother-infant interaction: A reinterpretation of past findings. *Developmental Review, 14,* 1–26.

Gray, V., Karmiloff-Smith, A., Funnell, E., & Tassabehji, M. (2006). In-depth analysis of spatial cognition in Williams syndrome: A critical assessment of the role of the LIMK1 gene. *Neuropsychologia, 44*(5), 679–685.

Green, J. A., Gustafson, G. E., Irwin, J. R., Kalinowski, L. L., & Wood, R. M. (1995). Infant crying: Acoustics, perception, and communication. *Early Development and Parenting, 4*(4), 161–175.

Green, J. A., Gustafson, G. E., & McGhie, A. C. (1998). Changes in infants' cries as a function of time in a cry bout. *Child Development, 69*(2), 271–279.

Green, J. E., Dorfman, A., Jones, S. L., Bender, S., Patton, L., & Schulman, J. D. (1988). Chorionic villus sampling: Experience with an initial 940 cases. *Obstetrics and Gynecology, 71,* 208–212.

Green, J. M. (1998). Postnatal depression or perinatal dysphoria? Findings from a longitudinal community-based study using the Edinburgh Postnatal Depression Scale. *Journal of Reproductive and Infant Psychology, 16*(2–3), 143–155.

Greenberger, E., O'Neil, R., & Nagel, S. K. (1994). Linking workplace and homeplace: Relations between the nature of adults' work and their parenting behaviors. *Developmental Psychology, 30,* 990–1002.

Greenfield, P., & Smith, J. H. (1976). *The structure of communication in early language development.* New York: Academic Press.

Greenleaf, P. (1978). *Children throughout the ages. A history of childhood.* New York: Barnes & Noble.

Greenough, W. T., Black, J. E., & Wallace, C. S. (1987). Experience and brain development. *Child Development, 58,* 539–559.

Greenspan, S. I. (2008). A dynamic developmental model of mental health and mental illness. . In A. Fogel, B. J. King, & S. Shanker (Eds.). *Human developompent in the 21st century: Visionary policy ideas from systems scientists.* Cambridge, UK: Cambridge University Press.

Greenspan, S. I. & Wieder, S. (1997). An integrated approach to interventions for young children with severe difficulties in relating and communicating. *Zero to Three, 17*(5), 5–17.

Grieser, D. L., & Kuhl, P. K. (1988). Maternal speech to infants in a tonal language: Support for universal prosodic features in motherese. *Developmental Psychology, 24*(1), 14–20.

Grieser, D. L., & Kuhl, P. K. (1989). Categorization of speech by infants: Support for speech-sound prototypes. *Developmental Psychology, 25,* 577–588.

Grimes, D. A. (1994). The morbidity and mortality of pregnancy: Still risky business. *American Journal of Obstetrics and Gynecology, 170,* 1489–1494.

Grimm, E. (1967). Psychological and social factors in pregnancy, delivery and outcome. In S. Richardson & A. Guttmacher (Eds.), *Childbearing: Its social and psychological aspects* (pp. 305–348). Baltimore: Williams & Wilkins.

Grobstein, C. (1988). *Science and the unborn.* New York: Basic Books.

Grodstein, F., Goldman, M. B., & Cramer, D. W. (1994). Infertility in women and moderate alcohol use. *American Journal of Public Health, 84,* 1429–1432.

Grolnick, W. S., Bridges, L. J., & Connel, J. P. (1996). Emotion regulation in two-year-olds. Strategies and emotional expression in four contexts. *Child Development, 67,* 928–941.

Grolnick, W. S., Cosgrove, T. J., & Bridges, L. J. (1996). Age-graded change in the initiation of positive affect. *Infant Behavior and Development, 19,* 153–157.

Gross, J., & Hayne, H. (1999). Young children's recognition and description of their own and others' drawings. *Developmental Science, 2*(4), 476–489.

Grossman, K., Grossman, K. E., Spangler, G., Suess, G., & Unzner, L. (1985). Maternal sensitivity and newborns' orientation responses as related to quality of attachment in northern Germany. *Monographs of the Society for Research in Child Development, 50* (Serial No. 209), 233–256.

Grossmann, T., Striano, T., & Friederici, A. D. (2006). Crossmodal integration of emotional information from face and voice in the infant brain. *Developmental Science, 9*(3), 309–315.

Grover, S., & Permezel, M. (1994). What's new?: Gynaecology. *Medical Journal of Australia, 161,* 330–331.

Gruen, A. (1987). The relationship of sudden infant death and parental unconscious conflicts. *Pre- and Perinatal Psychology Journal, 2,* 50–56.

Gruendel, J. M. (1977). Referential extension in early language development. *Child Development, 48,* 1567–1576.

Grunwaldt, E., Bates, T., & Guthrie, D. (1960). The onset of sleeping through the night in infancy. *Pediatrics, 26,* 667–668.

Grych, J. H., & Clark, R. (1999). Maternal employment and development of the father-infant relationship in the first year. *Developmental Psychology, 35*(4), 893–903.

Guerin, D. W., Gottfried, A. W., & Thomas, C. W. (1997). Difficult temperament and behaviour problems: A longitudinal study from 1.5 to 12 years. *International Journal of Behavioral Development, 21*(1), 71–90.

Guffanti, S., Grancini, F., Scalfaro, C., & Podesta, A. F. (2004). [Sudden infant death syndrome (SIDS)]. *Pediatr Med Chir, 26*(2), 96–104.

Guillain, A., Foxonet, C., Petersen, A., & Ramos, M. (1997). Socialization and cognition in children between the age of 18 and 24 months. *Early Development and Parenting, 6*(2), 59–71.

Gunnar, M. (1994). Psychoendocrine studies of temperament and stress in early childhood: Expanding current models. In J. E. Bates & T. D. Wachs (Eds.), *Temperament: Individual differences at the interface of biology and behavior* (pp. 175–198). Washington, DC: American Psychological Association.

Gunnar, M. R., & Barr, R. G. (1998). Stress, early brain development, and behavior. *Infants and Young Children, 11*(1), 1–14.

Gunnar, M. & Cheatham, C. L. (2003). Brain and behavior interface: Stress and the developing brain. *Infant Mental Health Journal, 24,* 195–211.

Gunnar, M., Leighton, K., & Peleaux, R. (1984). Effects of temporal predictability on the reactions of 1–year-olds to potentially frightening toys. *Developmental Psychology, 20,* 449–458.

Gunnar, M., Mangelsdorf, S., Larson, M., & Hertsgaard, L. (1989). Attachment, temperament, and adrenocortical activity in infancy: A study of psychoendocrine regulation. *Developmental Psychology, 25,* 355–363.

Gunnar, M., Senior, K., & Hartup, W. W. (1984). Peer presence and the exploratory behavior of eighteen- and thirty-month-old children. *Child Development, 55,* 1103–1109.

Gunnar, M. R., & Stone, C. (1984). The effects of positive maternal affect on infant responses to pleasant, ambiguous, and fear-provoking toys. *Child Development, 55,* 1231–1236.

Gurevich, R. (2009) How much does IVF cost? http://infertility.about.com/od/ivf/f/-ivf_cost.htm.

Guse, T., Wissing, M., & Hartman, W. (2006). The effect of a prenatal hypnotherapeutic programme on postnatal maternal psychological well-being. *Journal of Reproductive and Infant Psychology, 24*(2), 163–177.

Gusella, J. L., Muir, D., & Tronick, E. Z. (1988). The effect of manipulating maternal behavior during an interaction on three- and six-month-olds' affect and attention. *Child Development, 59,* 1111–1124.

Gustafson, G. E. (1984). The effects of the ability to locomote on infants' social and exploratory behaviors: An experimental study. *Developmental Psychology, 20,* 397–405.

Gustafson, G. E., & Green, J. A. (1989). On the importance of fundamental frequency and other acoustic features in cry perception and infant development. *Child Development, 60,* 772–780.

Gustafson, G. E., & Green, J. A. (1991). Developmental coordination of cry sounds with visual regard and gestures. *Infant Behavior and Development, 14,* 51–57.

Gustafson, G. E., Green, J. A., & Kalinowski, L. L. (1995, March). *Crying and vocalizing: A nascent system for communicating different meanings?* Poster presented at the meeting of the Society for Research in Child Development, Indianapolis, IN.

Gustafson, G. E., Green, J. A., & West, M. J. (1979). The infant's changing role in mother-infant games: The growth of social skills. *Infant Behavior and Development, 2,* 301–308.

Gustafson, G. E., & Harris, K. L. (1990). Women's responses to young infants' cries. *Developmental Psychology, 26,* 144–152.

Guthrie, H. A. (1979). *Introduction to nutrition.* St. Louis: Mosby.

Gutman, A., & Turnure, J. (1979). Mothers' production of hand gestures while communicating with their pre-school children under various task conditions. *Developmental Psychology, 15,* 197–203.

Guttmacher, A. (1973). *Pregnancy, birth and family planning: A guide for expectant parents in the 1970s.* New York: Viking Press.

Hack, M., Klein, N. K., & Taylor, H. G. (1995). Long-term developmental outcomes of low birth weight infants. *The Future of Children, 5,* 176–196.

Haden, C. A., Ornstein, P. A., Eckerman, C. O., & Didow, S. M. (2001). Mother-child conversational interactions as events unfold: Linkages to subsequent remembering. *Child Development, 72*(4), 1016–1031.

Hagekull, B. (2003). Early temperament and attachment as predictors of the Five Factor Model of personality. *Attachment & Human Development, 5*(1), 2–18.

Hagekull, B., & Bohlin, G. (2004). Predictors of Middle Childhood Psychosomatic Problems: An Emotion Regulation Approach. *Infant and Child Development, 13*(5), 389–405.

Hagekull, B., Stenberg, G., & Bohlin, G. (1993). Infant-mother social referencing interactions: Description and antecedents in maternal sensitivity and infant irritability. *Early Development and Parenting, 2,* 183–191.

Hagerman, R. J. (1996). Biomedical advances in developmental psychology: The case of fragile X syndrome. *Developmental Psychology, 32*(3), 416–424.

Haight, W., Masiello, T., Dickson, K. L., Huckeby, E., & Black, J. E. (1994). The everyday contexts and social functions of spontaneous mother-child pretend play in the home. *Merrill-Palmer Quarterly, 40,* 509–522.

Haight, W., & Miller, P. J. (1992). The development of everyday pretend play: A longitudinal study of mothers' participation. *Merrill-Palmer Quarterly, 38,* 331–349.

Haight, W. L., Wang, X., Fung, H. H., Williams, K., & Mintz, J. (1999). Universal, developmental, and variable aspects of young children's play: A cross-cultural comparison of pretending at home. *Child Development, 70*(6), 1477–1488.

Hains, S. M. J., & Muir, D. W. (1996). Effects of stimulus contingency in infant-adult interactions. *Infant Behavior and Development, 19,* 49–61.

Haith, M. M. (1980). *Rules that babies look by: The organization of newborn visual activity.* Hillsdale, NJ: Erlbaum.

Haith, M. M., Bergman, T., & Moore, M. (1977). Eye contact and face scanning in early infancy. *Science, 198,* 853–855.

Hala, S., Chandler, M., & Fritz, A. S. (1991). Fledgling theories of mind: Deception as a marker of three-year-olds' understanding of false belief. *Child Development, 62,* 83–97.

Haley, D. W., & Stansbury, K. (2003). Infant Stress and Parent Responsiveness: Regulation of Physiology and Behavior During Still-Face and Reunion. *Child Development, 74*(5), 1534–1546.

Hallock, M. B., Worobey, J., & Self, P. A. (1989). Behavioral development in chimpanzee *(Pan troglodytes)* and human newborns across the first month of life. *International Journal of Behavioral Development, 12,* 527–540.

Halonen, J. S., & Passman, R. (1978). Pacifier's effects upon play and separations from the mother for the one-year-old in a novel environment. *Infant Behavior and Development, 1,* 70–78.

Hamela-Olkowska, A., Marcyniak, M., Sienko, J., Czajkowski, K., Brandt, M., Jalinik, K., et al. (2003). [Sexuality in pregnant women]. *Med Wieku Rozwoj, 7*(3 Suppl 1), 175–180.

Hamilton, L. R. (1989). Variables associated with child maltreatment and implications for prevention and treatment. *Early Child Development, 42,* 31–56.

Hanawalt, B. A. (1993). *Growing up in medieval London: The experience of childhood in history.* New York: Oxford University Press.

Hanna, E., & Meltzoff, A. N. (1993). Peer imitation by toddlers in laboratory, home and day-care contexts: Implications for social learning and memory. *Developmental Psychology, 29,* 701–710.

Hannan, T. E. (1987). A cross-sequential assessment of the occurrences of pointing in three- to twelve-month-old infants. *Infant Behavior and Development, 10,* 11–22.

Hannon, E. E., & Trehub, S. E. (2005). Tuning in to musical rhythms: infants learn more readily than adults. *Proc Natl Acad Sci U S A, 102*(35), 12639–12643.

Hansen, M. (1993). Surrogacy contract upheld; California Supreme Courts says such agreements don't violate public policy. *American Psychological Association, 79,* 34.

Harding, C. G., & Golinkoff, R. M. (1979). The origins of intentional vocalizations in prelinguistic infants. *Child Development, 50,* 33–40.

Hardy, J. B., Aston, N. M., Brooks-Gunn, J., Shapiro, S., & Miller, T. L. (1998). Like mother, like child: Intergenerational patterns of age at first birth and associations with childhood and adolescent characteristics and adult outcomes in the second generation. *Developmental Psychology, 34*(6), 1220–1232.

Hardyck, C., & Petrinovich, L. F. (1977). Left-handedness. *Psychological Bulletin, 84,* 385–404.

Hareven, T. K. (1982). *Family time and industrial time.* New York: Cambridge University Press.

Hareven, T. K. (1985). Historical changes in the family and the life course: Implications for child development. *Monographs of the Society for Research in Child Development, 50* (Serial No. 211), 8–23.

Harkness, S., Super, C. M., Moscardino, U., Rha, J., Blom, M., Huitrón, B., et. al. (2007). Cultural models and developmental agendas. Implications for arousal and self-regulation in early infancy. *The Journal of Developmental Processes, 2*(1), 5–39.

Harley, K., & Reese, E. (1999). Origins of autobiographical memory. *Developmental Psychology, 35*(8), 1338–1348.

Harlow, H., & Harlow, M. (1965). The affectional systems. In A. Schrier, H. Harlow, & F. Stollnitz (Eds.), *Behavior of non-human primates* (Vol. 2). New York: Academic Press.

Harris, L. J., Spradlin, M. P., & Almerigi, J. B. (2007) Mothers' and fathers' lateral biases for holding their newborn infants: A study of images from the World Wide Web, , *Laterality, 12*:1, 64–86

Harris, M., Jones, D., & Grant, J. (1985). The social-interactional context of maternal speech to infants: An explanation for the event-bound nature of early word use? *First Language, 5,* 89–100.

Harris, P. L. (1989). *Children and emotion: The development of psychological understanding.* New York: Basil Blackwell.

Harris, P. L. (1998). Fictional absorption: Emotional responses to make-believe. In S. Br;araten (Ed.), *Intersubjective communication and emotion in early ontogeny. Studies in emotion and social interaction, 2nd series* (pp. 336–353). Cambridge, England: Cambridge University Press.

Harris, P. L., & Kavanaugh, R. D. (1993). Young children's understanding of pretense. *Monographs of the Society for Research in Child Development, 58,* 1–92.

Hart, B., & Risley, T. R. (1992). American parenting of language-learning children: Persisting differences in family-child interactions observed in natural home environments. *Developmental Psychology, 28,* 1096–1105.

Hart, S., Boylan, L. M., Carroll, S., Musick, Y., & Lampe, R. M. (2003). Brief report: Breast-fed one-week-olds demonstrate superior neurobehavioral organization. *Journal of Pediatric Psychology, 28*(8), 529–534.

Hart, S., Field, T., Del Valle, C., & Letourneau, M. (1998). Infants protest their mothers' attending to an infant-size doll. *Social Development, 7*(1), 54–61.

Hart, S., Field, T., Letourneau, M., & Del Valle, C. (1998). Jealousy protests in infants of depressed mothers. *Infant Behavior and Development, 21*(1), 137–148.

Harter, S. (1983). Developmental perspectives on the self-system. In P. H. Mussen (Series Ed.) & E. M. Hetherington (Vol. Ed.), *Handbook of child psychology: Vol. 4. Socialization, personality, and social development* (pp. 176–194). New York: Wiley.

Hartley, L. (1995). *Wisdom of the body moving.* Berkeley, CA: North Atlantic Books.

Hartmann, A. F., Radin, M. B., & McConnell, B. (1992). Parent-to-parent support: A critical component of health care services for families. *Issues in Comprehensive Pediatric Nursing, 15,* 55–67.

Hartmann, H., & Molz, G. (1979). Unexpected death in infancy. In J. Howells (Ed.), *Modern perspectives in the psychiatry of infancy* (pp. 360–395). New York: Brunner Mazel.

Hartmann, K., Viswanathan, M., Palmieri, R., Gartlehner, G., Thorp, J., Jr., & Lohr, K. N. (2005). Outcomes of routine episiotomy: a systematic review. *Jama, 293*(17), 2141–2148.

Harty, J. R. (1990). Pharmacotherapy in infantile autism. *Focus on Autistic Behavior, 5,* 1–15.

Harwood, R. L., Schölmerich, A., Schulze, P. A., & Gonzalez, Z. (1999). Cultural differences in maternal beliefs and behaviors: A study of middle-class Anglo and Puerto Rican mother-infant pairs in four everyday situations. *Child Development, 70*(4), 1005–1016.

Hass, J. K., & Walter, T. (2006–2007). Parental grief in three societies: Networks and religion as social supports in mourning. *Omega, 54*(3), 179–198.

Hatton, D. D., Bailey, D. B., Burchinal, M. R., & Ferrell, K. A. (1997). Developmental growth curves of preschool children with vision impairments. *Child Development, 68*(5), 788–806.

Hauser-Cram, P. (1996). Mastery motivation in toddlers with developmental disabilities. *Child Development, 67,* 236–248.

Hauser-Cram, P., Warfield, M. E., Shonkoff, J. P., Krauss, M. W., Upshur, C. C., & Sayer, A. (1999). Family influences on adaptive development in young children with Down syndrome. *Child Development, 70*(4), 979–989.

Hawley, P. H., & Little, T. D. (1999). On winning some and losing some: A social relations approach to social dominance in toddlers. *Merrill-Palmer Quarterly, 45*(2), 185–214.

Hay, D. F., Caplan, M., Castle, J., & Stimson, C. A. (1991). Does sharing become increasingly "rational" in the second year of life? *Developmental Psychology, 27*, 987–993.

Hay, D. F., Murray, P., Cecire, S., & Nash, A. (1985). Social learning of social behavior in early life. *Child Development, 56*, 43–57.

Hay, D. F., Pawlby, S., Sharp, D., Asten, P., Mills, A., & Kumar, R. (2001). Intellectual problems shown by 11–year-old children whose mothers had postnatal depression. *Journal of Child Psychology and Psychiatry, 42*(7), 871–889.

Hayne, H., Barr, R., & Herbert, J. (2003). The effect of prior practice on memory reactivation and generalization. *Child Development, 74*(6), 1615–1627.

Hayne, H., & Findlay, N. (1995). Contextual control of memory retrieval in infancy: Evidence for associative priming. *Infant Behavior and Development, 18*(2), 195–207.

Hayne, H., & Rovee-Collier, C. (1995). The organization of reactivated memory in infancy. *Child Development, 66*, 893–906.

Hazell, L. (1975). A study of 300 elective home births. *Birth and the Family Journal, 2*, 11–18.

Hazen, N. (1982). Spatial exploration and spatial knowledge: Individual and developmental differences in very young children. *Child Development, 53*, 826–833.

Hazlewood, V. (1977). The role of auditory stimuli in crying inhibition in the neonate. *Journal of Audiology Research, 17*, 225–240.

Health Watch (1997, January 7). *NBC Nightly News.* New York: NBC.

Healy, B. T. (1989). Autonomic nervous system correlates of temperament. *Infant Behavior and Development, 12*, 289–304.

Hebb, D. O. (1949). *The organization of behavior.* New York: Oxford University Press.

Heckhausen, J. (1988). Becoming aware of one's competence in the second year: Developmental progression within the mother-child dyad. *International Journal of Behavioral Development, 11*, 305–326.

Heiman, T. (2002). Parents of children with disabilities: Resilience, coping, and future expectations. *Journal of Developmental and Physical Disabilities, 14*(2), 159–171.

Heimann, M. (1989). Neonatal imitation, gaze aversion, and mother-infant interaction. *Infant Behavior and Development, 12*, 495–505.

Heimann, M., Ullstadius, E., Dahlgren, S. O., & Gillberg, C. (1992). Imitation in autism: A preliminary research note. *Behavioral Neurology, 5*, 219–227.

Heineman, T. & Ehrensaft, D., (Eds) (2006). *Building A Home Within: Meeting the Emotional Needs of Children and Youth in Foster Care.* Baltimore, MD: Brooks Publishing.

Heinicke, C. M. (1984). Impact of pre-birth parent personality and marital functioning on family development: A framework and suggestions for further study. *Developmental Psychology, 20*, 1044–1053.

Heinicke, C. M., Diskin, S. D., Ramsey-Klee, D. M., & Oates, D. S. (1986). Pre- and post-birth antecedents of 2–year-old attention, capacity for relationships, and verbal expressiveness. *Developmental Psychology, 22*, 777–787.

Heinicke, C. M., & Guthrie, D. (1992). Stability and change in husband-wife adaptation and the development of the positive parent-child relationship. *Infant Behavior and Development, 15*, 109–127.

Heinicke, C. M., & Lampl, E. (1988). Pre- and post-birth antecedents of 3– and 4–year-old attention, IQ, verbal expressiveness, task orientation, and capacity for relationships. *Infant Behavior and Development, 11*, 381–410.

Heinicke, C. M., & Westheimer, I. (1966). *Brief separations.* New York: Academic Press.

Heinze, S. D., & Sleigh, M. J. (2003). Epidural or no epidural anaesthesia: relationships between beliefs about childbirth and pain control choices. *Journal of Reproductive and Infant Psychology, 21*(4), 323–333.

Helmrath, T., & Steinitz, E. (1978). Death of an infant: Parental grieving and the failure of social support. *Journal of Family Practice, 6*, 785–790.

Helweg, L. A., Lundemose, J. B., & Bille, H. (1994). Overheating and sudden infant death: Temperature regulation in relation to the prone position, the possible pathogenesis of sudden infant death. *Ugeskrift For Laeger, 156*, 7193–7196.

Hemminki, E. & Meriläinen, J. (1996) Long-term effects of cesarean sections: Ectopic pregnancies and placental problems, *American Journal of Obstetrics and Gynecology,* 174:1569–1574.

Henriksson, K. M., & McNeil, T. F. (2004). Health and development in the first 4 years of life in offspring of women with schizophrenia and affective psychoses: Well-Baby Clinic information. *Schizophr Res, 70*(1), 39–48.

Henshaw, S. K. (1994). Recent trends in the legal status of induced abortion. *Journal of Public Health Policy, 15*, 165–172.

Hepper, P., Wells, D., & Lynch, C. (2005). Prenatal thumb sucking is related to postnatal handedness. *Neuropsychologia, 43*(3), 313–315.

Herault, J., Matineau, J., Petit, E., & Perrot, A. (1994). Genetic markers in autism: Association study on short arm of chromosome 11. *Journal of Autism and Developmental Disorders, 24*, 233–236.

Herbert, J., Gross, J., & Hayne, H. (2007). Crawling is associated with more flexible memory retrieval by 9–month-old infants. *Developmental Science, 10*(2), 183–189.

Hernandez, D. J. (1997). Child development and the social demography of childhood. *Child Development, 68*(1), 149–169.

Hernandez Blasi, C., & Bjorklund, D. F. (2003). Evolutionary developmental psychology: A new tool for better understanding human ontogeny. *Human Development, 46*(5), 259–281.

Herrick, K., Phillips, D. I., Haselden, S., Shiell, A. W., Campbell-Brown, M., & Godfrey, K. M. (2003). Maternal consumption of a high-meat, low-carbohydrate diet in late pregnancy: relation to adult cortisol concentrations in the offspring. *J Clin Endocrinol Metab, 88*(8), 3554–3560.

Hertenstein, M. J. (2002). Touch: Its communicative functions in infancy. *Human Development, 45*(2), 70–94.

Heshusius, L. (1994). Freeing ourselves from objectivity: Managing subjectivity or turning toward a participatory mode of consciousness? *Educational Researcher, 23*(3), 15–22.

Hess, E. H. (1959). Imprinting. *Science, 130,* 133–141.

Hesse, E., & van Ijzendoorn, M. H. (1998). Parental loss of close family members and propensities towards absorption in offspring. *Developmental Science, 1*(2), 299–305.

Hetherington, E. M., & Parke, R. D. (1993). *Child psychology: A contemporary viewpoint* (4th ed.). New York: McGraw-Hill.

Hewlett, B. S., Lamb, M. E., Shannon, D., Leyendecker, B., & Schölmerich, A. (1998). Culture and early infancy among central African foragers and farmers. *Developmental Psychology, 34*(4), 653–661.

Higgins, C. I., Campos, J. J., & Kermoian, R. (1996). Effect of self-produced locomotion on infant postural compensation to optic flow. *Developmental Psychology, 32*(5), 836–841.

Hildebrandt, K. H., Lake, M. A., & Parry, T. B. (1994). Infant coping with everyday stressful events. *Merrill-Palmer Quarterly, 40* (2), 171–189.

Hilder, A. S. (1994). Ethnic differences in the sudden infant death syndrome: What we can learn from immigrants to the UK. *Early Human Development, 38,* 143–149.

Hildyard, K. L., & Wolfe, D. A. (2002). Child neglect: Developmental issues and outcomes. *Child Abuse & Neglect, 26*(6–7), 679–695.

Hill, W. L., Borovsky, D., & Rovee-Collier, C. (1988). Continuities in infant memory development. *Developmental Psychobiology, 21,* 43–62.

Hines, M., Golombok, S., Rust, J., Johnston, K. J., Golding, J., Avon Longitudinal Study of, P., et al. (2002). Testosterone during pregnancy and gender role behavior of preschool children: A longitudinal, population study. *Child Development, 73*(6), 1678–1687.

Hirst, W. (1994). The remembered self in amnesics. In U. Neisser & R. Fivush (Eds.), *The remembering self: Construction and accuracy in the self-narrative* (pp. 253–276). Cambridge, England: Cambridge University Press.

Hobara, M. (2003). Prevalence of transitional objects in young children in Tokyo and New York. *Infant Mental Health Journal, 24*(2), 174–191.

Hobson, R. P. (1990). On the origins of self and the case of autism. *Development and Psychopathology, 2,* 163–181.

Hobson, R. P. (1991). Against the theory of "theory of mind." *British Journal of Developmental Psychology, 9*(1), 33–51.

Hobson, R. P. (1993). The emotional origins of social understanding. *Philosophical Psychology, 6,* 227–249.

Hobson, R. P., Chdambi, G., Lee, A., & Meyer, J. (2006). Foundations for self-awareness: An exploration through autism. *Monographs of the Society for Research in Child Development, 71*(2, Serial No. 284).

Hobson, R. P., & Meyer, J. A. (2005). Foundations for self and other: A study in autism. *Developmental Science, 8*(6), 481–491.

Hock, E., & DeMeis, D. K. (1990). Depression in mothers of infants: The role of maternal employment. *Developmental Psychology, 26,* 285–291.

Hodapp, R. M., Goldfield, E. C., & Boyatzis, C. J. (1984). The use and effectiveness of maternal scaffolding in mother-infant games. *Child Development, 55,* 772–781.

Hodnett, E. D., Downe, S., Edwards, N., & Walsh, D. (2005). Home-like versus conventional institutional settings for birth. *Birth, 32*(2), 151.

Hodnett, E. D., & Osborn, R. W. (1989). Effects of continuous intrapartum professional support on childbirth outcomes. *Research in Nursing and Health, 12*(5), 289–297.

Hofer, M. A. (1981). *The roots of human behavior: An introduction to the psychobiology of early development.* New York: Freeman.

Hoff, E. (2003). The Specificity of Environmental Influence: Socioeconomic Status Affects Early Vocabulary Development Via Maternal Speech. *Child Development, 74*(5), 1368–1378.

Hoff-Ginsberg, E. (1986). Function and structure in maternal speech: Their relation to the child's development of syntax. *Developmental Psychology, 22,* 155–163.

Hoff-Ginsberg, E., & Shatz, M. (1982). Linguistic input and the child's acquisition of language. *Psychological Bulletin, 92,* 3–26.

Hoffman, M. (1975). Developmental synthesis of affect and cognition and its implications for altruistic motivation. *Developmental Psychology, 11,* 607–622.

Holden, C. (1988). Family planning: A growing gap. *Science, 242,* 370–371.

Holden, G. W. (1983). Avoiding conflict: Mothers as tacticians in the supermarket. *Child Development, 54,* 233–240.

Holden, G. W. (1985). How parents create a social environment via proactive behavior. In T. Garling & J. Valsiner

(Eds.), *Children within environments: Towards a psychology of accident prevention* (pp. 160–186). New York: Plenum Press.

Holden, G. W., Thompson, E. E., Zambarano, R. J., & Marshall, L. A. (1997). Child effects as a source of change in maternal attitudes toward corporal punishment. *Journal of Social and Personal Relationships, 14*(4), 481–490.

Holland, R. L., & Smith, D. A. (1989). Management of the second stage of labor. A review (Part II). *South Dakota Journal of Medicine, 42,* 5–8.

Hollenbeck, A. R., Gewirtz, J. L., Seloris, S. L., & Scanlon, J. W. (1984). Labor and delivery medication influences parent-infant interaction in the first post-partum month. *Infant Behavior and Development, 7,* 201–210.

Holowka, S., & Petitto, L. A. (2002). Left hemisphere cerebral specialization for babies while babbling. *Science, 297,*1515.

Holt, S. A., Fogel, A., & Wood, R. W. (1998). Innovation in social games. In M. D. P. de Lyra & J. Valsiner (Eds.), *Construction of psychological processes in interpersonal communication: Vol. 4. Child development in culturally structured environments* (pp. 787–823). Norwood, NJ: Ablex.

Hong, K., & Townes, B. (1976). Infant's attachment to inanimate objects: A cross-cultural study. *Journal of the American Academy of Child Psychiatry, 15,* 49–61.

Honig, A. S. (2004). Longitudinal outcomes from the Family Development Research Program. *Early Child Development and Care, 174*(2), 125–130.

Honig, A. S., & Deters, K. (1996). Grandmothers and mothers: An intergenerational comparison of child-rearing practices with pre-schoolers. *Early Development and Parenting, 5*(1), 47–55.

Hooker, D. (1952). *The prenatal origin of behavior.* Lawrence: University of Kansas Press.

Hopkins, B., & Butterworth, G. (1997). Dynamical systems approaches to the development of action. In J. G. Bremner & A. Slater (Eds.), *Infant development: Recent advances* (pp. 75–100). Hove, England: Psychology Press/Erlbaum.

Hopkins, B., Janssen, B., Kardaun, O., & van der Schoot, T. (1988). Quieting during early infancy: Evidence for a developmental change? *Early Human Development, 18,* 111–124.

Hopkins, B., & von Wulfften Palthe, T. (1987). The development of state during early infancy. *Developmental Psychobiology, 20*(2), 165–175.

Hormann, E. (1977). Breast feeding the adopted baby. *Birth and the Family Journal, 4,* 165–173.

Hornik, R., & Gunnar, M. R. (1988). A descriptive analysis of infant social referencing. *Child Development, 59,* 626–634.

Hornik, R., Risenhoover, N., & Gunnar, M. R. (1987). The effects of maternal positive, neutral and negative affective communications on infant responses to new toys. *Child Development, 58,* 937–944.

Hoshi, N., & Chen, S. J. (1998). Emotion communication of Japanese mothers and their infants. *Research and clinical center for child development: Annual report 1997–1998, 21,* 27–34.

Hossain, Z., Field, T., Gonzalez, J., Malphurs, J., Del Valle, C., & Pickens, J. (1994). Infants of "depressed" mothers interact better with their nondepressed fathers. *Infant Mental Health Journal, 15,* 348–357.

Hossain, Z., Field, T., Pickens, J., Malphurs, J., & Del Valle, C. (1997). Fathers' caregiving in low-income African-American and Hispanic-American families. *Early Development and Parenting, 6*(2), 73–82.

Howard, J. (1978). The influence of children's developmental dysfunctions on marital quality and family interaction. In R. M. Lerner & G. B. Spanier (Eds.), *Child influences on marital and family interaction* (pp. 501–532). New York: Academic Press.

Howard, S. S. (1995). Treatment of male infertility. *New England Journal of Medicine, 332,* 312–317.

Howe, N. (1991). Sibling-directed internal state language, perspective taking, and affective behavior. *Child Development, 62,* 1503–1512.

Howe, N., & Rinaldi, C. M. (2004). 'You be the big sister': Maternal-Preschooler Internal State Discourse, Perspective-taking, and Sibling Caretaking. *Infant and Child Development, 13*(3), 217–234.

Howes, C. (1988). Relations between early child care and schooling. *Developmental Psychology, 24,* 53–57.

Howes, C. (1997). Children's experiences in center-based child care as a function of teacher background and adult:child ratio. *Merrill-Palmer Quarterly, 43*(3), 404–425.

Howes, C., Galinsky, E., & Kontos, S. (1998). Child care caregiver sensitivity and attachment. *Social Development, 7*(1), 23–36.

Howes, C., & Matheson, C. C. (1992). Sequences in the development of competent play with peers: Social and social pretend play. *Developmental Psychology, 28,* 961–974.

Howes, C., Phillips, D. A., & Whitebook, M. (1992). Thresholds of quality: Implications for the social development of children in center-based child care. *Child Development, 63,* 449–460.

Howes, C., & Smith, E. W. (1995). Children and their child care caregivers: Profiles of relationships. *Social Development, 4,* 45–59.

Howes, C., & Stewart, P. (1987). Child's play with adults, toys, and peers: An examination of family and child-care influences. *Developmental Psychology, 23,* 423–430.

Hrdy, S. B. (1999). *Mother nature: A history of mothers, infants, and natural selection.* Pantheon.

Hsieh, F. J., Shyu, M. K., Sheu, B. C., Lin, S. P., Chen, C. P., & Huang, F. Y. (1995). Limb defects after chorionic villus sampling. *Obstetrics and Gynecology, 85,* 84–88.

Hsu, H. C., Fogel, A., & Cooper, R. B. (2000). Infant vocal development during the first 6 months: Speech quality and melodic complexity. *Infant and Child Development, 9,* 1–6.

Hsu, H. C., & Fogel, A. (2001). Infant vocal development in a dynamic mother-infant communication system. *Infancy, 2* (1), 87–109.

Hsu, H., & Fogel, A. (2003) Social regulatory effects of infant nondistress vocalization on maternal behavior. *Developmental Psychology, 39*(6), 976–991.

Hsu, H., Fogel, A., & Messinger, D. (2001). Infant non-distress vocalization during mother-infant face-to-face interaction: Factors associated with quantitative and qualitative differences. Infant Behavior and Development, 24, 107–128.

Hubert, N. C., Wachs, T. D., Peters-Martin, P., & Gandour, M. J. (1982). The study of early temperament: Measurement and conceptual issues. *Child Development, 53,* 571–600.

Hudson, D. B., Campbell-Grossman, C., Fleck, M. O., Elek, S. M., & Shipman, A. (2003). Effects of the New Fathers Network on first-time fathers' parenting self-efficacy and parenting satisfaction during the transition to parenthood. *Issues Compr Pediatr Nurs, 26*(4), 217–229.

Hudson, J. A., & Sheffield, E. G. (1998). Déjà vu all over again: Effects of reenactment on toddlers' event memory. *Child Development, 69*(1), 51–67.

Hudson, V., & den Boer, A. (2004). *Bare branches: The security implications of Asia's surplus male population.* Cambridge, MA. MIT Press.

Huebner, C. E. (2002). Evaluation of a clinic-based parent education program to reduce the risk of infant and toddler maltreatment. *Public Health Nurs, 19*(5), 377–389.

Huffman, L. C., Bryan, Y. E., Carmen, R. del, Pedersen, F. A., Doussard-Roosevelt, J. A., & Porges, S. W. (1998). Infant temperament and cardiac vagal tone: Assessments at twelve weeks of age. *Child Development, 69*(3), 624–635.

Huffman, L. C., Bryan, Y. E., Pedersen, F. A., Lester, B. M., Newman, J. D., & Carmen, R. del. (1994). Infant cry acoustics and maternal ratings of temperament. *Infant Behavior and Development, 17,* 45–53.

Hughes, M. A., McCollum, J., Sheftel, D., & Sanchez, G. (1994). How parents cope with the experience of neonatal intensive care. *Children's Health Care, 23*(1), 1–14.

Huizink, A., Mulder, E., & Buitelaar, J. (2004). Prenatal stress and risk for psychopathology: Specific effects or induction of general susceptibility?. *Psychological Bulletin, 130*(1), 115–142.

Humphrey, M., & Kirkwood, R. (1982). Marital relationship among adopters. *Adoption and Fostering, 6,* 44–48.

Hunt, H. T. (1995). *On the nature of consciousness: Cognitive, phenomenological, and transpersonal perspectives.* New Haven, CT: Yale University Press.

Hunter, F. T., McCarthy, M. E., MacTurk, R. H., & Vietze, P. M. (1987). Infants' social-constructive interactions with mothers and fathers. *Developmental Psychology, 23,* 249–254.

Hunter, R. S., Kilstrom, N., Kraybill, E. N., & Loda, F. (1978). Antecedents of child abuse and neglect in premature infants: A prospective study in a newborn intensive care unit. *Pediatrics, 61,* 629–635.

Hunziker, U. A., & Barr, R. G. (1986). Increased carrying reduces infant crying: A randomized controlled trial. *Pediatrics, 77,* 641–648.

Hurd, Y. L., Wang, X., Anderson, V., Beck, O., Minkoff, H., & Dow-Edwards, D. (2005). Marijuana impairs growth in mid-gestation fetuses. *Neurotoxicol Teratol, 27*(2), 221–229.

Huston, A. C. (1994). Children in poverty: Designing research to affect policy. *Social Policy Report: Society for Research in Child Development, 8,* 1–11.

Huston, A. C., Anderson, D. R.., Wright, J. C., Linebarger, D. L., & Schmitt, K. L. (2001). Sesame Street viewers as adolescents: The recontact study. In S. M. Fisch & R. T. Truglio (Eds.), *"G" is for growing: Thirty years of research on children and Sesame Street Muppets* (pp. 131–143). Mahwah, NJ: Lawrence Erlbaum Associates, Inc.

Hutcheson, J. J., Black, M. M., & Starr, R. H. (1993). Developmental differences in interactional characteristics of mothers and their children with failure to thrive. *Journal of Pediatric Psychology, 18,* 453–466.

Huth-Bocks, A. C., Levendosky, A. A., Bogat, G. A., & von Eye, A. (2004). The Impact of Maternal Characteristics and Contextual Variables on Infant-Mother Attachment. *Child Development, 75*(2), 480–496.

Huth-Bocks, A. C., Levendosky, A. A., Theran, S. A., & Bogat, G. A. (2004). The Impact of Domestic Violence on Mothers' Prenatal Representations of Their Infants. *Infant Mental Health Journal, 25*(2), 79–98.

Huttenlocher, P., & Dabholkar, A. (1997). Regional differences in synaptogenesis in human cerebral cortex. *Journal of Comparative Neurology* (4), 387.

Huttenlocher, J., Haight, W., Bryk, A., Seltzer, M., & Lyons, T. (1991). Early vocabulary growth: Relation to language input and gender. *Developmental Psychology, 27,* 236–248.

Hyde, J. S., Essex, M. J., & Horton, F. (1993). Fathers and parental leave: Attitudes and experiences. *Journal of Family Issues, 14,* 616–623.

Hyde, J. S., Else-Quest, N. M., Goldsmith, H. H., & Biesanz, J. C. (2004). Children's Temperament and Behavior Problems Predict Their Employed Mothers' Work Functioning. *Child Development, 75*(2), 580–594.

Hyman, C. A., & Mitchell, R. (1977). A psychological study of child battering. *Health Visitor, 48,* 294–296.

Hyssala, L., Hyttinen, M., Tautava, P., & Sillanpaa, M. (1993). The Finnish family competence study: The transition to fatherhood. *Journal of Genetic Psychology, 154,* 199–208.

Illingworth, R. S. (1966). *The development of the infant and young child: Normal and abnormal* (3rd ed.). London: E. & S. Livingstone.

Illingworth, R. (1991). *Normal child: Some problems of the early years and their treatment* (10th ed.). London: Churchill Livingstone.

Imbens-Bailey, A., & Pan, B. A. (1998). The pragmatics of self- and other-reference in young children. *Social Development, 7*(2), 217–233.

Ingersoll, E. W., & Thoman, E. B. (1994). The breathing bear: Effects on respiration in premature infants. *Physiology and Behavior,* 56, 855–895.

Ingudomnukul, E., Baron-Cohen, S., Wheelwright, S., & Knickmeyer, R. (2007). Elevated rates of testosterone-related disorders in women with autism spectrum conditions. *Hormones & Behavior, 51*(5), 597–604.

Isabella, R. A. (1993). Origins of attachment: Maternal interactive behavior across the first year. *Child Development, 64,* 605–621.

Isabella, R. A. (1998). Origins of attachment: The role of context, duration, frequency of observation, and infant age in measuring maternal behavior. *Journal of Social and Personal Relationships, 15*(4), 538–554.

Isabella, R. A., & Belsky, J. (1991). Interactional synchrony and the origins of infant-mother attachment: A replication study. *Child Development, 62,* 373–384.

Isabella, R. A., Belsky, J., & von Eye, A. (1989). Origins of infant-mother attachment: An examination of interactional synchrony during the infant's first year. *Developmental Psychology, 25*(1), 12–21.

Ispa, J. (1981). Peer support among Soviet day care toddlers. *International Journal of Behavioral Development, 4,* 255–270.

Ispa, J. M., Fine, M. A., Halgunseth, L. C., Harper, S., Robinson, J., Boyce, L., et al. (2004). Maternal Intrusiveness, Maternal Warmth, and Mother-Toddler Relationship Outcomes: Variations Across Low-Income Ethnic and Acculturation Groups. *Child Development, 75*(6), 1613–1631.

Iverson, J. M., & Fagan, M. K. (2004). Infant Vocal-Motor Coordination: Precursor to the Gesture-Speech System? *Child Development, 75*(4), 1053–1066.

Iverson, J. M., & Goldin-Meadow, S. (2005). Gesture Paves the Way for Language Development. *Psychological Science, 16*(5), 367–371.

Izard, C. E. (1981, April). *The primacy of emotion in human development.* Paper presented at the meeting of the Society for Research in Child Development, Boston, MA.

Izard, C. E., & Abe, J. A. A. (2004). Developmental Changes in Facial Expressions of Emotions in the Strange Situation During the Second Year of Life. *Emotion, 4*(3), 251–265.

Izard, C. E., Haynes, M. O., Chisholm, G., & Baak, K. (1991). Emotional determinants of infant-mother attachment. *Child Development, 62,* 906–917.

Izard, C. E., Hembree, E. A., & Huebner, R. R. (1987). Infants' emotion expressions to acute pain: Developmental change and stability of individual differences. *Developmental Psychology, 23,* 105–113.

Izard, C. E., & Malatesta, C. Z. (1987). Perspectives on emotional development I: Differential emotions theory of early emotional development. In J. D. Osofsky (Ed.), *Handbook of infant development* (2nd ed., pp. 494–554). New York: Wiley.

Jack, K. E., & Chao, C. R. (1992). Female voluntary surgical contraception via minilaparotomy under local anesthesia. *International Journal of Gynecological Obstetrics, 39,* 111–116.

Jacklin, C. N., Wilcox, K. T., & Maccoby, E. E. (1988). Neonatal sex-steroid hormones and cognitive abilities at six years. *Developmental Psychobiology, 21,* 567–574.

Jackson, J. F. (1993). Human behavioral genetics, Scarr's theory, and her views on interventions: A critical review and commentary on their implications for African American children. *Child Development, 64,* 1318–1332.

Jacobson, J. L. (1981). The role of inanimate objects in early peer interaction. *Child Development, 52,* 618–626.

Jacobson, J. L., Boersma, D. C., Fields, R. B., & Olson, K. L. (1983). Paralinguistic features of adult speech to infants and small children. *Child Development, 54,* 436–442.

Jacobson, S. W. (1979). Matching behavior in the young infant. *Child Development, 50,* 425–430.

Jacobson, S. W., Fein, G. G., Jacobson, J. L., Schwartz, P. M., & Dowler, J. K. (1985). The effect of intrauterine PCB exposure on visual recognition memory. *Child Development, 56,* 853–860.

Jacobson, S. W., & Frye, K. F. (1991). Effect of maternal social support on attachment: Experimental evidence. *Child Development, 62,* 572–582.

Jacobson, S. W., & Jacobson, J. L. (2001). Alcohol and drug-related effects on development: A new emphasis on contextual factors. *Infant Mental Health Journal, 22*(3), 416–430.

Jacobson, S. W., Jacobson, J. L., O'Neill, J. M., Padgett, R. J., Frankowski, J. J., & Bihun, J. T. (1992). *Child Development, 63,* 711–724.

Jahromi, L. B., Putnam, S. P., & Stifter, C. A. (2004). Maternal Regulation of Infant Reactivity From 2 to 6 Months. *Developmental Psychology, 40*(4), 477–487.

Jahromi, L. B., & Stifter, C. A. (2007). Individual differences in the contribution of maternal soothing to infant distress reduction. *Infancy, 11*(3), 255–269.

Jaroszewicz, A. M., & Boyd, I. H. (1973). Clinical assessment of gestational age in the newborn. *South African Medical Journal, 47,* 2123–2124.

Jarvis, P. A., & Creasey, G. L. (1991). Parental stress, coping, and attachment in families with an 18–month-old infant. *Infant Behavior and Development, 14,* 383–395.

Jarvis, P. A., Myers, B. J., & Creasey, G. L. (1989). The effects of infants' illness on mothers' interactions with prematures at 4 and 8 months. *Infant Behavior and Development, 12,* 25–35.

Jelliffe, D. B., & Jelliffe, E. F. P. (1988). Breastfeeding: General review. In D. B. Jelliffe & E. F. P. Jelliffe (Eds.), *Programmes to promote breastfeeding* (pp. 3–11). Oxford, England: Oxford University Press.

Jennings, K. D. (2004). Development of goal-directed behaviour and related self-processes in toddlers. *International Journal of Behavioral Development, 28*(4), 319–327.

Jensen, M. (2005). Lower sperm counts following prenatal tobacco exposure. *Human Reproduction, 20*(9), 2559–2566.

Johnson, D. J., Jaeger, E., Randolph, S. M., Cauce, A. M., & Ward, J. (2003). Studying the effects of early child care experiences on the development of children of color in the United States: Toward a more inclusive research agenda. *Child Development, 74*(5), 1227–1244.

Johnson, H., Glassman, M. B., Fiks, K. B., & Rosen, T. S. (1987). Path analysis of variables affecting 36–month outcome in a population of multi-risk children. *Infant Behavior and Development, 10,* 451–465.

Johnson, J. L., McAndrew, F. T., & Harris, P. B. (1991). Sociobiology and the naming of adopted and natural children. *Ethology and Sociobiology, 12,* 365–375.

Johnson, L. G. (1983). Giftedness in preschool: A better time for development than identification. *Roeper Review, 5,* 13–15.

Johnson, M. H. (2000). Functional brain development during infancy. In J. G. Bremner & A. Fogel (Eds.), *Handbook of infancy research* (pp. 130–154). Oxford, England: Blackwell.

Johnson, M. H., Dziurawiec, S., Ellis, H., & Morton, J. (1991). Newborns' preferential tracking of face-like stimuli and its subsequent decline. *Cognition, 40,* 1–19.

Johnson, S. (1997). Young infants' perception of object unity: Implications for development of attentional and cognitive skills. *Current Directions in Psychological Science, 6,* 5–11.

Johnson, S., Slaughter, V., & Carey, S. (1998). Whose gaze will infants follow? The elicitation of gaze-following in 12–month-olds. *Developmental Science, 1*(2), 233–238.

Johnson, S. C., Ok, S.-J., & Luo, Y. (2007). The attribution of attention: 9–month-olds' interpretation of gaze as goal-directed action. *Developmental Science, 10*(5), 530–537.

Johnson, S. P., Bremner, J. G., Slater, A., Mason, U., Foster, K., & Cheshire, A. (2003). Infants' perception of object trajectories. *Child Development, 74*(1), 94–108.

Johnson, T. R. B., Besinger, R. E., & Thomas, R. L. (1989). The latest clues to fetal behavior and well-being. *Contemporary Pediatrics,* 66–84.

Jones, C. (1987). *Mind over labor.* New York: Viking.

Jones, C. P., & Adamson, L. B. (1987). Language use in mother-child and mother-child-sibling interactions. *Child Development, 58,* 356–366.

Jones, L. C., & Hermann, J. A. (1992). Parental division of infant care: Contextual influences and infant characteristics. *Nursing Research, 41,* 228–234.

Jones, L. C., & Thomas, S. A. (1989). New fathers' blood pressure and heart rate: Relationships to interaction with their newborn infants. *Nursing Research, 38,* 237–241.

Jones, N. A., Field, T., Fox, N. A., Davalos, M., Malphurs, J., Carraway, K., Schanberg, S., & Kuhn, C. (1997). Infants of intrusive and withdrawn mothers. *Infant Behavior and Development, 20,* 175–186.

Jones, O. (1977). Mother-child communication with prelinguistic Down's syndrome and normal infants. In H. R. Schaffer (Ed.), *Studies in mother-infant interaction* (pp. 76–109). London: Academic Press.

Jones, S. S. (1996). Imitation or exploration? Young infants' matching of adults' oral gestures. *Child Development, 67*(5), 1952–1969.

Jones, S. S., Collins, K., & Hong, H. W. (1991). An audience effect on smile production in 10–month-old infants. *Psychological Science, 2,* 45–49.

Jones, S. S., Raag, T., & Collins, K. L. (1990). Smiling in older infants: Form and maternal response. *Infant Behavior and Development, 13,* 147–165.

Jones, S. S., Smith, L. B., & Landau, B. (1991). Object properties and knowledge in early lexical learning. *Child Development, 62,* 499–516.

Josefsson, A., Berg, G., Nordin, C., & Sydsjo, G. (2001). Prevalence of depressive symptoms in late pregnancy and postpartum. *Acta Obstet Gynecol Scand, 80*(3), 251–255.

Judd, J. M. (1985). Assessing the newborn from head to toe. *Nursing '85, 15,* 34–41.

Juffer, F., & Rosenboom, L. G. (1997). Infant-mother attachment of internationally adopted children in the Netherlands. *International Journal of Behavioral Development, 20*(1), 93–107.

Juffer, F., Rosenboom, L. G., Hoksbergen, R. A. C., Riksen-Walraven, J. M. A., & Kohnstamm, G. A. (1997). Attachment and intervention in adoptive families with and without biological children. In W. Koops, J. B. Hoeksma, & D. C. van den Boom (Eds.), *Development of interaction and attachment: Traditional and non-traditional approaches* (pp. 93–108). Amsterdam: Royal Netherlands Academy of Arts and Sciences.

Jusczyk, P. W. (1985). The high-amplitude sucking technique as a methodological tool in speech perception research. In G. Gottlieb & N. A. Krasnegor (Eds.), *Measurement of audition and vision during the first year of postnatal life: A methodological overview* (pp. 414–438). Norwood, NJ: Ablex.

Jusczyk, P. W., Cutler, A., & Redanz, N. J. (1993). Infants' preference for the predominant stress patterns of English words. *Child Development, 64,* 675–687.

Jusczyk, P. W., Kennedy, L. J., & Jusczyk, A. (1995). Young infants' retention of information about syllables. *Infant Behavior and Development, 18*(1), 27–41.

Kagan, J. (1987). Perspectives on infancy. In J. D. Osofsky (Ed.), *Handbook of infant development* (2nd ed., pp. 1150–1198). New York: Wiley.

Kagan, J. (1989). *Unstable ideas.* Cambridge, MA: Harvard University Press.

Kagan, J., Arcus, D., Snidman, N., Feng, W. Y., Hendler, J., & Greene, S. (1994). *Reactivity in infants: A cross-national comparison.* Developmental Psychology, 30, 342–345.

Kagan, J., Kearsley, R., & Zelazo, P. (1978). *Infancy: Its place in human development.* Cambridge, MA: Harvard University Press.

Kagan, J., & Reznick, J. S. (1984). Cardiac reaction as an index of task involvement. *Australian Journal of Psychology, 36,* 135–147.

Kagan, J., Reznick, J. S., & Snidman, N. (1987). The physiology and psychology of behavioral inhibition in children. *Child Development, 58,* 1459–1473.

Kagan, J., Reznick, J. S., Snidman, N., Gibbons, J., & Johnson, M. O. (1988). Childhood derivatives of inhibition and lack of inhibition to the unfamiliar. *Child Development, 59,* 1580–1589.

Kagan, J., Snidman, N., & Arcus, D. (1998). Childhood derivatives of high and low reactivity in infancy. *Child Development, 69*(6), 1483–1493.

Kagan, J., Snidman, N., Kahn, V., & Towsley, S. (2007). The preservation of two infant temperaments into adolescence. *Monographs of the Society for Research in Child Development, 72*(2), 1–95.

Kaitz, M., Meirov, H., & Landman, I. (1993). Infant recognition by tactile cues. *Infant Behavior and Development, 16,* 333–341.

Kaler, S. R., & Kopp, C. B. (1990). Compliance and comprehension in very young toddlers. *Child Development, 61,* 1997–2003.

Kalmar, M. (1996). The course of intellectual development in preterm and fullterm children: An 8–year longitudinal study. *International Journal of Behavioral Development, 19*(3), 491–516.

Kanazawa, T., Shimizu, S., Kamada, J., Tanabe, H., & Itoigawa, N. (1997). Intelligence and learning disabilities in 6– to

8–year-old children weighing under 1,000 grams at birth. *International Journal of Behavioral Development, 20*(1), 179–188.

Kaplan, P. S., Bachorowski, J., & Zarlengo-Strouse, P. (1999). Child-directed speech produced by mothers with symptoms of depression fails to promote associative learning in 4–month-old infants. *Child Development, 70*(3), 560–570.

Kaplan, P. S., Dungan, J. K., & Zinser, M. C. (2004). Infants of Chronically Depressed Mothers Learn in Response to Male, But Not Female, Infant-Directed Speech. *Developmental Psychology, 40*(2), 140–148.

Kapoor, S. K., Amand, K., & Kumar, G. (1994). Risk factors for stillbirths in a secondary level hospital at Ballabgarh, Haryana: A case control study. *Indian Journal of Pediatrics, 61,* 161–166.

Karcew, S. (1994). Fetal consequences and risks attributed to the use of prescribed and over-the-counter (OTC) preparations during pregnancy. *International Journal of Clinical Pharmacological Therapy, 32,* 335–343.

Karlson, E. W., Mandl, L. A., Hankinson, S. E., & Grodstein, F. (2004). Do breast-feeding and other reproductive factors influence future risk of rheumatoid arthritis? Results from the Nurses' Health Study. *Arthritis Rheum, 50*(11), 3458–3467.

Karmel, M. (1959). *Thank you, Doctor Lamaze: A mother's experiences in painless childbirth.* Philadelphia: Lippincott.

Karmiloff-Smith, A. (2007). Atypical epigenesis. *Developmental Science, 10*(1), 84–88.

Karns, J. T. (2001). Health, nutrition, and safety. In J. G. Bremner & A. Fogel (Eds.), *Handbook of infant development* (pp. 438–460). Oxford, England: Blackwell.

Karr-Morse, R., & Wiley, M. S. (1997). *Ghosts from the nursery: Tracing the roots of violence.* New York: Atlantic Monthly Press.

Karrer, R., Monti, L., & Ackles, P. K. (1989, October). *Late ERP's of one-month-old infants in a visual oddball task.* Presented at the Society for Psychophysiological Research, New Orleans.

Karzon, R. G. (1985). Discrimination of polysyllabic sequences by one- to four-month-old infants. *Journal of Experimental Child Psychology, 39,* 326–342.

Kataria, S., Frutiger, A. D., Lanford, B., & Swanson, M. S. (1988). Anterior fontanel closure in healthy term infants. *Infant Behavior and Development, 11,* 229–233.

Katz, V. L., & Kuller, J. A. (1994). Recurrent miscarriage. *American Journal of Perinatology, 11,* 386–387.

Kaufman, R., & Adam, E. (2002). Findings in female offspring of women exposed in utero to diethylstilbestrol. *Obstetrics And Gynecology, 99*(2), 197–200.

Kaufmann, R., & Kaufmann, F. (1980). The face schema in 3– and 4–month-old infants: The role of dynamic properties of the face. *Infant Behavior and Development, 3,* 331–339.

Kavšek, M. (2004). Predicting later IQ from infant visual habituation and dishabituation: A meta-analysis. *Journal of Applied Developmental Psychology, 25*(3), 369–393.

Kawakami, K., Takai-Kawakami, K., Kurihara, H., Shimizu, Y., & Yanaihara, T. (1996). The effect of sounds on newborn infants under stress. *Infant Behavior and Development, 19,* 375–379.

Kaye, K. (1977). Toward the origin of dialogue. In H. R. Schaffer (Ed.), *Studies in mother-infant interaction* (pp. 75–120). New York: Academic Press.

Kaye, K. (1982). *The mental and social life of babies.* Chicago: University of Chicago Press.

Kaye, K., & Fogel, A. (1980). The temporal structure of face-to-face communication between mothers and infants. *Developmental Psychology, 16,* 454–464.

Kaye, K., & Marcus, J. (1978). Imitation over a series of trials without feedback. *Infant Behavior and Development, 1,* 141–155.

Kaye, K., & Wells, A. J. (1980). Mother's jiggling and the burst-pause pattern of neonatal feeding. *Infant Behavior and Development, 3,* 29–46.

Kedar, Y., Casasola, M., & Lust, B. (2006). Getting There Faster: 18– and 24–Month-Old Infants' Use of Function Words to Determine Reference. *Child Development, 77*(2), 325–338.

Keith-Speigel, P. (1983). *Children and consent to participate in research.* In G. B. Melton & M. J. Saks (Eds.), *Children's competence to consent* (pp. 179–211). New York: Plenum Press.

Keller, A., Ford, L. H., & Meacham, J. A. (1978). Dimensions of self-concept in preschool children. *Developmental Psychology, 14,* 483–489.

Keller, H., Chasiotis, A., Risau-Peters, J., Volker, S., Zach, U., & Restemeier, R. (1996). Psychobiological aspects of infant crying. *Early Development and Parenting, 5*(1), 1–13.

Keller, H., Lohaus, A., Kuensemueller, P., Abels, M., Yovsi, R., Voelker, S., et al. (2004). The Bio-Culture of Parenting: Evidence From Five Cultural Communities. *Parenting: Science and Practice, 4*(1), 25–50.

Keller, H., Yovsi, R., Borke, J., Kartner, J., Jensen, H., & Papaligoura, Z. (2004). Developmental Consequences of Early Parenting Experiences: Self-Recognition and Self-Regulation in Three Cultural Communities. *Child Development, 75*(6), 1745–1760.

Keller, M. A., & Goldberg, W. A. (2004). Co-Sleeping: Help or Hindrance for Young Children's Independence? *Infant and Child Development, 13*(5), 369–388.

Kelley, M. L., Smith, T. S., Green, A. P., Berndt, A. E., & Rogers, M. C. (1998). Importance of fathers' parenting to African-American toddler's social and cognitive development. *Infant Behavior and Development, 21*(4), 733–744.

Kelly, D. J., Quinn, P. C., Slater, A. M., Lee, K., Gibson, A., Smith, M., et al. (2005). Three-month-olds, but not newborns, prefer own-race faces. *Developmental Science, 8*(6), F31–F36.

Kelly, J. F., & Booth, C. L. (2002). The early child care study of children with special needs. In L. M. Glidden (Ed.), *International review of research in mental retardation, Vol 25* (pp. 71–106). San Diego, CA: Academic Press.

Kellman, P., & Spelke, E. (1983). Perception of partly occluded objects in infancy. *Cognitive Psychology, 15,* 483–494.

Kemper, T. L., & Bauman, M. L. (1993). The contribution of neuropathologic studies to the understanding of autism. *Neurological Clinics, 11,* 175–187.

Kendrick, C., & Dunn, J. (1980). Caring for a second baby: Effects on interaction between mother and firstborn. *Developmental Psychology, 16,* 303–311.

Kennedy, D., & Koren, G. (1998). Valproic acid use in psychiatry: Issues in treating women of reproductive age. *Journal of Psychiatry and Neuroscience, 23*(4), 223–228.

Kennedy, K. I., Fortney, J. A., Bonhomme, M. G., Potts, M., Lamptey, P., & Carswell, W. (1990). Do the benefits of breastfeeding outweigh the risk of postnatal transmission of HIV via breastmilk? *Tropical Doctor, 20,* 25–29.

Kent, R. D. (1981). Articulatory-acoustic perspectives on speech development. In R. Stark (Ed.), *Language development in infancy and early childhood* (pp. 105–106). New York: Elsevier.

Kermoian, R., & Campos, J. J. (1988). Locomotor experience: A facilitator of spatial cognitive development. *Child Development, 59,* 908–917.

Kern, M. E. (2008). Why do siblings often turn out very differently? . In A. Fogel, B. J. King, & S. Shanker (Eds.). *Human development in the 21st century: Visionary policy ideas from systems scientists.* Cambridge, UK: Cambridge University Press.

Kesmodel, U., Wisborg, K., Olsen, S. F., Henriksen, T. B., & Secher, N. J. (2002). Moderate alcohol intake in pregnancy and the risk of spontaneous abortion. *Alcohol and Alcoholism, 37*(1), 87–92.

Kessen, W., Haith, M., & Salapatek, P. (1970). Human infancy: A bibliography and guide. In P. H. Mussen (Ed.), *Carmichael's manual of child psychology* (3rd ed., pp. 808–856). New York: Wiley.

Kestenberg-Amighi, J. (2004). Contact and connection: A cross-cultural look at parenting styles in Bali and the United States. *Zero to Three, 24,* 32–40.

Ketting, E., & Visser, A. P. (1994). Contraception in the Netherlands: The low abortion rate explained. *Patient and Educational Counseling, 23,* 161–171.

Kiely, M., Drum, M. A., & Kessel, W. (1998). Early discharge: Risks, benefits, and who decides. *Clinical Perinatology, 25,* 539–553.

Kier, C. A., & Lewis, C. N. (1993). Sibling attachment: The development of a new infant-based measure (SPPIR). *Early Development and Parenting, 2,* 243–246.

Kilbride, H. W., Johnson, D. L., & Streissguth, A. P. (1977). Social class, birth order, and newborn experience. *Child Development, 48,* 1686–1688.

Killen, M., & Wainryb, C. (2000). Independence and interdependence in diverse cultural contexts. In S. Harkness & C. Raeff (Eds.), *Variability in the social construction of the child. New directions for child and adolescent development* (No. 87, pp. 5–21). San Francisco: Jossey-Bass, Inc.

Kisilevsky, B., Hains, S., Jacquet, A., Granier-Deferre, C., & Lecanuet, J. (2004). Maturation of fetal responses to music. *Developmental Science, 7*(5), 550–559.

Kisilevsky, B. S., Hains, S. M. J., Lee, K., Muir, D. W., Xu, F., Fu, G., Zhao, Z. Y., & Yang, R. L. (1998). The still-face effect in Chinese and Canadian 3– to 6–month-old infants. *Developmental Psychology, 34*(4), 629–639.

Kisilevsky, B., Hains, S., Lee, K., Xie, X., Huang, H., Ye, H., et al. (2003). Effects of experience on fetal voice recognition. *Psychological Science, 14*(3), 220–224.

Kisilevsky, B. S., & Muir, D. W. (1984). Neonatal habituation and dishabituation to tactile stimulation during sleep. *Developmental Psychology, 20,* 367–373.

Klaus, M. H., Kennell, J. H., Plumb, N., & Zeuhlke, S. (1970). Human maternal behavior at the first contact with her young. *Pediatrics, 46,* 187–192.

Klein, B. P. (1985). Caregiving arrangements by employed women with children under a year of age. *Developmental Psychology, 21*(3), 403–406.

Klein, P. S., Feldman, R., & Zarur, S. (2002). Mediation in a sibling context: The relations of older siblings' mediating behavior and younger siblings' task performance. *Infant and Child Development, 11*(4), 321–333.

Klein, R. P., & Durfee, J. T. (1976). Effects of stress on attachment behavior in infants. *Journal of Genetic Psychology, 132,* 321–322.

Kleitman, N. (1963). *Sleep and wakefulness.* Chicago: University of Chicago Press.

Klerman, L. V., & Goldenberg, R. L. (1999). Prenatal care: A new perspective. *Zero to Three, 19*(4), 3–8.

Klimes-Dougan, B., & Kopp, C. B. (1999). Children conflict tactics with mothers: A longitudinal investigation of the toddler and preschool years. *Merrill-Palmer Quarterly, 45*(2), 226–241.

Klinnert, M. D. (1984). The regulation of infant behavior by maternal facial expression. *Infant Behavior and Development, 7,* 447–465.

Klinnert, M. D., Emde, R. N., Butterfield, P., & Campos, J. J. (1986). Social referencing: The infant's use of emotional signals from a friendly adult with mother present. *Developmental Psychology, 22,* 427–432.

Klinnert, M. D., Gavin, L. A., Wamboldt, F. S., & Mrazek, D. A. (1992). Marriages with children at medical risk: The transition to parenthood. *Journal of the American Academy of Child and Adolescent Psychiatry, 31*(2), 334–342.

Kloeblen-Tarver, A., Thompson, N., & Miner, K. (2002). Intent to breast-feed: The impact of attitudes, norms, parity, and experience. *American Journal of Health Behavior, 26*(3), 182.

Klopfer, P. (1988). Metaphors for development: How important are experiences early in life? *Developmental Psychobiology, 21,* 671–678.

Knickmeyer, R., Baron-Cohen, S., Raggatt, P., Taylor, K., & Hackett, G. (2006). Fetal testosterone and empathy. *Hormones & Behavior, 49*(3), 282–292.

Knickmeyer, R., Baron-Cohen, S., Raggatt, P., & Taylor, K. (2005). Foetal testosterone, social relationships, and restricted interests in children. *Journal of Child Psychology and Psychiatry, 46*(2), 198–210.

Kochanska, G., Coy, K. C., Tjebkes, T. L., & Husarek, S. J. (1998). Individual differences in emotionality in infancy. *Child Development, 69*(2), 375–390.

Kochanska, G., Forman, D. R., & Coy, K. C. (1999). Implications of the mother-child relationship in infancy for socialization in the second year of life. *Infant Behavior and Development, 22*(2), 249–265.

Kochanska, G., Friesenborg, A. E., Lange, L. A., & Martel, M. M. (2004). Parents' Personality and Infants' Temperament as Contributors to Their Emerging Relationship. *Journal of Personality and Social Psychology, 86*(5), 744–759.

Kochanska, G., Tjebkes, T. L., & Forman, D. R. (1998). Children's emerging regulation of conduct: Restraint, compliance, and internalization from infancy to the second year. *Child Development, 69*(5), 1378–1389.

Koepke, J. E., & Bigelow, A. E. (1997). Observations of newborn suckling behavior. *Infant Behavior and Development, 20*(1), 93–98.

Koepke, J. E., Hamm, M., Legerstee, J., & Russell, M. (1983). Neonatal imitation: Two failures to replicate. *Infant Behavior and Development, 6,* 97–102.

Koester, L. S. (1994). Early interactions and the socioemotional development of deaf infants. *Early Development and Parenting, 3,* 51–60.

Koester, L. S., Brooks, L., & Traci, M. A. (2000). Tactile contact by deaf and hearing mothers during face-to-face interactions with their infants. *Journal of Deaf Studies and Deaf Education, 5*(2), 127–139.

Kogan, N., & Carter, A. S. (1996). Mother-infant reengagement following the still-face: The role of maternal emotion availability in infant affect regulation. *Infant Behavior and Development, 19,* 359–370.

Kojima, H. (1986). Becoming nurturant in Japan: Past and present. In A. Fogel & G. F. Melson (Eds.), *Origins of* nurturance: *Developmental, biological, and cultural perspectives on caregiving* (pp. 359–376). Hillsdale, NJ: Erlbaum.

Kolbert, K., & Miller, A. (1994). Government in the examining room. Restrictions on the provision of abortion. *Journal of Medical Women's Association, 49,* 153–155.

Konner, M. (1975). Relations among infants and juveniles in comparative perspective. In M. Lewis & L. A. Rosenblum (Eds.), *Friendship and peer relations* (pp. 108–140). New York: Wiley.

Konner, M. (1977). Infancy among the Kalahari Desert San. In P. H. Leiderman, S. R. Tulkin, & A. Rosenfeld (Eds.), *Culture and infancy* (pp. 680–699). New York: Academic Press.

Kontos, S., Howes, C., Shinn, M., & Galinsky, E. (1997). Children's experience in family child care and relative care as a function of family income and ethnicity. *Merrill-Palmer Quarterly, 43*(3), 386–403.

Koomen, H. M. Y., & Hoeksma, J. B. (1992). Maternal interactive behavior towards children with and children without cleft lip and palate. *Early Development and Parenting, 1,* 169–181.

Koops, W. (1996). Historical developmental psychology: The sample case of paintings. *International Journal of Behavioral Development,* 19(2), 393–413.

Kopp, C. B. (1982). Antecedents of self-regulation: A developmental perspective. *Developmental Psychology, 18,* 199–214.

Kopp, C. B. (1989). Regulation of distress and negative emotions: A developmental view. *Developmental Psychology, 25,* 343–354.

Kopp, C. B., & Vaughn, B. E. (1982). Sustained attention during exploratory manipulation as a predictor of cognitive competence in preterm infants. *Child Development, 53,* 174–182.

Korn, S. J., Chess, S., & Fernandez, P. (1978). The impact of children's physical handicaps on marital quality and family interaction. In R. M. Lerner & G. B. Spanier (Eds.), *Child influences on marital and family interaction* (pp. 285–308). New York: Academic Press.

Korner, A. (1987). Preventive intervention with high-risk newborns: Theoretical, conceptual, and methodological perspectives. In J. D. Osofsky (Ed.), *Handbook of infant development* (2nd ed. pp. 503–534). New York: Wiley.

Korner, A., Brown, B. W., Reade, E. P., Stevenson, D. K., Fernbach, S. A., & Thom, V. A. (1988). State behavior of preterm infants as a function of development, individual and sex differences. *Infant Behavior and Development, 11,* 111–124.

Kornfeld, J. R. (1971). Theoretical issues in child phonology. *Proceedings of the Seventh Annual Meeting of the Chicago Linguistics Society* (pp. 454–468). Chicago: University of Chicago Press.

Kornhaber, A., & Woodward, K. L. (1981). *Grandparent/grandchild: The vital connection.* Garden City, NY: Anchor Press.

Korte, D., & Scaer, R. (1990). *A good birth, a safe birth.* New York: Bantam.

Kotch, J. B., & Cohen, S. R. (1986). SIDS counselors' reports of own and parents' reactions to reviewing the autopsy report. *Omega Journal of Death and Dying, 16,* 129–139.

Kozer, E., Nikfar, S., Costei, A., Boskovic, R., Nulman, I., & Koren, G. (2002). Aspirin consumption during the first trimester of pregnancy and congenital anomalies: a meta-analysis. *Am J Obstet Gynecol, 187*(6), 1623–1630.

Krafchuk, E. E., Tronick, E., & Clifton, R. K. (1983). Behavioral and cardiac responsiveness to sound in preterm neonates varying in risk status: A hypothesis of their paradoxical reactivity. In T. Field & A. Sostek (Eds.), *Infants born at risk* (pp. 144–164). New York: Grune & Stratton.

Kramer, L., & Gottman, J. M. (1992). Becoming a sibling: "With a little help from my friends." *Developmental Psychology, 28,* 685–699.

Kramer, L., Perozynski, L. A., & Chung, T. Y. (1999). Parental responses to sibling conflict: The effects of development and parent gender. *Child Development, 70*(6), 1401–1414.

Kravitz, H., Goldenberg, D., & Neyhus, A. (1978). Tactual exploration by normal infants. *Developmental Medicine and Child-Neurology, 20*(6), 720–726.

Kremenitzer, J. P., Vaughan, H. G., Jr., Kurtzberg, D., & Dowling, K. (1979). Smooth-pursuit eye movements in the newborn infant. *Child Development, 50,* 442–448.

Kreppner, J. M., Rutter, M., Beckett, C., Castle, J., Colvert, E., Groothues, C., et al. (2007). Normality and impairment following profound early institutional deprivation: A longitudinal follow-up into early adolescence. *Developmental Psychology, 43*(4), 931–946.

Kretchmar, M. D., & Jacobvitz, D. B. (2002). Observing mother-child relationships across generations: Boundary patterns, attachment and the transmission of caregiving. *Family Process, 41*(3), 351–374.

Kropp, J. P., & Haynes, O. M. (1987). To identify general and specific emotion signals of infants. *Child Development, 58,* 187–190.

Kuchuk, A., Vibbert, M., & Bornstein, M. H. (1986). The perception of smiling and its experiential correlates in three-month-old infants. *Child Development, 57,* 1054–1061.

Kuczaj, S. A. (1978). Children's judgements of grammatical and ungrammatical irregular past-tense verbs. *Child Development, 49,* 319–326.

Kuczaj, S. A., & Maratsos, M. P. (1983). Initial verbs of yes-no questions: A different kind of general grammatical category. *Developmental Psychology, 19,* 440–444.

Kuczynski, L., & Kochanska, G. (1995). Function and content of maternal demands: Developmental significance of early demands for competent action. *Child Development, 66,* 616–628.

Kuczynski, L., Zahn-Waxler, C., & Radke-Yarrow, M. (1987). Development and content of imitation in the second and third years of life: A socialization perspective. *Developmental Psychology, 23,* 276–282.

Kuhl, P. K. (1981). Auditory category formation and developmental speech perception. In R. Stark (Ed.), *Language behavior in infancy and early childhood* (pp. 155–170). New York: Elsevier.

Kuhl, P. K. (1998). Language, culture, and intersubjectivity: The creation of shared perception. In S. Br;araten (Ed.), *Intersubjective communication and emotion in early ontogeny. Studies in emotion and social interaction, 2nd series* (pp. 297–315). Cambridge, England: Cambridge University Press.

Kulin, N. A., Pastuszk, A., Sage, S. R., Schick-Boschetto, B., Spivey, G., Feldkamp, M., Ormond, K., Matsui, D., Stein-Schechman, A. K., Cook, L., Brochu, J., Rieder, M., & Koren, G. (1998). Pregnancy outcome following maternal use of the new selective serotonin reuptake inhibitors. *Journal of the American Medical Association, 279,* 609–610.

Kuller, J. A., & Katz, V. L. (1994). Miscarriage: A historical perspective. *Birth, 21,* 227–228.

Kumar, T. C. (1994). The value and use of different contraceptive methods. *Human Reproduction, 9,* 578–585.

Kumari, A. S. (2001). Pregnancy outcome in women with morbid obesity. *Int J Gynaecol Obstet, 73*(2), 101–107.

Kurzweil, S. R. (1988). Recognition of mother from multisensory interactions in early infancy. *Infant Behavior and Development, 11,* 235–243.

Laakso, M. L., Poikkeus, A. M., & Lyytinen, P. (1999). Shared reading interaction in families with and without genetic risk for dyslexia: Implications for toddlers' language development. *Infant and Child Development, 8,* 179–195.

Labrell, F. (1994). A typical interaction behavior between fathers and toddlers: Teasing. *Early Development and Parenting, 3,* 125–130.

Laible, D. J., & Thompson, R. A. (2002). Mother-child conflict in the toddler years: Lessons in emotion, morality, and relationships. *Child Development, 73*(4), 1187–1203.

Lamb, M. E. (1977). The development of mother-infant and father-infant attachments in the second year of life. *Developmental Psychology, 13,* 637–648.

Lamb, M. E. (1978a). Influences of the child on marital quality and family interaction during the prenatal, perinatal and infancy periods. In R. M. Lerner & G. B. Spanier (Eds.), *Child influences on marital and family interaction* (pp. 259–289). New York: Academic Press.

Lamb, M. E. (1978b). Interactions between eighteen-month-olds and their preschool-aged siblings. *Child Development, 49,* 51–59.

Lamb, M. E. (1978c). Qualitative aspects of mother- and father-infant attachments. *Infant Behavior and Development, 1,* 265–277.

Lamb, M. E., & Bornstein, M. H. (1987). *Development in infancy* (2nd ed.). New York: Random House.

Lamb, M. E., Frodi, A. M., Frodj, M., & Hwang, C. P. (1982). Characteristics of maternal and paternal behavior in traditional and nontraditional Swedish families. *International Journal of Behavior and Development, 5,* 131–141.

Lamb, M. E., Gaensbauer, T. J., Malkin, C. M., & Schultz, L. A. (1985). The effects of child maltreatment on security of infant-adult attachment. *Infant Behavior and Development, 8,* 35–45.

Lamb, M. E., Pleck, J. H., Charnov, E. L., & Levine, J. A. (1987). A biosocial perspective on paternal behavior and involvement. In J. B. Lancaster, A. Rossi, J. Altmann, & L. R. Sherrod (Eds.), *Parenting across the lifespan: Biosocial perspectives* (pp. 66–87). Chicago: Aldine.

Lamb, M. E., Sternberg, K. J., & Prodromidis, M. (1992). Nonmaternal care and the security of infant-mother attachment: A reanalysis of the data. *Infant Behavior and Development, 15,* 71–83.

Lamb, M. E., Thompson, R., Gardner, W., Charnov, E., & Estes, D. (1984). Security of infantile attachment as assessed in the strange situation: Its study and biological interpretation. *Behavioral and Brain Sciences, 7,* 127–147.

Lambie, G. W. (2005). Child Abuse and Neglect: A Practical Guide for Professional School Counselors. *Professional School Counseling, 8*(3), 249–258.

Lampert, R. W., & Schochet, S. S. (1968). Demyelination and remyelination in lead neuropathy. *Journal of Neuropathology and Experimental Neurology, 27,* 527–545.

Landau, B., & Spelke, E. (1988). Geometric complexity and object search in infancy. *Developmental Psychology, 24,* 512–521.

Landesman-Dwyer, S. (1981). Maternal drinking and pregnancy outcome. *Applied Research in Mental Retardation, 3,* 241–263.

Landry, S. H. (1995). The development of joint attention in premature low birth weight infants: Effects of early medical complications and maternal attention-directing behaviors. In C. Moore & P. J. Dunham (Eds.), *Joint attention: Its origins and role in development* (pp. 223–250). Hillsdale, NJ: Erlbaum.

Landry, S. H., & Chapieski, M. L. (1989). Joint attention and infant toy exploration: Effects of Down's syndrome and prematurity. *Child Development, 60,* 103–118.

Landry, S. H., Chapieski, M. L., & Schmidt, M. (1986). Effects of maternal attention-directing strategies on preterms' response to toys. *Infant Behavior and Development, 9,* 257–269.

Landry, S. H., Garner, P. W., Swank, P. R., & Baldwin, C. D. (1996). Effects of maternal scaffolding during joint toy play with preterm and full-term infants. *Merrill-Palmer Quarterly, 42*(2), 177–199.

Landry, S. H., Smith, K. E., Miller-Loncar, C. L., & Swank, P. R. (1997). Predicting cognitive-language and social growth curves from early maternal behaviors in children at varying degrees of biological risk. *Developmental Psychology, 33*(6), 1040–1053.

Landry, S. H., Smith, K. E., Miller-Loncar, C. L., & Swank, P. R. (1998). The relation of change in maternal interactive styles to the developing social competence of full-term and preterm children. *Child Development, 69*(1), 105–123.

Landry, S. H., Smith, K. E., & Swank, P. R. (2006). Responsive Parenting: Establishing Early Foundations for Social, Communication, and Independent Problem-Solving Skills. *Developmental Psychology, 42*(4), 627–642.

Langkamp, D. L., & Harris, S. (1992). Predicting preschool motor and cognitive performance in appropriate-for-gestational-age children born at 32 weeks gestation. *Early Development and Parenting, 1,* 89–96.

Langlois, J. H., Ritter, J. M., Casey, R. J., & Sawin, D. B. (1995). Infant attractiveness predicts maternal behaviors and attitudes. *Developmental Psychology, 31,* 464–472.

Langlois, J. H., Ritter, J. M., Roggman, L. A., & Vaughn, L. S. (1991). Facial diversity and infant preferences for attractive faces. *Developmental Psychology, 27,* 79–84.

Langlois, J. H., Roggman, L. A., Casey, R. J., Ritter, J. M., Rieser-Danner, L. S., & Jenkins, V. Y. (1987). Infant preferences for attractive faces: Rudiments of a stereotype? *Developmental Psychology, 23,* 363–369.

Laplante, D. P., Zelazo, P. R., Brunet, A., & King, S. (2007). Functional play at 2 years of age: Effects of prenatal maternal stress. *Infancy, 12*(1), 69–93.

Largo, R. H. (1993). Early motor development in preterm children. In G. J. P. Savelsbergh (Ed.), *The development of coordination in infancy* (pp. 425–444). Amsterdam: Elsevier.

Larsson, I., & Svedin, C. G. (2002). Teachers' and parents' report on 3- to 6-year-old children's sexual behavior--a comparison. *Child Abuse & Neglect, 26*(3), 247–266.

Laughlin, C. D. (1991). Pre- and perinatal brain development and enculturation: A biogenetic structural approach. *Human Nature, 2,* 171–213.

Lavelli, M. & Fogel, A. (2002). Developmental changes in mother-infant face-to-face communication: Birth to 3 months. *Developmental Psychology, 38,* 288–305.

Lavelli, M. & Fogel, A. (2005). Developmental changes in the relationship between infant's attention and emotion during early face-to-face communication: The 2–month transition. *Developmental Psychology, 41,* 265–280.

Lavelli, M., & Poli, M. (1998). Early mother-infant interaction during breast- and bottle-feeding. *Infant Behavior and Development, 21*(4), 667–684.

Law, K. L., Stroud, L. R., LaGasse, L. L., Niaura, R., Liu, J., & Lester, B. M. (2003). Smoking during pregnancy and newborn neurobehavior. *Pediatrics, 111*(6 Pt 1), 1318–1323.

Lawrence, A., Lewis, L., Hofmeyr, G. J., Dowswell, T., & Styles, C. (2009). Maternal positions and mobility during first stage labour, *Cochrane Database of Systematic Reviews,* CD003934; 2

Lawson, K. R., Parrinello, R., & Ruff, H. A. (1992). Maternal behavior and infant attention. *Infant Behavior and Development, 15,* 209–229.

Lawson, K. R., & Ruff, H. A. (1984). Infants' visual following: The effects of size and sound. *Developmental Psychology, 20,* 427–434.

Lazar, I., & Darlington, R. (1982). Lasting effects of early education: A report from the Consortium for Longitudinal Studies. *Monographs of the Society for Research in Child Development, 47* (Serial No. 195), 1–151.

Leach, P. (1997). Infant care from infants' viewpoint: The views of some professionals. *Early Development and Parenting, 6*(2), 47–58.

Leadbeater, B. J., Bishop, S. J., & Raver, C. C. (1996). Quality of mother-toddler interactions, maternal depressive symptoms, and behavior problems in preschoolers of adolescent mothers. *Developmental Psychology, 32*(2), 280–288.

Leboyer, F. (1975). *Birth without violence.* New York: Knopf.

Lecanuet, J.-P., Granier-Deferre, C., Jacquet, A.-Y., Capponi, I., & Ledru, L. (1993). Prenatal discrimination of a male and a female voice uttering the same sentence. *Early Development and Parenting, 2,* 217–228.

Lee, C., & Bates, J. (1985). Mother-child interaction at age two years and perceived difficult temperament. *Child Development, 56,* 1314–1325.

Lee, K. T., Mattson, S. N., & Riley, E. P. (2004). Classifying children with heavy prenatal alcohol exposure using measures of attention. *Journal of the International Neuropsychological Society, 10*(2), 271–277.

Lee, M., Vernon-Feagans, L., Vazquez, A., & Kolak, A. (2003). The Influence of Family Environment and Child Temperament on Work/Family Role Strain for Mothers and Fathers. *Infant and Child Development, 12*(5), 421–439.

Lee, S., Ralston, H., Drey, E., Partridge, J., & Rosen, M. (2005). Fetal pain: a systematic multidisciplinary review of the evidence. *JAMA: The Journal Of The American Medical Association, 294*(8), 947–954.

Lee, V. E., Brooks-Gunn, J., & Schnur, E. (1988). Does Head Start work? A 1–year follow-up comparison of disadvantaged children attending Head Start, no preschool, and other preschool programs. *Developmental Psychology, 24,* 210–222.

Lee, V. E., Brooks-Gunn, J., Schnur, E., & Liaw, F. R. (1990). Are Head Start effects sustained? A longitudinal follow-up comparison of disadvantaged children attending

Head Start, no preschool, and other preschool programs. *Child Development, 61,* 495–507.

Lefebvre, F., Bard, H., Veilleux, A., & Martel, C. (1988). Outcome at school age of children with birth weights of 1,000 grams or less. *Developmental Medicine and Child Neurology, 30*(2), 170–180.

Leftwich, M., & Collins, F. (1994). Parental smoking, depression, and child development. *Journal of Pediatric Psychology, 19,* 557–569.

Leger, D. W., Thompson, R. A., Merritt, J. A., & Benz, J. J. (1996). Adult perception of emotion intensity in human infant cries: Effects of infant age and cry acoustics. *Child Development, 67,* 3238–3249.

Legerstee, M. (1991). Changes in the quality of infant sounds as a function of social and nonsocial stimulation. *First Language, 11,* 327–343.

Legerstee, M. (1992). A review of the animate-inanimate distinction in infancy: Implications for models of social and cognitive knowing. *Early Development and Parenting, 1,* 59–67.

Legerstee, M. (1997). Contingency effects of people and objects on subsequent cognitive functioning in three-month-old infants. *Social Development, 6*(3), 307–321.

Legerstee, M., & Bowman, T. G. (1989). The development of responses to people and a toy in infants with Down's syndrome. *Infant Behavior and Development, 12,* 465–477.

Legerstee, M., Pomerleau, A., Malcuit, G., & Feider, H. (1987). The development of infants' responses to people and a doll: Implications for research in communication. *Infant Behavior and Development, 10,* 81–95.

Legerstee, M., & Varghese, J. (2001). The role of maternal affect mirroring on social expectancies in three-month-old infants. *Child Development, 72*(5), 1301–1313.

Legerstee, M., & Weintraub, J. (1997). The integration of person and object attention in infants with and without Down syndrome. *Infant Behavior and Development, 20*(1), 71–82.

Le Goff, J. (1987). *The medieval world.* (L. G. Cochrane, Trans.). London, England: Collins and Brown.

Leiberman, A. F. (1977). Preschoolers' competence with a peer: Relations with attachment and peer experience. *Child Development, 48,* 1277–1287.

Leifer, G. (1999). *Thompson's introduction to maternity and pediatric nursing (3rd ed.)* Philadelphia: Saunders.

Leifer, J. S., & Lewis, M. (1983). Maternal speech to normal and handicapped children: A look at question-asking behavior. *Infant Behavior and Development, 6,* 175–187.

Leifer, M. (1980). *Psychological effects of motherhood: A study of first pregnancy.* New York: Praeger.

Leitch, D. B. (1999). Mother-infant interaction: Achieving synchrony. *Nursing Research, 48*(1), 55–58.

Lelorde, G., Barthelemy, C., Martineau, J., & Bruneau, N. (1991). Free acquisition, free imitation, physiological curiosity and exchange and development therapies in autistic children. *Brain Dysfunction, 4,* 335–347.

Lemche, E., Kreppner, J. M., Joraschky, P., & Klann-Delius, G. (2007). Attachment organization and the early development of internal state language: A longitudinal perspective. *International Journal of Behavioral Development, 31*(3), 252–262.

Lemery, K. S., & Goldsmith, H. H. (1999). Genetically informative designs for the study of behavioral development. *International Journal of Behavioral Development, 23*(2), 293–317.

Lemery, K. S., Goldsmith, H. H., Klinnert, M. D., & Mrazek, D. A. (1999). Developmental models of infant and childhood temperament. *Developmental Psychology, 35*(1), 189–204.

Lemmer, C. M. (1987). Early discharge: Outcomes in primiparas and their infants. *Journal of Obstetric and Gynecological Nursing,* 230–236.

Lempers, J. D., Flavell, E. R., & Flavell, J. H. (1977). The development in very young children of tacit knowledge concerning visual perception. *Genetic Psychology Monographs, 95,* 3–53.

Lenneberg, E. H. (1969). On explaining language. *Science, 164,* 635–643.

Leonard, R. (1993). Mother-child disputes as arenas for fostering negotiation skills. *Early Development and Parenting, 2,* 157–167.

Lesko, W., & Leski, M. (1984). *The maternity sourcebook.* New York: Warner Books.

Leslie, G. I., Gibson, F. L., McMahon, C., Tennant, C., & Saunders, D. M. (1998). Infants conceived using in-vitro fertilization do not over-utilize health care resources after the neonatal period. *Human Reproduction, 13*(8), 2055–2059.

Lester, B. M. (2005). *Why is my baby crying: The parents' survival guide for coping with crying problems and colic.* NY: Harper.

Lester, B. M., Boukydis, Z. C. F., Garcia-Coll, C. T., Hole, W., & Peucker, M. (1992). Infantile colic: Acoustic cry characteristics, maternal perception of cry, and temperament. *Infant Behavior and Development, 15,* 15–26.

Lester, B. M., & Dreher, M. (1989). Effects of marijuana use during pregnancy on newborn cry. *Child Development, 60,* 765–771.

Leung, E., & Rheingold, H. L. (1981). Development of pointing as a social gesture. *Developmental Psychology, 17,* 215–220.

Levitt, M. J., Weber, R. A., & Clark, M. C. (1986). Social network relationships as sources of maternal support and well-being. *Developmental Psychology, 22,* 310–316.

Levitt, P., Reinoso, B., & Jones, L. (1998). The critical impact of early cellular environment on neuronal development. *Preventive Medicine, 27*(2), 180–183.

Levy, G., & Haaf, R. A. (1994). Detection of gender-related categories by 10–month-old infants. *Infant Behavior and Development, 17,* 457–459.

Levy, H. L., Karolkewicz, V., Houghton, S. A., & MacCready, R. A. (1970). Screening the "normal" population in Massachusetts for phenylketonuria. *New England Journal of Medicine, 282,* 1455–1458.

Levy, T. M. (Ed). (2000). *Handbook of attachment interventions.* San Diego, CA: Academic Press.

Levy, Y. (1999). Early metalinguistic competence: Speech monitoring and repair behavior. *Developmental Psychology, 35*(3), 822–834.

Levy-Shiff, R. (1994). Individual and contextual correlates of marital change across the transition to parenthood. *Developmental Psychology, 30,* 591–601.

Levy-Shiff, R., Dimitrovsky, L., Shulman, S., & Har-Even, D. (1998). Cognitive appraisals, coping strategies, and support resources as correlates of parenting and infant development. *Developmental Psychology, 34*(6), 1417–1427.

Levy-Shiff, R., Goldschmidt, I., & Har-Even, D. (1991). Transition to parenthood in adoptive families. *Developmental Psychology, 27,* 131–140.

Levy-Shiff, R., Sharir, H., & Mogilner, M. B. (1989). Mother- and father–preterm infant relationship in the hospital preterm nursery. *Child Development, 60,* 93–102.

Lew, A. R., & Butterworth, G. (1995). The effects of hunger on hand-mouth coordination in newborn infants. *Developmental Psychology, 31,* 456–463.

Lewis, B. A., Singer, L. T., Short, E. J., Minnes, S., Arendt, R., Weishampel, P., et al. (2004). Four-year language outcomes of children exposed to cocaine in utero. *Neurotoxicol Teratol, 26*(5), 617–627.

Lewis, C., Kier, C., Hyder, C., Prenderville, N., Pullen, J., & Stephens, A. (1996). Observer influences on fathers and mothers: An experimental manipulation of the structure and function of parent-Infant conversation. *Early Development and Parenting, 5*(1), 57–68.

Lewis, M. (1995). Embarrassment: The emotion of self-exposure and evaluation. In J. P. Tangney & K. W. Fischer (Eds.) *Self-conscious emotions: The psychology of shame, guilt, embarrassment, and pride* (pp. 198–218). New York: Guilford Press.

Lewis, M. (2005). The Child and Its Family: The Social Network Model. *Human Development, 48*(1–2), 8–27.

Lewis, M., Alessandri, S. M., & Sullivan, M. W. (1992). Differences in shame and pride as a function of children's gender and task difficulty. *Child Development, 63,* 630–638.

Lewis, M., & Brooks-Gunn, J. (1979). *Social cognition and the acquisition of self.* New York: Plenum Press.

Lewis, M., & Feiring, C. (1978). The child's social world. In R. M. Lerner & G. B. Spanier (Eds.), *Child influences on marital and family interaction* (pp. 119–150). New York: Academic Press.

Lewis, M., & Feiring, C. (1989). Infant, mother, and mother-infant interaction behavior and subsequent attachment. *Child Development, 60,* 831–837.

Lewis, M., & Michalson, L. (1983). *Children's emotions and moods.* New York: Plenum Press.

Lewis, M., & Ramsay, D. S. (1995). Developmental change in infants' responses to stress. *Child Development, 66,* 657–670.

Lewis, M., & Ramsay, D. (2004). Development of self-recognition, personal pronoun use, and pretend play during the 2nd year. *Child Development, 75*(6), 1821–1831.

Lewis, M., Stanger, C., & Sullivan, M. W. (1989). Deception in 3–year-olds. *Developmental Psychology, 25,* 439–443.

Lewis, M., Sullivan, M. W., Ramsay, D. S., & Alessandri, S. M. (1992). Individual differences in anger and sad expressions during extinction: Antecedents and consequences. *Infant Behavior and Development, 15,* 443–452.

Lewis, M., Sullivan, M. W., Stanger, C., & Weiss, M. (1989). Self development and self-conscious emotions. *Child Development, 60,* 146–156.

Lewis, M., Young, G., Brooks, J., & Michalson, L. (1975). The beginning of friendship. In M. Lewis & L. Rosenblum (Eds.), *Friendship and peer relations* (pp. 305–341). New York: Wiley.

Lewis, M. D. (1993). Emotion-cognition interactions in early infant development. *Cognition and Emotion, 7,* 145–170.

Lewis, M. D. (1995). Cognition-emotion feedback and the self-organization of developmental paths. *Human Development, 38* (2), 71 102.

Lewis, M. D. (1993). Early socioemotional predictors of cognitive competency at 4 years. *Developmental Psychology, 29,* 1036–1045.

Lewis, M. D. (2008). Emotional habits of brain and behavior: A window on personality development. . In A. Fogel, B. J. King, & S. Shanker (Eds.). *Human development in the 21st century: Visionary policy ideas from systems scientists.* Cambridge, UK: Cambridge University Press.

Lewis, M. D., Koroshegyi, C., Douglas, L., & Kampe, K. (1997). Age-specific associations between emotional responses to separation and cognitive performance in infancy. *Developmental Psychology, 33*(1), 32–42.

Lewis, M. D., Lamey, A. V., & Douglas, L. (1999). A new dynamic systems method for the analysis of early socio emotional development. *Developmental Science, 2*(4), 457–475.

Lewis, M. D., & Ramsay, D. S. (1997). Stress reactivity and self-recognition. *Child Development, 68*(4), 621–629.

Lewis, S. E., & Nicolson, P. (1998). Talking about early motherhood: Recognizing loss and reconstructing depression. *Reproductive and Infant Psychology, 16,* 177–197.

Lewit, E. M., & Baker, L. S. (1995). Unintentional injuries. *Future of Children, 5,* 214–231.

Lewit, E. M., Baker, L. S., Corman, H., & Shiono, P. H. (1995). The direct cost of low birth weight. *Future of Children, 5,* 35–56.

Lewkowicz, D. J. (1988). Sensory dominance in infants: 1. Six-month-old infants' response to auditory-visual compounds. *Developmental Psychology, 24,* 155–171.

Lewkowicz, D. J. (1994). Limitations on infants' response to rate-based auditory-visual relations. *Development Psychology, 30,* 880–892.

Lewkowicz, D. J. (1996). Infants' response to the audible and visible properties of the human face: 1. Role of the lexical-syntactic content, temporal synchrony, gender, and manner of speech. *Developmental Psychology, 32*(2), 347–366.

Ley, R. G., & Koepke, J. E. (1982). Attachment behavior out of doors: Naturalistic observations of sex and age differences in the separation behavior of young children. *Infant Behavior and Development, 5,* 195–201.

L'Hoir, M., Westers, P., König, P., Visser, A., Guedeke, M., & Wolters, W. (1994). Parental management of infants born following a cot-death victim who were monitored compared to infants who, despite similar histories, were not monitored: A controlled study. *European Journal of Pediatrics, 153,* 694–699.

Li, R., Zhao, Z., Mokdad, A., Barker, L., & Grummer-Strawn, L. (2003). Prevalence of breastfeeding in the United States: the 2001 National Immunization Survey. *Pediatrics, 111*(5 Part 2), 1198–1201.

Liaw, F., & Brooks-Gunn, J. (1993). Patterns of low-birthweight children's cognitive development. *Developmental Psychology, 29,* 1024–1035.

Lickliter, R. (2008). Developmental dynamics: The new view from the life sciences. In A. Fogel, B. J. King, & S. Shanker (Eds.). *Human development in the 21st century: Visionary policy ideas from systems scientists.* Cambridge, UK: Cambridge University Press.

Lickliter, R., & Hellewell, T. B. (1992). Contextual determinants of auditory learning in Bobwhite quail embryos and hatchlings. *Developmental Psychobiology, 25,* 017–031.

Lieberman, A. B. (1992). *Easing Labor Pain: The Complete Guide to a More Comfortable and Rewarding Birth.* Harvard Common Press: Boston.

Lieberman, A. F. (1995). *Emotional Life of the Toddler.* NY: Free Press.

Lieberman, A. F., Padrón, E., van Horn, P., & Harris, W. W. (2005). Angels in the nursery: The intergenerational transmission of benevolent parental influence. *Infant Mental Health Journal, 26,* 504–520.

Lieberman, A. F., Weston, D. R., & Pawl, J. H. (1991). Preventive intervention and outcome with anxiously attached dyads. *Child Development, 62,* 199–209.

Lieberman, E., Lang, J. M., Frigoletto, F., Richardson, D. K., Ringer, S. A., & Cohen, A. (1997). Epidural analgesia, intrapartum fever, and neonatal sepsis evaluation. *Pediatrics, 99*(3), 415–419.

Lillard, A. S., & Witherington, D. C. (2004). Mothers' Behavior Modifications During Pretense and Their Possible Signal Value for Toddlers. *Developmental Psychology, 40*(1), 95–113.

Lindahl, L. B., & Heimann, M. (1997). Research report: Social proximity in early mother-infant interactions: Implications for gender differences? *Early Development and Parenting, 6*(2), 83–88.

Lindsay, J. A., Johnson, H. M., Wallace, F. M., & Soos, J. M. (1994). Can superantigens trigger sudden infant death? *Medical Hypotheses, 43,* 81–85.

Lindsey, E. W., & Mize, J. (2001). Contextual differences in parent-child play: Implications for children's gender role development. *Sex Roles, 44*(3–4), 155–176.

Lippit, JA. (2001, June/July) Policy and policy making for infants, toddlers, and their families: A primer for practitioners. *Zero to Three,* 4–8

Lipsitt, L. P. (1979a). Infants at risk: Perinatal and neonatal factors. *International Journal of Behavioral Development, 2,* 23–42.

Lipsitt, L. P. (1979b). The pleasures and annoyances of infants: Approach and avoidance behavior. In E. Thoman (Ed.), *The origins of the infant's social responsiveness* (pp. 105–119). Hillsdale, NJ: Erlbaum.

Lipsitt, L. P. (1981). Infant learning. In T. Field, A. Huston, H. Quay, L. Troll, & G. Finley (Eds.), *Review of human development* (pp. 256–279). New York: Wiley.

Lipsitt, L. P., Engen, T., & Kaye, H. (1963). Developmental changes in the olfactory threshold of the neonate. *Child Development, 34,* 371–376.

Lipsitt, L. P., Sturges, W. Q., & Burke, P. (1979). Perinatal indicators and subsequent crib death. *Infant Behavior and Development, 2,* 325–328.

Liptak, G. S., Keller, B. B., Feldman, A. W., & Chamberlain, R. W. (1983). Enhancing infant development and parent practitioner interaction with the Brazelton Neonatal Behavioral Assessment Scale. *Pediatrics, 72,* 71–78.

Little, A. B. (1988). There's many a slip 'twixt implantation and the crib (editorial). *New England Journal of Medicine, 319*(4), 241–242.

Little, J., & Vainio, H. (1994). Mutagenic lifestyles? A review of evidence of associations between germ-cell mutations in humans and smoking, alcohol consumption and use of "recreational" drugs. *Mutation Research, 313,* 131–151.

Lobo, M. A., Galloway, J. C., & Savelsbergh, G. J. P. (2004). General and Task-Related Experiences Affect Early Object Interaction. *Child Development, 75*(4), 1268–1281.

Lock, A. (1980). *The guided reinvention of language.* New York: Academic Press.

Lock, A. (2000). Preverbal communication. In J. G. Bremner & A. Fogel (Eds.), *Handbook of infancy research* (pp. 504–521). Oxford, England: Blackwell.

Locke, J. L. (1979). The child's processing of phonology. In W. A. Collins (Ed.), *Minnesota symposia on child psychology: Vol. 12. Children's language and communication* (pp. 1261–1289). Hillsdale, NJ: Erlbaum.

Locke, J. L. (1993). *The child's path to spoken language.* Cambridge, MA: Harvard University Press.

Lodish, H. F. (1995). Through the glass lightly. *Science, 267,* 1609–1611.

Loehlin, J. C. (1989). Partitioning environmental and genetic contributions to behavioral development. *American Psychologist, 44*(10), 1285–1292.

Loh, C.-C., & Vostanis, P. (2004). Perceived mother-infant relationship difficulties in postnatal depression. *Infant and Child Development, 13*(2), 159–171.

Lollis, S. P. (1990). Effects of maternal behavior on toddler behavior during separation. *Child Development, 61,* 99–103.

Lorenz, K. Z. (1952). The comparative method in studying innate behavior. *Symposium of the Society for Experimental Biology, 41,* 221–268.

Lorenz, K. Z. (1965). *Evolution and modification of behavior.* Chicago: University of Chicago Press.

Losoya, S. H., Callor, S., Rowe, D. C., & Goldsmith, H. H. (1997). Origins of familial similarity in parenting: A study of twins and adoptive siblings. *Developmental Psychology, 33*(6), 1012–1023.

Louik, C., Lin, A., Werler, M., Hernández-Díaz, S., & Mitchell, A. (2007). First trimester use of selective serotonin reuptake inhibitors and the risk of birth defects. *New England Journal of Medicine, 356*(26), 2675–2683.

Lounsbury, M. L., & Bates, J. E. (1982). The cries of infants of differing levels of temperamental difficultness: Acoustic properties and effects on listeners. *Child Development, 53,* 677–686.

Love, J. M., Harrison, L., Sagi-Schwartz, A., Van Ijzendoorn, M. H., Ross, C., Ungerer, J. A., et al. (2003). Child Care Quality Matters: How Conclusions May Vary With Context. *Child Development, 74*(4), 1021–1033.

Lowinger, S. (1999). Infant irritability and early mother-infant reciprocity patterns. *Infant and Child Development, 8*(2), 71–84.

Lozoff, B. (1998). Explanatory mechanisms for poorer development in iron deficient anemic infants. In *Nutrition, health, and child development* (Pan-American Health Organization Scientific Monograph No. 566) (pp. 1–89). Washington, DC: Pan-American Health Organization.

Lozoff, B., Klein, N. K., Nelson, E. C., McClish, D. K., Manual, M., & Chacon, M. E. (1998). Behavior of infants with iron-deficiency anemia. *Child Development, 69*(1), 24–36.

Lu, M. C. & Lu, J. S. (2007). Maternal nutrition and infant mortality in the context of relationality. Washington, DC: The joint center for political and economic studies health policy institute, www.jointcenter.org.

Lubic, R. W. (1999). Giving birth is powerful! *Zero to Three, 19*(4), 20–24.

Luby, J. L., Heffelfinger, A. K., Mrakotsky, C., Brown, K. M., Hessler, M. J., Wallis, J. M., et al. (2003). The clinical picture of depression in preschool children. *J Am Acad Child Adolesc Psychiatry, 42*(3), 340–348.

Ludemann, P. M. (1991). Generalized discrimination of positive facial expressions by seven- and ten-month-old infants. *Child Development, 62,* 55–67.

Ludemann, P. M., & Nelson, C. A. (1988). Categorical representation of facial expressions by 7–month-old infants. *Developmental Psychology, 24,* 492–501.

Ludington-Hoe, S. M., & Swinth, J. (1996). Developmental aspects of kangaroo care. *Journal of Obstetric, Gynecologic, and Neonatal Nursing, 25*(8), 691–703.

Ludwig, J., & Phillips, D. (2007). The benefits and costs of Head Start. *Social Policy Report, 21*(3), 3–19.

Lundy, B. L., Jones, N. A., Field, T., Nearing, G., Davalos, M., Pietro, P. A., Schanberg, S., & Kuhn, C. (1999). Prenatal depression effects on neonates. *Infant Behavior and Development, 22*(1), 119–129.

Lunt, R., & Law, D. (1974). A review of the chronology of eruption of deciduous teeth. *Journal of the American Dental Association, 89,* 872–879.

Lupe, P. J., & Gross, T. L. (1986). Maternal upright posture and mobility in labor: A review. *Obstetrics and Gynecology, 67*(5), 727–734.

Lyons, S. (1998). A prospective study of post traumatic stress symptoms 1 month following childbirth in a group of 42 first-time mothers. *Reproductive and Infant Psychology, 16,* 91–105.

Lyons, S. J., Henly, J. R., & Schuerman, J. R. (2005). Informal support in maltreating families: Its effect on parenting practices. *Children and Youth Services Review, 27*(1), 21–38.

Lyons-Ruth, K., Alpern, L., & Repacholi, B. (1993). Disorganized infant attachment classification and maternal psychosocial problems as predictors of hostile-aggressive behavior in the preschool classroom. *Child Development, 64,* 572–585.

Lyons-Ruth, K., Bronfman, E., & Parsons, E. (1999). Maternal frightened, frightening, or atypical behavior and disorganized infant attachment patterns. *Monographs of the Society for Research in Child Development, 64*(3), 67–96.

Lyons-Ruth, K., Connell, D. B., Grunebaum, H. U., & Botein, S. (1990). Infants at social risk: Maternal depression and family support services as mediators of infant development and security of attachment. *Child Development, 61,* 85–98.

Lyons-Ruth, K., Easterbrooks, M. A., & Cibelli, C. D. (1997). Infant attachment strategies, infant mental lag, and maternal depressive symptoms: Predictors of internalizing and externalizing problems at age 7. *Developmental Psychology, 33*(4), 681–692.

Lyra, M., & Ferreira, M. (1987, August). *Dialogue and the construction of the mother-infant dyad.* Paper presented at the International Society for Behavioral Development Conference, Tokyo, Japan.

Lyra, M. C., & Rossetti-Ferreira, M. C. (1995). Transformation and construction in social interaction: A new perspective on analysis of the mother-infant dyad. In J. Valsiner (Ed.), *Child development within culturally structured environments (Vol. 3). Comparative-cultural and co-constructionist perspectives* (pp. 316–351). Norwood, NJ: Ablex.

MacCallum, F., Golombok, S., & Brinsden, P. (2007). Parenting and child development in families with a child conceived through embryo donation. *Journal of Family Psychology, 21*(2), 278–287.

MacFarlane, A. (1975). Olfaction in the development of social preferences in the human neonate. In Ciba Foundation Symposium (Ed.), *Parent-infant interaction* (pp. 605–617). New York: Elsevier.

Mackner, L. M., Black, M. M., & Starr, R. H., Jr. (2003). Cognitive development of children in poverty with failure to thrive: A prospective study through age 6. *Journal of Child Psychology and Psychiatry, 44*(5), 743–751.

Madden, M. E. (1994). The variety of emotional reactions to miscarriage. *Journal of Women's Health, 21,* 85–104.

Madigan, S., Goldberg, S., Moran, G., & Pederson, D. R. (2004). Naive observers' perceptions of family drawings by 7–year-olds with disorganized attachment histories. *Attachment & Human Development, 6*(3), 223–239.

Madigan, S., Moran, G., & Pederson, D. R. (2006). Unresolved states of mind, disorganized attachment relationships, and disrupted interactions of adolescent mothers and their infants. *Developmental Psychology, 42*(2), 293–304.

Madsen, M. C., & Shapira, A. (1970). Cooperative and competitive behavior of urban Afro-American, Anglo-American, Mexican-American, and Mexican village children. *Developmental Psychology, 3,* 16–20.

Magid, K., & McKelvey, C. A. (1987). *High risk: Children without a conscience.* New York: Bantam.

Mahler, M., Pine, F., & Bergman, A. (1975). *The psychological birth of the human infant.* New York: Basic Books.

Main, M., & Cassidy, J. (1988). Categories of response to reunion with the parent at age 6: Predictable from infant attachment classifications and stable over a 1–month period. *Developmental Psychology, 24,* 415–426.

Main, M., & George, C. (1985). Responses of abused and disadvantaged toddlers to distress in agemates: A study in the day care setting. *Developmental Psychology, 21,* 407–412.

Main, M., Kaplan, N., & Cassidy, J. (1985). Security in infancy, childhood, and adulthood: A move to the level of representation. In I. Bretherton & E. Waters (Eds.), Growing points of attachment theory and research. *Monographs of the Society for Research in Child Development, 50* (Serial No. 209), 66–104.

Main, M., & Solomon, J. (1986). Discovery of an insecure disorganized/disoriented attachment pattern: Procedures, findings, and implications for the classification of behavior. In M. Yogman & T. B. Brazelton (Eds.), *Affective development in infancy* (pp. 95–124). Norwood, NJ: Ablex.

Main, M., & Weston, D. R. (1981). The quality of the toddler's relationship to mother and father: Related to conflict behavior and the readiness to establish new relationships. *Child Development, 52,* 932–940.

Malatesta, C. Z., Culver, C., Tesman, J. R., & Shepard, B. (1989). The development of emotion expression during the first two years of life. *Monographs of the Society for Research in Child Development, 54* (Serial No. 219), 1–104.

Malatesta, C. Z., Grigoryev, P., Lamb, C., Albin, M., & Culver, C. (1986). Emotion socialization and expressive development in preterm and full-term infants. *Child Development, 57,* 316–330.

Malatesta, C. Z., & Haviland, J. M. (1982). Learning display rules: The socialization of emotion expression in infancy. *Child Development, 53,* 991–1003.

Malatesta-Magai, C., Leak, S., Tesman, J., Shepard, B., Culver, C., & Smaggia, B. (1994). Profiles of emotional development: Individual differences in facial and vocal expression of emotion during the second and third years of life. *International Journal of Behavioral Development, 17,* 239–269.

Malphurs, J. E., Raag, T., Field, T., Pickens, J., & Nogueras-Pelaez, M. (1996). Touch by intrusive and withdrawn mothers with depressive symptoms. *Early Development and Parenting, 5*(2), 111–115.

Mandell, F., McAnulty, E., & Reece, R. M. (1980). Observations of paternal response to sudden unanticipated infant death. *Pediatrics, 65,* 221–225.

Mandler, J. M., & McDonough, L. (1998). On developing a knowledge base in infancy. *Developmental Psychology, 34*(6), 1274–1288.

Mandy, A., Gard, P. R., Ross, K., & Valentine, B. H. (1998). Psychological sequelae in women following either parturition or non-gynecological surgery. *Reproductive and Infant Psychology, 16,* 133–141.

Mangelsdorf, S. C. (1992). Developmental changes in infant-stranger interaction. *Infant Behavior and Development, 15,* 191–208.

Mangelsdorf, S. C., Plunkett, J. W., Dedrick, C. F., Berlin, M., Meisels, S. J., McHale, J. L., & Dichtellmiller, M. (1996). Attachment security in very low birth weight infants. *Developmental Psychology, 32*(5), 914–920.

Maratsos, M., Kuczaj, S., Fox, D., & Chalkley, M. (1979). Some empirical studies in the acquisition of transformational relations: Passives, negatives, and the past tense. In W. A. Collins (Ed.), *Minnesota symposia on child psychology: Vol. 12. Children's language and communication* (pp. 1242–1260). Hillsdale, NJ: Erlbaum.

March of Dimes (2009). Medical Costs for One Premature Baby Could Cover A Dozen Healthy Births. http://www.marchofdimes.com/aboutus/49267_55250.asp (retrieved January 3, 2010).

Marcos, H. (1995). Mother-child and father-child communication in the second year: A functional approach. *Early Development and Parenting, 4,* 49–61.

Marcos, H., & Chanu, M. K. (1992). Learning how to insist and clarify in the second year: Reformulation of requests in different contexts. *International Journal of Behavioral Development, 15,* 359–376.

Marcos, H., & Verba, M. (1990, April). *Referential communication with adults and infants in the second year.* Paper presented at the International Conference on Infant Studies, Montreal, Canada.

Marcovitch, S., Goldberg, S., Gold, A., & Washington, J. (1997). Determinants of behavioural problems in Romanian children adopted in Ontario. *International Journal of Behavioral Development, 20*(1), 17–31.

Marcovitch, S., & Zelazo, P. D. (1999). The a-not-b error: Results from a logistic meta-analysis. *Child Development, 70*(6), 1297–1313.

Marcovitch, S., Zelazo, P. D., & Schmuckler, M. A. (2002). The effect of the number of A trials on performance on the A-not-B task. *Infancy, 3*(4), 519–529.

Marcus, G. F., Pinker, S., Ullman, M., & Hollander, M. (1992). Overregularization in language acquisition. *Monographs of the Society for Research in Child Development, 57*(4), 1–182.

Markman, H. J., & Kadushin, F. S. (1986). Preventive effects of Lamaze training for first-time parents. A short-term longitudinal study. *Journal of Consulting Clinical Psychology, 54*(6), 872–874.

Marlier, L., Schaal, B., & Soussignan, R. (1998a). Bottle-fed neonates prefer an odor experienced in utero to an odor experienced postnatally in the feeding context. *Developmental Psychobiology, 33*(2), 133–145.

Marlier, L., Schaal, B., & Soussignan, R. (1998b). Neonatal responsiveness to the odor of amniotic and lacteal fluids: A test of perinatal chemosensory continuity. *Child Development, 69*(3), 611–623.

Martin, R. P., Noyes, J., Wisenbaker, J., & Huttunen, M. O. (1999). Prediction of early childhood negative emotionality and inhibition from maternal distress during pregnancy. *Merrill-Palmer Quarterly, 45*(3), 370–391.

Martin, S. L., Harris-Britt, A., Li, Y., Moracco, K. E., Kupper, L. L., & Campbell, J. C. (2004). Changes in Intimate Partner Violence During Pregnancy. *Journal of Family Violence, 19*(4), 201–210.

Martinez-Frias, M. L., Rodriguez-Pinilla, E., Bermejo, E., & Prieto, L. (1998). Prenatal exposure to sex hormones: A case-control study. *Teratology, 57*(1), 8–12.

Martini, M., & Kirkpatrick, J. (1981). Early interactions in Marquesas islands. In T. M. Field, A. M. Sostek, P. Vietze, & P. H. Leiderman (Eds.), *Culture and early interactions.* Hillsdale, NJ: Erlbaum.

Marvin, R., Cooper, G., Hoffman, K. & Powell, B. (2002). The Circle of Security project: Attachment-based intervention with caregiver–pre-school child dyads. *Attachment & Human Development, 4,* 107–124.

Masataka, N. (1992). Motherese in a signed language. *Infant Behavior and Development, 15,* 453–460.

Masataka, N. (1999). Preference for infant-directed singing in 2–day-old hearing infants of deaf parents. *Developmental Psychology, 35*(4), 1001–1005.

Mascolo, M. F., & Fischer, K. W. (1995). Development transformations in appraisals for pride, shame, and guilt. In J. P. Tangney & K. W. Fischer (Eds.), *Self-conscious emotions: The psychology of shame, guilt, embarrassment, and pride* (pp. 64–113). New York: Guilford Press.

Masur, E. F. (1993). Transitions in representational ability: Infants' verbal, vocal, and action imitation during the second year. *Merrill-Palmer Quarterly, 39,* 437–456.

Masur, E. F., & Rodemaker, J. E. (1999). Mothers' and infants' spontaneous vocal, verbal, and action imitation during the second year. *Merrill-Palmer Quarterly, 45*(3), 392–412.

Matas, L., Arend, R. A., & Sroufe, L. A. (1978). Continuity of adaptation in the second year: The relationship between quality of attachment and later competence. *Child Development, 49,* 547–556.

Matheny, A. P., Jr., Wilson, R. S., & Thoben, A. S. (1987). Home and mother: Relations with infant temperament. *Developmental Psychology, 23,* 323–331.

Mathews, T. J., Menacker, F., & MacDorman, M. F. (2002). Infant mortality statistics from the 2000 period linked birth/infant death data set. *Natl Vital Stat Rep, 50*(12), 1–28.

Matias, R., & Cohn, J. E. (1993). Are max-specified infant facial expressions during face-to-face interaction consistent with differential emotions theory? *Developmental Psychology, 29,* 524–531.

Maton, K., & Bishop-Josef, S. (2006). Psychological Research, Practice, and Social Policy: Potential Pathways of Influence. *Professional Psychology: Research & Practice, 37*(2), 140–145.

Maughan, B., Taylor, A., Caspi, A., & Moffitt, T. E. (2004). Prenatal Smoking and Early Childhood Conduct Problems: Testing Genetic and Environmental

Explanations of the Association. *Archives of General Psychiatry, 61*(8), 836–843.

Maun, A. R., Williams, R. S., Graber, B., & Myers, W. G. (1994). The passage of Florida's statute on assisted reproductive technology. *Obstetrics and Gynecology, 84,* 889–893.

Maurer, D. (1985). Infants' perception of facedness. In T. M. Field & N. A. Fox (Eds.), *Social perception in infants* (pp. 73–100). Norwood, NJ: Ablex.

Maurer, D., & Salapatek, P. (1976). Developmental changes in the scanning of faces by young infants. *Child Development, 47,* 523–527.

Mauthner, N. S. (1998). Re-assessing the importance and role of the marital relationship in postnatal depression: Methodological and theoretical implications. *Reproductive and Infant Psychology, 16,* 157–175.

Mayberry, R. I., Lock, E., & Kazmi, H. (2002). Linguistic ability and early language exposure. *Nature, 417*(6884), 38.

Mayer, S., & Musatti, T. (1992). Towards the use of symbol: Play with objects and communication with adults and peers in the second year. *Infant Behavior and Development, 15,* 1–13.

Mayes, L. C., Carter, A. S., & Stubbe, D. (1993). Individual differences in exploratory behavior in the second year of life. *Infant Behavior and Development, 16,* 269–284.

Mayes, L. C., Feldman, R., Granger, R. H., Haynes, O. M., Bornstein, M. H., & Schottenfeld, R. (1997). The effects of polydrug use with and without cocaine on mother-infant interaction at 3 and 6 months. *Infant Behavior and Development, 20*(4), 489–502.

Mayes, L. C., & Kessen, M. (1989). Maturational changes in measures of habituation. *Infant Behavior and Development, 12,* 437–450.

Maziade, M., Boudreault, M., Cote, R., & Thivierge, J. (1986). Influence of gentle birth delivery procedures an other perinatal circumstances on infant temperament: Developmental and social implications. *The Journal of Pediatrics, 108,* 134–136.

McBride-Chang, C., & Kail, R. V. (2002). Cross-cultural similarities in the predictors of reading acquisition. *Child Development, 73*(5), 1392–1407.

McCalin, M., & Mandell, F. (1994). Sudden infant death syndrome: The nurse counselor's response to bereavement counseling. *Journal of Community Health Nursing, 11,* 177–186.

McCall, R. B., & Carriger, M. S. (1993). A meta-analysis of infant habituation and recognition memory performance as predictors of later IQ. *Child Development, 64,* 57–79.

McCarty, M. E., Clifton, R. K., & Collard, R. R. (1999). Problem solving in infancy: The emergence of an action plan. *Developmental Psychology, 35*(4), 1091–1101.

McCarty, M. E., Clifton, R. K., & Collard, R. R. (2001). The beginnings of tool use by infants and toddlers. *Infancy, 2*(2), 233–256.

McClearn, G. E. (1970). Genetic influences on behavior and development. In P. H. Mussen (Ed.), *Child psychology* (3rd ed., Vol. 1). New York: Wiley.

McClure, V. S. (1989). *Infant massage: A handbook for loving parents.* New York: Bantam Books.

McConkie, R. A., & Iafolla, A. K. (1993). Medium-chain acyl CoA dehydrogenase deficiency: Its relationship to SIDS and the impact on genetic counseling. *Journal of Genetic Counseling, 2,* 17–27.

McCormick, C. M., & Maurer, D. M. (1988). Unimanual hand preferences in 6–month-olds: Consistency and relation familial-handedness. *Infant Behavior and Development, 11,* 21–29.

McCune, L. (1989, April). *Toward an integrative theory of early language acquisition: Evidence from longitudinal trends in vocal behavior.* Paper presented at the biennial meeting of the Society for Research in Child Development, Kansas City, MO.

McCune, L. (1995). A normative study of representational play at the transition to language. *Developmental Psychology, 31,* 198–206.

McCune-Nicholich, L. (1981). Toward symbolic functioning: Structure of early pretend games and potential parallels with language. *Child Development, 52,* 785–797.

McDonald, D. (1978). Paternal behavior at first contact with the newborn in a birth environment without intrusions. *Birth and the Family Journal, 5,* 123–132.

McDonald, M. A., Sigman, M., Espinosa, M. P., & Neumann, C. G. (1994). Impact of temporary food shortage on children and their mothers. *Child Development, 65*(2), 404–415.

McDonald, R., & Avery, D. (1983). *Dentistry for the child and adolescent* (4th ed.). St. Louis, MO: Mosby.

McDonnell, P. M., Anderson, V. E. S., & Abraham, W. C. (1983). Asymmetry and orientation of arm movements in three- to eight-week-old infants. *Infant Behavior and Development, 6,* 287–298.

McDonough, L., & Mandler, J. M. (1998). Inductive generalization in 9– and 11–month-olds. *Developmental Science, 1*(2), 227–232.

McElwain, N. L., Cox, M. J., Burchinal, M. R., & Macfie, J. (2003). Differentiating among insecure mother-infant attachment classifications: A focus on child-friend interaction and exploration during solitary play at 36 months. *Attachment & Human Development, 5*(2), 136–164.

McElwain, N. L., & Volling, B. L. (2004). Attachment security and parental sensitivity during infancy: Associations with friendship quality and false-belief understanding at age 4. *Journal of Social and Personal Relationships, 21*(5), 639–667.

McFarlane (2004*).* Elective cesarean birth: Issues and ethics of an informed decision *Journal of Midwifery & Women's Health, 49*(5), 421–429.

McGlaughlin, A., & Grayson, A. (1999). A prospective study of crying during the first year of infancy. *Journal of Reproductive and Infant Psychology, 17*(1), 41–52.

McGraw, M. B. (1935). *Growth: A study of Johnny and Jimmy.* New York: Appleton.

McGuire, J. (1988). Gender stereotypes of parents with two-year-olds and beliefs about gender differences in behavior. *Sex Roles, 19,* 233–240.

McIntosh, J. R., & Koonce, M. P. (1989). Mitosis. *Science, 246,* 622–628.

McKee, J. (1974). Selections from "Two legs to stand on." In J. Milgram & D. Sciarra (Eds.), *Childhood revisited* (pp. 41–55). New York: Macmillan. (Original work published 1955)

McKenna, J. J. (1987). An anthropological perspective on the sudden infant death syndrome: A testable hypothesis of the possible role of parental breathing cues in promoting infant breathing stability: I. *Pre- and Perinatal Psychology Journal, 2,* 93–135.

McKenna, J. J. (1988). An anthropological perspective on the sudden infant death syndrome: The neurological and structural bases of speech breathing and why SIDS appears to be a species-specific malady: II. *Pre- and Perinatal Psychology Journal, 2,* 149–178.

McKenna, J. J., & Mosko, S. (1994). Sleep and arousal, synchrony and independence, among mothers and infants sleeping apart and together (same bed): An experiment in evolutionary medicine. *Acta Paediatricia Supplement, 397,* 94–102.

McKenna, J. J., Mosko, S., Richard, C., Drummond, S., Hunt, L., Cetel, M. D., & Arpaia, J. (1994). Experimental studies of infant-parent co-sleeping: Mutual physiological and behavioral influences and their relevance to SIDS (sudden infant death syndrome). *Early Human Development, 38,* 187–201.

McKenna, J. J., & Volpe, L. E. (2007). Sleeping with baby: an internet-based sampling of parental experiences, choices, perceptions, and interpretations in a western industrialized context. *Infant and Child Development, 16*(4), 359–385.

McKenzie, B., & Over, R. (1983). Young infants fail to imitate facial and manual gestures. *Infant Behavior and Development, 6,* 85–95.

McKenzie, B. E., Skouteris, H., Day, R. H., Hartman, B., & Yonas, A. (1993). Effective action by infants to contact objects by reaching and leaning. *Child Development, 64,* 415–429.

McKenzie, B. E., Tootell, H. E., & Day, R. H. (1980). Development of visual size constancy during the first year of human infancy. *Developmental Psychology, 16,* 163–174.

McKim, M. K. (1987). Transition to what? New parents' problems in the first year. *Family Relations Journal of Applied Family and Child Studies, 36,* 22–25.

McLaughlin, B. (1983). Child compliance to parental control techniques. *Developmental Psychology, 19,* 667–673.

McLoyd, V. C. (1990). The impact of economic hardship on black families and children: Psychological distress, parenting, and socio-emotional development. *Child Development, 61,* 311–346.

McLoyd, V. C. (1998). Socioeconomic disadvantage and child development. *American Psychologist, 53*(2), 185–204.

McLoyd, V. C., & Wilson, L. (1991). The strain of living poor: Parenting, social support, and child mental health. In A. C. Huston (Ed.), *Children in poverty: Child development and public policy* (pp. 105–135). New York: Cambridge University Press.

McMahon, C. A., Tennant, C., Ungerer, J., & Saunders, D. (1999). Don't count your chickens: A comparative study of the experience of pregnancy after IVF conception. *Journal of Reproductive and Infant Psychology, 17*(4), 345–356.

McNeill, D. (1970). *The acquisition of language.* New York: Harper & Row.

McPherson, M. G. (1983). Improving services to infants and young children with handicapping conditions and their families: The Division of Maternal and Child Health as collaborator. *Zero to Three, 4,* 1–6.

McShane, J. (1980). *Learning to talk.* Cambridge, England: Cambridge University Press.

McTurk, R. H., McCarthy, M. E., Vietze, P. M., & Yarrow, L. J. (1987). Sequential analysis of mastery behavior in 6- to 12-month-old infants. *Developmental Psychology, 23,* 199–203.

Mead, M., & Newton, N. (1967). Cultural patterning of perinatal behavior. In S. Richardson & A. Guttmacher (Eds.), *Childbearing: Its social and psychological aspects* (pp. 76–104). Baltimore: Williams & Wilkins.

Mead, R. (1999, August 9). Annals of reproduction: Eggs for sale. *The New Yorker, 75,* 56–65.

Meade, C. S., & Ickovics, J. R. (2005). Systematic review of sexual risk among pregnant and mothering teens in the USA: Pregnancy as an opportunity for integrated prevention of STD and repeat pregnancy. *Social Science & Medicine, 60*(4), 661–678.

Meadow-Orlans, K. P., & Spencer, P. E. (1996). Maternal sensitivity and the visual attentiveness of children who are deaf. *Early Development and Parenting, 5*(4), 213–223.

Meares, R., Grimwalde, J., & Wood, C. (1976). A possible relationship between anxiety in pregnancy and puerperal depression. *Journal of Psychosomatic Research, 20,* 605–610.

Meder, A. (1989). Effects of hand-rearing on the behavioral development of infant and juvenile gorillas. *Developmental Psychobiology, 22,* 357–376.

Meer, A. L. H. van der, Weel, F. R. van der, & Lee, D. N. (1995). The functional significance of arm movements in neonates. *Science, 267,* 693–696.

Mehl, L., Peterson, G., Sokolsky, W., & Whitt, M. (1976). Outcomes of early discharge after normal birth. *Birth and the Family Journal, 3,* 101–107.

Meijer, A. M., & van den Wittenboer, G. L. H. (2007). Contribution of Infants' Sleep and Crying to Marital Relationship of First-Time Parent Couples in the 1st Year After Childbirth. *Journal of Family Psychology, 21*(1), 49–57.

Meins, E., Fernyhough, C., Russell, J., & Clark-Carter, D. (1998). Security of attachment as a predictor of symbolic and mentalising abilities: A longitudinal study. *Social Development, 7*(1), 1–24.

Melson, G. (1980). *The family as an ecosystem.* New York: Burgess.

Melson, G., & Cohen, A. (1981). Contextual influences on children's activity: Sex differences in effects of peer presence and interpersonal attraction. *Genetic Psychology Monographs, 103,* 243–260.

Melson, G., & Fogel, A. (1982). Young children's interest in unfamiliar infants. *Child Development, 53,* 693–700.

Melson, G., & Fogel, A. (1988, March). The development of nurturance in young children. *Young Children,* 57–65.

Melson, G., Fogel, A., & Toda, S. (1986). Children's ideas about infants and their care. *Child Development, 57,* 1519–1527.

Melson, G., Hsu, H. C., & Ladd, G. W. (1993). The parental support networks of mothers and fathers: A multidimensional approach. *Early Development and Parenting, 2,* 169–182.

Meltzoff, A. (1988). Infant imitation and memory: Nine-month-olds in immediate and deferred tests. *Child Development, 59,* 217–225.

Meltzoff, A., & Moore, M. K. (1989). Imitation in newborn infants: Exploring the range of gestures imitated and the underlying mechanisms. *Developmental Psychology, 25,* 954–962.

Meltzoff, A., & Moore, M. K. (1994). Imitation, memory, and the representation of persons. *Infant Behavior and Development, 17,* 83–99.

Meltzoff, A., & Moore, M. K. (1997). Explaining facial imitation: A theoretical model. *Early Development and Parenting, 6*(1), 179–192.

Meltzoff, A., & Moore, W. (1977). Imitation of facial and manual gestures by human neonates. *Science, 198,* 75–78.

Mennella, J. A. (1997). A cross-cultural perspective. *Nutrition Today, 32*(4), 144–151.

Mennella, J. & Beauchamp, G. (1993). Early flavor experiences: When do they start? *Zero to Three, 14*(2), 1–7.

Mennella, J., Jagnow, C., & Beauchamp, G. (2001). Prenatal and postnatal flavor learning by human infants. *Pediatrics, 107*(6), E88–E88.

Mercer, R. T., Ferketich, S., May, K., DeJoseph, J., & Sollid, D. (1988). Further exploration of maternal and paternal fetal attachment. *Research in Nursing and Health, 11,* 83–95.

Meredith, H. (1975). Somatic changes during human pre-natal life. *Child Development, 46,* 603–610.

Messer, D. J., Rachford, D., McCarthy, M. E., & Yarrow, L. J. (1987). Assessment of mastery behavior at 30 months: Analysis of task-directed activities. *Developmental Psychology, 23*(6), 771–781.

Messinger, D. S., Dolcourt, J., King, J., Bodnar, A., & Beck, D. (1996). The survival and developmental outcome of extremely low birthweight infants. *Infant Mental Health Journal, 17*(4), 375–385.

Messinger, D. S., & Fogel, A. (1998). Give and take: The development of conventional infant gestures. *Merrill-Palmer Quarterly, 44*(4), 566–590.

Messinger, D. S., Fogel, A., & Dickson, K. L. (1998). What's in a smile? *Developmental Psychology, 35*(3), 701–708.

Messinger, D., Fogel, A., & Dickson, K.L. (2001). All smiles are positive, but some smiles are more positive than others. *Developoomental Psychology, 37,* 642–653.

Messinger, D. S. & Lester, B. M. (2008) Prenatal substance exposure and human development. . In A. Fogel, B. J. King, & S. Shanker (Eds.). *Human developoment in the 21st century: Visionary policy ideas from systems scientists.* Cambridge, UK: Cambridge University Press.

Messmer, P. R., Rodriguez, S., Adams, J., Wells-Gentry, J., Washburn, K., Zabaleta, I., & Abreu, S. (1999). Effect of kangaroo care on sleep time for neonates. *Pediatric Nursing, 23*(4), 408–414.

Metosky, P., & Vondra, J. (1995). Prenatal drug exposure and play and coping in toddlers: A comparison study. *Infant Behavior and Development, 18,* 15–25.

Meyer, L., Mailloux, J., Marcoux, S., Blanchett, P., & Meyer, F. (1987). Maternal and neonatal morbidity in instrumental deliveries with the Kobayashi vacuum extractor and low forceps. *Acta Obstetrica et Gynecologica Scandinavica, 66*(7), 643–647.

Meyers, B. J., & Kaltenbach, K. (1992). Cocaine-exposed infants: Myths and misunderstandings. *Zero to Three, 12,* 1–5. Arlington, VA: National Center for Clinical Infant Programs.

Mezulis, A. H., Hyde, J. S., & Clark, R. (2004). Father Involvement Moderates the Effect of Maternal Depression During a Child's Infancy on Child Behavior Problems in Kindergarten. *Journal of Family Psychology, 18*(4), 575–588.

Michaelson, K. L., et al. (1988). *Childbirth in America: Anthropological perspectives.* South Hadley, MA: Bergin & Garvey.

Mick, E., Biederman, J., Faraone, S. V., Sayer, J., & Kleinman, S. (2002). Case-control study of attention-deficit hyperactivity disorder and maternal smoking, alcohol use and drug use during pregnancy. *Journal of the American Academy of Child & Adolescent Psychiatry, 41*(4), 378–385.

Middlemiss, W. (2003). Brief report: Poverty, stress and support. Patterns of parenting behaviour among lower income black and lower income white mothers. *Infant and Child Development, 12*(3), 293–300.

Miebert, C. J. (1991). Dimensions of subjectivity in parents' ratings of infant temperament. *Child Development, 62,* 352–361.

Milewski, A. E. (1976). Infant's discrimination of internal and external pattern elements. Journal of Experimental *Child Psychology, 22,* 229–246.

Miller, M., Bowen, J. R., Gibson, F. L., Hand, P. J., & Ungerer, J. A. (2001). Behaviour problems in extremely low birth-weight children at 5 and 8 years of age. *Child: Care, Health and Development, 27*(6), 569–581.

Miller, P. J., Mintz, J., Hoogstra, L., Fung, H., & Potts, R. (1992). The narrated self: Young children's construction of self in relation to others in conversational stories of personal experience. *Merrill-Palmer Quarterly, 38,* 45–67.

Miller, W. R. (1964). The acquisition of formal features of language. *American Journal of Orthopsychiatry, 34,* 862–867.

Mintzer, D., Als, H., Tronick, E. A., & Brazelton, T. B. (1985). Parenting an infant with a birth defect: The regulation of self-esteem. *Zero to Three, 5,* 1–7.

Mistry, R. S., Biesanz, J. C., Taylor, L. C., Burchinal, M., & Cox, M. J. (2004). Family Income and Its Relation to Preschool Children's Adjustment for Families in the NICHD Study of Early Child Care. *Developmental Psychology, 40*(5), 727–745.

Mitra, S. C., Ganesh, V., & Apuzzio, J. J. (1994). Effect of maternal cocaine abuse on renal arterial flow and urine output of the fetus. *American Journal of Obstetrics and Gynecology, 171,* 1556–1559.

Mix, K. S., Levine, S. C., & Huttenlocher, J. (1997). Numerical abstraction in infants. Another look. *Developmental Psychology, 33*(3), 423–428.

Miyake, K., Chen, S., & Campos, J. J. (1985). Infant temperament, mother's mode of interaction, and attachment in Japan: An interim report. In I. Bretherton & E. Waters (Eds.). *Growing points of attachment theory and research. Monographs of the Society for Research in Child Development, 50* (Serial No. 209), 276–297.

Molfese, V. J., DiLalla, L. F., & Bunce, D. (1997). Prediction of the intelligence test scores of 3 to 8 year old children by home environment, socioeconomic status, and biomedical risks. *Merrill-Palmer Quarterly, 43*(2), 219–234.

Molina, M., & Jouen, F. (1998). Modulation of the palmar grasp behavior in neonates according to texture property. *Infant Behavior and Development, 21*(4), 659–667.

Molnar, G. E. (1978). Analysis of motor disorder in retarded infants and young children. *American Journal of Mental Deficiency, 83,* 213–222.

Moon, C., Cooper, R. P., & Fifer, W. P. (1993). Two-day-olds prefer their native language. *Infant Behavior and Development, 16,* 495–500.

Moore, C., Angelopoulos, M., & Bennett, P. (1997). The role of movement in the development of joint visual attention. *Infant Behavior and Development, 20,* 83–92.

Moore, C., Mealiea, J., Garon, N., & Povinelli, D. J. (2007). The development of body self-awareness. *Infancy, 11*(2), 157–174.

Moore, G. A., Moore, G. A., & Calkins, S. D. (2004). Infants' Vagal Regulation in the Still-Face Paradigm Is Related to Dyadic Coordination of Mother-Infant Interaction. *Developmental Psychology, 40*(6), 1068–1080.

Moore, M. K., & Meltzoff, A. N. (2004). Object Permanence After a 24–Hr Delay and Leaving the Locale of Disappearance: The Role of Memory, Space, and Identity. *Developmental Psychology, 40*(4), 606–620.

Morales, M., Mundy, P., Crowson, M. M., Neal, A. R., & Delgado, C. E. F. (2005). Individual differences in infant attention skills, joint attention, and emotion regulation behaviour. *International Journal of Behavioral Development, 29*(3), 259–263.

Morales, M., Mundy, P., & Rojas, J. (1998). Following the direction of gaze and language development in 6–month-olds. *Infant Behavior and Development, 21*(2), 373–377.

Moran, G., Krupka, A., Tutton, A., & Symons, D. (1987). Patterns of maternal and infant imitation during play. *Infant Behavior and Development, 10,* 477–491.

Morange-Majoux, F., Cognot, P., & Bloch, H. (1997). Hand tactual exploration of textures in infants from 4 to 6 months. *Early Development and Parenting, 6,* 127–135.

Moreno, A., Posada, G., & Goldyn, D. (2006). Presence and quality of touch influence coregulation in mother-infant dyads. *Infancy, 9*(1), 1–20.

Moreno, A. J., Posada, G. E., & Goldyn, D. T. (2006). Presence and quality of touch influence coregulation in mother-infant dyads. *Infancy, 9*(1), 1–20.

Moreno, C., Ardanaz, E., Olivera, J. E., Castilla, J., & de Pedro, C. J. (1994). A temporal-spatial cluster of sudden infant death syndrome in Navarre, Spain. *European Journal of Epidemiology, 10,* 129–134.

Morgan, B., Finan, A., Yarnold, R., Petersen, S., Horsfield, M., Rickett, A., et al. (2002). Assessment of infant physiology and neuronal development using magnetic resonance imaging. *Child Care Health Dev, 28 Suppl 1,* 7–10.

Morrow, C. E., Bandstra, E. S., Anthony, J. C., Ofir, A. Y., Xue, L., & Reyes, M. B. (2003). Influence of prenatal cocaine exposure on early language development: Longitudinal findings from four months to three years of age. *Developmental and Behavioral Pediatrics, 24*(1). pp. 39–50.

Morrongiello, B. A., Fenwick, K. D., & Chance, G. (1990). Sound localization acuity in very young infants: An observer-based testing procedure. *Developmental Psychology, 26,* 75–84.

Morrongiello, B. A., & Rocca, P. T. (1987). Infants' localization of sounds in the horizontal plane: Effects of auditory and visual cues. *Child Development, 58,* 918–927.

Moscardino, U., & Axia, G. (2006). Infants' responses to arm restraint at 2 and 6 months: A longitudinal study. *Infant Behavior & Development, 29*(1), 59–69.

Moscucci, O. (2003). Holistic obstetrics: the origins of "natural childbirth" in Britain. *Postgrad Med J, 79*(929), 168–173.

Mosier, C. E., & Rogoff, B. (1994). Infants' instrumental use of their mothers to achieve their goals. *Child Development, 65,* 70–79.

Moustakas, C. (1994). *Phenomenological research methods.* Thousand Oaks, CA: Sage Publications.

Mueller, E., Bleier, M., Krakow, J., Hegedus, K., & Cournoyer, P. (1977). The development of peer verbal interaction among two-year-old boys. *Child Development, 48,* 284–287.

Mueller, E., & Brenner, J. (1977). The growth of social interaction in a toddler play group: The role of peer experience. *Child Development, 48,* 854–861.

Mueller, E., & Lucas, T. (1975). A developmental analysis of peer interaction among toddlers. In M. Lewis & L. Rosenblum (Eds.), *Friendship and peer relations* (pp. 65–90). New York: Wiley.

Mullen, M., Snidman, N., & Kagan, J. (1993). Free-play behavior in inhibited and uninhibited children. *Infant Behavior and Development, 16,* 383–389.

Mumme, D. L., Fernald, A., & Herrera, C. (1996). Infants' responses to facial and vocal emotional signals in a social referencing paradigm. *Child Development, 67,* 3219–3237.

Munakata, Y. (1997). Perseverative reaching in infancy: The roles of hidden toys and motor history in the AB task. *Infant Behavior and Development, 20*(3), 405–416.

Mundy, P., & Gomes, A. (1998). Individual differences in joint attention skill development in the second year. *Infant Behavior and Development, 21*(3), 469–482.

Mundy, P., Kasari, C., & Sigman, M. (1992). Nonverbal communication, affective sharing, and intersubjectivity. *Infant Behavior and Development,* 15, 377–381.

Munk-Olsen, T., Laursen, T. M., Pedersen, C. B., Mors, O., & Mortensen, P. B. (2006). New parents and mental disorders: a population-based register study. *Jama, 296*(21), 2582–2589.

Munn, P., & Dunn, J. (1989). Temperament and the developing relationship between siblings. *International Journal of Behavioral Development, 12,* 433–451.

Murai, N., Murai, N., & Takahashi, I. (1978). A study of moods in postpartum women. *Tohuku Psychologica Ioliak, 37,* 32–40.

Muris, P. (2006). The pathogenesis of childhood anxiety disorders: Considerations from a developmental psychopathology perspective. *International Journal of Behavioral Development, 30*(1), 5–11.

Murphy, C. M. (1978). Pointing in the context of a shared activity. *Child Development, 49,* 371–380.

Murray, A. D. (1988). Newborn auditory brainstem evoked responses (ABRs): Longitudinal correlates in the first year. *Child Development, 59,* 1542–1554.

Murray, L., Fiori-Cowley, A., Hooper, R., & Cooper, P. (1996). The impact of postnatal depression and associated adversity on early mother-infant interactions and later infant outcomes. *Child Development, 67*(5), 2512–2526.

Murray, L., & Trevarthen, C. (1985). Emotional regulation of interactions between two-month-olds and their mothers. In T. Field & N. Fox (Eds.), *Social perception in infants.* Norwood, NJ: Ablex.

Myers, B. J. (1982). Early intervention using Brazelton training with middle-class mothers and fathers of newborns. *Child Development, 53,* 462–471.

Myers, M., Fifer, W., Grose-Fifer, J., Sahni, R., Stark, R., & Schulze, K. (1997). " A novel quantitative measure of Trace-alternat EEG activity and its association with sleep states of preterm infants." *Developmental Psychobiology, 31,* 167–174.

Myers, B. J., Jarvis, P. A., & Creasey, G. L. (1987). Infants' behavior and their mothers and grandmothers. *Infant Behavior and Development, 10,* 245–259.

Myowa-Yamakoshi, M., & Takeshita, H. (2006). Do Human Fetuses Anticipate Self-Oriented Actions? A Study by Four-Dimensional (4D) Ultrasonography. *Infancy, 10*(3), 289–301.

Nachmias, M., Gunnar, M., Mangelsdorf, S., Parritz, R. H., & Buss, K. (1996). Behavioral inhibition and stress reactivity: The moderating role of attachment security. *Child Development, 67,* 508–522.

Nadel, J., Carchon, I., Kervella, C., Marcelli, D., & Plantey-Reserbat, D. (1999). Expectancies for social contingency in 2–month-olds. *Developmental Science, 2*(2), 164–173.

Nadel, J., & Fontaine, A. (1989). Communication by imitation: A developmental and comparative approach to transitory social competence. In B. H. Schneider & G. Attili (Eds.), *Social competence in developmental perspective* (pp. 131–144). The Netherlands: Kluwer Academic.

Nadel, J., & Tremblay-Leveau, H. (1999). Early perception of social contingencies and interpersonal intentionality: Dyadic and triadic paradigms. In P. Rochat (Ed.), *Early social cognition* (pp. 391–415). Mahwah, NJ: Lawrence Erlbaum Associates.

Naeye, R. (1980). Sudden infant death. *Scientific American, 242,* 56–62.

Nagan, H. Y., Miu, P., Ko, L., & Ma, H. K. (1990). Long-term neurological sequelae following vacuum extractor delivery. *Australia and New Zealand Journal of Obstetrical Gynaecology, 30*(2), 111–114.

Nagata, M., Nagai, Y., Sobajima, H., Ando, T., & Honjo, S. (2004). Depression in the early postpartum period and attachment to children--in mothers of NICU infants. *Infant and Child Development, 13*(2), 93–110.

Naigles, L. G., & Kako, E. T. (1993). First contact in verb acquisition: Defining a role for syntax. *Child Development, 64,* 1665–1687.

Nakano, S. (1995). Let your toddler journey to separation: Child separation and reconstruction of playful inter-actions in the Japanese mother and child. *Research and Clinical Center for Child Development, 17,* 23–44.

Nakata, T., & Trehub, S. E. (2004). Infants' responsiveness to maternal speech and singing. *Infant Behavior & Development, 27*(4), 455–464.

Nakazima, S. (1972). Phonemicization and symbolization in language development. In E. H. Lenneberg & E. Lenneberg (Eds.), *Foundations of language development: A multidisciplinary approach* (Vol. 1, pp. 306–332). New York: Academic Press.

National AIA Resource Center, (2005). Boarder Babies, Abandoned Infants, and Discarded Infants, http://aia.berkeley.edu/media/pdf/abandoned_infant_fact_sheet_2005.pdf (retrieved Jan. 4, 2010).

National Safety Council. (1987). *Accident facts.* Chicago: Author.

National Vital Statistics Reports, vol. 54, no. 8, Dec. 29, 2005.

Nazzi, T., Floccia, C., & Bertoncini, J. (1998). Discrimination of pitch contours by neonates. *Infant Behavior and Development, 21*(4), 779–784.

Nehlig, A., & Debry, G. (1994). Potential teratogenic and neurodevelopmental consequences of coffee and caffeine exposure: A review of human and animal data. *Neurotoxicology and Teratology, 16,* 531–543.

Neisser, U. (1991). Two perceptually given aspects of the self and their development. Special Issue: The development of self: The first three years. *Developmental Review, 11* (3), 197–209.

Nelson, C. A. (1985). The perception and recognition of facial expressions in infancy. In T. M. Field & N. A. Fox (Eds.), *Social perception in infants* (pp. 101–125). Norwood, NJ: Ablex.

Nelson, C. A. (1987). The recognition of facial expressions in the first two years of life: Mechanisms of development. *Child Development, 58,* 889–909.

Nelson, C. A. (1994). Neural bases of infant temperament. In J. E. Bates & T. D. Wachs (Eds.), *Temperament: Individual differences at the interface of biology and behavior*

(pp. 47–82). Washington, DC: American Psychological Association.

Nelson, C. A. (2007). A neurobiological perspective on early human deprivation. *Child Development Perspectives, 1*(1), 13–18.

Nelson, D. C. K., Egan, L. C., & Holt, M. B. (2004). When children ask, 'what is it?' What do they want to know about artifacts? *Psychological Science, 15*(6), 384–389.

Nelson, D. G. K., & O'Neil, K. (2005). How do parents respond to children's questions about the identity of artifacts? *Developmental Science, 8*(6), 519–524.

Nelson, J. R., Jr. (1982). The politics of federal day care regulations. In E. Zigler & E. Gordon (Eds.), *Day care: Scientific and social policy issues* (pp. 277–305). Boston: Auburn House.

Nelson, K. (1973). Structure and strategy in learning to talk. *Monographs of the Society for Research in Child Development, 38* (Serial No. 149), 1–136.

Nelson, K. (1978). How children represent knowledge of their world in and out of language: A preliminary report. In R. S. Siegler (Ed.), *Children's thinking: What develops?* (pp. 213–240). Hillsdale, NJ: Erlbaum.

Nelson, K. (1981). Individual differences in language development: Implications for development and language. *Developmental Psychology, 17,* 170–187.

Nelson, K., Rescorla, L., Gruendel, J., & Benedict, H. (1978). Early lexicons: What do they mean? *Child Development, 49,* 960–968.

Nelson, N. M., Enkin, M. W., Saigel, S., Bennett, K. J., Milner, R., & Sackett, D. L. (1980). A randomized clinical trial of the Leboyer approach to childbirth. *New England Journal of Medicine, 299,* 655–660.

Nettlebladt, P., Fagerstrom, C., & Udderberg, N. (1976). The significance of reported childbirth pain. *Journal of Psychosomatic Research, 20,* 215–221.

Network, N. E. C. C. R. (2002). Child-care structure - process - outcome: Direct and indirect effects of child-care quality on young children's development. *Psychological Science, 13*(3), 199–206.

Neumann, P. J., Gharib, S. D., & Weinstein, M. C. (1994). The cost of a successful delivery with in vitro fertilization. *New England Journal of Medicine, 331,* 239–243.

New England Center for Children (NECC) http://www.necc.org/autism_resources/fact_sheets.asp (retrieved Jan. 4, 2010).

Newman, D. L., Caspi, A., Moffitt, T. E., & Silva, P. A. (1997). Antecedents of adult interpersonal functioning: Effects of individual differences in age 3 temperament. *Developmental Psychology, 33*(2), 206–217.

NICHD Early Child Care Research Network (1996). Characteristics of infant child care: Factors contributing to positive caregiving. *Early Childhood Research Quarterly, 11,* 269–306.

NICHD Early Child Care Research Network (1997a). Child care in the first year of life. *Merrill-Palmer Quarterly, 43*(3), 340–360.

NICHD Early Child Care Research Network (1997b). Familial factors associated with characteristics of nonmaternal care for infants. *Journal of Marriage and the Family, 59,* 389–408.

NICHD Early Child Care Research Network (1997c). Poverty and patterns of child care. In G. J. Duncan & J. Brooks-Gunn (Eds.), *Consequences of growing up poor* (pp. 100–130). New York: Russell Sage.

NICHD Early Child Care Research Network (1998a). Early child care and self-control, compliance, and problem behavior in 24 and 36 months. *Child Development, 69*(4), 1145–1170.

NICHD Early Child Care Research Network (1998b). Relations between family predictors and child outcomes: Are they weaker for children in child care? *Developmental Psychology, 34*(5), 1119–1128.

NICHD Early Child Care Research Network (1999). Chronicity of maternal depressive symptoms, maternal sensitivity, and child functioning at 36 months. *Developmental Psychology, 35*(8), 1297–1310.

NICHD-Early Child Care Research Network. (2004). Type of child care and children's development at 54 months. *Early Childhood Research Quarterly, 19*(2), 203–230.

Nicolich, L. M. (1977). Beyond sensorimotor intelligence: Assessment of symbolic maturity through analysis of pretend play. *Merrill-Palmer Quarterly, 23,* 89–100.

Nichols, F. H., & Humenick, S. S. (1988). *Childbirth education: Practice, research, and theory.* Philadelphia: W. B. Saunders.

Niebyl, J. R., & Goodwin, T. M. (2002). Overview of nausea and vomiting of pregnancy with an emphasis on vitamins and ginger. *Am J Obstet Gynecol, 186*(5 Suppl Understanding), S253–255.

Ninio, A. (1979). The naive theory of the infant and other maternal attitudes in two subgroups in Israel. *Child Development, 50,* 976–980.

Ninio, A. (1980). Picture-book reading in mother-infant dyads belonging to two subgroups in Israel. *Child Development, 51,* 587–590.

Ninio, A. (1983). Joint book reading as a multiple vocabulary acquisition device. *Developmental Psychology, 19,* 445–451.

Nishida, T. K., & Lillard, A. S. (2007). The informative value of emotional expressions: 'Social referencing' in mother-child pretense. *Developmental Science, 10*(2), 205–212.

Nitschke, J. B., Nelson, E. E., Rusch, B. D., Fox, A. S., Oakes, T. R., & Davidson, R. J. (2004). Orbitofrontal cortex tracks positive mood in mothers viewing pictures of their newborn infants. *Neuroimage, 21*(2), 583–592.

Nwokah, E., Davies, P., Islam, A., Hsu, H., & Fogel, A. (1993). Vocal affect in three-year-olds: A quantitative acoustic analysis of child laughter. *Acoustical Society of America, 94,* 3076–3090.

Nwokah, E., & Fogel, A. (1993). Laughter in mother-infant emotional communication. *Humor, 6–2,* 137–161.

Nwokah, E., Hsu, H., Dobrowolska, O., & Fogel, A. (1994). The development of laughter in mother-infant communication: Timing parameters and temporal sequences. *Infant Behavior and Development, 16,* 23–25.

Oakes, L. M., Coppage, D. J., & Dingel, A. (1997). By land or by sea: The role of perceptual similarity in infants' categorization of animals. *Developmental Psychology, 33*(3), 396–407.

Oakes, L. M., Plumert, J. M., Lansink, J. M., & Merryman, J. D. (1996). Evidence for task-dependent categorization in infancy. *Infant Behavior and Development, 19,* 425–440.

Oakes, L. M., & Tellinghuisen, D. J. (1994). Examining in infancy: Does it reflect active processing? *Developmental Psychology, 30,* 748–756.

O'Brien, M., Asay, J. H., & McCluskey-Fawcett, K. (1999). Family functioning and maternal depression following premature birth. *Reproductive and Infant Psychology, 17*(2), 175–188.

O'Brien, M., & Huston, A. C. (1985). Development of sex-typed play behavior in toddlers. *Developmental Psychology, 21,* 866–871.

O'Connell, B., & Bretherton, I. (1984). Toddler's play, alone and with mother: The role of maternal guidance. In I. Bretherton (Ed.), *Symbolic play* (pp. 337–366). Orlando, FL: Academic Press.

O'Conner, M. J., Sigman, M., & Brill, N. (1987). Disorganization of attachment in relation to maternal alcohol consumption. *Journal of Consulting and Clinical Psychology, 55,* 831–836.

O'Connor, T., Ben-Shlomo, Y., Heron, J., Golding, J., Adams, D., & Glover, V. (2005). Prenatal anxiety predicts individual differences in cortisol in pre-adolescent children. *Biological Psychiatry, 58*(3), 211–217.

O'Connor, T. G., Caspi, A., Defries, J. C., & Plomin, R. (2003). Genotype-environment interaction in children's adjustment to parental separation. *J Child Psychol Psychiatry, 44*(6), 849–856.

Oehler, J. M., & Eckerman, C. O. (1988, April). *Regulatory effects of human speech and touch in premature infants prior to term age.* Presentation at the International Conference on Infant Studies, Washington, DC.

Ogunyemi, D., Hullett, S., Leeper, J., & Risk, A. (1998). Prepregnancy body mass index, weight gain during pregnancy, and perinatal outcome in a rural black population. *Journal of Maternal and Fetal Medicine, 7*(4), 190–193.

O'Hara, M. W. (1997). The nature of postpartum depressive disorders. In L. Murray & P. J. Cooper (Eds.), *Postpartum depression and child development* (pp. 3–31). New York: Guilford Press.

O'Hara, M. W., Schlechte, J. A., Lewis, D. A., & Varner, M. W. (1991). Controlled prospective study of postpartum mood disorders: Psychological, environmental, and hormonal variables. *Journal of Abnormal Psychology, 100*(1), 63–73.

Oken, E., Kleinman, K. P., Olsen, S. F., Rich-Edwards, J. W., & Gillman, M. W. (2004). Associations of seafood and elongated n-3 fatty acid intake with fetal growth and length of gestation: results from a US pregnancy cohort. *Am J Epidemiol, 160*(8), 774–783.

Oken, E., Taveras, E. M., Kleinman, K. P., Rich-Edwards, J. W., & Gillman, M. @. (2007) Gestational weight gain and child adiposity at age 3 years. *American Journal of Obstetrics & Gynecology, 196*(4), 322 e1–322.e8

Olds, S. B., London, M. L., & Ladewig, P. A. (1984). Nursing assessment of the newborn. *Maternal-newborn nursing: A family-centered approach* (pp. 660–707). Menlo Park, CA: Addison-Wesley.

O'Leary, J. (2007). Pregnancy and infant loss: supporting parents and their children. *Zero to Three, 27*(6) 42–49.

Oller, D. K. & Eilers, R. E. (1988). The role of audition in infant babbling. *Child Development, 59,* 441–449.

Olson, S. L., Bates, J. E., & Bayles, K. (1984). Mother-infant interaction and the development of individual differences in children's cognitive competence. *Developmental Psychology, 20,* 166–179.

Olson, S. L., Bates, J. E., & Kaskie, B. (1992). Caregiver-infant interaction antecedents of children's school-age cognitive ability. *Merrill-Palmer Quarterly, 38,* 309–330.

O'Neill, D. K. (1996). Seven-year-old children's sensitivity to a parent's knowledge state when making requests. *Child Development, 67,* 659–677.

Onzawa, K., Glover, V., Adams, D., Modi, N., & Kumar, R. C. (2001). Infant massage improves mother-infant interaction for mothers with postnatal depression. *Journal of Affective Disorders, 63*(1–3), 201–207.

Oppenheim, D., Sagi, A., & Lamb, M. E. (1988). Infant-adult attachments on the kibbutz and their relation to socioemotional development 4 years later. *Developmental Psychology, 24,* 427–433.

O'Reilly-Green, C., & Cohen, W. R. (1993). Pregnancy in women aged 40 and older. *Obstetrics and Gynecology, 20,* 313–331.

Örnkloo, H., & von Hofsten, C. (2007). Fitting Objects Into Holes: On the Development of Spatial Cognition Skills. *Developmental Psychology, 43*(2), 404–416.

Osofsky, J. (2007). *Young Children and Trauma: Intervention and Treatment.* NY: The Guilford Press.

Osofsky, H., Rosenthal, M., & Butterbaugh, G. (1999). Addressing infertility: Opportunities for the mental health professional to support families. *Zero to Three, 19*(4), 25–31.

Oster, H. (1978). Facial expression and affect development. In M. Lewis & L. A. Rosenblum (Eds.), *The development of affect* (pp. 43–75). New York: Plenum Press.

Oster, H., Hegley, D., & Nagel, L. (1992). Adult judgments and fine-grained analysis of infant facial expressions: Testing the validity of a priori coding formulas. *Developmental Psychology, 28,* 1115–1131.

Osterling, J., & Dawson, G. (1994). Early recognition of children and autism: A study of first birthday home videotapes. *Journal of Autism and Developmental Disorders, 24,* 247–257.

Ostrov, J. M., Gentile, D. A., & Crick, N. R. (2006). Media exposure, aggression and prosocial behavior during early childhood: A longitudinal study. *Social Development, 15*(4), 612–627.

Otaki, M., Durrett, M., Richards, P., Nyquist, L., & Pennebaker, J. (1986). Maternal and infant behavior in Japan and America: A partial replication. *Journal of Cross-Cultural Psychology, 17,* 251–268.

Oviatt, S. L. (1978, April). *Qualitative change in the language comprehension of 9– to 17–month-old infants: An experimental approach.* Paper presented at the International Conference on Infant Studies, Providence, RI.

Ozonoff, S., & South, M. (2001). Early social development in young children with autism: Theoretical and clinical implications. In J. G. Bremner & A. Fogel (Eds.), *Handbook of Infant Development* (pp. 72–96). Oxford, England: Blackwell.

Paiva, J. V., Hutto, C., Antunes, C., & Scott, G. (1994). Correlation between timing of rupture of amniotic membranes and risk of HIV-1 perinatal transmission *International Conference on AIDS, 10,* 307–308.

Palacios, J., & Sánchez-Sandoval, Y. (2006). Stress in parents of adopted children. *International Journal of Behavioral Development, 30*(6), 481–487.

Palkovitz, R. (1984). Parental attitude and fathers' interactions with their 5–month-old infants. *Developmental Psychology, 20,* 1054–1060.

Palmer, C. F. (1989). The discriminating nature of infants' exploratory actions. *Developmental Psychology, 25,* 885–893.

Palo, P., Piiroinen, O., Honkonen, E., Lakkala, T., & Aula, P. (1994). Transabdominal chorionic villus sampling and amniocentesis for prenatal diagnosis: 5 years' experience at a university centre. *Prenatal Diagnosis, 14,* 157–162.

Panneton, R. K., & DeCasper, A. J. (1986, April). *Newborns' postnatal preference for a prenatally experienced melody.* Paper presented at the International Conference on Infant Studies, Los Angeles, CA.

Papousek, H. (1967). Conditioning during early postnatal development. In Y. Brackbill & G. G. Thompson (Eds.), *Behavior in infancy and early childhood* (pp. 268–284). New York: Free Press.

Papousek, H., & Papousek, M. (1977). Mothering and the cognitive headstart: Psychobiological considerations. In H. R. Schaffer (Ed.), *Studies in mother-infant interaction* (pp. 63–88). London: Academic Press.

Papousek, H., & Papousek, M. (1987). Intuitive parenting: A dialectic counterpart of the infant's integrative competence. In J. D. Osofsky (Ed.), *Handbook of infant development* (2nd ed., pp. 302–331). New York: Wiley.

Papousek, M. (1989). Determinants of responsiveness to infant vocal expression of emotional state. *Infant Behavior and Development, 12,* 507–524.

Papousek, M. (1994). Melodies in caregivers' speech: A species-specific guidance towards language. *Early Development and Parenting, 3,* 5–17.

Papousek, M., Bornstein, M. H., Nuzzo, C., Papousek, H., & Symmes, D. (1990). Infant responses to prototypical melodic contours in parental speech. *Infant Behavior and Development, 13,* 539–545.

Papousek, M., & Papousek, H. (1981). Musical elements in the infant's vocalization: Their significance for communication, cognition, and creativity. In. L. P. Lipsitt & C. K. Rovee-Collier (Eds.), *Advances in infancy research* (Vol. 1, pp. 64–86). Norwood, NJ: Ablex.

Papousek, M., Papousek, H., & Bornstein, M. H. (1985). The naturalistic vocal environment of young infants: On the significance of homogeneity and variability in parental speech. In T. M. Field & N. A. Fox (Eds.), *Social perception in infants* (pp. 171–186). Norwood, NJ: Ablex.

Papousek, M., Papousek, H., & Symmes, D. (1991). The meanings of melodies in motherese in tone and stress languages. *Infant Behavior and Development,* 14, 415–440.

Papousek, M., & von Hofacker, N. (1995). Persistent crying and parenting: Search for a butterfly in a dynamic system. *Early Development and Parenting, 4*(4), 209–224.

Parfitt, R. R. (1977). *The birth primer.* Philadelphia: Running Press.

Park, K. A., & Waters, E. (1989). Security of attachment and preschool friendship. *Child Development, 60,* 1076–1081.

Park, S., Belsky, J., Putnam, S., & Crnic, K. (1997). Infant emotionality, parenting, and 3–year inhibition: Exploring stability and lawful discontinuity in a male sample. *Developmental Psychology, 33*(2), 218–227.

Parke, R. (1995). Fathers and families. In M. Bornstein (Ed.) *Handbook of Parenting* (Vol. 3, pp. 27–63). Mahwah, NJ, Erlbaum.

Parke, R., & Collmer, C. W. (1975). Child abuse: An interdisciplinary analysis. In E. Hetherington (Ed.), *Review of the child development research* (Vol. 5, pp. 87–102). Chicago: University of Chicago Press.

Parke, R. D., & Sawin, D. B. (1980). The family in early infancy: Social interactional and attitudinal analyses. In F. A. Pedersen (Ed.), *The father-infant relationship:* *Observational studies in the family setting* (pp. 244–268). New York: Praeger Special Studies.

Parke, R. D., & Tinsley, B. R. (1981). The father's role in infancy: Determinants of involvement in caregiving and play. In M. E. Lamb (Ed.), *The role of the father in child development* (2nd ed., pp. 310–329). New York: Wiley.

Parke, R. D., & Tinsley, B. R. (1987). Family interaction in infancy. In J. D. Osofsky (Ed.), *Handbook of infant development* (2nd ed., pp. 332–353). New York: Wiley.

Parker, B., McFarlane, J., & Soeken, K. (1994). Abuse during pregnancy: Effects on maternal complications and birth weight in adult and teenage women. *Obstetrics and Gynecology, 84,* 323–328.

Parks, W. (1996). Human immunodeficiency virus. In W. Nelson, R. Behrman, R. Kliegman, & A. Arving (Eds.), *Nelson's textbook of pediatrics (*15th ed., pp. 916–919). Philadelphia: Saunders.

Parmelee, A. H., Jr., Schulz, H. R., & Disbrow, M. W. (1961). Sleep patterns of the newborn. *Journal of Pediatrics, 58,* 241–250.

Parrinello, R. M., & Ruff, H. A. (1988). The influence of adult intervention on infants' level of attention. *Child Development, 59,* 1125–1135.

Parritz, R. H. (1996). A descriptive analysis of toddler coping in challenging circumstances. *Infant Behavior and Development, 19,* 171–180.

Parten, M. B. (1932). Social participation among preschool children. *Journal of Abnormal and Social Psychology, 27,* 243–269.

Pascalis, O., de Schonen, S., Morton, J., Deruelle, C., & Fabre-Grenet, M. (1995). Mother's face recognition by neonates: A replication and extension. *Infant Behavior and Development, 18,* 79–85.

Passman, R. H. (1977). Providing attachment objects to facilitate learning and reduce distress: Effects of mothers and security blankets. *Developmental Psychology, 13,* 25–28.

Passman, R. H., & Weisberg, P. (1975). Mothers and blankets as agents for promoting play and exploration by young children in a novel environment: The effects of social and non-social attachment objects. *Developmental Psychology, 11,* 170–177.

Patterson, C. J., Kupersmidt, J. B., & Vaden, N. A. (1990). Income level, gender, ethnicity, and household composition as predictors of children's school-based competence. *Child Development, 61,* 485–494.

Patterson, M. L., & Werker, J. F. (1999). Matching phonetic information in lips and voice is robust in 4.5–month-old infants. *Infant Behavior and Development, 22*(2), 237–247.

Patton, M. Q. (1990). *Qualitative evaluation and research methods* (2nd ed.). London: Sage.

Pauli-Pott, U., Mertesacker, B., & Beckmann, D. (2004). Predicting the development of infant emotionality from maternal characteristics. *Development and Psychopathology, 16*(1), 19–42.

Paulson, G., & Gottlieb, G. (1968). Developmental reflexes: The reappearance of foetal and neonatal reflexes in aged patients. *Brain,* 91, 37–52.

Paulson, R., Boostanfar, R., Saadat, P., Mor, E., Tourgeman, D., Slater, C., et al. (2002). Pregnancy in the Sixth Decade of Life: Obstetric outcomes in women of advanced reproductive age. *Journal of the American Medical Association, 288*(18), 2320.

Pawl, J. H. (1992). Interventions to strengthen relationships between infants and drug-abusing or recovering parents. *Zero to Three, 13,* 6–10.

Pearson, J. L., Hunter, A. G., Ensminger, M. E., & Kellam, S. G. (1990). Black grandmothers in multigenerational households: Diversity in family structure and parenting involvement in Woodlawn community. *Child Development, 61,* 434–442.

Pecheux, M. G., Labrell, F., & Pistorio, M. (1993). What do parents talk about to infants? *Early Development and Parenting, 2,* 89–97.

Peckham, C. S. (1993). Mother-to-child transmission of HIV: Risk factors and timing. *International Conference on AIDS, 9,* abstract no. PS-04–2.

Pedersen, D. R., & Moran, G. (1996). Expressions of the attachment relationship outside of the strange situation. *Child Development, 67*(3), 915–927.

Pedersen, F., Suwalsky, J. T., Cain, R. L., & Zaslow, M. J. (1987). Paternal care of infants during maternal separations: Associations with father-infant interaction at one year. *Psychiatry, 50,* 193–205.

Pedlow, R., Sanson, A., Prior, M., & Oberklaid, F. (1993). Stability of maternally reported temperament from infancy to 8 years. *Developmental Psychology, 29,* 998–1007.

Peduto, V. A., Musu, M., Gatto, G., & Ghilli, L. (1994). Sudden infant death syndrome (SIDS). Risk conditions and intervention strategies. *Minerva-Anesthesiology, 60,* 393–402.

Peiper, A. (1963). *Cerebral function in infancy and childhood.* New York: Consultants Bureau.

Pelaez-Nogueras, M., Field, T., Cigales, M., Gonzalez, A., & Clasky, S. (1994). Infants of depressed mothers show less "depressed" behavior with their nursery teachers. *Infant Mental Health Journal, 15,* 358–367.

Pelaez-Nogueras, M., Field, T. M., Hossain, Z., & Pickens, J. (1996). Depressed mothers' touching increases infants' positive affect and attention in still-face interactions. *Child Development, 67*(4), 1780–1792.

Pellegrini, A. D., & Smith, P. K. (1998). Physical activity play: The nature and function of a neglected aspect of play. *Child Development, 69*(3), 577–598.

Peña, I. C., Teberg, A. J., & Hoppenbrouwers, T. (1987). The Gesell developmental schedule in Hispanic low-birth weight infants during the first year of life. *Infant Behavior and Development, 10,* 199–216.

Perera, F., Rauh, V., Whyatt, R., Tang, D., Tsai, W., Bernert, J., et al. (2005). A summary of recent findings on birth outcomes and developmental effects of prenatal ETS, PAH, and pesticide exposures. *NeuroToxicology, 26*(4), 573–587.

Perlman, M., & Ross, H. S. (1997). The benefits of parent intervention in children's disputes: An examination of concurrent changes in children's fighting styles. *Child Development, 68*(4), 690–700.

Perris, E. E., & Clifton, R. K. (1988). Reaching in the dark toward sound as a measure of auditory localization in infants. *Infant Behavior and Development, 11,* 473–491.

Perris, E. E., Myers, N. A., & Clifton, R. K. (1990). Long-term memory for a single infancy experience. *Child Development, 61,* 1796–1807.

Perrucci, C., & Targ, D. (1988). Effect of plant closing on marriage and family life. In P. Voydanoff & L. Majka (Eds.), *Families and economic distress* (pp. 135–153). Newbury Park, CA: Sage.

Perry, B. (2005). Applying principles of neurodevelopment to clinical work with maltreated and traumatized children: The neurosequential model of therapeutics. In N. B. Webb (Ed.) *Working with traumatized youth in child welfare.* NY: The Guilford Press.

Peterson, C. (1999). Children's memory for medical emergencies: 2 years later. *Developmental Psychology, 35*(6), 1493–1506.

Peterson, C., & Bell, M. (1996). Children's memory for traumatic injury. *Child Development, 67,* 3045–3070.

Peterson, C., & Rideout, R. (1998). Memory for medical emergencies experienced by 1– and 2–year-olds. *Developmental Psychology, 34*(5), 1059–1072.

Peterson, G., & Peters, D. (1985). The socialization values of low-income Appalachian white and rural black mothers: A comparative study. *Journal of Comparative Family Studies, 16,* 75–91.

Petitto, L. (1985, October). *On the use of prelinguistic gestures in hearing and deaf children: Implications for theories of language acquisition.* Paper presented at the Tenth Annual Boston University Conference on Language Acquisition, Boston, MA.

Pettit, G. S., & Bates, J. E. (1984). Continuity of individual differences in the mother-infant relationship from 6 to 13 months. *Child Development, 55,* 729–739.

Phillips, D., & McCartney, K. (2005). *The Disconnect between Research and Policy on Child Care.* New York, NY, US: Cambridge University Press.

Phillips, D., McCartney, K., & Scarr, S. (1987). Child-care quality and children's social development. *Developmental Psychology, 23,* 537–543.

Phillips, R. D., Wagner, S. H., Fells, C. A., & Lynch, M. (1990). Do infants recognize emotion in facial expressions?:

Categorical and "metaphorical" evidence. *Infant Behavior and Development, 13,* 71–84.

Phipps, M. G., Blume, J. D., & DeMonner, S. M. (2002). Young maternal age associated with increased risk of postneonatal death. *Obstet Gynecol, 100*(3), 481–486.

Piaget, J. (1952). *The origins of intelligence in children.* New York: International Universities Press.

Piaget, J. (1954). *The construction of reality in the child.* New York: Ballantine Books.

Piaget, J. (1962). *Play, dreams and imitation in childhood.* New York: Norton.

Piaget, J., & Inhelder, B. (1969). *The psychology of the child.* New York: Basic Books.

Pickens, J. N., & Field, T. (1995). Facial expressions and vagal tone of infants of depressed and non-depressed mothers. *Early Development and parenting, 4,* 83–89.

Pieraut-Lebonniec, G. (1990). Reaching and hand adjusting to the target properties. In H. Bloch & B. I. Bertenthal (Eds.), *Sensory-motor organizations and development in infancy and early childhood* (pp. 301–314). Boston, MA: Kluwer Academic.

Pike, A., Iervolino, A. C., Eley, T. C., Price, T. S., & Plomin, R. (2006). Environmental risk and young children's cognitive and behavioral development. *International Journal of Behavioral Development, 30*(1), 55–66.

Pine, J. M., Lieven, E. V. M., & Rowland, C. F. (1997). Stylistic variation at the "single-word" stage: Relations between maternal speech characteristics and children's vocabulary composition and usage. *Child Development, 68*(5), 807–819.

Pipes, P. L. (1985). *Nutrition in infancy and early childhood* (2nd ed.). St. Louis: Mosby.

Pipp, S., Easterbrooks, M. A., & Brown, S. R. (1993). Attachment status and complexity of infants' self- and other-knowledge when tested with mother and father. *Social Development, 2,* 4–12.

Pipp, S., Easterbrooks, M. A., & Harmon, R. J. (1992). The relation between attachment and knowledge of self and mother in one- to three-year-old infants. *Child Development, 63* (3), 738–750.

Pipp, S., Fischer, K. W., & Jennings, S. (1987). Acquisition of self- and mother knowledge in infancy. *Developmental Psychology, 23,* 86–96.

Pipp-Siegel, S., Siegel, C. H., & Dean, J. (1999). Neurological aspects of the disorganized/disoriented attachment classification system: Differentiating quality of the attachment relationship from neurological impairment. *Monographs of the Society for Research in Child Development, 64*(3), 25–44.

Pistrang, N. (1984). Women's work involvement and experience of new motherhood. *Journal of Marriage and Family,* 433–446.

Placek, P. J. (1986). Commentary: Cesarean rates still rising. *Statistical Bulletin, 67,* 9.

Pleck, J. H. (1983). Husbands' paid work and family roles: Current research issues. In H. Lopata & J. H. Pleck (Eds.), *Research in the interweave of social roles: Vol. 3. Families and jobs* (pp. 575–605). Greenwich, CT: JAI Press.

Pleck, J. H., & Rustad, M. (1980). *Husbands' and wives' time in family work and paid work in 1975–1976 study of time use.* Unpublished paper. Wellesley College Center for Research on Women.

Plomin, R. (1990). The role of inheritance in behavior. *Science, 248,* 183–188.

Plomin, R. (1994). Nature, nurture, and social development. *Social Development, 3,* 37–53.

Plomin, R., DeFries, J. C. Craig, I. W., & McGuffin, P. (2003). *Behavioral genetics in the postgenomic era.* Washington, DC: American Psychological Association

Plomin, R., & Rutter, M. (1998). Child development, molecular genetics, and what to do with genes once they are found. *Child Development, 69*(4), 1223–1242.

Plomin, R., & Saudino, K. J. (1994). Quantitative genetics and molecular genetics. In J. E. Bates & T. D. Wachs (Eds.) *Temperament: Individual differences at the interface of biology and behavior* (pp. 143–171). Washington, DC: American Psychological Association.

Plowman, L., Stirling, U., & Stirling, S. (2004). "Hey, Hey, Hey! It's Time to Play": Children's interactions with smart toys. In J. Goldstein (Ed.), *Toys, games, and media* (pp. 207–223). Mahwah, NJ: Lawrence Erlbaum Associates, Inc.

Plunkett, J. W., Klein, T., & Meisels, S. J. (1988). The relationship of preterm infant-mother attachment to stranger sociability at 3 years. *Infant Behavior and Development, 11,* 83–96.

Pogarsky, G., Lizotte, A. J., & Thornberry, T. P. (2003). The delinquency of children born to young mothers: Results from the Rochester Youth Development Study. *Criminology, 41*(4), 1249–1286

Polansky, N. (1976). Analysis of research on child neglect: The social work viewpoint. In Herner and Co. (Eds.), *Four perspectives on the status of child abuse and neglect research* (pp. 602–638). Washington, DC: National Center on Child Abuse and Neglect.

Pollak, S. D., Vardi, S., Bechner, A. M. P., & Curtin, J. J. (2005). Physically Abused Children's Regulation of Attention in Response to Hostility. *Child Development, 76*(5), 968–977.

Pollitt, E., Garza, C., & Leibel, R. L. (1984). Nutrition and public policy. In H. W. Stevenson & A. E. Siegel (Eds.), *Child development research and social policy* (pp. 421–470). Chicago: University of Chicago Press.

Pollitt, E., Golub, M., Gorman, K., Grantham-McGregor, S., Levitsky, D., Schurch, B., Strupp, B., & Wachs, T. (1996). A reconceptualization of the effects of undernutrition on children's biological, psychosocial, and behavioral development. *Social Policy Report: Society for Research in Child Development, 10*(5).

Population Reference Bureau (2009) http://www.prb.org/pdf09/09wpds_eng.pdf.

Porcher, F. K. (1992). HIV infected pregnant women and their infants. Primary health care implications. *Nurse Practitioner, 17,* 46–54.

Porges, S. W. (2004). Neuroception: A subconscious system for detecting threats and safety. *Zero to Three, 24*(5), 19–24.

Porges, S. W., Doussard-Roosevelt, J., Shifter, C., McClenny, B., & Riniolo, T. (1999) Sleep state and vagal regulation of heart period patterns in the human newborn: An extension of the polyvagal theory. *Psychophysiology,* 36, 14–2.

Porreco, R. P., Harden, L., Gambotto, M., & Shapiro, H. (2005). Expectation of pregnancy outcome among mature women. *Am J Obstet Gynecol, 192*(1), 38–41.

Porter, R. H., Cernoch, J. M., & Perry, S. (1983). The importance of odors in mother-infant interactions. *Maternal Child Nursing Journal, 12*(3), 147–154.

Porter, R. H., Makin, J. W., Davis, L. B., & Christensen, K. M. (1992). Breast-fed infants respond to olfactory cues from their own mother and unfamiliar lactating females. *Infant Behavior and Development, 15,* 85–93.

Portes, P., Dunham, R., & Williams, S. (1986). Assessing child-rearing style in ecological settings: Its relation to culture, social class, early age intervention and scholastic achievement. *Adolescence, 21,* 723–735.

Posada, G., Carbonell, O. A., Alzate, G., & Plata, S. J. (2004). Through Colombian Lenses: Ethnographic and Conventional Analyses of Maternal Care and Their Associations With Secure Base Behavior. *Developmental Psychology, 40*(4), 508–518.

Posada, G., Gao, Y., Wu, F., Posada, R., Tascon, M., Schölmerich, A., Sagi, A., Kondo-Ikemura, K., Haaland, W., & Synnevaag, B. (1995). The secure-base phenomenon across cultures: Children's behavior, mothers' preferences, and experts' concepts. *Monographs of the Society for Research in Child Development, 244*(60), 27–40.

Post, S., Neimark, J, & Moss, O. (2007). *Why good things happen to good people: The Exciting New Research that Proves the Link Between Doing Good and Living a Longer, Healthier, Happier Life.* NY: Random House.

Poulin-Dubois, D., Serbin, L. A., & Derbyshire, A. (1998). Toddlers' intermodal and verbal knowledge about gender. *Merrill-Palmer Quarterly, 44*(3), 338–354.

Poulin-Dubois, D., Serbin, L. A., Kenyon, B., & Derbyshire, A. (1994). Infants' intermodal knowledge about gender. *Developmental Psychology, 30,* 436–442.

Powell, D. R. (2001). Early intervention and risk. In J. G. Bremner & A. Fogel (Eds.), *Handbook of infant development.* Oxford, England: Blackwell.

Powell, M. (1991). The psychosocial impact of Sudden Infant Death Syndrome on siblings. Committee of the Health Psychology Interest Group of the Psychological Society

of Ireland: Having babies: Issues in reproductive and infant psychology. *Irish Journal of Psychology, 12,* 235–247.

Power, T. G., Chapieski, M. L., & McGrath, M. P. (1985). Assessment of individual differences in infant exploration and play. *Developmental Psychology, 21,* 974–981.

Power, T. G., & Parke, R. D. (1986). Patterns of early socialization: Mother- and father-infant interaction in the home. *International Journal of Behavioral Development, 9,* 331–341.

Prange, M. T., Coats, B., Duhaime, A. C., & Margulies, S. S. (2003). Anthropomorphic simulations of falls, shakes, and inflicted impacts in infants. *J Neurosurg, 99*(1), 143–150.

Prechtl, H. F. R. (1977). *The neurological examination of the full term newborn infant* (2nd ed.). London: Heinemann.

Preisler, G. (1997). Social and emotional development of blind children: A longitudinal study. In V. Lewis & G. M. Collis (Eds.), *Blindness and psychological development in young children* (pp. 69–85). Leicester, England: BPS Books.

Pressman, E. K., DiPietro, J. A., Costigan, K. A., Shupe, A. K., & Johnson, T. R. B. (1998). Fetal neurobehavioral development: Associations with socioeconomic class and fetal sex. *Developmental Psychobiology, 33*(1), 79–91.

Pridham, K. F. (1998). Guided participation and development of care-giving competencies for families of low birth-weight infants. *Journal of Advanced Nursing, 28*(5), 948–958.

Prigogine, I., & Stengers, I. (Eds.) (1984). *Order out of chaos: Man's new dialogue with nature.* New York: Bantam Books.

Provence, S. (1982). Infant day care: Relationships between theory and practice. In E. F. Zigler & E. W. Gordon (Eds.), *Day care: Scientific and social policy issues* (pp. 33–35). Boston: Auburn House.

Provence, S., & Naylor, A. (1983). *Working with disadvantaged parents and children: Scientific issues and practice.* New Haven, CT: Yale University Press.

Prysak, M., Lorenz, R. P., & Kisly, A. (1995). Pregnancy outcome in nulliparous women 35 years and older. *Obstetrics and Gynecology, 85,* 65–70.

Puddifoot, J. E., & Johnson, M. P. (1999). Active grief, despair, and difficulty coping: Some measured characteristics of male response following their partner's miscarriage. *Journal of Reproductive and Infant Psychology, 17*(1), 89–93.

Puffer, R. R., & Serrano, C. V. (1973). *Patterns of mortality in childhood (PAHO Scientific Publication No. 262).* Washington, DC: Pan American Health Organization.

Pye, C. (1986). Quiche Mayan speech to children. *Journal of Child Language, 13*(1), 85–100.

Quinn, P. C., Cummins, M., Kase, J., Martin, E., & Weissman, S. (1996). Development of categorical representations for *above* and *below* spatial relations in 3– to 7–month-old infants. *Developmental Psychology, 32*(5), 942–950.

Quinn, T. C. (1995). The epidemiology of the acquired immunodeficiency syndrome in the 1990s. *Emergency Medical Clinics of North America, 13,* 1–25.

Rabain-Jamin, J., & Wornham, W. L. (1993). Practices and representations of child care and motor development among West Africans in Paris. *Early Development and Parenting, 2,* 107–119.

Radke-Yarrow, M., & Zahn-Waxler, C. (1984). Roots, motives, and patterns in children's pro-social behavior. In E. Staub, D. Bartal, J. Karylowski, & J. Reykowski (Eds.), *The development and maintenance of pro-social behaviors* (pp. 68–89). New York: Plenum Press.

Radke-Yarrow, M., Zahn-Waxler, C., Richardson, D. T., Susman, A., & Martinez, P. (1994). Caring behavior in children of clinically depressed and well mothers. *Child Development, 65,* 1405–1414.

Ragozin, A. S., Bashan, R. B., Crnic, K. A., Greenberg, M. T., & Robinson, N. M. (1982). Effects of maternal age on parenting role. *Developmental Psychology, 18,* 627–634.

Raiha, H., Lehtonen, L., Huhtala, V., Saleva, K., & Korven-ranta, H. (2002). Excessively crying infant in the family: Mother-infant, father-infant and mother-father interaction. *Child: Care, Health and Development, 28*(5), 419–429.

Raikes, H., Luze, G., Brooks-Gunn, J., Raikes, H. A., Pan, B. A., Tamis-LeMonda, C. S., et al. (2006). Mother-Child Bookreading in Low-Income Families: Correlates and Outcomes During the First Three Years of Life. *Child Development, 77*(4), 924–953.

Räikkönen, K., Pesonen, A., Järvenpää, A., & Strandberg, T. E. (2004). Sweet babies: Chocolate consumption during pregnancy and infant temperament at six months. *Early Human Development, 76*(2), 139–145.

Raine, A., Reynolds, C., Venables, P. H., & Mednick, S. A. (2002). Stimulation seeking and intelligence: A prospective longitudinal study. *Journal of Personality and Social Psychology, 82*(4), 663–674.

Rakoczy, H., Tomasello, M., & Striano, T. (2004). Young children know that trying is not pretending: A test of the 'Behaving-As-If' construal of children's early concept of pretense. *Developmental Psychology, 40*(3), 388–399.

Ramey, C. T., & Campbell, F. A. (1991). Poverty, early childhood education, and academic competence: The Abecedarian experience. In A. C. Huston (Ed.), *Children in poverty: Child development and public policy* (pp. 190–221). New York: Cambridge University Press.

Ramey, C. T., & Ramey, S. L. (1998). Early intervention and early experience. *American Psychologist, 53*(2), 109–120.

Ramey, S. L. (1999). Head Start and preschool education: Toward continued improvement. *American Psychologist, 54*(5), 344–346.

Ramig, P. R. (1993). High reported spontaneous stuttering recovery rates: Fact or fiction? *Language, Speech, and Hearing Services in Schools, 24,* 156–160.

Ramlau-Hansen, C., Thulstrup, A., Bonde, J., & Olsen, J. (2007). Parental infertility and semen quality in male offspring: A follow-up study. *American Journal of Epidemiology, 166*(5), 568–570.

Ramsay, D. S. (1980). Onset of unimanual handedness in infants. *Infant Behavior and Development, 3,* 377–386.

Ramsey, C. N., Abell, T. N., & Baker, L. C. (1986). The relationship between family functioning, life events, family structure, and the outcome of pregnancy. *Journal of Family Practice, 22,* 521–527.

Ransjo-Arvidson, A. B., Matthiesen, A. S., Lilja, G., Nissen, E., Widstrom, A. M., & Uvnas-Moberg, K. (2001). Maternal analgesia during labor disturbs newborn behavior: effects on breastfeeding, temperature, and crying. *Birth, 28*(1), 5–12.

Rapoport, R., Rapoport, R. N., & Strelitz, A. (1977). *Fathers, mothers and society: Toward new alliances.* New York: Basic Books.

Rappoport, D. (1976). Pour une naissance sans violence: Résultats d'une première enquête. *Bulletin de Psychologie, 29,* 552–560.

Rauh, V. A., Achenbach, T. M., Nurcombe, B., Howell, C. T., & Teti, D. M. (1988). Minimizing adverse effects of low birthweight: Four-year results of an early intervention program. *Child Development, 59,* 544–553.

Rautava, P., Koski, M. L., Sillanpaa, M., & Tuominen, J. (1992). The Finnish family competence study: Childbearing attitudes in pregnant nulliparae. *Acta Paedopsychiatrica, 55,* 3–8.

Raver, C. C. (1996). Relations between social contingency in mother-child interaction and 2–year-olds' social competence. *Developmental Psychology, 32*(5), 850–859.

Raver, C. C. (1996). Success at catching and keeping toddler's attention: An examination of joint attention among low-income mothers and their 2–year-olds. *Early Development and Parenting, 5*(4), 225–236.

Reardon, P., & Bushnell, E. W. (1988). Infants' sensitivity to arbitrary pairings of color and taste. *Infant Behavior and Development, 11,* 245–250.

Rebuffat, E., Groswasser, J., Kelmanson, I., Sottiaux, M., & Kahn, A. (1994). Polygraphic evaluation of night-to-night variability in sleep characteristics and apneas in infants. *Sleep, 17,* 329–332.

Recchia, S. L. (1997). Social communication and response to ambiguous stimuli in toddlers with visual impairments. *Journal of Applied Developmental Psychology, 18*(3), 297–316.

Reddy, V. (1991). Playing with others' expectations: Teasing and mucking about in the first year. In A. Whiten (Ed.), *Natural theories of mind: Evolution, development, and simulation of everyday mindreading* (pp. 143–158). Cambridge, MA: Basil Blackwell.

Reddy, V. (2000). Coyness in early infancy. *Developmental Science, 3*(2), 186–192.

Reddy, V. (2000). Mind knowledge in the first year: Understanding attention and intention. In J. G. Bremner

& A. Fogel (Eds.), *Handbook of infancy research* (pp. 155–181). Oxford, England: Blackwell.

Reeb, K. G., Graham, A. V., Zyzanski, S. J., & Kitson, G. C. (1987). Predicting low birthweight and complicated labor in urban black women: A biopsychosocial perspective. *Social Science and Medicine, 25,* 1321–1327.

Reed, G., & Leiderman, P. H. (1981). Age-related changes in attachment behavior in polymatrically reared infants: The Kenyan Gusii. In T. Field, T. M. Sostek, P. Vietze, & P. Leiderman, (Eds.), *Culture and early interactions* (pp. 85–101). Hillsdale, NJ: Erlbaum.

Reese, M. (1985). Moshe Feldenkrais's work with movement: A parallel approach to Milton Erickson's hypnotherapy. In J. K. Zeig (Ed.), *Ericksonian psychotherapy: Vol. 1: Structures* (pp. 213–229). New York: Brunner-Mazel.

Reilly, J., McIntire, M., & Bellugi, U. (1985, October). *Faces: The relationship between language and affect.* Paper presented at the 10th Annual Boston University Conference on Language Development, Boston, MA.

Reinecke, M. A., & Fogel, A. (1994). The development of referential offering in the first year. *Early Development and Parenting, 3,* 181–186.

Reiner, W. G., & Gearhart, J. P. (2004). Discordant sexual identity in some genetic males with cloacal exstrophy assigned to female sex at birth. *N Engl J Med, 350*(4), 333–341.

Reissland, N. (1988). Neonatal imitation in the first hour of life: Observations in rural Nepal. *Developmental Psychology, 24,* 464–469.

Reissland, N., & Harris, P. (1991). Children's use of display rules in pride-eliciting situations. *British Journal of Developmental Psychology, 9,* 431–435.

Reite, M., Kaemingk, K., & Boccia, M. L. (1989). Maternal separation in bonnet monkey infants: Altered attachment and social support. *Child Development, 60,* 473–480.

Remez, L. (1996). Few married women use a method in Côte d'Ivoire, but fertility is decreasing. *International Family Planning Perspectives, 22*(3), 130–132.

Rempel, L. A., & Rempel, J. K. (2004). Partner influence on health behavior decision-making: Increasing breastfeeding duration. *Journal of Social and Personal Relationships, 21*(1), 92–111.

Repacholi, B. M., & Gopnik, A. (1997). Early reasoning about desires: Evidence from 14– and 18–month olds. *Developmental Psychology, 33*(1), 12–21.

Reynolds, A. J. (1998). Developing early childhood programs for children and families at risk: Research-based principles to promote long-term effectiveness. *Children and Youth Services Review, 20*(6), 503–523.

Reznick, J. S., Kagan, J., Snidman, N., Gersten, M., Baak, K., & Rosenberg, A. (1986). Inhibited and uninhibited children: A follow-up study. *Child Development, 57,* 660–680.

Rheingold, H. L. (1982). Little children's participation in the work of adults: A nascent prosocial behavior. *Child Development, 53,* 114–125.

Rheingold, H. L., Cook, K. V., & Kolowitz, V. (1987). Commands activate the behavior and pleasure of 2–year-old children. *Developmental Psychology, 23,* 146–151.

Rheingold, H. L., Hay, D. F., & West, M. J. (1976). Sharing in the second year of life. *Child Development, 47,* 1148–1158.

Rhodes, J. E. (1993). Easing postpartum school transitions through parent mentoring programs. *Prevention in Human Services, 10,* 169–178.

Ricard, M., & Decarie, T. G. (1993). Distance-maintaining in infants' reaction to an adult stranger. *Social Development, 2,* 154–161.

Ricciuti, H. N. (1974). Fear and the development of social attachments in the first year of life. In M. Lewis & L. Rosenblum (Eds.), *The origins of fear* (pp. 39–58). New York: Wiley.

Ricciuti, H. N., & Poresky, R. H. (1972). Emotional behavior and development in the first year of life: An analysis of arousal, approach-withdrawal, and affective responses. In A. Pick (Ed.), *Minnesota symposia on child psychology* (Vol. 6, pp. 200–221). Minneapolis: University of Minnesota Press.

Richards, M. P. M. (1977). An ecological study of infant development in an urban setting in Britain. In P. Leiderman, S. Tulkin, & A. Rosenfeld (Eds.), *Culture and infancy: Variations in the human experience* (pp. 504–525). New York: Academic Press.

Richardson, D. K., Gray, J. E., Gortmaker, S. L., Goldman, D. A., Pursley, D. M., & McCormick, M. C. (1998). Declining severity adjusted mortality: Evidence of improving neonatal intensive care. *Pediatrics, 102*(4), 893–899.

Richardson, K. (2008). How dynamic systems have changed our minds. In A. Fogel, B. J. King, & S. Shanker (Eds.). *Human development in the 21st century: Visionary policy ideas from systems scientists.* Cambridge, UK: Cambridge University Press.

Rickman, M. D., & Davidson, R. J. (1994). Personality and behavior in parents of temperamentally inhibited and uninhibited children. *Developmental Psychology, 30,* 346–354.

Ricks, S. S. (1985). Father-infant interactions: a review of empirical research. *Family Relations, 34,* 505–511.

Ridgeway, D., Waters, E., & Kuczaj, S. A., II. (1985). Acquisition of emotion-descriptive language: Receptive and productive vocabulary norms for ages 18 months to 6 years. *Developmental Psychology, 21,* 901–908.

Rieck, M., Arad, I., & Netzer, D. (1996). Developmental evaluation of very-low-birthweight infants: Longitudinal and cross-sectional studies. *International Journal of Behavioral Development, 19*(3), 549–562.

Rieger, M., Pirke, K., Buske-Kirschbaum, A., Wurmser, H., Papousek, M., & Hellhammer, D. (2004). Influence of stress during pregnancy on HPA activity and neonatal behavior. *Annals Of The New York Academy Of Sciences, 1032,* 228–230.

Riese, M. L. (1987). Longitudinal assessment of temperament from birth to 2 years: A comparison of full-term and pre-term infants. *Infant Behavior and Development, 10,* 347–363.

Riley, C. A., & Trabasso, T. (1974). Comparatives, logical structures, and encoding in a transitive inference task. *Journal of Experimental Psychology, 17,* 187–203.

Ritter, J. M., Casey, R. J., & Langlois, J. H. (1991). Adults' responses to infants varying in appearance of age and attractiveness. *Child Development, 62,* 68–82.

Ritz, B., Yu, F., Fruin, S., Chapa, G., Shaw, G., & Harris, J. (2002). Ambient air pollution and risk of birth defects in Southern California. *American Journal Of Epidemiology, 155*(1), 17–25.

Rizzo, T. A., Metzger, B. E., Dooley, S. L., & Cho, N. H. (1997). Early malnutrition and child neurobehavioral development: Insights from the study of children of diabetic mothers. *Child Development, 68*(1), 26–38.

Robboy, S., & Jaubert, F. (2007). Neoplasms and pathology of sexual developmental disorders (intersex). *Pathology, 39*(1), 147–163.

Roberts, K., & Cuff, M. D. (1989). Categorization studies of 9– to 15–month-old infants: Evidence for superordinate categorization? *Infant Behavior and Development, 12,* 265–288.

Robertson, J., & Robertson, J. (1971). Young children in brief separation: A fresh look. *Psychoanalytic Study of the Child, 26,* 264–315.

Robertson, S. S. (1987). Human cyclic motility: Fetal-newborn continuities and newborn state differences. *Developmental Psychobiology, 20,* 425–442.

Robertson, S. S. (1990). Temporal organization in fetal and newborn movement. In H. Bloch & B. I. Bertenthal (Eds.), *Sensory-motor organizations and development in infancy and early childhood* (pp. 105–122). The Netherlands: Kluwer Academic.

Robertson, S. S., Bacher, L. F., & Huntington, N. L. (2001). The integration of body movement and attention in young infants. *Psychological Science, 12*(6), 523–526.

Robinson, C. H. (1978). *Fundamentals of normal nutrition* (3rd ed.). New York: Macmillian.

Robinson, J., Little, C., & Biringen, Z. (1993). Emotional communication in mother-toddler relationship: Evidence for early gender differentiation. *Merrill-Palmer Quarterly, 39,* 496–515.

Robinson, J. L., Kagan, J., Reznick, J. S., & Corley, R. (1992). The heritability of inhibited and uninhibited behavior: A twin study. *Developmental Psychology, 28* (6), 1030–1037.

Robson, A., & Cline, B. (1998). Developmental consequences of intrauterine growth retardation. *Infant Behavior and Development, 21*(2), 331344.

Rocha, N. A. C. F., dos Santos Silva, F. P., & Tudella, E. (2006). The impact of object size and rigidity on infant reaching. *Infant Behavior & Development, 29*(2), 251–261.

Rochat, P. (1987). Mouthing and grasping in neonates: Evidence for early detection of what hard or soft substances afford for action. *Infant Behavior and Development, 10,* 435–449.

Rochat, P. (1989). Object manipulation and exploration in 2– to 5–month-old infants. *Developmental Psychology, 25,* 871–884.

Rochat, P. (1992). Self-sitting and reaching in 5– to 8–month-old infants: The impact of posture and its development on early eye-hand coordination. *Journal of Motor Behavior, 24,* 210–220.

Rochat, P., Blass, E. M., & Hoffmeyer, L. B. (1988). Oropharyngeal control of hand-mouth coordination in newborn infants. *Developmental Psychology, 24,* 459–463.

Rochat, P., & Goubet, N. (1995). Development of sitting and reaching in 5– to 6–month-old infants. *Infant Behavior and Development, 18,* 53–68.

Rochat, P., Goubet, N., & Senders, S. J. (1999). To reach or not to reach? Perception of body effectivities by young infants. *Infant and Child Development, 8,* 129–148.

Rochat, P., & Hespos, S. J. (1997). Differential rooting response by neonates: Evidence for an early sense of self. *Early Development and Parenting, 6*(3–4), 105–112.

Rochat, P., & Morgan, R. (1995). Spatial determinants in the perception of self-produced leg movements by 3– to 5–month-old infants. *Developmental Psychology, 31,* 626–636.

Rochat, P., Querido, J. G., & Striano, T. (1999). Emerging sensitivity to the timing and structure of protoconversation in early infancy. *Developmental Psychology, 35*(4), 950–957.

Rochat, P., & Senders, S. J. (1990, April). *Sitting and reaching in infancy.* Paper presented at the Seventh International Conference on Infant Studies, Montreal, Canada.

Rocissano, L., Slade, A., & Lynch, V. (1987). Dyadic synchrony and toddler compliance. *Developmental Psychology, 23,* 698–704.

Rock, A. M. L., Trainor, L. J., & Addison, T. L. (1999). Distinctive messages in infant-directed lullabies and play songs. *Developmental Psychology, 35*(2), 527–534.

Rodholm, M., & Larsson, K. (1979). Father-infant interaction at the first contact after delivery. *Early Human Development, 3,* 21–27.

Rochat, T., & Richter, L. (2007). International adoption: Benefits, risks, and vulnerabilities. *Zero to Three, 27*(5), 23–29.

Roebuck-Spencer, T. M., Mattson, S. N., Marion, S. D., Brown, W. S., & Riley, E. P. (2004). Bimanual coordination in alcohol-exposed children: Role of the corpus callosum. *Journal of the International Neuropsychological Society, 10*(4), 536–548.

Rogers, S. J., & DiLalla, D. L. (1990). Age of symptom onset in young children with pervasive developmental disorders. *Journal of American Academy of Child and Adolescent Psychiatry, 29,* 863–872.

Roggman, L. A., Boyce, L. K., Cook, G. A., Christiansen, K., & Jones, D. (2004). Playing With Daddy: Social Toy Play, Early Head Start, and Developmental Outcomes. *Fathering, 2*(1), 83–108.

Roggman, L. A., Langlois, J. H., Hubbs-Tait, L., & Rieser-Danner, L. A. (1994). Infant day-care, attachment, and the "file drawer problem." *Child Development, 65,* 1429–1443.

Rogoff, B. (1990). *Apprenticeship in thinking: Cognitive development in social context.* New York: Oxford University Press.

Rogoff, B., Mistry, J., Goncu, A., & Mosier, C. (1993). Guided participation in cultural activity by toddlers and caregivers. *Monographs of the Society for Research in Child Development, 58* (8 Serial No. 236), 1–179.

Rogoff, B., Mosier, C., Mistry, J., & Goncu, A. (1989). Toddlers' guided participation in cultural activity. *Cultural Dynamics, 2,* 209–237.

Rogowski, J. (1998). Cost-effectiveness of care for very low birth weight infants. *Pediatrics, 102*(1), 35–43.

Rogowski, J. (1999). Measuring the cost of neonatal and perinatal care. *Pediatrics, 103*(5), 329–335.

Ronnqvist, L., & Hofsten, C. von. (1994). Neonatal finger and arm movements as determined by a social and an object context. *Early Development and Parenting, 3,* 81–94.

Rooks, J. P., Weatherby, N. L., Ernst, E. K. M., Stapleton, S., Rosen, D., & Rosenfeld, A. (1989). Outcome of care in birth centers. *New England Journal of Medicine, 321,* 1804–1811.

Roopnarine, J. L., Fouts, H. N., Lamb, M. E., & Lewis-Elligan, T. Y. (2005). Mothers' and Fathers' Behaviors Toward Their 3- to 4-Month-Old Infants in Lower, Middle, and Upper Socioeconomic African American Families. *Developmental Psychology, 41*(5), 723–732.

Rose, S. A., & Feldman, J. F. (1997). Memory and speed: Their role in the relation of infant information processing to later IQ. *Child Development, 68*(4), 630–641.

Rose, S. A., Feldman, J. F., & Wallace, I. F. (1988). Individual differences in infants' information processing: Reliability, stability, and prediction. *Child Development, 59,* 1177–1197.

Rose, S. A., Feldman, J. F., Wallace, I. F., & McCarton, C. (1989). Infant visual attention: Relation to birth status and developmental outcome during the first 5 years. *Developmental Psychology, 25,* 560–576.

Rose, S. A., Futterweit, L. R., & Jankowski, J. J. (1999). The relation of affect to attention and learning in infancy. *Child Development, 70*(3), 549–559.

Rose, S. A., Schmidt, K., & Bridget, W. H. (1976). Cardiac and behavioral responsivity to tactile stimulation in premature and full-term infants. *Developmental Psychology, 12,* 311–320.

Rosen, K. S., & Burke, P. B. (1999). Multiple attachment relationships within families: Mothers and fathers with two young children. *Developmental Psychology, 35*(2), 436–444.

Rosen, K. S., & Rothbaum, F. (1993). Quality of parental caregiving and security of attachment. *Developmental Psychology, 29,* 358–367.

Rosen, M. (2003). *Rosen Method Bodywork: Accessing the unconscious through touch.* Berkeley CA: North Atlantic Books.

Rosen, W. D., Adamson, L. B., & Bakeman, R. (1992). An experimental investigation of infant social referencing: Mothers' messages and gender differences. *Developmental Psychology, 28,* 1172–1178.

Rosenberg, M. (2009). China's One Child Policy, http://geography.about.com/od/-_populationgeography/a/onechild.htm, Nov. 4, 2009.

Rosenblatt, J. S. (1972). Learning in newborn kittens. *Scientific American, 277,* 18–25.

Rosenblith, J. F., & Sims-Knight, J. E. (1985). *In the beginning: Development in the first two years.* Belmont, CA: Brooks/Cole.

Rosenfield, J. A., Zahorik, P. M., Saint, W., & Murphy, G. (1993). Women's satisfaction with birth control. *Journal of Family Practice, 36,* 169–173.

Rosenstein, D., & Oster, H. (1988). Differential facial responses to four basic tastes in newborns. *Child Development, 59,* 1555–1568.

Rosenthal, N. K. (1991). The relation of peer interaction among infants and toddlers in family day care to characteristics of the child care environment. *Journal of Reproductive and Infant Psychology, Special Issues: International Perspective on Day Care for Young Children, 9,* 151–167.

Rosenthal, N. K. (1999). Out-of-home child care research: A cultural perspective. *International Journal of Behavioral Development, 23*(2), 477–518.

Rosett, H. L. (1980). The effects of alcohol on the fetus and offspring. In O. J. Kalant (Ed.), Alcohol and drug problems in women. *Neurobehavioral Toxicology and Teratology, 6,* 379–385.

Ross, H. S. (1996). Negotiating principles of entitlement in sibling property disputes. *Developmental Psychology, 32*(1), 90–101.

Ross, H. S., Conant, C. L., Cheyne, J. A., & Alevizos, E. (1992). Relationships and alliances in the social interaction of kibbutz toddlers. *Social Development, 1,* 1–17.

Ross, H. S., & Goldman, B. D. (1977a). Establishing new social relations in infancy. In T. Alloway, P. Pliner, & L. Krames (Eds.), *Attachment behavior* (pp. 225–239). New York: Plenum Press.

Ross, H. S., & Goldman, B. D. (1977b). Infant's sociability toward strangers. *Child Development, 48,* 638–642.

Ross, H. S., & Lollis, S. P. (1987). Communication within infant social games. *Developmental Psychology, 23,* 241–248.

Rossi, A. (1968). Transition to parenthood. *Journal of Marriage and the Family, 30,* 26–39.

Ross-Sheehy, S., Oakes, L. M., & Luck, S. J. (2003). The development of visual short-term memory capacity in infants. *Child Development, 74*(6), 1807–1822.

Rothbart, M. K. (1986). Longitudinal observation of infant temperament. *Developmental Psychology, 22,* 356–365.

Rothbart, M. K., & Derryberry, D. (1981). Development of individual differences in temperament. In M. E. Lamb (Ed.), *Advances in developmental psychology* (Vol. 1, pp. 191–230). Hillsdale, NJ: Erlbaum.

Rothbart, M. K., Derryberry, D., & Posner, M. I. (1994). A psychobiological approach to the development of temperament. In J. E. Bates & T. D. Wachs (Eds.), *Temperament: Individual differences at the interface of biology and behavior* (pp. 83–116). Washington, DC: American Psychological Association.

Rothbart, M. K., & Posner, M. I. (1985). Temperament and the development of self-regulation. In L. C. Hartlage & C. F. Telzrow (Eds.), *The neuropsychology of individual differences: A developmental perspective* (pp. 93–123). New York: Plenum Press.

Rothbart, M. K., Sheese, B. E., & Posner, M. I. (2007). Executive attention and effortful control: Linking temperament, brain networks, and genes. *Child Development Perspectives, 1*(1), 2–7.

Rounds, K. A. (1991). Early intervention services for very young children and their families under P.L. 99–457. *Special issues: Learning disabilities. Child and Adolescent Social Work Journal, 8,* 489–499.

Rovee-Collier, C., & Barr, R. (2000). Infant learning and memory. In J. G. Bremner & A. Fogel (Eds.), *Handbook of infancy research.* Oxford, England: Blackwell.

Rovee-Collier, C. K., Enright, M., Lucas, D., Fagan, J., & Gekoski, M. J. (1981). The forgetting of newly acquired and reactivated memories of 3–month-old infants. *Infant Behavior and Development, 4,* 317–331.

Rovee-Collier, C. K., Evancio, S., & Earley, L. A. (1995). The time window hypothesis: Spacing effects. *Infant Behavior and Development, 18,* 69–78.

Roy, T. S., Andrews, J. E., Seidler, F. J., & Slotkin, T. A. (1998). Nicotine evokes cell death in embryonic rat brain during neurulation. *Journal of Pharmacology and Experimental Therapy, 287*(3), 1136–1144.

Rubenstein, J., & Howes, C. (1976). The effects of peers on toddler interaction with mother and toys. *Child Development, 47,* 597–605.

Rubenstein, J., Howes, C., & Pedersen, F. A. (1982). Second order effects of peers on mother-toddler interaction. *Infant Behavior and Development, 5,* 185–194.

Rubin, G. B., Fagen, J. W., & Carroll, M. H. (1998). Olfactory context and memory retrieval in 3–month-old infants. *Infant Behavior and Development, 21*(4), 641–658.

Rubin, K. H., Hastings, P., Chen, X., Stewart, S., & McNichol, K. (1998). Intrapersonal and maternal correlates of aggression, conflict, and externalizing problems in toddlers. *Child Development, 69*(6), 1614–1629.

Rubinstein, A. J., Kalakanis, L., & Langlois, J. H. (1999). Infant preferences for attractive faces: A cognitive explanation. *Developmental Psychology, 35*(3), 848–855.

Ruda, M. A., Ling, Q.-D., Hohmann, R. G., Peng, Y. B., & Tachibana, T. (2000). Altered nocireceptive neuronal circuits after neonatal peripheral inflammation. *Science, 289*(5479), 628–630.

Ruff, H. A. (1978). Infant recognition of invariant forms of objects. *Child Development, 49,* 293–306.

Ruff, H. A. (1984). Infant's manipulative exploration of objects: Effects of age and object characteristics. *Developmental Psychology, 20,* 9–20.

Ruff, H. A. (1985). Detection of information specifying the motion of objects by 3– and 5–month-old infants. *Developmental Psychology, 21,* 295–305.

Ruff, H. A. (1986). Components of attention during infants' manipulative exploration. *Child Development, 57,* 105–114.

Ruff, H. A., & Kohler, C. J. (1978). Tactual-visual transfer in six-month-old infants. *Infant Behavior and Development, 1,* 259–264.

Ruff, H. A., & Lawson, K. R. (1990). Development of sustained, focused attention in young children during free play. *Developmental Psychology, 26,* 85–93.

Ruff, H. A., Lawson, K. R., Parrinello, R., & Weissberg, R. (1990). Long-term stability of individual differences in sustained attention in the early years. *Child Development, 61,* 60–75.

Ruff, H. A., Saltarelli, L. M., Capozzoli, M., & Dubiner, K. (1992). The differentiation of activity in infants' exploration of objects. *Developmental Psychology, 28* (5), 851–861.

Ruffman, T., Slade, L., & Crowe, E. (2002). The relation between children's and mothers' mental state language and theory-of-mind understanding. *Child Development, 73*(3), 734–751.

Ruffwarg, H. P., Muzio, J. N., & Dement, W. C. (1966). Ontogenetic development of the human sleep-dream cycle. *Science, 153,* 604–619.

Ruopp, R. R., & Travers, J. (1982). Janus faces of day care: Perspectives on quality and cost. In E. Zigler & E. Gordon (Eds.), *Day care: Scientific and social policy issues* (pp. 165–190). Boston: Auburn House.

Russell, M. J., Mendelson, T., & Peeke, H. V. (1983). Mothers' identification of their infant's odors. *Ethology and Sociobiology, 4*(1), 29–31.

Rutter, M. (1979). Maternal deprivation, 1972–1978; New findings, new concepts, new approaches. *Child Development, 50,* 283–305.

Rutter, M. (1987). Continuities and discontinuities from infancy. In J. D. Osofsky (Ed.), *Handbook of infant development* (2nd ed.). New York: Wiley.

Rutter, M., & O'Connor, T. G. (2004). Are There Biological Programming Effects for Psychological Development? Findings From a Study of Romanian Adoptees. *Developmental Psychology, 40*(1), 81–94.

Ryan, V., & Wilson, K. (1995). Non-directive play therapy as a means of recreating optimal infant socialization patterns. *Early Development and Parenting, 4*(1) 29–38.

Sachs, J., & Devin, J. (1976). Young children's use of age-appropriate speech styles in social interaction and role-playing. *Journal of Child Language, 3,* 81–98.

Sagi, A. (1981). Mothers' and non-mothers' identification of infant cries. *Infant Behavior and Development, 4,* 37–40.

Sagi, A., Donnell, F., van Ijzendoorn, M. H., Mayseless, O. & Aviezer, O. (1994). Sleeping out of home in a kibbutz communal arrangement: It makes a difference for infant-mother attachment. *Child Development, 65,* 992–1004.

Sagi, A., van Ijzendoorn, M. H., Scharf, M., Joels, T., Koren-Karie, N., Mayseless, O., & Aviezer, O. (1997). Ecological constraints for intergenerational transmission of attachment. *International Journal of Behavioral Development, 20*(2), 287–299.

Sagi, A., Lamb, M. E., Lewkowicz, K. S., Shoham, R., Dvir, R., & Estes, D. (1985). Security of infant-mother, -father, and -metapelet attachments among kibbutz-reared Israeli children. In I. Bretherton & E. Waters (Eds.), *Growing points of attachment theory and research. Monographs of the Society for Research in Child Development, 50* (Serial No. 209), 257–275.

Salapatek, P., & Banks, M. S. (1978). Infant sensory assessment: Vision. In F. D. Minifie & L. L. Lloyd (Eds.), *Communicative and cognitive abilities: Early behavioral assessment* (pp. 86–107). Baltimore: University Park Press.

Saldeen, P., & Saldeen, T. (2004). Women and omega-3 Fatty acids. *Obstet Gynecol Surv, 59*(10), 722–730; quiz 745–726.

Salk, L. (1973). The role of the heartbeat in relations between mother and infant. *Scientific American, 228,* 24–29.

Saltaris, C., Serbin, L. A., Stack, D. M., Karp, J. A., Schwartzman, A. E., & Ledingham, J. E. (2004). Nurturing cognitive competence in preschoolers: A longitudinal study of intergenerational continuity and risk. *International Journal of Behavioral Development, 28*(2), 105–115.

Sameroff, A. J. (1984). Developmental systems: Contexts and evolution. In P. H. Mussen (Ed.), *Handbook of child psychology: Vol. I. History, theory, and methods* (4th ed., pp. 237–294). New York: Wiley.

Sameroff, A. J., & Chandler, M. (1975). Reproductive risk and the continuum of caretaking casualty. In F. Horowitz (Ed.), *Review of child development research* (pp. 303–331). Chicago: University of Chicago Press.

Sameroff, A. J., & Emde, R. N. (1989). *Relationship disturbances in early childhood: A developmental approach.* New York: Basic Books.

Sameroff, A., & MacKenzie, M. (2003). Research strategies for capturing transactional models of development: The limits of the possible. *Development and Psychopathology, 15*(3), 613–640.

Sameroff, A. J., & Seifer, R. (1983). Familial risk and child competence. *Child Development, 54,* 1254–1268.

Sameroff, A. J., Seifer, R., & Elias, P. K. (1982). Sociocultural variability in infant temperament ratings. *Child Development, 53,* 164–173.

Samuels, C. A. (1985). Attention to eye contact opportunity and facial motion by three-month-old infants. *Journal of Experimental Child Psychology, 40,* 105–114.

Samuels, C. A., Scholz, K., & Edmundson, S. (1992). The effects of baby bath and massage by fathers on the family system: The Sunraysia Australia intervention project. *Early Development and Parenting, 1,* 39–49.

Samuels, H. R. (1980). The effect of an older sibling on infant locomotor exploration of a new environment. *Child Development, 51,* 606–609.

Samuelson, L. K., & Smith, L. B. (2005). They call it like they see it: Spontaneous naming and attention to shape. *Developmental Science, 8*(2), 182–198.

Sancier, B., & Mapp, P. (1992). Who helps working women care for the young and old? *Affiliate Journal of Women and Social Work, 7,* 61–62.

Sander, L. W. (1962). Issues in early mother-child interaction. *Journal of the American Academy of Child Psychiatry, 1,* 141–166.

Sander, L. W., Stechler, G., Burns, P., & Lee, A. (1979). Change in infant and caregiver variables over the first two months of life: Integration of action in early development. In E. B. Thoman (Ed.), *Origins of the infant's social responsiveness* (pp. 349–407). Hillsdale, NJ: Lawrence Erlbaum Associates.

Sandman, C. A., Wadhwa, P., Hetrick, W. H., Porto, M., & Peeke, H. V. S. (1997). Human fetal heart rate dishabituation between thirty and thirty-two weeks' gestation. *Child Development, 68*(6), 1031–1040.

Sansavini, A. (1997). Neonatal perception of the rhythmical structure of speech: The role of stress patterns. *Early Development and Parenting, 6*(1), 3–13.

Sansavini, A., Bertoncini, J., & Giovanelli, G. (1997). Newborns discriminate the rhythm of multisyllabic stressed words. *Developmental Psychology, 33*(1), 3–11.

Sansavini, A., Rizzardi, M., Alessandroni, R., & Giovanelli, G. (1996). The development of Italian low- and very-low-birthweight infants from birth to 5 years: The role of biological and social risks. *International Journal of Behavioral Development, 19*(3), 533–547.

Sardana, R. (1985). Examining for defects. *Nursing Mirror, 160,* 38–42.

Savage-Rumbaugh, S., Murphy, J., Sevcik, R. A., Brakke, K. E., Williams, S. L., & Rumbaugh, D. M. (1993). Language comprehension in ape and child. *Monographs of the Society for Research in Child Development, 58* (3–4, Serial No. 233), 1–221.

Savelsbergh, G. J. P., & van der Kamp, J. (1993). The coordination of infant's reaching, grasping, catching and posture: A natural physical approach. In G. J. P. Savelsbergh (Ed.), *The development of coordination in infancy* (pp. 289–317). Amsterdam: Elsevier.

Sawyer, D. (1999). *Birthing the self: Water-based methods for healing prenatal and birth trauma.* davidsawyer@ibm.net

Sawin, D., & Parke, R. (1979). Fathers' affectionate stimulation and caregiving behaviors with newborn infants. *Family Coordinator, 28,* 509–513.

Saylor, C. F., Boyce, G. C., & Price, C. (2003). Early predictors of school-age behavior problems and social skills in children with intraventricular hemorrhage (IVH) and/or extremely low birthweight (ELBW). *Child Psychiatry & Human Development, 33*(3), 175–192.

Scaife, M., & Bruner, J. S. (1975). The capacity for joint visual attention in the infant. *Nature, 253,* 265–266.

Scaramella, L. V., Conger, R. D., Simons, R. L., & Whitbeck, L. B. (1998). Predicting risk for pregnancy by late adolescence: A social contextual perspective. *Developmental Psychology, 34*(6), 1233–1245.

Scaramella, L. V., & Leve, L. D. (2004). Clarifying Parent-Child Reciprocities During Early Childhood: The Early Childhood Coercion Model. *Clinical Child and Family Psychology Review, 7*(2), 89–107.

Scarr, S. (1984). *Mother care/other care.* New York: Basic Books.

Scarr, S. (1992). Developmental theories for the 1990s: Development and individual differences. *Child Development, 63*(1), 1–19.

Scarr, S. (1993). Biological and cultural diversity: The legacy of Darwin for development. *Child Development, 64,* 1333–1353.

Scarr, S., & Eisenberg, M. (1993). Child care research: Issues, perspectives, and results. *Annual Review of Psychology, 44,* 613–632.

Scarr, S., & McCartney, K. (1983). How people make their own environments: A theory of genotype-environment effects. *Child Development, 21,* 391–402.

Scarr, S., & McCartney, K. (1988). Far from home: An experimental evaluation of the mother-child home program in Bermuda. *Child Development, 59,* 531–543.

Schachter, F. F. (1979). *Everyday mother talk to toddlers: Early intervention.* New York: Academic Press.

Schachter, F. S., & Stone, R. K. (1985). Difficult sibling, easy sibling: Temperament and the within-family environment. *Child Development, 56,* 1335–1344.

Schafer, G., Plunkett, K., & Harris, P. L. (1999). What's in a name? Lexical knowledge drives infant preferences in the absence of referential input. *Developmental Science, 2*(2), 187–194.

Schaffer, H. R., & Crook, C. K. (1979). Maternal control techniques in a directed play situation. *Child Development, 50,* 989–996.

Schaffer, H. R., & Crook, C. K. (1980). Child compliance and maternal control techniques. *Developmental Psychology, 16,* 54–56.

Schaffer, H. R., & Emerson, P. (1964). Patterns of response to physical contact in early human development. *Journal of Child Psychiatry and Psychology, 5,* 1–13.

Schanberg, S., Bartolome, J., & Kuhn, C. (1987, January). *Touching and the brain.* Paper presented at the American College of Neuropsychopharmacology, San Juan, Puerto Rico.

Scher, A., Epstein, R., & Tirosh, E. (2004). Stability and changes in sleep regulation: A longitudinal study from 3 months to 3 years. *International Journal of Behavioral Development, 28*(3), 268–274.

Scher, A., Zukerman, S., & Epstein, R. (2005). Persistent night waking and settling difficulties across the first year: Early precursors of later behavioural problems? *Journal of Reproductive and Infant Psychology, 23*(1), 77–88.

Schiffman, P. C., Westlake, R. E., Santiago, T. V., & Edelman, N. H. (1980). Ventilatory control in parents of victims of sudden-infant-death syndrome. *New England Journal of Medicine, 302,* 486–491.

Schindler, P. J., Moely, B. E., & Frank, A. L. (1987). Time in day care and social participation of young children. *Developmental Psychology, 23,* 255–261.

Schleidt, M., & Genzel, C. (1990). The significance of mother's perfume for infants in the first weeks of their life. *Ethology and Sociobiology, 11,* 145–155.

Schlesinger, M., & Langer, J. (1999). Infants' developing expectations of possible and impossible tool-use events between ages 8 and 12 months. *Developmental Science, 2*(2), 195–205.

Schmitt, K. L., & Anderson, D. R. (2002). Television and reality: Toddlers' use of visual information from video to guide behavior. *Media Psychology, 4*(1), 51–76.

Schmitz, S., Fulker, D. W., Plomin, R., Zahn-Waxler, C., Emde, R. N., & DeFries, J. C. (1999). Temperament and problem behavior during early childhood. *International Journal of Behavioral Development, 23*(2), 333–355.

Schmuckler, M. A. (1996). Visual-proprioceptive intermodal perception in infancy. *Infant Behavior and Development, 19,* 221–232.

Schneider, K. J. (1998). Toward a science of the heart: Romanticism and the revival of psychology. *American Psychologist, 53*(3), 277–289.

Schneider, M. L., Roughton, E. C., Koehler, A. J., & Lubach, G. R. (1999). Growth and development following prenatal stress exposure in primates: An examination of ontogenetic vulnerability. *Child Development, 70*(2), 263–274.

Schneider-Rosen, K., & Wenz-Gross, M. (1990). Patterns of compliance from eighteen to thirty months of age. *Child Development, 61,* 104–112.

Schölmerich, A., Fracasso, M. P., Lamb, M. E., & Broberg, A. G. (1995). Interactional harmony at 7 and 10 months of age predicts security of attachment as measured by Q-sort ratings. *Social Development, 4,* 64–68.

Schölmerich, A., Lamb, M. E., Leyendecker, B., & Fracasso, M. P. (1997). Mother-infant teaching interactions and attachment security in Euro-American and Central-American immigrant families. *Infant Behavior and Development, 20,* 165–174.

Scholz, K., & Samuels, C. A. (1992). Neonatal bathing and massage intervention with fathers, behavioral effects 12 weeks after birth of the first baby: The Sunraysia Australia Intervention Project. *International Journal of Behavioral Development, 15,* 67–81.

Schore, A. (2003). *Affect dysregulation and disorders of the self.* Norton.

Schreiber, J. (1977). Birth, the family and the community: A southern Italian example. *Birth and the Family Journal, 4,* 153–157.

Schuetze, P., & Eiden, R. D. (2006). The association between maternal smoking and secondhand exposure and autonomic functioning at 2–4 weeks of age. *Infant Behavior & Development, 29*(1), 32–43.

Schuetze, P., Lewis, A., & DiMartino, D. (1999). Relation between time spent in daycare and exploratory behaviors in 9–month-old infants. *Infant Behavior and Development, 22*(2), 267–276.

Schuetze, P., & Zeskind, P. S. (1997). Relation between reported maternal caffeine consumption during pregnancy and neonatal state and heart rate. *Infant Behavior and Development, 20*(4), 559–562.

Schulman-Galambos, C., & Galambos, R. (1979). Brain stem evoked response audiometry in newborn hearing screening. *Archives of Otolaryngology, 105,* 86–90.

Schum, T. R., Kolb, T. M., McAuliffe, T. L., Simms, M. D., Underhill, R. L., & Lewis, M. (2002). Sequential acquisition of toilet-training skills: a descriptive study of gender and age differences in normal children. *Pediatrics, 109*(3), E48.

Schum, T. R., McAuliffe, T. L., Simms, M. D., Walter, J. A., Lewis, M., & Pupp, R. (2001). Factors associated with toilet training in the 1990s. *Ambul Pediatr, 1*(2), 79–86.

Schwartz, A., Campos, J., & Baisel, E. (1973). The visual cliff: Cardiac and behavioral correlates on the deep and shallow sides at 5 and 9 months of age. *Journal of Experimental Child Psychology, 15,* 85–99.

Schwartz, C. E., Wright, C. I., Shin, L. M., Kagan, J., & Rauch, S. L. (2003). Inhibited and uninhibited infants "grown up": Adult Amygdalar response to novelty. *Science, 300,* 1952–1953.

Schwartz, P. (1983). Length of daycare attendance and attachment behavior in eighteen-month-old infants. *Child Development, 54,* 1073–1078.

Schweinhart, L. J., & Weikart, D. P. (1979, April). *Perry preschool effects in adolescence.* Paper presented to the biennial meeting of the Society for Research in Child Development, San Francisco, CA.

Sebire, N. J., Jolly, M., Harris, J. P., Wadsworth, J., Joffe, M., Beard, R. W., et al. (2001). Maternal obesity and pregnancy outcome: a study of 287,213 pregnancies in London. *Int J Obes Relat Metab Disord, 25*(8), 1175–1182.

Secret, M., & Sprang, G. (2001). The effects of family-friendly workplace environments on work-family stress of employed parents. *Journal of Social Service Research, 28*(2), 21–45.

Seifer, R., LaGasse, L. L., Lester, B., Bauer, C. R., Shankaran, S., Bada, H. S., et al. (2004). Attachment Status in Children Prenatally Exposed to Cocaine and Other Substances. *Child Development, 75*(3), 850–868.

Seifer, R., Sameroff, A. J., Anagnostopolou, R., & Elias, P. K. (1992). Mother-infant interaction during the first year: Effects of situation, maternal mental illness, and demographic factors. *Infant Behavior and Development, 15,* 405–426.

Seifer, R., Sameroff, A. J., Barrett, L. C., & Krafchuk, E. (1994). Infant temperament measured by multiple observations and mother report. *Child Development, 65,* 1478–1490.

Seifer, R., & Schiller, M., Sameroff, A. J., Resnick, S., & Riordan, K. (1996). Attachment, maternal sensitivity, and infant temperament during the first year of life. *Developmental Psychology, 32*(1), 12–25.

Seimyr, L., Edhborg, M., Lundh, W., & Sjogren, B. (2004). In the shadow of maternal depressed mood. Experiences of parenthood during the first year after childbirth. *J Psychosom Obstet Gynaecol, 25*(1), 23–34.

Seitz, V., Rosenbaum, L. K., & Apfel, N. H. (1985). Effects of family support intervention: A ten-year follow-up. *Child Development, 56,* 376–391.

Selby, J. M., & Bradley, B. S. (2003). Infants in Groups: A Paradigm for the Study of Early Social Experience. *Human Development, 46*(4), 197–221.

Self, P., & Horowitz, F. D. (1979). The assessment of the newborn infant. In J. Osofsky (Ed.), *Handbook of infant development* (pp. 240–268). New York: Wiley.

Seligman, M. E. P., & Maier, S. (1967). Failure to escape traumatic shock. *Journal of Experimental Psychology, 74,* 1–9.

Sell, E. J., Hill-Mangan, S., & Holberg, C. J. (1992). Natural course of behavioral organization in premature infants. *Infant Behavior and Development, 15*(4), 461–478.

Selman, R. L. (1980). *The growth of interpersonal understanding: Developmental and clinical analyses.* New York: Academic Press.

Serbin, L. A., Poulin-Dubois, D., & Eichstedt, J. A. (2002). Infants' response to gender-inconsistent events. *Infancy, 3*(4), 531–542.

Serifica, F. C. (1978). The development of attachment behaviors: An organismic-developmental perspective. *Human Development, 21,* 119–140.

Service, R. F. (1994). Barriers hold back new contraception strategies. *Science, 266,* 1489.

Service V., Lock, A., & Chandler, P. (1989). Individual differences in early communicative development: A social constructivist perspective. In S. Tetzchner, L. Siegel & L. Smith (Eds.), *The social cognitive aspects of normal atypical language development* (pp. 23–49). New York: Springer-Verlag.

Seto, A., Einarson, T., & Koren, G. (1997). Pregnancy outcome following first trimester exposure to antihistamines: Meta-analysis. *American Journal of Perinatology, 14*(3), 199–124.

Sewall, M. (1930). Some causes of jealousy in young children. *Smith College Studies in Social Work, 1,* 6–22.

Shah, D., & Sachdev, H. P. (2004). Maternal micronutrients and fetal outcome. *Indian J Pediatr, 71*(11), 985–990.

Shahmoon-Shanok, R. (1999). Adopting parenthood: An enduring transformation marking identity and intimacy capacities. *Zero to Three, 19*(4), 32–36.

Shand, N., & Kosawa, Y. (1985). Japanese and American behavior types at three months: Infants and infant-mother dyads. *Infant Behavior and Development, 8,* 225–240.

Shapira, A., & Madsen, M. C. (1969). Cooperative and competitive behavior of kibbutz and urban children in Israel. *Child Development, 40,* 609–617.

Sharan, P. (1988). One view of the cultural context for the study of childrearing in India. *Newsletter of the International Society for the Study of Behavioral Development, 13,* 1–3.

Shatz, M. (1978). The relationship between cognitive processes and the development of communication skills. In C. B. Keasey (Ed.), *Nebraska symposium on motivation.* Lincoln: University of Nebraska Press.

Shatz, M., & Gelman, R. (1973). The development of communication skills: Modifications in the speech of young children as a function of listener. *Monographs of the Society for Research in Child Development, 38* (Serial No. 152), 1–37.

Shea, A., Walsh, C., MacMillan, H., & Steiner, M. (2004). Child maltreatment and HPA axis dysregulation: Relationship to major depressive disorder and past traumatic stress disorder in females. *Journal of Psychoneuroendocrinology,* 24–36.

Sheppard, J. J., & Mysak, E. D. (1984). Ontogeny of infantile oral reflexes and emerging chewing. *Child Development, 55,* 831–843.

Sherrod, K. B., Crawley, S., Petersen, G., & Bennett, P. (1978). Maternal language to prelinguistic infants: Semantic aspects. *Infant Behavior and Development, 1,* 335–346.

Sherrod, K. B., Friedman, S., Crawley, S., Drake, D., & Dervieux, J. (1977). Maternal language to prelinguistic infants: Syntactic aspects. *Child Development, 48,* 1662–1665.

Sherrod, K. B., O'Conner, S., Vietze, P. M., & Altemeier, W. A. (1984). Child health and maltreatment. *Child Development, 55,* 1174–1183.

Shirley, M. M. (1931). *The first two years: A study of twenty-five babies: Vol. 1. Postural and locomotor development.* Minneapolis: University of Minnesota Press.

Shirley, M. M. (1933). *The first two years: A study of twenty-five babies (Vol. 3).* Minneapolis: University of Minnesota Press.

Shnider, S. (1981). Choice of anesthesia for labor and delivery. *Journal of Obstetrics and Gynecology, 58* (5 Suppl.), 24S-34S.

Shonkoff, J. P., Hauser-Cram, P., Krauss, M. W., & Upshur, C. C. (1992). Development of infants with disabilities and their families. *Monographs of the Society for Research in Child Development, 57,* 1–163.

Shore, C. (1986). Combinatorial play: Conceptual development, and early multiword speech. *Developmental Psychology, 22*(2), 184–190.

Shulman, S., Becker, A., & Sroufe, L. A. (1999). Adult-child interactions as related to adult's family history and child's attachment. *International Journal of Behavioral Development, 23*(4), 959–976.

Shwalb, B. J., Shwalb, D., & Shoji, J. (1994). Structure and dimensions of maternal perceptions of Japanese infant temperament. *Developmental Psychology, 30,* 131–141.

Shy, K. K., Luthy, D. A., Bennett, F. C., Whitfield, M., Larson, E. B., Belle, G. van, Hughes, J. P., Wilson, J. A., & Stenchever, M. A. (1990). Effects of electronic fetal-heart-rate monitoring, as compared with periodic ausculation, on the neurological development of premature infants. *New England Journal of Medicine, 322*(9), 588–593.

Sidebotham, P., & Heron, J. (2003). Child maltreatment in the 'children of the nineties:' The role of the child. *Child Abuse & Neglect, 27*(3), 337–352.

Siegel, D. (2001). *The developing mind: How relationships and the brain interact to shape who we are.* NY: The Guilford Press.

Siegal, L. S. (1981). Infant tests as predictors of cognitive and language development at two years. *Child Development, 52,* 545–557.

Siegal, M., & Storey, R. M. (1985). Day care and children's conceptions of moral and social rules. *Child Development, 56,* 1001–1008.

Sigman, M., Cohen, S. E., Beckwith, L., & Parmelee, A. H. (1981). Social and familial influences on the development of preterm infants. *Journal of Pediatric Psychology, 6,* 1–13.

Sigman, M., Cohen, S. E., Beckwith, L., & Parmelee, A. H. (1986). Infant attention in relation to intellectual abilities in childhood. *Developmental Psychology, 22,* 788–792.

Sigman, M., & Kasari, C. (1995). Joint attention across contexts in normal and autistic children. In C. Moore & P. J. Dunham (Eds.), *Joint attention: Its origins and role in development* (pp. 189–203). Hillsdale, NJ: Erlbaum.

Sigman, M., Neumann, C., Carter, E., Cattle, D. J., D'Souza, S., & Bwibo, N. (1988). Home interactions and the development of Embu toddlers in Kenya. *Child Development, 59,* 1251–1261.

Sigman, M., & Ruskin, E. (1999). Continuity and change in the social competence of children with autism, Down syndrome, and developmental delays. *Monographs of the Society for Research in Child Development, 64*(1), 1–139.

Silberner, J. (1986). Survival of the fetus. *Science News, 130,* 234–235.

Silver, M. (1985). Life after Tay-Sachs. *Jewish Monthly, 99,* 14–23.

Silverman, I., Dickens, S. E., Eals, M., & Fine, J. (1993). Perceptions of maternal and paternal solicitude by birth children and adoptees: Relevance for maternal bonding theory. *Early Development and Parenting, 2,* 135–144.

Simcock, G., & Hayne, H. (2003). Age-related changes in verbal and nonverbal memory during early childhood. *Developmental Psychology, 39*(5), 805–814.

Simons, R. L., Lorenz, F. O., Wu, C. I., & Conger, R. D. (1993). Social network and marital support as mediators and moderators of the impact of stress and depression on parental behavior. *Developmental Psychology, 29,* 368–381.

Singer, L. M., Brodzinsky, D. M., Ramsay, D., Steir, M., & Waters, E. (1985). Mother-infant attachment in adoptive families. *Child Development, 56,* 1543–1551.

Singer, L. M., Salvator, A., Guo, S., Collin, M., Lilien, L., & Baley, J. (1999). Maternal psychological distress and parenting stress after the birth of a very low-birth-weight infant. *Journal of the American Medical Association, 281*(9), 799–805.

Singer, L. T., Minnes, S., Short, E., Arendt, R., Farkas, K., Lewis, B., Klein, N., Russ, S., Min, M. O., & Kirchner, H. L. (2004). Cognitive outcomes of preschool children with prenatal cocaine exposure. *JAMA, 291*(20), 2448–2456.

Singh, G., Kogan, M., & Dee, D. (2007). Nativity/Immigrant status, race/ethnicity, and socioeconomic determinants of breastfeeding initiation and duration in the United States, 2003. *Pediatrics, 119,* S38–S46.

Singh, V. K., Warren, R. P., Odell, J. D., Warren, W. L., & Cole, P. (1993). Antibodies to myelin basic protein in children with autistic behavior. *Brain Behavior and Immunization, 7,* 97–103.

Siskind, V., Schofield, F., Rice, D., & Bain, C. (1989). Breast cancer and breastfeeding: Results from an Australian case-control study. *American Journal of Epidemiology, 130,* 229–236.

Sitskoorn, M. M., & Smitsman, A. W. (1995). Infants' perception of dynamic relations between objects: Passing through or support? *Developmental Psychology, 31,* 437–447.

Sitskoorn, M. M., & Smitsman, A. W. (1997). Perception of dynamic object relations in infancy. *Infant Behavior and Development, 20,* 141–150.

Sjogren, B., Edman, G., Widstrom, A. M., Mathiesen, A. S., & Uvnas-Moberg, K. (2004). Maternal foetal attachment and personality during first pregnancy. *Journal of Reproductive and Infant Psychology, 22*(2), 57–69.

Skarin, K. (1977). Cognitive and contextual determinants of stranger fear in six- and eleven-month-old infants. *Child Development, 48,* 537–544.

Skinner, B. F. (1938). *The behavior of organisms.* Englewood Cliffs, NJ: Prentice-Hall.

Slaby, R. G., & Frey, K. S. (1975). Development of gender constancy and selective attention to same-sex models. *Child Development, 46,* 849–856.

Slade, A. (1986). Symbolic play and separation-individuation: A naturalistic study. *Bulletin of the Menninger Clinic, 50,* 541–563.

Slade, A. (1987a). A longitudinal study of maternal involvement and symbolic play during the toddler period. *Child Development, 58,* 367–375.

Slade, A. (1987b). Quality of attachment and early symbolic play. *Developmental Psychology, 23,* 78–85.

Slade, A. (2005). Parental reflective functioning: An introduction. *Attachment and Human Development, 7,* 269–281.

Slade, E. P., & Wissow, L. S. (2004). Spanking in early childhood and later behavior problems: a prospective study of infants and young toddlers. *Pediatrics, 113*(5), 1321–1330.

Slama, R., Bouyer, J., Windham, G., Fenster, L., Werwatz, A., & Swan, S. (2005). Influence of paternal age on the risk of spontaneous abortion. *American Journal of Epidemiology, 161*(9), 816–823.

Slater, A., Morison, V., & Rose, D. (1984). Habituation in the newborn. *Infant Behavior and Development, 7,* 183–200.

Slater, A., von der Schulenburg, C., Brown, E., Badenoch, M., Butterworth, G., Parsons, S., & Samuels, C. (1998). Newborn infants prefer attractive faces. *Infant Behavior and Development, 21*(2), 345–354.

Slater, R., Cantarella, A., Gallella, S., Worley, A., Boyd, S., Meek, J., et al. (2006). Cortical Pain Responses in Human Infants. *Journal of Neuroscience, 26*(14), 3662–3666.

Slaughter, D. T. (1980). Social policy issues affecting infants. In B. Weissbourd & J. Musick (Eds.), *Infants: Their social environments* (pp. 150–178). Chicago: National Association for the Education of Young Children.

Slobin, D. (1970). Universals of grammatical development in children. In G. B. Flores d'Arcais & W. J. M. Levelt (Eds.), *Advances in psycholinguistics* (pp. 12–38). Amsterdam: North-Holland.

Smeeding, T. M., & Torrey, B. B. (1988). Poor children in rich countries. *Science, 242,* 873–877.

Smialek, A. (1978). Observations on immediate reactions of families to sudden infant death. *Pediatrics, 62,* 160–165.

Smidt-Jensen, S., & Hahnemann, N. (1988). Transabdominal chorionic villus sampling for fetal genetic diagnosis: Technical and obstetrical evaluation of 100 cases. *Prenatal Diagnosis, 8,* 7–17.

Smigel, K. L. (1988). Breast-feeding linked to decreased cancer risk for mother, child. *Journal of the National Cancer Institute, 80,* 1362–1363.

Smith, P. B., & Pederson, D. R. (1988). Maternal sensitivity and patterns of infant-mother attachment. *Child Development, 59,* 1097–1101.

Smith, R. (1999, March). The timing of birth. *Scientific American, 280*(3), 68–75.

Smith, S. L., Gerhardt, K. J., Griffiths, S. K., Huang, X., & Abrams, R. M. (2003). Intelligibility of Sentences Recorded from the Uterus of a Pregnant Ewe and from the Fetal Inner Ear. *Audiology & Neurotology, 8*(6), 347–353.

Smotherman, W. P., & Robinson, S. R. (1987). Prenatal expression of species-typical action patterns in the rat fetus. *Journal of Comparative Psychology, 101*(2), 190–196.

Smyth, J. M., & Pennebaker, J. W. (1999). Sharing one's story. In C. R. Snyder (Ed.), *Coping: The psychology of what works* (pp. 70–89). Oxford, England: Oxford University Press.

Snow, C. E. (1977). The development of conversation between mothers and babies. *Journal of Child Language, 4,* 1–22.

Snow, C. E. (1984). Parent-child interaction and the development of communicative ability. In R. Schiefelbusch & J. Pickar (Eds.), *The acquisition of communicative competence* (pp. 377–403). Baltimore: University Park Press.

Snow, M. E., Jacklin, C. N., & Maccoby, E. E. (1981). Birth-order differences in peer sociability at thirty-three months. *Child Development, 52,* 589–595.

Soderstrom, M., & Morgan, J. L. (2007). Twenty-two-month-olds discriminate fluent from disfluent adult-directed speech. *Developmental Science, 10*(5), 641–653.

Sodian, B., Thoermer, C., & Metz, U. (2007). Now I see it but you don't: 14–month-olds can represent another person's visual perspective. *Developmental Science, 10*(2), 199–204.

Sogaard, A. J., Kritz-Silverstein, D., & Wingard, D. L. (1994). Finnmark heart study: Employment status and parent-

hood as predictors of psychological health in women, 20–49 years. *International Journal of Epidemiology, 23,* 82–90.

Soken, N. H., & Pick, A. D. (1992). Intermodal perception of happy and angry expressive behaviors by seven-month-old infants. *Child Development, 63,* 787–795.

Soken, N. H., & Pick, A. D. (1999). Infants' perception of dynamic affective expressions: Do infants distinguish specific expressions? *Child Development, 70*(6), 1275–1282.

Sokolov, J. L. (1993). A local contingency analysis of the fine-tuning hypothesis. *Developmental Psychology, 29,* 1008–1023.

Solarz, A. (2001). Investing in Children, Families, and Communities: Challenges for an Interdivisional Public Policy. *American Journal of Community Psychology, 29*(1), 1.

Soliday, E. (2007). Infant feeding and cognition: Integrating a developmental perspective. *Child Development Perspectives, 1*(1), 19–25.

Sollie, D., & Miller, B. (1980). The transition to parenthood as a critical time for building family strengths. In N. Stinnet & P. Knaub (Eds.), *Family strengths: Positive models of family life* (pp. 19–36). Lincoln: University of Nebraska Press.

Søndergaard, C., Henriksen, T. B., Obel, C., & Wisborg, K. (2001). Smoking during pregnancy and infantile colic. *Pediatrics, 108,* 342–346.

Sorce, J., Emde, R., Campos, J., & Klinnert, M. (1985). Maternal emotional signaling: Its effect on the visual cliff behavior of 1–year-olds. *Developmental Psychology, 21,* 195–200.

Sorenson, E. R. (1979). Early tactile communication and the patterning of human organization: A New Guinea case study. In M. Bullowa (Ed.), *Before speech* (pp. 217–229). New York: Cambridge University Press.

Sostek, A. M., & Anders, T. F. (1977). Relationships among the Brazelton neonatal scale, Bayley infant scales and early temperament. *Child Development, 48,* 320–323.

Sostek, A. M., Smith, Y. F., Katz, K. S., & Grant, E. G. (1987). Developmental outcome of preterm infants with intraventricular hemorrhage at one and two years of age. *Child Development, 58,* 779–786.

Spangler, G., & Grossmann, K. E. (1993). Biobehavioral organization in securely and insecurely attached infants. *Child Development, 64,* 1439–1450.

Speltz, M. L., Endriga, M. C., Fisher, P. A., & Mason, C. A. (1997). Early predictors of attachment in infants with cleft lip and/or palate. *Child Development, 68*(1), 12–25.

Spemann, H. (1938). *Embryonic development and induction.* New Haven, CT: Yale University Press.

Spence, M. J., & Freeman, M. S. (1996). Newborn infants prefer the maternal low-pass filtered voice, but not the maternal whispered voice. *Infant Behavior and Development, 19,* 199–212.

Spence, S. H., Najman, J. M., Bor, W., O'Callaghan, M., & Williams, G. M. (2002). Maternal anxiety and depression, poverty and marital relationship factors during early childhood as predictors of anxiety and depressive symptoms in adolescence. *Journal of Child Psychology and Psychiatry, 43*(4), 457–470.

Speraw, S. R. (1994). The experience of miscarriage: How couples define quality in health care delivery. *Journal of Perinatology, 14,* 208–215.

Spieker, S. J., & Bensley L. (1994). Roles of living arrangements and grandmother social support in adolescent mothering and infant attachment. *Developmental Psychology, 30,* 102–111.

Spiker, D., Ferguson, J., & Brooks-Gunn, J. (1993). Enhancing maternal interactive behavior and child social competence in low birth weight, premature infants. *Child Development, 64,* 754–768.

Spinillo, A., Iasci, A., Dal-Maso, J., Di-Lenardo, L., Grella, P., & Guaschino, S. (1994). The effect of fetal infection with human immunodeficiency virus type 1 on birthweight and length of gestation. *European Journal of Obstetrics and Gynecology, 57,* 13–17.

Spinrad, T. L., Eisenberg, N., Gaertner, B., Popp, T., Smith, C. L., Kupfer, A., et al. (2007). Relations of maternal socialization and toddlers' effortful control to children's adjustment and social competence. *Developmental Psychology, 43*(5), 1170–1186.

Spinrad, T. L., Stifter, C. A., Donelan-McCall, N., & Turner, L. (2004). Mothers' regulation strategies in response to toddlers' affect: Links to later emotion self-regulation. *Social Development, 13*(1), 40–55.

Spitz, H. H. (1992). Does the Carolina Abecedarian early intervention project prevent sociocultural mental retardation? *Intelligence, 16,* 225.

Spitz, R. (1965). *The first year of life.* New York: International Universities Press.

Spock, B. (1957). *Baby and child care.* New York: Pocket Books.

Sroufe, L. A. (1979). Socioemotional development. In J. Osofsky (Ed.), *Handbook of infant development* (pp. 462–516). New York: Wiley.

Sroufe, L. A. (1983). Individual patterns of adaptation from infancy to preschool. In M. Perlmutter (Ed.), *Minnesota symposia on child psychology* (Vol. 16, pp. 165–182). Hillsdale, NJ: Lawrence Erlbaum.

Sroufe, L. A. (1989). Relationships, self, and individual adaptation. In A. J. Sameroff and R. N. Emde (Eds.), *Relationships disturbances in early childhood: A developmental approach* (pp. 70–94). New York: Basic Books.

Sroufe, L. A. (1995). *Emotional development: The organization of emotional life in the early years.* Cambridge, England: Cambridge University Press.

Sroufe, L. A., & Waters, E. (1976). The ontogenesis of smiling and laughter: A perspective on the organization of development in infancy. *Psychological Review, 83,* 173–186.

Sroufe, L. A., & Wunsch, J. P. (1977). The development of laughter in the first year of life. *Child Development, 43,* 1326–1344.

Stack, D. M. (2000). The salience of touch and physical contact during infancy: Unravelling some of the mysteries of the somaesthetic sense. In J. G. Bremner & A. Fogel (Eds.), *Handbook of infancy research* (pp. 268–292). Oxford, England: Blackwell.

Stack, D. M., & Arnold, S. L. (1998). Changes in mothers' touch and hand gestures influence infant behavior during face-to-face interchanges. *Infant Behavior and Development, 21*(3), 451–468.

Stack, D. M., & LePage, D. E. (1996). Infants' sensitivity to manipulations of maternal touch during face-to-face interactions. *Social Development, 5*(1), 41–55.

Stack, D. M., & Muir, D. W. (1992). Adult tactile stimulation during face-to-face interactions modulates five-month-olds' affect and attention. *Child Development, 63,* 1509–1525.

Stanton, A. N., Scott, D. J., & Downhan, M. A. (1980). Is overheating a factor in some unexpected infant deaths? *Lancet, 78*(5), 1054–1057.

Stark, R. E. (1978). Features of infant sounds: The emergence of cooing. *Journal of Child Language, 3,* 379–390.

Stark, R. E., Rose, S. N., & McLagen, M. (1975). Features of infant sounds: The first eight weeks of life. *Journal of Child Language, 2,* 205–222.

Starkey, D. (1981). The origins of concept formation: Object sorting and object preference in early infancy. *Child Development, 52,* 489–497.

Stattin, H., & Klackenberg-Larsson, I. (1991). The short and long-term implications for parent-child relations of parents' prenatal preferences for their child's gender. *Developmental Psychology, 27*(1), 141–147.

Stayton, D. J., Ainsworth, M. D. S., & Main, M. B. (1973). The development of separation behavior in the first year of life: Protest, following, greeting. *Developmental Psychology, 9,* 213–225.

Steele, H., Steele, M., Croft, C., & Fonagy, P. (1999). Infant-mother attachment at one year predicts children's understanding of mixed emotions at six years. *Social Development, 8*(2), 161–178.

Steele, H., Steele, M., & Fonagy, P. (1996). Associations among attachment classifications of mothers, fathers, and their infants. *Child Development, 67,* 523 540.

Stein, A., Cambell, E. A., Day, A., McPherson, K., & Cooper, P. J. (1987). Social adversity, low birth weight, and preterm delivery. *British Medical Journal, 295,* 291–293.

Stein, Z., & Susser, M. (1985). Effects of early nutrition on neurological and mental competence in human beings. *Psychological Medicine, 15,* 717–726.

Steiner, J. E. (1973). The gustofacial response: Observation on normal and anencephalic newborn infants. In J. F.

Bosma (Ed.), *Fourth symposium on oral sensation and perception*. (DHEW Publication No. NIH 73–546) (pp. 15–28). Bethesda, MD: Department of Health, Education, and Welfare.

Steiner, J. E. (1977). Facial expressions of the neonate infant indicating the hedonics of food-related chemical stimuli. In J. M. Weiffenbach (Ed.), *Taste and development* (pp. 204–219). Bethesda, MD: Department of Health, Education, and Welfare.

Stella-Prorok, E. M. (1983). Mother-child language in the natural environment. In K. E. Nelson (Ed.), *Children's language* (pp. 389–407). Hillsdale, NJ: Erlbaum.

Stenberg, C., Campos, J. J., & Emde, R. N. (1983). The facial expression of anger in seven-month-old infants. *Child Development, 54,* 178–184.

Stenberg, G., & Hagekull, B. (1997). Social referencing and mood modification in 1–year-olds. *Infant Behavior and Development, 20,* 209–217.

Sterman, M. B., & Hoppenbrouwers, T. (1971). The development of sleep-waking and rest-activity patterns from fetus to adult in man. In M. B. Sterman, D. J. McGinty, & A. M. Adinolfi (Eds.), *Brain development and behavior* (pp. 203–228). New York: Academic Press.

Stern, D. N. (1977). *The first relationship.* Cambridge, MA: Harvard University Press.

Stern, D. N. (1985). *The interpersonal world of the infant: A view from psychoanalysis and developmental psychology.* New York: Basic Books.

Stern, D. N. (1995). *The motherhood constellation.* New York: Basic Books.

Stern, D. N., Jaffe, J., Beebe, B., & Bennett, S. J. (1975). Vocalizing in unison and in alternation: Two modes of communication within the mother-infant dyad. *Annals of the New York Academy of Science, 263,* 89–100.

Stern, D. N., Spieker, S., Barnett, R. K., & MacKain, K. (1983). The prosody of maternal speech: Infant age and context related changes. *Journal of Child Language, 10,* 1–15.

Sternberg, R. J., & Davidson, J. E. (1985). Cognitive development in the gifted and talented. In F. D. Horowitz & M. O'Brien (Eds.), *The gifted and talented: Developmental perspectives* (pp. 37–74). Washington, DC: American Psychological Association.

Stettler, N., Stallings, V. A., Troxel, A. B., Zhao, J., Schinnar, R., Nelson, S. E., et al. (2005). Weight gain in the first week of life and overweight in adulthood: a cohort study of European American subjects fed infant formula. *Circulation, 111*(15), 1897–1903.

Stevens, B., Johnston, C., Franck, L., Petryshen, P., Jack, A., & Foster, G. (1999). The efficacy of developmentally sensitive interventions and sucrose for relieving procedural pain in very low birth weight neonates. *Nursing Research, 48,* 35–43.

Stevens, J. H. (1984). Black grandmothers' & black adolescent mothers' knowledge about parenting. *Developmental Psychology, 20,* 1017–1025.

Stevens, J. H. (1988). Social support, locus of control, and parenting in three low-income groups of mothers: Black teenagers, black adults, and white adults. *Child Development, 59,* 635–642.

Stevenson, M. R., & Black, K. N. (1988). Paternal absence and sex-role development: A meta-analysis. *Child Development, 59,* 793–814.

Stewart, A. (1983). Severe perinatal hazards. In M. Rutter (Ed.), *Developmental neuropsychiatry* (pp. 117–132). New York: Churchill Livingstone.

Stewart, D. E. (1994). Incidence of postpartum abuse in women with a history of abuse during pregnancy. *Canadian Medical Association Journal, 151,* 1601–1604.

Stewart, R. A. (1981). Supplementary foods: Their nutritional role in infant feedings. In J. Bond, L. Filer, G. LeVeille, A. Thomson, & W. Weil (Eds.), *Infant and child feeding* (pp. 101–128). New York: Academic Press.

Stewart, R. A. (1983). Sibling interaction: The role of the older child as teacher for the younger. *Merrill-Palmer Quarterly, 29,* 47–68.

Stewart, R. A., Mobley, L. A., Van Tuyl, S. S., & Salvador, M. A. (1987). The firstborn's adjustment to the birth of a sibling: A longitudinal assessment. *Child Development, 58,* 341–355.

Stiefel, G. S., Plunkett, J. W., & Meisels, S. J. (1987). Affective expression among preterm infants of varying levels of biological risk. *Infant Behavior and Development, 10,* 151–164.

Stifter, C. A., Bono, M., & Spinrad, T. (2003). Parent characteristics and conceptualizations associated with the emergence of infant colic. *Journal of Reproductive and Infant Psychology, 21*(4), 309–322.

Stifter, C. A., Coulehan, C. M., & Fish, M. (1993). Linking employment to attachment: The mediating effects of maternal separation anxiety and interactive behavior. *Child Development, 64,* 1451–1460.

Stifter, C. A., Fox, N. A., & Porges, S. W. (1989). Facial expressivity and vagal tone in 5– and 10–month-old infants. *Infant Behavior and Development, 12,* 127–137.

Stifter, C. A., & Moyer, D. (1991). The regulation of positive affect: Gaze aversion activity during mother-infant interaction. *Infant Behavior and Development, 14,* 111–123.

Stiles, J. (1995). The early use and development of graphic formulas: Two case study reports of graphic formula production by 2–to-3–year-old children. *International Journal of Behavioral Development, 18*(1), 127–149.

Stipek, D. (1995). The development of pride and shame in toddlers. In J. P. Tangney & K. W. Fischer (Eds.), *Self-conscious emotions: The psychology of shame, guilt, embarrassment, and pride* (pp. 237–252). New York: Guilford Press.

St. James-Roberts, I., Conroy, S., & Wilsher, K. (1998). Links between maternal care and persistent infant crying in the early months. *Child Care, Health, and Development, 24*(5), 353–376.

St James-Roberts, I., Goodwin, J., Peter, B., Adams, D., & Hunt, S. (2003). Individual differences in responsivity to a neurobehavioural examination predict crying patterns of 1–week-old infants at home. *Dev Med Child Neurol, 45*(6), 400–407.

St. James-Roberts, I., & Plewis, I. (1996). Individual differences, daily fluctuations, and developmental changes in amounts of infant waking, fussing, crying, feeding, and sleeping. Child Development, 67(5), 2527–2540.

St James-Roberts, I., Sleep, J., Morris, S., Owen, C., & Gillham, P. (2001). Use of a behavioural programme in the first 3 months to prevent infant crying and sleeping problems. *J Paediatr Child Health, 37*(3), 289–297.

Stockman, I. J., & Vaughn-Cooke, F. (1992). Lexical elaboration in children's locative action expressions. *Child Development, 63,* 1104–1125.

Stone, L. J., Smith, H., & Murphy, L. (1973). *The competent infant.* New York: Basic Books.

Stone, W. L., Lemanek, K. L., Fishel, P. T., Fernandez, M. C., & Altemeier, W. A. (1990). Play and imitation skills in the diagnosis of autism in young children. *Pediatrics, 86,* 267–272.

Stoneman, Z., Brody, G. H., & MacKinnon, C. (1984). Naturalistic observations of children's activities and roles while playing with their siblings and friends. *Child Development, 55,* 617–627.

Strassberg, Z., & Treboux, D. (2000). Interpretations of child emotion expressions and coercive parenting practices among adolescent mothers. *Social Development, 9*(1), 80–95.

Straus, M. A. (1995). *Beating the devil out of them: Corporal punishment in American families.* New York: Lexington Books.

Straus, M. A., & Kantor, G. K. (2005). Definition and measurement of neglectful behavior: Some principles and guidelines. *Child Abuse & Neglect, 29*(1), 19–29.

Straus, M. A., & Stewart, J. H. (1999). Corporal punishment by American parents: National data on prevalence, chronicity, severity, and duration, in relation to child and family characteristics. *Clinical Child and Family Psychology Review, 2*(2), 55–70.

Strauss, A., & Corbin, J. (1990). *Basics of qualitative research: Grounded theory procedures and techniques.* Newbury Park, CA: Sage.

Strauss, M. S., & Curtis, L. E. (1981). Infant's perception of numerosity. *Child Development, 52,* 1146–1152.

Streissguth, A. P., Barr, H. M., Sampson, P. D., & Bookstein, F. L. (1994). Prenatal alcohol and offspring development: The first fourteen years. *Drug and Alcohol Dependency, 36,* 89–99.

Striano, T. (2004). Direction of Regard and the Still-Face Effect in the First Year: Does Intention Matter? *Child Development, 75*(2), 468–479.

Striano, T., Henning, A., & Stahl, D. (2005). Sensitivity to social contingencies between 1 and 3 months of age. *Developmental Science, 8*(6), 509–518.

Striano, T., & Rochat, P. (1999). Developmental link between dyadic and triadic social competence in infancy. *British Journal of Developmental Psychology, 17,* 1–12.

Striano, T., & Rochat, P. (in press). Emergence of selective social referencing in infancy. *Infancy.*

Strobino, B. A., & Pantel-Silverman, J. (1987). First-trimester vaginal bleeding and the loss of chromosomally normal and abnormal conceptions. *American Journal of Obstetrics and Gynecology, 157,* 1150–1154.

Stroufe, L. A., Egeland, B., Carlson, E. A., & Collins, W. A. (2005). *The development of the person: The Minnesota study of risk and adaptation from birth to adulthood.* New York: The Guilford Press.

Stuchbery, M., Matthey, S., & Barnett, B. (1998). Postnatal depression and social supports in Vietnamese, Arabic, and Anglo-Celtic mothers. *Social Psychiatry and Psychiatric Epidemiology, 33*(10), 483–490.

Sugarman, S. (1982). The development of preverbal communication: Its contribution and limits in promoting the development of language. In R. Schiefelbusch & L. Pickar (Eds.), *Communicative competence: Acquisition and intervention* (pp. 410–449). Baltimore: University Park Press.

Sullivan, M. W., Rovee-Collier, C. K., & Tynes, D. M. (1979). A conditioning analysis of infant longterm memory. *Child Development, 50,* 152–162.

Sun, L. C., & Roopnarine, J. L. (1996). Mother-infant, father-infant and involvement in childcare and household labor among Taiwanese families. *Infant Behavior and Development, 19,* 121–129.

Suomi, S. J. (1987). Genetic and maternal contributions to individual differences in rhesus monkey biobehavioral development. In N. A. Krasnegor, E. M. Blass, M. A. Hofer, & W. P. Smotherman (Eds.), *Perinatal development: A psychobiological perspective* (pp. 397–420). New York: Academic Press.

Suomi, S. J., & Harlow, H. F. (1972). Social rehabilitation of isolate reared monkeys. *Developmental Psychology, 6,* 487–496.

Super, C. (1976). Environmental effects on motor development: The case of "African infant precocity." *Developmental Medicine and Child Neurology, 18,* 561–567.

Super, C. (1981). Behavioral development in infancy. In R. Munroe & B. Whiting (Eds.), *Handbook of cross-cultural human development* (pp. 95–128). New York: Garland.

Super, C., Herrera, M. G., & Mora, J. O. (1990). Long-term effects of food supplementation and psychosocial intervention on the physical growth of Colombian infants at risk of malnutrition. *Child Development, 61,* 29–49.

Surkan, P. J., Hsieh, C. C., Johansson, A. L., Dickman, P. W., & Cnattingius, S. (2004). Reasons for increasing trends in large for gestational age births. *Obstet Gynecol, 104*(4), 720–726.

Susman-Stillman, A., Kalkoske, M., Egeland, B., & Waldman, I. (1996). Infant temperament and maternal sensitivity as predictors of attachment security. *Infant Behavior and Development, 19,* 33–47.

Suwalsky, J. T., & Klein, R. P. (1980). Effects of naturally occurring nontraumatic separations from mother. *Infant Mental Health Journal, 1,* 196–201.

Swain, I. U., Zelazo, P. R., & Clifton, R. K. (1993). Newborn infants' memory for speech sounds retained over 24 hours. *Developmental Psychology, 29,* 312–323.

Swan, A. M. (1993). Helping children who stutter: What teachers need to know. *Childhood Education, 69,* 138–141.

Swets-Gronert, F. (1984, August). *Temperament in young children.* Paper presented at the European Conference on Development Psychology, Groningen, the Netherlands.

Swingley, D. (2007). Lexical Exposure and Word-Form Encoding in 1.5–Year-Olds. *Developmental Psychology, 43*(2), 454–464.

Swoboda, P. J., Kass, J., Morse, P. A., & Leavitt, L. A. (1978). Memory factors in vowel discrimination of normal and at-risk infants. *Child Development, 49,* 332–339.

Symons, D. K. (2001). A dyad-oriented approach to distress and mother-child relationship outcomes in the first 24 months. *Parenting: Science and Practice, 1*(1–2), 101–122.

Symons, D. K., & McLeod, P. J. (1994). Maternal, infant, and occupational characteristics that predict postpartum employment patterns. *Infant Behavior and Development, 17,* 71–82.

Szyf, M. (2007). The dynamic epigenome and its implications in toxicology. *Toxicol Sci, 100*(1), 7–23.

Takahashi, K. (1986). Examining the strange-situation procedure with Japanese mothers and 12–month-old infants. *Developmental Psychology, 22,* 265–270.

Tallandini, M. A., & Scalembra, C. (2006). Kangaroo Mother Care and Mother-Premature Infant Dyadic Interaction. *Infant Mental Health Journal, 27*(3), 251–275.

Tamis-LeMonda, C. S., & Bornstein, M. H. (1989). Habituation and maternal encouragement of attention in infancy as predictors of toddler language, play, and representational competence. *Child Development, 60,* 738–751.

Tamis-LeMonda, C. S., & Bornstein, M. H. (1990). Language, play, and attention at one year. *Infant Behavior and Development, 13,* 85–98.

Tamis-LeMonda, C. S., Bornstein, M. H., Baumwell, L., & Damast, A. M. (1996). Responsive parenting in the second year: Specific influences on children's language and play. *Early Development and Parenting, 5*(4), 173–183.

Tamis-LeMonda, C. S., Bornstein, M. H., Cyphers, L., Toda, S., & Ogino, M. (1992). Language and play at one year: A comparison of toddlers and mothers in the United States and Japan. *International Journal of Behavioral Development, 15,* 19–42.

Tan, L. E. (1985). Laterality and motor-skills in four-year-olds. *Child Development, 56,* 119–124.

Tanner, J. M. (1970). Physical growth. In P. H. Mussen (Ed.), *Manual of child psychology* (3rd ed., pp. 77–156). New York: Wiley.

Tanguay, P. E. (1990). Early infantile autism: What have we learned in the past 50 years? *Brain Dysfunction, 3,* 197–207.

Tardif, T. (1996). Nouns are not always learned before verbs: Evidence from Mandarin speakers' early vocabularies. *Developmental Psychology, 32*(3), 492–504.

Tardif, T., Gelman, S. A., & Xu, F. (1999). Putting the "noun bias" in context: A comparison of English and Mandarin. *Child Development, 70*(3), 620–635.

Tardif, T., & Wellman, H. M. (2000). Acquisition of mental state language in Mandarin- and Cantonese-speaking children. *Developmental Psychology, 36*(1), 25–43.

Taub, H. B., Goldstein, K. M., & Caputo, D. V. (1977). Indices of neonatal prematurity as discriminators of development in middle childhood. *Child Development, 48,* 797–805.

Taumoepeau, M., & Ruffman, T. (2006). Mother and Infant Talk About Mental States Relates to Desire Language and Emotion Understanding. *Child Development, 77*(2), 465–481.

Taylor, H., Baker, D., ALSPAC and the Study Team. (1997). Employment, parity, and single parenthood: Their impact on health in pregnancy. *Journal of Reproductive and Infant Psychology, 15,* 221–237.

Taylor, S. D. (1994). Demand for predictive genetic testing for Huntington's disease in Australia, 1987 to 1993. *Medical Journal of Australia, 161,* 351–355.

Technical Bulletin Number 189 (1994). Exercise during pregnancy and the postpartum period. *International Journal Gynecology and Obstetrics, 45,* 65–70.

Teitelbaum, P., Teitelbaum, O., Nye, J., Fryman, J., & Maurer, R. G. (1998). Movement analysis in infancy may be useful for early diagnosis of autism. *Proceedings of the National Academy of Sciences of the United States of America, 95,* 13982–13987.

Teitler, J. O. (2001). Father involvement, child health and maternal health behavior. *Children and Youth Services Review, 23*(4–5), 403–425.

Terjesen, N. C., & Wilkins, L. P. (1979). A proposal for a model of a sudden infant death syndrome act: Help for the "other" victims of SIDS. *Family Law Quarterly, 12,* 285–308.

Termine, N. T., & Izard, C. E. (1988). Infants' responses to their mothers' expressions of joy and sadness. *Developmental Psychology, 24,* 223–229.

Terr, L. (1994). *Unchained memories.* New York: Basic Books.

Tessier, R., Nadeau, L., Boivin, M., & Tremblay, R. E. (1997). The social behavior of 11– to 12–year-old children born as low birthweight and/or premature infants. *International Journal of Behavioral Development, 21*(4), 795–811.

Tessier, R., Tarabulsy, G. M., Larin, S., Josee, L., Gagon, M.-F., & Johanne, T. (2002). A home-based description of attachment in physically disabled infants. *Social Development, 11*(2), 147–165.

Teti, D. M., & Ablard, K. E. (1989). Security of attachment and infant-sibling relationships: A laboratory study. *Child Development, 60,* 1519–1528.

Teti, D. M., Bond, L. A., & Gibbs, E. D. (1988). Mothers, fathers, and siblings: A comparison of play styles and influence upon infant cognitive level. *International Journal of Behavioral Development, 11,* 415–432.

Teti, D. M., & Gelfand, D. M. (1991). Behavioral competence among mothers of infants in the first year: The mediational role of maternal self-efficacy. *Child Development, 62,* 918–929.

Teti, D. M., Gelfand, D. M., Messinger, D. S., & Isabella, R. (1995). Maternal depression and the quality of early attachment: An examination of infants, preschoolers, and their mothers. *Developmental Psychology, 31,* 364–376.

Teti, D. M., & Lamb, M. E. (1989). Socioeconomic and marital outcomes of adolescent marriage, adolescent childbirth, and their co-occurrence. *Journal of Marriage and the Family, 51,* 203–212.

Teti, D. M., Nakagawa, R. D., & Wirth, O. (1991). Security of attachment between preschoolers and their mothers: Relations among social interaction, parenting stress, and mothers' sorts of the attachment Q-set. *Developmental Psychology, 27,* 440–447.

Teti, D. M., O'Connell, M. A., & Reiner, C. D. (1996). Parenting sensitivity, parental depression and child health: The mediational role of parental self-efficacy. *Early Development and Parenting, 5*(4), 237–250.

Tharapel, A. T., Tharapel, S. A., & Bannerman, R. M. (1985). Recurrent pregnancy losses and parental chromosome abnormalities: A review. *British Journal of Obstetrics and Gynecology, 92,* 899–914.

Thelen, E. (1989). The (re)discovery of motor development: Learning new things from an old field. *Developmental Psychology, 25,* 946–949.

Thelen, E. (1990). Dynamical systems and the generation of individual differences. In J. Colombo & J. Fagen (Eds.), *Individual differences in infancy: Reliability, stability, prediction* (pp. 19–43). Hillsdale, NJ: Erlbaum.

Thelen, E., Bradshaw, G., & Ward, J. A. (1981). Spontaneous kicking in month-old infants: Manifestation of a human central locomotor program. *Behavioral and Neural Biology, 32,* 45–53.

Thelen, E., & Fogel, A. (1989). Toward an action-based theory of infant development. In J. Lockman & N. Hazen (Eds.), *Action in social context: Perspectives on early development* (pp. 23 64). New York: Plenum Press.

Thelen, E., Skala, K. D., & Kelso, J. A. (1987). The dynamic nature of early coordination: Evidence from bilateral leg movements in young infants. *Developmental Psychology, 23,* 179–186.

Thelen, E., & Smith, L. B. (Eds.) (1994). *A dynamic systems approach to the development of cognition and action.* Cambridge, MA: MIT Press.

Thelen, E., & Ulrich, B. D. (1991). Hidden skills. *Monographs of the Society for Research in Child Development, 56,* 1–106.

The Urban Institute. (2000, March). *Child care arrangements for children under five: Variation across states* (Series B, No. B-7, New Federalism: National Survey of America's Families). Washington, DC: J. Capizzano, G. Adams, & R. Sonenstein.

Thigpen, B. (2007). Outdoor play: Combating sedentary lifestyles. *Zero to Three, 28*(1), 19–23.

Thike, K. B., Wai, K. T., Oo, N., & Yi, K. H. (1993). Contraceptive practice before female sterilization. *Asia Oceania Journal of Obstetrics and Gynecology, 19,* 241–248.

Thoman, E. B. (1993). Obligation and option in the premature nursery. *Developmental Review, 13,* 1–30.

Thoman, E. B., Acebo, C., Dreyer, C. A., Becker, P. T., & Freese, M. P. (1979). Individuality in the interactive process. In E. B. Thomas (Ed.), *Origins of the infant's social responsiveness* (pp. 305–338). Hillsdale, NJ: Erlbaum.

Thoman, E. B., Barnett, C., & Leiderman, P. H. (1971). Feeding behaviors of newborn infants as a function of parity of the mother. *Child Development, 42,* 1471–1483.

Thoman, E. B., Leiderman, P. H., & Olson, J. P. (1972). Neonate-mother interactions during breast feeding. *Developmental Psychology, 6,* 110–118.

Thomas, A., & Chess, S. (1977). *Temperament and development.* New York: Brunner/Mazel.

Thompson, C. (1995). Umbilical cords: Turning garbage into clinical gold. *Science, 268,* 805–806.

Thompson, L. A., Fagan, J. F., & Fulker, D. W. (1991). Longitudinal prediction of specific cognitive abilities from infant novelty preference. *Child Development, 62,* 530–538.

Thompson, L. M., Murphy, P., O'Hara, J., & Wallymahmed, A. (1997). Levels of daily hassles and uplifts in employed and non employed pregnant women. *Journal of Reproductive and Infant Psychology, 15,* 271–280.

Thompson, R. A. (1998). Empathy and its origins in early development. In S. Br;araten (Ed.), *Intersubjective communication and emotion in early ontogeny. Studies in emotion and social interaction, 2nd series* (pp. 144–157). Cambridge, England: Cambridge University Press.

Thompson, R. A., Connell, J. P., & Bridges, L. J. (1988). Temperament, emotion, and social interactive behavior in the strange situation: A component process analysis of attachment system functioning. *Child Development, 59,* 1102–1110.

Thompson, R. A., & Lamb, M. E. (1982). Stranger sociability and its relationships to temperament and social experiences during the second year. *Infant Behavior and Development, 5,* 277–287.

Thorpe, K. J., Dragonas, T., & Golding, J. (1992). The effects of psychosocial factors on the mother's emotional well-being during early parenthood: A cross-cultural study of Britain and Greece. *Journal of Reproductive and Infant Psychology, 10,* 205–217.

Thorpe, L. A. & Trehub, S. E. (1989). Duration illusion and auditory grouping in infancy. *Developmental Psychology, 25,* 122–127.

Thurin, A., Hausken, J., Hillensji, T., Jablonowska, B., Pinborg, A., Strandell, A., et al. (2004). Elective single-embryo transfer versus double-embryo transfer in in vitro fertilization. *New England Journal of Medicine, 351*(23), 2392–2402.

Tian, Y., & Kanade, T. (2001, February). Recognizing Action Units for Facial Expression Analysis. *IEEE Transactions on Pattern Analysis & Machine Intelligence, 23*(2), 97.

Tideman, E., Nilsson, A., Smith, G., & Stjernqvist, K. (2002). Longitudinal follow-up of children born preterm: The mother-child relationship in a 19–year perspective. *Journal of Reproductive and Infant Psychology, 20*(1), 43–56.

Tiedemann, D. (1927). Tiedemann's observations on the development of the mental faculties of children (S. Langer, Trans.). *Pedagogical Seminary and Journal of Genetic Psychology, 34,* 205–230.

Tinsley, B. R., & Parke, R. D. (1984). Grandparents as support and socialization agents. In M. Lewis (Ed.), *Beyond the dyad* (pp. 89–102). New York: Plenum Press.

Titus, S. L. (1976). Family photographs and transition to parenthood. *Journal of Marriage and the Family, 38,* 525–530.

Titus-Ernstoff, L., Troisi, R., Hatch, E., Wise, L., Palmer, J., Hyer, M., et al. (2006). Menstrual and reproductive characterstics of women whose mothers were exposed in utero to diethylstilbestrol (DES). *International Journal of Epidemiology, 35*(4), 862–868.

Tizard, B., & Rees, J. (1974). A comparison of the effects of adoption, restoration to the natural mother, and continued institutionalization on the cognitive development of four-year-old children. *Child Development, 45,* 92–99.

Tizard, J., & Tizard, B. (1971). The social development of 2–year-old children in a residential nursery. In H. R. Schaffer (Ed.), *The origin of human social relations* (pp. 337–358). London: Academic Press.

Toda, S., & Fogel, A. (1989, April). *Infant behavior in the still-face situation at 3 and 6 months.* Paper presented at the Society for Research in Child Development, Kansas City, MO.

Toda, S., & Fogel, A. (1993). Infant response to the still-face situation at 3 and 6 months. *Developmental Psychology, 29,* 532–538.

Toda, S., Fogel, A., & Kawai, M. (1990). Maternal speech to three-month-old infants in the United States and Japan. *Journal of Child Language, 17,* 279–294.

Tomasello, M. (1995). Joint attention as social cognition. In C. Moore & P. J. Dunham (Eds.), *Joint attention: Its origins and role in development* (pp. 103–130). Hillsdale, NJ: Erlbaum.

Tomasello, M., Call, J., & Gluckman, A. (1997). Comprehension of novel communicative signs by apes and human children. *Child Development, 68*(6), 1067–1080.

Tomasello, M., & Farrar, M. J. (1986). Joint attention and early language. *Child Development, 57,* 1454–1463.

Tomasello, M., Mannle, S., & Kruger, A. C. (1986). Linguistic environment of 1– to 2–year-old twins. *Developmental Psychology, 22,* 169–176.

Tomasello, M., Savage-Rumbaugh, S., & Kruger, A. C. (1993). Imitative learning of actions on objects by children, chimpanzees, and enculturated chimpanzees. *Child Development, 64,* 1688–1705.

Tomlinson, M., Cooper, P., & Murray, L. (2005). The Mother-Infant Relationship and Infant Attachment in a South African Peri-Urban Settlement. *Child Development, 76*(5), 1044–1054.

Tortora, S. (2006). The dancing dialogue: Using the communicative power of movement with young children. NY: Brookes Publishing.

Toselli, M., Farneti, P., & Grossi, E. (2001). Role of motor imitation in traversability of surfaces by walking infants. *Percept Mot Skills, 93*(2), 523–530.

Toselli, M., Farneti, P., & Salzarulo, P. (1998). Maternal representation and care of infant sleep. *Early Development and Parenting, 7,* 73–78.

Totten, N. (2005). *New dimensions in body psychotherapy.* Open University Press.

Touraine, J. L., Sanhadji, K., & Firouzi, R. (1994). Susceptibility of human fetal cells to HIV infection, in vitro and in viol in the SICD-HU Model. *International Conference on AIDS, 10,* 307 (abstract no. PC0157).

Towers, C. V., Deveikis, A., Asrat, T., Nageotte, M. P., & Freeman, R. K. (1993). Role of "bloodless C section" to decrease maternal child HIV transmission: A pilot study. *International Conference on AIDS, 9,* 712 (abstract no. P0–C16–2978).

Trainor, L. J. (1996). Infant preferences for infant-directed versus noninfant-directed playsongs and lullabies. *Infant Behavior and Development, 19,* 83–92.

Trainor, L. J., Clark, E. D., Huntley, A., & Adams, B. A. (1997). The acoustic basis of preferences for infant-directed singing. *Infant Behavior and Development, 20*(3), 383–396.

Trainor, L. J., Wu, L., & Tsang, C. D. (2004). Long-term memory for music: infants remember tempo and timbre. *Dev Sci, 7*(3), 289–296.

Trainor, L. J., & Zacharias, C. A. (1998). Infants prefer higher-pitched singing. *Infant Behavior and Development, 21*(4), 799–806.

Trause, M. A. (1977). Stranger responses: Effects of familiarity, stranger's approach and sex of infant. *Child Development, 48,* 1657–1661.

Trause, M. A., Boslett, M., Voos, D., Rudd, C., Klaus, M., & Kennell, J. (1978). A birth in the hospital: The effect on the sibling. *Birth and the Family Journal, 5,* 207–210.

Trehub, S. E., Bull, D., & Thorpe, L. A. (1984). Infants' perception of melodies: The role of melodic contour. *Child Development, 55,* 821–830.

Trehub, S. E., Thorpe, L. A., & Morrongiello, B. A. (1987). Organizational processes in infants' perception of auditory patterns. *Child Development, 58,* 741–749.

Trehub, S. E., Unyk, A. M., & Trainor, L. J. (1993). Adults identify infant-directed music across cultures. *Infant Behavior and Development, 16,* 193–211.

Trevarthen, C. (1973). Behavioral embryology. In E. C. Carterette & M. P. Friedman (Eds.), *Handbook of perception: Vol. 3. Biology of perceptual systems* (pp. 61–78). New York: Academic Press.

Trevarthen, C. (1977). Descriptive analysis of infant communicative behavior. In H. R. Schaffer (Ed.), *Studies of mother-infant interaction* (pp. 227–270). London: Academic Press.

Trevarthen, C. (1980). Neurological development and the growth of psychological functions. In J. Sants (Ed.), *Developmental psychology and society* (pp. 46–95). New York: St. Martin's Press.

Trevarthen, C. (1998). The concept and foundations of infant intersubjectivity. In S. Br;araten (Ed.), *Intersubjective communication and emotion in early ontogeny. Studies in emotion and social interaction, 2nd series* (pp. 15–46). New York: Cambridge University Press.

Trevarthen, C., & Aitken, K. J. (2001). Infant intersubjectivity: research, theory, and clinical applications. *J Child Psychol Psychiatry, 42*(1), 3–48.

Trevarthen, C., Aitken, K., Papoudi, D., & Robarts, J. (1998). *Children with autism: Diagnosis and interventions to meet their needs* (2nd ed.). Philadelphia: Jessica Kingsley.

Trevarthen, C., & Hubley, P. (1978). Secondary intersubjectivity: Confidence, confiding and acts of meaning in the first year. In A. Lock (Ed.) *Action, gesture, and symbol: The emergence of language* (pp. 183–227). New York: Academic Press.

Trickett, P. K., & Susman, E. J. (1988). Parental perceptions of child-rearing practices in physically abusive and nonabusive families. *Developmental Psychology, 24,* 270–276.

Tronick, E. (2007) *The neurobehavioral and social-emotional development of infants and children.* NY: W.W. Norton and Co.

Tronick, E., Als, H., Adamson, L., Weise, S., & Brazelton, T. B. (1978) The infant's response to entrapment between contradictory messages in face-to-face interaction. *Journal of Child Psychiatry, 17,* 1–13.

Tronick, E. Z., Thomas, R. B., & Daltabuit, M. (1994). The Quechua Manta pouch: A caretaking practice for buffering the Peruvian infant against the multiple stressors of high altitude. *Child Development, 65,* 1005–1013.

Turkheimer, M., Bakeman, R., & Adamson, L. B. (1989). Do mothers support and peers inhibit skilled object play in infancy? *Infant Behavior and Development, 12,* 37–44.

Turkheimer, E., Haley, A., Waldron, M., D'Onofrio, B., & Gottesman, I. (2003). Socioeconomic status modifies heritability of IQ in young children. *Psychological Science, 14*(6), 623–628.

Ungerer, J., Brody, L., & Zelazo, P. (1978). Long-term memory for speech in 2– to 4–week-old infants. *Infant Behavior and Development, 1,* 177–186.

Ungerer, J., & Sigman, M. (1984). The relation of play and sensorimotor behavior to language in the second year. *Child Development, 55,* 1448–1455.

Ungerer, J., Zelazo, P. R., Kearsley, R. D., & O'Leary, K. (1981). Developmental changes in the representation of objects in symbolic play from 18 to 34 months of age. *Child Development, 52,* 186–195.

United Nations Department of Economic and Social Affairs (1986). *Demographic yearbook.* New York: United Nations.

United States Bureau of the Census. (1988). *Current Population Reports,* Series P-70, No. 20. Washington, DC: U.S. Government Printing Office.

United States Bureau of the Census (2009). http://www.census.gov/mail/www/-popclock.html.

U.S Department of Transportation, National Highway Traffic Safety Administration (2007). http://www-nrd.nhtsa.dot.gov/pdf/nrd-30/NCSA/RNotes/2007/809845.pdf (retrieved Jan. 4, 2010).

Uzgiris, I. C. (1983). Imitation in infancy: Its interpersonal aspects. In M. Perlmutter (Ed.), *Minnesota symposia on child psychology* (Vol. 17, pp. 1–32). Hillsdale, NJ: Erlbaum.

Uzgiris, I. C., & Hunt, J. M. (1975). *Toward ordinal scales of psychological development in infancy.* Champaign: University of Illinois Press.

Vahratian, A., Siega-Riz, A. M., Savitz, D. A., & Thorp, J. M., Jr. (2004). Multivitamin use and the risk of preterm birth. *Am J Epidemiol, 160*(9), 886–892.

Valdez-Menchaca, M. C., & Whitehurst, G. J. (1992). Accelerating language development through picture book reading: A systematic extension to Mexican day care. *Developmental Psychology, 28,* 1106–1114.

Valenzuela, M. (1997). Maternal sensitivity in a developing society: The context of urban poverty and infant chronic undernutrition. *Developmental Psychology, 33*(5), 845–855.

Valkenburg, P. M., & Vroone, M. (2004). Developmental changes in infants' and toddlers' attention to television entertainment. *Communication Research, 31*(3), 288–311.

van Beek, Y., & Samson, J. F. (1994). Communication in pre-term infants: Why is it different? *Early Development and Parenting, 3,* 37–50.

Vandell, D. L. (1979). Effects of a playgroup experience on mother-son and father-son interaction. *Developmental Psychology, 15,* 379–385.

Vandell, D. L., Hyde, J. S., Plant, E. A., & Essex, M. J. (1997). Fathers and "others" as infant-care providers: Predictors of parents' emotional well-being and marital satisfaction. *Merrill-Palmer Quarterly, 43*(3), 361–385.

Vandell, D. L., Owen, M. T., Wilson, K. S., & Henderson, V. K. (1988). Social development in infant twins: Peer and mother-child relationships. *Child Development, 59,* 168–177.

Vandell, D. L., & Ramanan, J. (1992). Effects of early and recent maternal employment on children from low-income families. *Child Development, 63,* 938–949.

Vandell, D. L., & Wilson, K. S. (1987). Infants' interactions with mother, sibling, and peer: Contrasts and relations between interaction systems. *Child Development, 58,* 176–186.

Vandell, D. L., Wilson, K. S., & Buchanan, N. R. (1980). Peer interaction in the first year of life: An examination of its structure, content, and sensitivity to toys. *Child Development, 51,* 481–488.

Van den Bergh, B. R., Mulder, E. J., Mennes, M., & Glover, V. (2005). Antenatal maternal anxiety and stress and the neurobehavioural development of the fetus and child: links and possible mechanisms. A review. *Neurosci Biobehav Rev, 29*(2), 237–258.

Van de Perre, P., Simonon, A., Hitimana, D. G., Dabis, F., Msellati, P., Mukamabano, B., Butera, J. B., Van-Goethem, C., Karita, E., & Lepage, P. (1993). Infective and anti-infective properties of breastmilk from HIV-1–infected women. *Lancet, 341,* 914–918.

Van de Walle, G. A., & Spelke, E. (1996). Spatiotemporal integration and object perception in infancy: Perceiving unity versus form. *Child Development, 67,* 2621–2640.

VanDoorninck, W. J., Caldwell, B. M., Wright, C., & Frankenburg, W. K. (1981). The relationship between twelve-month home stimulation and school achievement. *Child Development, 52,* 1080–1083.

van Geert, P. (1991). A dynamic systems model of cognitive and language growth. *Journal of Psychological Review, 98* (1), 3–53.

van Geert, P. (1993). A dynamic systems model of cognitive growth: Competition and support under limited resource conditions. In L. B. Smith & E. Thelen (Eds.), *A dynamic systems approach to development: Applications. MIT Press/Bradford Books series in cognitive psychology* (pp. 265–331). Cambridge, MA: MIT Press.

van Geert, P. (1998). We almost had a great future behind us: The contribution of non-linear dynamics to developmental-science-in-the-making. *Developmental Science, 1*(1), 143–159.

Van Giffen, K., & Haith, M. H. (1984). Infant visual response to Gestalt geometric forms. *Infant Behavior and Development, 7,* 335–346.

Van Hecke, A. V., Mundy, P. C., Acra, C. F., Block, J. J., Delgado, C. E. F., Parlade, M. V., et al. (2007). Infant Joint Attention, Temperament, and Social Competence in Preschool Children. *Child Development, 78*(1), 53–69.

van Hof, P., van der Kamp, J., & Savelsbergh, G. J. P. (2002). The relation of unimanual and bimanual reaching to crossing the midline. *Child Development, 73*(5), 1353–1362.

van Ijzendoorn, M. H., Goldberg, S., Kroonenberg, P. M., & Frenkel, O. J. (1992). The relative effects of maternal and child problems on the quality of attachment: A meta-analysis of attachment in clinical samples. *Child Development, 63,* 840–858.

van Ijzendoorn, M. H., & Kroonenberg, P. M. (1988). Cross-cultural patterns of attachment: A meta-analysis of the strange situation. *Child Development, 59,* 147–156.

van Ijzendoorn, M. H., Rutgers, A. H., Bakermans-Kranenburg, M. J., van Daalen, E., Dietz, C., Buitelaar, J. K., et al. (2007). Parental sensitivity and attachment in children with autism spectrum disorder: Comparison with children with mental retardation, with language delays, and with typical development. *Child Development, 78*(2), 597–608.

Varela, F. J., Thompson, E., Rosch, E. (1991). *The embodied mind: Cognitive science and human experiences.* Cambridge, MA: MIT Press.

Varendi, H., Porter, R., and Winberg, J. (1997). Natural odour preferences of newborn infants change over time. *Acta Paediatrica, 86,* 985–990.

Vaughn, B. E., Bradley, C. F., Joffe, L. S., Seifer, R., & Barglow, P. (1987). Maternal characteristics measured prenatally are predictive of ratings of temperamental "difficulty" on the Carey Infant Temperament Questionnaire. *Developmental Psychology, 23,* 152–161.

Vaughn, B. E., Deane, K. E., & Waters, E. (1985). The impact of out-of-home care on child-mother attachment quality: Another look at some enduring questions. In I. Bretherton & E. Waters (Eds.), Growing points of attachment theory and research. *Monographs of the Society for Research in Child Development, 50* (1–2, Whole No. 209), 110–135.

Vaughn, B. E., Egeland, B., Sroufe, L. A., & Waters, E. (1979). Individual differences in infant-mother attachment at twelve and eighteen months: Stability and change in families under stress. *Child Development, 50,* 971–975.

Vaughn, B. E., Grove, F. L., & Egeland, B. (1980). The relationship between out-of-home care and the quality of infant-mother attachment in an economically disadvantaged population. *Child Development, 51,* 1203–1214.

Vaughn, B. E., Kopp, C. B., & Krakow, J. B. (1984). The emergence and consolidation of self-control from 18 to 30 months of age: Normative trends and individual differences. *Child Development, 55,* 990–1004.

Vaughn, B. E., Kopp, C. B., Krakow, J. B., Johnson, K., & Schwartz, S. S. (1986). Process analyses of the behavior of very young children in delay tasks. *Developmental Psychology, 22,* 752–759.

Vaughn, B. E., Stevenson-Hinde, J., Waters, E., Kotsaftis, A., Lefever, G. B., Shouldice, A., Trudel, M., & Belsky, J. (1992). Attachment security and temperament in infancy and early childhood: Some conceptual clarifications. *Developmental Psychology, 28,* 463–473.

Vaughn, B. E., Taraldson, B. J., Crichton, L., & Egeland, B. (1981). The assessment of infant temperament: A critique of the Carey Infant Temperament Questionnaire. *Infant Behavior and Development, 4,* 1–18.

Velde, E. R., & Cohlen, B. J. (1999). The management of infertility. *New England Journal of Medicine, 340*(3), 224–226.

Venezia, M., Messinger, D. S., Thorp, D., & Mundy, P. (2004). The Development of Anticipatory Smiling. *Infancy, 6*(3), 397–406.

Ventura, S., Martin, J., Curtin, S., Menacker, F., & Hamilton, B. (2001). Births: Final data for 1999. *National Vital Statistics for 1999. 49*(1), 1–15.

Ventura, S. J., Mathews, T. J., & Curtin, S. C. (1998). Declines in teenage birth rates, 1991–97: National and state patterns. *National Vital Statistics Report, 47*(12), 1–17.

Vereijken, C. M. J. L., Riksen-Walraven, J. M., & Kondo-Ikemura, K. (1997). Maternal sensitivity and infant attachment security in Japan: A longitudinal study. *International Journal of Behavioral Development, 21*(1), 35–49.

Verlinsky, Y., & Kuliev, A. (1994). Human preimplantation diagnosis: Needs, efficiency and efficacy of genetic and chromosomal analysis. *Baillieres Clinical Obstetrics and Gynacology, 8,* 177–196.

Vertes, R. P. (1986). A life-sustaining function for REM sleep: A theory. *Neuroscience and Behavioral Reviews, 10*(4), 371–376.

Vibbert, M., & Bornstein, M. H. (1989). Specific associations between domains of mother-child interaction and toddler referential language and pretense play. *Infant Behavior and Development, 12,* 163–184.

Vohr, B. R., & Coll, C. T. G. (1985). Neurodevelopmental and school performance of very low-birth-weight infants: A seven-year longitudinal study. *Pediatrics, 76,* 345–350.

Völker, S. (2007). Infants' vocal engagement oriented towards mother versus stranger at 3 months and avoidant attachment behavior at 12 months. *International Journal of Behavioral Development, 31*(1), 88–95.

Volling, B. L., & Belsky, J. (1992). Infant, father, and marital antecedents of infant-father attachment security in dual-earner and single-earner families. *International Journal of Behavioral Development, 15,* 83–100.

Volling, B. L., & Elins, J. L. (1998). Family relationships and children's emotional adjustment as correlates of maternal and paternal differential treatment: A replication with toddler and preschool siblings. *Child Development, 69*(6), 1640–1656.

Volling, B. L., & Feagans, L. V. (1995). Infant day care and children's social competence. *Infant Behavior and Development, 18*(2), 177–188.

Von Hemel, J. O., Majoor-Krakauer, D. F., Jahoda, M. G. J., & Sachs, E. S. (1986). First trimester diagnosis from chorionic villi of a der(15), t(9;15), (q33;Q14)mat identified by DA/DAPI staining. *Journal of Medical Genetics, 23,* 89–90.

von Hofsten, C., Kochukhova, O., & Rosander, K. (2007). Predictive tracking over occlusions by 4–month-old infants. *Developmental Science, 10*(5), 625–640.

Von Hofsten, C., & Spelke, E. S. (1985). Object perception and object-directed reaching in infancy. *Journal of Experimental Psychology: General, 114,* 198–212.

Von Kries, R., Toschke, A. M., Koletzko, B., & Slikker, W., Jr. (2002). Maternal smoking during pregnancy and childhood obesity. *Am J Epidemiol, 156*(10), 954–961.

Vorhees, C. V., & Mollnow, E. (1987). Behavioral teratogenesis: Long-term influences on behavior from early exposure to environmental agents. In J. D. Osofsky (Ed.), *Handbook of infant development* (pp. 599–616). New York: Wiley.

Vreugdenhil, H., Slijper, F., Mulder, P., & Weisglas-Kuperus, N. (2002). Effects of perinatal exposure to PCBs and dioxins on play behavior in Dutch children at school age. *Environmental Health Perspectives, 110*(10), A593.

Vutyavanich, T., Kraisarin, T., & Ruangsri, R. (2001). Ginger for nausea and vomiting in pregnancy: randomized, double-masked, placebo-controlled trial. *Obstet Gynecol, 97*(4), 577–582.

Vygotsky, L. S. (1978). Mind in society. Cambridge, MA: Harvard University Press.

Vyt, A. (1993). Infant and parental pathways to pre-school cognitive competence. *Early Development and Parenting, 2,* 197–207.

Wachs, T. D. (1982). Early experience and early cognitive development: The search for specificity. In I. Uzgiris & J. Hunt (Eds.), *Research with scales of psychological development in infancy* (pp. 371–400). Champaign: University of Illinois Press.

Wachs, T. D. (1987). Specificity of environmental action as manifest in environmental correlates of infant's mastery motivation. *Developmental Psychology, 23,* 782–790.

Wachs, T. D. (1988). Relevance of physical environment influences for toddler temperament. *Infant Behavior and Development, 11,* 431–445.

Wachs, T. D. (1993). Nature of relations between the physical and social microenvironment of the two-year-old child. *Early Development and Parenting, 2,* 81–87.

Wachs, T. D. (2000). *Necessary but not sufficient: The respective roles of single and multiple influences on individual development.* Washington, DC: American Psychological Association.

Wachs, T. D., & Bates, J. E. (2000). Temperament. In J. G. Bremner & A. Fogel (Eds.), *Handbook of infancy research* (pp. 28–45). Oxford, England: Blackwell.

Wachs, T. D., Bishry, Z., Sobhy, A., McCabe, G., Galal, O., & Shaheen, F. (1993). Relation of rearing environment to adaptive behavior of Egyptian toddlers. *Child Development, 64,* 586–604.

Wachs, T. D., & Gandour, M. J. (1983). Temperament, environment, and six-month cognitive-intellectual development: A test of the organismic specificity hypothesis. *International Journal of Behavioral Development, 6,* 135–152.

Wachs, T. D., & Gruen, G. E. (1982). *Early experience and human development.* New York: Plenum Press.

Waddington, C. H. (1966). *Principles of development and differentiation.* New York: Macmillan.

Wade, J. (1996). *Changes of mind: A holonomic theory of the evolution of consciousness.* New York: State University of New York Press.

Wakefield, A., Murch, S., Anthony, A., Linnell, J., Casson, D., Malik, M., Berelowitz, A., Dhillon, M., Thomson, P., Valentine, A., Davies, S., Walker-Smith, J. (1998). Ileal-lymphoid-nodular hyperplasia, non-specific colitis, and pervasive developmental disorder in children. *The Lancet, 35,* 637–641.

Wakschlag, L. S., Chase-Lansdale, P. L., & Brooks-Gunn, J. (1996). Not just "Ghosts from the nursery": Contemporaneous intergenerational relationships and parenting in young African-American families. *Child Development, 67*(5), 2131–2147

Wakschlag, L. S., & Hans, S. L. (1999). Relation of maternal responsiveness during infancy to the development of behavior problems in high-risk youths. *Developmental Psychology, 35*(2), 569–579.

Wakschlag, L. S., Leventhal, B. L., Pine, D. S., Pickett, K. E., & Carter, A. S. (2006). Elucidating Early Mechanisms of Developmental Psychopathology: The Case of Prenatal Smoking and Disruptive Behavior. *Child Development, 77*(4), 893–906.

Wakschlag, L. S., Pickett, K. E., Cook, E., Jr., Benowitz, N. L., & Leventhal, B. L. (2002). Maternal smoking during pregnancy and severe antisocial behavior in offspring: A review. *American Journal of Public Health, 92*(6), 966–974.

Walden, T., Kim, G., McCoy, C., & Karrass, J. (2007). Do you believe in magic? Infants' social looking during violations of expectations. *Developmental Science, 10*(5), 654–663.

Walden, T. A., & Ogan, T. A. (1988). The development of social referencing. *Child Development, 59,* 1230–1240.

Waldenstrom, U. (1999). Effects of birth center care on fathers' satisfaction with care, experience of the birth and adaption to fatherhood. *Journal of Reproductive and Infant Psychology, 17*(4), 357–368.

Waletzky, L. (1979). Husbands' problems with breast-feeding. *American Journal of Orthopsychiatry, 49,* 349–353.

Walker, B. E., & Quarles, J. (1976). Palate development in mouse foetuses after tongue removal. *Archives of Oral Biology, 21,* 405–412.

Walker-Andrews, A. S., & Lennon, E. (1991). Infants' discrimination of vocal expressions: Contributions of auditory and visual information. *Infant Behavior and Development, 14,* 131–142.

Wallach, M. A. (1985). Creativity testing and giftedness. In F. D. Horowitz & M. O'Brien (Eds.), *The gifted and talented: Developmental perspectives* (pp. 99–123). Washington, DC: American Psychological Association.

Walton, G. E., Bower, N. J. A., & Bower, T. G. R. (1992). Recognition of familiar faces by newborns. *Infant Behavior and Development, 15,* 265–269.

Wang, Q. (2006). Relations of Maternal Style and Child Self-Concept to Autobiographical Memories in Chinese, Chinese Immigrant, and European American 3–Year-Olds. *Child Development, 77*(6), 1794–1809.

Wang, X., Dow-Edwards, D., Anderson, V., Minkoff, H., & Hurd, Y. L. (2004). In Utero Marijuana Exposure Associated with Abnormal Amygdala Dopamine D-sub-2 Gene Expression in the Human Fetus. *Biological Psychiatry, 56*(12), 909–915.

Ward, M. J., Vaughn, B. E., & Robb, M. D. (1988). Social-emotional adaptation and infant-mother attachment in siblings: Role of the mother in cross-sibling consistency. *Child Development, 59,* 643–651.

Warneken, F., & Tomasello, M. (2007). Helping and cooperation at 14 months of age. *Infancy, 11*(3), 271–294.

Wartner, U. G., Grossmann, K., Fremmer-Bombik, E., & Suess, G. (1994). Attachment patterns at age six in south Germany: Predictability from infancy and implications for preschool behavior. *Child Development, 65*(4), 1014–1027.

Wasik, B. H., Ramey, C. T., Bryant, D. M., & Sparling, J. J. (1990). A longitudinal study of two early intervention strategies: Project CARE. *Child Development, 61,* 1682–1696.

Wasserman, G. A., Allen, R., & Solomon, C. R. (1985). At-risk toddlers and their mothers: The special case of physical handicap. *Child Development, 56,* 73–83.

Waters, E. (1983). The stability of individual differences in infant attachment: Comments on the Thompson, Lamb, and Estes contributions. *Child Development, 54,* 516–520.

Waters, E., Vaughn, B., & Egeland, B. (1980). Individual differences in infant-mother attachment relationships at age one: Antecedents in neonatal behavior in an urban, economically disadvantaged sample. *Child Development, 51,* 208–216.

Watson, A. C., Painter, K. M., & Bornstein, M. H. (2001). Longitudinal relations between 2–year-olds' language and 4–year-olds' theory of mind. *Journal of Cognition and Development, 2*(4), 449–457.

Watson, J. S. (1973). Smiling, cooing, and "the game." *Merrill-Palmer Quarterly, 18,* 323–339.

Waxman, S. R., & Senghas, A. (1992). Relations among word meanings in early lexical development. *Developmental Psychology, 28,* 862–873.

Weatherill, R. P., Almerigi, J. B., Levendosky, A. A., Bogat, G. A., von Eye, A., & Harris, L. J. (2004). Is maternal depression related to side of infant holding? *International Journal of Behavioral Development, 28*(5), 421–427.

Weatherston, D. J. (2000, October/November). The infant mental health specialist. *Zero to Three,* 3–10.

Weaver, I. C., Cervoni, N., Champagne, F. A., D'Alessio, A. C., Sharma, S., Seckl, J. R., et al. (2004). Epigenetic programming by maternal behavior. *Nat Neurosci, 7*(8), 847–854.

Webster, J., Sweett, S., & Stolz, T. A. (1994). Domestic violence in pregnancy: A prevalence study. *Medical Journal of Australia, 161,* 466–470.

Wedenberg, E. (1956). Auditory tests on newborn infants. *Acta Oto-laryngologica, 46,* 446–461.

Weed, S., & Jensen, L. (1993). A second year evaluation of three abstinence sex education programs. *Journal of Research and Development in Education, 26,* 92–96.

Weinberg, M. K., & Tronick, E. Z. (1994). Beyond the face: An empirical study of infant affective configurations of facial, vocal, gestural, and regulatory behaviors. *Child Development, 65,* 1503–1515.

Weinberg, M. K., Tronick, E. Z., Cohn, J. F., & Olson, K. L. (1999). Gender differences in emotional expressivity and self-regulation during early infancy. *Developmental Psychology, 35*(1), 175–188.

Weinfield, N. S., Whaley, G. J. L., & Egeland, B. (2004). Continuity, discontinuity, and coherence in attachment from infancy to late adolescence: Sequelae of organization and disorganization. *Attachment & Human Development, 6*(1), 73–97.

Weinraub, M., Clements, L. P., Sockloff, A., Ethridge, T., Gracely, E., & Myers, B. (1984). The development of sex role stereotypes in the third year: Relations to gender labeling, sex-typed toy preference and family characteristics. *Child Development, 55,* 1493–1503.

Weinraub, M., & Lewis, M. (1977). The determinants of children's responses to separation. *Monographs of the Society for Research in Child Development, 42* (Serial No. 172), 1–127.

Weinraub, M., & Putney, E. (1978). The effects of heights on infant's social responses to unfamiliar persons. *Child Development, 49,* 598–603.

Weinraub, M., & Wolf, B. M. (1983). Effects of stress and social supports on mother-child interactions on single- and two-parent families. *Child Development, 54,* 1297–1311.

Weintraub, K. S., & Furman, L. N. (1987). Child care: Quality, regulation, and research. *Social Policy Report: Society for Research in Child Development, 2,* 27–68.

Weir, R., & Feldman, W. (1975). A study of infant feeding practices. *Birth and the Family Journal, 2,* 63–64.

Weir, R. H. (1966). Questions on the learning of phonology. In F. Smith & G. A. Miller (Eds.), *The genesis of language: A psycholinguistic approach* (pp. 112–140). Cambridge, MA: MIT Press.

Wellman, H. M., Cross, D., & Bartsch, K. (1986). Infant search and object permanence: A meta-analysis of the A-not-B error. *Monographs of the Society for Research in Child Development, 51* (3, Serial No. 214), 1–51.

Wellman, H. M., & Lempers, J. D. (1977). The naturalistic communicative abilities of two-year-olds. *Child Development, 48,* 1052–1057.

Welsh, M. C., Pennington, B. F., Ozonoff, S., Rouse, B., & McCabe, E. R. B. (1990). Neuropsychology of early-treated phenylketonuria: Specific executive function deficits. *Child Development, 61,* 1697–1713.

Wenckstern, S., Weizmann, F., & Leenaars, A. A. (1984). Temperament and tempos of play in eight month old infants. *Child Development, 55,* 1195–1199.

Wendland-Carro, J., Piccinini, C. A., & Millar, W. S. (1999). The role of an early intervention on enhancing the quality of mother-infant interaction. *Child Development, 70*(3), 713–721.

Wente, A., & Crockenberg, S. (1976). Transition to fatherhood: Pre-natal Lamaze preparation, adjustment difficulty and the adult husband-wife relationship. *Family Coordinator, 25,* 351–357.

Wentworth, N., & Haith, M. M. (1992). Event-specific expectations of 2– and 3–month-old infants. *Developmental Psychology, 28,* 842–850.

Were, E. O., & Karanja, J. K. (1994). Attitudes of males to contraception in a Kenyan rural population. *East African Medical Journal, 71,* 106–109.

Werker, J. F., & Lalonde, C. E. (1988). Cross-language speech perception: Initial capabilities and developmental change. *Developmental Psychology, 24,* 674–683.

Werker, J. F., & Tees, R. C. (1984). Cross-language speech perception: Evidence for perceptual reorganization during the first year of life. *Infant Behavior and Development, 7,* 49–63.

Werner, E. (1979). *Cross-cultural child development.* Monterey, CA: Brooks-Cole.

Werner, E. (1986, April). *The infant's view of planet Earth.* Paper presented at the International Conference on Infant Studies, Los Angeles, CA.

Werner, E., Bierman, J., & French, F. (1971). *The children of Kauai.* Honolulu: University of Hawaii Press.

Werntoft, E., & Dykes, A. K. (2001). Effect of acupressure on nausea and vomiting during pregnancy. A randomized, placebo-controlled, pilot study. *J Reprod Med, 46*(9), 835–839.

Wertsch, J. V., & Tulviste, P. (1992). L. S. Vygotsky and contemporary development psychology. *Developmental Psychology, 28,* 548–557.

West, M. J., & Rheingold, H. L. (1978). Infant stimulation of maternal instruction. *Infant Behavior and Development, 1,* 205–215.

Westbrook, M. (1978). Analyzing affective responses to past events: Women's reactions to a childbearing year. *Journal of Clinical Psychology, 34,* 967–971.

Weston, J. A., Coolton, M., Halsey, S., & Covington, S. (1993). A legacy of violence in nonorganic failure to thrive. *Child Abuse and Neglect, 17,* 709–714.

Wheeler, S. R. (1994). Psychosocial needs of women during miscarriage or ectopic pregnancy. *American Obstetrical and Gynecological Nursing Journal, 68,* 221–231.

Whiffen, V. E. (1988). Vulnerability to postpartum depression: A prospective multivariate study. *Journal of Abnormal Psychology, 97*(4), 467–474.

White D, Gros-Louis J, King A, Papakhian M, West M. (2007) Constructing culture in cowbirds (Molothrus ater). *Journal of Comparative Psychology. 121,* 113–122.

White, E. (1992). Foster parenting the drug affected baby. *Zero to Three, 13,* 13–16.

White, T., Matthey, S., Boyd, K., & Barnett, B. (2006). Postnatal depression and post-traumatic stress after childbirth: Prevalence, course and co-occurrence. *Journal of Reproductive and Infant Psychology, 24*(2), 107–120.

Whitehurst, G. J., & Vasta, R. (1975). Is language acquired through imitation? *Journal of Psycholinguistic Research, 4,* 37–59.

Whitehurst, G. J., Falco, F. L., Lonigan, C. J., Fischel, J. E., DeBaryshe, B. D., Valdez-Menchaca, M. C., & Caulfield, M. (1988). Accelerating language development through picture book reading. *Developmental Psychology, 24,* 552–559.

Whitelaw, N. C., & Whitelaw, E. (2006). How lifetimes shape epigenotype within and across generations. *Hum Mol Genet, 15 Spec No 2,* R131–137.

Whiten, A., & Milner, P. (1986). The educational experiences of Nigerian infants. In H. V. Curran (Ed.), *Nigerian children: Developmental perspectives* (pp. 260–280). London: Routledge & Kegan Paul.

Whitham, J. C., Gerald, M. S., Maestripieri, D. (2007). Intended receivers and functional significance of grunt and girney vocalizations in free-ranging femal rhesus monkeys. *Ethology, 113,* 862–874.

Whiting, B. (1974). Folk wisdom and child-rearing. *Merrill-Palmer Quarterly, 20,* 9–19.

Whiting, B., & Whiting, J. W. (1975). *Children of six cultures: A psychocultural analysis.* Cambridge, MA: Harvard University Press.

Whiting, J. (1981). Environmental constraints on infant care practices. In R. Monroe, R. Monroe, & B. Whiting (Eds.), *Handbook of cross-cultural development* (pp. 67–89). New York: Garland Publishing.

Whyatt, R. M., Rauh, V., Barr, D. B., Camann, D. E., Andrews, H. F., Garfinkel, R., et al. (2004). Prenatal insecticide exposures and birth weight and length among an urban minority cohort. *Environ Health Perspect, 112*(10), 1125–1132.

Whyte, H., Hannah, M. E., Saigal, S., Hannah, W. J., Hewson, S., Amankwah, K., et al. (2004). Outcomes of children at 2 years after planned cesarean birth versus planned vaginal birth for breech presentation at term: the International Randomized Term Breech Trial. *Am J Obstet Gynecol, 191*(3), 864–871.

Wicki, W. (1999). The impact of family resources and satisfaction with division of labor on coping and worries after the birth of the first child. *International Journal of Behavioral Development, 23*(2), 431–456.

Wideman, M. V., & Singer, J. E. (1984). The role of psychological mechanisms in preparation for childbirth. *American Psychologist, 39,* 1357–1371.

Widmayer, S. M., Peterson, L. M., Lerner, M., Carnahan, S., Calderon, A., Wingerd, J., & Marshall, R. (1990). Predictors of Haitian-American infant development at twelve months. *Child Development, 61,* 410–415.

Wiehe, V. R. (1989). Child abuse: An ecological perspective. *Early Child Development and Care, 42,* 141–149.

Wiesenfeld, A. R., Malatesta, C. Z., & DeLoache, L. (1981). Differential parental response to familiar and unfamiliar infant distress signals. *Infant Behavior and Development, 4,* 281–295.

Wigfield, R., Gilbert, R., & Fleming, P. J. (1994). SIDS: Risk reduction measures. *Early Human Development, 38,* 161–164.

Wijnroks, L. (1998). Early maternal stimulation and the development of cognitive competence and attention of preterm infants. *Early Development and Parenting, 7,* 19–30.

Wilcox, A. J., Weinberg, C. R., & Baird, D. D. (1995). Timing of sexual intercourse in relation to ovulation. Effects on the probability of conception, survival of the pregnancy, and sex of the baby. *New England Journal of Medicine, 333*(7), 1517–1521.

Wilcox, T., & Baillargeon, R. (1998). Object individuation in young infants: Further evidence with an event-monitoring paradigm. *Developmental Science, 1*(1), 127–142.

Wilkie, C. F., & Ames, E. W. (1986). The relationship of infant crying to parental stress in the transition to parenthood. *Journal of Marriage and the Family, 48,* 545–550.

Williams, D. (1999). *Like colour to the blind: Soul searching and soul finding.* London: Jessica Kingsley.

Wilson, M. N. (1986). The black extended family: An analytical consideration. *Developmental Psychology, 22,* 246–258.

Wilson, S. L. (2003). Post-Institutionalization: The Effects of Early Deprivation on Development of Romanian Adoptees. *Child & Adolescent Social Work Journal, 20*(6), 473–483.

WIN News (1992). Safe motherhood: New estimates show uneven progress. *Women's International Network News, 18,* 35–36.

Winick, M., Knarig, K., & Harris, R. (1975). Malnutrition and environmental enrichment by early adoption. *Science, 190,* 1173–1175.

Winnicott, D. (1971). *Playing and reality.* New York: Basic Books.

Winslow, M., & Guitar, B. (1994). The effects of structured turn-taking on disfluencies: A case study. *Language, Speech, and Hearing Services in Schools, 25,* 251–257.

Winston, R. M. L., & Handyside, A. H. (1993). New challenges in human in vitro fertilization. *Science, 260,* 932–936.

Wolf, D., & Gardner, H. (1979). Style and sequence in early symbolic play. In N. Smith & M. Franklin (Eds.), *Symbolic function in childhood* (pp. 64–92). Hillsdale, NJ: Erlbaum.

Wolff, P. H. (1966). The causes, controls, and organization of behavior in the neonate. *Psychological Issues, 5,* (Monograph No. 17).

Wolff, P. H. (1987). *The development of behavioral states and the expression of emotions in early infancy: New proposals for investigation.* Chicago: University of Chicago Press.

Wolff, P. H. (1993). Behavioral and emotional states in infancy: A dynamic perspective. In L. B. Smith & E. Thelen (Eds.), *A dynamic systems approach to development: Applications* (pp. 189–208). Cambridge, MA: MIT Press.

Wong, V., & Wong, S. N. (1991). Brainstem suditory evoked potential study in children with autistic disorder. *Journal of Autism and Developmental Disorders, 21,* 329–340.

Wood, J. J., Emmerson, N. A., & Cowan, P. A. (2004). Is early attachment security carried forward into relationships with preschool peers? *British Journal of Developmental Psychology, 22*(2), 245–253.

Wood, J. N., & Spelke, E. S. (2005). Infants' enumeration of actions: Numerical discrimination and its signature limits. *Developmental Science, 8*(2), 173–181.

Woodson, R., Drinkwin, J., & Hamilton, C. (1985). Effects of nonnutritive sucking on state and activity: Term-preterm comparisons. *Infant Behavior and Development, 8,* 435–441.

Woodson, R., & Hamilton, C. (1988). The effect of nonnutritive sucking on heart rate in preterm infants. *Developmental Psychobiology, 21* (3), 207–213.

Woodward, A. L. (1999). Infants' ability to distinguish between purposeful and non-purposeful behaviors. *Infant Behavior and Development, 22*(2), 145–160.

Woodward, A. L., & Hoyne, K. L. (1999). Infants' learning about words and sounds in relation to objects. *Child Development, 70*(1), 65–77.

Woodward, A. L., & Sommerville, J. A. (2000). Twelve-month-old infants interpret action in context. *Psychological Sciences, 11*(1), 73–77.

Woodward, A. L., Markman, E. M., & Fitzsimmons, C. M. (1994). Rapid word learning in 13– and 18–month-olds. *Developmental Psychology, 30*(4), 553–556.

Woolley, J. D., & Cox, V. (2007). Development of beliefs about storybook reality. *Developmental Science, 10*(5), 681–693.

Wooten, S. (1995). *Touching the body, reaching the soul: How touch influences the nature of human beings.* Santa Fe, NM: Rosen Method Center Southwest.

World Health Organization (1976). *New trends and approaches in the delivery of maternal and child care in health services.* (Tech. Rep. Series No. 600). Geneva: Author.

World Health Organization (1985). *The quantity and quality of breast milk.* Geneva: Author.

Worobey, J., & Belsky, J. (1982). Employing the Brazelton scale to influence mothering: An experimental comparison of three strategies. *Developmental Psychology, 18,* 736–743.

Worobey, J., & Blajda, V. M. (1989). Temperament ratings at 2 weeks, 2 months, and 1 year: Differential stability of activity and emotionality. *Developmental Psychology, 25,* 257–262.

Worobey, J., & Lewis, M. (1989). Individual differences in the reactivity of young infants. *Developmental Psychology, 25,* 663–667.

Wortley, P., Lindegren, M., & Fleming, P. (2001, May 11). Successful implementation of perinatal HIV prevention guidelines. *MMWR, 50*(RR06), 15–28.

Wright, L. (1994). Prenatal diagnosis in the 1990s. *Journal of Obstetrical and Gynecological Neonatal Nursing, 23,* 506–515.

Wu, G., Bazer, F. W., Cudd, T. A., Meininger, C. J., & Spencer, T. E. (2004). Maternal Nutrition and fetal development. *J. Nutr. 134,* 2169–2172.

Wu, S. S., Ma, C. X., Carter, R. L., Ariet, M., Feaver, E. A., Resnick, M. B., et al. (2004). Risk factors for infant maltreatment: A population-based study. *Child Abuse & Neglect, 28*(12), 1253–1264.

Wurmser, H., Rieger, M., Domogalla, C., Kahnt, A., Buchwald, J., Kowatsch, M., et al. (2006). Association between life stress during pregnancy and infant crying in the first six months postpartum: A prospective longitudinal study. *Early Human Development, 82*(5), 341–349.

Wynn, K. (1998). Numerical competence in infants. In C. Donlan (Ed.), *The development of mathematical skills. Studies in developmental psychology* (pp. 3–25). Hove, England: Psychology Press/Taylor & Francis.

Xie, H., Cairns, B. D., & Cairns, R. B. (2001). Predicting teen motherhood and teen fatherhood: Individual characteristics and peer affiliations. *Social Development, 10*(4), 488–511.

Xu, F., Spelke, E. S., & Goddard, S. (2005). Number sense in human infants. *Developmental Science, 8*(1), 88–101.

Yale Bush Center Infant Care Leave Project (1985). *Facts on parents in the workforce and infant care.* New Haven, CT: Author.

Yale, M. E., Messinger, D. S., Cobo-Lewis, A. B., & Delgado, C. F. (2003). The temporal coordination of early infant communication. *Developmental Psychology, 39*(5), 815–824.

Yale, M. E., Messinger, D. S., Cobo-Lewis, A. B., Oller, D. K., & Eilers, R. E. (1999). An event-based analysis of the coordination of early infant vocalization and facial actions. *Developmental Psychology, 35*(2), 505–513.

Yalom, I. D. (1968). Postpartum blues syndrome. *Archives of General Psychiatry, 28,* 16–27.

Yampolskaya, S., Greenbaum, P., & Berson, I. (2009). Profiles of child maltreatment perpetrators and risk for fatal assault: A latent class analysis. *Journal of Family Violence. 24*(5), Jul 2009, pp. 337–348.

Yarrow, L. J., Rubenstein, J. L., & Pedersen, F. A. (1975). *Infant and environment: Early cognitive and motivational development.* Washington, DC: Hemisphere Publishing.

Yates, D. J., & Bremner, J. G. (1988). Conditions for Piagetian stage IV search errors in a task using transparent occluders. *Infant Behavior and Development, 11,* 411–417.

Yeung, W. J., Sandberg, J. F., Davis-Kean, P. E., & Hofferth, S. L. (2001). Children's time with fathers in intact families. *Journal of Marriage & the Family, 63*(1), 136–154.

Yoder, P. J. (1989). Maternal question use predicts later language development in specific-language-disordered children. *Journal of Speech and Hearing Disorders, 54,* 347–355.

Yonas, A., Pettersen, L., & Granrud, C. E. (1982). Infants' sensitivity to familiar size as information for distance. *Child Development, 53,* 1285–1290.

Yoshikawa, H. (1999). Welfare dynamics, support services, mothers' earnings, and child cognitive development: Implications for contemporary welfare reform. *Child Development, 70*(3), 779–801.

Yoshikawa, H., & Hsueh, J. (2001). Child Development and Public Policy: Toward a Dynamic Systems Perspective. *Child Development, 72*(6), 1887.

Young, G., & Lewis, M. (1979). Effects of familiarity and maternal attention on infant peer relations. *Merrill-Palmer Quarterly, 25,* 105–120.

Young, G., Segalowitz, S. J., Misek, P., Alp, I. E., & Boulet, R. (1983). Is early reaching left handed? Review of manual specialization research. In G. Young, S. J. Segalowitz, C. M. Corter, & S. Trehub (Eds.), *Manual specialization and the developing brain* (pp. 337–353). New York: Academic Press.

Young, I. D., Rickett, A. B., & Clarke, M. (1986). Genetic analysis of malformations causing perinatal mortality. *Journal of Medical Genetics, 23,* 58–63.

Young, S. K., Fox, N. A., & Zahn-Waxler, C. (1999). The relations between temperament and empathy in 2–year-olds. *Developmental Psychology, 35*(8), 1189–1197.

Young, T., Turner, J., Denny, G., & Young, M. (2004). Examining external and internal poverty as antecedents of teen pregnancy. *Am J Health Behav, 28*(4), 361–373.

Youngblut, J. M., Loveland-Cherry, C. J., & Horan, M. (1993). Maternal employment, family functioning, and preterm infant development at 9 and 12 months. *Research in Nursing and Health, 16,* 33–43.

Younger, B., & Gotlieb, S. (1988). Development of categorization skills: Changes in the nature or structure of infant form categories? *Developmental Psychology, 24,* 611–619.

Younger, B. A., & Fearing, D. D. (1999). Parsing items into separate categories: Developmental changes in infant categorization. *Child Development, 70*(2), 291–303.

Younger, B. A., & Johnson, K. E. (2004). Infants' comprehension of toy replicas as symbols for real objects. *Cognitive Psychology, 48*(2), 207–242.

Zachry, W. (1978). Ordinality and interdependence of representation and language development in infancy. *Child Development, 49,* 681–687.

Zahn-Waxler, C., Radke-Yarrow, M., Wagner, E., & Chapman, M. (1992). Development of concern for others. *Developmental Psychology, 28,* 126–136.

Zahn-Waxler, C., & Robinson, J. (1995). Empathy and guilt: Early origins of feelings of responsibility. In J. P. Tangney & K. W. Fischer (Eds.) *Self-conscious emotions: The psychology of shame, guilt, embarrassment, and pride* (pp. 143–173). New York: Guilford Press.

Zahn-Waxler, C., Robinson, J. L., & Emde, R. N. (1992). The development of empathy in twins. *Developmental Psychology, 28,* 1038–1047.

Zaradic, P. A., & Pergams, O. R. W. (2007). JDP Forum: Videophilia: Implications for childhood development and conservation. *The Journal of Developmental Processes, 2*(1), 130–144.

Zarbatany, L., & Lamb, M. E. (1985). Social referencing as a function of information source: Mothers versus strangers. *Infant Behavior and Development, 8,* 25–33.

Zarling, C. L., Hirsch, B. J., & Landry, S. (1988). Maternal social networks and mother-infant interactions in full-term and very low birthweight preterm infants. *Child Development, 59,* 178–185.

Zaslow, M. J., & Eldred, C. A. (Eds.) (1997). The promise and limitations of parenting education for teen mothers on welfare: Lessons from the New Chance Observational Study. *Parenting behavior in a sample of young mothers in poverty: Results of the New Chance Observational Study.* Washington, D.C.: Child Trends.

Zeanah, C. H., Larrieu, J., Heller, S., & Valliere, J. (2005) Infant-parent relationship assessment. In C. H. Zeanah (Ed.) *Handbook of Infant Mental Health, 2nd Edition* (pp. 222–235). NY: The Guilford Press.

Zeanah, C. H., Smyke, A. T., Koga, S. F., & Carlson, E. (2005). Attachment in Institutionalized and Community Children in Romania. *Child Development, 76*(5), 1015–1028.

Zeanah P. D., Stafford B., Nagle G., Rice T. (2005, January). *Addressing Social-Emotional Development and Infant Mental Health in Early Childhood Systems.* Los Angeles, CA: National Center for Infant and Early Childhood Health Policy; Building State Early Childhood Comprehensive Systems Series, No. 12, 4–5.

Zebrowitz, L. A., & Montepare, J. M. (1992). Impressions of babyfaced individuals across the life span. *Developmental Psychology, 28,* 1143–1152.

Zeifman, D. M. (2004). Acoustic features of infant crying related to intended caregiving intervention. *Infant and Child Development, 13*(2), 111–122.

Zeitz, D. (1969). *Child welfare: Services and perspectives.* New York: Wiley.

Zelazo, N. A., Zelazo, P. R., Cohen, K. M., & Zelazo, P. D. (1993). Specificity of practice effects on elementary neuromotor patterns. *Developmental Psychology, 29,* 686–691.

Zelazo, P. R. (1976). From reflexive to instrumental behavior. In L. P. Lipsitt (Ed.), *Developmental psychobiology: The significance of infancy* (pp. 232–267). Hillsdale, NJ: Erlbaum.

Zelazo, P. R., Brody, L. R., & Chaikan, H. (1984). Neonatal habituation and dishabituation of head turning to rattle sounds. *Infant Behavior and Development, 7,* 311–321.

Zentner, M. R., & Kagan, J. (1998). Infants' perception of consonance and dissonance in music. *Infant Behavior and Development, 21*(3), 483–492.

Zeskind, P. S. (1980). Adult responses to cries of low and high risk infants. *Infant Behavior and Development, 3,* 167–178.

Zeskind, P. S., & Barr, R. G. (1997). Acoustic characteristics of naturally occurring cries of infants with "colic." *Child Development, 68*(3), 394–403.

Zeskind, P. S., & Iacino, R. (1984). Effects of maternal visitation to preterm infants in the neonatal intensive care unit. *Child Development, 55,* 1887–1893.

Zeskind, P. S., & Iacino, R. (1987). The relation between length of hospitalization and the mental and physical development of preterm infants. *Infant Behavior and Development, 10,* 217–221.

Zeskind, P. S., Klein, L., & Marshall, T. R. (1992). Adults' perceptions of experimental modifications of durations of pauses and expiratory sounds in infant crying. *Developmental Psychology, 28,* 1153–1162.

Zeskind, P. S., & Lester, B. M. (1981). Analysis of cry features in newborns with differential fetal growth. *Child Development, 52,* 207–212.

Zeskind, P. S., & Marshall, T. R. (1988). The relation between variations in pitch and maternal perceptions of infant crying. *Child Development, 59,* 193–196.

Zeskind, P. S., & Marshall, T. R. (1991). Temporal organization in neonatal arousal: Systems, oscillations, and development. In M. Weiss & P. Zelazo (Eds.), *Newborn attention: Biological constraints and the influence of experiences* (pp. 22–62). Norwood, NJ: Ablex.

Zeskind, P. S., Marshall, T. R., & Goff, D. M. (1992). Rhythmic organization of heart rate in breast-fed and bottle-fed newborn infants. *Early Development and Parenting, 1,* 79–87.

Zeskind, P. S., & Stephens, L. E. (2004). Maternal selective serotonin reuptake inhibitor use during pregnancy and newborn neurobehavior. *Pediatrics, 113*(2), 368–375.

Zeskind, P. S., Wilhite, A., & Marshall, T. R. (1993). Infant cry as a graded signal: Expiratory sounds alter mothers' perceptions. *Early Development and Parenting, 2,* 99–105.

Zevalkink, J., Riksen-Walraven, J. M., & Van Lieshout, C. F. M. (1999). Attachment in the Indonesian caregiving context. *Social Development, 8*(1), 21–40.

Zhu, J., Madsen, K., Vestergaard, M., Olesen, A., Basso, O., & Olsen, J. (2005). Paternal age and congenital malformations. *Human Reproduction, 20*(11), 3173–3177.

Zimmerman, F. J., Christakis, D. A., & Meltzoff, A. N. (2007). Associations between media viewing and language development in children under age 2 years. *J Pediatr, 151*(4), 364–368.

Zimmerman, F. J., Christakis, D. A., & Meltzoff, A. N. (2007). Television and DVD/video viewing in children younger than 2 years. *Arch Pediatr Adolesc Med, 161*(5), 473–479.

Zimmermann, P., Fremmer-Bombik, E., Spangler, G., & Grossmann, K. E. (1995, March). *Attachment in adolescence: A longitudinal perspective.* Poster presented at the Biennial Meeting of the Society for Research in Child Development, Indianapolis, IN.

Zimmerman, R. K., & Grebink, G. S. (1992). Childhood immunizations: A practical approach for clinicians. *American Family Physician, 45,* 1759–1772.

Zlatin, M. A. (1973). *Explorative mapping of the vocal tract and primitive syllabification in infancy: The first six months.* Purdue University Contributed Papers, Fall.

Zlochower, A. J., & Cohn, J. F. (1996). Vocal timing in face-to-face interaction of clinically depressed and nondepressed mothers and their 4–month-old infants. *Infant Behavior and Development, 19,* 371–374.

Zucker, K. J. (1999). Intersexuality and gender identity differentiation. *Annu Rev Sex Res, 10,* 1–69.

Zukow, P. G. (1980). A microanalytic study of the role of the caregiver in the relationship between and language acquisition during the one word period (Doctoral dissertation, University of California, 1980). *Dissertation Abstracts International, 42,* 18.

Zukow, P. G. (1986). The relationship between interaction with the caregiver and the emergence of play activities during the one-word period. *British Journal of Developmental Psychology, 4,* 223–234.

Zukow, P. G. (1990). Socio-perceptual bases for the emergence of language: An alternative to innatist approaches. *Developmental Psychobiology, 23,* 705–726.

Zukow-Goldring, P. (1996). Sensitive caregiving fosters the comprehension of speech: When gestures speak louder than words. *Early Development and Parenting, 5*(4), 195–211.

Zukow-Goldring, P. (1997). A social ecological realist approach to the emergence of the lexicon: Educating attention to amodal invariants in gesture and speech. In C. Dent-Read & P. Zukow-Goldring (Eds.), *Evolving explanations of development: Ecological approaches to organism-environment systems* (pp. 199–250). Washington, DC: American Psychological Association.

Name Index

Subject Index